COMPREHE~

LISBON, MADRID & THE COSTA DEL SOL '91-'92

by Darwin Porter
Assisted by Danforth Prince

PRENTICE
HALL
PRESS

NEW YORK • LONDON • TORONTO • SYDNEY • TOKYO • SINGAPORE

Ay

FROMMER BOOKS

Published by Prentice Hall Press
A division of Simon & Schuster Inc.
15 Columbus Circle
New York, NY 10023

ISBN 0-13-333121-0
ISSN 0899-2932

Manufactured in the United States of America

CONTENTS

MAPS

A Disclaimer

Readers are advised that prices fluctuate in the course of time and that travel information changes under the impact of the varied and volatile factors that affect the travel industry. The author and publisher cannot be held responsible for the experiences of the reader while traveling. Readers are invited to write the publisher with ideas, comments, and suggestions for future editions.

Inflation Alert

The author of this book has spent many hours researching to ensure the accuracy of prices appearing in this guide. As we go to press, we believe we have obtained the most reliable data possible. However, we cannot guarantee the tariffs quoted. In the lifetime of this edition—particularly in its second year (1992)—the wise traveler will add at least 20% to the prices quoted.

Currency Conversions

The currency conversions from Portuguese escudos to dollars and from Spanish pesetas to dollars, which appear in parentheses throughout these pages, were prepared on the basis of 147 escudos (written 147$) and 106.65 pesetas to $1 (U.S.). Because these rates change from day to day, depending on the relative values of both currencies on world markets, they may not be accurate by the time you travel. Use our currency conversions, therefore, only as a gauge of what you'll be spending, and check with a banker before you leave for Iberia to determine the actual rates of exchange at that time.

INTRODUCING IBERIA

1. SPAIN—LAND OF A LOST EMPIRE
2. PORTUGAL—IN ITS OWN RIGHT

As your jet descends over the port of Lisbon or sweeps above the golden plains of Castile on its way to Madrid, you'll be embarking on a unique travel adventure—the conquest of Iberia.

Long isolated from mainstream Europe by topography and its conquerers—the Pyrenees mountains and the Moors—Iberia developed and grew in its own individual, distinct way. Exotic is the word for it. Where else in Europe will you come across anything like the bold, sensuous rhythm of flamenco, the mournful wailing strains of fado, or the truly long, lazy siesta? And above all, there's the fascinating sport of bullfighting.

These are aspects of Iberia that every person has heard of or seen, but to experience them firsthand is something else, something no traveler should miss. But Iberia is much more than this—indeed, it is a continent in miniature.

1. Spain—Land of a Lost Empire

Castles, mostly in ruins, dot the Spanish countryside, hollow reminders of Spain's Golden Age, when it dispatched fleets to conquer the New World and return with its riches. Columbus sailed to America, Balboa to the Pacific Ocean. Cortés conquered Mexico for glory and the glory of the Church; Pizarro brought Peru into the Spanish fold.

The conquistadores too often revealed the negative side of the Spanish soul, the brutality in the name of honor and glory, but they also embodied the positive side, the belief that "the impossible dream" was possible—Don Quixote's tilting at windmills on the plains of La Mancha, and often conquering them.

It's difficult to see Spain today without recalling its golden past, for there are many reminders. Spain today is a perfect mixture of the old and the new, and its images constantly float by you—silvery olive trees in the south; mantilla-wearing Carmens in Andalusia; Moorish palaces; harsh Basque fishing villages along the northeast coast; the luxurious sandy beaches from the Costa de la Luz to the Costa Brava, thronged with bikini-clad tourists; the orange groves of Valencia; the hard-working industrial city of Barcelona, the largest of the Mediterranean ports; the elegance and serenity of Madrid.

So how can a traveler in Spain go wrong? Here you'll have the glories of the past and the excitement of the present.

2. Portugal—In Its Own Right

Portugal suffers from one of the most widespread misconceptions in European travel: that it's really "another Spain." This completely erroneous judgment exists even today, because Portugal is still relatively unknown and unexplored by the mass of foreign travelers who, at best, know only Lisbon and the famous resort of Estoril or Byron-praised Sintra.

Victorian guidebook writers called Portugal an "island," even though it's obviously connected to Spain. The marriage of this Iberian couple, which lasted for 60 years, was never successful. Spain was too large, too dominant, too intent on protecting its own interests, which conflicted with those of its reluctant bride. Although ruled by their powerful neighbor, the Portuguese staunchly maintained their identity during the captivity and eagerly waited for the moment when they could throw off the yoke and reassert their independence.

Despite its small size—only 140 miles in width, 380 miles in length—Portugal is one of the most rewarding adventures on the European docket. Exploring its towns, cities, villages, and countryside takes far longer than expected, because there is so much richness, such variety, along the way.

The people are the friendliest in Europe. The land they inhabit is majestic—almond trees in the African-looking Algarve; cork forests and fields of golden wheat in Alentejo; ranches that raise the brave black bulls in Ribatejo; the narrow, winding streets of the Alfama in Lisbon; ox-drawn carts crossing the plains of Minho; apron-clad *varinas* (the wives of the fishermen) carrying baskets of wiggling eels on their heads; and the vineyards of Douro.

Azaleas, rhododendrons, and canna grow for miles on end; the sound of fado drifts out of small cafés; windmills clack in the Atlantic breezes; rare, intricate *azulejos* (tiles) line churches and buildings; sardine boats bob in the bay; whitewashed houses gleam; and the sea . . . always the sea.

Kaleidoscopic scenery, sandy beaches, mild climate, and unique attractions such as Manueline architecture have contributed to the recent tourist boom in Portugal. But what has made the land initially popular with its many English visitors—and later the German and Scandinavian multitudes pouring into the Algarve—is its moderate tariffs, not only in the hotels and restaurants, but in the shops as well. Inflation, however, is the rule here too, and the people are hard-pressed. Nevertheless, Portugal is still a soothing breeze to those who've been to Rome and Stockholm lately.

Focusing on the unique features of each of these two Iberian capitals is one goal of this guide. The other is highlighting those special hotels and fine restaurants that will make your trip to Iberia memorable. And, after having explored the museums and monuments of Lisbon and Madrid, you can wind down with a beach holiday along the Costa del Sol.

GETTING ACQUAINTED WITH LISBON

Lisbon strikes most visitors as a series of images: narrow cobblestone streets; pastel-washed houses; cable cars clacking down to the river; black-shawled *fadistas* singing of unrequited love; floodlights illuminating an ancient castle; boats loaded with fresh seafood; mosaic-paved sidewalks; ferryboats plying the Tagus; laundry flapping in the wind; and the crowing of a rooster early in the morning.

This is Lisbon, an ancient city, whose people fancifully like to claim Ulysses as their founder. If this legendary figure did indeed possess a character of "experience, tenacity, and intelligence," then he is the appropriate father symbol for Lisbon, Europe's westernmost capital, sprawling across seven hills on the right bank of the Tagus.

HISTORY IN BRIEF

Those cynical of the Ulysses legend claim that the seafaring Phoenicians founded Lisbon (no history backs them up). In time, the Carthaginians sailed into the port. Romans occupied the city from the beginning of the third century B.C. to the fourth century A.D., during which time it was known as "Felicitas Julia." After Rome's decline, Lisbon was a Visigoth stronghold, then a Moorish city before it was liberated by the Catholic Portuguese from the north in 1147. But it wasn't until 1256 that Afonso III felt safe enough to move his court there, forsaking Coimbra, now a university city.

During the Age of Exploration some of the greatest names, such as Vasco da Gama and Magellan, embarked from Lisbon on their voyages of discovery. Like Ulysses, the captains of those long-ago crews had to contend with widely held beliefs that their ships would be consumed by huge sea monsters, or else be swallowed up by the fiery mouth (*boca*) of Hell.

In time, the discoveries and exploration, the opening of new worlds to the west and east, created a mother city of Lisbon, called in its Golden Age the "eighth wonder of the world." Ivory and slaves from Africa; spices, silks, rubies, pearls, and porcelain from China and the East Indies; ginger and pepper from the Malabar Coast—all these riches were funneled through the thriving port of Lisbon. Shopkeepers literally had more money than they knew how to spend. Their wives hired servants more for ostentation than need. The sea captain's spouse wore finery fit for a princess.

And then came the earthquake. At the peak of Lisbon's power, influence, and wealth, it suffered one of the greatest earthquakes of all time. Two-thirds of the city was destroyed. At 9:40 on the morning of November 1, 1755, most of the city's residents were at church, celebrating an important religious observance, All Saints' Day, when the earthquake struck. In minutes, the glory that was Lisbon became a thing of the past. The great earthquake was felt as far north as Scotland, causing damage even in North Africa. Ambassadors and slaves, merchants and sailors, courtesans and priests added to a death toll estimated at 20,000 to 60,000 people. A fire raged for nearly a week, destroying much that the quake had left undamaged, but thankfully sparing the heart of the Alfama district.

After the ashes had settled, the Marquês de Pombal, the prime minister, ordered that the dead be buried, the city rebuilt at once. To accomplish that ambitious plan, the king gave him the power of a virtual dictator.

What Pombal ordered constructed was a city of wide, symmetrical boulevards leading into handsome squares dominated by fountains and statuary. Bordering these wide avenues would be black-and-white mosaic sidewalks, the most celebrated in Europe.

LISBON TODAY

The mixture of the old (pre-earthquake) and the new (post-earthquake) was done so harmoniously that travelers consider Lisbon one of the most beautiful cities on earth.

Many who have never actually been to Lisbon know it well from watching World War II spy movies. It would be only natural, you'd assume, to see Hedy Lamarr slinking around the corner any moment. During World War II, Lisbon, officially neutral, was a hotbed of intrigue and espionage. It was also a haven for thousands of refugees. Many of those—such as deposed royalty—remained, settling into villas in Estoril and Sintra.

---

1. Orientation

THE DISTRICTS OF LISBON

As conceived by the Marquês de Pombal, the gateway to Lisbon is the **Praça do Comércio** (Commerce Square), also known as the Terreiro do Paço (Palace Grounds) in memory of the days when the royal court was located here before the earthquake destroyed it.

However, in the past century the English dubbed this same square **Black Horse Square,** and the name stuck (even some Portuguese refer to it in this way). The appellation is derived from the equestrian statue on the square of King José I, dating from 1775, the work of Machado de Castro, the leading Portuguese sculptor of his day. It was on this square in 1908 that the king, Carlos I, and his son, Prince Luís Filipe, were killed by an assassin's bullets.

To the east of the square lies the sector known as the **Alfama,** the ancient Moorish district of Lisbon spared from the earthquake. It is crowned by St. George Castle, once a Visigoth stronghold, although the present structure dates from the 12th century. This eastern quarter of Lisbon consists of narrow streets (some really stairways) and medieval houses, where neighbors could, if they wanted to, reach out and shake hands with the people next door. Old street lanterns and flower-draped balconies, barefoot children, and fishwives selling the latest catch from the sea add to the local color.

To the north of Black Horse Square lies the **Rossio,** more formally known as Praça Dom Pedro IV. A riot of neon, it draws the devotee of the sidewalk café, who sits talking, getting a shoeshine, and sipping the black, aromatic coffee of Angola. Again, tourists have bestowed a nickname on it: Rolling Motion Square. The undulating patterns of the black-and-white mosaic sidewalks certainly do give that impression.

A statue there honors Pedro IV, emperor of Brazil. The Estação do Rossio, the railway station on one side—one of the most bizarre in Europe—is built in what many have described as "Victorian Gothic" or "Neo-Manueline." Also opening onto the square is the Teatro Nacional Dona Maria II.

Proceeding north, you arrive at the Praça dos Restauradores, with an obelisk commemorating the Portuguese overthrow of Spanish domination in 1640.

Beginning here is Lisbon's main boulevard, the **Avenida da Liberdade** (Avenue of Liberty), dating from 1880. Graced with gardens, palm trees, and ponds with swans, it is often compared to Paris's Champs-Elysees or New York's Fifth Avenue. But those suggestions are misleading, as the Portuguese avenue maintains a distinctly original flavor. Along this most fashionable, mile-long promenade, you'll encounter many outdoor cafés, airline offices, restaurants, and shops.

Crowning the avenue is the Praça Marquês de Pombal, a heroic monument honoring the 18th-century prime minister who rebuilt Lisbon after the earthquake. Directly to the north is the magnificently laid-out Parque Eduardo VII, commemorating the visit of the English king to Portugal. It's one of the most attractive spots in all of Lisbon. In the northern section of the park is the Estufa Fria, one of the best greenhouses in Europe.

The commercial district ("downtown" Lisbon) is **Baixa,** a sector that is centered mainly between the Rossio and the Tagus. Its three principal streets are the Rua do Ouro (Street of Gold), Rua da Prata (Street of Silver), and the Rua Augusta. All three streets lead to the Praça do Comércio.

West of Baixa is the **Chiado,** higher up and considered more fashionable. Its main street is known as the Rua Garrett, in honor of a Portuguese poet, an appropriate commemoration, as this street has been the traditional gathering place for the literati. Today it contains some of the city's finest stores.

Looking down over the Chiado is **Bairro Alto** (the upper quarter). When visitors see the laundry flapping in the wind, the fishwives, and the narrow cobblestone streets, many think they're in the Alfama. Not so, but much of this district was, like the Alfama, spared from the destruction of the earthquake. It is of interest today because of its excellent fado cafés.

The western quarter of Lisbon is known as **Belém** (Bethlehem). In reality, it's a suburb, characterized by its world-famous landmark, the Tower of Belém, the point from which the explorers set out in the age of discovery (at Belém, the Tagus—after a long run beginning in Spain—pours into the sea). Opening onto the Praça do Império (Square of the Empire) is the Jerónimos Monastery, and down the street, on the Rua de Belém, is the Coach Museum.

Lisbon is connected to the working-class district, **Cacilhas,** which lies on the left bank of the Tagus, by the Ponte 25 de Abril. Built at a cost of $75 million, it is the longest and most expensive suspension bridge in Europe. Before it was opened, Lisbon was cut off from the south, except by ferryboat connections. The bridge is 7,473 feet long, its towers rising to a height of 625 feet. A herculean statue of Christ, his arms stretching out to the sky, stands watch over the southern banks of the Tagus. Tourists and Portuguese alike visit Cacilhas because of its seafood.

2. Flying to Lisbon

If you wish to fly directly to Lisbon from North America, as most visitors will, there are two major airlines that do so: **TAP AIR PORTUGAL** (the Portuguese international airline) and **Trans World Airlines (TWA).** TAP gives passengers the option of stopping midway across the Atlantic in the Azores. Flying TAP also makes baggage transfers and seat reservations on connecting flights within Portugal easier.

Within North America, TAP flies to Portugal from New York (JFK), New Jersey (Newark), Boston, Toronto, and Montreal. Within Portugal itself, TAP links nine cities with Lisbon.

TAP routes include flights from most of the major capitals of Western Europe. Its flights to Lisbon from London are especially good values, sometimes priced so attractively (with restrictions, as low as $320 in peak season, round-trip) that one might realistically combine a sojourn through Portugal with an inexpensive side trip to Britain.

Several ticket options exist for transatlantic TAP passengers. Winter bargains, when certain restrictions apply, are available between January and March, when Lisbon is arguably at its most serenely untrammeled.

Most passengers, however, prefer to travel in Portugal in the

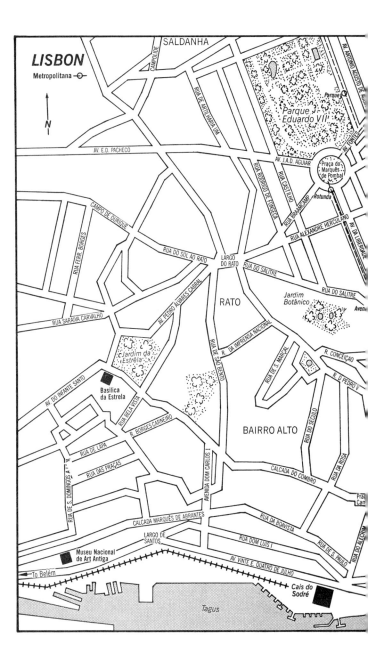

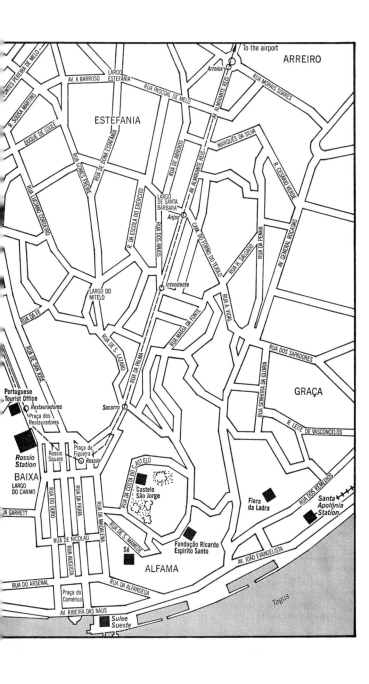

spring, summer, and autumn. At those times, TAP's most popular and lowest-priced ticket is called a midweek APEX fare. Its price varies with the season, but is competitive with similar fares carrying similar restrictions on other airlines. Tickets must be purchased 14 days before your departure. In some cases, passengers may be subject to a $100 penalty for any itinerary changes made after payment. At press time, a round-trip APEX ticket between New York and Lisbon in peak season cost $776 leaving and returning on a Monday through Thursday, and $826 leaving and returning on a Friday, Saturday, or Sunday. (A government tax of $16 will be added to these fares when you pay for your ticket.) For families, one strong attraction is the fact that children under 12 traveling with a parent pay 67% of the adult fare, and infants under 2 (if they remain on a parent's lap during the flight) pay 10% of the adult fare.

Travelers who prefer not to specify when they will return home, or who can't buy their tickets 14 days before takeoff, usually opt for an excursion fare. Costing more than either of the APEX options, it requires that passengers delay using the return halves of their tickets from 7 to 180 days. On this ticket, peak season lasts from June 1 to August 31.

TWA flies daily from New York's JFK to Lisbon, but with few of the benefits TAP can offer for side excursions to the Azores or within mainland Portugal. However, if your origin is Harrisburg, Pennsylvania, for example (or any of the other cities within TWA's North American network), TWA can book you on one of its flights into New York, then transfer your baggage within its JFK terminal onto the flight to Lisbon. Some passengers appreciate the convenience of continuing their trips on the same airline. As for fares, TWA matched TAP dollar for dollar on its APEX fares, and enforced many of the same requirements as TAP for its cheapest tickets.

From time to time all airlines, including TAP and TWA, offer special low-cost promotional fares. For instance, at press time, TWA was offering a less expensive "nonrefundable" ticket between New York and Lisbon, for the relatively modest price of $604. Unfortunately, it required a nonrefundable payment 30 days in advance, and change of any kind, for any reason, was prohibited. This, like other special promotions at both TWA and TAP, are offered for only a short time. The wise airline shopper should always be on the lookout for this type of special promotion, which appears and disappears on the computer screens of both TWA and TAP like fleeting snows upon the plains of Portugal.

For exact departure dates and up-to-the-minute tariffs, you can phone a reservations clerk at **TAP Air Portugal** (tel. toll-free 800/221-7370) or consult a travel agent. In Lisbon, for ticket sales, flight reservations, and information about the city and the country, you can get in touch with TAP at 3 Praça Marquês de Pombal (tel. 54-40-80).

For information about fares and departure times at TWA, call toll-free 800/221–2000.

BUCKET SHOPS

The name "bucket shops" originated in the 1960s in Britain, where mainstream airlines gave that (then perjorative) name to resalers of blocks of unsold tickets consigned to them by major transatlantic carriers. Bucket shop has stuck as a label, but it might be more polite to refer to such resalers as "consolidators." They exist in many shapes and forms. In its purest sense, a bucket shop acts as a clearing house for blocks of tickets that airlines discount and consign during normally slow periods of air travel.

Charter operators (see below) and bucket shops used to perform separate functions, but their offerings in many cases have been blurred in recent years. Many outfits perform both functions.

Tickets may be priced from 20% to 35% less than the full fare. Terms of payment vary—anywhere from 45 days prior to departure to last-minute sales offered in a final attempt by an airline to fill a disturbingly empty craft.

Bucket shops abound from coast to coast, but just to get you started, here are some recommendations.

Maharaja Travel, 518 Fifth Ave., New York, NY 10036 (tel. 212/391-0122 or toll-free 800/223-6862), has been around for 20 years, offering tickets to 400 destinations worldwide.

Access International, 101 W. 31st St., Suite 1104, New York, NY 10001 (tel. 212/333-7280 or toll-free 800/825-3633), may be the country's biggest consolidator. It specializes in thousands of discounted tickets to the capitals of Europe.

CHARTER FLIGHTS

Strictly for reasons of economy (never for convenience), some travelers are willing to accept the uncertainties of a charter flight to Iberia. Some charter companies have proven unreliable in the past, so check with your travel agent.

In a strict sense, a charter flight occurs on an aircraft reserved months in advance for a one-time-only transit to some predetermined point. Before paying for a charter, check carefully the restrictions on your ticket or contract. You may be asked to purchase a tour package and pay far in advance. You'll pay a stiff penalty (or forfeit the ticket entirely) if you cancel. Charters are sometimes canceled when the planes don't fill up. In some cases, the charter ticket seller will offer you an insurance policy to cover your own legitimate cancellation (for example, if you are hospitalized or there is a death in the family).

One charter flight operator is the **Council on International Educational Exchange** (Council Charters), 205 E. 42nd St., New York, NY 10017 (tel. 212/661-0311 or toll-free 800/223-7402). This outfit can arrange charter seats on regularly scheduled aircraft.

AIRPORT

Both foreign and domestic flights arrive at Lisbon's **Portela Airport,** which lies about four miles from the heart of the city. For all airport information, telephone 80-20-60 or 80-45-00.

From the airport, a **bus** (*Ligne Verte*) carries passengers into central Lisbon for 200$ ($1.35) per person. (Pay the driver directly.) The green-sided double-decker buses run every 15 minutes between the airport and Lisbon's northernmost train station, Santa Polonia, every day between 7 a.m. and 9 p.m.

If you have luggage, however, it's much easier (and not at all expensive) to take a **taxi** instead. These queue up, British style, in a usually well-organized line at the sidewalk in front of the airport. The average taxi fare from the airport to central Lisbon is 1,000$ ($6.80), including a surcharge for your suitcases and a tip.

***

3. Getting Around Lisbon

If all the attractions were on the Avenida da Liberdade, getting around Lisbon would be easy. As it is, many of the most charming nooks lie on streets too steep or too narrow for automobiles. Thus a good pair of walking shoes is essential for the explorer who really wants to get to know Lisbon.

Lisbon is endowed with an adequate public transportation system that is cheap, if not always convenient. At any rate, some form of public or private transportation is necessary, as most of the major attractions of Lisbon are in such suburbs or neighboring centers as Belém, Queluz, or Sintra. Also, many visitors prefer to anchor into hotels along the nearby Costa do Sol (Estoril, Cascais) and make frequent trips into Lisbon, so mastering the transportation network is essential—even for short-time visitors.

TAXIS

Taxis in Lisbon tend to be cheap and are a popular means of transport for all but the most economy-minded of tourists. The taxis are usually diesel-engine Mercedes, charging a basic fare of 110$ (75¢) for the first 400 yards. After that, you'll be assessed another 8$ (5¢) for each additional 180 yards, with a 20% additional night fare in effect from 10 p.m. to 6 a.m. The driver is allowed by law to tack on another 50% if your total luggage weighs more than 66 pounds. If you travel outside Lisbon, the driver is allowed to charge you 40$ (25¢) per kilometer. Most Portuguese tip about 20% of an already modest fare.

For visitors anchored at one of the Costa do Sol resort hotels, perhaps in Estoril or Cascais, taxi connections from Lisbon can be prohibitively expensive. Far preferable for Costa do Sol visitors is the electric train system (see below).

TRAMS AND BUSES

These are among the cheapest in Europe. The trolley cars, such as those that make the steep run up to the Bairro Alto, are usually painted a rich Roman gold. The double-decker buses, on the other hand, come from London and look as if they need Big Ben in the background to complete the picture. If you're trying to stand on the platform at the back of a jammed bus, by the way, you'll need both hands free to hold on.

Most short-term visitors to Lisbon won't bother with bulk purchases of bus and tram tickets, simply because they won't ride public transportation enough to make the savings worthwhile. If this is your case, you can pay the driver of any bus, cable car, or tram a flat rate of 110$ (75¢) and ride as far as you want to go. (Ask the driver or other passengers to tell you when you reach your destination.)

If you plan to be in Lisbon for an extended stay, however, you can buy blocks of bus and tram tickets from the kiosk at the base of the Santa Justa elevator on Rua Aurea. This kiosk also has schedules for the city's trams and buses. It is open Monday to Saturday from 9 a.m. to 6 p.m. A booklet of 20 "mini-tickets" costs 500$ ($3.40), or 25$ (15¢) each. If you opt for the bulk-ticket method, you have to be aware of Lisbon's different bus zones and their borders. Depending on the number of zones you need to cross, you must insert between one and five of these mini-tickets into a machine on the bus, which will stamp them, canceling them for future use. The driver will tell you how many mini-tickets you need to cancel, and then you can ride to your destination satisfied that you have saved a modest percentage on the price of your transport. However, you'll find that taxis are really a good value, and are a lot more convenient.

SUBWAYS

Lisbon's Metro stations are designated by large M signs, which are illuminated at night, but some readers have reported difficulty in locating the stations because of missing signs. If you plan to ride the subway only once or twice, you can buy a one-time passage for 50$ (34¢). If you plan on many subway rides during your sojourn in Lisbon, you can buy a booklet of 10 tickets for 375$ ($2.55), which works out to only 37.5$ (25¢) per ride. One of Lisbon's most popular (and crowded) subway lines runs from the Avenida da Liberdade to the Campo Pequeno, that brick bullring away from the center of the city. On *corrida* days, just before and after the bullfights, trains on that particular line are likely to be full.

TRAINS

Lisbon is connected with all the towns and villages along the Portuguese Riviera by a smooth-running electric train system. You can board the train at the waterfront Cais do Sodré station in Lisbon, heading up the coast all the way to Cascais, the end of the run.

Only one class of seat is offered, and the rides are cheap. For example, if you go from Lisbon to either **Estoril** or **Cascais,** the one-way fare is 120$ (80¢). The train trip takes about 45 minutes.

To get to **Sintra,** you must go to the Estação do Rossio railway station, opening onto the Praça Dom Pedro IV or the Rossio, where frequent connections can be made. The one-way fare is 110$ (75¢). The train trip takes about 1 hour.

Electrified trains to **Porto** in the north leave from Sta. Apolonia Station in Lisbon and take 3 hours. Reservations are absolutely necessary.

Express trains in summer depart Lisbon for the **Algarve** every day but Sunday. These leave from the Barreiro Station (across the Tagus—take one of the ferries departing frequently). Off-season service is reduced to four times weekly. The train trip takes 4 to 5 hours.

For information about rail travel in Portugal, telephone 87-60-25 or 87-70-92 in Lisbon.

FERRYBOATS

Long before the advent of the Ponte 25 de Abril (see below), the reliable ferryboats chugged across the Tagus, connecting the left bank with the right. They still do, and are as popular as ever. Many

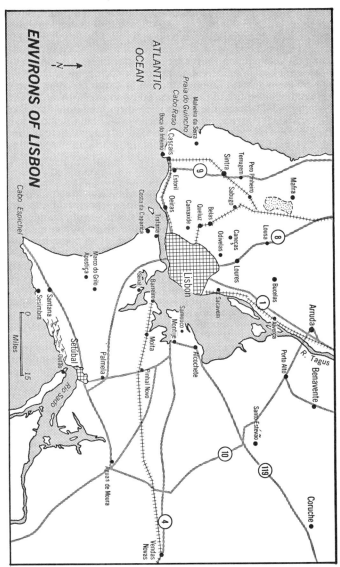

Portuguese find the bridge too expensive to traverse with their automobiles, so they leave their cars at home and take the ferryboat to work.

Most of the boats leave from the Praça do Comércio, and head for the towns of Barreiro and Cacilhas. Ferryboats leaving from the Praça do Comércio do not usually carry cars, only pedestrian passengers. The one-way fare on this ferryboat is 65$ (45¢) per passenger. If you have a car and want to use it on the opposite side of the Tagus, you'll have to take either the Ponte 25 de Abril Bridge or a different ferryboat, leaving from the Cais do Sodré, a short drive south of the Praça do Comércio. You'll pay between 100$ (70¢) and 200$ ($1.40) each way, depending on the size and weight of your car.

PONTE 25 DE ABRIL

As mentioned, this suspension bridge, the largest ever built in Europe, connects southeast Lisbon with Almada on its left bank and the district south of the Tagus. The price of your toll will depend on the distance between the axles and the weight of your car. The "normal" European car will usually average 85$ (60¢). The bridge is actually a lot more convenient than the aforementioned ferryboats, and you can use it to visit such cities as Setúbal in the south and Évora, the ancient Roman city in the east.

CAR RENTALS

So many of the scenic parts of Portugal are so isolated from a train or bus station that having a car is almost mandatory if you plan to do much serious touring. That way, you're a free agent, unhindered by the timetables of trains and buses, which often limit your excursions to places close to the beaten track.

Most visitors opt for an auto-rental plan providing weekly vehicle use with unlimited kilometers included in the overall price. Some of North America's major car-rental companies maintain branches at each of Portugal's most popular commercial and tourist centers, at rates that are usually competitive.

Avis has an office at the airport in Lisbon, plus as many as 10 other outlets throughout Portugal. If you reserve a car by telephone at least two days before you leave for Portugal, you'll qualify for Avis's least expensive rate of around $228 per week for a Renault 4 or Opel Corsa (which at press time were the two least expensive cars offered by most of the competition too). This rate includes full insurance, but the Portuguese government tacks on an additional 17% tax. Avis's main office is at 12-C Avenida Praia da Vittoria (tel. 56-11-77), but, once again, you'll do better if you reserve your car before leaving North America. For toll-free reservations and information, call 800/331–2112.

Hertz has an office in Lisbon at the airport (tel. 01/892-722) and also at 10 Avenida 5 de Outubre (tel. 01/579-027). For its smallest car (a Renault 4 or Opel Corsa), Hertz charges around $228 per week, with unlimited mileage and all insurance included (plus the obligatory 17% government tax), exactly the same as Avis. Within the Lisbon metropolitan area, Hertz maintains four different offices. As at its competitors, Hertz's least expensive prices are for clients who reserve at least two business days in advance from North America. For reservations and information, call toll-free by dialing 800/654–3001.

Your least expensive car-rental deal will probably be with **Budget Rent-a-Car,** whose insurance policies differ from those automatically offered at both Avis and Hertz. Budget includes a basic amount of collision damage insurance as an automatic part of each of its rental contracts, but leaves additional, all-encompassing collision insurance to the optional discretion of its clients. Budget offers a collision damage waiver (a policy that costs around $43.60 a week and allows you to waive responsibility for the cost of any repairs to the car if you damage it). If you don't buy the waiver, you can be charged up to 200,000$ ($1,360) worth of repairs.

Budget's least expensive car, a Renault 4, rents for a rock-bottom price of around $165.45 a week in midsummer (slightly less in wintertime). I strongly advise you to buy the optional insurance. Even if you do, the weekly total of car rental plus insurance will be around $210 a week, slightly less than for similar cars at Hertz or Avis.

One further way to save money (and this is a loophole intended only for readers who fully understand its consequences) is to pay for your car rental with a credit card from a company that agrees to pay the minimum deductible for repairs if you should have an accident. (Be sure that your original rental contract is imprinted with your credit card at the beginning of your rental.) If you fully understand the fine print of this arrangement, you may omit buying the extra insurance altogether. Be aware, however, that compensation from the credit-card company takes time, and you may have to pay some initial damage money and fill out some difficult paperwork before you are reimbursed. Check carefully with your credit-card backer for the details. American Express is the most visible of these, but by the time you read this, other credit-card companies may have followed Amex's lead. Also be aware that this loophole is available only at Budget, since Hertz and Avis require automatic purchase of collision damage waivers, which is included in the price of the rental. For reservations and information, call Budget's international department toll-free by dialing 800/472–3325. Budget has about a dozen offices scattered throughout Portugal. Its largest is the one at the Lisbon airport, which is open seven days a week. Budget's telephone number in Lisbon is 80-17-85.

Gas

Lisbon is well stocked with garages and gasoline pumps; some are open around the clock. If you're motoring in the provinces, it's best to fill up, as in some parts of the country gasoline stations are few and far between.

---

4. Lisbon Fact Facts

It's maddening to have your trip marred by an incident that could have been avoided if you'd been tipped off previously. Seeking medical care, getting your hair cut, or ferreting out the nearest toilet can at times become a paramount problem. Although I don't promise to answer all your questions, there are a variety of services in Lisbon that can ease your adjustment into the city.

The concierge in your hotel is a usually reliable dispenser of information, bullfight tickets, and general advice. However, should your hotel not be staffed with an English-speaking person, or should you desire more detailed answers to your questions, the following brief summary of basic information about Lisbon may prove helpful.

AMERICAN EXPRESS: The representative of American Express in Lisbon, **STAR Travel Service,** can accommodate most financial and travel needs. Its offices are at 4-A Avenida Sidónio Pais (tel. 53-98-71). It's open Monday to Friday from 9 a.m. to 12:30 p.m. and 2 to 6 p.m., closed Saturday and Sunday. The offices are near Pombal Square and are easily reached by bus. There you can buy tickets for tours, exchange currency, and cash American Express traveler's checks.

AREA CODES: The country code for Portugal is 351 and the city area code for Lisbon, Sintra, Estoril, and Cascais is 1. The area code for Porto is 2.

BABY-SITTERS: Check with the staff of your hotel for arrangements. Most first-class hotels can provide competent baby-sitters from lists that the concierge keeps. At smaller establishments, the sitter is likely to be the daughter of the proprietor. Rates are low. Remember to request a baby-sitter early—no later than the morning if you're planning on going out that evening.

BANKS: Check with your home bank before your departure, as many banks in Canada and the United States have affiliates in Lisbon. The majority of banks are open Monday to Friday from 8:30 a.m. to 3:30 p.m. Two major Portuguese banks are **Banco Portugues do Atlantico,** 112 Rua Aurea (tel. 346-13-21); the **Banco Espirito Santo e Comercial de Lisboa,** 195 Avenida da Liberdade (tel. 57-80-05). At the airport, the association of Portuguese banks keeps at least one of its many kiosks open 24 hours a day.

CIGARETTES: The price of American-brand cigarettes (which varies) is always high. Bring in at least 200 cigarettes as allowed by Customs. If you want to save money, try one of the Portuguese brands. Many smokers have found Portuguese tobacco excellent. One of Portugal's best-selling brands is S.G. Giant, costing 150$ ($1) per pack.

CLIMATE: The climate of Portugal is most often compared to that of California, with the rainfall occurring mostly in the winter and the summers tending to be dry. Where the border touches Spain's Galicia, Portugal is on the same latitude as New York—but there the resemblance ends, thanks to the mitigating force of the Gulf Stream.

For most tastes, spring through autumn is the best time for a Portuguese vacation. But many visitors head to the Algarve in the south in winter, when Northern Europeans find its average 60° temperatures a relief from their Arctic blasts. At Madeira, where summer temperatures are in the 70° range and winter temperatures in the 65° range, winter is high season.

From November through March, the average temperatures in

Lisbon and Estoril range between 46° and 65° Fahrenheit. June through August, the range is 60° to 82° Fahrenheit.

Lisbon's Average Daytime Temperature and Rainfall

	Jan	Feb	Mar	Apr	May	June	July	Aug	Sept	Oct	Nov	Dec
Temp. °F	57	59	63	67	71	77	81	82	79	72	63	58
Rainfall "	4.3	3.0	4.2	2.1	1.7	0.6	0.1	0.2	1.3	2.4	3.7	4.1

CLOTHING SIZES: See "Madrid Fast Facts" in Chapter VIII.

CURRENCY: Portugal is one of the most reasonably priced countries in which to travel in Europe. But first-time American visitors often panic at price quotations because Portugal uses the same dollar sign ($) to designate its currency. The Portuguese **escudo** is written as 1$00—the dollar sign between the escudo and the **centavo.** Banknotes are issued for 20, 30, 50, 100, 500, 1,000, 5,000, and 10,000 escudos. In coins of silver and copper, the denominations are 1, 2.50, 5, 10, 20, 50, and 100 escudos.

While currency conversions vary from day to day, in this guide we have used the rate of 147 escudos (147$) to $1(U.S.). Do check for the current conversion rate before you leave.

CUSTOMS: **When entering Portugal,** you may be asked how much tobacco you're bringing in: The limit is 200 cigarettes or 50 cigars. The following are allowed duty free: one still camera with five unexposed rolls of film, a small movie camera with two reels, a portable tape recorder, a portable record player with 10 "used" records, a portable typewriter, a portable radio, a portable musical instrument, and a bicycle (not motor bikes). You are allowed to bring in one tent and camping accessories (including a kayak not exceeding 18 feet), a pair of skis, two tennis rackets, a tackle set, and a small firearm (for hunting only) with 50 bullets. Be warned that even though Portuguese Customs considers it legal to import a firearm, the airline that transports it (and you) will be asked many questions when a weapon is found in your luggage. At the Portuguese border, you will be required to report your gun, fill out forms about it, and pay a cash deposit of 30,000$ ($204).

In addition to these items, a normal-sized bottle of wine and a half-pint of hard alcohol are permitted, as are a "small quantity" of perfume and a half-pint of toilet water.

When returning to the United States, citizens who have been outside the U.S. for 48 hours or more are allowed to bring in $400 worth of merchandise duty free—that is, if they have claimed no similar exemption within the past 30 days. Beyond this free allowance, the next $1,000 worth of merchandise is assessed at a flat rate of 10% duty. Goods that are valued at more than $1,400 require the payment of duty at a variety of different rates, which usually average around 12% for most tourist purchases. You can find out the rate you'll pay on specific items by referring to an up-to-date edition of *Tariff Schedules of the United States,* which is available at most libraries or at any U.S. Customs office. If you make purchases in Portugal, it's important to keep your receipts. On gifts that you mail from

Portugal to the U.S., you won't pay any duty if the value of the gift is under $50.

DENTIST: Place a call to **Centro de Medicina Dentaria,** 1 Calçada Bento da Rocha Cabral (tel. 68-41-91).

DOCUMENTS FOR ENTRY: Canadians, Americans, and the British need only a valid passport to enter Portugal.

ELECTRIC CURRENT: Many North Americans find that their plugs will not fit into sockets in Portugal or Spain, where the voltage is 200 volts AC, 50 cycles. In the unlikely event that you managed to force the plug of your appliance into the outlet, you would destroy your appliance, upset the hotel management, and possibly cause a fire. Don't try. Many hardware stores in North America sell the appropriate converters, and the concierge desks of most hotels will either lend you a converter and adapter or tell you where you can buy one nearby. If you have any doubt about whether you have the appropriate converter, ask questions at your hotel desk before you try to plug anything in.

EMBASSIES: If you lose your passport or have some other pressing problem, you'll need to get in touch with the **U.S. Embassy,** on the Avenida das Forças Armadas (à Sete Rios) (tel. 726-66-00). Hours are 8:30 a.m. to 12:30 p.m. and 1:30 to 5 p.m. If you've lost a passport, a photographer will be recommended who can provide the proper size photos for American passports.
    The **Canadian Embassy** is at Avenida da Liberdade 144 and 156, 1200 Lisboa (tel. 347-48-92), and is open Monday to Friday from 8:30 a.m. to 12:15 p.m. and 1:30 to 5 p.m.
    The **British Embassy,** 37 Rua São Domigos à Lapa, 1200 Lisboa (tel. 396-1122), is open Monday to Friday from 9:30 a.m. to 12:30 p.m. and 3 to 5 p.m.
    The **Embassy of the Republic of Ireland,** Rua de Imprensa A. Estrela s/n, 1200 Lisboa (tel. 396-1569) is open Monday to Friday from 9:30 a.m. to noon and 2:30 to 4:30 p.m.
    The **Australian Embassy,** Avenida da Liberdade 244 (second floor), 1200 Lisboa (tel. 52-33-50), is open Monday to Friday from 9 a.m. to noon.
    New Zealand does not maintain an embassy in Portugal.

EMERGENCIES: For the police (or for an ambulance) in Lisbon, telephone 115. In case of fire, call 32-22-22 or 60-60-60. The Portuguese Red Cross can be reached at 61-77-77.

FILM: This is so expensive that I suggest you bring in all that Customs will allow. There are no special restrictions on taking photographs, except in certain museums.

HAIRDRESSERS: Men are advised to go to any of the big barbershops in the deluxe hotels, such as the Ritz Inter-Continental in Lisbon. For women, two hairdressers in Lisbon are particularly recommendable: **Cabeleireiro Martins,** 31-1° Dt. Avenida Defensores de Chaves (tel. 54-89-33); and **Cabeleireiro Isabel**

Queiroz do Vale, 35-1° Avenida Fontes Pereira de Melo (tel. 54-82-38).

HOLIDAYS AND FESTIVALS: Watch those holidays and adjust your banking needs accordingly. Aside from the regular holidays such as Christmas, Portugal has a few all its own: Universal Brotherhood Day on January 1; a Memorial Day to the country's greatest poet, Camões, on June 10; Assumption Day, August 15; the anniversary of the republic, October 5; All Saints' Day on November 1; Independence Day on December 1; and the Feast of the Immaculate Conception on December 8. Good Friday and the Feast of Corpus Christi are also holidays, but their dates differ every year.

LANGUAGES: One writer suggested that Portuguese has "the hiss and rush of surf crashing against the bleak rocks of Sagres." If you don't speak it, you'll find French, Spanish, and English commonly spoken in Lisbon, along the Costa do Sol, and in Porto, as well as in many parts of the Algarve. In small villages and towns, hotel staffs and guides usually speak English.

LAUNDRY: Most hotels in this guide provide laundry services, but if you want your garment returned on the same day, you'll often be charged from 20% to 40% more. Simply present your maid or valet with your laundry or dry cleaning (usually lists are provided). *Note:* Materials needing special treatment (such as certain synthetics) should be called to the attention of the person handling your laundry. Some establishments I've dealt with in the past treated every fabric as if it were cotton.

Do-it-yourselfers in Lisbon may want to take their clothes to a self-service laundry, **Lavimpa,** 22-Á Avenida de Paris (tel. 89-03-88). Metro: Alvalade. The laundry is part of a chain.

LIBRARIES: If you're looking for a library for research or whatever, the **Biblioteca Nacional de Lisboa,** 83 Campo Grande (tel. 76-77-86), near University City, contains more than a million volumes (books, periodicals, non-book material). It is open from 9:45 a.m. to 5:30 p.m. Monday to Friday, mid-July to mid-September; from 9:45 a.m. to 8 p.m. Monday to Friday and from 9:45 a.m. to 5 p.m. on Saturday in winter. In addition, the **American Cultural Center** at 22-B Avenida Duque de Loulé (tel. 57-01-02) has a library of some 8,000 volumes and 132 periodicals. It is open from 2 to 6 p.m. on Tuesday, Wednesday, and Friday, to 7 p.m. on Monday and Thursday. Both libraries might request that you show your passport before using their collections.

LIQUOR LAWS: You have to be 18 years of age to drink liquor in the bars of Portugal. Liquor is sold in most markets, as opposed to package stores in most of the United States. In Lisbon you can drink until dawn. There's always some bar or fado club open serving alcoholic beverages.

MAIL DELIVERY: While in Portugal you may have your mail directed to your hotel (or hotels), to the American Express representative, or to General Delivery (*Poste Restante*) in Lisbon.

Your passport must be presented for mail pickups. The general post office in Lisbon is at Praça do Comércio (tel. 34-752-41 or 37-20-07).

MEDICAL CARE: Portugal does not have free medical service. The concierge at your hotel can usually put you in touch with a house doctor or summon one in case of emergencies. You can also call the **U.S. Embassy,** Avenida das Forças Armadas (à Sete Rios) (tel. 726-66-00), and ask the consular section there to give you a copy of its list of English-speaking physicians; or call the **British Hospital,** 49 Rua Savaiva Carvalho (tel. 60-20-20), where the telephone operator, staff, and doctors all speak English, naturally.

METRIC MEASURES: See "Madrid Fast Facts" in Chapter VIII.

NEWSPAPERS: The *International Herald Tribune* is sold at most newsstands in Lisbon, either in major hotels or else along the street. If you read Portuguese, the most popular centrist newspaper is the influential *Diario de Noticias.* To the right of center is *O Dia;* to the left of center is *O Dario.*

OFFICE HOURS: Hours in general are from 9 a.m. to 5 or 5:30 p.m. Most offices close between noon and 2 p.m. Most stores in Lisbon close between 1 and 3 p.m. Monday through Friday, and are closed all afternoon on Saturday and all day Sunday. The big shopping malls are open everyday of the year from 10 a.m. to midnight.

PETS: Pets brought into Portugal must have the okay of the local veterinarian and a health certificate from their home country.

PHARMACIES: The Portuguese government requires selected pharmacies (*farmácias*) to stay open at all times of the day and night. This is effected by means of a rotation system. Check with your concierge for locations and hours of the nearest drugstores, called *farmácias de serviço.* In general, pharmacies in Portugal are open Monday to Friday from 9 a.m. to 1 p.m. and 3 to 7 p.m.; Saturday from 9 a.m. to 1 p.m.; closed Sunday. A popular one is the **Farmácia Azevedos,** 31 Rossio (tel. 32-74-78).

POLITICS: The dust of the revolution has long settled. The Portuguese Republic, after years of dictatorship, is a democratic state, and tourists can travel without restrictions into every province of the land.

RADIO AND TV: In Lisbon there are two major TV channels— Channel I (VHF) and Channel II (UHF). Many foreign films are shown, often in English with Portuguese subtitles. Visitors to Portugal may want to listen to the radio every day at 8:15 a.m. when a 45-minute program—called "Holidays in Portugal"—is broadcast on the Metropolitan wavelength in English. Much helpful advice is offered for touring the country.

RELIGIOUS SERVICES: Portugal is a Catholic country, and

there are places of worship in every city, town, and village—far too numerous to document here. If you're a Protestant, a Baptist evangelical church exists in Lisbon. It's the **Igreja Evangélica Baptista de Lisboa,** 36-B Rua Filipe Folque (third floor) (tel. 53-53-62), with Sunday services in Portuguese at 10 and 11 a.m. and 7:30 p.m.; services are also at 7:30 p.m. on Wednesday. For Jewish visitors, services are usually held twice weekly at the **Shaare Tikua Synagogue,** 59 Rua Alexandre Herculano (tel. 68-15-92), on Friday at 7 p.m. and on Saturday at 10:30 a.m.

REST ROOMS: All major terminals (airports and railways) have such facilities, and Lisbon has several public ones. However, you can often use one at a café or tavern, as one of these establishments exists practically within every block. It is considered polite to purchase something, however—perhaps a small glass of wine.

SAFETY: Whenever you're traveling in an unfamiliar city or country, stay alert. Be aware of your immediate surroundings. Wear a money belt and don't sling your camera or purse over your shoulder; wear the strap diagonally across your body. This will minimize the possibility of your becoming a victim of crime. Every society has its criminals. It's your responsibility to be aware and alert even in the most heavily touristed areas.

TAXES: Since Portugal and neighboring Spain simultaneously joined the European Economic Community (EEC), or Common Market, on January 1, 1986, Portugal has imposed a value-added tax on most purchases made within its borders. Known in Portugal as the **I.V.A.,** its amount is almost always written into the bottom line of the bill for any purchase a foreign visitor might make. Hotel bills are taxed at 8%. Car rentals automatically include an additional 17% tax (less than in some other European countries). Such deluxe goods as jewelry, furs, and expensive imported liquors include a 30% built-in tax. Because a scotch and soda in a Portuguese bar carries this high tax, many imbibers have changed their choice of alcohol from scotch to Portuguese brandy and soda, or, more prosaically, beer.

To get a refund of the I.V.A. tax on those purchases that qualify (ask the shopkeeper), present your passport to the salesperson and ask for the special, stamped form. Present the form with your purchases at the booth marked for I.V.A. tax refunds at the airport. You will get your money refunded right there at the booth.

TELEGRAMS: At most hotels the receptionist will help you send a cable or telegram. If not, there is a cable dispatch service, open 24 hours a day, at **Marconi** (the Portuguese Radio Communications Office), 131 Rua S. Julião. To send telegrams from any telephone to points outside of Portugal, dial 183 to reach Marconi. To send telegrams within Portugal (and your language skills had better be good to handle this one), dial 113 from any telephone. Most foreign visitors leave the logistics of this to the concierge of their hotel, assuming that the hotel offers this service.

TELEPHONES: If you call locally in Lisbon, you can place your call at any telephone booth. Calls within Lisbon on pay phones begin at 20$ (15¢). However, you'll need some 5$, 10$, or 20$ coins if you plan to talk more than three minutes or telephone long distance in the country. For most long-distance telephoning, particularly transatlantic calls, go to the post office in Lisbon at the Praça dos Restauradores (tel. 37-00-51) or to the central post office in Praça do Comércio. Give an assistant there the number you wish, and the call will be made for you.

TELEX AND FAX: Ask your hotel for assistance.

TIME: Portugal is six hours ahead of the United States (eastern standard time). Daylight saving time (standard time plus one hour) is in effect from the last Sunday in March to the last Sunday in September.

TIPPING: The following tips on tipping are merely guidelines.

Hotels: The hotels add a service charge (known as *serviço*), which is divided among the entire staff. But individual tipping is also the rule of the day: 50$ (35¢) to the bellhop for errands run, 50$ (35¢) to the doorman who calls you a cab, 50$ (35¢) to the porter for each piece of luggage carried, 150$ ($1) to the wine steward if you've dined at your hotel, and 150$ ($1) to the chambermaid for stays of less than a week. However, in deluxe hotels, the chambermaid should get 400$ ($2.70) and the wine steward 300$ ($2.05) if you've dined at the hotel. Porters get 70$ (50¢) for each piece of luggage.

In first-class or deluxe hotels, the concierge will present you with a separate bill, outlining your little or big extras, such as charges for bullfight tickets. A gratuity is expected in addition to the charge, the amount depending entirely on the number of requests you've made.

Hairdressers: For a normal haircut, you should leave 50$ (35¢) behind as a tip to the barber. But if your hair is cut at the Ritz, don't dare leave less than 100$ (70¢). Beauticians get 150$ ($1); a manicurist, around 100$ (70¢).

Taxis: Figure on tipping about 20% of the regular fare for short runs. For longer treks—for example, from the airport to Cascais—15% is adequate.

Porters: The porters at the airport or train stations generally charge you 40$ (25¢) per piece of luggage. In addition, you should tip another 40$ (25¢).

Restaurants: Restaurants and nightclubs include a service charge and government taxes. As in the hotels, this is distributed among the entire staff, so extra tipping is customary. Add about 5% to the bill in a moderately priced restaurant, up to 10% in deluxe or first-class establishments.

Services: Hatcheck women in fado houses, restaurants, and nightclubs expect at least 50$ (35¢). Washroom attendants usually get no more than 25$ (15¢). The shoeshine boys of Portugal are the most undertipped creatures in Portuguese society. Here I recommend greater generosity, providing the shine was good.

TOURIST INFORMATION: The **Portuguese National Tourist**

Board is at 86 Avenida António Augusto de Aguiar in Lisbon (tel. 57-50-86). The public information section is housed at the Palácio Foz at Praça dos Restauradores (tel. 46-63-07 or 32-52-31), and at the Lisbon airport (tel. 88-59-74 or 89-42-48). For information or facts about Portugal before heading there, you can make contact with the **Portuguese National Tourist Office,** 590 Fifth Ave., New York, NY 10036 (tel. 212/354-4403).

HOTELS IN AND AROUND LISBON

In searching for a hotel, it's best to think of the Portuguese capital as "Greater Lisbon." Lisbon differs from most European capitals in that it can be visited on a day trip (or several day trips) from one of several attractive resorts along the Costa do Sol, such as Estoril or Cascais. Few capitals in Europe offer such resort-style accommodations so close to metropolitan life.

If you're arriving anytime between April 1 and October 1 and planning a fairly long stay, you may want to find an attractive resort hotel on the sea, venturing into Lisbon only for sightseeing excursions, fado singing, shopping, or whatever. If your stay is for only two or three days, you'll want to stay in Lisbon proper, as it takes more time to adjust to life in a resort hotel. And if your visit is in winter, you'll doubtless prefer a city lodging.

When staying along the Costa do Sol, the matter of transportation to Lisbon is taken care of by either renting a car or using the electric train system running from Cascais along the coast to Lisbon.

For easy reference, see the "Accommodations" index at the back of this book.

GOVERNMENT-CONTROLLED PRICES

In my selections—the majority of which are within Lisbon city limits—I have kept mainly to establishments the Portuguese government rates as "first-class." First-class hotels in Portugal, however, are moderate in price. Many would even be considered "budget" by some. In some cases, there is a slight distinction made between a first-class "A" hotel and a first-class "B" hotel. But often this is only a legal, technical difference that's of more interest to badge-wearing bureaucrats than to tourists.

At the reception desk of your hotel, you'll see (or should see) a sign on which the official tariffs are quoted. In Portugal, the Directorate of Tourism regulates the price a hotel owner may charge clients. To that official rate, a 10% charge is added for service, plus an additional 8% I.V.A. Usually, these add-ons are automatically quoted as part of the price before you check in, but ask to be sure.

OFF-SEASON DISCOUNTS

Off-season winter visitors find that the government requires hotels or inns along the coast—and especially in the southern province of the Algarve—to give you a reduction of at least 15% on room charges. Off-season is November to February. Many establishments, of course, grant greater reductions than this, often extending the time limit from mid-October to April 1. From November to March, hotels in Estoril grant reductions that average around 15%. Few Lisbon hotels grant off-season discounts; rates are the same year round.

The recommendations in this guide include a few of the older, more established lodgings, but generally the hotels are products of the 1960s, 1970s, and 1980s, and come complete with modern equipment and furnishings.

If the expense of a first-class accommodation is too much for a lean budget, you have an ample choice of smaller hotels where you can live inexpensively, the more so if you take all three meals at your lodging place.

---

1. Lisbon Hotels

When telephoning for information or reservations, the country code for Portugal is 351 and the area code for Lisbon—and for all the hotels listed in this chapter—is 01.

DELUXE HOTELS

The **Hotel Tivoli,** 185 Avenida da Liberdade, 1200 Lisboa (tel. 53-01-81 or toll-free 800/777-5848), is considered by the inner core of Portuguese society as the best hotel in Lisbon, and often serves as temporary home to dozens of the world's statesmen, diplomats, aristocrats, film stars, and writers. It rises from a convenient location on the most ostentatious avenue in town, a 10-minute walk uphill from the railway station, near the headquarters of Portugal's largest banks and newspapers.

The hotel was built early in the 1960s to replace a venerable 19th-century namesake legendary for World War II espionage and intrigue. The hotel today rises in a smooth sheath of stone slabs and glass. One of its many virtues is a very old walled and terraced garden, whose mature trees and gnarled wisteria were planted in the 19th century by the Marquês da Flor. Today, the garden also contains an outdoor swimming pool and tennis courts for the exclusive use of hotel guests and their friends, masses of well-tended flowering shrubs and exotic trees, a dove cote for the sheltering of cooing turtledoves, and one of the most delightful semiprivate bars in Lisbon. Black-vested waiters from the Tivoli Club serve drinks, salads, and sandwiches around the pool or within a stylish room draped from floor to ceiling in a striped fabric evocative of one of Napoleon's bivouac tents.

The hotel's enormous two-story lobby, entirely sheathed in slabs of brown Portuguese marble, is ringed with a balcony dotted with clusters of sofas and comfortable chairs.

Each of the 329 rooms (and 15 suites) contains private bathroom, direct-dial phone, radio, minibar, color TV, and mahogany reproductions of English-inspired furniture. With a breakfast buffet included, single rooms range from 24,000$ ($163.20) to 28,000$ ($190.40), doubles from 26,000$ ($176.80) to 33,000$ ($224.40). On the premises are two restaurants, including the sun-flooded O Zodiaco, where a daily luncheon buffet offers good value, and the more upscale O Terraço, whose penthouse location provides a view of Lisbon.

The **Ritz Inter-Continental,** 88 Rua Rodrigo da Fonseca, 1000 Lisboa (tel. 69-20-20), one of Lisbon's most prestigious accommodations, is now a part of Inter-Continental Hotels Corporation. You can't lose with a name like "the Ritz," especially when such a hotel lives up to its tradition. Close to everything, the 12-story modern structure faces the capital's Edward VII Park.

Four elevators serve the 300 rooms and 10 suites of the hotel, and an entire floor (30 rooms and 5 suites) has been allotted for the use of nonsmokers. Suites at the Ritz are top-drawer, furnished with antiques such as fringed canopy beds, fine Italian and Portuguese wood pieces, and inlaid desks and chairs. All the rooms are comfortable, spacious, and well kept, each with a balcony, marble bath with complete facilities and amenities, hair dryer, minibar, radio, color TV (both local and satellite), direct-dial phone, and air conditioning. The price for a single ranges from 38,000$ ($258.40) to 41,000$ ($278.80); a double rents for 42,000$ ($285.60) to 48,000$ ($326.40). A Continental breakfast and taxes are included. Suites, which include a sitting room and a dressing room, cost more.

The hotel offers a wide variety of dining choices in its three restaurants. In the Grill, classical music accompanies dinner, while music in the Varanda is furnished by Portuguese guitar players. In the Snack Ritz, guests can enjoy a fast and light meal in an agreeable atmosphere. Near the lobby is the Piano Bar.

An Executive Service Center is part of the hotel's facilities, for use by business people as a meeting place and working site.

The **Hotel Meridien,** 149 Rua Castilho, 1000 Lisboa (tel. 69-09-00), opened in 1985, takes advantage of the nearby Edward VII Park, whose verdancy is reflected in the wraparound windows that fill each of the bedrooms with Iberian sunshine. The air-conditioned lobby glitters with talc-white marble, polished chromium, and mirrors. A symmetrical entranceway frames the tile-bottomed fountains where the splashing rises to the top of the sunlit atrium.

You'll find lots of attractive and interesting public rooms, including a tearoom awash with Portuguese tiles, a ground-floor brasserie with a view of the park and the adjacent boulevard, and the formal glamorous Restaurant Atlantic. The hotel has a piano bar and a health club. The facilities are operated by a competent staff who combine French expertise with Portuguese capability.

The 331 handsomely furnished bedrooms rent for 40,000$ ($275.85) for a single, 48,000$ ($331.05) for a double, with breakfast and taxes included. Each room has air conditioning, radio, minibar, TV, and a private bathroom.

The **Lisboa-Sheraton Hotel & Towers,** 1 Rua Latino Coelho, 1000 Lisboa (tel. 57-57-57), is one of the tallest buildings in Portugal, rising 30 stories. Opened in 1972, the hotel boasts 400 bedrooms in a fine location on a prominent boulevard near Edward VII Park. The bedrooms have air conditioning, private bath, radio, color TV, direct-dial telephone, 24-hour room service, and, on the upper floors, some sweeping views of Lisbon. Singles range in price from 36,000$ ($248.30) to 48,000$ ($331.05); doubles from 42,000$ ($289.45) to 53,000$ ($365.50). The tariffs include tax and an American-style buffet breakfast. Crowning the tower-room complex is the Panorama Room and Bar overlooking the city, with a stunning view of old and new Lisbon. A buffet lunch and à la carte dinners are served in the Caravela Restaurant, and the Alfama Grill features regional Portuguese dishes. Among the facilities of the hotel are a health club, open-air heated swimming pool, shopping arcade, beauty parlor, and barbershop.

The **Hotel Alfa Lisboa,** Avenida Columbano Bordalo Pinheiro, 1000 Lisboa (tel. 726-2121), slightly removed from the commercial center of the city, lies on Lisbon's western edge, beside the avenue heading into the countryside toward Sintra. A stylishly modern five-star hotel that has gained popularity with business travelers, the hotel has a young and charming staff who work hard to make visitors comfortable. At the reception desk in the marble-floored lobby, you will be quoted rates of 17,000$ ($117.25) to 20,000$ ($137.95) for a single, 20,000$ ($137.95) to 24,000$ ($165.50) for a double, depending on the season, with taxes and breakfast included. The hotel contains 355 well-furnished bedrooms, each of which contains a minibar, air conditioning, color TV, telephone, and private bathroom.

Occupants of the hotel enjoy a selection of dining and drinking facilities. The most formal is the Pombalino Restaurant, with a decor based on that of a palatial 18th-century Portuguese manor house. A more popular, less expensive choice is A Aldeia, a coffee shop and restaurant decorated in regional and rustic Portuguese style. The Labirinto Bar, which features a pianist every night, is the hotel's most popular (and appealing) drinking spot.

The **Hotel Altis,** 11 Rua Castilho, 1200 Lisboa (tel. 52-24-96), is a five-star deluxe hotel with 225 rooms, including 13 suites, overlooking the city in the commercial and cultural center of Lisbon. Decorated on its outside with prominent horizontal bands of white marble, the hotel has a pleasant interior decor, personalized service, and a collection of meeting rooms that are frequently used by local corporations.

The bedrooms have air conditioning, direct-dial phones, minibars, radios, private bathrooms, and color TVs with satellite hookup. A new wing contains another 80 bedrooms, each with the same facilities as the older ones. Depending on the season, single rooms range from 24,000$ ($165.50) to 28,000$ ($193.10); double rooms from 28,000$ ($193.10) to 32,000$ ($220.70). Taxes, service, and buffet breakfast are included.

On the ground floor is a piano bar with live music. The Panoramic Bar and Grill Room on the top floor and the spacious Girassol Restaurant are attractive features that make your stay at the Altis a good one. The hotel also has a fully equipped health club, an indoor heated swimming pool, a coffee shop, and a disco.

FIRST-CLASS HOTELS

Tivoli Jardim, 7–9 Rua Julio Machado, 1200 Lisboa (tel. 53-99-71 or toll-free 800/777-5848), is the four-star hotel of the famous five-star Tivoli, recommended earlier in this section. Rising seven stories above landscaped grounds a few hundred yards off the Avenida da Liberdade, it offers many of the Tivoli's facilities, at somewhat less expensive prices. It also shares one of Lisbon's best-kept secrets—the walled and terraced garden that was originally laid out in the 19th century by the Marquês da Flor. On the premises are a bar and a dining room, and guests are free to meander across the parking lot for the more elegant facilities of the Hotel Tivoli. Each of the 119 bedrooms has a comfortably contemporary decor, usually with roughly plastered white walls and big windows. Each contains a color TV, minibar, direct-dial phone, air conditioning, radio, tile bathroom, and (in all but a few of the rooms) balcony. With Continental breakfast included, singles range from 12,500$ ($85) to 16,000$ ($108); doubles from 16,000$ ($108) to 19,500$ ($132.60).

There are public lounges and a cathedral-high, glass-walled lobby dominated by a ceiling-high tapestry in sunburst colors. The tile and marble floors are peacock blue and emerald green. The dining room is tasteful, with white brick walls and green tables, its wall niches filled with Portuguese ceramics. The main decorative piece is a convoluted bronze sculpture. Guests of the Tivoli Jardim can use the facilities of the Tivoli Club, described above.

The **Avenida Palace,** 123 Rua 1 de Dezembro, 1200 Lisboa (tel. 346-01-54), is Lisbon's leading hotel link to the past, a world reflected in crystal and antiques. The second-floor drawing room attracts those partial to the age of silk-brocade wall paneling, fringed velvet draperies, crystal chandeliers, marquetry tables, consoles, and hand-woven Portuguese carpets. Five tall windows in the dining room overlook the avenue. The location is noisy, right at the Rossio, minutes from fado clubs, restaurants, and some of Lisbon's major shops. Most of the 100 bedrooms have been redone. Each is furnished in a traditional, rather formal Portuguese style, with copies of 18th-century Portuguese antiques and artwork. Each accommodation contains a spacious bathroom, TV, minibar, radio, telephone, and air conditioning. Depending on the season, singles range from 18,000$ ($124.15) to 20,000$ ($137.95); doubles from 21,000$ ($144.80) to 23,000$ ($158.60). A buffet breakfast and taxes are included in the price.

Hotel Lisboa Plaza, Travessa Salitre 7 at Avenida da Liberdade, 1200 Lisboa (tel. 346-39-22), was originally constructed in

1953, but in 1988 it was literally ripped apart and reassembled under the skillful eye of one of Portugal's leading interior designers. Today, it contains many art-nouveau touches, including the embellishments of its façade and the 1900s-style bar. Adjacent to the bar is the Quinta Avenida restaurant, outfitted in shades of yellow and pink. The hotel contains 93 not-very-spacious but comfortably furnished bedrooms, each with TV (with satellite reception), minibar, air conditioning, phone, soundproof windows, and hair dryers. Depending on the season, singles range from 14,500$ ($98.60) to 19,000$ ($129.20); doubles from 17,000$ ($115.60) to 22,000$ ($149.60). An American-style buffet breakfast is included in the price.

A Converted Convent

A convent built in the 16th century, **York House,** 32 Rua das Janelas Verdes, 1200 Lisboa (tel. 396-24-35), was skillfully restored by a French lady, Mme Andrée Goldstein, and then sold to a Portuguese investor, Dr. José Tellas. It has been savored by discerning guests ever since. The location is on one of the tree-shaded streets up from the Tagus, next to the National Art Gallery. A great many professors, painters, and writers from both America and England wouldn't stay anywhere else.

You enter on a lower level, passing through iron gates, ascending steps past trailing vines and pepper trees into the patio where guests relax under fruit trees. The rooms overlook either this courtyard or the river below, with its parade of ships and tugs. The owners have ambitiously installed a private bath, telephone, and central heating in the 40 bedrooms, each of which has its own architectural shape and personality and its own selection of antiques. An additional 17 rooms, also with telephone, central heating, and private bath, lie across the street within a 17th-century town house whose accommodations have been restored in a comfortable and modern style. Guests from this residence cross the narrow street to use the restaurant and bar within the main building. The cost for a single room is 18,000$ ($124.15); for a double room, 20,400$ ($140.70). Breakfast, service, and taxes are included in the price. A luncheon or dinner in the dining room ranges from 2,500$ ($17.25) to 4,000$ ($27.60), depending on what you order from the à la carte menu.

The dining room has coved ceilings and whitewashed walls, enhanced by a touch of gilt wall sconces. There are several living rooms furnished in a personalized manner with old furniture, rare prints, high-backed leather and velvet armchairs, brass-studded chests, and fresh flowers brought in daily from the market.

Hotel Diplomático, 74 Rua Castilho, 1200 Lisboa (tel. 56-20-41), is a first-class hotel near the Ritz and Edward VII Park. The two-story-high lobby and lounge is dominated by a mural by George Bramdeiro. Spread among the 11 floors are 90 tastefully furnished and very comfortable bedrooms, each of which has modern furnishings, air conditioning, private bathroom, TV, telephone, and minibar. All but a handful have a small private balcony. Single rooms cost 14,000$ ($95.20), double rooms 16,500$ ($112.20), with buffet breakfast included. The hotel's restaurant, The Park, offers Portuguese regional specialties and an array of international dishes.

MIDDLE-BRACKET HOTELS

Hotel Príncipe Real, 53 Rua da Alegria, 1200 Lisboa (tel. 346-59-45), is a modern hotel, reached after a long, very steep climb from Avenida da Liberdade. Behind its rather impersonal façade lies a small world of fine living. It's a lot like a private villa, with a wood-burning fireplace, a bar with comfortable armchairs, a collection of handpainted tiles, a scattering of Oriental rugs, and Portuguese wood carvings.

Each of the 24 bedrooms has its own personality. Small but tasteful, each is enhanced by floral-patterned fabrics that offset the windows and comfortable beds. In addition to such niceties as fresh flowers and complementary fruit, each room has a private bathroom, satellite reception on color TVs, direct-dial phone, and 24-hour room service. Depending on the season, singles range from 13,000$ ($89.65) to 15,000$ ($103.45); doubles from 15,000$ ($103.45) to 18,500$ ($127.60). Breakfast, which is included in the price, is served every morning in a big-windowed room on the hotel's top floor, where a beamed ceiling slopes down toward a sweeping view of Lisbon.

The **Hotel Flórida,** 32 Rua Duque de Palmela, 1200 Lisboa (tel. 57-61-45), suits those desiring an anchor in the center of Lisbon life, convenient to boutiques, shops, restaurants, and discos. From the restaurant, you overlook the circular Praça de Marquês de Pombal, with its statue of the 18th-century prime minister and a bronze lion guarding the top flank of the Avenida da Liberdade. The hotel also has a bar, a large lounge on the second floor, and a glassed-in winter garden with potted plants.

The 111 bedrooms have private bath, radio, air conditioning, TV, and telephone. Depending on the season, single rooms range from 12,000$ ($82.75) to 13,000$ ($89.65), double rooms from 15,000$ ($103.45) to 17,200$ ($118.60), with service, taxes, and a buffet breakfast included.

The **Hotel Lutécia,** 52 Avenida Frei Miguel Contreiras, 1700 Lisboa (tel. 80-31-21), lies on the northern edge of Lisbon, within a shopping center. The hotel is set back from a busy thoroughfare, with a formal driveway entrance. The public lounges consume most of the first two floors. The Restaurant Panoramico is on the top floor, and there's a snack bar on the second floor.

This 12-story structure incorporates much comfort. There is air conditioning in its 151 rooms and suites, each unit has a private bath, and every guest has a private balcony. Twin beds are set against walls of fine-grained wood paneling, and the rooms all have color TV and a minibar. Singles cost 12,000$ ($82.75), doubles 15,250$ ($105.10), with service, taxes, and a buffet breakfast included.

The **Hotel Mundial,** 4 Rua Dom Duarte, 1100 Lisboa (tel. 86-31-01), is a modern hotel in the heart of Lisbon, close to the Alfama. The hotel is properly manicured and serviced by a capable staff. On the top floor is a dining room offering a panoramic view of Lisbon, with St. George Castle in the background.

Each of the 147 rooms is equipped with a tile bath, phone, radio, color TV with satellite reception, and air conditioning. Depending on the season, single rooms cost from 9,800$ ($67.60) to 12,000$ ($82.75), doubles from 12,000$ ($82.75) to 14,600$ ($100.70), with Continental breakfast and all taxes included. The most expensive rooms have a private terrace.

The **Dom Manuel I,** 187–189 Avenida Duque d'Avila, 1100 Lisboa (tel. 57-61-60), is for those who desire a high standard of living at a reasonable price. Its location is a little off-center, but not its taste. A little hotel, it has a rear lounge styled as in a fine private home, with an Aubusson tapestry, a raised fireplace, and sofas and armchairs. A window looks out onto a planter of subtropical greenery. The intimate mezzanine cocktail lounge, with decorative brass fixtures, overlooks the living room. The lower-level dining room is in the typically Iberian style, with leather armchairs, tall candle torchères, and a large stained-glass rose window.

The 64 bedrooms, although small, are consistently winning, each containing private bathroom, telephone, TV, and air conditioning. With taxes and a Continental breakfast included in the price, singles cost 12,000$ ($82.75); doubles 14,500$ ($100).

The **Hotel Rex,** 169 Rua Castilho, 1000 Lisboa (tel. 68-21-61), is a fine establishment in a desirable location, a few steps from the Ritz and the Hotel Meridien. It offers warmly decorated accommodations at prices far below those of its prestigious neighbors. Many of the rooms have a spacious balcony, with views over Edward VII Park and the baroque Manueline church on its far side.

From the large front windows of the elegant lobby, an unusual bronze statue of women bearing baskets is visible. The coffered wood-and-plaster ceiling adds the illusion of even greater height to the room. A panoramic restaurant on the hotel's top floor offers a view of one of Lisbon's most beautiful parks as well as of the city below.

Each of the 70 cozy bedrooms contains a private bathroom, minibar, TV, radio, air conditioning, telephone, and built-in bed (or beds). If you take one of the suites, you'll also enjoy a sitting room with its own breeze-swept terrace. Rooms are priced at 14,400$ ($99.30) for a single and 18,000$ ($124.15) for a double, with breakfast, service, and taxes included.

Hotel Fénix, 8 Praça Marquês de Pombal, 1200 Lisboa (tel. 53-51-21), enjoys a front-row position on the circular plaza dedicated to the 18th-century prime minister of Portugal. A modern hotel, which at press time was systematically upgrading many of its bedrooms, the Fénix is managed by the Iberian hotel chain, HUSA. From many of its 125 bedrooms you can view the trees on the avenues radiating out from the plaza below, and the greenery of Edward VII Park. Each contains telephone, air conditioning, TV with video movies, private bathroom, and minibar. By the time of your arrival, a diminishing handful of yet-to-be-renovated rooms may qualify for a 20% discount. The renovated bedrooms begin at 14,000$ ($96.55) for a single, 16,250$ ($112.05) for a double. Breakfast and taxes are included in the price.

BEST FOR THE BUDGET

The **Hotel Dom Carlos,** 121 Avenida Duque de Loulé, 1000 Lisboa (tel. 53-90-71), is a cool and inviting choice, set back from a busy boulevard and separated from the street by a small garden in which canna and daisies bloom. An all-modern, 73-room, glassed-in structure, the Dom Carlos lies just off Marquês de Pombal Square, in the center of Lisbon. Around the corner is a service station and a garage belonging to the hotel. A favorite spot is the cozy mezzanine bar, ideal for a rendezvous. The staff and management are attentive and courteous.

The bedrooms are paneled with a reddish South American wood. Cleverly compact, the rooms utilize built-in pieces well and come with air conditioning, TV, telephone, minibar, and private bathroom. With a Continental breakfast, service, and tax included, singles range from 8,750$ ($60.40) to 10,500$ ($72.40), doubles from 10,800$ ($74.50) to 13,000$ ($89.65), depending on the season.

Hotel Jorge V, 3 Rua Mouzinho da Silveira, 1200 Lisboa (tel. 56-25-25), wraps up comforts and little amenities and ties them with a ribbon of modest prices. Just off the Avenida da Liberdade, in the heart of the shopping district, the "George V" is both modern and comfortable. Built in 1963, it provides balconies for about half of the 49 rooms. Light sleepers may prefer the quieter chambers in the rear, although none of these has a balcony. You register in a miniature reception lobby, near a bar/lounge with comfortable chairs and sofas.

Each bedroom contains soft beds, built-in wardrobes, bedside tables and reading lights, telephone, a small tile-sheathed bath, and TV. All but two or three of the rooms have air conditioning. Depending on the season, singles cost from 7,200$ ($49.65) to 8,400$ ($57.95), doubles from 9,000$ ($62.05) to 10,800$ ($74.50), with breakfast and taxes included.

The **Albergaria da Senhora do Monte,** 39 Calçada do Monte, 1100 Lisboa (tel. 86-28-46), is perched on a hilltop belvedere in the Graça section, at a spot where knowing Lisboans like to take their guests for a view of their city. Once a small rambling apartment house, the hotel has been converted to provide unique guest bedrooms, each with a sense of style. Multilevel corridors lead to the 28 bedrooms; a few have a private terrace, and each has a private bathroom and a telephone. Decorator touches abound, as reflected by the grass-cloth walls, the tile baths (one with 18th-century *azulejos* rescued from an old villa), and solid bronze fixtures. With a Continental breakfast, taxes, and service included, a single rents for 9,000$ ($62.05), a double for 12,000$ ($82.75), and a suite for two occupants for 13,200$ ($91.05). The bar on the top floor has a sweeping view over the rooftops of Lisbon.

The **Hotel Presidente,** 13 Rua Alexandre Herculano, 1100 Lisboa (tel. 53-95-01) is located on a convenient, central corner near the Avenida da Liberdade and Edward VII Park. The Presidente is so clean-cut and modern that the effect is stark. Built in the early 1970s, the hotel is small enough to avoid staffs that overpower and intimidate. It contains only 59 comfortably unpretentious rooms, each of which has private bath, telephone, and air conditioning. By the time of your visit, thanks to an improvement program that was in effect at press time, the hotel might have added TV and minibar too. The rooms are compact, with chestnut-paneled walls and furniture more functional than stylish.

Depending on the season, with Continental breakfast included, single rooms rent for between 8,500$ ($58.60) and 10,200$ ($70.35), doubles for between 10,200$ ($70.35) and 12,250$ ($84.50). No meals other than breakfast are served.

The **Hotel Príncipe,** 201 Avenida Duque d'Avila, 1000 Lisboa (tel. 53-61-51), originally built early in the 1960s, is a favorite of visiting Spanish and Portuguese matadors. Each of the hotel's 67 large and simply furnished rooms contains private bathroom, TV, telephone, and radio. About half have air conditioning, and many of them open onto their own balconies. With Continental breakfast included, singles cost 7,800$ ($53.80), doubles 9,600$ ($66.20). The matadors seem to like the lobby-level bar and the hotel's pleasant dining room, located one floor above street level.

EVEN CHEAPER ACCOMMODATIONS

Built as an apartment house, the **Residência Horizonte,** 42 Avenida António Agusto de Aguiar, 1000 Lisboa (tel. 53-95-26), has an impressively proportioned flight of stone steps leading up from the busy tree-lined boulevard outside. As you enter, the lower-level reception area is at the bottom of a short flight of stairs. What used to be the elegant lobby of the building is a bit grim today. Nonetheless, the 52 rooms upstairs are clean, freshly scrubbed, and unpretentiously comfortable. A few of them have balcony and TV, and each contains a private bathroom and telephone. With breakfast included, single rooms cost 6,000$ ($41.35); doubles 7,200$ ($49.65). The units in the back are a little less sunny than those at the front, but they are also quieter.

The **Residência América,** 47 Rua Tomás Ribeiro, 1000 Lisboa (tel. 352-11-77), was built as a bank about 40 years ago and became a comfortable, simple hotel through later renovation. Each of the 56 bedrooms contains a private bath and a telephone. The 1950s-style accommodations all differ in layout and size. The quiet rooms in back are somewhat smaller and darker than those in the front. Prices quoted are from 5,500$ ($37.95) to 6,600$ ($45.50) for a single, and from 6,200$ ($42.75) to 7,400$ ($51.05) for a double, with breakfast included.

No visitor to the América should leave without checking out the seventh-floor bar, whose leatherette furniture has been there so long that by now it's back in style, giving a note of nostalgia to a stay here. There's a restaurant adjacent to the bar.

The **Residência Imperador,** 55 Avenida 5 de Outubro, 1000 Lisboa (tel. 352-4884), is located in the northern part of Lisbon, within a five-minute walk of the Gulbenkian museum. The front entryway, designed in Portuguese pinewood, is barely large enough for one's suitcase; however, the bedrooms and upper lounge are adequate in size. Opening onto balconies, the front bedrooms face a tiny private garden. The units are contemporary in concept, neatly planned with built-in beds and simple lines. Muted colors are used on the walls and in the fabrics. Each of the 43 rooms contains a telephone and a private bathroom. With breakfast included, single rooms cost 6,000$ ($41.40), double rooms 6,700$ ($46.20). On the top floor is an airy public room and terrace with a glass front where breakfast is served. Tram 1 or 21 and the Metro (Saldanha station) can whisk you into the city center.

2. A Belém Inn

Now a suburb of Lisbon, Belém once had its own share of greatness. Here the Portuguese built the ships to sail on their voyages of discovery. Today Belém still has its share of charm. It's an attractive little town in its own right, filled with regional restaurants. And since it happens to be the site of the major sight-seeing attractions near the Portuguese capital, it is rarely missed by visitors.

A BUDGET CHOICE

The **Hotel da Torre,** 8 Rua dos Jerónimos, 1400 Lisboa, Belém (tel. 363-01-61), is suitable primarily for those who want to be in Lisbon's museum belt. The renovated inn, which contains 52 rooms, rises three stories and is furnished in a comfortable regional style. The modern lobby contains sunken seating areas, overhead balconies, and an innovative design with many horizontal lines washed with sunlight from the big front windows.

Each of the accommodations contains a private bathroom, TV, and telephone, but air conditioning is confined to the public rooms, the wood-paneled bar, and the restaurant, where regional and international food is offered. Singles range from 7,000$ ($48.30) to 7,400$ ($51.05), doubles from 9,000$ ($62.05) to 10,000$ ($68.95), with breakfast and taxes included.

3. A Carcavelos Hotel

The **Hotel Praia-Mar,** 16 Rua do Gurué, Carcavelos, 2775 Parede (tel. 247-31-31), is a modern palace of angular design, with recessed balconies. A private world unfolds behind the plant-bordered walls separating the elliptical swimming pool from the street outside. Unlike some of the other hotels on the coast, the Praia-Mar is in a quiet neighborhood a few blocks from the four-lane highway cutting along the coast and a 10-minute walk south of the Carcavelos railway station. The lobby, fashioned from white marble, is somewhat sparsely furnished with upholstered leather armchairs, many of which face the large windows leading toward the sun-bathed swimming pool. There's a bar on the eighth floor and another in a secluded corner of the lobby.

Each of the 158 bedrooms has a balcony, usually with a view toward the sea, along with a pleasing combination of contemporary and Iberian-inspired furniture. Each contains a telephone and a private bathroom. Single rooms cost around 12,000$ ($82.75), doubles 13,500$ ($93.10), with breakfast, service, and taxes included. The restaurant on the hotel's eighth floor serves well-prepared meals costing from 3,500$ ($24.15).

4. Sintra Hotels

THE TOP HOTEL

The finest hotel in Sintra is the modern, airy **Hotel Tivoli Sintra,** Praça da República, 2710 Sintra (tel. 923-35-05 or toll-free 800/777-5848), opened in 1981. It lies only a few doors to the right of the National Palace. The hotel offers an abundance of modern conveniences, including a garage (most important in Sintra). However, the decorator stuck to the *típico* Portuguese style in the decor, and the combination of modern and traditional is successful.

Each of the 74 bedrooms is air-conditioned and contains a terrace or balcony, private bathroom, TV with English-language news broadcasts, minibar, radio, telephone, easy chairs for relaxing, and large comfortable beds. Balconies look out over a view of the elegant villas and forested hillsides of Sintra.

In high season, singles cost 13,200$ ($91.05), doubles 15,800$ ($108.95). Prices include a Continental breakfast; parking in the hotel's garage is free for guests. The hotel has a good restaurant and bar, a beauty parlor, a travel agency, and a cooperative staff.

A CONVERTED PALACE IN SETEAIS

The **Palácio de Seteais,** 8 Rua Barbosa do Bocage, 2710 Sintra (tel. 923-32-00), is a small palace converted in 1956 into an elegant hotel. Lodged in the hills adjoining Sintra—it is approached by an encircling avenue of shade trees and a clipped yew hedge—its twin formal buildings are linked by an ornate towering gate. The estate was built at the end of the 18th century by a Dutch gildemeister, then restored by the fifth Marquês de Marialva, who used it for lavish parties and receptions. Even its gardens are appropriate for its regal interior.

A lightness, a sense of joy, pervades the interior—there's nothing stuffy about this palace. You enter a long galleried hallway, with white columns and a balustraded staircase leading to the lower-level drinking salon and the L-shaped dining room. Along the corridors are several tapestries, groupings of antiques, and hand-woven Portuguese carpets.

Unfolding before you are a music salon, a sedate library, and a main drawing room overlooking the countryside so beloved by Byron. There are only 18 rooms, so reservations are imperative. Each contains a private bathroom and a telephone. Even the simplest chamber has taste, charm, and a form of grandeur that is carefully supervised by Portugal's finest hotel chain, the Tivoli group. In high season, the tariffs, with breakfast included, range from 30,000$ ($206.90) to 36,000$ ($248.30) for a double, 28,200$ ($194.50) for a single. Taxes and service are also included.

On the premises are a swimming pool, gardens, and two tennis courts.

Meals are events here; many Portuguese travel for miles just to dine here. (See the restaurant chapter immediately following.) Full-board rates are available, but many visitors prefer to sample other restaurants in Sintra during their stay as well.

5. Costa do Sol Hotels

ESTORIL HOTELS

About 15 miles west of Lisbon, Estoril—with its splendid, cabaña-studded beaches—is one of the most fashionable resorts of Europe. Raymond Postgate wrote that it has "everything Cannes has except a film festival."

Much of the history of Estoril is associated with Fausto Figueiredo and his deluxe Hotel Palácio. His vision of a chic seaside resort in Estoril predated World War I. And in the 1930s, with the opening of the hotel, Estoril began attracting a steady stream of international visitors. During World War II, spies—both Allied and Nazi—thronged through the rooms of the Palácio and the nearby casino.

Since rebuilt, the casino remains a potent attraction. In the center of the resort is the Parque Estoril with its sweep of palms and subtropical gardens extending from the casino to the shore road. But to many the major attraction of Estoril is its golf course.

A Deluxe Choice

Receiving guests since 1930, the **Hotel Palácio do Estoril,** Parque Estoril, 2765 Estoril (tel. 268-04-00), won its fame as a haven for royalty. The two-story entrance hall is grand indeed, with handsome furnishings, hand-woven carpets, and fine paintings. You walk along a series of intimate salons, with Wedgwood paneling, large chandeliers glittering with sparkling prisms, fluted pilasters, and arched windows opening onto the large garden and lawn. The main drawing room, with its classic columns and black-and-white marble floors, is a stately place for after-dinner coffee accompanied by soft piano music. The dining room is a proper backdrop for impeccable service and good-tasting food. There is also the Grill Four Seasons, an outstanding evening-only à la carte restaurant (open every night from 8 to 11 p.m., reservations necessary), where both Portuguese and French cuisine are served in an atmosphere of class and distinction. The center of pre-dinner life is the bar, also in neoclassic decor. On the pool terrace, under a border of shaped bougainvillea, guests gather for breakfast or a buffet lunch.

The 165 bedrooms are elegantly conservative, some with brass beds, a dressing table, and a double wardrobe. Many rooms have a balcony with a view of the pool. Each contains a private bathroom, air conditioning, TV, telephone, minibar, and lots of extras. In high season (mid-March through October), bed-and-breakfast rates for singles are 30,000$ ($206.90) to 34,800$ ($240), 32,400$ ($223.45) to 38,000$ ($262.05) for doubles, depending on the accommodation; service and taxes are included. Of course, the air-conditioned duplex suites overlooking the pool cost more. Off-season, all tariffs are lowered. Everything is run expertly, supervised by the general manager, Manuel Quintas.

The bonus—for golfers—is the 9- and 18-hole course in the foothills of Sintra, bordered by pine woods, about a three-minute drive from the hotel. Guests of the Palácio are granted a temporary membership. A further attraction is the seven tennis courts, three floodlighted for night games, located immediately next door to the hotel.

Fronting Estoril Park, the hotel is but a short walk from either the water or the casino.

The Middle Bracket

The tastefully modern little **Hotel Alvorada,** 3 Rua de Lisboa, 2765 Estoril (tel. 268-00-70), is directly opposite the grand entrance to the casino. What makes staying here so special is the attractiveness of the rooms, plus such facilities as a solarium and a private garage. The decor combines modern with provincial: carved country pieces, simple wall colors, wooden screens used as dividers, lounge chairs, and coffee tables. Each of the 55 rooms contains a private bathroom, color TV, and telephone. Depending on the season, single rooms range from 3,500$ ($24.15) to 6,600$ ($45.50), doubles from 5,000$ ($34.50) to 11,500$ ($79.30), with breakfast, service, and taxes included. A few of the rooms can be air-conditioned, although most visitors prefer to open their windows to the sea breezes instead. If you request air conditioning, it will cost an additional 2,000$ ($13.80) per day.

Estalagem Belvedere, 8 Rua Dr. António Martins, 2765 Estoril (tel. 298-91-63), built as a private villa during the Edwardian age, was converted into a charming hotel around 30 years ago. This English-owned establishment offers 24 bedrooms, each with a private bath and telephone, some with TV. Throughout the year, single rooms cost 6,700$ ($45.55), doubles from 8,100$ ($55.10) to 10,500$ ($71.40), with breakfast included. The hotel is in a gracious neighborhood of faded 19th-century residences, among century-old trees and gardens, about a five-minute walk uphill from the beach. There's a pool sunk into the garden, surrounded by a terrace. Inside, the comfortable public rooms contain Iberian furnishings, a cozy bar filled with rustic bric-a-brac, and a dining room serving dinner only, every night between 7:15 and 10 p.m.

A MONTE ESTORIL HOTEL

Monte Estoril, with its many hotels, is a satellite of Estoril, sprawling across the slope of a hill, offering vistas of the Bay of Cascais.

Right at the center of this hillside resort, within a white and moss-green tower jutting skyward above a neighborhood of 19th-century villas, is the **Hotel Zenith,** 1 Rua Belmonte, 2765 Estoril (tel. 268-02-02). On the premises you'll find a rectangular swimming pool, a ground-floor bar, and a wood-burning fireplace for nippy evenings. Each of the 48 bedrooms contains a TV, private bath, telephone, and radio. Those on the sea side have a little balcony; others, a bay window. The furnishings are tasteful and restrained. In high season, with breakfast included, singles cost 11,100$ ($76.55), doubles, 14,800$ ($102.05). During the low season, (between November and April) reductions of up to 50% are usually offered. English is spoken here. The hotel lies within a two-minute walk north of the main artery of Monte Estoril, the Strada Marginale, and about a five-minute walk north of the town's railway station.

CASCAIS HOTELS

Special Hotels

Estoril Sol Hotel, Parque Palmela, 2750 Cascais (tel. 28-28-31), faces the ocean on the eastern edge of Cascais, halfway between the center of Cascais and the center of Monte Estoril. It is the largest, most elaborate, and most all-encompassing resort hotel in the region. Considered a Portuguese showcase of glamor, service, and style, it contains 350 bedrooms and the largest dining room on the Costa do Sol. Built in 1969, it offers 20 floors of elegant bedrooms, each of which opens onto a balcony and about 80% of which have views of the sea. Depending on the season, singles range from 19,500$ ($132.60) to 23,000$ ($156.40); doubles from 22,500$ ($153) to 30,000$ ($204). Each of the accommodations contains conservatively traditional furnishings, air conditioning, a safe for locking up your valuables, TV with in-house movies, minibar, and telephone. *Warning:* In the lower rooms facing the sea, you'll be aware of the busy coastal traffic, so ask for a lodging on a higher floor. Facilities include an elegant grill room, a coffee shop, a health center, squash courts, at least five bars, a nightclub/disco, and a swimming pool with an adjoining café.

The Hotel Albatroz, 100 Rua Frederico Arouca, 2750 Cascais (tel. 28-28-21), takes its name from the wandering albatross, a bird noted as a master of gliding flight, capable of staying airborne on motionless wings for hours at a time. Positioned on a ledge of rocks just above the ocean, the hotel seems to float over the water like its namesake. This is the most delectable treasure along the Costa do Sol, a "good luck" choice whether you're seeking rooms or food.

The Albatroz is centered around a neoclassic villa built as a luxurious holiday retreat for the Duke of Loulé and acquired in the 19th century by the Count and Countess de Foz. Sometime in the present century it was converted into an inn, and in time received such guests as Anthony Eden, Cary Grant, the Duke and Duchess of Bedford, Claudette Colbert, William Holden, and Prince Rainier and Princess Grace visited on more than one occasion.

Today the hotel has benefited from a tastefully elegant refurbishing that incorporates a lavish use of tiles in garlanded patterns of blue and yellow, acres of white latticework, and expanses of panoramic glass, through which you can see dozens of fishing boats bobbing at anchor. The stone-trimmed main structure has been expanded with a series of balconied additions, each containing some of the 40 elegant bedrooms.

Depending on the season and the exposure, singles cost 15,000$ ($102) to 31,000$ ($210.80), doubles 18,000$ ($122.40) to 36,500$ ($248.20). An oval swimming pool nestles alongside the sun terrace between the new and old wings. Dining here is a worthwhile experience.

A unique resort hotel, the **Hotel do Guincho,** Praia do Guincho, 2750 Cascais (tel. 285-04-91), is the remake of a 17th-century fortress, standing high on a rocky coast, near Cabo da Roca on the westernmost tip of the European continent. The Portuguese regard it as a honeymooner's hotel, and, as such, it is not recommended for singles. Its stark-white exterior in no way reveals the opulence and high-fashion taste reflected inside. The inner court-yard is encircled by a colonnade of stone arches, with potted sub-tropical plants and flowers.

Inside, the stone coved ceilings, the Romanesque arches, the curving staircases, the heavy beams, and the baronial fireplaces have been preserved. Furnishings and trappings both handsome and har-monious add to the ambience. These include large gilt ecclesiastical sculptures, Portuguese tapestries, oil paintings, and hand-woven rugs.

Each of the 36 bedrooms contains a minibar, color TV, tele-phone, private bathroom, and air conditioning. Several have a balcony, and everywhere the thick stone of the walls and portals re-mind you of the purpose for which the place was originally built. High-season rates are in effect from April to the end of October. With breakfast included, singles cost 21,500$ ($148.30), doubles 27,000$ ($186.20). Half board can be arranged for an additional charge of 3,500$ ($24.15) per person per day.

Even if you can't stay here, try to visit for a meal, costing around 4,000$ ($27.60), plus wine. The spacious ocean-view din-ing room has regal touches, with hand-embroidered draperies, high-backed red chairs, and overscale antique armoires. The food is im-peccable, the service the same. Watching the maître d'hôtel flambé a peach is worth the trek up from Lisbon, which is 20 miles away.

The **Cidadela,** Avenida 25 de Abril, 2750 Cascais (tel. 28-29-21), is a gem. It is set on a knoll, with six floors of balcony bedrooms overlooking an enclosed garden and swimming pool. The lounges and dining room have been furnished with both restraint and good taste, plus a sense of the best of Portuguese decor. You may never make it to the beach once you discover the thatched bar and pool-side restaurant at one end of the garden. Two blocks from the center of Cascais, the "Citadel" offers 128 rooms, suites, or apartments, each of which contains a private bathroom, color TV with at least seven different channels, telephone, minibar, and balcony. In high season, single rooms cost 17,500$ ($119), double rooms 19,000$ ($129.20). An American-style breakfast is included in the price. The rear rooms, sheltered from the noise of traffic, are preferable. Suites and apartments are more expensive, of course. Half board can be arranged for an additional 3,000$ ($20.40) per person per day.

The Middle Bracket

One of the loveliest hotels in the region, the **Estalagem Se-nhora da Guia,** Strada do Guincho, 2750 Cascais (tel. 28-92-39), was a villa built in 1970 by heirs of the Sagres brewery fortune, who fled to Brazil, allowing the house to fall into ruin until it was rescued by the Ornelas family, who now own and run it. The thick walls, high ceilings, and elaborately crafted moldings give the impression of a much older structure, and the restoration has capitalized on that fact through use of antiques and period reproductions throughout.

Because of the villa's position on a bluff above the sea, the views are excellent. Breakfast is served buffet style under parasols at the edge of the swimming pool. Lunches and dinners are offered be-neath a ceiling of African hardwood in a formal dining room that remains cool even on the hottest days, thanks to its thick walls and terra-cotta floors.

Each of the establishment's 28 elegant bedrooms is tastefully furnished with copies of 18th-century Portuguese pieces, thick carpets, and louvered shutters. Each has a modern, spacious bathroom, a color TV, and a telephone, and room service is available throughout the day. Ten of the accommodations are air-conditioned. In high season, double rooms cost from 26,500$ ($182.75) to 30,000$ ($206.90), with breakfast included; suites cost 36,000$ ($248.30). Occupants of single rooms receive a token 500$ ($3.50) discount off the price of a double. An extra bed can be set up in any double room for 3,500$ ($24.15). Prices are reduced in off-season.

RESTAURANTS IN AND AROUND LISBON

1. DINING IN LISBON
2. DINING IN SINTRA
3. DINING IN BELÉM
4. DINING IN CASCAIS

Early British visitors spoke contemptuously of the Portuguese diet they encountered. They claimed the Portuguese sustained themselves on cod, but thrived on their dreams. Codfish, in fact, is the national dish, prepared in hundreds of ingenious ways. For instance, there's **bacalhau** (salted codfish). When you see the different ways it's cooked and how it's savored by the locals, you'll know why the Portuguese speak of bacalhau as *o fiel amigo* (faithful friend).

Another Portuguese specialty is **caldeirada,** described to visitors as a "fishermen's stew" or the "Portuguese bouillabaisse." This savory kettle of goodness is made with at least four different types of fish, even in simple establishments. The fish is cooked with onions and tomatoes, but many contain nearly a dozen different vegetables.

Portuguese **sardines,** packed in tins with olive oil, are shipped around the world. One of the best sardine dishes is sardinhas assadas (grilled). In the Alfama, some housewives cook the sardines over an open brazier in front of their doorways.

As you've gathered by now, the item to order in Portugal is fish. Even in the simplest tavern, it's likely to be fresh and abundant—all except shellfish. Portuguese **lagosta** (crayfish) was once served commonly throughout the land, almost as a side course. But in recent years catches have yielded less and less, and foreign markets have demanded more and more. Because the price of crayfish varies from day to day and is quite expensive, it is rarely listed on the menu, so inquire about the price before ordering it.

Meat tends to be inferior in Portugal, especially beef and veal. However, acorn-fattened porco (pork) is tender and packed with flavor. A real banquet is **porco alentejano** (pork in the style of the province of Alentejo—fried and coated with a savory sauce of clams and mussels, often accompanied by bay-leaf-flavored tomatoes and onions). Another good dish, popular in taverns with beer, is **bife na frigideria** (steak with mustard sauce), but you might want to forgo its usual accompaniment, a fried egg.

Many a peasant has staved off hunger with **tripe** cooked with fat white beans and flavored with bits and pieces of pungent sausage. **Iscas** is also good—calves' liver thinly cut and coated with onions.

A Portuguese specialty, with infinite regional variations, is **cozido** (a boiled dinner including beef and pork as well as cabbage, bacon, sausages, potatoes, and other greens—almost anything the chef has in abundance). Lamb is poor, but a savory treat is **cabrito** (roast kid), especially when it's prepared in the style of the province of Alentejo.

Portuguese **dining hours** are between 1 and 2 p.m. for lunch, between 7:30 and 9 p.m. for dinner. Of course, meals may be served both earlier and later at some establishments.

To help you select a restaurant by location, price range, or cuisine, there is a "Restaurant" index in the back of this book.

---

1. Dining in Lisbon

DELUXE CHOICES

Restaurante Aviz, 12-8 Rua Serpa Pinto (tel. 32-83-91), for many years reigned supreme as the most prestigious—and the finest—restaurant in Portugal. Today its position has been seriously challenged by other fast-rising establishments, and many readers have complained about the service, food, and prices. Nevertheless, it should be noted that many respected food critics still consider it the best choice in Lisbon.

Today you encounter an old-world aura as you enter the reception lounge for a before-dinner drink. There is a private-club atmosphere of green marble columns, black leather chairs, crystal chandeliers, and a pair of paintings of respectable nudes.

The dining room consists of three communicating salons. The two smaller rooms are more intimate, the larger one more animated. To begin your meal, try, if featured, the espadon fumé, razor-thin slices of smoked swordfish served with half a lemon wrapped in white gauze. Its delicacy is memorable. My most recent duck had an orange sauce that was bittersweet with shredded orange peel, and the dish was accompanied by light, crisp potato croquettes. Crêpes Avis, stuffed with ice cream, flambéed in kirsch, and covered with whipped cream, is a popular dessert. Sipping Portuguese coffee from tiny Vista Alegre cups is an appropriate way to conclude a meal.

Your bill, discreetly presented in a leather folder, is likely to come to 7,000$ ($48.25) or a whole lot more. The Aviz is open Monday to Friday from 1 to 3 p.m. and 8 to 10:30 p.m.; Saturday from 8 to 10:30 p.m.

Tagide, 18 Largo da Academia Nacional de Belas Artes (tel. 32-07-20), is a distinguished place to dine in the Chiado. Its situation is colorful—up from the docks, on a steep hill on a ledge overlooking the old part of Lisbon and the Tagus. Once the town house of a diplomat, then a leading nightclub, it is now one of Lisbon's leading restaurants. Some gourmets say it serves the finest food in town.

It's very old, with a museum look to it. You go up marble steps with shiny brass balustrades. The dining room has picture windows overlooking moored ships and the port. Set into the white plaster walls are overscale figures made of blue and white tiles, each depicting a famous queen. The chairs are provincial and the tablecloths have hand-crocheted edges. Glittering above are crystal chandeliers.

Both Portuguese dishes of quality as well as selections from the international repertoire are featured and beautifully served. For an appetizer, try the salmon pâté, cold stuffed crab, or smoked swordfish. Other specialties include suprême of halibut with coriander, pork with clams and coriander, and grilled baby goat with herbs. For dessert, I recommend the stuffed crêpes Tagide. Expect to spend from 5,000$ ($34.50) plus the cost of your wine. Food is served Monday to Friday from noon to 2:30 p.m. and 7:30 to 10:30 p.m.; Saturday from noon to 2:30 p.m. It's important to reserve a table in advance.

António Clara, 38 Avenida da República (tel. 76-63-80), another of the capital's best-rated restaurants, is in an exquisite turn-of-the-century villa that was once the home of one of Portugal's most revered architects, Miguel Ventura Terra. Built in 1890 by and for its designer, the interior has Ventura Terra's photograph hanging amid polished antiques and gilded mirrors. The angled and tiled wings of the villa seem to embrace visitors as they approach the Moorish-influenced façade.

Before going to the dining room, one of the loveliest in Lisbon, you can enjoy a drink in the 19th-century salon, where griffins snarl down from their position on the pink-shaded chandelier. In the dining room, the efficient staff make wine tasting a ceremony. Full meals, priced from 6,000$ ($41.40), include such specialties as smoked swordfish, cheese soufflé, paella for two, chateaubriand béarnaise, codfish Clara style, tournedos "symphony," and beef Wellington.

The restaurant is open Monday to Saturday, from 12:30 to 3 p.m. and 7:30 to 11:30 p.m. Reservations are very important. There's a ground-floor bar, accessible through its own entrance, where you can have an after-dinner drink.

Restaurante Clara, 49 Campo dos Mártires da Pátria (tel. 57-04-34), is an elegant hideaway in a green tile house on a quiet hillside amid decaying villas and city squares. It was opened a few years ago by a quartet of Portuguese businessmen. You might enjoy a drink under the ornate ceiling of the bar; at lunchtime, you may prefer a seat near the plants and fountain of the garden terrace. At night, an indoor location—perhaps near the large marble fireplace—is more appealing. A piano is played softly during dinner.

Menu specialties include tournedos Clara, stuffed rabbit with red wine sauce, four different kinds of pasta, codfish Clara, lobster crêpes, filet of sole with orange, pheasant with grapes, cheese soufflé, filet Wellington, and Valencian paella. Full meals, costing from 6,000$ ($41.40), are served Monday to Friday from noon to 3:30 p.m. and 7 p.m. to midnight; Saturday from 7 p.m. to midnight.

OTHER TOP RESTAURANTS

Escorial, 47 Rua Portas de S. Antão (tel. 346-44-29), has an exclusive club aura, rich in wood paneling from South America, opera-red carpets and tablecloths, plus sedate, but attentive, service. Near the Rossio, it offers excellent Portuguese cookery, attracting a steady clientele of business people and out-of-towners, even owners of fashionable villas out at Cascais. The English menu helps the foreigner. A good opener is steamed clams in the Cataplana style, followed by sea bass cooked "the Portuguese way." If you want something more festive, you can order a barbecue of lamb or spring chicken on the spit. It's good to finish off with a peach Melba. Expect to pay from 3,500$ ($24.15) to 5,500$ ($37.95) for a dinner here. Try to reserve a table for this centrally located establishment, right in the heart of the city. It's open seven days a week from noon to 1:30 a.m.

Michel, 5 Largo de Santa Cruz do Castelo (tel. 86-43-38), is the most fashionable restaurant in the Alfama. On a tiny plaza near St. George's Castle, this popular first-class restaurant serves Continental cuisine prepared under the watchful eye of Michel da Costa, the restaurant's Moroccan-born owner and chef. Tempting Continental specialties include smoked swordfish, several versions of codfish, seaweed-flavored sea bass, a succulent version of lamb chops (for two diners), and black bass "Don Fernando." One especially recommendable main dish is green-pepper duck. For dessert, the apple tart Michel is favored. The chef also specializes in his own version of the "new cuisine," as exemplified by a prosciutto-like specialty made from goose with a well-seasoned salad, or blinis with swordfish. The cost of a regular meal is around 4,000$ ($27.60) to 5,000$ ($34.50). Michel is open for business Monday to Friday from 12:30 to 3 p.m. and 8 to 11 p.m.; Saturday from 8 to 11 p.m. It is closed during most of August. Reservations are necessary.

Gambrinus, 25 Rua das Portas de Santo Antão (tel. 32-14-66), is an establishment whose stature among Lisbon's leading restaurants is justified. Intimate dining rooms are clustered around an open blue-tile kitchen, where expert chefs in starched white hats prepare fine meals, using large copper pots and a charcoal grill. The location is ideal for those who want to dine in the heart of the city, off the Rossio, near the railway station, and on a little square near the National Theater.

You can have your meal while sitting on leather chairs in the rear under a cathedral-beamed ceiling, or else select a little table beside a fireplace upon the raised end of the room. All is dominated by an impressionist tapestry along one wall. There is also an alcove with a stained-glass enclosure. For before-dinner drinks, a front bar beckons.

There is a diversified à la carte menu, plus specialties of the day. The soups are good, especially the bisque of shellfish. The shrimp, crab, and lobster dishes are the most expensive, but you might prefer conch with shellfish Thermidor or sea-bass minhota. If you don't fancy fish, and you like your dishes *hot,* ask for chicken piri-piri. The restaurant also offers elaborate desserts. Coffee with a 30-year-old brandy complements the meal perfectly. Expect to spend from 7,500$ ($51) to 10,000$ ($68). The restaurant is open seven days a week from noon to 2 a.m.

Lisbon's Oldest Restaurant

A prestigious star, the **Restaurante Tavares,** 37 Rua da Misericórdia (tel. 32-11-12), is Lisbon's oldest restaurant (founded in 1784). It has been favored since the 18th century by gourmet-minded politicians, diplomats, authors, and exiled royalty drawn to its personalized cooking and service.

The preferred street-level dining room is a salon of mirrors, with panels of ecru and gilt, crystal chandeliers, and sconces. As you sit in Louis XV–style armchairs, you can enjoy a small bouquet of flowers on your finely set table.

For an appetizer, you can choose presunto de Chaves (Chaves ham). Among the main dishes are santola (crab) recheada à Tavares, linguado (sole) Newburg, and the special beef of the house. At the start of your meal, you can ask the chef to whip up an Alp-high soufflé as a finale. Then top it off with a café filtro. Your final bill is likely to run 4,000$ ($27.60) to 6,000$ ($41.40) for a complete meal. Tavares is open Monday to Friday from 1 to 3 p.m. and 8 to 10:30 p.m.; Sunday from 8 to 10:30 p.m.

MODERATELY PRICED RESTAURANTS

What follows is a selection of restaurants that serve good food at moderate prices. Of course, if you order shellfish, such as lobster, you can expect to pay a lot of money.

Sua Excelência, 40-42 Rua do Conde (tel. 60-36-14), is the creation of Francisco Queiroz, who created his little dream restaurant with a refined, sedate atmosphere, attracting a discerning clientele. Outside you'll see no sign. There is only a large heavy door with a bell you ring to announce your arrival. The host will greet you with personalized hospitality. The atmosphere he has created is somewhat like a fashionable drawing room, with round tables in an intimate Portuguese provincial decor, cooled by the terra-cotta floor and high painted ceiling.

The host recites the day's specialties, some uncommon to Portugal. These include prawns piri-piri (not unreasonably hot), rollmop sardines, smoked swordfish, and clams in at least five different recipes. One unusual specialty is "little jacks," a small fish of which diners eat heads, tails, everything. It's served with a well-flavored paste made from two-day-old bread. You can also order sea-bass puffs with "doctored" rice. Meals cost 4,500$ ($31.05) and up. Sua Excelência is just a block up the hill from the entrance to the National Art Gallery, so it could be visited on a tie-in museum/luncheon adventure, although its ambience is more charming in the evening. It is open Monday, Tuesday, Thursday, and Friday from 1 to 2 p.m. and 8 to 10:30 p.m.; Sunday from 8 to 10:30 p.m.

Conventual, 45 Praça de Flores (tel. 60-91-96), is in many ways one of my favorite restaurants in Lisbon. This preference is influenced strongly by the taste and sensitivity of its gracious owner, Mrs. Dina Marquês. On one of the loveliest residential squares in town, behind a discreet, plain wood door, you'll see a display of old panels from baroque churches, religious statues, and bric-a-brac from Mrs. Marquês's private collection. A large, ornate silver incense burner that once scented the interior of a 17th-century church hangs over the bar. The restaurant is kept pleasantly cool by the old, thick stone walls and terra-cotta floor of the building.

Many of the delectably flavored recipes were invented or developed by the owner, among them a creamy coriander soup, stewed partridge in port, ox tongue in egg sauce, pork filet Portuguese style, steak with onion sauce and fried potatoes, and a tempting grilled monkfish in a herb-flavored cream sauce. Meals begin at 4,000$ ($27.60), and reservations are suggested. Food is served Monday to Saturday from 12:30 to 3:30 p.m. and 7:30 to 11:30 p.m.

Restaurante O Faz Figura, 15-B Rua do Paraíso (tel. 86-89-81), is one of the best and most attractively decorated dining rooms in Lisbon. Part of its atmosphere is provided by a veranda where you can order both lunch and dinner overlooking the Tagus. When reserving a table, ask for one there. The restaurant lies in the heart of the Alfama, and it offers faultless service and typical Portuguese food along with international specialties. A complete meal will cost around 4,000$ ($27.60). There is also a handsome cocktail bar. The restaurant serves Monday to Saturday from 12:30 to 3 p.m. and 8 p.m. to midnight.

A midday meal at **Casa do Leão,** Castelo de São Jorge (tel. 87-59-62), is a must when visiting the charmingly located Castle of St. George. It's in a low-slung stone building within the castle walls. You'll pass between a pair of ancient cannons before entering a sunflooded vestibule where the splashing from a dolphin-shaped foun-

---

IN THE KITCHEN AT QUELUZ

To feel like a king or queen, dine in the **Cozinha Velha,** Palácio Nacional, Queluz, Largo do Palácio (tel. 435-02-32). Housed in the former kitchen of the 18th-century Queluz Palace, it's the appropriate luncheon spot either before or after a visit to the palace. You enter through a small patio garden. The high vaulted ceiling with wide stone arches is intact, as is the tremendous walk-in central fireplace.

The cook's 15-foot marble table is still in use, although it's now laden with ready-to-serve delicacies: hors d'oeuvres, salads, fish mousse, and assorted cheeses, along with abundant flower arrangements. The ladderback chairs, torchère lights, 15-foot-high front door, the well-trained waitresses in regional dress, plus the superb food, make it well worth the trip.

You must order from an à la carte menu, which includes the house specialty, linguado (sole) Cozinha Velha. Other courses include a filet mignon with a béarnaise sauce, or the more traditional bife à Portugesa. A good meal is likely to cost at least 4,200$ ($28.95). Reserve a table in advance. The restaurant is open seven days a week from noon to 3 p.m. and 7:30 to 10 p.m.

tain and the welcoming voice of the uniformed maître d'hôtel provide the only sounds. Once seated in the spacious blue-tile dining room, you'll enjoy a panoramic view of the Alfama and the legendary hills of Lisbon. There's even a baronial fireplace, which in cold weather provides an intimate retreat for an apéritif.

Regrettably, this establishment is open only for lunch, which it serves daily from 12:30 to 3 p.m. Full meals, which range upward from around 5,000$ ($34), might include roast duck with orange slices or grapes, pork chops St. George style, codfish with cream, smoked swordfish from Sesimbra, and an array of the chef's daily specials. Reservations are suggested, especially in midsummer.

Chester, 87 Rua Rodrigo da Fonseca (tel. 65-73-47), near the Ritz Inter-Continental, is an attractive restaurant and bar, with a good cellar. Its specialty is grilled steaks. The pepper steak is tempting, as is the rib steak for two. Entrecôte with whisky sauce is hearty, and the fondue bourguignonne is prepared only for two persons.

The tab is likely to range from 3,500$ ($24.15) to 5,500$ ($37.95) for a complete meal. Service is efficient, and reservations are suggested. Chester's is open Monday to Saturday from 12:30 to 3 p.m. and 8:30 to 10:30 p.m. The restaurant lies on the building's street level, but many diners descend into the cozy cellar bar for a drink either before or after their meal.

Pabe, 27A Rua Duque de Palmela (tel. 53-74-84), is the Portuguese word for pub, and that's what this cozy English-style place is. Convenient to the Praça do Pombal, the pub has done its best to emulate English establishments. There's soft carpet on the floor, mugs hanging over the long bar, a beamed ceiling, coats-of-arms, and engravings of hunting scenes around the walls. Two saloon doors lead into a wood-paneled dining room, where you can sup on meat specially imported from the U.S. A chateaubriand for two is about the most expensive dish. If you prefer local fare, start off with a shrimp cocktail, then Portuguese veal liver or chicken breast with mushrooms, and finish with a sherbet, all for a cost of 4,000$ ($27.60). The crowd tends to be a well-groomed Portuguese set as well as resident Yanks and Britons. Pabe is open every day from noon to 1 a.m.

Casa da Comida, 1 Travessa de Amoreiras (tel. 68-53-76), has steadily gained in popularity. If you're in Lisbon between December and March, when the winters are mild but gray and rainy, this is among the best choices for dining in the city. A roaring fire will greet and warm you. Not only is the atmosphere most pleasant (at any time of the year), but the food is impeccably served and good-tasting. You enter by way of a step-down garden. The sole is delectable, and the meat, especially veal, is well prepared. Dinners begin at 4,000$ ($27.60). Hours are Monday to Friday from 12:30 to 3:30 p.m. and 7:30 p.m. to 1 a.m.; Saturday from 7:30 p.m. to 1 a.m.

BUDGET RESTAURANTS

The restaurants described below are patronized mainly by Portuguese, and one characteristic that these restaurants have in common, other than their low prices, is that the chefs are generous with their helpings. Added economy tip: Look for the chef's *prato do dia* (plate of the day)—invariably inexpensive and fresh. And some

Portuguese restaurants save you more by offering reductions for double portions that are shared.

Sancho, 14 Travessa dos Gloria (tel. 36-97-80), is a cozy, well-managed restaurant just off the Avenida da Liberdade, close to the Praça dos Restauradores. The decor is in a vaguely baronial Iberian style, with a beamed ceiling, a fireplace, and leather-covered wooden chairs. The walls are stuccoed and painted white, and the staff is both uniformed and polite. In summer, there is air conditioning. A gratinée fish soup is a classic opener. Shellfish is the specialty, and it's always expensive. Main dishes are likely to include a chef's special hake or pan-broiled Portuguese steak. If your palate is made of asbestos, order churrasco de cabrito (goat) au piri-piri. For dessert, try the crêpes Suzette or perhaps a chocolate mousse. Meals cost from 2,000$ ($13.60) and service is Monday to Saturday from noon to 3 p.m. and 7 to 10 p.m.

Restaurant Bota Alta, 35-37 Travessa da Queimada (tel. 32-79-59), sits at the very top of a steeply inclined street in the Bairro Alto, and boasts a clientele that eagerly crams into its two dining rooms, sometimes standing for hours at the bar waiting for a table. It has rustic artifacts as well as original art and photographs, lots of Lisbon-related gossip, and full meals costing from 1,800$ ($12.25) each. These might include beefsteak Bota Alta, several different preparations of codfish, and a frequently changing array of daily specials, including, for example, Hungarian goulash. The establishment is open Monday to Saturday from noon to 2:30 p.m. and 7 to 11:30 p.m.

Pap' Acôrda, 57-59 Rua da Atalaia (tel. 346-48-11), lies behind a façade that was originally a bakery, and welcomes one of Lisbon's most diverse collections of iconoclasts (of many life-styles and sexual persuasions) into its pink and white interior. Most visitors order a pre-dinner drink at the long and vaguely old-fashioned bar whose marble top dominates the front of the establishment. No one will object if you never get around to actually dining, but if you do, there are two different rooms in back, one of which is outfitted like a garden. Full meals cost 2,500$ ($17), and could include Spanish-style mussels, shellfish rice, sirloin steak with mushrooms, and a wide array of fish and shellfish dishes. The house specialty, after which the establishment was named, is a traditional dish incorporating coriander, bread, seafood, and eggs, called an acôrda. Pap' Acôrda is open Monday to Friday from 12:30 to 2:30 p.m. and 7:30 to 10:30 p.m., and Saturday from 7:30 to 10:30 p.m. Reservations are a good idea.

At **O Funil** (Funnel), 82-A Avenida Elias Garcia (tel. 76-60-07), recommendable for its *cozinha Portuguêsa,* you almost never find a free table at mealtimes. It's that popular.

The dining rooms are on two levels; the street-level one is tavern style, with the tables leg to leg. Most habitués, however, gravitate to the lower level, with its adjoining tiny bar. This is the kind of place where you ask for the *vinho de casa,* and it comes in two sizes of bottles. Wines of all the regions of Portugal are on the wine list, including green wines, ripe wines, and rosés.

The owners offer fresh fish and several meat dishes daily, with specialties of ameijoas (clams) à Funil, cabrito assado (roast goat), and bacalhau (cod) à Funil. To finish your meal, you can choose almond tart, walnut tart, almond cake, cheese, or French pudding, among other delicacies. A complete meal costs from 2,500$ ($17.25). The restaurant is open Tuesday to Saturday from noon to 3:30 p.m. and 7 to 10:30 p.m.; Sunday from noon to 3:30 p.m.

António Restaurante, 63 Rua Tomás Ribeiro (tel. 53-87-80), is just outside the center of the city, only a few blocks from Edward VII Park, in back of the Lisboa-Sheraton. Special touches here include pewter service plates, a blue-and-white tile motif, and an English menu. Each day the chef features a different soup, and clams are always a favorite opener. A Portuguese regional dish worth recommending is pork with a savory clam sauce, or try the chicken with clams. I'd also suggest the fresh sole and the swordfish. A very special dessert is António pudding. Expect to pay about 3,000$ ($20.70) for a really filling meal. Hours are noon to 4 p.m. and 7 to 10:30 p.m. seven days a week.

Restaurant A Colmela, 110 Rua da Emenda (tel. 37-05-00), is a center of healthy living and eating. Its health-conscious kitchen prepares two entirely separate types of cuisines (one vegetarian, the other macrobiotic). There is also a miniature shop where you can buy such natural foods as nuts, raisins, herbs, pastries, and black breads. It lies on the top floor of a corner building in the Chiado district, near the Plaza Camoẽs. You'll have to climb a well-scrubbed wooden staircase (accessible from a stone-floored passageway leading in from the street). At the top, there's a narrow hallway lined with shelves of books dealing with metaphysics as well as healthful

---

SEAFOOD ACROSS THE TAGUS

On the left bank of the Tagus, across the river from Lisbon, you'll find a very popular seafood restaurant, the **Floresta do Ginjal,** 7 Ginjal, in the harbor town of Cacilhas (tel. 275-00-87). To reach it, head for the Praça do Comércio or the Cais do Sodré, pay 65$ (45¢) per person, and catch one of the many ferryboats that depart every 10 or 20 minutes, depending on the time of day, for the opposite bank of the Tagus. Boat service begins very early in the morning and stops shortly after midnight every day. When you land at Cacilhas, cross the bridge and turn right on the street that runs parallel to the waterfront. Within a few moment's walk, you'll find this restaurant one floor above street level. The view opens onto the river scene of Lisbon. You ascend to the dining rooms via a staircase that's a veritable tunnel of assorted seashells embedded in the wall, a proper introduction to the array of fresh and well-prepared fish that will be set before you.

Family-owned and -run, the restaurant attracts a largely Portuguese trade drawn here to sample such regional dishes as caldeirada—the national dish. For dessert, a good Portuguese cheese is queijos serra (from the hills or farm). Almond cake is another favorite dessert. A complete meal begins at about 2,400$ ($16.55) and is available seven days a week from noon to 3 p.m. and 7 to 10:30 p.m.

living. A trio of dining rooms each has large windows and plenty of sunlight. Full meals cost from 850$ ($5.80). The restaurant is open Monday to Friday from noon to 8:30 p.m.; Saturday from noon to 3 p.m.

Restaurant Choupal, 9 Rua do Salitre (tel. 54-29-63), is a stylized taverna, one minute from the Avenida da Liberdade, where regional dishes are served family style. Its walls have aqua and olive tiles combined with wood paneling, the tables have bright cloths, and there is an English menu. The waiter brings a loaf of crusty bread and a little ceramic jar of mildly seasoned pâté with sweet butter to begin your meal. You might start with a shellfish soup or savory Spanish-style clams. Two main-dish specialties are roast chicken and lampreys, those tiny eels from the north of Portugal. The chef also does a special beef dish. A meal here will cost from 2,000$ ($13.60). The restaurant is open every day from 9 a.m. to midnight.

Xele Banana, 29 Praça das Flores (tel. 67-05-15), caters to a sophisticated and hip crowd of all possible persuasions. This stylish restaurant lies behind an anonymous-looking façade on a residential 18th-century square. The decor consists of green and brown murals of jungle plants evocative of the Brazilian rain forest against a cream-colored background of art-deco inspiration. Full meals cost around 3,000$ ($20.40) each, and might include oysters au gratin, rabbit mousse with walnuts, steak with Roquefort sauce, ox tongue with mushrooms, and several different preparations of partridge. Meals are served seven days a week from 12:30 to 3 p.m. and 8 to 11 p.m.

To reach **Xico Carreira,** Parque Mayer (tel. 346-38-05), you'll have to traverse the grounds of a famous but slightly seedy amusement park whose arcades, theaters, and restaurants open onto the Avenida da Liberdade. The restaurant is perched on a hillside overlooking the park below. Decorated with bullfight memorabilia, it is reached by a steep flight of zigzagging concrete steps. It charges 1,500$ ($10.20) for an unpretentious meal from a limited but inexpensive menu. Menu items include beef of the house, pork cutlets, and such Portuguese specialties as sardines and codfish with green sauce. The place is open seven days a week from noon to midnight. On Friday night, there's likely to be a fado performance.

Now more than 150 years old, the **Cervejaria Trindade,** 20-C Rua Nova de Trindade (tel. 32-35-06), owned by the makers of Sagres beer, is one of the oldest beer halls in Lisbon. Along with those steins of beer, you'll be given quite good small steaks, smothered in a mountain of crisp french fries. Also featured are clams (ameijoas) in a savory sauce. You'll be tempted to have more than one of the accompanying beers. Every day a different typical Portuguese dish is featured, including açorda de marisco (bread, panada, and seafood), carne de porco à Alentejana (pork and clams), and presunto de Chaves (ham from Chaves, a town near the northern border of Portugal). If the day is sunny, head for the open-air terrace. The cost of a regular lunch or dinner, featuring the typical dishes and including a large-size mug of beer, costs about 2,000$ ($13.80). Hours are seven days a week from noon to 2 a.m. *Note:* This beer hall was once a convent, and it survived the great earthquake of the 18th century.

INTERNATIONAL CUISINE

The sun has now set over much of the Portuguese empire, but the memory lingers on in a handful of its restaurants that brought the cuisines of other lands back for the home folks to sample. A good one is **Velha Goa,** 41-B Rua Tomás de Anunciação (tel. 60-04-46). India forcibly annexed the Portuguese colony of Goa in 1961. Against a backdrop of Oriental decor, Indian dishes are served at this pleasant restaurant where English is spoken. Typical Goanese dishes include curries—prawns, chicken Madrasta, and other specialties—but pork chops and beef are also served. All dishes are prepared according to the taste of the clients—that is, mild, pungent, and very pungent. Expect to pay 2,000$ ($13.80) to 2,500$ ($17.25). The restaurant is open Tuesday to Friday from noon to midnight; closed Saturday at lunchtime and all day on Monday. In the evening, the last order is accepted at 10:30 p.m. Connected to the restaurant is a bar.

A Gondola, 64 Avenida de Berna (tel. 77-04-26), is Lisbon's "Little Italy," serving what are perhaps the finest Italian specialties, such as ravioli and cannelloni, in town. The restaurant offers indoor dining as well as al fresco meals in the courtyard. Although the decor isn't inspired, the food makes the restaurant worth the trip out of the center. It's best reached by taxi (the street on which it sits crosses the Avenida da República). A full dinner is offered for about 3,200$ ($22.05) and up. This is quite a buy when you realize what you get. A first-course selection might include Chaves ham with melon and figs or liver pâté. For a second course, you're likely to face a choice—filet of sole meunière, grilled sardines with pimientos, or even red mullet. This is followed by yet another course, ravioli or cannelloni in the Roman style, or perhaps veal cutlet milanese. The banquet is topped off by fruit or dessert. The restaurant is open Monday to Friday from 12:45 to 3 p.m. and 7:45 to 10 p.m.; Saturday from 12:45 to 3 p.m.

FAST FOOD

The **Ritz Snackbar,** the Ritz Hotel, 77-C Rua Castilho (tel. 69-20-20, ext. 235), lies among the many satelite businesses surrounding the Ritz, but it is reached by a separate entranceway on a street bordering Edward VII Park. Its two bright and attractive levels are so popular among local office workers at midday that it is sometimes difficult to find a seat. From the Italian kitchen, you can select a pizza, pasta in a bolognese sauce, or lasagne. A hamburger platter is probably the most popular dish in the restaurant. Also in great demand are such ice cream dishes as an Afrodite and a Himalaya. Count on spending 2,000$ ($13.80) and up. The snack bar is open Monday to Saturday from noon to 1:30 a.m.

Hamburger House (The Great American Disaster), 32 Rua Duque de Palmela (tel. 52-12-66), is cramped and convivial. It occupies a big-windowed room one floor above street level, at the corner of one of Lisbon's busiest intersections, about a block from the Ritz Hotel. To reach it, you'll enter an anonymous-looking commercial arcade within a building devoted to Varig Airlines, then climb a flight of winding steps to the second floor. Hamburgers, depending on size and garnishes, range from 450$ ($3.05) to

700$ ($4.75); full meals, which can include more substantial fare such as platters of roast beef and daily specials, begin at around 1,000$ ($6.80). The place is open seven days a week from noon to 3 p.m. and 7 to 11 p.m.

GAY RESTAURANTS

Senhor Marques, 42 Rua da Horta Seca (tel. 32-85-19), lies on a residential street whose buildings are eerily quiet at night, within a trio of very old rooms whose ceilings are supported by the massive arches and beams of an 18th-century town house. Catering largely to a gay clientele, it serves apéritifs from a small bar raised several steps above the floor of the dining room. Specialties include shrimps with Pernod, grilled sole, fondue bourguignonne, Portuguese steak, and frog legs with curry. Full meals, priced from 2,500$ ($17), are served Monday to Friday and Sunday from 12:30 to 3 p.m. and 7:30 to 11 p.m., Saturday 7:30 to 11 p.m. Reservations are a good idea.

Restaurant Bizarro, 133 Rua da Atalaia 133 (tel. 371-899), enjoys a reputation as a likeable meeting spot for gay friends who appreciate its permissive charm. Lying on a narrow street of the Bairro Alto, it's an airy and spacious place with a sparse and spare decor and plenty of room between tables. A la carte meals cost from around 2,000$ ($13.60), although there is a fixed-price meal offered for just 1,600$ ($10.90). Your meal might include grilled red snapper, codfish prepared in three different ways, and filet of wild boar in red wine sauce. Bizarro is open everyday from 12:30 to 3 p.m. and 7 p.m. to midnight.

---

2. Dining In Sintra

The **Palácio do Seteais,** 8 Rua Barbosa do Bocage (tel. 923-32-00), lying about a mile from the center of Sintra, provides a background for one of the finest meals you're likely to be served in Portugal. The exquisite 18th-century palace can be reached only by car, taxi, or horse-drawn carriage. If you opt for a carriage, you'll find a convoy of them parked in the main square of Sintra, charging around 2,800$ ($19.30) for the mile-long ride. Taxis, although more prosaic, are cheaper.

Meals are served daily from 12:30 to 2:30 p.m. and 7:30 to 9:30 p.m. in the lower dining room, overlooking the hillside of villas and orchards. However, you may want to have a before-dinner drink in the loggia or the salon at the bottom of the grand staircase. Once seated, you are apt to have a bouquet of pink hydrangeas placed at your table. Serving stewards are skillful and polite.

For 5,600$ ($38.60), you can order a four-course meal, which begins with your choice of any or all of the 20 different kinds of hors d'oeuvres, such as shrimp, Russian salad, fish mousse, and egg in a gelatin pâté. The next course is fish, perhaps turbot Florentine (creamy with spinach and browned in the oven). Your following meat course will be abundant and tasty, with a wide choice of fresh vegetables. When the dessert cart is brought to your table, you'll be tempted by all of the creamy, fruit-stuffed pastries and cakes. In spring, the fresh strawberries from Sintra are the best in the world.

3. Dining in Belém

Restaurant S. Jerónimo, 12 Rua dos Jerónimos (tel. 64-87-97), is lighthearted and elegant. A visit to this restaurant could be combined with a trip to the famous monastery of the same name. The restaurant sits directly on the east side of the monastery, behind a big-windowed façade that floods the interior with sunlight. You'll be invited to enjoy an apéritif in a spacious cocktail lounge. The dining room is stylishly outfitted with bamboo accents and plants separating the tables.

The all-Portuguese menu contains such specialties as trout Hemingway style, two types of codfish, osso buco, grilled tournedos, shrimp with garlic, fish pâté with tartar sauce, and grouper with champagne. Full meals range upward from 3,000$ ($20.70), usually peaking at around 5,000$ ($34.50). The restaurant is open Monday to Saturday, from 12:30 to 3 p.m. and from 7:30 p.m. to 2 a.m. A Sunday buffet, held from 12:30 to 3:30 p.m., is considered an important event in Belém.

Dionysos', 124 Rua Belém (tel. 64-06-32), is a good Greek restaurant out in the suburb of Belém, an ideal place for lunch if you're visiting the Coach Museum or the monastery nearby. Of course, it's also open for dinner. At the latter, while ensconced at a crowded table under a beamed ceiling on the second floor, you can dine by candlelight, enjoying friendly service. You might begin with a Greek salad for two. The popular souvlaki is featured, and you can also select from a varied menu of fish and meat dishes, finishing with a homemade dessert. Meals cost from 2,800$ ($19.30). The restaurant is open seven days a week from 9 a.m. to 3 p.m. and 7 to 11 p.m. or midnight, depending on business.

4. Dining in Cascais

Restaurant Albatroz, 100 Rua Frederico Arouca (tel. 28-28-21), provides one of the finest dining experiences along the Costa do Sol. This elegantly decorated restaurant is part of the most famous inn along the coast (see my previous recommendation).

You can begin with an apéritif on the covered terrace, whose edges are balanced on the rocks high above the sea. Then you'll be ushered into a glistening dining room, where you can enjoy some of the finest cuisine in Portugal. Your repast might include poached salmon, partridge stew with applesauce, steak Albatroz, sole or lobster prepared as you like it, paella chef's style, lamb with walnuts, or a savory version of stuffed crab. For dessert, your choices will range from crêpes Suzette to an iced soufflé. Accompanying your meal will be a wide selection of Portuguese and international wines. Full meals, served seven days a week from 12:30 to 3 p.m. and 7:30 to 10 p.m., cost from 6,500$ ($44.80); reservations are necessary.

The most preferred "middle-bracket" restaurant is **Reijos,** 35 Rua Frederico Arouca (tel. 28-03-11). Your hosts are Portuguese-born Tony Brito and an American, Ray Ettinger, a purser for a transatlantic airline (he often brings in hard-to-get items by air, including curry from India and soy sauce from Hong Kong). The cuisine represents a blending of their two countries. For example, Reijos is the only place in Cascais where you can get Salisbury Steak. Portugal is represented by a codfish casserole à Reijos, which requires a 30-minute wait (and it's worth it). A delightful prelude to any meal is the shrimp pâté. The menu includes such items as an excellent roast beef as well as roast loin of pork served with rice and beans. The chef is also proud of his fresh seafood, featuring a "catch of the day"—usually sea bass, turbot, or red mullet. The restaurant has one of the most varied menus in town, right down to the homemade chutney and assorted condiments served with the authentic curries. The cost of a regular meal ranges from 2,500$ ($17.25) to 3,000$ ($20.70). Be sure to reserve your table, as this place is popular. It's open seven days a week from 12:30 to 3:30 p.m. and 7 to 9 p.m.

Modest tabs are also rung up at **La Gran Tasca Restaurant and Wine Bar,** 3 Rua Sebastião José de Carvalho e Melo (tel. 28-11-40). If a local person in Cascais were to recommend a restaurant to his visiting Portuguese cousin, it would probably be this one. It has good regional fare, the daily plats du jour announced on a blackboard out front. It's always crowded, and with good reason. There is a wine bar at the entrance where you can drink by the glass or bottle while enjoying tapas, always available at the bar. Try the clam soup, followed by maracana (clams and squid in a coconut-cream sauce) or maracanissimo (king prawns, angelfish, squid, and clams, also in a coconut-cream sauce). Besides these specialties, you can order steaks, poultry, or fish cooked to order from the à la carte menu. This is the type of place to which you are likely to want to return. You can dine well for about 2,000$ ($13.80); a glass of wine will cost around 160$ ($1.10), depending on the vintage. Located close to the Cascais railway station, the establishment is open Wednesday to Monday from noon to midnight.

SIGHTSEEING IN LISBON

Many visitors think seeing the sights of Lisbon can be accomplished by one quick visit to the Coach Museum in the parish of Belém. Not so, and if you limit yourself to just this one sight you'll be missing quite a lot. Lisbon is chock-full of sights, attractions you'll be glad you took the time to see, and that will give you a greater feeling and knowledge of this very individual country, Portugal. (For your reference, there is a "Sights and Attractions" index at the back of this book.)

Those on the strictest of schedules should really try to visit the following at least: (1) the Coach Museum, (2) the Jerónimos Monastery, (3) the Alfama, (4) the Castle of St. George (for the view if nothing else), (5) the National Art Gallery, and (6) the Gulbenkian Center for Arts and Culture.

However, if your time is so tight that you've allowed only one day for sightseeing in Portugal, head for the museum-filled area of Belém in the morning, then spend the afternoon enjoying Sintra.

For our exploration of all the major sights (and many esoteric but worthwhile ones), we'll begin in the old quarter.

1. The Alfama—A Walking Tour

The most *típico* district of Lisbon lies to the east of Black Horse Square. It's the old Moorish quarter of the city, the Alfama, partially spared by the earthquake of 1755, because its foundation was more solid than that of the rest of the capital. Here, narrow cobblestone streets stretch down to the Tagus from St. George Castle, crowning the hill.

Today the Alfama is the traditional home of stevedores, sailors, and fishermen. But in days gone by it was the aristocratic sector. Even today you can see coats-of-arms of noble families embedded in the façades of some of the houses.

Allow at least two hours for your walking tour of the Alfama. The streets are rarely suitable for a car; at times, you must walk up steep stone stairs.

A good point to begin your tour is the **Largo do Salvador** (a taxi can drop you off there), housing a 16th-century mansion that once belonged to the Count of Arcos. From there, turn down the **Rua da Regueira,** which leads to the **Beco do Carneiro,** the "cul-de-sac of rams." The lane couldn't be narrower. Families live in houses literally four feet (if that much!) apart. "Our lips easily meet high across the narrow street," wrote poet Frederico de Brito.

At the end of the alley, circle back via a flight of steps to your left to the **Largo de Santo Estevão,** named after the church on the site. Round the church and from the back proceed to the **Patio das Flores,** via a flight of steps, where you can see some of the most delightful little houses fronted with characteristic Portuguese tiles (*azulejos*). Walk down the steps to the **Rua dos Remédios,** cutting right to the **Largo do Chafariz de Dentro,** where you're bound to see the Alfama housewives busily gossiping in front of an old fountain and often walking with jugs of fresh water balanced on their heads.

From the square, you connect with the **Rua de São Pedro,** which is perhaps the most animated street in the Alfama. Strolling deep into the street, you'll probably eventually attract a trail of children, and will come upon women squatting on the street, bartering furiously with a rough-faced, barefoot *varina* (fishwife) over slices of giant swordfish.

You'll pass some local taverns, and adventurous sightseers will go inside to sample a glass of *vinho verde* (green wine). Later, back on the narrow street, you may pass an old fisherman with brown nets draped over his shoulder.

The Rua de São Pedro leads into the **Largo de São Rafael,** which convinces you the 17th century never ended. You pass a *leitaria* (dairy), which now sells milk in the bottle (cows used to be kept right inside, as the women of Alfama wanted to make sure their milk was fresh).

Right off the square is the **Rua de Judiaria,** so called because of the many Jews who settled there after escaping the Inquisition in Spain.

Go back to the Largo de São Rafael, crossing it to rejoin the Rua de São Pedro. Walk down that street to the intersection, forking left. You enter the **Largo de São Miguel,** its church richly adorned with baroque trappings. From there, walk up the **Rua da São Miguel,** cutting left onto the **Beco de Cardosa,** where from some flower-draped balcony overhead, a *varina* is bound to scream down hell and damnation to her street-urchin son if he doesn't come inside immediately.

As you pass the doorways, you'll see black-shawled old women grilling Setúbal sardines on braziers. The armies of cats that reside in the Alfama will easily devour any bones or heads left over. At the end of the alley, you connect with the **Beco Sta. Helena,** a continuation, which leads up several flights of steps to the **Largo das Portas do Sol.**

On this square is the **Museum of Decorative Art,** handsomely ensconced in one of the many mansions that used to grace the Alfama.

One of the most favored belvederes in the city opens onto the square. Called the **Santa Luzia Belvedere,** it's really a balcony to view the sea, overlooking the houses of the Alfama, as they sweep down in a jumbled pile to the Tagus.

Although best explored by day, the Alfama takes on a different spirit at night, when street lanterns cast ghostly patterns against medieval walls and the plaintive sound of the *fadista* is heard until the early morning hours in the traditional cafés.

---

2. Castle of St. George

Known as the "cradle" of Lisbon, the present castle is of Visigoth origin; before that, the site was most likely used as a Roman fortress. The castle is named after St. George in honor of the Portuguese and English alliance of 1386. Around the periphery of the fortress is a district of much interest, looking as if it were removed intact from the Middle Ages.

Before entering the grounds, pause at the **Castle Belvedere,** known as the "ancient window" looking over the city below. In the distance, you can see the best view of the "Bay of Straw," the hills of Monsanto and of Sintra, the Ponte 25 de Abril, the rusty-red rooftops of Lisbon, and the Praça do Comércio. The statue is of Afonso Henriques, the first king of Portugal, who is said to have lived here after he liberated the city from the Moors.

Inside the grounds, you can walk along in cool shade or in sunlight, watching the swans gliding by in the moat, peacocks craning their long necks, olive and cork trees fluttering in the wind. Pink flamingos, weeping willows, and oleander create a dreamy feeling until you stumble upon a cannon, reminding you of the castle's bloody history, the lives lost in battles on this hill.

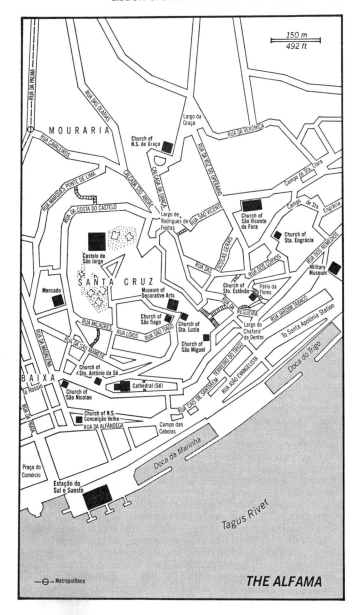

150 m
492 ft

RUA DA PALMA

MOURARIA

RUA DAS OLARIAS

RUA CAVALEIROS

RUA MARQUÊS PONTE DE LIMA

RUA DA COSTA DO CASTELO

CALÇADA STO ANDRÉ

CALÇADA DA GRAÇA

Largo da Graça

Church of N.S. de Graça

RUA DA VOZ DO OPERÁRIO

RUA DA VERÓNICA

RUA SÃO VICENTE

Largo de Rodrigues de Freitas

Church of São Vicente de Fora

Campo de Sta. Clara

Campo de Sta. Engrácia

Church of Sta. Engrácia

RUA DOS REMEDIOS

Castelo de São Jorge

SANTA CRUZ

Mercado

Museum of Decorative Arts

RUA DAS ESCOLAS GERAIS

RUA DOS CORVOS

Church of Sto. Estêvão

Pátio da Flores

Military Museum

RUA MILAGRES

RUA DA SÃO MAMEDE

RUA DA MADALENA

RUA LÓIOS

RUA SÃO TIAGO

Church of São Tiago

Church of Sta. Luzia

Church of São Miguel

RUA REGUEIRA

Largo do Chafariz de Dentro

RUA JARDIM TABACO

To Santa Apolónia Station

Doca do Trigo

B A I X A

To Rossio

RUA DO PRATA

Church of Sto. António da Sé

Cathedral (Sé)

Church of São Nicolau

TERREIRO DO TRIGO

RUA CAIS DE SANTARÉM

RUA JOÃO EVANGELISTA

Church of N.S. Conceição Velha

RUA DA ALFÂNDEGA

Campo das Cebolas

Doca da Marinha

Praça do Comércio

Estação do Sul e Sueste

Tagus River

—Θ— Metropolitana

THE ALFAMA

In the only room left of the ancient Royal Palace, the Alcáçova, you can wander in and study the details of Roman and Islamic tombstones.

The admission-free castle is open daily from 9 a.m. until sunset.

3. The Cathedral (Sé)

As European cathedrals go, this one is not wealthy with great art, but it does remain an enduring landmark. Its twin towers give it a fortress-like look, and the present structure is a mixture of architectural styles ranging from Romanesque to Gothic to baroque. Actually, the cathedral is a little bit of everything, having been changed and modified considerably after it suffered damage from two different earthquakes—one in 1344, the other in 1755.

It is said to have been built on the foundation of a mosque. After King Afonso Henriques liberated the city in the 12th century, the church was built as a triumphant gesture, the establishment of a Christian bastion. Lisboans speak of it as their mother church, the oldest one in the city.

Inside, the most interesting features are a rose window; the Gothic chapel of Bartolomeu Joanes dating from the 14th century; a "crib" by Machado de Castro, the leading Portuguese sculptor of the 18th century; the original nave and aisles; and the 14th-century tomb of Lopo Fernandes Pacheco. The church, at the Largo da Sé, within walking distance of the Praça do Comércio, may be visited from 9 a.m. to 5 p.m.

4. The Bairro Alto

Like the Alfama, the Bairro Alto (the upper city) preserves the characteristics of the Lisbon of yore. It was once called the heart of the city, probably for both its location and its houses, streets, and inhabitants. Many of its buildings were left intact during the 1755 earthquake. Today it is the home of some of the finest fado cafés in Lisbon, making it a center of nightlife, but it is also a fascinating place to visit during the day, when its lasting charm of narrow cobblestone streets and alleys, lined with ancient buildings, can be enjoyed.

The Bairro Alto, originally called Vila Nova de Andrade, was started in 1513, when part of the huge Santa Catarina farm was sold to the Andrade family, who sold the land as plots for construction. Early buyers were carpenters, merchants, and ship caulkers, who must have been astute businessmen: At least some of them immediately resold their newly acquired land to aristocrats, and little by little, noble families moved to the quarter. The Jesuits followed, moving from their modest College of Mouraria to new headquarters at the Monastery of São Roque, where the *Misericórdia* (social assistance to the poor) of Lisbon is still carried on today. As often happens, the Bairro Alto gradually became a working-class quarter. Today, the neighborhood is also the domain of journalists, since some of the big Portuguese newspapers have their plants here. Writers and artists have also been drawn here to live and work, attracted by the ambience and the good cuisine of local restaurants.

The area is a colorful one. From the windows and balconies, streamers of laundry hang out to dry, and here and there are cages of canaries, parrots, parakeets, and other birds. In the morning, the street scene is made up of housewives coming out from their homes to shop for food, probably attracted by the cries of the varinas (fishmongers) and other vendors, some pushing creaky, heavily laden carts, and some trudging by with baskets of fresh vegetables. Other women lounge in doorways or lean on windowsills to watch the world go by.

The Bairro Alto blooms at night, luring with fado, food, discos, and small bars. Lisbon's budget restaurants, the **tascas,** proliferate here, together with more deluxe eateries. Victorian-era lanterns light the streets, where people stroll leisurely along.

5. Belém

This western parish of Lisbon is forever linked to the glory of the Age of Exploration. Here, at the mouth of the Tagus, Vasco da Gama set out to blaze a new trail to India, Ferdinand Magellan to circumnavigate the globe, and Días to round the Cape of Good Hope, even if he didn't know it at the time.

THE TOWER OF BELÉM

Built between 1515 and 1521 at the point where the caravels, inspired by Henry the Navigator, were launched on their historic missions, Manuel the Fortunate erected the Tower of Belém. The quadrangular tower is the most distinctive landmark in Portugal. It was designed by Francisco de Arruda in a Manueline style that incorporates Gothic and Romanesque features, also betraying the debt the architect owed to the Moors during his years of work in Morocco. One historian claimed that the tower "seems to epitomize the hybrid yet highly original character of Portugal's people."

If you climb the stairs to the ramparts, you'll have a panoramic view of the Tagus, as well as the handsome villas in the hills. To reach the entrance door, you walk across a drawbridge. Inside, the rooms are sparsely furnished, except for a few antiques that include a circa-1500 throne-armchair with carved finials and an inset paneled with pierced Gothic tracery. Along the balustrade of the loggia are stone crosses symbolizing the Portuguese crusaders. On the tower is the coat-of-arms of Manuel I.

Fronting the Praça do Império is the **Fonte Luminosa** (Luminous Fountain), standing majestically between the Memorial to the Discoveries and the Jerónimos Monastery. Erected in 1940, the fountain attracts motorists from Lisbon who come out at night to watch the floodlit waterworks. To see the entire show takes nearly an hour, as there are about 75 original "liquid designs" from the water jets. On the Avenida Marginal, it is open Tuesday to Sunday, except holidays. From April 1 through September 30, hours are 10 a.m. to 6:30 p.m., during the rest of the year, from 10 a.m. to 5 p.m. The admission charge is 250$ ($1.70) between October and May; 400$ ($2.70) between June and September.

THE MEMORIAL TO THE DISCOVERIES

The Portuguese speak of it with pride as their Padrão dos Descobrimentos. Standing in the river, the monument was designed to stimulate the effect of a prow of one of the legendary caravels. Along the ramps of either side you'll see some of the more memorable explorers, such as Vasco da Gama. But occupying the most prominent position, at the meeting point of the ramps, is Henry the Navigator.

This memorial was unveiled in 1960 on the fifth centennial of the prince's death. Symbolized in the frieze are sailors, mapmakers, monks (always taken along on the missions of exploration), a kneeling Philippa of Lancaster (mother of Henry the Navigator), artists, cosmographers, and a man holding a flag with a cross representing the crusaders. At the highest point on the memorial is the 15th-century "arms of Portugal."

JERÓNIMOS MONASTERY

The extravagant, flamboyant architecture of Renaissance Portugal reached its pinnacle in this monastery, the **Mosteiro dos Jerónimos,** Praça do Império (tel. 61-70-20). Traditionalists assert that it was ordered built by Manuel the Fortunate to celebrate the opening of the route to India by Vasco da Gama. Certainly, it was paid for by the flourishing spice trade with the East.

Gothic elements romp with exotic Manueline motifs. The total effect was summed up by Howard La Fay: "Here, frozen forever in stone, is the blazing noontide of empire. Stylized hawsers writhe in the arches. Shells and coral and fish entwine on every column. Sanctuary lamps glow red above carved African lions."

Originally, a modest chapel founded by Henry the Navigator stood on these grounds; then the monastery was ordered built in 1502. Damaged but not destroyed by the earthquake of 1755, it was subsequently restored—the restoration a subject of controversy among architectural critics.

You enter through a magnificently sculpted doorway. To the right in the abbey are the tombs of Vasco da Gama and Luís Vaz de Camões, Portugal's greatest poet, whose fame rests on his *Os Lusíadas* ("The Portuguese"). Also allegedly buried here are the kings of Portugal's Golden Age, such as Manuel the Fortunate and Sebastian. The latter was a mystic and religious fanatic who perished with his army in a mad attempt to lead a crusade against the Muslims in Morocco in 1578.

The cloister is of exceptional style and beauty, and it's the most exciting part of a visit to the abbey. As you head down the corridors —observing that each pillar is sculpted in a different and original style—you'll be walking across the unmarked tombs of long-forgotten people. Later, you can climb to the second tier where monks of old paced in meditation. Opening onto the cloisters are the monks' cells (seven feet long, four feet wide).

Open Tuesday to Sunday (except holidays) from 10 a.m. to 6:30 p.m. in summer, to 5 p.m. in winter, the monastery charges no entrance fee to the church. Admission to the adjacent cloisters costs

250$ ($1.70) between October and May; 400$ ($2.70) between June and September. Hours are the same as for the church. Take bus no. 43 from Praça de Figueira or bus no. 27 or 49 from Praça Marquês de Pombal.

NATIONAL MUSEUM OF ARCHEOLOGY

This museum, called the Museu Nacional de Arqueologia in Portuguese, located in the wing of the abbey at the Praça do Império, was founded in 1893 by José Leite de Vasconcellos and has been in the Mosteiro dos Jerónimos since 1903. For many years this institution has been one of the most important in Portugal in the field of archeological and ethnological research.

The collections of ancient jewelry are outstanding, as are the Roman pavements and sculpture and the remains from many archeological sites, mainly Vaiamonte, Torre da Palma, and Tróia. The museum also has a fine nucleus of Portuguese ethnography and archeology and a valuable Egyptian collection. The Roman sculpture exhibition has the most significant objects in the museum's collection, and "Treasures of Portuguese Archeology" traces the history of jewelry and its development in the territory that became Portugal since Chalcolithic times (2000 B.C.) up to the Visigothic period. The museum also has various temporary shows.

It can be visited Tuesday to Sunday, except holidays, from 10 a.m. to 12:30 p.m. and 2 to 5 p.m. Admission is 250$ ($1.70).

THE PORTUGUESE MARITIME MUSEUM

The pageant and glory that was Portugal on the high seas is evoked for posterity in this maritime museum, Museu de Marinha, Praça de Império (tel. 362-0019), one of the most important museums of its kind in Europe. Appropriately, it is installed in the west wing of the Monastery of Jerónimos. It recalls, through the display of artifacts, ship models, full-size state barges, and traditional Portuguese fishing and traffic boats, Portugal's dependence on the sea. As a historical maritime museum, it has navy, merchant marine, fishing, and pleasure-craft sections. In the Royal State Barges Hall is an outstanding collection of magnificent barges built from the early 18th century up to the middle of the 19th century. The largest and most impressive one, displayed with 80 wax dummy oarsmen in gold and red jackets, was put into actual use during a state visit of Queen Elizabeth II of England to Lisbon in 1957. Also displayed are models of ships of Portugal's Golden Age, including the *caravela*, which were the most important ships of the discoveries, and *São Gabriel*, the flagship of Vasco da Gama, the great Portuguese navigator who discovered the sea route to India.

A special hall displays Queen Amélia's lodgings removed from the royal yacht of Carlos I, the king who was assassinated along with his son in the Praça do Comércio in 1908. In another hall is a remarkable display of 16th- and 17th-century Portuguese astrolabs, one of the most complete collections in the world, as well as replicas of nautical charts from the same period.

There are also exhibits from the Portuguese Fleet Air Arm, which was in operation from 1917 until the early 1960s, when an independent Portuguese Air Force was created. On display is the seaplane *Santa Cruz* and other mementos that recall the feat of naval aviators Sacadura Cabral and Gago Coutinho, who in 1922 made the first crossing of the South Atlantic by air, with astronomical navigation made possible by use of a modified sextant invented by Gago Coutinho. The sextant is in the museum. With that flight, the Portuguese were the first Europeans to arrive in Brazil by air, some 400 years after their forebears were the first to arrive by sea in the fleet of Pedro Álvares Cabral.

The museum is open Tuesday to Sunday, except holidays, from 10 a.m. to 5 p.m. Admission is 200$ ($1.35) for adults, 100$ (70¢) for students.

THE PLANETARIUM

Annexed to the Maritime Museum, but with a separate entrance lying across the courtyard, stands the 82-foot Planetarium called **Planetario C. Gulbenkian** (tel. 362-0002). In its sky theater, presentations of astronomical science can be viewed on Saturday and Sunday at 4 p.m. and 5 p.m. in English and French. Admission costs 250$ ($1.60) for adults, 125$ (80¢) for children. Children under six are not allowed inside. You can rent headphones (which you'll need to hear the accompanying lecture) for an additional 100$ (70¢). Take bus no. 27, 28, 29, 43, 49, or 51.

FOLK ART MUSEUM

Nowhere are the folk arts and customs of the Portuguese displayed more dramatically than here at the **Museu de Arte Popular,** Avenida de Brasília (tel. 61-12-82). The walls of the building, which previously housed the Regional Center during the 1940 Portuguese World's Exhibition, were painted by contemporary artists, some of the best in Portugal, including Carlos Botelho, Eduardo Anahory, Estrela Faria, Manuel Lapa, Paulo Ferreira, and Tomás de Melo (Tom). Their work is supplemented by enlarged photographs of the people of the provinces, with each individual region maintaining a separate personality. The establishment of the Folk Art Museum in 1948 was a result of a campaign for ethnic revival directed by António Ferro. The collections, including ceramics, furniture, wickerwork, clothes, farm implements, and painting, are displayed in rooms that correspond more or less to the provinces.

The room devoted to Entre-Douro and Minho has examples of various subjects related to different features of that area. There are flowers, musical instruments, goldsmith pieces, Barcelos painted pottery, and Vila Nova de Gaia painted earthenware dolls. Elaborate harnesses used for oxen are on display, along with farm implements. You can see models of regional boats, fishing tools, embroidered sweaters, Azurara stockings, rugs, a Viana do Castelo weaver's loom, and various items for the preparation of linen, for spinning, and for knitting. Bilros laces and fiancés' handkerchiefs are also on exhibit.

The exhibition from Tras-os-Montes gives a survey of the northeast area, based on its main activities. You'll see straw *escrinhos* (baskets), a Vila Real oxcart and a harrow for threshing corn, kitchen items, black earthenware, and a collection of rugs and bedspreads. *Chocalheiros* masks, worn by men called by the same name who appear on feast days, are interesting displays.

The Algarve, well-known to tourists, is represented by palm

mats and baskets, a water cart, horse trappings, fishing nets, and a manually operated millstone, plus line-cut chimneys.

The room devoted to Beiras contains a reproduction of the interior of a Monsanto country house, as well as a variety of wicker and straw baskets, fine Molelos black earthenware items, bedspreads, and rugs. Here, too, is a set of tools used in salt making from Aveiro. Of special interest is a *moliço*-catcher's boat. *Moliço* is seaweed dredged up and used as fertilizer.

The final room, containing displays from Estremadura and Alentejo, holds a variety of objects such as glazed pottery pieces from Leiria and Mafra; Nazaré fishing and clothing items, sculpture, and saints' registries; and a wax dummy modeling the garb of the *campino,* a herdsman who looks after the bulls on the plains. From Alentejo, you'll see a replica of a kitchen, glazed Redondo earthenware, Nisa earthenware, Estremoz polished and striped pottery, and earthenware painted dolls, together with items of shepherds' art and votive paintings.

The museum is open Tuesday to Sunday, except holidays, from 10 a.m. to 12:30 p.m. and 2 to 5 p.m. Admission is 200$ ($1.35). Buses no. 12 and 14 go there.

THE COACH MUSEUM

This is Lisbon's number-one sight-seeing attraction. In what was once a riding academy attached to the royal residence at Belém, Queen Amélia, seeing many of Portugal's greatest old coaches falling into disrepair, started the nucleus of the collection. But poor Amélia used a yacht—not a coach—when she fled with her son, Manuel II, following the collapse of the monarchy in Portugal.

Gathered here are the magnificent coaches, some royal, ranging from the 17th through the 19th centuries. Far superior in the scope and style of its collection to that of the Palacio Real in Madrid, the **Museu Nacional dos Coches** is acclaimed as the world leader.

At Praça Afonsô de Albuquerque, the museum (tel. 363-8022) is open Tuesday to Sunday, except Portuguese holidays, from 10 a.m. to 1 p.m. and 2:30 to 5:30 p.m. The entrance fee is 400$ ($2.70) between June and September; 250$ ($1.70) between October and May.

Among the more intriguing coaches is a 17th-century vehicle in which the Habsburg monarch, Philip II, rode to Lisbon in the era of Spain's domination. The most lavish trio—a collection of elegant gilded baroque carriages—was built in Rome for the Portuguese ambassador to the Vatican of Pope Clement XI in 1716. Less celebrated—but of much interest—is a *berlinda* belonging to the queen, Maria I. On the second floor, you'll find a collection of harnesses, saddles, armor, stirrups, and portraits from the deposed House of Bragança.

---

6. Other Museums of Lisbon

For art lovers, the two most important museums are the National Museum of Ancient Art and the newer Calouste Gulbenkian Museum.

NATIONAL MUSEUM OF ANCIENT ART

Although drawing fewer visitors than the Coach Museum, this is actually Portugal's greatest museum. It is the country's major showcase for both Portuguese and foreign paintings, exhibited along with an assemblage of French and Flemish tapestries; Portuguese embroidered carpets; antiques (many from the 15th century); a remarkable collection of gold and silver jewelry; and porcelain, pottery, and Oriental carpets. The museum, at 95 Rua das Janelas Verdes (tel. 396-41-51), is open Tuesday to Sunday, except holidays, from 10 a.m. to 1 p.m. and 2:30 to 5 p.m. The museum's cafeteria is also open from 10 a.m. to 5 p.m. The charge for admission is 200$ ($1.35) except Sunday, when it's free.

The most celebrated painting here is *The Temptations of St. Anthony* by Hieronymus Bosch, which was restored in the early 1970s by the José de Figueiredo Institute for the Examination and Preservation of Works of Art. In the west building, the best-known Portuguese work is the 15th-century polyptych found in the convent of St. Vincent de Fora. These panels were probably the masterpiece of Nuno Gonçalves, Portugal's painter who worked at the court of Afonso V, and are unique examples of early Renaissance collective portraits.

Notable foreign paintings include a *St. Catherine* and a *Salomé* (with the head of John the Baptist resting on a platter) by Lucas Cranach; plus works by Anthony Van Dyck, Sir Joshua Reynolds, Velázquez, Raphael, Andrea del Sarto (a remarkable self-portrait), Tiepolo, Guardi (a small Venetian scene), Poussin, Zurbarán (a whole room), Murillo, Ribera, Dürer (seek out his *St. Jerome*), Hans Holbein (*Virgin and Saints*), Memling, and Pieter Brueghel (*Charity Work*).

The collection is rich in Portuguese works, including canvases by Frey Carlos, a well-known artist of the Flemish-Portuguese School. The jewelry collection here stuns—everything from a processional cross from the Monastery of Alcobaça to a *custódia* removed from the Monastery of Belém. This latter monstrance was said to have been made in 1506 by Gil Vicente from the first gold brought back from the East by Vasco da Gama.

From the 18th century, a silver plate, the work of the Germain family, is considered the finest in the world. Weighing more than a ton, it was ordered by King Joseph I. The miracle is that this group was never melted down to fill up some later king's sagging treasury.

Among sculptural exhibits are works by Machado de Castro, the leading Portuguese sculptor of the 18th century and a master of terra-cotta relief.

CALOUSTE GULBENKIAN MUSEUM

Opened in the autumn of 1969, this museum houses what one critic called "one of the world's finest private art collections"—that of Armenian oil tycoon Calouste Gulbenkian, who died in 1955. The multimillion-dollar modern center, at 45 Avenida de Berna (tel. 73-51-31), is in a former private estate that belonged to the Count of Vilalva. It is open on Tuesday, Thursday, Friday, and Sunday from 10 a.m. to 5 p.m.; on Wednesday and Saturday from 2 to

7:30 p.m. (closed Monday and holidays), from June 1 to October 31. During the other months of the year, it's open Tuesday to Sunday, except holidays, from 10 a.m. to 5 p.m. The admission is 40$ (25¢).

The collections cover Egyptian, Greek, and Roman antiquities; a remarkable set of Islamic art including ceramics and textiles of Turkey and Persia, Syrian glass, books, bindings, and miniatures; Chinese vases; Japanese prints; and lacquer work. The European displays include medieval illuminated manuscripts and ivories, 15th- to 19th-century paintings and sculpture, Renaissance tapestries and medals, important collections of 18th-century French decorative arts, French impressionist painting, René Lalique jewelry, and glassware.

In a move requiring great skill of negotiation, Gulbenkian managed to make purchases of art from the Hermitage at Leningrad. Among his most notable acquisitions are two Rembrandts: *Pallas Athene* and *Portrait of an Aging Man.* Two other well-known paintings are a portrait of *Helen Fourment* by Peter Paul Rubens and Renoir's *Madame Claude Monet Lounging.* The French sculptor Jean Antoine Houdon is represented by a statue of *Diana.* Much of the collection of 18th-century silver—said to be the finest in the world—came from the sales by the Soviet government during its cash-raising activities of the 1920s. Much of it belonged to Catherine the Great, and many pieces from the French monarchs are also displayed.

As a cultural center, the Gulbenkian Foundation sponsors plays, films, ballet, and musical concerts, as well as a rotating exhibition of works by leading Portuguese and foreign artists.

CENTER FOR MODERN ART

Around the corner from the central main entrance to the Gulbenkian Museum, the **Centro de Arte Moderna,** Rua Dr. Nicolau de Bettencourt (tel. 73-43-09), is the first major permanent exhibition center of modern Portuguese artists to open in Lisbon. The center shares park-like grounds with the Gulbenkian Foundation and was, in fact, a gift left from the legacy of the late Armenian oil magnate.

Housed in a British-designed complex of clean lines and dramatically proportioned geometric forms, with a Henry Moore sculpture in front, the museum houses a collection of some 5,000 works of art. It displays the works of many modern Portuguese artists, some of which enjoy world reputations. Some of the paintings on exhibit were considered aggressively iconoclastic at the time of their execution.

Admission is 30$ (20¢). July to November, hours are 10 a.m. to 5 p.m. on Tuesday, Thursday, Friday, and Sunday, and from 2 to 7:30 p.m. on Wednesday and Saturday. November to July, it's open from 10 a.m. to 5 p.m. Tuesday to Sunday. Throughout the year, the museum is closed Monday and bank holidays.

MUSEUM OF DECORATIVE ART

The decorative arts school museum, **Fundação Ricardo do Espírito Santo Silva,** 2 Largo da Porta do Sol (tel. 86-21-83), is a foundation established in 1953 through the vision and generosity of Dr. Ricardo do Espírito Santo Silva, who endowed it with items belonging to his private collection and set up workshops in which nearly all activities related to the decorative arts are represented. The handsomely furnished museum is in one of the many mansions of the aristocracy that used to grace the Alfama. The principal aim of the foundation is the preservation and furtherance of the decorative arts by maintaining the traditional character and developing craftspersons' skills and culture. In the workshops, you can see how perfect reproductions of pieces of furniture and other objects are made in the purest styles. The foundation also restores furniture, books, and Arraiolos rugs.

The museum has been given the character of an inhabited palace; the esthetic value of the objects on display is enhanced by setting them in appropriate surroundings. Visitors can have a fairly accurate picture of what the interior of a posh Lisbon home in the 18th and 19th centuries might have been like. There are particularly outstanding displays of furniture, Portuguese silver, and Arraiolos rugs of the 17th through 19th centuries.

The museum is open Tuesday to Saturday from 10 a.m. to 1 p.m. and 2:30 to 5 p.m. Admission is 500$ ($3.40). Visitors must wait downstairs in the entrance hall, where an old coach sits, for a guide to show them through the three floors of rooms. To reach the museum and the foundation, take tram 28 or bus no. 37.

NATIONAL MUSEUM OF CONTEMPORARY ART

Founded in 1911, the **Museu Nacional de Arte Contemporânea**, 6 Rua Serpa Pinto (tel. 346-80-28), has collections of paintings and sculptures going back to 1850. The romantic and naturalistic schools of the 19th century, as well as more modern styles such as surrealism, neorealism, abstractionism, and neofiguratism, are represented here. This is perhaps the most important collection of 19th- and 20th-century Portuguese paintings and sculptures in the world, consisting of more than 2,500 works of art.

The collection is displayed in rooms of the old Monastery of Saint Francis, where the Lisbon Royal Academy of Arts opened in 1836, the first school and art gallery in the capital. The first three directors, famous painters Carlos Reis (1863–1940), Columbano (1857–1920), and Sousa Lopes (1879–1944), organized and exhibited the initial grouping. At that time, the museum was mainly an artistic workshop.

It is open Tuesday to Sunday from 10 a.m. to 5 p.m. Admission is 400$ ($2.70).

7. Lisbon Churches

Lisbon, past and present, lives on in its churches. The earthquake of 1755 destroyed many of them completely. Others were reconstructed—some better than others, according to the times.

CHURCH OF MADRE DE DEUS/MUSEU NACIONAL DO AZULEJO

One of Lisbon's most interesting buildings is the Church of Madre de Deus, which was founded as a simple monastery by Queen Leonora in 1509 and later enlarged in 1540 by King João (John) III. João V further embellished the church, but his reign ended five years before the great earthquake of 1755. The task of rebuilding, which was performed in the most opulent style of its day (and which retained many of the tiles of the earlier building), fell to the lieutenants of José I in the 18th century.

Today, both on the walls and in display cases, the church contains some of the most precious *azulejos* (glazed tiles) of any church in Lisbon, and as such, it has been declared a museum (The National Tile Museum/Museu Nacional do Azulejo) by the Portuguese government. The Manueline façade hardly reveals the lush decorations inside. At 4 Rua Madre de Deus (tel. 814-7747), the church/museum, with its sacristy and choir, is considered one of the most important ensembles of baroque decoration in Portugal. As you enter the church, you see walls lined with glazed tiles in clear blues and whites, the effect crowned by oil paintings framed in lavish baroque gilt. The guide will show you through the two-tiered cloisters. The rooms opening off the cloisters are lined with remarkable 16th- and 17th-century tiles, many from Delft. (Why anyone wanted to import tiles from Holland to azulejo-rich Portugal remains a mystery.) One of the highlights of the collection is a *Panel of the Great View of Lisbon* (done around 1730), a 120-foot-long panorama of pre-earthquake Lisbon. There are also temporary exhibitions of contemporary Portuguese ceramics, which change on a yearly basis. The museum charges an admission of 200$ ($1.35) and is open throughout the year Tuesday to Sunday from 10 a.m. to 5 p.m.

PANTHEON CHURCH OF ST. ENGRÁCIA

When a builder starts to work on a Portuguese house, the owner often chides him, "Don't take as long as St. Engrácia." Construction on this Portuguese baroque church began in the 17th century and it resisted the earthquake. Nevertheless, it was completed only in 1966. The completed product appears pristine and cold, and the state has fittingly turned it into a neoclassic Pantheon, containing memorial tombs to Portuguese greats as well as heads of state.

Memorials honor Henry the Navigator; Luís Vaz de Camões, the country's greatest poet, author of *Os Lusíadas,* an epic poem of Portugal's world history; Pedro Álvares Cabral, discoverer of Brazil; Afonso de Albuquerque, viceroy of India; Nuno Álvares Pereira, warrior and saint; and Vasco da Gama, of course.

Also entombed in the National Pantheon are presidents of Portugal: Sidónio Pais, assassinated in 1918; Marshal António Óscar de Fragoso Carmona, under whose government António de Oliveira Salazar began his climb to power; and Téofilo Braga, first president of the provisional government after the settling of the Republic. Several Portuguese writers are also interred here, including Almeida Garrett, the country's most outstanding writer of the 19th century; João de Deus, lyric poet; and Guerra Junqueiro, also a poet.

The National Pantheon, Campo de Santa Clara (tel. 87-15-29), is open to the public Tuesday to Sunday (except holidays) from 10 a.m. to 5 p.m. Admission is 50$ (35¢). Ask the guards to take you to the terrace for a beautiful view over the river.

A visit to the Pantheon can be combined with a shopping trip to the Flea Market (walk down the Campo de Santa Clara, heading toward the river).

ST. ROQUE CHURCH AND MUSEUM

The St. Roque Church (tel. 346-03-61) was founded in the closing years of the 16th century by the Jesuits. To reach it, head for the Largo Trindade Coelho.

The church, with its painted wood ceiling, contains a celebrated chapel honoring John the Baptist by Luigi Vanvitelli. The chapel was assembled in Rome in the 18th century with such precious materials as alabaster and lapis lazuli, then dismantled and shipped to Lisbon, where it was reassembled. It was ordered by the Bragança king João V nine years before the end of his reign in 1750. The marble mosaics look like a painting. You can also visit the sacristy, rich in paintings illustrating scenes from the lives of the Society of Jesus saints. The Jesuits held great power in Portugal, at one time virtually governing the country for the king.

The St. Roque Museum is visited chiefly by those wishing to see its collections of metal pieces and fabrics. A pair of gold and silver torch-holders, weighing about 840 pounds, is considered among the most elaborate in Europe. The gold embroidery from the 18th century is a rare treasure, as are the vestments. The paintings are mainly from the 16th century, including one of a double-chinned Catherine of Austria and another of the wedding ceremony of King Manuel. Look for a remarkable 16th-century *Virgin of the Plague,* and a polished conch shell from the 18th century that served as a baptismal font.

Hours for the museum are Tuesday to Sunday from 10 a.m. to 5 p.m. The church is open during the same hours, except that it is open on Monday as well. Admission is 25$ (20¢); free on Sunday.

ST. VINCENT OUTSIDE THE WALLS

This outstanding Renaissance church houses the Pantheon of the House of Bragança, the dynasty that ruled Portugal beginning with the collapse of Spanish domination in 1640 and lasting until 1910. A former convent, the church contains an estimated one million *azulejos* (glazed earthenware tiles). The sacristy is graced with Portuguese marble, jacaranda woodwork from Brazil, and an 18th-century ivory Christ from Goa.

When St. Vincent was first built between 1582 and 1627, it was outside the walls of Lisbon—hence, its name. The earthquake of 1755 caused its dome to collapse, and it was never replaced. At Largo de S. Vincente, it is open daily from 10 a.m. to 1 p.m. and 3 to 5 p.m., charging 120$ (80¢) for admission.

In the burial chamber is entombed the twice-married Maria II, who ascended to the Portuguese throne at the age of 15. Dom Carlos I is buried near his son, Luís Felipe, the latter only 19 when both were assassinated at the Praça do Comércio in 1908. Manuel II, who ruled for only two years, lived a life of exile in England, dying there in 1932, at which time his body was returned home to Lisbon.

The House of Bragança also ruled Brazil from 1822 to 1889. The coffin of Dom Pedro, the first emperor of that country (he abdicated in 1831), rests in this Pantheon. Finally, because there was no native burial ground for him, Michael, the last king of Rumania, was placed here in a handsome sarcophagus. King Michael of Rumania was forced to abandon his throne in the closing hours of 1947, and he lived in exile in Portugal until his death in 1953.

8. Queluz Palace

For most visitors, the **Palácio Queluz** is the first stop of their venture into the suburbs of Lisbon. And what a fortunate choice. One writer called it "the prettiest pink palace in the world, as well as the most important and charming example of rococo architecture in Portugal." The Portuguese government is so proud of the little 18th-century nugget that it houses foreign dignitaries in its Pavilion of Dona Maria I (former guests have included Eisenhower and Elizabeth II).

Queluz is most often described as Portugal's Versailles, but so lofty a comparison detracts from its true character. Essentially, it's a palace of faded pink walls that stands quietly in the bright sunshine looking out over beds of mauve-colored petunias. Its character has always been that of a summer residence, whose façade is rather simple and classic, although the interior is rich and ornate, overlooking beautiful gardens and ponds.

The palace was an adaptation of an old hunting pavilion of the Marquês Castelo Rodrigo, which came into the possession of the royal family in 1654. King Pedro III, husband of Maria I, liked it so much he decided to turn it into a summer residence, enlarging it and having it decorated with lavish interiors. What you see now is not the way it was, as the palace suffered greatly during the French invasions. Almost all the belongings were sent to Brazil with the royal family at the beginning of the 19th century.

The glassy Throne Room is most intriguing to visitors. You can stroll under the watchful eye of a guard through the dressing room of the queen, through the Don Quixote Chamber, and into the Music Salon, with its grand French piano and 19th-century harp.

The furnishings and general accoutrements are eclectic: Venetian chandeliers, Empire antiques, Florentine marbles, Delft plates, Macao screens, Austrian porcelain, Portuguese Chippendale and tapestries, and pieces made of jacaranda wood from Brazil.

After a royal tour, you can wind down by strolling through the handsomely laid-out gardens, with their lily-studded fountains, earthenware tiles, beds of flowers, and 18th-century statuary.

The palace is open daily except Tuesday from 10 a.m. to 1 p.m. and 2 to 5 p.m. (On the grounds is the Cozinha Velha, or old kitchen, a restaurant that is described in Chapter IV.) Admission to the palace is 200$ ($1.35) in the low season (from October to May) and 400$ ($2.72) in the high season (from June to September). If you just wish to visit the gardens, the admission is 40$ (25¢).

Queluz lies on the road to Sintra, about 9½ miles from Lisbon. To reach it by public transportation, take a train at Rossio Station in Lisbon. A one-way fare costs 85$ (60¢).

9. Sintra

Ancient Sintra, on the rugged slope of the Serra de Sintra, is the town Byron dubbed "glorious Eden." John Cam Hobhouse and Byron came this way in 1809 on their grand tour, and later Byron was to write his autobiographical poem, *Childe Harold,* in which he included his praise of the beauty of Sintra. Thus Sintra became a focus for a host of English visitors.

Byron and Robert Southey, another English poet, weren't the first to discover the wonders of this remarkable oasis. Its praises were sung centuries before by the Luís Vaz de Camões poem, *Os Lusíadas.*

Even before Portugal's Golden Age, Sintra was favored by the Moors, who selected it as a site of one of their greatest castles, which stands in ruins today crowning a hilltop. The castle fell to the Christian crusaders in 1147.

Today Sintra is virtually a suburb of Lisbon, favored by the aristocracy, even exiled royalty, who inhabit the elaborate villas—often compared to birthday cakes—studding the hills.

Sintra lies about 17½ miles northwest of Lisbon, and is reached by private car, on an organized tour, or else by frequent train service, about a 45-minute ride from the main railway station at Rossio in Lisbon. But connections are possible from such Costa do Sol resorts as Estoril and Cascais.

Much of Sintra's charm comes from its luxurious vegetation—camellias, ferns, mimosa, eucalyptus, lemon trees, strawberry beds, pink bougainvillea, red geraniums, and pine trees (and more lizards crawling up more damp tile walls than in any other place in Portugal). One publicist summed up the charm of the town quite well by saying, "It is indeed a fairytale setting and gives one the feeling that this is where Sleeping Beauty must have rested all those years."

THE NATIONAL PALACE

This royal palace (tel. 923-00-85) was constructed primarily during the reign of two Portuguese kings: João I (1385–1433) and Manuel I (1469–1521; known as "the Fortunate"). Subsequent additions were made in later centuries, and the palace continued to function as a royal palace until 1910, when Manuel II fled to exile in England.

Portuguese kings and queens summered here. Although the original Moorish palace that stood on this spot was torn down, the Muslim influence lived on when it was reconstructed. The introduction of the Gothic or Manueline style makes for a bizarre effect. Be sure to note the painted *azulejos* (tiles) that line many of the rooms, as these are considered the finest in Portugal. This is one of the most important Portuguese monuments.

The palace has been intimately linked to the lives and legends of many members of the Portuguese royal family. For example, Afonso V, king of Portugal from 1438 to 1481, was born at Sintra. He was named king only six years later. But to a later king, Afonso VI, the palace was a gloomy prison. Imprisoned by his brother (later Pedro II), he lost not only his throne but his wife. The ill-fated Afonso endlessly paced his cell until his death in 1683.

The Room of the Swans was favored by João I, part of its window decoration coming from what is now Spanish Morocco (Ceuta). One of the most interesting legends of the palace revolves around João I, who married Philippa of Lancaster (they were the parents of Henry the Navigator). As the oft-repeated tale goes, Philippa discovered her husband making love to one of her fair ladies-in-waiting. Although the English queen forgave her errant spouse, gossips speculated at length. Enraged, the king ordered that the room be redecorated, its ceiling adorned with magpies, these noisy birds symbolizing the chattering court. Hence, the nickname Room of the Magpies.

For many visitors, the Stag Room—also called the Heraldic Room—is the most expressive, with its coats-of-arms of the noble families of Portugal and scenes from the hunt. The Room of the Mermaids (sometimes known as Sirens) is also graceful. In the old kitchen there are two enormous original chimneys.

From many of the salons there are excellent vistas opening onto the hills surrounding Sintra. Tapestries, paintings, sheltered patios, softly falling water, potted plants, and long, dark corridors evoke the faded life of another era.

Tickets to the palace cost 400$ ($2.70) from June to September, 200$ ($1.35) from October to May. Purchase your ticket downstairs at a counter on the left, then walk up the stairway to the right and ring the bell to be let in. The palace is open daily, except Wednesday, from 10 a.m. to 5 p.m. (Ticket sales stop at 4:30 p.m.)

THE PALACE OF PENA

Some have called this the most romantic scenic spot in all of Portugal. The palace was built on a peak about 1,500 feet high, overlooking the Moorish castle on the opposite hill. Pena Palace (tel. 923-02-27) majestically looks down on Sintra from its regal throne. (Some actually walk to it from the town square, but others take a taxi or drive their own cars.)

The *National Geographic* labeled Pena Palace a "soaring agglomeration of towers, cupolas, and battlemented walls." A fantasy in the sky it truly is, constructed to the specifications of Ferdinand of Saxe-Coburg-Gotha, the consort of Queen Maria II.

Helping Ferdinand achieve his dream was Baron Eschwedge, a German architect. The baron attempted to re-create the aura of the Middle Ages; in some respects he succeeded, but it's "merely the mock." The present castle was built on the grounds of a monastery ordered erected in the early 16th century for Jerónimos monks by Manuel the Fortunate. What remains of the monastery is a cloister and a tiny ogival chapel (see its alabaster panel and stained-glass window).

Most critics satirize the interior of the palace, suggesting that it is Wagnerian or lacking in taste. Actually, it's quite fascinating, as it's been left almost intact since it was last occupied by the royal family in 1910. It was from this palace that the mother of Manuel II gathered her jewelry and most valuable possessions on a long-ago autumn day and was driven on a wild ride to Mafra, where she collected her son, the king, to flee with him into exile. Around the top of the hill is the **Parque de Pena,** mapped out between 1846 and 1850 under the direction of Ferdinand. It's acclaimed as one of the most majestic landscapes in Europe. Climb to the **Cruz Alta** for a panoramic view.

Tickets cost 400$ ($2.70). Hours are Tuesday to Sunday from 10 a.m. to 5 p.m.

10. A Bullfight Spectacle

Portuguese bullfights, of course, differ from the Spanish in that the matador doesn't kill the bull. This tradition dates from the 18th century when the son of the Duke of Arcos (bullfighting was then a nobleman's sport) lost his life in the arena. His father jumped into the ring and personally killed the bull. The dictator prime minister, Marquês de Pombal—worried about manpower needed to rebuild Lisbon after the earthquake—decreed that that was the last life to be sacrificed in the ring. From that day forth, the horns of the bull were bound with leather bandages known as *emboladas*.

The prohibition against killing the bull is always under fire from certain critics. For example, Jaime Saraiva, a commentator in Lisbon, was once quoted in the press as saying, "a bullfight without a kill is a great lie; it is not serious." But don't let his words keep you from attending a spectacle. The fight may not be "serious," but it is what Marvine Howe termed "one of the most beautiful equestrian displays in the world."

Warning: Even though the bull isn't killed in Portugal, it must be pointed out, in fairness, that many readers still find this spectacle nauseating and take strong exception to Howe's comment that it is "beautiful." The spears jabbed into the neck of the bull produce blood, of course, making the unfortunate animal visibly weaker. The so-called fight has been labeled no contest. One reader wrote, "The animals are frightened, confused, and badgered before they are mercifully allowed to exit. What sport!"

Bullfighting in Portugal doesn't enjoy the number of fans it has in Spain. It's estimated that only one-quarter of the populace attend the *corridas,* as opposed to three times that number in neighboring Spain.

Opening the corrida, the matadors parade in wearing their colorful suits, many unchanged in design for 200 years. They are followed by *cavaleiros,* the horseback-riding men who place darts in the bull, and the *forcados,* the troupe of men who tackle the bull. Traditionally, the latter wear jaunty green caps with red bands on their heads. They are attired in gold jackets and olive trousers, with red sashes around their waists, white stockings covering their calves.

At the sound of a trumpet, the gates open and out comes the cavaleiro on a horse he's most likely trained from its birth. The trick is to lead the galloping horse into the pathway of a rampaging bull —only to get the steed to swerve in time to prevent a head-on collision (which has happened). Darts are thrust into the bull's neck at this point to weaken him.

In Portugal, the bull is tackled by hand, the action known as a *pega*. A phalanx of eight forcados advances on the bull. One takes the angry animal by the horns; another may latch onto his tail; still another may grab the flesh hanging from the bull's chest, and so forth until the matador enters and finishes up the show.

The "season of the corridas" runs from Easter until early autumn, and in Lisbon, bullfights are presented at the Moorish **Campo Pequeno,** reached by the subway. Alternatively, you can attend the **Monumental de Cascais** (tel. 28-31-03) at one of the leading resorts on the Costa do Sol. Fights are usually scheduled for Thursday night and Sunday afternoon.

Seats are sold in three different categories: *sombra* (shade), *sombra y sol* (a seat in the sun for part of the fight, in the shade for the rest), and *sol* (a seat in the sun during the entire fight). Naturally, the shady seats are the most expensive.

11. Organized Tours

Any travel agent in Lisbon will book you on an organized tour. One of the most popular agencies is **STAR,** the Portuguese representative of American Express, at 4-A Avenida Sidónio Pais (main office, tel. 53-98-71). It lies close to the southern edge of Edward VII Park, near the starting point of most of its tours, the Marquês de Pombal Square. It also has a downtown branch office at 14 Restauradores Square (tel. 346-2501). A competing company, which offers basically the same tours at the same prices, is **Portugal Tours,** Rua D. Estefânia 124 (second floor) (tel. 52-06-20).

At the height of the season, from April 1 to October 31, most of STAR's tours are operated every day. St. George's Castle, Belém's Jerónimos monastery, the National Coach Museum—all are highlighted by different city tours that stress cultural, historical, or scenic attractions. A half-day tour of Lisbon, with a guided commentary, leaves daily at 9:30 a.m. and 2:30 p.m., for a cost of around 4,000$ ($27.20).

The most heavily booked excursion to the environs is the full-day tour to Pena or Mafra, Queluz, Sintra, and Estoril, with lunch included. Even if you don't take organized tours, this is a way to reach far-flung monuments—each of which lies inconveniently in different outlying regions—in as short a time as possible, leaving the hassle of navigation to an expert. The cost of the full-day tour is around 9,000$ ($61.20).

The longest and most ambitious of the day trips is a 12-hour journey north to the walled city of Óbidos, the fishing village of Nazaré, the legendary monastery of Batalha, and the pilgrimage site of Fátima. You won't have much time in any of these places (you'll be practically running from monument to monument), but if your time is short and you want to see as much of Portugal as possible, it might be worthwhile. The cost is around 10,000$ ($68) and includes lunch.

SHOPPING IN LISBON

1. SHOPPING MALLS
2. SHOPPING A TO Z

All the major Portuguese handcrafts get their best showing in Lisbon. Shopkeepers or their agents scan the country, as well as Madeira and the Azores, ferreting out the best work from the most skillful artisans and craftspeople. Owing to the versatility of the Portuguese and their ability to absorb other styles, handcrafts often betray exotic influences.

Although frowned upon in prestigious shops, bargaining is still a respectable custom throughout Lisbon. You'll have to let your intuition be your guide. A good rule of thumb to follow is to determine whether the shop is small enough to be owner managed. If it is, you might possibly work out a deal.

Shops are spread throughout the city, but the major area for browsing is the **Baixa,** the district forming downtown Lisbon. Its three principal streets are the Rua do Ouro (Street of Gold, with major jewelry shops), Rua da Prata (Street of Silver), and Rua Augusta. To the west is the more fashionable **Chiado,** the second major shopping district, whose main street is the Rua Garrett.

You'll find especially good buys in Portugal in handmade embroideries (blouses, tablecloths, napkins, and handkerchiefs) from the Madeira Islands and the Azores; cork products in every size, shape, and description, everything from placemats to cigarette boxes; decorative *azulejos* (glazed tiles); porcelain and china from Vista Alegre; Nazaré fishermen's sweaters; gold and silver filigree jewelry; Arraiolos carpets; local pottery; and fado records.

1. Shopping Malls

There are some 150 boutiques, shops, and snack bars installed in four of the five floors of the **Rossio Railway Station,** on the Praça Dom Pedro IV in the heart of downtown Lisbon. The fifth floor is where the trains arrive and depart. Banks of escalators whisk you from floor to floor, and shopping in the maze of small shops is easier than walking on the congested streets. Conveniently, the shops are open every day of the year from 9 a.m. to midnight. The street floor is deceivingly shabby—ignore it and take the escalator to the boutiques. You'll find apparel for men, women, and children, shops specializing in jewelry, fado records, whatever. There's a pharmacy for "naturalists," beauty parlors, hairdressers, bookstores, leather goods, sweaters, and Portuguese handcrafts.

The most spectacular shopping complex in Lisbon is the **Amoreiras Shopping Center de Lisboa,** the largest in Iberia and fourth largest in Europe. You can wander through this Oriental fantasy, exploring the contents of more than 300 shops and boutiques. A huge array of merchandise is offered for sale, including Portuguese fashions, leather goods, crystal, and souvenirs. In addition to several restaurants and snack bars, there is also a health center. The location is on a hill at the entrance to Lisbon, lying in back of the old reservoir called Aguas Livres. The blue-and-pink towers rise 19 stories and have already changed the skyline of Lisbon. The mall is open daily from 10 a.m. to midnight.

Most stores open at 9 a.m. and close at 1 p.m. for lunch; they generally reopen at 3 p.m. and shut down at 7 p.m. However, some proprietors prefer to close for lunch from noon to 2 p.m., so keep a watch out. Most stores in Lisbon and elsewhere in Portugal are open only half a day on Saturday—in the morning.

---

2. Shopping A to Z

ANTIQUE ALLEY

Along both sides of the narrow **Rua de São José** are treasure troves—shops packed with antiques from all over the world. Antique dealers from America come here to pick up bargains. You'll find ornate carvings or time-seasoned woods, brass, plaques, copper pans, silver candelabra, crystal sconces, and chandeliers, plus a wide selection of old wooden figures, silver boxes, porcelain plates, and bowls.

Rua Dom Pedro V is another street of antique shops, of which one of my personal favorites is **Solar,** 68–70 Rua Dom Pedro (tel. 346-55-22). It is stocked with architectural remnants (for example, fountains and garden ornaments) and antique tiles salvaged from some of Portugal's historic buildings and manor houses. The condition of the tiles varies, of course. Some go back as far as the 16th century. Don't expect bargains—long ago the prices of these museum-quality pieces hit stratospheric levels. The store also sells antique furniture and pewter ware. The store, like many of its neighbors, is open Monday to Friday from 10 a.m. to 1 p.m. and 3 to 7 p.m.; Saturday, 10 a.m. to 1 p.m.; closed Sunday. Manuel Leitão is the English-speaking owner.

ARRAIOLOS CARPETS

The fine woolen rugs made in the little town of Arraiolos have earned the place an international reputation. Legend says these rugs were first made by Moorish craftspeople expelled from Lisbon in the early 16th century. Those designs were said to be in imitation of those from Persia. Some of these carpets eventually found their way into museums.

In Lisbon, the showcase for the Arraiolos carpets is **Casa Quintão,** 30-34 Rua Ivens (tel. 346-58-37). Rugs here are priced by the square foot, according to the density of the stitching. Casa Quintão can also reproduce intricate Oriental or medieval designs in rugs or tapestries and create any custom pattern specified by a client. The shop also sells materials and gives instructions on how to make your own carpets and tapestry-covered pillows. The staff seems genuinely willing to help. Casa Quintão is open Monday to Friday from 9 a.m. to 1 p.m. from 3 to 7 p.m. Between October and May, it is also open Saturday from 9 a.m. to 1 p.m.

ART GALLERIES

The leading art gallery of Lisbon (and perhaps of all of Portugal) is **Galeria Sesimbra,** 77 Rua Castilho (tel. 56-02-91), which lies in a shop set into the foundation of the Ritz Hotel. It is operated by one of the most distinguished art dealers of Iberia, a well-traveled and distinguished Scotsman who long ago decided to make Portugal his home. Mainly Portuguese artists are displayed here, but foreign artists "who have lived in Portugal long enough to get a feeling for the country" are also exhibited. The finest of Portuguese paintings, sculpture, and ceramics, including the works of such critically acclaimed Spanish artists as Miró Turmo, are sold here. Among the gallery's best-known works are Agulha tapestries, composed of a controlled variation of stitching, giving it an aesthetic advantage over those made on looms. Sizes can range from 10 square feet to "the longest tapestry in the world." Extremely sophisticated, with clients from around the world, the gallery is open Monday to Friday from 10 a.m. to 7 p.m.; Saturday from 10 a.m. to 1 p.m.

Galeria 111, 113A Campo Grande (tel. 77-74-18), has been recognized since 1964 as one of the major art galleries of Lisbon. Some of the leading contemporary artists of Portugal are on display here in wide-ranging exhibitions of sculpture, paintings, and graphics. It is open Monday to Friday from 10 a.m. to 6 p.m.; Saturday from 10 a.m. to 1 p.m. It closes for two weeks in late August every year.

AZULEJOS (GLAZED TILES)

Founded in 1741, **Sant'Anna,** 95-97 Rua do Alecrim (tel. 32-25-37), is Portugal's leading ceramic center. In the Chiado section, Sant'Anna is known for its *azulejos* (glazed tiles). The Rua do Alecrim location is the showroom outlet; however, you can also visit the factory at 96 Calçada da Boa Hora, but you must call ahead and make an appointment. The craftspeople who create and decorate the tiles are among the finest in Europe, many of them following designs in use since the Middle Ages. Sant'Anna is open Monday to Friday from 9 a.m. to 7 p.m. without a lunch break; Saturday from 9 a.m. to 1 p.m.

Fábrica Cerâmica Viúva Lamengo, 25 Largo do Intendente (tel. 57-59-29), sells reproductions of old Portuguese pottery and tiles, including an interesting selection of planters and umbrella stands. When you reach the address, you'll know you're at the right place: its façade is decorated with these colorful *azulejos* with figures in their rich plumage and dress. Viúva Lamengo is open Monday to Friday from 9 a.m. to 1 p.m. and 3 to 7 p.m.

CORK PRODUCTS

For something typically Portuguese, try the **Casa das Cortiças,** 4 Rua Escola Politécnica (tel. 32-58-58). "Mr. Cork" became somewhat of a legend in Lisbon for offering everything conceivable that could be made of cork, of which Portugal controls a hefty part of the world market. Mr. Cork is gone now, but the store carries on. You'll be surprised at the number of items that can be made from cork, including a chess set or a checkerboard. Perhaps a set of six placemats in a two-toned checkerboard style will interest you. For souvenirs, the cork caravels (three-masted 15th- and 16th-century ships) are immensely popular. Other items include a natural cutting board and an ice bucket. The House of Cork is open Monday to Friday from 9 a.m. to 1 p.m. and 3 to 7 p.m.; Saturday from 9 a.m. to 1 p.m.

EMBROIDERIES

A good place to shop, **Madeira Superbia,** 75-A Avenida Duque de Loulé (tel. 53-79-68), is an outlet for one of the finest embroidery factories on the Madeira Islands. This showcase of the exquisite craft offers excellent—although not inexpensive—linens, tapestries, and women's apparel, such as embroidered blouses and petit-point handbags. High-quality linen and organdy are often imported from Switzerland and Belgium, then embroidered in Madeira. The collection of hand-embroidered pillowcases, tea cloths, napkins, and table centerpieces is exceptional. Placemats often come in organdy with a linen appliqué (some double-edged with shadow-work embroidery). Another popular item is monogrammed linen handkerchiefs. There are branches at the Ritz Hotel in Lisbon and the Hotel Estoril Sol in Cascais. The store is open Monday to Friday from 9 a.m. to 1 p.m. and 3 to 7 p.m.; Saturday from 9 a.m. to 1 p.m.

In the Chiado district, the **Casa Regional da Ilha Verde,** 4 Rua Paiva de Andrade (tel. 32-59-74), is the "Regional House of the Green Island." As such, it specializes in handmade items—especially embroideries—from the Azores. Every piece of merchandise is guaranteed to have been made by hand. Good buys are found in linen placemats with napkins. Some of the designs have been in use for centuries. Other gift items include products made of sperm whale teeth, such as cigarette holders, letter openers, and rings. The shop is open Monday to Friday from 9:30 a.m. to 1 p.m. and 3 to 7 p.m.; Saturday from 9:30 a.m. to 1 p.m.

FILIGREE

Filigree items are all the rage not only in Lisbon but all over Portugal. This art of ornamental openwork made of fine gold or silver wire dates back to ancient times. The most expensive items, often objets d'art, are fashioned from 19¼-karat gold. Depictions of caravels are one of the forms this art expression takes. However, less expensive trinkets are often made of sterling silver or sterling silver that has been dipped in 24-karat gold. Well on its way to being a century old, **Joalharia do Carmo,** 87-B Rua do Carmo (tel. 32-30-50), is the best place in Lisbon to shop for filigree work. Some of the gold pieces here have been further adorned with either precious or semiprecious stones. Joalharia do Carmo is open Monday to Friday from 9:30 a.m. to 1:30 p.m. and 3 to 7 p.m.; Saturday from 9:30 a.m. to 1:30 p.m.

LINENS

Principe Real, 12-14 Rua da Escola Politecnica (tel. 346-59-45), specializes in linens elegant enough to grace the tables of monarchs, including, in days gone by, Princess Grace of Monaco. This family-run store produces some of Europe's finest tablecloths and sheets in cotton, linen, and organdy. Although the Rockefellers have purchased items here from its owner and designer, the merchandise is not beyond the means of a middle-class tourist. About two dozen staff members can execute a linen pattern to match a client's favorite porcelain, or the owner can create one of her own designs. The store is open Monday to Friday from 9 a.m. to 1 p.m. and 3 to 7 p.m.; Saturday from 9 a.m. to 1 p.m.

PORCELAIN AND CHINA

Unparalleled for china and glassware, **Vista Alegre,** 18 Largo do Chiado (tel. 346-14-01), numbers diplomats and royalty, or whoever demands the very best, among its regular clientele. Of special interest to the casual shopper are statues made in Vista Alegre's factories in the town of Ilhavo. Amazingly lifelike, they depict characters in regional Portuguese costumes, as well as porcelain birds and flowers. Although beautiful, they are expensive. You'll spend less money ordering a set of dishes or porcelain fruit bowls. The shop is open Monday to Friday from 9:30 a.m. to 1:30 p.m. and 3 to 7 p.m.; Saturday from 9:30 a.m. to 1:30 p.m.

SILVER AND GOLD

The most distinguished silver- and goldsmith in Portugal is **W. A. Sarmento,** 251 Rua Aurea (tel. 32-67-74). The shop at the foot of the Santa Justa elevator provides Lisboans with treasured confirmation and graduation gifts, and is favored by diplomats, movie stars, and the Costa do Sol aristocracy. In 1970 Sarmento celebrated its 100th anniversary—it's remained in the hands of the same owners all the while. The store is open Monday to Friday from 9:30 a.m. to 1:30 p.m. and 3 to 7 p.m.; Saturday from 9:30 a.m. to 1:30 p.m.

Gold is considered a good buy in Portugal, as the government strictly regulates its sale, requiring jewelers to put a minimum of 19¼ karats in articles made of the precious metal. Sarmento specializes in lacy filigree jewelry in gold or silver. Just hold an earring or brooch up to the light and enjoy its intricacy and delicacy. Especially popular are small gold filigree caravels, which come in many prices. Less expensive filigree jewelry is made of silver and plated with gold. In this category earrings and cufflinks predominate. For the charm collector, Sarmento is a Roman holiday. Literally dozens of choices are offered.

SUEDE

A "one-couple" show is **Caprice**, 45 Rua Joaquim António de Aguiar (tel. 65-78-93), very close to the entrance of the Ritz Hotel. M. and Mme Gaulier sell a fine line of washable suede garments for men and women, including long coats, skirts, and suits. Philippe Gaulier's mother was a Lanvin stylist, and apparently he inherited a great deal of her taste. He and the English-speaking Mme Gaulier will present you with an assortment of Ultra-suede garments, particularly dresses and coats, that are wrinkle-free and machine washable. The suede comes in an interesting assortment of colors, including dark chocolate, pink, aqua, navy, and caramel. Other garments they sell are made of silk. The store is open Monday to Friday from 9:30 a.m. to 1 p.m. and 3 to 7 p.m.; Saturday from 9:30 a.m. to 1 p.m.

THIEVES' MARKET

This open-air street market—called the **Feira da Ladra**—is similar in character to the flea markets of Paris and Madrid. Almost every conceivable article is offered for sale in the street stalls. Vendors peddle their wares on Tuesday and Saturday (it's best to go in the morning when the pickings are riper).

In the Alfama district, about a five-minute walk from the waterfront, the market lies in back of the Military Museum, adjoining the Pantheon of São Vicente. Begin your shopping expedition at the Campo de Santa Clara. The hilly street with its tree-lined center is lined with portable stalls with individual displays.

You may pick up a valuable object here, but you'll have to search through an abundance of cheap clothing and useless junk to find it. The following types of merchandise are displayed: old brass door knockers with clasped hands, brass scales, brass beds, oil lamps, portable bidets, cowbells, old coins, Macao china, Angola woodcarvings, antique watches, meat grinders, broken torchiers, ships' lanterns, and gas lamps.

Not only can you bargain, you *should* bargain. After the stallkeeper quotes you the first price, assume a not-interested stance. Then the fun commences, the price (usually) sliding downhill like a toboggan ride.

LISBON AFTER DARK

Fado singing is Portugal's most popular and important art form, originating in the hearts and experiences of every Portuguese, whether a fisherman from Nazaré, a cork grower from the plains of Alentejo, or a metropolitan Lisboan. Every Portuguese has a point of view about fado: He or she sings it or has a favorite artist whose particular style speaks to him or her directly.

Fado ("fate" in Portuguese) is the true folk song of the people, not superimposed on them in the name of art or culture. It's in their blood. The songs are poignant, from the heart—sometimes tragic, sometimes wistful, even joyful at times, but usually melancholic, filled with nostalgia. The sound originates in Portugal, combining the Arabic "wail" with the throaty, almost guttural voice of the peasant.

Even if you don't understand the Portuguese language, fado speaks vibrantly for itself. Traditionally, fado is sung to the accompaniment of one or two guitars. These songs of sorrow have been heard for more than a century. The most famous singer of the 19th century was a beautiful gypsy, Maria Severa. Her electric and dynamic style won the attention of all the city, especially the Count of Vimioso, who loved her and made her "the toast of Lisbon." Her style of singing stimulated others and sparked a host of imitators. Upon her death, the reverence for her was so great and lasting that every female *fadista* to this day drapes herself in a black shawl in memory of Severa. This story is legendary, and many fans of fado tend to discount it as "fanciful."

North Americans first heard fado in New York City in a chic club, La Vie en Rose, when Portugal's best known *fadista,* Amalia Rodrigues, appeared. She rose from a lowly beginning—a barefoot urchin of the streets of Lisbon selling fruit to Alfama housewives—to fame and fortune and an international reputation.

There are more than 20 restaurants or cafés where fado is sung in Lisbon. There are two major areas where the wailing cry of fado can be heard nightly: the **Alfama** and the **Bairro Alto** (upper quarter). You can spend an entire evening—until dawn if you wish—"fado hopping" in Lisbon. You can begin with a meal around 9:30 p.m. and continue throughout the night, sipping the heady Portuguese wine and sinking deeper and deeper into a sweet melancholia. To begin your hop in the Alfama, go to the **Largo do Chafariz,** a little plaza about a block from the harbor. Three of Lisbon's top-ranking clubs are within a one- to five-minute walk from this point. The Bairro Alto fado district is found just off the **Largo de San Roque.**

There are other diversions as well: discos, nightclubs, vaudeville, opera, theater, and ballet. Motion pictures are shown in their original languages, with Portuguese subtitles. Local newspapers contain listings of what's on after dark. Or refer to a weekly copy of *What's On In Lisbon,* usually obtainable from your hotel concierge.

---

1. Fado Cafés

Lisboa à Noite, 69 Rua das Gáveas (tel. 346-85-57), is a re-creation of a 17th-century tavern, complete with several open rooms separated by thick stone arches. Near the kitchen is a stone well, yielding fresh water since the 17th century. The decor consists of leather and brass-studded chairs, blue tile walls, and old engravings and prints. At one time the club was a stable, but now glamor prevails, a proper backdrop for some of the best fado in Lisbon.

In winter, eucalyptus logs burn in an open fireplace. *Típico* touches are added by the collection of pewter candlesticks on a mantel, the hanging hams and strings of garlic in the open kitchen, and the old leather bottles. All of this forms a setting for the great *fadista,* Fernanda Maria, the owner of the café. When it comes time for Fernanda to perform, the air becomes charged with intensity.

Lisboa à Noite is not Lisbon's cheapest place to drink or dine, but it's worth every escudo. If you've already had dinner, you can drop in for two drinks, which will cost 2,000$ ($13.80) and will automatically be charged to your bill whether you consume them or not. Many visitors order dinner before the show begins. A la carte meals cost around 5,000$ ($34.50) each, and could include either codfish Fernanda Maria or steak Lisboa à Noite. The club is open for drinks and food Monday to Saturday from 8 p.m. to around 2 a.m. The music, by as many as four different artists a night, begins around 9:30 p.m. and lasts, with a few breaks, until 11:30 p.m. It's a good idea to reserve a table in advance, whether you plan to dine or not.

Parreirinha da Alfama, 1 Beco do Espérito (tel. 86-82-09), is an oldtime fado café, just a one-minute walk from the docksite of the Alfama. You can order a good regional dinner beginning early, but it's suggested that you go toward the shank of the evening and stay late. It's open every night of the week beginning at 7:30 p.m., although the crowds usually don't form until the music begins at 9:30 p.m. An à la carte dinner, which might include specialties from many different regions of Portugal, costs between 4,000$ ($27.60) and 5,000$ ($34.50). It's very important to reserve a table in advance. If you've already had dinner, you can order drinks priced at around 1,000$ ($6.90) each, and you may be encouraged to have more than one or two. The club closes around 2 a.m. The atmosphere is self-consciously *taverna,* with all sorts of Portuguese provincial oddities. The singers are first-rate.

A Severa, 49–61 Rua das Gáveas (tel. 346-40-06), is one of the oldest and most consistently successful fado houses in the Bairro Alto. Many *fadistas* who went on to greater fame got their start here. It's bistro-style, and you can either have drinks or order a complete Portuguese dinner with all the trimmings. The house specialty is chicken cooked in a clay pot. Whether you intend to dine here or not, it's wise to make a reservation, because tables are usually overcrowded by 9 p.m. A la carte dinners cost around 5,000$ ($34.50); if you only want to drink and listen to the music, you'll pay a minimum charge of 2,000$ ($13.80). This will get you either one drink of expensive non-Portuguese liquor, or two drinks of domestic liquor (beer, wine, or Portuguese brandy). Open every night of the week except Thursday, A Severa serves dinner from 8 p.m. until closing, which is usually around 2 a.m. Music begins at 10 p.m.

2. Cultural Evenings

Opera and ballet devotees may want to attend a performance at the **Teatro Nacional de São Carlos,** 9 Rua Serpa (tel. 36-84-08). This national theater was constructed in the 18th century. It books companies from around the world. The season begins in mid-December and extends through May.

In addition, there are several theaters presenting plays—both classic Portuguese and foreign—autumn through spring, but only in Portuguese. The most famous of these theaters is **Teatro Nacional de D. Maria II,** Praça Dom Pedro IV (tel. 337-22-46). Seats here usually cost from 500$ ($3.40) to 3,000$ ($20.40).

Recitals and concerts are held at various places in Lisbon, especially the **Estufa Fria** in Edward VII Park and the **Gulbenkian Arts Center,** 45 Avenida de Berna (tel. 77-91-31).

Chamber-music concerts and symphony presentations are performed at the **Teatro Municipal de São Luís,** 40 Rua António Maria Cardoso (tel. 36-52-59).

Major motion pictures are shown in Lisbon in their original languages, usually at one of the big cinema houses along Avenida da Liberdade. First-run movie houses include **São Jorge,** 175 Avenida da Liberdade (tel. 57-91-94), and **Tivoli,** 188 Avenida da Liberdade (tel. 57-05-95).

3. Discos of Lisbon

Banana Power, 51 Rua Cascais (tel. 64-84-85), is an old warehouse converted into a stylish disco in the Alcantara section, midway between Lisbon and the suburb of Belém. Hundreds of Lisboans, all young, pour in here to enjoy the recorded music, paying an entrance fee of 1,000$ ($6.90) for men and 500$ ($3.45) for women; a scotch and soda is around 750$ ($5.15). Go as late as your fatigue level will allow, since it doesn't open until 11 p.m., and usually doesn't begin jumping until midnight. Once the action begins, it lasts until 5 a.m., every night of the week except Monday. You can take tram 17 to the entrance from the Praça do Comércio, but since taxis are inexpensive, it's best to take one to the entrance, which has only a small sign announcing itself.

Ad Lib, 28 Rua Barata Salgueiro (tel. 56-17-17), is one of the most chic discos in Lisbon, advertising itself as a private club, but secretly willing to admit well-dressed outsiders (that means jackets and ties for men, appropriately glamorous costumes for women). Located on the seventh floor of a modern apartment building near the Ritz Hotel, it offers a shimmering sky-level view, acres of smoke-tinted mirrors and plants, and such sophisticated accents as stone Buddhas from Macao and flickering candles. The latest in recorded music from America, England, and Italy is played on the newest in sound equipment. You'll pay 7,000$ ($48.30) per person at the door, then around 750$ ($5.15) for a scotch and soda at the bar. Expensive and very beautiful, the club is open every night of the week from 11 p.m. to 5 a.m.

Whispers, Edifício Aviz, 35 Avenida Fontes Pereira de Melo, next to the Sheraton Hotel (tel. 57-54-89), is almost as glamorous as its neighbor Ad Lib. (Men should wear jackets and probably a necktie.) Located in the basement of a modern building, it welcomes its regular clients as well as whatever young, chic visitors happen to be in Lisbon at the moment. It's open every night from 11 p.m. to 5 a.m., charging 2,000$ ($13.80) at the door, and around 600$ ($4.15) for a scotch and soda.

Springfellows, 8B Avenida Oscar Monteiro Torres (tel. 793-29-44), is another fun and charming disco in Lisbon. Scattered over three different levels of a modern building downtown, it has a disc jockey who is held captive in an illuminated elevator that rises and descends between the floors. A relatively calm pub is on the second floor, while wild and frenzied dancing takes place on the top floor. Men pay 1,200$ ($8.30) at the entrance (women pay half price) on Friday and Saturday nights. Other nights, entrance is free. A whisky and soda costs 650$ ($4.50). The establishment is open Monday to Saturday from 11 p.m. to 5 a.m.

4. Bars In and Around Lisbon

Bachus, 9 Largo da Trindade (tel. 32-12-60), offers one of the capital's most convivial watering spots, as well as a restaurant. In an environment of Oriental carpets, fine hardwoods, bronze statues, intimate lighting, and polite uniformed waiters, you can hobnob with some of the most glamorous names in Lisbon. An organist provides live music from a cubbyhole beneath a winding staircase. Late-night suppers are served in the bar by candlelight. The array of drinks, costing from 650$ ($4.50), is international, and the place is a good one in which to unwind in privileged circumstances. Bachus is open seven days a week from noon to 2 a.m.

Metro e Meio, 174 Avenida 5 de Outubro (tel. 77-59-97), has as its façade a giant yellow ruler, with the entrance cut into it. The management rented a certain amount of space, but carpenters renovating the bar discovered many more rooms hidden for decades. The overall effect is grotto-like, with stone and brick arches, a maze of salons, and a central fireplace. The unusual decor is a mélange of artifacts—hand-loomed wool wall hangings, gilt mirrors, statues, hanging lamps, and Victorian fringed shades. Recordings are piped in, and sometimes there's a live pianist. Whiskies begin at 550$ ($3.80). Hours are Monday to Saturday from 6 p.m. to 2 a.m. Near the Gulbenkian Museum and the Campo Pequeno, the bar is a taxi ride from the center of town.

The **Panorama Bar,** 1 Rua Latino Coelho (tel. 57-57-57), lies on the uppermost floor of one of Portugal's tallest buildings, the 30-story Lisboa Sheraton Hotel. Consequently, the view by day or night includes the old and new cities of Lisbon, the mighty Tagus, and many of the towns on the river's far bank. Amid a decor of chiseled stone and stained glass and a polite, uniformed staff, you'll pay around 900$ ($6.12) for a whisky and soda. The bar is open Mon-

---

THE VALOR OF PORT WINE

Portuguese port wine is known in every country of the world. The English were the first foreigners to discover rich, blended port, which they've enjoyed since the 17th century. The wine comes from grapes grown in the mountainous Douro River Valley in the north of Portugal. After port is fortified with brandy, it is shipped out to the "ports" of the world from Porto, Portugal's second-largest city.

The soil and climate of the Douro are said to be unique in the world, hence the special taste of the wine. Vintage port is the best wine produced from an especially good year. Crusted port, another vintage-like wine, takes its name from the fact that its "crust" must be decanted before it can be drunk.

"Wood ports," matured in wooden casks, fall into three major types: ruby, white, and tawny, made from the blending of the grape yield over a period of many years, assuring a consistent quality. The ruby-colored port is the young wine, but as it ages it becomes tawny.

Owned and sponsored by the Port Wine Institute, the **Solar do Vinho do Porto,** 45 Rua São Pedro de Alcântara (tel. 32-33-07), contains many relics related to the history of port wine. You can stop here and order from its *lista de vinhos.* If you want a glass (*cálice*) you can get it, costing 75$ (50¢) to 650$ ($4.40) for an average drink. Of course, you can also order a vintage bottle of port if you'd like to make a night of it. The center is open Monday to Saturday from 10 a.m. to midnight.

day to Friday from 10 a.m. to 1:30 a.m.; Saturday and Sunday from 4 p.m. to 1:30 a.m.

Procópio Bar, 21-A Alto de San Francisco (tel. 65-28-51), could easily become your favorite watering hole in Lisbon—if you can find it. The street it lies on rarely appears on Lisbon maps. However, the location is just off Rua de João Penha, which itself is off the landmark Praça das Amoreiras. Low-ceilinged, dark, and cozy, it is a social center for many politicians and journalists, who unwind amid the turn-of-the-century memorabilia. Guests sit on red tufted velvet, enjoying the atmosphere of stained and painted glass, ornate brass hardware, and a piano awaiting an amateur player. It's like being in an intimate living room where the guests know each other. Drinks cost from 500$ ($3.40). Procópio is open daily except Friday, from 6 p.m. to 3 a.m.

Bora-Bora, 201 Rua da Madalena (tel. 87-20-43), is a Polynesian bar. This might seem out of context in Lisbon, but it's all the rage in Iberia these days. So if you have a yearning for the kind of fruited, flaming, rum-laced drinks you thought you'd left behind on the West Coast, you'll find imaginative variations here. The couches are comfortable and inviting, and you can take in the Polynesian art on the walls. Hamburgers and other fare are available as well. Snacks cost from 550$ ($3.75), and drinks from 500$ ($3.40). Hours are seven nights a week from 6 p.m. to 2 a.m.

Ray's Cocktail Bar and Lounge, 425 Avenida Saboia, Monte Estoril (tel. 268-01-06), is popular with American expatriates, many of whom make it their private club. It's a souped-up decorator extravaganza. Inside, you're likely to find an eclectic assortment of elements—a Fátima hand from Tangier, a ruby-colored glass newel post finial, chandeliers dripping with crystal, a black ostrich fan, antique benches, provincial chairs, and a heterogeneous mixture of modern art. Most strong libations cost 400$ ($2.75) to 500$ ($3.45). The bar is open seven days a week from 4 p.m. to 2:30 a.m. Ray's is midway between Estoril and Monte Estoril, within a 10-minute walk from the railway station of either town.

Estalagem Muchaxo, Praia do Guincho, in Guincho (tel. 28-50-221), is a unique and ideal place for a drink, with whiskies costing around 600$ ($4.10). You can also come here for lobster (very expensive) or even a room, but many prefer to drive out from Lisbon just to enjoy the jagged coastal rock, the Cabo da Roca, marking the westernmost point of Europe. The inn has a rustic atmosphere, with a rugged stone fireplace, Madeira wicker stools, and rows of waterside tables. The establishment is open every day from 10 a.m. to midnight. If you are captivated by the beauty of the spot (or the allure of your companion), the establishment will rent you one of its 24 rooms, with breakfast included, for between 7,500$ ($51.70) and 14,500$ ($100) a night, depending on the season and the accommodation.

GAY BARS

Xeque Mate Bar, Rua de Sao Marcal 170 (tel. 37-28-30), mingles the down-home earthiness of an English pub with the futuristic black and silver trappings of a high-tech disco. Set behind a discreet brass plaque on a steeply sloping street lined with elegant 18th-century villas, it imposes no cover charge. Beer costs from 350$ ($2.40), whisky and soda from 450$ ($3.05). The establishment was founded and is run by an English-born (Oxford) master of cerebe the most interculturally sophisticated gay bar in Lisbon. Xeque Mate is open seven nights a week from 10 p.m. to between 1:30 and 2:30 a.m. A taxi is recommended.

Memorial, Rua Gustavo de Matos Squeira 42 (tel. 396-88-91), is near the narrow streets of the Barrio Alto and is considered a "household word" among the gay community of Lisbon. This disco caters mostly to gay men. Both Spanish and Portuguese are spoken by most of the staff, and newcomers will usually be able to strike up a conversation with one of the regular clients. It's open Tuesday to Sunday from 10 p.m. to 4 a.m. You'll pay a cover charge of 800$ ($5.45), after which a beer costs 400$ ($2.70). Metro: Avenida.

Trumps, Rua da Imprensa Nacionale 104B (tel. 671-059), lies near (but not in) the Bairro Alto. Although it tries to cater to both heterosexual and homosexual tastes, most of its clientele is composed of male homosexuals. Contained within a large room on the street level of its building, it has a prominent dance floor, a spacious bar, and a staff that speaks French and Spanish. You'll pay 1,000$ ($6.80) at the door only on Friday and Saturday nights. A beer costs around 400$ ($2.70). Trumps is open Tuesday to Sunday from 11 p.m. to 3:30 a.m. Metro: Avenida; tram no. 20 or 24, or bus no. 15 or 39.

THE CAFÉ OF THE LITERATI

In the Chiado district behind an art-nouveau façade, **A Brasileira,** 102-A Rua Garrett (tel. 36-87-92), is one of the oldest coffeehouses in Lisbon. It's a 19th-century holdover, once a favorite gathering place of the literati. Today, like much of the world, the atmosphere has grown somewhat tatty, but the place remains a favorite with some diehard devotees. A demitasse of coffee, called a *bica,* costs about 120$ (82¢), and a simple glass of beer 220$ ($1.50). It's open Monday to Saturday from noon to 2 p.m. and 7 to 9 p.m. Guests sit at small tables on chairs made of tooled leather, while taking in the mirrored walls and marble pilasters. There is also a collection of paintings to admire. Old men go around offering to shine your shoes just as they did in the 19th century.

Outside, the street speaks of its past associations with men of letters. Garrett, a romantic dandy of the last century, was one of Portugal's leading poets (the street is named after him). The district itself, the Chiado, was named for another poet. On the square near the café, a statue honors António Ribeiro, a 16th-century poet. Yet another poet, Bocage of Setúbal, used to frequent this coffeehouse. When once accosted by a bandit, he is said to have replied, "I am going to the Brasileira, but if you shoot me, I am going to another world."

5. The Casino In Estoril

The magnet for international society along the Costa do Sol, the **Casino Estoril,** Praça José Teodoro dos Santos (tel. 268-45-21), is a contemporary structure, with walls of glass opening onto a wide formal garden stretching to the shore road. The magnetic attraction, of course, is the gaming room of the casino, which is open from 3 p.m. to 3 a.m. On Friday and Saturday, a private room for baccarat chemin de fer is open from 3 to 8 a.m. You can clear the official barrier by presenting your passport and purchasing a tourist card valid for one day for 400$ ($2.75), or a one-week card for 1,200$ ($8.30). Once upstairs, you can play American and French roulette, French banc, blackjack, baccarat punto banca, chemin de fer, craps, and cussec (a Chinese game). The casino also has a Bingo room and a slot-machine room. You're likely to rub elbows with deposed royalty. Men are required to wear jackets and ties in the gaming room.

In the **Grand Salon Restaurant,** you can sample a standard international dinner, where a three-course meal costs from around 5,000$ ($34.50), not including wine. If you prefer, you can dine in Estoril or Cascais, then drop in for drinks only, paying a minimum of 2,500$ ($17.25). This buys you either one or two drinks, depending on the cost of your particular beverage. The floor show begins every night at 11:15 p.m., and usually requires an advance reservation. It is a lavish production in the tradition of Paris or Las Vegas. You can count on an international array of show girls in glittery costumes—most often crowned with billowing feather headgear—strutting their stuff and demonstrating their curves.

AFTER LISBON—WHERE TO?

Every first-time visitor who comes to Portugal usually visits Lisbon, Estoril, and Sintra, and this small guide is aimed at those travelers. However, there are those who will want a deeper look at this most fascinating little country, particularly its beachfront, the Algarve, or such old cities of the north as Porto and Viana do Castelo. Nazaré is considered the country's most intriguing fishing village, and the old Roman city of Évora draws visitors west across the plains of Alentejo. Others will want to fly to the popular tourist island of Madeira off the coast of Africa, and perhaps as an offbeat adventure, the Azores, said to be the peaks of volcanoes on the lost continent of Atlantis. These islands are part of Portugal.

With that in mind, we publish a large guide devoted to Portugal, Madeira, and the Azores, documenting their many sightseeing attractions, along with hotels and restaurants in all price ranges, from budget to deluxe. Its philosophy is to help you get the best value for your dollar: *Frommer's Portugal, Madeira & The Azores.*

For information on this and other Frommer guides, please turn to the last two pages of this book.

GETTING ACQUAINTED WITH MADRID

In *The Sun Also Rises,* Hemingway described Madrid as "a white sky-line on the top of a little cliff away off across the sun-hardened country." Papa would not know the city today. The little pueblo that was Madrid continues to grow at a dramatic rate, expanding rapidly in land area and industrial development, sprouting suburbs of apartment houses for the burgeoning population.

On a plateau of the Sierra de Guadarrama, the capital of Spain is the highest in Europe, reaching a peak of 2,373 feet above sea level at its loftiest point. The sierra air is dry, almost crystal pure, the sky cerulean as painted by Velázquez.

As Spanish cities go, Madrid is still young. *Don Quixote* was known throughout the world when Philip II made Madrid the capital of Spain in 1606. The location was apt: Geographically, it was the heart of the Iberian peninsula.

On your way into Madrid from Barajas Airport, you're likely to see an aging *duena* shrouded in black—perhaps mourning for her husband who died in the Spanish Civil War in the late 1930s. The scene is one of the *tableaux vivants,* frozen in time and space.

As you near the center of the city, however, skyscrapers herald tomorrow's world. Flashy billboards implore everybody to *"bebe* Coca-Cola," or to wear Yankee-style Levi's for greater sex appeal.

Spain is in metamorphosis. Now that the country is justifiably called "the playground of Europe," authorities are forced to grant concessions to the hordes of invaders pouring across its borders or winging in from the skies. For example, ever-increasing numbers of visitors now stroll the streets of Madrid in summer shorts. In the not-too-distant past, such apparel would have given a skimpily clad visitor firsthand experience for an autobiography, "My Life in a Spanish Jail."

It is impossible to separate Madrid or Castile from the saga of the nation as a whole. It was from the barren, undulating plains of the country's heartland that the proud, sometimes arrogant, Castilians emerged. They were destined not only to unify the country, but to dominate it—and to go even further, carving out an empire that was to embrace the Aztecs and Incas, even the far-away Philippines.

In Castile you'll meet a survival-sharpened people. One scholar put it this way: "The Spaniards are a fierce, idealistic, generous people, capable of great sacrifice and heroism when driven by their proud and burning passions, but they are also intolerant, dogmatic, and individualistic." Regardless, know that Spaniards—whatever their backgrounds—are generally friendly, especially to their well-behaved guests. As hosts, they have great style and graciousness, and Spain today is among the most hospitable nations in Europe.

1. Orientation

No one ever claimed that knowing or getting around Madrid was easy. Many taxi drivers (usually from the provinces) are unfamiliar with the city as well, once they branch off the main boulevards.

Everything in the Spanish capital is spread out, and this may cause you initial difficulty until you get the feel of it. For example, on one typical night, you may want to sample the *tapas* (hors d'oeuvres) at a *tasca* on the Ventura de la Vega; dine at a restaurant opening onto the fairly far-off Plaza Mayor, witness an evening of flamenco near the Ritz Hotel, then head for your hotel at the gateway to Toledo. The easiest, most sensible and practical means of getting around to all these widely scattered places is by taxi (see "Getting Around Madrid").

THE DIFFERENT MADRIDS

The Spanish capital, as mentioned, is a fast-growing city, its development sporadic and largely haphazard. It can be described in many ways and from many points of view.

If you're interested in "Royal Madrid," you'll think of the **Palacio Real,** fronting the handsome **Plaza de Oriente,** with its Velázquez-inspired equestrian statue of Philip IV. The gardens and parks, the wide avenues appropriate for state receptions and parades took new significance with the restoration of the Spanish monarchy.

If you're a romanticist nostalgic for the 19th century, you'll watch in sadness as the mansions along the **Paseo de la Castallana** and its satellite streets are torn down to make way for modern offices and shops, deluxe hotels, apartment buildings. Thankfully, a few are still preserved and used today by foreign embassies.

If you're an artist or devotee of art, you'll spend most of your time at the great old **Prado,** treasure house of Spanish masterpieces, sheltering a once-royal collection of European art. If you're on a shopping spree, you'll gravitate to the **Gran Vía,** called the Avenida José Antonio during the long dictatorship of Franco, the main street of Madrid, with its stores, cinemas, and hotels, the latter both luxury and budget. The wide avenue—flanked with sidewalk cafés

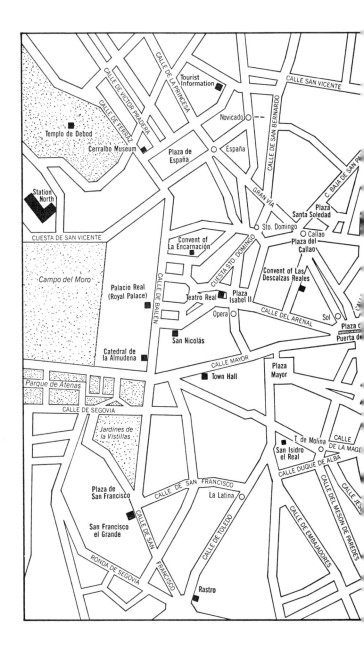

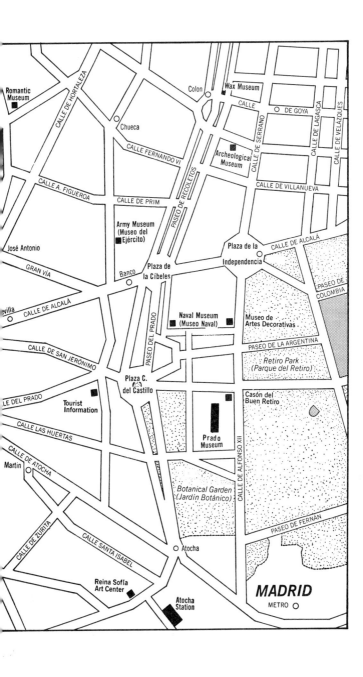

—ends at the **Plaza de España** with its Edificio España, one of the tallest skyscrapers in Europe. Or you'll wander past the multitude of shops, boutiques, coffeehouses, and couturiers' salons of the more prestigious **Calle de Serrano.**

If medieval Madrid intrigues you, you'll seek out the Moorish towers of the old quarter, looking for the *mudéjar* style of architecture. You'll photograph (in your mind, if not with your instant-shot camera), the **Plaza de la Villa,** and focus especially on the **Torre de los Lujanes.** According to tradition, Francis I of France was held captive at the tower after he was taken prisoner in Pavia, Italy.

The colonnaded and rectangular **Plaza Mayor,** one of the most harmoniously designed squares in Europe, recalls the Madrid of the 17th century. The scene of many an *auto-de-fé,* bullfight, or execution of a traitor, it is today one of the best spots in the city for a *paseo,* especially if you take time out from your walking to explore the adjoining shops, some of which sell sombreros. Later you can select a restaurant, perhaps one with a table opening right on the square.

If you walk through one of the vaulted porticoes of the Plaza Mayor to the south, down the street of *típico* restaurants and taverns —the **Calle de Cuchilleros**—you'll reach the **Calle de Toledo.** Then you'll be entering a speical world of Old Madrid, still preserved. Known as the *barrios bajos,* it is home to the Madrileño lowest on the economic scale. In some cities it would be called a ghetto or slum. But in Madrid the area abounds with such style— screaming gypsy *niños,* arcaded markets stuffed with meats and vegetables, shops, *tascas, cuevas,* that it retains great punch.

The real center of the city is the **Puerta del Sol** (the "Doorway" or "Gateway to the Sun"). Despite its grand appellation, it is a dull terminus of considerable traffic congestion and crime. Beginning at the Puerta del Sol, the **Calle de Alcalá** is the most traffic-choked artery in Madrid, a street that runs for more than 2½ miles. It is the avenue of Spanish bankers, and houses the Escuela y Museo de la Real Academia de Bellas Artes de San Fernando.

Madrid's greatest boulevard, its Champs-Élysées, begins at Atocha Railway Station. Heading north, it's called the **Paseo del Prado,** passing on its right the Botanical Gardens and the Prado Museum. It doesn't end, but changes its name at the **Plaza de la Cibeles,** dominated by the "cathedral of post offices" and a fountain honoring Cybele, "the great mother of the gods."

At Cibeles, the boulevard is henceforth the **Paseo de Carvo Sotelo,** and leads into the **Plaza de Colón.** At Colón, the **Paseo de la Castellana** begins. Seemingly endless, the Paseo de la Castellana stretches through a posh area spreading out on both sides and featuring apartment houses, restaurants, department stores, and hotels; it continues past the public ministries, up to the flourishing **Plaza de Castilla,** and then on to the huge **La Paz** hospital complex.

2. Flying to Madrid

The capital of Spain has the busiest and most convenient airport in the country. Until the recent entry of American Airlines into the busy transatlantic market to Madrid, the major airlines servicing Madrid from North America were Iberia and Trans World Airlines (TWA).

Iberia Airlines, the national carrier of Spain, offers more routes into and within Spain than any other carrier. It also gives its passengers a preview of the Spanish experience through such extras as travelogue films on Spanish architecture, art, and traditions. Iberia's routes include daily nonstop service to Madrid from New York, Chicago, Miami, and Los Angeles, and nonstop service to Barcelona (continuing on the same aircraft to Málaga) from New York several times a week. Within Spain, Iberia services dozens of large and medium-sized cities, making it the unparalleled leader for flights within Spain and to its offshore islands.

Many different ticket options exist, but tickets at each of the airlines are less expensive if you can reserve your seat and pay for your ticket at least 14 days in advance, schedule your return for between 7 and 60 days from your departure, and schedule both your departure and return for Monday through Thursday. A ticket with these provisions is called a weekday APEX (advance purchase excursion) fare. In high season (which stretches roughly between June and September), it will cost $776 round-trip, plus $16 tax. If you fly both directions on a Friday, Saturday, or Sunday, it will cost an additional $50. A similar ticket from Los Angeles to Madrid will cost $986 plus $16 tax, with $50 extra for weekend travel. Many other ticket options exist, including more expensive fares for business class and gran (first) class. Thanks to increased amenities and roomier seats (which extend backward into something resembling a bed), you can arrive in Madrid rested. For reservations and information, call Iberia toll-free from throughout North America by dialing 800/772-4642.

Iberia is not alone in flying from North America to Madrid. Its routes from New York are contested by **TWA,** which operates one daily nonstop flight to Madrid from its terminal at New York's JFK. Using its network, it can bring passengers from other North American airports into New York for transfers onto its night flight to Madrid. At press time, however, TWA's cheapest APEX fare, with tax included, cost $827 in high season, which is more than a similar ticket at Iberia. At both Iberia and TWA, there is a substantial penalty for altering the itinerary once the ticket is paid for. (At TWA, the penalty is 60% of the value of the ticket, so be sure of your dates before you accept an offer.) For more information, call TWA toll-free at 800/221-2000.

Spain-bound passengers living in America's southwestern and western states can profit from **American Airlines'** daily nonstop service to Madrid from Dallas, which isn't serviced by either TWA or Iberia. Departing every evening from Dallas at 5:30 p.m., American Airlines is able to funnel passengers into Dallas from throughout its vast North American network, sometimes making transfers more efficient and easier than through the overcrowded terminals of New York. At press time, with a 14-day advance purchase and a delay of between 7 and 60 days before your return home, American's least expensive high-season round-trip ticket from Dallas to Madrid cost $1,006. American charges a $50 supplement if you want to fly in both directions on a Friday, Saturday, or Sunday. This fare, of course, is substantially reduced in shoulder season (roughly speaking, in spring and autumn) and low season (most of the winter). American charges a $100 penalty for any changes in itinerary once the ticket is issued, although by industry standards, that penalty is relatively modest.

Unlike Iberia or TWA, American offers a youth fare from Dallas to Madrid (for persons aged 12 to 24) of $491 each way (with a $25 surcharge each way for travel on a Friday, Saturday, or Sunday). Though not substantially less than the transatlantic APEX fare, it at least favors last-minute departures, since its restrictions bypass the usual 14-day advance-booking requirement. The youth fare can't be reserved more than three days before departure in either direction.

Important news from American includes the establishment of a new daily nonstop route from Miami to Madrid (which had already received FAA approval but had not yet begun at the time of this writing) and the strong possibility of a daily nonstop route from Dallas/Fort Worth to Barcelona, scheduled to begin sometime during the lifetime of this edition. For more information and reservations, call American toll-free at 800/433-7300.

BUCKET SHOPS

For information about buying discounted airline tickets to Madrid through bucket shops, or "consolidators," see "Flying to Lisbon" in Chapter II.

CHARTER FLIGHTS

For information about flying to Madrid on charter flights, see "Flying to Lisbon" in Chapter II.

AIRPORT

Barajas is the international airport for Madrid, and it's divided into two separate terminals—one for international flights, another for domestic. A shuttle bus runs between the two. For Barajas Airport information, telephone 408-5200; for Iberia Airlines information, dial 411-2545.

Air-conditioned yellow buses take you from right outside the arrival terminal at Barajas to the underground bus depot under the Plaza Colón. You can also get off at several points along the way, provided you don't have your suitcases stored in the hold. The cost of the service is 250 pesetas ($2.35), and buses leave about every 20 minutes, either to or from the airport.

If you go by taxi into town, the approximate cost ranges from 1,800 pesetas ($16.90) to 2,100 pesetas ($19.75), depending on traffic. The driver is entitled to assess a surcharge (either direction) not only for the trip but for baggage handling. If you should step into a nonmetered limousine, it is important to negotiate the price in advance.

3. Getting Around Madrid

TRAINS

Madrid has three major railway stations. At the **Atocha,** Glorieta de Carlos V, you can book passage for Lisbon, Toledo, Andalusia, and Extremadura. Metro: Atocha. For trains to Barcelona, Asturias, Cantabria, Castilla-Leon, Pais Vasco, Aragon, Cataluña, Levante, Murcia, and the French frontier, go to **Charmartín** in the northern suburbs, at Agustin de Foxa. Metro: Charmatín. The third is **La Estacion del Norte** (Príncipe Pío), which is the main gateway for trains to northwest Spain (Salamanca and Galicia). Metro: Norte. For railway information, telephone 552-05-18.

Warning: In Madrid, don't wait to buy your rail ticket or make a reservation at the train station. By this time there may be no tickets left—or at least no desirable tickets. For most tickets, go to the principal RENFE office at 44 Alcalá (tel. 733-30-00). It is open Monday to Friday from 9 a.m. to 3 p.m. and 4 to 7:30 p.m.; Saturday from 9 a.m. to 1:30 p.m. Metro: Banco de España.

TAXIS

Fortunately, the cabs are moderately priced. At the start of a ride, the meter registers 105 pesetas ($1) (but that fare will surely have gone up by the time of your visit). An average ride costs about 500 pesetas ($4.70) to 600 pesetas ($5.65). There are extras as well. Trips to the railway station or to the bullring carry a supplement, plus an additional fee tacked on to the fare on Sunday and holidays. A ride to Barajas Airport carries a 150-peseta ($1.40) surcharge, plus 20 pesetas (20¢) per bag. It's customary to tip at least 10% or more of the fare.

A ride is usually an adventure, as Madrileño drivers go fast, occasionally (but not always) stopping at red lights.

Taxi-riding has some minor traps that visitors will do well to avoid. There are two types of taxis: black with horizontal red bands and white with diagonal red bands. Their rates are usually the same. However, many *unmetered,* unbanded taxis also abound in Madrid, their drivers renting their services as guides for the day or half day. But when business is slow, these guides sometimes operate as "gypsy" cabs, picking up unsuspecting passengers, taking them to their destinations, and charging them whatever they think the market will bear.

Beyond that pitfall, you must be careful to require that your driver start the meter when you enter the cab. Otherwise, the driver may "assess" the cost of the ride to your disadvantage.

SUBWAYS (METRO)

The system, first installed in 1919, is quite easy to learn, and you can travel in the underground if not comfortably, at least without any congestion or crushing, as in former years.

Line No. 7 is completely different from the rest, and as modern as some of Europe's newest underground systems. The future lines under construction will be the same type as No. 7.

The central converging point of the metro is at the **Puerta del Sol.** The subways begin their runs at 6 a.m., shutting down at 1:30 a.m. It's best to try to avoid traveling on the subways during the rush hours, of course. The fare is 65 pesetas (60¢). A 10-trip ticket costs 410 pesetas ($3.85). For information, call 435-22-66.

BUSES

A network of buses also traverses the city, fanning out to the suburbs. The route of each bus is clearly marked at each stop on a schematic diagram. Buses are fast and efficient, traveling down special lanes made for them all over the city. Both red and yellow buses charge 65 pesetas (60¢) per ride, although most of the yellow buses have the advantage of being air-conditioned. For information on buses from the airport into Madrid, refer to the "Airports" section, above.

Bus Terminals

Madrid has at least eight principal bus terminals, including the large **Estacíon Sur de Autobuses,** 17 Canarias (tel. 468-42-00). Metro: Palos de Moguer. Buses to the environs of Madrid, such as Toledo and Segovia, leave from numerous stations.

CAR RENTALS

If you're planning to tour Spain, a car will ease the burden considerably. However, don't plan to drive in Madrid: It's too congested. Even if you're limited to extensive touring in the environs of Madrid, you'll find that a rented car will come in handy, allowing you to stop off at that *típico* roadside tavern for *tapas* or to make that side detour to a medieval village. You'll be your own master, exploring at your leisure places not covered—or covered too hurriedly—on an organized tour.

Many of North America's biggest car-rental companies, including Avis, Budget, and Hertz, maintain offices in Madrid, both downtown and at the airport. Though several Spain-based car-rental companies will try to entice you, past letters from readers have shown that the resolution of billing irregularities and insurance claims tends to be less complicated when you stick to one of the U.S.-based car-rental firms.

Each of the big-three car-rental companies offers its least expensive rates to clients who reserve a car at least two days in advance from North America, keep the car for at least a week, and agree to return it to the original rental location. The fine print of their insurance policies, however, differs markedly, as you'll see below.

Avis is one of Spain's biggest car-rental franchises, with almost 100 branches throughout the country, including several in Madrid. If you reserve a car by telephone at least two days before you leave for Spain, you'll qualify for Avis's least expensive rate of around $240 per week for a cramped but convenient Opel Corsa Swing. This rate includes full insurance, but the Spanish government tacks on an additional 12% tax. In addition to the airport office (tel. 91/205-8532), Avis has a main downtown office at 60 Gran Vía (tel.

91/247-2048). Unlike some of its competition, Avis offers a limited number of cars with air conditioning, but they are frightfully expensive, costing around $675 plus tax per week, with unlimited mileage. For toll-free reservations and information within North America, call Avis at 800/331-2112.

Hertz has an office in Madrid at the airport (tel. 91/205-8452) and also downtown in the Edificio España, Gran Vía 88 (tel. 91/248-5803). For its smallest car (a Ford Fiesta or an Opel Corsa), it charges almost exactly the same rate as Avis (in Hertz's case, $241 per week, plus 12% tax), and enforces similar restrictions. For toll-free reservations and information from within North America, call Hertz toll-free at 800/654-3001.

Your least expensive car-rental deal will probably be with **Budget Rent-a-Car,** which also offers more lenient insurance policies than those automatically included at both Avis and Hertz. Budget includes a basic amount of collision damage insurance as an automatic part of each of its rental contracts, but leaves optional additional, all-encompassing collision insurance to the discretion of its clients. Budget offers a collision damage waiver at the time of rental to each of its clients. This policy costs between $48 and $63 a week, depending on the value of the car, and allows you to waive responsibility for the cost of any repairs if you damage it. If you don't buy the waiver and then have an accident, you'll be charged for up to $1,700 worth of repairs.

Budget's least expensive car, a Seat Marbella, rents for a rock-bottom price of $151.57 per week in midsummer (slightly less in wintertime), plus the obligatory government tax of 12%. If only for peace of mind, I advise most readers to buy the optional collision damage insurance, but even if you do, the weekly total of car rental plus insurance will be only $200 a week, plus tax—less than at Hertz or Avis. These prices may change by the time you're ready to reserve a car, so make some telephone calls before you commit yourself.

One further way to save money (and this is a loophole intended only for readers who fully understand its consequences) is to pay for your car rental with a credit card issued by a company that agrees to pay the minimum deductible for repairs if you should have an accident. (Be sure that your original rental contract is imprinted with your credit card at the beginning of your rental.) If you fully understand the fine print of this arrangement, you may omit buying the extra insurance altogether. Be aware, however, that compensation from the credit-card company takes time, and you may have to pay some initial damages in cash (or have them billed to your credit card) and fill out some difficult paperwork before you are reimbursed. Check carefully with your credit-card company for the details. American Express is the most visible of these, but other credit-card companies may soon follow Amex's lead. Also be aware that this loophole is available only at Budget, since Hertz and Avis require automatic purchase of their collision damage waivers.

For reservations and information, call Budget's international department toll-free from within North America by dialing 800/472-3325. In addition to its location at the Madrid airport (tel. 900/100-560), Budget's main Madrid office is at 49 Gran Vía (tel. 91/248-9040).

Gas

Gas is easily obtainable and is the normal fuel used in rented cars in Spain. The average Spanish vehicle—predominantly Seats or Fiats—gets close to 45 miles a gallon.

HITCHHIKING

This is no longer smiled upon as much as it used to be. Although, technically, it is legal, I don't recommend you stick out your thumb in the presence of the Civil Guard. More important, hitchhiking is an increasingly dubious and unsafe way to travel, with the inherent danger of simply not knowing what maniac is likely to pick you up. Take the bus or train—it's safer, easier, and faster.

---

4. Madrid Fast Facts

Whatever your needs or travel problems, you'll find that Madrid has the answer to them. The single question is: How do you find what you are seeking quickly and conveniently? In an emergency, of course, your hotel is your best bet. But some of the smaller hotels aren't staffed with personnel entirely fluent in English; and sometimes—even if they are—the person at the desk can be apathetic about something of vital interest to you.

What follows is an alphabetical listing of important miscellany —the data that can often be crucial to a visitor.

AMERICAN EXPRESS: For your mail or banking needs, try the American Express office at the corner of the Marqués de Cubas and the Plaza de las Cortés (tel. 429-57-75), across the street from the Palace Hotel. The office is open Monday to Friday from 9 a.m. to 5:30 p.m.; Saturday from 9 a.m. to noon.

AREA CODES: The telephone area code for Madrid is 91, if you are within Spain. If you're dialing Spain from North America, the country code for Spain is 34, the area code for Madrid is 1. (Do not dial 91 when calling Madrid from the United States.)

BABY-SITTERS: Nearly all major hotels in Madrid can arrange for baby-sitters. Usually, the concierge keeps a list of reliable sitters and will put you in touch with one of them, provided you give adequate notice. Rates vary considerably, but tend to be reasonable. More and more baby-sitters in Madrid speak English, but don't count on it. Chances are yours won't—although you can request it, of course.

BANKS: You get a better exchange rate at banks if you're exchanging dollars into pesetas than you do at any of the exchange bureaus around the city. Banks are open Monday to Friday from 9:30 a.m. to 2 p.m. (it's best to go after 10 a.m.). Many banks are also open on Saturday from 9:30 a.m. to 1 p.m.

CLIMATE: In Madrid, climate is subject to rapid change. July and August are the most uncomfortable months. In fact, the government virtually shuts down in August except for a skeleton crew, going into "exile" at the northeast Atlantic resort of San Sebastián.

The temperature can often reach a high of 91° Fahrenheit in July, 76° in September. In winter, it can plunge to 34° Fahrenheit, although it averages around 46°. In October (average temperature: 58° Fahrenheit), Madrid enjoys its "season." Hotel space is at a premium. Every bullfighter, doll manufacturer, Galician hotelier, Andalusian olive grower, or Santander vineyard keeper having business with the government descends on Madrid at this time. In the same month, wealthy Spanish aristocrats flock here from the secluded ducal palaces in Andalusia and Castile to savor the sophistication of the capital, its opera, theater, and endless rounds of parties and dinners. The air is clear, the sun kind; the restaurants and *tascas* (bars) overflow with Iberian joie de vivre.

In my view, however, the balmy month of May (average temperature: 61° Fahrenheit) is the best time for making your own descent on the capital.

Madrid's Average Daytime Temperature and Rainfall

	Jan	Feb	Mar	Apr	May	June	July	Aug	Sept	Oct	Nov	Dec
Temp. °F	42.8	45.1	49.1	53.8	61	68.4	75.2	74.3	68	58	48.2	43
Rainfall "	2	2	1.6	2	1.5	1.2	0.4	0.3	1.3	2	2.4	2

CLOTHING SIZES: For the most part, Spain uses the same sizes as the continent of Europe. The sizes of women's stockings and men's socks are international.

For Women

Junior Miss		Regular Dresses		Shoes	
U.S.	Spain	U.S.	Spain	U.S.	Spain
5	34	10	40	5	36
7	36	12	42	5½	36½
9	38	14	44	6½	37½
11	40	16	46	7½	38½
		18	48	8	39
		20	50	8½	39½
				9	40

For Men

Shirts		Slacks		Shoes	
U.S.	Spain	U.S.	Spain	U.S.	Spain
14	36	32	42	5	36
14½	37	34	44	6	37
15	38	36	46	7	38
15½	39	38	48	7½	39
15¾	40	40	50	8	40
16	41			9	41
16½	42			10	42
17	43			10½	43
				11	44
				12	45

Warning: This chart should be followed only as a very general outline. If possible, try on all clothing or shoes before making a purchase. You'll be glad you did.

CONSULATES AND EMBASSIES: If you lose your passport, fall seriously ill, get into legal trouble, or have some urgently serious problem, your embassy or consulate will probably have a mechanism to help you.

The **United States Embassy** is at 75 Calle de Serrano (tel. 576-3400). It's open Monday to Friday from 9:30 a.m. to 1 p.m.

The **Australian Embassy** is at 143 Paseo de Castellana (tel. 279-85-04) and is open Monday to Friday from 10 a.m. to 1 p.m.

The **British Embassy** is at 16 Fernando El Santo (tel. 319-0200) and is open Monday to Friday from 10 a.m. to 1 p.m. Residents of New Zealand address themselves to the British Embassy, when necessary.

The **Canadian Embassy** is at 35 Nuñez de Balboa (tel. 431-4300) and is open Monday to Friday from 9 a.m. to 1 p.m.

The **Embassy of the Republic of Ireland** is at 73 Claudio Coello (tel. 576-3500) and is open Monday to Friday from 10 a.m. to 1 p.m.

CRIME: Increased thefts in Madrid have resulted in a warning by the U.S. Embassy to American visitors, urging that you leave your passport and valuables in a hotel safe or other secure place while you visit sights of the city. Purse-snatching is prevalent, with the criminals working in pairs, grabbing purses from pedestrians, cyclists, and even from cars. If a car is standing still, a thief may open the door or break a window in order to snatch a purse or package, even from under the seat. A popular scam against Americans in Madrid involves one miscreant smearing the back of the clothing of the victim, perhaps with mustard or chocolate. An accomplice pretends to help the victim clean off the mess, meanwhile picking all pockets of valuables. The embassy statement advises: Don't carry a purse; keep your valuables in front pockets; carry only enough cash for the day's needs; be aware of who is around you; and keep a separate record of your passport number, traveler's check numbers, and credit-card numbers.

Whenever you're traveling in an unfamiliar city or country, stay alert. Be aware of your immediate surroundings. Wear a money belt and don't sling your camera or purse (if you must take it) over your shoulder. Wear the strap diagonally across your body. This will minimize the possibility of your becoming a victim of crime. Every society has its criminals. It's your responsibility to be aware and be alert, even in the most heavily touristed areas.

Every car can be a target, parked or just stopped at a light. Don't leave anything in sight in your car. Place valuables in the trunk when you park, and always assume that someone is watching you to see whether you're putting something away for safekeeping. Keep the car locked while you're driving and even for a one-minute stop.

CURRENCY: Spain's unit of currency is the peseta, worth about $.0094 (or less than 1¢ in U.S. coinage). One U.S. dollar is worth about 106.65 Spanish pesetas. (*Warning:* This is subject to change, of course, because the dollar and the peseta fluctuate on the world market. Check with your bank for up-to-date quotations.)

The abbreviation of peseta is pta. Pesetas are distributed in coin denominations of 1, 2, 5, 10, 25, 50, 100, and 200 pesetas. Paper money comes in bills of 100, 200, 500, 1,000, 5,000, and 10,000 pesetas.

Hotels usually offer the worst rate of exchange, while banks generally offer the best. But even banks charge a commission for the service, often $2 or $3, depending on the transaction.

CUSTOMS: Spain permits you to bring in most personal effects and the following items duty free: two still cameras with 10 rolls of film each, one movie camera, tobacco for personal use, one bottle each of wine and liquor per person, a portable radio, a tape recorder, a typewriter, a bicycle, golf clubs, tennis rackets, fishing gear, two hunting weapons with 100 cartridges each, skis, and other sports equipment.

Upon leaving Spain, American citizens who have been outside the U.S. for 48 hours or more are allowed to bring in $400 (U.S.) worth of merchandise duty free—that is, if they have claimed no similar exemption within the past 30 days. Beyond this free allowance, the next $1,000 worth of merchandise is assessed at a flat rate of 10% duty. If you make purchases in Spain, it's important to keep your receipts.

DENTIST: For an English-speaking dentist, get in touch with the **U.S. Embassy,** 75 Calle de Serrano (tel. 276-34-00), which has a list of recommended ones. If you have a dental emergency, you may have to call several dentists before you can get an immediate appointment.

ELECTRIC CURRENT: For information on using electrical appliances in Spain, see "Electric Current" in Section 4 of Chapter II.

EMERGENCIES: If you need the police, call 091. In case of fire, dial 080. For an ambulance, as in the case of an accident, telephone 230-7145.

FILM: Film is expensive in Spain; take in as much as Customs will allow. I suggest you wait to process it until you return home. However, if you can't wait, you can take your undeveloped film to the leading department store, **Galerias Preciados,** 28 Preciados, right off the Gran Vía (tel. 222-47-71). There you can have your film developed in two hours.

HOLIDAYS: They include January 1 (New Year's Day), January 6 (Epiphany), March 19 (Day of St. Joseph), Good Friday, Easter Monday, May 1 (May Day), June 10 (Corpus Christi), June 29 (Day of St. Peter and St. Paul), July 25 (Day of St. James), August 15

(Feast of the Assumption), October 12 (Spain's National Day), November 1 (All Saints' Day), December 8 (Immaculate Conception), and December 25 (Christmas). No matter how large or small, every city or town in Spain also celebrates its local saint's days. In Madrid it's on May 15 (Saint Isidro).

LANGUAGE: Spanish is the official language of the land, of course, and French is also widely spoken in parts. In Madrid more and more people, especially the younger ones, are learning English. Nearly all major hotels and top restaurants are staffed with English-speaking persons. However, out in the country it will help a lot if you were a language major in school.

LAUNDRY: In most first-class hotels recommended in this guide, you need only fill out your laundry and dry-cleaning list and present it to your maid or valet. Same-day service usually costs anywhere from 25% to 50% more. Madrid has a number of laundromats. Try, for example, **Lavandería Marcenado,** 15 Calle Marcenado (tel. 416-68-71), which is full service and open Monday to Friday from 9:30 a.m. to 1:30 p.m. and 4:30 to 8 p.m. Metro: Prosperidad. There's also **Lavanderiá Donoso Cortés,** 17 Calle Donoso Cortés (tel. 446-96-90), which is self-service. It's open Monday to Friday from 8:30 a.m. to 7:30 p.m., Saturday from 8:30 a.m. to 1 p.m. Metro: Quevedo.

LIQUOR: Almost anyone of any age can order a drink in Spain. I've seen gypsy shoeshine boys who looked no more than 8 years old go into a *tasca* and purchase a glass of wine with their newly acquired tip. Bars, taverns, and cafeterias generally open at 8 a.m., and many serve alcohol all day until around 1 or 2 a.m. Spain doesn't have many stores devoted entirely to selling liquor and wine. Rather, you can purchase alcoholic beverages in almost any market, along with cheese and other foodstuffs.

METRIC MEASURES: Here's your chance to learn metric measures before going to Europe.

Weights	Measures
1 ounce = 28.3 grams	1 inch = 2.54 centimeters
1 pound = 454 grams	1 foot = 0.3 meters
2.2 pounds = 1 kilo (1000 grams)	1 yard = 0.91 meters
	1.09 yards = 1 meter
1 pint = 0.47 liter	1 mile = 1.61 kilometers
1 quart = 0.94 liter	0.62 mile = 1 kilometer
1 gallon = 3.78 liters	1 acre = 0.40 hectare
	2.47 acres = 1 hectare

NEWSPAPERS: Most newsstands along the Gran Vía or kiosks at the major hotels carry the latest edition of the *International Herald Tribune.* Spain also has an American weekly, a magazine known as the *Guidepost,* packed with information about late-breaking events in the Spanish capital, tips on movies shown in English, musical recitals, and more. You may also want to become a regular reader of the *Iberian Daily Sun,* an English-language newspaper containing stories and listings of interest to visitors from North America and Britain as well as expatriates. If you're traveling south, look out for *Lookout* magazine, a quality production in English with stories focused primarily on Spain's Sun Coast, although the staff also runs articles of general interest to the traveler to Spain.

PASSPORTS: A valid one is all an American, British, Australian, or Canadian citizen needs to enter Spain. You don't need an international driver's license if renting a car. Your local one from back home should suffice.

PHARMACIES: Drugstores are scattered all over Madrid. If you're trying to locate one at an odd hour, note a list posted outside the door of any drugstore that's not open. On the list are the names and addresses of pharmacies that are in service. The Spanish government requires drugstores to operate on the rotating system of hours —thereby assuring you that some will be open at all times, even on Sunday at midnight. Two of the capital's largest pharmacies lie within districts heavily visited by foreign visitors. **Farmacia Gayaso,** 2 Arenal (tel. 521-2860), and the **Farmacia del Globo,** 46 Atocha (tel. 239-4600), usually have at least one employee who speaks English. For a 24-hour pharmacy, phone 098.

POLITICS: In its post-Franco era, Spain now has a constitutional monarchy, and it won't disturb you unless you disturb it.

POST OFFICE: If you don't want to receive your mail at your hotel or the American Express office, you can direct it to *Lista de Correos* at the central post office in Madrid. To pick up such mail, go to the window marked *Lista,* where you'll be asked to show your passport. The central post office in Madrid is housed in what is known as "the cathedral of post offices" at the Plaza de la Cibeles (tel. 521-81-95). An airmail postcard to the United States costs 64 pesetas (60¢) if sent from Spain, and an airmail letter up to 15 grams goes for 69 pesetas (65¢).

RELIGIOUS SERVICES: Most churches in Madrid are Catholic, and they're found all over the city. Catholic masses in English, however, are given in a church at 165 Alfonso XIII. For more information, call 233-20-32 in the morning. For an Anglican service, the British Embassy Church of St. George is at 43 Nuñez de Balboa (call 274-51-55 for worship hours).

The interdenominational Protestant Community Church is at 34 Padre Damian (tel. 723-04-41), offering weekly services in the Colegio de los Sagrados Corazones, while the Immanuel Baptist Church offers English-speaking services at 4 Hernández de Tejada (tel. 407-43-47).

A Christian Science church is at 63 Alonso Cano (tel. 259-21-35), and a Jewish synagogue is on Calle de Balmes (tel. 445-98-35). It opened in the late 1960s, the first one to do so since the expulsion of the Jews from Spain in 1492. Friday-night services begin at 7:30, while Saturday morning services are at 9:30 a.m.

REST ROOMS: Some are available, including those in Retiro

Park in Madrid and on the Plaza del Oriente across from the Royal Palace. Otherwise, you can always go into a bar or *tasca,* but you really should order something—perhaps a small glass of beer or even a bag of peanuts.

The Spanish designations for rest rooms are *aseos* or *servicios. Caballeros* are for men, and *damas* are for women.

SMOKING: In Spain virtually everyone smokes—on buses, in the Metro, everywhere. "No Fumar" signs are often ignored.

STORE HOURS: Major stores no longer take a siesta, and are open from 9:30 a.m. to 8 p.m. Monday to Saturday. However, smaller stores, such as "mama and papa" operations, still follow the old custom and do business from 9:30 a.m. to 1:30 p.m. and 4:30 to 8 p.m.

TAXES: Since Spain joined the Common Market (EEC) on January 1, 1986 (which it did simultaneously with Portugal), it committed itself to gradually eliminating most tariff barriers between itself and the rest of Europe. In consequence, internal sales taxes (known in Spain as I.V.A.) were immediately adjusted upward to 6% or 12%, depending on the commodity being sold. Most of the basic necessities of the Spaniard's life, including food and most wines, are taxed at 6%. The majority of goods and services, as well as rental cars, are taxed at the "ordinary" rate of 12%. Luxury goods such as jewelry, furs, motor yachts, and private airplanes also carry a 12% tax. The rental of rooms in hotels with government ratings of four or five stars is subject to a 12% tax; rooms in hotels rated three stars or less are levied a 6% tax. These taxes are usually (but not always) quoted as part of the hotel rates.

For drinkers and smokers, all imported liquors and all tobaccos (whether Spanish or foreign) are taxed at 6% or 12% (depending on the store), making the prices of vices just a little bit higher. Most drinkers solve the problem by switching from scotch to Spanish wines, Spanish beers, or Spanish brandies with soda.

If you buy goods worth a total of more than 10,000 pesetas ($94), you are eligible for a tax rebate of 6% or 12%, depending on the type of purchase. Major department stores will deduct the tax from your bill upon presentation of your passport. Small stores may provide you with a form to fill out that you must show with your purchase to Spanish Custom's I.V.A. desk at your departure point. If a shop does not have a form, save your receipts to show at the I.V.A. desk. The government will refund by mail the amount due in pesetas. Refunds take between 2 and 3 months.

TELEGRAMS: Cables may be sent at the central post office building in Madrid at the Plaza de las Cibeles (tel. 221-81-95). However, the phone number for international telegrams is 241-33-00.

TELEPHONES: If you don't speak Spanish, you'll find it easier to telephone from your hotel. Know, however, that this is often a very expensive way of doing it, as hotels impose a surcharge on every operator-assisted call. If you're more adventurous, you'll find street phone booths, known as *cabinas,* with dialing instructions in English. A three-minute local call can be made by inserting three coins of 5 pesetas (5¢) each. It may be best for long-distance calls—especially transatlantic ones—to go to the main telephone exchange, Locutorio Gran Vía, 30 Gran Vía, or Locutorio Recoletos, 37–41 Pº Recoletos. However, you may not be lucky enough to find an English-speaking operator. You will have to fill out a simple form that will facilitate the placement of a call.

TELEX AND FAX: You can send Telex and fax messages from the central post office building in Madrid, Plaza de las Cibeles (tel. 221-81-95), and from all major hotels.

TIME: Spain is six hours ahead of eastern standard time in the U.S. Daylight saving time (one hour ahead of standard time) is in effect from the last Sunday in March to the last Sunday in September.

TIPPING: It is not a problem if you follow certain guidelines, knowing that general rules are to be abandoned in the face of exceptional circumstances, such as someone performing a "lifesaving feat." Tipping is simplified in Spain, since the government requires hotels and restaurants to include their service charges—usually 15% of the bill—in their tariffs or in the price of their food items. However, that doesn't mean you should skip out of a place without dispensing some extra pesetas.

Hotels: A porter is tipped 50 pesetas (45¢) per piece of luggage handled, but never less than 100 pesetas (95¢), even if you have only one small suitcase. Maids are tipped 200 pesetas ($1.90) per week. In front-ranking hotels, the concierge will often submit a separate bill.

Hairdressers: Both barbers and beauticians should be tipped at least 15% of the bill.

Taxis: Add about 12% to the fare as shown on the meter. However, if the driver personally unloads or loads your luggage, increase that to approximately 20%.

Porters: At airports such as Barajas and major terminals, the porter who handles your luggage will present you with a fixed-charge bill.

Restaurants: In both restaurants and nightclubs, 15% is added to the bill. To that, you should add another 3% to 5%, depending on the quality of the service.

Service: The women who guard the washrooms get 25 pesetas (25¢), and theater ushers—at the bullfights or in movie houses or legitimate theaters—get from 25 pesetas (25¢) to 50 pesetas (45¢).

TOURIST OFFICE: The headquarters of the main tourist office for Spain is at 1 Calle Princesa (tel. 541-23-25), near the Plaza d'España. Its hours are Monday to Friday from 9 a.m. to 7 p.m.; Saturday from 9:30 a.m. to 1:30 p.m. A location more easily visited by most tourists is the branch that specializes in information only for Madrid and its surrounding regions, at 3 Plaza Mayor (tel. 266-54-77). It's open Monday to Friday from 10 a.m. to 2 p.m. and 4 to 7 p.m.; Saturday from 10 a.m. to 1:30 p.m. An additional tourist office is at 2 Duque de Medinaceli (tel. 429-49-51). There's also a branch of the tourist office in the arrivals hall of Barajas Airport (tel. 205-8656), which is open Monday to Friday from 8 a.m. to 8 p.m.; Saturday from 8 a.m. to 1 p.m.

For information before you go, get in touch with the National Tourist Office of Spain, 665 Fifth Ave., New York, NY 10022 (tel. 212/759-8822).

THE HOTELS OF MADRID

1. DELUXE HOTELS
2. OTHER TOP CHOICES
3. MODERATELY PRICED HOTELS
4. THE BUDGET RANGE

The hotel boom in Madrid has been spectacular: three-quarters of my recommendations are modern.

What about the relics of yesteryear? Except for those grand old ladies, the Ritz and the Palace (circa 1910–1912), most other older hostelries in Madrid haven't kept abreast of the times. A handful haven't added improvements or overhauled bedrooms substantially since the 1890s.

Traditionally, hotels in Madrid were clustered around the Atocha Railway Station and the Gran Vía. In my search for the most outstanding hotels in all price brackets, I've almost ignored these two popular, but noisy, districts. The newer hotels have been erected away from the center, especially on residential streets jutting off from the Paseo de la Castellana.

THE STAR SYSTEM

Spain officially rates its hotels by star designation. Five stars is the highest rating in Spain, signaling a deluxe establishment, complete with all the amenities and high tariffs associated with such accommodations.

Most of the establishments recommended in this guide are three- and four-star hotels falling into that vague "middle-bracket" category. Hotels granted one and two stars, as well as pensions (guesthouses), are far less comfortable, although they may be perfectly clean and decent places, but with limited plumbing and other physical facilities. The latter category is strictly for dedicated budgeteers.

For easy reference, see the "Accommodations" index at the back of this book.

Reminder: The telephone area code for Madrid is 91 if you're calling from within Spain. If you're dialing from North America, the country code is 34 and Madrid's code is 1.

---

1. Deluxe Hotels

The most famous hotel in Madrid is the **Ritz,** Plaza de la Lealtad, 28014 Madrid (tel. 521-28-57), offering all the luxuries and special attentions that world travelers have come to expect of a grand deluxe hotel. The director suggests that guests book very, very early, as rooms are hard to come by at this veritable citadel of gracious and snobbish living. An international rendezvous point, it has been handsomely updated and modernized, although efforts have been made to retain its Belle Époque character, unique in Europe. Acquired by Trusthouse Forte, the Ritz has undergone millions of dollars of "refreshing" to maintain its position as one of the leading hotels in the world.

One of *Les Grand Hôteles Européens,* it was built at the command of King Alfonso XIII, with the aid of Cesar Ritz, in 1908. It looks out onto the big circular Plaza de la Lealtad in the center of town, near the 300-acre Retiro Park, facing the Prado Museum and its extension, the Palacio de Villahermosa, and the Stock Exchange. The new hotels going up in Madrid simply can't match its elegance. The Ritz was constructed when costs were relatively low, and when spaciousness, luxury, and comfort were the orders of the day. This plush comfort will cost from 37,500 pesetas ($352.50) to 61,000 pesetas ($573.40) for a single room, and from 61,000 pesetas ($573.40) to 73,000 pesetas ($686.20) for a double, plus 12% tax. Suites, of course, cost more, and breakfast is extra. The marble baths are some of the finest I've seen in more than two decades of inspecting hotels in Europe.

Like the cognoscenti of old, who have long had a liking for the Ritz, today's guest likes its grandeur, comfort, service, and gracious living, including 24-hour room service. It's not only elegant in this thick-carpeted sense, but also quiet. In these days of casual attire, it's important to know that guests at the Ritz dress up, even for breakfast. This is not a "resort" hotel.

Each of the 156 bedrooms contains masses of fresh flowers, air conditioning, minibar, private bathroom, television with video movies and satellite reception, and telephone. The façade of the hotel is classed as a historic monument. No other hotel, except perhaps for the Palace, has a more varied history.

The five-star Ritz Restaurant is one of the most attractive in Europe. It is decorated in cream, blue, and gold, with paneled mirrors and 16th-century Flemish tapestries. Its chefs present an international menu, and its paella is said to be the best in Madrid. Except for champagne, the wine list is staunchly Spanish. Metro: Banco de España.

The **Park Hyatt Villa Magna,** 22 Paseo de la Castellana, 28046 Madrid (tel. 261-49-00 or toll-free in North America 800/233-

1234), is clad in slabs of rose-colored granite and set behind a bank of pines and laurels on the city's most fashionable boulevard. This is one of the finest and most sought-after hotels in Europe. It was already legendary as a supremely comfortable and elegant modern hotel when Hyatt International took over its management in 1990. Today, it is still getting better.

It was originally conceived when a handful of the elite teamed up to create a setting in which their special friends, along with an increasing array of discriminating international visitors, would be pleased to live and dine. They hired an architect, imported a French decorator (whose style has been described as a modern form of classicism), planted exquisitely arranged gardens, and put the staff through a rigidly intensive training program. The result is elegant and appropriately expensive.

Separated from the busy boulevard by a park-like garden, its façade has severely elegant contemporary lines. In contrast, its opulent interior recaptures the style of Carlos IV, with richly paneled walls, marble floors, and massive bouquets of fresh flowers. Through the lobby and elaborate drawing rooms pass almost every film star shooting on location in Spain. In the Mayfair cocktail lounge, sedate and leathery à la London, the bartender can mix any drink you conjure up.

This luxury palace offers 182 plush but dignified bedrooms, decorated in Louis XVI, English Regency, or Italian provincial style. Each has air conditioning, minibar, telephone, fresh flowers, and color TV with video movies and satellite reception (including news broadcasts beamed in from the U.S.). Depending on the season, single rooms range from 43,000 pesetas ($404.20) to 58,000 pesetas ($545.20), doubles from 53,000 pesetas ($498.20) to 71,000 pesetas ($667.40), plus tax. Breakfast costs extra. Metro: Rubén Dario.

Hotel Villa Real, 10 Plaza de las Cortés, 28014 Madrid (tel. 420-37-67), was until 1989, little more than a run-down, 19th-century apartment house auspiciously located across a three-sided park from the Spanish Parliament (Congreso de los Diputados). Its developers poured billions of pesetas into renovations to produce a charming and stylish hotel that is working hard to catch on with the cognoscenti of Spain. The eclectic façade combines an odd mixture of neoclassical and Aztec motifs, and in front of it wait footmen and doormen dressed in buff and forest-green uniforms. At press time, this hotel boasted a four-star rating by the Spanish government. (The only thing preventing a five-star upgrade was its lack of a formal restaurant.) The interior contains a scattering of modern paintings amid neoclassical moldings and details. The social center is the high-ceilinged, formal bar.

Each of the 115 accommodations contains a color TV with video movies and satellite reception, telephone, air conditioning, safe for the lockup of valuables, soundproofing, minibar, private bathroom, sunken salon filled with leather-upholstered furniture, and built-in furniture accented with burlwood inlays. Single rooms rent for 26,000 pesetas ($244.40), doubles cost 32,500 pesetas ($305.50), and suites for two begin at 59,000 pesetas ($554.60), plus tax. Breakfast is extra. Metro: Plaza de la Cibeles.

Next on the deluxe list is the **Eurobuilding,** 23 Calle Padre

Damián, 28036 Madrid (tel. 457-17-00). Even while this hotel was on the drawing boards, the rumor was that this five-star sensation of white marble would provide, in the architect's words, "a new concept in deluxe hotels." The Eurobuilding long ago lived up to its advance billing, reflecting a high level in taste and design. It is two hotels linked by a courtyard, away from the city center, but right in the midst of apartment houses, boutiques, nightclubs, first-class restaurants, tree-shaded squares, and the heart of the modern Madrid business world.

The more glamorous of the twin buildings is the main one, containing only suites, each of which was recently renovated in luxurious pastel shades and named Las Estancias de Eurobuilding. Drinks await you in the refrigerator. Gold-and-white ornately carved beds, background music, TV, a roomwide terrace for breakfast and cocktail entertaining—all are tastefully coordinated. Across the courtyard, the sister Eurobuilding contains less impressive—but still very comfortable—single and double rooms, each with a view from its private balcony of the formal garden and swimming pool below. In all, 540 accommodations are available, each with its own air conditioning, minibar, TV with video movies and satellite reception, telephone, security doors, and individual safes. Depending on the accommodation, single rooms range from 22,000 pesetas ($206.80) to 26,000 pesetas ($244.40), double rooms from 28,000 pesetas ($263.20) to 33,000 pesetas ($310.20). Suites cost 34,000 pesetas ($319.60) for single occupancy, 42,000 pesetas ($394.80) for double occupancy. Tax and breakfast are not included.

Shared by both buildings is the luxury restaurant, Balthasar, on the lower level behind a Turkish-inspired spindle screen. La Taberna, also on the premises, offers more rapid dining. Perhaps the ideal way to dine here is al fresco by the pool, enjoying a buffet luncheon. Metro: Cuzco.

The **Meliá Madrid,** 27 Princesa, 28008 Madrid (tel. 241-1988), is one of the most up-to-date, impressively modern, yet uniquely Spanish hotels in the country. Its 23 floors' worth of wide picture windows have taken a permanent position in the capital's skyline. Each of the 265 bedrooms is comfortably spacious, filled with contemporary furnishings, and usually offers sweeping views of the Madrid skyline. Each contains air conditioning, telephone, TV with video movies and many different channels from across Europe, and telephone. The chalk-white walls dramatize the flamboyant use of color accents; the bathrooms are sheathed in snow-white marble. Rates are 22,000 pesetas ($206.80) for a single room, 28,000 pesetas ($263.20) for a double; suites for two range from 40,000 pesetas ($376) to 70,500 pesetas ($662.70). Tax and breakfast are extra. The Restaurant Princesa is a subdued and restful spot. Equally popular is the Don Pepe Grill. The cuisine in both restaurants is international, including Japanese and Indian dishes. Metro: Rodríguez.

The **Miguel Angel,** 31 Miguel Angel (tel. 442-81-99), just off the Paseo de la Castellana, is sleekly modern and has quickly built a reputation for providing some of the finest accommodations in the Spanish capital. It has much going for it—location, contemporary styling, imaginative furnishings and art objects, an efficient staff, and plenty of comfort. Behind its façade is an expansive sun terrace on several levels, with clusters of garden furniture, surrounded by semitropical planting. The Farnesio bar is decorated in a Spanish Victorian style, and piano music is played from 8 in the evening. All the deluxe facilities are provided—an indoor heated swimming pool, saunas, hairdressers, and a drugstore. Art exhibitions are sponsored in the arcade of boutiques.

The 278 bedrooms contain color-coordinated fabrics and carpets and, in many cases, reproductions of classic Iberian furniture. Each is soundproof and air conditioned and has radio, TV, telephone, and minibar. Singles rent for around 17,500 pesetas ($164.50), doubles for 30,000 pesetas ($282), plus tax and the cost of breakfast. A well-managed restaurant on the premises is the Florencia, which serves a set lunch or dinner for 4,500 pesetas ($42.30). Dinner is also served in the Zacarias disco until around 3 a.m., which you can eat while watching an occasional cabaret or musical performance. Metro: Rubén Darío.

The **Wellington,** 8 Velázquez, 28001 Madrid (tel. 575-44-00), with its impressive antique-tapestried entrance, is one of Madrid's more sedate deluxe hotels, built in the mid-1950s but substantially remodeled since. In the Salamanca residential area near Retiro Park, the Wellington offers redecorated rooms, 325 in all, each air-conditioned and with color TV (with cable and movie channels), music, two phones (one in the bathroom), and a guest-operated combination safe. Units are furnished in English mahogany, and the bathrooms (one per accommodation) are modern and immaculate, with marble sheathing and fixtures. Doubles with private terraces (at no extra charge) are the choice accommodations. Singles cost 17,000 pesetas ($159.80), doubles 26,500 pesetas ($249.10), suites for two 30,000 pesetas ($282), plus tax. Breakfast costs extra.

In addition to an outdoor swimming pool, the Wellington offers 24-hour room service, a garage, beauty parlor, and same-day dry cleaning and laundry. An added bonus here is the El Fogón grill room, styled like a 19th-century tavern, where many of the provisions for the typically Spanish dishes are shipped in from the hotel's own ranch. The pub-style Bar Ingles is a warm and hospitable rendezvous spot. Metro: Retiro or Velázquez.

2. Other Top Choices

The **Palace,** 7 Plaza de las Cortes, 28014 Madrid (tel. 429-75-51), is the grand *dueña* of Spanish hotels. The establishment had an auspicious beginning, inaugurated by the late King Alfonso XIII in 1912. Covering a city block, it is superbly located, facing the Prado Museum and Neptune Fountain, in the historical and artistic area, within walking distance of the main shopping center and the best antique shops. Some of the city's most intriguing *tascas* and restaurants are only a short stroll away.

Architecturally, it captures the elegant pre–World War I "Grand Hotel" style, with an emphasis on space and comfort. Even though it is one of the largest hotels in Madrid, containing 508 accommodations, it retains a personal atmosphere. The rooms are conservatively traditional, with plenty of space for leisurely living, color TV, air conditioning, television, telephone, and large bathrooms with lots of extra amenities. Single rooms cost from 23,000 pesetas ($216.20) to 34,000 pesetas ($319.60), doubles from 29,000 pesetas ($272.60) to 43,000 pesetas ($404.20). Suites for two begin at 54,000 pesetas ($507.60). Tax and breakfast are extra.

The hotel is fully air-conditioned, with an impressive lobby, restaurant, grill room, and bar. A coffee shop in the main lobby is open daily from noon to 3 a.m. Metro: Banco de España or Anton Martin.

The **Princesa Plaza,** 3 Serrano Jover, 28015 Madrid (tel. 542-35-00), is a sprawling hotel designed like a series of massive rectangular solids set together. The concrete-and-glass façade overlooks busy boulevards in the center of Madrid. The interior contains a large assortment of conference rooms, an underground garage, a hairdressing salon, a restaurant, a bar, and a disco that opens every night at 8 p.m. Each of the 406 bedrooms is decorated in springtime colors and comfortably modern furniture, and has air conditioning, telephone, TV, and minibar. Single rooms cost 21,000 pesetas ($197.40), doubles 26,500 pesetas ($249.10), and suites for two range from 52,000 pesetas ($488.80) and up. Tax and breakfast are extra. Metro: Argüelles.

The **Castellana Hotel,** 49 Paseo de la Castellana, 28046 Madrid (tel. 410-02-00), is solid, spacious, and conservatively modern. This is one of the more reliable and stylish hotels in Madrid. Under the direction of the Inter-Continental hotel chain, it lies behind a barrier of trees on the most famous *paseo* of Madrid, within a neighborhood of elegant apartment houses and luxury hotels. Its sunflooded public rooms contain terrazzo floors, high ceilings, a collection of modern abstract murals pieced together from multicolored stones and tiles, and such conveniences as an airline reservations office, a travel agent who will book theater tickets, a handful of shops and boutiques, and a helpful concierge. Other facilities include La Ronda Bar, a coffee shop, an upscale restaurant, a health club with a gymnasium, and a massage and sauna room.

Most of the 305 accommodations have private balconies, and each contains a color TV with in-house video and reception of many different channels from across Europe, air conditioning, minibar, and phone. Single rooms cost from 28,000 pesetas ($263.20) to 32,000 pesetas ($300.80), doubles from 34,000 pesetas ($319.60) to 39,000 pesetas ($366.60). Suites for two begin at 53,000 pesetas ($498.20). Tax and breakfast are extra. Metro: Rubén Dario.

At the **Hotel Apartamento Escultor,** 3 Miguel Angel, 28010 Madrid (tel. 410-42-03), a large percentage of the accommodations contain bedrooms, sitting rooms, and dressing rooms—a combination that provides more space than many other hotels within this category. Although many of the accommodations within this apartment hotel contain fully equipped kitchenettes, these are unlocked only for prepaid visits of at least a week or more.

The apartments have their own charm and contemporary styling. Each has a minibar, color TV with video films, private bathroom, and air conditioning. Whether you opt for a traditional one room plus bath or one of the larger apartments, everything is compact, well-organized, and comfortable. Accommodations for one or two occupants range from 10,500 pesetas ($98.70) to 29,500 pesetas ($277.30) per night, plus tax and breakfast.

The hotel has a small and comfortable lounge where nighttime disco pulsates, and a modern restaurant, Vanity, seating 40 to 45 people. The hotel is fully air-conditioned and contains a garage. Metro: Rubén Dario.

The **Plaza Hotel,** 8 Plaza de España, 28013 Madrid (tel. 247-12-00), could be called the Waldorf-Astoria of Spain. A massive rose-and-white structure, it soars upward to a central tower 26 stories high. It is a landmark visible for miles around and one of the tallest skyscrapers in Europe, crowned by a panoramic disco, swimming pool, and sun terrace.

The hotel's 302 accommodations include both conventional singles and doubles as well as 82 luxurious suites, each of which contains a sitting room and lots of amenities. Each of the accommodations, regardless of its size, contains a telephone, expansive marble-covered bathroom, air conditioning, and color TV. Furniture is usually a standardized modern style, in such carefully harmonized colors as grey and mulberry. Single rooms cost 14,900 pesetas ($140.05), double rooms 18,500 pesetas ($173.90), and suites for two 29,000 pesetas ($272.60). Tax and breakfast are extra. Metro: Plaza de España.

Meliá Castilla, 43 Calle Capitán Haya, 28020 Madrid (tel. 571-22-11), is a mammoth hotel with 1,000 rooms and plenty of extra facilities. It qualifies, along with the already-recommended Palace, as one of the largest hotels in Europe. Built primarily to accommodate the huge conventions that sometimes take place here, Meliá Castilla also caters to the needs of the individual traveler. Everything is larger than life here: You need a floor plan to direct yourself around its precincts. The lounges and corridors of pristine marble are vast. As you wander around, you'll find a swimming pool, a shopping arcade, a coffee shop, a seafood restaurant, a restaurant specializing in paella and other rice dishes, cocktail lounges, a landscaped garden, saunas, a gymnasium, a parking garage, the Trinidad nightclub, even a showroom full of the latest model cars. In addition to these features, there's the restaurant/show, Scala Meliá Castilla.

As for the accommodations, each of the twin-bedded rooms comes equipped with private bath, minibar, radio, color TV, telephone, air conditioning, and modern furniture. Single rooms cost 23,500 pesetas ($220.90), double rooms 28,000 pesetas ($263.20), plus tax. Breakfast is included in the price. The Meliá Castilla is in the north of Madrid, about a block west of Paseo de la Castellana, a short drive from the Chamartín railway station. Metro: Cuzco.

Gran Hotel Reina Victoria, 7 Plaza del Angel, 28012 Madrid (tel. 531-45-00), is about as important to the legends of Madrid as the famous bullfighter Manolete himself. He used to stay here, giving lavish parties in one of the reception rooms and attracting mobs in the square below when he went out on his balcony for morning coffee. Since the recent renovation and upgrading of this property by Spain's Tryp Hotel Group, it's less staid and more impressive than ever. Guests enjoy the hotel's stylish and popular lobby bar, whose bullfight memorabilia and potent drinks add another attraction to an already memorable hotel.

Originally built in 1923, and named after the grandmother of the present King of Spain, Juan Carlos, the hotel sits behind an ornately eclectic stone façade, which the Spanish government protects as a historic monument. Although it's located in a congested neighborhood in the center of town, it opens onto its own verdant and sloping plaza, rich in tradition as a meeting place of intellectuals during the 17th century. Today the area is usually filled with flower vendors, older people catching rays of midafternoon sun, and young persons resting between bouts at the dozens of neighborhood tapas bars.

Each of the hotel's 201 bedrooms contains air conditioning, sound-resistant insulation, color TV with satellite reception, safe for valuables, minibar, and private bathroom with many amenities. With breakfast included, single rooms cost 12,500 pesetas ($117.50), doubles from 12,500 pesetas ($117.50) to 21,500 pesetas ($202.10), and triples from 21,500 pesetas ($202.10) to 28,000 pesetas ($263.20), plus tax. Metro: Tirso de Molina.

---

3. Moderately Priced Hotels

The **Emperatriz,** 4 López de Hoyos, 28006 Madrid (tel. 563-8088), lies just off the wide Paseo de Castellana, only a short walk from some of Madrid's most deluxe hotels, but it charges relatively reasonable rates. It contains 170 comfortably unpretentious bedrooms, each of which has a TV with reception of many different European channels, private bathroom, minibar, air conditioning, telephone, and mixture of both traditional and modern furniture. Single rooms cost 9,000 pesetas ($84.60), doubles 14,000 pesetas ($131.60), and suites for two 18,000 pesetas ($169.20). Tax and breakfast are extra. If one is available, ask for a room on the eighth floor, where you'll get a private terrace at no extra charge.

On the premises are a beauty salon, barbershop, and well-upholstered lounges where you're likely to meet fellow globe-trotting Americans. Metro: Rubén Dario.

The **Novotel Madrid,** 1 Calle Albacete (at the corner of Avenida Badajoz), 28027 Madrid (tel. 405-46-00 or toll-free in North America 800/221-4542), was originally intended to serve the hotel needs of a cluster of multinational corporations with headquarters 1½ miles east of the center of Madrid, but its rooms are so comfortable and its prices so reasonable that tourists have begun using it as well. It opened in 1986, with an enthusiastic staff. Its position on the highway, away from the maze of sometimes confusing inner-city streets, makes it especially attractive to motorists.

The hotel contains 236 bedrooms, each designed in a standardized format whose popularity in Europe has made it one of the hotel industry's most notable success stories. Each contains a well-designed bathroom, color TV with in-house movies, minibar, radio, phone, air conditioning, and soundproofing. The English-speaking staff is well-versed in both sightseeing attractions and solutions to most business-related problems. A copious breakfast buffet is included in the price of a room. Singles cost around 12,000 pesetas ($112.80), doubles 14,300 pesetas ($134.42), plus tax. Children under 16 stay free in their parents' room. (The sofa, once bolster pillows are removed, is transformed into a comfortable bed.)

Motorists should exit from the M-30 at Barrio de la Concepcion/Parque de las Avenidas, just before reaching the city limits of central Madrid, then look for the chain's trademark electric-blue signs. Metro: Concepcion.

The **Hotel Chamartín,** Estacion de Chamartín, 28036 Madrid (tel. 733-90-11), is a 378-room brick-sided hotel soaring nine stories above the northern periphery of Madrid. It's part of the massive modern shopping complex attached to the Chamartín railway station, although once you're inside your soundproof room, the noise of the railway station will seem far away. The owner of the building is RENFE, Spain's government-owned railway system, but the nationwide hotel chain that administers it is Entursa Hotels. The hotel lies 15 minutes by taxi from both the airport and the historic core of Madrid, and is conveniently close to one of the capital's busiest Metro stops. Especially oriented to the business traveler, it offers a currency exchange kiosk, a travel agency, a car-rental office, and a video screen in the lobby that posts the arrival and departure of all of Chamartín's trains. A coffee bar serves breakfast daily, and room service is available. A short walk from the hotel lobby, within the railway-station complex, are a handful of shops and movie theaters, a roller-skating rink, a disco, and ample parking.

With a buffet breakfast included in the price, single rooms cost 11,000 pesetas ($103.40), double rooms 14,700 pesetas ($138.18), plus tax. Metro: Chamartín.

The **Gran Hotel Colón,** 119 Avenida del Doctor Esquerdo, 28007 Madrid (tel. 273-0800), stands west of Retiro Park, a few minutes by subway from the center. It offers 390 comfortable yet moderately priced accommodations in one of the city's modern hotel structures. More than half of the accommodations have private balconies, and each contains air conditioning, TV, telephone, and comfortably traditional furniture, much of it built-in. Single rooms cost from 7,600 pesetas ($71.44) to 8,800 pesetas ($82.72), double rooms 11,100 pesetas ($104.34). Tax and breakfast are extra. To literally top everything off, there is a swimming pool on the roof, 11 stories up, where you can sunbathe with a view of the skyline of Madrid. Other assets of the hotel include two dining rooms, a covered garage, and Bingo games. One of the Colón's founders was an accomplished interior designer, which accounts for the unusual stained-glass windows and murals in the public rooms and the paintings by Spanish artists in the lounge. Metro: Condé Casal.

The **Residencia Bretón,** 29 Bretón de los Herreros, 28003 Madrid (tel. 442-83-00), is a modern 56-room hotel on a side street several blocks from the Paseo de la Castellana. It is well furnished with reproductions of Iberian pieces. As a *residencia,* it doesn't offer a major dining room, but it does have a little bar and breakfast room adjoining the reception lounge. Each of the rooms has air conditioning, telephone, TV, and minibar, as well as attractive wooden beds, wrought-iron electric fixtures, wall-to-wall curtains, comfortable chairs, and tilework painted with ornate designs in the bathrooms. Single rooms cost from 9,000 pesetas ($84.60) to

11,000 pesetas ($103.40), double rooms from 13,500 pesetas ($126.90) to 20,000 pesetas ($188), plus tax. Breakfast costs extra. Metro: Ríos Rosas.

The **Grand Hotel Tryp Velázquez,** 62 Calle de Velázquez, 28001 Madrid (tel. 275-28-00), faces an affluent residential street near the center of town. The art-deco façade conceals an interior so filled with well-upholstered furniture and richly grained paneling that it shows more of its 1947 origin than any 1930s kinship. Several public rooms lead off a central oval area; one of them includes a warm bar area.

As in many hotels of its era, the bedrooms (144 in all) vary, some large enough for entertaining, but all containing air conditioning, TV, telephone, and piped-in music. A room used for single occupancy costs 10,700 pesetas ($100.58); 14,000 pesetas ($131.60) for two persons. Breakfast is included in the tariffs. This is one of the most attractive medium-sized hotels in Madrid, with comfort and convenience. Parking is available on the premises. Metro: Retiro.

The **Cuzco,** 133 Paseo de la Castellana, 28046 Madrid (tel. 556-06-00), is popular with business people and American tour groups. It lies in a commercial neighborhood of big buildings, government ministries, spacious avenues, and the main Congress Hall. The Chamartín railway station is located within a 10-minute walk north of the hotel, so it's a popular and convenient address.

This 15-floor structure, set back from Madrid's longest boulevard, has been redecorated and modernized since it was completed in 1967. The architect of the Cuzco allowed for 330 spacious bedrooms, each with a separate sitting area. Each also has air conditioning, TV with video movies, private bathroom, and telephone. The decorator provided modern furnishings and patterned rugs. Single rooms cost 14,000 pesetas ($131.60), double rooms 18,000 pesetas ($169.20), and suites for two 25,000 pesetas ($235), plus tax and the cost of breakfast. Metro: Cuzco.

There is a bi-level snack bar and cafeteria. The lounge is a forest of marble pillars and leather armchairs, the ambience enhanced by contemporary oil paintings and tapestries. Facilities include a free parking lot, covered garage, beauty parlor, sauna, massage, gymnasium, and cocktail bar.

The **Hotel Claridge,** 6 Plaza Conde de Casal, 28007 Madrid (tel. 551-94-00), is a contemporary building beyond Retiro Park, about five minutes from the Prado by taxi. The air-conditioned bedrooms are well-organized and styled: small, compact, with coordinated furnishings and colors, air conditioning, TV, and phone. All 150 bedrooms have a private bathroom. A single rents for 6,500 pesetas ($61.10), a double for 8,700 pesetas ($81.80), plus tax and breakfast. You can take your meals in the hotel's cafeteria or just relax in the modern lounge. Metro: Conde Casal.

Hotel Alcalá, 66 Alcalá, 28009 Madrid (tel. 435-10-60), enjoys an enviable position on a busy boulevard near the northern edge of Retiro Park. It has 153 tastefully modern bedrooms, each with voluminous draperies, tile and wooden headboards, coordinated colors, private bathroom, minibar, TV with reception of many different European channels, telephone, and air conditioning. Depending on the facilities, single rooms range from 10,400 pesetas ($97.75) to 11,500 pesetas ($108.10), doubles 15,200 pesetas ($142.90), plus tax and the cost of breakfast. Facilities within the hotel include a two-level public lounge dotted with comfortable chairs, the ornate Restaurant Basque, a lower-level coffee shop, an underground garage, and a bright Toledo-red American bar opening off the lounge. Metro: Príncipe de Vergara.

The **Residência Liabeny,** 3 Salud, 28013 Madrid (tel. 532-52-06), lies behind a stone-sheathed rectangular façade in a prime location midway between the tourist highlights of the Gran Vía and the Puerta del Sol. Named after the original owner of the hotel, it contains seven floors and 177 comfortably contemporary bedrooms, each of which has a private bathroom, air conditioning, TV, and telephone. Single rooms cost 7,700 pesetas ($72.40) to 9,500 pesetas ($89.30), doubles 12,000 pesetas ($112.80), plus tax. Breakfast costs extra. Metro: Puerta del Sol, Callao, or Gran Vía.

4. The Budget Range

The **Hostal Residencia Don Diego,** 45 Calle de Velázquez, 28001 Madrid (tel. 435-07-60), lies in a combination residential/commercial neighborhood that is relatively convenient to many of the monuments of the city. The hostal is on the fifth floor of a building with an elevator. The vestibule contains an elegant winding staircase accented with iron griffin heads supporting its balustrade. The hotel is warmly inviting, filled with leather couches and a kind of comfortable, no-nonsense style of angular but attractive furniture. A bar stands at the far end of the main sitting room. Each of the 58 bedrooms contains a private bathroom and a telephone. Singles cost 6,000 pesetas ($56.40), doubles 8,000 pesetas ($75.20), plus tax. Breakfast is not included in the price. Metro: Colón.

The **Anaco,** 3 Tres Cruces, 28013 Madrid (tel. 522-46-04), is a modestly modern 39-room hotel, just off the shopping thoroughfare, Gran Vía. Opening onto a tree-shaded plaza, it attracts those seeking a resting place featuring contemporary appurtenances and cleanliness. The bedrooms are charmingly compact, with built-in headboards, reading lamps, and lounge chairs. Each room is air-conditioned and contains a private bathroom, TV, and telephone. Single rooms cost 4,700 pesetas ($44.20), doubles 8,200 pesetas ($77.10), and triples 11,000 pesetas ($103.40), plus tax. Breakfast is not included in the price. Useful tip: Ask for one of the five terraced rooms on the top floor, which rent at no extra charge. English is spoken. Nearby is a municipally operated garage. Metro: Gran Vía, Callao, or Puerta del Sol.

The **Aristos,** 34 Avenida Pío XII, 28016 Madrid (tel. 457-04-50), is a three-star hotel in an up-and-coming residential area of Madrid, not far from the Eurobuilding. Its main advantage is a garden in front, where you can lounge, have a drink, or order a complete meal. The hotel's restaurant, El Chaflán, is frequented by residents of the neighborhood in addition to hotel visitors. Each of the bedrooms has a small terrace, air conditioning, television, and telephone. All but four of the hotel's 24 bedrooms contain a private bathroom, and each has an uncomplicated collection of modern furniture. Single rooms cost 7,400 pesetas ($69.55), double rooms 11,500 pesetas ($108.10), plus tax. Bathless rooms rent for about 20% less. Suites for two cost from 13,000 pesetas ($122.20), plus tax. Breakfast is extra. Metro: Pio XII.

The **Tirol,** 4 Marqués de Urquijo, 28008 Madrid (tel. 248-19-00), a short walk from the Plaza de España and the swank Meliá Madrid Hotel, is a good choice for clean, unpretentious comfort. A three-star hotel, it offers single rooms for 6,500 pesetas ($61.10), double rooms for 8,100 pesetas ($76.15), and suites for two for 11,700 pesetas ($110), plus tax. Breakfast is extra. Each of the hotel's 97 accommodations contains a private bathroom, air conditioning, and telephone, and 8 of them have a private terrace. Furnishings are simple and functional. There's a cafeteria and a parking garage within the hotel. Metro: Argüelles.

The **Casón del Tormes,** 7 Río, 28013 Madrid (tel. 541-97-46), is an attractive three-star hotel around the corner from the Royal Palace and the Plaza de España. Set behind a red-brick four-story façade with stone-trimmed windows, it overlooks a quiet one-way street. The long narrow lobby contains vertical wooden paneling, a marble floor, and a bar opening off into a separate room. Each of the 61 accommodations contains air conditioning, TV, and telephone, and motorists appreciate the public parking lot near the hotel. Single rooms rent for 7,400 pesetas ($69.60), doubles for 9,700 pesetas ($91.20), plus tax, with breakfast included in the price. Metro: Plaza de España.

The **Hostal Embajada,** 5 Calle Santa Engracía, 28010 Madrid (tel. 447-33-00), is a three-star hotel about one block from the Plaza Alonso Martínez, a rather distinguished residential area. Still standing across the street is a great 19th-century palace. The Embajada has 65 rooms, most with bath and telephone. Depending on the plumbing, singles range from 6,000 pesetas ($56.40) to 7,200 pesetas ($67.70), doubles from 8,800 pesetas ($82.70) to 12,300 pesetas ($115.62), plus tax and breakfast. Metro: Alonso Martínez.

The **Residência Mercátor,** 123 Atocha, 28012 Madrid (tel. 429-05-00), is only a three-minute walk from the Prado. It draws a clientele seeking a good, modern hotel—orderly, well run, and clean, with enough comforts and conveniences to please the weary traveler. The public rooms are simple, outfitted in a vaguely modern type of minimalism. Some of the 89 rooms are more inviting than others, especially those with desks and armchairs. Most have a private bathroom and each has a telephone. Singles with bath cost 5,000 pesetas ($47), doubles with bath 10,000 pesetas ($94), plus tax and breakfast. Residents of bathless rooms receive a discount of about 25%. The Mercátor is a *residência*—that is, it offers breakfast only, and does not have a formal restaurant for lunch and dinner. However, it has a bar and cafeteria serving light meals such as *platos combinados* (combination plates). Happily, the hotel has a garage, and is within walking distance of American Express. Metro: Atocha or A. Martín.

The **Hotel Francisco I,** 15 Arenal, 28013 Madrid (tel. 248-43-14), offers 58 modern, clean rooms, each with a small private bathroom and telephone. With breakfast included, single rooms cost 5,500 pesetas ($51.70), doubles 7,200 pesetas ($67.70), plus tax. There's a pleasant lounge and a bar, and on the sixth floor you'll find a comfortable, rustically decorated restaurant where a set meal costs around 1,800 pesetas ($16.95). Metro: Puerta del Sol or Opéra.

The **Hotel Nuria,** 52 Fuencarral, 28004 Madrid (tel. 231-92-08), just three blocks from the Gran Vía, has some bedrooms with especially interesting views of the capital. Renovated in the late 1960s, the 80-room hotel offers single rooms for 3,000 pesetas ($28.20), double rooms for 5,300 pesetas ($49.80), with breakfast included. Tax is extra. Metro: Bilbao or Quevedo.

DINING IN MADRID

All the major Spanish cuisines, ranging from Galician and Asturian to Basque (the Basques are said to be the best cooks) to Andalusian and Levantine, are represented in Madrid, along with the traditional Castilian cuisine, which predominates.

At best, the cuisine of Spain is controversial. It inspires some to unqualified praise, others to fulmination.

The kitchens of Spain turn out a pungent, varied, and imaginative fare, including squid cooked in its own ink, Valencian paella, Andalusian gazpacho, grilled pink prawns, garlic soup (said to bestow longevity), and the tail of a bull.

For the versatile, adventurous diner, there is no problem. There are loads of temptation—such as *anguillas* (baby eels)—waiting to lure you. If not, the chefs of Spain are prepared to accommodate you with what has come to be known as an "international" cuisine. In any case, beware: If you overindulge in the dishes cooked in olive oil and the wines called "noble" but strong, chances are you'll come down with that traditional tourist malady euphemistically known as "Toledo tummy."

If you don't like garlic, instruct your waiter (*camarero*). If he or she doesn't speak English, say *"Sin ajo"* (pronounced ah-ho). Of course, many dishes of combined ingredients depend on garlic for their basic flavor. Two of these are Spain's best-known specialties, the **paella** of Valencia and the "liquid salad" or **gazpacho** of Andalusia. Both items vary greatly, depending on the skill of the chef and the quality of ingredients used.

At its worst, paella—the Spanish rice dish—is made with last night's leftovers. At its finest, it is cooked with such well-chosen items as tender chicken, artichoke hearts, prawns, clams, bits of sausage, peas, garlic, pimientos—all aromatically seasoned and served on saffron rice. Traditionally, paella is presented in a piping-hot black iron skillet.

Gazpacho is especially good in summer. Ideally chilled thoroughly, in the tradition of vichyssoise, it is a soup of olive oil, vinegar, garlic, fresh tomatoes, cucumber, peppers, croutons, and raw onions. Another soup in which the Spaniards excel is **sopa de pescado,** literally "soup of fish," varying from province to province, but usually a taste treat worth trying.

Another exciting taste treat originates in the province of Segovia. It is the roast suckling pig, so beloved by Hemingway. Called **cochinillo asado,** it is a rich-tasting—and richly priced—banquet. Roast lamb (**cordero asado**) also draws many admirers. Otherwise, meat dishes, especially beef, sometimes disappoint North Americans used to finer cuts.

In their fish dishes, the Spaniards are quite remarkable and most inventive. Thanks to speedy transportation facilities, inland cities such as Madrid receive daily supplies of fresh fish. Mountain river trout (**trucha**) is superb, as is the paralyzingly priced lobster (**langosta**). A great fish dish is **zarzuela de mariscos,** with hunks of prawn, lobster, and other shellfish.

Many restaurants in Spain feature a *menú del día*. The principle behind this set meal is to give a tourist a complete meal, including soup or hors d'oeuvres, a meat or fish dish, plus dessert, a small carafe of the house wine, service, and taxes—all for one standard charge.

Note: The chic dining hour in Madrid is 10 or 10:30. Quite conceivably you might get out by midnight.

For easy reference, see the "Restaurants" index in the back of this book.

1. The Leading Restaurants

Restaurant Jaun de Alzate, 18 Calle Princesa (tel. 247-0010), lies within what was originally built as a stable for the Duchess of Alba's Liria Palace. Although its address is technically on the Calle Princesa, a sign will direct you to an entrance on a narrow side street behind the Plaza de España. Inside, most of the decor's color comes from small vases of seasonal flowers, which offset an otherwise monochromatic room vaguely influenced by art deco.

The award-winning chef is Basque-born Iñaki Izaguirre, whom some observers compare to Salvador Dali, because of both his handlebar mustache and his almost surrealistic combination of unusual ingredients. Although ardently committed to the preservation of his Basque traditions, his culinary style was strongly influenced by the years he lived in England, Holland, and the U.S. A *menú del día* will cost around 6,700 pesetas ($62.98), while à la carte meals range upward from 8,000 pesetas ($75.20).

These specific offerings will almost certainly have changed by the time of your visit, but examples of Izaguirre's cuisine include a salad of pine nuts, fresh greens, and poached lobster with an olive oil dressing; sushi with chorizos sausage; rabbit meatballs and mango balls in cold almond soup; deep-fried crayfish tails marinated in béchamel sauce; deboned loin of lamb stuffed with sweetbreads and black truffles; and turbot stuffed with lobster in saffron sauce.

All the fish served in this restaurant come fresh every day from the wholesale fish market in the heart of the Basque country, San Sebastián, where a trusted employee selects the finest fish of the Cantabrian coast.

Izaguirre believes in food low in fat, cholesterol, and calories, but loaded with nutrition and bursting with flavor. The cross-cultural dishes here probably look as good as they taste, arranged on a platter as an artist would arrange colors on a palette. Reservations are very important, and meals are served every day of the year from 1:30 to 4 p.m. and 9 p.m. to midnight. Metro: Plaza de España.

Fortuny, 34 Fortuny (tel. 410-77-07), is the most elegant restaurant in Madrid, and also one of the best. Lying off the Paseo de la Castellana, the restaurant opened in 1986 in a 19th-century villa, originally the home of the Marqués Cuevas de Vera. Guests, who include expense-account gourmets and foreign visitors, often arrive by limousine. They are ushered across the courtyard and into the beautifully decorated, luxurious restaurant. Diners can choose to eat in the garden in fair weather. Otherwise, they will be seated in one of several different dining rooms, the most visible of which has a Louis XVI decor.

Imaginative appetizers include codfish ravioli Fortuny, and the menu is likely to feature grilled suckling lamb in its own juice (prepared for two diners), roast duck with fig ravioli, sea bass with shrimp tartare, steamed flatfish served with a sauce based on extract of Ceylon tea, and pork trotters in a hot sauce. The wine list is among the finest in Madrid. Meals cost from 6,500 pesetas ($61.10) to 9,000 pesetas ($84.60). The restaurant is open Monday to Friday from 1 to 4 p.m. and 9 p.m. to midnight; Saturday 9 p.m. to midnight. Reservations are essential. Metro: Rubén Dario.

Las Cuatro Estaciones, 5 Général Ibáñez Ibero (tel. 534-87-34), is placed by gastronomes and horticulturists alike among their favorite dining spots of Madrid. In addition to superb food, the establishment prides itself on the masses of flowers that change with the season, plus a modern and softly inviting decor that has delighted some of the most glamorous diners in Spain. Depending on the time of year, the mirrors surrounding the multilevel bar near the entrance reflect thousands of hydrangeas, chrysanthemums, or poinsettias. Even the napery matches whichever colors the resident botanist has chosen as the seasonal motif. Each person involved in food preparation spends a prolonged apprenticeship at restaurants in France before returning home to try their freshly sharpened talents on the taste buds of aristocratic Madrid.

A la carte meals cost from around 4,200 pesetas ($39.50) each. Representative specialties include crab bisque, fresh oysters, a petite marmite of fish and shellfish, imaginative preparations of salmon, a salad of eels, fresh asparagus with mushrooms in puff pastry with a parsley-butter sauce, a three-fish platter with *fines herbes,* brochette of filet of beef in pecadillo, and a nouvelle-cuisine version of blanquette of monkfish so tender it melts in your mouth. A "festival of desserts" includes whichever specials the chef has concocted that day, a selection of which is placed temptingly on your table.

Reservations are recommended for meals, which are served Monday to Friday from 1 to 4 p.m. and 9 p.m. to midnight. The restaurant is closed Saturday, Sunday, and the month of August. Metro: Cuatro Caminos.

Jockey, 6 Amador de los Ríos (tel. 419-24-35), is considered by many to be the finest restaurant in Spain. At any rate, it is the favorite of international celebrities, diplomats, and heads of state, and some of the more faithful patrons look upon it as their own private club.

The restaurant, with tables on two levels, isn't overly large. Wood-paneled walls and colored linen provide warmth. Against the paneling are a dozen prints of horses mounted by jockeys—hence the name of the place.

If you like your decisions made for you, two or more persons can order a *Menu Dégustation,* which is changed monthly and presumably includes an array of the most sophisticated and creative dishes produced by the chef. It's priced at around 8,000 pesetas ($75.20), while à la carte meals range in price from 6,000 pesetas ($56.40) to 8,500 pesetas ($79.90).

Since Jockey's establishment shortly after World War II, the chef has prided himself on coming up with new and creative dishes. Your meal might include such concoctions as a mousse of smoked eel with sardines, a salad of crayfish tails, hearts of artichokes with fresh duck liver in *cava* wine sauce, hake in green sauce, filet strips of sole served with fresh figs and chardonnay sauce, sautéed goose liver with fettuccini, or deboned duckling with figs in wine sauce. Desserts are appropriately sumptuous, including perhaps a cold mandarin soufflé. The restaurant is open Monday to Saturday from 1 to 4 p.m. and 9 to 11:30 p.m.; closed Sunday and during the entire month of August. Reservations are necessary. If you go early (within half an hour of opening), you'll have the dining room virtually to yourself. Metro: Cuzco.

El Cabo Mayor, 37 Juan Ramón Jiménez (tel. 250-87-76), in the prosperous northern edges of Madrid, is not far from the city-within-a-city of Chamartín Station. This is one of the best, most popular, and most stylish restaurants in Spain. The open-air staircase leading to the entranceway descends from a manicured garden on a quiet side street. You'll know you're here by the battalion of uniformed doormen who greet arriving taxis. The restaurant's decor is a nautically inspired mass of hardwood panels, brass trim, old-fashioned pulleys and ropes, a tile floor custom-painted into sea-green and blue replicas of the waves, and hand-carved models of fishing boats. In brass replicas of portholes, some dozen bronze statues honoring fishermen and their craft are displayed in illuminated positions of honor.

Full meals, costing 5,000 pesetas ($47) to 7,500 pesetas ($70.50), are served Monday to Saturday from 1:30 to 4 p.m. and 9 p.m. to midnight. The restaurant is closed Sunday and during the last two weeks of August. Menu choices include a superb version of paprika-laden peppers stuffed with fish, a salad composed of Jabugo ham and foie gras of duckling, fish soup from Cantabria (a province between the Basque country and Asturias), stewed sea bream with thyme, asparagus mousse, salmon in sherry sauce, and a loin of veal in cassis sauce. Desserts are appropriately sophisticated, among them a mousse of rice with pine-nut sauce. Because of the restaurant's popularity, reservations are recommended. Metro: Cuzco.

Horcher, 6 Alfonso XII (tel. 522-07-31), originated in Berlin in 1904. In a sudden move prompted by a tip from a high-ranking German officer that Germany was losing the war, Herr Horcher moved his restaurant to Madrid in 1943. The restaurant has continued its grand European traditions ever since.

A jacket and tie are imperative—as is a reservation. Your best chance of getting a seat is to go early. The restaurant is open Monday to Saturday from 1:30 to 4 p.m. and 8:30 p.m. to midnight. The service is excellent.

Where to start? You might try the seafood mousse. Wild duck salad also attains distinction. Both the venison stew in green pepper with orange peel and the crayfish with parsley and cucumber are excellent. Other main courses include veal scaloppine in tarragon. For dessert, the house specialty is crêpes Sir Holden, prepared at your table, with fresh raspberries, cream, and nuts, or you may prefer a Sachertorte. Expect to spend from 6,000 pesetas ($56.40) for a full meal. Metro: Retiro.

Valentin, 3 San Alberto (tel. 521-16-38), founded in 1892, has drawn a clientele from such widely varied categories as bullfighters, artists, high society, and movie stars, many of whose pictures can be seen on the walls. The restaurant's two rooms have a welcoming atmosphere, and its staff provides excellent service. Especially popular at lunchtime, Valentin's serves traditional Spanish food, with a special regional dish offered daily. You might have callos a la madrileña or fabada on a weekday, but on Saturday, if you're there for lunch, I recommend the paella. Main dishes also include grilled veal, fresh baked sea bass, "Valentin" sole, and perhaps the most famous (and most complicated) dish of Madrid, cocido Madrileño. A good dessert list and some fine wines add to the pleasure of dining here. Meals begin at 3,500 pesetas ($32.90). The restaurant, which is air-conditioned, is open every day of the year, from 1:30 to 4 p.m. and 8:30 p.m. to midnight. Metro: Gran Vía or Puerta del Sol.

Zalacaín, 4 Álvarez de Baena (tel. 261-48-40), is outstanding both in food and decor. It's reached by an illuminated walk from the Paseo de la Castellana, housed at the garden end of a modern apartment complex. In fact, it's within an easy walk of such deluxe hotels as the Luz Palacio, the Castellana, and the Miguel Angel. It's small, exclusive, and expensive. In an atmosphere of quiet refinement, you can peruse the menu, perhaps at the rust-toned bar. Walls are covered with textiles, and some are decorated with Audubon-type paintings. The menu is interesting and varied, often with nouvelle-cuisine touches, along with many Basque and French specialties. It might offer a superb sole in a green sauce, but it also knows the glory of grilled pigs' feet. Among the most recommendable main dishes are a stew of scampi in cider sauce; crêpes stuffed with smoked fish;

ravioli stuffed with mushrooms, foie gras, and truffles; Spanish bouillabaisse; and veal escalopes in orange sauce. For dessert, I'd suggest a luscious version of praline cream with hot chocolate sauce, or crêpes Zalacaín. Depending on what you order, many tabs climb as high as 8,500 pesetas ($79.90) to 11,000 pesetas ($103.40). The Zalacaín is open Monday to Friday from 1:30 to 3:30 p.m. and 9 to 11:30 p.m., Saturday 9 to 11:30 p.m. The restaurant is closed Sunday, the week before Easter, and all of August. Reservations are necessary, and men should wear jackets and neckties. Metro: Rubén Dario.

La Gamella, 4 Alfonso XII (tel. 532-45-09), established its gastronomic reputation shortly after it opened several years ago in less imposing quarters in another part of town. In 1988 its Illinois-born owner, former choreographer Dick Stephens, moved into the 19th-century building where the Spanish novelist Ortega y Gasset was born. Horcher's, one of the capital's legendary restaurants, lies just across the street. The design and decor of La Gamella invite customers to relax in russet-colored, high-ceilinged warmth. Mr. Stephens has prepared his delicate and light-textured specialties for the King and Queen of Spain as well as for many of Madrid's most talked-about artists and merchants, many of whom he knows and greets personally between sessions in his kitchens.

Typical menu items include a ceviche of Mediterranean fish, sliced duck liver in a truffle sauce, Caesar salad with strips of marinated anchovies, rolled and truffled capon in a strawberry sauce with mushrooms, a dollop of goat cheese served over caramelized endives, duck breast with peppers, a ragoût of fish and shellfish with Pernod, and an array of sophisticated desserts, among which is an all-American cheesecake. Full meals cost from 5,000 pesetas ($47) and are served Monday to Friday from 1:30 to 4 p.m. and 9 p.m. to midnight; Saturday 9 p.m. to midnight. La Gamella is closed during most of July, and Saturday and Sunday during August. Because of the intimacy and the small dimensions of the restaurant, reservations are important. Metro: Retiro.

El Cenador del Prado, 4 Calle de Prado (tel. 429-15-49) is deceptively elegant. In the simple anteroom, an attendant will check your coat and packages in an elaborately carved armoire, and you'll be graciously ushered into one of a trio of rooms. Two of the rooms, done in rich tones of peach and sepia, have thick cove moldings and English furniture in addition to floor-to-ceiling gilded mirrors. A third room, perhaps the most popular, is ringed with lattices and floods of sunlight from a skylight.

You can enjoy such well-flavored specialties as house-style crêpes with salmon and Iranian caviar and many other succulent dishes, including a salad of crimson peppers and salted anchovies, a casserole of snails and oysters with mushrooms, a ceviche of salmon and shellfish, soup studded with tidbits of hake and clams in a potato-and-leek base, sea bass with candied lemons, veal scallopini stuffed with asparagus and garlic sprouts, and medallions of venison served with a pepper-and-fig chutney. A la carte meals cost from 6,500 pesetas ($61.10) to 7,500 pesetas ($70.50). Reservations plus a jacket and necktie for men are recommended. Meals are served Monday to Friday from 1:45 to 4 p.m. and 9 p.m. to midnight; Saturday 9 p.m. to midnight. The restaurant is closed Sunday and during a two-week period in August. Metro: Puerta del Sol.

2. Other Top Restaurants

Armstrong's, 5 Jovellanos (tel. 522-42-30), combines excellent cuisine with a sense of lighthearted charm and big-city style. It is a pink-and-white labyrinth of street-level rooms that, until they were altered in 1986 by savvy English entrepreneur Ken Armstrong, served as a furniture showroom owned by a former cohort of Franco. Amid rich planting, Chinese Chippendale furniture, and the kind of hidden lighting and deep cove molding sometimes shown in *Architectural Digest,* you can enjoy a sophisticated array of international dishes. The clientele that has preceded you here has included the King and Queen of Spain and the Prince and Princess of Wales.

Brunch is offered every Saturday and Sunday from 10 a.m. to 4:30 p.m., along with the usual assortment of lunchtime dishes. A full brunch, which might feature a dish such as eggs Casanova, costs from 3,000 pesetas ($28.20). Other menu offerings, both at brunch and during regular lunch and dinner hours, include an elegant array of salmon and hake dishes, perhaps a luscious version of caviar-topped crêpes concocted from both fresh and smoked salmon; Waldorf salad; grilled breast of duck; beef Wellington, steak-and-kidney pie; a collection of stuffed baked potatoes (some containing caviar); and a full complement of wines, champagnes, and sherries. Other than brunches, full meals cost from 4,000 pesetas ($37.60) and are served daily from 1 to 4:30 p.m. and 8:30 p.m. to 1 a.m. Metro: Banco de España or Sevilla.

At first glance, **La Recoleta,** 9 Calle Recoletos (tel. 578-29-04), looks like a small delicatessen, where take-out food and an array of wines are displayed and sold. An inner room, however, contains the gastronomic hideaway of one of Spain's leading new female chefs, Belén Laguia. Her nouvelle Spanish cuisine and resuscitations of old Spanish recipes are a much-discussed topic of conversation in a Madrid eager for new culinary ideas.

You'll dine within a large pink room whose dozens of modern paintings make it appear a bit like an art gallery. (In fact, many of the paintings are for sale.) Waitresses in vaguely punk-rock costumes will take your order. The house-special drink is a Mexican-inspired Marguerita, which—with guacamole—is the restaurant's only concession to non-Spanish traditions.

Menu items lean toward flavorful elaborations of regional and time-tested Iberian recipes, including certain ones based on 18th- and 19th-century middle-class recipes that were unearthed by a culinary researcher from an obscure source in Murcia. Some of these include a *sopa escondida* (hidden soup) of boletus mushrooms covered in puff pastry, scrambled eggs with blood pudding and fried potato sticks, scrambled eggs with strips of duck meat from Navarre, veal sweetbreads in puff pastry, a *pastel de caza* (puff pastry encasing a stew of woodcock, hare, and wood pigeon), and grilled sea bass with alioli (garlic and oil) dressing. The bill will probably be around 5,000 pesetas ($47) per person, which is considered relatively modest for a restaurant of such innovative and high quality. Reservations are important. Meals are served Monday to Friday from 12:30 to 4 p.m. and 9 p.m. to midnight; Saturday 9 p.m. to midnight. Metro: Colón.

La Taberna de Liria, 9 Duque de Liria (tel. 541-4519), before being adopted by French-Spanish chef Juan López Castanier, was a restaurant specializing in grilled versions of Basque meats. Today, the enormous open grill—which sits within full view of the air-conditioned dining room—is used frequently by its new owner to produce sophisticated interpretations of Mediterranean dishes derived from all parts of the *Mare Nostrum.*

Full meals cost around 4,500 pesetas ($42.30) each, and might include exotic mushrooms in a warm salad, scrambled eggs with pickled sardines and an unusual winter vegetable (borage), carpaccio of bonito fish with sherry, grilled steak of bullock served with a piquant sauce, grilled sea bass with a garlic and saffron sauce (with the peeled and fried skin of the fish served as a side dish), and roasted young pigeon with fresh thyme. Hours are Monday to Friday from 1 to 3:45 p.m. and 9:15 p.m. to midnight; Saturday 9:15 p.m. to midnight. The restaurant is closed Sunday, holidays, and for the second half of August. Reservations are important. Metro: V. Rodríguez.

The success of **El Mentidero de la Villa,** 6 Santo Tomé (tel. 419-5506), is the result of a collaboration between a Spanish owner and a Japanese chef, each of whom infuses the menu with the best of their respective traditions. The decor is postmodern and includes softly tinted trompe l'oeil ceilings, exposed wine racks, ornate columns with unusual lighting techniques, and a handful of antique carved horses from long-defunct merry-go-rounds. Chef Kensito Sato prepares such dishes as veal liver in a sage sauce, a version of spring rolls filled with fresh shrimp and leeks, noisettes of veal with tarragon, filet steak with a mustard and brown-sugar sauce, medallions of venison with purées of chestnut and celery, and such desserts as a sherry trifle. Full meals cost around 5,000 pesetas ($47) and are served Monday to Friday from 1:30 to 4 p.m. and 9 p.m. to midnight. Annual closing is for the last two weeks of August. Metro: Alonso Martínez, Colón, or Gran Vía.

El Bodegón, 15 Calle Pinar (tel. 262-88-44), is imbued with the atmosphere of a gentleman's club for hunting enthusiasts—in the country-inn style. International globe-trotters are attracted here, especially in the evening, as the restaurant is near three deluxe hotels: the Castellana, the Miguel Angel, and the Luz Palacio. King Juan Carlos and Queen Sofia have dined here.

Waiters in black and white, with gold braid and buttons, bring dignity to the food service. Even bottled water is served champagne style, chilled in a silver floor stand. There are two main dining rooms—conservative, oak-beamed.

The following à la carte suggestions are recommended to launch your meal: cream of crayfish bisque or a cold, velvety vichyssoise. Main-course selections include grilled filet mignon with classic béarnaise sauce or venison à la bourguignonne. Other main-course selections include shellfish au gratin Escoffier, quails Fernand Point, a tartare of raw fish marinated in parsley-enriched vinaigrette, and smoked salmon. For dessert, try homemade apple pie. A complete meal here is likely to cost between 6,000 pesetas ($56.40) and 9,000 pesetas ($84.60). Hours are Monday to Friday from 1:30 to 4 p.m. and 9 p.m. to midnight; Saturday 9 p.m. to midnight. The restaurant is closed Sunday, holidays, and most of August. Metro: Rubén Dario.

El Amparo, 8 Puigcerda, at the corner of Jorge Juan (tel. 431-64-56), behind the cascading vines of its façade, is one of the most elegant gastronomic enclaves of Madrid. It sits beside a quiet alleyway close to a bustling commercial section of the center of the city. Inside, three tiers of roughly hewn wooden beams surround elegantly appointed tables where pink napery and glistening silver add cosmopolitan touches of glamour. A sloping skylight floods the interior with sunlight by day, and at night pinpoints of light from the high-tech hanging lanterns create intimate shadows. A battalion of uniformed and polite waiters serves well-prepared nouvelle-cuisine versions of cold marinated salmon with a tomato sorbet, cold cream of vegetable and shrimp soup, bisque of shellfish with Armagnac, ravioli stuffed with seafood, roast lamb chops with garlic purée, breast of duck, ragoût of sole, a platter of steamed fish of the day, and steamed hake with pepper sauce.

Full meals, which are priced from 6,500 pesetas ($61.10) to 7,500 pesetas ($70.50), are served Monday to Friday from 1:45 to 5:30 p.m. and 9 to 11:30 p.m.; Saturday 9 to 11:30 p.m. The restaurant is closed Sunday, the week before Easter, and most of August. Reservations are essential. Metro: Goya.

Los Porches, 1 Paseo Pintor Rosales (tel. 247-70-53), is open all year in a garden setting next to an Egyptian temple, the Templo de Debod, which once stood in the Nile Valley. The menu at Los Porches is typically and elaborately gourmet, in the tradition of many of Madrid's finest restaurants, including lobster salad or lobster soup, sea bass with aromatic fennel in puff pastry, venison in Rioja wine sauce, partridge prepared in the style of Toledo, roast baby lamb, or duck with pears and prunes. Lemon tart is the perfect dessert finish. Expect to pay 4,500 pesetas ($42.30) to 6,000 pesetas ($56.40) for a complete meal, available daily from 1 to 4 p.m. and 9 p.m. to midnight. Metro: Ventura Rodríguez.

La Bola, 5 Bola (tel. 247-69-30), is just north of the Te Teatro Real. If you'd like to savor the Madrid of the 19th century, then this *taberna* is an inspired choice. It's one of the few restaurants (if not the only one) left in Madrid that's painted with a blood-red façade. Once, nearly all fashionable restaurants were so coated. La Bola hangs on to tradition like a tenacious bull. Time has galloped forward, but not inside this restaurant, where the soft, traditional atmosphere, the gentle and polite waiters, the Venetian crystal, the Carmen-red draperies, and the aging velvet preserve the 1870 ambience of the place. Ava Gardner, with her entourage of bullfighters, used to patronize this establishment, but that was long ago, before La Bola became so well-known to tourists.

A specialty is the sopa Wamba, which is soothing to those who have had too much rich fare, made as it is with ham and rice in a broth over which chopped hard-boiled eggs are sprinkled. The roast chicken *(pollo asado)* and the sole meunière are always reliable, but more adventurous might be the filet of sole in whisky sauce; a stew of fresh mushrooms, baby eels, and garlic; or the heavily seasoned roast pork. Depending on your selections, the cost of a complete à la carte meal ranges from 2,500 pesetas ($23.50) to 4,000 pesetas ($37.60), although a fixed-price *menu del día* is offered for around 2,000 pesetas ($18.80). The restaurant is open daily from 1 to 4 p.m. and 9 to 11:45 p.m. Metro: Plaza de Espāna or Opéra.

El Pescador, 75 José Ortega y Gasset (tel. 401-12-90), is a well-patronized fish restaurant that has become a favorite of the Madrileños who appreciate the more than 30 kinds of fish prominently displayed in a glass case. Many of these are unknown in North America, and some originate off the coast of Galicia. Management air-freights them in, and prefers to serve them grilled *(à la plancha)*.

You might precede your main course with a spicy fish soup and accompany it with one of the many good wines served from northeastern Spain. If you're not sure what to order (even the English translations might sound unfamiliar), try one of the many varieties and sizes of shrimp. These go under the name of *langostinos, cigalas, santiaguinos,* and *carabineros.* Many of them are expensive and priced by the gram, so be careful when you order. Expect to spend from 4,000 pesetas ($37.60) to 5,500 pesetas ($51.70) per person. Pescador is open Monday to Saturday from 1:30 to 4 p.m. and 8:30 p.m. to midnight. It is closed Sunday and from mid-August to mid-September. Metro: Lista.

Lhardy, 8 Carrera de San Jerónimo (tel. 521-33-85), opened its doors in 1839. I'm told the food served today isn't as good as back then, but there's really no one around to verify that claim. This is a place with a great tradition as a gathering place of Madrid's literati, its political leaders, and the better-heeled members of the city's business community. Your consommé is likely to be presented in cups from a large silver samovar, if you drink it in the ground-floor tearoom. This adjoins a deli shop, where you can buy some of the delicacies you tasted at the bar or in the restaurant upstairs. There, the decor, known as "Isabella Segundo," gives off a definite aura of another era. Specialties of the house include an excellent roast beef and a *cocido,* the celebrated stew of Madrid. This might be served with a selection from the extensive wine cellar. Meals range from around 4,500 pesetas ($42.30). It is open Monday to Saturday from 1 to 3:30 p.m. and 9 to 11:30 p.m.; closed Sunday and holidays. In August, it is open only at lunchtime. Metro: Sevilla or Puerta del Sol.

El Espejo, 31 Paseo de Recoletos (tel. 308-23-47), offers good-tasting food and one of the most perfectly crafted art-nouveau decors in Madrid. If the weather is good, you can choose one of the establishment's outdoor tables, served by a battery of uniformed waiters who carry food across the busy street to a green area flanked with trees and strolling pedestrians. I personally prefer a table inside, within view of the tile maidens with vines and flowers entwined in their hair. You'll pass through a charming café/bar, where many visitors linger before walking down a hallway toward the spacious and alluring dining room. Dishes include vichyssoise, codfish omelet, shellfish terrine, grilled sole, escargots bourguignons, and crêpes Suzette. Full à la carte meals begin at 3,700 pesetas ($34.80) and are served every day of the week from 1 to 4 p.m. and 9:30 p.m. to midnight. Metro: Banco or Colón.

3. Basque Specialties

Alkalde, 10 Jorge Juan (tel. 576-33-59), has been known for decades for serving top-quality Spanish food in an old tavern setting. It's decorated like a Basque inn, with beamed ceilings and hams hanging from the rafters. You might begin with the cream of crabmeat soup, followed by gambas à la plancha (grilled shrimp) or the *cigalas* (crayfish). Other well-recommended dishes include *mero salsa verde* (brill in a green sauce), trout Alkalde, and chicken steak Alkalde. The dessert specialty is a copa Cardinal. For 4,000 pesetas ($37.60) and up, you can enjoy a very satisfying meal. A *menú del día* goes for around 3,000 pesetas ($28.20).

Upstairs is a large, *típico* tavern. Downstairs is a maze of stone-sided cellars, pleasantly cool in the summer, although the whole place is air-conditioned. Alkalde is open Monday to Friday from 1 to 4 p.m. and 8:30 p.m. to midnight; Saturday 1 to 4 p.m.; and Sunday 1 to 4 p.m. and 8:30 p.m. to midnight, but closed Sunday during July and August. Advance reservations are recommended. Metro: Retiro or Serrano.

Asador Errota-Zar, 32 Corazón de Maria (tel. 413-5224), is one of Madrid's best asadors. An asador is a Spanish restaurant that typically roasts meat on racks or spits over an open fire. (The technique is said to have been brought to the Basque country by repatriated emigrés who learned it in Argentina and Uruguay a century ago. Since then, the Basques have claimed it as their own, and presumably do it better than anyone else.) Asador Errota-Zar is contained behind the stucco and stone walls of an antique mill, and managed by Basque-born Segundo Olano and his wife Eugénia.

You might begin your meal with slices of pork loin, grilled spicy sausage, scrambled eggs with boletus mushrooms, a savory soup made from Basque kidney beans, or perhaps red peppers stuffed with codfish. Other dishes include stewed hake with clams in a marinera sauce, but the real specialties of the house are the succulent cuts of beef, fish, or pork that are first gently warmed, then seared, then cooked by the expert hand of Sr. Olano himself. The restaurant is at its most interesting when groups of friends arrive, sharing portions of several different appetizers among themselves before concentrating on a main course. Full meals cost around 4,000 pesetas ($37.60) to 5,000 pesetas ($47) each and are served Monday to Saturday from 1 to 4 p.m. and 9 p.m. to midnight; closed Sunday and the month of August. Metro: Alfonso XIII.

Gure-Etxea (Restaurant Vasco), 12 Plaza de la Paja (tel. 265-61-49), is housed in a stone-walled building that was the convent for the nearby Church of San Andrés before the Renaissance. Today, amid a decor enhanced by Romanesque arches, vaulted tunnels, and dark-grained paneling, you can enjoy selections from a small but choice menu. Specialties include vichyssoise, rape (a whitefish) in green sauce, Gure-Etxea's special filet of sole, and *bacalau al pil-pil* (codfish in a fiery sauce). Full meals cost from 3,000 pesetas ($28.20) to 4,500 pesetas ($42.30) and are served Monday to Saturday from 1:30 to 4 p.m. and 9 p.m. to midnight. The restaurant is closed Sunday and during most of August. Reservations in advance are a good idea. Metro: La Latina.

Arce, 32 Augusto Figueroa (tel. 522-5913), has brought some of the best modern interpretations of Basque cuisine to the palates of Madrid, thanks to the enthusiasm of owner/chef Inaki Camba and his wife Theresa. Within a comfortably decorated dining room designed for the unabashed enjoyment of food without unnecessary decorative frills, you can order full meals for around 5,000 pesetas ($47) each.

Your meal might include simple preparations of the finest available ingredients, where the natural flavors are designed to dominate your taste buds. Examples include a salad of fresh scallops, an oven-baked casserole of fresh boletus mushrooms with few seasonings other than the woodsy taste of the original ingredients, unusual preparations of hake, and seasonal variations of game dishes such as pheasant and woodcock. Arce is open Monday to Friday from 1:30 to 4 p.m. and 9 p.m. to midnight; Saturday 9 p.m. to midnight. The restaurant is closed Sunday, the week before Easter, and two weeks every August. Reservations are recommended. Metro: Colón.

---

4. Best for Seafood

O'Pazo, 20 Reina Mercedes (tel. 253-23-33), is a deluxe Galician restaurant, considered by the local cognoscenti as one of the top seafood places in the country. The fish is flown in daily from Galicia. It is decorated in a tasteful style for the distinguished clientele it caters to. In front is a cocktail lounge and bar, all in polished brass, with low sofas and paintings. The restaurant has carpeted floors, cushioned Castilian furniture, soft lighting, and colored-glass windows.

Most diners begin with assorted smoked fish or fresh oysters. The house specialty is hake Galician style, but you may prefer the sea bass, baked in the oven, and served with a mustard sauce. O'Pazo sole is also recommended. Your tab for a full meal is likely to be between 4,000 pesetas ($37.60) and 6,000 pesetas ($56.40). O'Pazo is open Monday to Saturday from 1 to 4 p.m. and 8:30 p.m. to midnight; closed Sunday and most of August. It lies north of the center of Madrid, near the Chamartín railway station. Metro: Chamartín or Alvarado.

Bajamar, 78 Gran Vía (tel. 248-59-03), is one of the best fish houses in Spain, and it's right in the heart of the city, near the Plaza de España. Both fish and shellfish are shipped in fresh daily by air from their points of origin, the prices depending on what the market charges. Lobster, king crab, prawns, soft-shell crabs, and the like are all priced according to weight. There is a large array of reasonably priced dishes as well. The setting is contemporary and attractive, the service is smooth and professional, and meals are served from 1 to 4 p.m. and 8 p.m. to midnight daily. The menu is in English. For an appetizer, I'd recommend half a dozen giant oysters or rover crayfish. The special seafood soup is a most satisfying selection, a meal in itself. Try also the lobster bisque. Some of the more recommendable main courses include turbot Gallego style, the special seafood paella, even baby squid cooked in its ink. Desserts are simple, including the chef's custard. Seafood dinners range in price from 4,500 pesetas ($42.30) to 6,000 pesetas ($56.40). Metro: Plaza de España.

VALENCIAN PAELLA

La Barraca, 29-31 Reina (tel. 232-71-54), is like a country inn —right off the Gran Vía. This Valencian-style restaurant is a well-managed establishment recommendable for its tasty provincial cooking. There are four different dining rooms, three of which lie one flight above street level, and they're colorfully cluttered with ceramics, paintings, photographs, Spanish lanterns, flowers, and local artifacts. The house specialty is paella à la valenciana, made with fresh shellfish. The portions are enormous—only the most ravenous will clean out the skillet. Other recommendable main dishes include roast suckling pig and roast leg of lamb. The sorbet makes a good finish. A complete meal, served every day from 1 to 4 p.m. and 8:30 p.m. to midnight, will cost from around 3,200 pesetas ($30.10). There's a fixed-price *menu del día*, which is usually priced at around 3,000 pesetas ($28.20). Advance reservations are a good idea. Metro: Gran Vía or Sevilla.

---

5. Dining in Old Madrid

Right on or near a corner of the historic and immense square, the **Plaza Mayor,** are clustered fine typical restaurants and taverns, as well as *tascas,* all of which quickly capture the spirit of Madrid's past. No matter which restaurant you favor with your patronage, you're likely to be entertained by the strolling bands of *tuna,* students dressed in Castilian capes with ribbons fluttering, guitars by their sides and tambourines for after-the-songfest collections.

The **Mesón del Corregidor,** 8 Plaza Mayor (tel. 266-50-56), shares the best vantage point on the Habsburg plaza. Tables are set out in fair weather, providing an unobstructed view of the entire square. In winter, you enter first a *típico tasca,* with hanging smoked hams, wrought-iron chandeliers, vintage wine bottles, and ceramics. It's a well-tended slice of the past, with stone and cobbled floors, stained glass, and a fireplace. The specialty of the house is a shellfish paella for two people. The chef also prepares a succulent, spicy roast suckling pig. Other typical dishes include baby eels, hake wrapped in ham, and tripe Madrid style. There's a fixed-price meal offered for around 2,000 pesetas ($18.80), and à la carte meals that cost between 2,800 pesetas ($26.32) and 4,000 pesetas ($37.60). The restaurant is open every day from 1 to 4 p.m. and 8 p.m. to midnight. Metro: Puerta del Sol.

Right down the steps is the even better-known **Las Cuevas de Luís Candelas,** 1 Cuchilleros (tel. 266-54-28). It is entered through a doorway under an arcade on the steps leading to Calle de Cuchilleros, the nighttime street of Madrid, teeming with restaurants, flamenco clubs, and rustic taverns. The restaurant is named after the legendary Luís Candelas, a bandit of the 18th-century—sometimes known as "the Spanish Robin Hood." He is said to have hidden out in this maze of *cuevas*. Although the menu is in English (the restaurant is very "touristy"), the cuisine is authentically Spanish. Specialties include the chef's own style hake. To begin your meal, another house dish is sopa de ajo Candelas, a garlic soup. Roast suckling pig and roast lamb, as in the other restaurants on the Plaza Mayor, are the featured specialties. Meals are served from 1 to 4 p.m. and from 8 p.m. to midnight every day. They average between 3,500 pesetas ($32.90) and 5,500 pesetas ($51.70). Reservations in advance are a good idea. Metro: Puerta del Sol.

Restaurant Aroca, 3 Plaza de los Carros (tel. 265-2626), is a simple tavern. Before the Civil War there were many like it, but few remain as authentic to its original as this one, which is considered a cultural anchor in a fast-changing society. Its allure lies in the fact that almost no changes have been imposed on either its menu or its cooking techniques in almost a century. It has had three different addresses since it was established as a wine shop in the 1880s, each staffed with different generations of the Aroca family, and almost always with a head chef named Maria. Its most recent setting—completely unchanged since the early 1960s—has plain white walls, dark wooden furniture, and framed photographs of famous customers. The food never varies, and is selected from an uncomplicated menu, including Ríoja wines. You can have a chunky version of seafood soup, boiled prawns served with aromatic mayonnaise, fried hake or filet of sole, lamb cutlets, fried chicken, and (when available) fresh Galician oysters. On the side, you can order a simple but refreshing tomato and lettuce salad, or an order of *croquetas* (fried dumplings studded with morsels of ham).

The owners, Manolo and Maria Aroca, charge around 2,300 pesetas ($21.60) for a *menú del día*. Aroca is open Monday to Saturday from 2 to 4 p.m. and 9 p.m. to midnight; closed Sunday and the month of August. The restaurant lies in the heart of old Madrid, a 10-minute walk southwest of the Plaza Mayor. Metro: La Latina.

6. International Cuisine

Once upon a time a foreign restaurant was hard to find in Madrid. It seemed the Spanish were perfectly content with their own cuisine. However, in recent decades a noticeable change has occurred. For change-of-pace dining, today's restaurant shopper will find a fair selection of foreign cuisine, including American food.

GERMAN
Edelweiss, 7 Jovellanos (tel. 521-03-26), is a German standby that has provided good-quality food and service at moderate prices since the war. You are served hearty portions of food, mugs of draft beer, and fluffy pastries. That's why there's always a wait at lunch. *Tip:* To beat the crowds, go for dinner at un-Spanish hours, say around 9 p.m., when tables are not at a premium. But even when it's jammed, service is almost always courteous. You can start with Bis-

marck herring, then dive into goulash with spätzle, or eisbein (pigs' knuckles) with sauerkraut and mashed potatoes, the most popular dish at the restaurant. Finish with the homemade apple tart. A complete meal is likely to cost 2,200 pesetas ($20.68) to 3,500 pesetas ($32.90). The decor is vaguely German, with travel posters and wood-paneled walls. No reservations are accepted in advance, and during peak dining hours the bar is likely to be full of clients waiting for tables. It's air-conditioned in summer. Hours are Monday to Saturday from 12:30 to 4 p.m. and 8:30 p.m. to midnight; closed Sunday and the month of August. Metro: Sevilla.

AMERICAN

A popular hangout for locals and visiting Yanks is **Foster's Hollywood,** 1 Calle Magallanes (tel. 448-91-65). It's a California-style hamburger extravaganza, a fashionable place to eat and be seen, serving, according to many travelers, "the best American food in Europe." This is an establishment that wholeheartedly celebrates the American dream. Outside, you can sit in a director's chair on the terrace, with the name of a movie star on the back. You will find this one of the most comfortable and best people-watching sites in Madrid, while you enjoy sangría or your back-home favorite beverage. Inside, it's nostalgia time, with bentwood chairs and many framed photographs and posters. Some Spaniards have encountered problems in eating the hamburgers, as would anyone not familiar with devouring food five inches high. Hamburgers weigh in at half a pound, and they vary from simple and unadorned to one with cheese, bacon, and Roquefort dressing; they are served with french fries and salad. Other Stateside treats are chili con carne, homemade apple pie, cheesecake, and, as once reported in the *New York Times,* "probably the best onion rings in the world." Tabs begin at 750 pesetas ($7.05). Hours are from 1 p.m. to 1:45 a.m. daily. Metro: Quevedo.

The same food is also available at Hollywood's other locations at 3 Apolonia Morales (tel. 457-79-11) in the Castellana area near the Eurobuilding; 16 Avenida de Brasil (tel. 455-16-88) for the Meliá Castilla hotels; 80 Velázquez (tel. 435-61-28) in the Serrano shopping area; 1 Tamayo y Baus (tel. 231-51-15), close to Plaza de Cibeles and the Prado; 100 Guzman el Bueno (tel. 234-49-23) in the University area; 2 Plaza Sagrado Corazón de Jesús (tel. 411-41-25), next to the National Music Auditorium; and 16 Calle del Cristo in Majadahonda (tel. 638-67-94), one of Madrid's best suburbs.

FRENCH

The **Chez Lou Crêperie,** 6 Pedro Muguruza (tel. 250-34-16), near the Eurobuilding Hotel in the northern sector of Madrid, stands near the huge mural by Joan Miró, which alone would be worth the trek up here. In this intimate setting, you get well-prepared and reasonably priced French food. The restaurant serves pâté as an appetizer, then a large range of crêpes with many different fillings. Folded envelope style, the crêpes are not tearoom size, and they're perfectly adequate as a main course. I've sampled several variations of crêpe, finding the ingredients nicely blended yet distinct enough to retain their identity. A favorite is the large crêpe stuffed with minced onions, cream, and smoked salmon. The ham and cheese is also tasty. Crêpes cost from 500 pesetas ($4.70) and up, and the price of your dessert and drink is extra.

Come here if you're seeking a light supper when it's too hot for one of those table-groaning Spanish meals. Chez Lou is open Tuesday to Sunday from 1 to 4 p.m. and 8 p.m. to midnight. Metro: Plaza de Castilla.

COMBINATION FARE AND CHINESE

At **Casablanca**, 29 Calle del Barquillo (tel. 521-1568), the theme is the famous movie of the late-late show, and memorabilia (such as posters of Bogart and Bergman) are scattered over the two levels of its premises. The cuisine served at the umbrella-covered tables is a combination of northern Spanish, Continental, and Japanese. The owner is Dick Angstadt, an American. It's open every day from 1:30 to 4 p.m. and 9 p.m. to 1 a.m., and charges around 3,500 pesetas ($32.90) for a full meal. Casablanca also has a *tapas* bar. Metro: Alonso Martínez.

Kuopin Restaurante Chino, 6 Valverde (tel. 532-3465), is an interesting Chinese restaurant, only 100 long strides from the busy Gran Vía. It's approached through a long hallway in an old Madrid building. Inside, you'll find the usual Chinese decor with large lanterns. Many of your fellow diners will be Chinese, a fairly good gauge of authenticity and value. The chef offers a special budget dinner for 750 pesetas ($7.05) featuring, for example, egg-drop soup, sweet-and-sour pork, and ice cream. Bread and a beverage are included. A la carte temptations include sweet corn, egg, and chicken soup; Cantonese shrimp; and roast pork. An à la carte dinner will cost 1,500 pesetas ($14.10) and up. Kuopin is open every day from noon to 4 p.m. and 8 p.m. to midnight. Metro: Gran Vía.

---

7. Specialty Restaurants

HEMINGWAY'S ROAST SUCKLING PIG

Ernest Hemingway made **Sobrino de Botín,** 17 Calle de Cuchilleros (tel. 266-42-17), famous. In the final two pages of his novel *The Sun Also Rises,* he had Jake invite Brett there for the Segovian specialty, washed down with Rioja Alta.

By merely entering its portals, you step back to 1725, the year the restaurant was founded. You'll see an open kitchen, with a charcoal hearth, hanging copper pots, an 18th-century tile oven for roasting the suckling pig, and a big pot of regional soup, the aroma wafting across the tables. The dining tables sit under time-aged beams, the wall literally covered with a mishmash collection of photographs, engravings, paintings, and bullfight memorabilia. Your host, Don António, never loses his cool—even when he has 18 guests standing in line waiting for tables.

A *menú de la casa* is served in autumn and winter at 3,300 pesetas ($31.02). The two house specialties are roast suckling pig and roast Segovian lamb. From the à la carte menu, costing from 4,000 pesetas ($37.60), you might try the "quarter-of-an-hour" soup, made with fish. Good main dishes include the baked Cantabrian hake and filet mignon with potatoes. The dessert list features strawberries (in season) with whipped cream. You can wash down your meal with Valdepeñas or Aragón wine, although most guests order sangría. Hours are daily from 1 to 4 p.m. and 8 p.m. to midnight. Annual vacation occurs during the week between Christmas and New Year's Day. Metro: La Latina or Opéra.

THE BEST STEAKS IN MADRID

Madrileños defiantly name **Casa Paco,** 11 Puerto Cerrada, just beside the Plaza Mayor (tel. 266-31-66), when someone has the "nerve" to put down Spanish steaks. They know that here you can get the thickest, juiciest, most flavorsome steaks in Spain—and at half the price you'd pay in Chicago. Señor Paco was the first Madrid restaurateur to seal steaks in boiling oil before serving them on plates so hot that the almost-raw meat continues to cook, preserving the natural juices.

Casa Paco isn't just a steakhouse. You can start with a fish soup and proceed to such dishes as grilled sole, baby lamb, Casa Paco cocido, or callos a la madrileña. You might top it off with one of the luscious desserts, but you can't have coffee here. Paco won't serve it, not necessarily for health reasons but because customers used to be inclined to linger over their cups, keeping tables occupied while people had to be turned away for lack of space.

In the Old Town, the two-story restaurant offers three dining rooms, and reservations are imperative. Otherwise, you face a long wait, which you can while away sampling the *tapas* (hors d'oeuvres) in the *tasca* in front. Around the walls are autographed photographs of such notables as Frank Sinatra. A typical meal will run about 3,800 pesetas ($35.70) and up. The tourist menu costs 1,500 pesetas ($14.10), but the real reason most people come here is to order one of the deliciously thick steaks, priced according to weight, and served sizzling hot on a wooden board. Food is served Monday to Saturday from 1:30 to 4 p.m. and 8:30 p.m. to midnight; closed Sunday and during most of August. Metro: Puerta del Sol, Opéra, or La Latina.

VEGETARIAN FARE

La Galette, 11 Conde de Aranda (tel. 576-0641), was one of Madrid's first vegetarian restaurants, and remains one of the best. Small and charming, it lies in a residential and shopping district in the exclusive Salamanca district, near the Plaza de la Independencía and the northern edge of Retiro Park. Its hours are Monday to Saturday from 2 to 4 p.m. and 9 p.m. to midnight. There is a limited selection of meat dishes, but the true allure lies in this establishment's imaginative use of vegetarian fare. Examples include baked stuffed peppers, omelets, eggplant croquettes, and even vegetarian "hamburgers." Some of the dishes are macrobiotic. The place is also noted for its mouth-watering pastries. A *menú de la casa* cost around 1,800 pesetas ($16.90). Metro: Retiro.

THE ATTRACTIONS OF MADRID

Tourist officials in Madrid often confide, "We spend so much fuss to get people to visit Madrid. But when we get them here, and they've seen the Prado and a bullfight, we send them off to El Escorial or Toledo." Too true—and regrettably so.

As European capitals go, Madrid is hard to know. Her mainstream attractions—tree-shaded parks, wide *paseos,* bubbling fountains, the art treasures of the Prado—are obvious. And, of course, it is this Madrid that the routine visitor sees quickly before striking out for the next adventure, usually to one of the satellites such as Segovia. But for the more determined traveler, willing to invest the time and stamina, the Spanish capital tucks away many hidden treasures.

For easy reference, see the "Sights and Attractions" index at the back of this book.

---

1. The Two Top Attractions

SPAIN'S GREATEST MUSEUM—THE PRADO

A. E. Hotchner wrote: "Ernest [Hemingway] loved the Prado. He entered it as he entered cathedrals." More than any other, one picture held him transfixed, "the girl whom he had loved longer than any other woman in his life," Hotchner relates—Andrea del Sarto's *Portrait of a Woman.*

The late American author wasn't alone in his passionate devotion to the Prado. Numerous citizens of Madrid go once or twice a month every month of their lives just to gaze upon their particular favorites (the reproductions at home are never adequate). But first-time visitors, with less than a lifetime to spend, will have to limit their viewing. That task is difficult, as the Prado owns more than 7,000 paintings and is ranked among the top three art museums of the world.

In an 18th-century neoclassic palace designed by Juan de Villanueva, the Prado has been considerably improved in the past few years, especially in its lighting. There will be work in progress for some time to come.

The most hurried trekker may want to focus attention on the output of three major artists: the court painters Velázquez and Goya, plus El Greco, who was in fact a Greek (born in Crete in 1541). But don't overlook the exceptional visions of Hieronymus Bosch, the 15th-century Flemish artist who peopled his canvases with fiends and ghouls and conjured up tortures that far surpassed Dante's Inferno. In particular, seek out his triptychs, *The Hay Wagon* and *The Garden of Earthly Delights*.

Most of the products of these artists are on the second floor. However, on the ground floor you'll find Goya's "black paintings" and his remarkable drawings.

The Prado's single most famous work is *Las Meninas*—the maids in waiting—the masterpiece of Velázquez.

In the Goya room is displayed his *Naked Maja*, certainly one of the most recognizable paintings in the West—said to have been posed for by the woman the artist loved, the Duchess of Alba. As a court painter to Charles IV and his adulterous queen, María Luisa, Goya portrayed all their vulgarity of person and mind—and got them to pay for the results.

Other paintings, by Raphael, Botticelli, Correggio, Titian, (Titzano), Pieter Brueghel, Murillo, Ribera, and Fra Angelico, will make the morning fade quickly into dusk.

The painting stirring up the most excitement in recent years is Picasso's *Guernica*. Long banned in Spain, the painting rested for years in the Museum of Modern Art in New York before it was returned. The Prado houses it in one of its satellites, behind the Ionic columns of the *Cason del Buen Retiro*, at the edge of nearby Retiro Park. (The *Cason's* main entrance is on the Calle Felipe IV, and your ticket allows you entrance to both the main body of the Prado and its satellites.) It's still considered a controversial work decades after he painted it to protest Generalíssimo Franco's participation in the Nazi bombing of Guernica (Gernika), an important center of Basque culture. Picasso requested that *Guernica* not be returned to Spain until the death of Franco and the "reestablishment of public liberties."

A much-belabored expansion plan that began in 1985 and is to be completed in 1991 has increased the Prado's display space. In the 1980s, one of Europe's most suspense-ridden art bequests was lavished upon Madrid by the Dutch-born Baron Hans Heinrich von Thyssen-Bornemisza. His collection was formerly housed in the baron's residence/museum in Lugano, Switzerland, the Villa Favorita. When added to the existing inventories within the Prado, the baron's collection (one of the largest and finest in Europe) will place the densest concentration of art masterpieces in the world into the small city neighborhood ringing the Prado. Its acquisition was considered one of Europe's most sensational art coups, one that Britain's Prince Charles and representatives of the Louvre wanted for themselves.

Beginning in 1991, the Thyssen-Bornemisza collection will be housed within the Villahermosa Palace, a 17th-century building located diagonally across the Plaza Canovas del Castillo from the Prado, a two-minute walk to the northwest. The collection will include works by El Greco, Velázquez, Goya, Frans Hals, Hans Memling, Rubens, Rembrandt, Sebastiano del Pompo, Watteau, Canaletto, and John of Flanders, as well as the only privately owned Dürer painting, *Christ Among the Doctors.* Picasso's *Harlequin with Mirror* is among that artist's important works in the collection, and there are also pictures by impressionist and post-impressionist painters, among them Degas, Renoir, Sisley, Van Gogh, Gauguin, Chagall, Monet, Cézanne, Toulouse-Lautrec, and Gris. Modern art is represented by such expressionists as Vlaminck, Pechstein, Heckel, Kirchner, Feininger, Nolde, and Kandinsky. The baron's recent acquisitions are concerned with American artists.

The museum, on the Paseo del Prado (tel. 420-2836), is open from Tuesday to Saturday from 9 a.m. to 7 p.m.; on Sunday and holidays, from 9 a.m. to 2 p.m. The Prado is closed on Monday, Christmas, and New Year's Day. The entrance fee is 400 pesetas ($3.75). Metro: Banco or Atocha; or bus no. 10, 14, 27, 34, 37, or 45.

THE BULLFIGHT

In art, literature, and life, the Spaniard is urgently concerned with the subject of death. The ritual killing of the bull, as reenacted in countless seasons of *corridas* from early spring until late October, sustains the Spanish soul. Perhaps it is in the back of the mind of some aficionados that the bull may not be the only one killed, that the matador may meet his "death in the afternoon."

Despite the fanfare and the fiesta mood enveloping the Plaza de Toros, bullfighting is a deadly serious business. Like a major industry, it supports a good part of the Spanish population—from the promoters, the *apoderados* biting down on their Havana cigars, to the poor soul who cleans up the horse dung and sells it as fertilizer.

In the way Americans growing up in the 1940s and 1950s dreamed of becoming movie stars, the Spanish boy often fantasizes about the acclaim, the shouts, and the cheers ringing in his ears in the bullring. For many a peasant boy born in poverty, bullfighting is his way to break out of the role life cast him in. A case in point is former matador El Cordobés, a poor boy who rose to become a symbol of wealth and glamour throughout Spain.

An aficionado, Ernest Hemingway wrote: "The bullfight is not a sport in the Anglo-Saxon sense of the word, that is, it is not an equal contest or an attempt at an equal contest between a bull and a man. Rather, it is a tragedy; the death of the bull, which is played, more or less well, by the bull and the man involved and in which there is danger for the man but certain death for the bull." Fortified by that definition, you may be ready to attend your first bullfight.

The day of the corrida is Sunday afternoon, although Madrid

may also hold fights on Thursday. It's becoming an increasing practice to stage an 11 p.m. Saturday *novillada,* in which amateur or inexperienced bullfighters test their skill against often "defective" bulls.

The spectacle of the bullfights opens with a parade—an exciting, dramatic experience, as the bullfighters stroll in their "suits of lights." This is followed by a matador's preliminary capework, often a *verónica,* in which he faces the bull for the first time. This act appears almost to be choreographed, and has been compared to a ballet.

The fight begins as *picadores* on horseback charge the bull to "pic" him with lances. The *banderilleros* are next, jabbing the beast with brightly ornamented *banderillas,* preparing the animal for the kill. A fight is considered much more enthralling if the bullfighter himself sticks in the darts.

After this ceremony, the matador faces the bull armed with a sword and a *muleta,* a scarlet cloth. The challenging of the bull—most hazardous—is a *natural.* After a series of such passes, the matador is ready for the kill, the so-called moment of truth.

The most skillful will kill the bull in one quick thrust, although many a leading matador has been forced to make repeated thrusts like a *novillero.* The more thrusts, the more hostile grows the reaction of the crowd toward the bullfighter. If he shows skill, the "lucky" matador will be rewarded with an ear (*òreja*) of the bull. The amateurish performer is likely to get a rotten tomato thrown in his face.

Madrid attracts the most skilled matadors in Spain to its 26,000-seat **Plaza de Toros,** 237 Calle de Alcalá (tel. 246-22-00). The height of the corrida season is the week of festivities around May 10, honoring San Isidore, patron of the city.

Major hotels sell bullfighting **tickets,** and they pride themselves on keeping blocks of unsold tickets for their guests. You can also purchase tickets at the Plaza de Toros (see above) Monday to Saturday from 10 a.m. to 2 p.m. and 4 to 6 p.m. This ticket office usually closes on Sunday, but remains open from 10 a.m. until the fight begins if a particular bullfight doesn't sell out. Since you'll never know until Sunday, the day of the fight, whether the box office will be open or not, it's best to get your tickets at least a day in advance.

Front-row seats are called *barreras. Delanteras* or third-row seats are available in both the *alta* (high) and the *baja* (low) sections. You can also request quite passable *filas,* which are adequate seats (but not special). In *sombra y sol* (shade and sun) seats, you'll spend part of the fight in the sun. The cheapest seats, not really recommended, are of the *sol* variety, in which you're exposed to the hot sun during the entire fight.

When a top-flight matador is performing, tickets disappear quickly—only to be resold at scalper's prices. Tickets cannot be obtained weeks in advance. As for ticket prices, they vary from fight to fight. Count on spending at least 250 pesetas ($2.35) for a just-passable seat, all the way up to 10,000 pesetas ($94) for the most desirable seat in the shade.

You can take the Metro to Ventas to reach the Plaza de Toros. To avoid a stampede, try to arrive at the ring early, and while you're at it, visit the Bullfight Museum (see below). After the fight, it's virtually impossible to get a taxi back into the city. Why not wait and have coffee at a nearby sidewalk table?

---

2. Five Top Sights

After wandering through the Prado and watching the blood and gore of the Plaza de Toros, you may be in a mood for more relaxed browsing through Madrid. What follows is a subjective listing of five additional attractions, in order of importance.

THE ROYAL PALACE

Alfonso XIII, grandfather of King Juan Carlos, and his queen, Victoria Eugénie, were the last to use the Palacio Real as a royal abode in 1931, before they fled into exile. Franco used the Royal Palace (also known as the Palacio de Oriente) for state functions and elaborate banquets for foreign dignitaries. But guides like to point out that he never sat on the king's chair in the Throne Room.

King Juan Carlos and Queen Sofia are more modest in their requirements. They have turned the Royal Palace over to history, choosing not to live there but in their much smaller suburban palace, the Zarzuela, named after the Spanish operetta or musical comedy.

On the landmark site of the former Alcázar of Madrid (destroyed by fire on the Christmas of 1734), the Royal Palace was launched in 1737. Its first tenant was Charles III, the "enlightened despot" of the House of Bourbon. In all, the number of rooms— many added at a later date—total around 1,800. Not all are open to the public, of course. Nor need they be, as the tour would then take a week.

Visitors are conducted on a guided tour of the **State Apartments,** the Tapestry Room, the Reception Salons, the Royal Armory, the Royal Pharmacy, and the Royal Library. If you're rushed—and want just a quick glimpse of the grandeur of the palace—then you'll want to confine your sightseeing to the State Apartments and the Reception Rooms. Metro stop: Opéra.

After your tour, you can skip across the courtyard to the **Royal Armory,** considered one of the most impressive in Europe. Recalling the days of jousting and equestrian warfare, many of the exhibits date from the reign of Charles V (Charles I of Spain) of the Habsburg Empire. Roughly, the collection spans about 200 years of the Spanish Empire.

Afterward, you can visit the **Royal Library,** with its leather-bound volumes—at least 190,000 different editions, many belonging to Spain's most famous kings and queens, such as Isabella I. The **Royal Pharmacy** also merits a visit. It was, in its heyday, the "cure-all" source for any ailment that plagued the royal family.

You can buy a combined ticket to the State Apartments, the Reception Salons, Armory, Library, and Gallery of Tapestries (*tapices*) for 500 pesetas ($4.70). If you don't want to see everything, you can visit only what you wish. For example, a single ticket to the Armory costs 100 pesetas (95¢).

The Palacio Real (tel. 248-74-04), on the Plaza de Oriente, is only a short walk from the Plaza de España. Hours are Monday to Saturday from 9:30 a.m. to 12:45 p.m. and 4 to 5:15 p.m.; Sunday from 9:30 a.m. to 12:15 p.m.

Worth a detour, the **Museo de Carruajes Reales** (Carriage Museum), on the palace grounds, charges an entrance fee of 100 pesetas (95¢). It's not as impressive as its more famous counterpart in Lisbon, but you can view the horse-drawn vehicles that Spanish aristocrats used in the days when a person was judged solely on appearance. Metro: Opéra, Ventura Rodríguez, or Plaza de España; or bus no. 1, 25, 33, or 39).

After your whirlwind tour, you can wind down by strolling through the **Campo del Moro,** the gardens of the palace.

THE ROYAL FACTORY OF TAPESTRIES

The making of tapestries—based on original designs by Goya, Francisco Bayeu (Goya's brother-in-law), and others—is still a flourishing art in Madrid. You can actually visit the factory where the *tapices* are turned out, and chat with the workers. Some of the hand-looms on which they work date back to the days of Goya.

The great Spanish artist sketched numerous cartoons that were converted into tapestries to adorn the walls of the Royal Palace not only in Madrid, but in Aranjuez and La Granja. One of the most famous, reproduced hundreds of times, is *El Cacharrero* (The Pottery Salesman).

Some craftspeople have copied the same design all of their lives, so that now they can work on it without thinking. Others, less cavalier, prefer to watch the design carefully through a mirror.

The factory—called **Real Fábrica de Tapices**—is at 2 Fuenterrabia (tel. 551-34-00). It may be visited Monday to Friday from 9:30 a.m. to 12:30 p.m.; closed weekends and the entire month of August. Admission is 50 pesetas (45¢) per person. Metro: Atocha or Pelayo.

LÁZARO GALDIANO MUSEUM

Deserving of far more visitors than it receives, this remarkable, compact, and art-stuffed museum at 122 Serrano (tel. 261-60-84) spans the centuries of artistic development with seeming ease.

An elevator takes you to the top floor of what was once one of the great mansions of Madrid. It belonged to José Lázaro Galdiano, a famous 20th-century patron of the arts. You weave your way from room to room (37 in all), descending the stairs as you go.

The collection begins with vestments, some dating from the 15th century. Along the way, you can stop and stare at an assemblage of weapons, daggers, and swords, some with elaborate handles dating from the 15th century. Seals, such as one belonging to Napoleon, are displayed; and there is a rare exhibition of Spanish fans, one possessed by Isabella II.

In Room XX are two Flemish paintings by the incomparable Bosch—rats crawling through the eyes of humans, and so on. In the following room (XXI) is a portrait of Saskia signed by Rembrandt, dating from 1634. In other salons, several of the major artists of Spain are represented: Velázquez, Zurbarán, El Greco, Valdés Leal, Murillo, and Ribera. Room XXV is the salon of English-speaking portraitists: Gainsborough, Sir Joshua Reynolds, Gilbert Stuart, and Constable. Many well-known works by Goya are in his salon (XXX), including some of the "black paintings" and portraits of Charles IV and his voluble spouse.

Other intriguing showcases are filled with 16th-century Limoges crystal, French and Italian ivory carving from the 14th and 15th centuries, and a 15th-century Maltese cross. In Room VI hangs a small portrait of the Savior as an adolescent, encased in green velvet. Although the museum attributes this painting to Leonardo da Vinci, some art historians dispute this claim.

The museum is open Tuesday to Sunday from 10 a.m. to 2 p.m.; closed Monday, holidays, and the month of August. The admission fee is 300 pesetas ($2.80). Metro: Rubén Dario or Avenida America; or bus no. 9, 16, 19, 51, or 89.

CONVENT OF LAS DESCALZAS REALES

What would you do if you were a starving nun surrounded by a vast treasure house of paintings, gold, jewelry, and tapestries? Sell them? Not possible. The order of the Franciscan Clarissas threw themselves upon the mercy of the government, which in turn opened the doors of the convent to the general public as a museum (with the pope's permission, of course). It's still an operational convent of approximately 30 sisters.

The collection includes tapestries based on Rubens's "cartoons," 16th- and 17th-century vestments, a silver forearm said to contain bones of St. Sebastian, and a statue of the Virgin wearing earrings, as is the custom in Andalusia. The most interesting chapel is dedicated to Our Lady of Guadalupe (the statue of the Virgin is made of lead).

One of the best paintings here is a *Virgin and Child* by Bernardino Luini of northern Italy; but the most valuable oil is Titian's *Caesar's Money,* worth millions of pesetas. The Flemish Hall contains other superb canvases—for example, one of a processional by Hans Baker.

The Convent of Las Descalzas Reales is open Tuesday to Friday from 10:30 a.m. to 12:30 p.m.; Saturday 10:30 a.m. to 12:30 p.m. and 4 to 5:15 p.m.; Sunday and holidays 11 a.m. to 1:15 p.m. It's closed Monday, New Year's Day, the week before Easter, May 1 and December 24 and 25. Admission is 300 pesetas ($2.80) for adults, 100 pesetas (95¢) for students. Entrance is free on Wednesday. From the Plaza de Callao, a satellite square of the Gran Vía, walk down a narrow street, Postigo de San Martín, to one of the most charming squares in Madrid, the Plaza de las Descalzas Reales. You'll see the convent (tel. 522-06-87) on your left. You must wait for a guided tour. Metro: Puerta del Sol, Callao, or Opéra.

THE PANTHEON OF GOYA

Emulating Tiepolo, Goya frescoed the **Church of San António de la Florida** in 1798. Although he depicted in part the miracles of St. Anthony of Padua, his work was nearly secular in its execution. Mirrors are placed to allow you to capture the beauty of the ceiling better. The figure of a woman draped in a cape is one of the most celebrated subjects in Goya's work.

Located at the northwestern edge of the city, near the western edge of the Parque Oeste, beyond the North Station, the hermitage is at Glorieta de San António de la Florida (tel. 542-07-22). Goya died in exile in Bordeaux, France, in 1828, but his bones were later removed from there and interred here in the memorial that he unknowingly created for himself. In transit, his head disappeared, presumably stolen by a souvenir hunter.

Some church officials once considered Goya's frescoes irreverent—hence, the hermitage not a fit place of worship. A twin of the 18th-century church was erected alongside it, and services are conducted there now. Facing both of them, go into the one on the right to pay your respects to Goya.

The pantheon is open Tuesday to Friday from 10 a.m. to 2 p.m. and 5 to 9 p.m. (until 8 p.m. in low season); Saturday and Sunday from 10 a.m. to 2 p.m. Entrance is free. Metro: Norte.

---

3. Other Sights

For the visitor who'd like to know Madrid more intimately, I've compiled the following list.

FINE ARTS MUSEUM

Right on Madrid's busy boulevard, an easy stroll from the Puerta del Sol, the **Museo de la Real Academia de Bellas Artes de San Fernando,** 13 Calle de Alcalá (tel. 522-00-46), is considered second only to the Prado in importance as a leading Spanish museum. It houses more than 1,500 paintings and 800 sculptures by such masters as Goya, Murillo, and El Greco, plus drawings by Rubens, Ribera, and Velázquez. The collection ranges from the 16th century to the present, and was started in 1744 when the academy was founded during the reign of King Philip V. The emphasis is on works of Spanish, Flemish, and Italian artists, and you can see masterpieces by the artists mentioned above, plus Zurbarán, Sorolla, Cano, and Coello. The museum is in the restored and remodeled palace of Juan de Goyeneche, a banker who had it constructed in 1710 in the Baroque style, later redone in the neoclassical style. It's open from 9 a.m. to 7 p.m. Tuesday to Saturday, to 2 p.m. on Sunday and Monday. Admission is 200 pesetas ($1.80). Metro: Sol or Sevilla.

THE MUSEUM OF BULLFIGHTING

At 237 Alcalá, in the Plaza de Toros de las Ventas (the Patio de Caballos), this **Museo Taurino** (tel. 255-18-57) ideally should be visited before you see your first Spanish bullfight, as it serves as a good introduction to "the tragedy" in the arena. It's located beneath the Moorish arcade of the largest bullfight stadium in Madrid. The complete history of the *torero,* as well as a lot of bullfighting trivia, is traced in pictures, historic bullfight posters, and scale models.

Works of art include a Goya painting of a matador, plus an exquisite bust, sculpted in bronze, of Manolete. The museum may be visited Tuesday to Friday from 9 a.m. to 2:30 p.m.; Sunday from 10 a.m. to 1 p.m. It also opens one hour before each bullfight. Entrance is free. Metro: Ventas.

THE HOUSE OF LOPE DE VEGA

Ironically, the Casa de Lope de Vega (tel. 429-92-16) stands on a street named after Cervantes (no. 11), his competitor for the title of the greatest writer of the Golden Age of Spain and a bitter enemy. The house is considered a *perfecta* reconstruction of the casa in which Lope de Vega lived, and it is furnished with pieces indigenous to his time (1562–1635). The Spanish writer, the major dramatist of Habsburg Spain, wrote more than 1,000 plays, many of which have been lost to history.

You'll be shown through the house, with its volumes upon volumes of manuscript reproductions, and then allowed to roam at random in the garden in back. The museum and memorial to Lope de Vega is open from 10 a.m. to 2 p.m. on Tuesday and Thursday, and the price of admission is 125 pesetas ($1.20). It is closed between mid-July and mid-September. Metro: Anton Martín.

MUNICIPAL MUSEUM

Perhaps more than any other museum in Madrid, the **Museo Municipal,** 78 Fuencarral (tel. 521-66-56), documents the explosion of Madrid from a sleepy and dusty backwater into a world-class city. It contains exhibits on local history, archeology, art, porcelain, plans, engravings, and photographs, all depicting the history of Madrid. In a churrigueresque baroque structure, the museum displays deal especially with the Bourbon Madrid of the 18th century, whose paseos with strolling couples are shown on huge tapestry cartoons. Paintings from the royal collections are here, plus period models of the best-known city squares and a Goya that was painted for the Town Hall. The museum is open Tuesday through Saturday from 10 a.m. to 1:45 p.m. and 5 to 8:45 p.m.; Sunday from 10 a.m. to 2:15 p.m. Admission is free. Metro: Tribunal.

THE CHURCH OF SAN FRANCISCO EL GRANDE

In lieu of a great cathedral, Madrid possesses this church (tel. 265-38-00), with a dome larger than that of St. Paul's in London. Constructed on the site of a much earlier church, San Francisco dates from the latter 18th century, owing much of its appearance to Sabatini, a celebrated architect of his day.

Its interior of Doric columns and Corinthian capitals is cold and foreboding, although 19th-century artists labored hard to adorn its series of chapels flanking the nave. The best painting—that of St. Bernardinus of Siena preaching—is by Goya.

You are conducted through the church by a guide, who notes the most outstanding artwork, especially the choir stalls dating from the 16th century. The church dominates its own square, the Plaza de San Francisco El Grande (1 San Buenaventura), and it may be visited Tuesday to Saturday from 11 a.m. to 1 p.m. and 4 to 7 p.m. In summer, the afternoon hours are 5 to 8 p.m. Metro: La Latina. You can also take bus no. 3 from the Plaza de España, which goes right to the church.

ARCHEOLOGICAL MUSEUM (MUSEO NACIONAL ARQUEOLOGICO)

For some reason, Iberian archeological museums tend to be dull—surprisingly, since so many civilizations (prehistoric, Roman, Visigothic, Muslim) have conquered the peninsula. An exception, however, to that generalization is this stately mansion in Madrid, a storehouse of artifacts from prehistoric times to the heyday of the baroque. One of the prime exhibits here is the Iberian statue *La Dama de Elche,* a piece of primitive carving—probably from the 4th century B.C.—that was discovered on the southeastern coast of Spain, as well as the splendidly polychromed *Dama de Baza* discovered in Granada Province, also from the same period.

Treasures from the discovery of some of the finest Punic relics in Europe on the Balearic island of Ibiza, many of them found in a Carthaginian and Roman necropolis, are on display. Excavations from Paestum, Italy, are shown: some of the statuary of Imperial Rome, including a statue of Tiberius enthroned and one of the controversial Livia, wife of Augustus. The collection of Spanish Renaissance lusterware, as well as Talavera pottery and Retiro porcelain, is shown to good advantage, along with some rare 16th- and 17th-century Andalusian glassware.

The "classic" artifacts are impressive, and the contributions from medieval days up through the 16th century are highly laudable. Many of the exhibits were ecclesiastical treasures removed from churches and monasteries. A much-photographed choir stall from Palancia—hand-painted and crude, but remarkable nevertheless—dates from the 14th century.

Worthy of a look are the reproductions of the prehistoric Altamira cave paintings discovered near Santander in northern Spain in 1868. Joseph Déchelette called them "the Sistine Chapel of Quaternary art." The original caves have been closed except to a carefully arranged handful of monthly visitors, so this is your chance to see an excellent copy.

The Archeological Museum lies within the same enormous building that houses the National Library. Its entrance is at 13 Calle de Serrano (tel. 403-65-59), and it can be visited Tuesday to Sunday (except holidays) from 9:30 a.m. to 8:30 p.m. The entrance cost is 200 pesetas ($1.90). Metro: Colón or Serrano; or bus no. 1, 5, 9, 14, 19, 51, 74, or M-2.

DECORATIVE ARTS MUSEUM (MUSEO NACIONAL DE ARTES DECORATIVAS)

In 62 rooms spread over several floors, this museum at 12 Montalbán, near the Plaza de las Cibeles (tel. 521-34-40), displays a rich collection of furniture, ceramics, and decorative pieces from all regions of Spain. It is especially rich in the 16th and 17th centuries, but the collection is eclectic, with many surprises—including bronzes from the Ming dynasty in China. You're greeted by an

18th-century Venetian sedan chair in the vestibule. This bit of whimsy is only a preview of what awaits you: Gothic carvings, tapestries, alabaster figurines, vestments, festival crosses, elaborate dollhouses, Andalusian antique glass, elegant baroque four-poster beds, a chapel covered with leather tapestries, even kitchens from the 17th century. Just keep climbing one flight of steps after another; the surprises continue until you reach the top floor of what must have been one of the grandest mansions in Madrid. Hours are Tuesday to Friday from 9:30 a.m. to 2:30 p.m.; Saturday and Sunday from 10 a.m. to 2 p.m.; closed Monday and holidays. Entrance costs 200 pesetas ($1.90). Metro: Banco de España; or bus no. 14, 19, 27, 34, 37, 45, or M-6.

ARMY MUSEUM (MUSEO DEL EJÉRCITO)

Behind the Prado, at 1 Calle Méndez Núñez (tel. 531-46-24), this museum has some outstanding exhibits from military history, including the original sword of El Cid. Isabella carried this same sword when she took Granada from the Moors. In addition, you can see the tent used by Charles V in Tunisia, along with relics of Pizarro and Cortés. The collection of armor is also exceptional. The museum contains a piece of the cross that Columbus carried with him when he discovered the New World, and weapons and memorabilia from the grisly Spanish Civil War.

The museum is housed in the Buen Retiro Palace, which dates from 1631 and was destroyed (and subsequently rebuilt in a smaller form) during the Napoleonic Wars. It's open Tuesday to Sunday from 10 a.m. to 2 p.m., and charges an entrance fee of 50 pesetas (45¢). Metro: Banco de España; or bus no. 15, 27, 34, 37, or 45.

NAVAL MUSEUM (MUSEO NAVAL)

The history of nautical science and the Spanish navy comes alive at 5 Paseo del Prado (tel. 521-04-19). For me, the most fascinating exhibit is the map the mate of the *Santa Maria* made to show the Spanish monarchs the new discoveries of land. There are also souvenirs of the Battle of Trafalgar. The admission-free museum is open Tuesday to Sunday from 10:30 a.m. to 1:30 p.m.; closed Monday and holidays. Metro: Banco de España; or bus no. 10, 14, 27, 34, 37, 45, or M-6.

MUSEUM OF SOROLLA

Sorolla is an acquired taste. He was born Joaquín in Valencia in 1863, and died in Madrid in 1923. In his day he was celebrated, as autographed portraits from King Alfonso XIII and U.S. President Taft reveal. From 1912, he and his family occupied this elegant Madrileño town house off the Paseo de la Castellana. Two years after his death, his widow turned it over to the government—and it is now maintained as a memorial to the painter, inaugurated in 1932.

Except for the faded furniture and portraits, much of the house remains as Sorolla left it, right down to his stained paint brushes and pipes. In the museum wing, however, a representative collection of the artist's paintings is displayed. All of the works owned by the museum can't be exhibited, however, because of the lack of space.

Although Sorolla painted portraits of Spanish aristocrats, he was essentially interested in "the people," often in their native costumes, such as those once worn in Ávila and Salamanca. He was especially fond of painting beach scenes on what is now the Costa Blanca. His favorite subjects are depicted either "before" or "after" their bath, and he was interested in the subtle variations of the Spanish sunlight. Once critic wrote that Sorolla "may fail to please certain individuals, contaminated by an unhealthy leaning towards things decadent, pessimistic and tragic."

Seek out not only the artist's self-portrait, but the paintings of Madame Sorolla and their handsome son.

Entered through an Andalusian-style patio, the museum is at 37 General Martínez Campos (tel. 410-15-84). It is open Tuesday to Sunday, from 10 a.m. to 2 p.m.; closed Monday and holidays. The entrance charge is 200 pesetas ($1.90). The house and garden alone are worth the trip. Metro: Rubén Dario or Iglesia; or bus no. 5, 7, 16, 40, 61, or M-3.

THE ROMANTIC MUSEUM (MUSEO ROMANTICO)

Of special interest and limited appeal, this museum attracts those seeking the romanticism of the 19th century. Decorative arts festoon the mansion in which the museum is housed: crystal chandeliers, faded portraits, oils from Goya to Sorolla, opulent furnishings, porcelain, jewelry, ceramics, even *la grande toilette*. Many of the exhibitions date from the days of Isabella II, the high-living, fun-loving queen who was forced into exile and eventual abdication of the throne (she lived in Paris until her death in 1904).

At 13 San Mateo (tel. 448-10-45), the Museo Romantico is open Tuesday to Sunday from 10 a.m. to 3 p.m.; closed Monday, holidays, and during August. The entrance fee is 200 pesetas ($1.90). Metro: Alonso Martínez; or bus no. 21, 37, 40, 48, or M-10.

TEMPLE OF DEBOD (TEMPLO DE DEBOD)

This Egyptian temple once stood in the Valley of the Nile, 19 miles from Aswan. When the new dam built there threatened to overrun its site with water, the Egyptian government agreed to have the temple dismantled and presented to the Spanish people. It was taken down stone by stone in 1969 and 1970, then shipped to Valencia. From that Mediterranean port, it was sent by rail to Madrid, where it was reconstructed and opened to the public in 1971. Photos upstairs in the temple depict its long history. It stands on Calle Ferraz, at the Paseo de Rosales, right off the Plaza de España, and can be visited daily from 10 a.m. to 1 p.m. and 4 to 7 p.m., except national and Catholic holidays. Entrance is free. Metro: Plaza de España or Ventura Rodríguez; or bus no. 1, 2, 44, or 74.

---

4. Parks and Gardens

THE RETIRO

It's the most prominent and famous park in Madrid, and sprawls over 350 acres. A reminder of the large forests that once stood proudly in Castile, it was originally a royal playground for the exclusive use of the Spanish monarchs and their guests. The huge palaces that stood there were destroyed in the early 19th century. Only the palace's former dance hall, the Cason del Buen Retiro (housing the modern works of the Prado, including Picasso's *Guernica*), and the building containing the army museum remain. The park is filled with numerous fountains (one is dedicated to an artichoke) and statues (one honors Lucifer, strangely heretical in Catholic Spain), and there is a large lake where soldiers meet their girlfriends during the hotter months. There are also a pair of exposition centers, the Velázquez and Crystal Palaces (built to honor the Philippines in 1887), and a lakeside monument, erected in 1922, to Alfonso XII. In summer, the rose gardens are worth the visit, and you'll find several places where you can have inexpensive snacks and drinks.

The park is technically open all day and night, but it's at its most popular (and most safe) between 7 a.m. and 8:30 p.m. Entrance is free, and hundreds of Madrileños, especially on hot midsummer days, are likely to be there too.

Across the Calle de Alfonso XII, abutting the southwest corner of the Retiro, are the famous **Botanical Gardens (Jardín Botanico)** 2 Plaza de Murillo (tel. 420-35-68). Founded by Carlos III, and in its present location since the 18th century, it contains more than 100 species of trees and 200 types of plants. It also contains a library specializing in botany and an exhibition hall. It's open daily from 10 a.m. to 8 p.m., charging 75 pesetas (70¢) per person. Metro: Atocha; or bus no. 10, 14, 19, 32, 37, or M-9.

THE CASA DE CAMPO

Most people aren't in Madrid too long before they hear about that once-royal park, the Retiro. But many visitors never make it to the former royal hunting grounds, the Casa de Campo, miles and miles of parkland lying south of the Royal Palace, across the Manzanares. You can see the gate through which the kings rode out of the palace grounds—either on horses or in carriages—and headed for the park. You, of course, will have to take less elegant transportation: the Metro to El Lago or El Batán.

The park has a variety of trees and a lake, which is usually filled with rowers. You can have drinks and light refreshments around the lake, or you can go swimming in an excellent municipally operated pool.

The Madrileños like to keep the place to themselves; on a hot night or a Sunday morning, the park throngs with people trying to escape the heat. If you have an automobile you can go for a drive, as the grounds are extensive. The park is open until around 11 p.m. It's cool, pleasant, refreshing—a cheap way to spend an evening.

5. Walking Tours of Medieval Madrid

TOUR NO. 1

This tour begins in the **Plaza Villa** (Metro: Opéra, Puerta del Sol, or La Latina), which lies beside the Calle Mayor, midway between the Royal Palace and the Puerta del Sol. In the center, note the bronze statue of Don Alvaro de Bazan, an admiral under Philip II best remembered for defeating the Turks at Lepanto. With your back to the Calle Mayor, you'll see the red-brick 17th-century façade of Town Hall (**Ayuntamiento de Madrid**) on your right. It was originally built as a prison, and today houses the Municipal Museum (refer to the previous section for a description). On the square's south side rises the depressingly somber stone and brick façade of the 15th-century **Torre de Los Lujanes,** whose simple granite entrance is one of Madrid's few remaining examples of Gothic architecture. Beside the tower, at 3 Plaza de la Villa, behind a Gothic/mudéjar archway, lies the tomb of Beatriz Galindo, nicknamed *La Latina* because she taught Latin to the adolescent Isabella I.

With your back to the Calle Mayor, you'll see two narrow streets, each stretching parallel to one another to the south. Take the one on the left (Calle del Cordon) and walk for one short block to the **Plaza del Cordon.** (There will not be, at this point, an abundance of street signs.) You'll find yourself amid a complex of unmarked 16th- and 17th-century municipal buildings, one of the nerve centers of Madrid, protected and patrolled by uniformed guards. Turn left at the entrance to the Plaza del Cordon, walk about 40 paces, and notice the convex, semicircular entrance to one of Madrid's noteworthy baroque buildings, the **Church of San Miguel** (4 San Justo), built by Giacomo Bonavia in the 18th century. A few steps further on, flanking the right side of the church, is the narrow alleyway, the Pasadizo del Panecillo, where 17th-century priests distributed bread to hungry paupers.

The grim, rather dingy-looking stone building facing the front of the church across the narrow street is one of the oldest houses in Madrid. Look for the heraldic shields carved into its fortress-like façade. Historical sources report that the legendary Isidro, patron saint of Madrid, worked as a servant in this baronial, much-faded residence, which today contains private apartments. (Its address, although you probably won't see a street sign until you reach the bottom of the hill, is the Calle del Doctor Letamendi.) Descend this cobble-covered street. (You'll have to retrace your route about 10 paces, and enter it from the edge of the Plaza del Cordon.) Follow it for one block until you cross the busy traffic of the Calle Segovia.

After crossing Calle Segovia, turn right, always descending the hill. In about three short blocks (the street will now ascend sharply), look to your left on the Costanilla de San Pedro and notice the mudéjar tower of the very old **Church of San Pedro,** which marks the border of Madrid's **Arab quarter.** Continue walking straight along Calle Segovia, ascending it one additional block, until you eventually stop for another view at the corner of the Costanilla de San Andrés. Although the houses in this neighborhood look small, they are considered among the most chic and expensive in Madrid. From afar, gazing across Calle Segovia, notice the **Plaza de la Cruz Verde,** whose centerpiece is a 19th-century baroque fountain. It commemorates the end of the Spanish Inquisition. In the background you'll see the massive brick tower of the Spanish Army's favorite church, the **Eglesia del Sacramento.** (Memorial services for soldiers killed in war or by terrorists are traditionally performed here.)

When you tire of the panorama, continue ascending the steep cobblestones of the Costanilla San Andrés. All around you (and especially to your right) rises the Arab quarter, although many newer buildings—erected during the past 200 years—now rise upon Arab foundations.

Very shortly, you'll reach the triangular and steeply sloping grounds of the **Plaza de la Paja,** whose lovely trees and calm give no hint that this was long ago the most important market in the region for animal fodder, chaff, and grain. (When the more imposing Plaza Mayor was completed in the early 1600s, the importance of the Plaza de la Paja waned considerably.) Today, the neighborhood dozes sleepily in the intense sunlight, waiting for nighttime to bring business to the several famous restaurants that ring its perimeter. To your left as you climb the ascending slope of the square is the former Bishop's Palace, and facing you at the top of the square is the simple but dignified San Andrés chapel. (The mortal remains of San Isidro himself, before they were moved to the Cathedral of Madrid, were buried here.) At the top of the square, follow the continuation of the Costanilla de San Andrés to the right side of the chapel. You'll discover that the chapel abuts the back side of a much more imposing church, the **Church of San Andrés.**

Your path will open onto the fountains of the **Plaza de Los Carros,** which is the first of four interconnected squares. Each has its own name and allure, and each melds confusingly into its neighbor. Descend the steps at the far edge of the Plaza de Los Carros, and turn left on the street identified as the Plaza de Puerta de Moros. You'll soon notice diagonally across the street the modern brick and concrete dome of the **Mercada de la Cebada.** Contained within its echoing interior are congregations of open-air markets, open Monday to Saturday from 8 a.m. to 2 p.m. and 5 to 8 p.m. Many sightseers take a break here to purchase supplies (meat, bread, cheese, fruit) for the makings of a picnic, or at least to enter for a dose of neighborhood color. The square has by this time changed its name once again to the **Plaza del Humilladero.**

You'll notice directly in your path the beginnings of two approximately parallel streets, one that forks to the left (the **Cava Baja**) and another to your right (the **Cava Alta**). Six hundred years ago, these streets defined the city limits of Madrid (to the right of the Cava Alta were open fields and rolling meadows). Take the Cava Baja, which is loaded with cafés, bars, and restaurants, selecting whichever you prefer for your refueling stop. One attractive possibility is the rustically decorated **La Chata,** Cava Baja 24 (tel. 266-1458). It has a restaurant in back, but far more popular is the stand-up bar where local residents chatter amid hanging Serrano hams and photographs of famous bullfighters. It's open Monday and Wednesday to Saturday from noon to 5 p.m. and 8 p.m. to midnight; Sunday 8 p.m. to midnight; closed Tuesday.

A bit further on, two of the oldest hotels in Madrid, similar to dozens of hotels in common use during the 1930s, lie on the left-hand side. Not recommended for readers of this guide, they are León de Oro (no. 12) and the Pousada del Dragon (no. 14). Neither has private bathrooms in the rooms, and neither is particularly clean or safe, but each is considered a touristic holdover from a bygone era.

The tour ends at the end of the Cava Baja, at the **Puerta Cerrado,** whose centerpiece is a simple white stone cross. If you're in the mood for refreshment at the end of your jaunt through medieval Madrid, cross the Puerta Cerrado and walk to the top of street on the opposite side (Calle Arco de Cuchilleros, with its continuation onto the Calle San Miguel), where dozens of tapas bars await your pleasure.

Approximate touring time: 2 ½ hours.

TOUR NO. 2

Old Madrid is best seen by walking, the only way to savor its unique charm. This tour begins on the **Gran Vía,** a street whose position as *the* boulevard of Madrid is being fast overtaken by the Paseo de la Castellana. Still the busiest street in Madrid, the shop-flanked Gran Vía was opened at the end of World War I. Until recently it was called Avenida de José António. Long before deluxe hotels started to sprout up on the Castellana, the hotels of the Gran Vía were the most expensive and elegant in the Spanish capital. The street ends at the Plaza de España, a vast square overshadowed by one of the tallest skyscrapers in Europe.

From the square, you can walk for two blocks northwest, on the busy Calle de la Princesa, turning to your left down the Calle Ventura Rodríguez. At number 17 is the **Cerralbo Museum** (tel. 247-36-46), which gives you a rare glimpse into the life of one of the most prestigious Spanish families of the 19th century. Graced with its own chapel and ballroom, it was donated to the city of Madrid by the last Marqués de Cerralbo. It contains a collection of furniture, armour, and ceramics, as well as some important paintings. The museum is open Tuesday to Sunday from 10 a.m. to 3 p.m.; closed Monday and during the entire month of August. Admission is 200 pesetas ($1.90). Metro: Plaza de España or Ventura Rodríguez; or bus no. 1, 2, 44, 74, C, M-5, or M-9.

Returning to the Plaza de España, head south down the wide stretches of Calle de Bailen until you reach the semicircular **Plaza de Oriente,** created in 1840, and centered around an equestrian statue of Felipe IV reading a proclamation, supposedly to the masses assembled in the square below. Immediately to the north and south of the Plaza de Oriente are a pair of satellite squares ringed with formal hedges and a collection of statues representing past Spanish monarchs. They were originally intended as ornaments for the cornice of the Royal Palace, but—because of the danger of falling stonework onto passersby below—they were relocated here. From here, you can explore the vast interiors of the **Palacio Nacional** (Royal Palace), described above, which faces you from across the traffic of the Calle de Bailen.

After your tour of the palace, head north on the narrow street that flanks the eastern edge of the Plaza de Oriente (Calle Pavia). In about two minutes, you'll arrive at the edge of the **Plaza de la Encarnación,** one of the most charming squares of Madrid. Sitting on this plaza is the **Convent de la Encarnación** (tel. 247-05-10), finished in 1616 during the reign of Philip III and his queen, Margaret of Austria. Only the façade remains of the original church, which was destroyed by a fire and rebuilt in 1767. The convent and the adjoining church can be visited Tuesday to Thursday, Saturday, and Sunday from 10:30 a.m. to 1 p.m. and 4 to 5:30 p.m.; Friday 10:30 a.m. to 1 p.m. Entrance is free on Wednesday, and 300 pesetas ($2.80) every other day. Metro: Opéra; or bus no. 3, 25, 33, or 39.

From the Plaza de la Encarnación, walk southeast along the Calle de Arrieta to the **Plaza de Isabel II** (note the dignified statue of the monarch in the center). At the plaza's southern edge, you can connect with the Calle del Arenal, which, heading east for seven or eight blocks, will funnel you into the **Puerta del Sol,** the "gateway to the sun," the historic heart of Madrid.

Approximate touring time: 4½ hours (including museum visits).

6. Kids' Madrid

The chances are that children and their desires will be shuttled aside when parents are confronted with the museums and architectural treasures of Madrid. The Spanish, however, have always loved children, creating diversions for them that many Spanish adults remember with great fondness in later years. Here is a sampling of some of them.

THE WAX MUSEUM

Famous personalities come to life, sometimes in eerily disconcerting ways, at the **Museo de Figuras de Cera,** 41 Recoletos (tel. 419-22-82). It charges 500 pesetas ($4.70) for adults and 300 pesetas ($2.80) for children. Some parents consider it a good way to imbue children with a sense of history. There are scenes depicting such events as Columbus calling on Ferdinand and Isabella, Romans battling with Celts, Arabs fighting with Spaniards, and characters from *Don Quixote.* Twentieth-century international figures aren't neglected either. Thus we see Jacqueline Onassis drinking champagne and Garbo all alone. The heroes and villians of World War II—everyone from Eisenhower to Hitler—are highlighted by the presence of Marlene Dietrich singing "Lili Marlene." The 400 figures that inhabit the 38 tableaux were created by out-of-work filmmakers, who succeeded best with backdrops, falling shortest in their depictions of contemporary celebrities. A film gives a 30-minute recap of Spanish history from the days of the Phoenicians to today. Admission to the small theater to see this show costs 100 pesetas (95¢). The waxworks is open daily from 10:30 a.m. to 1:30 p.m. and 4 to 8 p.m. Metro: Colón; or bus no. 5, 14, 27, 45, 53, M-6, or M-7.

AQUAPOLIS

Sixteen miles northwest of Madrid lies a watery attraction where your kids might happily intermingle with hundreds of other children. They can cool off at **Aquapolis,** Villanueva de la Canada, Carretera de El Escorial (tel. 815-69-86). Scattered amid shops, a picnic area, and a barbecue restaurant are water slides, wave-making machines, and tall slides that spiral children (and an occasional adult) into the swimming pool below. These water sports are available in summertime only, every day from 10 a.m. to 8 p.m. Admission costs 1,400 pesetas ($13.15) for adults and 900 pesetas ($8.45) for children. When the park is open, there's a free bus that runs every hour throughout the day, departing from the Calle Reyes, next to the Coliseum Cinema, on the eastern edge of the Plaza de España.

PARQUE DE ATRACCIONES

Madrid's Parque de Atracciones contains many diversions geared to the pleasure of children, as well as many others geared to more adult tastes. (For more information on the latter, see Chapter XIII.) It was created in 1969 to amuse the young at heart with an array of rides and concessions. The park is at its most popular in July and August, when it's open Tuesday to Friday from 6 p.m. to 1 a.m.; Saturday from 6 p.m. to 2 a.m.; and Sunday from noon to 1 a.m. Between September and March, hours are Saturday and Sunday from noon to 8 or 9 p.m., depending on business. Between April and June, hours are Tuesday to Friday from 3 to between 9 and 11 p.m., depending on business; Saturday and Sunday from noon to 8 or 9 p.m., depending on business. Admission costs 150 pesetas ($1.40) for adults, 50 pesetas (45¢) for children under nine. Most rides require between one and five tickets to board; tickets cost 50 pesetas (45¢) each, although you can buy an all-inclusive ticket, good for all rides, for around 1,200 pesetas ($11.30).

The park's numerous attractions include a tobaggan slide, a carousel, pony rides, an adventure into "outer space," a walk through a transparent maze, a visit to "jungleland," a motor-propelled series of cars disguised as a tail-wagging dachshund puppy, and a gyrating whirligig clutched in the tentacles of an octopus named "El Pulpo." The most popular rides are a pair of roller coasters named "7 Picos" and "Jet Star."

To get to the park take the cable car (Teleferico) described below. At the terminus of the cable car, a line of micro-buses awaits to complete your journey to the park. An alternative way to get there is to take a suburban train from the Plaza de España, which stops near an entrance to the park (the Entrada del Batán). Of course, the easiest way to get there is by taxi.

THE ZOO

Children are invariably delighted by the zoo, which in Madrid lies in the Casa de Campo, at the edge of the Parque de Atracciones. (The Parque de Atracciones is previewed separately both within this section and in Chapter XIII.) The zoo was developed in the 1970s using up-to-date theories about layout and planning. Sprawling over 50 carefully landscaped acres, it contains animals from Spain and throughout the world.

It allows you to see, through its division by continents, the wildlife of Africa, Asia, the Americas, and Europe, with about 2,500 animals on display. Most of the animals are in a simulated natural habitat, with moats separating them from the public. There's an area where small animals may be petted by children. The zoo is open daily from 10 a.m. to 7 p.m. (the last ticket is sold at 6 p.m.). Admission costs 875 pesetas ($8.25) for adults and 650 pesetas

($6.10) for children aged three to eight. Metro: Batán; or bus no. 33 or 65.

TELEFERICO

An alternative way to reach the zoo is via Madrid's *Teleferico* or cable car (tel. 241-19-97). It departs from the Paseo Pinter Rosales at the eastern edge of the Parque del Oeste (at the corner of the Calle Marqués de Urquijo) and will carry you high above two parks, railway tracks, and the Manzanares River to a spot near a picnic ground and restaurant in the Casa de Campo Park. (Weather permitting, there are good views of the Royal Palace along the way.) The ride takes 11 minutes and costs 400 pesetas ($3.75) round-trip or 275 pesetas ($2.60) one-way. Children under five ride free. Between March and October, the cable car runs every day between noon and 9 p.m. Between November and February, service is eliminated on Tuesday and Wednesday; service on Monday, Thursday, and Friday is from noon to 2 p.m. and 4 to 7 p.m.; and service on weekends and holidays is from noon to 7 p.m. Metro: Argüelles; or bus no. 1.

SHOPPING IN MADRID

Practically everything is available in Madrid, which 17th-century playwright Tirso de Molina called "a shop stocked with every kind of merchandise."

Madrid has been one of the major shopping centers of Spain ever since the court moved here. Today, its merchandise has expanded, and it is so diverse in its offerings that it has become one of the major cities for people "born to shop." So, whatever your travel schedule, try to budget some time for exploring some of the merchandise on display everywhere in Madrid.

It is estimated that there are more than 50,000 stores in Madrid alone, selling everything from its emerging high-fashion clothing (for both men and women) to flameco guitars to art and ceramics.

The *rebajas* (summer sales) start in July, and if you visit in August, you'll find prices lowered even more. These sales tie in with the time of the biggest tourist migration to Madrid.

If your time is limited and you want a quick overview of Madrid offerings, go to one of the big department stores (see below). Each of them carries a "bit of everything."

BEST BUYS

Spain has always been revered for the dedication of its craftspeople, many of whom still work in the time-honored, labor-intensive traditions of their grandparents. Your life-style, tastes, and individual needs will be your best gauge of what to buy, but it's hard to go wrong if you stick to the handcrafted objects that the Spanish have always executed so beautifully. These include handpainted tiles, sturdy ceramics, and fine porcelain. Shipping can be arranged by any reputable dealer, who will send the object to its destination swathed in protective padding.

Handwoven rugs, handmade sweaters, and intricate embroideries are also good buys. And you'll find some of the best leather in the world.

Jewelry—especially gold set with Majorca pearls, which have been produced in Spain for centuries—represents good value and unquestioned luxury.

Antiques, although no longer the giveaway bargains they were before World War II, are still available in Spain, and are sold in highly sophisticated retail outlets. Better suited to the budgets of many travelers, however, are the flea markets whose weekly bartering and haggling have become a celebrated and elaborate ritual in modern Madrid.

Spain, although hardly the center for haute couture that Milan and Paris are, is still making inroads into fashion. Its young designers are regularly featured in the fashion magazines of Europe. You'll also find some excellent shoes. *Warning:* Prices for shoes and quality clothing are generally more expensive in Madrid than in the United States.

1. Shopping Districts

Drawing on its historical origins as the most interesting part of Madrid, **the center of Madrid** has a dense concentration of all kinds of shops. Their sheer diversity is staggering, interspersing the most old-fashioned mom-and-pop outlets for salt, meat, fish, and staples with high-tech, high-fashion boutiques in the most current European style. The neighborhood's densest concentration of shops lies immediately north of the Puerta del Sol, radiating out from the Calle del Carmen, Calle Montera, and Calle de Preciados.

The Calle Mayor and Calle del Arenal district, although technically in the center (not far from the Puerta del Sol), still seems to exist as a separate shopping entity. Unlike their more stylish neighbors to the north, shops in this district tend toward the small, slightly dusty enclaves of coin and stamp collectors, family-owned souvenir shops, clockmakers, sellers of military paraphernalia, and (thanks to the nearness of the Teatro Real and the Music Conservatory) an abundance of stores selling musical scores for obscure orchestral works.

The **Gran Vía** was conceived, designed, and built in the 1910s and 1920s as a showcase for the best shops, hotels, and restaurants Madrid could offer. Since those days, its allure has been battered by the emergence of other shopping districts, yet the art-nouveau/art-deco glamor of the Gran Vía still survives in the hearts of most Madrileños. The bookshops here are among the best in the city, as are outlets for fashion, shoes, jewelry, furs, and handcrafted accessories from all regions of Spain.

Most visitors are so immediately enamored by the architectural symmetry of the **Plaza Mayor** that they overlook its neighborhood as a shopping opportunity. Within three or four blocks in each direction from the square you'll find more than the predictable concentration of souvenir shops. Under the arcades of the square itself are exhibitions of lithographs and oil paintings, and every Saturday and Sunday there's a loosely organized market of collectible stamps and coins. One of the city's headquarters for the sale of bolts of cloth, threads, and buttons lies amid the stores on the Calle Marqués Viudo de Pontejos, which runs east from the Plaza Mayor. Also running east of the square, on Calle de Zaragoza, are collections of silversmiths and small jewelry shops. On the more practical end of the spectrum, the Calle Posetas contains shops selling housewares, underwear, soap powders, and almost everything a householder would need to create a happy (and clean) home.

Near the **Carrera de San Jerónimo,** lying several blocks east of the Puerta del Sol, is Madrid's densest concentration of gift shops, craft shops, and antique dealers—a decorator's delight. Its most interesting streets include the Calle del Prado, Calle de las Huertas, and Plaza de las Cortés. Because of the nearness of some of Madrid's most expensive and posh hotels and the general upscale nature of the neighborhood, don't expect any bargains.

Lying a few blocks east of the Parque del Oeste, the verdant and well-heeled neighborhood of **northwest Madrid** is well stocked with luxury goods and staples for middle-class and upscale homes. Identified by its Metro stop, Argüelles, its main thoroughfare is Calle Princesa, which contains a bevy of shops selling shoes, handbags, fashions, gifts, and children's clothing. Thanks to the influence and presence of the nearby university, there's also a dense concentration of bookstores, especially within the Calle Isaac Peral and the Calle Fernando el Católico (which lie several blocks north and northwest, respectively, from the subway stop of Argüelles).

The **Salamanca district** is known throughout Spain as the quintessential upper-bourgeois neighborhood, as uniformly prosperous as anything you're likely to find in Iberia. Its shops are correspondingly exclusive. They include outlets run by interior decorators, furniture shops, fur and jewelry shops, Spanish couture, several department stores, and design headquarters whose output ranges from the solidly conservative to the high-tech *outré* of Europe. The main streets of this district are the Calle Serrano and the Calle Velázquez. The district lies northeast of the center of Madrid, a few blocks north of Retiro Park. Its most central Metro stops are Serrano and Velázquez.

---

2. A Shopping Mall

The **Mercado Puerta de Toledo** is one of Spain's most upscale, ambitious, and architecturally unusual shopping malls. More than 150 of the most glamorous names and merchandise in Spain are collected into a slightly rundown neighborhood just southwest of the historic center. Name-brand fashions and antiques are featured here—an unusual contrast for a building that served until very recently as Madrid's central fish market. Today, thanks to pesetas invested by the municipal government, the complex is perceived as a showcase for the very best of Spanish art and fashion. (Some observers have compared it to London's revitalized Covent Garden marketplace.) Almost half of the 150 stores are devoted to the sale of antiques, and many are outlets for the most sophisticated names in

Spanish fashion and design. Interspersed among the stores are museum-quality temporary expositions devoted to such subjects as the pottery of Talaverde or the Toledo-based art of metalworking.

Highly stylized and futuristic, the market rises five floors above a sun-flooded courtyard that contains an artistic rendering of a lunar clock and sun dial. You won't go hungry between shopping binges because of the many restaurants, tapas bars, and cafés within the premises.

Each of the individual shops maintains hours of its own choosing, but most of them do business Monday to Saturday from 10 a.m. to 8:30 p.m. Metro: Puerta de Toledo.

---

3. Department Stores

Despite the presence of innumerable charming boutiques scattered throughout the city, many Madrileños appreciate the congregation of thousands of items under one roof. Department-store shopping is definitely a Spanish *institución*. Many visitors also prefer the convenience of making all their purchases in one store, rather than running from boutique to boutique.

The largest and most glamorous of these stores is **El Corte Inglés,** which is considered by some shopping devotees to be one of Europe's best department-store chains. Despite the throngs of shoppers jamming the corridors and escalators, it manages to retain a cheerfully upper-crust image of a store loaded with desirable and practical goods. Salespeople rarely speak English, but they are so tuned in to the merchandise and to the needs of shoppers that they can often be of great help anyway.

El Corte Inglés sells all kinds of souvenirs and Spanish handcrafts, such as damascene steelwork from Toledo, flamenco dolls, and embroidered shawls. Some astute buyers report that it also sells glamorous fashion articles such as Pierre Balmain for about a third less than equivalent items in other European capitals. The chain has a multitude of services that foreign visitors appreciate, including interpreters, currency exchange facilities, and parcel delivery either to a local hotel or overseas. It will also arrange for all the necessary formalities regarding the VAT (Value Added Tax) refund. (For more information on this, refer to the "Fast Facts" section in Chapter VIII.)

There are almost 20 branches of this store scattered throughout Spain, with the largest outlet located in central Barcelona. Madrid, however, boasts several different branches, the flagship of which is at 3 Calle Preciados (tel. 232-8100), about a block from the Puerta del Sol. Metro: Puerta del Sol. Additional branches within Madrid lie at 76 Calle Goya (tel. 448-0804), on the northern end of the Paseo de la Castellana at the corner of Calle Raimunda Fernández Villaverda (tel. 456-50-20), and at 56 Calle Princesa (tel. 242-4800). Each is open Monday to Saturday from 10 a.m. to 9 p.m. (without interruption).

Fiercely competitive with El Corte Inglés is Madrid's other enormous department-store chain, the **Galerías Preciados,** 1 Plaza de Callao (tel. 522-6410). It is really two stores connected by an underground passageway. It's more Macy's than Lord & Taylor, slightly more downscale than its famous competitor, but with quite presentable ready-made clothing for men, women, and children. There's a top-floor snack bar and restaurant. Some good buys I've noted in the past include guitars, men's suede jackets and Spanish capes, and women's full-length suede coats. There's a tailoring department on the store's second floor, where men can have a suit made to order. The selection of fabrics—solids, herringbones, or stripes,—can be made into whatever style you prefer. Galerías Precíados is open Monday to Saturday from 10 a.m. to 8 p.m. Metro: Callao.

---

4. Flea Market

In addition to the thousands of conventional shops that call Madrid home, the Spanish capital has a strong tradition of open-air markets, whose haggling and informality have become part of Madrileño lore.

Foremost among these is the **Rastro** (which is translated as either flea market or thieves' market). Located on a meandering network of streets and plazas a few minutes' walk south of the Plaza Mayor, it will warm the heart of anyone attracted to fascinating junk interspersed with bric-a-brac and paintings. (Don't expect to find a Goya.) The neighborhood is also lined with permanent stores that are open, with exceptions, Tuesday to Sunday from 9:30 a.m. to 1:30 p.m. and 5 to 8 p.m. These sell a mixture of dusty junk and antiques, and should be visited during the week if you're seriously interested in buying (or just looking for) antiques. On Sunday, between 9 a.m. and 2 p.m., it seems that half of Madrid and many people from the surrounding countryside jostle each other through the narrow streets, searching for real and imagined bargains.

The flea market occupies a roughly triangular district of streets whose center is the Plaza Cascarro and the Ribera de Curtidores. As its name implies, thieves are rampant here, so proceed carefully. Metro: La Latina; or bus no. 3 or 17.

---

5. Shopping A to Z

ANTIQUES

Spain's imperial traditions and status-conscious bourgeoisie created a market for enormous amounts of furniture during the 19th century. Much of this is available today as highly desirable antiques. Other than at the flea market or within the newly erected Mercado de Puerta de Toledo shopping mall (see above), one of the densest concentration of antique stores is within the **Centre de Arte y Antiguedades,** 5 Calle Serrano (tel. 576-9682). Set within a mid-19th-century building, it has several unusual antique dealers (and a large carpet emporium as well). Each establishment maintains its own hours, but they tend to be open Monday to Saturday from 10:30 a.m. to 2 p.m. and 3 to 5:30 p.m. Metro: Retiro.

Another possibility is the **Centro de Anticuarios Lagasca,** 36 Calle Lagasca, which contains about a dozen shops specializing in antique furniture. The center is open Monday to Saturday from 10 a.m. to 1:30 p.m. and 5 to 8 p.m. Metro: Serrano or Velázquez.

ART GALLERIES

One highly successful entrepreneur on Madrid's art scene is the Ohio-born Edward Kreisler, whose **Galéria Kreisler,** 8 Calle Hermosilla (tel. 431-42-64), specializes in relatively conservative paintings, sculptures, and graphics. Metro: Serrano. Far less conservative is his **Jorge Kreisler Galéria,** 13 Calle Prim (tel. 522-05-34), which inventories the sculptures, paintings, and graphics of avant garde artists. Metro: Chuega.

Both galleries pride themselves on occasionally displaying and selling the works of artists who are critically acclaimed in Spain, and displayed in museums throughout the country. Both galleries are open Monday to Friday from 10:30 a.m. to 1:30 p.m. and 4:30 to 7:30 p.m.; Saturday 10:30 a.m. to 1 p.m.

Sr. Kriesler is not without competition from rising new galleries. One establishment that sells Goya prints from the artist's original plates, as well as many other engravings and etchings, is the **Calcografia Nacional,** 13 Calle Alcalá (tel. 532-1543). It's open Tuesday to Friday from 10 a.m. to 2 p.m.; Saturday 10 a.m. to 1:30 p.m. Metro: Sevilla.

BOOKSTORES

There are many bookstores all over the city, selling both English and Spanish-language editions, along with touring maps. One of Madrid's most popular booksellers, **Aguilar,** has three different outlets: 24 Serrano (Metro: Serrano; tel. 577-3674), 18 Goya (Metro: Velázquez; tel. 575-0640), and 154 Paseo Castellana (Metro: Cuzco; tel. 259-0967). It's open Monday to Saturday from 10 a.m. to 1 p.m. and 5 to 8 p.m.

Equally popular is the **Casa del Libro,** 29 Gran Vía (tel. 521-6657), which contains five floors of inventory, with various sections devoted to special-interest areas such as travel. It's open Monday to Saturday from 9:30 a.m. to 1 p.m. and 4:30 to 8:30 p.m. Metro: Gran Vía.

CAPES

Memories of Zorro have prompted some visitors to Madrid to search out similar attire. If you're looking for the perfect cape, head for **Capas Seseña,** 23 Calle Cruz (tel. 531-5510). Founded shortly after the turn of the century, it has been manufacturing and selling the finest wool capes for both men and women for many years. The wool comes from the mountain town of Béjar, near Salamanca. Prices begin at 55,000 pesetas ($517) for men and around 35,000 pesetas ($329) for women. The store is open Monday to Friday from 9:30 a.m. to 1:30 p.m. and 5 to 8 p.m.; Saturday 9:30 a.m. to 1:30 p.m. Metro: Sevilla or Tirso de Molina. A second outlet is located within the sophisticated new shopping mall at the Puerta de Toledo. (For more information, see "Shopping Mall" above.)

CERAMICS

Called "the first house of Spanish ceramics," the **Antigua Casa Talavera,** 2 Isabel la Católica (tel. 247-34-17), has wares that include a sampling of regional ceramic styles from every major area of Spain—Talavera, Toledo, Manises, Valencia, Puente del Arzobispa, Alcora, Granada, and Seville, among many others. Sangría pitchers, dinnerware, tea sets, plates, vases are all handmade, and the buyers work hard to find pieces with character. Inside one of the showrooms there's an interesting selection of tiles, painted with reproductions of everything from scenes from *El Quijote* to bullfights, dances, and folklore. There's also a series of tiles depicting famous paintings at the Prado. At its present location for more than 80 years, the shop is only a short walk from the Plaza de Santo Domingo. Metro: Santo Domingo.

CRAFTS

Handmade objects can be purchased in virtually any neighborhood of Madrid, but one of the city's most stylish outlets is one sponsored by the Spanish government as a showcase for the best of its national designs. **Artespana,** 3 Plaza de las Cortés, not far from the Palace Hotel and the Prado, collects within its duplex of showrooms a tempting collection of Spanish ceramics, furniture, and household items. It's open Monday to Friday from 10 a.m. to 1:30 p.m. and 4:30 to 8 p.m.; Saturday 10 a.m. to 1:30 p.m. Be sure to look at the additional merchandise in the establishment's basement. Metro: Cibeles.

EMBROIDERIES

Throughout the 19th and 20th centuries, the intricately detailed embroideries produced in Spain's Balearic Islands (especially Majorca) have been avidly sought out for inclusion in bridal chests and at elegant dinner settings. One outlet that stocks and sells them is **Casa Bonet,** 76 Calle Núñez de Balboa (tel. 575-0912). A few examples are displayed on the walls, but a true concept of the store's inventory comes when tablecloths, sheets, napkins, and pillowcases are unrolled on Spanish tables covered with velvet. You'll find a full range of cottons, linens, and polyesters here, many embroidered into patterns fit for a bride. The shop is open Monday to Friday from 9:45 a.m. to 2 p.m. and 5 to 8 p.m.; Saturday from 10:15 a.m. to 2 p.m. Metro: Núñez de Balboa.

ESPADRILLES

These are those wonderfully lighthearted shoes that no self-respecting Iberian fisherman would do without. Although many different styles exist, the tops are usually crafted from canvas and the soles from tightly woven hemp. (The hemp is first woven into ropes, then stitched in oval patterns into what is eventually used as a sole.) Despite their humble origins, some consumers consider espadrilles perfect for beachwear and occasionally as a kind of casually chic shoe to wear to summer parties. If you want to stock up on this kind of Iberian accessory, head for **Casa Hernanz,** 18 Calle de Toledo (tel. 266-5450). Located on a busily trafficked street a brisk walk south of the Plaza Mayor, it has been in business for more than 150 years. In addition to espadrilles, the shop sells shoes in other styles and hats. The staff is cordial, but they don't speak English. Hours are Monday to Friday from 9 a.m. to 1:30 p.m. and 4:30 to 8 p.m.; Saturday 10 a.m. to 2 p.m. Metro: Puerta del Sol, Opéra, or La Latina.

FANS AND UMBRELLAS

Fans and umbrellas have traditionally been inventoried and sold from the same shops in Spain. A true mistress of the fan-bearing art can convey a multitude of messages through the way she manipulates her fan, and part of the fun of a trip to Spain is the attempt to figure out the various signals. One well-known shop that can supply you with all the ingredients you'll need for your own Spain-inspired flirtation is **Casa de Diego,** 12 Puerta del Sol (tel. 522-566-43). Fans sold here range from plain to fancy, from plastic to exotic hardwood, from cost-conscious to lavish, in an assortment that will probably tempt you to become (at least during a candlelit evening or two) a bit more *espagnole.* Hours are Monday to Saturday from 9:45 a.m. to 1:30 p.m. and 4:30 to 8 p.m. Metro: Puerta del Sol.

FASHION

The dowdiness of Franco-era Spain has disappeared as designers typified by Paloma Picasso have transformed the fashion landscape. The array of desirable boutiques is endless, but a representative list might include the following.

For Women

One of the most popular retail outlets is **Herrero,** Precíados 16 (tel. 521-2990), whose sheer size and buying power make it an attractive choice for women's clothing. Additional outlets can be found at number 7 (same phone) and number 23 (tel. 521-2722) on the same street. All three branches are open Monday to Saturday from 10:45 a.m. to 2:15 p.m. and 4:30 to 8:15 p.m. Metro: Puerta del Sol or Callao.

Modas Gonzalo, 43 Gran Vía (tel. 247-1239), is a boutique with a baroque and gilded atmosphere reminding you of the 1940s. However, its fashions for women are strictly up-to-date. It's open Monday to Saturday from 10 a.m. to 1:30 p.m. and 4:30 to 8 p.m. Metro: Callao, Puerta del Sol, or Santo Domingo.

Don Carlos, 92 Serrano (tel. 575-7507), strictly maintains its status as a boutique, with a limited but tasteful array of carefully chosen clothing for women, and a somewhat smaller selection for men. Open Monday to Saturday from 10 a.m. to 2 p.m. and 5 to 8:30 p.m. Metro: Núñez de Balboa.

Jesús de Pozo, 28 Calle Almirante (tel. 531-6676), markets the collections of one of the most fashionable designers for women in Spain. The fabrics are beautiful and the garments expensive, but when they make you look gorgeous, perhaps it's worth it. It's open Monday to Saturday from 10 a.m. to 1:30 p.m. and 5 to 8 p.m. Metro: Colón.

For Men

Although it may be dead in many other western capitals, the art of custom tailoring is alive and thriving in Madrid. A tried and tested establishment is **Valdivia,** 86 Gran Vía (tel. 247-9640). Located within the Edificio España (the Plaza Hotel building) at the Plaza de España, it has won the respect and patronage of many Spanish diplomats and businessmen. Mariano Valdivia inherited his skill and business from his father. His staff can produce a suit in four or five working days, if you're available for fittings. The shop offers a choice of fabrics in many weights, which can be crafted into different styles.

Sr. Valdivia has expanded his shop to include women's clothing, blouses, and overcoats, and a collection of garments shipped in from Paris. The prices are relatively reasonable for this ready-to-wear, but the establishment still caters mostly to men. The shop is open Monday to Friday from 9 a.m. to 2 p.m. and 4 to 6 p.m. Metro: Plaza de España.

FOOD AND WINE

Each of the capitals of Europe has its own legendary gourmet shop where you can eat, drink, and carry away succulent tidbits for consumption at home or on your picnic. Madrid's best-established shop, **Mallorca,** 59 Calle Velázquez (tel. 431-9909), was originally established in 1931 as an outlet for a specific kind of pastry called an *ensaimada.* Consumed as part of the coffee-drinking ritual throughout Madrid, it's still the store's most famous product. (They emerge ultrafresh every hour from the establishment's ovens.) There are also a tempting array of cheeses, canapés, roasted and marinated meats, sausages, about a dozen kinds of pâtés, and a mind-blowing array of tiny pastries, tarts, and chocolates.

Don't overlook the displays of wine and brandies. There is also a stand-up tapas bar, where clients stand three deep, sometimes sampling the wares before they buy larger portions to take away. Hostesses of chic cocktail parties, and marauding families organizing picnics, sometimes make take-out from Mallorca the gastronomic focal point of their events. Tapas cost from 100 pesetas (94¢) to 200 pesetas ($1.90) per *racion* (portion).

The 59 Calle Velázquez branch of Mallorca (Metro: Velázquez) and the five other branches maintain the same hours: seven days a week from 9 a.m. to 9 p.m. The other branches are at 6 Calle Serrano (Metro: Serrano; tel. 577-1859), 39 Calle Juan Pérez Zúñiga (Metro: Blvd. Concepcion; tel. 267-1807), 7 Calle Bravo Murillo (Metro: Alvarado; tel. 448-9749), 39 Calle Comandante Zorita (Metro: Calle Caminos; tel. 253-5102), and 48 Calle Alberto Alcocer (Metro: Cuzco or Colombia; tel. 458-7511).

HATS AND HEADGEAR

Founded in 1894, **Casa Yustas,** 30 Plaza Mayor (tel. 266-50-84), is an extraordinary hat emporium, especially popular in this day of strange headgear. If your sessions with the analyst have revealed a hangup for unusual hats, you can satisfy your inclinations here. Picture yourself as a Congo explorer, a Spanish sailor, an officer in the Kaiser's army, a Rough Rider, a priest, even Napoleon. Hats are priced at between 600 pesetas ($5.65) and 12,000 pesetas ($112.80). The store is open Monday to Friday from 9:45 a.m. to 1:30 p.m. and 4:30 to 8 p.m.; Saturday 9:45 a.m. to 1:30 p.m. Metro: Puerta del Sol.

JEWELRY

Madrid has more than its share of predictably upscale jewelers, but one establishment noted for producing relatively inexpensive jewelry with taste and whimsy is **Yannes,** 37 Calle Goya (tel. 435-3105). It's open Monday to Saturday from 10 a.m. to 1:30 p.m. and 5 to 8:30 p.m. Metro: Velázquez.

LEATHER

Loewe, 8 Gran Vía (tel. 577-6056), has been the most elegant leather store in Spain since 1846. Its gold-medal-winning designers have always kept abreast of changing tastes and styles, but there remains a timeless chic to much of their inventory. The store sells luggage, handbags, and jackets for men and women (in leather or suede). Much of the inventory is in the supple and soft shade of medium brown for which the store is known. The store is open Monday to Saturday from 9:30 a.m. to 2 p.m. and 4 to 8:30 p.m. Metro: Banco de España. Keeping the same hours is a second outlet at 26 Serrano (tel. 577-60-560). Metro: Serrano.

Less expensive is **Patricia,** 45 Calle Lagasca (tel. 276-2330), which specializes in leather purses, handbags, clothes, and shoes. It's open Monday to Saturday from 10 a.m. to 1:30 p.m. and 5 to 8 p.m. Metro: Serrano.

MUSICAL INSTRUMENTS

If you're looking to buy a Spanish guitar, a piano, a string or wind instrument, or simply a record, CD, or pieces of sheet music, head for **Real Musical,** 1 Carlos III (tel. 241-3009). It's open Monday to Friday from 9:30 a.m. to 2 p.m. and 5 to 8 p.m.; Saturday 9:30 a.m. to 2 p.m. Metro: Opéra.

PERFUMES

The seductive arts have never been ignored in Spain, and one of the tools used for that purpose is perfume. Women hoping to tame their bulls might consider heading for the **Perfumería Padilla,** 17 Preciados (tel. 522-66-83), which sells a large and competitively priced assortment of Spanish and international scents for women. It's open Monday to Friday from 9:45 a.m. to 1:45 p.m. and 5 to 8 p.m.; Saturday from 10 a.m. to 2 p.m. Metro: Puerta del Sol. The store maintains another branch at 7 Calle del Carmen (tel. 521-55-08).

Urquiola, 1 Mayor (tel. 521-59-05), has one of the most complete stocks of perfume in Madrid, with both national and imported brands. It also has a wide, tasteful selection of gifts and costume jewelry. It's open Monday to Friday from 10 a.m. to 2 p.m. and 4:45 to 8:30 p.m. Metro: Puerta del Sol.

PORCELAIN

Some visitors prefer the thick and rustic pottery and stoneware that Spanish artisans churn out by the thousands at potters' wheels throughout the country. Others search out only the delicately realistic porcelain sculptures whose elongated limbs and whimsically yearning expressions were probably inspired by the mannerist paintings of El Greco. Foremost among the manufacturers of this style of porcelain sculpture is Lladró.

Many different shops have concessions to sell Lladró porcelain. One that is especially well-suited to the tastes of foreign visitors to Spain is run by an Ohio-born entrepreneur, Edward Kreisler. **Kreisler,** 19 Calle Serrano (tel. 276-5338), is an official distributor of both Lladró and Nao porcelains and Majorca pearls. It also sells damascene jewelry from Toledo and a selection of Spanish soaps and perfumes. The shop is open Monday to Saturday from 10:30 a.m. to 2 p.m. and 5 to 9 p.m. Metro: Serrano.

Another, even more imposing, outlet for Lladró is a store devoted almost exclusively to its distribution. **Lladró,** 2 Calle Quintana (tel. 247-7147), is open Monday to Friday from 10 a.m. to 2 p.m. and 5 to 8 p.m.; Saturday 10 a.m. to 2 p.m. It has a large inventory and can usually tell you about new designs and new releases the Lladró company is planning for the near future. Metro: Argüelles.

TOYS

One of Madrid's most enduring outlets for children's toys is **Sánchez Ruíz,** 47 Gran Vía (tel. 541-5313). In addition to the inventories of dolls, toys, and games, you'll find gift items appreciated by adults. The store is open Monday to Saturday from 10:30 a.m. to 2 p.m. and 4:30 to 8:30 p.m. Metro: Callao or Santo Domingo.

MADRID AFTER DARK

The Madrileños are called *gatos* (cats) because of their excessive fondness for prowling around at night. If you're going to a club, the later you go, the better. If you arrive too early, you'll probably have the place to yourself.

In recent years, nightlife in Madrid has changed more dramatically than in any other capital of Europe. There is something going on at night to interest virtually everyone. The young people of Madrid rarely seem to stay home watching television. They are out exploring the many nocturnal facets of their city.

Nightlife is so plentiful in Madrid that the city can be roughly divided into "night zones." The most popular district—both traditionally and from the standpoint of tourist interest—is the **Plaza Mayor/Puerta del Sol** districts. These areas can also be dangerous (muggings, for example), so explore them with caution, especially late at night. The area is filled with tapas bars and *cuevas* (drinking "caves"). Here it is customary to begin a tasca crawl, going from tavern to tavern, sampling the wine in each, along with a selection of tapas. The major streets for such a crawl are Cava de San Miguel, Cava Alta, and Cava Baja. You can order *pinchos y raciones* (tasty snacks and tidbits).

Gran Vía's nightlife is confined mainly to cinemas and theaters. Most of the after-dark action takes place on little streets branching off the Gran Vía.

Another area much frequented by tourists is the section around **Plaza de Isabel II** and **Plaza de Oriente,** site of the Royal Palace. Both are in the center of Madrid. Many restaurants and cafés flourish in this area, including the famous Café de Orient.

Chueca, embracing such streets as Hortaleza, Infantas,

Barquillo, and San Lucas, is the gay nightlife district, with many clubs. Cheap restaurants, along with a few striptease joints, are also found here. Again, this area can be dangerous at night; be alert for pickpockets and muggers.

For university students, the area of **Argüelles-Moncloa** sees most of the action. However, if it's a weeknight and there are classes tomorrow, most students head home by 11 p.m. Many discos are found in the area, along with ale houses and fast-food joints. The area is bounded by Pintor Rosales, Cea Bermúdez, Bravo Murillo, San Bernardo, and Conde Duque.

1. The Performing Arts

There is within Madrid a wide variety of large-scale theaters, opera companies, and ballet groups. To discover the specific cultural events being performed during your visit, pick up a copy of *Guía del Ocio* for 75 pesetas (70¢) at any city newsstand. The sheer volume of cultural offerings might stagger you, but for a highly distilled presentation, see below.

Tickets to dramatic and musical events usually range in price from 700 pesetas ($6.60) to 1,500 pesetas ($14.10), with discounts of up to 50% on certain days of the week (usually Wednesday and early performances on Sunday). The concierge at most major hotels can usually get you tickets to specific concerts. He or she will, of course, charge a considerable markup, part of which will be passed along to whichever agency originally booked the tickets. You'll save money if you go directly to the box office. If the event of your choice is sold out, you may be able to get tickets (with a considerable markup attached to them) at the **Galicia Localidades** at the Plaza del Carmen (tel. 531-27-32). Metro: Puerta del Sol. This agency also markets tickets to bullfights and sports events. It is open Tuesday to Sunday (except holidays) from 10 a.m. to 1 p.m. and 4:30 to 7:30 p.m.

The following is a grab bag of nighttime diversions that might amuse and entertain you.

DRAMATICS

Madrid offers many different theater performances, but they'll be useful to you only if your Spanish is fluent. If it isn't, check the *Guía del Ocio* for performances by English-speaking companies on tour from Britain, or select a concert or subtitled movie instead.

The largest theater in Madrid is the **Teatro Calderon,** 18 Atocha (tel. 239-1333), with a seating capacity for 1,700 spectators. It's known for its popular reviews, performances of popular Spanish plays, and flamenco. Metro: Tirso de Molina.

More prestigious is the **Teatro de la Comedia,** 14 Calle Príncipe (tel. 521-4931), site of the *Compania Nacional de Teatro Clasico.* Here, more than anywhere else in Madrid, you're likely to see performances from the classic repertoire of great Spanish drama. Metro: Sevilla.

The **Teatro Español,** 25 Calle Príncipe (tel. 429-6297), is funded by Madrid's municipal government. Its repertoire is a time-tested assortment of great and/or favorite Spanish plays. Metro: Sevilla.

Teatro María Guerrero, 4 Tamayo y Baus (tel. 419-4769), also funded by the government, works in cooperation with its sister theater, the Teatro Español (see above) to stage performances of works by such classic Spanish playwrights as García Lorca and Lope de Vega. The theater was named after a much-loved Spanish actress. Metro: Banco d'España or Colón.

There are at least 30 other theaters, including one devoted almost entirely to performances of children's plays, the Sala La Bicicleta, in the Ciudad de los Niños at the Casa de Campo. Dozens of other plays are staged by nonprofessional groups in such places as churches. All that are open to the public will be listed in *Guía del Ocio.*

MUSIC

Auditorio Nacional de Musica, 136 Calle Príncipe de Vergara (tel. 337-0200), sheathed in slabs of Spanish granite, marble, and limestone and capped with Iberian tiles, is the ultramodern home of both the National Orchestra of Spain and the National Chorus of Spain. Standing just north of Madrid's Salamanca district, it is viewed today as a major addition to the competitive circles of classical music in Europe. Inaugurated in 1988, it is devoted exclusively to the performance of symphonic, choral, and chamber music. In addition to the *auditorio principal* (Hall A), whose capacity is almost 2,300, there's a hall for chamber music (Hall B) and a small auditorium for intimate concerts seating 250 spectators or less. Each hall is musically independent of its neighbor, permitting simultaneous performances with no sound interference. The lofty space of the main hall is noteworthy for having absolutely no sound-absorbing materials of any kind (such as carpeting or curtains). This, and a smooth-finished wooden ceiling, give it a sound that experts say is distinctive. Metro: Cruz del Rayo.

Auditorio del Real Conservatorio de Musica, Plaza Isabel II (tel. 337-0100), a few steps from the Royal Palace and the Opera House, sometimes presents its students in admission-free musical concerts. More regularly, however, are both Spanish and visiting musical ensembles whose performances (which take place in an auditorium seating only around 400) are sometimes sold out long in advance.

The **Fundación Juan March,** 77 Calle Castello (tel. 435-4240), sometimes holds free weekly concerts at lunchtime, although the advance schedule is notoriously difficult to predict. Metro: Núñez de Balboa.

One theater whose schedule might include everything from punk-rock musical groups to the more highbrow warm-weather performances of visiting symphonic orchestras is the **Auditorio del Parque de Atracciones.** It can hold 3,500 spectators and is within the most complete amusement park in Spain (the Parque de Atracciones; see below).

There are another 30 formally designated concert halls within Madrid, plus dozens of impromptu concerts organized on short notice—sometimes in churches—throughout the capital. Other types of concerts occur as part of the regular program in bars.

OPERA

Operas in Madrid have traditionally been performed in the **Teatro Real** (Royal Theater), Plaza de Isabel II, (tel. 248-14-05), the neoclassical opera house that faces the Royal Palace behind an ornate bronze statue of the music-loving Queen Isabel II. When it was inaugurated by her in 1850, it was intended exclusively for operatic performances, but for many years it shared its premises with the National Orchestra and National Chorus in a never-ending battle for space and scheduling.

All of this ended, however, when the *Auditorio Nacional de Musica* (see above) provided a new home for Spain's symphonies and choruses, leaving the Teatro Real for the almost exclusive use of opera. Renovations and enlargements, scheduled for completion during the lifetime of this edition, have transformed the elegant but antiquated building into one of the finest and most acoustically sophisticated opera houses in Europe, all the while retaining the neoclassical opulence for which the building is famous. Metro: Opera. At press time, box-office information had not yet been finalized, so for last-minute ticket information, refer to the *Guía del Ocio*.

BALLET

Ballet, Spanish style, is presented at the **Centro Cultural de la Villa,** Plaza de Colón (tel. 573-6080). Tickets go on sale five days before the event, and performances are usually presented at two evening shows, 8 and 10:30 p.m. Tickets, when available, average around 1,000 pesetas ($9.40) each. Metro: Serrano or Colón.

FLAMENCO

The strum of a guitar, the sound of hands clapping rhythmically, and you know that flamenco is about to start. Soon, colorfully dressed women, occasionally men, flounce onto the stage to swirl in time with the music. The staccato beat of castanets and the tapping of heels make the rafters ring. Flamenco—the incomparable Spanish performing art.

Flamenco personifies the blood and guts of Andalusia, where it originated. Nowadays, gypsies have virtually taken over the art form, making flamenco part of their own folklore. Their fire and flair add another dimension to an already passionate dance.

The performers sit in a half circle upon a stage, with the lead or head dancer at one end. At the left and right rear, the male singers and dancers await their turn. To the accompaniment of guitars, castanets, and rhythmic clapping, each performer does a solo, occasionally uniting with another partner—strutting, tapping, clapping, and stamping their feet with inner tension and barely suppressed pride. The songs are chanted in a passionate, tense tone, almost Arabic in origin. Age doesn't keep an artist off the center stage. Flamenco singers *(cantores)* seem to perform forever.

Many of the major flamenco clubs in Madrid are patronized almost exclusively by foreigners searching for a glimpse of an earlier era. For that privilege you'll pay dearly, but some visitors still consider it worth the expense.

Café de Chinitas, 7 Torija (tel. 248-5135), is one of the swank-iest and most expensive flamenco spots in town. In the old part of Madrid, between the Opéra and the Gran Vía, it features the dancer La Chunga and the guitarist Serranito. They join with about 40 other artists to make up the *cuadro*. The show starts at about 11 p.m., running until 3:30 a.m. The minimum, which entitles you to a drink at a table, is 4,000 pesetas ($37.60). You can also go for din-ner and then stay for the show. A fixed-price dinner costs 9,000 pesetas ($84.60) and is served from 9:15 p.m. to 12:30 a.m. The café is open Monday to Saturday throughout the year. You sit in an elongated room at tables with fair visibility. The stage is at the far end of the room. The decor is amorphously elegant, sometimes in questionable taste, and doesn't quite live up to the promise of the building's exterior. You enter through a staircase lined with bull-fighting memorabilia. Reservations in advance are recommended. Metro: Santo Domingo.

Corral de lo Morería, 17 Morería (tel. 265-8446), is in the Old Town, the *Morería*—meaning a quarter where Moors reside. It sizzles more in its flamenco than in its skillet. The place is open nightly from 9 p.m. to at least 3 a.m. Strolling performers, colorful-ly costumed, get the proceedings under way around 11 p.m., but they are there only to warm up the audience. A flamenco showcase follows, with at least 10 dancers who initiate the stage for the star, who always appears late and with an almost hyperbolic drama.

The management has devised ways of putting tables in the most unlikely places; reserve near the front and go early if you really want a ringside table. The show and an à la carte dinner, which is served any time after 9:30 p.m., costs 7,000 pesetas ($65.80). If you've already eaten (which is what I usually prefer to do), your first drink will cost from around 2,700 pesetas ($25.38). Metro: La Latina or Puerta del Sol.

Zambra, in the Hotel Wellington, 8 Velázquez (tel. 435-5164), is a subterranean supper club within the hotel premises. Some of the best flamenco singers and dancers of Spain appear here before enthusiastic audiences. The doors open Monday to Saturday at 9:30 p.m. for dinner. The show is scheduled to begin at 10:15 p.m., although it is occasionally delayed, perhaps for dramatic effect. It ends around 3 a.m. With dinner included, the show costs 6,500 pesetas ($61.10) per person. Without dinner, a view of the show and your first drink costs around 3,000 pesetas ($28.20). Reserva-tions are a good idea. Metro: Velázquez.

If you're still on the flamenco trail, you might try **Arco de Cuchilleros,** 7 Cuchilleros (tel. 266-5867). Lots of single men and women come here. A flamenco show with a girlie twist is often pre-sented. All in all, it's fun to be here, if you don't take the proceedings too seriously. The one-drink minimum costs from 2,800 pesetas ($26.30). The establishment is open for business ev-ery day from 10:30 p.m. to 2:30 a.m. Metro: Puerta del Sol.

ZARZUELA

For an authentic Spanish experience, you can attend a *zarzuela,* a Spanish operetta with turn-of-the-century music, lots of Iberian panache, bright costumes, and what usually turns out to be a pre-dictably sentimental plot with plenty of schmaltz. Sometimes, the theaters sandwich flamenco numbers and musical revues between excerpts from the time-tested librettos.

One of the best places to view this musical theater is the **Teatro Nuevo Apolo,** 1 Plaza Tirso de Molina (tel. 527-3816). Within its imperially ornate walls is the headquarters of the renowned Antologia de la Zarzuela company. Metro: Tirso de Molina.

Another company performs at the **Teatro Lirico Nacional de la Zarzuela,** 4 Calle Jovellanos (tel. 429-1286), near Cibeles Square. It also produces ballets and an occasional opera. Metro: Banco de España.

Another possibility is the occasional zarzuela that is deliberately interspersed with other types of musical performances at the **Teatro Monumental,** 65 Atocha (tel. 227-1214). This theater is the permanent home of the Spanish Radio and TV Orchestra and the Spanish Radio and TV Chorus (RTVE), whose style ranges from the seriously classical to the far more frivolous. Metro: Anton Martín.

---

2. Clubs and Discos

CABARET AND "SPECTACLES"

Madrid's nightlife is no longer steeped in prudishness, as it was (at least officially) during the Franco era. You can now see glossy cabarets and shows with lots of nudity. Madrid's most visible manifestation of this is **Scala Meliá Castilla,** 43 Calle Capitan Haya (entrance at 7 Rosario Pino; tel. 450-4400), serves dinners, but few of its patrons show up only for the food. The allure is the show—girls, glitter, and the gloss of ballet, a gaggle of musicians, and a graceful duo of ice skaters. Sunday to Thursday, there are shows at 9 p.m. (for guests who want dinner) and at 10:30 p.m. (for spectators who want only to drink and see the show). The show with dinner costs 7,500 pesetas ($69) per person, the late show costing 3,500 pesetas ($32.90) with a first drink included. On Friday and Saturday, a bargain "teatime" show is presented for 2,000 pesetas ($18.80) at 5 p.m.; a dinner show at 8:30 p.m. for 7,500 pesetas ($32.90), and a late show at 12:30 a.m., costing 3,500 pesetas ($32.90) with a first drink included. Reservations are needed. Metro: Cuzco.

More subtle, and sometimes vastly more poignant, is **Les Noches de Cuple,** 51 Calle La Palma (tel. 532-7115). It's a nostalgic cabaret of a type that is fading fast. Its entrance is on a crowded street barely wide enough for the pedestrians and cars that compete for space. Like everything else in Madrid, the show begins very late and ends when dawn begins to trickle through to the cobblestones of the gutters and alleyways. Inside, a long room with a vaulted ceiling and a tiny stage are the forum for the still-charming former beauty Señora Olga Ramos, who conducts an evening of Iberian song. The charm of her all-Spanish act is increased by the discreet humor of an octogenarian accompanist with an ostrich-feather tiara and a fuchsia-colored boa. There's no cover charge, but your first drink will cost 2,400 pesetas ($22.55). If you want dinner, it will cost 5,500 pesetas ($51.70). Each additional drink will cost around 900 pesetas ($8.45). Dinner is served between 9:30 p.m. and midnight (don't go too early), and the show usually begins around midnight. The establishment is open Monday to Saturday until 2:30 a.m. Even if you don't speak Spanish, the kitsch, the unabashed camp, and the sometimes lavish sentimentality of the evening will give you something to remember. Metro: Noviciado.

JAZZ CLUBS

Clamores, 14 Calle Albuquerque (tel. 445-7938), is the largest jazz club in Madrid, accommodating some 450 people. With dozens of small tables and a huge bar in its somewhat dark interior, the club serves beer, whisky, wine, and the best Catalán champagne to go with the music of bands from Spain and the rest of Europe. The club is open every day from 3 p.m. to 3 a.m. (until 4 a.m. Friday and Saturday), and the best jazz usually begins after 11:30 p.m. When music is playing, there's a 300-peseta ($2.80) surcharge on the price of each drink. Without the surcharge, beer costs 300 pesetas ($2.80), whisky with soda around 700 pesetas ($6.60). Monday night is *salsa* night, and the place is transformed into something akin to what you'd see in Brazil. Metro: Bilbao.

Whisky Jazz, 7 Diego de Léon (tel. 261-1165), is a hideaway for jazz enthusiasts just a block away from the U.S. Embassy. If you arrive at the right time, you'll be presented with one of the best showcases of jazz in all of Spain. In the interior of the two-story brick building is a stairway leading to an open mezzanine that projects out over a downstairs bar. The walls and a glass case contain intriguing jazz memorabilia, including autographs and photos from its heyday in Chicago and New Orleans. The entrance price begins at 800 pesetas ($7.50), but could go much higher, depending on which group is performing. Hours are Monday to Saturday from 9 p.m. to 3:30 a.m. Metro: Núñez de Balboa.

Café Berlin/Oba-Oba, 4 Jacometrezo, carries a double whammy thanks to its dual nature. In its basement lies Oba-Oba (tel. 531-0640), whose specialty is Caribbean-and Brazilian-inspired jazz, to which an animated clientele dances the *lambada,* the *salsa,* and an occasional *pasadoble.* If you doubt that you'll be able to master these steps in a single evening, don't be shy—there will almost certainly be someone there to teach you. Upstairs, the Café Berlin (tel. 531-0810) has live jazz concerts that pack spectators tightly inside whenever the music is playing. There's no admission charge to either establishment, but you'll pay around 700 pesetas ($6.60) for each drink. They're both open from 6 p.m. until 4 or 5 a.m., sometimes even later. Here, like everywhere else, it's most crowded after 11 p.m.

Café Populart, 22 Huertas (tel. 429-8407), is known in town for hiring competent and exciting jazz groups that encourage the audience to dance. Run by an engaging entrepreneur named Arturo, it specializes in Brazilian, Afro-bass, reggae, and "new African wave" music. It's open from 6 p.m. to 4 or 5 a.m. every day, charging 350 pesetas ($3.30) for a beer and 500 pesetas ($4.70) for a whisky with soda when live music isn't playing. (When the music starts, prices of drinks are nearly double.) Metro: Anton Martín or Sevilla.

DISCOS

Some discos are spectacular, complete with the latest sound systems and lasers. Others are little cellar dives where the owner plays records to special but fickle late-night claques who desert him the next day for a newer club. Be assured of one thing: It's a matter of *gato* pride that no disco worth its entrance charge will be crowded and hot until at least 11 p.m.

Joy Eslava, 11 Arenal (tel. 266-54-40), is housed in an old theater whose walls have been painted almost entirely black, and it may be one of the most electronics-conscious nightspots in Madrid. It's filled with up-to-date lighting and sound equipment and a prominent array of bars, with imitation lasers that shoot bursts of light into almost every corner. If you don't feel like dancing, comfortable chaises longues are scattered throughout the establishment. Libations cost from 1,100 pesetas ($10.35) each, and there's a cover charge of 1,300 pesetas ($12.20). Joy is open from 11:30 p.m. to 7 a.m. every day, unless it happens to be closed for a private party. Metro: Sol or Opéra.

Mau-Mau, 23 Padre Damian (tel. 457-94-23), lies within the Eurobuilding complex, an appropriately glamorous location for one of the most glamorous clienteles of Madrid. You can order a whisky and soda for between 2,000 pesetas ($18.80) and 3,000 pesetas ($28.20), but the preferred drink on many nights is a bottle of champagne. Anyone with hopes of being included in the *tout Madrid* category will eventually make his or her appearance within Mau-Mau's gloriously luxurious interior. Management requires that men wear jackets, except on Sunday and between July 1 and late September. There is no admission charge. The club is open every night from midnight to 5 a.m. Metro: Colombia.

Bocaccio, 16 Marqués de la Enseñada (tel. 419-10-08), is considered one of the most elegant discos in the Spanish capital, known for a clientele of show-biz entrepreneurs, pretty women, and an occasional mogul. This is no rock-and-roll palace, but rather a stylish triumph of art-nouveau design. Tufted red velvet crescent-shaped banquettes seat attractive young and older people. Serving them are regally attired bartenders who become part of the show. The place is open every day from 7 p.m. to 5 a.m., charging 1,600 pesetas ($15.04) after 10 p.m. Whisky and soda costs from 750 pesetas ($7.05).

---

3. Tascas and Tapas Bars

Madrileños know that they cannot live by culture alone; food and love are just as important in the nocturnal life of the city.

In spite of Madrid's notoriously late hours, the denizens of the night usually begin their evenings as early as 8 p.m. by tasca-hopping and tapas-tasting. Since dinner is served in Madrid at the fashionably late hour of 10:30 p.m., the ingestion of some kind of nourishment is the only thing that both staves off starvation and keeps the social gears smoothly oiled. From 8 p.m. onward, the tuned-in Madrileño might enter one or several *tascas* (taverns), drinking a *chato* (small glass of vino) and eating *tapas,* literally, "covers." Tapas are Spanish hors d'oeuvres, usually displayed on the counter of the bar, sometimes behind a glass or plastic display case, usually at eye level. Most often they include crunchy fried fish, cold tortillas (omelets), squid, *gambas* (shrimp), olives, sausages, salads, mushrooms, even the tail of a bull. Each of the major tascas is noted for two or three specialties, which you'll usually find prominently displayed or advertised (often in chalk on a blackboard). Although most have waiter service at the tables—if they have tables at all—it is less expensive to order your tapas and drinks at the bar. Some of my favorite taverns—scattered about in interesting and colorful parts of Madrid—are listed below.

António Sánchez, 13 Mesón de Parades (tel. 239-78-26), was named in 1850 after the founder's son, who was killed in a bullfight. Memories of the bullfighter abound here, chief of which is the stuffed head of the animal that gored young Sánchez. Also featured on the darkly paneled walls are three valued works by the Spanish artist Zuloaga, who had his last public exhibition in this restaurant shortly before he died. A limited array of tapas, including garlic soup, is served with the Valdepeñas wine that a barman will draw from a barrel. A restaurant in the back serves Spanish food with a vaguely French influence. Tapas generally cost from 200 pesetas ($1.90) to 600 pesetas ($5.65) each. Hours are Monday to Saturday from noon to 4 p.m. and 8 p.m. to midnight; Sunday from noon to 4 p.m. The establishment lies in a warren of narrow streets near the Plaza Tirso de Molina Metro.

Taberna Toscana (Tuscan Tavern), 22 Ventura de la Vega (tel. 429-6031), is not particularly ornate or fashionable-looking on the outside. Inside, however, its theme is that of a country inn, with terrazzo floors, rustic stools and tables, and hand-held beams from which hang hams, sheaves of wheat, and garlic pigtails. Nearly two dozen tapas are set out at the bar. Tasty and highly recommended are kidneys in sherry sauce and snails in hot sauce. Tapas range from 100 pesetas (95¢) to 1,200 pesetas ($11.30), and a glass of beer or wine from around 85 pesetas (80¢). Metro: Sevilla.

Café Bar Los Galayos, 1 Plaza Mayor (tel. 265-6222), with rows of outdoor tables, occupies one of the prime locations on the Plaza Mayor, right at one of the inside corners. If you prefer to drink inside, away from the streaming sunlight, there's a popular stand-up bar of elaborately molded hardwoods. You'll recognize the place by its forest-green façade, which, even under the weathered arcades of 16th-century Spain, looks somewhat like a English Victorian storefront. Tapas range in price from 150 pesetas ($1.40) to 2,000 pesetas ($18.80) for the most elusive and expensive shellfish. A beer costs 110 pesetas ($1.05) at the stand-up bar and a few pesetas more at one of the tables. There's also a restaurant if you're in the mood for a more formal dinner, but many visitors prefer to munch on whatever tapas appeal to them, considering the variety and the ambience part of their evening's entertainment. Los Galayos is open every day from 8 a.m. to 1:30 a.m. Metro: Puerta del Sol.

El Anciano Rey de los Vinos, 19 Bailén (tel. 248-5052), may look like many other stand-up wine bars in Madrid, but the difference is in its connection with the fun-loving sister of Queen Isabela Segundo who, late in the 19th century, used to slip away from the nearby Royal Palace for a tipple of wine whenever she could find an appropriate disguise as a commoner. Today the curved wooden bar is jammed during many parts of the day with crowds of talking and gesticulating Madrileños out for a glass (or carafe) of one of the four house wines. These range from dry to sweet, and cost (as does a beer) from 80 pesetas (75¢) per glass. The simple tapas cost from 75 pesetas (70¢) to 350 pesetas ($3.30) each. The establishment is open from 10 a.m. to 3 p.m. and 5:30 to 11 p.m., every day except Wednesday. Metro: Opéra.

Cervecería Alemana, 6 Plaza Santa Ana (tel. 429-7033), was intended as a German beer hall when it was originally established a century ago, but it became undeniably Spanish somewhere along the way. Young Madrileños are fond of stopping off for a mug of draft beer at 85 pesetas (80¢) or a glass of wine at 80 pesetas (75¢). In the old days you might have seen Hemingway, accompanied by the celebrated bullfighter Luís Miguel Dominguin, occupying one of the tables. (Ask the waiter to point out where he traditionally sat.) Opening directly onto one of the liveliest little plazas of Madrid, it clings to its turn-of-the-century traditions. Here you can sit at one of the tables, leisurely sipping your beer or wine, as the waiters make no attempt to have you drink up and press on. The beer hall draws a wide assortment of people, but the dress is decidedly casual. To accompany your brew, try the fried sardines, a Spanish omelet, or perhaps a *racion* of the establishment's shrimp or crayfish. Tapas cost from 80 pesetas (75¢) to 800 pesetas ($7.50). The establishment is open every day except Tuesday, from 10 a.m. to 12:30 a.m. (to 1:30 a.m. on Friday and Saturday). Metro: Alonso Martínez or Sevilla.

Cervecería Santa Bárbara, 8 Plaza de Santa Bárbara (tel. 319-0449), is a popular outlet for a beer factory. And although beer isn't a beverage traditionally associated with Spain, the clientele here seems to enjoy it immensely. The interior is quite large, dominated by a long counter, cooled with spinning ceiling fans and illuminated with globe lighting. There are long communal tables that are tended by waiters, although many guests prefer to stand at the bar. You go here for beer, of course: *la cerveza negra* (black beer)—which costs 120 pesetas ($1.15)—or the slightly less expensive *cerveza dorada* (golden beer). The brew is best accompanied by homemade potato chips, a plate of which costs around 185 pesetas ($1.75). Fresh shrimp, lobster, crabmeat, and barnacles are also served. The establishment is open every day from 11 a.m. to 11 p.m. Metro: Alonso Martínez; or bus no. 3, 7, or 21.

Casa Sierra, 1 Calle de Gravina (tel. 521-1290), with smoke stains on the 19th-century frescoed ceiling, zinc bar, and dozens of oak barrels of vintage sherries and ports, is one of the most atmospheric gathering places in town. You won't find any tables or chairs —only a sawdust-covered floor, dozens of gossiping neighbors of all ages, and a gruff but friendly greeting from the barman. Plates of tapas cost from 375 pesetas ($3.50); beer, from 85 pesetas (80¢). The establishment is open from noon to 4 p.m. and 8 p.m. to midnight every day except Wednesday. Metro: Chuega.

Balmoral, 10 Calle Hermosilla (tel. 431-41-33), is unashamedly Anglo-Saxon. Its exposed wood and comfortable chairs evoke something you'd expect to find in London. Its clientele tends toward journalists, politicians, army brass, owners of large estates, bankers, diplomats, and an occasional literary star. *Newsweek* magazine once dubbed it "one of the best bars in the world." Beer costs around 325 pesetas ($3.05), whisky with soda around 700 pesetas ($6.60). No food, other than tapas, is served. It's open every day of the week from 7:30 p.m. to 2 a.m. Metro: Serrano.

Los Motivos, 10 Ventura de la Vega (tel. 429-6729), offers about two dozen different platters of tasty tapas every evening. It's one of the most frequented bars in Madrid; its smart and relatively sophisticated crowd of Madrileños start filing in nightly around 8 p.m. It's decorated like an old tavern: hand-hewn beams, strings of garlic, wine bottles hanging from the ceiling, and crude wood stools and tables. The food at the bar is under glass—so it's most sanitary. Tapas range in price from 325 pesetas ($3.05) to 1,400 pesetas ($13.16), while a glass of beer costs from 80 pesetas (75¢) and a glass of wine from 60 pesetas (55¢). The establishment is open Monday to Saturday from noon to 4 p.m. and 8 p.m. to midnight. There's also a restaurant on the premises, serving a simple *menú del día* for 900 pesetas ($8.45). Metro: Puerta del Sol or Sevilla.

Hispano, 78 Paseo de la Castellana (tel. 411-48-76), is a popular place. Every day, especially at the end of a workday, it's crowded with a clientele that includes everyone from office workers to entrepreneurs, as well as a scattering of stylish women. It's open every day from 7:30 p.m. to 3 a.m., charging an average of 800 pesetas ($7.50) for a whisky with soda. Metro: Nuevos Ministerios.

Cock, 16 de la Reina (tel. 576-28-69), attracts some of the most visible artists, actors, models, and filmmakers in Madrid, including award-winning Spanish director Almodovar, who is rumored to be here frequently. The decoration is elaborately antique, perhaps in deliberate contrast to its clientele. Drinks cost around 600 pesetas ($5.65) each, and are served Monday to Saturday from 9 p.m. to 3 a.m. Metro: Gran Vía.

Sesamo (Sesame), 7 Príncipe (tel. 429-65-24), despite its rustic and bohemian appearance (or perhaps because of it), has hosted Truman Capote and many other celebrated persons. Styles and cultural heroes rise and fall, but Sesamo seems to go on forever. Its two cellar rooms are reached via a long flight of steps. Downstairs, you'll find seats gathered around tiny tables. Guests have been known to bring their guitars or banjos, spontaneously singing folk songs, laments of love, or political protests. When no one in the audience is particularly musical, management provides a piano player. Like virtually everything else in Madrid, the action here doesn't get going until around 11 p.m. If you're with a group, it's customary to order a pitcher of sangría for 800 pesetas ($7.50). Otherwise, a pint of beer costs 275 pesetas ($2.60). It's open every day from 6 p.m. to 2 a.m. Metro: Sevilla or Puerta del Sol.

Mesón del Champiñon, 17 Cava San Miguel (tel. 248-6790), is a place where the barmen keep a brimming bucket of sangría behind the long stand-up bar as a thirst-quencher for the many people who crowd in. The name of the establishment translates as "mushroom," and that is what you see delineated in various sizes along sections of the vaulted ceilings. A more appetizing way to experience a *champiñon* is to order a *racion* of grilled, stuffed, and salted mushrooms, served with toothpicks. A portion costs 400 pesetas ($3.75) at the bar, and 475 pesetas ($4.45) at a table. Beer, at 225 pesetas ($2.10) a glass, is the preferred accompaniment, but if you prefer, a whisky with soda costs around 500 pesetas ($4.70). The pair of tiny, slightly dank rooms in the back is where Spanish families jam in for the organ music produced by a stalwart musician performing in one corner. Champiñon is open from 1:30 p.m. to 6 a.m. every day of the week. Metro: Sol, Opéra, or La Latina.

---

4. Conventional Bars

Some visitors can't quite get into the hustle-bustle of the *típica tasca,* preferring the more sedate elegance of a conventional bar. What follows is a random sampling of some of the most interesting bars—each one attracting a widely diverse clientele, many quite fashionable. The Palace Bar, Mr. Pickwick's, and Nuevo Oliver are all suitable for two women traveling together.

The **Palace Bar,** the Palace Hotel, 7 Plaza de las Cortés (tel. 429-75-51), basks in its tradition as *the* place in the capital for upper-crust Madrileños and international travelers from around the globe. In his Hemingway biography, A.E. Hotchner called it "the nerve center of Madrid social intrigue, where every women looks like a successful spy." The panels of grained marble, the soft lounge chairs, and the alert and polite waiters are appropriate for the turn-of-the-century glamour of the Palace. Many a governmental policy has been made here, and many a female film star has preened her feathers in front of an admiring audience. The atmosphere is deliberately relaxed and cordial. A brand-name scotch costs from 1,100 pesetas ($10.35). The Palace Bar is open every day from noon to 2:30 a.m. Metro: Banco de España.

Viva Madrid, 7 Calle Manuel Fernández y González (tel. 467-4645), with its lushly ornate tiled façade and the animated crowd that sometimes spills out onto the sidewalk during peak hours, is an establishment that's hard to resist. It lies within a neighborhood of narrow streets loaded with marauding *gatos* searching for friendship, love, and fulfillment (sometimes successfully), near the Plaza Santa Ana. A congenial mixture of students, artists, foreign tourists, and visiting Yanks cram into its turn-of-the-century interior, where tilework murals and carved animals contribute an undeniable charm. Beer costs from 500 pesetas ($4.70). The place is open Sunday to Friday from noon to 1:30 a.m.; Saturday from noon to 2 a.m. Metro: Anton Martín.

Los Gabrieles, 17 Calle Echegaray (tel. 429-6261), is in the heart of one of Madrid's most pulsating concentrations of bars, restaurants, and nightclubs, but even if it were more isolated, a view of its lavishly tiled walls would be worth a special detour. Throughout most of the 19th century, the building served as the sales outlet for the sherries of a Spanish wine merchant. In the 1980s, its two rooms were transformed into a bar and café, open daily from 12:30 p.m. to 2:30 a.m. You can buy a glass of beer for 200 pesetas ($1.90) during the day and 325 pesetas ($3.05) at night, while admiring elaborately detailed scenes of courtiers courting, dancers dancing, flautists piping, and Andalusian maidens flirting with rigidly attentive *caballeros* on village streets. Metro: Tirso de Molina, Sevilla, or Sol.

Nuevo Oliver, 12 Almirante (tel. 521-0147), attracts a youthful, sophisticated crowd in an atmosphere a lot like a private drawing room or a members-only club. The street-floor room evokes a stage setting by one of London's gifted designers. There's a pastoral mural on the ceiling, a formal fireplace, and recessed alcoves containing shelves of books. The walls support old paintings and engravings. The color scheme is aged Mediterranean: faded red, sienna, bronze, and gold. At the bottom of a winding staircase, there's a lower level ringed with couches. Often, someone plays the piano softly in the background. You pay 850 pesetas ($7.80) for a whisky with soda and 600 pesetas ($5.50) for a beer at a table; slightly less at the stand-up bar. Music begins most evenings about 30 minutes after midnight. It's open every evening from 4 p.m. to 6 a.m. Metro: Chueca.

Balneario, 37 Juan Ramón Jiménez (tel. 458-2420), serves gratifyingly potent drinks within an enclave of fresh flowers, white marble, and the kind of stone bathtub that might have been used by Josephine Bonaparte. Near the Chamartín Station in one of the capital's northern edges, it's one of the most stylish and upmarket bars in Madrid. Many guests precede a meal at the previously recommended restaurant El Cabo Mayor with a drink here. The two establishments share a portion of well-tended garden a few steps away. Tapas such as endive with smoked salmon, asparagus mousse, and anchovies with avocados cost from 400 pesetas ($3.75) to 1,500 pesetas ($14.10) each. Drinks start at 350 pesetas ($3.30), but could easily cost around 700 pesetas ($6.60) if you prefer whisky with soda. The establishment is open Monday to Friday from noon to 2:30 a.m.; Saturday to 3 a.m. Metro: Cuzco.

Chicote, 12 Gran Vía (tel. 532-6737), created by the now-legendary Sr. Chicote, once attracted thousands of English-speaking Hemingway fans. The writer used it as a setting for his only play, *The Fifth Column*. Hemingway would sit here night after night entertaining his friends. The bar still attracts writers, musicians, and artists, and is open Monday to Saturday from 1:30 p.m. to 2:45 a.m. Whisky with soda costs around 650 pesetas ($6.10). Metro: Gran Vía.

Mr. Pickwick's, 48 Paseo Pintor Rosales (tel. 248-5185), is a re-creation of the world of Dickens: timbered ceilings, high-backed settles, framed prints of the author's most famous characters, hunting horns, tiny nooks with a china collection, pewter mugs, an English fireplace, and even a brass horse collection. It's a pleasant place at which to have a mug of beer—either at the tiny bar or at one of the small tables. Most drinks, accompanied by olives and peanuts, are 650 pesetas ($6.10). The pub is open every day from at least 6 p.m. (and sometimes earlier, depending on the mood of the owner) to 1:30 a.m. The pub lies within a corner building where its *paseo* meets the Calle del Marqués de Urquijo. Metro: Argüelles.

The **Sportsman British Pub,** 65 Alcalá (tel. 276-6908), is an attractive English-style club near the central post office. At the section near the entrance is a long bar area with comfortable, padded elbow rests. The walls are covered with photographs of celebrities, including Rita Hayworth and Ava Gardner. Beer, depending on its brewer, costs from 450 pesetas ($4.25) to 550 pesetas ($5.15) after

8:30 p.m. (when there's usually live piano music) and a few pesetas less during the afternoon. The pub is open Monday to Saturday from noon to 2 a.m. The restaurant, The Paddock, is in back, with a bulletin board that seems to indicate that this is a gathering place for British expatriates. The restaurant serves meals Monday to Saturday from 1 to 4 p.m. and 9:30 to 11:45 p.m. Metro: Retiro.

Maravillas New Age Center, 33 Calle San Vicente Ferrer (tel. 532-79-87), is a new-wave bar where youthful clients in costumes bordering on punk rock listen to occasional live concerts of folk music, pop music, or jazz. The schedule is unpredictable. Drinks cost around 550 pesetas ($5.15) each. The place is open every day from 10 p.m. to 5:30 a.m. Metro: Tribunal.

---

5. Special Drinking Experiences

In an old tavern, just a short walk from the Goya Pantheon, **Casa Mingo,** 2 Paseo de la Florida (tel. 247-1098), has been known for its Asturian cider, both the still and the bubbly kind, for decades. There's no formality here, with customers sharing big tables under the vaulted ceiling in the dining room. Cider is served at Casa Mingo in the old manner. The waiter or bartender holds the glass as low as he can in his left hand, and the bottle of still cider as high as he can in his right, and then pours the cider. A few drops may fall on the ground, but it's all part of the rite. The perfect accompanying tidbit is a piece of the local Asturian *cabrales* (goat cheese), but the roast chicken is *the* specialty of the house, with an unbelievable number of helpings served daily. Casa Mingo started roasting chicken when it was considered an unusual delicacy in Spain. Other specialties include *chorizo* (sausage) braised in cider, or perhaps a potato omelet. The price of chicken and cider is 1,100 pesetas ($10.35). In summer, the staff places some tables and wooden chairs outdoors on the sidewalk. Or, if you prefer, you can stand at the bar, under the huge casks of wine and cider that line the walls. The establishment is open daily from 10 a.m. to midnight. Metro: Norte.

Café Gijón, 21 Paseo de Recoletos (tel. 521-54-25), was founded in 1888 by a man named Garcia, who named it after a port in his northern province of Asturias. It has become so entwined since then with the lives of Spanish writers and artists that it is considered a part of the cultural fabric of Madrid.

A spacious and airy room, it contains none of the bedevilments that plague many modern cafés, such as slot machines, video games, and sports events broadcast on television sets. Artists and writers (some looking like Spanish versions of Tennessee Williams) still patronize this café, which sits behind a barrier of trees on a park-like extension of one of Madrid's most prestigious boulevards. Many clients spend hours over one cup of coffee. The dozen-or-so waiters have each been employed for many years and know a lot about many of their regular clients. Along one side of the café is a stand-up bar. In summer, you can sit amidst the greenery of the sidewalk outside, enjoying, say, a *blanco y negro* (black coffee with ice cream). Whisky and soda costs 550 pesetas ($5.05) and beer 250 pesetas ($2.35) at a table, slightly less at the bar. The Gijón is open Monday to Saturday from 9:30 a.m. to 2:30 a.m. Meals are served in the basement-level restaurant Monday to Saturday from 1 to 4 p.m. and 9 p.m. to midnight. Metro: Banco, Colón, or Recoletos.

6. Gay Nightlife

Spain has witnessed an explosion of gay life since the 1970s, perhaps as a reaction against the omnipresent pressures of *machismo* and traditional models of feminity. Many gay Spaniards agree, however, that the ghetto-style segregation of gay men from gay women simply doesn't apply with the rigid boundaries you might have expected, and that in the most sophisticated clubs, all forms of sexual proclivities mix comfortably together.

Hanoi, 81 Hortaleza (tel. 319-66-72), is a stylish and minimalist assemblage of stainless steel, curving lines, and space-age angles. Its clientele is fun, young, attractive, and articulate. The mood is amusedly permissive, and the crowd blends comfortably with both heterosexual and homosexual expressions. There's a small restaurant in the rear, a bevy of male and female models who seem to be in constant attendance, eight video screens showing adventure shows from some long-defunct TV series, and up-to-date music. No matter who you are, you will probably have fun in Hanoi. The establishment is open every day from 9:30 p.m. to 3:30 a.m., but probably becomes more densely populated with gay men and women after 1 a.m. A drink will cost from 600 pesetas ($5.50). Metro: Alonso Martínez.

No Sé los Digas a Nadie, 7 Calle Ventura de la Vega (tel. 420-29-80), defines itself as a women's entertainment center, although it seems to attract an almost equal number of men to its two floors hidden behind a black garage door on this street of budget restaurants. It is open Sunday to Wednesday from 7 p.m. to 1:30 a.m.; Thursday to Saturday from 7 p.m. to 2:30 a.m. Inside there's an art gallery, a bar/café, a staff with information on women's activities in Madrid, and live or recorded music every evening after 11 p.m. Metro: Puerta del Sol.

Black & White, Calle Gravina at the corner of Libertad, (tel. 231-11-41), lies on a not-very-safe street in the center of town. A guard will open the door to a large room painted, as its name implies, in black and white. There's a disco in the basement. The street-level bar, however, is the premier gathering spot for gay men in Madrid. Old movies are shown against one wall, and all kinds of men, from many different worlds within Madrid, are likely to come in. Metro: Chueca.

Café Figueroa, 17 Augusto Figueroa, corner of Hortaleza (tel. 521-16-73), is a turn-of-the-century café where the clients are mainly gay men and women, many of whom know each other. It's open daily from 3 p.m. to 2 a.m. Metro: Chueca.

Cruising, 5 Perez Galdos (tel. 521-5143), is a bar with an open and vaguely permissive aura, where many gay men congregate. It's open from 7:30 p.m. to 3:30 a.m. every day. Beer costs 350 pesetas ($3.30). Metro: Chueca.

Duplex, 64 Hortaleza (tel. 531-37-92), attracts a young crowd of disco-loving gays, both men and women. It has a modern decor, a disco with recent and very danceable music, and an amply stocked bar. It's open daily from 10 p.m. to 5 a.m. There's no cover charge, and beer costs 350 pesetas ($3.30) Metro: Chueca.

---

7. More Entertainment

MOVIES AND FILMS

Spanish film director José Luís Garci has written that no other city in the world treats films and the pronouncements of publicity agents with greater respect than Madrid. Recent cinematic releases from Paris, New York, Rome, and Hollywood come quickly to Madrid, where an avid audience often waits in long lines for tickets. Most foreign films are dubbed into Spanish, unless they're indicated as *"V.O."* (original version).

The premier theaters of the city are the enormous, slightly faded movie palaces of the Gran Vía, whose huge movie marquees announce in lurid colors whichever romantic or adventure *espectaculo* happens to be playing at the moment.

Madrid boasts at least 90 legitimate movie houses (many of which have several theaters under one roof), and many others running pictures for adults only. All listings are contained in the previously recommended *Guía del Ocio,* the *Guía de Diario 16* (also available at newsstands), or within the film listings of Madrileño newspapers.

If you want to see a film while in Madrid, one of the best places is **Alphaville,** with four different theaters at 14 Calle Martín de los Heroes (tel. 248-72-33). It shows English-language films with Spanish subtitles. Metro: Plaza de España.

The movie houses on the Gran Vía, dear to the heart of thousands of Madrileños simply because of their endurance power and their enormous marquees, include the **Rex,** 43 Gran Vía (tel. 247-1237); the **Palácio de la Musica,** 35 Gran Vía (tel. 521-62-09); and the **Coliseum,** 78 Gran Vía (tel. 247-66-12). All are reached by taking the Metro to Gran Vía.

For classic revivals and foreign films, check out the listings at Filmoteca in the **Cine Doré,** 3 Santa Isabel (tel. 227-3866). Movies here tend to be shown in their original language. Tickets cost around 200 pesetas ($1.90). There's a bar and a simple restaurant. Metro: Antón Martín.

AMUSEMENT PARK

Famous throughout Spain, and the site of more than the typical barrage of motorized thrills, the **Parque de Atracciones,** Casa de Campo (tel. 463-2900), is a combination of Coney Island and Copenhagen's Tivoli Gardens. Madrileños refer to it as "Disneylandia." Created almost overnight in 1969 to amuse the young at heart, it lies in the former royal hunting grounds of western Madrid. At the core of the park is an illuminated tower from which fall cascades of water into the surrounding reflecting pool.

You can take an elevator up to the tower's observation platform. There are dozens of motorized rides (see the "Kids' Madrid" section in Chapter XI).

Adults, however, are not left out of the fun. You can take a leisurely trip in a boat on a circuitous canal, become breathless on one of the rides (*Uranus* or *Jungla* seem to attract as many adults as children), or attend a performance at the open-air Greek-style *teatro*, depending on the schedule of plays and weather permitting. The semicircular theater has cast-cement seats facing a cement shell that reverberates sound back from the outdoor stage. The apron has a reflecting pool and illuminated fountains. The popular entertainment is strictly potluck—everything from Spanish ballet to a flamenco singer. The park is at its most popular in July and August, when it's open Tuesday to Friday from 6 p.m. to 1 a.m., Saturday from 6 p.m. to 2 a.m., and Sunday from noon to 1 a.m. Between September and March, hours are Saturday and Sunday from noon to 8 or 9 p.m., depending on business. Between April and June, hours are Tuesday to Friday from 3 to between 9 and 11 p.m., depending on business; Saturday and Sunday from noon to 8 or 9 p.m., depending on business. Admission costs 150 pesetas ($1.40) for adults, 50 pesetas (45¢) for children under nine.

The Metro stop for the Parque de Atracciones is Batan, but for additional information on how to get to the park, refer to the "Kids' Madrid" section in Chapter XI.

GAMBLING CASINO

Casino Gran Madrid is at km 28,300 de la Ctra. Nacional VI-Madrid-La Coruña, Apdo 62, Torrelodones (tel. 856-1100). Even non-gamblers sometimes make the trek here from the capital; the casino's many entertainment facilities are considered by some to be the most exciting thing around. Its scattered attractions include two restaurants, four bars, and a nightclub. The casino is open Sunday to Thursday, from 5 p.m. to 4 a.m.; to 5 a.m. on Friday, Saturday, and holiday evenings. For an entrance fee of 700 pesetas ($6.60) you can sample the action in the gaming rooms, including French and American roulette, blackjack, punto y banco, baccarat, and chemin de fer.

An à la carte restaurant in the French Gaming Room offers international cuisine, with dinners costing from 6,000 pesetas ($56.40). A buffet in the American Gaming Room will cost around 2,200 pesetas ($20.70). The restaurants are open from 9:30 p.m. to 2 a.m. The casino is about 17 miles northwest of Madrid, along the Madrid-La Coruña N-BI highway. If you don't feel like driving, the casino has buses that depart from 6 Plaza de España every afternoon and evening at 4:30, 6, 7:30, 9, and 11:30 p.m. Note that between October and June, men must wear jackets and ties. Jeans and tennis shoes are forbidden in any season. To enter, European visitors must present an identity card, and non-European visitors must present a passport.

ONE-DAY TRIPS FROM MADRID

Some of the most interesting and varied scenery and attractions in Europe lie in the satellite cities and towns ringing Madrid. These include Toledo with its El Greco masterpieces, a monastery considered the eighth wonder of the world (El Escorial), castles that "float" in the clouds (Segovia), and palaces of the Bourbon dynasty at La Granja.

If your time is short, go at least to **Toledo,** which captures the ages of Spain in miniature. Many tourists combine the tour of Toledo with a stopover at the royal palace of **Aranjuez.**

1. Toledo

The ancient capital of Spain looms on the horizon like an El Greco painting, seemingly undisturbed by the ages. The See of the Primate of Spain, the ecclesiastical center of the country, Toledo is medieval, but well preserved. (For a preview of the city much as it is today, see El Greco's *View of Toledo* at the Metropolitan Museum of Art in New York City.)

The Tagus River loops around the granite promontory on which Toledo rests, surrounding the Imperial City on three sides like a snake.

Toledan steel, known as early as the 1st century B.C., has sliced its name down through the ages. Many a Mexican or Peruvian—if he had lived—could attest to the deadly accuracy of a Toledan sword. But except for its steel and damascene work, the lack of major industrial activity has kept Toledo a virtual museum. Many of its buildings are intact, having survived countless battles, the most recent being the bloody fighting the city witnessed in the Spanish Civil War. It is not uncommon for mansions to preserve their original coats-of-arms in their façades.

The natural fortress that is Toledo is a labyrinth of narrow and precipitous streets, decaying palaces, towers, and squares—all of them tourist-trodden.

The Spanish government has seen fit to preserve all of Toledo as a "national monument." One critic labeled the entire city "a gallery of Art," with every style represented from Romanesque to Moorish to Gothic (best exemplified by the cathedral) to Renaissance.

Essentially, Toledo is a blending of the widely diverse cultures that made Spain what it is today: Roman, Visigothic, Moorish, Jewish, and Christian. Perhaps for that reason, Tirso de Molina, the 17th-century dramatist, called Toledo, "the heart of Spain." He named three of his dramas *Los Cigarrales de Toledo,* which brings us to a most important suggestion: Before you leave the Imperial City, you should—preferably in the late afternoon—traverse the **Carretera de Circunvalación,** that most scenic of roads across the left bank of the Tagus. Along the slopes of the hills, you'll find the *cigarrales,* the rustic houses. From this side of the river, you can obtain the best panorama, seeing the city in perspective as El Greco did. With luck, you'll be perched on some belvedere as the sun goes down. Then you'll know why Toledo's sunsets are called violet.

Toledo lies 44 miles south of Madrid. You can reach it by car, of course, although public transportation includes both train and bus. However, the train delivers you outside the city, and you must take a bus into the heart of Toledo, depositing yourself at the Plaza of Zocodover. From Madrid, Toledo-bound buses leave from the Estación Sur de Autobuses, 17 Calle Canarias (take the Metro to Palos de Moguer). Trains (at least 10 per day) depart from Estación de Atocha; the trip to Toledo takes 1½ hours.

You can see all of the major sightseeing attractions in one day, provided you arrive early and stay late.

THE CATHEDRAL

Built at the flowering peak of the Gothic era of architecture, the Cathedral of Toledo, Arco de Palacio (tel. 22-22-41), is one of the greatest in Europe. It was erected principally between the years 1226 and 1493, although there have been later additions. The monument is a bastion of Christian architecture, but a great deal of the actual construction work was carried out by the Moors, master builders themselves.

The cathedral witnessed many prime moments in Spanish history—such as a proclamation naming "Juana la Loca" (the insane daughter of Isabella I) and her husband, Philip the Handsome, heirs to the throne of Spain.

Inside, the Transparente—the altar completed in 1732 by Narcisco Tomé—is considered a landmark in European architecture. Lit by a "hole" cut through the ceiling, this production includes angels on fluffy clouds, a polychrome "Last Supper," and a Madonna winging her way to heaven.

Dating from the 16th century, the iron gate of the cathedral is in the plateresque style. Works of art include the *Twelve Apostles* by El Greco and paintings by Velázquez, Goya, Morales, and Van Dyck. El Greco's first painting in Toledo was commissioned by the cathedral. Called *El Expolio,* it created a furor when the devout saw the vivid coloring of Christ's garments. The artist was even hauled into the courts. Many elaborately sculpted tombs of both the nobility and ecclesiastical hierarchy are sheltered inside.

Don't fail to visit the Gothic cloister, the Capilla Mayor, and the Renaissance-style Choir Room (elaborate wood carvings), and you should see the rose windows, preferably near sunset. In the Treasure Room is a 500-pound monstrance, dating from the 16th century and said to have been made, in part, from gold that Columbus brought back from the New World. To celebrate Corpus festivities, the monstrance is carried through the streets of Toledo. The Mozarabic Chapel dates from the 16th century and contains paintings by Juan de Borgoña (a mass using Mozarabic liturgy is still conducted here).

The treasures of the cathedral can be visited in summer Monday to Saturday from 10:30 a.m. to 1 p.m. and 3:30 to 7 p.m.; Sunday from 10:30 a.m. to 1:30 p.m. and 4 to 7 p.m. In winter, the cathedral closes an hour earlier in the evening. Admission is 300 pesetas ($2.80). The cathedral stands directly east of Plaza del Ayuntamiento in the heart of Toledo.

MUSEO DE SANTA CRUZ

Dating from the 16th century and built in the form of a Greek cross, the plateresque hospice has been turned into a **Museum of Fine Arts and Archeology,** Calle de Cervantes (tel. 22-10-36). As a hospital, it was originally founded by Cardinal Mendoza. It is of such beautiful construction—especially its paneled ceilings—that it's a question of the "frame" competing with the pictures contained inside.

In the Fine Arts Museum are 18 paintings by El Greco (*The Burial of Count Orgaz* is a copy of his masterpiece). *The Assumption of the Virgin* is his most important canvas here. Other works are by Ribera and Goya. Flemish tapestries, antique furnishings, and jewelry round out the exhibit.

In the Archeological Museum the past ages of Toledo are peeled away: prehistoric, Iberian, Roman (note the mosaics), Moorish, Visigothic, and Gothic. The museum is an easy walk from the Plaza de Zocodover in the very heart of Toledo.

Santa Cruz is open Monday to Saturday from 10 a.m. to 6:30 p.m.; Sunday 10 a.m. to 2 p.m. Admission is 200 pesetas ($1.90).

EL GRECO'S HOUSE AND MUSEUM

The famous painter Domenicos Theotocopoulos, called El Greco because he was born in Crete, arrived in Toledo in 1577, living there with Doña Jerónima, a noted beauty (either wife or mistress) until his death in 1614. His living quarters stood in the

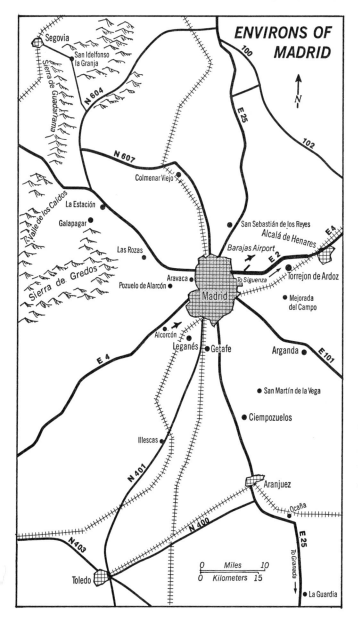

ENVIRONS OF MADRID

Segovia

San Idelfonso la Granja

Sierra de Guadarrama

N 604

N 607

Colmenar Viejo

Valle de los Caídos

La Estación

Galapagar

San Sebastián de los Reyes

Alcalá de Henares

Barajas Airport

Las Rozas

Sierra de Gredos

Aravaca

To Sigüenza

Torrejon de Ardoz

Pozuelo de Alarcón

Madrid

Mejorada del Campo

Alcorcón

Leganés   Getafe

Arganda

E 101

E 4

San Martín de la Vega

Ciempozuelos

Illescas

N 401

Aranjuez

Ocaña

N 400

E 25

To Granada

N 403

Toledo

Miles   10

Kilometers   15

La Guardia

antiguo barrio judío, or the old Jewish quarter, on Calle Samuel Levi in the heart of Toledo. It is believed that the painter moved to this site in 1585.

Samuel Ha-Levi, chancellor of the exchequer to Pedro the Cruel, is said to have built a series of houses here, forming a complex in the 14th century. These little interconnected houses were often called "apartments." Ha-Levi had subterranean passages dug to hide his treasury, and a Don Enrique de Villena, it is said, practiced alchemy in these underground cellars.

The apartments or houses were torn down in the late 19th century, but many people in Toledo say El Greco's house or apartment was rescued. Perhaps it was, but critics aren't sure. What emerged, nevertheless, was identified for visitors as "Casa del Greco." Eventually, a neighboring house was incorporated to shelter a museum with 19 pictures by El Greco.

Visitors are admitted into the studio of El Greco, containing a painting by the artist. Especially interesting are the garden and kitchen. The house may be visited in summer Tuesday to Sunday from 9:30 a.m. to 2 p.m.and 3:30 to 7 p.m.; in winter, Tuesday to Sunday from 9:30 a.m. to 1:45 p.m. and 5:30 to 6 p.m. The admission fee is 200 pesetas ($1.90).

THE CHURCH AND CLOISTERS OF SAN JUAN DE LOS REYES

This church at 21 Calle de los Reyes Católicos (tel. 22-38-02), was founded by King Ferdinand and Queen Isabella to commemorate their triumph over the Portuguese at Toro in 1476. Its construction was started in 1477, according to the plans of architect Juan Guas. It was finished, together with the splendid cloisters, in 1504, dedicated to St. John the Evangelist, and used, from the very beginning, by the Franciscan Friars. It is a perfect example of Gothic-Spanish-Flemish style.

San Juan de los Reyes was restored after being damaged in the invasion of Napoleon and abandoned in 1835. Actually, the national monument has been entrusted again to the Franciscans since 1954. The price of admission is 75 pesetas (70¢). You can visit the church from 10 a.m. to 2 p.m. and 3:30 p.m. to 7 p.m. daily (it closes an hour earlier in winter).

THE CHURCH OF SANTO TOMÉ

Except for its mudéjar tower, this little 14th-century chapel, on Calle de Santo Tomé (tel. 21-02-09), is rather unprepossessing. But by some strange twist it was given the honor of exhibiting El Greco's masterpiece, *The Burial of Count Orgaz*. Long acclaimed for its composition, the painting is a curious work in its blending of realism with mysticism. To view the painting, you have to purchase a ticket for 85 pesetas (80¢).

The church is open daily from 10 a.m. to 1:45 p.m. and 3:30 to 6:45 p.m. in summer, closing an hour earlier in winter; closed on Christmas and New Year's Day.

THE ALCÁZAR

The characteristic landmark dominating the skyline of Toledo is the Alcázar, Plaza de Zocodover in the very center of the city. It attracted worldwide attention during the siege of the city in 1936. Nationalists held the fortress for 70 days until relief troops could respond to their plea for help, arriving on September 27, 1936.

The most famous event surrounding that battle was a telephone call the Republicans placed to the Nationalist leader inside. He was informed that his son was being held captive and would be executed if the Alcázar were not surrendered. He refused to comply with their demands, and his son was sacrificed.

The Alcázar was destroyed, and the one standing in its place today is a reconstruction, housing an Army Museum (tel. 21-39-61) with a monument out front to the heroes of that 1936 siege. The price of admission is 150 pesetas ($1.40). Entrance is daily from 9:30 a.m. to 2 p.m. and 4 to 7 p.m. It closes at 6 p.m. in winter.

THE TRÁNSITO SYNAGOGUE

Down the street from El Greco's museum on the Paseo del Tránsito is the once-important worshipping place for the large Jewish population that used to inhabit the city, living peacefully with both Christians and Arabs. This 14th-century building is noted for its superb stucco and its Hebrew inscriptions. There are some psalms along the top of the walls and on the east wall a poetic description of the temple. The building of the synagogue was ordered by the chancellor of the exchequer to King Pedro el Cruel (Peter the Cruel), Don Samuel Ha-Levi. The name of the king appears clearly in a frame in the Hebrew inscription.

The synagogue is the most important part of the **Museo Sefardi,** which was inaugurated in 1971 and contains in other rooms tombstones with Hebrew epigraphy dating from before 1492, as well as other art pieces. The museum and synagogue can be visited Tuesday to Saturday from 10 a.m. to 1:45 p.m. and 4 to 5:45 p.m.; Sunday 10 a.m. to 2 p.m. Admission is 200 pesetas ($1.90). For information, telephone 22-36-65.

---

2. Aranjuez

On the Tagus River, 29 miles south of Madrid on the N-400, Aranjuez strikes visitors as a virtual garden. It was mapped out by the royal architects and landscapers of Ferdinand VI in the 18th century. The natural setting has been blended with wide boulevards and fountain- and statuary-filled gardens.

Surrounded in late spring by beds of asparagus and heavily laden strawberry vines, Aranjuez exudes the spirit of May. But for some visitors autumn best reveals the royal town. It is then that the golden cypress trees cast lingering shadows in countless ponds, evoking a painting by Santiago Rusiñol Prats.

Aranjuez can easily be reached by public transportation from Madrid, either bus or train. Buses, about seven a day, leave from Madrid at the Estación Sur de Autobuses, 17 Calle Canarias. Trains leave from the Atocha Station in Madrid, depositing you at the rail station in Aranjuez, which lies one kilometer (less than a mile) from the center. If you arrive by train, you'll have to wait for a bus (but the schedules are erratic). It might be best to make the 15-minute walk into town. If you are visiting Aranjuez and want to go to Toledo, you can return to the station at Aranjuez. There are frequent trains heading for Toledo; the ride takes about 40 minutes.

Once at Aranjuez, you can buy a ticket for 400 pesetas ($3.75), entitling you to visit the three most important sights in town, the **Royal Palace** and the adjoining **Jardín de la Isla** (Garden of the Island), and the **Casita del Labrador** in the Jardín del Príncipe. The first sight visited will sell you a comprehensive ticket.

THE ROYAL PALACE

Since the beginning of a united Spain, the climate and natural beauty of Aranjuez have attracted Spanish monarchs, notably Ferdinand and Isabella and Philip II, who managed to tear himself away from El Escorial. But the Palacio Real, lying immediately west of the center, in its present form dates primarily from the days of the Bourbons, who used to come here mainly in the autumn and spring, reserving La Granja, near Segovia, for their summer romps. The palace was also favored by Philip V and Charles III.

Fires have swept over the structure numerous times, but most of the present building was finished in 1778. William Lyon, writing in the Madrid weekly, the *Guidepost,* called its dominant note one of ". . . deception: in almost each of its widely varying rooms there is at least one thing that isn't what it first appears." Mr. Lyon cites assemblages of mosaics that look like oil paintings; a trompe l'oeil ceiling that seems three-dimensional, although it is flat; and a copy of a salon at the Alhambra Palace at Granada.

In spite of these eye-fooling tricks, the palace is lavishly and elegantly decorated. Especially notable are the dancing salon, the throne room, the ceremonial dining hall, the bedrooms of the king and queen, and a remarkable Salón de Porcelana (Porcelain Room). Paintings include works by Lucas Jordán and José Ribera.

Visiting hours in summer are 10:30 a.m. to 2:30 p.m. and 3:30 to 6:30 p.m.; winter hours are 10 a.m. to 1 p.m. and 3 to 6 p.m.; closed on Tuesday year round. Individual admission is 300 pesetas ($2.80), unless you purchased the comprehensive ticket. The beautiful gardens around the palace remain open all day.

JARDÍN DE LA ISLA

The gardens appear somehow forgotten, their mood melancholic. They lie to the east of the Palacio Real, adjoining a royal ornamental garden, called Parterre. From the Parterre, two bridges lead to the "garden of the island." The "Non Plus Ultra" fountain is dazzling, although one observer found the black jasper fountain of Bacchus "orgiastic." Under linden trees, the fountain of Apollo is romantic, and others honor the king of the sea and Cybele, goddess of agriculture. The most delightful stroll is along an avenue of trees, called Salón de los Reyes Católicos, which lies along the river.

CASITA DEL LABRADOR

"The little house of the worker," reached along Calle de la Reina, is a classic example of understatement. Actually, it was modeled after Petit Trianon at Versailles. If you visit the Royal Palace in the morning, you can spend the afternoon here in the northeast part of town. Those with a car can motor to it through the tranquil **Jardín del Príncipe,** with its black poplars.

The little palace was built in 1803 by Charles IV, who later abdicated in Aranjuez. The queen came here with her youthful lover, Godoy (whom she had elevated to the position of prime minister), and the feebleminded Charles didn't seem to mind a bit. Surrounded by beautiful gardens, the "bedless" palace is lavishly furnished in the grand style of the 18th and 19th centuries. The marble floors represent some of the finest workmanship of that day. The brocaded walls emphasize luxurious living—and the royal bathroom is a sight to behold (in those days, royalty preferred an audience). The clock here is one of the treasures of the house. The site is open daily from 10 a.m. to sunset. If you didn't purchase the comprehensive ticket, the separate admission cost is 200 pesetas ($1.90).

---

3. El Escorial

In the Guadarrama mountain resort of El Escorial, about 30 miles northwest of Madrid, stands the imposing **Monastery of San Lorenzo el Real del Escorial,** 1 Calle José Antonio (tel. 890-50-11). Many refer to it as the eighth wonder of the world. Both a palace and a monastery, it was ordered built south of the town by Philip II to commemorate the triumphs of his forces at the Battle of San Quentin in 1557. Escorial was dedicated to St. Lawrence, the martyred saint burned to death. Dozens of tour companies, including American Express, run organized tours to El Escorial. You can also take a do-it-yourself tour by either train or bus. RENFE runs at least two dozen trains a day to El Escorial from either Atocha or Chamartín stations in Madrid, the trip taking half an hour. The train station at El Escorial lies one mile outside the center. Autocares Herranz buses provide shuttle service from the center into town. Buses to El Escorial are also operated by Autocares Herranz, with offices in Madrid at 10 Calle Isaac Peral (tel. 243-36-45). You can pick up a schedule here and purchase a ticket if you'd like to go by bus to El Escorial. The bus will let you off at Plaza Virgen de Gracia, which is only a block to the east of the monastery.

The original architect of El Escorial in 1563 was Juan Bautista de Toledo. After his death the monumental task was assumed by the greatest architect of Renaissance Spain, Juan de Herrera, who completed it in the shape of a gridiron in 1584.

The severe lines of the great pile of granite strike many as being as austere as the pious Philip himself. The architectural critic, Nikolaus Pevsner, called it "overwhelming, moving no doubt, but frightening."

The Palace, Pantheon, Chapter House, and Library, as well as the satellite Casita del Principe and Casita del Infante, may be visited daily Tuesday to Sunday from 9:30 a.m. to 1 p.m. and 3:30 to 6:30 p.m. The admission ticket including the Palace, Pantheon, Chapter House, and Library costs 400 pesetas ($3.75), but for 500 pesetas ($4.70) you are granted admission to all sights.

In the **Charter Hall** is one of the greatest art collections in Spain outside of the Prado, the canvases dating primarily from the 15th to the 17th centuries. Among the most outstanding works are El Greco's *The Martyrdom of St. Maurice,* Titian's *Last Supper,* Velázquez's *The Tunic of Joseph,* Van der Weyden's *Crucifixion,* and another version of Bosch's *The Hay Wagon* (see also a remarkable tapestry based on a painting by "El Bosco" as the Spanish call this artist); there are also works by Ribera, Tintoretto, and Veronese.

The **Biblioteca** contains one of the most important libraries in the world, its estimated number of volumes in excess of 50,000. The collection, started by Philip II, ranges far and wide: Muslim codices; a Gothic "Cántigas" of the 13th century from the reign of Alfonso X (known as "The Wise King"); and signatures from the Carmelite nun, St. Teresa of Jesús, who conjured up visions of the devil and of angels sticking burning hot lances into her heart.

For many sightseers, the highlight of the tour is a visit to the **Apartments of Philip II,** containing many of the original furnishings of the monarch. He died in 1598, in the "cell for my humble self" that he ordered built. He desired quarters that were spartan, and so they remain today—graced by a painting by Bosch, a copy he made of his *The Seven Capital Sins,* now at the Prado.

The **Apartments of the Bourbons** reflect different tastes and style, a complete break from the asceticism imposed by the Habsburg king. They are richly decorated, with a special emphasis on tapestries (many resembling paintings) based on Goya and Bayeu cartoons at the Royal Factory in Madrid.

From a window in his bedroom, a weak and dying Philip II could look down at the services being conducted in the **Basilica.** As the dome clearly indicates, the church was modeled after Michelangelo's drawings of St. Peter's in Rome. Works of art include a crucifix by Benvenuto Cellini, choir stalls by Herrera, and sculpted groups of father and son (Charles V and Philip II), along with their wives, flanking the altar.

The **Royal Pantheon,** burial place of Spanish kings from Charles V to Alfonso XII, is under the altar. (The Bourbon king, Philip V, is interred at La Granja, and the body of Ferdinand VI was placed in a tomb in a Madrid church). In the octagonal mausoleum you'll see the tombs of queens who were mothers of kings.

On the lower level rests one of the curiosities of El Escorial: a "wedding cake" tomb for royal children. The Whispering Hall, with its odd sound effects, is also intriguing.

If time (and interest) remain, you can visit Casita del Príncipe (Prince's Cottage), a small but elaborately decorated 18th-century palace that was a hunting lodge. The so-called cottage was built for Charles III by Juan de Villaneuva. Near the gateway is a cafeteria. *Warning:* It is almost impossible to visit both the monastery and the prince's cottage in the morning—at least before the casita closes for lunch. Most visitors see the monastery in the morning, have lunch somewhere at El Escorial, then save the cottage for an afternoon visit. It is at Calle de la Reina s/n (tel. 891-03-05), lying south of the town, near the train station. Admission is 300 pesetas ($2.80). Hours are from 10 a.m. to 1 p.m. and 3:30 to 6:30 p.m.; closed Tuesday. Separate admission is 100 pesetas (95¢), unless you purchased the comprehensive ticket at the monastery.

4. The Valley of the Fallen

The Spanish call it the *Valle de los Caídos*. Inaugurated five miles from El Escorial by Generalísimo Franco in 1959, it is a heroic-size monument to the Spanish dead of the Civil War, both the Nationalists and the Republicans. "El Caudillo" had wanted to honor only the Nationalist soldiers, but was prevailed upon to change his mind in the interest of the country's unity.

For two decades workers tunneled out an already-existing gorge in the Sierra de Guadarrama, making room for a basilica and a mausoleum. Crowning the Rock of Nava is a gargantuan cross, nearly 500 feet high, stretching its crossbars a distance of 150 feet. You can take a funicular at the foot of the cross. Service is daily from 10:30 a.m. to 1:15 p.m. and 4 to 8:45 p.m., and the cost of the ride is 200 pesetas ($1.90).

Directly below the cross is an underground basilica, decorated with mosaics. The body of José Antonio, the founder of the Falangist party, was finally interred here. His burial at the monastery of El Escorial sparked a wave of protest from the monarchists, who objected to the Spanish leader's "nonroyal" birth. El Caudillo, as Franco was called, is also buried here. To reach the basilica, you must first walk through a series of six chapels. The site is open Tuesday to Sunday from 9:30 a.m. to 7 p.m., charging no admission.

5. Segovia

In Old Castile, Segovia is one of the most romantic of Spanish cities, its glory of another day. Isabella I was proclaimed Queen of Castile here in 1474. Segovians live with the memory of the time when their star was in the ascendancy.

The capital of a province of the same name, it lies on a slope of the snow-capped Sierra de Guadarrama mountains, between two ravine-studded valleys and the Eresma and Clamores Rivers (actually streams). As it appears on the horizon, dominated by its Alcázar and its Gothic cathedral, Segovia is decidedly of the Middle Ages.

The city was of strategic importance to the Roman troops, and one of its greatest monuments, the Aqueduct, dates from those times. The skyline is characterized by the Romanesque belfries of the churches and the towers of its old and decaying palaces.

The Upper Town is mainly encased by its old walls; but the part outside the walls is of interest too, especially for views of the Alcázar.

If you go by automobile, the ride between Madrid and Segovia to the northwest will be 54 miles by one road, 63 miles by another. At Villalba, the road forks and you have a choice of routes. Consider taking the southern one to reach it, returning via the northern route, but budgeting enough time for a stopover at La Granja (see below).

If you're without a car, you can take a morning train leaving from Atocha Station in Madrid. You will be delivered to the train station in Segovia, where you can board a bus to the Plaza Mayor, the heart of the city. At least 11 trains a day connect Madrid with

Segovia. You can also go by bus, the service provided by La Sepúlveda, 11 Paseo de la Florida, in Madrid. Metro: Norte.

THE ALCÁZAR

If you've ever dreamed of castles in the air, then all the fairy-tale romance of childhood will return when you view the Alcázar, Plaza de la Reina Victoria Eugenia (tel. 43-01-76). Many have waxed poetic about it, comparing it to a giant boat sailing through the clouds. See it first from down below, at the junction of the Clamores and Eresma Rivers. It is on the west side of Segovia, and you may not spot it when you first enter the city, but that's part of the surprise.

The castle dates back many hundreds of years—perhaps to the 12th century. But a large segment of it—notably its Moorish ceilings—was destroyed by fire in 1862. Over the years, under an ambitious plan, the Alcázar has been restored.

Inside you'll discover a facsimile of Isabella's dank bedroom. It was at the Alcázar that she first met Ferdinand, preferring him to the more "fatherly" king of Portugal. But she wasn't foolish enough to surrender her "equal rights" after marriage. In the Throne Room, with its replica chairs, you'll note that both seats are equally proportioned. Royal romance continued to flower at the Alcázar. Philip II married his fourth wife, Anne of Austria, here.

After you inspect the polish on some medieval armor inside, you may want to walk the battlements of this once-impregnable castle, whose former occupants poured boiling oil over the ramparts onto their uninvited guests below. Or you can climb the tower, originally built by Isabella's father as a prison, for a supreme view of Segovia. (In particular, note the so-called pregnant-woman mountain.) The fortress is open daily from 10 a.m. to 7 p.m.; it closes at 6 p.m. in winter. Admission is 225 pesetas ($2.10).

THE ROMAN AQUEDUCT

This aqueduct, an architectural marvel, is still used to carry water, even though it was constructed by the Romans almost 2,000 years ago. It is not only the most colossal reminder of Roman glory in Spain, but also one of the best-preserved Roman architectural achievements in the world. It consists of 118 arches, and in one two-tiered section—its highest point—it soars 95 feet. You'll find no mortar in these granite blocks, brought from the Guadarrama mountains. The Spanish call it *El Puente,* and it spans the Plaza del Azoguejo, the old market square, stretching out to a distance of nearly 800 yards. When the Moors took Segovia in 1072, they destroyed 36 arches. However, Ferdinand and Isabella ordered that they be rebuilt in 1484. There are no visiting hours; you can see it anytime night or day. It's an integral landmark of Segovia.

"THE LADY OF THE CATHEDRALS"

This 16th-century structure lays claim to being the last Gothic cathedral built in Spain. Fronting the historic Plaza Mayor, the Cathedral of Segovia on Calle Marqués del Arco stands on the spot where Isabella I was proclaimed Queen of Castile. It's affectionately called *la dama de las catedrales.* Inside, it contains numerous treasures such as the Blessed Sacrament Chapel (created by the flamboyant Churriguera), stained-glass windows, elaborately carved choir stalls, and 16th- and 17th-century paintings, including a *reredos* portraying the deposition of Christ from the cross by Juan de Juni. Older than the cathedral are the cloisters, belonging to a former church destroyed in the "War of the Communeros." The museum of the cathedral contains jewelry, paintings, and a rare collection of antique manuscripts, along with the inevitable vestments. If you want to visit the cloisters, the museum, and the chapel room, the charge is 150 pesetas ($1.40). The cathedral is open daily from 9:30 a.m. to 7 p.m.

6. La Granja

San Ildefonso de la Granja was the summer palace of the Bourbon kings of Spain, who imitated the grandeur of Versailles in Segovia province. Set against the snow-capped Sierra de Guadarrama, the slate-roofed palace dominates the village that grew up around it (nowadays a summer resort).

The founder of La Granja was Philip V, grandson of Louis XIV and the first Bourbon king of Spain (his body, along with that of his second queen, Isabel de Fernesio, is interred in a mauseoleum in the Collegiate Church). Philip V was born at Versailles on December 19, 1683, which partially explains why he wanted to re-create that atmosphere at Segovia.

At one time a farm stood on the grounds of what is now the palace—hence the totally inappropriate name *granja,* meaning farm in Spanish.

The palace was built in the first part of the 18th century. Inside you'll find valuable antiques (many in the Empire style), paintings, and a remarkable collection of tapestries of Flemish design and others based on Goya cartoons from the Royal Factory in Madrid.

Most visitors, however, seem to find a stroll through the gardens more to their liking, so allow adequate time for it. The fountain statuary is a riot of gods and nymphs cavorting with abandon, hiding indiscretions behind jets of water. The gardens are studded with chestnuts and elms.

Charging an admission fee of 300 pesetas ($2.80), the royal palace can be visited Tuesday to Saturday from 10 a.m. to 1:30 p.m. and 3 to 5 p.m.; Sunday 10 a.m. to 2 p.m. A spectacular display comes when the water jets are turned on. The gardens, however, are open daily from 10 a.m. to 8 p.m., charging an admission of 150 pesetas ($1.40) if visited separately from the palace. La Granja lies seven miles from Segovia. You can take a 15-minute bus ride from Segovia. About a dozen buses a day leave from Paseo Conde de Sepúlveda at Avenida Fernández Ladreda in Segovia (tel. 42-77-25).

THE COSTA DEL SOL

The most popular beach strip in Spain—and Europe's most spectacular real-estate boom—begins at the port of Algeciras and stretches eastward all the way to Almería. Against the backdrop of once-pagan Andalusia, the Sun Coast curves gently along the Mediterranean, studded with beaches, sandy coves, lime-washed houses, high-rise apartments, tennis courts, golf courses, swimming pools, and hotels of every type and description.

Sun-seekers from all over Europe and North America are drawn to the mild climate and virtually guaranteed sunshine. You can bathe in the sun year round, but in January and February only Northern Europeans dare the sea. The less hardy splash in sheltered, heated pools. The mean temperature in January, the coldest month of the year, is 56° Fahrenheit. In August, the hottest month, the mean temperature is about 75° Fahrenheit, as prevailing sea breezes mercifully keep the heat down.

Once the Sun Coast was only a spring-to-autumn affair. Now, so many shivering refugees have descended from the cold cities of northern Europe that the strip is alive year round. From June through October, however, "alive" isn't the half of it. All year, bullfights, flamenco, and fiestas crowd its calendar. Holy Week in

Málaga, for example, is among the most stunning celebrations in Spain, rivaling that of Seville. And then there's Málaga's winter festival, packed with cultural and sporting events ranging from horse racing to folk songs and dances. On August fiesta days, Málaga's bullfights are second to none. There are hundreds of good and independent restaurants along the Sun Coast for those desiring to escape from their hotel dining rooms. I'll preview only a sampling of the many, many possibilities.

First, a word about the food specialties of the area. In this part of the Mediterranean, fish (such as whitebait), chopitos, and anchovies are the major part of the banquet. Particular specialties include fish soup *(sopa de pescade)*, a fisherman's rice dish of crayfish and clams *(arroz à la marinera)*, and grilled sardines *(espetones de sardinas)*. In all of Andalusia, soothing gazpacho is a refreshing opener to many a meal. Of course, everything's better when washed down with the renowned wines of Málaga, including Pedor Ximénez and Muscatel.

1. Getting There and Getting Around

FLYING TO MÁLAGA

Several different airlines consider the routes from North America into Spain among their most visible and desirable moneymakers, particularly with the surge in Spanish tourism of the last decade. Unfortunately for visitors to the Costa del Sol, all but a few of these routes end in Madrid, and transfers through Madrid's busy international airport can be uncomfortable and time-consuming.

Of the airlines that fly to Madrid, including **Iberia, TWA,** and **American,** only Iberia offers direct flights from North America to Malaga. These depart as often as five times a week from New York's JFK, usually touching down briefly in Barcelona before continuing on (with no change of aircraft) to the beaches of the Costa del Sol. In addition to its direct service from New York to Malaga, Iberia also has daily nonstop service to Madrid from Chicago, Miami, and Los Angeles, as well as nonstop service to Barcelona from New York several times a week. As the national carrier of Spain, Iberia offers more routes into and within Spain than any other carrier. It also provides its international passengers with a preview of the Spanish experience through travelogue films on Spanish architecture, art, investments, and traditions. In addition to its international flights, Iberia and its subsidiary, **Aviaco,** have many daily flights to Málaga, some of which are designed to correspond to the arrivals of transatlantic flights into Madrid on competing airlines.

Regular and Special Airfares

More information about airlines and airfares to Madrid can be found in the "Flying to Madrid" section of Chapter VIII. The usual round-trip fare from Madrid to Málaga is $226. However, there are two possible money-saving fares. Iberia offers a $135 round-trip "add-on" fare on a *limited* number of their flights. This fare can only be purchased in the U.S., requires a Saturday night stopover in Málaga and use of the return portion of the ticket within 3 months, and has a 50% penalty for a change of dates. An even better deal, however, is available to those traveling on an APEX ticket on either Iberia, TWA, or American who want to travel directly on to Málaga from the U.S. after landing in Madrid. This additional "leg" costs only $54 but, like the APEX fare to which it is connected, it requires a 14-day advance purchase and a 7-day minimum or 60-day maximum stay in Málaga. Transfers of luggage are easier on Iberia, because, of those airlines, only Iberia flies to Málaga; a TWA or American passenger would have to change airlines in Madrid. If you don't plan to stop in Madrid, this $54 fare is far less than you'd pay to take the train or rent a car.

In high season (which stretches roughly between June and September), a ticket from New York to Málaga will cost $846 round-trip, with tax included. If you fly both directions on a Friday, Saturday, or Sunday, it will cost an additional supplement of $50. (At press time, the direct New York to Málaga service wasn't available on Saturday or Sunday, so flights on those days would require a somewhat inconvenient transfer in Madrid.) A similar ticket from Los Angeles to Málaga (via Madrid) will cost $1,134.70, tax included, with a $50 supplement for weekend travel. Passengers have the right to request changes in this ticket once it's issued, at a cost of $100 per change.

If you're prepared to completely forfeit your ticket if you need to make changes of any kind, Iberia will sell you an even more rigid round-trip ticket between New York and Málaga in the height of midsummer for $674, tax included. This ticket requires an instant purchase, a stay abroad of between one and three weeks, and an absolutely unbreakable clause preventing alterations of any kind. If you're sure of your travel plans, it's probably worth the risk in view of the cheaper price. Its availability, however, was stringently limited to only a handful of tickets, which are not available on every flight. It will be to your advantage to be as flexible as possible in your choice of flight dates, since tickets sold out on one day might be available on an alternative date.

Many other ticket options exist, including more expensive fares for business class and gran (first) class. Thanks to increased amenities and roomier seats (which extend backward into something resembling a bed), you can arrive in Málaga well rested.

Iberia also offers, only to passengers who opt to fly transatlantic on one of its aircraft, a **Visit Spain** ticket, which includes in its price the right to stop at 30 different Spanish cities (including Málaga) within a two-month period. The price for a ticket, which includes mainland Spain and the Balearic Islands, is $249. For a similar ticket that includes the faraway Canary Islands, there's an additional $50 surcharge.

For reservations and information, call Iberia toll-free from throughout North America by dialing 800/772-4642.

BY RAIL AND BUS

In addition, Málaga maintains good rail connections with Madrid (at least five trains a day). The trip takes from 8 to 10 hours. Many visitors arrive by train after having explored the Andalusian city of Seville. There are at least three trains a day connecting Seville with Málaga, a four-hour run. It's also possible to go from Madrid to Málaga by bus. Three major coaches make the nine-hour run from Madrid to Málaga daily.

TRAVELING THE COAST

Once at Málaga, you can go by train along the coast as far west as the resort of Fuengirola. There is rail service every 50 minutes between Málaga and Fuengirola. The run to Torremolinos takes only 30 minutes by train. For train information, there is a RENFE office in Málaga at 2 Calle Strachan (tel. 21-31-22). Here you can not only get information but also purchase tickets. Hours are Monday to Friday from 9 a.m. to 1:30 p.m. and 4:30 to 7:30 p.m.

If you're in Málaga and plan to go to Marbella, you'll need to take a bus. The two resorts are connected by bus links, leaving about every 30 minutes in either direction. The ride from Málaga to Marbella takes about 1½ hours. It's also possible to get to Nerja by bus from Málaga in about 1½ hours. The Málaga bus depot lies just behind the RENFE offices, opening onto Po. de los Tilos.

If you're planning to rent a car and drive along the coast, exercise extreme caution. The impossibly overcrowded highway running along the Costa del Sol is considered one of the most dangerous in the world in terms of accidents. One of the major reasons the highway is so dangerous is that many of the drivers (some unfamiliar with driving on the right-hand side) are drunk on Spanish wine. However, if you want to chance it, you may want to arrange your car rental in advance with one of the major companies with toll-free numbers in the United States. For more details about rentals, and the financial advantages of reserving a car in advance, refer to Chapter VIII.

---

2. Málaga

One of the most important seaports on the Mediterranean, Málaga is the major city of the Costa del Sol and the second-largest city of Andalusia. At the foot of Mount Gibralfaro, it is marked by orange trees, flower markets, and fishing boats. The best way to see the city in true 19th-century style is in a horse-drawn carriage. If possible, visit the vegetable and fish markets.

Málaga's winter climate ranks as one of Europe's most idyllic, perhaps sufficient explanation for the luxuriant vegetation in the city's parks and gardens. Truly, **El Parque,** dating from the 19th century and filled with many botanic species, ranks among the most handsome parks in Spain.

Málaga lies 341 miles from Madrid and 135 miles from Sevilla. Its **Tourist Information Office** is at 5 Larios (tel. 21-34-45). The telephone area code for Málaga is 952.

WHAT TO SEE

Málaga is not especially known for its art treasures, even though Pablo Picasso was born here in 1881. The **Fine Arts Muse-**

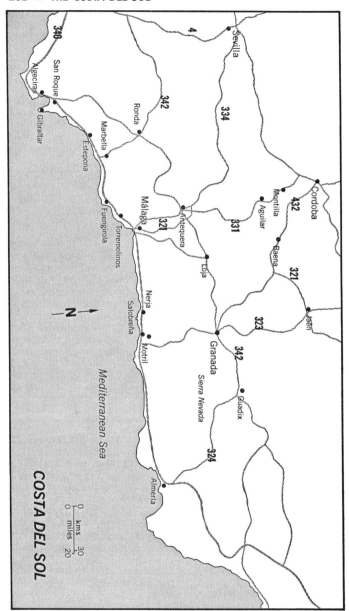

COSTA DEL SOL

Mediterranean Sea

um (Bellas Artes), 6 San Agustín (tel. 21-83-82), owns two of his
works, an oil painting and a watercolor, both done when he was a
teenager. Hours are Monday to Friday from 10:30 a.m. to 1:30 p.m.

and 5 to 8 p.m.; Saturday and Sunday from 10:30 a.m. to 1:30 p.m. Admission is 250 pesetas ($2.35). The location is behind the cathedral.

The city proudly possesses a trio of historical sights, including the **Alcazaba,** the remains of the ancient palace of Málaga's former Moorish rulers. Towers encircle two walled precincts. In ruins, it is considered an outstanding example of Moorish-Spanish architecture. Troops loyal to Isabella and Ferdinand fought a savage battle with the Arabs to take it. When the Catholic monarchs conquered Málaga, they lodged at the castle. Right in the center of town, it offers spectacular views. Wander at your leisure through the open patios, tile-lined pools, and flower gardens. Inside is an **Archeological Museum,** Plaza de la Aduana (tel. 21-60-05), containing artifacts found in prehistoric caves in Málaga province. Other exhibits document cultures ranging from Greek to Phoenician to Carthaginian. Hours are Monday to Saturday from 10 a.m. to 1 p.m. and 5 to 8 p.m.; Sunday from 10 a.m. to 2 p.m. In winter the museum closes at 7 p.m. on weekdays. Admission is 20 pesetas (20¢).

The **cathedral** at Plaza Obsipo of Málaga was begun in 1528. Its 300-foot tower stands as a lone sentinel, without a mate. Although never finished, the cathedral took so long to build that it's a mélange of styles, roughly classified as "Spanish Renaissance." Inside, seek out in particular its ornate choir stalls. It is open Monday to Saturday from 10 a.m. to 1 p.m. and 4 to 7 p.m., charging no admission.

Finally, as the sun is setting, head for **Gibralfaro Castle,** on a hilltop overlooking Málaga and the Mediterranean bay. It too is what's left of an ancient Moorish fortress. Originally, it is believed, the Phoenicians built a fortress on this site, but the present castle is of Arab construction and dates from the 7th century.

At Pizzara, about 25 miles northwest of Málaga near the village of Zalea, the **Museo Hollander** (tel. 48-31-63), operated by New York natives Gino and Barbara Hollander, contains a wealth of material, including tools and weapons from neolithic and paleolithic sites in Spain, historic clothing, and more than 100 pieces of 15th-to 18th-century Spanish furniture. The Hollanders built their own palatial home and museum here, using bricks, tiles, and carved ceiling beams from a 15th-century palace in Córdoba. The 40 massive doors date mostly from 1492. The museum can be visited by appointment only, as the Hollanders take turns guiding visitors through the house and the stables in which a series of small rooms and artisans' shops show what life was like in other days. Admission is free, but a maximum of eight are admitted at any one time.

After sightseeing, head back to town and do some shopping on Calle Larios and its satellite alleys, all containing stores brimming with Spanish handcrafts.

CRIME ALERT

Málaga is the unfortunate winner of a recent survey that declared it to have the highest crime rate in Spain. By far the most common complaint is purse-snatching, with an estimated 75% of the crimes committed by juveniles. The related problem of stolen passports reported to the U.S. consular office in Fuengirola has become a common story in this town where the pickings are rich from a floating population serviced by an understaffed police force.

As a warning to travelers, I stress that all precautions should be taken, including buttoning wallets and valuables into pockets (a money belt is an even better idea). Drive with your doors locked and your windows rolled up (many incidents occur while motorists are waiting at traffic signals with their windows down).

In an era of changing social structures, when you are likely to be perceived as a "have" traveling in an area of "have-nots," it is wise to take special care of your valuables. Don't flaunt your possessions, especially jewelry. With the right precautions taken, you can still have a carefree holiday, and the crime wave sweeping across Málaga need not darken the spirit of your traveling time spent there.

WHERE TO STAY

For such a large city in a resort area, Málaga has a surprising lack of hotels. The best ones in all price ranges are documented below.

The Upper Bracket

The **Málaga Palacio,** 1 Cortina del Muelle, 29015 Málaga (tel. 21-51-85), is the leading three-star hotel in a city that, frankly, lags behind in its innkeeping. The hotel is thrust right in the core of the city, opening directly on a tree-lined esplanade, near the cathedral and harbor. The building, containing 224 rooms, is built flat-iron style, rising 15 stories and crowned by an open-air swimming pool and refreshment bar. Most of the balconies open onto views of the port. Down below you can see graceful turn-of-the-century carriages pulled by horses. Each bedroom is air-conditioned and has TV, minibar, phone, and private bath. In high season, a twin or double rents for 15,000 pesetas ($141) daily, 12,000 pesetas ($112.80) for a single. Breakfast is extra. The bedrooms are traditionally furnished. The street-floor lounges mix antiques with more modern furnishings. Parking is available next to the hotel, and other facilities include hairdressers for both men and women, a cafeteria, boutiques, and a beauty salon.

Medium-Priced Hotels

Hotel Guadalmar, Urbanización Guadalmar, Carretera de Cádiz, km 238/9, 29080 Málaga (tel. 23-17-03), is a nine-story resort hotel five miles from the center of the city with its own private beach, about a mile from the airport. All 196 rooms open onto a swimming pool and garden. Each well-furnished accommodation is spacious, with a private sea-view balcony, air conditioning, minibar, phone, TV, and private bath. One person pays 8,500 pesetas ($79.90) daily; two people, 10,500 pesetas ($98.70). Children under 12, in addition to staying free in the same room with their parents, are provided with such extra advantages as a swimming pool and playground, plus baby-sitters, cribs, and even a special menu. Breakfast costs extra. Take your meals in the dining room, La Bodega, which opens onto the sea and is decorated in a rustic theme. For a live combo to listen and dance to, go straight to La Corrida.

Parador Nacional de Gibralfaro, Monte Gibralfaro, 29016 Málaga (tel. 22-19-02), is a government-owned hotel/restaurant perched high on a hill near the ancient castle, with a view of the sea, the city, the mountains, and beaches. It's an unusual combination of taste, beauty, moderate cost, and comfort. To get the picture, imagine a building of rugged stone with long arched open corridors and bedrooms furnished with hand-loomed fabrics. Each of the 12 bedrooms comes with a private bath, air conditioning, TV, phone, minibar, a sitting area, and a terrace bedecked with garden furniture. The price for all this is 10,500 pesetas ($98.70) for a double, 8,600 pesetas ($80.84) for a single. To reach the parador, take the coast road, Paseo de Reding, which becomes Avenida Casa de Pries and finally Paseo de Sancha. Turn left onto Camino Nuevo and follow the small signs the rest of the way. Do not attempt to walk down to the heart of Málaga, however. It's not safe: Many readers have been mugged. (*Note:* Book well in advance for all paradores.) The location is 1½ miles north of the center.

Parador Nacional del Golf, Torremolinos, 29080 Apartado 324 Málaga (tel. 38-12-55), is another tasteful resort hotel created by the Spanish government. Surrounded by an 18-hole golf course on one side, the Mediterranean on another, it is arranged hacienda style, with several low tile buildings. You're greeted by chirping birds and grounds planted with flowers. Here, too, all 60 bedrooms have a private balcony, with a view of the green, the circular swimming pool, or the water. Each has air conditioning, TV, and minibar. The furnishings are attractive. There are no single rooms, but you can rent doubles and twin-bedded rooms costing 12,000 pesetas ($112.80) to 14,000 pesetas ($131.60), depending on the season. Long tile corridors lead to the public rooms, graciously furnished lounges, and a bar and restaurants. The parador is less than 2 miles from the airport, 6½ miles from Málaga, and 2½ miles from Torremolinos.

Hotel Los Naranjos, Paseo de Sancha, 29016 Málaga (tel. 952-22-43-16), is one of the more reasonably priced (and safer) choices in the city. Serving breakfast only (which costs extra), this is a well-run and maintained hotel lying just outside the heart of town on the eastern side of Málaga past the Plaza de Torres or bullring. It is in the vicinity of the best beach in Málaga, Baños del Carmen. The hotel offers 41 air-conditioned rooms, each in contemporary styling with private bath or shower, TV, and phone. Singles rent for 8,500 pesetas ($79.90) daily, with doubles peaking at 10,500 pesetas ($98.70). The public rooms of the hotel are decorated in the typical Andalusian style, with colorful tiles and ornate wood carving.

Luxury in Loja

An hour's drive northeast of Málaga, **La Bobadilla,** Finca La Bobadilla, 18300 Loja (Granada), Apartado 53 (tel. 958/31-18-61), is the most luxurious retreat in the south of Spain. A secluded oasis, it lies in the foothills of the Sierra Nevada near the town of Loja, which is 44 miles north of Málaga. La Bobadilla is a 13-mile drive from Loja. The hotel complex is built like an Andalusian village, a cluster of whitewashed *casas* constructed around a tower and a white church. Every *casa* in this re-created village is rented to guests, complete with a roof terrace and balcony overlooking the olive-grove-studded district. Each accommodation is individually designed, from the least expensive doubles to the most expensive King's Suite, the latter with plenty of room for bodyguards. The hotel rents only 35 bedrooms to its pampered coterie of international guests.

Room and breakfast cost 22,500 pesetas ($211.50) daily in a single, 32,000 pesetas ($300.80) in a double. With a salon added, the double rate goes up to 34,000 pesetas ($319.60). Suites are even more expensive.

Set on 700 acres of private unspoiled grounds, the hotel village stands on a hillside, red roofed and white painted, blending in with its landscape. Superb craftsmanship is reflected at every turn, from the wrought-iron gates to the Andalusian fountains. The hotel breeds its own domestic animals, and grows much of its own food, including fruit and vegetables. Even the king of Spain has dined at La Finca, which serves both a Spanish national and an international cuisine. El Cortijo, on the other hand, specializes in a regional cuisine.

The hotel service is perhaps the finest in all of Spain. Facilities include two tennis courts, horseback riding, archery, outdoor swimming pool, heated indoor swimming pool, Jacuzzis, Finnish sauna, Turkish steam bath, and fitness club, to name only a few. Concerts, featuring flamenco, are presented on Friday and Saturday nights. If you get bored in this lap of luxury, you can always drive to Granada in only an hour. Should you decide to marry your companion here, you'll find a chapel with an organ 30 feet high with 1,595 pipes.

WHERE TO DINE

Café de Paris, 8 Vélez Málaga (tel. 22-50-43), brings elegance and a refined French cuisine to Málaga. The location is in La Malagueta, the district surrounding the Plaza de Toros or bullring of Málaga. This is the domain of the proprietor and chef de cuisine, José García Cortés, who has worked at many important dining rooms before carving out his own niche. There are some critics who have suggested that the chef's cuisine is pitched too high for the taste of the average *malagueño* patronizing this establishment, at least too high for the pocketbook. By that, reference is made to such costly items as caviar, game (including partridge), or foie gras often featured on the menu.

Much of his cuisine has been adapted from classic French dishes to please the Andalusian palate. Menus are changed frequently, reflecting both the chef's imagination and the availability of produce in the Málaga markets. You might on any given night be served such dishes as crêpes gratinée (filled with baby eels) or local white fish baked in salt (it doesn't sound good but is excellent). Meat Stroganoff is made here not with the usual cuts of beef but with ox meat. Save room for the creative desserts. Try, for example, a citrus-flavored sorbet made with champagne. One pleased diner pronounced the custard apple mousse "divine." Meals cost from 5,000 pesetas ($47). Reservations are needed, and hours are Monday to Saturday from 1:30 to 4 p.m. and 8:30 p.m. to midnight. The restaurant is closed Sunday and from June 21 to July 21.

A waterside restaurant, **Antonio Martín,** 4 Paseo Marítimo (tel. 22-21-13), is favored by known Spanish families, local executives, and the expatriate colony. Antonio, who opened the place in 1886, is gone now, but his children have kept alive his traditions and his name. Three dining rooms are clustered under a peaked wooden ceiling with natural brick walls. The most rustic dining room is Rincón de Ordóñez, in honor of one of Spain's top matadors. On the wall is the head of the last bull Ordóñez killed before his retirement, as well as the suit last worn by him. In summer, the shaded harbor-front terrace is the ideal place to dine. Shellfish soup is the traditional opener, or you might prefer the special hors d'oeuvres. A paella of shellfish, chicken, and meat is the chef's specialty. Other specialties include sirloin steak on a skewer and golden mackerel cooked in a coating of salt. I also recommend the grilled swordfish and the stewed oxtail. Custard with whipped cream is the standard dessert. For a good meal, expect to pay anywhere from 3,000 pesetas ($28.20) to 5,500 pesetas ($51.70). Service is rapid and attentive. It's usually crowded, so reservations are necessary. Hours are Tuesday to Sunday from 1 to 4 p.m. and 8 p.m. to midnight. The location is near the Plaza de Toros.

Parador Nacional del Gibralfaro, Monte Gibralfaro (tel. 22-19-02), is preferred for its view. Government owned, it sits on a mountainside high above the city. You can look down into the heart of the Málaga bullring, among other things. Meals are served in the attractive dining room or under the arches of two wide terraces, providing views of the coast. Featured are hors d'oeuvres parador—your entire table literally covered with tiny dishes of tasty tidbits. Another specialty is an omelet of chanquetes, tiny whitefish popular in this part of the country, or chicken Villaroi. If you stick to the set menu, a complete dinner will cost from 3,000 pesetas ($28.20). Food is served from 1 to 4 p.m. and 8:30 to 11 p.m. daily.

Another government-owned restaurant is the **Parador Nacional del Golf,** Apartado 324, Málaga (tel. 38-12-55). Its indoor/outdoor dining room opens onto a circular swimming pool, golf course, and private beach. The interior dining room, furnished with reproductions of antiques, has a refined country-club atmosphere. Pre-lunch drinks at the sleek modern bar tempt golfers and others, who then proceed to the covered terrace for their Spanish meals, served from 1:30 to 4 p.m. and 8:30 to 11 p.m. daily. Meals cost from 3,500 pesetas ($32.90).

Refectorium, 146 Avenue Juan Sebastián Elcano (tel. 29-45-93), lies outside of town near the Playa de El Palo beachfront, about three miles east of the Plaza de Toros or bullring. It stands on the east side of the bridge spanning Arroyo Jaboneros. Although finding it may involve a bit of a search, the result is worth it. Refectorium is removed from the typical tourist hustle and bustle of the coast. It offers dining with the flair of old Spanish tradition, in an atmosphere of brick-red terra-cotta floors, old wooden beams, and white stucco walls. The cuisine has a certain old-fashioned flair, and the servings are more than generous, so take that into consideration when ordering.

You might begin with a typical soup of the Málaga district, called *ajo blanco con uvas* or cold almond soup flavored with garlic and garnished with big muscatel grapes. A classic opener—also popular in the north of Spain—are garlic-flavored mushrooms seasoned with bits of sweet-tasting ham. The fresh seafood is generally a delight, including *rape* or angler fish. Lamb might be served with a savory saffron-flavored tomato sauce, and you might finish with a homemade dessert, such as rice pudding. Meals cost from 2,500 pesetas ($23.50), and service is Tuesday to Sunday from 1 to 4 p.m. and 8 p.m. to midnight. It's best to call ahead for a table on weekends.

DRINKS AND TAPAS

El Boquerón de Plata, 6 Alarcon Lujan (tel. 22-20-20), has long been one of the most frequented bars of Málaga. You go there for good Spanish wine and tapas. If you're a local, the latest gossip will be the order of the day. Most guests have a beer and a helping of the prawns. The fish depends on the catch of the day—it's invariably fresh. A plate of the day ranges from 350 pesetas ($3.30). A beer costs 100 pesetas (95¢). Hours are 10 a.m. to 3 p.m. and 6 to 10 p.m. daily. *Warning:* There are two other places in the region using the same name.

La Tasca, 12 Calle de Marín García (tel. 22-20-82), is *not* the place to go if you're looking for a quiet and mellow tasca where no one ever raises his or her voice. The most famous bar in Málaga, this is really a hole in the wall, but it has style, conviviality, and a large staff crowded behind the bar to serve the sometimes strident demands of practically everyone in Málaga, many of whom bring their children with them. You can have a choice of beer from the tap, wine, and an array of tapas. Try the croquettes (*croquetas*) and pungent shish kebabs laced with garlic and cumin. If you see an empty seat, try to commandeer it politely. Otherwise you'll stand in what might be awestruck observation of the social scene around you. Hours are noon to 1:30 p.m. and 7 to 10:30 p.m. daily. The bar lies between Calle Larios and Calle Nueva.

Bar Loqüeno, 12 Calle de Marín García (tel. 22-30-48), offers basically the same tapas as its neighbor, La Tasca. The entrance is behind a wrought-iron and glass door that leads into a stucco-lined room decorated in a "local tavern style" with a vengeance. There are enough hams, bouquets of garlic, beer kegs, fish nets, and sausages to feed an entire village for a week. There's hardly enough room to stand, and you'll invariably be jostled by a busy waiter shouting "calamari" to the cooks in the back kitchens. A glass of wine costs 125 pesetas ($1.20). It is open daily from noon to 4 p.m. and 7 p.m. to midnight.

3. Nerja

In 1959 five young men put Nerja on the map. At a point some 32 miles east of Málaga, near the hamlet of Maro, they discovered one of the great **prehistoric caves** of Europe. Nicknamed "the buried cathedral," the cave, about 350 yards long, is a series of intertwining galleries and passageways, reaching its highest point—about 200 feet—in what is called the Cataclysm Hall.

Paleolithic paintings of goats, deer, and horses were discovered here, as was a skeleton of a Cro-Magnon man. Rich in stalagmites and stalactites, the caves are open from 10 a.m. to 1:30 p.m. and 4 to 7 p.m. daily in winter. Summer hours are daily from 9:30 a.m. to 9 p.m. Admission is 150 pesetas ($1.40). In August, music festivals are presented in the Hall of the Cascade, its floors the bottom of an ancient lake. Buses run from the center of Nerja to the caves every hour, costing 50 pesetas (45¢). The caves lie three miles from the resort of Nerja.

Before the discovery of the caves, the sleepy village of Nerja was known for its fabulous belvedere, the **Balcony of Europe,** commanding one of the most spectacular positions along the Costa del Sol. Nerja, perched on a cliff on the slopes of the Sierra Almijara, is a town of narrow streets and whitewashed houses. Below the town are plenty of hidden coves for swimming. Nerja lies 33 miles east of Málaga and 341 miles from Madrid. Its **Tourist Information Office** is at 4 Puerta del Mar (tel. 52-15-31). Nerja's telephone area code is 952.

WHERE TO STAY

Medium-Priced Hotels

On the outskirts of town, **Parador Nacional de Nerja,** Playa de Burriana, 29780 Nerja (tel. 52-00-50), takes the best of modern motel designs and blends them with a classic Spanish ambience of beamed ceilings, tile floors, and hand-loomed draperies. It's built around a flower-filled courtyard with a splashing fountain. On the edge of a cliff, this government-owned hotel stands in a setting of lawns and gardens, its social life centering around a large swimming pool. There is, as well, a sandy beach below, reached by an elevator. The 73 air-conditioned bedrooms are spacious and furnished in an understated but tasteful style. Each has a private bath, TV, minibar, and phone. Maximum rates are charged from March 1 to October 31 and at the end of December. Singles rent for 9,500 pesetas ($89.30) daily, with doubles costing 12,000 pesetas ($112.80). However, for one of the doubles with a Jacuzzi, the charge is 13,500 pesetas ($126.90). Breakfast costs extra.

Hotel Monica, Playa de la Torrecilla, 29780 Nerja (tel. 52-11-00), looks something like a three-pronged propeller if you view it from the air. At ground level as you approach the entrance, you see that it has North African arches and green-and-white panels. This is the newest and the most luxurious hotel in Nerja. You'll find this four-star establishment in an isolated position about a 10-minute walk from the Balcony of Europe, on a low-lying curve of beachfront. The glistening white marble in its imaginative lobby is highlighted with such neo-baroque touches as elaborately detailed cast-iron balustrades, curved marble staircases, and bas-reliefs, paintings, and sculptures. Some of the stairwells even contain over-size copies, set in tiles, of the beach scenes of Claude Monet. A nautical theme is carried out in the bar with brass navigational instruments, models of clipper ships, and comfortable sofas. Both of the hotel's restaurants have outdoor terraces or patios for indoor/outdoor dining. A curved swimming pool was built into a terrace a few feet above the beach.

The 234 comfortable bedrooms offer private balconies and numerous other amenities such as air conditioning, TV, and phone. Doubles rent for 12,500 pesetas ($117.50) daily, and singles go for 9,500 pesetas ($89.30). Breakfast is extra.

The Budget Range

Comfortable accommodations at **Hostal Fontainebleau,** 5 Calle Alejandro Bueno, 29780 Nerja (tel. 52-09-39), are provided by four young people from England, Kerry and Neil Anderson, Angela Harrington, and Simon Sanderson. All in their 20s, they operate this hotel with a family atmosphere. Each of the 22 pleasantly furnished rooms has private bathroom, wall-to-wall carpeting, air conditioning, local and Gibraltar radio, tea- and coffee-making facilities, and telephone.

Singles cost 3,500 pesetas ($32.90) daily, doubles or twins 5,000 pesetas ($47); some rooms suitable for three people are available at 5,500 pesetas ($51.70). All rooms open onto a fountain patio. For an extra charge you can order a traditional cooked breakfast in the restaurant or have a Continental breakfast on the patio, weather permitting. The hotel has laundry, drying, and ironing facilities and a foreign exchange desk open seven days a week. You can also watch satellite TV in the air-conditioned cozy residents' lounge.

You can order drinks on the rooftop terrace from May to October and in the Fountain Bar, which resembles a British pub and offers pub food and snacks. From the pub you enter the three restaurant areas featuring a barbecue and all British home-style cooking. A three-course table d'hôte daily menu costs 1,500 pesetas ($14.10), including bread and wine. The Hostal is about a 10-minute walk from the main beach, Playa Burriana, and a 5-minute walk from the center of town. The hotel is open year round.

WHERE TO DINE

Established in 1966, **Pepe Rico Restaurant,** 28 Almirante Ferrándiz (tel. 52-02-47), is today one of the finest places for food in Nerja. It's run by Robert and Kathy Holder, who also rent apartments. It is a white building right on the street, with grill windows and little balconies. The rooms open onto a large rear balcony, overlooking a flower-filled courtyard. Dining is in a tavern room, half wood paneled, with handmade wooden chairs, plaster walls, and ivy vines. These vines creep in from the patio, where you can also order meals al fresco. Only dinner is served, and it's offered daily, except Tuesday, from 7:30 to 10 p.m. The restaurant is closed from the end of October until the middle of December.

Holder himself does the cooking with the help of one chef. The menu is international and offers a separate specialty of the day, which might be a Spanish, German, Swiss, or French dish. These range from the Holders' own cold almond-and-garlic soup to Andalusian gazpacho, available only in the summertime. The list of hors d'oeuvres is impressive—including Pepe Rico salad, smoked swordfish, and prawns pil-pil (with hot chili peppers). Main dishes include filet of sole Don Pepe, rosada Oriental style, prawns Café de Paris, and Robert's steak dishes. Considering the quality of the food, the prices are reasonable, from 3,000 pesetas ($28.20) for a full meal.

Portofino, 4 Puerta del Mar (tel. 52-01-50), may offer just the ambience you're looking for, particularly if you crave well-prepared food, a sweeping view of the sea, and a tasteful but whimsical decor stressing strong sunlight and different shades of pink and white. The open hearth greets you near the front entrance. Dinner, served daily from 7 to 10:30 p.m., can be eaten either behind the shelter of large sheets of glass or on the open terrace at the edge of the bay. Specialties include salade de chevre chaud (a salad garnished with goat cheese and baked in an apple); red mullet with tomatoes, black olives, and anchovies; entrecôtes; pork simmered in mustard sauce; filet of sole à l'Orientale; and calves' kidneys sautéed in Madeira; plus such tempting desserts as tarte Tatin (apple crumble enriched with butter and caramel) and gratin de fruits in a sweet sauce. A *menú del día* costs 1,600 pesetas ($15.05), while à la carte meals usually cost upward of 3,000 pesetas ($28.20). The Portofino is open only from March to November.

Restaurant Rey Alfonso, Paseo Balcón de Europa (tel. 52-01-95), boasts a panoramic dining room, found at the bottom of a flight of stairs skirting some of the most dramatic rock formations along the coast. It is one of the most popular restaurants in Nerja. The menu doesn't hold many surprises, but the view, ambience, and clientele make it worthwhile.

The establishment welcomes customers into the bar area if they don't want a full meal. If they do, menu specialties include paella valenciana, Cuban-style rice, five different preparations of sole (including everything from grilled to meunière), several versions of tournedos and entrecôte, beef Stroganoff, fondue bourguignonne, crayfish in whisky sauce, and for dessert, crêpes Suzette. Meals here begin at around 3,000 pesetas ($28.20). The establishment is open from 1 to 4 p.m. and 8 to 11 p.m. daily except Wednesday.

Casa Luque, 2 Plaza de los Martíres (tel. 52-10-04), looks more like a dignified private villa than a restaurant, especially since its impressive canopied and balconied façade opens onto a sycamore-lined village square a few steps from the Balcón de Europa. The interior has an Andalusian courtyard that may make you want to linger over your meal, which might include pâté maison, shoulder of ham, ossobuco, pork filet, hot pepper chicken Casanova, a full array of grilled meats, and a limited selection of fish, including grilled Mediterranean grouper. Full meals, served Tuesday to Sunday from 1 to 4 p.m. and 7 p.m. to midnight, begin at 2,700 pesetas ($25.40) and will be supervised by the watchful eye of the owner. The restaurant is closed January 15 to February 15.

Restaurant de Miguel, 2 Calle Pintada (tel. 522-996), was established several years ago by the son of a Nerja resident. At first, it was patronized only by local families hoping for their friend to succeed. Since then, however, mostly because of the excellent food, the place has attracted a devoted coterie of foreign visitors and expatriate residents of the Costa del Sol. It sits in the center of town near the busiest traffic intersection, behind a plate-glass aquarium loaded with fresh lobsters, fish, and shellfish. Its not-very-large air-conditioned interior is one of the most decidedly upscale places in Nerja, with white marble floors, elegant crystal and porcelain, and crisply ironed white napery. Full meals cost from 3,500 pesetas ($32.90) and include a full array of international dishes. Examples include cream of shrimp soup flavored with cognac, tournedos with a sauce made from goat's cheese, sea bass with Pernod and fennel, a wide selection of beef and steak dishes, and imaginative concoctions composed from the cornucopia of fish from the aquarium. The restaurant is open every day except Wednesday from 1 to 3 p.m. and 7 to 11 p.m.

---

4. Torremolinos

On a rocky promontory in the heart of the Costa del Sol, this resort dominates a magnificent bay at the foot of the Sierra Mijas. This international tourist center achieved prominence because of its five-mile-long beach, one of the finest along the Mediterranean, although its level of pollution has long been under press attack.

If you get up at daybreak and go to the beach, you'll see the fishermen bringing in their nets. But by 10 a.m. the sun worshippers have taken over. Many stay on the beach all day, depending on vendors who come around selling snacks and drinks. The once-sleepy fishing village pulsates with life in its high-rise apartments, hotels of every hue, discos, flamenco clubs, wine *bodegas,* boutiques, restaurants, and numerous bars—some with such unlikely names as "Fat Black Pussycat."

The original village runs along **Calle de San Miguel,** still distinctively Andalusian despite its boutiques and restaurants. Reached past a zigzag of buildings leading down to the beach, **La Carihuela** was the old fishermen's village—it still is, if you ignore the hotels and apartments. Opposite is **Montemar,** a smart residential quarter of villas and gardens. For a slice of old Andalusia, see the **El Calvario** area, with its whitewashed houses, donkeys, and street vendors.

In the evening the sidewalk café life flourishes. You can spend an entire evening along the traffic-free **Calle del Cauce,** with its open-air restaurants and bars (sample before-dinner *tapas,* Spanish hors d'oeuvres, here).

If you want to do some shopping, you won't be disappointed: the best stores of Barcelona and Madrid operate branches in Torremolinos.

Torremolinos lies 9 miles from Málaga and 76 miles from Algeciras. Its **Tourist Information Office** is at 517 La Nogalera (tel. 38-15-78). The **telephone area code** for Torremolinos is 952.

WHERE TO STAY

At first, everything in town looks like a hotel, a restaurant, a bar, or a souvenir shop—and that's about it. Actually, considering its number of visitors, Torremolinos doesn't have as many hotels as you'd expect. That's because many European visitors rent apartments on short-term leases during their vacation stays. Hotels are clustered not only in Torremolinos but in nearby Benalmádena Costa (see below). Many of the hotels in Torremolinos are filled with package-tour groups. The quality of accommodations is wide ranging, everything from upper-bracket choices (but nothing to equal the luxury of some of the Marbella hostelries) to cheap *hostals* (some of the latter seem popular with revelers who like to party until dawn on cheap wine). The best advice if you're planning to make Torremolinos your center in the Costa del Sol is to pick and choose carefully among the hotels, looking for one compatible with your interests and, most definitely, your pocketbook.

The Upper Bracket

Considered the best hotel in town, **Castillo de Santa Clara,** 1 Calle Suecia, 29620 Torremolinos (tel. 38-31-55), is an angular modern palace built in 1975 above the cliffs that separate Torremolinos from its satellite village of La Carihuela. It was designed so that about half of the 284 accommodations lie below the terraced gardens. Into these gardens were sunk a pair of curvaceous swimming pools, whose waters are shaded with exotic cacti, palms, and well-maintained flower beds.

The public rooms are sheathed almost entirely in russet-colored marble, the expanses of which are relieved with sculpted terra-cotta bas-reliefs, scattered copies of Chippendale antiques, and nautical accessories. On the premises are a sauna, gymnasium, nightclub, tennis court, and elevator that takes you down the cliffs to the beach.

Each bedroom is air-conditioned and has a private bath and a wood-trimmed balcony along with TV and phone. Single rooms rent for 14,200 pesetas ($133.50) daily; doubles, 16,000 pesetas ($150.40).

Meliá Costa del Sol, Paseo Marítimo, 29620 Torremolinos (tel. 38-66-77), is operated by a popular hotel chain in Spain. There are two Meliá hotels in Torremolinos, but this one is preferred by many clients because of its more central location. It is practically twice the size of the smaller hotel, offering a total of 540 modern and well-maintained bedrooms. Each of these is air-conditioned with TV and phone. Singles begin at 7,200 pesetas ($67.70); doubles, 10,500 pesetas ($98.70). However, the hotel is popular with package-tour groups, and you may not feel a part of things if you're here as an individual. Facilities include a garden, swimming pool, disco, shopping arcade, and hairdressing salon.

Meliá Torremolinos, 109 Avenida Carlotta Alessandri, 29620 Torremolinos (tel. 38-05-00), is the more luxurious of the two Meliá hotels, with better service too. This five-star hotel has its own garden, swimming pool, and tennis courts. Its rooms, 281 in all, each have a private bath or shower, phone, and TV, and are well furnished and maintained. Singles cost 8,500 pesetas ($79.90) daily, doubles 13,500 pesetas ($126.90). The hotel also has a good restaurant, serving meals for 3,000 pesetas ($28.15). Visitors are received from April to October only. The hotel stands on the western outskirts of Torremolinos on the road to Cádiz.

Don Pablo, Paseo Marítimo, 29620 Torremolinos (tel. 38-38-88), is one of the most desirable hotels in Torremolinos. It's a modern building, a minute from the beach, surrounded by its own garden and playground areas. There are two unusually shaped open-air swimming pools, with terraces for sunbathing and refreshments, and a large indoor pool as well. The surprise is the glamorous interior, which borrows heavily from Moorish palaces and medieval castle themes. Arched tile arcades have splashing fountains, and life-size stone statues of nude figures in niches line the grand staircase. At lunch a help-yourself buffet is spread before you.

The 443 bedrooms have air conditioning, phones, hi-fi channels, minibar, and sea-view terraces; a TV costs extra. Singles rent for 8,100 pesetas ($76.14) daily and doubles for 11,700 pesetas ($110), plus tax. A Continental breakfast is included in the price. Facilities include a tennis center with seven courts, floodlights, and top coaching. The hotel has a full day-and-night entertainment program, including keep-fit classes, dancing at night to a live band, and a disco. Piano music is also played in a wood-paneled English lounge, and the hotel has video movies shown on a giant screen every night.

Hotel Cervantes, Calle de las Mercedes s/n, 29620 Torremolinos (tel. 38-40-33), is a four-star hotel a seven-minute walk from the beach. It has its own garden and is adjacent to a maze of patios and narrow streets of boutiques and open-air cafés. The Cervantes is self-contained, with many facilities, including a sun terrace, sauna, massage, two pools (one covered and heated), hairdressers, gift shop, TV and video lounge, games such as billiards, table tennis, and darts, and a card room. A restaurant, a bar with an orchestra and entertainment programs, and a coffee shop are among the attractions. The hotel is fully air-conditioned. The 397 bedrooms have streamlined modern furniture, many with sea-view balconies. All the units have baths, phones, music, safes, TVs (on request), and spacious terraces. Singles rent for 9,200 pesetas ($86.50), doubles for 14,000 pesetas ($131.60). You can enjoy lunch or dinner at the hotel for 2,200 pesetas ($20.70) and up. Los Molinos Grill on the top floor offers excellent grill meals.

Aloha Puerto Sol, 45 Via Imperial, 29620 Torremolinos (tel. 38-70-66), stands on the seashore in the residential area of El Saltillo. Away from the noise in the center of Torremolinos, it offers 380 spacious rooms facing the sea and beach, protected by the Benalmádena Marina. One of the most modern hotels along the Costa del Sol, it offers rooms with air conditioning, TV, minibar, and phone. In addition, each accommodation has a sitting room. Two people are charged 12,000 pesetas ($112.80) daily. Singles rent for 8,200 pesetas ($77.10). In this resort setting, guests are given a choice of two restaurants and four bars. During the day you can lounge around two swimming pools, one heated. Spanish evenings at El Comodoro, one of the bars on the premises, last well into the early morning.

The Middle Bracket

Hotel Edén, Las Mercedes, 29620 Torremolinos (tel. 38-46-00), below the new town, is built on many levels on a cliff (the entrance is on the eighth floor). Two elevators take you down to the bedrooms—a "descent into the catacombs," as one reader put it. The 96 bedrooms have private terraces overlooking rooftops and climaxed by a vista of the Mediterranean. In a double with a complete private bath facing the beach, you pay 7,500 pesetas ($70.50) daily, with taxes and service included. In a single with bath, the rate is 6,500 pesetas ($61.10). The rooms are utilitarian and comfortable. Each has a private phone but no air conditioning. On the lower level is a swimming pool and an adjoining terrace. An open veranda restaurant overlooks the sea.

Sidi Lago Rojo, 1 Miami, 29620 Torremolinos (tel. 38-76-66), stands in the heart of the still-preserved fishing village of La Carihuela, only 150 feet from the beach with its waterside fish restaurants and bars. The hotel, the finest place to stay in the fishing village, has its own surrounding gardens and swimming pool, along with terraces for sunbathing and a refreshment bar. The modern hotel offers 144 studio-style rooms, tastefully appointed with contemporary Spanish furnishings, tile baths, and terraces with views. Other facilities include radios, phones, and air conditioning. Some rooms have minibar, and TV is optional. All rooms are doubles, costing 6,800 pesetas ($63.90) to 9,500 pesetas ($89.30). The bar is a popular gathering point, with a sophisticated decor. In the late evening there is disco dancing. The hotel also has a good restaurant.

Budget Hotels

Near the coastal road, **Las Palomas,** 1 Carmen Montes, 29620 Torremolinos (tel. 38-50-00), is one of the most attractive of the resort hotels built on the Málaga edge of Torremolinos. It has a formal entrance opening into spacious lounges. Tile corridors lead to dining rooms and cocktail lounges.

The 303 bedrooms each have balcony and private bath and phone. Rooms are not air-conditioned. You pay 5,800 pesetas ($54.50) daily in a single room, 8,500 pesetas ($79.90) in a double. Breakfast is extra. Lunch or dinner costs an extra 2,200 pesetas ($20.70). The hotel has dancing every night to records, a tennis court, two pools (one heated), plus a sauna. It lies 200 yards from the beach.

Miami, 14 Calle Aladino, 29620 Torremolinos (tel. 38-52-55), near the Carihuela section, is like one of those houses movie stars used to erect in Hollywood in the 1920s. It may even bring back memories of Vilma Banky and Rod La Rocque. Its swimming pool is isolated by high walls and private gardens. In the rear patio fuchsia bougainvillea climbs over arches. A tile terrace is used for sunbathing and refreshments. The country-style living room contains a walk-in fireplace, plus lots of brass and copper. The double rate is 5,000 pesetas ($47) daily, 3,200 pesetas ($30.10) for a single, including tax. The 27 bedrooms are furnished with style, each traditional and comfortable. Every accommodation has its own balcony, phone, and private bath. Breakfast, the only meal served, costs extra.

Amaragua, Los Nidos 23, 29620 Torremolinos (tel. 38-47-00), is right on the beach in the middle of the residential area of Torremolinos-Montemar, with a total of 198 rooms (12 of which are suites), all with complete bath, terrace, and sea view. The hotel has lounges, television, a bar, three large swimming pools (one heated), gardens, water sports, a children's playground, a sauna, parking facilities, and a tennis court. In a double with private bath, the rate is 7,000 pesetas ($65.80) daily, 5,000 pesetas ($47) in a single with shower bath. Rooms have no air conditioning, but do contain private phones. Breakfast costs extra.

WHERE TO DINE

Right in the heart of Torremolinos, **El Caballo Vasco,** Calle Casablanca, La Nogalera (tel. 38-23-36), is the best place to dine among the independent restaurants. It serves the deservedly popular Basque cuisine from the top floor of a modern building complex that is reached by an elevator. Picture windows lead to a terrace. As a prelude to your repast, you might try melon with ham or fish soup. Generous portions of tasty, well-prepared seafood are served, including prawns in garlic sauce and codfish Basque style. The meat dishes are of uniformly good quality, and you get some imaginative interpretations not usually found on menus along the Costa del Sol —pork shanks Basque style and oxtail in a savory sauce. For timid diners, one of the safest bets is chicken in sherry sauce. It's also one of the least expensive main courses. A complete meal, served Tuesday to Sunday from 1 to 4 p.m. and 8 p.m. to midnight, will cost from 2,500 pesetas ($23.50) to 3,500 pesetas ($32.90). Reservations aren't usually needed.

Frutos, Carretera de Cádiz, km. 235, Urbanización Los Alamos (tel. 38-14-50), stands next to the Los Alamos service station about a mile and a quarter from the center of Torremolinos. Malagueños frequent the place in droves, as they like its old-style cooking. Here the cooking is Spanish with a vengeance; nothing is made fancy for the occasional tourist who might wander in. The portions are large, and the food good—if you don't mind a bit of a wait on crowded days. Service can be hectic at times, but chances are you'll be pleased.

Many diners like to begin with ham and melon, followed by fresh seafood, likely to be something from the day's catch. Perhaps *rape* (angler fish) will be served, or else *mero* (grouper), which rarely appears fresh on any menu along the coast. Maybe you'll be in for a garlic-studded leg of lamb or oxtail prepared with a savory ragoût. It's wise to reserve a table and hope that it will be available upon your arrival. Hours are normally 1 to 4:30 p.m. and 8 p.m. to midnight daily, except in July through September, when the restaurant is closed on Sunday night. A set menu is offered for 1,400 pesetas ($13.15), but most diners order à la carte, with meals costing from 1,800 pesetas ($16.90) to 3,000 pesetas ($28.20).

Mesón Cantarranas, Avenida de Benalmádena s/n (tel. 38-15-77), is reached by heading out the road to Arroyo de la Miel and Benalmádena to the western end of the Torremolinos bypass. The restaurant, housed in a former olive mill dating from 1840, is set back from the Arroyo de la Mile-El Pinillo highway. Here you feel you're dining in a country inn. Perhaps you'll arrange for a table on the terrace in the rear, overlooking the olive grove. At this restaurant "of the singing frogs," you can, naturally, order frogs' legs, but you might prefer a hefty portion of roast suckling pig or roast baby lamb. Daily specials are featured, and they are often from the sea, including bream. Squid is cooked in its own ink, and the hake prepared Cantabrian style is invariably good. For dessert, the poached pears in red wine are always tempting, but there are many other selections as well. Hours are daily from noon to 4 p.m. and 8 p.m. to midnight, and reservations are a good idea. Meals cost from 2,500 pesetas ($23.50).

Seafood at La Carihuela

Casa Prudencio, 41 Carmen (tel. 38-14-52), is the leading seafood restaurant on the beach at Carihuela. It packs in diners like sardines, but its devotees don't seem to mind the wait. The decor is rustic, with indoor dining service. However, in summer the favored place is a reed canopy-covered open-air terrace where you dine elbow to elbow. The owner orchestrates and choreographs the waiters to a fast and nervous pace. Service is haphazard, but friendly. For an appetizer, a soothing gazpacho is ideal. Most diners are fascinated by the specialty of the house, lubina à la sal (salted fish). Cooked in an oblong pan, the fish is completely covered with white salt, which is then scraped away in front of the diner anxious to get to the well-flavored, tender white flesh inside. Other main-course dishes are swordfish, shish kebab, and a special paella. For dessert, try the fresh strawberries. A typical à la carte meal is likely to cost from 2,500 pesetas ($23.50), while a special budget menu goes for only 1,200 pesetas ($11.30). The restaurant is open Tuesday to Sunday from 1 to 5 p.m. and 7:30 p.m. to midnight. Call to reserve a table.

El Roqueo, 35 Carmen (tel. 38-49-46), is one of the best restaurants in this fishermen's village. Right near the beach, it is the perfect place for a seafood dinner. Spanish families often fill up some of the tables, gorging themselves on an array of fresh fish. Spaniards often order the bottled wine, whereas many tourists prefer a pitcher of sangría. Diners may begin with a savory *sopa de mariscos,* or fish soup. Some of the more expensive dishes are priced by the gram and can be expensive, so order carefully. A special is fish baked in rock salt. Grilled seabass is a favorite, as are grilled shrimp. For dessert, why not that Spanish standard, a carmelized flan (custard)? Meals cost from 2,200 pesetas ($20.70) to 3,000 pesetas ($28.20), and it's best to call for a table. Service is daily except Tuesday (also closed in November) from 1 to 4 p.m. and 7 p.m. to midnight.

Foreign Food

Vietnam Sur, Playamar, 9 Bloque (tel. 38-67-37), will wake up your taste buds after you've had a lazy day on the beach. The food here is best shared, so you should arrive with as many friends as possible. Chopsticks are the norm as you begin with spring rolls served with mint and a spicy sauce for dipping. The food is inexpensive, and the Vietnamese use a lot of vegetables in their food. Two chef's specials are fried stuffed chicken wings and beef with rice noodles. The wine list is short and moderately priced. Service is Monday, Tuesday, and Thursday to Saturday from 7 p.m. to midnight; Sunday 1 to 4 p.m. and 7 p.m. to midnight; closed Wednesday. Meals cost from 1,500 pesetas ($14.10). The restaurant, which has a terrace for dining, is closed in January and February.

Marrakech, Carretera de Benalmádena 7 (tel. 38-21-69), offers an excellent Moroccan cuisine in the midst of a rather garish decor. Some of the more famous dishes of the Maghreb are served here, including couscous, tagine (meat pies), and various kebabs, usually made with lamb. The stuffed pastries make a fitting dessert if you like them on the sweet side. Service is Monday and Wednesday to Saturday from 12:30 to 4:30 p.m. and 7:30 p.m. to midnight. Reservations are a good idea. Meals cost from 1,800 pesetas ($16.90) and up.

NIGHTLIFE

Torremolinos has more nightlife activity than any other spot along the Costa del Sol. The earliest action is always at the bars, which are lively most of the night, serving drinks and *tapas* (Spanish hors d'oeuvres). Sometimes it seems there are more bars in Torremolinos than people, so you shouldn't have trouble finding one you like. *NOTE:* Some of the bars are open during the day as well.

Bars and Tapas

Bar El Toro, 32 San Miguel (tel. 38-65-04), is for bullfight aficionados. Kegs of beer, stools, and the terrace in the main shopping street make it perfect for drinking a before-dinner sherry or an after-dinner beer. As a special attraction, the staff prepares a bullfight poster, with your name between those of two famous matadors, for 500 pesetas ($4.70). Drinks at your table begin at 150 pesetas ($1.40) for beer or 380 pesetas ($3.55) for a pitcher of sangría. In the very center of Torremolinos, the bar is open daily from 8 a.m. to midnight.

Bar Central, Plaza Andalucia, Bloque 1 (tel. 38-27-60), offers coffee, brandy, beer, cocktails, limited sandwiches, and pastries, served on a large, French-style covered terrace if you prefer. Open Monday to Saturday from 8 a.m. to midnight, it's a good spot to meet congenial people. Drinks cost from 70 pesetas (65¢) for a beer or 300 pesetas ($2.80) for a hard drink.

La Bodega, 38 Calle San Miguel (tel. 38-73-37), relies on its colorful clientele and the quality of its tapas to draw customers, who seem to seek this place out above the dozens of other tascas within this very popular tourist zone. You'll be fortunate to find space at one of the small tables, since many clients consider the bar food plentiful enough for a satisfying lunch or dinner. Once you begin to order one of the platters of fried squid, pungent tuna, grilled shrimp, or tiny brochettes of sole, you might not be able to stop. Most tapas cost 150 pesetas ($1.40) to 600 pesetas ($5.65). Bar and tapas service is from noon to midnight seven days a week.

Discos

Piper's Club, Plaza Costa del Sol (tel. 38-29-94), is the leading disco in town, and it's decorated tongue-in-cheek. It resembles a subterranean world, suggesting the caves at Nerja. Spread over many levels, with connecting ramps and tunnels, it has several dance floors, splashing water in reflecting pools, strobe lightning, and an aggressive set of international records to amuse its packed audience. It's very much the 1960s in aura and ambience. The club is open from 6 to 10:30 p.m. daily, when admission is 500 pesetas ($4.70). It reopens at 11 p.m.—charging 1,000 pesetas ($9.40) Sunday to Thursday, 1,200 pesetas ($11.30) on Friday and Saturday—and closes at 4:30 a.m. Your first drink is included in the price. After that, a beer costs 250 pesetas ($2.35).

Gatsby, 68 Avenida Montemar (tel. 38-53-72), stands on a major traffic-choked boulevard and, wisely, has its own private parking. Taking its theme from Fitzgerald's 1920s, Gatsby has a loud, distortion-free sound system. The illumination employs strobes and spots, as you dance to the disc selections. Entrance for the daily "matinee," from 6 to 10:30 p.m., is 500 pesetas ($4.70). From 11:30 p.m. to 4:30 a.m. the price is 1,000 pesetas ($9.40). One drink is included in the price of admission.

Piano Bars

Intermezzo Piano Club, 2 Plaza del Remo (tel. 38-32-67), is by far the most sophisticated bar in Carihuela, the little fishing village at the foot of Torremolinos. The sea is visible from the front door, and the interior opens generously into a large, almost square room whose focus is a shiny black piano. Its curves are repeated in the upholstered bar area, which is skillfully lit with a series of dramatically placed spotlights. The decor might be called a combination of Victorian and ultramodern. There's a small dance floor for those who want to follow the live music, which is presented from 10 p.m. to 3 a.m. every day of the week. Drinks range upward from 400 pesetas ($3.75).

The Gay Life

Torremolinos has the largest cluster of gay life, including bars and restaurants, of any resort along the coast of southern Spain. Gay men (and to a lesser degree, women) flock to Torremolinos, especially from England, Germany, and the Scandinavian countries. Gay bars seem to huddle together in clusters. The most outstanding of these is in **Pueblo Blanco,** which is like a little village of its own. Young men bar-hop here with gay abandon.

Much gay life sprawls across the development of **La Nogalera,** which is like a village within a village, with a wide scattering of restaurants, bars, souvenir shops, and apartment complexes. The restaurants here, even those that draw a large gay clientele, tend to be mixed. Notable among these is **El Comedor,** Calle Casablanca (tel. 38-38-81), which offers both regional and international cuisine. It is good enough to be rated in several Spanish gourmet guides. Many Basque specialties are also featured, and you can enjoy dishes such as sole in port wine sauce. The dessert specialty is *leche frita*—literally "fried milk," but actually a sort of sweet croquette. On some nights the restaurant draws an interesting mix of straight and gay couples, each paying from 2,200 pesetas ($20.70) per person for a meal. The restaurant is open every night except Wednesday from 7 p.m. to midnight. The restaurant is also closed from January 15 to March 1.

The leading gay disco is called **Bronx,** Edificio Centro Jardín (tel. 38-73-60). It is open every night from 10 p.m. to 6 a.m., charging an entrance fee of 1,000 pesetas ($9.40), with beer going for 350 pesetas ($3.30).

One of the most popular gay bars in La Nogalera is called simply **"Men's Bar,"** La Nogalera 714 (tel. 38-42-05). Crowded most nights, it charges 350 pesetas ($3.30) for a beer.

The best bar, in the opinion of some of its patrons, in Pueblo Blanco (mentioned earlier) is **La Gorila,** Pueblo Blanco 33 (no phone), which has good music and a usually congenial crowd. It's open daily from 9 p.m. to 3 a.m., charging 350 pesetas ($3.30) for a beer.

---

5. Benalmádena-Costa

Where Torremolinos ends and Benalmádena-Costa begins is hard to say. Benalmádena-Costa has long since become a resort extension on the western frontier of Torremolinos, and it's packed with hotels, restaurants, and tourist facilities.

The **Tourist Information Office** is at Castillo de Bil-Bil (tel. 44-13-63). The Benalmádena-Costa **telephone area code** is 952.

WHERE TO STAY

Hotel Torrequebrada, Carretera de Cádiz, km 220, 29630 Bendalmádena (tel. 44-60-00), is the newest and most impressive five-star luxury hotel along the Costa del Sol, opening onto the beach. It offers a wide range of facilities and attractions, including one of the largest casinos in Europe along with a world-class golf course. In addition, it has an array of restaurants, bars, pools, gardens, nightclub, health club, beach club, and tennis courts. You'll almost need a floor plan to navigate your way around the complex. Nine levels of underground parking solve that problem for motorists. The hotel is furnished in muted Mediterranean colors, and both antique and modern furniture are used.

The hotel offers 350 handsomely furnished and coordinated bedrooms and suites in two 11-story towers. All accommodations have large terraces with sea views, 12-channel satellite TV, minibars, air conditioning, and direct-dial phones, as well as private safes. Doubles rent for 18,500 pesetas ($173.90) to 20,500 pesetas ($192.70) daily, with singles paying from 15,000 pesetas ($141) to 16,000 pesetas ($150.40).

A specialty restaurant, Café Royal, overlooks the gardens and the sea, enjoying a five-fork rating for its international cuisine. At garden level, the Pavilion provides buffet and cafeteria service throughout the day.

Less than two miles north of Torremolinos, the **Tritón,** 29 Avenida António Machado, 29491 Benalmádena-Costa (tel. 44-32-40), is a beachfront Miami Beach–style resort hotel colony in front of the marina of Benalmádena-Costa. It features a high-rise stack of air-conditioned bedrooms as well as an impressive pool and garden area. Surrounding the swimming pool are subtropical trees and vegetation, plus thatched sun-shade umbrellas. The 196 bedrooms have roomwide windows opening onto sun balconies, and each has a private bath, TV, phone and minibar. Singles cost 14,000 pesetas ($131.60), doubles 18,500 pesetas ($173.90).

Among the public rooms are multilevel lounges and two bars with wood paneling and handmade rustic furniture (one has impressive stained-glass windows). For food, there's the main dining room with its three-tiered, mouth-watering display of hors d'oeuvres, fruits, and desserts; a barbecue grill; plus a luncheon terrace where ferns and banana trees form the backdrop. The Tritón also offers tennis courts, a Swedish sauna, and a piano player in the bar.

CASINOS

Casino Torrequebrada, 266 Carretera de Cádiz, Benalmádena-Costa (tel. 44-25-45), is a major casino that offers blackjack, chemin de fer, punto y banco, and two kinds of roulette to its formally dressed clientele. On the premises are a restaurant, bar, disco, and nightclub. It is open from 8 p.m. to 4 a.m. daily. Gamblers are charged an entrance fee of 600 pesetas ($5.65). Once inside, you can also patronize a disco from 9:30 p.m. to 2 a.m. for an entrance fee of 3,500 pesetas ($32.90), which includes your first drink.

---

6. Fuengirola

This will be the Torremolinos of the future. It is already a formidable challenger. About 10 miles to the west of its rival, Fuengirola and its adjacent resort village of Los Boliches are already deep into their development. Good sandy beaches against a hilly backdrop of pine woods couldn't escape attention for long—and didn't. Crowning the town are the ruins of the 10th-century **Sohail Castle,** built by the Caliphs of Córdoba and later rebuilt by Charles V as a defense against Berber pirates.

The **Tourist Information Office** is at Plaza de España (tel. 47-85-00). Fuengirola's **telephone area code** is 952.

WHERE TO STAY

A luxurious resort, **Byblos Andaluz,** Urbanización Mijas Golf, 29640 Fuengirola (tel. 47-30-50), is a hotel and health spa with lavish rooms, in a magnificent setting. The grounds contain shrubbery, a white minaret, Moorish arches, tile-adorned walls, and an orange-tree patio inspired by the Alhambra grounds, 97 miles away. Two 18-hole golf courses designed by Robert Trent Jones, tennis courts, spa facilities, a gymnasium, and swimming pools bask in the Andalusian sunshine. The spa is a handsome classic structure, Mijas Thalasso Palace.

The 144 rooms and suites are elegantly and individually designed and furnished in the Roman, Arabic, Andalusian, and rustic styles. Private sun terraces and lavish bathrooms add to the comfort. Each has air conditioning, TV, phone, and minibar. Singles cost 20,000 pesetas ($188), doubles 30,000 pesetas ($282). Breakfast is extra.

The hotel has a restaurant, El Andaluz, serving low-calorie menus as well as regional cuisine. Le Nailhac Restaurant features gourmet cuisine created from local products. Dinners cost from 5,000 pesetas ($47). Terrace dining is available in both restaurants, and the San Tropez Bar, opening onto a poolside terrace, has music nightly, with flamenco dancers, singers, and musicians presenting programs weekly. The Byblos Andaluz is three miles from Fuengirola and six miles from the beach.

Las Pirámides, Paseo Marítimo, 29640 Fuengirola (tel. 47-06-00), is a complex under pyramidal roofs favored by travel groups from the north of Europe. It's a city-like resort 50 yards from the beach, with seemingly every kind of divertissement: flamenco shows on the large patio, a cozy bar and lounge, traditionally furnished sitting rooms, a Belle Époque coffee shop, a poolside bar, and a gallery of boutiques and tourist facilities, such as car-rental agencies. All 320 rooms are air-conditioned, with slick modern styling, as well as private bath and terrace. Each room has a phone. Singles pay 9,000 pesetas ($84.60), doubles 11,500 pesetas ($108.10). Breakfast is extra.

WHERE TO DINE

When you enter **Restaurant Ceferino,** 1 Rotonda de la Luna, Pueblo López (tel. 464-593), your first view will be of a small bar area (where you might want to linger) and an open kitchen whose pots and bubbling stocks are visible for anyone to see. The air-conditioned dining room is small enough to accommodate only about two dozen diners, who sit amid a straightforward Iberian decor of stucco, brick, and a scattering of tiles. The chef is Sr. Ceferino Garcia Jiménez, who claims his fascination with cuisine began when he helped prepare meals as a child in his family home in Guadalajara. Since then, he has prepared dinners for kings, statesmen, and glamorous resort guests in both Spain and South America. Full meals cost from 3,000 pesetas ($28.20) each, and might include an avocado-based gazpacho; stuffed crêpe Ceferino filled with spinach, pine kernels, and smoked salmon; venison with muscatel sauce; grilled turbot with roe; Norwegian salmon in shrimp sauce; and braised duck with spinach pudding and pears. Service is excellent. Because of the restaurant's small size, reservations are important, especially in the evening. The restaurant is open every day from 1 to 4 p.m. and 8 p.m. to midnight. Annual closing is during January.

El Jardín Escondido, 28 Avenida Acapulco, Los Boliches (tel. 475-683), means "hidden garden," which justifies the difficulty you might have in finding it. Set within an Iberian chalet in the district of Los Boliches, its garden gate opens to reveal a charming oasis of gastronomic skill and comfort. Its owners are Dutch-born Dirk Simonsz and his partner, Louise Sutton, who almost singlehandedly direct the kitchen and dining room. Don't come here expecting a rapid meal. The rhythms of the place impose a leisurely pace, which, if you order a bottle of wine and enjoy your companion, can be wonderful. There's a small bar near the entrance, an indoor dining room filled with pink accessories, fresh flowers and potted palms, and a collection of tables set up within the scents and colors of the garden.

The ambitious menu encompasses a full array of French and Spanish selections. These include such temptations as cream of walnut and zucchini soup, filet of swordfish in a saffron cream sauce, filet of sea bass in an Asturian cider sauce, and chicken breast rendered more pungent with a savory orange and ginger sauce. Dessert could include a grapefruit sherbet or rich pastries.

Full meals cost from 3,000 pesetas ($28.20) and are served Monday to Saturday from 1:30 to 3:30 p.m. and 7:30 to 11:30 p.m.

Annual closing is between January 15 and February 15. Advance reservations are a good idea.

Don Pe', 19 Calle de la Cruz (tel. 478-351), lies amid a cluster of less desirable restaurants in the center of Fuengirola. Because of its quality, it seems to get more repeat business than most of its competitors. During hot weather, many visitors prefer to dine within the courtyard, whose roof can be mechanically retracted to allow in the air and light. During cold weather, the staff builds a fire in a hearth.

The menu lists specialties in three different languages and includes a selection of game dishes such as medallion of venison in wine sauce accompanied with red cabbage, roast filet of wild boar, and duck with orange sauce. The ingredients are imported especially for the restaurant from the forests and plains of nearby Andalusia. Less powerful dishes include peppers stuffed with prawns, fresh salmon covered with an herb sauce, and even an alpine version of fondue bourguignonne.

Full meals cost from 2,500 pesetas ($23.50) and are served Monday to Saturday from 1 to 3:30 p.m. and 7 to 11:30 p.m. Between early July and the end of September, only dinner is served. Reservations, especially at dinnertime, are very important.

El Tomate, 19 Calle El Troncon (tel. 463-559), occupies a deep and narrow town house in the heart of town, just around the corner from the rear side of the old Fuengirola market. Its owner is the hard-working German-born chef Micheal Lienhoop, who infuses his cuisine with the best traditions of both northern and southern Europe. Full meals cost from around 2,600 pesetas ($24.45), and might include a succulent version of marinated salmon; fresh tomato soup laced with gin; filet of hake floating atop a layer of sauce concocted from cream, mustard, and fresh dill; a savory version of pork in a red wine and mushroom sauce; and an always-popular German perennial, sauerkraut with bacon and sausage. Dinner is served daily from 7 p.m. to midnight. Reservations are a good idea.

Widely known for good food, **Don Bigote** (Mr. Mustache), 39 Francisco Cano at Los Boliches (tel. 47-50-94), was a deserted century-old sardine factory and a row of fishermen's cottages before its transformation into one of the most popular restaurants in the area. In summer, a splashing fountain in the garden patio makes the right background for the Italian menu. In cooler weather you have a choice of dining in one of the attractively decorated dining rooms, each furnished in a regional style. You might enjoy a before-dinner drink under the rafters in the lounge bar. The chefs turn out a most recommendable cuisine. Meals begin at 3,000 pesetas ($28.20) unless you order the set meal at 2,000 pesetas ($18.80). Dinner is served from 7 p.m. to midnight daily.

7. Mijas

It's called "White Mijas" because of its bone-white Andalusian houses. Just five miles from Fuengirola above the Costa del Sol, the village is a gem, standing at the foot of a sierra. From its lofty perches 1,400 feet above sea level, a panoramic vista of the Mediterranean unfolds. Along its narrow, cobblestone streets have walked Celts, Phoenicians, and Moors. You'll do better hiring a "burrotaxi." In a park at the top of Cuesta de la Villa, you see remnants of a Moorish citadel dating from 833. Shops threaten to inundate the village, selling everything from original art to olive-wood jewelry. Incidentally, Mijas possesses the only square bullring in Spain.

The **telephone area code** for Mijas is 952.

WHERE TO STAY

Hotel Mijas, Urbanización, 29650 Mijas (tel. 48-58-00), is one of the special hotels along the coast with a view of the sea and surrounding mountains. Designed hacienda style, it is perched on the side of a hill, with a semi-enclosed flower patio, a terrace with white wicker furniture and a view, a swimming pool, a tennis court, and a lounge that's Castilian in decor. The living room is furnished with fine antiques and inlaid chests, even a framed fan collection. All 100 excellently furnished bedrooms contain a private tile bath, air conditioning, and room phone. Doubles rent for 12,500 pesetas ($117.50), singles 9,000 pesetas ($84.60), plus tax. Breakfast is extra. Other facilities include a sauna, gymnasium, and beauty parlor. Barbecues are held in the open air. The location is in the center of the village, lying about five miles from the nearest beach. Entertainment is provided in season in the evening, and during the day guests can enjoy the 18-hole Mijas golf course.

Novotel Mijas, Carretera de Fuengirola-Mijas, km 4, Apartdao 20, 29650 Mijas (tel. 52/48-64-00; for reservations in North America call toll-free 800/221-4542), was built by one of Europe's most successful hotel chains, the French-based ACCOR group. Novotel Mijas is considered one of the model hotels of the region. It offers a welcome comfort and many amenities for relatively reasonable prices. It sits about a half mile inland from the seafront, midway between Mijas and Fuengirola. It was designed in a blend of modern and functional architecture with Andalusian accents, including a roof of terra-cotta tiles, walls of chiseled sandstone and thick stucco, and a grove of palm trees that shelter its façade and the waters of a large outdoor pool. Each of the 130 comfortably standardized bedrooms contains air conditioning, TV, radio, private bathroom, phone, and minibar. With a breakfast buffet included, singles cost 10,000 pesetas ($94), doubles 13,000 pesetas ($122.20). On the premises are a gym, a sauna, a well-managed first-class restaurant, and a bar remaining open 24 hours a day. The hotel also offers illuminated tennis courts and a convention center suitable for conferences of up to 200 people. Even the swimming pool is enriched with minerals for the closest approximation of a spa. A minibus transports guests without charge back and forth from the nearby beaches and golf courses.

WHERE TO DINE

Club el Padrastro, Paseo del Compás (tel. 48-50-00), is aptly named. In Spanish *padrastro* is a curious word, meaning both "stepfather" and "hangnail." However, it also suggests height, a commanding position—which you'll appreciate after climbing the 77 steps to reach the restaurant, although it's more sensible to take the elevator at the town parking lot. The location is in the center of

Mijas. After you've scaled the heights, a swimming pool and an art-fully decorated restaurant await you. Before dinner, order a drink under pine trees by the pool, enjoying the view. Inside, picture windows on two levels also open onto the panorama, and soft music plays. The food is quite good. Specialties include fish soup Padrastro, bass with fennel, and a special flambé Padrastro. The tab here is likely to run 2,200 pesetas ($20.70) to 3,300 pesetas ($31), although special budget meals are offered for 1,000 pesetas ($9.40) and 1,500 pesetas ($14.10). No reservations are taken. Hours are noon to midnight daily.

Restaurant El Cañuelo, 32 Calle Málaga (tel. 485-298), set within a carefully renovated medium-sized house, lies at the edge of Mijas and might be one of the first things you see as you enter the town. It contains a small bar and a pair of dining rooms that serve surprisingly good food in a town where much of the competition specializes almost exclusively in fast deep-fried food and steak-and-kidney pie. Owned and directed by partners Alex Hunter and John Brians, it offers a frequently changing menu based on regionally available ingredients. Examples include fettuccini in a salmon and cream sauce, filet steak with green peppercorns or with a mushroom sauce, seafood crêpes, a Cajun-style fish kebab, roast chicken with barbecue sauce, and even a Texas-inspired chili. The restaurant is open daily Tuesday to Sunday from 11:30 a.m. to 3:30 p.m. and 7:30 to 11 p.m. Full meals cost from 2,000 pesetas ($18.80) each.

---

8. Marbella

In the shadow of what was once an Arab fortress, Marbella is definitely chic, attracting a fashionable crowd of movie people and socialites. Many mansions and villas are found hereabouts.

About halfway between Málaga and Gibraltar, Marbella is at the foot of the Sierra Blanca, which keeps the climate mild. Its best beaches are the 600-yard-long Fuerta and the 800-yard-long Fontanilla. But actually Marbella is one long beach, taking in about 17 miles of sand from Guadalmina to Cabopino. Some 60 beachfront complexes and hotel clusters line this stretch. The beach resorts have elaborate swimming pools and all the trappings; the beachfronts are open to the public. From national highway N340, you'll see different roads signposted leading to the various beaches.

You don't need to get dressed to go to lunch either, as many of these beaches have bar-restaurants called *chiringuitos*. Right on the beach, these places sell cold beer throughout the day and often grill freshly caught fish for your lunch. Women often go topless on these beaches, but total nudity is prohibited. However, nudists still disrobe at some of the more isolated places at the eastern stretch of beach. Sports, such as waterskiing, shark fishing, and tennis, are popular. The even more athletically inclined dance until dawn.

At some point, take a walk in the old part of town, still partially enclosed by walls. The view of whitewashed houses, studded with potted flowers, along narrow streets makes for pleasant strolling. Then stop off at a café on the Plaza de los Naranjos (oranges) for a drink.

Marbella lies 35 miles west of Málaga and 47 miles east of Algeciras, a total of 373 miles from Madrid.

Its **Tourist Information Office** is at 1 Miguel Cano (tel. 77-14-42). Marbella's **telephone area code** is 952.

WHERE TO STAY

Since the setting is so ideal—pure Mediterranean sun, sea, and sky, plus the scent of Andalusian orange blossoms in the air—some of the best hotels along the Costa del Sol are found in Marbella.

Luxury Resort Hotels

Los Monteros, Carretera de Cádiz, km 187, 29600 Marbella (tel. 77-17-00), is one of the most tasteful and imaginative resort complexes along the Costa del Sol. Between the coastal road and its own private beach, it attracts those seeking intimacy and luxury. No cavernous lounges exist here; instead, many small tasteful rooms, Andalusian/Japanese in concept, are the style. The hotel offers various salons with open fireplaces, a library, a bar, terraces, and four restaurants on different levels, opening onto flower-filled patios, gardens, and fountains.

The 169 bedrooms are brightly decorated, with lightly colored lacquered furniture, private baths, and terraces. Each is air-conditioned, with TV, phone, and minibar. The hotel charges 35,000 pesetas ($329) daily for a single, 44,000 pesetas ($413.60) for a double, including breakfast. Free to guests of the hotel is the nearby 18-hole golf course, Río Real. Other facilities include several swimming pools, a beach club that has a heated indoor pool, 10 tennis courts, 5 squash courts, a riding club and school, plus a fully equipped gymnasium with sauna, massage, and Jacuzzi.

Within the precincts, Grill El Corzo is one of the finest grill rooms along the coast. The grill, done up in Toledo red, is on the first floor. Wall-size scenic murals are in the background, and tables are bedecked with bright cloths and silver candlesticks. Soft, romantic music is played nightly. Meals cost from 6,000 pesetas ($56.40). The cuisine is a pleasing combination of French and Spanish. The hotel lies 400 yards from a beach and four miles east of Marbella.

Hotel Don Carlos, Jardines de las Goldondrinas, Carretera de Cádiz, km 192, 29600 Marbella (tel. 83-11-40), one of the most dramatically alluring hotels along the coastline, rises on a set of angled stilts above a forest of pines. Between it and its manicured beach, considered the best in Marbella, are 130 acres of award-winning gardens replete with cascades of water, a full-time staff of 22 gardeners, and thousands of subtropical plants. There's far more to this hotel than the modern tower that rises above the eastern edge of Marbella. Its low-lying terraces and elegant eating and drinking facilities attract high-powered conferences from throughout Europe, as well as individual nonresident diners from along the Mediterranean coast.

You can dine amid splashes of bougainvillea beside an oversized swimming pool bordered with begonias and geraniums or in La Pergola, where ficus and potted palms decorate the hundreds of lattices. A hideaway, Los Naranjos, has a sun-flooded atrium with mosses and orange trees. A grand piano on the marble dais provides diverting music. Fixed-price meals here go for 4,500 pesetas

($42.30) each. Meals in the other restaurants, including grills or elaborate buffets in the semi-outdoor beachfront cabaña, cost about half as much.

Among the bars scattered around the various terraces and marble-lined hideaways of the public rooms, the most popular offers an English-inspired décor of exposed hardwoods, a panoramic view of the sea, plenty of sofas, a dance floor, and a musical trio.

Each of the 234 air-conditioned accommodations has its own panoramic balcony, lacquered furniture, a private bath done in honey-colored marble, a phone, satellite TV, and minibar. Single rooms rent for 20,600 pesetas ($193.65) to 22,300 pesetas ($209.60), doubles 25,600 pesetas ($240.65) to 27,000 pesetas ($253.80). Tax and breakfast are extra. The golf course, saunas, gym, and tennis courts are free for the use of hotel guests. A complete selection of water sports, plus horseback riding, is available at an extra charge to guests.

Hotel Puente Romano, 2½ miles west of Marbella at Carretera de Cádiz, km 167, 29600 Marbella (tel. 77-01-00), was originally built as a cluster of vacation apartments, a fact that influenced the attention to detail and the landscaping that surrounds it. In the early 1970s a group of entrepreneurs transformed it into one of the most unusual hotels in the south of Spain, sitting close to the frenetic coastal highway, midway between Marbella and Puerto Banús.

Once inside the complex, guests wander through a maze of arbor-covered walkways. Along the route, they pass cascades of water, masses of vines, and a subtropical garden. Nestled amid the lushness are well-upholstered indoor/outdoor bars and restaurants. Three of these overlook a terra-cotta patio, bordered at one end by the stones of a reconstructed Roman bridge, the only one of its kind in southern Spain. The edges of a free-form swimming pool are bordered by trees and vines and a drain-away waterfall, making it look something like a Tahitian lagoon.

The 185 Moorish-style accommodations are each a showcase of fabrics, accessories, and furniture. Each of the air-conditioned rooms has a semi-sheltered balcony with flowers, color TV, private bath, direct-dial phone, minibar, and electronic safe. Singles cost 28,000 pesetas ($263.20), doubles 35,000 pesetas ($329). Breakfast is extra.

If you're wondering who your fellow guests might be, the King of Spain, Barbara Striesand, Björn Borg, Stevie Wonder, Julio Iglesias, the Kennedys, and the President of Ireland have all enjoyed the pleasures of this establishment. Not the least of these are a sandy beach with an array of water sports, tennis courts, nightclub, and a cluster of boutiques.

Meliá Don Pepe, Finca Las Merinas, 29600 Marbella (tel. 77-03-00), occupies six acres of tropical gardens and lawns between the coastal road and the sea. Fully air-conditioned, its 202 well-furnished bedrooms, with private baths and wall-to-wall carpeting, face either the sea or the Sierra Blanca mountains. Each has a private bath, phone, TV, and minibar. A single rents for 20,000 pesetas ($188), a double for 31,000 pesetas ($291.40). The facilities are so vast you could spend a week here and not use them all. They include four swimming pools, tennis courts, a Swedish sauna, a collection of boutiques, even a bridge clubroom, along with lounges, bars, and restaurants. La Farola grill provides international à la carte cuisine, with meals costing from 5,000 pesetas ($47). Other facilities include a yacht harbor along the beach and a golf course.

Marbella Club, Carretera de Cádiz, km 178, 29600 Marbella (tel. 77-13-00), is a deluxe hotel with private beach club on the road from Marbella to Gibraltar. Begun in 1953 by Prince Alfonso von Hohenlohe, the hotel has grown into a luxurious holiday resort favored by people with taste from all over the world. It's a place of peace and quiet for guests seeking relaxation at the edge of the sea and for nature lovers. Twelve bungalows between the beach and the organically structured green spaces seem to be set in a park. The bungalows contain two or three bedrooms with living rooms, private gardens, and swimming pools. Other accommodations consist of 76 double rooms and 24 suites. All units have baths, phones, air conditioning, TV, music, and minibars. The charge for single occupancy is 28,000 pesetas ($263.20) daily; for two people, 32,500 pesetas ($305.50). Breakfast is extra.

Andalucia Plaza, Urbanización Nueva Andalucia, 29660 Apartado, 21 Nueva Andalucia Marbella (tel. 81-20-00), is a resort complex on a grand scale. On the mountain side of the coastal road between Marbella and Torremolinos, twin buildings are linked by a reception lounge and formal gardens. On the sea side is the hotel's beach club. Far more than a 300-foot strip of sand, it has sunbathing terraces, tennis courts, a sauna, gymnasium, open-air swimming pool, even an enclosed all-weather pool. And there's a 1,000-yacht marina, where you can rent one of the vessels and go deep-sea fishing. The public rooms in the hotel buildings are spacious and lavishly decorated. Equally luxurious are the 415 air-conditioned bedrooms furnished in the classic Castilian manner, utilizing reproductions. Each room has a TV, minibar, and phone. Single travelers pay 12,500 pesetas ($117.50) daily; two people, 15,000 pesetas ($141). Breakfast is extra. The location is four miles west of the center of Marbella.

The Middle Bracket

Hotel El Fuerte, Avenida El Fuerte s/n, 29600 Marbella (tel. 77-15-00), is the most recommendable hotel in the center of Marbella. With a balconied and angular façade, it's right on the waterfront, its palm-fringed swimming pools set across the street from a sheltered lagoon and wide-open beach. A handful of terraces, some shaded by flowering arbors, provide hideaways for quiet drinks. A restaurant with a panoramic water view and a bar are part of the facilities. The 262 comfortable, contemporary bedrooms all contain baths, minibars, phones, TVs, piped-in music, and air conditioning, with terraces and sea views. Singles rent for 11,000 pesetas ($103.40) daily; doubles, for 13,000 pesetas ($122.20). Breakfast is extra. The hotel has a coffee shop, two restaurants, and two bars. Facilities for leisure activities include a swimming pool, a floodlit tennis court, mini-golf, and two squash courts.

Estrella del Mar, Carretera de Cádiz, km 190.5, 29600 Marbella (tel. 83-12-75), is a tasteful resort hotel between Marbella and Torremolinos, with its own seafront swimming pool and sandy beach. The 98 bedrooms of Estrella del Mar, attractively furnished, have flower-filled balconies. Each has a private bath and phone, but no air conditioning. A single rents for 7,000 pesetas ($65.80), a double for 11,000 pesetas ($103.40). Breakfast is extra. The main lounge, with its reproductions of Castilian antiques, is two stories high. Meals are taken in the informal dining room in the main building. You can try a dish created in the hotel: Called fondue Marbella, it features an assortment of Mediterranean fish served with sauces ranging from tartar to curry. The hotel, open only from March to November, stands 200 yards from the beach.

Hotel Guadalpin, Carretera 340 Cádiz-Málaga, km 186, 29600 Marbella (tel. 77-11-00), is right on the rugged coast, only 50 yards from the beach (one mile from the center of Marbella). You can live at this 85-room hotel for 9,100 pesetas ($85.54) daily in a double room with private bath. For a single with a full bath the rate is 6,700 pesetas ($63), but only 10 rooms are available in this category. Breakfast is extra. Each room has a private bath and phone.

Guests spend many hours relaxing around two swimming pools, or they walk along a private pathway lined with fir trees to the Mediterranean. The dining room has large windows overlooking the patio and pool, and the main lounge has been designed in a ranch style with round marble tables and occasional leather armchairs arranged for conversational groups. The bar area of the spacious lounge is brick and natural wood, making it warm and attractive. Each room has not only two terraces, but a living room and bedroom combined. Most of the rooms are furnished in "new ranch" style.

WHERE TO DINE

La Fonda, 10 Plaza Santo Cristo (tel. 77-25-12), is considered both a gem of 18th-century Andalusian architecture and a gastronomic citadel of renown. It is the Costa del Sol extension of one of the most famous restaurants in Europe, the Madrid-based Horcher's. (For more information, refer to Chapter X.) The restaurant was the outgrowth of a simple inn, which had been originally created by interconnecting a trio of town houses in Old Marbella. Today, a central patio with a murmuring fountain, a series of colonnaded loggias, carefully chosen Andalusian *azulejos* (glazed tiles), beamed ceilings, open fireplaces, grill-covered windows, and checkerboard-patterned marble floors have been respectfully maintained. What is new, however, is the professionalism and sophistication that exudes from virtually everything here.

Some of the most beautiful faces (and some of the richest) come here regularly for long and languid dinners.

The cuisine is international, and so is the crowd. Overseeing the many tables with skill and Iberian panache is Ramón Ballesteros, personal representative of the Horcher family and director of the restaurant. Menu specialties change every four months or so, but might include fish terrine with herb sauce, avocado pancakes with prawns, guinea fowl or partridge, coq au vin, blanquette de veau, and chicken Kiev. Full meals cost from 4,500 pesetas ($42.30). Dinner is served Monday to Saturday from 8 p.m. to midnight. Reservations are imperative.

Restaurante La Meridiana, Camino de la Cruz, at Las Lomas (tel. 77-61-90), is inland from the coastal highway across from the Puente Romano complex. The restaurant has become famous for its cuisine, its service, and its intimate ambience. You enter through a tropical garden to reach the large dining area, where you'll be seated in one of the elegant sections and greeted with a complimentary fish pâté and fresh bread. The dishes come from the kitchen temptingly presented, with colorful accompaniments, turning them into small works of art—some à la nouvelle cuisine, others from the chef's special repertoire—all aimed at pleasing the eye as well as the palate.

You can choose from a menu that offers many fish, game, beef, pork, and lamb courses, including hare stuffed with duck liver, raisins, and Málaga wine; filet of dorado with purée of green and red peppers; medallions of lobster Florentine with béarnaise sauce; partridge sausages with chestnut purée; and wild duck with shallots. For dessert, I suggest the capricho Meridiana, which varies through the "caprice" of the chef, but is sure to have fine and fresh ingredients such as fruit of the season. Expect to pay from 5,500 pesetas ($51.70) per person.

Don't worry about your car: The restaurant has valet parking. It's open from 1:30 to 3:30 p.m. and 8:30 p.m. to midnight daily. The location is behind Mezquita Arabe.

La Hacienda, Urbanización Hacienda Las Chapas, Carretera de Cádiz, km 193 (tel. 83-11-16), is a tranquil choice, enjoying a reputation for serving some of the best food along the Costa del Sol. In cooler months you can dine inside in the rustic tavern before an open fireplace. However, in fair weather meals are al fresco, served on a patio partially encircled by open Romanesque arches. The chef is likely to offer calves' liver with truffled butter, lobster croquettes (as an appetizer), and roast guinea hen with cream, minced raisins, and port. A baked Alaska finishes the repast quite nicely, although you may prefer an iced soufflé. Even for such good food, the bill is high: 5,500 pesetas ($51.70) to 6,000 pesetas ($56.40) for a complete meal. In summer, only dinner is served, and reservations are important. Hours are Wednesday to Sunday from 8:30 to 11:30 p.m.; in August, the restaurant is also open on Monday. In winter, both lunch and dinner are offered Wednesday to Sunday from 1 to 3:30 p.m. and 8:30 to 11:30 p.m. La Hacienda is closed from November 15 to December 20. The location is eight miles east of Marbella.

La Dorada, Coral Beach, Carretera de Cádiz, km 176 (tel. 821-034), lies midway between Marbella and Puerto Banús, in a location beside the main road that diners from either resort can easily find. When properly illuminated and filled with chattering (and upscale) guests, its interior gives new meaning to the term "nautical decor." Entirely covered in glowing and carefully varnished vertical planks, it has a soaring ceiling supported by an enormous wood-sheathed column entwined by a circular staircase. To contribute to its likeness as an oceangoing yacht, a huge brass ship's propeller hangs motionless near the ceiling.

Several different dining rooms are available, including one called "the foredeck," whose glass walls show off a view of a nearby garden.

The setting is appropriate for the splendid fish dishes that emerge fresh from the kitchen. Prices are correspondingly expensive, around 6,000 pesetas ($56.40) per person, for the types of seafood delicacies that are considered high gastronomy throughout

Iberia. They include some taste-bud-awakening slices of Spanish ham served with an apéritif of fine sherry, a mixed fish fry, clams served in a garlic-laced broth, grilled grouper(*mero*), fresh salmon marinated in dill sauce, and a dazzling array of shellfish. There are also many varieties of fish baked in a salt crust (which keeps the flesh moist and flaky), prepared on the grill, stewed in a casserole, sautéed, boiled, or served any way you prefer. Because of its popularity, the restaurant usually requires reservations, especially at night. Lunch is served from 1 to 4 p.m., dinner from 8 p.m. to midnight. It's closed Sunday in winter.

Marbella Hill Club Restaurant, Urbanización Jardines Colgantes (tel. 82-40-85), lies in the hills north of Marbella. From its windows, you'll appreciate its sweeping views down to the sea. The ambience is sophisticated, airy, and polite, centered within a simple but stylish decor of green and white accessories. Partners Fabio Mezzasalna and Benito Palacio charge from 4,000 pesetas ($37.60) for a full meal, which might include dishes from a Mediterranean repertoire of French, Spanish, and Italian cuisine. The menu changes with the availability of the ingredients, and might include vichyssoise, a salad of avocado and duckling, quenelles of fish with lobster sauce, a ragoût of crayfish with tarragon, and John Dory in puff pastry with spinach and hollandaise sauce. The establishment is open daily except Tuesday from 1 to 4 p.m. and 8:30 p.m. to midnight.

The cuisine of **Hostería del Mar,** 1-A Avenida Canovas del Castillo (tel. 77-02-18), is known throughout the region as being both delicious and highly unusual. It has been called the most consistently good restaurant in the region—a judgment that many loyal clients agree with. Part of its excellence stems from the many years that the Spanish co-owners, Rafael Aguero and Roberto Pecino, worked as restaurateurs in Toronto, Canada, where they acquired a vivid concept of what international diners would enjoy.

You'll be seated within a dining room decorated in shades of fern green and cream, accented with wooden columns, a blue and terra-cotta floor, decorative ceiling beams, and handpainted porcelain. In summer, a tree-shaded patio is set with tables for additional seating. Full meals cost around 4,000 pesetas ($37.60) and might include calves' sweetbreads in a mustard sauce, clams stuffed with ratatouille, roast duck with a sauce made from roasted figs and cassis, Catalán-style shrimp with chicken, and stuffed quails with spinach, mushrooms, and pâté. Desserts are appropriately sumptuous, and include a selection of cold soufflés. The restaurant, which lies at the beginning of the bypass road that runs beside the Hotel Meliá Don Pepe, is open Monday to Saturday for dinner, from 7:30 p.m. to midnight.

As soon as you enter **Santiago,** 5 Avenida Duque de Ahumada (tel. 77-43-39), the bubbling lobster tanks give you an idea of the kinds of dishes available. The decor, the stand-up tapas bar near the entrance, and the summertime patio join together with fresh fish dishes to make this one of the most popular eating places in town. On my most recent visit, I arrived so early for lunch that the mussels for my mussels marinara were just being delivered. The fish soup is well prepared, well spiced, and savory. The sole in champagne comes in a large serving, and the turbot can be grilled or sautéed.

On a hot day, the seafood salad, garnished with lobster, shrimp, and crabmeat and served with a sharp sauce, is especially recommended. For dessert, I suggest a serving of Manchego cheese. A complete meal, served from 1 to 3 p.m. and 8 p.m. to midnight daily, will cost 3,500 pesetas ($32.90) and up. It's necessary to make a reservation.

Calycanto, 9 Avenida Cánovas del Castillo (tel. 77-19-59), at the west end of the bypass road, is a restaurant built in *cortijo* style, standing in its own grounds. The garden is the setting for meals in summer, while winter service is in a large room with a log fire. The menu offers a number of good dishes, and the wine list is extensive, with good table wines as well as vintage products. Vegetarians can be happy here, with such main dishes as vegetable mousse pudding and, of course, crisp salads. Try the tagliatelle, asparagus mousse, and endives Roquefort. For your main course, you might choose guinea fowl or an interesting fish dish with grapes. Meals cost from 3,000 pesetas ($28.20). The restaurant is open from 1:30 to 4 p.m. and 8 p.m. to midnight daily, but only for dinner in July and August.

NIGHTLIFE

In sheer volume, Marbella doesn't have the wide variety of after-dark clubs and bars that Torremolinos does, but it does offer some nighttime entertainment. And the center of Costa del Sol gambling is nearby.

Disco and Music Clubs

Long a leading disco along the Costa del Sol, **Pepe Moreno,** Carretera de Cádiz, km 186 (tel. 77-02-79), enlivens the Marbella nightlife scene. A disc jockey seems to play the right music at the right moment. It has a Spanish decor and ambience. Admission is 1,800 pesetas ($16.90), and it's usually open daily from 11 p.m. to 4 a.m. Drinks cost from 800 pesetas ($7.50).

Ana María, 4-5 Plaza del Santo Cristo (tel. 77-56-46), offers an elongated tapas bar crowded with garrulous locals and a frequently changing collection of singers, dancers, and musicians, who present everything from flamenco to popular songs. Entrance is 2,200 pesetas ($20.70), and drinks begin at 800 pesetas ($7.50). Hours are nightly from 11 p.m. to dawn seven days a week, except it closes on Monday from November to March.

Casino

On the outskirts of Marbella, **Casino Nueva Andalucia Marbella,** Urbanización Nueva Andalucia (tel. 78-08-00), is the most exciting nightlife complex along the Costa del Sol. To the west of Marbella, it offers just about everything—including terrace dining, swimming pools, a beach, a nightclub, and gaming rooms. The casino features French and American roulette, blackjack, punto y banco, craps, and chemin de fer. The club stays open all year. An admission card is available upon presentation of your passport and the payment of a fee—600 pesetas ($5.65) for one day. The casino is open from 8 p.m. to 5 a.m. daily. There's also a boite offering recorded music from 10 p.m. to 1:30 a.m., charging an admission fee of 3,500 pesetas ($32.90). You can dine in the Casino Restaurant, raised a few steps up from the gambling floor, for about 3,500 pesetas ($32.90), with wine and service included. Everybody should dress according to the high standards of the casino.

9. San Pedro De Alcántara

In a little resort suburb west of Marbella are found some of the most tranquil oases along the Costa del Sol. The San Pedro de Alcántara telephone area code is 952.

WHERE TO STAY

The moderately priced **Golf Hotel Guadalmina,** Hacienda Guadalmina, Carretera N-340, 29670 San Pedro de Alcántara (tel. 78-14-00), is a large country club–type resort, where the first tee and 18th green are both right next to the hotel. The golf course is open to both residents and nonresidents. An informal place, it is really a private world on the shores of the Mediterranean. You reach it by a long driveway from the coastal road. Three seawater swimming pools attract those seeking the lazy life; the tennis courts appeal to the athletic. The 80 bedrooms—most of them opening onto the pool/recreation area and the sea—are attractive in their traditional Spanish style. Each has air conditioning, TV, minibar, phone, and private bath. A single rents for 13,000 pesetas ($122.20), a double for 17,000 pesetas ($159.80). Breakfast and tax are extra.

The hotel offers two excellent dining choices—one a luncheon-only reed-covered poolside terrace overlooking the golf course and the sea, the other an interior room in the main building, with a sedate clubhouse aura. Informality and good food reign. The location is 50 yards from the beach, 8 miles east of Marbella, and 1¼ miles from the center of San Pedro de Alcántara.

Cortijo Blanco, Carretera de Cádiz, km 172, 29670 San Pedro de Alcántara (tel. 78-09-00), is a self-contained little world of whitewashed walls, tile roofs, fountains, courtyards, bell towers, wrought-iron balconies, and a maze of cottages linked by dozens of patios filled with tall subtropical vines and vegetation. All 162 bedrooms face the main garden, dominated by a good-sized swimming pool. Each room has a private bath and phone, but no air conditioning. Doubles cost 5,500 pesetas ($51.70) daily; singles, 3,800 pesetas ($35.70). Evening meals are a gracious affair as you sit in high-backed, carved red-and-gilt Valencian chairs; lunch is served around the covered pergola with its luxuriant vegetation. The hotel lies 600 yards from the beach.

WHERE TO DINE

Garuda de Oro, Carretera de Cádiz, km 166.5 (tel. 782-743), an Indonesian restaurant, is named after the mythical bird/dragon of the Spice Islands, the Garuda. Its menu reflects the diversity of the Asian island nation, and lists dishes from China, India, and the vast number of possibilities in between. The best way to taste the culinary possibilities of Indonesia is to order a special rice table (*Rijsttafel*), which includes between 18 and 25 different dishes.

The dining room is accented with parasol-shielded lights and South Seas puppets. Individual items include saté (small shish kebabs) of pork, beef, and chicken, sometimes served with a delicious peanut sauce; chicken, egg, and lemon soup; different versions of vegetables; and aromatic stews. Each is accompanied by rice from a large bowl that is periodically replenished. Full meals cost from 2,500 pesetas ($23.50) and are served Monday to Saturday from 1 to 4 p.m. and 8 to 11 p.m. Reservations in advance are a good idea, especially after 10 p.m. The restaurant lies just outside the city limits of San Pedro, beside the road leading to Estepona.

10. Puerto Banús

This marine village, five miles east of Marbella, is a favorite resort of celebrities from all over the world. Almost overnight the village was created in the traditional Mediterranean style. There is no sameness here. Each building appears different in design, yet everything blends into a harmonious whole. Yachts can be moored at your doorstep. If you don't have a yacht, you can take one of the 15 buses a day connecting Puerto Banús with Marbella. Along the harborfront is an array of sophisticated bars and restaurants, all of which are expensive.

Try, if you can, to wander through the back streets as well, past elegant archways and grilled patios. The rich and elegant rent apartments in this village for the winter season. In all, Puerto Banús is like a Disney World concoction of what a Costa del Sol fishing village should looklike. The **telephone area code** for Puerto Banús is 952.

WHERE TO STAY

Marbella-Dinamar, Urbanización Nueva Andalucia, Carretera de Cádiz, km 175, 29660 Puerto Banús (tel. 81-05-00), is an exotic resort oasis, right on the seafront just 500 yards from the beach and four miles east of Marbella. The architecture and decor are Moorish-inspired, with stark white walls and arches. At the rear, the lounges, facing the sea, have a light, airy mood. The patio, adjoining the bar, is tropical Victorian, with ornate white wicker armchairs. The large swimming pool is oddly shaped and surrounded by a tile terrace, lawns, and palm trees. The 117 bedrooms, conventionally furnished, contain all the modern necessities, including TV, phone, private bath, and air conditioning. Most of them open onto a sea view. Rates are 12,000 pesetas ($112.80) daily in a single, 15,000 pesetas ($141) in a twin-bedded room. Breakfast is extra. Another facility is a heated and covered swimming pool directly connected to the main building. The tennis courts are floodlit at night, and nearby is one of the best all-around golf courses along the Costa del Sol.

WHERE TO DINE

La Taberna del Alabardero, Muelle Benabola (tel. 81-27-94), lies directly on the harborfront, within full view of the hundreds of strolling pedestrians whose numbers seem to ebb and flow like the tides. You can dine inside its big-windowed interior, but you might have more fun at one of the dozens of outdoor tables, where the only clue to the upper-crust status is the immaculate napery, well-disciplined waiters, and discreet twinkle of some very expensive jewelry among the blue jeans or formal attire of the prosperous and fashionable clientele. An armada of private yachts bobs at anchor a few feet away. Full meals cost from 4,000 pesetas ($37.60), and might include crêpes stuffed with chunks of lobster and crayfish, hake and small clams served in a Basque-inspired green sauce, filet of duck's breast with green peppercorns or with orange sauce, and a sophisticated array of desserts. The establishment is open from 1 to 4 p.m. and 8 p.m. to midnight. It's closed every Sunday in winter and at lunchtime from mid-July to mid-September.

An excellent Italian restaurant is **Don Leone,** 45 Muelle Ribera (tel. 81-17-16). Many Costa del Sol visitors drive over just for dinner. If you decide to do likewise, you'll find Don Leone right at dockside. The decoration is attractive, with many luxurious touches. You can dine inside or out. The wine list is one of the best along the coast. To begin your repast, you might order the house minestrone, which is invariably good. Pasta dishes, made on the premises, are featured in various savory sauces, including bolognese and a clam sauce. Lasagne is also a regular item on the menu. Veal parmigiana and roast baby lamb are among the better meat courses, and there are also some well-prepared fish dishes. Count on spending 4,000 pesetas ($37.60) or more for a meal. The restaurant is open from 1 to 4 p.m. and 8 p.m. to 12:30 a.m. daily. Closed from November 20 to December 20. It tends to get crowded, so reserve a table.

THE BEST BARS

Sinatra Bar, 2 Muelle Ribera (tel. 81-48-25), is a center for people watching. Here residents of the nearby apartments meet for drinks late in the evening. The preferred spot, if the weather is right, is on one of the chairs set out on the sidewalk. Only a few feet away, rows of luxury yachts await your inspection. Tables are usually shared, and piped-in music lets you hear Sinatra's voice. Hard drinks range from 650 pesetas ($6.10). Snacks such as the "Mama-burger" are served throughout the night. Open from 9 p.m. to 4 a.m. daily.

Hollywood Bar, 14 Muelle Ribera (tel. 81-68-12), offers a place to sit and examine the yachts bobbing a few feet away and the pedestrians who may be admiring the boats as much as you are. The establishment contains a green and white decor of arched awnings and terra-cotta tiles focused around a series of collages of the best shots of the Hollywood stars of yesteryear. Monroe and Chaplin mark the entrance to the toilets. Beer costs from 200 pesetas ($1.90), with hard drinks going for 500 pesetas ($4.70) and up. The bar is open daily from 9:30 a.m. to 2 a.m.

11. Sotogrande

Sotogrande, a residential tourist development, sprawls across 4,400 acres—one of the most luxurious resorts along the whole

Costa del Sol. Across from the Rock of Gibraltar, it represents elegant Andalusia at its best.

The area appeals to the well-heeled sportsperson, one who doesn't mind crossing an ocean and/or a continent to play the two Robert Trent Jones golf courses. (There's a nine-hole executive course for the less energetic.) It lies 17 miles from Algeciras and 69 miles from Málaga. Sotogrande's **telephone area code** is 956.

This is a large complex with many facilities, some of which are in the members-only category. However, the **Hotel Sotogrande,** Carretera N. 340, km 131, 11310 Sotogrande (tel. 79-21-00), is open to the general public, containing 44 handsomely furnished double rooms and two luxurious suites. On the half-board plan, the rate in a double room is 22,000 pesetas ($206.80) to 26,000 pesetas ($244.40) daily, from 14,500 pesetas ($136.30) to 16,500 pesetas ($155.10) in a single.

The Hotel Sotogrande serves breakfast, lunch, and dinner. Light snack meals and bar service are available at the hotel as well at Sotogrande Golf Club Restaurant.

Next to the hotel, there are six tennis courts, a large swimming pool, a children's play area, and a hairdressing salon. Guests may also hire horses from nearby stables, and polo is enjoyed throughout the summer season by players and spectators alike on Sotogrande's two polo grounds.

AFTER MADRID—WHERE TO?

If you want a deeper look at Spain, and plan to visit its other fascinating cities, including Granada, Cordoba, Seville, and Barcelona, you'll need our companion guide, *Spain on $50 a Day*. This larger guide is devoted to the country's many sightseeing attractions, and provides wide coverage of hotels and restaurants. It explores the country in depth, and its philosophy is to help you get the most for your dollar. Special features of the book include detailed sections on the Balearic Islands (including Majorca, Ibiza, and Minorca), Gibraltar, and the Canary Islands.

For information on this and other Frommer guides, please turn to the last two pages of this book.

INDEX

GENERAL INFORMATION

SIGHTS AND ATTRACTIONS

Costa del Sol

FUENGIROLA
Sohail Castle, 221

MÁLAGA
Alcazaba, 203
Archeological Museum, 203
Cathedral, 203
El Parque, 201

Fine Arts Museum, 201–3
Gibralfaro Castle, 203
Museo Hollander, 203

NERJA
Balcony of Europe, 209
Prehistoric caves, 208–9

Lisbon

Alfama walking tour, 57–8
Bairro Alto (Upper City), 60–1
Bullfights, 74–5
Calouste Gulbenkian Museum, 66–7
Castle Belvedere, 58
Castle of St. George, 58–60
Cathedral (Sé), 60
Center for Modern Art, 67
Church of Madre de Deus/Museu
Nacional do Azulejo, 69

Museum of Decorative Art, 67–8
National Museum of Ancient Art, 66
National Museum of Contemporary
Art, 68
Pantheon Church of St. Engrácia,
69–70
Queluz Palace, 71–2
St. Roque Church and Museum, 70
St. Vincent Outside the Walls, 70–1

Lisbon Environs

BELÉM
Coach Museum, 65
Folk Art Museum, 64–5
Jerónimos Monastery, 62–3
Memorial to the Discoveries, 62
National Museum of Archeology, 63
Planetarium, 64

Portuguese Maritime Museum, 63–4
Tower of Belém, 61–2

SINTRA
National Palace, 72–4
Palace of Pena, 73–4

Madrid

Aquapolis, 155–6
Archeological Museum, 148

Army Museum, 149
Bullfights, 141–3

Madrid Day-Trip Areas

ACCOMMODATIONS

Costa del Sol

Key to Abbreviations: B = Budget; D = Deluxe; FC = First Class; M = Moderately priced; A = Apartment Hotel

Lisbon

Lisbon Environs

Madrid

RESTAURANTS

Costa del Sol

Lisbon

KEY TO ABBREVIATIONS: *B* = Budget; *D* = Deluxe (Top Restaurants); *FC* = First Class (Other Top Restaurants); *M* = Moderately priced

Lisbon Environs

Madrid

NOW, SAVE MONEY ON ALL YOUR TRAVELS!
Join Frommer's™ Dollarwise® Travel Club

Saving money while traveling is never a simple matter, which is why the **Dollarwise Travel Club** was formed 31 years ago. Developed in response to requests from Frommer's Travel Guide readers, the Club provides cost-cutting travel strategies, up-to-date travel information, and a sense of community for value-conscious travelers from all over the world.

In keeping with the money-saving concept, the annual membership fee is low—$18 for U.S. residents or $20 for residents of Canada, Mexico, and other countries—and is immediately exceeded by the value of your benefits, which include:

1. Any TWO books listed on the following pages.
2. Plus any ONE Frommer's City Guide.
3. A subscription to our quarterly newspaper, *The Dollarwise Traveler.*
4. A membership card that entitles you to purchase through the Club all Frommer's publications for 33% to 50% off their retail price.

The eight-page **Dollarwise Traveler** tells you about the latest developments in good-value travel worldwide and includes the following columns: **Hospitality Exchange** (for those offering and seeking hospitality in cities all over the world); **Share-a-Trip** (for those looking for travel companions to share costs); and **Readers Ask . . . Readers Reply** (for those with travel questions that other members can answer).

Aside from the Frommer's Guides and the Gault Millau Guides, you can also choose from our Special Editions. These include such titles as **California with Kids** (a compendium of the best of California's accommodations, restaurants, and sightseeing attractions appropriate for those traveling with toddlers through teens); **Candy Apple: New York with Kids** (a spirited guide to the Big Apple by a savvy New York grandmother that's perfect for both visitors and residents); **Caribbean Hideaways** (the 100 most romantic places to stay in the Islands, all rated on ambience, food, sports opportunities, and price); **Honeymoon Destinations** (a guide to planning and choosing just the right destination from hundreds of possibilities in the U.S., Mexico, and the Caribbean); **Marilyn Wood's Wonderful Weekends** (a selection of the best mini-vacations within a 200-mile radius of New York City, including descriptions of country inns and other accommodations, restaurants, picnic spots, sights, and activities); and **Paris Rendez-Vous** (a delightful guide to the best places to meet in Paris whether for power breakfasts or dancing till dawn).

To join this Club, simply send the appropriate membership fee with your name and address to: Frommer's Dollarwise Travel Club, 15 Columbus Circle, New York, NY 10023. Remember to specify which single city guide and which two other guides you wish to receive in your initial package of member's benefits. Or tear out the next page, check off your choices, and send the page to us with your membership fee.

FROMMER BOOKS
PRENTICE HALL PRESS
15 COLUMBUS CIRCLE
NEW YORK, NY 10023
212/373-8125

Date_____

Friends:

Please send me the books checked below.

FROMMER'S™ GUIDES

(Guides to sightseeing and tourist accommodations and facilities from budget to deluxe, with emphasis on the medium-priced.)

☐ Alaska. $14.95		☐ Germany $14.95
☐ Australia $14.95		☐ Italy $14.95
☐ Austria & Hungary $14.95		☐ Japan & Hong Kong. $14.95
☐ Belgium, Holland & Lux-		☐ Mid-Atlantic States $14.95
embourg $14.95		☐ New England $14.95
☐ Bermuda & The Bahamas . . . $14.95		☐ New York State. $14.95
☐ Brazil $14.95		☐ Northwest $14.95
☐ Canada $14.95		☐ Portugal, Madeira & the Azores. $14.95
☐ Caribbean $14.95		☐ Skiing Europe $14.95
☐ Cruises (incl. Alaska, Carib, Mex, Ha-		☐ South Pacific $14.95
waii, Panama, Canada & US). . $14.95		☐ Southeast Asia $14.95
☐ California & Las Vegas. $14.95		☐ Southern Atlantic States $14.95
☐ Egypt $14.95		☐ Southwest $14.95
☐ England & Scotland. $14.95		☐ Switzerland & Liechtenstein $14.95
☐ Florida $14.95		☐ USA $15.95
☐ France. $14.95		

FROMMER'S $-A-DAY® GUIDES

(In-depth guides to sightseeing and low-cost tourist accommodations and facilities.)

☐ Europe on $40 a Day $15.95		☐ New York on $60 a Day $13.95
☐ Australia on $40 a Day $13.95		☐ New Zealand on $45 a Day. $13.95
☐ Eastern Europe on $25 a Day . $13.95		☐ Scandinavia on $60 a Day. $13.95
☐ England on $50 a Day $13.95		☐ Scotland & Wales on $40 a Day $13.95
☐ Greece on $35 a Day $13.95		☐ South America on $35 a Day. $13.95
☐ Hawaii on $60 a Day $13.95		☐ Spain & Morocco on $40 a Day $13.95
☐ India on $25 a Day $12.95		☐ Turkey on $30 a Day $13.95
☐ Ireland on $35 a Day $13.95		☐ Washington, D.C. & Historic Va. on
☐ Israel on $40 a Day $13.95		$40 a Day $13.95
☐ Mexico on $35 a Day. $13.95		

FROMMER'S TOURING GUIDES

(Color illustrated guides that include walking tours, cultural and historic sites, and other vital travel information.)

☐ Amsterdam $10.95		☐ New York. $10.95
☐ Australia $9.95		☐ Paris $8.95
☐ Brazil $10.95		☐ Rome $10.95
☐ Egypt $8.95		☐ Scotland $9.95
☐ Florence $8.95		☐ Thailand $9.95
☐ Hong Kong $10.95		☐ Turkey. $10.95
☐ London. $8.95		☐ Venice. $8.95

TURN PAGE FOR ADDITONAL BOOKS AND ORDER FORM

0690

FROMMER'S CITY GUIDES

(Pocket-size guides to sightseeing and tourist accommodations and facilities in all price ranges.)

- ☐ Amsterdam/Holland........$8.95
- ☐ Athens.................$8.95
- ☐ Atlanta................$8.95
- ☐ Atlantic City/Cape May $8.95
- ☐ Barcelona $7.95
- ☐ Belgium $7.95
- ☐ Boston $8.95
- ☐ Cancún/Cozumel/Yucatán ...$8.95
- ☐ Chicago $8.95
- ☐ Denver/Boulder/Colorado
   Springs...............$7.95
- ☐ Dublin/Ireland..........$8.95
- ☐ Hawaii $8.95
- ☐ Hong Kong $7.95
- ☐ Las Vegas $8.95
- ☐ Lisbon/Madrid/Costa del Sol..$8.95
- ☐ London................$8.95
- ☐ Los Angeles............$8.95
- ☐ Mexico City/Acapulco $8.95
- ☐ Minneapolis/St. Paul.......$8.95
- ☐ Montréal/Québec City $8.95
- ☐ New Orleans $8.95
- ☐ New York......................$8.95
- ☐ Orlando.......................$8.95
- ☐ Paris.........................$8.95
- ☐ Philadelphia...................$8.95
- ☐ Rio $8.95
- ☐ Rome $8.95
- ☐ Salt Lake City $8.95
- ☐ San Diego $8.95
- ☐ San Francisco $8.95
- ☐ Santa Fe/Taos/Albuquerque $8.95
- ☐ Seattle/Portland.................$7.95
- ☐ Sydney $8.95
- ☐ Tampa/St. Petersburg $8.95
- ☐ Tokyo $7.95
- ☐ Toronto.......................$8.95
- ☐ Vancouver/Victoria...............$7.95
- ☐ Washington, D.C.................$8.95

SPECIAL EDITIONS

- ☐ Beat the High Cost of Travel ...$6.95
- ☐ Bed & Breakfast—N. America $11.95
- ☐ California with Kids $14.95
- ☐ Caribbean Hideaways $14.95
- ☐ Manhattan's Outdoor
   Sculpture...............$15.95
- ☐ Motorist's Phrase Book (Fr/Ger/Sp).....$4.95
- ☐ Paris Rendez-Vous...............$10.95
- ☐ Swap and Go (Home Exchanging) $10.95
- ☐ The Candy Apple (NY with Kids) $12.95
- ☐ Travel Diary and Record Book $5.95

- ☐ Honeymoon Destinations (US, Mex & Carib) $14.95
- ☐ Where to Stay USA (From $3 to $30 a night) $10.95
- ☐ Marilyn Wood's Wonderful Weekends (CT, DE, MA, NH, NJ, NY, PA, RI, VT) $11.95
- ☐ The New World of Travel (Annual sourcebook by Arthur Frommer for savvy travelers) ..$16.95

GAULT MILLAU

(The only guides that distinguish the truly superlative from the merely overrated.)

- ☐ The Best of Chicago $15.95
- ☐ The Best of France........$16.95
- ☐ The Best of Hong Kong $16.95
- ☐ The Best of Italy $16.95
- ☐ The Best of London........$16.95
- ☐ The Best of Los Angeles...........$16.95
- ☐ The Best of New England $15.95
- ☐ The Best of New York..............$16.95
- ☐ The Best of Paris.................$16.95
- ☐ The Best of San Francisco $16.95
- ☐ The Best of Washington, D.C. $16.95

ORDER NOW!

In U.S. include $2 shipping UPS for 1st book; $1 ea. add'l book. Outside U.S. $3 and $1, respectively.
Allow four to six weeks for delivery in U.S., longer outside U.S.
Enclosed is my check or money order for $_____

NAME_____

ADDRESS_____

CITY_____ STATE_____ ZIP____

0690

Politico's Guide to

THE
HISTORY OF
BRITISH
POLITICAL
PARTIES

Politico's Guide to

THE
HISTORY OF
BRITISH
POLITICAL
PARTIES

DAVID BOOTHROYD

First published in Great Britain 2001
Published by Politico's Publishing
8 Artillery Row
Westminster
London
SW1P 1RZ

Tel 020 7931 0090
Fax 020 7828 8111
Email publishing@politicos.co.uk
Website http://www.politicos.co.uk/publishing

First published in hardback 2001

A catalogue record for this book is available from the British Library.
ISBN 1 902301 59 5
Printed and bound by Creative Print and Design, Wales.

Contents

I believe that without party, Parliamentary government is impossible

– Benjamin Disraeli, 3 April 1872

Preface

At a time when political campaigning is increasingly dominated by single-issue pressure groups, and loyalty to a political party is in many quarters looked down upon as at best a mental weakness, it is appropriate to remind ourselves of the contribution to United Kingdom politics that has been made by our political parties over the centuries. This book was finished in the last month of the twentieth century, a century in which the idea of the mass party had become a central feature of our political system.

Voters may be cynical about all parties, but there is no great increase in support for the independent in politics. The success of Martin Bell in the 1997 general election happened only because two large parties decided to withdraw in his favour. In the eighteenth and early nineteenth centuries, people could and did get elected to Parliament on a single policy and gave support to whichever party appeared to help them. The last such member was Sir Edward Watkin, MP for Hythe in 1874–95. Sir Edward was a strong supporter of a Channel Tunnel and moved through all parties to try to get his scheme approved. Since this time, anyone who wishes to play a role in politics must commit themselves to a political party.

Only three parties out of the more than 250 in this book have ever formed a government in the United Kingdom. Many of the entries are for parties with no hope of election of their supporters to any office. The very existence of many small parties is a monument to the vanity of their leaders, and the suggestion that a few dozen constantly feuding Trotskyites could possibly lead a revolution in an advanced European democracy is an absurdity.

To my knowledge a book such as this has not previously been attempted. F. W. S. Craig published brief outlines of the smaller parties in *Minor Parties at British Parliamentary Elections 1885–1974* (Macmillan, London and Basingstoke, 1975), though this book concentrates on their election candidates rather than history. Many political parties are contained in the *Directory of British Political Organizations* (Longman, London, 1994) by Paul Mercer but the second edition is not easily available as a result of legal action taken by one of the organisations; a third edition is being published by Politico's in 2001. *The Encyclopaedia of British and Irish Political Organizations* (Pinter, London, 2000) by Peter Barberis, John McHugh and

Mike Tyldesley also contains much useful information but its high price makes it inaccessible to most readers.

This book actually began as a post I sent to the Usenet network on the Internet in June 1996, possibly still to be found in cyberspace with Message-ID <9606091516125240@election.demon.co.uk>.

Finding information on the smaller political parties has been difficult. Newspapers have rarely reported their activities, especially not since the great decline in political reporting in the 1970s and 1980s. The existence of the Internet will help small parties campaign electronically, and the creation of the Register of Political Parties may assist in tracing them in future.

Readers may be asking themselves what defines a political party. During the formation of PEOPLE, which ultimately became the Green Party, one of the founders investigated and discovered that there was no official definition and that all one needed to do was to start to act like a political party. Following from this, there are entries below for some organisations (such as Third Position) which do not consider themselves political parties, but which do share many of the attributes associated with political parties.

The scope of this book is political parties active within the United Kingdom, which since 1922 has included Northern Ireland, and from 1801 to 1922 encompassed the whole of Ireland. This means including Irish Nationalist and Republican parties who do not wish to be part of the United Kingdom. I apologise to these parties if they feel they should not belong here, but the book would not be complete without them. The linking factor for all entries is the United Kingdom Parliament and elections to it. Not all parties contest elections but, common sense being more important than consistency, I have included significant parties which are electorally inactive.

The notes below each entry may need some justification. The Number on Register indicates whether a party is registered with Companies House as a political party. Electoral statistics refer to elections to the United Kingdom Parliament only; this is because details of these elections are easily available from 1832 onwards, and considering one set of elections only ensures consistency. The highest percentage vote for each party (together with the actual number of votes polled) is given because most parties are small; the significance of the statistic is that it shows how close they were to electing a member. Wherever possible the highest vote cited is that obtained after near-universal franchise in 1918.

I must express my thanks to the many members and former members of political parties who helped in the research for the book, whilst making clear that the responsibility for each entry is my own. A special word of thanks should also go to Nicholas Whyte, who read all the entries for Irish parties and offered useful corrections. This book would have been much more difficult to compile were it not for the invaluable series of reference books published by the late F. W. S. Craig, and it is to be regretted that his successors Colin Rallings and Michael Thrasher have not maintained the same level of interest in smaller parties.

Much of the research for the book was done in various libraries and I would like to thank the staff of Westminster Public Libraries, the British Library Newspaper Library, and the London Library for their help and assistance. Thanks are also due to Iain Dale at Politico's Publishing for his decision to publish the book.

DAVID BOOTHROYD
Westminster, October 2000

The author would be delighted to receive any information or corrections on the entries in the book, preferably by email to david@election.demon.co.uk.

Definitions

anti-Semitism: hostility towards Jewish people, or support for discrimination against Jews.

Catholic Disabilities: a set of legal measures restricting the involvement of Roman Catholics in public life, imposed after the Reformation. Pressure to remove such laws increased throughout the eighteenth century.

Comintern: *see* 'Internationals'.

communism: political system in which substantially all property is in common ownership, so that the central apparatus of the state can distribute wealth equally and thereby break down class barriers. Technically, communism as defined by Karl Marx is the final stage at which class barriers disappear and the state withers away.

corporate state: system of government in which each sector of industry is grouped together as an economic unit under the control of the state. This policy is favoured by some fascist thinkers. The best explanation of how it would apply in Britain is given in *The Greater Britain* by Oswald Mosley (1934 new edition), pages 34–48.

deposit: the sum of money which all candidates must leave with the Returning Officer. The deposit was set at £150 in 1918, and was returned only to candidates who were elected or polled over 12.5% of the vote. In 1985 the deposit was increased to £500 but the threshold for retaining it was reduced to 5% of the vote. Retention of the deposit is therefore a test of electoral credibility.

devolution: the act of a government in creating subsidiary administrations covering a part of its territory.

electoral truce: the arrangement during the Great War and the Second World War by which the three main parties agreed not to nominate candidates for by-elections in seats held by the others. The texts of the electoral truces were printed in *Chronology of British Parliamentary By-elections*

1833–1987 by F. W. S. Craig, pages 361–2.

environmentalism: political philosophy placing care for the natural resources of the Earth at the centre of its policies.

fascism: system of government in which the state is paramount and the individual must submit to the power of the state, usually expressed through a single leader.

integration: proposal for future constitutional arrangement of Northern Ireland. Integration would mean that Northern Ireland would be a full part of the United Kingdom, with the same constitution as England.

'Internationals': a series of international associations of left-wing parties. The First International was formed in London on 28 September 1864 but fell into factionalism and disintegrated in 1881. The Second International, also known as the Socialist International, was formed in Paris in 1889 and (after several reformations) is still in existence. The Labour Party and the Social Democratic and Labour Party are affiliates. The Third International, also known as the Communist International or Comintern, was formed in Moscow in 1919 and was under Soviet control. The Fourth International, formed in Périgny, France in 1938, was organised by supporters of Leon Trotsky.

loyalism: belief in loyal support for the United Kingdom Crown. The term is usually applied to those in Northern Ireland allied to paramilitary groups supporting continued British rule.

multilateralism: belief that the United Kingdom should enter into negotiations with potential enemies in order to reach an agreement that both sides' nuclear weapons may be decommissioned.

national socialism: a system of government in which the state is all-powerful and seeks to maintain a racially pure nation, usually subservient to a single charismatic leader.

nationalism: support for policies which increase the unity of a nation and preserve it from the domination of other nations. Scottish, Welsh and Irish nationalism means a belief that these countries should be autonomous and not part of the United Kingdom. British nationalism is a belief in the racial unity of the people of the British Isles and opposition to immigration by those of other racial backgrounds.

nationalisation: policy of bringing major companies into public ownership. Advocates of this policy believe that such companies, when directed by the government, can be made to serve the nation as opposed to their shareholders.

nazism: *see* National Socialism.

pacifism: opposition to the use of war and conflict to solve disputes between nations.

power-sharing: system of government in which two communities are involved. In relation to Northern Ireland the term means a government including both unionists and nationalists.

proportional representation: electoral system in which the number of seats a party wins is in direct proportion to the number of votes they receive.

protectionism: policy of increasing duties on foreign goods in order to damage their competitiveness with respect to goods manufactured in this country.

republicanism: support for a constitution in which the head of state is elected. This term is usually used with respect to Ireland, in which it means favouring the establishment of a nation consisting of the whole of Ireland with no link to Great Britain.

social credit: political system advocating reforms to the banking system in order to provide prosperity for all without nationalisation.

socialism: political system in which government acts to remove unfairness, so as to prevent society from falling into division. Some hold that this requires common ownership of the key points, or all, of the economy.

(Many dictionaries and encyclopaedia make the mistake of defining socialism by reference to section four of Clause IV of the Labour Party constitution as it was in 1918–95.)

syndicalism: policy advocating that the working-class take direct action to abolish capitalism and institute a workers' state based on production units.

tariff reform: policy whereby goods exported within the British Empire would be given preferential tariffs, and high tariffs would be added to foreign goods, in order to protect domestic industry threatened by foreign imports.

trotskyite: supporter of the policies of Leon Trotsky.

unilateralism: belief that the United Kingdom should decommission its nuclear weapons irrespective of the actions of other countries.

unionism: belief that Ireland (or Northern Ireland) should be part of a United Kingdom with Great Britain.

BRITISH POLITICAL PARTIES A–Z

Action Party

Website: http://www.geocities.com/CapitolHill/3759/ [This is the website of the 'Friends of OM', an organisation of ex-members of the various parties formed by Sir Oswald Mosley]

Parliamentary elections won: 0

Number of candidacies: 0

The Action Party was the name taken by Sir Oswald Mosley's **Union Movement** from January 1973. 'Action' as a political slogan had been associated with Sir Oswald Mosley for very many years, having been the name of a **New Party** journal in October 1931. Sir Oswald himself had retired from active politics in 1966 and the party was led by Jeffrey Hamm, Mosley's Private Secretary. The Action Party did not contest any Parliamentary elections, though it did nominate six candidates for the Greater London Council in 1973.

The party renamed itself the Action Society in 1978 and is still in existence as a publishing house. It campaigns for a power bloc based on Europe and the British Commonwealth of Nations.

Agricultural Party

Only vote: J.L. Anderson (Fife Eastern, 1933 (2/2)) – 4,404 votes, 14.6%

Parliamentary elections won: 0

Number of candidacies: 1

This party was formed at a meeting addressed by Lord Beaverbrook in Norwich in January 1931. The meeting had been called by J.F. Wright, a leading member of the National Farmers' Union in Norfolk; originally it was intended to organise in Norfolk only and called itself the Norfolk Farmers Party. After one week it became the Agricultural Party and organised nationwide.

As a Beaverbrook venture, it was also a supporter of Empire Free Trade (see **Empire Free Trade Crusade**) and received publicity in the *Daily Express*; Viscount Rothermere was also a supporter and both he and Beaverbrook were members of the party's executive. The party campaigned for protectionism for agriculture by increasing tariffs and duties on non-Empire food imports.

When Beaverbrook made peace with the **Conservative Party** on 27 March 1931, the Agricultural Party was included: Neville Chamberlain wrote to Lord Beaverbrook to confirm that the Conservative Party would support measures to increase agricultural production, if necessary by imposing protective tariffs. On 30 March, J. F. Wright declared that 'We are no longer rebels' and pledged support for the Conservative Party.

In 1933 the party fought a by-election in East Fife after Beaverbrook objected to the lack of progress on imperial preference at the Ottawa Imperial Economic Conference. East Fife was a fairly but not overwhelmingly agricultural area and the call for a meat tax did not carry many voters. Though the party saved its deposit, activity declined swiftly after this by-election; the party had lost the support of the National Farmers' Union and had been abandoned by the press; the by-election was Beaverbrook's last attempt to challenge the Conservatives at the polls.

It appears that the party continued in existence until the late 1940s.

Air Road Public Safety White Resident

See **Public Safety Democratic Monarchist White Resident**.

Albion Party

Only vote: J. R. Muir (Cheshire, Tatton, 1997) – 126 votes, 0.3%.
Parliamentary elections won: 0
Number of candidacies: 1

The Albion Party was formed in August 1996 by Richard Muir, a self-employed businessman and former journalist living in central London. Albion Party policies favour decentralisation, and the party opposes UK membership of the European Union. Its social policies have a libertarian flavour; its economic ones, a co-operative flavour. Richard Muir had been planning to fight his local seat, but gave it up in order to fight Tatton against Neil Hamilton. The party appears to have been disbanded.

All Party Alliance

Highest vote: J. Creasey (Oldham West, 1968 (13/6)) - 3,389 votes, 13.2%.

Parliamentary elections won: 0

Number of candidacies: 4

John Creasey, a crime and adventure novelist who was one of the founders of the British Crime Writers Association and had been a Liberal Parliamentary candidate, formed this movement in 1967. The Alliance called for power-sharing by all-party government with proportional representation in Parliament and the cabinet. Creasey started fighting by-elections during the second Wilson government under the banner of the Alliance.

Creasey polled well enough to save his deposit at Oldham West in June 1968 but then stopped fighting elections. In the early 1970s the movement changed its name to Evolution to Democracy/All Party Alliance; in April 1973, the Alliance merged with a body called The Organisation led by Colin Campion to form the **Independent Democratic Alliance**. John Creasey died on 9 June 1973.

Alliance

Highest vote: M. O. J. Taylor (Cornwall, Truro, 1987 (12/3)) – 30,599 votes, 60.4%

Parliamentary elections won: 54

Number of candidacies: 1,294

This was the term popularly used to describe the Liberal/Social Democratic Party Alliance. Aspects of the history of these parties are included under their own entries but it will be convenient to discuss the relationship between the two here.

When the **Social Democratic Party** was formed in March 1981, there was an immediate expectation of some form of electoral link with the **Liberal Party**. A joint policy programme, 'Fresh Start for Britain', was agreed in June 1981. At the SDP's first by-election contest in Warrington in July 1981, the Liberal Party stood down and Roy Jenkins fought as 'Social Democratic Party with Liberal support'.

Proposals for a formal alliance went to the Liberal Assembly which voted to support the pact on 16 September. The two parties agreed to fight the next general election on a common platform, and to arrange between themselves which seats were to be contested by which party. The term 'Alliance' was first used in the Croydon North West by-election of October 1981, the first to be fought under the formal pact, apparently as an unofficial title thought up by the Liberal Party President, Richard Holme.

The negotiation of the Alliance caused some difficulties for candidate selection as the Liberal Party had already chosen a number of prospective candidates by the time the Alliance was agreed. As is usual for political parties, these early candidates were in the seats the Liberals were closest to winning. Negotiations on the share-out of seats took most of 1982, and eventually the Liberal candidates in seats re-allocated to the SDP were given the ill-defined job of 'Parliamentary spokesperson'.

In the event, at the 1983 general election, 322 Liberals and 311 Social Democrats were made official Alliance candidates. The division caused some opposition from Liberals, especially in the north of England. In three constituencies (Hammersmith, Liverpool Broadgreen and Hackney South and Shoreditch) the local Liberal Association refused to accept the SDP candidate (in two cases, a sitting MP) and put up a candidate of their own. In Liverpool Broadgreen, the unofficial Liberal eventually polled more votes than the official SDP candidate.

The Alliance manifesto for the 1983 general election was negotiated by a series of joint policy panels. Two of these panels found a consensus hard to reach: on industrial relations, the SDP favoured statutory controls on trade unions whereas the Liberals sought a non-statutory approach, and on defence, the Liberals were opposed to deployment of Cruise nuclear missiles whereas the SDP was opposed to unilateralism. The final manifesto included statutory controls on trade unions but made no pledge on Cruise missiles.

The question of the leadership of the Alliance also caused difficulties. Roy Jenkins, leader of the SDP, was firmly in favour of the Alliance having a 'Prime Minister Designate', and as a former senior minister he was the natural choice. However, his appearances during the general election proved uninspiring and under a fortnight before polling day an attempt was made to get him to stand down. He refused, but the Alliance strategy meeting decided that Liberal leader David Steel should be more prominent during the remainder of the campaign.

The result of the election reversed the previous balance of the two Alliance parties in Parliament, with only six SDP members and 17 Liberals. Roy Jenkins, who supported moves to merge the two parties into a single organisation, stood down as leader of the SDP and was replaced by David Owen, who was known to be a firm supporter of the SDP remaining a separate party and who regarded the Alliance merely as an electoral pact.

As a result of the difficulties between the two parties in 1983, a Joint Leaders' Advisory Committee for the Alliance was created; in 1985 it became the Alliance Strategy Committee. Joint working between the parties was however limited in the run-up to the 1987 election. In 78 seats, local constituency members of both parties participated in Parliamentary selections open to candidates of both parties (called 'joint open selection'). In 60 more seats which were allocated to the SDP, local Liberal Party members were allowed to vote in the selection.

Policy formulation again hit problems over defence policy. A joint commission had been established but when it was leaked that the commission would recommend abandoning Trident and would not commit the Alliance to replacing Polaris, David Owen openly insisted that Britain must retain nuclear weapons. A new compromise was produced in which British nuclear weapons would be part of an Anglo-French unit, but the Liberal Assembly voted to reject this idea by 652 to 625. Policy committees of the two parties tried many compromises and it was not until the end of 1986 that a defence policy was agreed. The public perception that David Owen's insistence had forced David Steel to give way gave rise to satirical depictions of Owen as dominating Steel.

The range of Alliance policies was launched in January 1987 in *The Time has Come*, which was the basis for the 1987 election manifesto *Britain United: The Time has Come*. Even more than in 1983 the dual leadership looked cumbersome: 'the two Davids' appeared together at practically all Alliance news conferences during the election, which invited the media to look for differences of policy and emphasis in their answers to the same questions. While Alliance strategy was to look forward to a Parliament in which no party had a majority, in separate interviews a week before polling day, David Steel ruled out Alliance co-operation with a minority Conservative government, while David Owen appeared to do the same with regard to Labour.

The Alliance's painfully hammered out defence policy again came under strain during the election campaign itself when under attack by the Conservatives: David Owen said that they could be persuaded to retain Trident, and David Steel said he personally would be prepared to authorise use of nuclear weapons.

The final results of the 1987 election showed the Alliance falling back slightly compared with 1983. On the Sunday after the election, David Steel announced that he had called a meeting of Liberal Party officers to set out options for merging the Liberal Party with the SDP into one organisation; David Owen immediately declared he would oppose any such suggestion and would not play any part in a merged party. The SDP executive backed its leader but only by 18 votes to 13, and proposed that the Alliance simply elect a single leader while continuing as two parties.

In August 1987, when the SDP membership voted in favour of continuing discussions with the Liberals on a merger, David Owen resigned as leader and was replaced by Robert Maclennan (who, although personally opposed to merging the parties, was willing to follow the majority). Negotiations on the shape of the merged party continued through the autumn of 1987 and a draft constitution was agreed on 2 December 1987, largely based on that of the old SDP.

Negotiations on the policy of the new party proved more difficult. A joint policy statement published on 13 January 1988 was immediately rejected by Liberal MPs, who identified a large number of vote-losing policies, and was dropped. A new policy statement which was acceptable was produced soon after and a Special Liberal Assembly accepted the merger on 24 January 1988; the SDP council accepted on 31 January. The **Social and Liberal Democrats** were formally launched on 3 March 1988.

Alliance Party of Northern Ireland

Address: 88 University Street, Belfast BT7 1HE

Email address: info@alliance.org

Web site: http://www.allianceparty.org

Number on Register: 14

Highest vote: Dr J. T. Alderdice (Belfast East, 1987) – 10,574 votes, 32.1%

Parliamentary elections won: 0

Number of candidacies: 91

The Alliance Party grew out of the New Ulster Movement, formed during the February 1969 Stormont elections to support the moderate Unionist Prime Minister Terence O'Neill. In April 1970 the New Ulster Movement reformed as the Alliance Party, campaigning for support for the constitutional position of Northern Ireland in the United Kingdom irrespective of religious differences. The party had a fairly low profile in its early years.

In 1972 two moderate Unionist members of the Northern Ireland House of Commons, and a moderate Nationalist, joined the new party, and it picked up some of the support which had previously gone to the **Northern Ireland Labour Party**. The party gained one United Kingdom MP through secession – Stratton Mills joined from the **Ulster Unionists** in 1972, though he did not seek re-election in 1974. Alliance seeks to portray itself as cross-community, and the Alliance vote appears to be mostly middle-class.

Alliance won 13.6% of the vote in the 1973 local elections, but fell to 9.2% in theNorthern Ireland Assembly elections the next month, securing eight seats. The party, especially its leader Oliver Napier, played a large part in framing the negotiations at Sunningdale. Napier was made Head of the Office of Law Reform on the 'Sunningdale' Executive, and Bob Cooper was Head of the Department of Manpower Services. Perhaps because of the party's support for Sunningdale, its headquarters were blown up on the day before the February 1974 general election.

The Alliance vote increased throughout the 1970s. It polled 9.8% in the Northern Ireland Constitutional Convention elections of 1975, and within the Convention argued for a strong cross-community Assembly with law-making powers, exercised through committees which matched

9

the political balance in the Assembly as a whole. However, it believed a single-party government could be possible if the political situation developed, and opposed the establishment of a Council of Ireland (as envisaged by the Sunningdale Agreement) – both policies which would appeal to unionists. The party had its peak vote of 14.4% in the 1977 district council elections.

The Alliance general election vote reached a peak in 1979 at just under 83,000 votes. The party was within 1,000 votes of winning Belfast East where the Unionist vote was almost evenly split – a seat it had itself predicted it would win. The increased political tension of the hunger strikes in the early 1980s damaged the chances of a moderate party and its vote fell. Alliance strongly supported the Conservative government's policy of 'rolling devolution' in 1982, and it won 10 seats in the Northern Ireland Assembly elections that October.

Alliance support fell again in the 1983 general election and the party's candidate polled 5%, losing his deposit, in the European Parliament elections of 1984. Oliver Napier resigned the leadership of the party on 24 September 1984 and was succeeded by John Cushnahan, but the Alliance vote continued to fall in the district council elections of 1985 – especially outside Belfast. The party's backing of the Anglo-Irish Agreement in 1985 may have further cost it some Unionist support, as shown by its low vote in the by-elections of January 1986.

None the less the party stuck to its policy and opposed the Unionist policy of adjourning all meetings of local authorities, as part of their campaign against the Anglo-Irish Agreement. The 1987 general election saw the party increase its vote to 10% though John Cushnahan did poorly in North Down; he resigned the leadership on 7 September. In the leadership contest that followed, the party's economics spokesperson Seamus Close was unexpectedly defeated by a consultant psychiatrist who had not held elected office, John Alderdice.

On Alderdice's initiative, the party held talks with senior political figures in Great Britain and the Republic of Ireland in early 1988. The party welcomed the launch of the **Social and Liberal Democrats** and eventually agreed a common manifesto with the SLD and the Progressive Democrats of the Republic of Ireland in order to fight the 1989 European Parliament elections, in which the party polled 5.2%.

The party found new competition when the **Conservative Party** began organising in Northern Ireland, at first unofficially but with official backing from November 1989. The Conservatives built up a large and active branch in North Down, Alliance's best constituency, which began to dent the Alliance vote in the district council elections of 1989 – though elsewhere its vote increased.

Alliance joined in the 'Brooke Talks' from April 1991 along with the other three main constitutional parties (**Ulster Unionists, Ulster Democratic Unionists**, and **Social Democratic and Labour Party**) and managed to agree with the two Unionist parties on devolution. The party did well in the district council elections of 1993 and stood to profit further when the Northern Ireland Conservatives' popular leader Dr Laurence Kennedy retired from politics. Oliver Napier came a strong third in a by-election in North Down in 1995.

After the IRA ceasefire in September 1994, Alliance councillors on Belfast City Council successfully proposed a motion that called upon the loyalist paramilitaries to end violence. The Party sent a delegation to the Republic of Ireland sponsored Forum for Peace and Reconciliation and took part in other cross-party talks. It supported Prime Minister John Major's decision to call an election in order to secure entry to the all-party talks.

In the Forum elections of 1996, Alliance polled 6.5% and won one constituency seat each in Belfast East and South, North Down, Strangford and East Antrim. After the confrontation between the Orange Order and local residents at Drumcree in July 1996, Alliance made a complaint against the Ulster Unionists and the Ulster Democratic Unionists for allying themselves with loyalist paramilitaries, and supported the suspension from the talks process of **Sinn Féin** and the **Ulster Democratic Party** which had been linked with terrorist murders.

Alliance leader Dr John Alderdice was made a life peer in a list of working peers in August 1996, nominated by the Liberal Democrats. The party's vote fell slightly in the 1997 general election to 8.0%. After participating in the all-party talks, the party was delighted to find that the 1998 Belfast Agreement contained many aspects which had been Alliance Party policy. Its chances in the subsequent Northern Ireland Assembly election were dented by the **Northern Ireland Women's Coalition** but it still won six seats.

Lord Alderdice, a day after resigning as party leader, was appointed by the Northern Ireland Secretary as the initial Presiding Officer of the Assembly and eventually became Speaker. The current Alliance Party leader is Sean Neeson.

Anti-Common Market Free Trade Party

Highest vote: D. W. Bundy (Hertfordshire South West, 1979 (13/12)) – 288 votes, 0.8%
Parliamentary elections won: 0
Number of candidacies: 6

The Anti-Common Market Free Trade Party was the name taken by the **United Anti-Common Market** candidates from June 1979. The party's policy was opposition to British membership of the European Communities. It contested a few seats in by-elections in 1979–83. In 1982 it reversed the order in its name to the Free Trade Anti-Common Market Party. The party appears to have disbanded shortly after 1983.

Anti-Federalist League

Highest vote: M. C. Howson (Staffordshire Moorlands, 1992) – 2,121 votes, 3.4%
Parliamentary elections won: 0
Number of candidacies: 18

Dr Alan Sked, Lecturer in International History at the London School of Economics, formed the Anti-Federalist League in early November 1991 after writing to *The Times* to appeal for those opposed to the European Union to form a party campaigning for British withdrawal. The formation was shortly before the Maastricht Conference at which the European Union was to negotiate its future structure.

The new organisation was based on the Anti-Corn Law League of the mid-nineteenth century, and the League was first envisaged as a cross-party group: Dr Sked appealed to members of other parties who were opposed to a federal structure for the European Union to join. The **Labour Party** however banned its Parliamentary candidates from joining within a month of its foundation.

In response to the Maastricht Treaty, the League decided to nominate candidates in the forthcoming election of 1992. It fought 16 seats, mostly in London and the south of England, some held by senior Conservative ministers (Dr Sked himself fought Bath against **Conservative Party** Chairman Chris Patten). The League, and the issue of European policy, did not have a high profile in the election and the candidates polled a total of just over 5,000 votes. The highest vote went to a candidate who had been well known as a Conservative councillor.

The issue of the Maastricht Treaty became more prominent after the election when the government introduced a Bill to ratify it. With a large number of Conservative MPs opposed to the Treaty voting with the opposition, the government suffered several defeats in Parliament and appeared vulnerable. The Anti-Federalist League nominated Dr Sked to stand in two by-elections in Conservative-held seats in summer 1993 – Newbury and Christchurch. In both seats he polled well in a crowded field, coming in above all other minor party candidates and polling more than half of the Labour vote.

The League reorganised as the **UK Independence Party** on 3 September 1993, adopting a more formal party structure.

Anti H-Block

Highest vote: R. G. Sands (Fermanagh and South Tyrone, 1981 (9/4)) – 30,493 votes, 51.2%
Parliamentary elections won: 2
Number of candidacies: 2

In 1980–1, IRA and INLA prisoners held in the Maze Prison went on hunger strike in a protest at the removal of 'special status' for members of paramilitary organisations. The leader of the strike was the Officer Commanding IRA prisoners in Long Kesh (the former name of the Maze Prison, still widely used in Ireland), Bobby Sands.

When a by-election was caused in the nationalist-majority Fermanagh and South Tyrone constituency, Sands was nominated as an Anti H-Block/Armagh Political Prisoner candidate. No other nationalist or republican stood to split the vote and he went on to win the by-election. Twenty-seven days later, without any concessions by the government,

Bobby Sands died. The second by-election was won by his election agent, Owen Carron, standing as an Anti H-Block/Proxy Political Prisoner candidate.

The Anti H-Block movement was essentially a front organisation for Sinn Féin which was not at that stage contesting elections. Sinn Féin resumed its electoral strategy soon after and Carron was their candidate in the 1983 general election.

Anti-Partition of Ireland League of Great Britain

Highest vote: W. McGuinness (Glasgow Gorbals, 1950) – 1,959 votes, 4.7%

Parliamentary elections won: 0

Number of candidacies: 5

In 1948, the Irish Taoiseach John Costello announced that the Irish Free State was to declare itself a Republic and leave the Commonwealth. In order that citizens of the Republic of Ireland should not be treated as foreigners in the United Kingdom, the Labour government introduced the Ireland Bill. The Bill also put the partition of Ireland on a permanent basis by declaring that no change would be made in Northern Ireland's consti-tutional position without the endorsement of the Stormont Parliament.

As a result of these constitutional developments, Irish nationalists formed the Anti-Partition of Ireland League. In 1948 this League formed a Great British branch to act as a focus for Irish nationalist campaigning. It fought four seats in the 1950 election, and one in 1951, all of which had large Irish populations and were held by Labour MPs who had voted for the Ireland Bill. The candidates all claimed that on other issues they were Labour supporters, and one also supported Scottish nationalism.

The Anti-Partitionists never made the breakthrough which had been achieved by T. P. O'Connor, who sat as an Irish **Nationalist** for a Liverpool seat for 44 years, and the League was disbanded in the 1950s.

Anti-Waste League

Highest vote: M. F. Sueter (Hertford, 1921 (16/6)) – 12,329 votes, 68.9%.

Parliamentary elections won: 2

Number of candidacies: 4

Viscount Rothermere, the millionaire newspaper proprietor, made several attempts to form his own party. The Anti-Waste League was the first of these, announced in January 1921 in the *Sunday Pictorial* after a campaign against government waste (this was a time of recession). It advocated a reduction of government (including local government) spending to return the country to solvency. The real aim of the league was to break up the Lloyd George **Coalition**. Rothermere himself was President of the League.

The Anti-Waste League managed to win two by-elections from the Conservatives in June 1921. Conservative MP Esmond Harmsworth (Viscount Rothermere's son) became leader of its Parliamentary group and Chairman of the League, though he retained the Conservative whip. The League was closely associated with Horatio Bottomley's Independent Parliamentary Group and one MP elected under the auspices of that group was also a League member.

Horatio Bottomley was convicted of fraud in summer 1922 and expelled from the House of Commons, damaging the League by association. Pressure for reduced government spending had already resulted in the establishment of the Committee on National Expenditure under the ex-cabinet minister Sir Eric Geddes. In February 1922 this committee recommended savings of £75 million.

The waning of support forced a change of strategy by the Anti-Waste League in the 1922 election when it supported individual candidates from other parties instead of putting up candidates of its own. The League was wound up after the 1922 election; most of its supporters rejoined the **Conservative Party**.

Bean Party

See **New Millennium Bean Party**

Belfast Labour Party

See **Northern Ireland Labour Party**.

British and Commonwealth Party

Highest vote: M. S. Blair (Stratford, 1963 (15/8)) – 281 votes, 0.8%
Parliamentary elections won: 0
Number of candidacies: 2

This party was formed by Miles Blair, a farmer from Kidderminster, in 1963. Blair had resigned from the Conservatives in around 1955, and formed his own party to campaign for action against the overseas trade deficit. The party wanted to increase trade with the Commonwealth and to form an integrated Commonwealth defence policy. It opposed British membership of the European Communities and excessive interference by the USA.

Miles Blair fought the Stratford by-election of August 1963, caused by the resignation of John Profumo, and Kidderminster in the 1964 election, polling badly in both cases.

British Democratic Party

Parliamentary elections won: 0
Number of candidacies: 0

The British Democratic Party was formed in early 1979 by Anthony Reed-Herbert, a Leicester solicitor who had been a Conservative before becoming a leading local member of the **National Front**. The party was based on the Leicester branch of the National Front which mostly followed Reed-Herbert into the new party, but attempted to distance itself from the extremist image of the far-right.

The anti-racist campaigns of the late 1970s and early 1980s hit the party's organisation. A Granada Television programme in 1981 exposed the party's activity in stockpiling guns and its links with the **British Movement.** Shortly afterwards Anthony Reed-Herbert emigrated to Ireland and the party became dormant. In 1982 the remnants merged with the New National Front to form the **British National Party.**

British Empire Party

Only vote: T. David (Glamorganshire, Ogmore, 1951) – 1,643 votes, 3.4%
Parliamentary elections won: 0
Number of candidacies: 1

The British Empire Party was formed in 1951 by P. J. Ridout, a pre-war member of the **Imperial Fascist League** who had been implicated in anti-Semitic violence. In the 1951 general election, the party nominated Trefor David, a blacksmith and former **Plaid Cymru** member from Bridgend, to fight the Ogmore constituency. Though David claimed support from miners, having previously been a miner himself, the local newspaper highlighted the fascist past of Ridout when he spoke at one of David's meetings.

The party's newspaper ceased publication the following year and the party appears to have disbanded then.

British Fascisti (British Fascists)

Parliamentary elections won: 0
Number of candidacies: 0

This group was formed by Rotha Lintorn Orman in 1923, shortly after Mussolini had become *Duce* of Italy. Miss Lintorn Orman claimed that she was inspired on hearing the news of the Labour Party's attendance at a meeting of the Socialist International; being opposed to 'international and class-war tendencies', she placed an advertisement suggesting the formation of British Fascists. She knew little of Mussolini save for the fact that he was firmly anti-socialist.

A declaration of aims was issued in June 1923 committing the group to patriotism and upholding the constitution. Many of those involved with the group were from military backgrounds and the internal organisation resembled an army unit. The Grand Council of the British Fascisti included Sir Charles Burn, the Conservative MP for Torquay. The group's activities centred on supporting Conservative candidates in elections.

A split occurred in October 1924 when about 100 members who were anti-Semitic and endorsed Mussolini's conception of the fascist state formed the National Fascists, but this group proved short of finance and was wound up in 1928. In 1925 the British Fascisti issued a manifesto which set out its aim of resisting communist revolution by force.

During the General Strike of 1926, the British Fascisti offered assistance to the strikebreakers, but the Home Secretary objected to the group's policy of a corporate state and demanded it change its name. Rotha Lintorn Orman was opposed to these demands and those who were prepared to agree resigned from the group. The group did however change its name to the British Fascists in 1927 and concentrated on promoting unionism in Northern Ireland.

In 1932 Sir Oswald Mosley offered the group merger terms with the **New Party** which were rejected by only one vote, after pressure from Rotha Lintorn Orman who did not trust Mosley (thinking him a communist). A number of senior members joined the **British Union of Fascists** on its formation, taking with them a copy of the British Fascists' membership list; the ex-British Fascist members went on to play an important role in the BUF.

The remaining British Fascists were strongly opposed to the BUF and a number of members shouted abuse at BUF headquarters during a Jewish demonstration against the BUF in July 1933. In retaliation, fifty BUF members wrecked the British Fascists' headquarters. By 1934 the group was in financial difficulties and Mosley again opened negotiations on a merger, but Miss Lintorn Orman again vetoed them. Later that year the group was forced into bankruptcy by Colonel Henry Wilson, who had lent it £500. It never fought a Parliamentary election, though two members won seats on Stamford Borough Council as independent fascists in 1924. One was Arnold Leese, who went on to lead the **Imperial Fascist League**.

British Movement

Website: (for the British National Socialist Movement): http://www.hail.to/bnsm/

Highest vote: J. C. C. Jordan (Birmingham, Ladywood, 1969(26/6)) – 282 votes, 3.0%

Parliamentary elections won: 0

Number of candidacies: 3

The British Movement grew out of an organisation called the National Socialist Movement, formed on 20 April 1962 by Colin Jordan and John Tyndall who had been expelled *de facto* from the **British National Party** (*see* British National Party (1960–7)). Jordan, Tyndall and two others were at that time on trial for organising 'Spearhead', their private army in the British National Party; their Old Bailey trial in December 1963 ended in jail sentences of between three and nine months.

Jordan and Tyndall fell out with each other in 1963 when both wanted to marry Françoise Dior, a French heiress who had joined the Movement the previous year (she eventually chose to marry Jordan). The split resulted in each expelling the other, and though Jordan retained the name, Tyndall took most of the membership to his new organisation the **Greater Britain Movement**.

As an explicitly National Socialistic group, the National Socialist Movement was left out of the negotiations for the formation of the **National Front** in 1967 at the insistence of A. K. Chesterton. It took the name British Movement in the summer of the following year. Colin Jordan became National Chairman and chose himself to stand as the British Movement's only Parliamentary candidate, fighting West Midlands constituencies in a 1969 by-election and the 1970 and February 1974 general elections. In May 1975 he was jailed for shoplifting and resigned as National Chairman, being replaced by Michael McLaughlin. With the change of leader, the Movement established its base in the north-west of England. In 1976 Colin Jordan left the Movement.

The Movement encouraged military training for its members, and organised its own camps. It had a uniformed Leader Guard. These measures won the loyalty of many of its members, but the Movement remained small and was swiftly taken over by a violent element which formed links with the underground neo-Nazi movement in other countries; they organised around the National Socialist Group. In the mid 1970s the National Front organiser Martin Webster recruited many of these members, taking advantage of the confusion caused by the change of leader.

The Movement in turn hoped to attract former members of the National Front to join it after the NF's difficulties following the 1979 general election, but this hope was unfulfilled. British Movement activities were severely curtailed in the early 1980s when Ray Hill, a BM activist, became an anti-fascist and operated as a saboteur, provoking internal disputes; he also revealed that the group was planning to bomb the 1981 Notting Hill Carnival.

The Movement began to fracture in 1982. One faction joined with the New National Front created by John Tyndall, to form the **British National Party** (*see* British National Party (1982–)). The Movement attempted to fight Peterborough in the 1983 general election using the description 'Labour' but could not find enough valid nominating signatures. Michael McLaughlin resigned as National Chairman that autumn and closed the Movement's offices in Shotton in North Wales.

The Movement was wound up in 1984; the next year one member from Yorkshire, Stephen Frost, revived it. It is now known as the British National Socialist Movement.

British National Party (1960–7)

Highest vote: J. E. Bean (Southall, 1964) – 3,410 votes, 9.1%

Parliamentary elections won: 0

Number of candidacies: 4

The first British National Party was formed in February 1960 by the merger of the White Defence League (formed 1956 by Colin Jordan), and the **National Labour Party**. Both the White Defence League and the National Labour Party were the result of defections from the **League of Empire Loyalists**. The party took the motto 'For Race and Nation', was anti-Semitic and advocated repatriation of black and Asian immigrants in order to preserve the northern European character of the United Kingdom.

The founding President was Andrew Fountaine, a former Conservative from Norfolk; Colin Jordan was National Organiser. Jordan formed a private army for the party, based on the German Nazi Party's SA ('Brownshirts'), which he called 'Spearhead'. The police (and later, the *People* newspaper) were aware of the group and observed its manoeuvres, resulting eventually in a charge of organising a paramilitary group against Colin Jordan, his deputy John Tyndall, and two other members.

On 11 February 1962, John Bean and Andrew Fountaine moved a resolution at the BNP's National Council opposing Jordan's approach of associating the party with Nazi Germany. The resolution was passed but Jordan refused to step down. In response, Bean and Fountaine set up a new British National Party with four out of five members of the old party, and kept on the party's journal *Combat*. Colin Jordan then established the National Socialist Movement on 20 April 1962; he had been expelled *de facto* from the BNP. The National Socialist Movement later became the **British Movement**.

Shorn thereby of its National Socialist supporters, the British National Party then attempted to build up a local base by fighting elections; in the 1964 election, John Bean fought Southall and obtained 9% of the vote (then the highest vote gained by any far-right candidate since the war). Three seats were fought in 1966, all in areas with a high immigrant population. The most significant was Smethwick which the Conservatives had won in 1964 by running an anti-immigration campaign, but where the MP was increasingly toning down the message; here the party polled poorly.

The British National Party was at this time the largest of the far-right parties, and the only one which had good electoral experience. It had however a perpetual shortage of funds and this led it to seek a merger with other far-right groups; in early 1967 a merger with the **League of Empire Loyalists** was agreed, forming the **National Front**.

British National Party (1982–)

Address: PO Box 287, Waltham Cross, Hertfordshire EN8 8ZU

Website: http://www.bnp.net

Number on Register: 17

Highest vote: D. M. King (Tower Hamlets, Bethnal Green and Bow, 1997) – 3,350 votes, 7.5%

Parliamentary elections won: 0

Number of candidacies: 128

The present British National Party is the ultimate result of a split in the **National Front** following its poor performance in the 1979 general election. John Tyndall, then responsible for NF tactics, was removed from power within the NF and formed a breakaway organisation called the New National Front. The New National Front became the British National Party in 1982 after it absorbed a faction from the disintegrating **British Movement** and the small **British Democratic Party**.

In the 1983 election the party fought 54 seats, succeeding in qualifying for an election broadcast, but failing to attract mass support. The party was clearly less popular than the National Front. The serious splits in the NF in the mid 1980s left the BNP as the largest and most prominent far-right party, though it was still weak: in the 1987 election it fought only two seats. The party had financial difficulties in the late 1980s.

Increased political concern over Europe and a moderate **Conservative Party** possibly provided the far-right with an opportunity in the early 1990s and the BNP had a revival. It opened its office and bookshop in Welling in 1989, East London having become a promising area for the party.

After concerted local activism over several years, the party won a council by-election in Millwall Ward of Tower Hamlets in September 1993, helped by local grievances and an even division of votes between Labour and the Liberal Democrats. Anti-racist campaigners flooded the area in the full council elections of 1994 and the seat was lost, but the BNP vote rose. The Welling office, linked by anti-racist organisations to a rise in racist attacks in the area, had meanwhile become the target for mass demonstrations calling for the party to be banned. There was violence on

16 October 1993 when police prevented demonstrators from approaching the building.

The police claimed the party was contacting supporters of various English and Scottish football clubs in a recruitment campaign in summer 1993. In December 1993 the BNP moved to expel Combat 18, a violent neo-Nazi group, and its political ally (the National Socialist Movement) after an article in Combat 18's magazine *The Order* criticised John Tyndall's leadership; the move to distance the party from violence was also partly motivated by a desire to become more voter-friendly. Combat 18 later beat up some BNP local election candidates and latterly the BNP has described Combat 18 as a 'state-sponsored pseudo-gang'.

BNP policy developed in the mid 1990s in parallel with the party's attempt to make itself more respectable. The party has become more welcoming to the market economy though it advocates protectionism. It fought 56 seats in the 1997 election, enough to get a five-minute televised election broadcast (which was censored by some broadcasters). The party saved three deposits in 1997, in the East End and in Dewsbury.

The party made a big effort to fight every region except Wales in the 1999 European Parliamentary elections, campaigning for British withdrawal from the European Union. It was hindered by the refusal of some postal workers, supported by their union, to deliver its freepost election addresses, and by the Soho, Brixton and Brick Lane bombings during the campaign which were immediately blamed on the far right. The BNP polled just over 100,000 votes nationwide.

Founder Chairman John Tyndall was ousted in a leadership struggle in December 1999 by his former deputy Nick Griffin. The British National Party's candidate for Mayor of London, accountant Michael Newland, polled 2%, while the party's list of candidates polled 2.9% in the Greater London Authority elections in 2000. This was approximately half the support given to the National Front at its peak in the 1977 Greater London Council elections.

British People's Party

Highest vote: H. St J. B. Philby (Hythe, 1939(20/7)) – 576 votes, 2.6%
Parliamentary elections won: 0
Number of candidacies: 2

This party was formed in February 1939 by John Beckett, a former **Independent Labour Party** MP who had joined the **British Union of Fascists** and left it with William Joyce in 1937, and the Marquess of Tavistock, later the 12th Duke of Bedford. It had grown from a monthly journal called the *New Pioneer* of which Beckett was the editor and Viscount Lymington the proprietor; Lymington, attempting to avoid war with Germany, had established several pacifist organisations which inaccurately claimed left-wing origins.

The BPP's approach was a fusion of pacifism in its foreign policies, and social credit for its domestic economic policies. The party recruited several ex-BUF and ex-ILP members and in June 1939 fought the Hythe by-election (the candidate was the father of spy Kim Philby). In 1940 Beckett was interned and the organisation became dormant, though it was not proscribed.

Shortly after VE day an attempt to unite the BPP with a revivalist anti-Semitic group called the National Front after Victory was scuppered by the Board of Deputies of British Jews, which prompted Lord Vansittart to hold a debate in the House of Lords in February 1946 denouncing attempts to recreate fascism. The party changed its policy after the war, to favour monetary reform and reconstruction of agriculture. It fought the Combined English Universities by-election of March 1946, but was disbanded in 1954.

British Socialist Party

Highest vote: [excluding candidates who received Labour Party endorsement] J. D. MacDougall (Glasgow Tradeston, 1918) – 3,751 votes, 19.4%
Parliamentary elections won: 0
Number of candidacies: 6

The British Socialist Party was formed in 1911 as an amalgamation of the forces who opposed the 'Labour alliance' between political socialists and the trade union movement which had led to the formation of the **Labour Party**. By far the largest element was the **Social Democratic Federation** led by H. M. Hyndman; some **Independent Labour Party** branches also affiliated. At the end of its first year it had 15,000 members but it swiftly declined.

The party fought three by-elections in 1913–14, but by 1914 the BSP had fewer members than were in the old SDF. It conceded the argument and sought affiliation to the Labour Party, which was granted in 1916. The party suffered splits over support for the Great War. In April 1915, a small and very pro-war group formed the Socialist National Defence Committee; this group abandoned any links with the BSP in March 1916.

When a leading member of the BSP started publishing an anti-war newsletter, most of the older members, led by H.M. Hyndman, were determined to oppose the party's pacifist tendencies. Finding the majority of the party firmly anti-war they left to form the **National Socialist Party**, taking the party's official newspaper *Justice*.

The British Socialist Party gave support to the October Revolution in Russia and declared its allegiance to the Communist (Third) International in preference to the Second International. Despite this, it remained affiliated to the Labour Party and, in the 1918 election, four of its seven candidates had Labour Party endorsement. Due to British participation in the Russian civil war the party was unable to send delegates to the first sessions of the Communist International, but did convene meetings from June 1919 for various other groups believed to be sympathetic, with the object of securing unity.

As the BSP was the largest group in these discussions, some other participants were wary of being outvoted – notably the Workers' Socialist Federation led by Sylvia Pankhurst. When, in June 1920, the Workers' Socialist Federation reformed itself as the Communist Party (British Section of the Third International) and left the negotiations, the BSP called a Unity Conference for 31 July – 1 August 1920. The Conference voted to establish the **Communist Party of Great Britain** and the BSP immediately voted to merge with it.

The BSP had acquired a Member of Parliament in June 1920 when

Cecil L'Estrange Malone joined from the **Coalition** Liberals, and he went on into the Communist Party, but the party's London County Councillors and many of its leading Parliamentary candidates did not.

British Union of Fascists (and National Socialists)

Website: http://www.geocities.com/CapitolHill/3759/ [This is the website of the 'Friends of OM', an organisation of ex-members of the BUF and other parties formed by Sir Oswald Mosley]

Highest vote: S. Allen (Leeds North East, 1940 (13/3)) – 722 votes, 2.9%

Parliamentary elections won: 0

Number of candidacies: 3

After the failure of the **New Party** in the 1931 election, Sir Oswald Mosley went to Italy to study 'the new movements', and returned a convinced fascist. He first attempted to unify and take over the existing fascist organisations (hence the choice of the name British Union of Fascists), but was only partly successful. The party was launched on 1 October 1932. Mosley was insistent from the start that it should operate as a major political party, with large numbers of paid party staff. He supported the party from his own resources but also sought funds from elsewhere. Early funding was given by Mussolini, who persuaded press baron Lord Rothermere to back the party.

The party held mass meetings and rallies to promote its cause, but suffered from opposition both from the left (especially the **Communist Party of Great Britain**) and from other fascists (*see* **British Fascisti** and **Imperial Fascist League**). In autumn 1933, the party bought the lease on a former teacher training college in Chelsea which was renamed The Black House and served as a headquarters and barracks for the party's black-shirted stewards. The 'blackshirts' became the most distinctive part of the BUF. Ironically, in view of later events, they received their physical training from the East End Jewish boxer Teddy 'Kid' Lewis who had been a New Party candidate in the 1931 election.

At a rally at Olympia on 7 June 1934, the mass brawling between the BUF and anti-fascist demonstrators left the party indelibly associated with political violence and extremism. Shortly afterwards Rothermere cancelled his support, influenced also by the 'Night of the Long Knives' in Germany on 30 June and by the party's growing anti-Semitism and dictatorial leanings. Membership of the BUF declined and the party increasingly took up local and sectional issues rather than promoting fascism generally.

Sensing that fascist views were becoming unacceptable in high society, Mosley established the January Club in 1934 as a dining club which would bring in experts to discuss the political situation. Many members left when they realised the real function of the Club was to promote Fascist ideas and it was wound up in 1936. The BUF was unable, because of its loss of members, to contest the 1935 election. Mosley used the slogan 'Fascism next time' to hide the party's lack of organisation. In 1936, the party announced 19 prospective Parliamentary candidates, saying it intended to fight 100 seats.

As a result of the influence of William Joyce, the party added the words 'and National Socialists' to its name in 1936, and decided to hold more rallies and marches and fewer speeches. Left-wing counter-demonstrations, however, prevented a march through Cable Street in the East End of London on 4 October of that year. In 1937 the BUF fought three East End seats in the London County Council elections, polling a fifth of the vote on average. The party later fought local elections in several parts of the country, though only one freakish success saw a councillor elected. After the LCC elections of 1937, the party was forced to lay off most of its employees and this prompted a breakaway by William Joyce and his supporters to form the **National Socialist League**.

The BUF did not, in the event, contest a Parliamentary election before the outbreak of war – which cancelled an expected 1939 general election. It fought three by-elections in the first year of war, calling for peace by negotiation. Initially Mosley was received with little reaction, but at Middleton and Prestwich in May 1940 he was physically assaulted.

A week later, on 23 May 1940, Sir Oswald Mosley and many leading party members were arrested and interned because of a security scandal involving the leak of secret correspondence between Winston Churchill and President Roosevelt. Mosley and the BUF were not personally involved in the scandal, but it tipped the balance for the War Cabinet in favour of widespread internment of the far right. The allegation that BUF members were security risks appears to have been largely untrue, but in July 1940 the BUF was proscribed under Defence Regulation 18b.

The BUF was primarily motivated by Italian fascism and not German national socialism; it advocated the construction of a corporate state involving 24 trade groups, with the Prime Minister permitted to rule by decree. Anti-Semitism had been apparent among some of Sir Oswald Mosley's followers even before the formation of the BUF; it was openly expressed by the BUF in 1934 and was increasingly prominent as the 1930s wore on.

For Sir Oswald Mosley's post-war political ventures, see **Action Party** and **Union Movement**.

Càirdeas

See **Highlands and Islands Alliance**.

Campaign for a More Prosperous Britain

Highest vote: T. L. Keen (Portsmouth North, October 1974) – 527 votes, 1.0%
Parliamentary elections won: 0
Number of candidacies: 34

This organisation was formed in 1974 by Thomas Keen, a property developer from Oldham, as a campaign to keep the **Labour Party** out of government. Candidates of the Campaign stressed that they were not seeking votes for themselves, but advising electors not to vote for the Labour Party or **Communist Party of Great Britain** candidates.

In the February 1974 election, Harold Smith, an associate of Thomas Keen, opposed Harold Wilson in his Huyton constituency. In October 1974, Keen himself stood in 11 separate seats and Smith in 12; two other candidates fought Keighley and Glasgow Govan. All the seats fought were marginals which Labour needed to win to form a government, and most were in the north of England.

Keen also fought some by-elections in the mid 1970s and early 1980s, sponsored by the CFMPB. In the early 1980s, the Campaign appears to have been dissolved; in the 1983 election, Keen fought five Labour marginals calling for tactical voting to defeat the Labour candidate.

Campaign for Social Democracy (1973–4)

Highest vote: J. Martin (Tottenham, February 1974) – 763 votes, 2.4%
Parliamentary elections won: 0
Number of candidacies: 4

The Campaign for Social Democracy was formed in September 1973 by Dick Taverne MP, who had in March 1973 successfully sought re-election in his Lincoln Parliamentary seat after resigning from the **Labour Party**. Taverne's candidature in Lincoln was sponsored by the Lincoln Democratic Labour Association (*see* **Democratic Labour**).

The CSD sought to build a radical non-doctrinaire social democratic movement. In the February 1974 election, it fought four seats including that of the leading left-wing Labour shadow cabinet member, Tony Benn. It polled poorly. One of the candidates, John Binns, had previously been a Labour MP for the seat he fought; he had the lowest vote of all.

When it appeared that the Labour Party was going to be in government for some time, thereby postponing a split in the Labour Party which the CSD believed would bring it members, the Campaign was wound up.

Chartist

Highest vote: F. E. O'Connor (Nottingham, 1847) – 1,257 votes, 32.3% [two-member seat]
Parliamentary elections won: 1
Number of candidacies: 23

In the winter of 1837, there was a depression and a wave of unemployment; the unemployed were subject to the Poor Law Amendment Act of 1834 which restricted the poor relief available to them. Political agitation grew for democratic reform and on 8 May 1838 William Lovett drafted a Bill called the 'People's Charter' which set out six demands: universal male suffrage, equal electoral districts, vote by ballot, annually elected

Parliaments, payment of members of Parliament, and abolition of the property qualifications for membership.

Irish orator Feargus O'Connor campaigned throughout the country to promote the Charter and in 1839 a conference drafted a petition to Parliament in its support. The petition was presented and rejected that July. An armed uprising was suppressed in November and its leaders transported to Australia; from then on, the Chartist movement was entirely peaceful. A second petition gathered about three million signatures in 1842, but the impetus to reform was slowed by a more buoyant economy. There was a third petition in 1848, with 5,706,000 signatures, of which 1,975,496 were genuine.

Chartist candidates were seen in the General elections of 1841 (eight), 1847 (nine) and 1852 (four), and one stood in 1857 and 1859. Only Feargus O'Connor ever won a seat as a Chartist candidate, though a supporter of Chartist demands won Macclesfield in 1847 as a Liberal. All but one of the Chartists' demands have since been enacted.

Christian Alliance

Highest vote: J. Floyd (Bradford, North, 1990 (8/11)) – 219 votes, 0.6%
Parliamentary elections won: 0
Number of candidacies: 6

This Alliance was formed by David Black, a Christian campaigner from Reading. Black opposed abortion and campaigned for family values; he was also opposed to British membership of the European Communities. Black's first candidacy was in the Pontypridd by-election of February 1989 but he was rarely seen during the campaign. He fought five by-elections in 1989–90, usually finishing bottom of the poll; in Bradford North in November 1990, an associate also stood. Black usually described himself as 'Christian Alliance' but in Mid Staffordshire (March 1990) his description was 'Christian Patriotic Alliance – Save Britain Campaign.'

Christian Democratic Party

Address: 123 Oldham Road, Middleton, Greater Manchester M24 1AV

Email address: christinemwest@hotmail.com

Number on Register: 18

Parliamentary elections won: 0

Number of candidacies: 0

This party was formed in 1999. It aims to promote Christian morals and has fought local elections.

Christian Peoples Alliance

Address: PO Box 932, Sutton SM1 1HQ

Email address: info@cpalliance.net

Website: http://www.cpalliance.net

Number on register: 59

Parliamentary elections won: 0

Number of candidacies: 0

This party emerged from the Movement for Christian Democracy, an all-party pressure group formed in 1990 by two MPs (one Liberal Democrat, one Conservative). In 1999 the MCD formed the Christian Democrat Electoral Committee to survey its members about how to respond to proportional representation, concluding that a party of Christian inspiration within a European Christian Democratic tradition would have support.

The MCD then called a meeting which formed the Christian Peoples Alliance. The Movement for Christian Democracy remains a non-party organization and the two are independent. Initially the Alliance campaigned in London. On 19 January 2000 it announced that Ram Gidoomal would be its candidate for Mayor of London; despite the lack of media coverage, he came fifth and the party's list polled 3.3% across London (enough to win a seat but for the legal 5% threshold).

In summer 2000 the Alliance announced that it intended to organise nationwide and a launch meeting was held on 14 October 2000. The party supported a candidate from the 'Alliance for Preston' at the November 2000 Preston by-election.

Coalition

Highest vote: Rt Hon. D. Lloyd George (Caernarvon District of Burghs, 1918) – 13,993 votes, 92.7% [candidate standing as Coalition Liberal]

Parliamentary elections won: 524

Number of candidacies: 610

In May 1915, in response to stagnation in the Great War and criticism from the Conservative opposition, the Liberal Prime Minister Asquith formed a Coalition government including **Liberals**, **Conservatives** and the **Labour Party**. The Coalition proved a fractious alliance, and in December 1916 David Lloyd George replaced Asquith as Prime Minister. Labour's relations with the Coalition were put under strain when Arthur Henderson was forced to resign in 1917, though there were Labour members of the government until the end of the war.

When, in May 1918, Major-General Frederick Maurice criticised the preparation of troops on the Western front, Asquith's supporters backed Maurice and a deep fissure opened up between Liberals who supported Asquith and those who followed Lloyd George and the Coalition. At the end of the war, Labour were opposed to the continuation of the Coalition in peacetime and left it.

In the 1918 general election the Coalition fought as a single unit, with a letter of support sent out by Lloyd George and the then Conservative leader Balfour to all official coalition candidates. This letter was known as the 'Coupon'. It was sent to 362 Conservatives, 159 Liberals (14 of whom rejected it), 18 members of the **National Democratic and Labour Party**, two members of the Labour Party (with three more considered as unofficially endorsed by the Coalition), and one Independent. The Coalition won a big victory at this election. After the election, 9 Liberals who had not received the coupon accepted the Coalition whip.

In the early post-war years the Coalition had a great deal of popularity. From 1919 to 1920 there was an attempt to form a 'Centre Party' by which the Coalition Liberals and Conservatives would merge to form a single party. A memo was sent to the two party leaders (Bonar Law and Lloyd George) in early 1920 calling for such a move, signed by 93 Coalition MPs. Though the leaders were apparently well disposed, opposition from grassroots members of each party forced them to put off any proposed merger.

Conservatives in the country had increasing difficulties in supporting the Coalition which, led by a Liberal Prime Minister, was pursuing mostly Liberal policies. In 1922, they were angered by a scandal over Lloyd George's sale of honours to finance his own party, and an unnecessary confrontation with Turkey which threatened war. Conservative MPs met at the Carlton Club on 19 October, encouraged by winning the Newport by-election the previous day, and broke off the Coalition. Lloyd George immediately resigned as Prime Minister.

Common Wealth Movement

Highest vote: E. R. Millington (Chelmsford, 1945 (26/4)) – 24,548 votes, 57.5%
Parliamentary elections won: 4
Number of candidacies: 35

Common Wealth was formed on 26 June 1942 by the merger of two short-lived organisations: Forward March, formed in 1940 by Liberal MP Sir Richard Acland, and the 1941 Committee, formed by J. B. Priestley. The 1941 Committee was aimed at securing an efficient war effort and was funded by Edward Hulton of *Picture Post*. Sir Richard Acland had been converted to socialism in 1936 and wanted the war run as a moral crusade. In the event, most of those who joined from the 1941 Committee left Common Wealth shortly after it started.

The policy of Common Wealth was an idealistic Christian socialism, and it proposed devolution and common ownership of factories – as opposed to nationalisation – in supporting the ideal of service to the community. One of the party's rallying cries was the implementation of the Report on Social Insurance and Allied Services by Sir William Beveridge. In foreign affairs the party advocated friendship with the USSR, and half of its candidates favoured a European Federal Union. Common Wealth supporters tended to be people of the middle class who were put off by Labour Party machine politics. It did however apply for affiliation to the **Labour Party** in 1944, but was rejected.

Common Wealth fought several by-elections during the war, when the electoral truce prevented Labour from standing. It declared it intended to contest all by-elections where a 'reactionary' candidate was not already opposed by a 'progressive'. It won three seats: Eddisbury (April 1943) where the candidate benefited from his family connections with the Liberal Party, Skipton (January 1944) by inheriting the Labour vote, and Chelmsford (April 1945).

In the 1945 election Common Wealth nominated 23 candidates, trying only to fight seats where Labour had no chance. In several of these seats there was no official Labour candidate. However, it won only Chelmsford. Eddisbury MP John Loverseed had joined the Labour Party and Skipton's Hugh Lawson stood down to allow Labour to fight.

Sir Richard Acland resigned from the Movement in September 1945 to join the Labour Party, and though the organisation continued, it was only as a discussion group. Ernest Millington, the Chelmsford MP, took the Labour whip from April 1946.

Commonwealth Labour Party

Only vote: Rt Hon. H. C. Midgley (Belfast South, 1945) – 14,096 votes, 30.3%

Parliamentary elections won: 0

Number of candidacies: 1

The Commonwealth Labour Party was formed by Harry Midgley, who was one of the founders of the **Northern Ireland Labour Party** and had led the party in the 1930s. Midgley, a Protestant trade unionist, had been against partition in 1921 but later became a firm unionist. The Northern Ireland Labour Party had adopted a policy of having no policy on the constitutional status of Northern Ireland, but was never able completely to avoid the issue.

Midgley had lost his Stormont seat in the 1938 general election when he supported the Spanish Republic; his mainly Catholic constituents supported Franco and a Nationalist candidate stood against him. He won a by-election in December 1941 in a loyalist constituency and attempted to persuade the Northern Ireland Labour Party to endorse partition.

In December 1942, after the party refused, Midgley broke away to form the Commonwealth Labour Party as a unionist party representing Labour interests. He was appointed Minister of Public Security in the Northern Ireland government of Sir Basil Brooke in May 1943, the first non-member of the Ulster Unionist Party to be appointed to a position in the Stormont administration.

Midgley later became Northern Ireland Minister for Labour, but felt obliged to resign after the surrender of Germany in May 1945, when he fought the 1945 Stormont election against a Unionist candidate. He retained his seat, though five other candidates in seats in or near Belfast were unsuccessful. Midgley then fought the Belfast South seat in the 1945 UK general election. In 1947 Midgley joined the **Ulster Unionist Party** and the Commonwealth Labour Party was disbanded.

Commonwealth Land Party

Highest vote: J. W. G. Peace (Hanley, 1931) – 946 votes, 2.7%

Parliamentary elections won: 0

Number of candidacies: 2

The origins of this party were in January 1919 when Graham Peace formed the Commonwealth League. Peace had been inspired by the book *Progress and Poverty*, published in 1879 by American economist Henry George. George proposed that all other taxes be abolished and replaced by a single tax on the 'economic rent' of bare land (i.e. from the use of the land, but not from developments on it). The **Scottish Land Restoration League** had also promoted Henry George's theories in British politics.

One early member was Robert Outhwaite who had been Liberal MP for Hanley from 1912 but had been deselected and lost his seat in the 1918 general election. Outhwaite had joined the **Independent Labour Party** and added to the ideas of Henry George the suggestion that when the land tax was imposed, the effect was the restoration of land to the people. By this argument, he was opposed to land nationalisation.

The Commonwealth League adopted the name Commonwealth Land Party in September 1923. In the 1931 election, the party nominated Graham Peace and an associate to fight two urban Potteries constituencies.

Peace died in April 1947, and the party was renamed the Common Land Party, but it appears to have gone out of existence in 1954.

Communist League

Address: 47 The Cut, London SE1 8LL

Email address: 101515.2702@compuserve.com

Highest vote: A. N. Buchanan (Manchester Central, 1992) – 167 votes, 0.5%

Parliamentary elections won: 0

Number of candidacies: 5

This party was formed in December 1987 by Brian Grogan and Jonathan Silberman, who had been expelled from the Socialist League (*see* **International Marxist Group**) due to doctrinal differences. The League rejects the Trotskyite theory of 'permanent revolution' and models its economic proposals on the policies of Fidel Castro in Cuba. It is allied to the Socialist Workers Party of the USA and distributes that party's publications.

The League owns the Pathfinder bookshop (where it has its headquarters) and has its best organisation in London, Manchester and Sheffield. It fought three seats in the 1992 election, and two in 1997, and it has fought local elections. In 1999 the party began discussions with German allies to create the New Communist [Marxist-Leninist] Party. Jonathan Silberman fought the Lambeth and Southwark seat for the Greater London Assembly in May 2000, polling 0.5%.

Communist Party of Britain (1988–)

Address: 3 Ardleigh Road, London N1 4HS

Email address: cp-of-britain@mcr1.poptel.org.uk

Website: http://www.myspace.co.uk/cp-of-britain/

Number on Register: 49

Highest vote: M. Goldman (Hackney South and Shoreditch, 1997) – 298 votes, 0.9%

Parliamentary elections won: 0

Number of candidacies: 3

The Communist Party of Britain has its origins in the Communist Campaign Group, formed in 1985 within the **Communist Party of Great Britain** (*see* Communist Party of Great Britain (1920–91)) around the editorial board of the *Morning Star* newspaper. The Communist Campaign Group sought to retrieve the Communist Party of Great Britain from the eurocommunist section which had grown to dominate it. They were opposed to the distancing of the party from the USSR and a class analysis of British politics.

By 1987 it was apparent that the eurocommunist control of the CPGB was solid and the Communist Campaign Group called a congress to re-establish a British branch of the Third International. This congress was held in April 1988 and voted to form the Communist Party of Britain. The party immediately adopted the constitution used by the CPGB and when it formulated its policy, the party published it (April 1989) under the title *The British Road to Socialism* which had been used for CPGB policy statements since 1950.

The British Road to Socialism of the Communist Party of Britain envisions a Parliamentary majority for a left-wing Labour government, which is supported by a communist-led mass membership. In accordance with this analysis the party advocates a vote for the **Labour Party** where it is not itself standing. The party retains the allegiance and support of the *Morning Star.*

The Communist Party of Britain was slow to begin fighting elections. It fought South Wales Central in the 1994 European Parliament elections, but did not fight Parliamentary elections until 1997. The three seats fought in that contest were in Hackney, Newcastle upon Tyne and South Wales. The party's list for London members in the Greater London Assembly came bottom of the poll with 0.4% in May 2000.

Communist Party of England (Marxist-Leninist)

See **Revolutionary Communist Party of Britain (Marxist-Leninist) (1979–)**.

Communist Party of Great Britain (1920–91)

Address: (for New Politics Network) 6 Cynthia Street, London N1 9JF

Website: http://www.democratic-left.org.uk

Highest vote: S. Saklatvala (Battersea North, 1924) – 15,096 votes, 50.9%

Parliamentary elections won: 4

Number of candidacies: 597

The Communist Party of Great Britain was formed as a result of the Russian Revolution. A congress of Communist parties had been called in Moscow in 1919–20, which was later termed the Third International. On their return, the British delegates called a Unity Convention on 31 July – 1 August 1920 at which the Communist Party of Great Britain was formed. The convention was attended by 160 delegates, of whom 96 had been sent by the **British Socialist Party**, which provided a large base on which the party could be built.

Until 1924, Communist candidates could and did receive **Labour Party** endorsement. The party had some early and localised electoral success, but suffered throughout its life by being tied to the USSR which it refused to criticise; as was widely suspected at the time, the party was receiving a large subsidy from the USSR.

In 1928 the party was ordered to cease its attempts to join with Labour and denounced Labour's leadership. This policy was reversed in the mid 1930s as the party campaigned for a 'United Front' against fascism. The Moscow influence was most graphically demonstrated in 1939 when the party went from initial support for war with Germany to complete opposition within a few weeks: the Nazi-Soviet pact meant that Communist parties were for the time being in alliance with Germany.

The Communists prospered in Britain later in the war when the USSR were allies and communism did not seem unpatriotic. Two Communists were elected in the 1945 election (for the coal-mining seat of West Fife, and Mile End in the bomb-damaged East End). Both seats were lost in 1950, when the Communists criticised the Labour government as indistinguishable from the Conservatives. The invasion of Hungary in 1956 provoked mass resignations from the party.

The last good electoral performance by a Communist was clearly a personal vote for Jimmy Reid, leader of the Upper Clyde Shipbuilders' work-in, in the February 1974 general election. The well-distributed Communist-owned newspaper the *Daily Worker* (from 1966 the *Morning Star*) provided a ready outlet for the party's campaigning.

The Communist Party of Great Britain had a long internal debate on whether to adopt a 'eurocommunist' stance (meaning independence from the Soviet Communist Party), beginning in the late 1960s. Like most other western European communist parties, it had condemned the Soviet invasion of Czechoslovakia in 1968. The rise of the eurocommunists and their accommodation by the leadership prompted a group of Stalinist members (estimated to be 700 strong) to break away in 1977 to form the **New Communist Party of Britain**.

The eurocommunist section of the CPGB was responsible for publishing the theoretical journal *Marxism Today* which achieved a wide circulation outside the party and established a reputation in the 1980s for independent left-wing thought. In 1983 the eurocommunists attempted without success to take editorial control of the *Morning Star*, the editorial board of which was the main body of Third International loyalists.

In 1985, the eurocommunists were clearly in control of the Communist Party and those who remained loyal to the Third International line began a separate organisation around the *Morning Star* editorial board. On 15 November 1987 the Communist Party of Great Britain severed its links with the paper, and in April 1988 the Third International loyalists established the **Communist Party of Britain**.

The Communist Party of Great Britain then produced a new policy and on 22 November 1991 voted by 135 to 72 to reform as Democratic Left; the party was disbanded two days later. It abandoned an electoral strategy, save for advocating tactical voting against Conservative candidates to secure left unity, and described itself not as a political party, but as an organisation of like-minded individuals. The Communist Party had some councillors in the mining areas of Fife and their supporters formed the **Communist Party of Scotland**.

Democratic Left published the newspaper *New Times* which had a wide circulation and support from some trade unions. In December 1999, Democratic Left was wound up, and *New Times* ceased publication in summer 2000. The large assets of the movement were transferred to the New Politics Network, which aims to provide a forum for best practice in politics to be discussed.

Communist Party of Great Britain (1989–)

Address: BCM Box 928, London WC1N 3XX

Email address: office@cpgb.org.uk

Website: http://www.cpgb.org.uk

Number on Register: 53 (as Weekly Worker)

Highest vote: M.W. Fischer (Rhondda, 1992) – 245 votes, 0.5%

Parliamentary elections won: 0

Number of candidacies: 5

This party, regarding itself as the continuation of the original CPGB, has its origins in a factional journal called *Leninist*. This journal was published from November 1981 by Leninist members of the Communist Party of Great Britain (*see* **Communist Party of Great Britain (1920–91)**) together with the youth wing of the **New Communist Party of Britain**, which had been expelled from the NCPB on 9 December 1979 for 'ultra-leftism'. This group had been influenced by developments in the Turkish Communist Party.

As the Communist Party of Great Britain moved more towards revisionism, the publishers of *Leninist* saw an opportunity for themselves. A conference in November 1989 voted to form a distinct revolutionary wing of the Communist Party. The organisation retitled itself the Provisional Central Committee of the Communist Party of Great Britain. The party is Provisional because it declares that its aim is to re-establish the old broadly-based Communist Party; it took back the banner of the CPGB when the original party liquidated itself in 1991.

While the party contests elections, it is a revolutionary party. It fought four seats in the 1992 general election, and the 1993 Newbury by-election. It publishes the *Weekly Worker* and was forced to fight the 1999 European Parliament elections under this title, the term 'Communist Party' having been awarded to the **Communist Party of Britain** by the Registrar of Political Parties.

In order to further its goal of recreating a mass Communist Party, the party actively involves itself with other far-left groups, including the various Trotskyite groups. It promotes left alliances such as the **Scottish Socialist Alliance** and the London Socialist Alliance, formed to fight the Greater London Authority elections of 2000. A member of the party, Anne Murphy was selected as sixth on the London Socialist Alliance's list.

Communist Party of Ireland (Marxist–Leninist)

Highest vote: P. D. P. Kerins (Belfast West, October 1974) – 203 votes, 0.5%

Parliamentary elections won: 0

Number of candidacies: 3

This party was formed in 1965 as the Irish branch of the international Maoist Communist movement formed by Hardial Bains, a counterpart of the Communist Party of England (Marxist-Leninist) (*see* **Revolutionary Communist Party of Britain (Marxist-Leninist) (1979–)**). The party supported Irish republicanism and therefore organised throughout the whole of Ireland. It fought the Monaghan by-election for the Dáil in November 1973, and three seats at the October 1974 election in Northern Ireland – Belfast West and two border seats. Only one of their candidates got more than 200 votes.

The party also nominated two candidates in Belfast West in the 1975 elections for the Northern Ireland Constitutional Convention, who came bottom of the poll. Activity appears to have ceased shortly after though the party may still be in existence.

Communist Party of Scotland

Address: 2 Merkland Street, Glasgow G11 6DB.

Parliamentary elections won: 0

Number of candidacies: 0

When the **Communist Party of Great Britain** was disbanded on 24 November 1991, those Scottish members who had opposed the decision began moves to re-establish the party in Scotland. The Communist Party of Scotland was formally launched on 26 January 1992 in Glasgow, with the support of the Communist Party's councillor on Fife Regional Council.

The party was affiliated to the Scottish Constitutional Convention which proposed the devolution scheme eventually used to create the Scottish Parliament. While the party has continued to sponsor Councillor William Clarke, who has increased his majority in Ballingry and Lochore Ward, it has not contested Parliamentary or Scottish Parliamentary elections. It opened a headquarters building in Partick, Glasgow, in April 1993, and publishes *Scottish Marxist Voice*.

Conservative (and Unionist) Party

Address: Conservative Central Office, 32 Smith Square, London SW1P 3HH

Email address: ccoffice@conservative-party.org.uk

Website: http://www.conservatives.com

Number on Register: 3

Highest vote: E. E. Gates (Middleton and Prestwich, 1940 (22/5)) – 32,036 votes, 98.7%

Parliamentary elections won: 14,837

Number of candidacies: 25,201

The origins of the present-day Conservative Party are in 1679, when a parliamentary group supporting the Duke of York's claim on the throne (and therefore opposing a bill to exclude him) were given the nickname 'Tories' – an anglicised form of the Irish Gaelic word 'Toraidhe', meaning pursuer. The term 'Tories' had first been applied to Irish cattle-rustlers.

Under Queen Anne, the Tories became identified with resistance to religious toleration and dominated the ministry, but the Whigs managed to get control of the government shortly before her death and ensured the succession for George I of Hanover who in turn guaranteed Whig dominance. The Tory leader Bolingbroke fled to France in 1715, and until the accession of George III in 1760, the Tories were identified with the Jacobites and excluded from office.

George III sought to appoint a government which would be loyal to him personally, and did not believe in the old system of appointing governments which balanced the interests of the leading peers. His closest political friend was the Earl of Bute, a Tory, and the King forced the Duke of Newcastle to include Bute in his government. When Newcastle lost a cabinet battle and resigned, Bute was made the first Tory Prime Minister.

His government was phenomenally unpopular. Bute was Scottish and an outsider, and at a time of war imposed new taxes. The radical John Wilkes started *The North Briton* to attack Bute's government, and Bute declared his administration would be a temporary one. He resigned after less than a year, but remained in the King's favour until he voted to keep the Stamp Act in 1766.

A succession of Whig governments followed; the Commons remained largely in Whig control and George III gathered more experience. In 1770 the Whig government fell apart and the King appointed the Tory Lord North as Prime Minister. Unlike the Earl of Bute, North was a good politician who could persuade the House of Commons (in which he sat) to back him.

North's government was dominated by foreign affairs, especially the growing trouble in the American colonies. His instinct was to conciliate with the colonies but he underestimated the depth of their anger, and the King's determination to maintain the supremacy of Parliament led to war. North was forced by the King to carry on the war even when he knew it was hopeless, and wished to resign, but the King still preferred him to any alternative government.

After the anti-Catholic Gordon riots of 1780, it was clear North's government was failing at home and the final victory of the Americans at Yorktown led him to insist on resigning in 1782. Only a year later, North was the leading Tory in a Tory/Whig coalition with Charles James Fox.

This coalition was not welcome to the King who detested Fox, and he had only agreed to it after the young Tory William Pitt declined to form a government.

In December 1783, the King dismissed the Fox–North coalition after bringing about its defeat in the House of Lords, and again asked Pitt to form a government; this time Pitt accepted, though only 24 years and 205 days old. Few expected the government to last as it did not have a majority in Parliament, but though it suffered several defeats, the majority against the government fell.

Pitt called a general election in March 1784, and won with a majority of 120. This was unexpectedly high but was clearly boosted by the use of state funds to help the government election campaign. Under Pitt the government finances were brought into sound order and an efficient taxation system put in place. He was defeated in his attempt to reform the corrupt electoral system.

When George III suffered a bout of insanity in 1788, Pitt delayed moves to appoint the Prince of Wales Regent, arguing it was for Parliament to decide who should be Regent, and insisted on a regency of restricted powers. Fortunately for Pitt, the King recovered and secured his ministry. Pitt's personal following was small but he helped dominate the Commons by splitting the opposition in 1794: the Whigs supporting the Duke of Portland joined the government.

Pitt was less effective in his conduct of foreign affairs, being forced to sue for peace in the wars with France of 1793–96. The failed rebellion in Ireland in 1798 and fears of the spread of the French revolution led the government to pass the Act of Union with Ireland in 1800. Pitt knew this would require a removal of the legal disabilities on Roman Catholics, but could not persuade George III to accept any moves; this prompted his resignation in the new year of 1801.

Pitt was followed by Addington, a much weaker figure ('Pitt is to Addington', it was said, 'as London is to Paddington'). Yet Addington enjoyed early success in the war with France and in further improving Pitt's taxation system. His weakness was in Parliament and two years after his appointment he asked Pitt to return to government; Pitt declined to return to a subordinate position.

In 1803 war broke out again with France and a rising in Ireland killed the Irish Chief Justice, giving Addington a reputation for incompetence. Pitt began to lead a campaign against the government, convinced he could do better, and his campaign forced Addington's resignation in May 1804. Pitt returned but his health was already failing and his second government was weak. In January 1806 Pitt died.

George III was unable to find a Tory who could take over a secure government and was forced to appoint the Whig 'Ministry of All the Talents'. This government again pressed the King for the relief of Catholic disabilities and was dismissed; the next Prime Minister was the Whig Duke of Portland, but he led a Tory government.

Portland was only a figurehead and he did very little, allowing dangerous feuds to build up within the cabinet. The failure of efforts to suppress Napoleon in Spain led George Canning, Foreign Secretary, to accuse Viscount Castlereagh, Secretary of State for War and the Colonies, of being responsible; before Portland had acted the cabinet had formed two factions and eventually the two men fought a duel.

The Duke of Portland was already ill and resigned less than a month before his death in October 1809. The King rejected Canning and appointed Spencer Perceval, who shared his position on Catholic disabilities, as Prime Minister. Perceval spent the first two years of his government amid crisis: mistakes in the war, and financial difficulties caused by the war, were followed by the final descent of the King into mental illness.

Perceval handled the crises effectively and when the Prince of Wales was made Prince Regent, he remained in office – despite disappointing the Prince Regent over the amount of the funds for the Royal Household. Conditions were improving when Perceval was assassinated on 11 May 1812 by John Bellingham, a trader who blamed the government for his imprisonment in Russia several years previously. After Perceval's death the government lost a censure vote in Parliament.

To form a strong administration, the Prince Regent appointed the Earl of Liverpool – an experienced cabinet minister – to replace Perceval. Liverpool was especially experienced in foreign affairs and directed the final years of the war with France effectively; he was also able to direct the simultaneous war against the USA which broke out in June 1812. After British forces burned the White House, the war stagnated and ended in a return to pre-war conditions.

45

Napoleon was defeated in 1814, and to stimulate British agriculture in peacetime Liverpool introduced the Corn Laws which forbade the import of foreign corn until the price reached a set level. This legislation was to cause the party considerable difficulty in years to come. Peace appeared to have gone when Napoleon escaped from Elba, but the Battle of Waterloo in June 1815 totally defeated him.

Public celebration at the victory was shortlived, as the economy began to suffer. The government was defeated in its attempt to keep income tax, which had been imposed to pay for the war, and had to borrow to finance its spending. Bad harvests hit agriculture and manufacturing industry went into recession; there was a resurgence of the 'Luddite' riots of those who believed machinery was taking their jobs. Liverpool dealt with the riots repressively, as he had done previously.

There was discontent over political matters as well as the economic situation. A mass meeting in Manchester calling for extension of the right to vote was broken up and 11 people killed in August 1819, and Liverpool reacted by introducing the 'six Acts' which suppressed seditious meetings and publications. The political situation remained tense until the economy improved in 1823.

Liverpool opposed Catholic emancipation and spoke against an emancipatory bill in 1821, helping to defeat it. Another attempt in 1825 would have resulted in his resignation, had the Lords not voted against. Liverpool retained office until he was paralysed by a cerebral haemorrhage in 1827. George Canning was invited to form a government; he found he needed to have Whig support and a coalition was formed.

Canning was distrusted by his fellow Tories for his Whig background and the Duke of Wellington, among others, began to oppose government measures. Barely three months later, Canning died and Viscount Goderich took over; he was told by the King not to bring forward any reforms of Parliament or emancipation of Catholics. A divided cabinet and the King's restrictions made effective government impossible and Goderich resigned in January 1828.

Following two weak leaders, the next Tory to be Prime Minister was a very strong figure. The Duke of Wellington had been Commander of the Army from the end of the Napoleonic Wars and tried to lead a long-term stable government. Wellington disliked political conflict and when William

Huskisson, a supporter of George Canning, opposed a government bill, Wellington sacked him and all the other Canningites.

Wellington finally had to deal with the Catholic emancipation issue, when the Catholic Daniel O'Connell won a by-election in County Clare. A rebellion in Ireland threatened if O'Connell was excluded from Parliament, and this ensured that the Bill to remove Catholic disabilities passed without much opposition. However, Wellington refused to move on reform of Parliament. He was outspoken on the subject in Parliament, which made his government very unpopular in the country.

In 1830, at the suggestion of John Wilson Croker MP, the Tory party changed its name to Conservative. A general election in July 1830 went against Wellington, and in November 1830, after a Commons defeat on the Civil list, Wellington resigned – helping to prevent an opposition motion on reform. The new King, William IV, appointed a Whig government under Earl Grey strongly committed to reform. Wellington, as leader of the Opposition, continued his campaign against reform.

These tactics backfired. The first Reform Bill was defeated in Committee and the government called an election on the issue of reform, resulting in a landslide victory for the Whigs. The second Reform Bill passed easily through the Commons but was blocked by the Lords, resulting in riots. A third Bill was allowed to progress in the Lords but the Conservative opposition tried to delay it in Committee. The Whigs began to pressure the King to create more Whig peers to pass the Bill and Wellington faced public opposition – his house was twice stoned.

William IV's initial refusal to create peers led to the government's resignation. Wellington found himself unable to form a government and was forced to give a pledge not to hinder the Reform Bill. 100 Conservatives abstained on the Third Reading of the Bill and it passed. A reformed system was bound to harm Conservative election chances and the government immediately called a general election on the new basis, winning a huge majority.

With their diminished strength in Parliament, the Conservatives were unable to form a government when Grey resigned in July 1834. When Grey's successor Lord Melbourne was dismissed in November 1834, Wellington was again appointed Prime Minister by William IV, hoping to hold the post only until the leading Commons Conservative Sir Robert

Peel could take over; Peel returned from holiday in Italy and became Prime Minister a month later.

Peel could not hope to govern with the Commons as hostile as it was and called a general election, outlining his policies in the 'Tamworth Manifesto'. The Manifesto mentioned the electoral difficulty of the Reform Bill but hoped to win the confidence of the voters; Peel declared his acceptance of the Reform Bill as a final settlement. This helped the Conservatives in the election but they failed to win a majority, leading to defeats and Peel's resignation in April 1835.

The Conservatives were kept in opposition by the Whig victory at the 1837 general election, but they made gains. In 1839 they came close to defeating the Whigs in a vote, prompting the resignation of the government, but Peel was unable to form an administration because of Queen Victoria's refusal to dismiss her Whig Ladies of the Bedchamber, and the Whigs returned.

After some Whig incompetence in foreign affairs, Peel successfully moved a motion of no confidence in May 1841 and went on to prove that the Conservatives could win a general election. He returned to office, having immediately to deal with a recession which was prompting riots. Peel reintroduced income tax to help the national finances, and controlled the Bank of England's issue of banknotes to curb inflation.

Peel believed in conciliating feelings in Ireland and increased the grant to the Catholic seminary at Maynooth, which did not find favour with many Conservatives. The failure of the Irish potato crop from 1845 faced Peel's government with a difficulty. To relieve the famine would need foreign food imports but these were forbidden by the Corn Laws originally introduced during the Napoleonic Wars. Peel tried to persuade the cabinet to repeal the Corn Laws but failed and resigned in December 1845.

The Whigs failed to form a government, and Peel returned determined to repeal the laws regardless of the effect on the Conservative Party. Though he managed to get the agreement of almost all the cabinet, two thirds of Conservative MPs voted against him; soon after the repeal was agreed, he was defeated and resigned, leaving a split party. Peel's supporters were designated **Liberal Conservatives** and usually supported the Liberal government of Lord John Russell. The remainder were known as 'Protectionists'.

The 1847–52 Parliament was a very confused one with shifting allegiances. The Peelites continued after Peel's death in 1850 under the Earl of
Aberdeen; an invitation to the Protectionist Earl of Derby to form a
government in 1851 could not be followed up, because Derby could not
obtain Peelite support. Early in 1852, Derby did form a government
without the Peelites, though he was forced to choose his Cabinet from
little-known figures.

Derby had gambled that he could win a general election, but despite
gaining seats he failed to get a majority independent of the Peelites.
Figures in his government were hated by the Peelites, especially
Chancellor of the Exchequer Benjamin Disraeli, and the budget introduced in December 1852 was voted down by them in combination with
the Liberals, prompting the government's resignation. Peel's successor, the
Earl of Aberdeen, formed a coalition with the Liberals, which managed to
hold together surprisingly well in difficult times.

The Conservatives had enough strength in Parliament to defeat
Aberdeen over the inefficient conduct of the Crimean War, but not
enough to form their own government in 1855. Three years later, the Earl
of Derby accepted office, again hoping to divide the other factions. He
survived longer this time, but again failed to win a majority at the 1859
general election and was then defeated on a vote of no confidence. By this
point, the remaining Peelites had finally severed links with the
Conservatives and became Liberals. This helped stabilise politics at the
expense of harming Conservative chances.

The Conservative Party was in opposition for seven years, facing a
Liberal government with a safe majority. Though an effective leader of the
Opposition in the Commons, Benjamin Disraeli had no chance of
defeating the government. Only when the Liberals split over Parliamentary
reform did the Conservatives get an opportunity, as anti-reform Liberals
joined the Conservatives to vote down Lord John Russell's proposals in
June 1866. The Earl of Derby formed his third minority government.

Despite their coming to office because of opposition to reform, it was
clear to the Conservatives that some move needed to be made as public
anger mounted over lack of progress. Benjamin Disraeli, who led for the
government in the House of Commons, introduced a moderate Reform
Bill; after being strengthened, the Bill passed in 1867: Derby claimed it had

'dished the Whigs'. Shortly afterwards he made way for Disraeli, though this was only a caretaker government until a general election on the reformed system could be held.

Despite the limited time, Disraeli was determined to put forward a programme of reforming legislation. He allowed the Post Office to buy up telegraph companies and moved executions of sentences of death inside prisons, as well as making further changes to the electoral system. At the reformed general election of November 1868, the Liberals won but with a majority less than many expected.

Disraeli in opposition was at first quite inactive, as he revised the Conservative Party's policies in order to make them more relevant to the new reformed political situation; he also created Conservative Central Office. From 1872 he took firm charge and set out a distinct policy for the party of defence of the monarchy and established Church, and solidification of the Empire, with cautious measures of social reform.

Disraeli refused to lead a minority government when invited in 1873, and waited until the 1874 general election which he won. The early actions of his government were pioneering reforms of trade union law, but problems arose over the government's tactical alliance with Turkey. Turkish forces violently suppressed an uprising in Bulgaria in 1876, and Liberal leader Gladstone attacked the government for its complicity.

The Foreign and Colonial Secretaries both resigned from the cabinet when war broke out between Russia and Turkey, unable to support Disraeli's attempts to give military assistance to Turkey. The crisis was resolved at the Congress of Vienna in July 1878, from which Disraeli brought back 'peace with honour'. However, Gladstone's 'Midlothian campaign' against the government's policy eventually won public opinion over and the Conservatives lost the 1880 general election.

Disraeli died in 1881 and the Marquess of Salisbury (Lords) and Sir Stafford Northcote (Commons) became joint leaders of the Conservative Party. This meant a more cautious style after Disraeli's social radicalism. The Liberals introduced a further electoral reform, giving the vote to many of the working class for the first time, but before the details of the new system could be put in place the Conservatives combined with the Irish **Home Rulers** to defeat the government on part of the 1885 budget.

Salisbury was invited to form a government by Queen Victoria, who had grown to detest Gladstone, and he reluctantly accepted. In a fevered pre-election atmosphere the Conservatives put forward moderately progressive legislation on working-class housing, as well as other measures which they hoped would be popular. At this time the Conservatives were being supported by the Irish **Nationalists**, who had grievances over the policy of the previous Liberal government, and Nationalist leader Charles Parnell called on Irishmen in Great Britain to vote Conservative.

There was a knife-edge result at the 1885 general election: the Conservatives and Irish Nationalists obtained the same number of seats as the Liberals. Gladstone chose this moment to disclose his personal support for Home Rule and the Nationalists immediately voted the Salisbury government out; Gladstone's support for Home Rule forced the Conservatives to oppose it, a policy they had been inclining towards in any case.

Divisions among the Liberals quickly surfaced and the Home Rule Bill was defeated; a general election on the 'Irish Question' was called. Home Rule was not popular in Great Britain and the Conservatives (who in most case stood down where there was a **Liberal Unionist** candidate) won the most seats. Salisbury became Prime Minister again but dependent on Liberal Unionist support.

While Salisbury was able to dominate foreign affairs, at which he was experienced and acted as his own Foreign Secretary, his policy at home was heavily influenced by Liberal Unionists. He usually left his ministers to get on with the job so that he could concentrate on the Empire where he vigorously defended British interest (Salisbury believed Britain should be an independent power and opposed international alliances). This government created elected county councils and abolished fees for primary education.

After six years of government, Salisbury called a general election. The Liberals had reconstructed after their loss in 1886 and won a majority in consort with the Irish Nationalists; Salisbury waited to be defeated in Parliament before resigning. He did not hesitate to oppose Home Rule in the House of Lords, where the defection of the Liberal Unionists had severely depleted Liberal strength, and the bill was easily defeated.

After that defeat, Salisbury expected the government to resign, and when it did not the Lords continued to veto much of the legislation proposed by

Gladstone and the Earl of Rosebery. This made effective government impossible and when a minor censure vote was carried in the Commons the government did resign. The Marquess of Salisbury returned as Prime Minister in 1895, forming a government including Liberal Unionists, and won a general election to give the government a large majority.

Salisbury was again preoccupied with the Empire, though he did not enjoy total success. Afrikaners, known as Boers, formed a South African republic, which threatened British interests in the area, and Colonial Secretary Joseph Chamberlain backed the 'Jameson Raid', an incompetent attempt to seize control organized from the Cape Colony. The inquiry into the Jameson Raid dogged the government for two years and could have been more damaging if the Liberals had pursued it.

The raid and subsequent attempts to keep British influence in South Africa spurred Afrikaner nationalism, and on 9 October 1899 the South African republic issued an ultimatum to Britain to withdraw troops from its borders. The government sent up to half a million troops to crush about 65,000 Boers, at great cost. In the first part of the Boer War, the Boers besieged three British garrisons, but the sieges were lifted to the delight of the British public.

In October 1900 it appeared that the war was nearly won and the Conservatives called a general election in the midst of much jingoism; it was nicknamed the 'khaki election'. The Liberals were divided and the party was re-elected with a slightly reduced majority. After the election it became clear that the war was not going well as Boer resistance continued to halt British advances. World opinion was condemnatory of a large Empire's persecution of a small nation.

Superior numbers eventually won and the Boers made peace in May 1902. Shortly afterwards Salisbury, in ill health, handed over to Arthur Balfour – his nephew. Balfour was an unpopular choice as Prime Minister as his initial appointment had been criticised for nepotism (the expression 'Bob's your uncle' comes from the Marquess of Salisbury's christian name). He had also just passed the Education Act of 1902, which faced fierce opposition from nonconformists by bringing their schools under local education authority control.

Balfour had a special concern for education and founded several universities. However, his administration was severely split over the tariff reform campaign of Joseph Chamberlain, the Colonies Secretary. Chamberlain proposed that the British Empire raise tariffs on foreign goods, while lowering them on imports from within the Empire, in order to unite the Empire and create a powerful world trading unit.

Tariff reform won many supporters and almost as many enemies. When Balfour refused to declare himself on either side, Chamberlain resigned from the government to fight in the party at large, and won good support. Several MPs who opposed the scheme and supported free trade resigned to join the Liberals. Balfour sometimes had to lead Conservative MPs out of Parliament rather than vote on Liberal motions concerning free trade.

Balfour disagreed with Salisbury's policy on alliances and negotiated the *entente cordiale* with France in 1904, but by 1905 the party's divisions were making government difficult. Balfour stayed on in office for longer than many expected, but in December 1905 he acknowledged the divisions and resigned, partly in the hope of causing Liberal divisions before a general election.

There were none and the party suffered a catastrophic defeat in the January 1906 election, winning only 156 seats. Balfour himself was defeated and a safe seat had to be found for him in a by-election. He retained the leadership (Joseph Chamberlain suffered a stroke in 1906) but was an ineffective leader of the Opposition, despite obtaining near unity on the tariff issue – the free trade minority was so small it accepted defeat. As the Marquess of Salisbury had done in 1892–5, Balfour decided to use the party's House of Lords majority to wreck Liberal legislation.

The party was careful to weigh up the likely popularity of a bill. It did not block the Trade Disputes Act of 1906 which reversed an anti-trade union court judgment and was very much welcomed. However, in 1908 the Lords destroyed the key points of the government's programme. This proved popular in the country and the Conservatives began to win some spectacular by-elections (such as Peckham in March 1908).

The ease with which the Lords thwarted the government led to over-confidence. When the budget foresaw increased taxation (including new land taxes) to pay for social reforms, the Conservative Party denounced it. A Budget Protest League was formed in the country, and after 70 full days in the House of Commons debating the budget, the Finance Bill went to the Lords.

Conservative peers decided to block the Bill, over-ruling objections that to do so was unconstitutional, and it was rejected by 350 to 75. The amendment that was carried declared that the government had no right to introduce a measure for which no consent was obtained from the voters at the previous election, but amid the Liberal outrage over the Lords' actions, this was forgotten. The Liberals called a general election, stating the issue was 'the peers versus the people'.

In Great Britain the Liberals and Conservatives won roughly the same number of seats, but the addition of Labour and Irish Nationalists gave the Liberal government a sizeable majority, and the Conservatives were forced to agree that the budget had received the assent of electors. Meanwhile the Liberals instituted a reform of the powers of the House of Lords to prevent it challenging an elected government.

The Liberals called a Constitutional Conference to discuss options on Lords reform but in November 1910 it collapsed without agreement, and a second general election was called. Sensing that tariff reform was still unpopular, at this election the Conservatives promised to submit the policy to a nationwide referendum before implementing it; this proposition failed to win many voters but did outrage the most fervent tariff reformers.

The result of the December 1910 election was almost the same as that in January and the Liberals put to the new Parliament their proposals for Lords Reform in the Parliament Bill. Conservative peers agitated to block this attempt to reduce their powers, but Prime Minister Herbert Asquith informed Balfour that the King had agreed to create sufficient Liberal peers to pass the Bill if it were blocked. Balfour pressed his peers to abstain, but it was only through the decision of 37 Conservatives to support the Bill that it was passed, 114 'die-hards' voted against.

Balfour resigned the leadership in November 1911. A further split on tariff reform threatened, as the two main contenders to be his successor were Austen Chamberlain (son of Joseph Chamberlain and just as enthusiastic for tariff reform) and Walter Long, who was cautious about the question. Andrew Bonar Law was agreed as a compromise leader to head off the division. He swiftly moved to formally merge the Conservatives with the Liberal Unionists, the distinction between the two having virtually disappeared several years before.

Bonar Law helped unite the party around an attack on the Liberals for increasing tax, disestablishing the Church in Wales, and the Marconi scandal where leading Liberals were accused of making a personal profit from government contracts to the Marconi company. However, the key issue of the period after 1911 was again Home Rule for Ireland, now that the Parliament Act had removed the Lords veto.

Home Rule passed the Commons in 1912, which meant that it could become law in 1914 under the provisions of the Parliament Act. Bonar Law was himself from an Ulster family and declared he would support Ulster's resistance to Home Rule, and privately called upon the King to dismiss the cabinet in September 1912 for disloyalty. Home Rule was indeed passed for the third time by the Commons early in 1914, but the Liberal government held an all-party conference to discuss a compromise.

There were no results to this discussion by the time of the outbreak of the Great War, and while given Royal Assent, Home Rule was postponed for the duration. The outbreak of war also delayed the expected general election which the Conservatives would probably have won, but it increased the Conservatives' popularity as they had previously called for a more anti-German policy and higher defence expenditure.

The party therefore campaigned during the early months of the war for a more vigorous war effort, and was successful in damaging the Liberal government's credibility so that Asquith had to form a coalition government. The Conservatives were very much junior partners as Liberals retained all the key positions, and Bonar Law was even excluded from the initial formulation of the Inner War Council.

Conservative unrest at the conduct of the war did not stop, and reached a peak in late 1916. After a large backbench rebellion, Conservative cabinet ministers met and passed a resolution demanding a reconstruction of the government, and Asquith was forced to resign. The King asked Bonar Law to form a government but Law suggested that David Lloyd George – who was campaigning for a reconstruction on the same lines – would be the most popular choice.

The Conservatives had a bigger role in the Lloyd George government and criticisms of the war effort subsided. From the summer of 1918 the war was going well and attention began to turn to the post-war political situation, which would require an immediate general election on near-universal franchise. The Conservatives had reason for optimism but the unknown effect of the new voters made them cautious, and Bonar Law agreed with Lloyd George that the **Coalition** should fight the election as a single unit.

When the election happened in December 1918, Lloyd George and Bonar Law sent out a letter ('the coupon') to all official Coalition candidates. It was agreed to limit the number of Liberals receiving the coupon to about 150, which meant that few Conservatives did not receive one. The Coalition won a great victory, and only 30 out of the 362 Coalition Conservatives lost; 50 non-Coalition Conservatives also won – though many of those actually gave support to the Coalition.

The Conservatives were happy to remain in the Coalition in the immediate post-war years, as Lloyd George was firmly against the Russian Revolution and sent irregular British forces (the 'Black and Tans') to suppress the Sinn Féin rising in Ireland. Suggestions were made that the Coalition partners formally merge, and surprisingly Bonar Law agreed. Objections from Coalition Liberal MPs prevented any progress.

Bonar Law retired due to ill health in March 1921, to be succeeded by Austen Chamberlain. By this time, Coalition feeling was fading and the performance of the Coalition in by-elections was disappointing. Lloyd George had never been a popular figure for Conservatives, who remembered it was he who proposed the 1909 budget, and though Chamberlain always defended the Coalition he was a weak leader.

Attacks on the Coalition increased through 1922 with the 4th Marquess of Salisbury publishing a manifesto for anti-Coalition Conservatives in June. The campaign reached a climax in October when Lloyd George needlessly confronted Turkey, threatening war. On 18 October the Conservatives unexpectedly won a by-election in Newport while the Liberal did badly, and Conservative MPs meeting at the Carlton Club the next day voted to end the Coalition by 185 to 88. The need for the leadership to remain in touch with backbench MPs resulted in the formation of the Conservative Private Members Committee, still popularly known as the '1922 Committee'.

Chamberlain then resigned as leader and was replaced by Bonar Law, who had made a recovery from illness, and was immediately appointed Prime Minister following Lloyd George's resignation. A general election was called, in which many local Conservative associations agreed to co-operate with Lloyd George's supporters. In a very confused election, the Conservatives won a clear majority after running a strong anti-socialist campaign. They could count on the support of most of the 51 Lloyd George Liberals.

Many leading Conservatives who had supported the Coalition refused to serve under Bonar Law and he was in poor health, lasting only until May 1923 when he was diagnosed with throat cancer. Stanley Baldwin, a Worcestershire industrialist, won the leadership over the Foreign Secretary, the Marquess of Curzon. Baldwin was a supporter of tariff reform and saw it as the issue to unite the party, but Law's manifesto in 1922 had specifically ruled it out.

Baldwin therefore felt a new general election had to be called in order to obtain a mandate for tariff reform. The election happened earlier than he had wanted, in December 1923. Tariff reform remained unpopular in the country though it provided a cause to unite the Conservatives. The Conservative vote was almost the same as in 1922, but the other parties increased their vote and the result was that no party obtained a majority. The Conservatives remained the largest single party and Baldwin remained as Prime Minister.

Baldwin refused to consider forming an anti-Labour coalition and would not drop tariff reform, which resulted in the Liberals supporting a Labour motion of no confidence and the defeat of the government. It is likely Baldwin did not fight too hard against a Labour government because he felt it would not last long, and this proved to be the case: a Liberal motion to establish a Select Committee into the dropped prosecution of a communist newspaper was declared an issue of confidence, so the Conservatives backed it and defeated the government.

Baldwin had dropped tariff reform shortly after the formation of the Labour government, and formulated a new set of policies which would appeal to the mass electorate. The party was helped by the revelation of a document purporting to be a letter from the Communist International to British Communists calling for insurrection; most Conservatives felt it must be genuine and justified their fears of a Labour government.

The Conservatives won a huge majority, largely at the expense of the Liberals. Stanley Baldwin became Prime Minister again, and immediately invited Winston Churchill (who had left the party over the tariff issue in

1904 and had later been a Lloyd George Liberal) to be Chancellor of the Exchequer. The government proved to be a surprisingly reformist one, starting with the provision of pensions for widows and injured workers. Baldwin opposed a private member's bill to restrict trade union political funds which he thought would damage industrial relations.

However, the government's decision to return to the Gold Standard (fixing the value of the pound in terms of other currencies) at a high rate, damaged the export trade. Mine owners found their coal exports too expensive and cut miners' wages; Baldwin stepped in to subsidise the wages in July 1925 but when a Royal Commission recommended the end of the subsidy, he left it to the mine owners and the unions to agree what to do.

Negotiations failed in May 1926 and the miners went on strike, while the Trades Union Congress called a general strike in their support. Baldwin remained calm, denouncing the general strike as unconstitutional in a broadcast. He let Churchill publish a highly patriotic newspaper (the *British Gazette*), and after nine days the strike collapsed. The government then moved to make general strikes illegal.

Economically, Baldwin's government proved to be surprisingly interventionist. It nationalised the BBC, set up the Central Electricity Generating Board, and moved to reorganise the cotton industry. Another reform for which the government was reponsible was the lowering of the age of female franchise to 21, coming in at the next general election. However, the government became unpopular as the economy suffered from the high exchange rate.

In spring 1929 the government's term came to an end and Baldwin called a general election. Though the Conservatives won the most votes, Labour obtained more seats, and the party decided to resign before Parliament met. The loss of the election caused some tension in the party, and a serious division opened up in autumn 1929 when Baldwin committed the party to support Labour's policy on India. Many in the party were opposed to the decision to allow more self-government to India and Winston Churchill resigned from the Shadow Cabinet in protest.

The issue which caused more strife than any other during this period was the campaign by the newspaper publishers Lord Beaverbrook and Viscount Rothermere for 'Empire Free Trade', a revised version of tariff reform (*see* **Empire Free Trade Crusade**). Beaverbrook campaigned for the Conservative Party to adopt his policy, but while sympathetic, Baldwin ultimately refused. Beaverbrook's response was to agitate for Baldwin's dismissal in his newspapers.

By the spring of 1931, the campaign against Baldwin was at its height, when a by-election in Westminster St George's resulted in a straight fight between a Baldwin supporter and a candidate backed by Beaverbrook. At a public speech, Baldwin denounced the press lords for seeking 'power without responsibility', a telling phrase which helped the Conservatives hold the seat; shortly afterwards a truce was negotiated between Beaverbrook and Conservative Party Chairman Neville Chamberlain.

The party was campaigning on the issue of the economy at a time of difficulties caused by the stock-market crash. The party's leaders were summoned back from holiday to discuss the crisis of August 1931, and when the Labour government resigned Baldwin was happy to agree to serve under Ramsay MacDonald in a National government. He saw the National government as a temporary measure; others welcomed the division of the Labour Party.

Conservative pressure resulted in a decision to call a general election to obtain a 'doctor's mandate' (i.e. permission to do what was necessary to provide for economic recovery) for the National government. Such a mandate would also ease disputes over the tariff issue and severely damage the Labour Party electorally, and in early October 1931 the Cabinet agreed to call an election.

The result was the biggest landslide in electoral history for the National government and especially for the Conservatives, who won 470 seats. Advocates of high tariffs won an early victory when a general tariff of 10% was introduced in 1932 and an Imperial Economic Conference was called at Ottawa for that autumn. The conclusions of the conference were not all the 'Empire Free Traders' wished but they went some way towards their demands, forcing the free trade Liberals out of the government.

Meanwhile, concern over foreign affairs and defence came to the fore as Adolf Hitler became Chancellor of Germany. Popular feeling towards reduced military expenditure led to the Conservatives unexpectedly losing a by-election at East Fulham in October 1933, and the government was wary of offering increased spending which might prove unpopular with voters.

As the National government included **Liberal National** and **National Labour** members, the Conservatives were unable totally to control the legislative programme and reformist measures were being proposed. Baldwin personally believed in mild reformism and welcomed the existence of the National government as a justification for introducing it. He was supported by those Conservative MPs who had won their seats because of the pact. Five Conservative MPs who did not share this feeling resigned the whip in May 1935.

Ramsay MacDonald resigned as Prime Minister the next month and Baldwin was appointed to continue the National government. He called a general election in November 1935 and won easy re-election, though the Conservative domination of the National government was becoming ever more clear; an unsuccessful move was made in 1936 to rename the party 'National' and unite government supporters.

Foreign affairs came to dominate the government after the 1935 election. Winston Churchill had already begun a campaign for rearmament to confront Hitler, and public anger forced Baldwin to repudiate a plan to partition Ethiopia, drawn up by Foreign Secretary Sir Samuel Hoare in December 1935 after Mussolini's Italy invaded. Hoare resigned but was reappointed only a few months later. Early in 1936 Baldwin gave in to Churchill's campaign for a Minister to co-ordinate defence, but failed to appoint Churchill to the role, much to everyone's surprise.

Baldwin was in poor health in 1936 but was able to handle the abdication crisis calmly. In May 1937 he resigned as Prime Minister, and was succeeded by Chancellor of the Exchequer Neville Chamberlain. It was the Conservative Party's misfortune to choose someone with little experience of foreign affairs at this time. Chamberlain believed that patient negotiation with the European dictators would defuse any crisis.

Chamberlain's policy of negotiation caused Foreign Secretary Anthony Eden to resign in February 1938 in protest at the intention to negotiate with Mussolini. Eden's objection to the lack of principle seemed borne out when, under the Anglo-Italian Agreement of April 1938, Britain accepted Italian domination of Ethiopia and declared that it would not intervene in the Spanish Civil War.

In September 1938 Hitler's demand that Czechoslovakia cede the Sudetenland to Germany suddenly threatened European war. Chamberlain saw Hitler three times in an attempt to avert war, and finally made an agreement at Munich which conceded almost all of Hitler's demands and dismantled the defences of the rest of Czechoslovakia, obtaining in return a statement from Hitler that it represented his last territorial claim in Europe and a declaration renouncing the use of war to solve disputes.

Chamberlain returned home to a hero's welcome, echoing Disraeli's response on the Congress of Vienna. He did not entirely trust Hitler and increased the rearmament programme, but strongly defended his policy against attacks from the Labour Party and Conservative critics. However, Hitler demonstrated in March 1939 that his assurances were meaningless when he invaded the rest of Czechoslovakia. The policy of appeasement was dropped and Britain, together with France, gave assurances to Poland, which would be Hitler's next territorial demand.

Compulsory military service was introduced in April 1939 and rearmament was accelerated. The Nazi-Soviet pact of August 1939 clearly presaged an attack on Poland and Parliament was recalled to pass special legislation in preparation for war. German forces invaded Poland on 1 September 1939 but Chamberlain delayed acting; on 2 September the cabinet demanded he send an ultimatum to Germany. No response came and on 3 September Britain declared war.

The cabinet was reconstructed and Winston Churchill was appointed First Lord of the Admiralty, but it remained a National government. The early period of the war contained little actual fighting and in April 1940 Chamberlain made a speech declaring that Hitler had 'missed the bus' – i.e. his opportunity to advance in the war. This declaration was embarrassingly proved wrong within days when Hitler invaded and conquered Denmark and Norway.

There had been a small British mission to Norway and its failure prompted a motion of no confidence in the House of Commons. Many Conservative MPs voted against the government's conduct of the war or abstained; though the government won, the majority was 81. Chamberlain's loss of support necessitated a reconstruction of the government and he invited Labour to participate; Labour refused to join the government under Chamberlain because of his previous support for appeasement.

Chamberlain decided to resign and Labour declared in favour of joining a coalition under Winston Churchill only; on the same day that Churchill was appointed Prime Minister, German forces invaded France. Churchill became leader of the Conservative Party from October 1940. As a war leader to unite the nation, Churchill proved ideal and he was able to unite the party also, in spite of having been a rebel for the previous decade, because his warnings had been proved right.

Churchill's conduct of the war was very personal and he devoted almost all his attention to it, leaving most domestic policy to Clement Attlee. He did not always consult with colleagues (for example over his negotiations with President Roosevelt). After the achievement of retrieving British forces at Dunkirk and resisting the Luftwaffe in the Battle of Britain, the nation had cause for optimism.

There were few Conservative critics of the government during the Second World War. A large number of MPs voted against the Catering Wages Bill in February 1943 believing it was socialistic, but most major arguments over domestic policy were won by the Conservative side. The vast scheme of social insurance proposed by Sir William Beveridge was delayed until after the war though many Conservatives were in favour of it. The most important domestic reform during the war was the responsibility of a Conservative minister. This was R. A. Butler's Education Act 1944.

As the war moved towards victory for the Allies over Germany, Churchill offered to keep the coalition in place until the surrender of Japan – which he believed was still more than a year away. Attlee refused and after VE day Labour left the coalition. Churchill then formed a caretaker Conservative government and called an election at which he hoped to use his immense personal popularity to win re-election. The Conservative Party manifesto was strongly progressive, and included a 'comprehensive health service'.

Most commentators expected a Conservative victory with a comfortable majority, and the eventual result of a landslide Labour victory was shocking to the Conservative Party. It took the opportunity to have a thorough review of its policies, led by several young thinkers who were to hold important cabinet positions in years to come. The result of the review, *The Right Road for Britain*, was published in 1949. Meanwhile the party amalgamated with the Liberal Nationals with whom it had been in alliance since 1931.

There was a good sense of party unity in the immediate post-war years. This was helped by such factors as Aneurin Bevan's 1948 outspoken attack on the party for being 'lower than vermin' – Conservative associations formed 'Vermin Clubs' to publicise the speech. Yet the party was dismayed by its failure to make a recovery in by-elections. Only one seat was gained from Labour, and that was a highly untypical election. The party's failure to win Hammersmith South in February 1949 was particularly illustrative of the disappointing by-election results.

With its new policies (and helped by a redistribution of seats) the party made a spectacular recovery at the February 1950 general election at which the Labour majority was reduced to 5 seats. It was clear this Parliament would not last long and the party's MPs harried the Labour government, defeating it on a sudden division in the first month of the Parliament. The party moved frequent censure motions – in February 1951 there were three in one month.

After other defeats Attlee called an election for October 1951. Labour's campaign to try to portray the Conservatives as warmongers failed to catch the public mood. Though Labour won slightly more votes, the Conservatives won a small overall majority and Churchill returned as Prime Minister. In forming his cabinet, Churchill picked figures who were in sympathy with the moderate policies now advocated by the party.

The new government's policies were in practice very similar to those of the previous Labour government, and spending on education, health and housing increased. The government denationalised the iron and steel industries and road haulage but left the other nationalised industries untouched. It is surprising the right of the party did not make any major objections to the conduct of the government; the only significant rebellion was that of 40 MPs who opposed the government's plan to withdraw a British military base at the Suez Canal.

Churchill suffered a severe stroke in June 1953 which was concealed from the public, but he recovered and retained office through his eightieth birthday in November 1954. He retired in April 1955 only when pressed to do so by the cabinet; Anthony Eden, who had been Foreign Secretary, was the natural successor (and had been for some time). Eden immediately called a general election and managed to increase the Conservative majority to 60.

The Eden government hit problems almost immediately. An economic crisis required an emergency budget in October 1955 which increased indirect taxes and cut spending. Eden seemed a weak leader, and an editorial in the *Daily Telegraph* in January 1956 called for 'the smack of firm government' from him.

Eden had formed a particular hatred for President Nasser of Egypt, thinking him a dictator who would not be appeased. When Nasser nationalised the Suez Canal, Eden made an alliance with France and Israel to retake the Canal and possibly depose Nasser. He expected Labour support, but though Labour had initially backed the government it would not support military action.

British and French forces went into action at the end of October 1956 by bombing Egyptian airfields, prompting the resignation of junior minister, Anthony Nutting, in protest. A paratroop landing began on 5 November but the next day, fears for the sterling exchange rate forced a ceasefire. The troops withdrew in December without any concessions from Egypt; 15 Conservative MPs abstained in a motion of no confidence after this humiliation.

Eden's health broke down with the strain of the crisis and he went to recuperate in Jamaica; shortly after returning he resigned as Prime Minister. This time there were two potential successors – R. A. Butler and Harold Macmillan – and a series of consultations with leading figures in the party was required to choose between them. Macmillan won as he was thought safer and more charismatic in a television age.

Macmillan moved to repair relations with the US which had been damaged by the Suez affair (about which the US was not told), and succeeded in negotiating a collaboration on defence. The economy was doing well when Macmillan took over, and he declared 'some of our people have never had it so good' in July 1957. However, the boom was getting out of control with a danger of inflation. To deflate the economy, public spending was cut.

Chancellor of the Exchequer Peter Thorneycroft proposed a further cut of £30 million in January 1958 but Macmillan, who had been committed to ending poverty and unemployment of the sort he saw in his first constituency of Stockton-on-Tees between the wars, objected, and the cabinet refused. Thorneycroft and his two junior ministers resigned. Macmillan, refusing to cancel a planned trip to Africa, dismissed the resignations as 'little local difficulties' though he was very concerned privately.

The economy continued to grow in the late 1950s and after successful diplomacy, Macmillan called a general election for October 1959. The Conservatives played up the good economic conditions and warned that Labour would ruin them, and won a landslide majority of 100. The impressive electoral performance of the Conservatives continued and the party won a by-election from Labour in 1960.

Macmillan took an active part in foreign affairs, cautiously supporting the process of decolonisation in Africa and forming a relationship with President Kennedy after his election in 1960. Kennedy was related to Macmillan by marriage and often telephoned him for advice. The government also applied to join the European Economic Community in 1961, which required the imperialist wing of the party to accept that the era of Empire was over.

The economy began to overheat in 1961 and the Chancellor had to introduce a 'pay pause', restricting wage rises; this prompted an increase in strikes. Meanwhile the government established the National Economic Development Council, popularly known as Neddy, where trade unions, the government and employers met to discuss economic planning. Economic difficulties lay behind the government's stunning loss of the Orpington by-election in March 1962.

When the government ran into political difficulties, they were exacerbated by Macmillan's panicked reaction in July 1962, when he sacked 6 Cabinet ministers in an attempt to make his government look newer. However, the government still made an easy target for the new wave of satire, which began in the early 1960s. A strong press campaign forced Macmillan to dismiss Sir Thomas Galbraith, who was accused of being too close to one of his civil servants who had been discovered to be a Soviet spy, though an inquiry eventually cleared him.

General de Gaulle vetoed the application to join the EEC in January 1963, destroying the government's long-term economic policy and depressing Macmillan. That summer the party was hit by a further scandal when the Secretary of State for War, John Profumo, had to admit to lying about a relationship with a prostitute and resigned. Macmillan had been in office for six years and was looking out of touch, being much older than the new Labour leader, Harold Wilson.

On the eve of the Conservative Party conference in October 1963 Macmillan entered hospital, where his doctors feared he had cancer. He resigned the leadership of the Conservative Party in a letter addressed to the Foreign Secretary, the Earl of Home, which was read out at the conference. The traditional process of consultation with senior party figures to produce a leader took place in public view.

There were several potential candidates for the leadership. Macmillan moved to block R. A. Butler, and eventually the surprise figure of the Earl of Home emerged as the most acceptable choice. The time had gone when a Prime Minister could operate from the House of Lords so Home disclaimed his peerage, becoming Sir Alec Douglas-Home, and was elected to the Commons for Kinross and West Perthshire in a by-election. The leadership campaign caused some wounds and several senior Conservatives refused to serve under Douglas-Home.

Douglas-Home took over with at the most a year to go before the general election. He would not have enough time to make major changes but adopted a reflationary economic policy and abolished resale price maintenance (a system allowing manufacturers to set the final price for their goods). This last measure was criticised by some Conservatives for its effect on small shops.

When time ran out, Douglas-Home called the election for October 1964. After 13 years in government the Conservative programme seemed to have nothing very new. While the economy was doing reasonably well, the Labour Party pointed to the rising Balance of Payments deficit caused by Douglas-Home's consumer boom. Labour won the election but the Conservatives managed to run them closer than many had expected: the overall majority was only 5.

Douglas-Home moved to reform the process for election of the party leader so that the party's MPs elected the leader by ballot. His own conduct of the Opposition ran into criticism and he resigned in July 1965. The first contest under the new procedure resulted in a victory for Edward Heath, who became the first Conservative Party leader from relatively modest origins. Heath had led the application to join the EEC and was the youngest leader since Disraeli.

Heath reviewed party policy quickly, knowing that a new election would not be far away. A reorganisation of the party's structure was also begun but was not complete by the time of the 1966 general election. The party had not reorganized sufficiently to get rid of the same sense of thirteen wasted years which had resulted in the 1964 election being lost, and Labour had been a competent government; Labour won with a landslide.

The Conservative Party began to get more popular as the Labour government suffered splits and economic disasters such as devaluation. The party began to win by-elections with some amazing swings in 1968. Edward Heath kept the party on a relatively moderate course, and when Enoch Powell made a speech opposing immigration which added to racial tension, Heath dismissed him from the shadow cabinet.

Shortly before the 1970 election the shadow cabinet met at the Selsdon Park Hotel in Croydon to settle the policy for the manifesto. The result of this conference was a new policy opposing intervention in industry and advocating lower public spending and taxes, more selective welfare payments and legislation to restrict the power of trade unions. This policy was a step away from the consensus which had shaped post war Labour and Conservative governments.

The Conservatives won a surprise victory in the 1970 general election, helped by a campaign which especially targeted women voters. However, the new government suffered a tragic blow when Iain Macleod, one of the brightest thinkers, died only a month after being appointed Chancellor of the Exchequer. The Industrial Relations Act was passed in 1971 to restrict trade unions, but caused mass protests and a wave of strikes; few unions complied with the requirement to register, introduced by the Act.

Heath's declaration against intervention in industry was forgotten in 1971 when Rolls-Royce, an important defence contractor, collapsed. The key parts of the business were nationalised. Unemployment increased and exceeded one million in January 1972. In the middle of the political and economic pressure, the government abruptly reversed its policy and began to intervene in industry after passing the Industry Act 1972. Under threat of a strike the government conceded a pay demand of the National Union of Mineworkers, and government spending began to increase. Inflation was held down by a statutory incomes policy (which the 1970 election manifesto had specifically ruled out).

The government applied to enter the European Communities again, and with the departure of General de Gaulle the application was granted. This was a considerable success for the government. The rise in violence in Northern Ireland was dealt with by abolishing the Northern Ireland Parliament and instituting direct rule from London.

Severe economic difficulties resulted from the sudden rise in oil prices after the Six Days War of October 1973. As fuel supplies dwindled, the miners made another large pay claim and banned overtime to campaign for it. The government was forced to restrict fuel and electricity to three days in every week, and when talks to resolve the miners' dispute failed, an all-out strike was called.

To Heath this seemed an attempt to intimidate an elected government by industrial force and he called a snap general election saying the issue was 'Who Governs Britain?' Most opinion polls gave the Conservatives a small lead, but the eventual result on 28 February 1974 was that Labour won slightly more seats in a Parliament where no one had an overall majority.

Heath held talks with Jeremy Thorpe, leader of the Liberal Party, but opposition from grassroots Liberals prevented a deal to give the government a majority and he resigned. In opposition, the Conservatives adopted one significant new policy on reforming local government funding to abolish the rating system, and managed to defeat the minority Labour government on a Commons motion to reform rates in June 1974.

The main appeal of the Conservatives in the second 1974 general election was radically different from the first: in place of the need to confront the unions, the party now appealed for 'Government of National Unity', and dropped the Industrial Relations Act. Though Labour won by only a narrow majority, the Conservative vote was the lowest since universal franchise. The loss of the second election opened up questions over whether Heath should continue to be leader, and he instituted a review of the election process which looked likely to be followed by an election.

In the event, he was challenged by Margaret Thatcher, after a minor change in the system. Mrs Thatcher had emerged as one of the most effective right-wing speakers and had been behind the proposed change of the rating system. Heath was known to be under threat, but his defeat in the first round by 130 to 119 was an unexpected humiliation and he withdrew. Mrs Thatcher then went on to win the second round. She appointed William Whitelaw, the leading moderate, as Deputy leader and his advice helped ensure party unity. As the first woman leader of a major party Mrs Thatcher's public image was unique and striking, enhanced by a gibe from the USSR against 'the Iron Lady' which she turned around and proclaimed.

Intellectually, Mrs Thatcher was strongly guided by Sir Keith Joseph, with whom she had served in Heath's Cabinet. They came to support the new economic theory of monetarism and free enterprise. Converting the Conservative Party to these beliefs was a long process and had to be conducted with sensitivity.

Under Mrs Thatcher's leadership the party put forward a policy statement – *The Right Approach* – in October 1976 which declared that the state had no role in intervening in industry. Heath had supported a Scottish Assembly, but Mrs Thatcher dropped this commitment and opposed the Labour government's devolution plans; this decision cost the resignation of the Shadow Scottish Secretary and his deputy but was popular with Scottish Conservatives.

The Conservative Party in Parliament began to harry Labour, with its small majority. The government's need to seek a large loan from the International Monetary Fund was a severe defeat and the party moved into a substantial opinion poll lead from late 1976, winning several by-elections. At a time of a rising vote for the far right, Mrs Thatcher mentioned her own concern at being 'swamped' by immigrants and pledged to control immigration, while supporting laws against racial discrimination.

A wave of industrial action made the Labour government very unpopular in the winter of 1978–9 and justified the Conservative policy to restrict the powers of trade unions. After the defeat of the referendums on devolution in Scotland and Wales, the Labour government lost the support of the **Scottish National Party**, and a Conservative motion of no confidence was passed by one vote on 28 March 1979, precipitating a general election.

The Conservatives won with an overall majority of 43 seats and Mrs Thatcher became the first woman Prime Minister. One of the first actions in government was to cut income tax, partially compensated for by a rise in Value Added Tax. In the first year the government passed measures to allow council tenants to buy their homes. Mrs Thatcher demanded, and won, a rebate in the British contribution to the European Communities.

Economically the period was difficult. Inflation, which had been 10% at the start of the government, increased to over 20% soon after and the increase in interest rates pitched the economy into recession which particularly damaged manufacturing industry. There were riots in many inner city areas in 1980–1. At the height of the recession, the 1981 budget went against the advice of 364 leading economists and increased taxes, causing consternation to those who did not share Mrs Thatcher's enthusiasm for monetarism.

The cabinet had originally been very similar to that of Edward Heath, but progressively Mrs Thatcher promoted her supporters and dismissed her critics, who attracted the nickname 'wets'. The party suffered in opinion polls but was helped by the confusion and unpopularity of the Labour Party; the advent of the Liberal/Social Democratic Party **Alliance** saw a three-way fight for public opinion.

At the beginning of April 1982 the political situation was suddenly transformed by the Argentine invasion of the Falkland Islands, a British dependency which they had a territorial claim over. Initially the invasion was embarrassing and the Foreign Secretary took responsibility and resigned, but within days a Royal Navy Task Force was despatched to retake the Islands. The Falklands War saw Mrs Thatcher becoming a very patriotic symbol and when the Argentine forces surrendered on 14 June the Conservative Party was in a clear lead.

After the harsh medicine of the first few years, the economy did improve, recession ended and inflation fell back to single figures. Mrs Thatcher went to the country in June 1983 and won re-election with a landslide majority of 144, a triumphant vindication of her policies. The party easily weathered a sex scandal which forced the resignation of Trade and Industry Secretary Cecil Parkinson in October 1983.

After some changes to trade union law in the first term, the government took further action in 1984. Civil servants working for the Government Communications Headquarters (GCHQ) were banned from membership of all trade unions save for the staff association. Closure of coal mines prompted the National Union of Mineworkers to call an all-out strike in

March 1984, but without a ballot, making the action illegal. The government had anticipated this action and built up coal stocks; power supplies were never threatened and the miners eventually returned to work without any concessions.

Mrs Thatcher was the target of an IRA bomb at the 1984 Conservative Party conference in Brighton. She escaped injury, but 5 leading Conservatives were killed and many others injured. Her Shadow Northern Ireland Secretary, Airey Neave, had been assassinated in March 1979 just before the election. Mrs Thatcher was determined not to make concessions to terrorism, though she did conclude the Anglo-Irish Agreement in November 1985 to allow discussion with the Republic of Ireland over Northern Ireland affairs.

One of the central policies identified with Mrs Thatcher was developed almost by accident. The party had not been committed to denationalising industries in 1979 but had sold several; for one of these, the government had invited applications from the public for shares and found it was surprisingly popular. This approach was then used for the much bigger privatization of 51% of British Telecom in 1984 and provoked a phenomenal response, doing much to achieve the Conservative ideal of a share-owning democracy.

Mrs Thatcher was so dominant of the government that her personality began to create problems. In January 1986 Defence Secretary Michael Heseltine resigned, after failing to persuade the government to support a bid by Italian helicopter manufacturers to take over Westland helicopters of Britain; Mrs Thatcher and the rest of the cabinet favoured a bid from the American manufacturer, Sikorsky. This scandal also cost the job of Trade and Industry Secretary Leon Brittan who was complicit in the leak of a letter discrediting Heseltine. Heseltine denounced Mrs Thatcher's conduct of her cabinet and became an unofficial candidate for the leadership of the party thereafter.

Further privatisations happened through the mid 1980s bringing in substantial revenue; the economy performed well and in 1987 the Chancellor was able to reduce income tax by 2%. This was a prelude to a general election in June 1987, at which the party won re-election in another landslide, obtaining an overall majority of 101. This election saw the Conservatives lose seats in Scotland and the north of England, and Mrs

Thatcher declared that she hoped to use the new term to help the inner cities.

There had been little difficulty in ensuring Conservative Party unity during Mrs Thatcher's government, partly because of the advice provided by her Deputy leader, William Whitelaw. Whitelaw was forced to resign due to health problems in 1988 and some believed that it was the loss of his guidance which caused problems. The economy was in such a strong surplus that Nigel Lawson, the Chancellor of the Exchequer, cut income tax rates again in the 1988 budget. The budget, applauded at the time, caused an unsustainable boom and interest rates had to be put up.

The Conservatives fell behind in the opinion polls in the spring of 1989, and lost the European Parliament elections of 1989. The campaign was run on a theme of scepticism about European Community institutions, which fitted in with a speech Mrs Thatcher had made in Bruges in September 1988 attacking plans for a European superstate.

Mrs Thatcher was known to be hostile to the scheme for European Monetary Union, but other cabinet members forced her to accept conditions for British entry to the Exchange Rate Mechanism which was to prepare for it. In July 1989 she demoted Foreign Secretary Sir Geoffrey Howe, who had been behind the rebellion, and her close work with her economics adviser Sir Alan Walters (equally hostile to monetary union) resulted in the resignation of Chancellor Nigel Lawson in October 1989.

A little-known backbench MP challenged Mrs Thatcher for the Conservative leadership in November 1989; although he was easily beaten, this was a sign of growing discontent. In spring 1990, there were a series of protest marches in traditional Conservative areas, over the government's new system for local government taxation to replace the rates which charged everyone, regardless of means, the same rate. Although the scheme was officially called the Community Charge, almost everyone began calling it the Poll Tax. In the middle of the protests there was a 21% swing to Labour in the Mid Staffordshire by-election.

Though Mrs Thatcher opposed it, Britain entered the Exchange Rate Mechanism in October 1990, but this did not stop Sir Geoffrey Howe from resigning in protest at Mrs Thatcher's tone in a Commons statement on Europe. Howe invited others to challenge her leadership and Michael Heseltine, who had been regarded as a natural candidate, decided to stand.

Mrs Thatcher came four votes short of the required majority to win on the first round and after consultation with her colleagues was told she could not win; she resigned so that others could enter the contest.

Heseltine was edged out of the contest by John Major, who had been Chancellor of the Exchequer for just a year. Major had Mrs Thatcher's backing in the contest but proved to be a moderate leader; he had experienced poverty in his youth and was committed to breaking down class barriers. He immediately announced a review of the Community Charge and eventually agreed to replace it with a graduated system.

Major marked a return to a less ideological approach after Mrs Thatcher. His one distinct new policy in his first year was the 'Citizen's Charter', an agreement between government services and the public over the standard of service to be expected. He negotiated an option not to participate in certain European Community schemes which were unpopular with the Conservative Party at the Maastricht Conference of December 1991, but the Treaty of Maastricht was still opposed by many 'Eurosceptics'.

The high interest rates imposed to curb inflation caused a recession in the early 1990s. The 1992 budget cut income tax but had to borrow a huge amount to pay for it, and immediately afterwards Major called a general election. Though circumstances were hostile, the Conservative campaign raised fears about Labour which resonated with the public and the party won an unexpected victory.

Shortly after the election the government had a disastrous setback when international pressure on the pound forced the government to withdraw from the Exchange Rate Mechanism. Conservative Eurosceptics regarded it as a very welcome development, and were inspired to oppose the government bill to enact the Treaty of Maastricht. The government suffered several defeats and was eventually forced to declare it an issue of confidence in order to get the bill passed.

The departure from the Exchange Rate Mechanism destroyed the government's economic policy and ensured that the public gave it no credit for the economic recovery. The government did get the blame for unpopular measures such as the imposition of tax on domestic fuel. It moved into a severe opinion poll deficit, helped by a succession of personal scandals prompted by a speech from John Major which was interpreted as calling for more morality.

John Major's government did see considerable success in Northern Ireland. The government had agreed a new statement with the Irish government in December 1993 and invited the parties to all-party talks, including Sinn Féin, if the IRA declared a ceasefire. A ceasefire was declared in September 1994 and the peace process took a move forward. Unfortunately the progress was not fast enough for the IRA, which broke off its ceasefire in February 1996.

Conservative divisions over Europe continued at every opportunity, and when in November 1994 the government put forward a bill to increase the contribution to the European Union, eight Conservative MPs voted against. Deciding to confront the rebels, Major removed the Conservative whip. This produced none of the expected contrition; the rebels launched their own manifesto. They were granted the Conservative whip again in April 1995 without having made any concessions.

John Major's inability to stamp his authority on the party led to discontent over his leadership. After attacks from Conservative MPs, he suddenly announced he would fight for re-election. The Eurosceptic Welsh Secretary John Redwood resigned to challenge him; Major won by 218 to 89. This victory secured the leadership but did not stop the attacks.

The Conservative Party's opinion poll rating recovered only slowly from their lowest point, with the Labour Party providing a vigorous opposition; more scandals enveloped the party in an aura of 'sleaze'. The party continued to be divided over the attitude to be taken to European Monetary Union; increasing numbers of MPs wanted to rule it out but John Major insisted on remaining in the negotiations and deciding later whether to join.

The election was delayed until the latest date but time ran out in March 1997. Labour won the election in a landslide and the Conservative vote fell to its lowest since 1832. Major immediately resigned and was succeeded by William Hague, who became the youngest leader since William Pitt. Hague adopted a policy of ruling out participation in the European single currency for the next Parliament, and his broadly sceptical approach to the European Union was encapsulated in the phrase 'In Europe but not run by Europe'. Hague's leading moderate rival for the leadership, Kenneth Clarke, refused to serve under him because of this policy.

Hague reviewed the party's internal structure and created a constitution for the party. The membership was given a say in the election of the party leader. The party remained behind in opinion polls and local elections but won an unexpected victory at the 1999 European Parliament elections. The party campaigned against the Labour government's increases in indirect taxes, a campaign which won many converts when hauliers and farmers blockaded oil refineries in a protest over the cost of petrol in September 2000.

The 2000 party conference saw an unofficial confrontation between those members who wished the party to be more welcoming to sectors of society which the party had not traditionally reached (such as the gay community), and those who campaigned for traditional morality. The former group was led by Michael Portillo, formerly a staunch supporter of Mrs Thatcher, who had reassessed his politics after losing his seat in the 1997 election.

The Ulster Unionist Council (*see* **Ulster Unionist Party**) which was formed in 1905 as the party's Northern Ireland affiliate, disaffiliated from the Conservative Party in 1974. Pressure by Conservative members throughout the UK forced the central party headquarters to set up a Conservative organisation in Northern Ireland in 1989, but this branch has not succeeded in building a large vote.

Co-operative Party

Address: Victory House, 10–14 Leicester Square, London WC2H 7QH

Website: http://co-op-party.org.uk

Number on Register: 2

Highest vote: [excluding candidates who received Labour Party endorsement] A. E. Waterson (Northamptonshire, Kettering, 1918) – 10,299 votes, 45.7%

Parliamentary elections won: 1

Number of candidacies: 11

The Co-operative Party was formed in October 1917 by the Co-operative Union, originally as the Central Co-operative Parliamentary Representation Committee. It did not consider itself bound by the electoral truce during the Great War and fought the Prestwich by-election in February 1918, obtaining a quarter of the vote. In 1918 the Co-operative

Congress upgraded the status of the Committee and retitled it the National Co-operative Parliamentary Representation Committee.

In the 1918 election the party fought ten seats in urban areas, in the midlands, north of England and central Scotland. In no seat did it oppose the **Labour Party**. It won Kettering, and the successful candidate took the Labour whip at Westminster. The party adopted the name Co-operative Party after the Co-operative Congress of 1919. All Co-operative Party candidates since the 1918 election have received Labour Party endorsement.

The Co-operative Party originally aimed to secure direct representation of Co-operators in Parliament, and the establishment of a Co-operative Commonwealth where common ownership ensured production for use, not for profit. In 1927 a formal written agreement with the Labour Party was entered into. It has been revised at intervals ever since. *See also* Labour and Co-operative.

Cornish Nationalist Party

Address: Roseland, Trewollock Lane, Gorran Haven, St Austell, Cornwall PL26 6NT
Email address: trelispen@care4free.net
Highest vote: J. C. A. Whetter (North Cornwall, 1983) – 364 votes, 0.7%
Parliamentary elections won: 0
Number of candidacies: 2

The Cornish Nationalist Party was formed in 1975 by Dr James Whetter, formerly the leader of **Mebyon Kernow**. The party seeks recognition of the Cornish flag and teaching of Cornish history and language in schools. In 1978, mindful of the party's support for conservation of the Cornish environment, it attempted to agree a pact with the **Ecology Party** whereby the parties would not oppose each other. This pact was not concluded.

Dr Whetter has been the party's only Parliamentary candidate; he stood in the 1979 and 1983 general elections, and the 1984 European Parliamentary election. Difficulties of finance have prevented the party from fighting since then but it remains active.

Corrective Party

Address: 116 Eastcombe Avenue, London SE7

Highest vote: Miss L. C. L. L. R. Whiplash (Eastbourne, 1990 (18/10)) – 216 votes, 0.5%

Parliamentary elections won: 0

Number of candidacies: 9

The Corrective Party was formed in 1988 by Lindi St Clair to campaign for the rights of prostitutes and to modernise the laws relating to sex. The party fought several by-elections in the late 1980s and early 1990s with Miss St Clair as candidate, but ambitious plans for the 1992 general election had to be pulled back after a court case in which the Inland Revenue successfully sued Miss St Clair for tax on her earnings. The case resulted in her bankruptcy, and the party undertook no campaigning activity until the bankruptcy was discharged in 1997.

Countryside Party

Address: The Croft, Sunnyside, Culloden Moor, Inverness IV2 5EE

Number on Register: 158

Parliamentary elections won: 0

Number of candidacies: 0

The formation of this party was announced on 24 May 2000. It was initiated by Jim Crawford, the Northern Director of the Countryside Alliance. The party campaigns for greater support for the countryside and strongly opposes any restriction on fox hunting.

Crofter

Highest vote: [excluding candidates who received Liberal endorsement] Dr. G. B. Clark (Caithness, 1885) – 2,110 votes, 63.4%

Parliamentary elections won: 4

Number of candidacies: 18

The highlands of Scotland have for many centuries been populated by

77

tenant farmers called crofters, who are the tenants of parts of huge estates owned by absentee landlords. By the nineteenth century the area was over-populated in relation to the opportunities for earning a living, and the landlords often resorted to desperate tactics, including eviction, to get the most from their land. In the 1880s, deer forests had become the most profitable use of land and rents were raised for those still operating crofts.

In 1885 the crofters were enfranchised by the third Reform Act and started Parliamentary agitation for greater protection. The main form this took was the promotion of unofficial **Liberal** candidates favouring Crofter interests, though after 1886 Liberal associations tended to support crofter demands. Dr Gavin Brown Clark, who sat as a Crofters MP from 1885 to 1900 had previously been associated with the First International and was a **Labour** candidate in 1918.

The Crofters' cause was popular and in 1885 they returned four candidates who had been refused Liberal endorsement. Their pressure won the establishment of a Royal Commission, which produced an 1886 Act of Parliament giving the crofters security of tenure and a Commission to fix rents.

Crofter candidates continued appearing in elections until 1895, and several won seats on county councils when these were created in 1889. **The Highland Land League**, a crofters' support organisation, also sponsored candidates at the 1918 election.

Cymru Annibynnol [Independent Wales Party]

Address: Plas Cwm Coed, Usk Road, Tredunnoc, Gwent NP15 1PE

Email address: independent_wales@compuserve.com

Website: http://www.independentwales.com

Parliamentary elections won: 0

Number of candidacies: 0

When **Plaid Cymru** President Dafydd Wigley said his party would 'never ever' campaign for independence for Wales, the Independent Wales Movement (formed by those who put nationalism in front of Plaid

Cymru's agenda) decided to establish itself as a separate party. The Independent Wales Party was officially formed at the Owain Glyndwr Parliament House in Machynlleth on 31 January 2000.

The party declared it would not fight elections to the UK Parliament which were 'irrelevant' to its agenda, but it vowed to contest every seat in elections to the National Assembly for Wales. An initial suggestion that it adopt the name Plaid Genedlaethol Cymru [National Party of Wales] was rejected on the grounds that this was too close to Plaid Cymru.

The party has the allegiance of two Gwynedd County Councillors, Owain Williams and Evie Griffith.

Cymru Goch [Red Wales]

Address: PO Box 661, Wrexham LL11 1QU

Email address: yfanergoch@yahoo.co.uk

Website: http://www.fanergoch.org

Parliamentary elections won: 0

Number of candidacies: 0

This party was formed in 1987 to fight for a free socialist Wales. It believes in grassroots socialism and community resistance to produce workers' control. In 1994 it nominated Sian Williams in the European Parliament elections in South Wales East. In the National Assembly for Wales elections of 1999 it joined with other socialists to form the United Socialists who fought three constituencies and one region.

Death Off Roads, Freight on Rail

Highest vote: Miss H. M. Anscomb (Hampshire North West, 1997) – 231 votes, 0.4%

Parliamentary elections won: 0

Number of candidacies: 7

This movement was formed by Helen Anscomb, a teacher of classics from Highclere in Berkshire. Miss Anscomb had battled against new road schemes in the courts and won an injunction against the planned route of the M40. In the 1983 general election she stood against Margaret Thatcher in Finchley, and went on to fight four by-elections in 1983 and 1984, under the campaign pledge to send freight by rail transport.

After fighting Enfield Southgate (December 1984) Miss Anscomb left the electoral scene, though she continued to fight against new road building. She returned to contest the Truro by-election in March 1987, caused by the death of Liberal MP David Penhaligon, whose car was in collision with a freight lorry. She also fought Hampshire North West in the 1997 general election (against Sir George Young, then Transport Secretary) under the title 'Newbury Bypass Stop Construction Now'.

Democratic Labour

Address: Lord Taverne, House of Lords, London SW1A 0AA

Highest vote: D. Taverne (Lincoln, 1973 (1/3)) – 21,967 votes, 58.2%

Parliamentary elections won: 2

Number of candidacies: 5

The full title of Democratic Labour was the Lincoln Democratic Labour Association. It was formed by ex-Labour MP Dick Taverne after he had fallen out with his Lincoln Constituency Labour Party over the issue of British membership of the European Communities, to which the CLP were opposed. The CLP had voted to ask him to stand down at the next election (at the time, this was the prescribed method for de-selecting a Labour MP).

On 6 October 1972, Taverne resigned from the **Labour Party** and from Parliament in order to seek re-election in Lincoln, and set up the Lincoln Democratic Labour Association to organise his supporters. Initially he said that he hoped eventually to rejoin the Labour Party, though *The Times* attempted to entice him to establish a new centre party for Labour moderates. The **Liberal Party** decided to give their support to Dick Taverne, and he went on to win the by-election in March 1973 as a vindication of his independence. Shortly afterwards he formed the **Campaign for Social Democracy** as a national campaign.

Dick Taverne was defeated at Lincoln in October 1974, and did not fight the seat again. However, Democratic Labour fought local elections and had control of Lincoln City Council from 1973 to 1979. The Lincoln Democratic Labour Association sponsored a different candidate in 1979 against Taverne's advice, though he campaigned for the Association. The Association also fought Brigg and Scunthorpe.

The Association was wound up after the 1979 election in which both its candidates lost their deposits. The social club established by the Association closed in 1987.

Democratic Left [Great Britain]

See **Communist Party of Great Britain (1920–91).**

Democratic Left [Ireland]

Website: http://www.connect.ie/users/dl/

Highest vote: S. Lynch (Belfast North, 1992) – 1,386 votes, 3.9%

Parliamentary elections won: 0

Number of candidacies: 2

This party was formed in February 1992, originally under the name New Agenda, by a faction within **The Workers' Party** (*see* The Workers' Party [Ireland]). The leader of the party, Proinsias de Rossa TD, wanted The Workers' Party to renounce its links to the Official IRA and he attracted the support of five out of the six Dáil deputies of The Workers' Party; when the rest of the party refused, he established a breakaway group called New Agenda. It took the name Democratic Left on 28 March 1992.

In the 1992 United Kingdom general election the party fought two seats; in November they suffered a slight reverse in the Dáil election and returned only four deputies. The party entered the Irish government in December 1994, in the 'Rainbow Coalition' with Fine Gael and the Irish Labour Party.

Party organisation in Northern Ireland appears to have been more difficult. The party obtained a derisory vote in the Forum elections of 1996 and in local elections of 1997 won only one seat (in Dungannon). It fought neither the 1997 general election nor the 1998 Northern Ireland Assembly elections. In the Republic of Ireland, the group agreed a merger into the **Irish Labour Party** in November 1998; the merged party was launched on 24 January 1999.

Democratic Monarchist Public Safety White Resident

See **Public Safety Democratic Monarchist White Resident**.

Democratic Party (1942–5)

Highest vote: W. R. C. Foster (Portsmouth Central, 1945) – 561 votes, 2.1%
Parliamentary elections won: 0
Number of candidacies: 5

The Democratic Party was formed by Major Norman Leith-Hay-Clark in 1942. The party called for support for free enterprise and efficient organisation of business, with employees encouraged by profit-sharing. It also called for the limitation of excessive individual incomes. Democratic Party members included some converts from Conservatism, although many were very young servicemen. It fought five seats at the 1945 election but performed badly, and shortly after the election it was renamed the Independent Democratic Party. It was reported to be still active in the early 1960s, investigating individual cases of hardship.

Democratic Party (1969–71)

Highest vote: D. L. Donnelly (Pembrokeshire, 1970) – 11,824 votes, 21.5%
Parliamentary elections won: 0
Number of candidacies: 7

This party was a short-lived venture formed by Desmond Donnelly, who had been Labour MP for Pembrokeshire. Donnelly resigned the Labour whip in January 1968, and was expelled from the **Labour Party** two months later. The Labour Party disaffiliated the Pembrokeshire

Constituency Labour Party which had supported its MP, and a struggle over the assets of the CLP ended in the High Court.

In May 1969 Donnelly announced the formation of the Democratic Party, which had an anti-socialist policy. Donnelly also supported British intervention in the Vietnam war. The party fought two by-elections in 1969, and five seats in the 1970 election, but only Desmond Donnelly retained his deposit.

In April 1971, Desmond Donnelly joined the **Conservative Party** and severed his contacts with the Democratic Party which was subsequently disbanded. Desmond Donnelly committed suicide in April 1974.

Democratic Party (1998–)

Address: Enigma House, Enigma Business Park, Malvern, Worcestershire WR14 1GD

Email address: democraticparty@compuserve.com

Website: http://www.ourworld.compuserve.com/homepages/democraticparty

Number on Register: 22

Only vote: Earl of Burford (Kensington and Chelsea 1999 (25/11)) – 182 votes, 0.9%

Parliamentary elections won: 0

Number of candidacies: 1

The Democratic Party was formed in 1998 by several people who believed there was a role for a party placing democracy as its paramount belief. The party asserts that its members come from across the political spectrum. It has opposed the planting of genetically modified crops and called for transport policies which are more favourable to the motorist.

The party did not contest the European Parliamentary elections of 1999, stating that it wished its members to help the **UK Independence Party**, though it has since criticised that party for its internal dispute and for moving to the right. In November 1999, the party invited the Earl of Burford, who had grabbed the headlines by protesting in the House of Lords chamber against the exclusion of hereditary peers, to fight the Kensington and Chelsea by-election. The party leader is Geoff Southall.

Democratic Unionist Party

See **Ulster Democratic Unionist Party**.

Dog Lovers Party

Only vote: A. A. Waugh (North Devon, 1979) – 79 votes, 0.1%

Parliamentary elections won: 0

Number of candidacies: 1

This party was invented by the author and columnist Auberon Waugh in 1979. Jeremy Thorpe, former leader of the Liberal Party, was fighting for re-election while accused of conspiracy to murder Norman Scott, a man who claimed to have had an affair with him; as part of the alleged conspiracy, Scott's dog had been shot in an apparent attempt to frighten him.

Waugh was a columnist on *Private Eye* which had led a campaign against Thorpe, and lived in Somerset not far from Thorpe's constituency; he agreed with *Private Eye* editor Richard Ingrams to stand against Thorpe. The name Dog Lovers Party was chosen to embarrass Thorpe, and Waugh's election address attacked the Liberal Party for treating Thorpe as a hero. Thorpe eventually won an injunction to prevent the distribution of this address as prejudicial to his trial.

Waugh won only 79 votes but had the satisfaction of seeing Thorpe lose his seat to the Conservatives. He later sat in the public gallery during Thorpe's trial, which resulted in an acquittal on all charges, and wrote about the case in *The Last Word* (Michael Joseph, 1980).

Ecology Party

Highest vote: Dr N. Thomas (Ogmore, 1983) – 1,161 votes, 2.9%

Parliamentary elections won: 0

Number of candidacies: 172 (including Northern Ireland Ecology Party and Ecology Party/Women for Life on Earth candidates)

The Ecology Party was formed when **PEOPLE**, the ecological movement established in February 1973, found that the media persistently referred to it as the 'People's Party', and decided to change its name. The new name was adopted in early 1975, shortly after the October 1974 general election, with green as the new party colour.

The party found it more difficult to organise in the late 1970s than it had been earlier in the decade, as public concern over the environment moved from world wide concern to issues closer to home. The increase in the activity of environmental pressure groups did not lead to a great recruitment to the Ecology Party. The party fought only one by-election in the 1974–9 Parliament, and polled only 0.5%. While its electoral performance was limited, the party did take the opportunity to frame a constitution and elect a chairman and national secretary.

At the Ecology Party's 1978 conference, the party was urged to concentrate on only ten candidates at the impending general election, but eventually decided to fight more than 50 seats so that the party would get a televised election broadcast. This was a very bold step given the small membership, but eventually 53 candidates were nominated in the 1979 general election. The party made its election broadcast professionally, featuring the party Vice-chairman, Jonathan Porritt.

The party polled nearly 40,000 votes, an average of 1.5% for each candidate; the highest was 2.8% in South Worcestershire. More importantly the increased coverage of the party brought in many more members – the party had so little organisation that many of the applications went unopened for months. The party managed to find enough funds to nominate three candidates in the European Parliament elections in June 1979, who polled well.

After the poor organisation of the 1970s, in the early 1980s the party concentrated on setting up a proper national office and on building links to the nuclear disarmament movement which was growing in importance. The party won a seat on Cornwall County Council in 1981 with a majority of 1 vote, and fought most Parliamentary by-elections until 1982 when preparation for the 1983 general election became a priority.

The party managed to nominate 109 candidates for the 1983 election, including one in Northern Ireland (*see* **Northern Ireland Ecology Party**), and three joint candidates with **Women for Life on Earth** who organised the Greenham Common peace camp. Good media coverage was obtained though the average vote for each candidate fell.

Organisation of the party continued to improve after 1983, and eventually a larger office was found, and an office manager and press officer employed. In the 1984 European Parliamentary election the party had 16 candidates and polled 73,000 votes; the highest percentage was 4.7% in Hereford and Worcester. This seemed to establish a general trend for the party to poll more votes in European Parliamentary elections.

At the party's 1985 conference it was decided to adopt the name **Green Party** which was becoming used generally for environmental campaigning.

Empire Free Trade Crusade

Highest vote: E. A. Taylor (Paddington South, 1930 (30/10)) – 11,209 votes, 37.4%

Parliamentary elections won: 1

Number of candidacies: 2

The Empire Free Trade Crusade was started by newspaper proprietor Lord Beaverbrook in the *Daily Express* in June 1929, shortly after the Conservatives had lost the 1929 election on a moderate policy. The Crusade invited individual members in December 1929. The Crusade was closely allied to the **United Empire Party** which was formed shortly afterwards by Beaverbrook together with his brother Viscount Rothermere.

Beaverbrook's policy of Empire Free Trade was based on his long-standing desire to preserve and maintain the British Empire. Under Empire Free Trade, all duties and tariffs would be abolished between the Dominions of the Empire, in order to make the bonds of Empire closer and create a powerful worldwide economic unit. Candidates of the Crusade offered themselves to the electors as 'Empire Crusaders' and the Crusade was intensely patriotic.

It took until the beginning of 1930 for the Empire Free Trade Crusade to be able to accept subscriptions, and in the meantime preparations for the launch of the United Empire Party were undertaken. When Stanley Baldwin gave assurances as to future Conservative policy, Beaverbrook decided that the United Empire Party should be disbanded and subscriptions returned, though Rothermere (who had wider objectives) kept the party in existence.

In October 1930 Baldwin appeared to Beaverbrook to be going back on his assurances and he determined to try to get rid of him. The Empire Free Trade Crusade fought the Paddington South by-election, managing to win the seat by taking the larger part of the Conservative vote in an ultra-safe Conservative seat. In February 1931 the Crusade and the United Empire Party nominated a candidate to fight the Islington East by-election, but here the party merely split the Conservative vote to allow Labour to win.

The showdown for Baldwin's leadership came in March 1931 at a by-election in the ultra-safe Conservative Westminster St George's constituency, when Beaverbrook and Rothermere sponsored an unofficial Conservative candidate (not a candidate of the Empire Free Trade Crusade). Baldwin fought the by-election vigorously and the official Conservative won. Shortly afterwards the Labour government fell and the National Government was formed. Ernest Taylor, the Paddington South MP, took the Conservative whip at this time. The Crusade was wound up after the 1931 election.

English National Party (1966–80?)

Highest vote: J. B. Barbour (Banbury, October 1974) – 547 votes, 1.1%

Parliamentary elections won: 0

Number of candidacies: 7

This party was formed by Dr Frank Hansford-Miller under the name John Hampden New Freedom Party in 1966, being named after a celebrated Parliamentarian of the pre-Civil War era. It changed its name to the English National Party in the summer of 1974. The party considered itself the English equivalent of **Plaid Cymru** or the **Scottish National Party** and formed friendly links with them.

The English National Party was boosted to prominence when John Stonehouse, Labour MP for Walsall North, joined it in 1975, though Stonehouse was later jailed for fraud. Dr Frank Hansford-Miller fought both the 1974 elections and several by-elections during 1974–9, ending up by joining the fight at Jeremy Thorpe's North Devon constituency in 1979. There was only one other party member who stood as a Parliamentary candidate, though the party also sponsored local election candidates, particularly in London.

The policy of the party could appear bizarre, in such proposals as a 16 lane Thames Tunnel to link existing motorways. The overall flavour was of a centre-right party, and it favoured abolition of income tax and an end to local authority housing, as well as establishment of an English Parliament. The party was not racist, but did seek a spiritual rebirth of English faith.

In the 1981 Greater London Council elections, Dr Frank Hansford-Miller and his wife fought on behalf of the Abolition of Rates Coalition.

English National Party (1999–)

Address: Quires Green, Willingale, Ongar, Essex CM5 0QP

Number on Register: 102

Parliamentary elections won: 0

Number of candidacies: 0

This party was founded by Robin Tilbrook in 1999. It believes that devolution to Scotland and Wales has undermined British national sentiment, and there is a strong likelihood of the United Kingdom being dissolved. It therefore calls for the creation of an all-England Parliament in preparation. The party is currently in the process of formation with an interim leadership, though a manifesto has been issued.

This manifesto reveals a party of broadly libertarian outlook, believing in the defence of the monarchy and the nation state. It is patriotic but not racist, with some tendency towards protectionism.

Equal Parenting Party

Address: 38–40 Gloucester Road, London SW7 4QU

Email address: tonyC@equalparenting.org

Website: http://www.equalparenting.org

Number on Register: 90

Only vote: P. May (Kensington and Chelsea, 1999 (25/11)) – 24 votes, 0.1%

Parliamentary elections won: 0

Number of candidacies: 1

This party was formed in July 1999 under the leadership of Tony Coe, as a development of the Equal Parenting Campaign. The Campaign had already entered the political arena when it sponsored Julian Fitzgerald as a candidate in the June 1999 by-election in Leeds Central.

The party declares itself a single-issue party, campaigning for both parents to be treated equally under law after a divorce or separation. It believes a situation where the parent with care enjoys all parental rights over the children and the absent parent has none, is damaging to children and unjust. The party has friendly links with the pressure group Families Need Fathers.

At the Kensington and Chelsea by-election of November 1999, the party nominated Peter May to contest the seat.

Fancy Dress Party

Highest vote: K. J. Davenport (Dartford, 1987) – 491 votes, 0.9%

Parliamentary elections won: 0

Number of candidacies: 5

This party was formed in 1979 by a group of former students at Dartford Grammar School and Dartford Boys' Technical High School who had become disillusioned with politics during the 1974 election. The party nominated John Beddoes, a 21-year-old van driver, to fight the Dartford seat in the 1979 general election and chose the name of the party in order to liven up the election (the challenge being welcomed by candidates of the larger parties). Among the policies of the party was reducing the size of the unemployment figures by using smaller type.

John Crockford, who had been Beddoes's election agent, fought the 1983 election and the party has continued to nominate candidates in each election since. It is a tradition for the candidates to wear a variety of costumes, in keeping with the party's name.

Federation of Labour (Ireland)

Parliamentary elections won: 0
Number of candidacies: 0

The Federation of Labour was formed by Jack Beattie, a **Northern Ireland Labour Party** member of the Northern Ireland House of Commons from 1925. Beattie was a firm anti-partitionist and had adopted such an independent line at Stormont that he was expelled from the Northern Ireland Labour Party in August 1934, after refusing to move the writ at Stormont for a by-election in Belfast Central – which the Northern Ireland Labour Party hoped to win from the Irish **Nationalists**.

Jack Beattie was re-elected as Independent Labour in his own constituency in the 1938 Stormont general election. In 1942 he was readmitted to the Northern Ireland Labour Party, in time to win the Westminster seat of Belfast West in a February 1943 by-election. In January 1945 Beattie and James Collins (a former member of the Irish Nationalists who had joined the Northern Ireland Labour Party in January 1942) formed the Federation of Labour (Ireland) as a nationalist Labour party.

The party nominated Collins in the Falls division of Belfast in the 1945 Northern Ireland general election; he polled 20% of the vote, being beaten by Harry Diamond (*see* **Republican Labour Party**) and an Irish Nationalist. Jack Beattie was re-elected but did not stand as a candidate of the party. The Federation of Labour joined the Irish **Labour Party** (see Labour Party [Ireland]) in April 1949, forming the nucleus of its Northern Ireland Council.

Fellowship Party

Address: Woolacombe House, 141 Woolacombe Road, Blackheath, London SE3 8QP

Highest vote: R. S. Mallone (Greenwich, 1971 (8/7)) – 792 votes, 3.6%

Parliamentary elections won: 0

Number of candidacies: 14

This party was formed on 11 June 1955 in London. The four principal founders were John Loverseed (a former **Common Wealth** MP who had been a Battle of Britain pilot), Eric Fenner, Kathleen Lonsdale and Lady Clare Annesley (a former Labour Parliamentary candidate). Loverseed and Fenner had fought London seats as anti-H bomb candidates in the May 1955 election. Party policies include non-violence, socialism and environmentalism; the party's anti-nuclear campaign led to the formation of the Campaign for Nuclear Disarmament in 1958.

The most persistent party candidate is Ronald Mallone, a retired lecturer in Literature and Liberal Studies who has been General Secretary of the party for many years. Mallone has fought Parliamentary elections in Greenwich and Woolwich many times since 1959, as well as local elections for Greenwich Borough Council, the Greater London Council and Inner London Education Authority.

Past Fellowship Party Presidents have included Donald Swann, Rowland Hilder, Frank Merrick and Sidney Hinkes; Vice Presidents have included Sybil Morrison, Stuart Morris, Vera Brittain, Albert Belden, Sybil Thorndike, Benjamin Britten and Glenn Paige.

For the Anglo-Irish Agreement

Highest vote: P. Barry (East Londonderry, 1986 (23/1)) – 2,001 votes, 6.1%

Parliamentary elections won: 0

Number of candidacies: 4

All Ulster Unionists were bitterly opposed to the Anglo-Irish Agreement, which was made at Dublin in December 1985. All 15 Unionist MPs (of whom 11 were members of the **Ulster Unionist Party**, 3 were **Ulster Democratic Unionist Party** members, and one was from the **Ulster**

Popular Unionist Party) resigned their seats to fight for re-election and an anti-Agreement mandate.

Faced with an unexpected almost province-wide election, the other Northern Ireland parties decided to concentrate their efforts on only their best seats, and this left four constituencies where no one other than the incumbent Unionist MP had applied for nomination papers. With no other candidate this would result in an unopposed return and no poll, so the Unionists decided to force a poll by nominating one of their members as a dummy 'For the Anglo-Irish Agreement' candidate.

This candidate, whose real name was Wesley Robert Williamson, changed his name for the purposes of the election to Peter Barry, the name of the Minister for Foreign Affairs in the Republic of Ireland at the time of the elections. He retained his deposit in three constituencies.

Free Trade Anti-Common Market Party

See **Anti-Common Market Free Trade Party**.

Free Trader

Highest vote: G. R. Bethell (Holderness, January 1910) – 4,661 votes, 48.0%

Parliamentary elections won: 0

Number of candidacies: 11

During the Boer War of 1899–1902, the United Kingdom faced opposition from world opinion and found itself isolated. When Joseph Chamberlain returned from negotiating the peace settlement, he developed a policy whereby goods exported within the Empire would be given preferential tariffs, and high tariffs would be added to foreign goods. The tariffs would serve to help protect domestic industry threatened by cheaper foreign imports.

This policy was known as tariff reform and Chamberlain resigned his cabinet post to campaign for it within the **Conservatives** and **Liberal Unionists**. Tariff reform attracted fervent opposition from those who followed Adam Smith in believing free trade encouraged greater efficiency.

Conservative leader Arthur Balfour refused to commit himself between the two.

Chamberlain succeeded in converting the Unionist grassroots membership to tariff reform and from 1904 several Unionist MPs who supported free trade left the party to join the **Liberals** (who were firm believers in free trade). In the 1906 election, a number of incumbent Unionists who supported free trade were deselected and fought as Unionist Free Traders. These candidatures continued to appear at by-elections and general elections until the Great War, though increasingly local Liberal Associations were the real sponsors of the candidates.

Glow Bowling Party

Highest vote: C. G. Beasley (Ealing Acton and Shepherds Bush, 1997) – 209 votes, 0.4%
Parliamentary elections won: 0
Number of candidacies: 5

This party was invented by the First Leisure Corporation for the 1997 general election, in an attempt to promote its chain of bowling arcades. Five candidates were nominated who promoted comedic policies; they were connected in some way to the local bowling arcade (for example, in Maidenhead the candidate was the contract Disc Jockey).

Greater Britain Movement

Parliamentary elections won: 0
Number of candidacies: 0

John Tyndall fell out with Colin Jordan, his colleague in the National Socialist Movement (*see* **British Movement**) in 1963. After attempting to expel Jordan he left, taking with him most of the members, and established the Greater Britain Movement in 1964. The name was probably taken from Sir Oswald Mosley's 1932 book *The Greater Britain*.

The Greater Britain Movement differed from the National Socialist Movement in being more concerned with British nationalism than National Socialism, but its members had come from the National Socialist

Movement. Some were suspected of involvement in racist attacks and Martin Webster, John Tyndall's Deputy, was sent to jail for assaulting President Jomo Kenyatta of Kenya in 1964.

It was for the Greater Britain Movement that John Tyndall founded the journal *Spearhead* (formerly the name of the **British National Party**'s paramilitary wing – *see* British National Party (1960–7)). The Greater Britain Movement had no more than 138 members at its peak. The Movement did not contest Parliamentary elections.

In 1967 the British National Party merged with the **League of Empire Loyalists** to form the **National Front**, which immediately became the largest and best organised party of the far right. Leading members of the National Front were divided over whether the Greater Britain Movement should be allowed to join: A. K. Chesterton was in favour, impressed by Tyndall's writing, but Andrew Fountaine was opposed. When Chesterton won this early NF power struggle, Greater Britain Movement members were allowed to join the NF as individual members. Eventually all had joined and the Greater Britain Movement was disbanded in 1968.

Green Party

Address: 1a Waterlow Road, London N19 5NJ

Email address: greenpartyuk@gn.apc.org

Website: http://www.greenparty.org.uk

Number on Register: 46

Highest vote: H. Bewley (Vauxhall, 1989 (15/6)) – 1,767 votes, 6.1%

Parliamentary elections won: 0

Number of candidacies: 486 (including 7 joint candidates with the Plaid Cymru)

The **Ecology Party** changed its name to the Green Party on 21 September 1985, partly in an attempt to stop other parties appropriating the 'Green' tag which was by then widely used for all environmental campaigns. The party meanwhile set about researching and developing its economic policy by launching The Other Economic Summit (TOES) which was organised by the party Chairman Paul Ekins, though it was independent of the party. The Summit's recommendations were drawn upon when the party wrote its 1987 election manifesto. Shortly afterwards the Summit was renamed the New Economics Foundation and is still in existence.

Green Party local election results had shown a steady increase in votes during the mid 1980s but the party leadership suffered a split over proposed reforms to the party constitution. When the pro-reformers held a meeting to co-ordinate their activities in May 1986, the party council tried to suppress what they perceived as attempted subversion.

The party nominated 133 candidates in the 1987 election, a bigger advance than it might first appear because of the increase in the deposit from £150 to £500. The national total of nearly 90,000 votes represented an increase in the average vote from 1.0% to 1.4%, still below the high point of 1979.

The Green Party seemed to benefit from the confusion and division in the Liberal/SDP Alliance after the 1987 election. In the 1988 local elections the party won two seats on Stroud Borough Council, and the next month two Liberal councillors defected to the party. The party obtained a large boost from a quite unexpected source, when Prime Minister Margaret Thatcher made a speech to the Royal Society in September 1988 about threats to the environment, repeating some of the same message in her party conference speech the next month.

The Green Party was brought into front-line politics in the early summer of 1989 when it announced what looked at the time a risky strategy of contesting every seat at the European Parliament elections. In a few weeks the party built up a considerable following, eventually polling 15% of the vote, enough to save the deposits of all their candidates. On the same day, the party saved a Parliamentary deposit for the first time in a by-election in Vauxhall. Most of the Green vote at this election seems to have come from former Alliance voters disillusioned with their parties' disorganisation. In 1990, the Green Party's Scottish branch became a separate political party (*see* **Scottish Green Party**).

Opinion-polling organisations recorded the Green Party vote from the time of the European elections, and the party was taken seriously as an electoral threat by the other main parties, which consequently stressed their own environmental policies. In the 1990 local elections the party's candidates averaged 8%, but soon afterwards it was exposed to ridicule when former television football commentator David Icke, a frequent spokesman on behalf of the party, declared he was the son of God. As the **Liberal Democrats** were resurrected, the Green Party eventually fell back out of the national poll ratings by the end of 1990.

In the early 1990s the issue of whether to adopt a more conventional political party structure was raised among the traditionally non-hierarchical Green Party activists. The 1991 conference voted to create a smaller Executive to replace the large and unwieldy Party Council structure. From the 1992 general election, the party has designated two 'Principal Speakers', one male and one female; there is a limit on the term one can serve as a principal speaker, in order to stop a *de facto* leader emerging.

In the early 1990s the party also experimented with joint candidates with **Plaid Cymru**, but this proved shortlived. When Jonathan Porritt supported a Plaid Cymru candidate and not the Green Party in the 1994 European Parliament elections, his membership was suspended and he eventually left the party.

The party fought 234 seats in the 1992 election, but it was clear that the European Parliamentary election success would not be repeated. In fact the average vote per candidate fell. However, unlike previous elections, the highest votes for the party were in inner-city seats. The mid to late 1990s saw the party beginning to win a firm base of support in local elections, particularly in Stroud and the student wards of Oxford. The party gained four seats in the May 1996 local elections, and 18 in May 1999.

The 1997 general election saw the party concentrate on its better constituencies rather than trying to fight everywhere. Only 89 candidates were sponsored; they won 62,000 votes, but the average was still only 1.4%. The party had consistently performed better in European Parliamentary elections, not just in 1989, and when the regional list system of proportional representation was introduced for the 1999 elections the party was optimistic about its chances.

Helped by increasing public concern over genetically modified foods (long a party campaign) and an award-winning party election broadcast, the party polled 568,000 votes and won two seats (in the South East and in London). In 2000 the party saw a breakthrough in the Greater London Assembly, helped by the endorsement of independent Mayoral candidate Ken Livingstone. The party's list of candidates polled 11%, winning three seats, and Darren Johnson was appointed as the Mayor's Environment adviser.

Green Party development seems to be in the direction of many European Green parties, where the party is an ecologically concerned alternative to the mainstream parties of the left.

Green Party of Northern Ireland

Address: 537 Antrim Road, Belfast BT15 3BU

Email address: nigreens@belfast.co.uk

Website: http://www.belfast.co.uk/greens/

Highest vote: P. F. Doran (Upper Bann, 1990 (15/6)) – 576 votes, 1.6%

Parliamentary elections won: 0

Number of candidacies: 2

The Green Party of Northern Ireland was formed on 12 February 1990 by Peter Doran, a former member of the Irish Green Party, and Peter Emerson, formerly a member of the **Northern Ireland Ecology Party**. It was initially independent of both the London and Dublin based organisations. Doran fought the Upper Bann by-election of June 1990, but there were no candidates after that until the 1996 Northern Ireland Forum elections. The party was relaunched in 1993 as an autonomous unit of the **Green Party** of England and Wales.

The party fought only one seat at the 1997 general election (Belfast North). In the 1998 Northern Ireland Assembly elections (in which it fought three seats), the party advocated a vote for the **Northern Ireland Women's Coalition** where there was no NIGP candidate.

Highland Land League

Highest vote: G. J. Bruce (Inverness-shire and Ross and Cromarty, 1918) – 2,930 votes, 26.8%

Parliamentary elections won: 0

Number of candidacies: 4

The Highland Land League was formed in August 1909 at a meeting in Glasgow, using the name of an organisation which had existed from 1887 to the mid 1890s. The League had essentially the same aims as the

Crofters: it sought the restoration of deer forests to the people, abolition of plural farms, and land nationalisation. They also pledged to defend crofters who were threatened with eviction, and supported Scottish Home Rule.

In August 1918 the League announced that it would link up with the **Labour Party**, and that September the Labour Party's Scottish Advisory Council agreed to co-operate with the League in selecting candidates and financing campaigns. The League nominated four candidates in the Scottish highlands in the 1918 election, all of whom were members of the Labour Party. It was claimed by the Scottish Advisory Council of the Labour Party that Highland Land League candidates were official Labour candidates, though it seems doubtful that this was actually the case.

The League's activities wound down in the early 1920s and appear to have been absorbed into the Labour Party. L. MacNeill Weir, who fought Argyll for the League in 1918, was Labour MP for Clackmannan and East Stirlingshire from 1922 to 1931 and from 1935 until his death, and served as Ramsay MacDonald's Parliamentary Private Secretary and biographer.

Highlands and Islands Alliance (Càirdeas)

Address: Midoxgate House, Fearn, Ross-shire IV20 1RP

Email address: Lorraine_Mann@cali.co.uk

Number on Register: 25

Parliamentary elections won: 0

Number of candidacies: 0

The search for a new political system in Scotland after the creation of the Scottish Parliament led to the formation of this Alliance by Lorraine Mann and a large number of prominent campaigners. Lorraine Mann was Convenor of Scotland Against Nuclear Dumping, which campaigned on radioactive waste management. The Alliance is a regional community-based party, seeking to defend the interests of the highlands and islands (Orkney, Shetland, and the Hebrides) of Scotland; it supports the use of Gaelic. The Gaelic name of the Alliance, Càirdeas, has a meaning incorporating friendship, fellowship, relationship, goodwill and alliance.

In the Scottish Parliament elections of 1999 the Alliance put forward a list of candidates for the Highlands and Islands region. The list was pioneering in that the candidates were in groups of two, intended by the Alliance to share the job of Member of the Scottish Parliament if elected (because the Alliance believed it was impossible to represent the community while living in Edinburgh). This innovation, and the strong organisation of the Alliance, gave it reasonably good media coverage during the elections, but the result was disappointing: the list polled only 2,600 votes (1.3%), possibly due to the Returning Officer's decision not to accept job-share nominations.

Lorraine Mann is at the time of writing challenging this decision in an Employment Tribunal.

(Irish) Home Ruler

Highest vote: J. Mitchel (Tipperary, 1875 (16/2)) – 3,311 votes, 81.6%

Parliamentary elections won: 170

Number of candidacies: 230

The Home Rule movement had its origins in the Home Government Association formed by Isaac Butt in 1870. The policy of the Association was to recreate an Irish Parliament within the United Kingdom. Butt, a Protestant, had been a Peelite MP for Youghal in succession to the **Irish Confederation** in 1852–7, and popularised the slogan 'Home Rule'. After some promising but unsuccessful by-elections, two Home Rule candidates were returned unopposed in February and June 1871, followed by Butt – also unopposed – in September 1871.

In 1873 the Home Government Association was dissolved and the Home Rule League was formed, again under the leadership of Butt. The League fought 80 seats in the 1874 general election, winning 60, a clear majority in Ireland. Butt became leader of its Parliamentary group but in 1877 lost this position to the more militant Charles Stuart Parnell who was deliberately disruptive of Parliamentary proceedings in order to raise the Irish question.

There was an agricultural crisis in 1878 in Ireland which threatened a return to famine; it prompted the setting up of the Irish Land League, which would oppose farmers' evictions by force. Many moderate Home

Rulers were opposed but Parnell accepted the post of President of the League (even though opposed to the League's policy of secession from the United Kingdom Parliament).

Spurred on by the Land League the Home Rulers pressed for land reform and gained a measure of success in 1881, but it did not satisfy the more radical members of the Land League. Parnell violently denounced the outcome and was jailed – in his absence the Land League campaign ended in violence. The Land League itself was suppressed, and Parnell released through the intervention of one of the moderate Home Rule MPs, William O'Shea.

A successor to the Land League was quickly established (the National League). Parnell succeeded in making sure the National League accepted his political leadership. This made Parnell a very powerful figure and the likelihood that the Home Rulers would hold a significant number of seats in the new Parliament, after the extension of the franchise, led to other parties attempting to gain their support. Parnell refused overtures from the radical Liberals, but agreed with the Conservatives and voted down the Liberal government's budget in June 1885. This forced the resignation of the government.

In the 1885 election the Home Rule movement was reconstituted as the Irish Nationalists (*see* (Irish) **Nationalist**).

Humanist Party

Address: 261 Archway Road, Highgate, London N6 5BS

Email address: hpuk@ndirect.co.uk

Website: http://www.humanistparty.org.uk

Number on Register: 26

Highest vote: Miss S. Ellis (Camden, Hampstead and Highgate, 1987) – 134 votes, 0.3%

Parliamentary elections won: 0

Number of candidacies: 5

This small party was formed on 8 March 1984, when the international Humanist Movement encouraged its affiliates to become politically active. The party is based on New Humanism, a philosophy which places human beings as its central value. The highest moral value of New Humanism is:

'When you treat others as you would have them treat you, you liberate yourself'. The movement is internationalist and supports employee co-ownership of business, as well as active non-violence.

The Humanist Party fought a few seats in London in the 1987 general election. The party has recently had a renaissance: it fought one seat (Hampstead) in the 1997 election, a regional seat for the Scottish Parliament in 1999, and two regions in the European Parliament elections of June 1999. A single candidate for the Greater London Assembly in 2000 won 1.3% of the vote in Lambeth and Southwark, the party deploring the tendency towards personality politics.

Early in 2000 the party gave support to a move to bring an international legal case against the Prime Minister and other senior governmental figures over the NATO military action in Kosovo the previous year.

Imperial Fascist League

Parliamentary elections won: 0
Number of candidacies: 0

The Imperial Fascist League was formed by Brigadier-General D. Erskine Tulloch in November 1928, originally intended as a patriotic anti-socialist organisation. In 1930, Arnold Leese became the largest personality in the League. Leese was a retired veterinary surgeon from Stamford, Lincolnshire, who had moved to Guildford, and was a virulent anti-Semite conspiracy theorist.

Leese rejected Sir Oswald Mosley's invitation to join the **British Union of Fascists**, thinking him what he termed a 'kosher fascist' – an agent of the Jewish conspiracy placed within the fascist movement to discredit it. In November 1933, a group of 150 BUF members violently broke up an IFL meeting. The IFL was itself involved in violence against Jews in the East End in the mid 1930s, with a secret squad led by Charles W. Gore and P. J. Ridout.

In 1936, Arnold Leese and his publisher were tried for seditious libel after publishing a pamphlet which claimed Jews were guilty of ritual murder; he was found guilty of the lesser crime of creating a public mischief and given six months hard labour after failing to pay a fine. The disappearance of Arnold Leese from the scene led to the IFL becoming moribund.

The IFL had close ties to Nazi Germany during the late 1930s though it received no financial support. After the outbreak of war, the organisation renamed itself the Angles Circle in order to fend off proscription. Arnold Leese was critical of many German policies and declared his primary allegiance was to King and country, though many of his followers disagreed with him and were interned. In June 1940 Leese was himself ordered to be interned, and in reaction to the insult to his patriotism he went on the run for four months before being captured.

Independent Democratic Alliance

Highest vote: G. Jarratt (Batley and Morley, February 1974) – 828 votes, 1.7%

Parliamentary elections won: 0

Number of candidacies: 6

This alliance was formed in April 1973, ostensibly as a merger of the **All Party Alliance** led by John Creasey and The Organisation led by Colin Campion, though Creasey died a few months after its formation. The Organisation had itself been formed in May 1972.

The alliance fought six seats and helped three other independent candidates in the February 1974 election. It stated that its aim was to secure democratic government controlled by the people, but it is fair to say that it was a centre-right organisation. The alliance appears to have lost some members to the **United Democratic Party** which was formed before the October 1974 election, possibly disbanding in 1974.

Independent Labour Party

Address: Keir Hardie House, 49 Top Moor Side, Leeds LS11 9LW

Website: http://www.theilp.org.uk

Highest vote: [excluding candidates who secured Labour Party endorsement]G. Buchanan (Glasgow, Gorbals, 1935) – 22,860 votes, 75.0%.

Parliamentary elections won: 12

Number of candidacies: 117

One of the earliest democratic socialist parties, the ILP had its origins among socialist activists, mostly in the north of England. The party was formed at a conference in Bradford on 13 January 1893, with the name 'Independent' being chosen to differentiate from those MPs who described themselves as **Liberal/Labour**.

The party's founder Chairman was J. Keir Hardie, who had been elected as an Independent Labour MP for West Ham South in the 1892 election. In its early years the ILP merged with several small socialist and labour parties that had operated previously (including the **Scottish Parliamentary Labour Party**), and succeeded in building strength at local elections. It fought 28 seats throughout the country at the 1895 general election, polling respectably in some urban centres, but Hardie lost his seat.

The ILP played a strategic role in the formation of the **Labour Representation Committee** in 1900 and was immediately affiliated to it, having previously campaigned for a socialist party with trade union links. The ILP continued to hold its own conferences, and had separate policies which its delegates and MPs were expected to argue for within the **Labour Party**. As the Labour Party did not have individual membership until 1918 the ILP provided much of the party's activist base.

Relationships between the ILP and the Labour Party were tense from the start. Many in the ILP believed the Labour Party was too timid and four senior Labour Party figures resigned from the ILP council in 1909 after criticism. In 1911, some branches of the ILP affiliated to the **British Socialist Party** which opposed co-operation with the trade unions. The ILP opposed the Great War and its members resisted conscription – resulting in a large branch in Dartmoor prison.

On some occasions, Labour Party endorsement was withheld from ILP candidates; this happened at a 1912 by-election, and in 1918 when relations were strained due to the trade unions' attack on the ILP's seats on the Labour Party National Executive Committee. In 1920 the party rejected, after the plea of Ramsay MacDonald, a proposal to affiliate to the Third International; through the inter-war period, the communists alternately denounced the ILP as capitalistic then attempted to take it over.

When Labour took office in 1924, differences between it and the ILP became more serious as the ILP looked on the government as a great disappointment. The ILP's response was to formulate its own radical programmes for Labour governments, but these policies were rejected by the Labour leadership.

During the second Labour government in 1929–31, 37 Labour MPs were sponsored by the ILP and they provided much of the left opposition to the leadership. The 1930 ILP conference decided that where ILP policies were in conflict with the Labour Party, its MPs should break the whip to support the ILP. This clearly opened up the question of whether the ILP could continue to affiliate, but the charismatic ILP leader Jimmy Maxton defended affiliation quotably at the ILP's 1931 Scottish conference: replying to a delegate who said he could not ride two horses at the same time, Maxton said 'if my friend cannot ride two horses, what's he doing in the bloody circus?'

In the 1931 election, the ILP refused to sign a form accepting the Standing Orders of the Parliamentary Labour Party and as a consequence its 19 official candidates (plus 5 others who were ILP members nominated by other organisations) fought the election without official Labour Party endorsement. Five members were successful and formed an ILP group in Parliament. In 1932 the ILP held a special conference and voted to disaffiliate; shortly afterwards the Labour Party conference expelled the ILP.

This decision caused a decline in ILP membership but the party remained very active in opposing fascism, sending some members to fight for the Republicans in the Spanish Civil War (one of whom was George Orwell). The party again considered and ruled out affiliation to the Comintern, but supported the United Front and Popular Front – attempts to unite Communists with other left-wing parties.

The ILP won four seats in 1935 but one of the MPs soon resigned and joined the Labour Party. The party narrowly missed out on winning by-elections during the Second World War when it was not bound by the electoral truce, though in general this was a time of revival in the party's electoral fortunes. In the 1945 election it held its seats though one was very marginal.

The death of Jimmy Maxton in July 1946 severely damaged the party. Though it held Maxton's seat in a very close by-election, all three MPs rejoined the Labour Party the next year, with most of the membership. The party remained active throughout the 1950s and 1960s, campaigning on international issues: it supported de-colonisation, and opposed nuclear arms. The party gained members as a result of the **Communist Party of Great Britain**'s loss of support in the mid 1950s.

In the 1970s the party reassessed its views on the Labour Party and decided that it should take a constructive approach. In 1975 the party renamed itself Independent Labour Publications, and became a left-wing pressure group within the Labour Party. It was active in many campaigns, including that for party democracy. After the fall of communism in Eastern Europe in 1989, the ILP reviewed socialist politics and produced a new programme for democratic social change.

The ILP currently works as an educational trust and publishes *Democratic Socialist*.

Independent Nuclear Disarmament Election Committee

Highest vote: M. H. Craft (Twickenham, 1964) – 1,073 votes, 1.9%
Parliamentary elections won: 0
Number of candidacies: 2

This shortlived committee was formed in April 1962 by members of the Campaign for Nuclear Disarmament who wished to stand unilateralist candidates. The leading personalities were Pat Arrowsmith and Vanessa Redgrave. The committee sponsored two candidates in the 1964 election, but was dissolved soon after, when the results were poor.

Independent Opposition [Ireland]

Highest vote: J. J. Ennis (Athlone, 1857) – 100 votes, 66.7%
Parliamentary elections won: 17
Number of candidacies: 23

The Independent Opposition was formed by Charles Gavan Duffy, a former member of the Young Ireland movement and the **Irish Confederation**. Shortly before the Confederation's revolt of August 1848,

Gavan Duffy was arrested and held until the following year. In the 1852 election he won New Ross as a **Liberal**, and in the House of Commons organised 50 Irish members (most of whom were Liberals) to oppose any government which did not support the Irish Tenant League. The 1852 Parliament was a very close one and the governments of Aberdeen and Palmerston were dependent on a coalition between Peelites (*see* **Liberal Conservatives**) and the Liberals, a situation which maximised the influence of the Independent Opposition.

Gavan Duffy retired from politics in poor health in 1855, and the Independent Opposition waned, but survived to fight 19 seats in the 1857 election, winning 13 (4 were unopposed returns). The overall result of the 1857 election was a substantial majority for the Liberals and the influence of the Independent Opposition was therefore much less; it was wound up.

Independent Wales Party

See **Cymru Annibynnol**.

International Communist Party

Highest vote: D. O'Sullivan (Newham North West, 1992) – 100 votes, 0.4%

Parliamentary elections won: 0

Number of candidacies: 4

The International Communist Party was originally a minority group operating inside the **Workers' Revolutionary Party** who regarded the leadership as betraying the principles of Trotsky and the Fourth International. On 9 November 1985, Dave Hyland organised the group and made contacts with the administration of the Fourth International, as a result of which the WRP was suspended as the official British representatives of the International on 16 December 1985.

At the Eighth Congress of the Workers' Revolutionary Party on 8 February 1986, the WRP leadership refused admission to Hyland's group, which then found another venue and established themselves as the Workers' Revolutionary Party (Internationalist). Early in March 1986, the

International Committee of the Fourth International expelled the WRP and accepted the Workers' Revolutionary Party (Internationalist) as the official British section.

The party swiftly adopted the name International Communist Party. It fought four seats at the 1992 election. In 1995 it reformed as the **Socialist Equality Party**.

International Marxist Group

Highest vote: B. Heron (Birmingham Stechford, 1977 (31/3)) – 494 votes, 1.4%

Parliamentary elections won: 0

Number of candidacies: 4

The International Marxist Group grew out of a split in the Revolutionary Socialist League (*see* **Socialist Party**) in 1961. Most of those who disagreed with the leadership of Ted Grant had joined with Gerry Healy (*see* **Workers' Revolutionary Party**), but six people based in Nottingham rejected Healy and, calling themselves the International Group, published their own journal, called *The Internationalist,* which was loyal to the Fourth International.

This group was the *de facto* British section of the (Trotskyite) Fourth International from its foundation, though many still recognised the Revolutionary Socialist League. In 1964 the United Secretariat of the Fourth International forced the two groups to merge, though in practice they continued to operate separately and soon came into conflict.

The International Group was at the time attempting entrism into the **Labour Party** Young Socialists under the auspices of the Socialist Labour League and was therefore competing with the RSL's Militant tendency. In 1965 the Socialist Labour League was expelled from the Labour Party, with the RSL doing nothing to prevent it. The lack of action from the RSL led the International Group to form a faction, which was usually called the International Marxist Group and was led by Pat Jordan, to challenge Ted Grant's leadership.

The faction fight prompted the Fourth International to downgrade both the Revolutionary Socialist League and the International Group to 'sympathisers'. This demotion caused the RSL to sever all its links with the

International, and left the International Group as the only organisation in Great Britain connected to the United Secretariat of the Fourth International.

The International Group formed the International Marxist Group in November 1966 as the British section of the Fourth International. Following Fourth International policy, it again attempted entrism into the Labour Party. The first target was the Nottingham City Labour Party and the IMG succeeded in electing one of its members, Ken Coates, as President. The IMG was instrumental in setting up the Vietnamese Solidarity Campaign in 1966 which campaigned for support for the North Vietnamese. A number of IMG members, including Ken Coates, resigned in October 1967 when the group supported an unofficial dock strike to which the Transport and General Workers' Union leadership was opposed.

The IMG gave up entrism to the Labour Party in 1969, but retained its front organisations – in 1971 it had no fewer than thirty, or one for every 11 of its members. It suppported the idea of unity among the far left and, being notably more libertarian than others, collaborated with some libertarian groups to publish *Black Dwarf* in 1968-70. This co-operation ceased when the IMG formed its own youth organisation (the Spartacus League); after *Black Dwarf* was discontinued, the group published *Red Mole*.

From 1971 the group also promoted the slogan 'Victory to the IRA' through its front organisation the Anti-Internment League. A group of IMG members formed the Troops Out Movement in 1973. The Group sponsored three candidates in the February 1974 election, and also fought the 1977 by-election in Birmingham Stechford; all its candidatures were in inner-city areas.

In the mid 1970s the IMG's belief in left unity led it to set up **Socialist Unity**. In 1976 the party took an interest in the newly established **Scottish Labour Party** but was rebuffed by the leadership of that party. The last IMG election candidate was in the 1979 European Parliament elections when Tariq Ali fought London West; by the early 1980s the party had become more interested in the struggle of the left in the Labour Party, and resumed entrism after a favourable interpretation of Tony Benn's challenge for the Deputy leadership in 1981.

The IMG took the name Socialist League in late 1982, though it was popularly known as Socialist Action after its newspaper. A split emerged in

1985 caused by rival factions in the Unified Secretariat of the Fourth International; the main group renamed itself Socialist Action. In 1987 the group expelled two members who formed the **Communist League**, but by this time there was little organisation left.

Irish Civil Rights Association

Highest vote: J. P. McFadden (Hammersmith North, October 1974) – 633 votes, 1.9%

Parliamentary elections won: 0

Number of candidacies: 7

The Irish Civil Rights Association was formed in Dublin in December 1972 as an international branch of the Northern Ireland Civil Rights Association which had organised the civil rights campaign in the late 1960s. The policy of the Association was anti-partitionist and it campaigned for a phased withdrawal of British troops from Northern Ireland, the end of internment, and an amnesty for political prisoners. A British branch of the organisation was formed almost immediately.

In the October 1974 election, the British branch decided to nominate Parliamentary candidates – seven stood in areas with a large Irish population. The decision to contest the election was not approved by the executive of the Association and the branch was expelled on 2 October 1974. It did not contest any more elections.

Irish Confederation

Highest vote: T. C. Anstey (Youghal, 1847) – 109 votes, 61.9%

Parliamentary elections won: 2

Number of candidacies: 4

The Irish Confederation grew out of the literary and political Young Ireland movement of the mid nineteenth century. On 27 July 1846, William Smith O'Brien led the Young Ireland movement in withdrawing from the Repeal Association (*see* **Repealer**) which had repudiated the use of force. In January 1847 the Irish Confederation was formed, which called for Irish independence and more effective famine relief.

In the August 1847 general election, Confederate candidates fought four seats, winning two (Youghal and one of the County Limerick seats). The next year, the organisation attempted a peasants' uprising in County Tipperary which was easily suppressed. The leaders of the group were convicted of high treason and transported to Australia. One of the Confederation's leaders, Charles Gavan Duffy, had been in jail at the time of the revolt and so escaped transportation; he later formed the **Independent Opposition**.

Irish Freedom Movement

See **Revolutionary Communist Party (1981–97)**.

Irish Independence Party

Highest vote: P. J. Fahy (Mid-Ulster, 1979) – 12,055 votes, 18.4%

Parliamentary elections won: 0

Number of candidacies: 4

This party was the product of a breakaway by a part of the **Social Democratic and Labour Party** which was more traditionally nationalist and less willing to seek accommodation within the United Kingdom than the SDLP leadership. It was launched in October 1977. The principal founders were Fergus McAteer, an SDLP member of Derry City Council, and Frank McManus, former **Unity** MP for Fermanagh and South Tyrone. Another leading figure was John Turnly who had been an SDLP member for North Antrim on the Northern Ireland Constitutional Convention in 1975–6; he was a Protestant and was murdered on 4 June 1980 by the Ulster Freedom Fighters loyalist group.

Irish Independence Party policy was to seek British withdrawal from Northern Ireland as a first step, followed by negotiations with the Republic of Ireland on inclusion of Northern Ireland. The party wished to see an electoral pact among anti-unionist parties at elections, but no progress was ever made on that wish.

The party fought four seats in the 1979 election, three in border areas, but saved only one deposit and was beaten by the SDLP wherever it stood. The party slightly increased its vote in the 1981 district council elections but did not fight the 1982 Northern Ireland Assembly election due to its opposition to the policy of devolution. At the same time, **Sinn Féin** returned to fighting elections and absorbed much of the party's vote. The IIP won only four seats in the 1985 district council elections, and ceased activity shortly after.

Irish Parliamentary Party

See **Nationalist**.

Irish Republican Socialist Party

Address: 392 Falls Road, Belfast BT12
Email address: IRSP-WEB@IRSM.ORG
Website: http://irsm.org/irsm.html
Parliamentary elections won: 0
Number of candidacies: 0

The Irish Republican Socialist Party was formed on 10 December 1974 as a result of the expulsion of Séamus Costello and his supporters from the Republican Clubs movement (*see* **The Workers' Party** [Ireland]). Costello was opposed to the decision to wind down the Official IRA and created the terrorist Irish National Liberation Army (INLA). The IRSP represents the political wing of this organisation. It was supported for a time by the former **Unity** MP for Mid-Ulster, Bernadette Devlin.

The INLA's first campaign targeted members of Republican Clubs who had proposed that party's 1972 change of strategy. The INLA and the IRSP were the subject of attacks from late 1975, when the Official IRA broke its ceasefire (though Republican Clubs claimed the Provisional IRA was responsible). The party sponsored a candidate for the Dáil of the Republic of Ireland in a June 1976 by-election and the 1977 general election. Séamus Costello was murdered in 1977.

The INLA began to co-operate with the Provisional IRA and **Sinn**

Féin from the late 1970s. Many senior Sinn Féin members had attended Séamus Costello's funeral, and the 1980–1 hunger strike in the Maze Prison was organised jointly by the INLA and the IRA. Three INLA prisoners died. During the hunger strike, two IRSP candidates were elected to Belfast City Council on a platform of support for the H-Block prisoners.

The IRSP did not fight the 1982 Northern Ireland Assembly election; it did fight six seats in the Republic of Ireland's February 1982 general election but only one in November 1982. The government of the Republic of Ireland proscribed the INLA on 5 January 1983.

In 1987 a bitter internal feud in the INLA arose after a 'supergrass' trial collapsed. The feud resulted in the creation of the Irish People's Liberation Organization (IPLO) which attacked and murdered many of the IRSP's leading figures; from that time, the level of INLA violence was low. The party did not participate in the talks process which led to the Good Friday Agreement (which it opposed); however, the INLA declared a ceasefire on 22 August 1998. Communications from the INLA are channelled through the IRSP.

The IRSP, as its name suggests, is much more dogmatic than the Workers' Party or Sinn Féin and considers itself to be to the left of both. It declared itself a revolutionary Marxist party at its 1984 Ard Fheis [conference] and does not believe in a Parliamentary road to socialism; this, along with its republicanism, explains its reluctance to contest elections.

Islamic Party of Britain

Address: PO Box 844, Oldbrook, Milton Keynes MK6 2YT

Email address: islamparty@breathemail.net

Website: http://www.islamicparty.faithweb.com

Highest vote: D. M. Pidcock (Bradford North, 1990 (8/11)) – 800 votes, 2.2%

Parliamentary elections won: 0

Number of candidacies: 5

This party was a result of experience gained during a campaign for state recognition of Muslim schools, centred on Batley in West Yorkshire. The Islamic Party was publicly launched on 13 September 1989 at the London

Central Mosque. Contrary to some reports the controversy over the book *The Satanic Verses* had little to do with the party's formation; the party felt Muslims handled the issue badly and set out its stance on the issue in *Satanic Voices* by David Pidcock.

The Islamic Party states that it seeks to offer viable alternatives to the present economic and monetary system by analysing problems from an Islamic perspective. It does not seek election in order to secure representation for Muslims, but to offer Islamic alternative solutions to problems in society to the whole population, including non-Muslims.

A central campaign for the party has been opposition to the interest-based banking system, and it also calls for state funding for Muslim schools and for protection against religious discrimination and vilification. Reports that the party is anti-Semitic are incorrect: it believes that the historic impact of anti-Semitism must be considered.

The party leader from its foundation has been David Pidcock, an English-born convert from Roman Catholicism to Islam. Pidcock fought the Bradford North by-election of 1990, and was one of four candidates in the 1992 election. The party recognized that most Muslims voted Labour in that election; it hopes that disillusionment has set in since 1997 and will therefore be fighting more elections.

John Hampden New Freedom Party

See **English National Party**.

Labour and Co-operative

Highest vote: Mrs H. Slater (Stoke-on-Trent North, 1951 (31/3)) – 23,103 votes, 75.5%
Parliamentary elections won: 299
Number of candidacies: 521

Since the **Co-operative Party** has been affiliated to the Labour Party, joint candidates of the two have run as Labour and Co-operative candidates. They are however, committed to the Labour Party manifesto.

Labour and Trade Union Party

Highest vote: P. Hadden (Belfast South, 1992) – 875 votes, 2.6%.

Parliamentary elections won: 0

Number of candidacies: 3

This party was the Northern Irish section of the organisation originally formed as the Revolutionary Socialist League, and popularly known as the Militant tendency (*see* **Socialist Party** (1996–)). It was originally known as the Labour and Trade Union Group. The Group fought Belfast East in the 1983 election and outpolled the **Social Democratic and Labour Party**. It fought two seats in the 1992 election, at Mid-Ulster and Belfast South.

On 5 March 1993 Militant Labour Northern Ireland was formed, possibly as a replacement for the Labour and Trade Union Party.

Labour Northern Ireland

Address: 16 Garland Heights, Lurgan, Northern Ireland

Email address: secretary@labourni.org

Website: http://www.labourni.org

Only vote: N. J. A. Cusack (Belfast South, 1997) – 292 votes, 0.7%

Parliamentary elections won: 0

Number of candidacies: 1

When Prime Minister John Major announced the creation of an elected Forum to determine entry into the all-party talks in Northern Ireland, the Labour and socialist organisations of Northern Ireland quickly united around a common manifesto to fight the elections. This alliance was called 'Labour' and won just under 1% of the vote, enough to secure it tenth place overall. Two seats were given to each of the parties in the top ten. 'Labour' also sponsored Niall Cusack in Belfast South at the 1997 general election, who won 0.7% of the vote.

The party saw its aim at the talks as being representation of non-sectarian trade unionists. It supported the talks process and the Belfast Agreement. As the talks were coming to an end the party decided to establish itself formally and it was launched at the Silverwood Hotel in Lurgan on 28 April 1998. The constitution declared that it was a socialist party, with its primary objective being to re-establish a Northern Ireland Labour Party.

In the Northern Ireland Assembly elections the party fought most constituencies but won only 0.3% of the vote.

Labour Party

Address: Millbank Tower, London SW1P 4GT

Email address: labour-party@geo2.poptel.org.uk

Website: http://www.labour.org.uk/

Number on Register: 1

Highest vote: J. Milner (Leeds South East, 1929 (1/8)) – 11,804 votes, 95.8%

Parliamentary elections won: 6,023

Number of candidacies: 13,643

The early history of the Labour Party is included in the entry for the **Labour Representation Committee**. Twenty-nine LRC candidates were elected in the 1906 general election, and on the meeting of the Parliament, decided to rename itself as the Labour Party. This declaration of independence as a political party had however only limited effect in the House of Commons: many Labour MPs owed their positions to the pact with the Liberals, and were definitely closer to the Liberal government policies than to the Conservative opposition.

The party did bring its pressure to bear in Parliament and succeeded in reversing the Taff Vale judgment (*see* Labour Representation Committee) by passing the Trades Disputes Act 1906 with Liberal support. The moderate measures which the party was forced to propose led to some discontent outside Parliament especially in the affiliated **Independent Labour Party**.

Any chance that the Labour Party would move to distance itself from the Liberal government was ended when the Liberals, led largely by Chancellor of the Exchequer David Lloyd George, adopted a policy of social reform in 1908. The high point of this policy was the 1909 'People's Budget' in which old age pensions were provided; the radical nature of this budget provoked the Conservative-dominated House of Lords to reject it and thus precipitate a constitutional crisis in which Labour was forced to support the Liberals.

Support of the Labour Party by the trade union movement had increased steadily through the Parliament, and the biggest boost came in 1909 when the Miners Federation of Great Britain affiliated. The miners had been the strongest opponents of the establishment of a separate political party in 1899; their recruitment brought a large number of **Liberal/Labour** Parliamentary seats to the party.

At the same time, the Labour Party suffered a major defeat in the courts. A member of the Amalgamated Society of Railway Servants named Osborne, objected to paying into a union fund to support Labour MPs (who were not paid from public funds) and had the fund declared illegal. The Osborne judgment removed at a stroke the main source of Labour Party financial support and threw the party into disarray.

The two 1910 elections, both of which were dominated by the constitutional question, saw a further Labour advance, even while the Liberals lost seats overall. 39 seats were won in both, and as in 1906, the party won only rarely when facing Liberal opposition. The close ties with the Liberals provoked the establishment in 1911 of the **British Socialist Party**, which opposed the alliance of socialists with trade unionists.

Pressure on the Liberals resulted in the introduction, in 1911, of a state salary for MPs, and in 1913, the Osborne judgment was reversed with the Trade Union Act, which created a system surviving ever since: political funds were permitted, but had to be kept separate from the general fund, and individual trade union members were permitted to opt out of paying into the political fund.

The main political battle at this time was over constitutional and foreign affairs, principally Irish Home Rule and later, the international situation. Labour was, as a party, not very interested in these issues but inclined to support Irish Home Rule. Foreign affairs discussions had generally been left to the socialist societies who were by and large pacifist; MPs with dockyard constituencies tended strongly to support the navy estimates, in defence of their local position.

When the Great War broke out in August 1914, the Labour Party initially opposed British involvement. After war was declared, the party was split with many MPs feeling instinctively the need to support British forces, whereas the ILP leadership was strongly anti-war. When the party decided not to oppose the new spending needed for the war, Ramsay MacDonald resigned as leader of the Parliamentary Labour Party.

Unity was ensured by campaigning against the worst effects of war on the home population – profiteering, inflation and unemployment. When a Coalition government was formed in 1915, Arthur Henderson was invited to join it; Labour MPs opposed participation but the party's National Executive Committee approved and Henderson accepted – becoming the first Labour cabinet minister. However, the government's hope that Labour ministers would diminish opposition to conscription and trade disputes was not borne out.

David Lloyd George was more favourable to Labour when he became Prime Minister in 1916. He offered state control of mines and shipping, and more effective food rationing, and the Labour Party again participated in the Coalition. ILP opposition led the trade unions to vote to reduce the ILP representation on the NEC at the 1917 Labour Party conference.

An international Socialist Congress was organised in Stockholm in 1917. The Labour Party decided to send delegates, knowing that a German delegation would also attend. The Cabinet summoned Henderson to explain this attitude but kept him waiting outside while it debated; this was known as the 'doormat incident' and precipitated Henderson's resignation from the government on 12 August 1917. Lloyd George made sure to replace him with another Labour member, George Barnes. (In the event the government refused exit visas for the conference delegation.)

In 1917 the party began to redraft its constitution. As a quid pro quo for the loss of socialist seats on the NEC, a socialist statement of aims and values was incorporated, as drafted by Sidney Webb. It pledged the party to seek the common ownership and public control of all sectors of industry. The new constitution, providing also for individual membership, was approved early in 1918. A policy statement adopted in June 1918 was also the work of Sidney Webb and his wife Beatrice.

When the War ended, the Parliamentary Labour Party was broadly favourable to continuing in the Coalition but a special conference voted against it; while some ministers resigned, several others including George Barnes retained office and were expelled from the party as a consequence.

The party campaigned optimistically in the general election, the first with universal franchise for men, and for women over 30. It had 365 candidates – many more than ever before.

The results were disappointing. The tide of public opinion was strongly with the **Coalition** which Labour had just left, and Conservative and Liberal supporters of the Coalition rarely fought each other. 57 Labour MPs were returned, more than in 1910 but only just. Some of the party's most prominent members were defeated after campaigns against their war record, including Ramsay MacDonald and Philip Snowden.

Labour's performance in local elections improved quickly after 1918, when the economy went into recession, and the party won control of many Metropolitan boroughs in London in 1919. The party also won a series of by-elections against the Coalition candidates which contemporaries regarded as impressive, though it is less so in retrospect.

The period around 1920 also clearly set the party on to a moderate course. Labour rejected the attempted affiliation of the **Communist Party of Great Britain**. There was a great deal of trade union militancy in 1921, especially by miners who were demanding nationalisation, and there was talk of a general strike. The growing political importance of the Trades Union Congress led to greater attempts at co-ordination by the Labour Party.

With the end of the wartime Coalition, and a widespread sense that Lloyd George had failed to deliver on his pledges, Labour expected to do well in the 1922 general election. Fifty more candidates were nominated and many more local Labour Parties were established in the early 1920s. The party won nearly 30% of the vote, coming in second place even if the two Liberal wings were counted together. 142 Labour MPs were returned, including almost all those who had lost in 1918.

Ramsay MacDonald became the first designated leader of the Parliamentary Labour Party, and leader of the Opposition, defeating J. R. Clynes in a ballot. MacDonald was the candidate of the ILP left, and it proved a surprise to them when he promoted moderate policies.

MacDonald, having supported the decision to refuse Communist affiliation, found himself having to fend off attempted entrism. Communists could still be selected as official Labour candidates, and even where they were not it was usual for the Communist to run as 'Labour' anyway. Two Communists sat in the 1922 Parliament.

A snap general election was called by the Conservatives in late 1923 in an attempt to get a majority for tariff reform. This policy was still unpopular and Labour scrambled to nominate 427 candidates; despite the reunification of the Liberals, Labour once again won second place and 191 Labour MPs were returned. The Conservatives, though they had more MPs than any other party, failed by some way to win a majority.

Labour's leadership declared itself ready to assume office, placing the responsibilty of deciding which party should be in government on the Liberals. Asquith felt that he must vote out the Conservatives because of the Liberal Party's firm opposition to tariff reform. Liberal MPs supported a Labour motion of no confidence when Parliament met, and the King sent for Ramsay MacDonald to form a government.

MacDonald's cabinet making showed some doubts about the abilities of his colleagues. He acted as his own Foreign Secretary and brought in Conservatives and Liberals to act as Ministers in the Lords (there being no Labour peers until MacDonald recommended the creation of three, on assuming office). The government had virtually no support in the Lords, and depended on the Liberals in the Commons, so was not expected to last long.

In these circumstances the government decided not to try bold and far-reaching measures, but to attempt to govern competently and persuade the electorate that Labour was a 'safe' government. The first Labour budget, introduced by Philip Snowden, was 'vindictive against no class and against no interest', reducing indirect taxes and tariffs.

The most notable legislation of the first Labour government was the Housing (Financial Provisions) Act which provided grants for the construction of council houses. The government also helped to negotiate a deal to ease German reparations, defusing a potential crisis over French occupation of the Ruhr. Soviet Russia was recognised and negotiations for a treaty were started.

The fall of the government was over a minor matter. The Communist newspaper *Worker's Weekly* urged troops to disobey orders to fire on workers in trade disputes. The Attorney-General prosecuted the editor for sedition but, after pressure from left-wing Labour MPs, withdrew the prosecution. It looked like Communist influence and the Conservatives put down a motion of censure; the Liberals put an amendment to refer the issue to a Select Committee.

MacDonald declared that both the motion and the amendment were issues of confidence, giving the Conservatives their opportunity: by their supporting the Liberal amendment, the government was defeated and MacDonald called a general election. With 514 candidates, the party was better organized than ever, and campaigned on its record.

However, all issues in the 1924 election were suddenly overshadowed on 25 October by the publication of what purported to be a letter from Grigory Zinoviev, Chairman of the Communist International, to the Communist Party of Great Britain, calling for subversion to ensure the treaty between Britain and Soviet Russia was made. Zinoviev declared the letter a forgery and Labour suspected a conspiracy (the letter was published without MacDonald's authority). It is now generally accepted that the letter was forged.

The general election resulted in the defeat of the government and the return of the Conservatives with a large majority, but there was a silver lining to the cloud of defeat: the Labour vote increased in real and percentage terms, and though 40 seats net were lost, it was the Liberal Party which was comprehensively defeated.

Ramsay MacDonald's personal popularity suffered after 1924. He had tried to do to much in government and had not consulted effectively with the TUC. MacDonald sensed a further need to remove all traces of Communist influence from the Labour Party, and the 1925 conference banned Communists from individual membership, but TUC militancy was not due to Communist influence.

In 1925 the Conservative government returned Britain to the Gold Standard at the pre-war rate, overvaluing the currency and damaging exports. This created a crisis in the coal industry and mine owners decided to reduce wages. The miners, feeling victimised, went on strike, and the TUC called a general strike in sympathy. The strike collapsed after nine days and the miners were eventually forced back to work; afterwards there was very little industrial militancy as the labour movement realised they could only advance by constitutional means.

MacDonald had by now incurred the open opposition of the ILP, which proposed a new economic policy. The leadership view persisted because the major unions were wary of the ILP's approach. MacDonald's moderation did however win converts to the party and his days as an anti-war outsider were being forgotten. As the Parliament moved towards its end Labour had a good organisation in all parts of the country.

When an election was called in May 1929, the party had some form of organisation in practically every constituency. 569 Labour candidates fought and campaigned on the economy, highlighting the need to cut unemployment. Labour's campaign struck a chord as there were consistently over 1,000,000 unemployed, and for the first time Labour won more seats than any other party, even though it was 1% behind the Conservatives in terms of share of vote.

Again dependent on Liberal support, Labour took office. To deal with unemployment a three-member committee was set up under Lord Privy Seal J. H. Thomas. However, unemployment started to rise, and the radical proposals of Oswald Mosley (one of the committee's members) were rejected by the rest of the government. Mosley resigned in May 1930 and started a campaign to win over the Labour Party. Narrowly failing at the 1930 conference, he left to form the **New Party**.

The second Labour government's legislative programme was derailed by the need to obtain the support of the Liberals in the Commons, and by the Conservative domination of the Lords. There was a government defeat on an electoral reform bill, and the government was forced to compromise on a proposed tax on land values.

It was the effect of the economic crisis that brought the government down. Overseas investment in London began to be withdrawn in May 1931 after an Austrian bank collapsed. The government's Economy Committee reported on 31 July 1931 that there would be a deficit of £120 million in April 1932, because of the increased cost of unemployment benefits, the rise in interest rates, and the fall in tax revenues.

The government attempted to negotiate loans from US banks but was told that it needed to reduce expenditure before the loan would be agreed. The government reluctantly agreed to cut civil service and forces pay, but the proposal to cut unemployment benefit was rejected. Ramsay MacDonald went to the King to offer the resignation of the Labour government.

Labour ministers were astonished when MacDonald returned to announce he had accepted the King's invitation to form a coalition National government with the Conservatives and Liberals. Very few ministers joined the National government, and it became clear that they were leaving the Labour Party: the TUC General Council and the remaining ex-cabinet ministers called a meeting which agreed to go into opposition. MacDonald was formally expelled on 28 September.

The new National government called a snap election in October 1931, seeking a 'Doctor's Mandate' to bring about economic recovery. The campaign was dominated by bitter attacks on Labour by the National leaders, especially Philip Snowden who described Labour policy as bolshevism run mad.

With the National government obtaining the united support of the other parties, the non-Labour vote was effectively unified. Labour's share of the vote was 31% but the National government had 67% – enough to win almost every seat. Labour returned only 46 MPs, and had now lost the support of the ILP which refused to sign the Labour Party's Standing Orders. Almost all the senior Labour Party members were defeated, including Arthur Henderson, the party leader.

George Lansbury, the most prominent left-winger, was the most senior ex-minister to survive and became Parliamentary leader in 1932. Lansbury was in his seventies and a weak leader. He was also a firm pacifist, which would cause problems later. The Parliamentary party was dominated by miners and the General Council of the TUC reconstituted its National Joint Council (which liaised with the Labour Party) as the National Council of Labour: many considered its resolutions binding on the Labour Party.

The 1931 general election result was swiftly shown to be a freak when Labour began to regain seats in by-elections. One by-election win stunned the political world: East Fulham, in October 1933, in which the Labour candidate made pacifism a central campaign theme. The party had an unexpected triumph in the London County Council elections of 1934 in which it gained control of the council under the leadership of Herbert Morrison.

Lansbury's dedication to pacifism ran up against the rearmament of Nazi Germany, and the aggression of fascist Italy. At the 1935 Labour Party conference, Lansbury agonised over what to do, but eventually decided that pacifism must win out. He was followed on the platform by Ernest Bevin, leader of the Transport and General Workers' Union, who denounced Lansbury for 'hawking your conscience round from body to body asking to be told what you ought to do with it'. Conference voted heavily against pacifism and Lansbury resigned in tears.

Clement Attlee, who had served as a minister in both Labour governments, was appointed as temporary leader. He therefore led the party in the November 1935 general election. Foreign affairs were raised in the election, but the National government was again united against Labour. The Labour vote increased to 38%, higher than in 1929, but there were only 154 Labour MPs elected. On the positive side most of the leading members who had been defeated in 1931 returned.

The first act of the party in the new session was to re-elect Attlee as full leader. This was something of a surprise given Attlee's self-effacement, but he had won the confidence of Labour MPs. Some thought that he would not be in office for very long. In fact, he served for the next twenty years and is still the longest-serving leader of the Labour Party.

Civil war in Spain in 1936 provided an opportunity for those in the Labour movement who believed in rearmament to press their cause. The National Council of Labour strongly backed rearmament, as did the TUC, and the Labour Party conference was forced along. From 1937 the Labour Party in Parliament supported rearmament.

However, the Labour Party was wary of directly supporting the International Brigades which had gone to help the Republicans in Spain. Their formation had been initiated by the Communists, and Labour was opposed to joint working with Communists. The left of the Labour Party called for a 'United Front' including all parties of the left (Communists, ILP, and Labour) to oppose fascism.

The Labour leadership determined to block 'United Front' sentiment and changed the system of election for the National Executive to give constituency parties a set number of seats in order to weaken the left. The new Executive disaffiliated the Socialist League, which had been the main body of United Front supporters.

Sir Stafford Cripps, who had led the United Front campaign, slightly revised the proposal to create the 'Popular Front' and launched a large-scale campaign within the party. Cripps' campaigning led to his expulsion, along with several supporters including Welsh ex-miner Aneurin Bevan, in 1939; the Popular Front did however attract many constituency Labour Parties.

At the time of the Munich conferences Labour had issued statements opposing any concessions to Hitler, and privately urged the National government to change policy. Outbreak of war faced the party with the dilemma of whether to participate in a coalition government. It decided not to, because to do so would mean accepting Chamberlain's leadership and policies, though Labour readily agreed to a new electoral pact.

The decision to stay in opposition proved to be a good one. The initial period of the war was marked by very little actual fighting and a great deal of complacency by war planners, which was shown when Hitler invaded and conquered Scandinavia in a matter of days in April 1940. The Labour opposition put down a motion of no confidence in the government's conduct of the war.

Parliament did not back the motion, but the abstention of many Conservative MPs showed that support was ebbing. Chamberlain asked Attlee whether Labour would join a coalition government under him or another Prime Minister; after consultation with the National Executive, Attlee replied that Labour would only join under a new leader. Churchill was the only Prime Minister acceptable to Labour because of his opposition to appeasement.

Attlee became Lord Privy Seal and Deputy Prime Minister, and Arthur Greenwood was also appointed to the War Cabinet. A Parliamentary seat was found for Ernest Bevin so a leading trade unionist could be Minister of Labour and National Service from October 1940, and Herbert Morrison's experience in London was put to good use as Home Secretary.

With Churchill concentrating on the war effort, Attlee played the key role in planning domestic policy. Some Labour-inspired social legislation was passed though the need to secure agreement from the Conservatives made it difficult. The implementation of the Beveridge Committee recommendations for a comprehensive welfare state was put off, prompting a rebellion of almost all Labour MPs who were not in the government.

The eventual defeat of Germany in 1945 left Labour needing to decide whether to continue the coalition. Sentiment in the party was opposed to a continuation of the coalition in peacetime, as in 1918, though Attlee wished to delay the election until the autumn to allow for more preparation. Churchill determined to hold the election early to try to capitalise on his personal popularity.

Labour's proposals for widespread social reform were published in its manifesto *Let us Face the Future*. The campaign was marked by Churchill's surprising claim that the Labour ministers with whom he had been in government only two months previously would have to fall back on 'some sort of Gestapo', and claims about the influence to be exerted by Harold Laski as Chair of the National Executive Committee.

Few paid any attention to infant opinion polls in 1945, which pointed to a big Labour victory. When the results were declared, Labour won a majority of 146 over all other parties. This gives an exaggerated impression of the votes cast because population movements made the electoral system favourable to Labour.

Attlee as Prime Minister was a revelation. He ran a crisp cabinet, using his wartime experience to get business through. Under his direction the government first nationalised the Bank of England and the coal industry, then civil aviation, electricity generation, railways, gas, and iron and steel. Beveridge was implemented and the National Health Service created. The money for these reforms came from retention of the high taxation which had been necessary during the war.

While the grassroots of the Labour Party welcomed the reforms, they were less pleased with the Attlee government's foreign policy. Many had looked forward to a 'socialist foreign policy' of friendliness with the Soviet Union, but Ernest Bevin as Foreign Secretary allied the UK with the USA in opposition to Stalin's expansionism. Several Labour MPs continued to dissent and eventually five were expelled when they associated themselves too closely with communism.

The Labour government made only minor reforms to the constitution. The delaying power of the Lords was reduced from two years to one year, and the University representation in the Commons ended, but the redistribution of seats could not be anything but damaging to the party. The government sustained its popularity and held all by-elections it was defending (save one, though this had been won by the ILP in 1945).

Attlee went to the country in February 1950. The swing against the government was not great (3.3%) but the redistribution exaggerated the effect on its number of seats. Labour won, but with an overall majority of

5. Adversity did not help party unity, and when the Chancellor imposed charges on NHS spectacles and dentures in order to pay for the Korean War, Aneurin Bevan resigned from the cabinet. He was followed by two others – Harold Wilson and John Freeman. Several other senior ministers were ill and resigned.

The need to have a government with a secure majority led Attlee to call another election in October 1951. The campaign was dominated by foreign affairs and Labour accusations that the Conservatives were 'warmongers'; this claim was refuted and backfired. Though Labour won more votes than the Conservatives, they won fewer seats.

Bevan became the leader of a faction of left-wingers within the party. They voted against the new Conservative government's defence estimates, when the official Labour line was to abstain. At the 1952 conference, Bevanites won six out of the seven seats for constituency Labour Parties on the National Executive, but Bevan's support among Labour MPs was much less.

The government's decision to build a hydrogen bomb split the party. Bevan believed that the bomb should only be built if guarantees were given about its use and campaigned for this policy in Parliament, opposing Attlee. The Labour whip was withdrawn from Bevan in March 1955 but eventually restored when he agreed to apologise: the result was a great deal of bitterness within the party.

At this time a general election was called by the Conservatives. The campaign was much less heated than 1951, but there were several public sector strikes during it and Labour suffered from its links with the trade unions. Clement Attlee was by now over 70 and rather tired after coping with Labour divisions; it was not a surprise to find Labour had been defeated, with a swing of about 2% to the Conservatives.

Attlee resigned shortly after the election. He had held on to the leadership for so long partly in order to prevent Herbert Morrison, who had been the obvious candidate, from being chosen as his successor. Morrison's best time had gone and he was easily defeated in the ballot of Labour MPs to choose the new leader. The winner was Hugh Gaitskell, who had been Chancellor at the end of the 1945–51 government.

Swiftly Gaitskell was able to unify the party by firm opposition to the Conservative government's action against Egypt over the Suez Canal.

Aneurin Bevan fully agreed and was appointed in 1957 as Shadow Foreign Secretary. At the 1957 Labour Party conference, Bevan astonished his supporters by denouncing the calls for nuclear disarmament, which he believed would leave the country without any international allies.

Labour entered the 1959 general election with optimism. It had rebuilt its local organisation after 1955 and presented a popular media campaign which was more impressive than the Conservatives'. Gaitskell himself believed he would win. It was a crushing blow when rising prosperity delivered an increased Conservative majority.

The defeat raised fundamental questions over the party's role. Gaitskell believed that the party's commitment to nationalisation had cost it votes (though in the 1959 manifesto, only road freight and steel were identified for nationalisation), and moved to alter the party constitution to remove the commitment in section 4 of Clause IV to the 'common ownership of the means of production, distribution and exchange'. This move attracted vehement opposition and eventually produced only a new 'statement of principles' alongside Clause IV. The 'statement of principles' was quickly forgotten.

Gaitskell also came under pressure on defence policy. Bevan died in 1960, and the increasing power of the left narrowly passed a unilateralist motion at the 1960 conference – prompting Gaitskell to declare he would 'fight, and fight, and fight again' to save the party. He spent the next year campaigning to reverse the decision and succeeded in doing so at the 1961 conference.

Growing Conservative unpopularity helped the party to an opinion poll lead in the early 1960s. Surprising the party, Gaitskell opposed the government's application to join the European Communities and therefore did a great deal to heal the division with the left. It was at this time that Gaitskell suddenly died, universally mourned within the party as the next Prime Minister.

The leadership election saw a fight between Harold Wilson, broadly on the left, and George Brown, on the right. Brown's emotional personality encouraged Labour MPs to vote for Harold Wilson, who appealed as a classless technocrat. Wilson's speech to the Labour conference of 1963 said that the white heat of the technological revolution would sweep away old ways of working and trade union organisation.

Harold Wilson was one of the best leaders of the opposition, in putting together a coherent campaign which could appeal to anyone. The Conservatives delayed the election for as long as possible in order to build their fightback, but in the end called the election for October 1964. Labour won a very narrow majority after a campaign led presidentially by Harold Wilson.

It was clear that the Parliament could not last long, as Labour lost a by-election in Leyton in January 1965 while attempting to get a seat for the Foreign Secretary, Patrick Gordon Walker, who had been defeated in the general election. The government had to govern carefully. Wilson separated out long-term economic planning from the Treasury and put George Brown in charge. The government decided to keep the pound's value high and increased interest rates.

The government's economic planning helped tackle inflation without causing unemployment and by the end of 1965 opinion polls were showing Labour ahead. After a favourable by-election in Hull in January 1966, Wilson called an election to try to obtain a majority. Labour's slogan 'You know Labour Government works' proved effective and the party won a landslide victory.

Almost immediately afterwards the economy turned. The government tried to freeze wages and prices voluntarily and then was forced to do so compulsorily, in order to tackle inflation, and unemployment rose over the winter of 1966–67. The attempt to decide long-term economic planning apart from the Treasury effectively ended. Interest rates were forced up to defend the pound, but unsuccessfully. In November 1967 the government decided to reduce the value of the pound.

Devaluation was a policy the government had insisted since 1964 it would not follow. However, when Wilson explained it on television, he seemed to be selling its advantages and claiming credit for a victory; this boosted his reputation for changing his beliefs while attempting to mislead the public.

Devaluation also forced public spending cuts which had previously been resisted; most of the cuts were in defence. The government also imposed a charge for NHS prescriptions. Government popularity plunged and it suffered huge swings against it in by-elections. Almost every section of the population had some grievance against the government; trade unionists were especially angry about the continued wage freeze and voted their condemnation of legislation 'curtailing basic union rights' at the 1968 Labour conference.

Trade union power was also seen over the government's attempt to change industrial relations law. A white paper called *In Place of Strife* published in January 1969 proposed giving the government the power to delay strikes and insist on a ballot of union members, but was opposed by right-wing MPs from trade unions as well as the left. It had to be dropped.

The economy began to improve in late 1969, with devaluation having helped exporters. Labour began improving in opinion polls and saved seats in by-elections which would previously have been lost. Taking an optimistic reading from local elections in May 1970, Wilson called a general election, and once again led it almost as a personal popularity crusade. Opinion polls throughout the campaign gave Labour leads.

The result of the general election was a nasty shock. There was a swing to the Conservatives of nearly 5%, giving a majority of 31. Some looked for excuses for the loss in a single month's bad trade figures published two days before polling day. Harold Wilson was still respected within the Labour Party not to be challenged for the leadership.

Voters seemed to tire of Edward Heath's government quickly, without any great campaigning from a Labour Party still trying to get over the defeat. 1971 saw some good results in local elections and by-elections. The party had to consider its response to the government's application to join the European Communities. Though the Labour government had applied to join in 1967, and the negotiating briefs used by the Conservatives had been prepared before the election, the National Executive Committee decided to oppose entry. Harold Wilson made clear his own opposition was on the basis of the terms offered.

A sizeable part of the Labour Party did not agree with opposition to the European Communities. When Parliament voted, 69 Labour MPs defied a three-line whip to vote in favour – including the Deputy leader, Roy Jenkins. This prompted an unsuccessful challenge to Jenkins's position the next month. In April 1972 the shadow cabinet agreed that there should be a nationwide referendum before entry. This prompted the resignation of Jenkins from the deputy leadership, and of two shadow cabinet members who supported him.

Unity within the Labour movement was ensured when the Conservative government passed the Industrial Relations Act, restricting the power of trade unions. The TUC decided not to comply with the Act and a series of strikes resulted. As the Conservatives broke their pledge and introduced a statutory pay policy, mineworkers began action in support of their pay claim.

This action helped Labour to portray itself as the party which could bring industrial peace. The snap election of February 1974 saw a left-wing Labour manifesto pledging a 'Social Contract' between government and unions. Unlike previous Wilson-dominated elections, the campaign promoted the Labour 'team'. Like 1970 there was an unexpected result, but unlike 1970 the surprise was that Labour did much better. Though it did not have a majority, Labour had more seats than anyone else, and formed a minority government.

One of the most experienced cabinets for an incoming government was appointed, and the miners went back to work in days when their pay claim was granted. The government aimed to get the country back on its feet swiftly and succeeded in bringing forward some important legislation (though often defeated on the detail), before Harold Wilson called another election in October in the hope of getting a majority.

With a small swing, Labour managed to win a majority – but only 5 seats. Having renegotiated the terms of membership of the European Community, the promised referendum was held in June 1975. However the cabinet had decided to support continued membership. A special conference of the party maintained opposition, and members at every level were allowed to campaign on both sides. The result of the referendum was a two-to-one vote in favour of continued membership.

Shortly after Harold Wilson's sixtieth birthday in March 1976, he suddenly announced his resignation. After three ballots, Wilson's preferred successor James Callaghan won; he was the candidate of the moderate right, but with a firm trade union base. Roy Jenkins, who had performed badly in the election, accepted a job as President of the European Commission.

The economy came under pressure in summer 1976, as the pound suddenly fell in value. A loan from the International Monetary Fund had to be negotiated; this was a considerable defeat and the government's popularity suffered. The IMF loan came with conditions: the government had to cut spending, which would inevitably offend the left. The loan was agreed during the Labour Party conference, provoking an angry confrontation between left-wing delegates and the Chancellor, Denis Healey.

Serious political difficulties struck the government over its programme for devolution to Scotland and Wales. Many Scottish and Welsh MPs were opposed to devolution and when the bill to devolve went through Parliament, it became bogged down. A 'guillotine motion' to cut short debate was lost when Labour MPs rebelled. In order to guarantee a majority, the government negotiated a deal with the Liberals.

The economy started to recover in late 1977 as inflation began to fall, without rising unemployment. The 'social contract' included a voluntary pay policy, and the trade unions began to look forward to the end of restrictions. Devolution was made law but subject to a referendum. Labour began to lead in opinion polls in summer 1978 and expectation grew of an early election.

Callaghan surprised everyone when he announced in September 1978 there would be no election. He hoped that a further year of pay restraint would give a much stronger economy and he tried to set a limit of 5% on pay rises. Trade unions never gave any indication of being prepared to agree to the pay policy and engaged in a series of strikes over the winter, which became known as the 'winter of discontent'. The 'social contract' had failed to bring industrial peace.

Referendums on devolution were held at the beginning of March 1979. In Wales devolution was defeated by more than four to one and was dropped. In Scotland the majority went in favour but the Yes vote was not the 40% of the electorate required. This lost Labour the support of the **Scottish National Party** MPs and the cumulative effect of by-election losses meant that a Conservative motion of no confidence on 28 March 1979 was passed by one vote. Callaghan called an election.

Labour's vote in the 1979 general election held up well in raw terms, actually increasing from that gained in October 1974, but the Conservative vote went up much more. Nationally there was a swing of 5% to the Conservatives who won an overall majority of 43. The left of the party regarded the defeat as inevitable given what they believed was a 'betrayal' of the party's socialism by the government. The left demanded changes in the Labour Party constitution to put more power in the hands of members.

A new policy statement called *Peace, Jobs, Freedom* was agreed in September 1980 as an attempted compromise between the left and right. At the 1980 Labour Party conference, the left succeeded in requiring Labour MPs to be reselected by their local parties (having objected to many Labour MPs as being out of touch with local views), and changing the system for electing the party leader so that trade unions and individual members would have a vote. The details were left to be settled later.

Within a fortnight after the conference, James Callaghan resigned as leader. This meant a new election on the old system of Labour MPs only having a vote, which helped the right-wing candidate, Denis Healey. However, Healey barely campaigned at all, and offended many of his supporters by taking them for granted. It has been suggested that some right-wing MPs voted for the left-wing candidate because they hoped to strand Labour with an unelectable leader before leaving the party. Whatever the explanation, Michael Foot won an unexpected victory in the election.

The special conference to settle the details of the new leadership election system was held in 1981. This produced an electoral college favoured by the left where the trade unions took 40% of the vote, constituency parties 30%, and Labour MPs 30%. The next day, four former cabinet ministers announced the formation of the Council for Social Democracy, which later became the **Social Democratic Party**. From 1981 to 1982, a total of 28 Labour MPs joined the new party.

In the middle of the infighting, the left-wing ex-cabinet minister Tony Benn announced he would challenge Denis Healey for the deputy leadership, to which Healey had been elected unopposed after losing the leadership. A bitter campaign distracted the party during the summer of 1981, at the end of which Healey won by less than 1%. The Labour Party conference also adopted a range of left-wing policy demands.

The Labour opinion poll rating slumped as the SDP/Liberal **Alliance** bandwagon rolled. From the Falklands War of 1982 the Conservatives recovered much ground. The party's internal split began to take on a different character, with those around Michael Foot becoming known as the 'soft left' to distinguish them from the 'hard left' who continued to press for reforms.

Labour Party divisions and the hard left proved to be electorally unappealing in the Bermondsey by-election of February 1983. Left-wing Labour candidate Peter Tatchell had been selected but was denounced by Michael Foot; Tatchell was eventually allowed to stand but was given little support when the press launched a vicious campaign against him. The by-election was lost to the Liberals on an unprecedented turnover of votes.

Some shadow cabinet members tried to get Michael Foot to stand down after Bermondsey, but he kept his job after a good performance in the next by-election at Darlington. Few expected a good performance in the 1983 general election, at which there was a great deal of chaos in Labour's organisation (three different defence policies were outlined). The party's vote slumped to 28% and the Conservatives won an overall majority of 144. The one consolation in the election was that Labour managed to keep just ahead of the Alliance.

Foot immediately stepped down as leader, and was followed by Neil Kinnock who had been an effective Shadow Education Secretary and was from the soft left. A young and dynamic leader put Labour briefly into an opinion poll lead early in 1984, but the lead was lost because of public concern over the violent scenes surrounding the miners' strike of 1984–5.

At the 1985 Labour Party conference, Neil Kinnock attacked the Labour council in Liverpool which was under the control of the Militant tendency (*see* **Socialist Party** (1996–)). The leading members were expelled from the party in the spring of 1986, and the determination of Kinnock to oppose the infiltration of Militant helped the party at a time when the Conservatives were growing unpopular. The party won a by-election from the Conservatives in Fulham in April 1986, the first gain for 15 years, by playing up the candidate's local roots and moderate politics.

The left remained strong in constituency parties, especially in London. Newspapers ran campaigns attacking local authorities as 'loony left', and at a by-election in Greenwich in February 1987 the Labour candidate faced a strong press campaign and lost the seat to the SDP. This by-election was very much in mind at the opening of the 1987 general election when it still appeared possible the Alliance would overtake Labour.

Labour's campaign was very different from 1983. The party had a new logo (a red rose), and the campaign was professionally organised with television broadcasts promoting Neil Kinnock personally. The party was attacked for its unilateralist defence policy and for wanting to increase taxes, and in the event only increased its vote to 32%.

It was obvious to the leadership that the party's policies were not attractive to voters and the 1987 conference agreed to review them. The hard left accused the leadership of not believing in the policies they were supposed to be promoting and challenged for the leadership and deputy leadership in 1988, but were easily defeated. In the midst of the in-fighting the party lost a safe seat (Glasgow Govan) to the Scottish National Party.

The policy review reports were adopted, giving the party a more defensible set of policies. Just in time for the 1989 European Parliament elections, the party took the lead again and won the elections. Neil Kinnock and his allies began a series of reforms to the party, including reducing the trade union block vote at Labour Party conferences and centralising the membership system.

Early in 1990 the party won the Mid Staffordshire by-election with a 21% swing and established huge opinion poll leads. The party supported the decision to send UK forces to participate in the Gulf War, but suddenly lost its lead when the Conservative Party replaced Margaret Thatcher with John Major in November 1990. Through 1991 the general election loomed and Conservative and Labour were evenly balanced.

John Major delayed the election until the last moment but called it after a tax-cutting budget. Labour unveiled a 'Shadow Budget' showing how its commitments could be afforded, but the Conservatives used their own calculations to claim that people on modest earnings faced huge tax rises. The last opinion polls showed a slight Labour lead but from the first results in the general election it was clear that the Conservatives were winning, and they won a small overall majority.

Neil Kinnock's personality had come under attack in the election, and he resigned immediately afterward. John Smith, on the centre-right, won the leadership election easily. He appointed two young and effective shadow cabinet members to key posts, Gordon Brown as Shadow Chancellor and Tony Blair as Shadow Home Secretary. Labour moved into an opinion poll lead very quickly, helped by 'Black Wednesday' when the government's economic policy collapsed.

Tony Blair proved an effective Shadow Home Secretary, and voters began to trust that a Labour government would keep law and order – an area in which the party had previously been weak. John Smith managed to persuade the party conference to end the use of trade union votes in candidate selection in 1993, a significant internal victory. By spring 1994 the party had a strong opinion poll lead and did well at the local elections that year.

John Smith died suddenly on 11 May, a tragedy which affected the party deeply. In a good-natured leadership election, Tony Blair was chosen after Gordon Brown agreed not to stand. Blair proved very popular and the party's opinion poll rating soared; there was a swing of 29% in the Dudley West by-election of December 1994. Blair immediately moved to rewrite Clause IV of the party constitution, a move agreed at a special conference in 1995.

In 1996 the party unveiled a series of five pledges for the general election, given away on 'pledge cards' that encouraged voters to 'keep this card to make sure we keep our promises'. More by-elections were gained and the party began to improve its vote even when it had started in third place. The Labour Party conference was spectacularly united with little sign of the party in-fighting of previous years.

Labour fought another very closely controlled election campaign and made sure not to allow the Conservatives to sustain an attack. The party won 44% of the vote and a swing of over 10%, giving it a majority of 179 – the highest ever Labour majority and also the greatest majority for any party since 1924. Tony Blair became the youngest Prime Minister since 1812.

The new government took some key decisions very early. The Chancellor gave the Bank of England operational independence to set interest rates, while the Education Secretary risked alienating youth support by ending the student grant and imposing fees for university tuition. Yet the government remained popular and managed to achieve a swing to Labour in a by-election in Beckenham in November 1997.

Labour's main electoral concern began to be the very low turnout of Labour voters, especially in the party's heartlands. Local elections in 1998 had an overall turnout of 29%, one of the lowest ever, and only 19% of voters recorded their votes in the Leeds Central by-election in June 1999.

The party did well to hold off the Scottish National Party in the first elections to the Scottish Parliament in May 1999.

Labour did less well in Wales, where the popular choice for leader among Labour Party members was defeated in the selection under an electoral system seemingly chosen for this object. The party lost several utterly safe seats to **Plaid Cymru** and failed to win an overall majority in the National Assembly for Wales.

It was largely a poor turnout of Labour voters which enabled the Conservatives to win the European elections of 1999; when Labour ran a populist campaign in the Eddisbury by-election shortly afterwards, the party marginally improved on its 1997 election performance.

The vote for the left in Labour Party internal elections increased as a consequence of concerns over the control exercised by the party over selections. The Labour Party in London adopted a similar system to that used in Wales, in a successful attempt to stop the popular left-wing former leader of the Greater London Council, Ken Livingstone, from being selected as Labour candidate for Mayor of London; Livingstone then stood as an independent and won – beating the official Labour candidate into third place.

The government's huge majority helped it overcome backbench revolts over cuts in benefits for single mothers and a series of measures from the Home Office which were criticised for illiberality. The government saw success in the Northern Ireland talks in 1998 and passed a measure ending the automatic right of hereditary peers to seats in the House of Lords. The economy remained buoyant throughout the period.

Labour's record eight-year spell in the lead in opinion polls ended suddenly in September 2000, when the nation was almost brought to a halt by protestors against increased fuel costs who blockaded petrol supplies. Though the price rises which sparked the protest were caused by the world oil price, most of the rise since the 1997 election had been due to increased imposed tax by the government.

★

In 1912 the Irish Trades Union Congress voted to establish a separate Labour Party for Ireland. This resolution was repeated in 1913, and a party was established (*see* **Labour Party [Ireland]**). As a consequence of that decision and the Labour Party officially declaring itself in support of Home Rule, activity in Ireland ceased, and in 1919 the Socialist International granted the Irish Labour Party the status of a separate delegation.

This decision meant that the Labour Party did not organise in Northern Ireland, though the **Northern Ireland Labour Party** was formed as a sister organisation and its candidates almost always secured Labour Party endorsement. With the advent of direct rule, this party lapsed and the **Social Democratic and Labour Party** became Labour's sister party in Northern Ireland, a situation which has proved contentious among Labour-inclined unionists.

Labour Party [Ireland]

Address: 17 Ely Place, Dublin 2, Ireland

Email address: webminder@labour.ie

Website: http://www.labour.ie

Highest vote: J. Beattie (Belfast West, 1951) – 33,174 votes, 50.0%

Parliamentary elections won: 1

Number of candidacies: 5

The Irish Labour Party was formed in a similar way to the British Labour Party, by a vote of the Irish Trades Union Congress in 1912. The party was established in Clonmel by James Connolly, James Larkin and William O'Brien. It did not fight the 1918 election in order that the issue of Irish nationalism could be resolved. It has been the representative of the Socialist International in the Irish Free State/Republic of Ireland since 1919, and has been part of several coalition governments.

The party formed branches in Northern Ireland after a 1948 split in the **Northern Ireland Labour Party**. Several members of the Northern Ireland Labour Party, especially in West Belfast, resigned from that party, opposed to its stance of supporting the partition of Ireland. The Irish Labour Party also gathered the support of a small Socialist Republican group which had won the Belfast Falls seat in the 1945 Stormont elections.

In the 1950 general election the Irish Labour Party fought Down South and Belfast West. It failed to make a big dent in the Unionist majority in Down South, but came within 4,000 votes of winning Belfast West. Here the candidate was Jack Beattie, the incumbent MP (*see* **Federation of Labour**), who won back his seat by 25 votes in 1951.

The party also fought some Stormont elections in heavily nationalist areas from 1950, though it did not oppose candidates of the Northern Ireland Labour Party. The defeat of Jack Beattie in Belfast West in 1955 and the poor performance of its candidates in 1958 restricted Irish Labour Party activity, though it persisted in nominating Gerry Fitt for Belfast Dock constituency for Stormont in 1962 and saw him elected. Fitt was effectively an independent since the party had no other significant personalities and little interest in Northern Ireland.

In 1964 Fitt joined the **Republican Labour Party** and Irish Labour Party activity in Northern Ireland ended.

Labour Party of Scotland

Only vote: G. McLean (Dundee East, 1973 (1/3)) – 1,409 votes, 3.2%
Parliamentary elections won: 0
Number of candidacies: 1

This party was the result of a breakaway by members of the **Scottish National Party** in Dundee in the early 1970s. It fought the Dundee East by-election of 1973, and won a vote larger than the Labour majority over the SNP, though it is questionable whether voters were clear about its origin. The party was dissolved later that year and its members returned to the SNP, which won Dundee East in the February 1974 general election.

Labour Party '87

Parliamentary elections won: 0
Number of candidacies: 0

This Northern Ireland group brought together the several Labour groups and parties which had operated separately before. The largest parts of the new party were the **Northern Ireland Labour Party** and the **United**

Labour Party; the Labour Party of Northern Ireland, formed in 1985, and a local Labour Party operating in Newtownabbey were also included in the party when it was formed in March 1987.

The party hoped to have friendly relations with the British and Irish Labour Parties, but without any direct connection; it did not favour any change to the constitutional arrangements of Northern Ireland but did seek a devolved bicameral assembly elected by proportional representation. The party's candidate won only 0.2% in the European Parliament elections of June 1989, bottom of the poll and beaten by a candidate describing himself as 'Labour for Representative Government'.

In early 1996, a loose coalition of Labour and socialist organisations, councillors and individuals was established to fight the Northern Ireland Forum elections, in which Labour '87 participated and eventually merged. See **Labour Northern Ireland**.

Labour Representation Committee

Highest vote: D.J. Shackleton (Clitheroe, 1906) – 12,035 votes, 75.9%

Parliamentary elections won: 34

Number of candidacies: 71

In 1899, the Doncaster branch of the Amalgamated Society of Railway Servants passed a resolution proposed by Thomas Steels, which called on the Trades Union Congress to convene a special conference of trade unions, co-operative societies and socialist bodies, to make arrangements to secure direct representation of labour interests in Parliament. The resolution was sent to the union's annual conference, and then passed to the TUC.

At the TUC in Plymouth in September 1899, the motion was the subject of heated debate. It was opposed by the Miners who had already formed close relationships with the Liberals (*see* **Liberal/Labour**), but eventually passed by 546,000 to 434,000, with about 300,000 abstentions. The special conference was held at the Memorial Hall in Farringdon Street, London, on 27–28 February 1900, and was attended by 129 delegates representing 568,177 workers. It voted to set up a Committee which would promote Parliamentary candidates sponsored by its affiliates, and form a distinct Labour party in the House of Commons.

The founding theory of the Labour Representation Committee, that labour interests could best be represented by uniting the trade unions with the socialist societies, had been put into effect before without much success (*see* **Labour Representation League**). The Labour Electoral Association of 1890 failed to get any co-operation from the trade unions, and the 1893 TUC had created a Parliamentary fund but only two unions had contributed. The LRC did however have the support of the three most influential socialist organisations: the **Independent Labour Party** the **Social Democratic Federation**, and the Fabian Society.

The LRC was pitched into an election for which it was unprepared within a few months of its foundation. Its 15 candidates contained many who had fought their seats before, without the benefit of a national organisation and most increased their vote. Two seats were won, but Richard Bell in Derby owed his position to the decision of the Liberals to fight only one of the two seats there, and Keir Hardie in Merthyr owed his election to the fact that one of the sitting Liberal MPs supported the Boer War, to which the Welsh miners were opposed.

During the 1900–6 Parliament, the party was helped in consolidating its base in the Trade Union movement by the Taff Vale judgment, in which the Amalgamated Society of Railway Servants was ordered to compensate the Taff Vale Railway for losses caused by a strike. A change in the law was needed to reverse the Taff Vale judgment and the Labour party was the best vehicle to press for the change.

The LRC began to form local conferences of trade union branches in promising constituencies, the beginnings of local Labour parties. When a by-election was called in Liberal-held Clitheroe in June 1902, the LRC immediately announced that it would stand, and the strong support from the trade unions in the area meant that no Liberal candidate could be found; the seat was gained unopposed on 1 August.

The LRC won a by-election in Woolwich in March 1903, with candidate Will Crooks sponsored by the Woolwich Trades Council, and in July 1903, for the first time, an LRC candidate beat both the Conservatives and the Liberals in a three-cornered contest in a by-election in the Barnard Castle division of Durham. However, when the LRC candidate came third in the Norwich by-election of January 1904, Richard Bell MP sent a telegram of congratulation to the Liberal who had won the seat. Bell was subsequently deemed to have left the party.

The rise of the LRC and its ability to win seats had been noted by the Liberals. The Liberal Chief Whip, Herbert Gladstone, began secret negotiations with the LRC's secretary, Ramsay MacDonald, in 1903 when it seemed possible that the Unionist government would collapse over the tariff reform split. They eventually agreed an unofficial pact whereby LRC and Liberal candidates would not oppose each other. Only Keir Hardie was kept fully informed about the pact, and many local labour associations were keen to put up a candidate despite the pact (local Liberal associations were similarly eager to fight).

This early planning meant that the LRC was well prepared for the 1906 election, and eventually had 52 candidates in place. Only 18 had Liberal opposition, usually unofficial; Lancashire was the area with the most efficient co-operation. There was no co-operation at all in Scotland. The main issues at the election were those which divided the Liberals from the Unionists and on these, the LRC was strongly in favour of the Liberal approach; this explains why the Labour candidates found it easy to pick up the Liberal vote.

The 1906 election was a Liberal landslide, and this helped the LRC to win 29 seats. Where an LRC candidate was opposed by a Liberal, success was much rarer. The substantial number of members led to the Parliamentary party electing its own officers and whips when Parliament assembled after the election, and to go with this new formal status, the Labour Representation Committee adopted the name The **Labour Party**.

Labour Representation League

Highest vote: T. Burt (Morpeth, 1874) – 3,332 votes, 85.1%

Parliamentary elections won: 5

Number of candidacies: 23

After the formation of the Trades Union Congress in 1868, the initial enthusiasm of trade union leaders led to the creation in 1869 of the Labour Representation League. The League aimed to promote the registration of working men as voters irrespective of their opinions, but also to secure the return of working men to Parliament – and failing that, of others who were friendly to their aims.

Many of the leading trade unionists supported the League and it sponsored George Odger in a by-election at Southwark in 1870: Odger beat the Liberal candidate and nearly won the seat. The League then fought the London School Board elections of 1870; one candidate (Benjamin Lucraft, a cabinetmaker) was elected. The League attempted to form itself as a nationwide organisation, but it was always concentrated in London.

The League had a difficulty in relating to the **Liberal Party**. Its by-election candidates would sometimes withdraw if the Liberal candidate gave assurances of support. Some supporters insisted that the League must fight, even if it meant handing the seat to the Conservatives, in order to pressure the Liberals. In the 1874 general election, 13 candidates were sponsored by the League, of whom two (Thomas Burt and Alexander Macdonald) won seats. They were the first Labour members of Parliament.

However, by 1874 the Labour Representation League had come under total control of the trade unions, rather than becoming the political party it had been intended to be. The Conservative government lifted several restrictions on unions in the mid 1870s; ironically, this drove the League further into an alliance with the Liberals. A manifesto issued in 1875 formally stated that the League was allied to the Liberal Party.

At the general election of 1880, the League existed only on paper, and sponsored five candidates. It was wound up in 1881.

League of Empire Loyalists

Highest vote: Miss L. M. C. Greene (Lewisham North, 1957 (14/2)) – 1,487 votes, 4.0%
Parliamentary elections won: 0
Number of candidacies: 4

This group was the first substantial far right party established after the Second World War. It was formed in April 1954 by A. K. Chesterton (the cousin of author G. K. Chesterton) who had been a regional organiser for the **British Union of Fascists** as well as the author of the BUF official biography of Sir Oswald Mosley and several BUF pamphlets. The party grew out of a newspaper called *Candour* which Chesterton started in 1953, using money donated by R. K. Jeffery, a reclusive millionaire based in Chile.

Chesterton's control over the League was absolute and he ran it in the same way as he had advocated the BUF be run. The League did not organise its own rallies and meetings, but disrupted other groups' events. This disruption included blowing bugle horns at the Conservative Party conference, throwing sheep entrails at Jomo Kenyatta, and invading the 1958 Lambeth Conference of the Anglican communion. The League was a rearguard action against the end of Empire and regarded the Conservative governments of the 1950s as traitors. It had 3,000 members at its peak in 1958.

The League fought the Lewisham North by-election of February 1957 with a good candidate who won 4% of the vote. The death of the League's benefactor, R. K. Jeffery in 1961, and a loss of members starting in the late 1950s, hindered the party and eventually forced it to stop the publication of *Candour*. There were a number of defections of leading activists who were disillusioned with Chesterton's leadership and the League's extreme conservatism, and wished to join more radical organisations (see **British National Party** (1960-67), **British Movement**, **National Labour Party** (1958-60) and **Patriotic Party**).

In the 1964 election the party put forward three candidates (standing as 'Independent Loyalists') who polled very poorly, but showed Chesterton how easy it was to raise money while fighting elections. The success of the Labour Party in increasing its majority at the 1966 election after UDI in Rhodesia depressed Chesterton, and convinced him that the far-right groups must unite, and from the autumn of 1966 a working party eventually agreed terms for a merger with the British National Party. The merged party, which was formed on 7 February 1967, was the **National Front**.

Left Alliance

Address: 22 Montague Crescent, Leeds LS8 2RF

Website: http://www.leftalliance.org.uk

Number on Register: 27

Only vote: C. Hill (Leeds Central, 1999 (10/6)) – 258 votes, 2.0%

Parliamentary elections won: 0

Number of candidacies: 1

This Alliance was formed in 1999 in Leeds. The left-dominated Leeds North East Constituency Labour Party had been suspended by the **Labour Party** at the end of 1997, prompting several councillors and Labour Party activists to resign from that party and form the Left Alliance. The Alliance also includes members of the **Socialist Party**, **Socialist Workers' Party**, **Socialist Alliance** and the **Green Party**.

The Alliance fought the Leeds Central by-election of June 1999, and nominated a list of candidates in the Yorkshire and Humber region in the 1999 European Parliament elections. It fought four wards in the 1999 local elections, and 10 wards in 2000, all in the City of Leeds.

Liberal Conservative

Sir Robert Peel, the Conservative Prime Minister from 1841, became convinced by autumn 1845 that the Corn Laws (prohibiting the import of foreign corn below a certain price, to aid British farmers) must be repealed. When he announced this policy to the cabinet, it split and forced him to offer his resignation as Prime Minister. However, Lord John Russell was unable to form a **Liberal** administration, so Peel stayed in office and pushed repeal of the Corn Laws through Parliament.

The landed element in the **Conservative Party** was firmly in support of the Corn Laws because of their farming interests, and after repeal they defeated Peel in the House of Commons in June 1846. This convinced Peel to break with his party and support the incoming Liberal administration of Lord John Russell and its policy of free trade. Russell continued to be dependent on Peelite support after the 1847 election.

Peel attracted a large body of personal supporters though they were a minority of the Conservative Party. These followers were generally known as Peelites or as Liberal Conservatives. They remained in existence after Peel's death in a riding accident in 1850, with the Earl of Aberdeen acknowledged as the leader. However, the Peelites were always a fluid group and some returned to backing the Conservatives very quickly. Because of this it is impossible to state with any certainty who was or was not a Peelite candidate.

After Lord John Russell was defeated in the House of Commons and resigned in 1852, the Earl of Derby formed a Protectionist administration, but failed to gain a majority at the 1852 general election. The Earl of Aberdeen took over as the Peelite Prime Minister of a coalition of Liberals, Peelites and a Radical, and survived until 1855 when forced to resign over poor prosecution of the Crimean War.

Shortly after the 1859 general election, the remaining Peelites voted the minority Conservative government out of office and finally made the formal switch to the Liberal Party.

Liberal Democrats

Address: 4 Cowley Street, London SW1P 3NB

Email address: libdems@cix.co.uk

Website: http://www.libdems.org.uk

Number on Register: 4

Highest vote: D.D. Rendel (Newbury, 1993 (6/5)) – 37,590 votes, 65.1%

Parliamentary elections won: 74

Number of candidacies: 1,315

The Liberal Democrats were formed, originally under the name Social and Liberal Democrats, from a merger between the **Liberal Party** (*see* Liberal Party (1679–1988)) and the **Social Democratic Party** (*see* **Social Democratic Party** (1981–8)) in 1988. The proposal to merge the two parties, which had previously been co-operating in 'the **Alliance**', was controversial especially within the SDP, and public support for the centre parties had been damaged by the internal disputes after the 1987 election.

David Steel, who had led the Liberal Party from 1976, declared that he would not stand for the leadership of the merged party. The leadership election was fought between Alan Beith, regarded as more traditionally Liberal, and Paddy Ashdown, a former Marine Captain who had come to prominence as the constituency MP for Westland Helicopters during the 1986 scandal. The campaign was quite bitter with one Liberal MP making a savage attack on Ashdown which Beith was forced to repudiate; Ashdown eventually won by 41,401 votes to Beith's 16,202.

The party initially took the short title 'The Democrats', but this name failed to catch on with the public. Opinion poll ratings showed the party slipping and when candidates from the SLD and the continuing SDP both fought the Richmond by-election of February 1989, they split the vote and cost the centre a likely gain. Worse was to follow in the European Parliament elections of June 1989, when the party polled only 6% of the vote, with the Green Party outpolling it by more than two to one.

Members of the party who were originally in the Liberal Party strongly believed that the name of the party should incorporate the word 'Liberal', and at the party's conference in September 1989 a motion to consider a change in the short title from 'The Democrats' to 'Liberal Democrats' was passed; a postal ballot of party members in October 1989 agreed the change. In 1993 the party adopted this title as their full official name.

An electoral recovery began the following year. The local elections of 1990 were very bad for the Conservatives and the Liberal Democrats managed to gain seats. The party made its first by-election gain in October 1990, helped by a weak Conservative candidate and tactical voting. A further seat was won in March 1991 in the Ribble Valley, when the party used local discontent over the Community Charge ('Poll Tax').

A minor scandal over the revelation of an extra-marital affair of the Liberal Democrat leader Paddy Ashdown had little effect, except in gaining a sympathy vote when revealed shortly before the 1992 general election. The party went into the election still polling below the Alliance's 1987 share, but steadily increased in support through the campaign and ended with 18% of the vote and 20 seats – having made four gains in the south west of England.

After the election, Paddy Ashdown declared that he wished to avoid being trapped in the Westminster system, and spent most of the year visiting diverse communities and individuals throughout the country, eventually writing up his experiences in a book *Beyond Westminster*. At about this time he also took up the cause of British military involvement in the civil war in Bosnia/Herzegovina, on the side of the Bosnian government.

The increasing unpopularity of John Major's Conservative government helped the party to record two stunning by-election wins in summer 1993 in previously safe Conservative seats – Newbury and Christchurch; the party briefly overtook the Conservatives in the opinion polls as a result of the publicity. The party finally won seats in the European Parliament elections of 1994, in Cornwall and Plymouth West, and Somerset and Devon North. A likely further seat in Devon and East Plymouth was lost owing to confusion with a freak candidate running as a 'Literal Democrat'.

The election of Tony Blair as leader of the Labour Party caused the party difficulty even before it was finally confirmed. The party managed to win the Eastleigh by-election, held at the same time as the European Parliament elections, but Labour fought an active campaign; the party's candidate in the simultaneous Newham North East by-election joined the Labour Party on the eve of poll.

After Tony Blair was elected, the Labour Party's popularity increased, partly at the expense of the Liberal Democrats. A by-election in Littleborough and Saddleworth, a Conservative held seat where Liberal Democrats and Labour had both been close in past elections, provoked a bitter campaign, in which Labour attacked the Liberal Democrat candidate for supporting decriminalisation of cannabis and raising taxes. The Liberal Democrats won but the Labour vote had increased by much more.

In response to the new popularity of the Labour Party and that party's new definition of its aims, the Liberal Democrats formally abandoned their policy of declaring themselves equidistant from the Conservatives and Labour in September 1995. Despite this move, Conservative MP Emma Nicholson defected to the party just after Christmas 1995; she was followed by another, Peter Thurnham, in October 1996.

The party's campaigning message was revised in the run-up to the 1997 general election. The demand for proportional representation in Parliament was reduced in prominence, and the party concentrated on its pledges to increase the tax on cigarettes to provide funds for the National Health Service, and to increase the basic rate of income tax to fund education. The party concluded an agreement with the Labour Party on constitutional reform shortly before the election, providing for a referendum on proportional representation.

The party succeeded in electing 46 MPs in the 1997 election, though its vote share was slightly less than in 1992. Work with Labour in opposition paid off: in July 1997, the Labour government formed a cabinet committee containing Liberal Democrat leaders to discuss constitutional reform issues. The party had a morale-boosting by-election win in November 1997: the general election result in Winchester was successfully challenged by the defeated Conservative MP, forcing a rerun in which the Liberal Democrat majority increased from 2 to 21,556.

Liberal Democrat local election performance held up during the Labour government, with advances in the north of England where Labour lost ground in its heartlands. The party won control of Liverpool City Council in 1998 and of Sheffield in 1999. In the 1999 elections for the Scottish Parliament and National Assembly for Wales, the party slightly increased its vote; the Labour Party in Scotland formed a coalition with the Liberal Democrats called the 'Partnership of Principle'. Performance in the European Parliament elections, fought under proportional representation, was less inspiring.

These were the last elections fought by Paddy Ashdown who announced his retirement in January 1999. Charles Kennedy, the best-known of the leadership contenders won, pledging to continue co-operation with Labour; he narrowly beat Simon Hughes, who was opposed. Though Charles Kennedy was criticised for a laid-back leadership style, the party won the Romsey by-election in May 2000.

Liberal/Labour

Highest vote: T. Burt (Morpeth, 1874) – 3,332 votes, 85.1%.
Parliamentary elections won: 111
Number of candidacies: 212

In the late 1860s, two innovations spurred on the political development of Labour: in 1867 the second Reform Act enfranchised manual workers, and the trade union movement was able to be organised legally (the annual Trades Union Congress began in 1868). The pressure for Parliamentary representation led to local trade unions sponsoring individual Liberal candidates, who campaigned mainly on issues suggested by the trade union. They were known as Liberal/Labour, often abbreviated to 'Lib/Lab'.

Four such candidates appeared at the 1868 election, though all were unsuccessful. There were 15 candidates at the 1874 election and two were elected – Thomas Burt at Morpeth and Alexander Macdonald at Stafford, both of whom were sponsored by miners' unions. There were three MPs elected in 1880. These candidates were sponsored by the **Labour Representation League**, which had started as an attempt to form an independent party but gravitated towards alliance with the **Liberal Party**.

The third Reform Act in 1884 gave most heads of household the vote, and for the first time the majority of voters were working-class. This spurred more candidates and 11 were elected in 1885. However, it became apparent that the Liberal Party was generally unwilling to adopt working-class candidates, for this required them to fund most of the election expenses and might mean paying a salary (which Members of Parliament did not receive from public funds until 1911).

By 1888 pressure for setting up an independent organisation for Labour candidates led to the establishment of the **Scottish Parliamentary Labour Party**, which was joined by a Lib/Lab (R.B. Cunninghame Graham), a Liberal/**Crofter** and a straight Liberal MP, though they kept the Liberal whip. Cunninghame Graham fought the 1892 election as a SPLP candidate, and though unsuccessful, two Labour candidates were elected independently of the Liberal Party. One of these MPs, J. Keir Hardie, shortly afterwards formed the **Independent Labour Party**.

The 1899 Trades Union Congress carried a motion proposed by the Amalgamated Society of Railway Servants, to call a special congress to decide whether to launch a Labour party. This move was fiercely opposed by those unions who had succeeded in electing many Lib/Labs, particularly the miners whose local concentration of voters helped them. However, the motion passed and the Labour Representation Committee (*see* **Labour Party**) was established in February 1900; by 1903 it had the affiliation of trade unions representing 956,000 workers – nearly two thirds of the total trade union membership.

In the 1906 election, there were more LRC than Lib/Lab MPs and the

Labour Party quickly soaked up the remaining unions which had opposed affiliation. The Miners' Federation of Great Britain finally joined in 1909, and only nine Lib/Labs sat in the 1910–18 Parliament. At the end of the war, they finally made the decision either to join the Labour Party or to remain as Liberals.

Though the Lib/Labs appear in hindsight to be an intermediate stage in the political development of Labour, some of the Lib/Lab MPs became noted Parliamentary figures – Thomas Burt sat for Morpeth from 1874 until 1918, and William Abraham ('Mabon') was MP for Rhondda from 1885 to 1920.

Liberal National (1931–48)

Highest vote: Rt Hon. G. Lambert (South Molton, 1931) – 25,700 votes, 88.0%

Parliamentary elections won: 91

Number of candidacies: 155

The roots of the Liberal Nationals were in June 1931 when three right-wing **Liberal** MPs (Ernest Brown, Sir Robert Hutchison and Sir John Simon) resigned the Liberal whip, no longer being able to tolerate Liberal support for the minority Labour government. The single event which sparked their move was a speech by the Chancellor of the Exchequer Philip Snowden, attacking the Liberal Party, after what the three believed was a capitulation to the government on the 1931 Finance Bill. The three made it clear that they were seceding from the Liberal Party in Parliament but not in the country.

That August, when the Labour government resigned and a National coalition government was appointed, a number of Liberal members were appointed to government positions. Owing to the illness of Liberal leader David Lloyd George, he was left out of negotiations and found himself opposed to the coalition for which his party had signed up.

This was the opportunity for a realignment in the Liberal Party. Six members, most related to David Lloyd George, formed an independent group opposed to the National government; 25 acknowledged Deputy leader Sir Herbert Samuel as *de facto* leader, and 23 Liberal MPs, mostly right-wing, joined with the three earlier rebels under the leadership of Sir

John Simon, describing themselves as Liberal Nationals. The three different types of Liberal did not oppose each other at the 1931 general election and the Liberal Nationals were included on the official list of Liberal candidates. In general, Liberal Nationals at the 1931 election were not opposed by Conservatives, and 35 MPs were returned in 1931.

The formal Liberal National Council was established in July 1932. When, in September 1932, the Imperial Economic Conference in Ottawa adopted imperial preference tariffs (raising duties on imports from outside the empire), the Liberal members of the government resigned due to their longstanding commitment to free trade. The Liberal Nationals retained their posts, however, and when most Liberal MPs went on to the opposition benches in May 1933, the Liberal Nationals remained on the government side.

Distinction between the Liberals and Liberal Nationals at this time was difficult and several Liberal MPs remained on the government benches for some time before formally accepting the Liberal National whip. Both branches served in the coalition government during the Second World War, and in the 1945 election the two groups did not oppose each other (though Conservatives did oppose Liberals).

The winding-up of the National Labour Organisation, and generally weak state of the Conservative Party in Parliament, led to a formal proposal for a merger of the local organisations of the Conservatives and Liberal Nationals, as a result of which the Woolton–Teviot agreement was signed in May 1947. Next year, the party was renamed the National Liberal Party. *See* **National Liberal and Conservative**.

Liberal Party (1679–1988)

Highest vote: Rt Hon. D. Lloyd George (Carnarvon District, 1918) – 13,993 votes, 92.7%
Parliamentary elections won: 8,281
Number of candidacies: 18,683

The Liberal Party is the oldest in the nation. It was formed originally in 1679 as a loose group of Members of Parliament who wished to exclude the Duke of York from the succession to the throne on account of his being a Roman Catholic, a battle which the group lost (the Duke became

King James II). The group acquired the name 'Whig', a term originally applied to Scottish horse-thieves and non-conformists; their opponents were given the equally insulting name of 'Tories' (Irish cattle-rustlers). When James II was forced to flee the country, both groups combined to invite William and Mary of Orange to the throne in the 'Glorious Revolution' of 1688.

After the revolution, the Whigs were dominated by those noble families who were supportive of the monarchy; they held most government offices under William III and Queen Anne despite rarely having a majority in Parliament, partly because of skilled leadership. The Act of Union with Scotland was passed when the administration threatened an economic blockade, and with it came an assurance that the Crown would pass to the Electors of Hanover.

The Whigs lost office in 1711, but when George I became King in 1714 he dismissed the leading Tories and called a general election in which the influence of the Crown helped to buy a Whig majority. The government then increased the maximum life of a Parliament from three to seven years, further extending Whig influence.

A Whig split then occurred with Robert Walpole going into opposition. He won the backing of the Prince of Wales, and when the 'South Sea Bubble' financial scandal ruined the administration, Walpole returned to office in 1721 and became the first 'Prime Minister' – an undisputed leader of the government. Walpole insisted on remaining in the House of Commons, making that House the more important.

Walpole's government managed the economy well and was popular. He served for over twenty years, though he lost the support of George II (as the Prince of Wales had become) in 1737, when he compromised on the civil list. He was finally ousted because of war with Spain from 1739, which was conducted badly, but his eventual successor, Henry Pelham, was a close ally. George II initially distrusted Pelham and plotted to replace him, forcing a temporary resignation in February 1746.

Pelham's successor after his death in 1754 was his brother, the Duke of Newcastle. Newcastle had a brief and unhappy ministry which suffered from his incompetence in foreign affairs. The Duke of Devonshire was a figurehead Prime Minister for a few months in a government dominated by William Pitt the elder, but King George II's dislike for Pitt led to Pitt's dismissal when the

Duke of Cumberland (George II's son) refused to serve as Commander-in-Chief of the Army under him. Devonshire resigned in protest.

Newcastle returned to government after a two-month stalemate, and persuaded the King to accept Pitt back as Secretary of State (Southern Department); within the month Cumberland was defeated by the French army and dismissed by the King for making peace. However, Pitt and Newcastle were not united and Pitt's initiative to liberalise the habeas corpus law was blocked by Newcastle; Newcastle also attempted to conduct his own foreign policy, for which Pitt was responsible.

Throughout the mid eighteenth century the Whigs made up both the government and the opposition, with Tories suspected of disloyalty and Jacobite sympathies. George II consistently appointed ministers from the 'old Whig' faction. The accession of George III in 1760 destroyed this cliquish system. A general election automatically followed the accession of a new sovereign, and George III forbade Newcastle from using public funds to support his re-election. This led to diminished Parliamentary support for the government.

Newcastle resigned in May 1762 after a dispute with George III over the funding of war with Spain. The King appointed the Earl of Bute as the first Tory Prime Minister. Being thrust into opposition helped promote unity among the Whigs. Though Bute resigned as Prime Minister within a few months, his influence continued to guide the King.

George Grenville, and later the Marquess of Rockingham, formed short lasting ministries after Bute's resignation, though the King really wished to appoint Pitt with whom he had been friendly. King George III blamed Grenville for riots by weavers over silk imports, and Rockingham found it difficult to govern with Pitt in opposition. Pitt was eventually appointed Prime Minister in July 1766 after accepting George III's terms, but immediately made a mistake by accepting a peerage and destroying his base in the Commons.

The government of the Earl of Chatham, as Pitt became, was disrupted by his illness; he suffered a mental breakdown because of the pressure and defeats in the Commons. Eventually he was forced to resign while he recovered, to be succeeded by the rather lazy Duke of Grafton. Grafton made a blunder in insisting that the radical, John Wilkes, not be admitted to Parliament despite his repeated election in Middlesex.

Grafton resigned following dissension within his administration in January 1770 and the new Prime Minister, Lord North, was a moderate Tory. Some Whigs (such as Grafton) served in North's administration but the support of leading Whigs for American independence ensured that George III kept them out of office. It was not until the victory of the American colonies at Yorktown in October 1781 that Lord North's pleas to allow him to resign were accepted.

There were a series of short-lived governments after North, under the Marquess of Rockingham and the Earl of Shelburne, and then a Whig/Tory coalition between Charles James Fox and Lord North under the figurehead Duke of Portland. King George III finally dismissed this government when the India Bill, promoted by leading Whig Charles James Fox was defeated in the House of Lords. Despite the knowledge that he had no majority in the Commons the King appointed Tory William Pitt (son of the Earl of Chatham) as Prime Minister.

Pitt's government won an immediate general election and stayed in office until 1801. The Whigs suffered from the use of government funds and influence to help government supporters, and from the mutual hatred between Charles James Fox and George III. Fox became a supporter of the Prince of Wales, who shared his dislike for the King.

When a bout of madness struck the King in November 1788, Fox insisted that the Prince would have to become Regent, while Pitt defended the right of Parliament to choose. This was an about-turn for Fox, who had made his key policy the limit of royal power. The Tory majority fought hard to dilute the powers to be given to the Prince under the Regency, knowing that the Prince would dismiss Pitt and appoint Fox as Prime Minister. The Regency Bill had to be withdrawn when the King's recovery was reported in February 1789, and the Tory majority increased at the 1790 general election.

The chances of a new Whig government were damaged in July 1794 when the Duke of Portland and his supporters joined Pitt's administration. Portland disagreed with Fox's criticism of the government over the war with revolutionary France, which he considered despotic. The remainder under Fox consisted of fewer than 60 MPs, and was further diminished when many stopped attending Parliament. George III dismissed Fox from the Privy Council in 1798 for his support of the sovereignty of the people.

After Pitt's resignation in 1801, the Addington government proved much less effective and Fox, together with Lord Grenville, led the opposition. After the government's majority began to fall, Addington resigned. Lord Grenville wished to form a government with Fox, but the King's objection to Fox continued and Pitt was reappointed. Pitt was ill however and died in January 1806; the King was forced to appoint Grenville without any restrictions on the composition of the cabinet.

Fox was therefore appointed Foreign Secretary, in what was termed the 'Ministry of all the talents'. He served until his death in September. The Ministry did not survive long, because it attempted to remove legal disabilities on Catholics after the union with Ireland. The King was set against this policy and rejected Grenville's demands to speak freely in Parliament on the subject. Grenville therefore resigned.

The Duke of Portland, who had been figurehead Prime Minister for the Fox/North coalition 24 years previously, returned as a Whig Prime Minister leading a Tory government. Grenville became leader of the Opposition with Lord Howick (later Earl Grey) taking over the leadership of Fox's supporters. Portland's hands-off approach led to a feuding cabinet which lasted only two years, and on his departure Spencer Perceval was appointed as another Tory.

Perceval attempted to form a coalition with the Whigs, but his outspoken opposition to any Catholic relief was a condition that both Grenville and Grey were unwilling to accept, and there were too few cabinet places on offer. Whig opposition continued. Not even the final madness of the King and the consequent Regency helped the Whigs, for the Prince Regent was unable to agree the details of government appointments; Perceval stayed in office.

Perceval's assassination in 1812 led to a further invitation to leading Whigs to join the government, but just at that time Grenville and Grey split over Grenville's support for the continuation of war with Napoleon. The Whigs continued in opposition to the new Tory Prime Minister, the Earl of Liverpool, and the split became permanent in 1817 when Grenville supported suspension of *habeas corpus*, while Grey attacked it. Grenville then moved to the cross-benches and Grey led the small Opposition.

After the death of George III, the Prince Regent became King George IV. The new King's attempt to divorce his Queen, Caroline of Brunswick, via a Parliamentary 'Bill of Pains and Penalties' was strongly opposed by Earl Grey, making Grey a permanent enemy of the new King – though popular in the country which sympathised with the Queen.

Whigs remained in opposition until the retirement of the Earl of Liverpool through ill health in 1827. George Canning, the new Tory Prime Minister, had been a Whig who switched to the Tories after meeting William Pitt, and was not trusted by many other Tories, and they resigned when he was appointed. He agreed a pact with the Whig Lord Lansdowne, and formed a coalition government – though not including Grey.

Canning's government was continued by Viscount Goderich after Canning's death, though George IV vetoed the appointment of any more Whigs, and eventually divisions over appointments within the government forced it to resign. A Tory government under the Duke of Wellington took office. In 1830 the King died and was succeeded by his brother as William IV; despite his own Tory sympathies, William IV had no dislike of Grey.

Parliamentary reform had become an important campaign for Grey after unrest in the country. At the state opening of Parliament in November 1830 he made a speech demanding reform; when Wellington totally rejected any reform, the public was outraged and the government destabilised. It lost a vote in the Commons later that month and resigned; William IV sent for Grey.

Immediately Grey began work on a Bill to reform the electoral system, which passed Second Reading by only one vote. A defeat in Committee led Grey to the belief that the Bill would not pass, and he called a general election on the issue of reform. The 1831 general election was a landslide Whig victory and the second Reform Bill passed the Commons, only to be defeated in the Lords – prompting riots.

A third Reform Bill was again passed in the Commons, and Grey asked the King to create more Whig peers so that it would pass in the Lords. A hostile amendment to the bill was however passed and the King's refusal to create peers resulted in the resignation of the government. The Duke of Wellington was unable to form a government and Grey returned with a pledge to create peers. The threat was enough to force the Tories to back down and the Reform Act was passed.

As soon as possible, Grey called a general election on the new reformed system. It resulted in a landslide victory. The government pressed ahead with more reforms, including to the poor law system and to factory regulations. Lord Melbourne replaced Grey as Prime Minister in July 1834 but William IV dismissed him in December – giving in to his Tory sympathies. However, Sir Robert Peel was unable to win a new general election and after a series of defeats in Parliament, Melbourne returned in April 1835.

Melbourne was not a reformer like Grey but did much to help Queen Victoria when she succeeded to the throne in 1837 at the age of 18. He resigned when nearly defeated in May 1839 but the Queen's insistence on keeping all her Ladies of the Bedchamber (who were Whigs) was unacceptable to Conservative leader Sir Robert Peel. Melbourne remained Prime Minister until losing a vote of no confidence by 1 in May 1841.

It was about this time that opponents took to calling the Whigs 'Liberals' to imply laxity of morals. Increasingly this insult was adopted and proclaimed by its targets. Lord John Russell, who had led the party in the House of Commons since 1834, became the undisputed leader from 1845. Russell campaigned for the total repeal of the Corn Laws, introduced at the time of the Napoleonic wars to control imports. The Corn Laws kept food prices high and were unpopular; food was also running out in Ireland because of the failure of the potato crop.

Though Sir Robert Peel was personally in favour of the repeal of the Corn Laws, he was unable to convince the Conservative cabinet and resigned, but Russell was unable to form a government. Peel returned and repealed the Corn Laws with Liberal support, but the opposition of most Conservatives. When he was defeated on another issue in June 1846, Russell did take over as Prime Minister.

Russell was however unable to secure a stable majority. Peel and his supporters sometimes backed the government (*see* **Liberal Conservative**), but the Foreign Secretary Viscount Palmerston became a loose cannon who acted without Russell's authority. Palmerston was eventually sacked, but only to defeat the government on an amendment to the Militia Bill in February 1852. Russell considered this an issue of confidence and resigned.

A shortlived Conservative government proved not to be viable despite making gains in a general election and securing Palmerston's support. The Liberals combined with the Peelites and the Irish **Independent Opposition** to bring it down, and a coalition of Peelites and Liberals took office under Peel's successor the Earl of Aberdeen. Aberdeen still needed the support of the Irish members in order to win votes.

The government was to split over the issue of further reform of the electoral system. Viscount Palmerston was firmly opposed and nearly resigned when Lord John Russell produced another Reform Bill, but the outbreak of the Crimean War led to it being dropped. The war went badly and when a motion to establish a Committee of Inquiry was passed in January 1855, Aberdeen resigned.

Palmerston was appointed as Prime Minister and improved the war effort; peace was eventually agreed in February 1856. When defeated in Parliament in March 1857, Palmerston called a general election and won a large majority. However, this did not save him from a defeat in February 1858 over an amendment personally critical of him.

Taking advantage of the Liberal divisions, the Earl of Derby formed a minority Conservative government. Attempting to outflank the Liberals, Derby promoted a Reform Bill which Palmerston opposed and had defeated in the Commons. Derby however failed to win a majority at the general election and a motion of no confidence immediately afterwards brought Palmerston back. The Liberal Party as a formal entity was established on 6 June 1859 by 274 Liberal MPs as a fusion of the factions led by Palmerston, Lord John Russell and the Radical John Bright.

Palmerston was in office for six years in a government dominated by foreign affairs. It had to face the American Civil War, in which the government sympathised with the Confederacy – though it acceded to US pressure not to recognise their sovereignty. Palmerston's determination to make Britain a dominant world power was however damaged by his non-intervention in Schleswig-Holstein when Prussia and Austria invaded.

The House of Lords censured the government for this lack of action and Palmerston took the opportunity to call an election at which his majority was increased, but Palmerston died before Parliament met. Lord John Russell – now Earl Russell – returned as Prime Minister and promoted a new Reform Bill, but Palmerston's supporters combined with anti-reform Conservatives and voted against the Bill. Russell resigned and the Liberals went into opposition in 1866.

In office, the Conservatives under the Earl of Derby and Benjamin Disraeli embarked on reforms of their own. Derby said his electoral reform

Bill had 'dished the Whigs', but the first general election on a reformed system gave a large Liberal majority. William Gladstone, who had started his political career as a Tory but came over to the Liberal Party with the Peelites, became Prime Minister in December 1868.

Gladstone's first government disestablished the Church of Ireland and established free elementary education provided by the state – though Gladstone was forced to give the Church of England a privileged status, which offended the traditional nonconformist supporters of the party. A move to reform land ownership in Ireland faced opposition from the Radicals under John Bright who thought it not powerful enough. An attempt to reform trade union law in 1871 in fact banned unions from peaceful picketing and was greeted with resentment by the trade union movement.

All this division cost the party support. Gladstone called a snap election in January 1874, campaigning for the repeal of income tax which he hoped would unite the party. It failed and Disraeli's Conservatives won a majority; Gladstone was tired of trying to hold the party together and resigned as Liberal leader in January 1875.

The new leader was the Marquess of Hartington, who was not a well-known figure. Whenever Gladstone made a speech, Hartington would be overshadowed. The party took the advantage of a lengthy spell in opposition to reform its own constitution and the National Liberal Federation was formed in 1877 in Birmingham. This body organised the annual party Assemblies and organised local associations.

Gladstone sprang back on the political scene when he became horrified at Disraeli's alliance with the Ottoman Empire, which had perpetrated atrocities in suppressing a rebellion in Bulgaria. Gladstone travelled the country making speeches in what was known as the 'Midlothian campaign', because he moved to fight the Midlothian constituency.

A general election was called in spring 1880 and gave the Liberals a majority. Hartington was still the leader but Gladstone had effectively won the campaign, and when he equivocated on whether he would support a Hartington government, it became clear he would have to become Prime Minister. Radical hopes for the new government were not borne out by the composition of the cabinet and the many reforms of the first Gladstone government were not followed through.

Gladstone also had to cope with the problems of Ireland. From the early 1870s the Home Rule movement had come to dominate Irish politics and its adherents were being disruptive in Parliament. When the government promoted the Irish Land Bill, giving tenant farmers security, a large part of the party believed this was encouraging Parnell and the **Home Rulers**. The murder of the new Chief Secretary and Under-Secretary for Ireland in Phoenix Park by nationalists seemed to justify such fears.

The one reforming measure passed by the government was the 'third Reform Act' which gave practically all male heads of household the vote in boroughs. The government had been hoping the Conservatives would oppose this measure but they did not, instead insisting on a redistribution of seats at the same time to minimise any Liberal advantage.

In February 1885 the government suffered a catastrophic embarrassment when news was brought that General Gordon, who had been besieged in Khartoum, had been killed with all his forces only three days before relief arrived. Gladstone had been urged to send a relief mission quickly but had delayed. Soon after, the government lost a vote on an amendment to the budget when Conservatives joined with the Irish Nationalists, and resigned.

Instead of an immediate general election, the Marquess of Salisbury formed a minority Conservative government with the support of the Irish. After some reforming Acts he called a general election which resulted in a dead heat between Conservative and Irish **Nationalists** on one side, and Liberals on the other. During the campaign, the Liberals were divided by Joseph Chamberlain's radical programme of free education, land reform and redistributive taxation; Gladstone refused to enter the fight.

Gladstone then determined to win the Irish Nationalists over to him by leaking his own decision, arrived at some years before in secret, that Home Rule was the best policy for Ireland. Immediately the Conservatives were voted out of office and Gladstone returned (January 1886). However, Gladstone's Home Rule bill was opposed by Joseph Chamberlain who resigned from the cabinet; 93 Liberal MPs voted against it and the Bill was defeated by a majority of 30. Gladstone called a general election.

Chamberlain then split from the party entirely to form the **Liberal Unionists** who allied with the Conservatives. The Liberals lost an unprecedented number of seats in the general election, as the Conservative and Liberal Unionists won a landslide victory. An attempt to reunite the party failed in 1887. Though Chamberlain was a radical, most of the Liberal Unionists were economically conservative, and their permanent removal encouraged radicals to develop a programme of social reform for the party. Gladstone did not always agree with these policies.

The Liberals fought the 1892 general election with confidence, expecting a large majority. They won, but only narrowly. Gladstone, now in his early 80s, took office a fourth time, but his concentration was on the Irish question and a new Home Rule bill. Many Liberal MPs wished to promote domestic reforms but found Parliamentary time taken up by the Irish question.

Defection of the Liberal Unionists had hit the party particularly hard in the House of Lords, and the Lords rejected the Home Rule Bill when it was sent to them in September 1893. Gladstone considered whether to run a popular anti-Lords campaign but could find little support. The Lords meanwhile pressed on and severely amended most of the government's programme. Non-appearance of reforming measures led several radical MPs (including David Lloyd George) to resign the whip.

Gladstone finally had enough in January 1894 when forced to accept increased spending on the navy. The only Liberal acceptable to Queen Victoria was the Earl of Rosebery, which caused inevitable friction with the Commons leader Sir William Harcourt. Rosebery was lukewarm in his support for Home Rule but was enthusiastic about a campaign for Lords reform, having served in the Lords for his whole political career. He found it increasingly difficult to conduct government from the Lords.

In June 1895, a minor censure vote was passed on the Secretary of State for War. Rosebery, weary of office, resigned; the incoming Unionist government called a general election which it won with a majority of over 150. Rosebery swiftly resigned the party leadership as well, giving way to an uneasy collaboration between Sir William Harcourt and the Earl of Kimberley. Harcourt's failure to criticise the government's disastrous attempt to seize power in the Transvaal forced him out in early 1899.

It was the growing confrontation in South Africa which dominated politics for the next four years. The Liberals divided between those such as Herbert Asquith and Sir Edward Grey who were fully supportive of the war, and the radicals such as David Lloyd George who objected to imperialism and to the immense cost of the war. This section was nicknamed 'pro-Boers' by their opponents. Sir Henry Campbell-Bannerman, the Liberal leader, at first did not take sides, but eventually opposed the war because of atrocities, including concentration camps, which the British forces were committing.

Taking advantage of the Liberal split, the Unionists called a general election in October 1900 when the war seemed to be nearly won; in a time of patriotism, the Liberals were defeated even more heavily than in 1895. The war turned out to last nearly two years longer, and Campbell-Bannerman's denunciation of the 'methods of barbarism' by which it was conducted struck a chord. Some Unionist legislation promoted unity among Liberals, such as the Education Act 1902 which abolished School Boards and put local authorities in charge (a move opposed by nonconformists).

The rise of the **Labour Representation Committee** led the party to decide to seek an electoral pact. The party was worried that opposing Labour would divide the vote in some of the Liberal heartlands where local Liberal associations were very weak. A secret pact was agreed with Ramsay MacDonald in 1903 that the parties would not oppose each other. Though the infancy of Labour makes it seem that the pact helped it more, it probably secured more Liberal seats in London.

Meanwhile, the Unionists gifted a popular campaign to their opponents with Chamberlain's campaign for tariff reform. Free trade had long been a Liberal principle and several Unionist MPs joined the Liberals in 1904 over the issue. It proved easy for the Liberals to win public support by pointing to the likely rise in food prices under tariff reform. Many candidates took a loaf of bread on to the hustings to provide a visual prop.

The Unionist government was growing very weak and divided by 1905 and took advantage of a brief inter-Liberal dispute over Home Rule to resign, hoping to stir up trouble in the allocation of government offices. However there was no trouble and the government immediately called a general election at which the pact with Labour held.

Even the most optimistic Liberals were surprised at their success in the January 1906 election. The outgoing Unionist Prime Minister was defeated, and the overall majority (counting Labour and Nationalists) was 356. The new government used this majority to good effect in passing some far-reaching legislation. The total would have been more had the

Lords not blocked some bills entirely; Lords' obstructiveness was tempered only by the likely popularity of the legislation.

Campbell-Bannerman, an old man, resigned in April 1908 due to ill health and was succeeded by Asquith, a much younger figure and more in sympathy with radical hopes. Asquith's budget, compiled shortly before he became Prime Minister, provided the first state old age pensions, and to follow him as Chancellor he appointed the most effective radical of all, David Lloyd George.

Lloyd George's 1909 budget was introduced as a 'war budget' to wage war on poverty, and became known as the People's Budget. It raised taxes and imposed some new ones, in order to pay for the pension and for more Dreadnoughts for the Navy. Lloyd George's rhetoric in support of his budget was at times quite violent, especially in a speech at Limehouse at the end of July. After lengthy consideration in the Commons, the budget went to the Lords which rejected it completely amid accusations that the budget was socialist.

Asquith denounced the Lords' actions as unconstitutional and called a general election to obtain popular approval for action against the Lords. With Labour and Nationalist support, the Liberals won and the budget passed. Eventually the Liberals decided on three reforms: the removal of any Lords input into the budget process, any Bill to become law if passed by the Commons in three successive years, and the maximum length of Parliaments to be reduced to five years.

The Unionists agreed to attend a Constitutional Conference to work out a compromise, but this conference ended in stalemate. Asquith then went to the country again to get a mandate for their suggested reforms, and won the December 1910 general election with almost exactly the same result. The Parliament Act 1911, embodying the reforms, passed under threat of creation of enough Liberal peers to see it through.

This was a reform too limited for many Liberals and Asquith faced criticism for alleged conservatism. He was also opposed to the growing women's suffrage campaign and there was pressure to reduce the defence estimates. The removal of the Lords' veto allowed Home Rule for Ireland to pass but Asquith permitted Ulster to opt out. The Lloyd George-inspired disestablishment of the Church in Wales also passed using the Parliament Act.

The sudden outbreak of the Great War in August 1914 forced the postponement of Home Rule in Ireland. Not all the cabinet supported the decision to declare war and two members resigned; there was much opposition in Parliament also, though Foreign Secretary Sir Edward Grey persuaded the majority. There was no great criticism of the war effort until the western front became bogged down.

Through 1915 there were demands for a coalition government because of a claimed shortage of shells; eventually Asquith agreed and invited the Conservatives and Labour to join a coalition in May 1915. This decision was opposed by the grassroots membership who did not see why the party should accept Conservative input. Their suspicion seemed borne out when the Conservatives forced the government to introduce conscription, and a budget introduced a series of import tariffs.

Asquith's position became extremely difficult through 1916 as Lloyd George increased in popularity, while objections to Asquith from the Conservatives mounted. Criticism of the government in *The Times* in December 1916 forced Asquith to resign, and Lloyd George took over. The division between Asquith and Lloyd George became formal, and each side established its own organisation and whips; Asquith Liberals effectively went into opposition though Asquith was reluctant to lead them.

In May 1918 a former War Office civil servant, Frederick Maurice, claimed that the government had been lying about the number of troops in France. Asquith demanded a Select Committee and the Commons vote on this motion provided the guide for both parts of the party as to which side each individual Liberal MP was on. By this time the war was going well and preparations were being made for a general election.

After the Armistice, an election was swiftly called, but Lloyd George had decided that it should be fought by the Coalition as a single unit. Asquith's supporters inevitably faced Conservative opposition, but Lloyd George's did not. The result was a landslide victory for the **Coalition**; only 36 non-Coalition Liberals were returned. Asquith was not among them. Many other senior ex-ministers were also defeated.

Nominally the party was one, but in practice it had separated into two, and this fact was recognised in March 1920, when the non-Coalition Liberals began to pass resolutions opposing the coalition. In May, the National Liberal Federation expelled Lloyd George and his supporters.

This had the effect of destroying the local Liberal associations in many constituencies, and Liberal strength in local government began to dissolve. The more radical figures throughout the party were beginning to defect to Labour.

Asquith returned to the Commons in a by-election in Paisley in February 1920. He again provided little actual leadership. At the 1922 general election, there were 334 Liberal candidates (Lloyd George's supporters fighting as National Liberals). The party won only 62 seats – losing some that it had held in 1918 to Labour, and only winning where it could get a straight fight with a Conservative.

A reunion of the Liberal party was clearly needed: the two wings had concentrated on attacking each other in the general election. The initiative was taken by Lloyd George but Asquith reacted coolly as Lloyd George's group continued voting with the Conservatives in Parliament. Reunification only happened when the Conservative government intervened by calling an election on whether to introduce a protective tariff – the same policy which had caused the 1906 Liberal landslide.

When reunification happened it was agreed very easily, with Asquith retaining the leadership. There was remarkably little tension in the 1923 general election campaign, and the Liberal Party polled just under 30% of the vote to win 159 seats. This gave the party the balance of power and the crucial decision about whether to support Labour into office.

Asquith decided to put Labour in, on the grounds that the conditions were safe: the Liberals would remain in control. All but 10 Liberal MPs supported a Labour motion of no confidence when Parliament met, and the party provided general support for the Labour government when it was established. This alignment lost the party the backing of those moderate conservatives who had supported the party in order to keep Labour out. Accusations that the party was in league with Labour could not be defeated by pointing to separate Liberal policy because the party did not have a settled policy.

The Liberal vote slumped in by-elections in 1924. The party did not have the funds to pay for an election campaign, but it had to threaten one in order to control the Labour government. It was still unprepared when the Labour government declared that a Liberal motion to establish a Select Committee on the withdrawn prosecution of a communist newspaper was an issue of confidence. The Conservatives backed the motion and therefore brought down the government.

This resulted in a new general election at which the party performed disastrously. By bringing down Labour it had lost any moderate Labour support and it still did not have any distinct policy. Liberals won only 18% of the vote, and returned only 40 MPs. Asquith lost again and went to the Lords; Lloyd George became leader in the Commons.

Lloyd George decided that the party needed policies to campaign for, and used his own campaign fund to pay for the research. When, towards the end of the Parliament, a series of radical proposals were produced, the party's vote began to pick up and it won several by-elections. The new policies included government planning for industry, and vast public works to conquer unemployment.

The party entered the 1929 election confident that it would bounce back after the defeat of 1924: it was united, had policies which were winning support, and had a degree of momentum. The results were another disappointment. Though the party improved its vote, it was only by 6%; it won only 59 seats. It had lost 17 seats to Labour and now had virtually none in industrial areas. Immediately after the election the party lost another when William Jowitt, MP for Preston, accepted a job in the Labour government and switched parties.

Unlike 1924 the Liberals did not have to vote for Labour in order for the government to survive, and therefore had slightly more freedom. The party did have the same basic problem – whether to be moderate Conservatives or moderate Labour supporters. It was left unresolved and the party often found its MPs split three ways. The right-wing of the Liberals became especially disenchanted and three MPs resigned the whip in June 1931.

The situation was transformed by the resignation of the Labour government and the formation of the National coalition. Lloyd George was seriously ill and unable to participate in the negotiations, but the Deputy leader of the party, Sir Herbert Samuel, became Home Secretary and the Marquess of Reading Foreign Secretary. The move to enter the coalition was popular with Liberal members, but the party still split, with the more right-wing MPs forming the **Liberal Nationals**.

Liberals were strongly opposed to the decision to call a general election.

Two of Lloyd George's family resigned from junior government posts. Despite the National government including Conservatives and Liberals, most Liberals (though not Liberal Nationals) were opposed by Conservatives. Because the coalition had its own policy, the Liberal policy was suppressed. 32 'Samuelite' Liberals and 4 of Lloyd George's family were elected; Lloyd George and his family became opposition MPs when Parliament met.

It soon became apparent that the Liberals were at the whim of a Conservative-dominated government. They voted against the government's Import Duties Bill in March 1932, using an 'agreement to differ' to keep their ministers. Grassroots members grew increasingly hostile to the government and began nominating anti-government candidates in by-elections.

Conservative pressure for tariff reform led the government to call an Imperial Economic Conference. When some progress towards tariff reform was made at this conference, the Liberal ministers resigned. They remained officially government supporters though in practice they increasingly opposed government legislation. A motion was passed at the Liberal Assembly in May 1933 calling on the party to go into opposition, and at the beginning of the new session in Parliament in November 1933, the party took its place on the opposition benches. In doing so it shed several MPs who became Liberal Nationals.

This move did little to staunch the loss of support. Many more went over to Labour. The 1935 election was yet another disaster, with only 161 candidates who polled less than 7% of the vote. 21 Liberal MPs were returned. Sir Herbert Samuel was defeated and Sir Archibald Sinclair became leader.

The Liberals rejected the idea of the 'United Front' to oppose fascism in 1937 because of their opposition to nationalisation. Yet there was no great Liberal challenge independent of other parties. Liberals were defined in terms of their reaction to the other parties' proposals. Most Liberals opposed the Munich agreement in 1938, but the party was evenly divided on the introduction of conscription in early 1939.

At the outbreak of war, the Liberal Party supported the war effort. Liberal ministers were appointed to the coalition government when Churchill replaced Chamberlain, though not in the War Cabinet. Some grassroots members were against the electoral truce and when by-elections occurred in 1943, two senior Liberals resigned from the party so that they could fight the Conservatives – both lost, but only narrowly. Meanwhile the most left-wing Liberal MP, Sir Richard Acland, formed a new left-wing party and resigned (see **Common Wealth**).

The Liberals did have an input on public policy when the academic, Sir William Beveridge, conducted an inquiry into Social Insurance, and recommended a comprehensive welfare state. Beveridge later became a Liberal MP. His plan was a central element of the Liberal campaign in the 1945 general election, in which he was the Chairman of the Campaign Committee. The party polled only 9% and returned 12 MPs – though one was to all intents and purposes a Conservative.

A full reconstruction of the party was begun and a proper fundraising effort was arranged, which gave the party sufficient means to fight a large number of seats at the 1950 general election. A great effort was put into the Liberal campaign at this election, though without full confidence: the party arranged insurance at Lloyds in case of a large number of lost deposits.

It was a wise precaution as 319 deposits were lost. The problems of the Liberals were not merely in organisation but in finding a role; only nine MPs now remained. Worse, the new Parliament was not going to be a long one and the party had exhausted its resources. The 1951 election saw only 109 Liberal candidates and six MPs; even this was an exaggerated picture as five of the MPs had not had Conservative opposition. Winston Churchill, who had been a Liberal in 1904–23, offered the party some positions in his new government. Clement Davies, who found himself the Liberal leader, refused.

The first sign that Liberal fortunes were changing came in a by-election four days before Christmas 1954 in Inverness. No Liberal had fought the seat in 1951 but in the by-election the Conservative majority over Liberal was only 1,300. A few months later came the 1955 general election. Though the party found only one more candidate than in 1951, and held the same number of seats, the election did mark the first occasion since 1929 that the party's vote had risen.

Further by-elections were offering hope to the party. Frank Owen, who had been MP for Hereford, did well in a by-election there in February

1956. At almost the same time, the party found a new leader who could inspire potential voters – Jo Grimond, MP for Orkney and Shetland. At about this time there was a further series of defections, with Dingle Foot and Lady Megan Lloyd George joining Labour. The irrelevance of the Liberals in the 1950s was shown by Robert McKenzie's book *British Political Parties*, which dealt with Conservative and Labour over 650 pages, and relegated the Liberals to a two-page appendix.

After the death of a Liberal MP, the party lost the Carmarthen seat to Lady Megan Lloyd George, standing for Labour in February 1957, but the run of good by-election results began again. At Rochdale in February 1958 the party came into second place in a seat not previously fought since 1950, helped by a well-known candidate (TV reporter Ludovic Kennedy).

In March 1958, the party won a seat from the Conservatives at Torrington in Devon. The majority was small (219 votes) but it was the first time the party had gained a seat since March 1929. This result got the party noticed and helped raise morale, and money. The 1959 general election saw 216 Liberal candidates who polled 6%, but the party won the same number of seats: North Devon was won but Torrington was lost.

More good by-election results began in 1961 at Paisley, but the result which produced a sensation was at Orpington in March 1962. The Liberal candidate, Eric Lubbock, turned a Conservative majority of 14,760 into a Liberal one of 7,855 in one of the biggest turnovers of votes since the war. One opinion poll immediately after showed the Liberals as the most popular party in the country, but the boost proved temporary.

At the 1964 general election the Liberals called on voters to 'Think for Yourself' and vote for a classless non-ideological progressive party. The Liberal vote increased to 11% and the party gained three seats overall on 1959. Another seat was gained in a by-election in March 1965 though this was the only good performance. The gain of three seats at the 1966 general election was more a product of Conservative unpopularity than increasing Liberal strength.

Jo Grimond resigned the leadership in 1967, to be succeeded by Jeremy Thorpe a dynamic campaigner and the son of a former Conservative MP. He had to manage the growing problem of the Young Liberals who were advocating policies more closely associated with the far left – unilateralism and withdrawal from NATO, support for strikes and workers' control of industry. Thorpe condemned the Young Liberals when they damaged cricket grounds in a protest over a South African tour and the then Chairman was voted out of office.

Liberal performance was unimpressive in the late 1960s with one exception – a by-election in Birmingham Ladywood in June 1969. This Labour stronghold was won by a technique known as 'community politics' whereby the party took up local grievances over deficiencies in government services. Ladywood was however an exceptional area.

The 1970 general election put the party back a long way when its vote fell and half the seats were lost. Jeremy Thorpe was nearly beaten in North Devon. However, the party bounced back very quickly by capitalising on voter discontent with both the Conservative and Labour Parties. A local government revival became obvious in 1971–2.

The first by-election to be won was Rochdale in October 1972. Though exceptional (because the Liberal candidate, Cyril Smith, had previously been involved in the local Labour Party), it began a wave of enthusiasm for the party. Two months later came an unexpected win on a huge turnover of votes at Sutton and Cheam. Three more seats were won before the end of the Parliament, giving a sense of momentum.

Liberal policy attempted to offer a radical vision which would attract those disillusioned by both Conservative and Labour. The party supported a permanent incomes policy to tackle inflation, with a surcharge on corporation tax for companies who broke it, and an integration of the tax and benefits system so that all citizens had a guaranteed minimum income.

A general election occurred early but the party was prepared and fielded more candidates than it had ever managed before. The party polled 6,000,000 votes, nearly 20% of the total, but found that this mass vote won only 14 seats. Liberals had long called for a proportional voting system but the 1974 results made this more of a crusade.

The result of the 1974 election was a hung Parliament. Conservative Prime Minister Edward Heath tried to negotiate a pact with Jeremy Thorpe, but without success. Thorpe was personally prepared to agree but other Liberal MPs were not and the party's grassroots members would have been outraged. Despite this opposition, the Liberal Party did campaign for a 'Government of National Unity' in June 1974; Labour would not have participated in such a government.

Moderate Labour MP Christopher Mayhew defected to the Liberals in July 1974. Having proved they could attract a mass vote, the party was confident in the October 1974 general election, called by the minority Labour government in an attempt to get a majority. The party's 'Government of National Unity' call was taken up by the Conservatives, which made it more difficult to attract Labour votes.

Virtually every seat was contested for the first time, which made the eventual result look better than it actually was: a fall in the vote to 18.8% in Great Britain. One seat was gained but two were lost. There was no new string of by-election successes in the new Parliament, and in fact the party began to lose deposits.

Just at this time, a bizarre scandal broke when Liberal leader Jeremy Thorpe was accused of a plot to murder a man claiming to have had an affair with him. Thorpe denied the allegations but they hit the party's vote and eventually he resigned. Jo Grimond took over as acting leader while the party organised a contest in which, for the first time in a major UK political party, the individual members decided the outcome. David Steel, an experienced campaigner and former TV reporter, won the contest at the young age of 37.

The Labour government lost its majority in Parliament in 1976 and after a defeat in 1977, a vote of no confidence loomed. James Callaghan knew that the Liberals did not want an early election, and arranged a deal with David Steel whereby Liberal MPs backed Labour in return for a role in examining government legislation before it was introduced, and government support for direct elections for the European Parliament – with a free vote on a proportional electoral system.

This vote went against, which cast doubt on whether the party membership would support the pact. The party's vote suffered as voters identified it with the unpopular Labour government, and its candidates were sometimes beaten by the **National Front**. The 'Lib-Lab pact' lapsed at the end of July 1978, allowing Steel to declare that autumn that the party would vote against Labour in a motion of confidence because an election was needed.

The House of Commons voted no confidence in the government on 28 March 1979 with Liberal support. The next day the party won a by-election in Liverpool Edge Hill from Labour. This gave the party a boost at the outset of the general election campaign, but it was clear the party was still in difficulties. The manifesto put constitutional reform at its head, specifically proportional representation and devolution.

The Liberal vote fell to 14% and the party lost three seats – including that of Jeremy Thorpe, who was about to go on trial for conspiracy to murder (he was eventually found not guilty). This was not a good result but it was not the disaster that would have happened if a 1977 general election had been called. The party seemed to do better in elections during a Conservative government and the party's vote increased in several by-elections.

Having long hoped for a reorganisation of British politics, the Liberals found that the left-wing trend in the Labour Party produced one in 1981. The mass breakaway from Labour to form the **Social Democratic Party** led the party immediately to negotiate a common policy statement, and from the time of the Liberal Assembly in September 1981, a formal alliance. See **Alliance** for the history of their co-operation.

The Alliance was very popular, though there was some discontent among Liberals (Cyril Smith, MP for Rochdale, memorably called for the SDP to be strangled at birth). By-election success followed quickly in Croydon North West, traditionally a Conservative-Labour marginal, though the candidate was a traditional Liberal.

Unfortunately for the SDP and Liberals the bandwagon stalled at the time of the Falklands War, the novelty of the Alliance having worn off. The party could still be helped by dissention within other parties, as in the Bermondsey by-election of February 1983. Here, a new left-wing Labour candidate was denounced by the Labour Party leader but eventually stood amid an unprecedented tabloid campaign; the Liberal candidate managed to identify himself as the main challenger and won with a vote increased by over 50% since the 1979 general election.

At the 1983 election, only 17 Liberals and six SDP MPs were elected despite the Alliance winning a popular vote of 26%. This numerical superiority of Liberal MPs in the Alliance fuelled those within the party who were sceptical about collaboration and suspected David Steel of being far more happy in the company of the SDP than of Liberals. It looked as if the Liberals were providing most of the support for the Alliance, but the SDP most of policies.

Liberal discontent surfaced over defence policy where the party was traditionally anti-nuclear. Opposition to unilateralism had been one of the main factors in prompting the formation of the SDP, and when the Alliance declared in favour of retaining nuclear weapons as part of an Anglo-French unit, the Liberal Assembly rejected the policy.

Two by-elections were gained by Liberals during the 1983 Parliament, at Brecon and Radnor in July 1985 (where Mrs Thatcher's personality was the central issue of the campaign) and Ryedale in May 1986. Tragedy struck the party when David Penhaligon, Liberal MP for Truro, was killed in a car accident in December 1986. An effective campaigner, Penhaligon was regarded as the likely next leader of the party.

At the 1987 general election, the Labour Party was rejuvenated and not so extreme as before, which damaged the Allliance in its aspiration to replace Labour as the main opposition to the Conservatives, but helped the party appeal for tactical votes to be given to it where Labour still had no chance. Though there does not seem to have been much response from Labour voters, the party did well in rural Scotland through tactical voting from **Scottish National Party** supporters. This was one reason why, despite a fall in the vote, the party retained 17 seats – gaining and losing three at the same time.

Immediately after the election David Steel began moves to merge the Liberals and the SDP. Unlike the SDP, the vast majority of Liberals supported the merger which was agreed early in 1988, the merged party eventually becoming the **Liberal Democrats**. A small minority of members disagreed and have continued to organise under the original name (see **Liberal Party** (1988–)).

Liberal Party (1988–)

Address: Pine Grove Centre, 1A Pine Grove, Southport PR9 9AQ

Email address: secgen@libparty.demon.co.uk

Website: http://www.libparty.demon.co.uk

Number on Register: 28

Highest vote: S. R. Radford (West Derby) – 4,037 votes, 9.6%

Parliamentary elections won: 0

Number of candidacies: 138

When the Liberal Party voted to merge with the **Social Democratic Party** in 1988, a minority of members (of which the most prominent was Michael Meadowcroft, a former Liberal MP) decided that the Liberal Party had left them and re-established it. They claim the official inheritance of the party, but found organisation difficult in their early years.

The party fought 73 seats in the 1992 election but only Michael Meadowcroft saved his deposit. In no seat did the party outpoll the **Liberal Democrats**. The party has built up local bases in Slough, Peterborough, Exeter and especially Liverpool. In the 1997 election, Cllr Steve Radford unexpectedly won second place in Liverpool West Derby, and the party saved one other deposit.

The party advocates a radical and distinctly left-wing policy including unilateral nuclear disarmament, opposition to nuclear power, more community ownership of industry, and devolution of health care to local control. As purists for proportional representation by the single transferable vote, they opposed the recommendations of the Jenkins Committee for a mixed member system in October 1998.

Liberal Unionist Party

Highest vote: J.T. Middlemore (Birmingham, North, 1910(D)) – 5,189 votes, 84.0%.

William Gladstone, Liberal Prime Minister in the early 1880s, slowly became convinced that the right answer to the 'Irish question' (i.e. the constitutional settlement in Ireland) was the establishment of a devolved Irish Parliament. He worked behind the scenes to make this option acceptable to the whole of his party, but in June 1885, before this was complete, his government was defeated on the budget by a combination of **Conservatives** and Irish **Nationalists**. The general election that followed gave Conservatives and Irish Nationalists combined the same number of seats as the Liberals, and in an attempt to form a government, Gladstone announced his conversion to Home Rule.

Gladstone's decision forced the Conservatives to declare their opposition and when he presented his Home Rule Bill in June 1886, it was defeated with 93 Liberal MPs voting against it alongside the Conservatives. Gladstone called another election, but as it was clear that he would not be deposed as Liberal leader, those Liberals opposed to Home Rule fought the election as Liberal Unionists. Their acknowledged leader was Joseph Chamberlain, who had been President of the Board of Trade in 1882–85.

The Liberal Unionists returned approximately 77 MPs in 1886, who supported the **Conservative** government throughout the Parliament; they pressured the Conservatives to adopt measures of social reform but did not themselves take office. In the 1892 election, the Gladstone Liberals and Irish Nationalists secured a majority and Gladstone was able to get a Home Rule Bill through the Commons, though it was defeated in the Lords (which forced Gladstone's resignation). The Lords then blocked all government legislation and when a minor censure vote in the Commons was passed, the government resigned and another election was called; the Conservatives and Liberal Unionists won and jointly formed an administration.

The Unionist coalition held through the 1900 election, which it again won with a big majority. The Unionists split over the campaign for tariff reform from 1903. Though the leader of the campaign for tariff reform was Joseph Chamberlain, the campaign gathered support from both wings of the coalition. In the 1906 and two 1910 elections it was becoming increasingly difficult to distinguish which candidates were Liberal Unionists and which Conservatives, and movement between the wings was common. In 1912 the two formally merged and created the **Conservative and Unionist Party**.

Liberal Unionism was always strongest around Birmingham where there was a great deal of personal loyalty to the Chamberlain family.

Liverpool Protestant Party

Highest vote: the Rev. H. D. Longbottom (Liverpool Kirkdale, 1931) – 7,834 votes, 24.7%
Parliamentary elections won: 0
Number of candidacies: 3

The Orange movement in Liverpool usually supported Conservative candidates, but in 1903 a separate political party was formed by the Rev. George Wise. The party concentrated on municipal elections (in which it saw some success), though between 1931 and 1945 it fought the Liverpool

Kirkdale Parliamentary seat. The religious basis for the party appears to have been the Protestant Reformers' Church. The party was strongly anti-socialist.

The party had councillors until the late 1960s and was still contesting local elections in the early 1970s, but had disbanded by 1979.

Mebyon Kernow (the Party for Cornwall)

Address: c/o Dick Cole, Shell Cottage, Moorland Road, Indian Queens, St Columb, Cornwall TR9 6HN

Email address: dickcole@tinyworld.co.uk

Web site: http://www.mebyon.kernow.eu.org

Number on Register: 29

Highest vote: C. F. Murley (Cornwall, St. Ives, 1979) – 1,662 votes, 4.0%

Parliamentary elections won: 0

Number of candidacies: 9

Mebyon Kernow [Sons of Cornwall] was formed on 6th January 1951 at Redruth by twenty Cornish people who had previously been active in a cultural organisation called Tyr ha Tavas [Land and Language]. Initially it was a non-political organisation seeking to preserve the Celtic character of Cornwall and pressing for more self-government, with membership open to all people including members of other political parties. By the 1960s a majority of Cornish MPs were members. The party first fought a Parliamentary election in 1970, though only one candidate appeared then, and in both 1974 elections.

In the mid 1970s the party became more political and declared itself in favour of full self-government for Cornwall, though by constitutional means. The party suffered the defection of Dr James Whetter (who had been its candidate in Truro in 1974) to form the **Cornish Nationalist Party** in 1975, but continued to grow stronger.

In the 1979 election the party fought three of the five Cornish Parliamentary seats, 19 wards in district councils, and the European Parliament constituency of Cornwall and Plymouth. The European Parliament election was a considerable success for the party, as Richard Jenkin (now the party's life President) polled nearly 6% of the vote.

After fighting two seats in the 1983 general election, the mid 1980s to the mid 1990s was a lean period for the party as it concentrated on local and European Parliamentary elections. In several areas it managed to win seats and has held some of them ever since. Dr Loveday Jenkin fought the 1994 European Parliament elections, and in the 1997 general election, the party fought four out of the five Cornish seats. It did not oppose Liberal Democrat candidate Andrew George in St Ives who supported the party's aims.

Mebyon Kernow was central in setting up the cross-party Cornish Constitutional Convention in July 1997. Since the general election the party has adopted the English alternative 'the Party for Cornwall' and it has expanded its local base, naming Parliamentary candidates early before the election. The party has links with **Plaid Cymru** and now campaigns for self-government with a legislative Cornish Assembly with at least the same powers as the Scottish Parliament.

Mebyon Kernow's leader since 1997 has been Dick Cole.

Militant Labour

See **Socialist Party**.

Moderate Labour Party

Highest vote: B. Marshall (Nottinghamshire Mansfield, 1987) – 1,580 votes, 3.0%.
Parliamentary elections won: 0
Number of candidacies: 2

The Moderate Labour Party was launched in late January 1987 in Mansfield by a group of former Labour councillors together with some defectors from the Liberal/SDP **Alliance** and independents. The launch was attended by the wife of the Labour MP for Mansfield, Don Concannon. Concannon was retiring at the subsequent general election but was dismayed by the choice of a left-wing Labour candidate to succeed him; however, he did not announce publicly which way he was going to vote.

The party was linked to the Union of Democratic Miners which had been formed by miners in the Nottinghamshire coalfield who remained at work during the strike by the National Union of Mineworkers in 1984–5. The party fought local elections in Mansfield in 1987 without success. It then fought Mansfield and one other constituency at the 1987 general election where left-wing Labour candidates had been selected. In Mansfield their candidate nearly split the Labour vote enough to allow the Conservative to win. Nothing has been heard of them since and it appears that the party was wound up soon after 1987.

Monster Raving Loony Party

See **Official Monster Raving Loony Party**.

Mudiad Gweriniaethol Cymru [Welsh Republican Movement]

Only vote: I. Davies (Glamorganshire, Ogmore, 1950) - 631 votes, 1.3%.

Parliamentary elections won: 0

Number of candidacies: 1

The Welsh Republican Movement was formed as a result of a split in **Plaid Cymru** in 1949. Its members, who were mostly from industrial South Wales, wished the Blaid to take up more social issues rather than the Welsh language and culture which had dominated its campaigns. The Movement began with about 50 members but gathered others who had left the **Independent Labour Party** or the **Labour Party**.

The Welsh Republican Movement campaigned for the establishment of a Welsh socialist republic, using its English-language journal *Welsh Republican*. The party rejected all royalist institutions and was firmly nation-alistic, in contrast to Plaid Cymru's policy of self-government (members were fined for burning the Union flag).

The movement fought Ogmore in 1950, but then turned away from electoral politics. Its members returned to Plaid Cymru or the Labour Party.

National

Highest vote: I.M. Horobin (Southwark Central, 1931) – 15,913 votes, 65.3%

Parliamentary elections won: 11

Number of candidacies: 22

At the end of July 1931, the government's Economy Committee issued a warning that the next year's budget was £120 million in deficit. The Labour government set out to try to find the money either in loans from other countries or in spending cuts, but on 23 August the cabinet rejected a proposed cut in unemployment benefit and the government decided to resign. Labour ministers expected Prime Minister Ramsay MacDonald to lead them in opposition, but instead he returned from Buckingham Palace inviting them to join him in a 'National Government' which would include Conservatives and Liberals. Only a few ministers accepted.

The National Government was formed and governed until the formation of the wartime coalition in May 1940. The whole of the **Conservative Party** took part, and the whole of the **Liberal Party** (with the exception of David Lloyd George and his family) was involved from formation until 1933. In addition a group of **Liberal Nationals** was formed, who continued to support the National government throughout, and Labour supporters were organised in the **National Labour Organisation**.

There were also many non-party supporters of the National government and when fighting elections, they offered themselves as National candidates. In the 1931 and 1935 elections, four such candidates were nominated. Sir John Anderson also used the 'National' label when he won Combined Scottish Universities in 1938 after the death of Ramsay MacDonald.

'National' candidacies were used during the Second World War in order to find seats in Parliament for non-party men appointed to the coalition government, of whom the most famous was the former BBC Director-General Sir John Reith (elected unopposed for Southampton in February 1940). These MPs were effectively conservatives who did not wish to join the Conservative Party. Several accepted office in the 'Caretaker' Conservative ministry formed by Winston Churchill after the dissolution of the coalition, and none of the ten 'National' candidates in the 1945 election was opposed by a Conservative. The two National members who survived the 1945 election retired at the end of the Parliament.

National Association of Discharged Sailors and Soldiers

Highest vote: R. H. Barker (Yorkshire (WR), Sowerby, 1918) − 8,287 votes, 37.0%

Parliamentary elections won: 1

Number of candidacies: 4

This association had its origins in a meeting at Blackburn in September 1916. It was at first linked to the labour and trade union movement, though this connection began to disappear during 1918. In the 1918 election, local branches of the NADSS in three Leeds constituencies joined with the other ex-servicemen's organisations (the **National Federation of Discharged and Demobilised Sailors and Soldiers** and the Comrades of the Great War) to nominate a candidate.

In addition, in the Sowerby constituency the local branch of the NADSS was persuaded by local Conservatives to nominate a candidate. In Sowerby the sitting MP was a Liberal whom the **Coalition** whips intended to be a Coalition Liberal candidate; they therefore ordered the local Conservatives not to oppose him and issued a coupon to him, which he repudiated. Deciding that the seat had to be fought by a conservative, the local party noticed that a leading local NADSS member was a strong conservative and persuaded the NADSS to nominate him.

This candidate, Major Robert Barker, won the seat. In making his maiden speech he declared 'I am here as the soldiers' candidate' though his attitude in Parliament was generally to support the Coalition. He retired at the end of the Parliament.

National Democratic and Labour Party (1915–21)

Highest vote: C.B. Stanton (Merthyr Tydfil, Aberdare, 1918) – 22,824 votes, 78.6%
Parliamentary elections won: 9
Number of candidacies: 28

This party was a product of efforts to bolster support for the Great War among the labour movement. It was originally formed as the Socialist National Defence Committee in April 1915, being a breakaway from the **British Socialist Party**. In November 1915, the by-election in Merthyr Tydfil caused by the death of Keir Hardie saw a straight fight between a pro-war and an anti-war Labour candidate: the latter had the official endorsement, the former won the seat.

The Socialist National Defence Committee was renamed the British Workers' National League in March 1916. A year later, the National was dropped, and in May 1918 it adopted the name National Democratic and Labour Party though it was known popularly as the National Democratic Party. The party fought 26 seats in the 1918 election, when it portrayed itself as a patriotic working-class party in support of the **Coalition** government; 18 candidates of the party received Coupons, and nine were elected (all of whom had received the Coupon).

The party provided a haven for those Labour ministers in the Coalition who did not agree with the **Labour Party**'s decision to sever all connections with it, and its acknowledged leader was George Barnes (though he in fact fought as a Coalition Labour candidate). The Coalition tended to put NDP candidates up in strong Labour areas and against anti-war Labour MPs.

In December 1921 the party reverted to the name British Workers' League and ceased electoral activity, becoming a patriotic propaganda group. Sitting NDP MPs sought re-election at the 1922 election as **National Liberals.** In late 1925 the British Workers' League became known as the Empire Citizens' League, but within a few years, it had been disbanded.

Support for the NDP was strongest among the trade unions which supported the war, notably the dockers in the Liverpool area, the

Musicians' Union, parts of the Textile workers, and parts of the Miners' Federation of Great Britain.

National Democratic Party (1915–21)

See **National Democratic and Labour Party** (1915–21).

National Democratic Party (1963–?)

Highest vote: E. N. I. Bray (Southampton Itchen, 1970) – 9,581 votes, 21.9%
Parliamentary elections won: 0
Number of candidacies: 8

This far-right party was formed by Dr David Brown in January 1963, with its main base of membership coming from the Racial Preservation Society of which Dr Brown was Chairman. The party held discussions about a merger with the **British National Party** (*see* British National Party (1960–7)) in 1966 but these foundered because of Brown's insistence on his leadership and on the banning of the (national socialistic) **Greater Britain Movement** from membership.

Dr Brown fought his home seat of Ipswich at each election from 1964 until February 1974, unusually for a minor party candidate increasing his vote at the first three. In the 1970 election the party fought three other seats and saved its deposit in Southampton Itchen where the Speaker was not being opposed by other major parties.

With the rise of the **National Front** as the biggest far-right party, the National Democratic Party lost most of its members. A merger with the National Front was discussed from late 1970 (which led to the party's decision not to field a candidate in the Marylebone by-election), but the National Front Directorate refused to allow a mandate for discussions. Later the party established a series of fora between itself and activists within the **Conservative Party**, the Monday Club and the Anglo-Rhodesia Society.

No more candidates were nominated after 1974 and it appears that the party was wound up in the mid 1970s.

National Democratic Party
[Northern Ireland] (1964–70)

Highest vote: Dr A. McDonnell (Antrim North, 1970) – 4,312 votes, 7.4%

Parliamentary elections won: 0

Number of candidacies: 2

The National Democratic Party was an early sign of discontent among the nationalist community with the existing Irish **Nationalist** party. It derived from the National Unity group within the Irish Nationalists which was formed in 1959. In 1964, National Unity called a conference in Belfast which formed a 'National Political Front', which brought together Nationalist MPs and grassroots members who wanted a more democratic movement. The National Political Front fell apart later that year when the group failed to contest the Fermanagh and South Tyrone constituency in the 1964 general election, a plan favoured by the Nationalist MPs.

After the dissolution of the National Political Front, its grassroots members formed the National Democratic Party. Unlike the Irish Nationalist movement it had a card-carrying membership and a formal organisation. It fought four seats in the 1965 Stormont elections, winning one unopposed. The party was generally left-wing although not tied to any specific ideology; its strongest organisation was in Belfast.

In the 1969 Stormont elections, the party fought seven seats but was unsuccessful. It fought two seats in the 1970 UK general election. When the **Social Democratic and Labour Party** was formed, the National Democratic Party greeted it with enthusiasm, and after its conference in October 1970 the central party organisation was disbanded. Several prominent SDLP members, such as Eddie McGrady and Dr Alasdair McDonnell, were formerly in the National Democratic Party.

National Democratic Party (1995–)

Address: BCM NATDEMS, London WC1N 3XX

Email address: natdems@swnd.freeserve.co.uk

Website: http://www.natdems.org.uk

Number on Register: 82

Highest vote: S. Edwards (West Bromwich West, 1997) – 4,181 votes, 11.4%

Parliamentary elections won: 0

Number of candidacies: 26

This party name was adopted in 1995 by the **National Front** (see National Front Flag Group (1985–95)), though the group refers to itself in all its literature as 'National Democrats'. The National Democrats were formed from the majority faction in the National Front, as an attempt to modernise and make more respectable the face of far-right politics.

The party fought 23 seats at the 1997 general election, saving its deposit in the Speaker's seat where there was no major party opposition. The leader of the National Democrats is Ian Anderson. The party has been forced to register with the Registrar of Political Parties as 'National Democratic Resistance' because the words 'National' and 'Democrat' are reserved and may not be claimed exclusively.

National Farmers' Union

Address: 164 Shaftesbury Avenue, London WC2H 8HL

Email address: NFU@nfu.org.uk

Website: http://www.nfu.org.uk

Highest vote: H.J.Winn (Yorkshire (ER), Howdenshire, 1922) – 7,021 votes, 39.5%.

Parliamentary elections won: 0

Number of candidacies: 10

The NFU was originally formed by a group of Lincolnshire farmers on 2 September 1904 as the Lincolnshire Farmers' Union. One member, Colin Campbell, pledged to organise the union on a nationwide basis; it was launched as the National Farmers' Union of England and Wales on 10

December 1908. The next year, the NFU established a Central Parliamentary Committee and a Parliamentary Fund to contest elections.

The first candidate of the NFU was nominated by a local branch for a by-election in Ross, Herefordshire, in May 1918. The candidate had failed to secure the official Conservative nomination, and polled a third of the vote in a straight fight. In 1918 the national offices of the NFU were moved from Lincoln to London. In the 1918 general election, the NFU nominated six candidates, one of whom was also sponsored by the **National Party** (*see* National Party (1917–21)). Four saved their deposits.

The NFU successfully lobbied the **Coalition** government in 1920 to enforce a minimum price for home-grown wheat and compensate growers who had been underpaid. In the 1922 election the party sponsored three candidates of its own who saved their deposits but did not get elected, along with four Conservatives, all of whom were elected. This seems to have led the NFU to change strategy to sponsoring Conservative candidates: it sponsored four in 1923, three of whom were successful, and two each in 1924 and 1935 who were all successful. NFU-sponsored MPs were frequently independent-minded on agricultural issues though they were expected to obey the Conservative whip.

From 1945, the NFU adopted a policy of strict neutrality between the political parties and ceased supporting individual candidates.

National Federation of Discharged and Demobilised Sailors and Soldiers

Highest vote: A. W. Brooksbank (Liverpool Everton, 1918) – 5,779 votes, 47.6%

Parliamentary elections won: 0

Number of candidacies: 32

This Federation was formed in April 1917 at a meeting sponsored by James Hogge, a left-wing Liberal MP, at the National Liberal Club. The Federation's aim of promoting the welfare of ex-servicemen was specifically directed towards the Military Service (Review of Exceptions) Bill which aimed to reclassify those invalided out of the army so that they were again engaged in the services, a bill which caused immense anxiety and proved to be implemented incompetently.

The Federation intended to contest elections and first fought a by-election in Liverpool in June 1917, polling a quarter of the vote. In the 1918 general election, the National Executive Committee approved five candidatures, and local branches sponsored a further 26 (of which three were jointly nominated with the **National Association of Discharged Sailors and Soldiers** and the Comrades of the Great War). Several of these candidates polled substantial votes, although none of them was elected.

James Hogge resigned as President in January 1919. The Federation had initially banned officers from membership, except if they were commissioned from the ranks, and though this ban was lifted in June 1919 the anti-officer feeling persisted for many years. The removal of the ban helped ease moves towards a merger of the ex-servicemen's organisations, though the Federation's membership was initially hostile.

Earl Haig, the former wartime commander, helped to persuade members of the Federation to accept merger with the National Association of Discharged Sailors and Soldiers, and the Comrades of the Great War. The British Legion was eventually selected as the name of the new organisation at a Unity conference on 14–15 May 1921.

National Fellowship

Only vote: E.D. Martell (Bristol South East, 1963 (20/8)) – 4,834 votes, 19.0%
Parliamentary elections won: 0
Number of candidacies: 1

The National Fellowship was formed by Edward Martell on 1 January 1962, being his second attempt to establish a political party (*see* **People's League for the Defence of Freedom**). The aim of the party was 'to restore Britain's greatness by leading a return to sane government and a national morality based upon Christian principles'. The party was part of the Freedom group which included the People's League for the Defence of Freedom.

Martell promoted the National Fellowship through his newspaper *The New Daily*, which he sponsored through the Free Press Society and the

Anti-Socialist Front. The New Daily was fervently patriotic and promoted free enterprise while attacking trade unions. Martell had a non-unionised workforce which he paid more than other printing workers.

The National Fellowship entered the electoral arena in August 1963. Tony Benn, having renounced his peerage, was fighting a by-election in Bristol South East, which the Conservatives were boycotting. Edward Martell, declaring that the socialist candidate had to be opposed, offered himself as a 'National Fellowship Conservative' candidate (he produced a Conservative Party membership card when challenged). He attempted, only half successfully, to inherit the Conservative vote in the constituency.

The National Fellowship was effectively superseded in 1966 when Martell formed the **National Party** (*see* National Party (1966)).

National Front (1967–90)

Highest vote: M. G. A. Webster (West Bromwich, 1973(24/5)) – 4,789 votes, 16.0%

Parliamentary elections won: 0

Number of candidacies: 550

The National Front was originally formed in 1967, the result of a merger of the **League of Empire Loyalists** and the **British National Party** (see British National Party (1960–67)). The **Greater Britain Movement** joined the next year. National Front politics were far-right, nationalistic, and racist. The party advocated forced repatriation of all black and Asian immigrants, and any white spouse of an immigrant. Economically it was protectionist, though opposed to big business and the financial system (favouring instead small businesses and co-operatives).

The NF vote grew in the years after its formation, helped by factors such as Enoch Powell's 'Rivers of Blood' speech and the admission of the Ugandan Asians. In 1974 John Kingsley Read managed to oust John Tyndall as Chairman, but when the courts reversed his attempt to expel Tyndall, Read and his populist supporters left and formed the **National Party** (*see* National Party of the United Kingdom (1975–)). The departure of these members and the simultaneous problems in the **British Movement** led to the NF's Martin Webster organising a recruiting campaign among the paramilitary element which had supported the BM.

The strongest time for the NF was in the mid 1970s; the party polled over 100,000 votes in London at the 1977 Greater London Council elections. The Labour Party even devoted a party political broadcast to campaigning against the NF in December 1977. The rise of the far right prompted the extreme left to establish groups such as the Anti-Nazi League which confronted the Front's marches and rallies. The NF nominated more than 300 candidates in the 1979 general election but did badly as the conventional right soaked up much of its support.

When blame for the poor performance fell on John Tyndall, he was removed from all positions and eventually left to form the New National Front, which later became the **British National Party** (*see* British National Party (1982–)). Martin Webster, the national organiser for the NF, became the effective leader of the National Front for the early 1980s. There was another breakaway in 1981 when the Constitutional Movement, a group opposed to the Nazi associations of NF leaders, left the Front and eventually became the **Nationalist Party**.

The NF dismissed its national organiser, Martin Webster, on 10 December 1983, as a result of attacks made on him by John Tyndall and opposition from members who supported the theories of Otto Strasser (see **National Front Flag Group** (1985–95)), and he was expelled in February 1984.

The NF found a cause célèbre in 1984–5 when one of its youth leaders, Patrick Harrington, enrolled at the Polytechnic of North London. Anti-fascist students campaigned against his admission and the lecturers of the college refused to teach him, but after the NF won a court case, the college authorities were forced to accept him and he was taught on his own for several terms.

Soon after the Harrington case, the NF suffered a split. Supporters of Strasserite policies formed the National Front Flag Group, taking its name from the party newspaper *The Flag*. The remaining members expelled the Flag Group in 1986, and when the Flag Group contested elections as 'National Front' they described themselves as 'Official National Front'. In the 1987 election they nominated no candidates, citing the increase in the deposit required from all candidates as the reason, though electoral unpopularity was probably the key factor. At the Vauxhall by-election of June 1989, both the Official NF and the Flag Group nominated candidates.

The Official NF itself split in 1990, with one part renouncing fascism (*see* **Third Way**), and another retreating from public view. (*see* **Third Position**).

National Front (1995–)

Address: PO Box 279, Beckenham BR3 4ZT.

Email address: nfpress14@mailcity.com

Website: http://www.natfront.com

Number on Register: 150

Highest vote: G.S. Hutchins (Hillingdon, Hayes and Harlington, 1997) - 504 votes, 1.2%.

Parliamentary elections won: 0

Number of candidacies: 8

This group was formed by those members of the National Front (*see* **National Front Flag Group**) who disagreed with the proposal to reform as the National Democrats. It has organised marches against asylum seekers in Margate, Kent (at which 300 marched) and annually protests against the march to commemorate 'Bloody Sunday', hoping to expose it as a front for the IRA. The Front fought six seats at the 1997 election, and two by-elections since, and is led by Stephen Rowland.

National Front Constitution Movement

See **Nationalist Party**.

National Front Flag Group (1985–95)

Highest vote: G.E. Cartwright (Dudley East, 1992) – 675 votes, 1.2%

Parliamentary elections won: 0

Number of candidacies: 18

The Flag Group was formed within the **National Front** (see National Front (1967–90)) in April 1985 by Ian Anderson. Anderson was the leader of a faction within the National Front who partly derived their politics from those of Otto Strasser, who had been the main opposition to Adolf Hitler within the German Nazi Party. The Strasserites advocated a corporate state to break up financial power, to which the Flag Group added historical British concepts such as a return to agrarianism.

The main National Front expelled members of the Flag Group in 1986, officially recognising the split in the Front. The Flag Group fought Bristol East in the 1987 election. Shortly afterwards it resumed using the name National Front, and fought the Vauxhall by-election of June 1989, being outpolled by the Official National Front.

The Flag Group fought the Mid Staffordshire by-election of 1990 and 14 seats in the 1992 general election. On 20 May 1995, the National Front National Directorate passed a resolution to reform as the **National Democratic Party** (*see* National Democratic Party (1995–)). A minority group did not go along with the decision to seek to make the party more mainstream and respectable – see **National Front (1995–)**.

National Health Service Supporters Party

Only vote: Dr C. A. Abell (Mid Staffordshire, 1990 (22/3)) – 102 votes, 0.2%

Parliamentary elections won: 0

Number of candidacies: 1

The NHS Supporters Party is the archetype of the failed single-issue party. It was established by Dr Christopher Tiarks, who had stood as an 'Independent – Protect the Health Service' candidate and polled a fairly healthy 847 votes in the June 1989 Vale of Glamorgan by-election. The party was formed in December 1989, announced plans to fight 50 seats (the fifty-first through to the hundredth most marginal Conservative seats) at the next general election. However, at the first by-election fought by the party (Mid Staffordshire in March 1990), the party's candidate came ninth in the poll and barely made three figures. The party swiftly lost momentum and disappeared entirely.

National Independence Party

Highest vote: M. P. Coney (Haringey, Tottenham, 1974(F)) – 1,373 votes, 4.4%

Parliamentary elections won: 0

Number of candidacies: 3

This party was formed in the late 1960s by John Davis, a former associate of Andrew Fountaine (a leading member of the **National Front**). It was run on similar lines to the National Front, with many fewer members, but received a boost in July 1972 due to the defection of John O'Brien and his supporters. O'Brien, who was Chairman of the National Front from February 1971, was disturbed by evidence he had gathered of links between the National Front and neo-Nazi organisations and decided to copy the NF membership list and circulate them with an invitation to join the NIP.

The NIP fought two by-elections in December 1972 in Sutton and Cheam and Uxbridge, but polled poorly and was easily beaten by the National Front in Uxbridge where both stood. The NIP then concentrated on north London. It managed to obtain over 20% in Tottenham in the 1973 Greater London Council elections, and in the February 1974 general election, managed to outpoll the National Front in the same constituency. The same candidate was elected to Haringey Borough Council in May 1974 but this was the last time the NIP fought an election and the party was wound up in about 1975.

Some NIP members may have gone on to join the **National Party** (*see* National Party of the United Kingdom (1975–)), but most joined the **Conservative Party**.

National Labour Organisation (1931–45)

Highest vote: S. T. Rosbotham (Lancashire, Ormskirk, 1931) – 30,368 votes, 75.0%

Parliamentary elections won: 25

Number of candidacies: 47

National Labour was the organisation which was set up by the supporters of the National government who had come from the Labour Party. In the

August 1931 political crisis, Labour Prime Minister Ramsay MacDonald failed to get cabinet agreement to cut unemployment benefit and the government felt forced to resign. King George V asked MacDonald to form a National government, and a conference of the three party leaders on 24 August 1931 produced a workable agreement.

MacDonald's invitation to his Labour colleagues to join this government met with few acceptances. Chancellor of the Exchequer Philip Snowden and Dominions Secretary Jimmy Thomas remained in post, but only 15 of 260 Labour MPs joined. The National Labour Organisation was hurriedly established shortly afterwards. Those who had joined National Labour were expelled from the Labour Party at its 1931 conference.

In October 1931 Macdonald called a general election. National Labour issued a separate election manifesto, but as in 1918, the National coalition decided which party should nominate candidates in which seats. National Labour nominated 20 candidates, though several found they were splitting the National vote and had to stand down. National Labour did well to see 13 members elected, given the scratch organisation. Despite National Labour's very small proportion of the National vote, Ramsay MacDonald retained the premiership until he was forced through ill health to resign. In the 1935 general election, National Labour again nominated 20 candidates, of whom 8 were elected.

National Labour was popularly perceived as a contradiction in terms; the government was essentially a Conservative one and the Labour movement was uniformly against it. Nevertheless, when Ramsay MacDonald's son Malcolm MacDonald won a by-election in 1936 and received a congratulatory letter rejoicing in the defeat of Labour, he replied angrily that Labour had won the by-election.

During the Second World War, the Labour Party entered the coalition government, and this left National Labour looking more and more like a Conservative 'stooge' party. On 14 June 1945, at the start of the 1945 general election campaign, the National Labour Organisation was wound up. The four sitting National Labour MPs who wished to seek re-election fought that election as either **National** candidates or Independents. Only one survived, later becoming a Conservative MP.

National Labour Party (1958–60)

Only vote: W. Webster (St Pancras North, 1959) – 1,685 votes, 4.1%

Parliamentary elections won: 0

Number of candidacies: 1

The National Labour Party was formed in May 1958 by John Bean and John Tyndall, who had left the **League of Empire Loyalists** the previous year. They were opposed to the League's extreme conservatism and wished to establish a national socialist political party. The party published *Combat*, edited by John Tyndall, and was anti-Semitic and racist.

One of the party's leading members was Andrew Fountaine, a Norfolk farmer who had been expelled from the Conservative Party for making an anti-Semitic speech. He was an independent candidate in a by-election in South West Norfolk in March 1959 and the party helped with his publicity; he polled 2.6%. He became President of the party shortly after the by-election.

John Bean had a local base in Southall and concentrated his efforts in publicising the party there, though he opted out of fighting elections. In the 1959 general election, the party fought St Pancras North, polling 4% of the vote. The **Labour Party** successfully obtained an injunction in late 1959 to prevent the party using the name 'Labour', prompting the party to reorganise.

In 1960, the party merged with the White Defence League formed in 1956 by Colin Jordan as another breakaway from the League of Empire Loyalists; the merged party was the **British National Party** (see British National Party (1960–67)).

National Labour Party (1981–4?)

Highest vote: J. W. King (Kent, Ashford, 1983) – 456 votes, 1.0%

Parliamentary elections won: 0

Number of candidacies: 2

This party was a result of the split from the **National Front** in the early 1980s by John King, who had been National Front candidate for

Rochester in 1979, and his wife Ann. They were the party's only Parliamentary candidates. The party took a Powellite stance on immigration but also advocated economic reforms: it accepted the need for some state ownership of industry, and called for a revised form of taxation so that 10% income tax was payable on gross wages, with a 5% stamp to pay for health care, pensions and benefits.

The party fought the Bermondsey by-election of 1983, and Ashford in the 1983 general election, but then ceased organisation.

National Liberal (1920–3)

Highest vote: G. Lloyd George (Pembrokeshire, 1922) – 21,569 votes, 69.0%

Parliamentary elections won: 53

Number of candidacies: 151

When David Lloyd George became Prime Minister in 1916, his predecessor Herbert Asquith went into opposition with his supporters among the Liberal MPs. In the 1918 general election, Lloyd George's adherents in the party received 'coupons' and supported the **Coalition**. In May 1920, the National Liberal Federation (under the control of Asquith) expelled Lloyd George and his supporters, forcing them to set up their own organisation.

In many constituencies, particularly in Wales and Scotland, the local Liberal association supported Lloyd George. Most sitting Coalition Liberal MPs were able to carry the support of their local association. In many other constituencies, Lloyd George Liberal associations were formed in 1920–22. The organisation was strongest in London; elsewhere many associations fell apart shortly after their first meeting.

Lloyd George had to find other means of financial support for his party since the Asquith group had retained the central party funds. He turned to the sale of honours, and a sliding scale of charges for OBEs, knighthoods, baronetcies and peerages was discreetly circulated. A number of honours were indeed sold, and some of the recipients proved to be of dubious probity. When the honours sale was exposed in June 1922, angering the Conservatives, Lloyd George was forced to set up a Royal Commission.

In September 1922, the country was brought to the verge of a needless war with Turkey, further enraging the Conservatives. At a meeting in the Carlton Club on 19 October the Conservatives broke off the Coalition and Lloyd George resigned. The incoming Prime Minister, Andrew Bonar Law, called a general election at which Lloyd George's Liberals fought as National Liberals.

Given the recent coalition, the **Conservatives** and National Liberals were fairly close and there was much pressure for them to co-operate, though no national agreement was reached. In 159 seats, there were local agreements; in 55 seats both parties nominated candidates, and in the remaining 389 seats there was neither conflict nor co-operation. In all, 151 National Liberals were nominated, and 53 seats were won.

During the 1922 Parliament, the National Liberal MPs tended to support the Conservative government, though Lloyd George tried to push for a Liberal reunification. On 13 November 1923, Prime Minister Stanley Baldwin announced a new election on the issue of tariff reform, to which Liberals had always been opposed. A hasty reunification of the **Liberal Party** was agreed and the Liberals fought the 1923 election as one party.

National Liberal and Conservative
(joint candidate of the Conservative Party and the National Liberal Organisation, 1947–68)

Highest vote: J. A. L. Duncan (Angus and Kincardineshire, 1955) – 23,967 votes, 72.7%

Parliamentary elections won: 88

Number of candidacies: 235

On 9 May 1947, the **Liberal National's** and the **Conservative Party** signed the Woolton–Teviot agreement by which they agreed to amalgamate their constituency associations. The following year, the name of the Liberal Nationals was changed to the National Liberal Organisation. The National Liberals continued to exist as a Parliamentary party, in full alliance with the Conservatives, and they did not issue separate election manifestos.

Candidates sponsored by the National Liberal Organisation actually used varying descriptions in their own campaigns. The most common was 'National Liberal and Conservative', though some candidates used 'Liberal and Conservative'. The potential for confusion with Liberal candidates led to an exchange of correspondence between Winston Churchill and the Liberal Party during the early stages of the 1950 general election.

At the 1950 election, the National Liberals sponsored 55 candidates, 9% of the total number of Conservatives, and 16 members were returned. The activity of the National Liberals decreased as time went on, taking a particularly steep dive during the early 1960s. After the 1966 general election the Parliamentary party had only three members; the party relinquished its office at the House of Commons. The National Liberal Organisation was wound up in 1968 and incorporated into the Conservative Party.

Several significant Conservative personalities came originally from the National Liberals, such as Michael Heseltine and John Nott. The most prominent National Liberal and Conservative member was Dr Charles Hill, formerly known as the 'Radio Doctor'.

National Party (1917–21)

Highest vote: H.P. Croft (Bournemouth, 1918) - 14,048 votes, 66.3%
Parliamentary elections won: 2
Number of candidacies: 29

The National Party was formed by **Conservative** MP Henry Page Croft in the late summer of 1917, and immediately attracted the support of seven other Conservative MPs. The party advocated a reactionary right-wing policy in contrast to the Conservative Party's acquiescence to the Liberals in the **Coalition**, including protectionist tariffs, raising the age of conscription to 50, closing all German owned businesses, and air raids against Germany.

Several of the National Party's MPs rejoined the Conservatives within a few months and this factor combined with deaths and retirements to leave only two incumbents fighting the 1918 general election – Page Croft and Sir Robert Cooper. Neither of them was opposed by the Conservatives, though most of the party's 24 other candidates were nominated against Conservative opposition. During the campaign, the party made a special point of attacking the sale of honours. Page Croft and Cooper were re-elected but the party won no other seats.

The party went on to fight two by-elections in 1919 and 1920, but after poor results it ceased to organise as a political party in April 1921. Page Croft and Cooper both rejoined the Conservative Party and the organisation was renamed the National Constitutional Association.

National Party (1966–68)

Only vote: D. C. T. Bennett (Warwickshire, Nuneaton, 1967(9/3)) – 517 votes, 1.2%
Parliamentary elections won: 0
Number of candidacies: 1

This party was formed by Edward Martell in September 1966, as a continuation of the **National Fellowship** which he had formed in 1962. The party was anti-socialist and pro-free trade. It fought the Nuneaton by-election of March 1967. Its candidate was Air Vice-Marshal Donald Bennett, a Second World War hero who had established the Pathfinder Force, was briefly a **Liberal** MP, and later went on to campaign against British membership of the European Communities.

Martell was declared bankrupt in June 1968 and his political organisations had to be disbanded.

National Party of Scotland

Highest vote: Miss E. Campbell (Glasgow, St. Rollox, 1931) – 3,521 votes, 15.8%
Parliamentary elections won: 0
Number of candidacies: 14

In the 1920s, there were several nationalist and Home Rule bodies in Scotland which had varying emphases, but none had formed themselves as a political party and fought elections. Campaigners for Home Rule were divided between those supporting the establishment of a Home Rule party (on the model of the Irish **Nationalists**) and those favouring pressure on the existing parties. The culturally based Scots National League called for independence for Scotland and prompted a 1926 breakaway called the Scottish National Movement, but this Movement had a small membership.

The largest Home Rule body was the Scottish Home Rule Association, formed in 1918, which hoped that a Labour government would bring in home rule. When Labour formed a minority government in 1924, George Buchanan MP introduced a Home Rule Bill which had government support but was talked out by the Conservatives. After the government fell, a Scottish National Convention was called by the Scottish Home Rule Association with the support of 29 of the 36 non-Unionist Scottish MPs. The Convention produced a devolution scheme, but in 1927 and 1928 a bill based on its proposals promoted by Labour MP James Barr was again talked out.

As a consequence, John MacCormick of the Glasgow University Scottish Nationalist Association called a meeting of all those supporting the establishment of a new party. The meeting was presided over by R.B. Cunninghame Graham, who had played a prominent part in the establishment of the **Scottish Parliamentary Labour Party** in 1888. In April 1928, the meeting established the National Party of Scotland with a nationalist policy. The party first fought a by-election in January 1929 and two seats in the 1929 general election.

In a by-election during the 1929–31 Parliament, the party managed to save its deposit for the first time, and of its five candidates in the 1931 election, only two lost their deposit – narrowly. A Home Rule movement initiated by former Conservatives, the **Scottish Party**, was formed in October 1932; the NPS candidate in the East Fife by-election of February 1933 received a questionnaire from this group.

John MacCormick, wishing for unity, made contact with the Scottish Party and tried to persuade them to merge. When the Scottish Party fought the Kilmarnock by-election in November 1933, the National Party of Scotland endorsed their candidate. The path towards merger was helped by the expulsion of many of the more radical nationalist and republican members of the NPS, one of whom was the poet C.M. Grieve (Hugh MacDiarmid).

The National Party of Scotland and the Scottish Party merged in April 1934 to form the **Scottish National Party**.

National Party of the United Kingdom

(1975–8)

Highest vote: M. Lobb (City of London and Westminster South, 1977 (24/2)) – 364 votes, 1.8%

Parliamentary elections won: 0

Number of candidacies: 2

The National Party was the eventual product of a split in the **National Front** in 1974. As the NF vote grew, it chose to broaden its range of speakers to include some recent converts from other parties who were able to portray its policies in a more populistic fashion, by contrast with the existing leaders who had a history of involvement in neo-Nazi organisations. In the autumn of 1974, this group of populists had made advances in internal National Front elections and shortly after the October 1974 general election, the populist John Kingsley Read was elected NF Chairman, defeating John Tyndall.

Tyndall and his supporters campaigned against the populist group throughout 1975 to such extent that the populists decided to expel Tyndall, but when this was done by unconstitutional means Tyndall went to the High Court and got the decision reversed. This court case prompted the populist leaders John Kingsley Read, Roy Painter, Richard Lawson and Gordon Brown to form the National Party on 29 December 1975. Gordon Brown was the owner of the National Front's headquarters and attempted to evict them, but before this could be done or the membership lists copied, the NF won another court battle to stop the National Party using its membership lists in any way.

The anti-populist faction in the NF had taken contingency measures to ensure the loyalty of its branches in the event that the populists seceded, and they succeeded in keeping the majority of membership in the NF. When the National Party held its inaugural meeting at Chelsea in February 1976, it had an attendance of 187. The party fought the Coventry North West by-election of March 1976, but was soundly beaten by the NF candidate; it did manage in May 1976 to win two local council seats in Blackburn, where John Kingsley Read was based.

A National Party candidate was fielded in the City of London and

199

Westminster South by-election of February 1977, but again the performance was poor and the NF outpolled them. The party fought 22 seats at
the May 1977 Greater London Council elections, averaging less than 400
votes each. One of the National Party's founders, Roy Painter, was
attempting to rejoin the **Conservative Party** by this stage, and the party
sank into oblivion before the 1979 general election. Some members may
have gone on to join the **Nationalist Party**.

National Prohibition Party

Only vote: S. M. Holden (Stepney, Whitechapel and St George's, 1923 (8/2)) – 130 votes,
0.9%
Parliamentary elections won: 0
Number of candidacies: 1

This party was formed at a convention in London in December 1887 and
formed the British affiliate to the World Prohibitionist Federation. It
campaigned for the prohibition of all alcoholic drink, though it did not
consider an electoral strategy as the primary campaign.

The party fought a by-election in Whitechapel in 1923, but its candidate
(who had fought Accrington as an unofficial Labour candidate in 1906)
was badly received on the hustings and polled very poorly. It continued to
organise until 1949 when its journal *Prohibitionist* ceased publication, and
the party appears to have disbanded then.

National Socialist League (1937–9)

Parliamentary elections won: 0
Number of candidacies: 0

This organisation was formed by William Joyce after his resignation from
the **British Union of Fascists** in 1937. At its establishment, it also had
the support of former **Independent Labour Party** MP John Beckett,
though in 1939 he resigned to form the **British People's Party**. The total
membership was estimated at 60 at foundation, dwindling quickly to 20.
The League had a virulent personal opposition to Sir Oswald Mosley.

The League was funded by a retired stockbroker and his sister, Alec and Ethel Scrimgeour, who had been admirers of Joyce in the BUF. The League rented an office in Vauxhall Bridge Road and opened a shop in Bristol. The League's public meetings were often disrupted by anti-fascist demonstrators and Joyce's preferred response was violence (the Bristol shop sold rubber truncheons).

In August 1939, as war with Germany loomed, the government recalled Parliament to pass the Emergency Powers Act which included provisions for internment. Joyce was tipped off two days before that the provisions would be brought into effect on 26 August, and immediately wound up the League to go to Germany where he became a propaganda broadcaster.

The National Socialist League called for a syndicalist fascist state and British alliance with Germany and Italy against the Soviet Union. While expressing admiration for Hitler, speakers for the League were adamantly insistent on its Britishness.

National Socialist Party (1916–20)

Highest vote: T. Kennedy (Kirkcaldy Burghs, 1923) – 14,221 votes, 54.4%

Parliamentary elections won: 11

Number of candidacies: 16 (including those who obtained Labour Party endorsement)

In 1916 the **British Socialist Party** suffered a split over the issue of British participation in the Great War. Roughly one third of the membership, who were on the whole the older members, patriotically supported the allied war aims and established the National Socialist Party as a breakaway. They were led by H. M. Hyndman, who had formed the **Social Democratic Federation** in 1881, which had in 1911 given birth to the British Socialist Party.

The NSP affiliated to the **Labour Party** from 1918, and in the 1918 election nominated four candidates – but only Dan Irving in Burnley secured Labour Party endorsement. Two NSP candidates won, Irving and Jack Jones in West Ham and Silvertown, and Jones took the Labour whip from February 1919.

In August 1920, after the British Socialist Party had reformed as the **Communist Party of Great Britain**, the National Socialist Party returned to the name Social Democratic Federation. It sponsored several Parliamentary candidates in the years 1921–4 and had at its peak in the 1923 Parliament, four members. After the 1924 general election, the Federation ceased to sponsor candidates, though its sitting members continued to be MPs and their candidatures were sponsored by their constituency parties.

It should be noted that the National Socialist Party had absolutely no connection with the ideology called 'national socialism'. The split in the British Socialist Party allowed the **Independent Labour Party** to supplant it in London as the principal body for the left wing of the Labour movement.

National Teenage Party

Highest vote: D. E. Sutch (Huyton, 1966) – 585 votes, 0.9%

Parliamentary elections won: 0

Number of candidacies: 2

David Sutch, the lead singer of the pop group Screaming Lord Sutch and the Savages, decided to fight the 1963 by-election in Stratford-upon-Avon caused by the resignation of the former War Minister, John Profumo. He formed the National Teenage Party to organise his campaign (though he was 22 at the time). A key campaign pledge was to lower the voting age to 18.

Sutch came bottom of the poll but was not deterred from continuing his political career. He attempted to fight Harold Wilson at Huyton in the 1964 election but his nomination papers were invalid; he fought the seat in 1966 and polled under 1%.

When the voting age was reduced to 18 in 1970, Sutch wound up the party. In the early 1970s he founded two short lived parties, the Young Ideas Party and the Go To Blazes Party, before establishing the **Official Monster Raving Loony Party** in 1983.

National Union of Small Shopkeepers

Highest vote: T. Lynch (Derby North, 1962 (17/4)) – 886 votes, 2.7%

Parliamentary elections won: 0

Number of candidacies: 3

This organisation was formed as a trade union in 1943, but did not affiliate to the Trades Union Congress. It had national headquarters in Nottingham. In March 1959, the Union nominated its President, Tom Lynch, to fight a by-election in Harrow East; it also fought two by-elections in 1962 and 1968 with the same candidate. The Union was opposed to increases in postal rates and to the Selective Employment Tax, and called for an all-party National government. In the 1968 Bassetlaw by-election, a public meeting in support of Tom Lynch was addressed by a Conservative Wiltshire County Councillor.

(Irish) Nationalist

Highest vote: J. D. Sheehan (Kerry Eastern, 1885) – 3,769 votes, 99.2%

Parliamentary elections won: 793

Number of candidacies: 1,007

The Irish Nationalist movement was established in 1885 as a further development of the Home Rule movement (*see* **Home Ruler**). It did not exist as a single party; Nationalist candidates were selected at meetings of members of several nationalist bodies. The most prominent of these organisations were the National League, formed in October 1882 by Charles Parnell as the successor to the Land League, and the United Irish League, formed in 1898 by William O'Brien.

Charles Parnell was undisputed leader of the Irish Nationalists from their foundation, and with the extension of the franchise in 1884 it was clear that he would lead a large Parliamentary party in the next Parliament. In fact, the Irish Nationalists won almost every seat at every election in the southern part of Ireland until 1916.

The **Conservatives** approached Parnell for support in ousting the **Liberal** government, and in June 1885 they combined to defeat the government on the budget, forcing Gladstone's resignation. When Gladstone refused to give a pledge of Home Rule for Ireland, Parnell advised Irish Nationalists in Great Britain to vote Conservative in the 1885 election. The result gave Conservatives and Irish Nationalists combined the same number of MPs as the Liberals.

Shortly after the election, Gladstone announced his support for Home Rule and the Conservatives declared against it; the Irish Nationalists then voted out the Conservative government and supported Gladstone. However, a large part of the Liberal Party rebelled on granting Irish Home Rule and formed a **Liberal Unionist** group. This resulted in the defeat of the government's Home Rule Bill and the fall of the government. The Conservatives and Liberal Unionists won the subsequent 1886 election.

On Christmas Eve 1889, Nationalist MP Captain William O'Shea filed a divorce suit against his wife, citing Charles Parnell as co-respondent; the accusation was true and the suit was undefended. Revelation of Parnell's affair led to a long debate within the Nationalists on whether to expel him, which Parnell lost; he and his followers split with the party (see **Parnellite Nationalist**) and the anti-Parnellite majority formed the Irish Nationalist Federation.

The Liberal Party under Gladstone won the 1892 election with a majority enough to pass Home Rule through the House of Commons, but the bill was blocked in the House of Lords. In 1900 the two wings of Irish Nationalism were reunited when the Parnellite John Redmond was elected to lead the Parliamentary party. The frustration of seeing Home Rule blocked by British politics led to the growth of terrorist and republican organisations such as the Irish Republican Brotherhood and **Sinn Féin** in the early years of the twentieth century.

After the Parliament Act was passed in 1911, the House of Lords veto was removed and the Liberal government passed Home Rule in 1914, but the advent of the Great War meant that it did not come into effect until peacetime. The revolutionary republican organisations refused to accept the delay and at Easter 1916 an armed uprising was attempted. The brutal suppression of this uprising, and executions of sentence of death upon its leaders led to a wave of sympathy for the republicans, and the constitutional nationalist movement lost support. In the 1918 election the

Nationalists returned only 6 members in Ireland compared with 73 abstentionist Sinn Féiners.

The nationalists played little part in the negotiations for partition of Ireland, but remained active in opposing partition in border areas, and its members of the Northern Ireland Parliament boycotted its first session (1921–5). The nationalist movement did occasionally organise in Great Britain: it fought several elections in Liverpool, and T. P. O'Connor was MP for Liverpool Scotland from 1885 to his death in 1929.

There were nationalist members of the Northern Ireland ('Stormont') Parliament until its dissolution, but as a permanent minority they were ineffective and only once did the Unionists permit them to pass a piece of legislation (Wild Birds Protection Act (N.I.) 1931). It has been claimed there was a tacit understanding that the Nationalists would confine themselves to Stormont elections, while Sinn Féin would fight Westminster elections. The strongest Nationalist support during this time was in the rural border areas. Catholic voters in Belfast tended to back various republican or Labour candidates.

Throughout the existence of the Stormont Parliament, the Nationalist movement did not have a central headquarters. They did not publish an agreed programme until 1964. In December 1959, a pressure group called National Unity was formed in order to campaign for a unified and dynamic Nationalist campaign, which was resisted by the leadership of the movement. Too late did the Nationalists realise that their support was ebbing, and they were superseded by the establishment of the **National Democratic Party** (see National Democratic Party [Northern Ireland] (1964–70)) and its successor the **Social Democratic and Labour Party**.

One Nationalist candidate stood in the 1973 election to the Northern Ireland Assembly, but since then there have been no candidacies.

Nationalist Party (1980–5?)

Highest vote: B. F. Franklin (Barnet, Hendon North, 1983) – 194 votes, 0.5%

Parliamentary elections won: 0

Number of candidacies: 7

The Nationalist Party was one of the products of the disintegration of the

National Front after its poor performance at the 1979 general election. The group was originally formed inside the National Front in about 1978 as the National Front Constitutional Movement, by Andrew Fountaine, a Norfolk landowner and former Conservative, who opposed the Nazi associations of the NF leaders John Tyndall and Martin Webster, as well as the links with football hooliganism and violence.

In 1980 the National Front Constitutional Movement separated from the National Front, and in the 1981 Greater London Council elections it fought 23 seats. The Movement renamed itself the Constitutional Movement in summer 1981, and fought the Croydon North West by-election that October. The party adopted the name Nationalist Party in 1982 and fought five seats at the 1983 election. It fought the Enfield Southgate by-election of 1984 but, after poor results, no more candidates were nominated. The party appears to have been wound up.

Nationalist Unity

See **Opposition Unity**.

Natural Law Party

Address: Roydon Hall, Roydon Hall Road, East Peckham, Tonbridge, Kent TN12 5NH

Email address: info@natural-law-party-org.uk

Website: http://www.natural-law-party.org.uk

Number on Register: 30

Highest vote: Ms. L. J. Blair (Glasgow Maryhill, 1997) – 651 votes, 2.2%.

Parliamentary elections won: 0

Number of candidacies: 526

The Natural Law Party was formed a few days before the calling of the 1992 general election by followers of the Maharishi Mahesh Yogi, who promotes Transcendental Meditation as a basis of world harmony. Natural Law Parties were formed in most other democracies at about this time. The party emerged from nowhere to stand 310 candidates, fighting nearly half of all the seats. The party claimed to have selected candidates as a result of psychometric tests. Late in the campaign it claimed to have abandoned its own election campaign and formed an alliance with all parties opposed to single-party rule.

Most people treated the NLP as a bit of light relief, especially when they practised 'Yogic Flying' (involving bouncing up and down with folded legs), and claimed to be able to eliminate taxes, but the party has pointed to a plummeting crime rate in Merseyside as a solid achievement of following Natural Law. Their candidates in general came at the bottom of the poll and received derisory votes, but they have continued to fight by-elections. In the 1997 election the party's activity was somewhat reduced compared with 1992.

The party leader is Dr Geoffrey Clements, who stood as a candidate for the Mayor of London, coming bottom of the poll with 0.3% of the vote.

New Agenda

See **Democratic Left [Ireland]**.

New Britain

Address: 13 Cooper's Row, London EC3N 5BQ

Number on Register: 62

Highest vote: J. P. Pratt (Bournemouth East, 1977 (24/11) − 1,127 votes, 4.7%

Parliamentary elections won: 0

Number of candidacies: 9

This small right-wing political group was formed by Dennis Delderfield in 1976. Delderfield was a Common Councilman of the Corporation of London, elected as an Independent, in 1971–8, 1982–92 and 1995–8. The party's policy was extreme conservatism and its candidates campaigned for the return of capital punishment and a halt to immigration (supporting voluntary repatriation for immigrants). New Britain was supported by the Christian Affirmation Campaign, which was a fundamentalist movement strongly opposed to what it regarded as the World Council of Churches' support for communist régimes in Africa.

Dennis Delderfield fought his home seat of City of London and Westminster South in the February 1977 by-election, and in November 1977 the party's candidate in the Bournemouth East by-election polled a respectable vote. However, the candidate in the Ilford North by-election of March 1978 was revealed, after nominations closed, to be a convicted child abuser, and his endorsement was withdrawn. In the rest of the Parliament the party found no suitable by-elections and it fought only two seats in the 1979 general election.

After the 1979 election the party effectively absorbed the **United Country Party** of Edmund Iremonger, and a small anti-devolution group calling itself the Keep Britain United Party. The party fought two by-elections in the 1979 Parliament and two seats in the 1983 election, but then disappeared from public activity.

It emerged again to fight five seats in the 1994 European Parliament elections, polling well enough to save its deposit in one seat and nearly in another. It then fought the Dudley West by-election of December 1994, though there it did not do well.

The party's key policy from the 1990s has been opposition to British membership of the European Union. In the November 1997 Beckenham by-election, the party's candidate was formerly the **Referendum Party** candidate for the constituency, who managed to secure the endorsement of the **UK Independence Party** (several leading members of the UKIP were formerly members of New Britain). Dennis Delderfield remains the National Chairman.

New Communist Party of Britain

Address: PO Box 73, London SW11 2PQ

Email address: ncp@clara.net

Website: http://www.geocities.com/CapitolHill/2853/homepage.htm

Parliamentary elections won: 0

Number of candidacies: 0

In 1977, the **Communist Party of Great Britain** (*see* Communist Party of Great Britain (1920–91)) was divided over its future direction due to the rise of a Eurocommunist element which sought to divide the British party from the official Soviet line. A new draft of the party's programme *The British Road to Socialism* was debated from February until the 35th Congress in November, when it was adopted.

The programme was wide enough for most of the party, but a group led by Sid French refused to accept the repudiation of 'democratic centralism' and formed the breakaway New Communist Party of Britain. The party had approximately 700 members at formation.

Its youth wing began to show an interest in developments in the Communist Party in Turkey, which the leadership considered incompatible with the party's aims; it also adopted a different policy on peace. It was expelled in December 1979 and eventually formed the **Communist Party of Great Britain (Provisional Central Committee)** (*see* Communist Party of Great Britain (1989–)).

The New Communist Party does not fight elections, but generally calls on voters to support Labour (save in the European elections of 1999 when it called for a boycott). It publishes the *New Worker*.

New Conservative Party

Highest vote: J. E. Dayton (Harrow West, 1960 (17/3)) – 1,560 votes, 4.7%

Parliamentary elections won: 0

Number of candidacies: 4

This party was formed by John Dayton in March 1960 when he fought the Harrow West by-election with a British nationalistic policy. He polled nearly 5% of the vote and was encouraged by this to start the *Watching Brief* newsletter and then to stand in the Bolton East by-election in November of that year, while a colleague fought the simultaneous by-election of Mid Bedfordshire. However, these two by-elections saw a much more modest showing.

In May 1961 Dayton renamed his party the True Conservative Party, but this was dissolved in the autumn when he launched the Patriotic Front for Political Action. Under Patriotic Front auspices, Dayton fought the Oswestry by-election of November 1961, polling 2.8%. *Watching Brief* ceased publication soon afterwards, and in February 1962 John Dayton wound up the Patriotic Front and joined the Labour Party.

New Millennium Bean Party

Address: 6 Flint House, Moorland Road, Sandfields Estate, Port Talbot SA12 6JX

Number on Register: 141

Highest vote: C. Beany (Aberavon, 1992) – 707 votes, 1.8%

Parliamentary elections won: 0

Number of candidacies: 3

Barry Kirk, a charity fund-raiser from Port Talbot in South Wales, has dubbed himself 'Captain Beany' – a human baked bean. He fought the by-election in Neath in April 1991 under the banner of the Bean Party in an attempt to raise money for Catherine Williams, then a pupil at Sandsfield Comprehensive School in Port Talbot, who needed a new electric wheel-chair. His main campaign issue was a call for more government spending on charities.

Kirk then changed his legal name to Captain Beany and fought his home constituency (Aberavon) in the 1992 and 1997 elections, as well as South Wales West in the 1994 European Parliament elections. His nomination paper for the elections for Mayor of London in 2000 was ruled invalid.

New Party

Highest vote: S. Davies (Merthyr Tydfil, Merthyr, 1931) – 10,834 votes, 30.6%

Parliamentary elections won: 0

Number of candidacies: 25

Sir Oswald Mosley, who had begun his political career as a Conservative MP in 1918 but joined the **Labour Party** in 1924, was appointed Chancellor of the Duchy of Lancaster in the Labour government of 1929 with a brief to deal with the unemployment problem. Finding that he had insufficient authority to carry out the radical proposals he considered necessary, and that a policy paper he put to the cabinet was rejected, Mosley resigned on 19 May 1930.

After resignation, Mosley expanded on his proposals in a resignation speech and in a document published in July 1930, popularly known as the

'Mosley Manifesto'. Support in the grassroots of the Labour Party led Mosley to take his campaign to the 1930 Labour Party conference, which narrowly rejected the proposals. On 8 December 1930 an expanded version of the Mosley Manifesto was published, signed by 16 Labour MPs and A.J. Cook, General Secretary of the Miners' Federation of Great Britain.

Mosley made his break with the Labour Party on 28 February 1931 and launched the New Party on the following day. The New Party attracted the initial support of six Labour MPs, but two of these resigned after only one day to sit as independents. With a scratch organisation, the New Party fought the Ashton-under-Lyne by-election of April 1931, the candidate being Allan Young, who had been Mosley's private secretary in government. He polled 16%, splitting the Labour vote to allow the Conservative candidate to win.

The New Party advocated a 'National Policy' to meet the economic crisis, including the granting of wide powers to the government subject only to general control by Parliament, a five-member cabinet without portfolio, and isolationism of industry within the Commonwealth. The party followed Keynesian economics in suggesting investment in housing schemes to provide work and clear the slums.

Mosley's determination to retain control of New Party policy, and his tendencies towards dictatorship, led to the resignation of several leading members (including John Strachey and Allan Young) in July 1931. Later in 1931, two more MPs (one Conservative and one Liberal) joined the party. In the 1931 general election, the party fought 24 seats, but only Mosley himself (fighting Stoke, the seat held by his first wife) and a candidate facing only Labour opposition in Merthyr Tydfil, polled well. The New Party's candidates came from a wide-range of backgrounds, including a Jewish East End ex-boxing champion and a retired Liberal MP.

After the election, Sir Oswald Mosley went on a study tour of 'the new movements' in Italy and Germany and returned convinced that a fascist policy was the best way of meeting the economic crisis. Some parts of the New Party, especially its youth movement NUPA, had already adopted fascist policies. In 1932 Mosley set about uniting the existing fascist organisations, and when the **British Union of Fascists** was formed, the New Party merged with it.

Northern Ireland Ecology Party

Highest vote: M.H. Samuel (North Antrim, 1983) – 451 votes, 1.0%

Parliamentary elections won: 0

Number of candidacies: 2

This party was formed in 1981 by Malcolm Samuel, as the Northern Ireland branch of the **Ecology Party** of Great Britain. He fought North Antrim in the 1982 Northern Ireland Assembly elections and in the 1983 general election; in 1987 he fought East Londonderry. In 1988 the party was renamed Northern Ireland Green Party. After winning some support in Coleraine and Down in the 1989 local government elections, the party fought the 1989 European Parliament elections, polling 1.2% – the highest vote for green politics in Northern Ireland.

The party appears to have been wound up in 1990 when the **Green Party of Northern Ireland** was formed.

Northern Ireland Green Party

See **Northern Ireland Ecology Party.**

Northern Ireland Labour Party

Highest vote: H.C. Midgley (Belfast, West, 1923) – 22,255 votes, 47.1%

Parliamentary elections won: 0

Number of candidacies: 60

This party was formed as the Belfast Labour Party in 1919, in the immediate aftermath of the Great War. The Belfast Labour Party was a development of the Labour Representative Committee which had fought four seats in Belfast in the 1918 general election. Two of these candidates had been opposed by 'Labour Unionist' candidates sponsored by the **Ulster Unionist Labour Association**.

The main base of support for the Labour Representative Committee and the Belfast Labour Party was the Belfast Trades Council, which had been the only Irish affiliate to the **Labour Party** before the Great War.

The Trades Council had been disaffiliated when the Irish Labour Party (*see* **Labour Party [Ireland]**) was formed in 1913, but was still a bastion of unionism.

The Belfast Labour Party fought Belfast West in the 1923 general election and came close to winning. The party adopted the name Northern Ireland Labour Party in 1924 and was granted affiliation by the Labour Party, which had accepted the partition of Ireland as a solution of the constitutional problem. From this time, candidates of the party for Westminster elections usually received Labour Party endorsement.

The party was non-sectarian and did not take a collective stance on the constitutional question. This left individual candidates who felt strongly to take their own line, and eventually resulted in breakaways by the unionist former leader Harry Midgley (*see* **Commonwealth Labour Party**) and the nationalist Jack Beattie (*see* **Federation of Labour**).

Compared with the British Labour Party, the Northern Ireland Labour Party suffered from a deficiency in terms of its support from the Trade Unions, few of which affiliated to it. In addition, union members had to sign in to join the union political fund (a provision repealed in Great Britain in 1930). There was usually a small group of Northern Ireland Labour Party members at Stormont who attempted to co-operate with the Unionists in running that Parliament effectively, but were rebuffed.

The party suffered a split in 1948 over the issue of partition. The majority of the party supported making the border permanent, prompting the West Belfast members to resign and join the Irish Labour Party. After the Labour government at Westminster passed the Ireland Act 1949, the Labour Party provided a grant to the party and seconded an organiser, apparently in the hope that the party could win Westminster seats.

However, in the 1949 Northern Ireland general election, called by the Unionists on the issue of the constitution, opinion was highly polarised and the party lost both the seats it had held. The party adopted a staunch anti-republican stance after the IRA campaign of the mid 1950s, and in consequence won the votes of many Protestant workers – enough to take four Belfast seats at the 1958 Stormont elections.

In 1964 the party promoted a bill at Stormont to ban religious discrimination, a stance which the party hoped would win it Catholic support. Its effect was to alienate Protestant support, and after an obscure internal split the party lost two seats at the 1965 election. In 1969 the Unionists launched a large-scale attack on the party as having nationalist and republican tendencies and it lost another seat.

The party lost its link with the Labour Party after the **Social Democratic and Labour Party** was formed and was recognised as the Northern Irish representative of the Socialist International. With the demise of Stormont the party lost its prominence and candidacies during the 1970s were rare. The last candidate stood in South Antrim in the 1982 Northern Ireland Assembly election.

Since the demise of the party, various attempts have been made either to reform a Northern Ireland Labour Party, or to persuade the Labour Party in London to organise in Northern Ireland. The remnants of the party merged with the **United Labour Party** in 1987 to form **Labour '87**.

Northern Ireland Unionist Party

Address: Room 358, Parliament Buildings, Stormont, Belfast BT4 3XX.

Email address: info@niup.org

Website: http://www.niup.org

Number on Register: 64

Parliamentary elections won: 0

Number of candidacies: 0

This party derives from a split among the **United Kingdom Unionist Party** members of the new Northern Ireland Assembly in December 1998. UKUP leader Robert McCartney MP wanted the party to withdraw from the Assembly if Sinn Féin took seats in an all-party Executive, opposed by the four other UKUP members. A special meeting called by Robert McCartney in December 1998 removed the four members from all positions and privileges within the UKUP.

In January 1999, the four members announced they had left the UKUP and formed the Northern Ireland Unionist Party. One of the founders, Roger Hutchinson, was expelled in December 1999. Cedric Wilson is the party leader. At the South Antrim by-election in September 2000 the party withdrew its candidate and urged voters to support the **Democratic**

Unionist Party candidate; if it had not done so, the **Ulster Unionist** would probably have won.

Northern Ireland Women's Coalition

Address: 52 Elmwood Avenue, Belfast BT9 6AZ.

Email address: niwc@iol.ie

Website: http://www.niwc.org

Number on Register: 33

Highest vote: Miss J. E. Morrice (North Down, 1997) – 1,240 votes, 3.4%.

Parliamentary elections won: 0

Number of candidacies: 3

The Women's Coalition was formed in 1996 by Professor Monica McWilliams and Pearl Sagar, shortly before the Northern Ireland Forum elections. Some members of the Women's Coalition had met in various cross-community groups campaigning for peace, and the two principal founders were from the different communities of Northern Ireland.

The Coalition won two seats in the province-wide top-up section of the 1996 Forum elections, enabling it to take part in the negotiations leading up to the Belfast Agreement of 1998. It is a centrist body within Northern Ireland politics, not taking an explicit stance on the constitutional question but advocating problem-solving by building a consensus and negotiation.

The Coalition fought three seats in the 1997 general election, but lost its deposit in each. It strongly supported the Good Friday Agreement in the June 1998 referendum and won two seats in the Northern Ireland Assembly elections soon after, regarded as a very good performance. A leading member, May Blood, received a life peerage in 1999.

Official Monster Raving Loony Party

Address: The Dog and Partridge, Yateley, Hampshire GU46 7LR

Website: http://freespace.virgin.net/raving.loony/

Number on Register: 56

Highest vote: L. D. Sutch (Rotherham, 1994(5/5)) – 1,114 votes, 4.0%

Parliamentary elections won: 0

Number of candidacies: 97

The full name of this party is The Official Monster Raving Loony Party as it wishes to distinguish itself from all the other parties which occasionally come up with loony policies. It was set up in 1983 by David 'Screaming Lord' Sutch, a rock musician who had been contesting elections since 1963 under the banner of first the **National Teenage Party**, then later as the Young Ideas Party and the Go To Blazes Party.

The efforts of this party to liven up elections are greatly appreciated by many. The party asserts that all those who do not vote in an election should be counted as its supporters. The main political impact the Monster Raving Loonies have had was to beat the **Social Democratic Party** in the first 1990 Bootle by-election – this poor result finally convinced SDP leaders that there was no mileage in continuing the party and directly led to it being wound up.

David Sutch changed his first names from David Edward to Lord David in 1988; his autobiography, *Life as Sutch*, was published in 1993. He committed suicide in June 1999. The current leadership is shared between Alan 'Howling Laud' Hope and his cat, Mandu. Alan Hope has been an elected Loony councillor in Honiton for several years and served as Mayor of Honiton in 1997–8.

Official National Front (1986–90)

See **National Front (1967–90)**.

Opposition Unity

Highest vote: Miss J. B. Devlin (Mid Ulster, 1970) – 37,739 votes, 53.5%

Parliamentary elections won: 3

Number of candidacies: 9

Otherwise known as Nationalist Unity, but usually just as Unity, this label was used by a number of nationalist candidates in Northern Ireland from the mid 1960s. All these candidates were in border areas and the movement was strongest to the west of the Bann. As with the Irish **Nationalists**, there was no formal organisation to the Unity movement: candidates were adopted at 'Unity conventions' which were open to the broad nationalist movement.

Unity candidates only fought United Kingdom Parliamentary elections, leaving the Northern Ireland ('Stormont') Parliament to the Nationalists. There was some co-operation between the two organisations, and Edward McAteer (leader of the Nationalists at Stormont 1964–9) was Unity candidate for Londonderry in 1970. Unity had its first and biggest success in the Mid-Ulster by-election of April 1969 when its candidate, 21-year-old psychology student Bernadette Devlin, beat the widow of the former **Ulster Unionist** MP in a straight fight.

The movement held the seat, and gained Fermanagh and South Tyrone in the 1970 general election. It was notable that none of the other nationalist parties opposed Unity candidates at this election, though the Northern Ireland Labour Party, the Ulster Liberal Party and three independent candidates did. Bernadette Devlin abandoned the movement shortly after her re-election and her constituency supporters established an independent socialist association to support her.

Frank McManus, the remaining MP, launched the Unity Movement as a formal organisation in April 1973. It issued a manifesto calling for amnesty for political prisoners, disbanding the Royal Ulster Constabulary, and repeal of repressive legislation. **The Social Democratic and Labour Party** was not prepared to defer to the movement, and in the February 1974 election the movement lost Fermanagh and South Tyrone when an SDLP candidate split the vote. There was only one other candidate at that election, who was soundly beaten, and no candidates appeared after then. A faint echo of the Unity Movement was found with the election of Lisnaskea publican Frank Maguire as an Independent Republican in Fermanagh and South Tyrone in October 1974.

Parnellite Nationalist

Highest vote: T. C. Harrington (Dublin Harbour, 1892) – 4,482 votes, 76.5%
Parliamentary elections won: 25
Number of candidacies: 87

Charles Stewart Parnell, the leader of the Irish **Nationalists**, had begun an affair with the wife of William O'Shea, another Nationalist MP, in 1880. On 24 December 1889, O'Shea petitioned for divorce and cited Parnell as co-respondent, creating a scandal. As O'Shea was known to be a supporter of Joseph Chamberlain, most Irish Nationalists assumed the divorce suit was a political ploy to discredit Parnell.

The divorce suit was however, undefended and in November 1890 the court found against Parnell and Mrs O'Shea. Confirmation of Parnell's adultery outraged **Liberal** leader Gladstone and the British nonconformist allies of Irish Nationalism, who demanded that he be removed from leadership. This put the Nationalists in a dilemma: keep Parnell and jeopardise the chances of obtaining Home Rule from a Liberal government, or expel him at the urging of Britain. Eventually the majority sided against Parnell, and the Catholic Church in Ireland declared him morally unfit for leadership.

Parnell's supporters then took their cause to the Irish people and stood candidates against the official Nationalists, endorsing Parnell's increasingly radical approach. This split continued after Parnell's death in October 1891, John Redmond becoming the Parnellite leader. The Parnellites were strongest in Dublin and on the west coast. In the 1892 general election nine Parnellites were elected. Unlike the official Nationalists, Parnell's supporters went into opposition in 1893 when the Home Rule Bill was defeated, and they increased their numbers to 12 in the 1895 general election.

By 1900 the two wings of Irish Nationalism were moving increasingly together and the Chairman of the (anti-Parnellite) Irish Nationalist

Federation, John Dillon, agreed to join a reunited Nationalist party under the leadership of John Redmond – who had impressed many people on both sides of the Irish Sea with the quality of his speeches. Despite the slight difference over approach (anti-Parnellites being more moderate than Parnell's supporters), there was no significant ideological divide between the two wings.

Party of Associates with Licensees

Highest vote: A. Farrell (Surrey, Guildford, 1983) – 425 votes, 0.8%
Parliamentary elections won: 0
Number of candidacies: 4

This party was formed by a group of Surrey public house landlords in 1983, shortly before the general election. They campaigned against inflexible licensing laws and excessive duties on alcoholic drinks. Four candidates were nominated in the general election, including one (Brian Wareham, landlord of the Cricketers', Ash, and the King Alfred, Godalming) against then Prime Minister Margaret Thatcher in Finchley.

No more elections were fought and it appears no formal organisation for the party was ever established.

Patriotic Front for Political Action

See **New Conservative Party**.

Patriotic Party

Highest vote: A. R. Braybrooke (Fulham, 1964) – 632 votes, 1.8%
Parliamentary elections won: 0
Number of candidacies: 3

The Patriotic Party was formed under the name The True Tories by Major-General Richard Hilton in 1962. Hilton was a former member of the **League of Empire Loyalists** and his organisation adopted a similar nationalistic policy. Many senior members were ex-military men: the Deputy Chairman was Major Arthur Braybrooke, a former Liberal Parliamentary candidate.

The True Tories took the name Patriotic Party shortly before the 1964 general election, in which two candidates were sponsored. During the course of the campaign, the party split, with Major Braybrooke (one of the candidates) continuing the organisation. Major-General Hilton and his supporters left and re-established The True Tories; he later became a sponsor of the National Youth Movement of the **British National Party** (*see* British National Party (1960–7)). The party polled poorly at the 1964 election, and when Major Braybrooke stood again in 1966, he barely scraped 100 votes.

When the **National Front** was formed in 1967, both the Patriotic Party and The True Tories merged with it.

Peelites

See **Liberal Conservative**.

PEOPLE

Highest vote: Mrs. A. L. Whittaker (Coventry North West, February 1974) – 1,542 votes, 3.9%

Parliamentary elections won: 0

Number of candidacies: 9 (+3 affiliated)

Concern about the environment greatly increased in the early 1970s. In summer 1972, Tony and Lesley Whittaker, solicitors in Warwickshire, were prompted by an article in *Playboy* magazine by biologist Paul Ehrlich to begin discussing their concerns over the ecological future with friends in the Napton Bridge public house. Eventually, one of the participants of these discussions called a formal meeting in the premises of the bankrupt Herbert-Ingersoll machine-tool company in Daventry.

The first meeting adopted the name The Thirteen Club, the number of attendees. They read and distributed writings of Paul Ehrlich and others, but by the end of the year the club had split over the question of whether political action was needed. The club had written to the existing political parties about the problem, but received unhelpful replies and decided that the only thing left was to form a new political party.

In January 1973, the four members of The Thirteen Club who supported political action (Tony Whittaker, Lesley Whittaker, Mike Benfield and Freda Sanders) placed an advertisement inviting people wishing to be candidates for their party to come forward. The name on the advertisement was 'PEOPLE' and this was chosen as the name for the new party when it was officially formed in February 1973.

The founding principles of PEOPLE were taken from a book called *Blueprint for Survival* which had profoundly influenced The Thirteen Club: minimum disruption of ecological processes, maximum conservation of materials and energy, a population in which recruitment equals loss, and a social system in which individuals can enjoy rather than feel restricted by the first three conditions. The party formulated its *Manifesto for a Sustainable Society* later in 1973 based on the principles.

PEOPLE fought five constituencies with its own candidates in the February 1974 election, and supported two other affiliated candidates with similar aims to the party. It had several encouraging votes. One of its candidates was Edward Goldsmith, proprietor of *Ecologist* magazine and brother of Sir James Goldsmith, who later formed the **Referendum Party**. In the October 1974 election, the party had four candidates and one affiliate but did noticeably less well.

The party was disappointed that many environmental and pacifist pressure groups failed to ally with it, preferring to work within the existing political parties. Some of the socialist members left to join the Socialist Environment and Resources Association after divisions emerged at the party's conferences of 1974 and 1975.

Poor results in the October 1974 election were ascribed by some to the media's persistent misnaming of PEOPLE as 'The People's Party', which sounded like a far-left movement. The party's colours of coral and turquoise sometimes came out as red and blue. In 1975 the party renamed itself the **Ecology Party**.

People's League for the Defence of Freedom

Only vote: E. D. Martell (East Ham North, 1957 (30/5)) – 2,730 votes, 12.2%

Parliamentary elections won: 0

Number of candidacies: 1

The People's League for the Defence of Freedom was formed by Edward Martell in March 1956. Martell, a former **Liberal** member of the London County Council (Bethnal Green South West, 1946–9), had played a leading part in Liberal preparations for the 1950 general election in which he fought Hendon North. He resigned from the Liberals in the early 1950s to launch a series of anti-socialist and pro-free market crusades.

There were all-out newspaper strikes in 1955 and 1956, during which Martell's printing firm continued to produce his own publications and other magazines under contract. This was achieved by a non-union workforce who were paid over the union rates. Martell had become a nationally recognised figure in 1954 when he had organised the Winston Churchill Birthday Fund.

The People's League fought the East Ham North by-election of May 1957 with Martell as candidate. He polled well for a minor party candidate, nearly saving his deposit. After the by-election, Martell turned again to the printing industry, though the People's League apparently continued in existence. When Martell returned to politics in 1962, it was to form the **National Fellowship**.

Plaid Cymru (the Party of Wales)

Address: 51 Cathedral Road, Caerdydd, Cymru CF1 9HD

Number on Register: 7

Website: http://www.plaidcymru.org

Highest vote: D. W. Wigley (Caernarfon, 1992) – 21,439 votes, 59.0%

Parliamentary elections won: 21

Number of candidacies: 420 (including 7 joint candidacies with the Green Party)

Plaid Cymru, the party which campaigns for Welsh self-government, was a result of developments immediately after the Great War. Nationalists in

Wales had not been organised before the war (though a Welsh Home Rule Bill had been proposed by Liberal MP E. T. John in 1914), but were spurred on by the successful establishment of the Irish Free State.

The first meeting to organise nationalism was held in Caernarfon by Hugh Robert Jones in September 1924. To obtain intellectual support Jones contacted Saunders Lewis, a lecturer in Welsh at University College, Swansea, to invite him to join. Lewis had converted to Catholicism and was influenced by Maurice Barrès and Charles Maurras, French writers who believed that people should have a profound attachment to their native areas.

Lewis had already formed a secret group called Mudiad Cymreig [Welsh Movement] in South Wales and used the ideas of this group in his proposals for the planned new party. Barrès and Maurras also believed that people should not be taken away from their native traditions and following this theory, Lewis sought the deindustrialisation of south Wales and a return to agriculture.

At a meeting on 5 August 1925 at the Maesgwyn Temperance Hotel in Pwllheli, six men formed Plaid Genedlaethol Gymreig [National Party of Wales]. The founding President was the Reverend Lewis Valentine, with H. R. Jones as full-time General Secretary and organiser. Valentine was the first Parliamentary candidate, polling 1.6% in Caernarvonshire in 1929, but the initial base of the party's support was in middle-class academia. Saunders Lewis obtained 30% of the vote in the University of Wales in 1931.

At first, Plaid Cymru meetings were in Welsh only, and it intended that any of its candidates who were elected would not take their seats. However, grassroots members found that the abstentionist policy was a vote-loser and in 1930 they passed a resolution to get rid of it – against the advice of Saunders Lewis who had taken over as President that year. In January 1932 the party issued an English-language publication for the first time.

In 1936, Saunders Lewis, Lewis Valentine and D. J. Williams were arrested and tried for setting fire to an RAF bombing school which was being built at Penyberth on the Lleyn peninsula; on 19 January 1937 they were convicted and sentenced to nine months' imprisonment. The trial gathered the Blaid great sympathy (it was transferred to London after a local jury could not agree), though some of that was thrown away when the party boycotted the coronation of King George VI.

In the late 1930s, Plaid Cymru advocated neutrality in the Spanish Civil War and had some sympathy for António Salazar and Benito Mussolini, nationalistic European dictators. During the Second World War the party opposed conscription due to its pacifism. Plaid Cymru's concern with Welsh culture and language, and its North Wales base, tended to blind it to the industrial difficulties in South Wales in the 1930s depression, but during two by-elections early in 1945 the Blaid concentrated on post-war regeneration.

By the end of the war, the Blaid's policy was finalised as seeking self-government for Wales. Broadly, the Blaid seeks preservation of the Welsh language and culture; its social policies are distinctly left-wing and at times socialist. Gwynfor Evans was chosen to lead Plaid Cymru in 1945, and in the late 1940s the Blaid embarked on a campaign to give the Welsh language equal status with English.

Plaid Cymru's vote and activity increased slowly and steadily after the Second World War. In order to help it target voters more effectively, in 1951 the party did not oppose other candidates who it believed were sincere supporters of Welsh self-government. The Blaid found its best results in heavily Welsh-speaking areas in west Wales, and elsewhere its candidates almost always lost their deposits.

By 1954 the party was in a position to give strong support to the 'Parliament for Wales' campaign, drawing heavily on the tactics of the **Scottish Covenant Association**. There were 250,000 signatures on a petition to support the Parliament for Wales Bill, but only six of the 36 Welsh MPs gave their support.

The 1959 general election saw Plaid Cymru contesting more than half of the Welsh constituencies for the first time, and saving six deposits. However, the result was a disappointment at the time. The Blaid had hoped to win a large vote against the flooding of Trenywern Valley in Meirionnydd to create a reservoir for the people of Liverpool, which no Welsh authority was able to stop, but Gwynfor Evans's vote in Merionethshire increased by less than 1%.

Having made a stand in all parts of Wales, Plaid Cymru looked for an issue to campaign upon; it emerged when the 1961 census showed that the

Welsh-speaking population had fallen to 25%. Saunders Lewis gave a radio lecture on 'Tynged yr Iaith' [The Fate of the Language] which argued that preservation of the language was more important than self-government. This led to the formation of Cymdeithas Yr Iaith Gymraeg [Welsh Language Society] at a Plaid Cymru Summer School in 1962. Cymdeithas thereafter could take the direct action which was inappropriate for a political party, enabling the Blaid to develop its industrial policy confident that the language issue was well fought elsewhere.

The 1964 general election saw 23 Plaid Cymru candidates, the Blaid deciding that to fight fewer seats than in 1959 would look like a retreat. Again this led to a dispersal of effort: the Plaid Cymru vote fell and 21 candidates lost their deposits. A modernising campaign was started within the Blaid, around the journal 'Cilmeri'. Before there could be any results the 1966 general election was called: the Blaid vote fell again, and in a result bad for morale, Elystan Morgan (who had joined the **Labour Party** after losing an election for Vice-President) won Cardiganshire for Labour.

In Carmarthenshire, where Plaid Cymru had a rare good performance during the 1966 general election, there was a by-election only a few months after. Gwynfor Evans had fought the seat in 1964 and 1966 and was chosen for the by-election (he lived there and had served on Carmarthenshire County Council since 1945). He used local issues, such as the closure of mines and railway lines and new taxes, to offer the electorate a choice 'between Wilson and Wales'. On 14 July Carmarthen gave him a majority of nearly 2,500 over Labour.

Demonstrating that it could win was important to the Blaid. Another useful development was the refining of an effective campaigning 'machine' which could be deployed in other by-elections. An early opportunity came in March 1967 at Rhondda West, where the Blaid had done relatively well in the 1950s. Though Labour won, the Blaid had the satisfaction of reducing the majority from 67% to 9%. July 1968 saw another South Wales by-election, this time in Caerphilly. Much the same arguments were made by the Blaid candidate, with the same result: a much reduced Labour majority.

Opposition to the investiture of the Prince of Wales in summer 1969 was instinctive, but probably cost the Blaid some support in the run-up to the 1970 general election. The party's successes had given it the opportunity to fight every seat for the first time, and its vote rose to 11.5%, but Gwynfor Evans lost in Carmarthen.

The early 1970s were a frustrating time for Plaid Cymru. There was a by-election early in 1972 in Merthyr Tydfil, following the death of pro-self-government MP S. O. Davies, where the Plaid Cymru vote rose from under 10% to 37%. However local authority elections had mixed results. The February 1974 general election saw the Blaid winning two seats in north-west Wales which it has held ever since, and Gwynfor Evans only failed in Carmarthen by 3 votes.

In October 1974 Carmarthen was won back, and in the Parliament that followed, devolution for Wales was put on the statute book by the Labour government. Unfortunately, anti-devolution Labour MPs had inserted an amendment requiring 40% of the electorate to support it in a referendum before the scheme came into operation. When the referendum was held on 1st March 1979, there was a four-to-one vote against. Despite this, Plaid Cymru MPs backed the government in the vote of no confidence shortly after, when they won compensation for slate miners suffering lung diseases.

The Blaid lost Carmarthen back to Labour in the 1979 general election. A further campaign of direct action was launched when the Conservative government appeared to go back on the commitment to establish a Welsh-language television channel, forcing a second rethink and the establishment of S4C in 1982. Despite this success, its vote appeared to be stuck at less than 8% of the Welsh total during the 1980s.

The election of Dafydd Elis Thomas to the Presidency in 1984 signalled a change to the left. Plaid Cymru supported the striking miners and became increasingly socialist, while changing its language policy to campaign for equal status for Welsh and English. The Blaid won the Ynys Môn seat in 1987, helped by the retirement (after a scandal) of the sitting Conservative MP.

A local agreement between Plaid Cymru and the Green Party was negotiated in the early 1990s. The Monmouth by-election of May 1991 was fought by a joint candidate, as were all the Gwent seats in the 1992 general election. This election saw a small advance in the total Plaid Cymru vote, but was enlivened by the unexpected win in the Ceredigion and Pembroke North constituency: the Blaid had been in fourth place before. An endorsement by the local Green Party had also been agreed in Ceredigion and the newly elected MP Cynog Dafis therefore claimed to be the first Green MP.

The European Parliamentary elections of 1994 were a triumph for Plaid Cymru despite its failure to win any seats. For the first time ever, Plaid Cymru took second place with 17% of the vote: the increase was largely caused by the campaign of Plaid Cymru President Dafydd Wigley in the North Wales seat, which he came within 7% of winning. In 1995 Plaid Cymru won control of Gwynedd County Council in the local authority elections.

Disappointingly the 1997 general election showed the increase had stalled. Plaid Cymru actually polled fewer votes, despite the increase in turnout, than it had in 1994. However, the election of a Labour government offered the renewed opportunity of devolution. A second referendum was held in September 1997, and after a tense night the result went in favour by 0.6% on a turnout barely over 50%. The Blaid attributed the lack of enthusiasm to the weakness of the devolution scheme and pressed in Parliament for the National Assembly for Wales to be given extra powers, including the right to vary taxes, which had been granted to the Scottish Parliament.

At its conference in September 1998, Plaid Cymru added the English alternative the Party of Wales to its name, reaching out to non-Welsh-speakers. The party's campaign for the National Assembly election made much of the moderation of the Labour Party. When Labour attacked the Blaid for being separatists, Plaid Cymru President Dafydd Wigley reminded the electorate that the Blaid had never used the term 'independence' (Saunders Lewis had written in 1926 that it would be materialistic and cruel). Aided by Labour's internal difficulties over the election of a leader and by a proportional voting system, the Blaid made an immense breakthrough in the National Assembly for Wales election in 1999, winning 17 seats including some South Wales valley constituencies which previously looked impossible for them.

Bolstered by the retention of the Ceredigion Parliamentary seat in a by-election, Plaid Cymru moved a motion of no confidence in the First Secretary of the National Assembly for Wales in February 2000. The motion was carried, resulting in the resignation of Alun Michael and appointment of Rhodri Morgan. Illness caused the resignation of Dafydd Wigley from the Presidency shortly afterwards; his successor is Ieuan Wyn Jones.

Plaid Genedlaethol Cymru [National Party of Wales]

See **Plaid Cymru (the Party of Wales)**.

Pro-Assembly Ulster Unionist

Highest vote: R. H. Bradford (North Down, February 1974) – 21,943 votes, 35.1%
Parliamentary elections won: 0
Number of candidacies: 7

On 20 March 1973, a year after the dissolution of the Northern Ireland ('Stormont') Parliament, the United Kingdom government put forward a white paper entitled *Northern Ireland Constitutional Proposals*. The white paper proposed a 78-member Assembly elected by single transferable vote, with a cross-community power-sharing Executive. The White Paper proposals were enacted in the Northern Ireland Constitution Act 1973 and elections scheduled for June 1973.

The **Ulster Unionists** were divided as to whether to co-operate with the Assembly. 73 candidates were selected by local Unionist Associations for the Assembly elections; a fortnight before polling day a list of the 40 candidates supportive of the White Paper and Brian Faulkner's leadership was published. These candidates were often referred to as 'Pledged' Unionists (pledged to support the White Paper), and 22 were successful in the election.

Brian Faulkner became Chief Executive of the Assembly on 1 January 1974. Three days later the Ulster Unionist Council voted to reject the White Paper and Faulkner resigned as their leader. The Assembly had been in operation for only a month when a United Kingdom general election was called. The Ulster Unionist Council formally allied itself with the **Ulster Democratic Unionist Party** and the **Vanguard Unionists**, forming the **United Ulster Unionist Council**, which fought all twelve Northern Ireland seats on an anti-Assembly platform. Faulkner's supporters were then forced to fight the election as Pro-Assembly Ulster Unionists. Despite opposing the leadership of the Ulster Unionists, the Pro-Assembly Ulster Unionists remained part of the Ulster Unionist Council.

Due to the surprise calling of the election, the Pro-Assembly Ulster Unionists were only able to contest seven seats. Disastrously, they failed to win any of them and lost two deposits. The Northern Ireland Assembly collapsed in May 1974 in the face of strikes organised by loyalists determined to bring it down; an Assembly by-election had already been called and went ahead in June 1974, in which the Pro-Assembly Ulster Unionist candidate saw her vote halved.

With another United Kingdom general election imminent, Faulkner decided to organise his supporters on a more formal basis outside the Ulster Unionist Council, and established the **Unionist Party of Northern Ireland** in September 1974.

Pro Euro Conservative Party

Address: 40 Smith Square, London SW1P 3HL

Number on Register: 55

Website: http://www.proeuro.co.uk

Only vote: J. C. C. Stevens (Kensington and Chelsea, 1999(25/11)) – 740 votes, 3.8%

Parliamentary elections won: 0

Number of candidacies: 1

After the loss of the 1997 general election, caused partly by tensions within the **Conservative Party** over further European integration, the party adopted a more eurosceptic policy which it felt was more in tune with its activists. This policy dismayed some of the Conservative Members of the European Parliament who supported a policy of further European integration, including membership of the single currency as soon as possible. In 1998 several of the most pro-European MEPs were not reselected for the 1999 European Parliamentary elections.

Two MEPs, John Stevens and Brendan Donnelly, decided at this time to look at the possibilities of setting up their own pro-European party, and commissioned private opinion polls to estimate the support such a party would get. When this news was leaked during the 1998 Conservative Party conference, the Conservative Party seemed ready to expel them, but they managed to keep the whip temporarily. The results of the polls were apparently encouraging and in January 1999 the Pro Euro Conservative Party was launched, with Stevens as leader.

In the event, the party did very badly at the June 1999 elections. Despite contesting every region, with some high-profile candidates, they polled only 138,000 votes nationwide, less than 1.5% of the vote, and were far-off winning any seats. John Stevens also contested the Kensington and Chelsea by-election in November, where they had polled their highest vote in June; they had the highest vote of all the minor parties, beating the **UK Independence Party**.

Pro–Life Alliance

Address: PO Box 13395, London SW3

Number on Register: 35

Website: http://www.prolifealliance.org.uk

Highest vote: J. A. Deighan (Paisley South, 1997 (6/11)) – 578 votes, 2.5%

Parliamentary elections won: 0

Number of candidacies: 58

This party was formed in 1996 under the leadership of Bruno Quintavalle. The party campaigns for absolute respect of human life from fertilisation to natural death, and therefore opposes abortion, embryo experimentation, and euthanasia. The party contested 55 seats in the 1997 election, enough to qualify for 5 minutes of TV time, but broadcasters refused to show pictures of abortion and the central portion had to be censored. The party unsuccessfully challenged this decision in the UK courts and afterwards launched a case at the European Court of Human Rights, which has yet to be decided.

Pro-Life Alliance candidates in general polled poorly in the general election. Its highest votes were in areas with a substantial Catholic population in west Scotland. It also fought five out of the eight regions in the

Scottish Parliament election.

The party mounted an unsuccessful legal move to prevent an operation to separate the siamese twins Jodie and Mary in autumn 2000.

Progressive Democratic Party

Address: 12 Manor Drive, Mill Hill, London NW7 3NE.
Website: http://www.progdemparty.org.uk
Number on Register: 36
Parliamentary elections won: 0
Number of candidacies: 0

This party was formed in 1999 by Mashud Stewart who proposed to offer more democracy to the British people. The members of the party vote on a series of positions and the nine most popular become party policy. The party opposes British membership of the European Union, and supports basing strong defence on the reintroduction of national service. It rejects the policy of first use of nuclear weapons.

Among the policies put forward for approval by the party's members are independence for Ulster, refusal of entry for refugees or asylum seekers, making abortion illegal and ending street homelessness by providing free accommodation which the homeless must take.

Progressive Liberal Party

Email address: liberalparty@hotmail.com
Website: http://www.raf.cwc.net
Parliamentary elections won: 0
Number of candidacies: 0

The Progressive Liberal Party was formed in 1999 to campaign for a fairer democracy, and to promote an ethical society. Constitutional reform is an important part of the party's programme, and it opposes British membership of the European Union. The party's social liberalism is shown by its support for the legalisation of cannabis and for repeal of laws discriminating against lesbians and gay men. It has fought local elections in Norwich, but failed to find sufficient assenting electors to stand a candidate in the Kensington and Chelsea by-election of November 1999.

Progressive Unionist Party of Northern Ireland

Address: 182 Shankill Road, Belfast BT13 2BL.

Number on Register: 65

Website: http://www.pup.org/

Highest vote: D. W. Ervine (Belfast South, 1997) – 5,687 votes, 14.4%

Parliamentary elections won: 0

Number of candidacies: 3

This party grew out of the Independent Unionist Group, formed in the Shankill Road area of Belfast in 1978 by Alderman Hugh Smyth, and calling for a 153-seat Parliament for Northern Ireland. The Independent Unionist Group took the name Progressive Unionist Party in 1979, but was still very small: when the Independent Unionist MP James Kilfedder (*see* **Ulster Popular Unionist Party**) decided in January 1980 to form his own party, he initially chose the same name, unaware of this party's existence.

The party seeks to represent the working class and declares itself Labour-oriented. Hugh Smyth has been a Belfast City Councillor since 1973 and had taken up issues promoted by loyalist groups, particularly the Ulster Volunteer Force. After the IRA ceasefire of August 1994, which happened when he was Lord Mayor of Belfast, he urged the loyalist groups to take the opportunity for peace. A combined loyalist ceasefire was called in October 1994 and the Progressive Unionist Party immediately joined in negotiations with nationalist politicians for a political settlement.

The party had not entered many elections, save in the City of Belfast, until the 1996 Northern Ireland Forum when it won 3.5% of the vote across the province, giving it two seats. Its co-operation with the peace process gave it a wider platform and in the 1997 general election it fought three seats around Belfast, saving its deposit in each. The party welcomed the Good Friday Agreement and tried to persuade the Orange Order to back it.

Two seats were won by the PUP in the Northern Ireland Assembly elections of June 1998. In the Assembly its members voted for David Trimble as First Minister, and have criticised the Democratic Unionists for obstructiveness. PUP principal spokesman David Ervine came fifth in the European Parliamentary elections of 1999.

In August 2000 the party's offices were attacked after a confrontation between the Ulster Defence Association and the Ulster Volunteer Force.

Protestant Unionist Party

See **Ulster Democratic Unionist Party**.

Public Safety Democratic Monarchist White Resident

Highest vote: W. G. Boaks (Peckham, 1982 (28/10)) – 102 votes, 0.5%

Parliamentary elections won: 0

Number of candidacies: 28

This was one of the names used by the famous by-election campaigner Bill Boaks. Lieutenant-Commander William Boaks (1904–86) had been a Royal Navy officer. He first fought an election at Walthamstow East in 1951, and then in a by-election in Walthamstow West in 1956 (after Clement Attlee had been made an Earl). In the mid-1970s Boaks was a candidate at most by-elections, invariably coming bottom of the poll.

Boaks was devoted to campaigning for road safety and became a well-known character in Wimbledon (to where he retired), frequently seen riding a bicycle festooned with slogans. Unlike other transport campaigners he was strongly opposed to buses and was alleged to hold them up deliberately by delaying on pedestrian crossings.

In the Glasgow Hillhead by-election of March 1982, Boaks set a new record low by polling only five votes: in order to stand at all, he had had to persuade ten local voters to sign his nomination papers. His last election campaign was in Birmingham Northfield in October 1982.

In a supreme irony, his death in April 1986 was due to the after-effects of a serious road accident.

Radical Alliance

Highest vote: R. W. Gott (Kingston-upon-Hull North, 1966 (27/1)) – 253 votes, 0.5%
Parliamentary elections won: 0
Number of candidacies: 2

This pacifist movement was formed in August 1965 after the founders, including Pat Arrowsmith, had met in the Campaign for Nuclear Disarmament. The Alliance was particularly opposed to the Vietnam War, which the Labour government was supporting and considering sending British troops to participate in. Richard Gott, a leader-writer on the *Guardian* newspaper, was sponsored by the Alliance to fight the Hull North by-election of January 1966 where Labour were widely expected to lose a marginal seat; his campaign inspired newspaper reporters covering the election but he obtained a derisory vote.

Pat Arrowsmith went on to oppose the Foreign Secretary, Michael Stewart, in Fulham at the 1966 general election but did no better. The Alliance was disbanded shortly after the election.

Rainbow Alliance

Address: c/o George Weiss (WPB), 21 Perrins Walk, London NW3 6TH
Email address: wpb@idiot.dircon.co.uk
Website: http://www.algroup.co.uk/wpb/rainbowalliance.htm
Highest vote: Mrs. C. D. Payne (Kensington and Chelsea, 1988 (14/7)) – 193 votes, 0.8%
Parliamentary elections won: 0
Number of candidacies: 49

As the name suggests, the Rainbow Alliance is not one single party but a loose association of groups on the fringe of politics. Some are less than serious. The Alliance was brought together in the mid 1980s by George Weiss, aka Captain Rainbow, who fought several by-elections in the 1983–7 Parliament under the banner of Captain Rainbow's Universal Party.

The Alliance supported candidates in most by-elections between 1986 and 1988, but dropped out of sight after Epping Forest (December 1988) until 1992. In the 1992 general election it sponsored three fringe candidates in Hampstead and Highgate, one as Rainbow Ark Voters Association, and the other two declaring Rainbow Connection.

In 1997 it fought 31 seats, mostly in London and the south-east, some with celebrity candidates. Its candidates used the name Rainbow Dream Ticket Party.

Raving Loony Green Giant Party

Highest vote: S. B. F. Hughes (Devon, Honiton, 1992) – 1,442 votes, 2.3%

Parliamentary elections won: 0

Number of candidacies: 9

This was a result of a split in the **Official Monster Raving Loony Party**, with the departure of Stuart Basil Fawlty Hughes, who had been the party's candidate in Honiton in 1987. After fighting two by-elections in the early 1990s, the party sponsored seven candidates throughout the United Kingdom in the 1992 general election. Stuart Basil Fawlty Hughes rejoined the main group in the mid 1990s.

Red Front

See **Revolutionary Communist Party (1981–97)**.

Referendum Party

Democracy Movement

Address: 2 Beaufort Mews, London SW6 1PF

Website: http://www.democracy-movement.org.uk

National Association of Referendum Party Supporters Groups

Address: 44 Kingston Street, Cambridge CB1 2NU

Email Address: narpsg@damak.freeserve.co.uk

Website: http://www.damak.freeserve.co.uk/narpsg.htm

Referendum Party

Highest vote: J. W. Titford (Harwich, 1997) – 4,923 votes, 9.2%

Parliamentary elections won: 0

Number of candidacies: 547

The formation of this party was announced in October 1994 by multi-millionaire industrialist Sir James Goldsmith, and the party was formed a year later and formally launched on 27 November 1995. The party was explicitly single-issue; the one policy was the holding of a referendum giving voters a choice on continued UK membership of the European Union. After funding the Yes campaign in the 1975 referendum, Sir James had become convinced that the European Union would lead to economic disaster.

After a one-day conference in Brighton on 19 October 1996, the party unveiled its proposed referendum question on 28 November: 'Do you want the UK to be part of a federal Europe, or, do you want the UK to return to an association of sovereign nations that are part of a common trading market?' Though the party proclaimed itself neutral, its campaigning was entirely eurosceptical.

Sir James Goldsmith provided extensive resources to the party, possibly up to £20 million. It gathered the support of several public figures, including Lord Tonypandy, who as George Thomas had been Speaker of the House of Commons. When the eurosceptic Conservative MP Sir George Gardiner was deselected, he joined the party for the last few weeks of the 1992–7 Parliament.

The party fought 547 constituencies in the 1997 election, not contesting those constituencies where a candidate from the major parties was considered by the party already to favour its central policy. Overall, it polled more than 800,000 votes, 2.6% of the national total, and lost 505 deposits (the highest number of lost deposits for a single party in one general election). The largest part of its vote appears to have come from former Conservative voters, and the appearance of the party was blamed by some Conservatives for the loss of several seats at the election.

Sir James Goldsmith had always insisted that the 1997 election would be the only one his party would fight, claiming that the process of European unification would become irreversible before the following general election. He died less than three months after polling day. After his death, the leadership of the party drastically cut down its activity and renamed itself the Referendum Movement, declaring it was a pressure group and would not contest elections.

This decision was highly controversial with the membership. Many of the party's active campaigners joined the **UK Independence Party** at this stage; some joined the **Democratic Party** (*see* Democratic Party (1998)). Robin Birley, a former Referendum Party candidate and stepson of Sir James Goldsmith, became Chairman of the Referendum Movement in April 1998, and a further grant to the Movement was made by the Goldsmith family. In January 1999 the Referendum Movement merged with the Euro Information Campaign, which had been formed by the millionaire Yorkshire businessman and ex-Conservative, Paul Sykes. The merged body named itself the Democracy Movement.

Some of the supporters of the Referendum Party favour the continued establishment of the party and organise around the National Association of Referendum Party Supporters Groups. This group sponsored a Referendum Party candidate in the Kensington and Chelsea by-election of November 1999.

(Irish) Repealer

Highest vote: J. O'Connell and J. O'Brien (Limerick City, 1847) – 583 and 537 votes, 93.8%

Parliamentary elections won: 71

Number of candidacies: 91

In 1800, the British government took fright at the possibility of the French Revolution transferring to Ireland and passed the Act of Union, abolishing the Irish Parliament in return for Irish representation at Westminster. The Catholic population of Ireland was divided on whether to support the Union, but united in demanding that the government get rid of various Acts (such as the Test Act) preventing their participation in public life. The Test Act was finally repealed in 1828.

Daniel O'Connell, a leader of the campaign for Catholic emancipation, won a by-election in County Clare in July 1828, becoming the first Catholic to win a Parliamentary seat in Ireland. He was still disqualified from membership of the House of Commons but his victory forced the Prime Minister (the Duke of Wellington) to pass the Emancipation Act which enabled Catholics to take their seats. In 1835 O'Connell helped bring down the Conservative government and supported a Whig administration which he hoped would promote social and economic reform in Ireland. In the event, many of the reforms were blocked by the Conservative-dominated House of Lords.

By 1839 it was clear to O'Connell that supporting the Whigs was doing no good and he formed the Repeal Association to campaign for repeal of the Act of Union. Candidates supporting repeal had already appeared in elections, especially in the 1832 general election, and the Repeal Association helped to campaign for them. In support of the Repeal Association O'Connell held mass meetings throughout Ireland, which the authorities attempted to suppress: troops prevented a meeting in Clontarf, near Dublin, in October 1843. O'Connell was arrested for seditious conspiracy and was in jail for three months in summer 1844.

Despite the failure of the attempt to campaign peacefully, O'Connell declared that the Repeal Association would not use force. This resulted in the Young Ireland movement under William Smith O'Brien leaving the

Repeal Association in July 1846 (*see* **Irish Confederation**). Daniel O'Connell died in May 1847, and the failure of the Confederation's uprising in 1848 destroyed the Repeal Association's public support.

Republican Clubs

See **The Workers' Party [Ireland]**.

Republican Clubs – The Workers Party

See **The Workers Party [Ireland]**.

Republican Labour Party

Highest vote: G. Fitt (Belfast West, 1970) – 30,649 votes, 52.8%
Parliamentary elections won: 2
Number of candidacies: 3

The Catholic population of Belfast had, by the 1950s, established a tradition of supporting various unofficial Labour and republican candidates in elections to the Northern Ireland ('Stormont') Parliament. Harry Diamond had been elected to Stormont for the Belfast Falls constituency first as a Socialist Republican in 1945, then later fought as an Irish Labour Party candidate. Gerry Fitt, a member of the Irish Labour Party, had formed the Dock Labour Party in Belfast Dock constituency and won the seat in the 1962 Stormont elections.

In 1964, the two MPs decided to unite and formed the Republican Labour Party. The party was socialist and supported non-violent republicanism. The party sponsored Harry Diamond to fight the Belfast West constituency in the 1964 general election, and he managed to beat the **Northern Ireland Labour Party** for second place.

In the 1966 general election, the much younger Gerry Fitt stood in Belfast West with the benefit of no competing Northern Ireland Labour Party or Republican candidate, and narrowly won the seat from the Unionists. In the House of Commons he took the Labour whip and attempted to raise awareness among British Labour MPs of the problems in Northern Ireland.

The party took part in the civil rights campaign of 1968–9, but Harry Diamond lost the Belfast Falls constituency in the 1969 Stormont elections. This was compensated for by Paddy Kennedy's victory in Belfast Central, winning the seat from the **National Democratic Party** (**see** National Democratic Party [Northern Ireland] (1964–70)).

On 21 August 1970, Gerry Fitt became leader of the **Social Democratic and Labour Party** and many members followed him into the new party. Paddy Kennedy refused to join the SDLP and became leader of Republican Labour. In July 1971 he withdrew from Stormont, and the party's six Belfast Corporation Councillors also withdrew. After the introduction of internment without trial in August 1971, the party was prominent in the campaign of civil disobedience, which included non-payment of rates and a forty-eight-hour hunger strike outside 10 Downing Street.

In the elections to the Northern Ireland Assembly of June 1973, Paddy Kennedy was the party's only candidate. He fought Belfast West, but polled only 4.2% of the first preference vote. He retired from active politics and the party appears to have been dissolved soon afterwards.

Republican Sinn Féin

Address: Dáithí Ó Conaill House, 223 Parnell Street, Dublin 1, Ireland.

Email address: saoirse@iol.ie

Website: http://www.come.to/RepublicanSF

Parliamentary elections won: 0

Number of candidacies: 0

At the 1986 Ard Fheis [conference] of Sinn Féin, the party's President Gerry Adams successfully proposed that the party should take up any seats it won in the Dáil of the Republic of Ireland. This decision was regarded by some members of the party, especially those living in the Republic of Ireland, as acceptance of partition. This group broke away and established Republican Sinn Féin which declared it would continue to support the armed struggle against British occupation of the north of Ireland.

The founding President of Republican Sinn Féin was Ruairí Ó Brádaigh, who had been President of Sinn Féin from 1970 to 1983, and its Vice President was Dáithí Ó Conaill who had been a leading republican strategist and Vice President of Sinn Féin from 1974. The party has firmly opposed any attempts at accommodation with the United Kingdom government. It rejected the Downing Street Declaration of December 1993 and opposed the Belfast Agreement of April 1998.

The party promotes the Éire Nua [New Ireland] policy in which Ireland would be governed as a federation of its four provinces, with the maximum decentralisation of power. It supports separation of Church and state and a neutral, non-aligned, Ireland. Because of its abstentionist policy it has not contested elections.

Republican Sinn Féin has been linked with the terrorist group the Continuity IRA which exploded a large bomb outside a hotel in Enniskillen, County Fermanagh, in July 1996. The Continuity IRA has been the only republican group not to declare a ceasefire.

Revolutionary Communist Party (1944–9)

Only vote: J. R. Haston (Glamorganshire, Neath, 1946 (15/5)) – 1,781 votes, 4.6%
Parliamentary elections won: 0
Number of candidacies: 1

In the aftermath of the Fourth International, organised by supporters of Leon Trotsky in Périgny, France, in 1938, attempts were made to found viable Trotskyite groups in Britain. The Fourth International officially recognised the Revolutionary Socialist League, which was attempting entrism within the **Labour Party**. However, an independent group called the Workers' International League had a larger membership and the Revolutionary Socialist League had difficulty organising.

In March 1944, a conference of members of both organisations in London resulted in a merger to establish the Revolutionary Communist Party. The merger was instituted by the Fourth International. Jock Haston became the leader of the party, but throughout its life it suffered from intense factionalism. When Haston and his supporters said that a small post-war economic boom was possible, the International's leadership wrote to the RCP's central committee informing it that there would be no economic recovery.

Haston was also opposed to the policy of entrism, which the International advised the party to engage in. He fought the Neath by-election of May 1946 as an RCP candidate. A faction within the RCP, led by Gerry Healy, was prompted by the International to organise against the RCP leadership; because of the policy of 'democratic centralism', the International could intervene in their support. Healy and his supporters began to engage in complete entrism from 1947.

One section of the RCP did not follow the Fourth International line that the USSR was a workers' state which had degenerated, and instead denounced it as 'state capitalist'. This group was led by Tony Cliff, and eventually broke with the remnants of the RCP to form the Socialist Review Group (*see* **Socialist Workers' Party**).

By December 1948, the Healy faction had clearly won the RCP's internal struggle, and Jock Haston and his supporters accepted that the party could not continue as an independent body. It was wound up in July 1949 and an official statement said that its members would join the Labour Party. Jock Haston renounced Trotskyism and resigned from the Fourth International in June 1950.

Revolutionary Communist Party (1981–97)

Highest vote: D. P. Hallsworth (Merseyside, Knowsley North, 1986 (13/11)) – 664 votes, 2.1%

Parliamentary elections won: 0

Number of candidacies: 33 (including Irish Freedom Movement and Workers Against Racism candidates)

The origins of this party were in the International Socialists (*see* **Socialist Workers Party**) in the early 1970s. In 1969, the International Socialists adopted a strategy called 'turn to the class' in which the movement attempted to build a working-class base by encouraging its student members to take industrial work, and forming workplace branches. Opponents of this process formed the 'Right Faction' of the International Socialists.

In 1973 this faction established the Revolutionary Communist Group, and in March 1974 they were expelled by the International Socialists. The Revolutionary Communist Group, like the International Socialists, was a Trotskyist organisation, though it neither had nor sought the official backing of the Fourth International; it set out its policies in a document published in January 1975. In 1977 the Revolutionary Communist Group itself split, resulting in the formation of the Revolutionary Communist Tendency – which became the Revolutionary Communist Party in 1981.

The party fought Lambeth Central in the 1981 Greater London Council elections, as well as sponsoring three candidates in East London using its front organisation, Workers Against Racialism. It fought an active campaign in the Bermondsey by-election of February 1983, when journalists from the party's newspaper *Next Step* attended press conferences organised by other parties. Chief among the early preoccupations for the party was the constitutional future of Ireland: the party supported IRA terrorism.

The 1987 election saw the party campaign under the name Red Front. It put forward 14 candidates, all in Labour seats in large cities, but none exceeded 1.4% of the vote. The 1992 election saw 8 candidates, this time under the party's formal name, together with one candidate each from the Irish Freedom Movement and Workers Against Racism.

The party magazine, *Living Marxism*, was established in 1988 and achieved a wide circulation outside the party, partly by adopting a series of policy positions out of keeping with the traditional far left. The party supported those who argued that AIDS was not caused by the Human Immunodeficiency Virus. It strongly sympathised with the Serb positions in the succession of wars in former Yugoslavia in the 1990s. Later on, *Living Marxism* developed a strong interest in a distinctive kind of libertarianism. It opposed restrictions on firearm ownership and attacked the environmental movement.

At the beginning of 1997 *Living Marxism* relaunched as *LM* and the Revolutionary Communist Party was wound up. *LM* magazine was forced into bankruptcy in 1999 when ITN and one of its journalists won a libel suit over a claim that they had misrepresented the truth about a Bosnian Serb-run camp during the Bosnian civil war.

Revolutionary Communist Party of Britain (Marxist–Leninist) (1979–)

Address: 170 Wandsworth Road, London SW8 2LA

Website: http://www.rcpbml.org.uk/

Number on Register: 139

Highest vote: A. D. Rifkin (Portsmouth South, October 1974) – 612 votes, 1.2%

Parliamentary elections won: 0

Number of candidacies: 16

This party was formed as the Communist Party of England (Marxist-Leninist). It had its origins in a movement called the Internationalists formed in 1963 by Hardial Bains in Vancouver, Canada. In August 1967, Hardial Bains' supporters in the UK formed the English Internationalists; in March 1972 this became the Communist Party of England (Marxist-Leninist).

The party's policy was communism of a Maoist variety. It began contesting elections in 1973, when it fought two by-elections. Six candidates were sponsored in the February 1974 election, and eight in October 1974. The candidates were mostly in south London, the south coast, and university areas. The party ceased fighting elections after the October 1974 general election. The party renamed itself the Revolutionary Communist Party of Britain (Marxist-Leninist) in March 1979.

The party was supportive of the government of Albania during the time of communist control, and sharply critical of Soviet and Chinese communism which it regarded as revisionist. It continues to organise, though mainly around its bookshop and the *Workers' Weekly* newspaper.

Revolutionary Workers' Party

Parliamentary elections won: 0

Number of candidacies: 0

This party is the British representative of the Posadist tendency. The Posadists had broken away from the United Secretariat of the (Trotskyite)

Fourth International in 1962, and the party was formed in early 1963. Posadists were named after their founder, Juan Posadas, a Latin American who took the Marxist belief in the inevitable self-destruction of capitalism one stage further. Posadists believe that the continuance of capitalism will lead to a nuclear war, which socialists will inevitably win. It has not fought elections.

Rizz Party

Address: 23 Howitt Road, London NW3 4LT
Highest vote: C. Rizz (Hampstead and Highgate, 1997) – 101 votes, 0.2%
Parliamentary elections won: 0
Number of candidacies: 3

This party was formed by Captain Rizz, a musician living in Hampstead. He allied with the **Rainbow Alliance** in 1992 to fight Hampstead and Highgate, calling for a relaxation of radio licensing to free the airwaves, and for lifting of restrictive licensing laws. The party also campaigned for 'home rule for Hampstead, Highgate and everywhere else'. Rizz came bottom of the poll.

In 1997 Rizz fought three constituencies but only two (Dulwich and West Norwood, Hampstead and Highgate) were on behalf of his party; in the other (Lewisham East) he won his highest vote as the candidate of the Rainbow Dream Ticket Party (*see* Rainbow Alliance). However, he was bottom of the poll in all three.

Scottish Covenant Association

Parliamentary elections won: 0
Number of candidacies: 0

The Scottish Covenant was a product of the 'Scottish National Assembly', a conference first organised in 1947 by John MacCormick (*see* **National Party of Scotland**). The Scottish National Assembly declared its aim as being to promote the spiritual and economic welfare of the Scottish nation, and soon edged towards a policy of devolution. A draft scheme was published in 1948, followed in 1949 by the full Scottish Covenant. The Covenant itself was firmly loyal to the Crown, but called for a Parliament for Scotland with legislative authority.

The backers of the Covenant then sought signatures from the people of Scotland: there were 50,000 within a week, and in February 1950 the number exceeded 1,000,000. The eventual total was over 2,000,000 though some of these were not authentic. Many well-known personalities signed, and some important political figures from all parties. The kidnapping of the Stone of Destiny from Westminster Abbey in December 1950 was partly undertaken in order to win publicity for the Covenant.

Early in 1951, when a general election looked close, the Scottish Covenant Association was formed to bring the movement together. Despite its mass support, the Association was divided as to whether to nominate candidates. In the 1950 general election it had seemed likely that the committee organising the Covenant would endorse candidates who agreed with it, but in the event no decision was taken. At the 1951 general election the Association had threatened to fight large numbers of seats, but eventually withdrew. To have begun fighting elections would have split the movement as many of its members were involved in other political parties.

The Scottish Covenant Association continued local activism as a pressure group throughout the 1950s though with decreasing influence (losing out partly to the **Scottish National Party)**. It appears to have disbanded in the early 1960s.

Scottish Green Party

Address: 14 Albany Street, Edinburgh EH1 3QB

Email address: info@scottishgreens.org.uk

Website: http://www.scottishgreens.org.uk

Highest vote: D. G Mellor (Paisley South, 1990 (29/11)) – 918 votes, 3.5%

Parliamentary elections won: 0

Number of candidacies: 28

The Scottish branch of the **Green Party** was separated from the English and Welsh party in 1990 and formed as an independent political party; it is therefore a full member of the Federation of European Green Parties. The independence of the parties reflects the Scottish party's commitment to Scottish independence, though the party took part in the Scottish Constitutional Convention from March 1989 which sought agreement on a devolution scheme.

In the 1992 general election, the party fought 19 of the 72 Scottish seats, a smaller proportion than was contested by the Green Party in England and Wales, and polled slightly fewer votes where it did stand. Local elections had shown that the party's largest bases were in the middle-class wards of Edinburgh and the Highlands, where well-known local personalities dominated politics (the party won a Regional Council seat in Highland in 1990). In the 1997 general election, the party therefore concentrated its efforts, standing in only five seats in these areas. However, only one candidate exceeded 1% of the vote.

The party's opportunity came in May 1999 with the Scottish Parliament and its use of the Additional Member System of voting. The party left alone the constituency seats but entered candidates for all the 'top-up' regions. Throughout the country, it polled 4%, and in the Lothian Region (including Edinburgh), nearly 7%. This was enough to win one seat, and Robin Harper became the first elected Green Parliamentarian in the whole of the United Kingdom. The party consolidated its success in the European Parliament elections a month later, polling 6% on average. Its best result was 13.8% in Edinburgh Central.

The party has set out five principles which guide it: ecological wisdom, radical democracy, social justice, non-violence and egalitarianism. Its 1997 general election manifesto advocated land reform, food co-operatives to supply local shops, a national plan for the reduction of traffic, and a Basic Income Scheme to simplify the benefits system.

Scottish Labour Party (1906–9)

Highest vote: J. Burgess (Montrose Burghs, 1908 (12/5)) – 1,937 votes, 29.4%
Parliamentary elections won: 0
Number of candidacies: 2

After the general election of 1906, the **Scottish Workers' Representation Committee** took the name Scottish Labour Party. This change of name also prompted the party to establish local branches. The party's relations with the **Labour Party** were sometimes strained as the Labour Party had also run candidates in Scotland (two of whom were elected in 1906).

In January 1908 the Scottish Labour Party conference voted to affiliate to the Labour Party. Despite the affiliation, the party fought two by-elections in 1908 at which its candidates did not receive Labour Party endorsement. This situation was not sustainable in the long term and at the party's ninth conference in January 1909 a motion was passed to merge with the Labour Party.

Scottish Labour Party (1976–9)

Highest vote: J. Sillars (Ayrshire South, 1979) – 12,750 votes, 31.4%
Parliamentary elections won: 0
Number of candidacies: 4

The formation of this party was first suggested by James Sillars, who had been Labour MP for South Ayrshire from 1970. Sillars was a left-wing MP who was a very strong advocate of Scottish Home Rule, and felt held back by the cautious approach of the **Labour Party**. In the referendum on continued membership of the European Communities in 1975, Sillars was one of the main spokesmen for the No campaign in Scotland, while the Labour Prime Minister supported a Yes vote, prompting him again to suggest the formation of a separate party.

Sillars made his move in January 1976, shortly after the publication of a white paper outlining government plans for a limited Assembly for Scotland with neither tax nor industrial policy responsibilities. He was joined by John Robertson, MP for Paisley, by Alex Neil, the Research Officer for the Labour Party in Scotland, and by Dan Skene, a member of the Scottish Executive of the Labour Party. The Scottish Labour Party was formally launched on 18 January 1976 in Glasgow.

At first, the Labour Party did not withdraw the whip from Sillars and Robertson, partly because of the political situation in Parliament where Labour had an overall majority of only 1 seat. On 26th July, the two voluntarily resigned the Labour whip four days after the Chancellor of the

Exchequer announced £1 billion of spending cuts. Sillars claimed the inheritance of the socialism of Keir Hardie and Tom Johnston, and the Scottish Labour Party campaigned for a real legislative Parliament for Scotland.

At the Party's first congress at Stirling in October 1976, it became apparent that the far left – the **International Marxist Group** – was attempting to infiltrate the party. The leadership refused to admit one delegation and expelled four others who were believed to be IMG affiliated, which prompted about one-third of the other delegates to walk out in sympathy.

The party saw only limited success in elections during the late 1970s. Two of Sillars's local supporters won seats on Cumnock and Doon Valley District Council in the elections of May 1977, but apart from one seat on Clydebank District Council this was the party's only success. No seats were won in the regional council elections of 1978 and the party's candidate in the Glasgow Garscadden by-election polled only 583 votes.

Sillars used his prominence and skill as an orator to campaign for devolution, forming a double-act with anti-devolutionist Tam Dalyell in the March 1979 referendum campaign. The party joined in the 'Yes for Scotland' campaign with supporters of devolution from some other parties. Despite the loss of the referendum on which an artificial threshold of 40% of the electorate had been imposed, Sillars and Robertson supported the Labour government in the subsequent vote of no confidence. John Robertson stood down at the end of the Parliament but Sillars sought re-election and the party nominated two other candidates.

In a close campaign, James Sillars came close to retaining his seat, but the other two candidates suffered badly lost deposits. The 'one-man band' situation this revealed led Sillars to leave the party shortly after the 1979 election, and it was subsequently disbanded. He was approached by members of the **Scottish National Party** who invited him to join; shortly after the 1980 district council elections, he did. Sillars later claimed that he only joined after the SNP did badly, in order that his move not be perceived as opportunistic. Most other members of the Scottish Labour Party also joined the SNP and some have risen to high office in that party.

Scottish Land Restoration League

Highest vote: J. S. Maxwell (Glasgow Blackfriars and Hutchesontown, 1885) – 1,156 votes, 14.4%

Parliamentary elections won: 0

Number of candiacies: 5

The American economist Henry George proposed in *Progress and Poverty* (published in 1879) that all other taxes be abolished and replaced by a single tax on the 'economic rent' of bare land (i.e. from the use of the land, but not from developments on it). After the depression of the mid 1870s the idea found a great deal of support in Scotland, where large amounts of land were owned by absent landlords.

Early in 1884, Henry George went on a lecture tour to Scotland to publicise his book. As a result of this tour, a group of supporters in Glasgow formed the Scottish Land Restoration League in February 1884. The League advocated that the economic product of the land be restored to the people, and the largest part of its supporters were working-class; its Scottish organiser was Richard McGhee, who was later an Irish **Nationalist** MP.

After the third Reform Act of 1884, most heads of households had the vote and the Land Restoration League fought five constituencies in and around Glasgow. Two of the League's candidates won over 10% of the vote but the three others had derisory totals. It did not fight elections thereafter though it did support Keir Hardie in the Mid Lanark by-election of April 1888.

The League appears to have renamed itself the Scottish Single Tax League soon after, and in 1904 this became the Scottish League for the Taxation of Land Values.

Scottish Militant Labour

Highest vote: T. Sheridan (Glasgow Pollok, 1992) – 6,287 votes, 19.3%

Parliamentary elections won: 0

Number of candidacies: 10 (including 9 as part of the Scottish Socialist Alliance)

Scottish Militant Labour was formed on 9 December 1991 and launched on 30 January 1992. It was the first section of the Militant tendency (*see* **Socialist Party** (1996–)) to abandon the policy of entrism and fight elections on its own, an action which clearly anticipated the similar decision in England and Wales which led to the formation of Militant Labour in 1993. The party was supportive of Scottish independence, in order to create a socialist Scottish republic.

In the 1992 election, Scottish Militant Labour nominated its leader, Tommy Sheridan, to fight the Glasgow Pollok seat. Sheridan had become a prominent campaigner from 1988 as the organiser of the Scottish Anti-Poll Tax Union, and because of his links with the Militant tendency had been expelled from Glasgow Pollok Constituency Labour Party in that year. At the time of the election, Sheridan was serving a sentence of six months' imprisonment in Saughton gaol, Edinburgh, after defying a court order banning him from attending warrant sales of the goods of people convicted of failing to pay the Community Charge (commonly called the Poll Tax).

Sheridan polled very well at the election and secured second place with nearly a fifth of the vote. This success was followed a month later by Sheridan winning a seat on Glasgow District Council. In the 1994 European Parliamentary elections, Sheridan fought the Glasgow seat and came third with 12.7% of the vote.

The 1995 unitary council elections saw a patchy performance by the party. While Tommy Sheridan retained his seat with 48% of the vote and there were good performances in some other Glasgow wards, there were few candidates outside Glasgow, and where they stood they did poorly (Dundee was the only other substantial base).

In 1996 the party began negotiations with other organisations on the broad left in Scotland, leading to the formation of the **Scottish Socialist Alliance** shortly before the 1997 general election. Of the Scottish Socialist Alliance's 16 candidates, 8 were sponsored by Scottish Militant Labour and they consistently polled better than the other candidates of the Alliance (though this may be explained by the fact that they fought the most promising constituencies in Glasgow).

The Scottish Socialist Alliance worked well in practice, without any major doctrinal differences, and in 1998 Scottish Militant Labour proposed that it be solidified into a single party. This proposal was accepted and the **Scottish Socialist Party** was formed that summer.

Scottish National Party

Address: 6 North Charlotte Street, Edinburgh EH2 4JH, Scotland

Email address: snp.hq@snp.org.uk

Website: http://www.snp.org

Number on Register: 6

Highest Vote: D. J. Stewart (Western Isles, 1974(F)) – 10,079 votes, 67.1%

Parliamentary elections won: 40

Number of candidacies: 672

In February 1934 the **National Party of Scotland** agreed to merge with the **Scottish Party**, bringing together the devolutionist and nationalist tendencies of Scottish politics and creating the Scottish National Party. The strain of unity meant that many members from the extreme wings of the party left soon after the unification. This was especially true of the extreme nationalists, as the SNP's policy highlighted Home Rule and downplayed independence.

The SNP fought eight seats in the 1935 general election. Though its candidates in the central belt did not obtain much support, in rural areas the party saved three deposits and polled nearly 30% in the Western Isles. The insistence on a moderate policy was continued by SNP leader John MacCormick, though members continued to leave when they failed to find the party sufficiently exciting (membership dwindled to only 2,000 in 1939).

Though losing members the SNP was gaining credibility. Its members were openly involved in cross-party organisations, and in 1938 the Scottish Liberal Association (which had favoured self-government since 1912) concluded a pact with the SNP whereby the SNP was allowed to fight twelve seats without Liberal opposition. The SNP leadership decided to capitalise on the extensive connections of SNP members by calling an all-party convention to discuss Scottish Home Rule, but outbreak of war in 1939 prevented it being held.

The war presented the SNP with a difficulty over its attitude to conscription and pacifism. A resolution had been passed in 1937 opposing conscription except when practised by a Scottish government, and taking this lead, the Chair of Aberdeen SNP, Douglas Young decided to become a cause célèbre. He was charged with resisting conscription and in a long court battle was eventually convicted and sent to jail. The party did not consider itself bound by the electoral truce and fought the Argyll by-election of April 1940, polling 37.2% in a straight fight with the Conservatives.

Meanwhile, John MacCormick attempted to come to an arrangement with the Labour Secretary of State for Scotland in the coalition government, Tom Johnston, who was known privately to favour Home Rule. The two sides of the argument came together at the SNP's annual conference in June 1942. Douglas Young proposed a pacifistic motion, which was narrowly passed, while John MacCormick's motion to cease fighting elections and try to build a cross-party consensus was rejected.

MacCormick then left the party and formed the Scottish Union – which later formed the **Scottish Covenant Association**. Douglas Young was elected as the new Chairman of the SNP and the party took a much more nationalistic stance thereafter, re-engaging with some of the members it had lost in the 1930s.

This stance, and exploitation of wartime grievances such as the conscription of Scottish women to work in English factories, began to pay dividends in by-elections. Douglas Young came within 2,000 votes of winning Kirkcaldy in February 1944. On 12 April 1945, the SNP's Secretary Dr Richard McIntyre, was elected as Member of Parliament for Motherwell with a majority of 617 over Labour. Breaking with tradition, Dr McIntyre presented himself at the House of Commons to take his seat without sponsors; he was ordered to return the next day and two Labour MPs agreed to act as his sponsors.

Dr McIntyre's success proved shortlived, as Parliament was dissolved after the end of the war and the electoral truce came to an end; in a normal fight he managed to beat the Conservatives but lost to Labour by nearly 8,000 votes. Six of the party's other seven candidates lost their deposits. The next year, the party adopted a new constitution written largely by Dr McIntyre; it was a firmly left-wing document which, while it did not give a definite programme for an independent Scotland, did outline the principles which were influencing the SNP at the time. The party declared that, if it won the majority of seats in Scotland, its members would withdraw and form a new Parliament for Scotland.

Despite having had an MP, the SNP took a back seat in the debate over the constitutional future of Scotland at the beginning of the 1950s. The devolutionist Scottish Convention, founded by ex-SNP leader John MacCormick, was much more popular. Dr McIntyre saw his share of the poll in Motherwell fall to below 10% in the 1950 election, at which only three SNP candidates stood; in 1951 there were only two.

By 1959 the party was recovering and gaining ground in Perthshire; it fought five constituencies in the general election of that year. A November 1961 by-election in Glasgow Bridgeton, once held by Independent Labour Party leader James Maxton, revived the party further. An uninspiring Labour candidate led the SNP to portray itself as the inheritor of the Maxton tradition, and though Labour won, the SNP almost beat the Conservatives for second place. SNP candidate Ian Macdonald then gave up his farm to work unpaid as the SNP's National Organiser.

In June the next year, another by-election came in West Lothian. Here the Labour candidate was an aristocratic radical who seemed out of place in a depressed urban area, and SNP candidate William Wolfe campaigned hard on the issue of the local shale oil industry. He easily outpolled both the Conservative and Liberal candidates and came a clear second; but more importantly he put together a nucleus of activists around which a mass campaigning party could be built. In fact, at the SNP's 1963 conference, one quarter of all delegates were from West Lothian.

In February 1964, William Wolfe (then Vice Chairman of the party) offered the Scottish Liberal Association a similar pact to that agreed in 1938. This time the Liberals declined, though they tried to avoid standing candidates where the SNP was intending to fight. There were eventually 15 SNP candidates in the 1964 general election; the party therefore fought more than one fifth of all Scottish constituencies.

The unofficial pact with the Liberals paid off, for in the four seats which the two parties both fought, the average SNP poll was almost half the average for all candidates. The party saved only three deposits, however, and lost the second place it had been cultivating in Perth and East Perthshire. By contrast William Wolfe's vote in West Lothian increased on the by-election.

When a second general election followed after only 18 months, the rapid increase in SNP membership (from 2,000 in 1962 to 42,000 in 1966) allowed the party to fight 23 seats. In the area around the Forth and Tay estuaries the party fought every seat and saved every deposit. The SNP's increased vote contrasted with the Liberals who slumped in Scotland in 1966.

Early in 1967 another chance by-election offered the party an opportunity – Glasgow Pollok, the most marginal Labour–Conservative seat. SNP candidate George Leslie proved a good orator and fought a glamorous campaign, using the endorsement of Sean Connery. Eventually the Conservatives won, largely because much of the Labour vote was diverted to the SNP. Pollok marked the point at which the SNP became a credible party.

September 1967 saw a very timely by-election in Hamilton. The by-election was caused by the resignation of the sitting MP to a well-paid quango job, and the Labour candidate (emerging from a disputed selection) was very weak: a National Union of Mineworkers nominee in a constituency where almost all the mines had closed. SNP candidate Winnie Ewing was a left-winger (unlike George Leslie), and managed to exploit grievances over an economy on the verge of devaluation. She won the by-election with a majority of 1,799.

Victory in Hamilton sent shockwaves through Scotland. All sorts of unexpected groups started making pro-devolution hints; the Conservative Party formed a 'Constitutional Committee' to work out a devolution scheme, under former leader Sir Alec Douglas-Home, and the Labour government eventually set up the Royal Commission on the Constitution (over-ruling the Scottish Secretary Willie Ross). The SNP vote continued to rise, and in the 1968 local elections, it was projected that the SNP would outpoll all other parties. An opinion poll in May 1968 put the SNP at 43%.

The growing local government presence of the SNP forced it to examine its policies on a wider range of issues than it had previousl considered. Many SNP councillors were inexperienced and it showed. A series of policy study groups formulated a left-wing agenda which faced opposition from the activists determined to get independence first. Internal splits and the recovery of other parties meant the SNP's vote fell in the 1969 local elections to 22%, and a by-election in Glasgow Gorbals (the safest seat in Scotland) saw Labour hold off the challenge in October.

For the first time the SNP intended to contest all the Scottish seats at the 1970 election. In the event it fought 65 out of 71, leaving alone three

Liberals and being unable to fight two Glasgow seats; Rutherglen was left to an unofficial candidate. Standing candidates against most Liberals ended all talks of a pact (despite four out of six Scottish Liberal MPs being in favour).

The results were disappointing. Hamilton was lost to Labour – the same uninspiring candidate who had lost the by-election – by over 8,500 votes. The brightest part of the 1970 election for the SNP was their success in the unique Western Isles constituency, where the 35-year veteran Labour MP was defeated by Donald Stewart. There were also seven second-places. Progress was already being made by the SNP in 1971, when Dr Richard McIntyre cut the Labour majority in a by-election in Stirling and Falkirk.

In September 1972 the party launched a campaign which managed to unite the issue of nationalism with economic advancement. Oil and gas-fields had been discovered under the North Sea, and production forecasts seemed to increase by the week. The slogan 'It's Scotland's Oil!' was coined, though the campaign was always more profound than the slogan: the SNP campaigned for a programme to spread the economic benefit so as not to create upheaval on the north-east coast.

Early 1973 saw a by-election in Dundee East, a Labour-held seat which had seen an SNP lost deposit in 1970. Gordon Wilson was only 1,141 votes behind Labour. In the autumn of that year there were two by-elections on the same day. Most SNP effort went into Glasgow Govan. The campaign was enlivened by the publication, the week before the poll, of the Report of the Royal Commission on the Constitution. The Royal Commission recommended a devolved system. On 8 November, Margo Macdonald won Govan with a majority of 571.

The SNP therefore went into the February 1974 general election in a spirit of optimism. Both Labour and the Conservatives had dropped their commitments to devolution. The party polled 22% of the vote and won seven seats – gaining four from the Conservatives and two from Labour – though it lost Govan back to Labour. A return of the SNP threat led the incoming Labour government to reconsider its position and a white paper on devolution was published in September.

This development did not slow the SNP's advance, and one opinion poll showed it in the lead during the campaign leading to the October 1974 election. In the end it polled 30% and won four more seats, all from the

Conservatives. In the very close 1974–9 Parliament it proved useful to have a sizeable presence.

The referendum on membership of the European Communities in June 1975 presented the SNP with a dilemma. Many leading members were privately in favour of membership, though most voters were believed to be against. Unity was achieved by campaigning under the slogan 'No – on anyone else's terms'. This was partly a tactical move as it appeared possible that Scotland could vote No while the overall vote went Yes – adding to the case for self-government. When Scotland voted 60% Yes, the policy was reversed and in later years the party became enthusiastically pro-Europe.

On 27 November 1975 the government finalised its devolution proposals in a White Paper which promised a very weak Assembly. Willie Ross, the hardline anti-devolution Scottish Secretary, left office in April 1976 and a devolution bill was introduced in November 1976. However, opposition from anti-devolution Labour MPs stalled its progress in February 1977 and the government was forced to start again that November.

Meanwhile the SNP suffered an internal divide over strategy. At the SNP's 1976 conference, Douglas Henderson MP demanded that the party force an early general election, which he believed would result in an SNP win. This demand was opposed by others who thought this would lead to the fall of a government committed to devolution. A proposal to support the devolution bill was carried by 594 to 425. There was a tension between the SNP MPs and other senior figures in the party not in Parliament.

The internal divisions found their way into SNP campaigning. A by-election in Glasgow Garscadden in April 1978 was easily held by Labour, and two further by-elections in Hamilton (May) and Berwick and East Lothian (October) showed a swing to Labour. Though the SNP made progress in the district council elections of 1978, it was only a modest advance at a time of high government unpopularity.

Anti-devolution Labour MPs forced the government to include a referendum on whether the devolution Act would come into effect, and required that at least 40% of the electorate vote Yes in order to count as a positive result. The referendum was held on 1 March 1979, but resulted in only 32.85% of the electorate voting Yes. When the Labour government proposed further talks on devolution the SNP insisted that the Act be put into operation and put down a motion of no confidence in the government.

The Conservatives then put down their own motion of no confidence which took precedence, knowing the SNP was now bound to support it. During the debate (28 March 1979) Labour Prime Minister James Callaghan drew attention to the expected drop in SNP support by observing 'it's the first time in recorded history turkeys have been known to vote for an early Christmas'. With SNP support the motion was carried by one vote, though some SNP MPs privately opposed it.

As expected the SNP suffered badly in the general election. Its share of the Scottish vote fell to 17.3% and it lost all but two of its MPs. In the aftermath of the defeat the running in the SNP was made by the left. The '79 Group' was formed to campaign for a socialist and republican Scotland, urging the party to campaign among the working-class who had been the most likely to vote Yes in 1979. The 79 Group was joined in 1980 by Jim Sillars (see **Scottish Labour Party** (1976–9)).

When five 79 Group members, Sillars among them, were elected to the SNP executive in 1981, SNP policy changed to supporting unilateralism and withdrawal from NATO. The 79 Group also organised an incompetent civil disobedience campaign including an attempted occupation of the intended site for the Scottish Assembly. The SNP leadership then took action by banning all organised groups from membership; some 79 Group members were expelled in 1982 (among them Alex Salmond, a future party leader).

The highly publicised struggle with the 79 Group further damaged SNP support and its vote dropped to 11.8% in the 1983 general election. It was lucky to retain the two seats it held. Facing the suggestion that their best time had passed, the 1984 SNP conference endorsed the idea of a Scottish Constitutional Convention to form a consensus between the parties.

Largely as a product of the unpopularity of Mrs Thatcher and the Conservatives, the SNP vote increased to 14% in the 1987 election. This was a bittersweet occasion for the party: it lost the two seats it had to Labour, but won three seats from the Conservatives. The SNP's gains in 1987 appear to have much to do with tactical voting by previous Alliance voters.

A reaction to the continued Conservative control over Scotland which heavily rejected them in 1987 was the launch, on 6 July 1988, of the 'Claim of Right', a declaration of Scottish sovereignty. In November, Jim Sillars won the Glasgow Govan by-election from Labour, helped by an inept Labour candidate who seemed to illustrate the SNP's argument that Labour MPs were not fighting adequately for Scotland. Sillars jibed at Scotland's Labour MPs: 'the feeble 50 are now the frightened 49'.

The loss of Govan forced Labour to revisit its previous reaction to SNP advances. The Scottish Labour Party signed the Claim of Right and decided to take part in the Constitutional Convention which was being set up. This move forced the SNP to withdraw: their demand for the Convention had been partly an attempt to put pressure on Labour, but they did not want to find themselves tied to the same policy as Labour.

Labour's increasing use of nationalist rhetoric and support for the Convention stopped the SNP advance from going further. Though the SNP vote at the June 1989 European elections was 25.6%, a by-election in Glasgow Central on the same day was easily held by Labour.

Gordon Wilson, who despite his defeat at Dundee East in 1987 had retained the SNP leadership, retired in 1990. On 22 September Alex Salmond was elected as the new leader at the age of 35. Salmond, having been involved with the 79 Group, was a supporter of proposals to shift the SNP leftwards; this was a populist move at a time when the Labour Party was moderating.

The 1992 general election was, in general, a disappointment to the SNP. It had the endorsement of the *Scottish Sun* from January 1992, and the party's vote rose to 21.5%, but it lost Govan back to Labour and made no other gains. The party's confident slogan 'Free by 93' proved an embarrassment, though the party was able to make some gains in the district council elections of May 1992.

There was a steady advance in SNP support during the 1992 Parliament. A month after winning 26.7% in the regional council elections of 1994, the party won a second seat in the European Parliament in the 1994 elections. Its vote rose to 32.6% – higher than October 1974. At the end of the same month, Kay Ullrich ran Labour very close in the by-election in Monklands East caused by the death of Labour leader John Smith.

May 1995 saw a by-election in Perth and Kinross, where the SNP had been only 2,000 votes behind the Conservatives in the general election. This was the first by-election at which the SNP were challenging in a Conservative-held constituency. In the circumstances where the government was almost unprecedentedly unpopular, the SNP won the by-election easily, with Labour also increasing its vote.

In the 1997 election the SNP increased its vote by only 0.5%, but it gained three seats from Conservatives who were undergoing their worst election result in Scotland ever. In the incoming Labour government's referendum on devolution, the SNP backed a Yes vote and co-operated with Labour and the Liberal Democrats in the campaign. The party's popularity surged in the opinion polls after the referendum vote in favour of devolution, but the Labour Party managed to restore its lead in time for the first election to the Scottish Parliament.

During the Scottish Parliament election campaign, the SNP pledged to use the tax-varying power of the Parliament to increase income tax by 1p in the pound, which it described as 'the penny for Scotland'. Labour attacked the plan to raise taxes and campaigned hard against the SNP policy of independence for Scotland, and managed to win easily the largest number of seats. The SNP polled 29% on the first ballot, but gained only one seat from Labour on top of the six seats won at the 1997 general election.

Alex Salmond unexpectedly resigned as leader in 2000, and was succeeded by John Swinney, who beat Alex Neil by 547 to 268 votes.

Scottish (Parliamentary) Labour Party (1888–94)

Highest vote: R. Smillie (Mid Lanarkshire, 1894 (5/4)) – 1,221 votes, 13.8%
Parliamentary elections won: 0
Number of candidacies: 4

In the mid 1880s, Keir Hardie was an advanced Liberal who had founded two miners unions and was working for them full time, when the Liberal MP for the mining area of Mid Lanarkshire resigned. He applied to be **Liberal Party** candidate for the by-election but was rejected, and decided to fight the election anyway on the platform of 'independent working-class representation'.

Though polling only 8.4%, Hardie's campaign obtained the support of a wide range of bodies: the **Highland Land League** and **Scottish Land Restoration League**, the Glasgow Trades Council and Scottish Home Rule Association. Immediately after the by-election, Hardie set about forming the Scottish Parliamentary Labour Party, and it was launched at a conference in Glasgow on 25 August 1888.

Hardie's Liberal Party connections helped him to recruit R. B. Cunninghame Graham (Liberal MP for North West Lanarkshire) as honorary President of the party. Dr Gavin Brown Clark (**Crofter** MP for Caithness-shire) was one of two Vice Presidents, and Charles Conybeare (Liberal MP for Camborne) also held office within the party. Though the party was officially called Scottish Parliamentary Labour Party, it was usually referred to internally and externally as the Scottish Labour Party.

The party's policy was socialistic (advocating nationalisation of banks, mining and the railways) and it sent Keir Hardie as its delegate to the Second International in Paris in 1889, but it was cautious: it wanted to build up a large political Labour party and then make it firmly socialist. Though many leading Scottish trade unionists were supporters of the party, it had no formal link with them: initially the **Scottish United Trades Council Labour Party** intended the party to be represented on its executive, but it was excluded after only a few months. It also had links with Irish nationalism and with the Scottish Home Rule Association and supported a federal-type constitution.

In about 1890, R. B. Cunninghame Graham was selected as Liberal candidate for Glasgow Camlachie, but his continual attacks on the Liberal Party's policy and support for the Scottish Parliamentary Labour Party led to his being dropped as candidate in February 1892, a few months before the 1892 general election. The Scottish Parliamentary Labour Party then adopted him as its candidate, but with only 11.9% of the vote he failed to retain his seat. One other candidate in a similar seat (a convert from **Liberal Unionism**) polled nearly as well though the party's third candidate in Dundee polled poorly.

In January 1893, the party passed a resolution to prohibit members of other political parties from holding office, and Clark and Conybeare were forced to resign. This move was partially inspired by the foundation of the **Independent Labour Party**, but also by difficulties with having members of different parties involved. One Vice President, John Ferguson, supported Liberal candidates in accordance with Irish **Nationalist** policy. The decision cost the party heavily as the MPs had been heavy contributors to party funds. Despite this loss the party continued to campaign and expand. Another by-election in Mid Lanarkshire was held in April 1894, at which Robert Smillie received twice as many votes as Keir Hardie had six years previously.

Keir Hardie had been elected as founder Chairman of the ILP and it was natural that the two parties began to co-operate. At the Scottish Parliamentary Labour Party's conference on 26 December 1894, a motion to dissolve the party and merge into the Independent Labour Party was carried unanimously.

Scottish Party

Only vote: Sir A. M. MacEwen (Kilmarnock, 1933 (2/11)) – 6,098 votes, 16.9%
Parliamentary elections won: 0
Number of candidacies: 1

The nucleus of the Scottish Party was originally a group within the Glasgow Cathcart Conservative Association who favoured Home Rule for Scotland. In 1930 this group had prompted the establishment of the Scottish National Development Council to attract development funds, which was originally a private venture but later obtained government funding.

The group of Cathcart Conservatives sought the establishment of a devolved Parliament within the United Kingdom, and as such were opposed to the nationalism of the **National Party of Scotland**; they were also opposed to the left-wing tendency within the NPS. In October 1932 the Scottish Party was formed as a breakaway, inspired by a succession of attacks on the infant Home Rule movement by Scottish industrialists.

Though called a political party, the Scottish Party at first organised more as a think tank and pressure group. It sent questionnaires to the candidates at the East Fife by-election of February 1933 to ask them to what extent they agreed with the party's policy. The party had some high-profile supporters, including the 6th Duke of Montrose, Professor Andrew Dewar Gibb (Regius Professor of Scots Law at Glasgow University), and Sir Alexander MacEwen.

Despite being in separate parties, members of the National Party of Scotland (led by its founder John MacCormick) made contact with the Scottish Party, with a view to joint working. MacCormick had acted in a personal capacity to advise the party on policy. These moves were helped when the National Party of Scotland endorsed Sir Alexander MacEwen, the Scottish Party's candidate in the Kilmarnock by-election of November 1933. His poll of nearly 17% was higher than the NPS had yet achieved.

In April 1934, merger terms with the National Party of Scotland were agreed and the merged party was named the **Scottish National Party**.

Scottish Prohibition Party

Highest vote: E. Scrymgeour (Dundee, 1929) – 50,073 votes, 29.2%
Parliamentary elections won: 4
Number of candidacies: 10

The story of the Scottish Prohibition Party begins and ends with Edwin Scrymgeour. A former member of the **Independent Labour Party**, Scrymgeour was a very religious man who urged his supporters to 'vote as you pray'. He was very active in the Independent Order of Good Templars as a campaigner for prohibition.

In November 1901, a split in the Good Templars resulted in Scrymgeour forming the Scottish Prohibition Party in Dundee. Scrymgeour became Organising Secretary of the party. The party's activities were very closely centred in Dundee where Scrymgeour lived, and the party found an audience there in the large working-class population. The party was reformed in 1904 and the next year Scrymgeour was elected under the party's sponsorship to Dundee Town Council. In recognition of his left-wing politics, he was given support by Dundee Trades Council and the **Labour Representation Committee**.

Scrymgeour first fought the Dundee constituency in a Parliamentary by-election in May 1908, but came bottom of the poll, and lost support from the Labour movement as he had opposed a Labour candidate. In the two 1910 general elections he increased his vote, and in 1917 a wartime by-election saw him win a fifth of the vote in a straight fight with Liberal MP Winston Churchill, who was being required to seek re-election. At this election the party secured the support of many among Dundee's Irish population, for whom Scrymgeour's firm support of Irish nationalism was attractive.

In 1918 the franchise was extended to women, who were more supportive of the temperance and prohibition movement. The **Labour Party** put up two candidates in the two-member seat, with Churchill fighting as a **Coalition** Liberal. Scrymgeour managed to come third in the race, outpolling one of the Labour candidates, having obtained the local support of the Irish League.

When Scrymgeour backed the Anglo-Irish Treaty in 1921 he obtained the maximum level of Irish support. From 1922, the Labour Party in Dundee decided, in view of Scrymgeour's Labour history and popular support, and the electoral danger posed by the Communist Party, in future to nominate only one candidate, and give strong unofficial support to Scrymgeour in the hope that Labour voters would use their other vote for him.

This tactic worked in the 1922 general election, with Scrymgeour topping the poll owing to support from 'plumpers' (those voting for one candidate only). In Parliament he resisted many entreaties from the Parliamentary Labour Party asking him to join, though he invariably voted with them on all matters except prohibition. During the second Labour government of 1929–31, Scrymgeour became increasingly disenchanted with the Labour Party and allied with James Maxton and the Independent Labour Party group.

Scrymgeour was swept away in the Conservative landslide election of 1931, then decided at the age of 65 to retire from politics (he took a job as Chaplain at two Dundee hospitals). Without Scrymgeour as candidate, the party lost much of its appeal and it was disbanded in January 1935.

Scottish Republican Socialist Party

Address: 1148 Argyll Street, Glasgow G3 8TE.

Only vote: A. H. Tennent (Glasgow Queen's Park, 1982 (2/12)) – 39 votes, 0.2%

Parliamentary elections won: 0

Number of candidacies: 1

The Scottish Republican Socialist Party had its origins in a group called Scottish Republican Socialist Clubs which was formed in 1973. The group had organised several clubs in central Scotland, intended for members who supported nationalism and were socialists (some were members of the **International Marxist Group**). The clubs had links to Irish republicanism but were only loosely organised.

In 1979 a sizable part of the membership of the Scottish Republican Socialist Clubs fell out with the majority of the group over organisation, and formed the Scottish Republican Socialist League, which had a more formal structure. The 79 Group within the **Scottish National Party** was formed within the Scottish Republican Socialist League.

By 1982, members who had remained in Scottish Republican Socialist Clubs, and those who had joined the Scottish Republican Socialist League joined together to establish the Scottish Republican Socialist Party. The party campaigned for an independent workers' Republic of Scotland, in which there would be workers' control of industry.

The party fought the Glasgow Queen's Park by-election of December 1982, but performed dismally: it polled only 39 votes, and came bottom of the poll, though it recognised the candidature was to raise awareness without any chance of winning. From November 1998 the party affiliated to the **Scottish Socialist Party** and renamed itself the Scottish Republican Socialist Movement; not every member agreed, and some who did not joined the Scottish National Party.

Scottish Socialist Alliance

Highest vote: T. Sheridan (Glasgow Pollok, 1997) – 3,639 votes, 11.1%

Parliamentary elections won: 0

Number of candidacies: 17

This alliance between several parties and activists of the far left in Scotland was organised in 1996, in planning for the 1997 election. The members had been involved in the Scottish section of a group called the 'Socialist Movement', which had been formed after a conference in Chesterfield in October 1987. As such it contained members of various left-wing organisations, and people who were left-wing but not members of any organisation. The Communist Party of Great Britain (*see* **Communist Party of Great Britain** (1989–)) was a member.

By far the largest force in the Alliance was **Scottish Militant Labour**. The Alliance fought 16 constituencies in Scotland in the 1997 general election, all in the central industrial belt. Eight of the candidates were Scottish Militant Labour members, who monopolized the working-class areas of Glasgow where the party's vote was strongest. The party polled nearly 10,000 votes in total, with Scottish Militant Labour taking the six highest votes.

The Alliance's popularity increased with the election of a Labour government, which it attacked as being English dominated. At the Paisley South by-election in November 1997, the Alliance increased its vote substantially.

In summer 1998, Scottish Militant Labour successfully proposed that the Alliance relaunch as a united **Scottish Socialist Party**. A number of the smaller groups in the Alliance were opposed to this move.

Scottish Socialist Federation

Only vote: J. Wilson (Edinburgh Central, 1892) – 434 votes, 7.3%

Parliamentary elections won: 0

Number of candidacies: 1

John Leslie, an Irish-born insurance agent living in Edinburgh, called a conference there in December 1888 for members of the **Social Democratic Federation**, the Socialist League (a breakaway from the SDF), and diverse other groups. This conference voted to form the Scottish Socialist Federation to promote unity and campaign for socialist policies.

Leslie was Secretary of his local branch of the **Scottish Parliamentary Labour Party** and knew the value of working with other groups. The Scottish Socialist Federation and the **Scottish United Trades Councils Labour Party** jointly nominated John Wilson, an Edinburgh shale miner, to fight the Edinburgh Central constituency at the 1892 general election.

The Socialist League's Scottish branches ceased operating in about 1893 and the Scottish Socialist Federation was later incorporated into the Social Democratic Federation.

Scottish Socialist Party

Address: PO Box 980, Glasgow G14 9QQ

Website: http://www.scotsocialistparty.org

Number on Register: 50

Only vote: Ms S. Blackall (Hamilton South, 1999 (23/9)) – 1,847 votes, 9.5%

Parliamentary elections won: 0

Number of candidacies: 1

The Scottish Socialist Party was launched in September 1998 when the various left groups in the **Scottish Socialist Alliance** were united into one single party. The party gained an early convert when Hugh Kerr, an MEP who had been expelled from the **Labour Party** in December 1997, joined it soon after its formation. Its first major contest was at the North East Scotland European Parliamentary by-election in November 1998, when Harvey Duke polled 2%.

In the Scottish Parliamentary elections of 1999, party leader Tommy Sheridan unexpectedly won a list seat in Glasgow, and the party outpolled the **Liberal Democrats** there. In the Parliament, Tommy Sheridan has promoted a bill to end warrant sales as a means of recovering a debt, which passed at second reading when Labour MSPs made their support clear (over the objections of the Executive).

Scottish Unionist Party

Address: PO Box 2420, Glasgow G40

Number on Register: 40

Only vote: J. W. Reid (Hamilton South, 1999 (23/9)) – 113 votes, 0.6%

Parliamentary elections won: 0

Number of candidacies: 1

The formation of the Scottish Unionist Party was sparked by the Anglo-Irish Agreement of November 1985. The Agreement created as much hostility among the Orange movement in Scotland as it did in Northern Ireland and caused a fissure between them and the **Conservatives**, the party they had traditionally supported. Early in 1986 the Scottish Unionist Party was formed to campaign on the issue.

The founder Chairman, Bill McMurdo, said the party intended to fight nine seats in the 1987 general election, including that of the then Secretary of State for Scotland, Malcolm Rifkind. However, in the event no candidates were nominated and the party merely campaigned against the Conservatives.

The party fought only local elections until the creation of the Scottish Parliament. It put forward lists for three out of the eight regions (Glasgow, Central Scotland, and West of Scotland) but with only five candidates in total, and no list reached 1% of the vote. The party then nominated Jim Reid to fight the Hamilton South by-election of September 1999, but failed to make any sort of breakthrough.

Scottish United Trades Councils Labour Party

Highest vote: H. H. Champion (Stirlingshire, 1892) – 991 votes, 15.8%

Parliamentary elections won: 0

Number of candidacies: 4

From around 1850, delegates from various local trades in major Scottish cities started meeting in organised trades councils to discuss local issues.

These trades councils were involved in political campaigns from the start, including discussions of legislation and campaigns opposing MPs who were unfavourable. The Edinburgh Trades Council ran candidates for the Edinburgh School Board in 1879 and established a fund to fight Town Council elections in 1886.

On 8 September 1891, a conference was held at Edinburgh at which the Scottish United Trades Councils Labour Party was formed. The party had a socialist policy and it invited the **Scottish Parliamentary Labour Party** to send representatives to its executive, but soon after formation this invitation was withdrawn, and local organisation was based solely on the trades councils.

Another conference was held in Glasgow in March 1892 to organise the party and prepare for the impending general election. This conference adopted policies including the 8-hour day, universal adult suffrage, three-year Parliaments, payment of MPs, nationalisation of the mining and railway industries and of land, and 'local option' (the temperance demand for local authorities to veto sales of alcoholic drinks).

The party put forward four candidates at the 1892 general election in areas where the local trades council was strong. One candidate was also endorsed by the **Scottish Socialist Federation**. The SUTCLP's candidates found it difficult to make headway as all of them were intervening in Unionist–Liberal battles, and the party's base soon began to deteriorate. Two of the most active trades councils (Dundee and Greenock) had never affiliated, and the Edinburgh Trades Council disaffiliated in October 1892.

Despite the claimed affiliation of 30 branches, the party was formally dissolved in March 1893. An attempt to revive it was made that October by Chisholm Robertson of the Stirlingshire miners and H. H. Champion of Aberdeen Trades Council, but failed to get off the ground.

Scottish Workers Representation Committee

Highest vote: A. E. Fletcher (Glasgow Camlachie, 1900) – 3,107 votes, 41.7%
Parliamentary elections won: 0
Number of candidacies: 8

The Scottish Workers Representation Committee was formed in a very similar way to the **Labour Representation Committee**. A conference of delegates from trades unions, some of the larger trades councils, Co-operative societies, and from the **Independent Labour Party** and the **Social Democratic Federation**, was held in Glasgow in January 1900.

The Committee had the benefit of the backing of the miners, denied to the Labour Representation Committee/Labour Party until 1909; Robert Smillie, a miner, was the first Chairman. Its first electoral performance was strong: a candidate in the Camlachie division of Glasgow polled over 40%, where Smillie had taken only 10% as an ILP candidate at the previous election.

In 1903 it was proposed that the Committee should work with the Labour Representation Committee but this suggestion did not produce any effective co-ordination. The Committee managed to increase its vote in two by-elections in North East Lanarkshire, and in the 1906 general election put forward five candidates. All were miners in mining seats. However, all its candidates were in three-way contests as the committee was not included in the non-opposition pact with the Liberals.

Immediately after the general election, the committee paralleled the Labour Representation Committee by changing its name to the Scottish Labour Party (*see* **Scottish Labour Party (1906–9)**).

Sinn Féin

Address: 51/53 Falls Road, Belfast

Website: http://www.sinnfein.ie/

Number on Register: 11

Highest vote: J. McBride (Mayo West, 1918) – 10,195 votes, 86.7%

Parliamentary elections won: 86

Number of candidacies: 214

In 1901, Arthur Griffith became editor of *The United Irishman*, an Irish nationalist newspaper. Griffith used his editorship to promote his policy of direct resistance to British rule in Ireland: while the Irish Nationalists attempted to press Parliament to pass a Home Rule bill, Griffith called for Irish members not to take their seats but to form a National Council in Ireland. This policy was called Sinn Féin in Irish, the translation being 'We Ourselves'.

Griffith had created the Cumann na n Gaedheal [Society of Gaels] in 1900 to link nationalist and republican groups, and the Cumann announced its support for Sinn Féin in 1902. As knowledge of the policy grew, the name was eventually transferred to refer to the (still unofficial) party which supported the policy in about 1905. To accommodate this change the Cumann na n Gaedheal united with Dungannon Clubs, a cultural group formed by republicans in Ulster, and formed the Sinn Féin League in September 1907. The Sinn Féin League became a political party in 1908.

In January 1908, the **Nationalist** MP for North Leitrim, Charles Dolan, joined Sinn Féin and felt obliged to seek re-election in his constituency. In a straight fight with a Nationalist he polled only 27% of the vote. After this election the party began a long period of internal division over the belief of Arthur Griffith that Ireland should continue to have the British monarch as King. A large proportion of members who were also in the Irish Republican Brotherhood (commonly called the Fenians) were opposed to this policy and managed to gain control of Sinn Féin from about 1914.

The Easter Rising of 1916 was organised by the Irish Republican Brotherhood and its offshoot, the Irish Citizen Army, and not by Sinn Féin (Arthur Griffith had no advance knowledge), but was popularly ascribed to them after the event. The action of the British government in having 15 of the leaders of the rising shot by firing squad created immense public sympathy for a rebellion which had had little support at the time, and Sinn Féin was forced both by its republican members and by the weight of public opinion to reform as a republican organisation early in 1917.

At this time Sinn Féin began contesting elections in support of its policy of an independent Ireland. In the first, in Roscommon North on 3 February 1917, Count George Plunkett easily won the seat from the Irish Nationalist while interned in Oxford Gaol. In May 1917, Sinn Féin won Longford South with a candidate (Joseph McGuinness) who was in Lewes Gaol for his part in the Easter Rising. Four more by-election gains followed before the end of the war, with the Nationalists only able to hold three seats against a Sinn Féin opponent.

The 1918 general election offered an opportunity for Sinn Féin to seek a mandate from the whole of Ireland. It fought all but two seats (Down

North and Dublin University), and the extent of the collapse of the Irish Nationalists was such that 25 Sinn Féin seats were won unopposed. Where there was a contest, Sinn Féin almost always defeated the Irish Nationalist, and in the final results it had 73 seats compared with only 7 held by Irish Nationalists (one of which was in England). 36 of those elected were in gaol at the time; some later escaped.

In accordance with its policy the Sinn Féin members convened the first Dáil Éireann in Dublin and organised the provisional government of Ireland. The army of this government was made up of members of the Irish Volunteers, the force established by the Irish Republican Brotherhood. In August 1919 the Volunteers were required by the Dáil Éireann to swear allegiance to the Dáil, and therefore became the Irish Republican Army. The Irish Republican Army retains its original name in Irish: Oglaigh na h Éireann translates as Irish Volunteers.

The IRA launched a war of independence against the British over the years 1919–21, and public opinion was further outraged by the behaviour of the irregular British forces (called 'Black and Tans' from the colour of their uniform) brought in to replace the police. The British government passed the Government of Ireland Act 1920 which partitioned Ireland and created two Parliaments, but the Southern Ireland House of Commons was elected unopposed: Sinn Féin took all seats except Dublin University. The Sinn Féin members, together with one member who had been elected to the Northern Ireland House of Commons, formed the second Dáil Éireann.

Continued resistance forced the United Kingdom government to sue for peace, and a truce was agreed on 11 July 1921. Negotiations for a permanent peace began that October, and on 6 December a Treaty was agreed with Michael Collins (Minister of Finance in the provisional government). The treaty granted to Southern Ireland a Parliament with full authority, but formally still in the British Empire, with a requirement that its members pledge allegiance to the King. The northern six counties were allowed to opt out. Such a treaty was bound to be controversial.

Ireland descended into civil war in 1922, with members of the IRA who opposed the Treaty forming the 'Irregulars' and fighting against those who had only a few months before been their comrades. In 1923 the Irregulars were defeated, while the rest of the IRA became the official Army of the Irish Free State. Sinn Féin split in two.

The Sinn Féin policy of abstention held in relation to the Northern Ireland House of Commons, and after the first election in 1921 it did not fight elections there. In 1924 Sinn Féin nominated seven candidates in Northern Ireland in the general election, but polled poorly. In the two-member Fermanagh and Tyrone constituency, which two Irish Nationalists had won in previous elections, Sinn Féin polled only 13%.

From the late 1920s Sinn Féin had a very low profile. Pro-Treaty members formed Fine Gael and most anti-Treaty members left in 1927 to form Fianna Fáil. The IRA split from the party and gave to its army council the responsibility for its political leadership. The party only resurrected in the late 1940s, after the proclamation of the Irish Republic, which removed a significant part of the party's campaign. The IRA again began to form links with Sinn Féin, and at the 1951 Ard Fheis [Conference] the IRA managed to win control of Sinn Féin. Opposition to partition became the central part of the party's campaigning.

On 17 October 1954 the IRA attacked the Royal Inniskilling Fusiliers' Barracks at Omagh, County Tyrone. The attack was repulsed and eight members of the IRA arrested. For the 1955 United Kingdom general election, Sinn Féin fought all 12 seats in Northern Ireland, five of the candidates being participants in the Omagh raid; three other candidates were also in gaol for other activities. Though polling poorly in Belfast, border areas gave strong support. Two of the Omagh raiders were elected.

Though the two seats were eventually given to Unionists (convicted prisoners being disqualified), the success showed the potential for support for a republican military campaign. The IRA began such a campaign ('the Border Campaign') in December 1956, and though it lasted until 1962 it was a military failure. The leadership of the IRA and Sinn Féin changed strategy thereafter to build a socialist and republican coalition among working-class nationalists.

By 1969, the IRA leadership was dominated by Marxist strategists. At the January 1970 Ard Fheis, the IRA Chief of Staff, Cathal Goulding, proposed that Sinn Féin drop its abstentionist policy and fight elections to the Dáil, Stormont and the United Kingdom Parliament in order to win seats. He carried the majority but a substantial minority withdrew to form the Provisional IRA. For the history of those that remained, *see* **The Workers' Party [Ireland]**.

The Provisionals quickly supplanted the Official IRA, which by its inaction in the face of loyalist intimidation had fallen into contempt by the nationalist population of Northern Ireland. The level of violence increased and in August 1971 the Northern Ireland government introduced internment without trial. This move was intended to remove key IRA personnel but was instead used indiscriminately, both creating extreme resentment among nationalists and allowing the internees to train together.

In March 1972 Sinn Féin produced a new policy called Éire Nua [New Ireland] under which Ireland would be governed by four Parliaments, one in each of the provinces, with the maximum decentralisation. It called for the abolition of Stormont and announcement of British withdrawal. The United Kingdom government secretly flew three Provisional IRA leaders to talks in July 1972 but found their offer unacceptable.

The incoming Labour government in 1974 lifted the proscription on Sinn Féin which had been imposed by the Stormont government, in the hope that Sinn Féin would fight the elections to the Constitutional Convention in 1975, but Sinn Féin decided not to fight and invited its supporters to abstain. Sinn Féin members were involved in discussions with the government in 1975 when the IRA called a brief ceasefire.

Security operations and the stagnating political situation led to a decreasing level of IRA activity in the late 1970s. Sinn Féin found a popular campaign when IRA and INLA prisoners in the H-Blocks of the Maze prison went on hunger strike to restore special political status in 1980–1 (*see* **Anti H-Block**). The leader of IRA prisoners at Long Kesh (the former name of the Maze prison, widely used in Ireland), Bobby Sands, was elected while on hunger strike, as MP for Fermanagh and South Tyrone, and two other prisoners won seats in the Dáil Éireann in June 1981. Sands and nine other hunger strikers died.

leadership of Sinn Féin had by this time passed to its members from the north. They dropped the Éire Nua policy at the 1981 Ard Fheis, which they saw as a sop to loyalists (the Ulster Parliament would probably have a unionist majority), and in 1982 the Ard Fheis required Sinn Féin candidates to pledge support to the armed struggle.

Sinn Féin fought the 1982 Northern Ireland Assembly elections on an abstentionist platform after failing to convince other nationalists to boycott the elections. It polled 64,000 votes, just over 10% of the total, but won only 5 seats. Shortly after the elections, leader of the Greater London Council, Ken Livingstone invited two Sinn Féin Assembly members to talks in London, but the Conservative government banned them from travelling.

Sinn Féin fought 14 seats at the 1983 general election, achieving their target of more than 100,000 votes. The party gained Belfast West, where the former **Social Democratic and Labour Party** leader, Gerry Fitt was opposed by his old party, but was unlucky to lose Mid-Ulster by only 78 votes. Fermanagh and South Tyrone was lost when an SDLP candidate intervened. The Belfast West MP, Gerry Adams was soon after elected President of Sinn Féin.

The 1985 local council elections were the first in which Sinn Féin participated. It largely kept its share of the vote from 1983 and won 59 seats. The Anglo-Irish Agreement of November 1985 was partly a product of British concern over the popularity of Sinn Féin, and the party had a difficult time in the by-elections forced by unionist MPs in January 1986.

At the 1986 Sinn Féin Ard Fheis, the leadership moved to change the constitution to allow its candidates to take their seats at the Dáil. This proposal was accepted by 429 votes to 161, but the former southern leadership were unable to accept this recognition of the Dáil and resigned to form **Republican Sinn Féin**. Very few grassroots members joined the breakaway.

Sinn Féin were under pressure at the 1987 general election from the SDLP in Belfast West. The Anglo-Irish Agreement had strengthened co-operation between the British and Republic of Ireland governments but not on a republican agenda, which did not help the party, and its vote fell by 2%: Gerry Adams held on to Belfast West by 2,000 votes.

Abortive talks were held between the SDLP and Sinn Féin early in 1988, as part of an attempt to unite republicans with nationalists, but the SDLP found the Sinn Féin policy outdated. Broadcasting of interviews with Sinn Féin speakers was banned in late 1988 by the British government, and an attempt was made to end Sinn Féin's presence in local government by requiring all candidates to sign a declaration against violence, but these moves horrified civil libertarians while failing to affect the Sinn Féin vote. It won 11.2% in local elections in 1989.

At the same time, a series of IRA attacks hit civilian targets. The Sinn

Féin Ard Fheis of 1989 called on the IRA to avoid harming civilians, and when two Australian tourists in Holland were murdered in mistake for British army officers, the Sinn Féin President said the mistake was inexcusable. Sinn Féin was not invited to participate in the all-party talks initiated by the British government in 1991, which Adams described as 'a non-starter'.

The 1992 general election saw the SDLP gain Belfast West by 589 votes because of unprecedented tactical voting by loyalist residents of the Shankill Road area. The overall Sinn Féin vote fell again to 10%. The election results did damage to Sinn Féin's credibility. In the immediate aftermath it was revealed that senior Sinn Féin members had met with Presbyterian clergymen and Edward Daly, Catholic Bishop of Derry, who had criticised IRA violence.

Early in 1993 the Sinn Féin President Gerry Adams held talks with John Hume, leader of the SDLP, arranged by Catholic priests in Derry. These talks were publicly revealed the month before local elections, in which the Sinn Féin vote increased to 12.4%. The talks continued and produced a broad agreement on a peace process on 25 September 1993, showing Sinn Féin could contribute effectively.

A month later, Gerry Adams carried the coffin of an IRA member killed when a bomb he was planting exploded prematurely; nine Protestant civilians had died in the explosion, and unionists were cynical about whether republicans were helping peace. Soon afterwards, the British government were embarrassed when a secret communications channel to the IRA was revealed shortly after Prime Minister John Major had said it would 'turn his stomach' to talk to terrorists.

Sinn Féin responded cautiously to the Downing Street Declaration of December 1993, asking for clarification. By summer 1994 it became clear that the IRA was considering a ceasefire, and on 31 August it announced a 'total cessation of military operations'. Mass celebration broke out in republican areas and within a few months the reporting restrictions were lifted; official talks with British civil servants began in December 1994.

Progress on peace talks was slow through 1995, with Sinn Féin demanding all-party talks and the Unionists demanding that IRA weapons be handed in beforehand. On 9 February 1996 the IRA cessation was ended with a large bomb at Canary Wharf in London, which seemed to take Sinn Féin by surprise. The resumption of IRA activities did not end the peace process, with the British government announcing a 110-member elected Forum from which the delegates to all-party talks would be selected.

Sinn Féin were strongly against the Forum but participated in the elections, winning 15.5% of the vote and 17 seats. The members were refused entry to the talks and boycotted the Forum. Sinn Féin had topped the poll in Belfast West and Mid-Ulster, and nearly did so in two other areas – West Tyrone and Belfast North. This increase in support gave rise to optimism for the 1997 general election.

The run-up to the election was full of speculation about the future of the peace process, and whether a further cessation would be proclaimed by the IRA. In that context Sinn Féin appealed for votes for peace, and won 16% of the vote. Gerry Adams regained Belfast West and Martin McGuinness, the party's chief negotiator, gained Mid Ulster. Neither broke the party's abstentionist policy, and the Speaker of the House of Commons introduced more stringent regulations about the services they were able to use as MPs. Soon after, the party won its first seat in the Dáil since the 1920s.

On 19 July 1997 the IRA announced the restoration of its cessation of military activity. Sinn Féin accepted the principles set out by Senator George Mitchell, the Chairman of the all-party talks, and entered the negotiations that September. It was briefly expelled early in 1998 when the British government announced that it had evidence of IRA involvement in two recent murders, but readmitted after a month.

The conclusion of the talks was welcomed by Sinn Féin. The Belfast Agreement contained many aspects unpalatable to republicans but the party negotiators accepted it as a basis for a transition to Irish unity. 96% of delegates to a special Ard Fheis voted in favour of the Agreement and altered the constitution to allow Sinn Féin members to take their seats in the new Northern Ireland Assembly.

The Agreement received the overwhelming support of the nationalist community in a referendum on 22 May and elections to the Assembly were held on 25 June. Sinn Féin polled well, increasing its vote to 17.6% and winning 18 seats. The party was strongly critical of a small number of members who were opposed to the Agreement and joined Republican

Sinn Féin or the 32-County Sovereignty Committee. The Omagh bomb of August 1998, carried out by the 'Real IRA' (linked with the 32-County Sovereignty Committee) was deplored by Sinn Féin.

Formation of the all-party Executive was delayed when Unionists insisted on the decommissioning of IRA arms before entering government with Sinn Féin. In an atmosphere of lack of progress, Sinn Féin won 17.3% in the June 1999 European Parliament elections, nearly outpolling the **Ulster Unionist** candidate. An attempt to form the Executive in July 1999 collapsed when the Unionists boycotted it, and a review of the Agreement was organised.

The review concluded in December. The IRA appointed a representative to the International Decommissioning Body, and the Unionists agreed to the formation of the Executive. Martin McGuinness and Bairbre De Brún were chosen as the Sinn Féin ministers. The Executive was suspended in February 2000 but resumed when the IRA agreed to put its weapons 'verifiably beyond use'.

Social and Liberal Democrats

See **Liberal Democrats**.

Social Credit Party of Great Britain

Higher vote: W. Townend (Leeds South, 1935) – 3,642 votes, 11.0%

Parliamentary elections won: 0

Number of candidacies: 2

John Hargrave, a stretcher-bearer during the Great War, became a convinced pacifist and was expelled from the Scout movement. He reacted by forming the Kindred of Kibbo Kift as a pacifist youth movement in about 1920. This movement was small and became smaller when it split in 1925, the departing group becoming the Woodcraft Folk.

Partly in response to the split, Hargrave developed an interest in the 'social credit' theories of C. H. Douglas. Douglas advocated reform of the banking system in order to make up the gap between rising prices and rising wages; these reforms would provide a 'national dividend' to every citizen as of right. Douglas believed this method could achieve prosperity for all without nationalisation.

Hargrave reformed the Kindred of Kibbo Kift as the Green Shirt Movement for Social Credit in 1933, receiving the endorsement of C.H. Douglas. Two years later, on the eve of the 1935 general election, the Green Shirt Movement retitled itself the Social Credit Party of Great Britain. It fought Leeds South in the election and nearly saved its deposit. Most of the party's vote appears to have come from the **Labour Party**.

The passing of the Public Order Act 1936, intended to obstruct fascism, caused the party problems by banning the use of the Green Shirt uniform in political campaigns. Activity was suspended during the Second World War, but barely resumed afterwards. Hargrave himself fought Stoke Newington in the 1950 election but polled very poorly. The *Official Gazette of the Social Credit Party* ceased publication on 11 May 1951 and it appears the party was wound up that year.

Social Democratic and Labour Party

Address: 611c Lisburn Road, Belfast BT9 7GT

Website: http://www.sdlp.ie

Number on Register: 8

Highest vote: J. Hume (Foyle, 1997) – 25,109 votes, 52.5%

Parliamentary elections won: 15

Number of candidacies: 98

The SDLP is the main constitutional nationalist party in Northern Ireland. It was formed on 21 August 1970 by seven Stormont MPs and Senators. Three MPs had been elected as independent supporters of the civil rights movement in 1969 (John Hume, Ivan Cooper and Paddy O'Hanlon); Paddy Devlin was one of two **Northern Ireland Labour Party** MPs; Gerry Fitt and Senator Paddy Wilson were from the **Republican Labour Party**, and Austin Currie was an Irish **Nationalist**. Gerry Fitt was named as the leader of the party.

The aim of forming the party was to obtain the unity of Ireland by consent, and the party was to campaign for civil rights for all and for redistribution of wealth. It aimed to secure the support of all constitutional nationalists, but while the **National Democratic Party** gave it full support, the Republican Labour Party was divided.

On 16 July 1971 the SDLP members withdrew from Stormont, declaring that the party was withdrawing consent from the Northern Ireland institutions of government after they were refused an official inquiry into the riots in Derry. The Party attempted to organise an unofficial Assembly at Dungiven Castle later that year. When the Unionist government introduced internment without trial, the SDLP organised a civil disobedience campaign, encouraging non-payment of taxes.

After the dissolution of Stormont, the SDLP called for joint rule of Northern Ireland by Britain and Ireland, with an assembly to govern locally. The party therefore welcomed the 1973 white paper which proposed an Assembly elected by proportional representation together with a Council of Ireland. It won 22% of the vote in the elections for the Northern Ireland Assembly in June 1973, confirming that it had grown to dominate nationalist politics.

When the Executive was formed, the SDLP filled four out of the eleven portfolios, including Gerry Fitt as Deputy Chief Executive. The collapse of the Executive in the face of the Ulster Workers' Council strike led the party bitterly to attack the British government for failing to confront loyalist paramilitaries. The party's share of the vote held through the 1974 general elections though it won only one seat.

After the inconclusive Constitutional Convention of 1975, the SDLP held talks with members of the **Ulster Unionist Party**, which were intended to be secret. Nothing emerged, and a 1977 policy document was interpreted as a more heavily nationalist statement. Paddy Devlin opposed the policies as a move away from socialism and was expelled from the party.

Through the late 1970s the SDLP grew steadily more disillusioned over the Labour government and Northern Ireland Secretary Roy Mason. In March 1979 the SDLP leader Gerry Fitt refused to vote for the Labour government in the vote of confidence, explaining that his loyalty to the nationalist community outweighed his loyalty to the Labour movement. The one vote made the difference and the government fell.

In the ensuing general election the party increased its majority in Belfast

West, but the other seats it targeted had increased Unionist majorities. The overall vote fell to 18.2%, but the next month John Hume was elected to the European Parliament with 24.6% of the vote.

On 25 October 1979 the Secretary of State for Northern Ireland announced that he was calling a new Constitutional Conference on government of Northern Ireland. The party's official response objected to the Conference's lack of any real Irish dimension. This response dismayed Gerry Fitt, who resigned from the party saying it had lost its commitment to socialism; John Hume was swiftly elected as the new leader.

Despite its reservations, the SDLP eventually decided to participate in the Conference, having won some concessions on the scope of discussion; the conference was inconclusive. The hunger strike by IRA and INLA prisoners in the Maze put the party in a dilemma; it called for concessions to the prisoners but not full political status. The party decided not to fight the Fermanagh and South Tyrone by-election, producing accusations from some members that the party was effectively allying itself with the IRA. The local council elections at this time showed the party's vote down.

Following the unsuccessful Constitutional Conference, the Northern Ireland Secretary announced the establishment of a Northern Ireland Assembly in a scheme of 'rolling devolution'. The SDLP denounced the scheme as unworkable and fought the elections in October 1982 on a policy of creating an all-Ireland Council to discuss unity (it pledged not to take its seats in the Assembly). The party won 18.8% of the vote, dented slightly by the competition of **Sinn Féin** for nationalist votes. One of its seats was lost when Séamus Mallon was disqualified by virtue of his membership of the Senate of the Republic of Ireland.

The New Ireland Forum, containing the three largest parties in the Republic and the SDLP, opened in May 1983 shortly before the general election; support for the Forum was the key point of the SDLP's manifesto. The party's vote fell slightly to 17.9%; it lost Belfast West to Sinn Féin when Gerry Fitt fought as an Independent Socialist, but John Hume was elected for Foyle (containing the City of Derry).

On 3 May 1984 the New Ireland Forum reported, favouring a unitary 32-county Ireland but setting out options for a federation and for joint rule of Northern Ireland. The report had strong support from the USA, other European Community member states, and the Labour Party, but Margaret

Thatcher's outspoken denunciation of all options in the report was unexpected.

The SDLP vote held firm in the 1985 local elections despite Sinn Féin's involvement. The Anglo-Irish Agreement of November 1985 was welcomed by the party as the beginning of reconciliation, though the party's hopes for a talks process were in vain. When all the unionist MPs resigned to seek re-election, the SDLP concentrated on four seats in border areas; Séamus Mallon won Newry and Armagh when some Sinn Féin voters switched to the party.

That gain was consolidated in the 1987 general election, when the party also won South Down by a similar campaign. The group of three MPs became effective in speaking for the nationalist population, and soon after the election it became clear that nationalists were growing disillusioned with the progress of the Anglo-Irish Agreement. John Hume again called on unionists to negotiate at the SDLP conference in November 1987.

Beginning in January 1988 Hume and other SDLP figures held unsuccessful talks with Gerry Adams of Sinn Féin, hoping to persuade him to end support for violence. Engagement with Sinn Féin was popular with the party's grassroots and its vote rose at the 1989 local council and European Parliament elections (then the best performance by the party).

The party welcomed the British government's declaration that it had no selfish, strategic or economic interest in Northern Ireland and participated in the 'talks about talks' called by the Northern Ireland Secretary Peter Brooke. It now called for government by six commissioners, three elected locally, and one each nominated by the British government, the Irish government, and the European Commission. This approach was rejected by unionists.

Presence of the SDLP in talks from which Sinn Féin was excluded was a useful campaigning tool and the party targeted Belfast West in the 1992 general election, winning the seat by 589 votes. It also moved ahead of Sinn Féin to take second place in Fermanagh and South Tyrone. The talks collapsed in November 1992, and SDLP pressure to revive them went unfulfilled.

John Hume began a process of talks with Gerry Adams of Sinn Féin in spring 1993. Other members of the party became concerned that they were not being consulted on what was being discussed, which risked giving Sinn Féin credibility. While welcoming the Downing Street Declaration in December 1993 the SDLP felt too many concessions had been made to unionists; John Hume backed the Sinn Féin call for clarification.

The 1994 European Parliament elections showed the party vote increasing again, and John Hume came close to outpolling Ian Paisley. The IRA ceasefire of 31 August 1994 vindicated the Hume–Adams talks but at the same time allowed Sinn Féin to campaign for votes for peace to be given to it; throughout the rest of 1994 and 1995 the party pressed for swift progress. Proposals for a pact with Sinn Féin were made in 1995 but ruled out while Sinn Féin continued to be abstentionist.

Resumption of IRA violence in February 1996 led the party to call for all-party talks in order to force a restoration of the ceasefire. The British government's plan for an elected Forum was opposed by the party, and though it fought the elections (polling 21.4%), its members swiftly withdrew after the confrontation between the Orange Order and local residents in Portadown.

The 1997 general election saw the party lose Belfast West to the invigorated Sinn Féin, and the party did poorly in Mid-Ulster and West Tyrone largely due to a strong Sinn Féin performance. However, the overall performance of 24.1% was good. In the local elections a month later, Sinn Féin again made gains at the expense of the SDLP.

After campaigning for all-party talks for so long, the SDLP naturally played a central part in the Stormont talks in 1998 and strongly supported the Belfast Agreement. It received its reward in the new Northern Ireland Assembly elections by topping the poll for the first time, even if it did not win the most seats. Séamus Mallon was elected Deputy First Minister Designate, after John Hume declined, owing to his workload.

John Hume pressed Sinn Féin to try to secure decommissioning of IRA arms in order to get an all-party Executive formed. The party therefore welcomed the formation of the Executive in December 1999, in which it had three members.

Social Democratic Federation

Highest vote: [excluding candidates who secured Labour Representation Committee endorsement] D. D. Irving (Accrington, 1906) – 4,852 votes, 38.3%

Parliamentary elections won: 0

Number of candidacies: 37 (including 2 who were endorsed by the Labour Representation Committee)

The formation of the Social Democratic Federation, the first socialist political party in Britain, was almost entirely due to Henry Mayers Hyndman. Hyndman, who had begun as Disraelian Conservative, became converted to socialism on reading a French translation of Marx's *Capital* in 1880. Early the next year, he began a campaign in a small newspaper called *Radical* for the formation of a new Radical Party under Joseph Cowen, then Liberal MP for Newcastle-upon-Tyne.

Hyndman then formed the Democratic Federation at a series of conferences of which Cowen was Chairman, concluding in June 1881. The Democratic Federation was small to begin with but grew considerably in 1883–4, as part of the interest in radical economics sparked off by Henry George (*see* **Scottish Land Restoration League**). In 1883 the Federation set socialism as its object and in February 1884 changed its name to the Social Democratic Federation.

Almost as soon as the SDF had been established, it split, when Hyndman fell out with William Morris; Morris left to form the Socialist League. The SDF nominated three candidates in the 1885 general election; John Burns won 5.4% in Nottingham West, but the other two polled dismally. Shortly after the election the reason for these two candidatures was revealed: the Federation had accepted £340 indirectly from the **Conservatives** in order to stand. The Conservatives hoped (in vain, as it turned out) that SDF candidates would split the Liberal vote. This was known as the 'Tory Gold' affair and cost the SDF the support of many of the members it shared with the Fabian Society. The SDF's candidates had only been intended as propaganda.

Hyndman's own character led to more splits. He made enemies easily, was anti-Semitic and strongly unionist, and even opposed trade unions and the eight-hour day. This last led to a split in February 1888 when H.H.

Champion, a champion of the eight-hour day, stood in a by-election in Deptford. Hyndman repudiated him, and though Champion eventually withdrew from the election, he formed his own independent Labour Party.

The split did not go wider, partly because the SDF decided to stop the attacks on the defectors, but mostly because it soon began to follow the strategy ('new unionism') Champion and others were advocating. The involvement with trade unions especially helped the party in Lancashire, and Hyndman won 12.4% in Burnley when he stood there in the 1895 general election. The SDF was regarded as especially strong on the issue of unemployment.

The SDF also had considerable strength in east London, especially in the Bow and Bromley division of Poplar. In an 1899 by-election, the Liberal had been given a free run and been easily defeated, but when George Lansbury stood as an SDF candidate in the 1900 general election he did noticeably better. West Ham was another strong SDF area by this time. In both, this strength was achieved through alliances with local labour.

When the **Labour Representation Committee** foundation conference was called, the SDF sent four delegates who moved an unsuccessful motion to establish a party based on the recognition of class war. Two SDF candidates (George Lansbury and Will Thorne) were given **Labour Party** endorsement in the 1900 general election. However, the SDF frequently attacked the Labour Party for compromising on socialism, and when Hyndman (who saw the LRC as an opportunity to convert trade unions to socialism in the long run) temporarily retired from politics, the SDF voted to withdraw at its conference in August 1901.

This same conference saw links being forged with the 'impossibilist' movement which wanted a pure form of socialism, and which was already present in some branches of the SDF. Unfortunately, Harry Quelch, the leading figure in the SDF, fell out with the main London branch containing impossibilists in 1903 and the branch was expelled at that year's conference, eventually joining the **Socialist Labour Party** (*see* Socialist Labour Party (1903–80)). A further group of impossibilists, led by Jack Fitzgerald, remained but were expelled the next year; Fitzgerald then formed the **Socialist Party of Great Britain**.

At the 1906 general election the SDF nominated eight candidates. In spite of staying out of the LRC it had participated in local labour alliances, and did not oppose any LRC candidates, but it was not part of the pact with the Liberals and all eight faced Liberal opposition. In several seats its share of the vote was respectable but it did not come close to winning.

In August 1907, in recognition of its development as a political party, the SDF adopted the name Social Democratic Party. Several attempts were made to get the party to affiliate to the Labour Party, but the majority of the party did not believe the Labour Party had the full support of the trade union movement. The party fought nine seats in the January 1910 general election, but the results showed it had lost support since 1906; shortage of funds led it to concentrate on only two seats in December 1910 – both in the Lancashire stronghold.

In October 1911, the Social Democratic Party merged with a number of other organisations which took a similar view of the Labour Party to form the **British Socialist Party**.

Social Democratic Party (1907–11)

See **Social Democratic Federation**.

Social Democratic Party (1981–90)

Highest vote: R. A. R. Maclennan (Caithness and Sutherland, 1987) – 12,338 votes, 53.6%
Parliamentary elections won: 15
Number of candidacies: 639

The origin of the Social Democratic Party was in the desire of Roy Jenkins to return to British politics after the end of his term as President of the European Commission. After Labour's defeat in the 1979 general election, it quickly became clear to Jenkins that he could not return to the **Labour Party**, as it moved to the left. In November 1979, Jenkins gave the annual Dimbleby Lecture on the BBC, and used it to call for a realignment of politics and the creation of a new party of the radical centre.

The chance of such a party being formed had a boost in 1980 when the Labour Party conference voted for a left-wing policy document and to change the mode of election of Labour Party leaders to an electoral college including constituency parties and trade unions. Three ex-cabinet ministers, David Owen, Shirley Williams and Bill Rodgers, began to hint in August 1980 that they were considering whether to leave the party, in a manifesto published in the *Guardian*. It has been claimed that Michael Foot's unexpected election as leader of the Labour Party in 1980 was aided by some MPs who intended to join a new party, and wished the Labour Party to be as unelectable as possible.

Roy Jenkins joined the 'Gang of Three' in January 1981 after the end of his term on the European Commission. The day after a special Labour Party conference had agreed on a much larger than expected share for trade unions in leadership elections, the four gathered at David Owen's home in Limehouse and issued a declaration in support of social democratic policies. The Council for Social Democracy was quickly formed to co-ordinate preparations for a new party.

Over the period from the end of January to the end of March 1981, the supporters of the Limehouse Declaration (initially 11 Labour MPs, growing to 13) disentangled from the Labour Party. One Conservative, Christopher Brocklebank-Fowler, also joined. The party was formally launched at the Connaught Rooms in London on 26 March.

Opinion polls in the spring of 1981 showed a strong measure of support for the SDP. The party was anxious to enter the fight, but the first by-election was in the unpromising northern industrial town of Warrington in July 1981. By this time a common policy programme had been agreed with the **Liberal Party** and Roy Jenkins fought the seat as an SDP candidate with Liberal support.

In the event Jenkins did not win, but with 42.4% of the vote he came very close. Through the summer of 1981 two more Labour MPs joined the party, followed by seven more after the Labour Party conference, which saw the narrow defeat of Tony Benn's challenge for the deputy leadership. At the end of November 1981, Shirley Williams won the Crosby by-election on a huge turnover of votes, becoming the first elected SDP MP, and in December 1981 opinion polls put the **Alliance** parties (as they now were) leading both Conservative and Labour by 27%.

Six more Labour MPs joined the SDP up to January 1982, giving the party 30 seats in all; it had 70,000 members and received funding from

David Sainsbury, Finance Director of J. Sainsbury superstores. Roy Jenkins was unofficially acknowledged as the leader of the party, though it was not until he won the Glasgow Hillhead by-election of March 1982 that he had a seat in Parliament. A ballot for the leadership was then held, with Jenkins defeating David Owen by 26,256 to 20,864.

The SDP had resisted the argument that MPs who joined it should resign their seats and fight for re-election under their new label. One MP insisted on consulting his electorate: Bruce Douglas-Mann, in Mitcham and Morden. Unfortunately for him the by-election occurred in the middle of the Falklands War and the seat was lost to the Conservatives.

After the Falklands the polls showed the Alliance vote falling away and the party lost its novelty. Anticipating an election in autumn 1982 the party spent much of its advertising budget, and ran out of money by April 1983. By-election victories became rarer and a poor candidate in Darlington in March 1983 threw away an initial lead to come third. One SDP MP who had lost a selection battle for his boundary-changed seat, resigned from the party.

In the 1983 general election the Alliance polled 26%. The SDP, with slightly fewer candidates than the Liberals, polled fewer votes; only four of the MPs who had joined it kept their seats. The party held one of its by-election gains, and gained one additional seat from the Conservatives. To go from 30 seats to 6 was a shock. David Owen immediately announced he was standing for the leadership, prompting Roy Jenkins to stand down without a contest.

Suggestions were made by Liberals at this time that the Alliance parties should merge, but David Owen was firmly opposed and the 1983 SDP conference voted to support this approach. Owen became much more of a dominant leader than Jenkins had, by setting up a 'Co-ordinating Committee' meeting in his office; this helped to bypass the SDP National Committee. Bill Rodgers and Shirley Williams, having lost their seats in 1983, were inevitably cut out of the day-to-day workings.

June 1984 saw a by-election gain in Portsmouth South, off-setting a disappointing performance in the European elections the same day. Membership of the SDP, which had consistently fallen from 1981, began to increase from 1984, with many non-members giving money to help the party. Most of the SDP's members were from London and the home counties.

In the run-up to the 1987 general election, strains began to occur between the Alliance parties over policy issues, specifically defence. Owen resisted all attempts at forming joint Alliance organisations, and insisted on keeping distinctive SDP policies. He forced the Liberals to back down over their unilateralist defence policy in 1986.

The SDP won a morale-boosting by-election victory in Greenwich in February 1987. SDP candidate Rosie Barnes, had not been involved in politics before joining the SDP, and the campaign managed to highlight the Labour candidate's left-wing approach. Four months later, this was also a theme in the general election campaign. The SDP's 1987 election campaign was more difficult than 1983, as the joint leadership of the Alliance looked unwieldy; unlike 1983 there was no Labour collapse and Alliance surge in the last week.

With a drop of 3% on 1983, the SDP lost two of its seats: Roy Jenkins was beaten by Labour in Glasgow Hillhead, and Ian Wrigglesworth relinquished Stockton South to the Conservatives (who had only failed to win in 1983 because their candidate was revealed to have been in the **National Front**). Greenwich was held but Portsmouth South was narrowly lost.

Immediately after the 1987 election results were known, pressure grew for a merger of the SDP with the Liberal Party. David Owen at once declared he would oppose any merger and would not join a merged party, and obtained the narrow backing of the SDP Executive. To pacify pro-merger sentiment he reluctantly agreed to a single leader for the Alliance parties.

When a ballot of the whole SDP membership in August 1987 found that it favoured participation in merger talks, Owen resigned the leadership. Only one SDP MP favoured merger (Charles Kennedy) but he was unwilling to take the leadership; eventually Robert Maclennan, who personally opposed merger but went along with the majority, was chosen.

A constitution for the new merged party was completed at the beginning of December 1987, and, after a false start, a policy statement was agreed the next month. The SDP Council accepted the merger terms on 31 January 1988, and 65% of the membership endorsed them in a ballot. The Social and Liberal Democrats were launched on 3 March 1988, inheriting two SDP MPs, the party's offices and funds, and most of its membership.

Meanwhile, David Owen had reformed the SDP with the support of two other MPs. Starting with around 10% in the opinion polls, the 'continuing SDP' quickly declined. It lost its deposit in the first by-election it fought (Kensington, July 1988). It did have one extremely good performance when it nearly won the Richmond (Yorkshire) by-election in February 1989. Had it not been for the split between the SDP and the SLD, the seat would have been won.

After a disastrous performance in the 1989 county council elections and European Parliament elections, when it lost deposits everywhere, the SDP announced that it was no longer a national party and could not fight all seats. May 1990 saw the party come bottom of the poll in Upper Bann. A week later came the Bootle by-election in which the SDP candidate polled less than half as many votes as the **Official Monster Raving Loony Party** candidate.

The next month the SDP national committee suspended the constitution and the three SDP MPs sat as Independent Social Democrats in Parliament. The party was formally wound up in July 1990. Some local organisation remains to this day, though in sharp decline.

Socialist Alliance

Address: 101 Lazyhill Road, Aldridge, Walsall WS9 8RS

Website: http://www.londonsocialistalliance.org.uk

Only vote: W. E. Bennett (Tottenham, 2000 (22/6)) – 885 votes, 5.4%

Parliamentary elections won: 0

Number of candidacies: 1

In the aftermath of the 1997 general election victory of the **Labour Party**, the far left began to hold talks on a unity pact. Formal steps were taken in London, which led to the launch of the unofficial London Socialist Alliance on 4 February 1998. This meeting was addressed by one Labour MEP, and received letters of support from two others as well as two who had been expelled from the party. Representatives of the Communist Party of Great Britain, Socialist Outlook, Workers' Power, the Socialist Party of England and Wales, and the Alliance for Workers' Liberty attended, along with some former members of the **Socialist Labour Party**.

Late in 1998 a working agreement was reached nationally and the Socialist Alliance was launched publicly on 9 March 1999. The two largest constituent organisations of the Alliance are the **Socialist Party** (*see* Socialist Party (1996–) and the **Socialist Workers Party**. The **Communist Party of Great Britain** (*see* Communist Party of Great Britain (1989–)) is also a member.

Other members of the Alliance come from a broad background. The Independent Labour Network was formed by Ken Coates, an MEP who had been expelled from the Labour Party in January 1998. The Alliance for Workers' Liberty, popularly known as *Socialist Organiser* after its newspaper, is a Trotskyite group which has been allied at various times with many other far-left groups, and has attempted entrism into the Labour Party. Socialist Outlook is the British section of the Unified Secretariat of the Fourth International, formed originally as a breakaway from the Socialist League (*see* **International Marxist Group**).

Two other small groups that are part of the Alliance came from expelled members of the Socialist Workers' Party. Workers' Power had been known as the 'Left faction' of the International Socialists but were expelled in 1975, while the International Socialist Group were expelled in 1994.

It appears the Alliance intended to pool resources to fight the 1999 European Parliament elections, but the challenge failed to appear save for the West Midlands region where a Socialist Party-dominated list polled less than 1% of the vote. The Alliance's strongest area was London and it began planning at an early stage for the Mayoral election.

The independent candidacy of Ken Livingstone allowed the Alliance to fight the Greater London Assembly seats on a platform of supporting the Mayor. However, the London Socialist Alliance did not have the support of the Socialist Party, which had decided to back an alternative list (the Campaign Against Tube Privatisation) for the Londonwide top-up section. The one Socialist Party candidate could not be officially endorsed by the London Socialist Alliance.

The Alliance then fought the Tottenham by-election of June 2000, at which it accused the Labour candidate of abandoning socialist principles.

Socialist Equality Party

Address: PO Box 1306, Sheffield S9 3UW

Email address: sep@socialequality.org.uk

Website: http://www.socialequality.org.uk

Highest vote: Miss J. E. Hyland (Barnsley East, 1996 (12/12)) – 89 votes, 0.5%

Parliamentary elections won: 0

Number of candidacies: 5

This party was formed in 1996 as the British Section of the (Trotskyite) Fourth International, though it is substantially the reformation of the **International Communist Party**. It fought the Barnsley East by-election in December 1996, and four seats at the 1997 election. It publishes the *International Worker*.

Socialist Labour Party (1903–80)

Highest vote: A. McManus (Halifax, 1918) – 4,036 votes, 15.4%

Parliamentary elections won: 0

Number of candidacies: 3

This party was formed by branches of the **Social Democratic Federation** who were attracted by the thinking of Daniel De Leon, leader of the Socialist Labour Party in the USA. De Leon wanted trade unions to be the building block for a socialist state and a strong socialist party to fight elections. The Scottish divisional council of the SDF began publishing its own journal from August 1902 in support of De Leonism.

In June 1903 the Scottish divisional council seceded and formed the Socialist Labour Party, with the support of a small number of members expelled from the SDF in London. Its organisation was based in Scotland and it failed to catch on in London, but branches soon developed in the industrial cities of northern England. Three candidates were nominated in the 1918 general election in northern English seats.

On hearing of the second Russian Revolution, the Socialist Labour Party welcomed the news. The party became involved in the discussions leading to the formation of the **Communist Party of Great Britain** but left them over its opposition to the party affiliating to the **Labour Party** (eventually this affiliation was rejected); part of the membership formed the Communist Unity Group which seceded in order to join the Communist Party in 1920.

The party suffered after 1920 from competition with the Communists. Its organisation declined and party journals no longer appeared regularly; no conference was held between 1932 and 1945, and various internal splits emerged and carried off members. The last publication of the party appeared in 1980.

Socialist Labour Party (1996–)

Address: 9 Victoria Road, Barnsley, South Yorkshire S70 2BB

Website: http://www.socialist-labour-party.org.uk

Highest vote: I. Khan (East Ham, 1997) – 2,697 votes, 6.8%

Parliamentary elections won: 0

Number of candidacies: 70

This party was formed by Arthur Scargill, President of the National Union of Mineworkers, after the **Labour Party** changed the wording of the Objects clause (Clause IV) of the party constitution in 1995. Scargill was opposed to a change which removed the commitment to common ownership of the means of production. The party was officially launched on May Day 1996, though broke cover early to contest a by-election in the miners' heartland at Hemsworth.

The party advocates a traditionalist socialist platform, including a 35-hour-week, a £6 per hour minimum wage and retirement at 55 on full pay. As one of the broadest-organised far-left parties, it has suffered from attempts at entrism by (among others) the **Communist Party of Great Britain** (*see* Communist Party of Great Britain (1992–)) and Militant Labour (*see* **Socialist Party**) which have been firmly opposed.

The party has extensive links in trade union politics, to the extent of its members holding the leadership of two of the smaller unions (NUM and ASLEF). The party publishes *Socialist News*. It has the support of a number of well-known figures, including Imran Khan, solicitor for the family of murdered black teenager Stephen Lawrence, and film-maker Ken Loach (who directed the party's election broadcast in 1997).

Attempts by other far-left groups to operate entrism into the party have been rebuffed and the party has always insisted on its independence, giving no support to the various left alliances put together in the late 1990s. Recent elections have seen its vote squeezed.

Socialist Party (1996–)

Address: PO Box 24697, London E11 1YD

Website: http://www.socialistparty.org.uk

Highest vote [excludes members who were selected as Labour Party candidates or who stood as independents.]: D. J. Nellist (Coventry, South, 1997) – 3,262 votes, 6.5%.

Parliamentary elections won: 0

Number of candidacies: 20

The present-day Socialist Party is probably still best known as 'Militant', the name of its newspaper, having formerly organised as the Militant tendency. The prime force in establishing the party was Ted Grant, a South African-born Trotskyite. Grant had effectively been the Deputy leader of the **Revolutionary Communist Party** (*see* Revolutionary Communist Party (1944–9)) and had reluctantly followed Gerry Healy into entrism in the **Labour Party** in 1949–50.

Healy's departure from the Fourth International in 1953 led the International to try to re-establish a British section. In 1955 the Committee for the Regroupment of the British Section of the Fourth International had been formed, and in 1956 it merged with other former members of the Revolutionary Communist Party to form the Revolutionary Socialist League; the International Secretariat of the Fourth International recognised it as its British section in 1957.

Ted Grant's views were not however in accord with the Fourth International (which he regarded with suspicion after its destruction of the Revolutionary Communist Party). His influence eventually prompted his opponents to leave the group; in 1961 most returned to backing Gerry Healy (*see* **Workers Revolutionary Party**), but a small section in Nottingham formed their own group (see **International Marxist Group**). The United Secretariat of the Fourth International forced this group to reunite with the RSL in 1964 but unification failed to happen in practice; in 1965 the Fourth International downgraded the RSL to the status of 'sympathizers', and in retaliation the RSL severed all links with it.

Though he opposed Gerry Healy's politics, Ted Grant had come to agree with him on the tactic of entrism (though for different reasons). He had seen Healy operate it and therefore knew some of the pitfalls. He also identified Liverpool as the ideal place to begin the process. Unlike other far-left groups, the RSL identified local government as a crucial forum for promoting their politics: it believed that local government was the base of reformism within the Labour movement, and therefore that it was up to the Marxist councillor to demonstrate that reformism 'cannot resolve the contradictions of capitalism'. In short, the group went into local government in order to prove it would not work.

The RSL did well in its organisation. Ted Grant was even selected as prospective Parliamentary candidate for Liverpool Walton in 1959 (though the NEC refused endorsement and he stood down). By 1964 the RSL was ready to launch what it termed 'an entrist propaganda newspaper' and *Militant* was chosen as the title. The first issue was published during the 1964 general election.

Militant's greatest strength tended to come from the youth wing of the Labour Party (indeed, it was subtitled 'the Marxist paper for Labour and youth'). Its growth in the 1960s owed a great deal to the extent to which the Labour government attracted left-wing opposition, and also to the greater freedom granted by the Labour Party to the Labour Party Young Socialists. In 1969, the LPYS conference supported a 'Charter for Young Workers' reflecting Militant policy. In 1970, Militant took control of the LPYS National Committee.

As a result of these advances *Militant* the newspaper went weekly instead of monthly and was printed on presses owned by the tendency. Commercial printing became a big source of funds: local Labour Parties either willingly or unwittingly contributed by choosing to print election material there.

The effect of this entrism did not go unnoticed by officials in the Labour Party. The National Agent, Reg Underhill, compiled a report on the extent of entrism from various far-left groups in late 1975, and high-lighted Militant as the greatest threat. However, the left of the Labour

Party, which frequently found Militant an ally, managed to stop any action being taken. Andy Bevan, a Militant member, was appointed National Youth Officer of the Labour Party in 1976 using this link.

Militant members could and did get selected as Labour Party candidates. David White was elected as Greater London Council councillor for Croydon Central in 1973, and he and two others were unsuccessful Parliamentary candidates in 1979. It was not until the 1979–83 Parliament that Militant attained its greatest power within the Labour Party. The Labour group on Liverpool City Council came under Militant control from 1981 and the 1982 City Council elections were fought on Militant policy; in 1983 Labour won control of the council.

The rise of Militant also prompted increasing efforts to stop them. Reg Underhill, after his retirement as Labour Party National Agent, compiled a new report on its activities. Six Militant members had been selected as prospective parliamentary candidates by late 1981. Labour leader Michael Foot overcame his reluctance (caused by previous moves to expel him) and ordered an inquiry, which in June 1982 reported that Militant was in conflict with the Labour Party constitution.

The 1982 Labour Party conference determined that members of Militant were not eligible for Labour membership, and a process of expulsion of Militant members was begun. The Labour Party acted with caution, fearing legal action by Militant, but a move to stop the expulsions failed; in February 1983 the five members of the editorial board of *Militant* were expelled. It was too late to deal with the Parliamentary candidates, though in the end only five ran in 1983: two were elected.

Militant ran Liverpool City Council as it had intended. Its first budget in 1984 involved an illegal deficit. In 1985, running out of money, the council initially refused to set a rate and lost £106,000 of interest; this loss was the source of the District Auditor's claim against councillors who had voted for the Militant strategy. The financial difficulties caused the council to give its 31,000 workforce 90 days' notice of redundancies at the end of September 1985 – an action which was seized on by Labour leader Neil Kinnock in his conference speech. Eventually, a loan from Swiss banks was obtained.

An investigation of the Liverpool District Labour Party was called, and recommended the expulsion of the leading Militant members; these expulsions went through the Labour Party NEC in the summer of 1986. However, as Labour entered the 1987 general election, Militant's strength was not significantly reduced: the expulsions had only affected a handful of high-profile figures. A third Militant member was elected as a Labour MP in 1987 and the tendency very nearly won several selections for safe seats.

Pressure for action against grassroots Militant members forced the Labour Party to establish the National Constitutional Committee to speed up the expulsion process. Special inquiries were ordered on constituency parties under Militant control. Though denounced by Militant and others on the left of the Labour Party as a 'witch-hunt', the expulsions severely reduced Militant's strength.

In spring 1991 the Labour MP for Liverpool Walton, Eric Heffer, died. The Labour Party's selection of Peter Kilfoyle over Militant member Lesley Mahmood for the seat enraged Militant, as Kilfoyle had led the NEC inquiry into Liverpool in the mid 1980s. Mahmood was expelled shortly after the selection and fought the by-election under the title 'Walton Real Labour' – the first time a Militant candidate had opposed the Labour Party. She polled 6.5%, saving her deposit but not coming close to the Labour total.

In summer 1991 the Labour Party decided to take action against the two remaining Militant MPs (one had died in 1990). They were suspended from Labour Party membership in September and expelled in December. In the meantime, Militant was coming to the conclusion that the game was up with the Labour Party; in October, Militant's conference decided to establish a separate party in Scotland – see **Scottish Militant Labour**.

The decision to abandon entrism forced Militant to part with its founder, Ted Grant, in 1992; Grant later formed a group called Socialist Appeal. Militant Labour was launched on 25 March 1993. It was slow to fight elections, concentrating on its heartlands where it had built a personal vote while within the Labour Party. On the eve of the 1997 general election Militant Labour changed its name to the Socialist Party, and *Militant* became *The Socialist*. The Socialist Party fought 19 seats; Dave Nellist, a former MP, saved his deposit in his old constituency.

Militant politics originally showed a preoccupation with economics and employment rights. The central demand was for the nationalisation of the

200 largest monopolies (no lesser figure was deemed acceptable). Unlike many other far-left groups it disdained contact with social movements such as feminism and gay rights, and did not join in the anti-fascist fight of the 1970s. On occasion an issue would be taken up after the Trades Union Congress had raised it. Militant was also opposed to nuclear disarmament, believing capitalists would not destroy the working-class which was being so productive for them.

Since 1992 this approach has changed and the Socialist Party has campaigned on issues it formerly ignored. A front organisation, Youth Against Racism in Europe, was set up in 1992 and played a large part in organising the October 1993 march to close the headquarters of the **British National Party**. Socialist Party policy now calls for the establishment of a Parliament for Wales and strengthened local government. The party also trumpets the record of the Militant-run Liverpool City Council.

The Party has benefited from the decision of some left-wing Labour councillors disillusioned with the Labour leadership to join it. It has seen some success in local elections, particularly in Coventry, where Dave Nellist now leads a group of three city councillors. In a spectacular by-election gain, Ian Page won the party a seat on Lewisham Borough Council in 1999.

Following the example of Scotland, where Scottish Militant Labour joined with several other groups to form the **Scottish Socialist Alliance**, the Socialist Party formed a part of the **Socialist Alliance** from 1999. However, it disagreed with the London Socialist Alliance and backed the Campaign Against Tube Privatisation list for the London Member section of the Greater London Assembly elections in 2000; this meant that Socialist Party candidate Ian Page, was only an unofficial London Socialist Alliance candidate in the Greenwich and Lewisham constituency.

Socialist Party of Great Britain (1904–)

Address: 52 Clapham High Street, London SW4

Email address: spgb@worldsocialism.org

Website: http://www.worldsocialism.org/spgb

Number on Register: 51

Highest vote: J. L. Read (Bethnal Green, 1959) – 899 votes, 2.4%

Parliamentary elections won: 0

Number of candidacies: 24

The Socialist Party is the longest-lived of socialist parties. It was formed in a breakaway from the **Social Democratic Federation** of members opposed to the perceived reformism of the SDF leadership, and the party was established on 12 June 1904 by Jack Fitzgerald, a self-educated Irish bricklayer. The party's standpoint is a pure form of Marxist socialism that rejects any reforms to capitalism; it therefore opposes all other left-wing organisations, as well as the concept of party leaders. The party viewed the USSR as state capitalist.

The party believes that socialism will be established through democracy after the majority of the electorate are in favour of it, and so it contests elections. It has usually nominated one or two candidates at each general election, but 14 seats were fought at the 1964 and 1967 Greater London Council elections. In 1997 the Socialist Party fought five seats, the most it has ever fought in a general election. The party urges its supporters to write 'socialism' on their ballot papers where there is no SPGB candidate.

The party has fought elections as The Socialist Party since 1989, because it perceived 'of Great Britain' to be nationalistic. The party's support for the overthrow of communist governments in Eastern Europe prompted a minority of members in north London to form an opposition faction. Members of this faction were expelled from the party in 1991 and established another party using the name **Socialist Party of Great Britain** (*see* Socialist Party of Great Britain (1991–)).

Socialist Party of Great Britain (1991–)

Address: 71 Ashbourne Court, Woodside Park Road, London N12 8SB
Parliamentary elections won: 0
Number of candidacies: 0

This party was formed by members of the **Socialist Party** (*see* Socialist Party of Great Britain (1904–)) who opposed the party's support for the overthrow of communist governments in Eastern Europe in 1989. These members considered the party was turning reformist and had accepted the need for a leadership, infringing cardinal principles of the party.

These members, who were mostly in the party's North West London and Camden/Bloomsbury branches, were expelled in May 1991 and reconstituted the party under the original name on 11 June 1991 – claiming the inheritance of the party formed in 1904.

Socialist Unity

Highest vote: R. Ahsan (Birmingham Ladywood, 1977 (18/8)) – 534 votes, 3.5%
Parliamentary elections won: 0
Number of candidacies: 13

Socialist Unity was an initiative of the **International Marxist Group**, which it launched in 1977. The IMG had been in favour of building bridges to other groups, and by 1977 it was prepared to argue that differences between the Trotskyist groups were sufficiently small for them to join in a single movement. The IMG hoped to secure wide support, but the largest Trotskyist group, the **Socialist Workers' Party**, refused to participate. The two principal groups to join, apart from the IMG, were Marxist Worker and Big Flame.

Socialist Unity fought the Birmingham Ladywood by-election of August 1977, but with a Socialist Workers' Party candidate also fighting, the vote was split. Socialist Unity comfortably outpolled the SWP in Birmingham Ladywood, and it was consistently to do so throughout. A Socialist Unity candidate came second with 19% of the vote in a local by-election in Spitalfields in October 1977. Many candidates were sponsored in the 1978 local elections, but their performance was damaged by the SWP splitting the vote.

Ten Socialist Unity candidates fought the 1979 general election, all in depressed inner-city areas. Socialist Unity also supported a candidate nominated by the Troops Out Movement (a creation of the IMG) against the Northern Ireland Secretary. None polled more than 1.9%. The IMG then recognised that the initiative had been a failure and it was wound up so that the IMG could concentrate on resuming entrism into the **Labour Party**.

Socialist Worker

See **Socialist Workers' Party**.

Socialist Workers' Party

Address: PO Box 82, London E3.

Website: http://www.swp.org.uk

Number on Register: 68

Highest vote: D.W. Hayes (Newcastle upon Tyne, Central, 1976(4/11)) – 184 votes, 1.9%

Parliamentary elections won: 0

Number of candidacies: 8

In 1949, Tony Cliff was a member of the Revolutionary Communist Party (*see* **Revolutionary Communist Party** (1944–9)) who was growing increasingly critical of the conduct of the USSR. While most in the party accepted the official Trotskyite view that the USSR was a degenerate workers' state, Cliff argued that it had become 'state capitalist'. He circulated a pamphlet to all RCP members in 1949, and when the party folded, formed the Socialist Review Group. It had 33 members at formation.

The Socialist Review Group did follow the Trotskyite approach of entrism into the **Labour Party**. Cliff pursued his thinking with Michael Kidron, to arrive at a theory that the cost of arming the armed forces deprives the economy of investment funds which might otherwise cause over-heating; the implication of this theory was that militarism was an economic tool of capitalism.

The group grew slowly, benefiting little from the many resignations from the **Communist Party of Great Britain** in 1956. In 1960 the group launched *International Socialism* magazine and two years later changed its name to the International Socialists; by this time, the group had launched its newspaper under the title *Industrial Worker*. In 1964 this became *Labour Worker*. The paper concentrated on reports from industrial disputes.

In 1965 the International Socialists ceased entrism, convinced that a major fight was about to break out between the Labour Party and the trade unions. As an independent group it hoped that shop stewards would provide a working-class base on which a revolutionary party could be built. Membership began to increase from under 400 in 1964 to around 1,000 in 1968 as the party benefited from the growth of the left among students; despite its preoccupation with trade union matters, the place where the International Socialists were strongest was the London School of Economics.

Labour Worker was retitled *Socialist Worker* in 1968, as Tony Cliff attempted to reorientate the group towards a more traditional Leninist revolutionary approach; democratic centralism was adopted in order to deal with any internal opposition (there were a number of resignations from the group because of this). Rank and file groups were encouraged in individual trade unions; the first was in the National Union of Teachers.

In 1969 the International Socialists instituted a 'turn to the class' in an attempt to form an extensive working-class base. In the first stage this meant encouraging its student members to find industrial jobs. Sales of *Socialist Worker* increased dramatically in the early 1970s, helped by good journalism from Paul Foot and good editing by Roger Protz. The group formed workplace branches from 1973.

Tony Cliff's impatience to form a mass-membership revolutionary party caused problems. He wanted readers of *Socialist Worker* to write for the paper, and when Roger Protz refused, he was dismissed, in April 1974. He hoped to double the number of workplace branches in a year, but the branches were very weak. The group began to nominate Parliamentary candidates in suitable by-elections in 1976; they fought as 'Socialist Worker' candidates.

In January 1977 the International Socialists took the name Socialist Workers' Party. The movement was already declining at this stage, the decline encouraged by intense sectarianism which led the party to oppose all collaboration. Membership only began to increase when the party launched the Anti-Nazi League in November 1977; as an attempt at a front organisation it was remarkably successful in attracting support from outside the SWP and a large membership.

SWP sectarianism led it to reject participation in the International Marxist Group's **Socialist Unity** initiative and it deliberately opposed Socialist Unity candidates in 1978. It became convinced that the way forward was through front organisations, and established the Women's Voice group in an attempt to attract feminists to the party; when instead, the group tried to input feminist ideas into SWP theory, it was closed down.

In 1979 SWP rhetoric about elections being a choice between 'Tweedledum and Tweedledee' led it to decide not to nominate candidates. More than ever before, SWP politics became centred on the idea that trade union agitation for wage increases was inherently political and part of the class struggle; whenever a strike failed this was put down to the workers being held back by reformist trade union officials who felt they were middle class.

The SWP's 'Rank and File' strategy was ended in 1982, with the winding up of its workplace branches and specialist newspapers. The preoccupation with industrial relations and the class struggle continued, though the party argued that the workers were less able to take action because of fears over unemployment. Sales of *Socialist Worker* increased in the 1980s when opposition to the Conservative government helped recruitment. The Anti-Nazi League, which had lapsed in the early 1980s, was revived in 1992.

SWP policy developed in 1992, when it argued for a general strike in order to protest at the announcement of the closure of most of the country's deep coal mines. After a long internal debate the party voted in favour of fighting elections in 1998. It fought five seats for the Scottish Parliament in 1999. In England and Wales the party joined with the **Socialist Alliance** and sponsored the vast majority of the London Socialist Alliance candidates for the Greater London Assembly in 2000.

Spare the Earth Ecology Party

Highest vote: T. A. Layton (Hove, 1983) – 524 votes, 1.1%

Parliamentary elections won: 0

Number of candidacies: 4

This party was formed by Tommy Layton, a retired wine merchant from Hove who had become a writer on food and travel and was opposed to acid rain, lead in petrol, heavy lorries and the pollution of the Mediterranean Sea. Layton fought Hove in the 1983 and 1987 elections, polling a respectable vote for what was in essence a one-member party. He also fought by-elections in Chesterfield (March 1984) and Portsmouth South (June 1984).

The Worker's Party [Ireland]

Website: http://www.workers-party.org/

Highest vote: T. French (Upper Bann, 1986 (23/1)) – 6,978 votes, 19.2%

Parliamentary elections won: 0

Number of candidacies: 71

The Workers' Party is the current name of the organisation sometimes known as Official Sinn Féin. In 1962, the Irish Republican movement declared that the military campaign it had run since 1956 was over, and set about trying to change the direction of the movement from paramilitarism to a peaceful but revolutionary socialist movement for Irish unity. This prompted a split with those who wished to continue the armed struggle and were opposed to ending abstentionism.

The Republican movement played a large part in the Northern Ireland Civil Rights Association in the late 1960s. The Republican movement was banned in 1967 by the Northern Ireland (Unionist) government. The increasing confrontation and demands from the nationalist community for more action led to those committed to armed struggle forming Provisional Sinn Fein (*see* **Sinn Féin**), and the Provisional IRA in 1969. The non-provisional part of the movement then became known as Official Sinn Féin.

In May 1972, 'Official Sinn Féin' and the official IRA declared that violence would lead to a spiral of killings and frustrate moves towards Irish unity, and the official IRA was eventually disbanded. The Secretary of State for Northern Ireland lifted the ban on the party in April 1973 in order that it could fight the Northern Ireland Assembly elections, in which it stood 10 candidates but failed to win a seat. In the February 1974 general election the movement fought four seats, and in October 1974 added a fifth candidate. During this period, the party described its candidates as 'Republican Clubs' nominees; this reflected the main base of its support.

A Trotskyite section in the republican movement, led by Séamus Costello, was opposed to the decision to dismantle the official IRA and he was expelled in 1975; he went on to form the **Irish Republican Socialist Party** with Bernadette McAliskey, former **Unity** MP for Mid-Ulster.

On 21 February 1977, the 'Official Sinn Féin' Ard Fheis [conference] voted to add the title 'The Workers' Party' to its name, and from this time candidates in the Irish Republic described themselves as 'Sinn Féin/The Workers' Party'; in Northern Ireland candidates became 'Republican Clubs/The Workers' Party'. The party fought seven seats in the 1979 election but saw its vote fall.

After successes in the Republic of Ireland that had seen three Dáil seats won, the party adopted the name 'The Workers' Party' as its sole title, on 30 September 1982. The party had opposed the IRA hunger strike and went on to establish links with Communist Parties in several countries. The party's share of the vote in Northern Ireland during the 1980s and 1990s showed a steady fall.

In 1992 there was a split in the party, with moderate members led by the Dáil Deputies forming an organisation called New Agenda, later taking the name **Democratic Left** (*see* **Democratic Left [Ireland]**). The one remaining Deputy who did not join lost his seat in the 1992 general election.

Third Position

Address: BCM ITP, London WC1N 3XX
Website: http://www.thirdposition.org/intro.shtml
Parliamentary elections won: 0
Number of candidacies: 0

This organisation was a product of the break-up of the **National Front** (*see* National Front (1967–90)), formed by the majority faction within the 'Official National Front'. It consisted of the members of the Official National Front who believed in the 'political soldiers' theory, of whom the central figure was Derek Holland. The organisation declares itself a revolutionary nationalist movement, which believes the political party system is corrupt, useless and evil; it does not contest elections as it regards democracy as a cancer which has destroyed the British Isles, and believes in street activism and community politics.

The organisation has international links with similar organisations throughout the world. In the UK it campaigns for the state to be the only institution allowed to issue money, the restoration of the guild system and a return to the land, which would be nationalised and shared with the British peoples. The movement opposes abortion and homosexuality, and calls for repatriation of non-Europeans; it would withdraw from the European Union, NATO and the United Nations.

Third Position is the publisher of *The Voice of St George* newspaper, but has very few open communications. It holds training schools for its activists, including some on a farm in northern Spain. In 1999, it was revealed that a chain of charity shops were connected to Third Position, a part of the organisation's belief in 'Counter Power'.

Third Way

Address: PO Box 1243, London SW7 3PB

Email address: thirdway@dircon.co.uk

Website: http://www.thirdway.org

Number on Register: 69

Highest vote: Ms. J. Trueman (Havering, Hornchurch, 1997) – 259 votes, 0.6%

Parliamentary elections won: 0

Number of candidacies: 2

This party is definitely not to be confused with Prime Minister Tony Blair's search for the 'third way'. It was formed in 1990; one of the founders was Patrick Harrington, who had previously been a member of the 'Official National Front' (*see* **National Front (1967–90)**) but then renounced fascism. Though Third Way describes itself as 'Radical centre', its advocacy until 1997 of an end to mass immigration and a voluntary repatriation programme has led many to place it on the far-right.

Third Way's policies are libertarian, with support for co-operatives; it is also a supporter of environmentalism. The party was formerly opposed to British membership of the European Union, and advocated a vote for the **Referendum Party** in 1997 where there was no Third Way candidate, but now believes in reform as opposed to withdrawal.

Three candidates stood in the London local elections of 1994, one polling 17% in a ward in Hornchurch; a single candidate in the European Parliament elections a month later won 2% in a much larger constituency. Third Way fought two seats at the 1997 general election, but these candidates polled dismally. The party built up its strength over many years to win 22% in Cuffley, Hertfordshire, in local elections in May 2000.

Tory

See **Conservative and Unionist Party**.

True Conservative Party

See **New Conservative Party**.

Twenty-First Century Party

Highest vote: C. R. Palmer (Forest of Dean, 1997) – 80 votes, 0.2%
Parliamentary elections won: 0
Number of candidacies: 6

The Twenty-First Century Party was formed in 1992 by a student from the Forest of Dean called Colin Palmer, to campaign for increased spending on events to mark the turn of the millennium. Palmer has since bought a Lordship of the Manor and refers to himself as Lord of Manton. He fought his home seat in 1992 and 1997 and four by-elections in the 1992–7 Parliament.

UK Independence Party

Address: 80 Regent Street, London W1R 5PE
Website: http://www.independenceuk.org.uk
Number on Register: 42
Highest vote: N. P. Farage (Salisbury, 1997) – 3,332 votes, 5.7%
Parliamentary elections won: 0
Number of candidacies: 215

The UK Independence Party was formed on 3 September 1993 at the London School of Economics, as a reformation of the **Anti-Federalist League**. The party seeks to prevent Britain becoming part of a federal Europe and proposes British withdrawal from the European Union, though it differed from the **Referendum Party** in having a full programme of policies in all fields which may or may not be contingent on withdrawal. It is non-sectarian and though it has a nationalist flavour, the whole tone is right-wing liberal.

When Sir James Goldsmith announced his intention to use his funds to finance an anti-EU campaign, the UKIP approached him with an invitation to join it, but received no answer; he was put off by the party's outright opposition to any forms of European supranational organisation, instead seeking to limit the EU to being a free trade organisation.

The UKIP has seen some substantial votes in by-elections but was eclipsed by the Referendum Party as the main anti-European force in the 1997 election. The party leader from formation until 1997 (and former leader of the Anti-Federalist League) was Dr. Alan Sked, Lecturer in International History at the LSE – once a Liberal Parliamentary candidate. Dr Sked severed his links with the party and denounced it in January 1999, when it declared that any members elected to the European Parliament would take their seats.

In the 1999 European Parliamentary elections the party benefited from lack of competition, and had a striking success in winning three seats under the proportional representation system. Its strongest poll was in the South-West region, affected by the crises in agriculture and fishing. However, only a few months after the election, a bitter feud broke out within the party over internal democracy.

The split resulted in a vote of no confidence against party leader Michael Holmes MEP, who resigned and left the party on 20 March 2000. Jeffrey Titford MEP was elected as the new leader. There were reports in summer 2000 of attempts by far-right parties to link to the UKIP.

Ulster Democratic Party

See **Ulster (Loyalist) Democratic Party**.

Ulster Democratic Unionist Party

Address: 91 Dundela Avenue, Belfast BT4 3BU

Website: http://www.dup.org.uk/

Number on Register: 9

Highest vote: The Rev. I. R. K. Paisley (North Antrim, 1986 (23/1)) – 33,937 votes, 97.4%

Parliamentary elections won: 21

Number of candidacies: 50

The genesis of the present-day Democratic Unionist Party was a group calling itself Ulster Protestant Action which was formed in 1959 to campaign for preferential treatment for Protestants in employment, and for freedom to organise parades and demonstrations. Ulster Protestant Action nominated four candidates for Belfast Corporation in 1964, two of whom were elected, under the label Protestant Unionist.

In 1966 Ulster Protestant Action became the Protestant Unionist Party, hoping to gather strength from those opposed to the moderate leadership of the **Ulster Unionists**. Its two councillors were re-elected in 1967. At the 1969 Stormont general election, it fought against six prominent moderate Unionists, polling nearly 21,000 votes. This strong showing helped to overthrow Northern Ireland Prime Minister Terence O'Neill shortly after the election.

When O'Neill and one of his supporters resigned from Stormont in 1970, the Rev. Ian Paisley and the Rev. William Beattie, the party's leader and Deputy leader, won their seats in the by-elections. Two months later the two stood in the Westminster general election and Paisley won Antrim North from the official Unionist.

The Protestant Unionist Party was wound up and the Ulster Democratic Unionist Party created on 30 October 1971, when Unionist Stormont MP Desmond Boal joined up. Boal advocated the creation of a left-wing party which would appeal to working-class loyalists (and had wanted to call it the Ulster Loyalist Party), though Ian Paisley remained the leader and ensured the party retained its social conservatism.

The DUP firmly opposed power-sharing and worked together with the Vanguard Unionists (*see* **Vanguard Unionist Progressive Party**) in what was called the Loyalist Coalition from 1973. In the Northern Ireland Assembly elections the coalition won 23.6%, with the DUP ahead of Vanguard with eight seats. The party had advocated integration with a Greater Ulster Council to look after the province; it laid special emphasis on local control of law and order.

When the official Unionist Party repudiated Sunningdale, the DUP, Vanguard and the Ulster Unionist Party created the **United Ulster Unionist Council** as a wider coalition of all those unionists opposed to the Sunningdale Agreement. Sheltering under the UUUC allowed the DUP to build up. Two of the UUUC candidates in the 1974 general elections were from the DUP – Ian Paisley and John McQuade, fighting Belfast West. Paisley made his own seat safe.

Sunningdale collapsed in the summer of 1974 in the face of a paralysing strike by the Ulster Workers' Council. The incoming Labour government held elections to a Constitutional Convention in 1975, in which the UUUC again fought as a single unit, advocating single-party majority rule; with 14.8% of the vote, the DUP won 12 seats. In the Convention, the DUP proved to be more opposed to power-sharing than was Vanguard, which proposed a voluntary coalition.

The Constitutional Convention ended in deadlock and two years later the UUUC was dissolved when the Ulster Unionists withdrew in opposition to a further strike by the Ulster Workers' Council. This led to the DUP fighting against the Ulster Unionists in the 1977 district council elections and attacking them as untrustworthy. The DUP won 12.7% of the vote. Despite falling out with the Ulster Unionists, the DUP still favoured an electoral pact for the general election, but found that the traditional independence of local unionist associations prevented it.

The DUP therefore fought three Unionist-held constituencies in the 1979 general election, in addition to the two seats it had fought before. It gained two seats, Belfast East and Belfast North, with narrow majorities. A month later the DUP's strong line against membership of the European Communities paid off, when Ian Paisley headed the poll for the European Parliament with 29.8% of the vote.

The incoming Conservative government's Northern Ireland Secretary, Humphrey Atkins, invited the four main constitutional parties to a conference to discuss a political settlement. The DUP decided, unlike the Ulster Unionists, to go to the conference in order to oppose power-sharing, though the conference was deadlocked. When the Prime Minister held talks with the Irish government, the DUP organised an 'Ulster Declaration' on 9 February 1981, similar to the Covenant launched by Sir Edward Carson in 1912.

The DUP polled more votes than the Ulster Unionists in the 1981 local elections, doubling its share at the previous elections. The three DUP MPs were suspended from the House of Commons when they shouted down the Northern Ireland Secretary after the assassination of Ulster Unionist MP Robert Bradford, in November 1981.

Elections to the Northern Ireland Assembly, created by the Conservative government in an attempt to devolve power, were held in October 1982. The DUP polled 23.0% on a platform of support for an Assembly which would scrutinise government decisions. It negotiated a partial pact with the Ulster Unionists for the 1983 general election, whereby the two parties agreed not to oppose each other in some seats where a split in the vote might let a republican or nationalist win.

In the general election, the DUP was disappointed by its performance in losing Belfast North and only gaining one other seat (Mid-Ulster). However, Ian Paisley's personal popularity was undiminished and he again topped the poll in the 1984 European Parliament elections with 33.6% of the vote. That this was a personal vote was demonstrated by the local government elections of 1985 in which the DUP polled 24.3%.

The Anglo-Irish Agreement of November 1985 was a big spur to Unionist unity. The DUP and the Ulster Unionists jointly organised the 'Ulster Says No' campaign against the Agreement; all unionist MPs sought re-election to Parliament and all three DUP MPs were re-elected with huge majorities. A pact was organised with the Ulster Unionists for the by-elections and the 1987 general election; attempts by the DUP in East Antrim to oppose the Ulster Unionist were blocked by the party's executive.

DUP rejection of any talks with the British government unless the Anglo-Irish Agreement was suspended, did not preclude 'talks about talks' which were held in early 1988. With the Ulster Unionists, the DUP rejected the idea of any talks with the Irish government until there was an internal settlement in Northern Ireland, involving majority rule.

Support for the DUP fell in the 1989 local council elections, as did Ian Paisley's vote in the European Parliament elections a month later. The alliance with the Ulster Unionists threatened the DUP's distinctiveness, and the party voted at its conference on 25 November 1989 to fight all safe unionist seats. For the period of the 'talks about talks', however, the party continued to collaborate with the Ulster Unionists.

At the 1992 general election, the DUP challenged the Ulster Unionists in Strangford and East Antrim, being challenged itself in North Antrim. No seat came close to changing hands. The DUP vote fell again in the 1993 local government elections. The party presented peace proposals in September 1993 called *Breaking the Log-Jam,* but opposed talks with the

Social Democratic and Labour Party until the Hume–Adams talks between the SDLP and **Sinn Féin** were ended.

The Downing Street Declaration of December 1993 was described by the DUP as a sell-out and the party organised a 'Save Ulster' campaign; its 1994 European election campaign attempted to make the election a referendum on approval of the Downing Street Declaration. Ian Paisley's vote fell by 0.7%. The IRA ceasefire was greeted with scepticism and the party attempted to create a pan-Unionist front to counter the pan-Nationalist front of the SDLP and Sinn Féin. The Unionist commission however attracted little support outside the DUP.

DUP scepticism about IRA intentions seemed to be confirmed by the return to violence in February 1996, and it boycotted the 'proximity talks' which were held soon after. It welcomed the creation of the Northern Ireland Forum and won 18.8% of the vote in the elections, but withdrew for a time from the multi-party talks which followed, in protest against the blocking of the Orange parade at Drumcree.

When the party returned to the talks, it campaigned for the expulsion of the parties allied to loyalist paramilitaries. It was also opposed to the choice of Senator George Mitchell as Chair of the Talks. While the party was angry with the Ulster Unionists over their attitude to the talks, it had to withdraw its general election candidates in Belfast North and West Tyrone, where there was a danger of a split vote letting in a nationalist. The DUP lost Mid-Ulster to Martin McGuinness of Sinn Féin in the general election of 1997.

The DUP's scepticism over the talks turned to outright opposition in July 1997, when it failed to get the assurances it was seeking from the British government over decommissioning of terrorist weapons. It held several meetings with the government, attempting to change the basis of the talks, but was unsuccessful. On the eve of the agreement, a DUP press conference was heckled by members of the **Ulster Democratic Party** and **Progressive Unionist Party**.

Campaigning against the Belfast Agreement in the referendum, the DUP claimed that a majority of unionists had voted No. It won 18.1% in the subsequent Northern Ireland Assembly elections. In January 1999 the party announced that it was to open an office in Liverpool which would organise the party on the mainland and contest local elections.

When the Executive was formed in December 1999, the DUP took up its entitlement to two ministers, despite its opposition to power-sharing. The DUP ministers did not attend meetings of the Executive. After further concessions to Sinn Féin on decommissioning, the party announced that it would rotate the ministerial positions among its Assembly members; the Executive decided to restrict circulation of government papers to them.

As unionist opposition to the Agreement increased, the party won the South Antrim seat in a September 2000 by-election.

Ulster (Loyalist) Democratic Party

Address: 36 Castle Street, Lisburn, County Antrim BT27 4XE

Email address: info@udp.org

Website: http://www.udp.org

Highest vote: G. J. McMichael (Upper Bann, 1990 (17/5)) – 600 votes, 1.7%

Parliamentary elections won: 0

Number of candidacies: 2

The launch of this party in June 1981 was an initiative of the Ulster Defence Association, the largest loyalist paramilitary group in Northern Ireland. After a failed attempt in 1977 to recreate the Ulster Workers' Council strike of three years earlier which had brought down the Sunningdale Agreement, the UDA had set up the 'New Ulster Political Research Group' to develop a political strategy. This group suggested Northern Ireland be given independence within the European Union, a radical suggestion which was rejected by the UDA leadership.

When the New Ulster Political Research Group was wound up in 1981, John McMichael (Deputy leader of the UDA) formed the Ulster Loyalist Democratic Party. McMichael fought the Belfast South by-election of March 1982, polling 1.3%; the low level of support for the party was confirmed when two candidates in Belfast North in the October 1982 Northern Ireland Assembly elections won only 3.0%; the party did not nominate candidates in the 1983 general election. Two candidates in the 1985 local elections polled very badly.

The Anglo-Irish Agreement produced a surprising response from the party, when in February 1986 it urged that Sinn Féin participate in a constitutional conference. A fully worked out strategy, *Common Sense*, was published in January 1987 arguing for a proportionally elected Assembly with a written constitution, and an all-party executive. John McMichael was assassinated in December 1987, and other leading members of the party have been murdered.

In 1988 the party declared that it was independent and had no links with the UDA, and in December 1989 it dropped the title 'Loyalist' to rename itself the Ulster Democratic Party. Gary McMichael, son of John, was the party's candidate in the May 1990 Upper Bann by-election and polled 600 votes. One leading figure in the party urged unionists in Belfast West to vote for the **Social Democratic and Labour Party** in order to defeat Gerry Adams of Sinn Féin. At the 1993 local government elections, Gary McMichael won a seat on Lisburn Borough Council.

The party's leaders went to talk to loyalist prisoners after the IRA ceasefire in 1994, and helped to negotiate the Combined Loyalist Military Command ceasefire a few months later. The party supported peace talks and met the British and Irish governments; when the IRA resumed violence, it urged calmness from loyalists. At the Northern Ireland Forum elections of May 1996, the party won 2.2% of the total vote, mostly in Greater Belfast.

Deciding not to contest the 1997 general election, the party entered the talks process when it began soon afterwards. It withdrew from the talks when it was on the point of being expelled in January 1998 after a series of killings by the Ulster Freedom Fighters; when it returned in late February, it again supported the process and attacked the anti-Agreement Unionist parties. Michael Stone, who had attacked an IRA funeral in 1988, appeared at a party rally to support its campaign for a Yes vote in the referendum of May 1998.

Disastrously, the party did not win any seats in the Northern Ireland Assembly elections of June 1998; Gary McMichael came closest, being the runner-up for the last seat in Lagan Valley. The inability of the party to play any direct part in the Assembly was thought to have prompted some of its members to join smaller loyalist groups. The Ulster Freedom Fighters, linked with the UDA, have twice threatened to break off their ceasefire in 2000.

In August 2000, rivalry between the Ulster Defence Association and the Ulster Volunteer Force (*see* **Progressive Unionist Party**) broke into violence; a member of the UDA and a member of the UVF were murdered and both parties' offices were attacked.

Ulster Popular Unionist Party

Highest vote: J. A. Kilfedder (North Down, 1986 (23/1)) – 30,793 votes, 79.2%
Parliamentary elections won: 4
Number of candidacies: 4

This was a small party formed by supporters of James Kilfedder, who was an **Ulster Unionist** MP who resigned the whip to sit as an Independent Unionist MP for North Down in 1977. In January 1980, after his 1979 general election victory over the official Unionist candidate, he formed the Ulster Progressive Unionist Party. This party changed its name when Kilfedder discovered that the name was used by a fringe party allied to loyalist terrorists (*see* **Progressive Unionist Party**). In the House of Commons, Kilfedder received the Conservative whip.

The party, as well as sponsoring Kilfedder himself, also fought local elections in North Down. It won five seats in the 1981 local elections while in a temporary pact with the **Unionist Party of Northern Ireland**. When James Kilfedder fought the Northern Ireland Assembly elections of October 1982, his large vote failed to transfer to other UPUP candidates. Kilfedder was elected Speaker of the Assembly.

Kilfedder was opposed by a rebel integrationist at the 1987 election and his majority fell; his constituency was the strongest area for the **Conservative Party** when it decided to organise in Northern Ireland, despite his own links with the Conservatives at Westminster. He was re-elected over Conservative opposition in 1992 with an increased majority.

The party did not survive Kilfedder's death in 1995; one of the party's councillors joined the **United Kingdom Unionist Party**, another the **Ulster Democratic Unionist Party**, and another fought the 1996 Forum elections as 'Independent Democratic Unionist Party'.

Ulster Unionist Labour Association

Highest vote: T. H. Burn (Belfast St. Anne's, 1918) – 9,155 votes, 74.7%

Parliamentary elections won: 3

Number of candidacies: 3

In order to counter the challenge to **Ulster Unionist** candidates in working-class Protestant areas of Belfast, Unionist leader Sir Edward Carson set up this association within the Ulster Unionist Council, in June 1918. The Association was strongly anti-socialist.

Three candidates of the Association fought the 1918 general election and won seats, without opposition from official Unionists. The same three won seats in the Northern Ireland Parliament in 1921, but they did not form a group separate from the Ulster Unionists.

The Association still exists though it no longer sponsors candidates.

Ulster Unionist Party

Address: Unionist Headquarters, 3 Glengall Street, Belfast BT12 5AE

Email address: uup@uup.org

Website: http://www.uup.org/

Number on Register: 5

Highest vote: Rt Hon. J. D. Taylor (Strangford, 1986 (23/1)) – 32,627 votes, 94.2%.

Parliamentary elections won: 69

Number of candidacies: 99

The roots of the Ulster Unionist Party were in the Ulster Unionist Council which was formed in March 1905. This body was intended to co-ordinate Unionist activity and sponsor candidates at a time when the unionists were fighting against Home Rule for Ireland. The Council was affiliated to Conservative Central Office and therefore part of the **Conservative Party**.

The initial campaign of the Unionists was against any form of Home Rule, especially under the leadership of Sir Edward Carson from 1911. However, when the violent British reaction to the Easter Rising led to the ascendency of Sinn Féin throughout Catholic Ireland, the attention turned to trying to exclude the bulk of the unionist population in Ulster from the inevitable settlement in the rest of the country.

The Government of Ireland Act 1920 provided for six of the nine Ulster counties to form a province of the United Kingdom, with three included in the devolved Southern Ireland. The Unionists accepted this policy reluctantly (there were a substantial number of unionists in Monaghan, Donegal and County Dublin) and at the cost of Sir Edward Carson, who retired. Sir James Craig (later created Viscount Craigavon) became Prime Minister of Northern Ireland in 1921.

The Unionists regarded the Northern Ireland Parliament as 'a Protestant Parliament for a Protestant people'. They changed the electoral system from multi-member single-transferable vote to single-member first past the post after the 1925 election. Viscount Craigavon had been Prime Minister for nearly 20 years when he died. A backbench revolt in 1943 forced his successor, John Andrews, to leave office after three years, but the next incumbent, Sir Basil Brooke, served another 20 years. Brooke persuaded Clement Attlee to insert a clause in the Ireland Act 1949, that no change would be made in the constitutional arrangements for Northern Ireland without the consent of the Northern Ireland Parliament.

In 1963, Terence O'Neill became Prime Minister and decided to try to involve the nationalist community in public life. He visited a catholic Secondary school in April 1964, and on 14th January 1965 invited Séan Lemass – the Republic of Ireland Taoiseach – to Belfast. O'Neill called a general election soon afterwards and increased the Unionist vote, winning over many liberals who had not previously voted.

O'Neill's invitation did however cause severe strain within Unionism. He had to fight hard to get cabinet approval for reforms, and sacked the hardline Minister of Home Affairs, William Craig, in December 1968. In 1969, O'Neill called a general election in order to get a mandate for reforms; though the Unionists won, it was not a sufficient endorsement and he resigned in April 1969. Civil unrest escalated under his successor, James Chichester-Clark, and British troops had to intervene.

Chichester-Clark resigned in March 1971 due to backbench opposition. His successor, Brian Faulkner, tried to set up a wider administration including a member of the **Northern Ireland Labour Party** and (unprecedentedly) a catholic, Gerard Newe. However, the introduction of internment and the 'Bloody Sunday' killings in January 1972 led to more security trouble and the eventual end of the Northern Ireland Parliament in March 1972, when Faulkner refused to hand over control of law and order.

Shortly before, William Craig had formed a pressure group called Ulster Vanguard to campaign against direct rule. When Craig formed Vanguard into a political party (*see* **Vanguard Unionist Progressive Party**) he and a number of his supporters resigned from the party. Elections to the Northern Ireland Assembly, conducted by proportional representation in June 1973, saw the Unionists divided between those in favour of the government's white paper and power-sharing, and those against.

Brian Faulkner supported power-sharing, and entered into negotiations with other parties at Sunningdale in Berkshire; an agreement was reached and a power-sharing Executive was formed on 1 January 1974. However, the Ulster Unionist Council meeting on 4 January voted against the proposals for a Council of Ireland betweeen the Northern Ireland Executive and the Republic of Ireland by 427 to 374 and Faulkner resigned (*see* **Pro-Assembly Ulster Unionist**).

The Ulster Unionists then formed a coalition with the **Ulster Democratic Unionist Party** and the Vanguard Unionists, called the **United Ulster Unionist Council**. The object of this coalition was to oppose the Sunningdale Agreement. The UUUC fought the February 1974 general election as a single bloc, and won all but one seat with an overall total of 51.1%. The UUUC MPs did not join the Conservatives as the Ulster Unionists had previously done; this thwarted Conservative Prime Minister Edward Heath's hope of remaining in office. The Ulster Unionist Council was still connected to the 'National Union' until 1986.

The Northern Ireland Executive collapsed in the face of a strike organised by the Ulster Workers' Council in May 1974. The UUUC continued and lost only one seat in the October 1974 election (unfortunately, that of their leader Harry West), and fought the elections to the Constitutional Convention in May 1975 again as one unit campaigning for majority rule. The Convention was inconclusive.

In 1977, when loyalists tried to organise a new strike similar to that in 1974, the Ulster Unionists objected and left the UUUC. The six Unionist

MPs acted as an independent group in Parliament, and managed to put pressure on the by now minority Labour government to grant extra seats to Northern Ireland, in compensation for the end of Stormont. While the bill to give effect to this recommendation went through, the Ulster Unionists preserved the Labour government in office.

After Royal Assent, the party was more attracted by the Conservative proposals for two-tier local government and four MPs voted for the no confidence motion on 28 March 1979. In the ensuing general election the party lost two seats in Belfast to the DUP. The party's result in the European Parliament elections a month later was disappointing, with party leader Harry West running behind John Taylor. Taylor was eventually elected; West had to resign. James Molyneaux was elected as the new leader.

The Ulster Unionists' optimistic reading of Conservative policy was not borne out and they boycotted a Constitutional Conference called by the new Northern Ireland Secretary. The party regarded attempts at negotiation with the Republic of Ireland government with extreme suspicion. In the 1981 local elections the DUP managed to outpoll the party. Robert Bradford, the Ulster Unionist MP for Belfast South, was assassinated by the IRA on 14 November 1981. While grieving for him, the party campaigned in favour of more security measures. It retained the seat in a by-election, easily beating the DUP.

The party broadly opposed the creation of the Northern Ireland Assembly under the Conservative government's 'rolling devolution' programme, thinking it a potential revival of power-sharing and Sunningdale. In the Assembly election in October 1982 the party won 29.7% of the vote, regaining first place from the DUP. A limited agreement was made with the DUP for the 1983 general election, so that the unionist vote was not split in three seats.

1983 was a very successful election for the party; it won 11 seats, gaining one from the DUP, though it again did badly at the European Parliament elections in June 1984, where Ian Paisley topped the poll. However, the inter-unionist competition ended when the Anglo-Irish Agreement forced the two parties to co-operate. The party lost one seat when all its MPs sought re-election in opposition to the Agreement, due to tactical voting among nationalists.

An electoral pact across all constituencies in the 1987 election masked any competition between the parties, though the party was disappointed to see Enoch Powell lose his seat in South Down. After the election, the party did not allow its block on participation in talks to stop them taking part in 'talks about talks' with the government, at which it tried unsuccessfully to replace the Anglo-Irish Agreement.

The Unionist vote increased slightly at the 1989 local government and European Parliament elections, and the party comfortably held the Upper Bann seat in a May 1990 by-election at which the Conservatives, who began to organise in Northern Ireland, badly lost their deposit.

A series of inter-party talks began in 1991, at which the party proposed a devolved system, hoping to persuade the government to drop the Anglo-Irish Agreement. Differences with the DUP led to the breakdown of the full electoral pact, but the DUP challenge in two seats in the 1992 general election was fended off easily. The Unionists were more enthusiastic about using the talks to try to find a solution, incurring DUP criticism.

In a narrow Parliament, the Unionists agreed to support the Conservative government's Maastricht Treaty Bill; the government later conceded a Unionist demand and created a Northern Ireland Select Committee. The Downing Street Declaration of December 1993 was constructed partly to reassure the party, though a leak of the proposed framework for talks in February 1995 was denounced as biased towards nationalists and had to be rewritten.

In 1995 James Molyneaux, who had led the Unionists since 1979, was challenged by a little-known student who was recognized as a 'stalking horse' for a more credible challenger. He survived, though stood down shortly afterwards; David Trimble was unexpectedly elected to succeed him. Trimble was anxious to make unionism a modern force.

The Ulster Unionists welcomed the creation of the elected Northern Ireland Forum and won 24.2% in the elections. It withdrew from the talks in protest at the Royal Ulster Constabulary block on the Orange Order parade at Drumcree in July 1996, and on return in September, pressed for a requirement of IRA decommissioning before Sinn Féin could participate in the talks.

In the 1997 general election the party did well to win the West Tyrone seat, which many had expected to go to the **Social Democratic and**

Labour Party. The party executive transferred the decision on tactics in the talks to the 'talks team', which faced criticism from some Ulster Unionist MPs. The Good Friday Agreement, while welcomed by the leadership, was approved by the executive by only 55 to 23, and seven out of the party's ten MPs opposed it.

The party was disappointed to come second to the SDLP in terms of popular vote in the Northern Ireland Assembly elections, though it won more seats. David Trimble became First Minister-Designate in the Northern Ireland Executive and won the Nobel Peace Prize for his work in securing the Good Friday Agreement. A declaration that the party would not agree to devolution before the actual decommissioning of IRA arms prevented the formation of the Executive; in December 1999 a compromise was agreed in which the IRA agreed to open contacts with the decommissioning body.

The party faced some anger over the decision to accept office in a government which included Sinn Féin, without any actual decommissioning; the Executive had to be suspended in February 2000 because of a post-dated letter of resignation David Trimble had been forced to give, but resumed when the IRA agreed to international inspection of its arms dumps. Unionist opinion however, appears to be moving against the Agreement, and the party lost the South Antrim by-election to the DUP in September 2000.

Union Movement

Highest vote: Sir O. E. Mosley, Bt. (Kensington North, 1959) – 2,821 votes, 8.1%.

Parliamentary elections won: 0

Number of candidacies: 8

After the end of the Second World War, Sir Oswald Mosley was reluctant to resume an active role in politics. His supporters were organised in several groups: the 18b Detainees Aid Fund, formed to help those interned during the war, the League of Ex-Servicemen, formed by ex-**British Union of Fascists** member Jeffrey Hamm, and the Union of British Freemen, formed by Victor Burgess in 1945, were dominated by Mosley's supporters.

Supporters contacted Mosley and organised the Mosley Book Clubs in

1946, which distributed a newsletter from that November. It took until February 1948 for Mosley to be persuaded to accept the leadership of a new group; on 8 February 1948, the 47 Mosley Book Clubs united with the 18b Detainees Aid Fund, the League of Ex-Servicemen and the Union of British Freemen to create the Union Movement.

Mosley had used the war to read widely on European civilisation and had developed a new policy of 'Europe a Nation'. Under this policy, a common European government would take responsibility for foreign and defence policy, finance and scientific development. National Parliaments would have power over social and cultural matters. Colonialism would end, but with a system of apartheid throughout Africa.

This policy was taken up by the Union Movement, but received little support or publicity. When the Union Movement ran campaigns against immigration (principally from Eastern Europe, though as early as 1952 the party was highlighting black and Asian immigration), the media often gave it bad publicity. Mosley's insistence that he had left fascism behind was not believed, and in 1951 he left England for Ireland, later moving to Paris.

The Union Movement began to direct its activity towards those areas of London into which most immigrants were settling – Brixton and Notting Hill. The Notting Hill race riot of August 1958 led Mosley to fight the 1959 general election there. Mosley expected to get one third of the vote on the basis of a flawed canvass, and when he polled only 8% he tried to get the result declared void in the courts.

Two by-elections fought by the party in 1961–2 were disappointing. In 1962 Mosley invited John Bean and Colin Jordan of the **British National Party** (*see* British National Party (1960–67)) to be national organisers of the Union Movement, but they refused. At a conference in Venice on 4 March 1962, Mosley tried to form a united National Party of Europe, together with fascists from other countries, though little joint working resulted.

Mosley had been effectively banned from the BBC since 1934 and resented the lack of opportunities to promote the party. Four Union Movement candidates fought in 1966; Mosley, in Shoreditch and Finsbury, polled the highest though with only 4.6%. Mosley retired from politics later in the year at the age of 70. The movement declined after then, fighting only one more by-election, and reformed in 1973 as the **Action Party**.

Unionist Party of Northern Ireland

Highest vote: P.J. McLachlan (Belfast East, October 1974) – 14,417 votes, 27.0%
Parliamentary elections won: 0
Number of candidacies: 5

This party was launched on 4 September 1974 by former Northern Ireland Prime Minister Brian Faulkner, who had previously supported the **Pro-Assembly Ulster Unionist** candidates. After the failure of the Assembly, Faulkner hoped that the party would become the mainstream Unionist party. The hurried organisation of the party, the month before a general election, meant it fought only two seats.

The UPNI's performance was not encouraging. It lost its deposit in North Down and polled only 27% in Belfast East. In the elections to the Constitutional Convention in May 1975, the UPNI's 18 candidates polled 7.7%, arguing for power-sharing in a strong regional government. It won five seats but the failure of the Convention to produce agreement prompted Brian Faulkner to retire from active politics.

When the **United Ulster Unionist Council** split up in 1977, the UPNI hoped to conclude an electoral pact with the **Ulster Unionists**, but was unable to reconcile policy over power-sharing, to which the Ulster Unionists were firmly opposed. It fought three Belfast seats in the 1979 general election but all three candidates lost their deposits.

The party went into a coalition with the **Ulster Popular Unionist Party** in the 1981 local elections but did badly there also. The party was wound up soon after these elections.

United Anti-Common Marketeers

Parliamentary elections won: 0
Number of candidacies: 0

This group was formed by a number of the non-party No campaigners from the 1975 referendum. The two leading figures, Donald Bennett and Oliver Smedley, had been Liberal candidates. The group did not fight Parliamentary elections, but did nominate five candidates at the 1979

European Parliament elections. Donald Bennett had the highest vote, winning 6.1% in the Cotswolds. Immediately after the election the group reformed as the **Anti-Common Market Free Trade Party**.

United Country Party

Highest vote: E. A. L. Iremonger (Chichester, 1979) – 863 votes, 1.5%
Parliamentary elections won: 0
Number of candidacies: 2

The formation of the United Country Party was announced on 13 February 1979 by Edmund Iremonger and the television astronomer Patrick Moore, who were near neighbours in Selsey, West Sussex. Iremonger had been a member of the **Conservative Party** and was a past Chairman of the West Sussex branch of the Freedom Association.

The United Country Party favoured a reduction in taxation, especially death duties, and argued for restrictions on the power of trade unions: it opposed the 'closed shop' and supported managers' right to dismiss an employee without trade union intervention. It also favoured stricter immigration laws. Though expressing admiration for Mrs Thatcher, the party was wary of the rest of the Conservative Party.

Hoping to nominate four candidates, it eventually fought only two seats at the 1979 election. In the face of poor results, it amalgamated with the **New Britain Party** soon afterwards.

United Democratic Party

Highest vote: C. J. Curry (Cambridge, October 1974) – 885 votes, 1.7%
Parliamentary elections won: 0
Number of candidacies: 13

This party was a product of right-wing dissatisfaction with the **Conservative Party** of the early 1970s. Several candidates had fought the February 1974 general election as independent or unofficial Conservative candidates. Shortly after the election, when it was obvious another election would be held soon afterwards, a group of these candidates joined together to form the United Democratic Party. United Democratic Party policy was right-wing, and some members stressed their opposition to British membership of the European Communities.

The party picked up some members from the **Independent Democratic Alliance** and fought thirteen seats in the October 1974 general election. All the seats were in East Anglia or the south of England, including all seats in Somerset, where the party's leader James Tippett lived. The highest poll was in Cambridge, where the candidate was a well-known manager of a local high technology company.

The party appears to have been disbanded soon after. One of its members contested several by-elections in the 1974–9 parliament as an independent.

United Empire Party

Highest vote: A. C. Critchley (Islington East, 1931 (19/2)) – 8,314 votes, 27.2% [Joint candidate with the Empire Free Trade Crusade]

Parliamentary elections won: 0

Number of candidacies: 3

This party was formed by Lord Beaverbrook, the proprietor of the *Daily Express*, in February 1930, in order to campaign for the policy of 'Empire Free Trade' (tariff-free trade within the British Empire, but increased tariffs on foreign goods). He was supported by Viscount Rothermere, proprietor of the *Daily Mail* and Beaverbrook's cousin.

Beaverbrook met with Conservative leader Stanley Baldwin in March 1930 to discuss policy, and obtained satisfactory assurances such that he decided to disband the party and return subscriptions. However, Rothermere determined to continue the party and expanded its policy: it now campaigned for subsidies for British agriculture and cuts in public spending, and against Indian self-government, and diplomatic relations with the USSR.

A United Empire Party candidate was nominated in the Bromley by-election of September 1930, coming third with almost a quarter of the vote, and nearly splitting the Conservative vote enough to allow the Liberal candidate to win. However, there was friction with the parallel

Empire Free Trade Crusade, when the local branch of the United Empire Party put up a candidate against the Empire Crusader in Paddington South in October 1930. A joint candidate was agreed for the Islington East by-election in February 1931, though this candidate merely succeeded in allowing Labour to retain the seat.

In the 1931 general election, the United Empire Party supported the National government, and as the Conservatives tended to support tariff reform, the party was wound up shortly afterwards.

United English National Party

Highest vote: A. S. Ashby (Derby South, October 1974) – 793 votes, 1.5%

Parliamentary elections won: 0

Number of candidacies: 3

In the early summer of 1974, a number of members of the **National Front** in Leicester, led by the former Chairman John Kynaston, resigned and joined with members of the local Enoch Powell supporters group to form an organisation they called the English National Party. On 7 August 1974, the English National Party went to Derby to merge with a small local group called the United Party; the merged party was the United English National Party.

The party fought Derby South in the October 1974 general election, winning 1.5% of the vote. It continued to organise in Derby and fought both seats there in 1979, but against National Front opposition. The National Front outpolled both candidates easily. It appears the party was wound up soon afterwards.

United Kingdom Independence Party

See **UK Independence Party**.

United Kingdom Unionist Party

Address: 10 Hamilton Road, Bangor, Co. Down BT20 4LE

Website: http://www.ukup.org

Number on Register: 10

Only vote: R. L. McCartney (North Down, 1997) – 12,817 votes, 35.1%

Parliamentary elections won: 1

Number of candidacies: 1

Robert McCartney MP won the 1995 North Down by-election fighting as a 'United Kingdom Unionist' on an integrationist platform, and his campaign attracted a number of local supporters. In 1996, the government decided to hold an election to the all-party talks process in Northern Ireland by means of a party list, and so McCartney registered the United Kingdom Unionist Party, in order to fight the elections for himself and his supporters.

The party was broadly successful in these elections, winning a constituency seat for McCartney in North Down, and two seats province-wide; one of these went to Conor Cruise-O'Brien, a former minister in the Republic of Ireland government from the Irish Labour Party. However, it was sceptical over the talks process and like the **Ulster Democratic Unionist Party** it withdrew in July 1997.

Membership applications were invited from December 1997, putting the party in a position to campaign against the Belfast Agreement and to fight the Northern Ireland Assembly elections of June 1998. It won five seats in this election, regarded at the time as a notably good performance. However, a dispute with Robert McCartney led all four other Assembly members to resign to form the **Northern Ireland Unionist Party** in December 1998.

During the by-election campaign in 1995, Robert McCartney declared his intention to apply for the Labour whip, and though this was refused, he generally supported the **Labour Party** on issues not relating to Northern Ireland. Since July 1998 the party has been allied to the **UK Independence Party**.

United Labour Party

Only vote: B. P. Caul (Belfast South, 1982 (4/3)) – 303 votes, 0.7%

Parliamentary elections won: 0

Number of candidacies: 1

Formed in 1978, this party was the first attempt to restart a non-sectarian Labour Party in Northern Ireland after the disintegration of the **Northern Ireland Labour Party**. The formation was partly instigated by Paddy Devlin, a founder member of the **Social Democratic and Labour Party** who had been expelled from that party in 1977 after accusing it of dropping socialism.

The party's stance on the constitutional future of Northern Ireland was to seek consent for measures which promoted reconciliation. Paddy Devlin polled 1.1% in the European Parliament elections of June 1979, and a candidate in the Belfast South by-election of March 1982 won 0.7%.

In 1987 the party merged with the remnants of the Northern Ireland Labour Party, the Labour Party of Northern Ireland and a local group in Newtownabbey to form **Labour '87**.

United Ulster Unionist Council

Highest vote: The Rev. I. R. K. Paisley (Antrim North, October 1974) – 43,186 votes, 72.6%.

Parliamentary elections won: 21

Number of candidacies: 24

When the **Ulster Unionists** voted to reject the Council of Ireland proposed under the Sunningdale Agreement on 4 January 1974, they formed an alliance with the two other unionist parties opposing the Agreement – the **Ulster Democratic Unionist Party** and the **Vanguard Unionist Progressive Party**. This alliance became the United Ulster Unionist Council and operated as an effective electoral pact at the February 1974 general election, winning all but one seat.

A conference was held in April 1974, at which the UUUC agreed its support for a majority-rule administration, elected using proportional representation in smaller constituencies. The Council was opposed to any suggestion of a Council of Ireland. The UUUC gave support to the Ulster Workers' Council strike of May 1974, which succeeded in bringing down the Sunningdale administration.

When Harry West, leader of the Unionists in Parliament, lost his seat in October 1974, the leadership was taken by James Molyneaux. The Council fought the 1975 Northern Ireland Constitutional Convention elections on a common platform, but a split emerged in 1976 when William Craig, leader of Vanguard, proposed a voluntary coalition with the Social Democratic and Labour Party.

Early in 1977, the UUUC's Steering Committee formed an 'Action Council' which initiated links with paramilitary groups and attempted to organise a strike similar to that of 1974. The Ulster Unionists disowned this action and the UUUC broke up in May 1977.

United Ulster Unionist Movement

See **United Ulster Unionist Party**.

United Ulster Unionist Party

Highest vote: J. Dunlop (Mid Ulster, 1979) – 29,249 votes, 44.7%
Parliamentary elections won: 1
Number of candidacies: 2

When William Craig, the leader of the **Vanguard Unionist Progressive Party**, suggested in the Northern Ireland Constitutional Convention in 1976 that a voluntary coalition could be formed between Unionists and the **Social Democratic and Labour Party**, the opponents of such a policy (most of the party) formed the United Ulster Unionist Movement as an internal campaign against it.

The name of the movement was suggested by its policy of seeking to build a united party covering all Unionists. By 1977 it became apparent this was not possible and Ernest Baird, the leader of the Movement, announced it was to re-establish itself as a political party. The United Ulster Unionist

Party was formed in time to fight the 1977 local council elections in which it won 3.2% of the vote.

The party attracted the allegiance of one of the three Vanguard MPs, John Dunlop (Mid Ulster). In the 1979 general election, in addition to John Dunlop's re-election, Ernest Baird fought Fermanagh and South Tyrone. The **Ulster Unionists** did not oppose John Dunlop and he won easily, but Ernest Baird was outpolled by the Unionist candidate; his splitting of the unionist vote allowed the Republican MP to win.

The party nominated only seven candidates in the 1981 local council elections, of whom five won. However, this appears to have been due to personal votes; all of the party's 12 candidates in the Northern Ireland Assembly elections of 1982 were defeated. John Dunlop did not seek re-election in 1983 and the party was wound up. A number of the party's members subsequently joined the Ulster Unionists.

United Unionist Assembly Party

Parliamentary elections won: 0
Number of candidacies: 0

This party was formed by three members of the Northern Ireland Assembly in 1998. All three had been elected as Independent Unionists opposed to the Belfast Agreement, and banded together in order to have an organisation at Stormont.

Unity

See **Opposition Unity**.

Vanguard Unionist Progressive Party

Highest vote: The Rev. R. J. Bradford (Belfast South, October 1974) – 30,116 votes, 59.2%
Parliamentary elections won: 6
Number of candidacies: 6

A succession of moderate **Ulster Unionist** leaders from the mid 1960s provoked discontent among some Unionists. William Craig, Minister of Home Affairs in the Stormont administration, was sacked by Terence O'Neill in December 1968, after claiming pressure had been brought by the British government to introduce reforms. In 1972, when abolition of the Northern Ireland Parliament was suggested, Craig set up Ulster Vanguard, a pressure group within the Unionists, to oppose direct rule.

Direct rule turned into a reality at the end of March 1972 and Vanguard held mass rallies to campaign against it. However, a policy statement in favour of an independent Northern Ireland cost some support. The advent of elections by proportional representation to the Northern Ireland Assembly in 1973, led Craig to break with the Unionists and establish the Vanguard Unionist Progressive Party.

In the elections, Vanguard won 10.5% of the vote. It opposed the Sunningdale Agreement on a power-sharing administration and joined the **United Ulster Unionist Council** in January 1974. Three out of twelve UUUC candidates in the February 1974 general election were nominees of Vanguard, and all gained seats (two previously held by pro-Agreement Unionists, one by Bernadette Devlin). The three seats were kept in the October general election.

In the elections to the Northern Ireland Constitutional Convention in May 1975, again as part of the UUUC, Vanguard polled 12.7%. However, despite the party's strong opposition to power-sharing, William Craig supported the idea of a voluntary coalition between Unionists and the **Social Democratic and Labour Party**. This idea was rejected by the bulk of the membership who resigned to form the United Ulster Unionist Movement, later the **United Ulster Unionist Party**.

William Craig remained leader of Vanguard and promoted David Trimble, a young constitutional law lecturer, to be his Deputy leader. The loss of members was so severe that the party did not fight the 1977 local council elections, and in February 1978 the party rejoined the Ulster Unionists, reverting to being a pressure group.

Vectis National Party

Only vote: R. W. J. Cawdell (Isle of Wight, 1970) – 1,607 votes, 2.8%
Parliamentary elections won: 0
Number of candidacies: 1

This party was formed in November 1969 in a meeting at Ryde, Isle of Wight. Vectis is the Latin name for the Isle of Wight, and the party sought for the Isle the same status as the Isle of Man. During the postal strike of January 1971, with the agreement of the Island's postmaster, the party sold Isle of Wight postage stamps. Other campaigns of the party were for Isle of Wight television and radio stations.

The party fought the 1970 general election, but failed to make a breakthrough. It only narrowly lost a local election in 1971, but the difficulty in persuading voters to break with traditional allegiances disillusioned many of its members, and activity was wound down in the mid 1970s. There has been some pressure for the party to reform.

It should be noted that the Isle of Wight was a Kingdom between approximately AD 534 and 687. The sovereignty was sold to the English Crown for 4000 marks in 1293, and the party believed this was unconstitutional.

Volunteer Political Party

Only vote: S. M. Gibson (Belfast West, October 1974) – 2,690 votes, 6.0%
Parliamentary elections won: 0
Number of candidacies: 1

This party was the political wing of the Ulster Volunteer Force, one of the largest loyalist paramilitary organisations in Northern Ireland. It was formed in September 1974, shortly after the Ulster Workers' Council strike which brought down the power-sharing Sunningdale Executive, and nominated one candidate in the October 1974 general election, in Belfast West.

The party received some support from the Ulster Defence Association in that election, but appears to have been wound up afterwards. Hugh

Smyth, who had helped to found the party, fought the Northern Ireland Constitutional Convention election of 1975 as an Independent. He later formed the **Progressive Unionist Party**.

Weekly Worker

See **Communist Party of Great Britain (1989–)**

Welsh Republican Movement

See **Muudiad Gweiniaethol Cymru**

Wessex Regionalist

Highest vote: T. M. Thatcher (Westbury, 1979) – 1,905 votes, 3.0%
Parliamentary elections won: 0
Number of candidacies: 19

The Wessex Regionalists were formed by Alex Thynne (later Thynn), then Viscount Weymouth and now the Marquess of Bath. The party was similar to the Cornish **Mebyon Kernow** in seeking an increased regional identity for the west country but not independence. It began as a very informal group. Alex Thynne fought Westbury in the February 1974 general election.

The 1979 election saw seven candidates. The movement was formally organised in November 1981 and fought ten seats in 1983. After the 1984 European Parliament elections, where only one candidate stood, the movement did not nominate any candidates until 1997 when a single candidate fought Portsmouth North.

Whig

See **Liberal Party (1679–1988)**.

Women for Life on Earth

Highest vote: Ms R. Johnson (Henley, 1983) – 517 votes, 1.1%

Parliamentary elections won: 0

Number of candidacies: 4

Women for Life on Earth was the group which organised the Greenham Common women's peace camp. The camp began at the conclusion of the 'Walk for Life' from Cardiff to Greenham Common, when four women chained themselves to the fence in protest at the media's lack of coverage of the issue. The camp became women-only in 1982.

In the 1983 election, Women for Life on Earth nominated four candidates on a unilateralist and pacifist platform; three of the candidates were also endorsed by the **Ecology Party**.

Women's Party

Only vote: Miss C. H. Pankhurst (Smethwick, 1918) – 8,614 votes, 47.8%

Parliamentary elections won: 0

Number of candidacies: 1

The Women's Party was formed by Christabel Pankhurst in November 1917, with the support of the Women's Social and Political Union (which had led the suffragette movement before the Great War). At this stage, the battle for votes for women had been won, and Christabel Pankhurst nursed a desire to be the first woman MP. The Women's Party effectively succeeded the WSPU.

The party's policy supported equal pay and equal divorce laws for women, but also campaigned in the economic sphere, where it called for the abolition of trade unions. It was also a fervently 'patriotic' party. This meant removal of all officials 'of enemy blood', control of essential industries only by those of 'British blood', and prevention of Germans being naturalised. Some of the rhetoric of the party echoed the 'hidden hand' accusations of anti-Semitism.

Christabel Pankhurst was offered the chance to fight a seat in Wiltshire without any **Coalition** opposition, but chose instead to fight Smethwick where **Labour** was well-organised. The Conservative candidate who had been selected there was persuaded to stand down, and she was the unofficial Coalition candidate for the seat. She narrowly lost.

Early in 1919, Christabel Pankhurst announced her candidacy for the Abbey division of Westminster, where the sitting Conservative MP was expected to retire. However, the party was already declining, and lost funding which it had been receiving from the British Commonwealth Union. Though it was still meeting in May 1919, later that year it was disbanded.

Workers Against Racism

See **Revolutionary Communist Party (1981–97)**.

Workers' Party [Great Britain]

Highest vote: D. P. Roberts (Leicester South, 1983) – 161 votes, 0.3%
Parliamentary elections won: 0
Number of candidacies: 4

This party was a breakaway from the **Workers' Revolutionary Party** in early 1979. Leaving behind the Trotskyite beliefs of the WRP, it took a pure Leninist outlook and was critical of all other far-left groups. It therefore supported martial law in Poland and the Chinese government's suppression of the Tienanmen Square protest. It fought two seats in the 1979 and 1983 general elections and is now known as the International Leninist Workers' Party.

Workers' Party of Scotland

Only vote: M. Lygate (Glasgow Gorbals, 1969 (30/10)) – 72 votes, 0.5%
Parliamentary elections won: 0
Number of candidacies: 1

This party was formed in autumn 1966 in Edinburgh by former members of the **Communist Party of Great Britain** who supported Scottish nationalism. The party advocated the creation of a Socialist Republic of Scotland. Obtaining a minuscule vote in a 1969 by-election, leading member Matt Lygate was sent to jail for armed robbery in 1972. The party supported the Khmer Rouge movement in Cambodia.

Workers' Revolutionary Party

Highest vote: B. Lavery (Pontefract and Castleford, February 1974) – 991 votes, 2.2%

Parliamentary elections won: 0

Number of candidacies: 124

When the Fourth International leadership got its way and forced the **Revolutionary Communist Party** (see Revolutionary Communist Party (1944–9)) to become an entrist organisation, the members met in 'The Club' under the leadership of Gerry Healy. 'The Club' broke with the official Fourth International in 1953, when it objected to the views of the secretary Michael Pablo, and established a new 'International Committee of the Fourth International'.

'The Club' recruited a large number of former members of the **Communist Party of Great Britain**, after the Soviet invasion of Hungary in 1956. In May 1959, Gerry Healy formed the Socialist Labour League, also intended to be entrist but proscribed by the **Labour Party** almost immediately. Despite this, the Socialist Labour League eventually grew to control the Young Socialists from 1964; the Labour Party responded by dissolving the Young Socialists.

This forced the Socialist Labour League to abandon entrism and attempt to form its own party. The League, following Trotskyite belief, expected an imminent economic crisis and mass unemployment which would build the movement; in 1968 it established the All Trades Union Alliance and in 1969 it began publication of the daily *Workers' Press* newspaper.

As a general election approached in November 1973, the Socialist Labour League became the Workers' Revolutionary Party, and in the February 1974 general election fought nine seats. Considerable media attention was given to the actress Vanessa Redgrave, who had joined the party and was a candidate. In the summer of 1974, the WRP's claims of an

337

imminent military coup were rejected by some members, who were expelled.

The party appears to have received funding from Libya and Iraq during the 1970s and this money, together with the wealth of Vanessa and Corin Redgrave, enabled the party to fight 60 seats in the 1979 general election. This entitled it to a party election broadcast, given by Corin Redgrave, who spoke on the need to fight the armed state. The party polled only 12,600 votes.

In October 1985, the WRP suffered a deep split when Gerry Healy was accused of misusing his position to obtain sexual favours. The split resulted in two Workers' Revolutionary Parties, that including Gerry Healy being known as the Workers' Revolutionary Party (Newsline). Gerry Healy, together with Corin and Vanessa Redgrave, left the party in November 1986 to form the Marxist Party. The WRP (Newsline) continued nominating candidates.

The other faction in the split of 1985 was known as the Workers' Revolutionary Party (Workers' Press). This group lost a faction almost immediately (*see* **International Communist Party**) and, after further factionalism, was dissolved in 1996; most of its members appear to have joined the **Socialist Labour Party**.

Phonlogical Acquisition

Can you see the common error pattern? (If you see it, but you don't know how to describe it in phonological terms, Chapter 1's review should be of use.) You might also be wondering about a different question·

Q2. *At what ages are these errors typically observed in English-learning children?*

… which is a very important question, particularly for guiding parents and educators, and for diagnosing language delays, but it will be fairly secondary in this text. Zack's phonology in tables (1) and (2) is quite typical for his age, but children differ quite widely in their rates of production mastery – for example, a monolingual child's first word can be reported anywhere between at least eight and 18 months or later.

Beyond the speech of individual children, this textbook is also concerned with many other broader questions – questions that naturally emerge as soon as you have seen a few different data sets like Zack's. Here are two of them:

Q3: *Is phonology learned by imitating ambient speech? Or do children 'invent' their own phonologies?*

Q4: *What do child phonologies have in common with adult phonologies? How similar are they, and how different, and how can we explain their similarities and differences?*

These questions are two facets of the most central question for any theory of phonological acquisition: *why* do children speak the way they do? There are many possible answers – feel free to imagine as many as you can now! – but the most common immediate answer to the question *'How do children learn to speak?'* is that they imitate the people around them. Zack's sample, however, already suggests that that response is somewhat beside the point – children may be <u>trying</u> to imitate their parents or older siblings, but we can be fairly certain that Zack did not hear anyone else producing *briefcase* or *Christopher* as he did in (1). So to understand these patterns we must be looking for something beyond imitation, for some learning mechanism(s) that can understand why a child's phonology is sometimes rather distant from its eventual target, and how that distance is shortened and changed over the course of development.

As for Q4, one of this text's biggest goals is to present you with many striking similarities between phonological process in child speech and those found elsewhere: in the target languages that children are learning, as well as in other target languages they have never experienced, and in the speech of other learners and populations. Throughout the book, we will build up a theory in which the explanations for Zack's errors relate them to all these other phonologies. It's not just that he's small, tired or inexperienced. There are more exciting explanations! As for the differences: we will have to face them from time to month.day.) As you skim this data, ask yourself what kinds of questions you might want to answer about Zack's speech:

(1)	Zack at ages 2;3.23–2;4.26 (data from Smith, 2010)				
	Target	*Child*		*Target*	*Child*
	briefcase	['bi:dəteitə]		*clean*	[tin]
	special	['pɛdu]		*Christopher*	['tidəwə]
	screwdriver	['tu:deidə]		*grandpa*	['dæmba:]
	fleece	[fi:t]		*three*	[fi:]
	glove(s)	[dʌb]		*throw*	[fəu]
	bring	[bɪn]		*grape(s)*	[de:p]

To start with:

Q1: *What is systematic about the differences between the child and adult pro-nunciations of these words?*

Question (1) is the starting point of this textbook: describing what is <u>systematic</u> about the *non-target* productions in child speech. We will call these non-target productions *errors*, but note that *error* here does NOT mean 'speech error' in the adult sense: Zack is not assumed to be saying [tin] meaning *clean* the way you might accidentally say ['sɪməmɪm] meaning *cinnamon*. Instead, this term *error* simply means a child's production that deviate from the adult target form they are acquiring – much more on this idea to come.

In this sample, Zack's errors show many systematic deviations from the ambient English around him, which we will start to describe in phonological terms in the next few chapters. He deletes sounds (the 's' in *special*); he changes sounds (the 'v' in *glove* which becomes a 'b'); he adds sounds (the vowel in the middle of *briefcase*); and sometimes he does multiple changes at once (look at the pronuncia-tion of /θɹ/ in *throw* and *three*). You may also be able to see that there are common patterns to these errors: for example, seeing how Zack pronounces the word-initial segments of *grandpa*, *glove* and *grape* will give you a hint as to how he pronounces the beginning of *clean* and *Christopher*, and that hint is right:

(2)	*grandpa*	['dæmba:]		*clean*	[tin]
	glove(s)	[dʌb]		*Christopher*	['tidəwə]
	grape(s)	[de:p]			

assembled as a potential resource for those studying other aspects of language, child development or learning theories, such as cognitive and developmental psychologists, applied linguists and teachers focused on second language learning, speech language pathologists and specialists in communication disorders. My hope is that once a reader has absorbed this text, they will be ready to start reading the primary literature on phonological acquisition, particularly in the linguistic but also developmental psychology traditions, and perhaps know where to look for more detailed answers to their specific questions.

This text also has a main theoretical focus: analysing children's productive phonology with a constraint-based grammar, namely Optimality Theory (OT).[3] The text assumes no background in OT: rather, the goal of this book is to use common patterns and properties of child phonology to motivate some basics of the OT framework. Chapters 3 through 5 provide the bulk of this argumentation: describing child data using production constraints, competition and optimization of surface outputs, and comparisons with the typology of adult languages. If this is all nonsense to you right now, that's just fine – Chapters 3 through 5 will build up the theory, piece by piece. It starts from the beginning, but it does get advanced, and exercises are provided throughout.

Given this theoretical focus, it should be clear from the outset that this book does not provide an introduction to other phonological theories, nor their application to acquisition data. There will be some limited comparing and contrasting with alternatives, but they will predominantly serve to help evaluate OT's strengths and weaknesses in capturing child phonologies. The goal of this myopic approach is to equip the reader with sufficient grounding in this one theory to assess its merits in light of a wide range of phonological data, both from children and adults. For a textbook on phonological acquisition that considers several different theoretical perspectives, see Johnson and Reimers (2010), and also the further readings section.

2   A Teaser of What this Textbook Is About

So what exactly is this exciting child production data that this textbook is all about? Here is a teaser from Zack, who was transcribed by his grandfather producing the following English words over the course of a month when he was two. (Throughout this book, we will give ages in a standard format – year;

---

[3] With respect to origins: OT was brought into being most notably in a manuscript circulated as Prince and Smolensky (1993), also published as a book in 2004, as well as McCarthy and Prince (1993) and (1995).

Preface

1 The Goals and Intended Audiences of this Textbook

This section lays out the aims and intended audience of this textbook. Hopefully you have turned to this page before committing yourself to understanding the rest; if not, at least you will soon know what you have gotten yourself into.

This is a textbook for readers who have already taken an introduction to linguistics, including a unit on rule-based phonology. It assumes that the reader is acquainted with the basic concepts and working hypotheses underlying phonological study in the generative tradition. Chapter 1 skims over these concepts as a quick refresher, but students who need more than that should probably start elsewhere (a couple of excellent introductory phonology textbooks are listed in the further readings at the end of this chapter). This text also assumes you can read IPA (International Phonetic Alphabet) transcriptions of speech, as the IPA is the international gold standard for attempting to accurately describe speech sounds on the printed page. If you have used the IPA before but forget some of the symbols' meanings, there are charts to consult! The official IPA chart is provided at the end of this chapter,[1] and the further readings section gives you a link to an online version of the chart where you can also listen to each symbol's sound.

The textbook's empirical focus is the typical development of monolingual children's phonological production. In other words, it concerns how typically-developing children produce the sound patterns of their mother tongue from about 12–14 months to five- to six-years-old. Although Chapter 8 also discusses the childhood acquisition of more than one phonology (simultaneously or sequentially), Chapter 2 is primarily focused on infant speech perception, and atypical development of phonology is treated from time to time.[2]

Given this empirical scope, this book may hopefully be useful not only to students of phonology, acquisition and/or linguistics. It was also

---

[1] Although note that a few non-IPA-but-standard transcription conventions will be used, particularly in the transcription of North American English vowels.

[2] A couple of other regrettable omissions: this text barely deals with the acquisition of vowels (except in Section 6.2 and that chapter's further reading section), and has nothing to say about the acquisition of phrasal phonology, intonation or tone.

Contents

For MJM, RMT and JRT

First published 2016 by
PALGRAVE

Palgrave in the UK is an imprint of Macmillan Publishers Limited, registered in England, company number 785998, of 4 Crinan Street, London, N1 9XW.

Palgrave Macmillan in the US is a division of St Martin's Press LLC, 175 Fifth Avenue, New York, NY 10010.

Palgrave is a global imprint of the above companies and is represented throughout the world.

Palgrave® and Macmillan® are registered trademarks in the United States, the United Kingdom, Europe and other countries.

ISBN 978-0-230-29376-2   hardback
ISBN 978-0-230-29377-9   paperback

This book is printed on paper suitable for recycling and made from fully managed and sustained forest sources. Logging, pulping and manufacturing processes are expected to conform to the environmental regulations of the country of origin.

A catalogue record for this book is available from the British Library.

A catalog record for this book is available from the Library of Congress.

Typeset by MPS Limited, Chennai, India.

Printed in China

PHONOLOGICAL ACQUISITION

CHILD LANGUAGE AND CONSTRAINT-BASED GRAMMAR

ANNE-MICHELLE TESSIER

Department of Linguistics, University of Alberta

 macmillan education

 palgrave

time, and we will attempt to highlight and generalize about them, but our explanations for these divergences will be rather more piecemeal.

At the same time, there are other data areas to explore and worry about, such as:

Q5: *How many of a child's production errors result from limitations in motor control and/or perception?*

Q6: *How does a child's mental dictionary affect the rate and nature of their phonological learning?*

Although these questions are not the heart of this textbook, they are always nearby – because children and their phonology are clearly grounded in the real world, and this real world affects their phonological knowledge. There are indeed pressures and demands made by the tongue and the ear that are specific to children; there is motor planning and gestural co-ordination to be learnt, there are sequences that are more or less likely to be misperceived in particular contexts. In Zack's sample, there is the lateral sound at the end of target *special*, which he pronounces as a back vowel ['pɛdu] – and there is good reason to suspect that that error is the result of misperceiving that dark 'l' as a vowel.[4] There are also practical limitations of known vocabulary (which we will refer to frequently as a *mental lexicon*) and memory capacity that no doubt affect production, and which might particularly affect any experimental work done with young children. Our discussion will return to these questions from time to time, especially in Chapters 7 and 8.

And since this text is about learning, and also about studying learning, we should also be directly asking questions like:

Q7: *What learning mechanisms can explain or at least describe how children get from their initial state to an adult-like grammar within a few years?*

Q8: *What are the best empirical methodologies for determining what children know about their phonology and when they know it? How do we ask experimental questions about phonological development of very young children?*

By the end of this text, you will be ready to look at new data, and ask these questions yourself – maybe pilot an experiment, maybe study the speech of younger family members and so on.

---

[4] For one thing, adults learning English as a second language often misperceive dark l as a vowel, in the same way – and in fact some Scottish English dialects may well be merging the two (see Stuart-Smith et al., 2013).

3   How the Chapters Are Organized and How to Use Them

This book's chapters are organized to match the order of topics in a semester-long advanced undergraduate course in phonological acquisition (as the author has taught it many times.) However, many chapters could be used on their own or in combination with others.

The first two chapters are introductory in nature: Chapter 1 is a refresher on phonological concepts and representations; Chapter 2 is a crash course on infant speech perception. Each of these chapters can be read on their own. Chapters 3 through 6 present child phonology at the levels of the syllable (Chapter 3), the word (Chapter 4) and the segment (Chapters 5–6) in turn. At the same time, they motivate the OT framework at each of these levels; in order to understand their theory-building arguments, they should be read in sequence. The next three chapters discuss the connection between a child's nascent phonology and their learning of words (Chapter 7), morphemes (Chapter 8) and multiple languages (Chapter 9). These chapters have much less OT and more broad theoretical discussion; they assume the basics of Chapters 3–6 but are not otherwise inter-dependent. Chapter 10 introduces some aspects of OT learning theories – that is how the learner <u>actually learns</u>. It introduces no new empirical data, and in principle could be read with only Chapters 1 and 3 as background.

Many chapters contain exercises interspersed within the text. Some of these ask you to look at some data and come up with generalizations before you continue to read; others provide technical exercises to let you check that they have understood the tools immediately under discussion. In addition every chapter ends with exercises, which come in two types. Some are problem sets with data to analyse, intended to solidify basic concepts, while others are more open-ended discussion questions. Every section also ends with a further reading section.

For a textbook, this text has a lot of footnotes. For the researcher interested in a topic under discussion, they may be very valuable; for a student who is taking their first pass through the material, they can always be ignored.

4   On the Languages of This Textbook

Especially for non-linguists, this book contains lots of language data from potentially-unfamiliar languages. The first time any such language is introduced, its name is followed by a description of its language family, and one or more of the primary countries in which it is spoken, for example 'This data comes from French (Gallo-Romance, spoken in e.g. France, the Democratic Republic of Congo and Canada).'

Acknowledgements

To truly acknowledge all the help that went into this textbook would require an equally-long companion text entitled 'How Did Anyone Write a Textbook Before the Internet?' As a poor substitute, I thank the following alphabetized colleagues for data, corrections, suggestions, references and discussion (as well as the additional contributors I will remember the day after this manuscript goes to press): Hildy Barca, Melissa Baese-Berk, Michael Becker, Andries Coetzee, Robert Daland, Lila Daskalaki, Lisa Davidson, Michael Dow, Ashley Farris-Trimble, Annahita Farudi, Ilaria Frana, Maria Gouskova, Kara Hawthorne, Eva Juarros Daussa, Shigeto Kawahara, Tara McAllister Byun, Kevin McGowan, Rachel McGraw, Paula Menendez-Benito, Monika Molnar, Tuuli Morrill, Benjamin Munson, Elena Nicoladis, Johanne Paradis, Yvan Rose, Michelle Sims, Willem Visser, Sophie Wauquier and Tania Zamuner. Sadly, I can hold none of them responsible for whatever egregious misrepresentations and errors have crept in despite their best efforts.

I thank all the students who have taken my classes – at the University of Alberta, the University of Michigan and the LSA 2013 Summer Institute – especially those whose looks of bewilderment bordering on despair quickly taught me what was <u>not</u>, in fact, a clever explanation. I thank several anonymous reviewers for many excellent suggestions, corrections and improvements; and the absurdly patient professionals at Palgrave, especially Paul Stevens, Aléta Bezuidenhout and Kitty van Boxel. For careful technical proofreading, I thank Blake Allen, Kayla Day, Zachary Jaggers, Elizabeth Robertson, Amanda Rysling and Pocholo Umbal; and Stephanie Archer and Anja Arnhold for additional close reading and suggestions. I am also grateful to the Faculty of Arts at the University of Alberta for granting me sabbatical leave in the fall of 2013 during which much of this manuscript was actually written.

I acknowledge a special debt to Heather Goad, John McCarthy and Joe Pater, for showing me how to teach phonology and its acquisition over many years. And finally I thank Marcin Morzycki for writing his own book during the semester before my sabbatical, thereby ensuring that I would have to write this one or else risk looking bad.

1 Background I: A Phonological Refresher

1.1 The Basics of Phonology

To begin with: what is *phonology*? To be more precise, we will usually be talking about the phonology of either a language or a speaker – and our working definition will be that a phonology is a characterization of all the mental representations and unconscious knowledge that speakers have about abstract speech sounds. Studying phonology, then, is studying the nature of this knowledge, and also the characterization of this knowledge.

We will often talk about this abstract knowledge in terms of phonological *generalizations*. To exemplify: one generalization about Zack's speech from the Preface is that he begins all of his words with only one consonant, and never with two consonants side-by-side. At the same time, a different generalization about English as spoken by the native speaker adults around him is that words begin with two or three consonants in a row all the time! By looking at Zack's own version of English words, we can see that he systematically modifies all words beginning with more than one consonant so that they are consistent with his own pattern – the 'sp' of *special* comes out as just [p], the 'fl' of *fleece* as just [f], and so on. The task of a phonological grammar is to capture a speaker or population's generalizations, explicitly enough that an algorithm plugged into some otherwise-dumb computer could approximate the phonological knowledge of a human language speaker.

Most phonological grammars (and all the ones we will use in this text) operate on representations of two kinds: stored forms in the mental lexicon, called *underlying representations* (URs), and forms that can actually be produced by a speaker or heard by a listener, called *surface representations* (SRs). This text will also refer to these URs and SRs respectively as *inputs* and *outputs*, and the mapping from one to the other is illustrated as /input/ → [output]; note the / / vs [ ] notation. The grammars we will use in this textbook are ones in which you can feed the grammar <u>any</u> input and it will always generate[1]

---

[1] This property – though certainly not always cached out in this format – is the source of the term *generative linguistics*, associated as you probably already know with the pioneering work of Noam Chomsky.

a *legal* output – that is, an output that a native speaker would judge to be a possible surface form in the language. If you give it input /blɛp/, and it is a phonology of English, it will simply return [blɛp] again, because that string of sounds is a well-formed possible English word. If you give it /pɛlb/, though, it will map that input onto some modified form to accord with English phonological generalizations, perhaps as [pʰɛɫ]. In this way, you might think of a phonological grammar as a language-specific filter. The job of phonologists is to spell out how these filters work: what building blocks they are composed of, how they differ between languages, and what kinds of structures they can rule out or in (and eventually why). When studying acquisition, phonologists take on the further tasks of describing how these filters become language-specific (through learning), and how children use them and refine them in the years before they have acquired a fully-adult grammar.

To build a phonological grammar, we first need to understand the objects that it manipulates: what are these underlying and surface representations made of? The basic phonological building blocks of URs and SRs are *segments*. Segments are abstractions away from the raw acoustic signal of speech, made into manageable mental chunks that we can manipulate with the grammar. To see the value of this approach consider the two *spectrograms* below, which together represent much of the raw acoustics of the author saying an English sentence. If you are not familiar with reading spectrograms, these will be rather messy and hard to interpret. The only crucial aspects of the graph are that the x-axis measures time in milliseconds, and the y-axis indicates the strongest resonating frequencies[2] measured in Hertz, and overall intensity of the sound, indicated by the darkness of each bar.

(1a)   'She borrowed a plastic yellow bin...

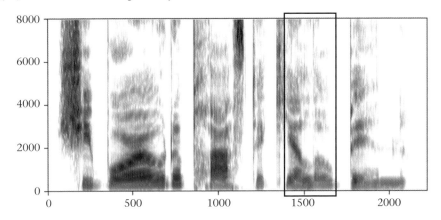

---

[2] Which you may already know are called *formants*.

(1b)   '... to hold extra pin cushions and a trock'

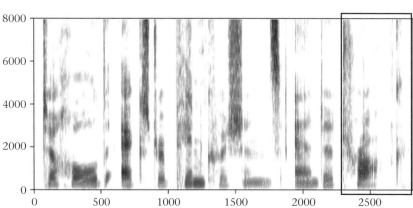

Let us just consider the two boxed portions of the sentence, which correspond to the word *yellow* in the (1a) spectrogram and *trock* in (1b). (Yes, *trock*
is not a real word of English, on which there will be more in a minute.) It is
somewhat hard to process this visual representation, with its continuous time
dimension and myriad phonetic dimensions. But from a phonological viewpoint, one basic question is: how many segments does each word contain?
If we examine each spectrogram for steady-state periods of sound, expecting some noise during the transitions, then we can perhaps come up with a
rough approximation of the words' segments. Below this has been done for
zoomed-in spectrograms of *yellow* and *trock,* where each segment has been
transcribed with an IPA symbol.

(2a)   *yellow*, segmented:

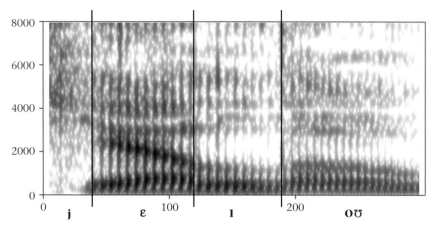

(2b)   *trock*, segmented[3]:

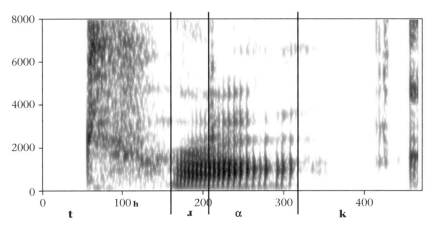

Segments are thus at least a method of abstracting away from continuous phonetics to more discrete phonology. Phonologists (and others) have also found some compelling evidence that grammars and speakers manipulate their phonologies at the level of the segment, so it is not just a convenient notation. These arguments will be developed as we go. Note also that the fact of *trock* not being an English word has caused us no difficulty in segmentation and transcription – and that is precisely the point, that is that phonology is about the legality of speech sound interactions in a language, not just the particular words that happen to occur in your mental dictionary (which we will usually refer to as the mental *lexicon*). This issue will also be raised many times in the pages that follow.

Exercise 1: Identify all the letters in the English words of (1) which correspond to multiple IPA symbols, and vice versa.

A phonological grammar is a mechanism for regulating phonological segments, their parts and their combinations. The first kind of phonological knowledge we will ascribe to our grammar is *phonotactics*, by which we will mean the regulations that describe how segments can or can't be strung together. It is the phonotactics of English that tell you that *trock* could be a word, as in our previous example, but for example **tlock* could not – English word-initial phonotactics rule out the sequence #[tl].[4] You also know, via English phonotactics, that *trock*'s second segment is a voiceless [ɹ] and that the similar second segment in *plastic* is a voiceless [l], while *borrow* and *yellow*

---

[3] The second symbol 'h' indicates that the segment [t] was *aspirated*. If you have forgotten what this term means, read on . . .

[4] # is a word boundary sign.

have a voiced [ɹ] and [ɬ] respectively. Note, however, that this knowledge is usually completely unconscious – you almost certainly knew nothing overt about voiced and voiceless versions of 'r' and 'l' until you encountered them in a linguistics class, but you were already devoicing 'r' and 'l' whenever appropriate for your dialect without knowing you were doing it.

How does a phonological grammar capture this knowledge? There are many theories, which actually turn out to have rather different consequences. For example, an English grammar could contain a *rule* that maps word-initial /tl/ onto something else (see 3) – this would mean picking a way of fixing #tl so it conforms to English, for example:

(3a) /t/ → [k] / # __ l   (Turn /t/ into [k] when word-initial and followed by l)

(3b) /0/ → [ə] / # t __ l   (Epenthesize a schwa between word initial t and l)

Alternatively, the grammar could have a *constraint* that says 'No Word-initial [tl]', which would mean relying on other bits of the grammar to decide what to do about an input /#tl/ should it appear. In this textbook, our first crucial choice will be to use constraints to capture phonological patterns like this, so we will spend some time justifying that choice in later chapters.

One other big job for the phonological grammar is to regulate sound sequences via *alternations* when they are concatenated by multiple *morphemes*, that is the meaningful building blocks of words and phrases. An English example of alternation which you have probably seen before comes from our plural morpheme, which has multiple phonological forms. Returning to the nonsense noun *trock*: whatever a trock is, if you have more than one trock, you have two … [tɹɑks] (*trocks*).[5] And if you found another one that needed storage, you would probably want to get more … [bɪnz] (*bins*). Both words end with a morpheme meaning 'plural', but the phonology of English dictates two different surface *allomorphs* [-z] and [-s] in these two phonological environments. In the grammars that we will build in this textbook, the same kinds of constraints that tell you why *tlock couldn't be an English word also tell you that *trock*'s plural is *trock*[s] and not *trock*[z].

1.2   Phonology at and below the Segmental Level

While *segments* are a very useful phonological unit for analysis and study, phonologies also organize their segments according to many different subsegmental properties. To see which of these properties are important for phonological purposes, let us consider one basic way that they are used: defining a language's phonological *categories*.

---

[5] This game of fill in the blank is in fact a common experimental device; see Chapter 8.

One classic example of a property used to categorize phonological segments is *voice onset time* (VOT). In the simple case of a stop followed by a vowel, VOT indicates the number of milliseconds between the burst of air caused by releasing the stop and the beginning of vocal fold vibrations for the vowel. If voicing begins exactly when the stop is released, VOT is zero. If it is negative, voicing had already begun during the stop's closure; if it is positive, then the stop was followed by a period of voiceless *aspiration* before vowel voicing began.

Here are two spectrograms of two English words within that previous phrase, with an arrow indicating the period of aspiration in each case (very little in the first, a fair bit in the second):

(4a)   *bin*

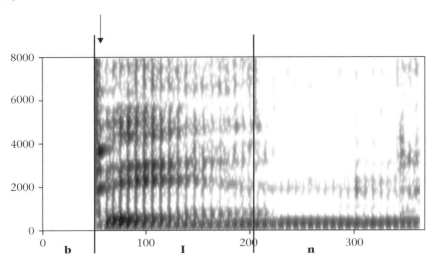

(4b)   *pin*

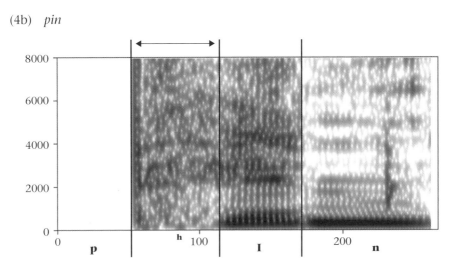

For these particular two tokens, the VOT for the initial segment in (4a) was measured at around five milliseconds, while the VOT for the initial segment of (4b) is 50 milliseconds. Whatever the precise difference, the phonological question is whether English speakers treat these two segments as same or different. In this case, the difference in their VOT causes you to perceive two different words: (4a) is *bin* and (b) is *pin*, so these two labial stops belong to two different phonological categories. (We refer to any such useful pair of words like *pin~bin* that highlight the contrast between two categories in a language as a *minimal pair*.)

In comparison, many English dialects distinguish two different *lateral* ('l'-like) segments: the alveolar, non-velarized [l] of *plastic* and the velarized [ɫ] of *hold*. Unlike the difference in VOT of 5 vs 50 milliseconds, though, the segments in *plastic* and *hold* belong to a single English category; there are no minimal pairs like *hold* vs **ho[l]d* or *plastic* vs **p[ɫ]astic*, and English speakers cannot change the meaning of a word by replacing one lateral with the other. Instead, the English distribution of alveolar vs velarized laterals is *predictable*. Comparing just these two words, you might come up with a prediction as to the *contexts* in which lateral can be used: for example, before a [d] laterals are velarized (as in *hold*), but after word-initial [p] (as in *plastic*) they are not. Of course, this analysis is only built from two data points, and it is so specific that you should suspect it is missing some broader generalizations (keep reading!).

The traditional terminology is that /p/ and /b/ are different English *phonemes*, whereas alveolar [l] and velarized [ɫ] are both *allophones* of a single English phoneme /l/. What is crucial in this textbook is the notion of predictability: part of the phonological grammar's job is to predict which of the allophones from a single category can occur in any specific phonological context. It is also crucial to note that phonemic or allophonic status is language-specific: the question of whether two different segments are part of two different categories (i.e. different phonemes) or a single category (i.e. both allophones of a single phoneme) is answered differently from language to language. As one quick example: nasalizing a vowel in English doesn't change the vowel's category – so that the vowels in *lap* [læp] and *lamb* [læ̃m] are allophones of the same phoneme /æ/ – whereas in French nasalized and oral versions of the same vowels are often different phonemes, as shown in minimal pairs like *beau* [bo] 'beautiful' and *bon* [bõ] 'good'.

The descriptions given so far of a segment's properties have been fairly grounded in articulatory terms: voice onset time, vowel nasalization and velarization[6] are all measurable phonetic aspects of a sound. In a

---

[6] Which means some raising of the tongue body or *dorsum*: not very detectable on a spectrogram although possibly discernable as movement or 'pinching' of F3 relative to F2, and definitely detectible if you happen to have an ultrasound recording.

phonological grammar, however, these articulatory properties do not all have the same status, and it is therefore useful to describe segments and their properties using a formal language of *phonological features*. Many of these features should not be news to you, but many of them also have definitions that span multiple categories in the IPA chart, so some discussion is necessary.

In the case of the phonetic property of voice onset time, there are a couple of different phonological features that we might need for describing cross-linguistic categories. One feature is *aspiration*, which distinguishes between the long positive VOT at the beginning of 'pin' and the short or nearly-zero VOT at the beginning of 'bin', meaning that their true IPA transcriptions might be [pʰɪn] and [b̥ɪn] or [pɪn] respectively. In some environments, aspiration is a predictable feature – meaning that for example in the context [s__ɪn] (as in *spin*), the English grammar will judge [p] or [b̥] as grammatical but [pʰ] as ungrammatical. The other most common phonological feature that involves VOT is *voicing*, which in languages like Spanish and Dutch will distinguish either of these 'voiceless' English stops from a truly prevoiced [b], where voicing begins during the closure, resulting in a negative VOT.

A long phonological tradition has argued that features give us insight into how languages arrange their phonemes, allophones, contexts and predictability.[7] Our quick discussion of *spin* (where aspiration of 'p' is banned) vs *pin* (where 'p' aspiration is obligatory) suggested that these aspirated and unaspirated allophones of English /p/ are in *complementary distribution*, only one appearing in each potential English phonological context. A more interesting point is that other pairs of English segments with similar distributions: *stick* vs *tick*; *scoff* vs *cough*, where again the s_V context requires an unaspirated allophone [p, t, k] and the #_V contexts requires an aspirated one, [pʰ tʰ kʰ]. Why these three? Not only are {p,t,k} all voiceless stops, they are also the language's *only* voiceless stops – in other words, they form the English *natural class* of voiceless stops. So rather than listing the unrelated behaviours of three phonemes, the English phonology can make broader generalizations like 'voiceless stops are aspirated word-initially' (and so on, describing other environments).

Given the wealth and complexity of phonological processes, it is not surprising that several different sets of phonological features have been proposed. This textbook is not designed to provide much insight into choosing between their specifics, and our feature set will lack many necessary bits, but it will

---

[7] To see this history in its original unfoldings, see: Trubetzkoy (1939); Jakobson (1941); Jakobson, Fant and Halle (1952); Jakobson and Halle (1956); Chomsky and Halle (1968).

make use of a crucial, small set of feature types that most phonologists would recognize. Here we will present them by trying to introduce as little confusing detail as possible. Let's begin with features describing *place of articulation*:

(5)

Place features		
Major/Primary Place	Minor/Secondary Place	
labial	+/–labiodental	
coronal	+/–anterior	[+ant] = dental, alveolar [–ant] = postalveolar, retroflex
	note: palatal = [coronal AND dorsal]	
dorsal	+/–low	[–low] = velar [+low] = uvular
pharyngeal		
glottal		

Note that the major place features are *monovalent* in this table, meaning they are simply attributes that a segment does or does not have – you can be labial or not, those are the only two options. Those minor places features within a major place class, however, are treated as *bivalent*, so that for example all [coronal] segments can in principle be specified as either [+/–anterior].

Turning to *manner* features: these are sometimes the hardest for students to get a handle on, so the table in (6) adapts a way of laying them out from Hayes (2009):

(6)

Manner features						
stops	*affricates*	*fricatives*	*nasals*	*liquids*	*glides*	*vowels*
[-sonorant]			[+sonorant]			
[-delayed release]	[+delayed release]					
	[+/-strident]					
[-continuant]			[+continuant]			
			[-approximant]	[+approx.]		
				[-vocalic]	[+vocalic]	
					[-syllabic]	[+syllabic]

The first big distinction in manner is [+/–sonorant], distinguishing the *obstruents* from the *sonorants*; we will have much more to say about this property of *sonority* in later chapters. Notice that most other manner features are only defined for a subset of the manners discussed here; note too that the status of nasals as [+continuant] is a rather non-standard assumption here (you will eventually see why in Chapter 5). There are also a few missing features here: two that we will need are [+/–lateral], [+/–tap] (or flap) and [+/–trill]. Finally, we will also use the feature [+/–nasal] which can be used to describe any consonant or vowel.

The *laryngeal* features we will use include [+/– voice], [+/–aspirated] and [+/–constricted glottis], the last of which describes sounds such as *ejectives*, 'tense' consonants (see Chapter 5), and *creaky* vowels.

Beyond the manner information above, we will have fairly little to say about *vowel* features, simply because this text is quite vague about the acquisition of vowels. However, we will use the terms [+/–high], [+/–low], [+–back] and [+/round] to describe them, in accordance with their location in the vowel space (see again the IPA vowel chart on page **28**). Note also that in Chapter 6.2 we will spend some time discussing how the place features of consonants and vowels line up. In addition, we will need to be able to refer to two *prosodic* qualities of segments as features: [+/–long], which distinguishes phonemically long vowels and geminate consonants, as well as [+/–stress] (which is not that common a feature, and very possibly for good reason, but is used in e.g. Hayes, 2009). These will appear when necessary.

To re-iterate: this text is not especially committed to the details of any particular featural description, but there are times when we will have evidence from child phonology to prefer one version to another. If this is your first time using phonological features to understand speech patterns, you will want more background, for which see the chapter's further readings. If you are not sure whether you need more or not, make sure to use the exercises here and at the end of the chapter to evaluate.

Exercise 2: Using the features just introduced, how could you describe the English ban on #tl ? That is, what features are not allowed in that word-initial sequence?

Exercise 3: Now look at this larger set of data, listing possible and impossible word-initial segments in the author's dialect. Can you give a more general featural account of what features cannot co-occur word-initially?[8] It's not a completely simple pattern, but you can get started …

---

[8] Some speakers may also judge *dwin* or *gwin* as bad enough to be impossible, and may judge *bwin* as good enough to be possible. We do have rather few #dw words in English – e.g. *dwarf, dwell* and the name *Duane*; #gw is really only found in names like *Gwenneth* so its status may be truly marginal. While we have no native words with #bw, some speakers may be too familiar with Spanish words like *bueno* to keep the English judgments crisp.

(7)

prick	brick	trick	drip	crick	grit
plot	blot	*tlick	*dlip	click	glock
*bwick	*pwit	twin	dwindle	quick	Gwin

This question is designed to show you two things: first, that featural description makes more sense out of a list of facts like (7) than was previously possible, and second, that features are often not well-suited to explaining *all* the details of a phonological phenomenon, such as the intricacies of place dissimilation among word-initial consonant sequences. Both of these claims will be reinforced throughout our study of child phonology, and we will build a grammar that uses features to describe patterns, but uses other mechanisms to describe the relative importance of each pattern and their individual (principled) exceptions.

Exercise 4: Below are examples of alveolar and velarized English laterals, in just four environments. What's the distribution of the two laterals?

(8)

alveolar[l]		velar [ɫ]	
light	police	wilting	shrill
lavender	delirium	alpine	cudgel
lopsided	igloo	wholesome	elemental
lasagne	resolution	palm	impossible
lewd	clubs	bulbs	school

First *describe the phonological environment* of each column – that is, find a phonological context that includes all the members of each column, without including any members of any other column. Secondly, *describe the context for each lateral allophone*, and then see if you can describe the two allophone's contexts each with a single description. If not, how close can you get?

1.3   Phonology above the Segmental Level

This section moves on to larger groupings of speech sounds above the segment, called *prosodic* units, which the phonological grammar can constrain and organize. This textbook will be primarily interested in the acquisition of three prosodic units: *syllables*, *feet* and words.

1.3.1   Syllables

To begin with the smallest of these units: what's a syllable? One place to begin is the notion of words containing multiple 'beats'. Just as we perceive a beat to music, we can also ask how many beats a word has (though people's intuitions on this matter differ in their strength and reliability.)

Consider these sets of English words: how many beats would you say each one has? And can you identify any linguistic element that you are tracking with these beats?

(9)	a)	*banana*	*canasta*	*Canada*	*activate*
	b)	*America*	*Northumbria*	*Indonesia*	*avocado*
	c)	*proliferation*	*organization*	*inescapable*	*inescapably*
	d)	*diversification*	*discombobulation*	*onomatopoeia*	*originality*
	e)	*ease*	*rough*	*grease*	*squeeze*
		foe	*foal*	*fold*	*folds*
	f)	*baby*	*shady*	*elbow*	*singlet*
		obey	*chalet*	*portray*	*barrette*

Your intuitions about how many *beats* are in these words also track how many *syllables* there are – and in all of these cases, the common predictor of the number of beats is the number of *vowel segments* there are. The examples in (3) in particular suggest that the number of consonants is fully irrelevant[9]: for example the set *foe ~ foal ~ fold ~ folds* ends with between zero and three consonants, yet we perceive all four words as taking the same amount of 'time', in having just only 'beat'.

Thus, we have the foundation of a syllable, indicated with the Greek letter sigma σ: a perceived grouping of speech sounds, organized as a single timing unit around (most often) a vowel, called the syllable's *nucleus*. Beyond their obligatory nuclei, syllables often have consonants on either side of them: segments before the nucleus are part of the *onset* and those after the nucleus are the *coda*. This structure is illustrated by means of a tree diagram like the ones in (10), but whenever we can (which will be most of the time)

---

[9] Although this isn't always true – keep reading on to the data in (11).

the text will boil down this structure simply by using periods to indicate syllable breaks, e.g. [ɛɫ.boʊ].

(10)

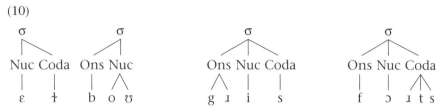

Many aspects of syllable structure are relevant to the early stages of phonological acquisition, especially in languages like English, so we will now review some. One complication is that it's not always vowels that give a word its beats and so gives the syllables their nuclei. In your estimation, how many syllables are in the following words?

(11)   *bought   bottom   bottle   bottler*
       mitt   mitten   middle

In the case of words like *bottom* and *mitten*, which segments make up the second syllable? In their transcription, no vowel seems to be in evidence – instead, the nucleus of these syllables seems to be the *nasal* consonants [m] and [n]. Similarly, *bottle* and *middle* both end with a syllable whose nucleus is the velarized lateral, whether [bɑɾɫ] or [ba?ɫ] or similar. And what about words like *her* or *earl* or *world*? For speakers of *rhotic* dialects, these monosyllabic words appear to contain *no* vowels, their single nucleus is [ɹ]. While nasal and lateral consonants are fairly reluctant nuclei – showing up in limited contexts, very often word-finally – [ɹ] is nucleus enough to sit in the middle of a syllable, surrounded by typical onsets and also codas.

(12)

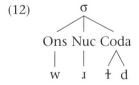

Quiz time: can you find a natural class that describes all and only the English consonants that can act as nuclei? Look back at the manner features in table (6), and you should be able to find one ... they are the *sonorants*.[10] Cross-linguistically, we find that phonologies differ in their requirements for syllable nuclei – but in every language, vowels are the *most* likely nuclei and always the most preferred.

---

[10] What about glides? It is probably right to assume that if a glide is put in nuclear position, it simply becomes a vowel.

Like its nuclei, English also imposes many restrictions on onsets and codas that relate to *sonority,* a concept which we will now examine in greater detail. Beyond the obstruent/sonorant divide, sonority is a rather more fine-grained scale, which orders the manners roughly top-to-bottom on the IPA chart:

(13)   *A sonority scale*[11]

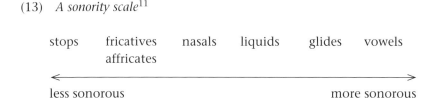

stops	fricatives	nasals	liquids	glides	vowels
	affricates				

←————————————————————————————→

less sonorous   more sonorous

Now what is the use of this sonority scale for English syllables? Let us consider which manners of consonants can occur in onset *clusters,* meaning the adjacent consonants within an onset, like the [gɹ] of *grease.* This [gɹ] is part of the very common sequence of stop + liquid, as we saw in all those examples in (7).

If you try to come up with other English onset cluster types, in terms of their natural classes, you will notice that nearly all such clusters *rise in sonority* – that is, the first member is less sonorous than the second. Recall that the nucleus is restricted to a set of *sonorous* segments – and prefers to contain a vowel, the most sonorous manner there is! Overall, then, can we say that syllables represent the peaks and troughs of sonority throughout a word?

Often, but not always. In English, although most onset clusters rise in sonority, there is a special cluster type that violates this profile. You may be able to think of it off the top of your head – in fact, there was an example of one such cluster in the previous sentence. Consider:

(14)   *special   student   school*
    spray   strife   squeeze

These cases show a <u>drop</u> in sonority between the first and second consonants: [s] is a fricative, already not very sonorant, but [p, t, k] as voiceless stops are even less so. This exception to the sonority rise generalization should perhaps give us pause – how good a generalization is it, really? Notably, it is only this one fricative [s] that can occur before stops in onset clusters – but more compellingly, it turns out that <u>many</u> languages allow [s]+stop onsets but otherwise obey the sonority rise restrictions (in other languages like German it is the very similar [ʃ]+stop that is given special sonority privileges).

---

[11] More detail may sometimes be necessary to include in this scale: for instance, voiceless obstruents are less sonorous than their voiced counterparts; high vowels are less sonorous than low ones.

Much phonological ink has been spilled trying to understand the correct characterization of the [s]-exception to onset sonority profiles; for now we simply note that s-initial onsets are special.

The last note about syllabification concerns cross-linguistic variation. Phonologies around the world differ greatly in terms of syllable *shape* – to use two famous examples, Hawaiian has no onset clusters or codas at all, while Polish can build words which begin with such cluster surprises as [fʂtʂɲɛʂ] and [mgwa].[12] Many languages show slight variations on the English theme – Spanish for example shares many onset clusters with English, but it does prohibit [s]+stop onsets (see the next exercise). But regardless of differences in syllable inventories, one universal appears to be that languages never use syllabification *contrastively*. In other words: given as string of segments, two grammars might syllabify them differently, or rule them out entirely because they are unsyllabifiable, but no grammar will allow two different syllabifications <u>which mean different things.</u>

All other things being equal, that is. As for when things are not equal: see next section.

Exercise 5: The fact that Spanish does not allow [s]+stop onsets is reflected in several English/Spanish cognates: for example, *Spain* vs *España* [ɛspaɲa] and *school* vs *escuela* [ɛskwela]. Given this fact, figure out how these Spanish words must be syllabified – that is, where their first syllable ends and their second syllable begins.

Exercise 6: Do you remember the constraint against word initial [tl] clusters, or its more general version, as revealed from looking at (7)? With that in mind, now look at some other English words, as pronounced in the author's dialect:

(A)   *mattress*   *mantra*   *atlas*   *antler*
     [mætɹɪs]   [mæ̃ntɹɑ]   [æʔlɪs]   [æ̃nʔlɚ]

How do you think they are syllabified? That is, where do their syllable breaks fall? How does your knowledge of the constraint against #[tl] figure into this reasoning? Can it be tweaked to help explain the distribution of t vs glottal stop in these words?

Exercise 7: How many syllables do you think there are in *opener* and *lightener?* How many in *world* and *squirrel?* English speakers tend to disagree on such items, and it's probably the case you can produce them all with two

---

[12] meaning 'you (sg.) will initiate', and 'fog, mist' respectively.

different numbers of syllables. Try transcribing the two different versions, and try thinking about why there might be two syllabifications.

1.3.2   Stress and Feet

Having just learnt that syllabification is not contrastive look at the pairs of words below, which have nearly the same segments in them, and therefore the same English syllabification:

> (15)   *record* (ancient object for playing music)   *record* (to encode information)
>   *address* (a precise location)   *address* (to direct speech at someone)
>   *convict* (a person found guilty)   *convict* (to find someone guilty)

How do these words differ? Their segmental transcriptions are slightly different, but speakers also have an intuition that there is a more fundamental difference between the two columns of words. The difference might be described as one of 'emphasis', or in the terms of the previous section, as which of the beats is the strongest. The phonological term for this word-internal emphasis or strongest beat is *stress*.

Even though native speakers perceive word stress quite easily and unconsciously, the raw acoustic reflex of a word's stress – that is, the measurable properties that distinguish *REcord* the noun and *reCORD* the verb – are rather complicated. To be very brief: stress is a property of a syllable (at least of its nucleus), and when compared phonetically to their unstressed counterparts, stressed syllables are typically longer, higher in pitch, and higher in amplitude (louder), though the relative importance and reliability of these phonetic cues are different between languages.

Stress is a fundamental part of organizing speech sounds, in many if not most phonological grammars, but its role in defining the meaning of words is very variable. In some languages the position of stress in a word is just as unpredictable as a phoneme: that is, all words are in some sense like *record*, where speakers must memorize which syllable gets stressed. In such languages, like Russian, stress can create minimal pairs: for example ['muki] '*torments (nom. pl.)*' vs [mu'ki] '*flour (gen. sg.)*'. Notice that stress is best transcribed with a superscript straight apostrophe, placed <u>before</u> the stressed syllable.[13]

---

[13] This IPA transcription for stress is safer than placing an accent on the stress vowel itself, as in recórd, because that accent is the IPA symbol for high tone and confusion can ensue.

On the other hand, many languages have much more predictable stress patterns – here stressed and unstressed syllables are like allophones, and the phonological grammar determines which one is chosen in each location of the word. Predicting the placement of stress involves many moving parts, but it will be crucial to the child data we will look at. (Notably, English falls somewhere in the middle of this stress continuum – with no purely contrastive stress or minimal pairs, but far from a purely predictable stress pattern either – making its acquisition all the more complicated.)

So what are the properties involved in predicting stress? First, stress is almost always an 'edge-oriented' phenomenon. In some languages this is very obvious: look at these representative words from Persian (an Indo-Aryan language spoken in Iran) and Hungarian (Ugro-Finnic) and describe their stress pattern:

(16)

Persian stress (data adapted from Windfuhr, 1997)			
dæst	*hand*	of'tad	*fell*
dæs'tɛ	*handle, bunch*	ofta'dɛ	*fallen*
mærda'nɛ	*manly, men's*	kɛ'tab	*book*
sæb'zi	*greenness, vegetables*	kɛtab'ha	*books*
di'gær	*other (adj.)*	ruzna'mɛ	*newspaper*
digæ'ran	*others*	haftɛ'gi	*weekly*

(17)

Hungarian stress[14]			
['ʃaːrgɒ]	*yellow*	['tɛlihold]	*full moon*
['ɛrdøː]	*forest*	['tyːzoltoːʃaːg]	*fire department*
['tørveːɲeʃ]	*legal*	['pɒrɒditʃom]	*tomato*
['pɒlotɒ]	*castle*	['eːksiːnkeːk]	*sky blue*
['ʃyːrgøːʃ]	*urgent*	['øsːɛkøtːɛteːʃ]	*connection*

Describing the location of surface stress in these languages is easy: every initial syllable is stressed in Hungarian, while every word-final syllable is stressed

---

[14] Data from M. Molnar, p.c.

in Persian.[15] But this is a much broader pattern: generally, word edges are the most likely place for stress to occur. As we will see in Chapter 2, the edge-oriented property of stress also turns out to be very crucial to how infants learn to parse out new words from fluent speech. As we have already seen, though, English stress is not so well behaved as Persian or Hungarian: the noun *record* looks like it follows the Hungarian pattern, and the verb *record* seems to follow the Persian pattern.

There are also many languages with more than one stress per word (called *iterative* stress); English is definitely such a language, and in longer words we can begin to see more predictable patterns to our stress-assigning phonology. Here are two fairly long words: *Mississippi* and *onomatopoeia*. Determine how many syllables each one has, and which ones get stressed. If you are not convinced you're doing it right, imagine the word was your pet's name, and you were trying to call him or her back to you from very far away. What syllable would you sing out the longest? That one is definitely stressed. So, for example: 'MississIIIIIIIIIIIIIIIIIIIIIIIIIIIIIIIIIIIIIIpi!'

Here are the full words with their stressed syllables marked in IPA. (For the moment we are using the primary stress mark on every stressed syllable 'σ, but we will refine this soon.)

(18) ['mɪ.sɪ.'sɪ.pi] ['ɑ.nə.'mæ.tɪ.'pi.jə]

Think about some other English words with the stress pattern as Mississippi: *Alabama, Aberystwyth, coronation, elemental, institution, influential, margarita, perturbation, sentimental*; something similar is found in *alligator, helicopter, elevator, Halliburton* and *Tonypandy*. Words with six syllables are rather less common – and those that follow the pattern of *onomatapoeia* are place names, such as *Apalachicola*.

This stress pattern could be worded many different ways, but one description is that every *odd* syllable is stressed: that is the first, third, fifth syllable and so on. It turns out that this *alternating* stress pattern is derived from the interaction of more basic constraints – and those constraints are crucial to how children build up early words with many syllables, so let us delve into them a little closer.

To see how English iterative stress might be constructed, we turn to two languages that you have probably never heard of. First look at the stress

[15] In fact, the placement of Persian stress is a little more complicated because 'phrasal' stress, for example in the vocative, can overrule stress in the first word of a phrase, and certain functional morphemes are stressless; see discussion in Windfuhr (1997). For recent discussion and argumentation about Hungarian stress, see Blaho and Szeredi (2011).

pattern of Garawa (a language native to northeastern Australia) – what generalizations can you make?

(19)	Garawa (data from Furby, 1974)	
	['ja.mi]	*eye*
	['wat.jim'pa.u]	*armpit*
	['ja.ka'la.ka'lam.pa]	*loose*
	['am.pa'la.in'mu.kun'ji.na]	*at our many*

These words contain two, four, six and eight syllables, and each word bears stress on the first, third, fifth, seventh syllables ... and so on. Now examine stress in a completely unrelated language, Tiriyó (a Cariban language spoken in Brazil and Surinam):

(20)	Tiriyó (data from Meira, 1998)			
	pa'waːna	*friend*	[ə'kəːrə'puːkə]	*species of otter*
	pa'koːro	*house*	[i'kaːpu'ruːtu]	*cloud*
	i'jaːra'maːta	*his/her chin*	[a'poːto'maːta'təːkə]	*you all help!*
	[a'maːta'kaːna]	*species of toucan*		

Here we see words with three, five and seven syllables, with stresses on the second, fourth and sixth syllables![16]

Although they differ from English dramatically in other ways, Garawa and Tiriyó phonology show a commonality in their stress patterns: syllables generally alternate strong, then weak, then strong and so on. In other words, all three languages' phonologies use *rhythmic* stress – and this turns out to be a very common pattern.

So why is iterative stress rhythmic? The guiding idea we will use here is that syllables are grouped into a prosodic unit made up of two syllables, called a *foot*, and that it is actually these *feet* that receive stress. Each foot is rhythmically asymmetric: if it is weak-strong it is an *iamb*; if it is strong-weak it is a *trochee*.[17] With these assumptions, Garawa builds trochees, and Tiriyó builds iambs.

---

[16] For what happens in Garawa words of odd-numbered syllables, or Tiriyó words of even-numbered syllables, see Hayes (1995) and many references therein.

[17] You may remember these terms from a poetics class – for example, the term *iambic pentameter* describes the rhythm of Shakespeare's poetry, with five iambs (i.e. weak-strong feet) per line.

When we represent phonological string with foot structure, we use parentheses to group syllables together regardless.

(21)   [('mɪ.sɪ).('sɪ.pi)]   [('ɑ.nə).('mæ.tɪ).('pi.jə)]

We can now finally say something more predictable about English – that it must build *trochees*. If the grammar were building iambs, they would be stressed like [(mɪ.'sɪ)(sɪ.'pi),] which most English speakers find hard even to pronounce reliably.

Now let's go back to a different type of predictable but *non-iterative* stress pattern: Dakota (a Siouan language spoken in the Midwestern US and Canada), and Polish. Where does the *main* or *primary* stress fall in these two languages? (As before, main stress is marked with the superscript [']; we now include *secondary* stress with a subscript [ˌ] before the target syllable.)

(22)	Dakota (data from Shaw, 1985; Kyle, 1994)			
	wak'sa	*he cut it (absolute)*	wa'mijetʃiksa	*you cut it for me*
	wa'kiksa	*he cut his own*	wa'witʃʰajetʃiksa	*you cut it for them*
	wa'kitʃiksa	*he cut it for him*	wa'wawitʃʰajetʃiksa	*you cut something for them*
	wa'jetʃiksa	*you cut it for him*		

(23)	Polish: (data from Newlin-Łukowicz, 2012: 273, 275 see also Rubach and Booij, 1985)[18]			
	'dvujka	*two*	rɛ'pɔrtɛr	*reporter (nominative)*
	'dvutakt	*two-stroke (engine)*	ˌrɛpɔr'tɛra	*reporter (genitive)*
	lis'tɔvnɨ	*letter (adjectival)*	ˌrɛpɔrtɛ'rɔvi	*reporter (dative)*
	lis'tɔnɔʃ	*mailman*	ˌzaraˌpɔrtɔ'vanɨ	*report (past part. nom.)*
	ɔ'ɕɛmsɛt	*eight hundred*	ˌzaraˌpɔrtɔva'nɛmu	*report (past, dative)*

---

[18] Exceptions to this stress pattern appear in a small set of borrowings, and words with a conditional suffix; see Newlin-Łukowicz (2012).

These two languages, like many pairs we have seen, appear as mirror images of each other: Dakota is consistently stressed on its second syllable, and Polish's main stress falls on its second last (or *penultimate*) syllable.

Our reason to focus on these two patterns is their edge-orientations: across languages, predictable non-iterative stress is nearly always on the syllable at the edge of a word, or one syllable in from the edge. Can you explain that pattern more insightfully by making reference to feet? Try to do so in your own words before reading on.

* * *

To summarize thus far: we have seen three dimensions of difference between stress patterns. The first is which edge of the word feet (and therefore stressed syllables) are built. A second difference is between iterative and non-iterative systems, which we might think of as whether or not the grammar continues stacking up more feet after the first one. A third difference is what kind of foot the grammar builds: building a trochee at the right edge or an iamb at the left edge will result in stress on the second or second-last syllable, as in Dakota or Polish.[19]

We will need to understand one other crucial dimension along which stress system differ: the fact that not all feet contain two syllables. Below are some words from Hopi (a Northern Uto-Aztecan language of Arizona), whose main stress pattern involves a foot built at the left edge of the word. But the precise location of stress varies: sometimes the first syllable is stressed, and sometimes the second. Figure out the pattern that predicts which of the first two syllables are stressed before reading on.

(24)		Hopi stress (Whorf, 1946; Hayes, 1981: 77–79)[20]				
	a)	'tuː.van.gu	*usually throws*	b)	i.'ta.mu.mi	*towards us*
		'iː.sa.wuj	*coyote*		hi.'mut.ski	*shrub (nom.)*

Continued

---

[19] A crucial note: we also find languages that frequently stress the third-last syllables, and occasionally the third-last alone. One common understanding of this pattern is that it combines the desire to stress the second last syllable of the 'available' syllables, so to speak, combined with a pressure to not stress the last syllable – this is in fact the case with four syllable words in Tiriyó as in (20). For more on this, see especially Hayes (1995).

[20] This data has been simplified with regards to what happens when the word has only two syllables; see Hayes (1995: 261).

'at.kja.miq	*all the way to the bottom*		i.'ta.muj	*we/us*
'paː.hut	*spring water*		ka'wajo	*horse*
'as.kwa.li	*thank you*		nu'vakwahu	*eagle*

The deciding factor is the shape of the word's first syllable. When the word begins with CV or V, stress falls on the second syllable (24a), just as in every word of Dakota in (22). This makes it look like the language is building an iamb at the left edge of the word. But when the word begins with CV: or CVC (24a), stress falls on the first syllable. It therefore appears that the longer syllables CV: or CVC are making up a foot *all on their own*. In languages like Hopi (and many others), syllables are divided into two types, called *heavy* and *light*, with reference to how much segmental material is included in their nucleus and coda (because they pattern together in this and other ways, the nucleus and coda of a syllable are referred to together as the *rime*.) To build a foot in *weight-sensitive* or *quantity-sensitive* languages, you don't need two whole syllables necessarily, just two units of weight. Since Hopi builds iambs, words whose first syllable is *light* (24b) get their stress on the second syllable of a two-syllable foot, (V.'CV) or (CV.'CV). But when the first syllable is heavy (24a), it acts as a foot all on its own and so bears stress: ('CVC) or ('CVV).[21]

To finish with edge-oriented stress: compare the stress pattern of *helicopter* and *coronary*. If you underlined their stressed syllables as you did for *Mississippi*, you would still find that all three have two trochees, and yet we feel that their stress is different. Why? *Primary* vs *secondary* stress. To wit:

(25)   [(ˌmɪ.sɪ)('sɪ.pi)]   vs   [('hɛ.lɪ)(ˌkɑp.tɚ)]
        [(ˌɑ.nə)(ˌmæ.tɪ)('pi.jə)]   [('kʰɔ.ɹɪ)(ˌnɛ.ɹi)]

Again, English seems fairly permissive as to the location of main stress. But many languages are more picky: the Garawa words from (19) are now transcribed with both levels of stress:

(26) | Garawa, again (data from Furby, 1974) | |
| ['ja.mi] | *eye* |
| ['wat.jim̩.pa.u] | *armpit* |

Continued

---

[21] You can't hear that CV: or CVC is stressed on the first or second or anything, because stress is heard across the syllable – we know that the language is iambic only because of how it stresses the CVCV feet. For other properties of trochees vs iambs and quantity-sensitive systems, see Hayes (1995) and many references therein.

['ja.ka.la.ka.lam.pa]	*loose*
['am.pa.la.in.mu.kun.ji.na]	*at our many*

Now we can see that the main stress always resides on one of the edgemost feet: Garawa's first foot is the main one. This is again a cross-linguistic pattern: for example, the *second* foot is never consistently chosen for main stress.

A final aspect of word-level prosodic patterning that we will consider is a language's smallest possible phonological word, also known as the *Minimal Word*. In some languages a word or a class of words must be at least two syllables long; nothing monosyllabic is grammatical (such is the case for example for verbs in Mohawk, as described in Michelson, 1988). In English, we can get away with one syllable, but not just any one – here are some minimally-small grammatical words, compared to some ungrammatical ones:

(27)	Some small grammatical and ungrammatical English words								
bee	[bi]	*bay*	[bej]	*bit*	[bɪt]	*bet*	[bɛt]		*[bɪ]
boo	[bu]	*bow*	[boʊ]	*but*	[bʌt]	*put*	[pʊt]		*[bʌ]
				bin	[bɪn]	*Ben*	[bɛn]		*[bɛ]
				bun	[bʌn]	*book*	[bʊk]		*[bʊ]

The generalization is that to be a one syllable English word, you must have either a coda, or a *long* or *tense*[22] vowel in the nucleus. Why should this be? How do we represent this ban?

The key to seeing how the Minimal Word relates to this section is that most languages can only build up higher prosodic units from smaller units: to build a syllable, you need at least one segment (a nucleus); to build a foot, you need some syllables (on how many see below), and to build a word, you

---

[22] The featural system of vowels that we built at the beginning of this chapter did not include the feature [+/–tense], though it turns out to be a crucial one in English phonology, at least. There is clearly a phonetic length component to this abstract feature – the vowels that are considered [+tense] and which can hold up a minimal word on their own are all produced with much longer durations in English than their [tense] counterparts. In many English varieties the distinction is usually also one of quality, for example [i] vs [ɪ], but in for example Southern British English varieties the vowels in *ship* and *sheep* can be [i] and [iː] – see for example values in Boersma and Escudero (2001).

need a foot. In languages like Mohawk mentioned above, feet have to contain two syllables – this means that if every word must contain a foot, no word can be just monosyllabic. In English, however, you *can* get monosyllabic words – so it must be the case that English like Hopi is *quantity-sensitive*, and that a single syllable can make up a foot, so long as that syllable's *rime is heavy* (i.e. contains either a coda or a tense nucleus).

1.4   Two Conceptual Issues

Now that we have taken a whirlwind tour through some basic aspects of phonology, you know our starting place. If any terms or concepts in the previous section have been completely foreign to you, now is the time to take a break and do some additional reading before continuing (recommendations are made at the end of the chapter). One exception is the notion of using *constraints* to describe phonological pattern. If you are familiar with rules like /p/ → [p^h] / # __ V, but not with any notion of constraints to do the work of such rules, don't worry; Chapters 3–5 will get you up to speed. But before we move onto children, two bigger-picture issues need to be addressed.

1.4.1   Competence vs Performance

In a previous linguistic class or context, you have probably come across the distinction between linguistic *competence* or knowledge on the one hand, and linguistic *performance*, being all the behaviour reflecting that knowledge, on the other. This textbook treats competence and performance as distinct in the traditional Chomskyian sense, and this text is about learning phonological *competence*. The question is: since competence is something unconscious in our minds, how do we get at it and study it?

The first way is *introspection*, simply asking native speakers or learners for their linguistic intuitions. This on-demand introspection can answer some questions very simply and directly – 'could *bnick* be an English word?' – but is not maximally effective in many contexts. At the very least, requests for introspection or intuitions will not get us closer to answering the question 'does a four month old know that *bnick* could not be a English word?'

A second way might be called pure observation: simply recording everything a native speaker or learner says, in as carefully-observed a context as possible. From there we must make some inferences: perhaps that everything they say represents something(s) they know to be grammatical, and everything they do not say represents something(s) they know to be ungrammatical (or whose ungrammaticality they are not yet sure of). This might also be a very good way of answering some questions – for example, 'can you pronounce the cluster [bl] in word-initial position?' or 'do you understand that a question like "Are you hungry" requires an answer of something like *yes* or *no*?' – but again, observation is not going to suffice as a method of answering the question 'do you know that *bnick* could not be an English word?' And even seeing that you can pronounce 'cats' and 'dogs' with the right voiced and voiceless final fricative *alternation* does not shed any clear light on whether you or your grammar 'know' in any sense that *ca*[tz] could not be an English word.

To access competence – in all learners, but particularly infants and very young children – researchers must use some cunning techniques to determine what is known and what is accidental, and what the nature of that knowledge is. These issues motivate researchers to use a wide range of data collection and experimental methods, many of which we will discuss at the ends of chapters throughout the book. And whenever we examine learning data of any sort, we will always need to consider carefully its methods, and how competence vs performance are being tapped.

1.4.2   Perception and Production

Using a phonology is not just about producing the words and segments of your language – it's also about perceiving them when produced by other people. At some basic level this is very central to studying learning: to acquire your phonology, you listen to other people using theirs, and figure out what they are doing so that someday you can approximate it.

It's probably already intuitively clear to you that your native language experience affects not only how you produce speech but how you hear it. When hearing people speak a completely foreign language on the radio for instance, it is extremely hard to pick out the words within the stream of speech, and an entire conversation can seem like one big long undifferentiated sound mass. Contrast that with the ease of picking out word breaks in a nonsense poem like *Jabberwocky*[23] – even if you've never heard it before, you perceive subtle aspects of English spoken phonology that tell you where one word ends and another begins.

The fact is that your experience with your first language (or languages, and also experience with later ones to some extent), has a tremendous influence on your experience of speech – in a crucial sense you are also a native 'listener' of your mother tongue(s). Thus we have to keep in mind that learners are acquiring both, and as you are about to see, phonological acquisition is

---

[23] Being a poem by C.S. Lewis, which begins 'Twas brillig, and the slithy toves/ Did gyre and gimble in the wabe: All mimsy were the borogoves/ And the mome raths outgrabe'.

preceded by a lot of perceptual learning. The next chapter introduces you to a wild area of research, pioneered in the 1970s and 1980s and still finding astonishing results in recent years: the area of *infant speech perception*, studying what children can perceive, discriminate and expect about their language(s) long before they have functioning productive phonologies – between birth and up until their second birthday. After reading Chapter 2, you will never look at drooling babies the same way again.

1.5   Further Reading

The International Phonetic Alphabet

(In addition to the full chart on page **28** of this chapter)
   An interactive version of the IPA chart with sound files for each sound is available at: http://web.uvic.ca/ling/resources/ipa/charts/IPAlab/IPAlab.htm

Introductions to phonology, especially to segments and features

Hayes, Bruce. 2009. *Introductory Phonology*. Oxford: Blackwell.
Flynn, Darin. 2012. *Phonology: The Distinctive Features of Speech Sounds*. Ms., University of Calgary. Available at: http://www.ucalgary.ca/dflynn/files/dflynn/flynn12_distinctive_features.pdf
   – *this book is all about features, and while they will not always match the specific features adopted in this book, it provides a wealth of data.*

Other perspectives on and introductions to child phonology

Johnson, Wyn and Reimers, Paula. 2010. *Patterns in Child Phonology*. Edinburgh, Scotland: Edinburgh University Press.
Kiparsky, Paul and Menn, Lise. 1977. On the acquisition of phonology. In John Macnamara (ed.) *Language Learning and Thought*. New York: Academic Press. 47–78.
Rose, Yvan and Inkelas, Sharon. 2011. The Interpretation of Phonological Patterns in First Language Acquisition. In Colin J. Ewan, Elizabeth Hume, Marc van Oostendorp and Keren Rice (eds) *The Blackwell Companion to Phonology*. Malden, MA: Miley-Blackwell. 2414–2438.
Vihman, Marilyn M. 2014. *Phonological Development*. 2nd edition. Oxford: Basil Blackwell.

Exercises

   Q1: As discussed with respect to English vs French nasal vowels: pho-
       nemes are language-specific. *What consequences does that have for*

learning? What might a child be able in principle to learn about phonemes and allophones when they don't yet know any words?

Q2: Let's return once more to the English ban on [tl]. From the exercise at the end of 1.3, you may now realize that it's a ban on [tl] within *onsets,* and from the data in (7) you may have a way of defining a more general ban on stop+liquid sequences that share *place of articulation* (though that doesn't tell us why [tr] and[dr] are ok).

With all this in mind, here are some further questions to answer about this constraint:

> *(a) Should our representation of this constraint make reference to the fact that the [l], were it to appear after [t], would be voiceless? Does it make any difference?*
>
> *(b) English also doesn't have any [fw], [zl] or [ðl] clusters in onsets. Can you write a constraint to ban them as well? Can they be subsumed into a more general constraint that will also ban all the problematic clusters in (7)?*

Q3: Here are a few examples of the way Finnish has borrowed some English and French words into its phonology. (Data from Suomi, 2004: 94–95; Suomi, Toivanen and Yitalo, 2008: 71, and Tuuli Morrill, p.c.) Examine how they differ from the originals, and then read the question below:

Finnish borrowing	English gloss		Finnish borrowing	English gloss
[bɪt:ɪ]	*bit*		[mɑkɑsɪ:nɪ]	*store* (from French '*magasin*')
[hɪt:ɪ]	*hit*		[mɔ:t:ɔrɪ]	*motor*
[pɔp:ɪ]	*pop*		[kɛtsʊp:ɪ]	*ketchup*
[pɪn:ɪ]	*pin*		[sɔsɛt: ɑ]	*sauce*
[fɑnɪ]	*fan*			
[nɛt:ɪ]	*net*			

What accounts for the major difference between the first row of Finnish borrowings and their English source words? One possibility is that these words are too small to meet the Finnish *minimal word* requirement (as discussed in Section 1.3) *If that were so, what might be the size minimum for a Finnish word? And how does the second column support or challenge this explanation?*

THE INTERNATIONAL PHONETIC ALPHABET (revised to 2005)

CONSONANTS (PULMONIC)   © 2005 IPA

	Bilabial	Labiodental	Dental	Alveolar	Postalveolar	Retroflex	Palatal	Velar	Uvular	Pharyngeal	Glottal
Plosive	p b			t d		ʈ ɖ	c ɟ	k ɡ	q ɢ		ʔ
Nasal	m	ɱ		n		ɳ	ɲ	ŋ	N		
Trill	B			r					R		
Tap or Flap		ⱱ		ɾ		ɽ					
Fricative	ɸ β	f v	θ ð	s z	ʃ ʒ	ʂ ʐ	ç ʝ	x ɣ	χ ʁ	ħ ʕ	h ɦ
Lateral fricative				ɬ ɮ							
Approximant		ʋ		ɹ		ɻ	j	ɰ			
Lateral approximant				l		ɭ	ʎ	L			

Where symbols appear in pairs, the one to the right represents a voiced consonant. Shaded areas denote articulations judged impossible.

CONSONANTS (NON-PULMONIC)

Clicks		Voiced implosives		Ejectives	
ʘ	Bilabial	ɓ	Bilabial	ʼ	Examples:
ǀ	Dental	ɗ	Dental/alveolar	pʼ	Bilabial
ǃ	(Post)alveolar	ʄ	Palatal	tʼ	Dental/alveolar
ǂ	Palatoalveolar	ɠ	Velar	kʼ	Velar
ǁ	Alveolar lateral	ʛ	Uvular	sʼ	Alveolar fricative

OTHER SYMBOLS

ʍ	Voiceless labial-velar fricative	ɕ ʑ	Alveolo-palatal fricatives
w	Voiced labial-velar approximant	ɺ	Voiced alveolar lateral flap
ɥ	Voiced labial-palatal approximant	ɧ	Simultaneous ʃ and x
ʜ	Voiceless epiglottal fricative		
ʢ	Voiced epiglottal fricative	Affricates and double articulations can be represented by two symbols joined by a tie bar if necessary.	k͡p t͡s
ʡ	Epiglottal plosive		

DIACRITICS   Diacritics may be placed above a symbol with a descender, e.g. ŋ̊

̥	Voiceless	n̥ d̥	̤	Breathy voiced	b̤ a̤	̪	Dental	t̪ d̪
̬	Voiced	s̬ t̬	̰	Creaky voiced	b̰ a̰	̺	Apical	t̺ d̺
ʰ	Aspirated	tʰ dʰ	̼	Linguolabial	t̼ d̼	̻	Laminal	t̻ d̻
̹	More rounded	ɔ̹	ʷ	Labialized	tʷ dʷ	̃	Nasalized	ẽ
̜	Less rounded	ɔ̜	ʲ	Palatalized	tʲ dʲ	ⁿ	Nasal release	dⁿ
̟	Advanced	u̟	ˠ	Velarized	tˠ dˠ	ˡ	Lateral release	dˡ
̠	Retracted	e̠	ˤ	Pharyngealized	tˤ dˤ	̚	No audible release	d̚
̈	Centralized	ë	̴	Velarized or pharyngealized	ɫ			
̽	Mid-centralized	e̽	̝	Raised	e̝	(ɹ̝ = voiced alveolar fricative)		
̩	Syllabic	n̩	̞	Lowered	e̞	(β̞ = voiced bilabial approximant)		
̯	Non-syllabic	e̯	̘	Advanced Tongue Root	e̘			
˞	Rhoticity	ɚ a˞	̙	Retracted Tongue Root	e̙			

VOWELS

Where symbols appear in pairs, the one to the right represents a rounded vowel.

SUPRASEGMENTALS

ˈ	Primary stress	
ˌ	Secondary stress	ˌfoʊnəˈtɪʃən
ː	Long	eː
ˑ	Half-long	eˑ
̆	Extra-short	ĕ
ǀ	Minor (foot) group	
‖	Major (intonation) group	
.	Syllable break	ɹi.ækt
‿	Linking (absence of a break)	

TONES AND WORD ACCENTS

LEVEL			CONTOUR		
e̋ or ˥	Extra high		ě or ˩˥	Rising	
é or ˦	High		ê ˥˩	Falling	
ē or ˧	Mid		e᷄ ˦˥	High rising	
è or ˨	Low		e᷅ ˩˨	Low rising	
ȅ or ˩	Extra low		e᷈ ˧˦˧	Rising-falling	
↓	Downstep		↗	Global rise	
↑	Upstep		↘	Global fall	

2 Background II: Infant Speech Acquisition

2.1 Methodologies: Speech Experiments with Infants

How can we study what infants know about the sounds of their language before they can reliably produce any recognizable linguistic utterances? Researchers primarily in psychology have invented a variety of ingenious methods, and here we will discuss two basic ones.

At birth, what can a baby do to indicate their awareness of the world around them? One very helpful reflex in babies with normal neurological development is the impulse to suck: when something touches their palate, they will begin to suck – and when a baby is interested in something while sucking, they will suck faster or more intensely. Thus sucking provides a method of studying linguistic *discrimination*. For example: to test whether a baby can discriminate the sound sequence [ba] from [pa], we could give them a pacifier to suck on, play them many successive *trials* in which they hear [ba] over and over, and then switch the stimulus (i.e. start playing [pa] instead) and watch whether they show a behavioural response to the change, that is whether they start sucking faster.[1]

To measure this behaviour accurately, participating babies are given a pacifier containing a *pressure transducer*, which calculates the rate of sucks per second in real time. This means that the timing of the stimulus switch can be determined online: the first sound A is played until the baby's sucking slows to a rate below a certain threshold, for example at half as fast as their initial baseline rate, indicating that they have *habituated* to A (and so are presumably bored), at which point the stimulus is switched from A to a second sound B. After playing A and B to many babies, we can determine whether infants from a certain population (i.e. at the same age and the same L1) reliably show interest via sucking when A is replaced by B and not otherwise. If they do, then we know that these babies can tell the two sounds apart – though of course we cannot know precisely what they make of the difference or how it is represented in their minds. This paradigm is

---

[1] Eimas et al. (1971) found that even one-month-olds already show this [ba] ~ [pa] discrimination!

referred to as *high-amplitude sucking*, and it can be used to study discrimination in babies who are only a few days old up until three or four months.

Starting around age four months, the dominant type of experimental method used to study speech perception tracks the infants eye gaze and/or head turns, as a measure of their relative interest in different speech sounds. Much of this research uses some variant of the *Head Turn Preference Procedure* (see especially Kemler Nelson et al., 1995; see also e.g. Fernald, 1985; Jusczyk and Aslin, 1995, and many others). In this type of experiment, infants will be usually held on an adult's lap (or sometimes propped up in a modified seat); they are first oriented to look forwards (at the green light in Figure 1), and then are exposed to different sounds playing from speakers on one side or the other:

(1)   Illustrated set-up of Head Turn Preference Procedure (HTPP): Adapted from Kemler Nelson et al., (1995): figure 1.

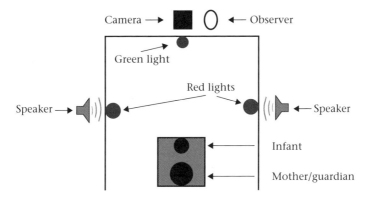

In one simple design, each trial begins by attracting the infant's attention to the left or right with a flashing light (depicted as red above). When the child has oriented their head to the relevant side, the light stops flashing and either sound A or B begins to play, and the sound continues until the baby looks away. After multiple trials, the sum of *total* looking times for all A trials vs. B trials will determine whether each infant showed a preference for A or B – and so again, across multiple infants we can determine whether infants at a particular age prefer one of A or B. In some head turn studies, testing is preceded by a *training* session. In one kind of training, infants are passively exposed to some stimuli X, which might influence their later preferences for A vs B in testing.[2]

---

[2]In another kind of training, infants learn an association between a switch in stimuli and some visual reward – e.g., every time A is replaced by B, a mechanical bear begins to dance. In testing, the switch between A and B will be followed by a *delayed* reward, and the resulting data is whether infants consistently turn their head to look at the reward *before* the bear begins dancing (for more on this head turn procedure, see Werker and Tess, 1983, 1984).

Depending on the stimuli, variants of the head turn preference procedure can be used successfully with children as old as 24 months.[3]

If total looking times are skewed towards for example A, we can conclude that infants both can *discriminate* between A and B, and furthermore that something about A is *more interesting* than B. With this type of design, multiple possibilities can be explored: is A preferable because of the infant's experience thus far listening to their native language(s)? is A preferable because of a universal bias beyond language-specific experience? Was the infant trained in a way that would lead them to prefer A? Of course, knowing that A is preferred over B does not ensure that the difference between A and B that interests experimenters is the same difference that interests infants – but at least we know that on the whole they can discriminate the contrast in some way. It is also not immediately clear whether looking longer to A rather than B is evidence that A was more interesting because it matched something in their experience, called a *familiarity* effect, or whether A was more interesting because B matched their experience and was therefore boring, called a *novelty* effect. Both familiarity and novelty effects are seen in various head turn studies (for more discussion, see especially Houston-Price and Nakai, 2004).

Before we look at some results, let's consider some practical details about high-amplitude sucking and head turn studies. The first question is how many data points you can gather from a very young infant: the answer is not very many, and experimental designs are created to collect meaningful data even if each infant is only exposed to a few trials, or studied for only a few minutes of overall looking time. Even so, many young infants are not able to complete a study before they get bored and stop sucking, fall asleep, throw up, 'fuss out' and squirm from their parent's lap, or otherwise abandon science; often twice as many babies are brought into the lab as there are eventual participants in the study. There are also many criteria to control for when choosing participants: infants are usually required to have been carried full-term, to be typically developing physically, and to have no reported hearing deficits – and of course to have the desired language exposure background.

Another crucial question is the nature of coding: how is it decided whether a baby turned their head or not? Typical standards are that a baby must turn their head 20 or 30 degrees away from the central midpoint. This is measured by asking either naïve researchers (who are blind to the goals of the study), or automated computer software, to track the number of milliseconds during which the baby turns their head past this 20 or 30 degree threshold. Since babies often get distracted, head turns away from the relevant speaker which last less than two seconds are usually considered momentary blips in

---

[3] For another kind of looking paradigm, Sequential Looking, see Cooper and Aslin (1994).

attention: while these periods are not counted in an infant's total looking time on that trial, they also do not terminate the trial, and if the infant looks back within that two second window, the clock restarts and the trial continues. A related technical issue is the possible confound of adult influence, in those cases where the parent is holding the infant on their lap. In such studies, the mother wears headphones that play masking noise or music, so they hear nothing of the baby's stimuli. (Work out for yourself why this is important!) For more information on infant speech perception methodologies, see the further readings section.

2.2   Speech Perception in the First Year of Life

2.2.1   Earliest Perception: Intonation and Prosody

Preferential sucking studies have revealed how fast infants learn about speech. At the earliest possible ages of study – a few hours after birth! – infants display a preference for their mother's voice (DeCasper and Fifer, 1980), and by at least three or four days, they prefer languages that sound like their native language in general prosodic or rhythmic terms (see e.g. Bertoncini et al., 1988; Nazzi, Bertoncini and Mehler, 1998; Ramus, Nespor and Mehler, 1999).

These nearly-magical skills are less shocking because we know that infants can perceive some properties of ambient speech from within the womb during the third trimester before birth (Bredberg, 1985). What they can hear has no specific segmental detail, but rather a rough contour with degrees of louder and softer, lower and higher pitched buzzing: imagine listening to someone talking in the other room, when you can tell whether they are answering a question or asking it, but not the precise words they are using.[4] As a result, it appears that infants show a general preference for the language they have been hearing through the uterine wall, compared to language with very different prosodic structures. For instance, English-listening babies prefer to listen to English over Japanese, which does not organize its pitch according to word-level stress like English (recall Chapter 1.3), but they cannot yet discriminate between English and German, which also uses stress. A related result (Bertoncini et al., 1988) is that newborns can discriminate between CV syllables that differ in their vowels ([bɑ] vs [bu]) but not in their consonants ([bɑ] vs [dɑ]). This too is evidence that infants are at first sensitive to prosodic

---

[4] In lab settings, we can approximate this general type of sound distortion by using a *low-pass filter.*

and rhythmic elements of speech – because these factors are carried in large part by the vowels and not the consonants.

In their first few months, babies also begin to show a preference for *infant-directed speech* or IDS.[5] Fernald (1984, 1985) provided key early evidence of this preference in four-month-olds, and Cooper and Aslin (1990) also found this preference (with a different task) even in four-week-olds.

How is IDS different from adult-directed speech? Well, just imagine to yourself the way you change your voice when you speak to a very young infant. First, you will usually not use particularly esoteric or impressive verbiage – content is often limited to observations such as *'Hello, baby! I see you, baby! Helllooooo!'* and so on. But think also about (i) the *pitch* of your voice, which is overall higher and can also rise and fall dramatically; (ii) your *speech rate*, which slows considerably; and (iii) your use of pauses, which probably group your utterances into short, few-word chunks. (As to which of these properties the infants seem to be tracking, see especially Fernald and Kuhl, 1987.)

One important result is that IDS pitch differences are not just preferred by English-learning babies, or even babies learning stress-timed languages. In fact, studies have now found that four-month-olds (and older babies) prefer IDS even when their L1 uses considerable pitch changes as part of word meaning – as in tone languages like Mandarin – and indeed they prefer IDS to adult speech in a language they have never heard before (see Werker, Pegg and McLeod, 1994 on babies learning Canadian English vs. Cantonese; see also Kitamura et al., 2002, on the similarities between IDS in American English vs. another tonal language, Thai). Additionally, it seems clear that infants prefer female speech to male speech at this age, but they still prefer male IDS to male adult-directed speech (Pegg, Werker and McLeod, 1992).

There have been some questions raised over the years as to the crucial or necessary role of IDS in language acquisition; some ethnographic studies report cultures in which children are not considered as conversational partners until they begin to speak themselves, and so are not the recipients of infant-directed speech. However, the prosodic markers of IDS have now been very widely reported among urban communities around the world, as well as in more 'traditional' rural contexts (see survey in Broesch and Bryant, to appear). For a larger-scale study of different languages and their IDS patterns, see especially Fernald et al. (1989).

---

[5] IDS is also sometimes referred to as 'motherese', although IDS is a rather more accurate term. For one thing, you don't have to be a mother, or indeed a woman, to use it.

2.2.2   Perception of Phonemes and Allophones

In the next several months of life, infants learn to discriminate segments in a language-specific way: first their vowels, and then their consonants. But what is language-specific in their abilities is that they *stop* discriminating contrasts, if they are not part of their ambient language! This is a remarkable finding, so let's look at some real-life examples.

Table (2) below gives three pairs of sounds that many languages use as separate phonemes: front vs. back rounded vowels as in French; dental vs. retroflex stops as in Hindi; and voiced vs. voiceless unaspirated stops as in Thai:

(2)		Some phonemic contrasts		
		Feature	*IPA*	*Gloss*
	a)	French round vowels	[+front]:	[lu]	'wolf'
			[-front]	[ly]	'read (past)'
	b)	Hindi coronal stops	dental	[t̪al] [d̪ɑl]	'beat' (n.) 'lentil'
			retroflex	[ʈal] [ɖɑl]	'postpone' 'branch'
	c)	Thai unaspirated stops	[+voice]	[bâː] [dàː]	'crazy' 'curse'
			[-voice]	[pâː] [taː]	'aunt' 'eye'

In English, none of the contrasts in (2) are phonemic: they cannot build minimal pairs or carry a difference in meaning. English has back round vowels like [u] in (2a) but no <u>front</u> rounded ones; and it uses coronal stops [t] and [d], which are typically produced as alveolar but occasionally as dentals like in (2b), but no retroflexes. As for (2c), while both of these sounds appear in English words, they are in *complementary distribution* (recall Chapter 1) so that in any phonological context, only one or the other is grammatical. Thus, native English speakers who have no experience with languages like French, Hindi or Thai are pretty poor at discriminating these contrasts – for example, the two Hindi stops can both just sound like odd versions of an English [d].

But what about infants? A few decades of experimental work has established that between four and six months of age, infants are able to discriminate most such language contrasts, <u>regardless of their ambient L1</u>: that is, babies who have only heard English are nevertheless able to discriminate French or German [u] vs. [y], and Hindi [ḍ] vs [d].[6] By roughly six months, though, vowel perception becomes sensitive to L1 experience: now English-learning babies do <u>not</u> discriminate [u] and [y], while German-learning babies still do (Polka and Werker, 1994)! A few months later, by eight to ten months, consonant perception is similarly reduced, so that English learning babies no longer discriminate [ḍ] and [d], which Hindi-learning babies keep doing (Werker and Tees, 1983, 1984). The same loss of discrimination is found at eight to ten months for the non-phonemic difference between English [b] and unaspirated [p] in (2c) (Pegg and Werker, 1997) – and this last key result suggests that these older infants are attending to the phonological <u>contrasts</u> in their L1, that is those that could potentially carry meaning in words.[7]

So by their first birthday, infants appear to have mostly honed their perceptual abilities to detect phonemic differences in their own language, and to ignore other sub-phonemic, novel or allophonic differences among speech sounds. This is a considerable feat of mental processing and representation. But how are they doing it? Here we will look at two experimental clues.

The first comes from Maye, Werker and Gerken (2002), who exposed two groups of six- and eight-month-old English-learning babies to a continuum of tokens between [da] and unaspirated [ta], meaning the same (2c) contrast which the six-month-old infants should still perceive differently. Both groups of babies heard the same eight tokens, but as the graph below shows, they heard different <u>numbers</u> of each one. In this graph, the x axis represents the eight steps on the continuum – 1 beginning with a definite voiced stop like [da] and 8 beginning with a definitely voiceless unaspirated stop as in [ta], with the six remaining steps in between. The y axis represents the <u>frequency</u> of presentation of each token for the two groups, distinguished by a dark vs. light line. Infants in the light line condition heard tokens 4 and 5 most often (16 times each) while tokens 2 and 7 near the end of the continuum were only played four times each. Compare that experience to the infants in the dark line condition, who heard tokens 2 and 7 16 times each, and tokens 4 and 5 only four times. Think about what these distributions might teach an infant about their language's use of VOT before reading on …

---

[6] However, not *all* contrasts are so easily detected: see e.g. Narayan et al. (2010).
[7] Although most contrasts follow this trajectory towards language-specific perception, it does appear that there are some non-native contrasts that may remain discriminable both for older infants and even adults – see question 2 at the end of the chapter.

(3) Bimodal vs unimodal VOT token distribution:
     (Adapted from Maye, Werker and Gerken, 2002: figure 1)

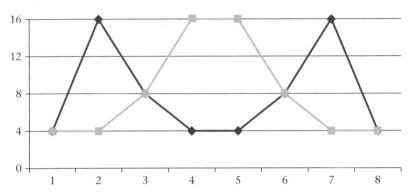

The two conditions in this study were designed to simulate the kind of expo-sure infants would hear in a language that has one vs. two VOT categories within this continuum. The dark line condition are receiving evidence consistent with two VOT categories (a *bimodal* distribution), suggesting that the ambient language includes one phonetic category somewhere around token 2 and another centred around token 7. On the other hand, the light line *unimodal* group mostly hears tokens in the middle of the continuum, with only one peak (or *mode*) in frequency – this would be expected if all of these tokens are part of the same category, cen-tred in the middle of the continuum.

Notice that despite this difference in the number of categories, both groups heard the same raw number of tokens 3 and 6 (see how the lines cross?), namely eight tokens each. So these tokens were used in testing to ask whether the dif-ference in other token's frequencies has affected their behavioural reaction to tokens 3 and 6. The big question of interest was whether infants thought that 3 and 6 belong to the same category. Had training influenced their behaviour when exposed to these two tokens? Note that training was really short – only two minutes of passive listening to random tokens from the continuum, matching these dark and light line distributions.

To answer this question in testing, infants heard two kinds of trials: *static* ones, hearing either token 3 or 6 over and over again, and *alternat-ing* ones that switched back and forth between tokens 3 and 6. The result was that the infants who were exposed to a unimodal (light line) distribu-tion did not show different behaviour between static vs. alternating trials, but the infants in the bimodal group did show a difference.[8] Remember that

---

[8] In particular, the bimodal babies showed more interest in the static trials than the alternating ones. This should probably be interpreted as a *familiarity* effect: static trials represented a single example of a category that they had extracted in training, that was therefore familiar, while alternating trials represented two categories in rapid succes-sion, back and forth, possibly being too much for the infant to handle.

in training, all babies heard these two tokens <u>the same number of times</u>; thus it seems that young infants' patterns of discrimination between different acoustic tokens – deciding, in essence, whether they are drawn from one or two categories – was based on the statistical distribution of *other* tokens along the same acoustic dimension. If infants can scale up this kind of statistical input tracking, these distributions could therefore help them build phonetic and phonemic categories in a language-specific way.

The second clue comes from a comparison of young English-learning infants' reactions to place contrasts among synthesized tokens, along a continuum of places of articulation where each token differed roughly the same amount from its neighbours in raw acoustic terms (Werker and Lalonde, 1988). This continuum of 16 steps is illustrated in (4), and above each token is given the label given to these synthetic consonants by English- and Hindi-speaking adults: two categories in English, labial and coronal, and three in Hindi, labial, dental and retroflex:

(4) Schematic representation of continuum used by Werker and Lalonde (1988)
     (Adapted from their figure 3)

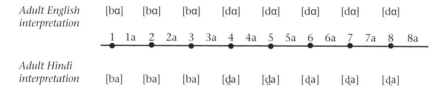

One crucial result from Werker and Lalonde's experiment two shows the following difference in behaviour. At six to eight months, English-learning infants were still able to discriminate between tokens with dental and retroflex place, specifically tokens 5a [d̪a] and 6a [ɖa]; recall that this contrast is not used in English but the adult's labelling shows it <u>is</u> phonemic in Hindi. However, infants at the same age did NOT discriminate between tokens 6a and 7a. While this pair of tokens is equally-different than the last, the difference between 6a and 7a is not phonemic in Hindi – notice the Hindi-speaking adults categorized them both as retroflex – and in fact these two steps on the continuum are not categorized as different phonemes in any known language.

Put together with the Maye et al. (2002) data, these results suggest both that infants are able to compute statistics over the raw tokens of speech sound they are listening to – but also that they bring certain biases to the learning task (see also further readings at the end of the chapter).

2.2.3 Perception of Phonotactics

Moving up a bit in the phonological hierarchy: what about combinations of those phonemic sounds whose categories they have established? Are infants at these same ages yet aware of language-specific phonotactics? Can they demonstrate knowledge of the fact that *bnick* could not be an English word while *blick* could – even before they have learned many <u>real</u> words?

To look for this kind of phonotactic knowledge, studies have again used preferential head turns and looking times: simply playing lists of words that share phonotactic properties, and seeing whether infants at different ages prefer one or the other. As with the phonemic discrimination studies above, the results also indicate a change during the second half of the first year of life. By about ten to 12 months, infants appear to be very sensitive to the possible sound patterns of their native language – they prefer grammatical but unfamiliar (low-frequency) words over ungrammatical ones, even when comparing two fairly similar languages (i.e. English-learning children prefer English words over Dutch ones; Jusczyk, Cutler and Redanz, 1993). Furthermore, infants distinguish between well-formed words based on their phonotactic or distributional *probability*, both in terms of segments and prosody.[9] In the latter category, for instance, English learning infants prefer lists of trochaic words (bisyllables with a strong-weak stress pattern) rather than lists of iambic (weak-strong) words (Jusczyk. Luce and Charles-Luce, 1994). This robust finding correlates well with the ambient English lexicon – because even though English contains many iambs ('balloon,' 'guitar,' 'surprise' ...) an overwhelming majority of English bisyllables are trochees ('baby,' 'kitten,' 'sleepy,' 'bottle' ...; for some overwhelming stats, see Cutler and Carter, 1987, also Cutler and Norris, 1988). At the same time, there is also considerable evidence that infants at these ages are better at perceiving differences in some prosodic positions than others – in particular, that segments at the beginning of words are better discriminated than those at the word ends (see survey of evidence in Zamuner, 2009).

2.3   Word Segmentation in the First Year of Life

So now we know that infants are startlingly knowledgeable about the sound patterns of their native language by their first birthday – and to accomplish this task, we suspect they are tracking a tremendous amount of information about the speech around them. One logical next question is how infants are using this knowledge. When they are not in an infant speech perception lab,

---

[9] Often the term *phonotactics* is used to refer exclusively to describe sequences of segments and subsegmental features, but here it is being used in a broader sense to refer to all the static generalizations about grammatical co-occurrences of sounds, including for example the relative ordering of stressed and unstressed syllables.

are they doing something with their perceptual knowledge of phonemic categories and phonotactics? In particular, are infants starting to learn *words?*

As a first step, we can ask whether infants are performing *word segmentation*: not necessarily associating meanings with words, but simply locating the boundaries between words in the speech stream. If you have been immersed in a second language learning environment, you may have experienced a word segmentation breakthrough, listening to an unparseable stream of speech and suddenly finding that words begin to 'pop out' of the noise at you. Knowing the phonotactics of a language is a great boost towards this segmentation. For example, if you know that a language's phonology prohibits syllable-initial *[bn, then hearing a [b] followed by an [n] means that that [b] cannot be the beginning of that word. If you also know that the phonology prohibits coda-onset clusters of *[...b.n...] as well, then you have probably found a word boundary, in which [b] ends one word and [n] begins the next. This kind of small observation could be collected with many others, to start segmenting or 'chunking' the speech stream into well-formed phonological units, and perhaps also recognizing the most frequent chunks as proto-words.

So: what evidence do we have of infants' word segmentation skills?

One set of amazing studies by Jusczyk, Houston and Newsome (1999) showed that English learning infants can, in fact, segment words out of running speech by at least 7.5 months – and they appear to be sensitive again to the probabilities of different stress patterns, that is not just what is grammatical, but what is frequent. In one of these studies, infants heard words with either trochaic or iambic stress patterns – first in isolation and then embedded many times in stories. When the training words were trochaic – such as <u>**can**</u>*dle* or <u>**pre**</u>*sent* – English 7.5-month-olds preferred to listen to stories containing these training words, compared to equivalent stories with untrained words. However, when training words were iambic – such as *gui<u>**tar**</u>* or *sur<u>**prise**</u>* – infants showed no preference for these words in testing. As just mentioned, English two-syllable words are much more likely to be Sw trochees rather than wS iambs, and so it seems that infants at this very early age are only able to segment the frequent (Sw) prosodic pattern out of running speech. The final impressive piece of this study is that the trochee-only segmentation strategy is overcome by ten months, at which point English-learning infants also show a preference for passages containing iambic training words like *guitar*.[10] (For more suggestive experimental evidence, see especially Mattys et al., 1999.)

---

[10] Note that this asymmetry does not ever go away entirely – because English-speaking adults still use stressed syllables as a strong indicator of a word's beginning, when listening to running speech. For this evidence, see especially Cutler and Norris (1988).

Discovering that infants are able to begin word segmentation before they turn one still leaves open the question of how infants have learned their phonotactics to do this segmentation. How can they know that for example English words are not usually iambs?

First of all: do they learn this from words produced in isolation? One data-rich corpus study of eight mothers talking to nine to 15-month-olds (Brent and Siskind, 2001) reports that roughly 9% of infant-directed utterances consist of single word utterances – and this study also found a correlation between the frequency with which mothers used individual words in isolation, and their children's knowledge of those words later on (see discussion question at the end of the chapter). On the other hand, Woodward and Aslin (1990) found that even when parents were asked to teach their infants a new word, they presented the new word in isolation on average only 20% of the time. The upshot, then, is that some words might be learned in isolation, but surely not all of them.

A related strategy might be to learn words at the very beginnings and endings of utterances, where at least one side of the word is bounded by silence. This seems plausible because infant-directed speech includes very short sentences and longer pauses compared to adult-directed speech; Fernald and Simon (1984)'s study of German IDS found that these pauses were almost always at sentence boundaries. Thus, very young infants may also be learning additional words from their appearance at prosodic boundaries (i.e. phrase-initially or finally); Seidl and Johnson (2008) found that in the lab, such boundary alignment helps infants learn novel words.

However, some groundbreaking studies have found that young infants at this same age – around eight months – can segment nonsense words, embedded in a continuous speech stream, without ever hearing them in isolation or at prosodic boundaries. Saffran, Aslin and Newport (1996) familiarized infants with a synthesized speech stream of nine CV syllables, grouped into three nonsense words shown in (5a), and repeated over and over without pauses for two minutes in a random[11] order (5b). The syllables were all prosodically-controlled – all had the same duration, stress, flat pitch and so on – so that the only cue to word boundaries was the statistical distribution of syllables:

(5)   Saffran, Aslin and Newport (1996)
      Experiment 2 familiarization (emphasis explained below)

a)   'words': [pabiku] [tibudo] [golatu] [daropi]
b)   sample string in familiarization: [...pabi**kugo**latudaropitibudogolatupabi**kuda**ropi...]

---

[11] Random except that no word could be repeated twice in a row.

The distributional clues to word boundaries (in this experiment, but also in the real world) can be described in terms of *transitional probabilities* at the syllable level. Calculating such probabilities can be done by asking: for every sequence of two syllables, A then B, what is the probability of B following A? Since every syllable is used only once in the (5a) words, these probabilities are very different depending on whether A and B are within the same word, or whether A ends one word and B begins the next. For example: if the last syllable you heard is [ti], the next syllable *has* to be [bu] because [ti] only occurs in the word [ti.bu.do]. Thus, the transitional probability of [bu] following [ti] is 1: it happens 100% of the time. But if the last syllable you heard is [**ku**], then there are three possible next syllables – [ku] only appears at the end of [pabiku], so the next word could start [ti...] or [go...] or [da...]. Given that the choice of each next word is random, the transitional probability of each sequences is 0.33: 33% of the time [ku] will be followed by [go] (like it is near the beginning of 6b), another 33% of the time by [da] (as near the end of 6b) and the remaining 33% by [ti].

If you can monitor the difference between syllable-to-syllable probabilities of 100% (within words) vs. 33% (across word boundaries), then you will eventually be able to chunk this stream in (5b) into the individual words of (5a). But are eight-month-old infants able to track anything like these transitional probabilities? In the second of Saffran et al., (1996)'s experiments, after familiarization (which was only two minutes long, remember!), infants' preferences were then tested. In every testing trial, a three-syllable sequence was repeated over and over: either a 'real' word, repeated in (6a) below, or a 'part word' as in (6b). Part words were created by taking the last syllable of a familiarization word and adding to it the first two syllables of a different familiarization word – [tudaro], for example, is built from the last syllable of [gola**tu**] and the first two of [**daro**pi]. In part words, the transitional probability between the two first syllables was much lower than in real words, since in the familiarization stream this sequence [tu-da] would have only occurred across word boundaries:

(6)   Saffran, Aslin and Newport (1996) Experiment 2 testing:

a)   Real words from familiarization: [pabiku]   [tibudo]
     Transitional probabilities: [pa-bi] – 1   [ti-bu] – 1
                                             [bi-ku] – 1   [bu-do] – 1

b)   Novel partword: [tudaro]   [pigola]
     Transitional probabilities: [tuda] – 0.33   [pi-go] – 0.33
                                             [daro] – 1   [go-la] – 1

The exciting result was that eight-month-olds did indeed show a difference between the two types of testing words: in particular, they showed a *novelty* effect, preferring to listen to the part words rather than the real words. (In this study, preference was indicated by looking times: the recording for each trial was played as long as an infant looked in a particular direction, so that the infant controlled the length of the trial with their looking.)[12]

Of course, this experimental setting is not the same as any real world environment, as even the most boring story teller does not talk to infants by repeating four words 45 times each for two minute stretches. Nevertheless – as with Maye, Werker and Gerken (2002)'s study with VOT distributions – this experiment provides evidence that infants can, in principle, track transitional probabilities among syllables in running speech. They may well therefore be using this ability to start learning about words and phonotactics in tandem.

2.4 Methodology: Vocabulary Development in the Pre-Phonological Period

Eventually, all these sound pattern generalization and segmentation skills get put to use in preparing for real communication – and a child finally learns some words. At first, infants and toddlers can recognize and to some extent understand many more words than they can produce, so we refer to their *receptive* and *productive* vocabularies separately.

Especially in English, there have been some very large scale studies of lexical development, which have resulted in month-by-month norms and ranges for the number of words that infants know and use. A widely-adopted tool for assessing this progress is the MacArthur-Bates Communicative Inventories (CDI: Fenson et al., 1994a, 1994b), which asks <u>parents</u> to report their children's receptive and productive vocabulary of their child. Since the CDI has been administered to the parents of thousands of children, the tool also includes normalized data for comparing boys' and girls' scores – starting with the earliest word knowledge at eight months, all the way to 2;6. (For debate about the pros, cons and validity of this questionnaire approach and its norming data, see e.g. Feldman et al., 2000; Fenson et al., 2000.) The MacArthur CDI has been translated into more than 50 languages around the world[13] although in most

---

[12] Note that the words in (7) were those used in one of two conditions – another set of infants had the same experimental design but different syllables used, and the same novelty effect was seen, so the result cannot easily be explained as a particular item confound, for example that eight-month-olds are somehow entranced by the 'word' [pigola].
[13] For a survey of the known translations as of 2010, see http://www.sci.sdsu.edu/cdi/documents/AdaptationsSurvey7-5-11Web.pdf

cases it has been tested and validated with far fewer children than the English studies, so data collection and norming is an ongoing process. Overt tests asking children about their own receptive vocabulary are not typically used until around age two and a half (see especially the Peabody Picture Vocabulary Test: PPVT, Dunn and Dunn, 2007), but by that age children are of course producing speech as well, as we will discuss extensively in our later chapters. Another way to assess receptive vocabulary is by tracking an infant's eye gaze: at least by 14 months, infants will fixate their gaze on the picture of an object if they know and hear its label ('*Where's the dog?*': see Swingley, 2009 and references therein).

The acquisition of novel words has also been studied extensively in laboratory settings, and the connections between these laboratory tasks and development in real worlds contexts (both of phonology and vocabulary) have been the subject of much research and some considerable debate. One now-classic paradigm for studying novel word learning in the lab is the Switch procedure pioneered in Werker et al. (1998) and Stager and Werker (1997). In this word-learning task, infants are trained on two sound-meaning associations between a nonce word and a novel object: for example, training trials might consist either of infants hearing [lɪf] repeatedly while seeing a colourful crown on a screen, or hearing [nim] repeatedly while seeing a plastic molecule-like object. Then, in a testing 'switch' trial, infants' eye gaze is measured when they hear [lɪf] mismatched with the molecule object. If infants look significantly longer on this trial, this novelty effect provides evidence that they had learned the connection between [lɪf] and the crown – a precursor to knowing that [lɪf] *means* 'colourful crown.' In a simpler variant of the Switch procedure, infants are trained on a single sound-object pairing, and tested afterwards to see whether they notice either a novel sound string or a novel object. Another related task (Schafer and Plunkett, 1998) exposes infants to two sound-object pairs in training trials where the object image is displayed on one of two screens. In testing, both images are displayed and one of the two labels is played, and infants' looking times at the matching vs. mismatching image is measured.

We now know from a large body of such word-learning studies that this 'fast mapping' connecting a sound string with an object develops over the second year of life. By 12 months, infants have learned enough about words (or at least nouns) to reject sounds like [mmmmm] or individual sounds like [l] as labels for objects (MacKenzie, Graham, and Curtin, 2011). And by 17–20 months, infants succeed in learning two minimal pair labels for novel objects (see especially Werker et al., 2002; also Nazzi, 2005), even in word-final position by 18 months (Levelt, 2012), although some perceptual asymmetries remain (Altvater-Mackensen, van der Feest and Fikkert, 2013).

The biggest fascination, however, is about what happens between these two ages. At 14 months, infants will detect a 'switch' in testing between highly dissimilar words like [lɪf] and [nim] – but they will <u>not</u>

detect a difference between minimal pairs like [bɪn] and [dɪn] (Stager and Werker, 1997; Pater, Stager and Werker, 2004). This is particularly interesting since infants can reliably discriminate English phonemes [b] and [d] by eight months, and indeed earlier. In addition, 14 months is a prime time for children to begin learning real words, even lots of real words, in the real world setting! Nevertheless, adding images and objects to the mix in a laboratory context appears to <u>suppress</u> their ability to keep [bɪn] and [dɪn] straight.

Many studies have replicated this lack of phonetic detail in laboratory word learning at around 14 months, and there have been many attempts to understand and explain it (see discussion in Thiessen, 2007). What is now clear is that various additional support in the lab learning context improves discrimination between minimal pairs in word learning: for example, pre-exposing infants to the novel objects before they learn their labels (Fennell, 2012), or introducing the labels in the linguistic context of a phrase, as in *'Look, it's a [dɪm]'* (Fennell and Waxman, 2010), lets even 14-month-olds detect the mismatch of a switch trial. The phonetic context of the contrast can also improve their word learning: Archer, Ference and Curtin (2014) found that 14-month-olds could detect a switch trial if the minimal pair had its contrast in the onset of a medial stressed syllable: [leˈdona] vs. [leˈbona] but <u>not</u> when the contrast was word-initial and stressed: [ˈdolena] vs. [ˈbolena]. One of the authors' potential explanations for this difference is the acoustic salience of the minimal contrast in medial stressed position – that the initial unstressed [le] before [...ˈdona] and [...ˈbona] might provide a context that highlights the [b]~[d] distinction enough to support label-object matching (see also Curtin, 2009).[14]

Perhaps these isolated lab word learning experiments seem very far from an infant's daily experience? One intriguing result from Werker et al. (2002) was a correlation between 17-month-olds' ability to detect a switch trial in the lab and the size of their receptive vocabulary in English – which does suggest that such lab word learning tasks are tapping some of the same skills that babies are using to build their real-world lexicon. We will eventually return to the connections between word and phonological learning among toddlers and older children in Chapters 7 and 8.

---

[14] In their stimuli, Archer et al. found that the difference between the F2 transitions from stop to following vowel in [bo] vs. [do] were greater in the medial stressed items, compared to when these CV syllables were stressed word-initially. This aligns well with the result that F2 is the key indicator of place-of-articulation for English stops (Delattre, Liberman and Cooper, 1955), suggesting that the place contrast is easier to discern in word-medial position.

2.5   The Beginnings of Speech Production

We have seen thus far in this chapter that children's *perception* speech develops very quickly during the first months of life, and that even a 12-month-old is in many ways already 'listening' like an adult, from a purely phonological standpoint. On the speech *production* side, however, development does not get going quite so fast.

The earliest language-related productions are not words but rather *babble*, meaning strings of speech sounds produced repetitively and seemingly without a communicative intent or linguistic referent.[15] Typically this begins (by about seven to ten months) with one or a few *canonical babble* utterance shapes – such as a single CV or VCV sequence, where the Cs include stops and often also nasals. Over the course of a few months, the range of sounds used in babble may widen to include other manner types such as fricatives and glides; infants often also begin to babble with sounds not observed in their target language.[16]

Here are some sample babbles involving labial Cs from one child learning Dutch. Before reading on, try describing the phonological properties of these babbles, and any evidence of development over the three months sampled:

(7)	Dutch babble: excerpted from Elbers (1982): table 9	
Age	Samples	
0;7	ˈmabababəwəbabaˈba baːbaːbaːbəbaːbaːmbaː	baˈbə aˈwaː
0;8	pfpfpfff aːaːaːaːˈbə	əbˈə pffpffpffff
0;10	papapapvvv həpəpəpəpfff bapapapapapa bapfuf	papf bəpʙ[17]ː haːaːaː

---

[15] Prior to real babble, infants will produce a number of language-like sounds, variously referred to with terms like '*cooing*' and '*marginal babble*', during which babies establish basic control of phonotation, macro-level tongue movement, and perhaps the beginnings of true vowels (see discussion in Kimbrough Oller, 2000: chapter 1).

[16] This availability for pre-linguistic sounds outside the target language's inventory seems to have led Jakobson (1941/1968) to the fairly extreme claim that infants in the babbling stage made 'an astonishing quantity and diversity of sound productions'; current knowledge suggests a rather more modest amount of non-target options.

[17] This is the IPA symbol for a bilabial trill.

The strongest generalization in this dataset concerns place of articulation: the overwhelming majority of consonantal babbles here are labial.[18] Some features may be becoming more freely combinable over these months: notice that at seven and eight months, each babble is either voiced or voiceless in its entirety, while by ten months voiceless [p], [f] and voiced [b], [v] are combined. Notice also the use of non-target segments, like the bilabial trill, and also non-target sequences like stop-fricative [pff].

To consider babbling data from a different perspective: here are the relative frequencies of consonantal sounds recorded from three English-learning children during the last month before their onset of meaningful words:

(8) | Relative frequency of consonants in one month of late-stage English babbles (Data from Stoel-Gammon and Cooper, 1984: table 1)[18]

Child (age range)	Total consonants	% Occurrence		
		30–40%	10–20%	1–9%
D (0; 11–1; 0)	405	[d]	[b n w j]	[m s x ð r]
S (0; 10–0–11)	453	[d]	[b g m]	[n β h j **r** l]
W (0; 11–1; 0)	512	[d]	[b t s z]	[m ʃh w j]

The overwhelming preponderance of [d]s across all three children is rather striking; notice also that two of the three children used alveolar trills, and fricatives not found in English.

Adding vowels to the analysis of babbling: a large body of babbling research argues that the Cs and Vs used adjacently in babble are reliably found to share place of articulation (i.e. front vowels and coronal consonants; round vowels and labial consonants) at higher than chance levels, for a variety of languages such as English, French, Japanese and Swedish (see especially Davis and MacNeilage, 1995, 2000).[19]

In the later stages, infants begin to produce *variegated babble*, involving two or more Cs at different places of articulation as well as multiple Vs:

---

[18] To some extent this is an artifact of this particular data set, but even in a more complete corpus labial place is often the most common in early babbles.

[19] For possible phonological connections, see Chapter 6.2.

(9)	Examples of variegated babble (Data from Keren-Portnoy et al., 2009)		
	Child (Age)	*Sample babbles*	
	A (0;10)	[bagebagebageba]	
	L (1;1)	boto]	[botobo]
		[bodo]	
	L (1;2)	[dokodoko]	[towotopodo]
		[petapeta]	

An interesting point to consider is that the babbles in (9) are from children who were learning Italian. Could you tell? (See exercise 4 at the end of the chapter!)

Cross-linguistic evidence does suggest that while babbling has broad universal tendencies, even the earliest proto-linguistic vocalizations may show some influence of language-specific tendencies (e.g. de Boysson-Bardies et al., 1989; de Boysson-Bardies and Vihman, 1991). As children get closer to the onset of meaningful language, their babbles can show considerable overlap with words (sometimes making it hard to tell the difference) and there are often remnants of babble in early phonological patterns (e.g. Vihman et al., 1985; Locke, 1989).

Another example from a diary study of Alice (Jaeger, 1997) involves one specific, unusual strategy used in some earliest words. Between 1;6 and 1;8, Alice's English vocabulary was very small (roughly 20 words) and the handful of words that followed this unusual output pattern are illustrated in (10) below:

(10)	A subset of Alice's lexicon, 1; 6–1; 8 (Data from Jaeger, 1997: table 1)[20]		
	food	[kak̚ŋ]	*stocking*	[tat̚n]
	bottle	[pap̚m]	*doggie (all animals)*	[tak̚ŋ]

The IPA transcriptions here indicate that the medial stop was orally unreleased, but followed by nasal plosion – that is a syllabic nasal, articulated at the same place as the preceding stop. Some dialects of English use such sequences in words like *chicken* [tʃɪk̚ŋ] but Jaeger notes that neither of Alice's parents nor her surrounding speech community used such forms. So where

---

[20] Stress and tone diacritics have been suppressed to make the data more readable; see Jaeger (1997).

did she get this strategy? The source seems to be a late stage of Alice's self-generated babble, in which she reported produced nonsense strings like [ta:t͡nta:t͡n] with loud nasal plosion – and which eventually she imported into her earliest referential attempts at words.[21] Once Alice's lexicon grew, however, this CVCn pattern was abandoned – and in the meantime, many others emerged and grew into a larger phonological system. (For much more about babbling and proto-phonology, see further readings).

The earliest words in production – the very simplest *'mama'* or anything similar – typically appear in somewhere between eight and 16 months – but there is a tremendous range of variability in early word use and production.[22] Many parents report wildly different developmental timelines for different children in the same family, with the same language environment.

And once real words do emerge: what do they typically sound like? This question of early phonological productions will now be our subject for most of the rest of this textbook.

2.6   Further Reading

Readings About Speech Perception Studies

Also available (at least at time of publication) is a video demonstration from the Infant Language Lab at Johns Hopkins University, explaining the high amplitude sucking, head turn preference and preferential looking procedure: https://www.youtube.com/ watch?v=EFlxiflDk_o.

Feldman, Naomi, Myers, Emily, White, Katherine, Griffiths, Thomas and Morgan, James. 2013. Word-level information influences phonetic learning in adults and infants. *Cognition* 127: 427–438.

Jusczyk, Peter W. 1997a. *The Discovery of Spoken Language*. Cambridge, MA: MIT Press.

Jusczyk, Peter W. 1997b. Finding and remembering words: Some beginnings by English-learning infants. *Current Directions in Psychological Science* 6(6): 170–174.

Walley, A. C. 2005. Speech perception in childhood. In D. B. Pisoni and R. E. Remez (eds) *Handbook of Speech Perception*. Oxford: Blackwell. 449–468.

Readings About Lexical Learning and Infant Speech Perception

Thiessen, E. D. 2007. The effect of distributional information on children's use of phonemic contrasts. *Journal of Memory and Language* 56: 16–34.

---

[21] see also Chapter 7.5

[22] It is reported that the author's first recognizable (i.e. non-onomatopoeic) word was not mama but rather shoe, despite quite liking her mother.

Readings About Babbling

These readings take a wide range of perspectives on infant vocalizations before phonology begins – including the role of hearing, both for hearing and deaf infants.

Davis, Barbara L. and MacNeilage, Peter F. 1995. The articulatory basis of babbling. *Journal of Speech, Language and Hearing Research* 38: 1199–1211.

Elbers, L. (1982) Operating principles in repetitive babbling: A cognitive continuity approach. *Cognition* 12: 45–63.

Kimbrough Oller, D. and Eilers, R. E. 1988. The role of audition in babbling. *Child Development* 59(2): 441–449.

Petitto, Laura Ann and Marentette, Paula F. 1991. Babbling in the manual mode: Evidence for the ontogeny of language. *Science* 251: 1493–1496.

Stoel-Gammon, Carol. 1989. Prespeech and early speech development of two late talkers. *First Language* 9: 207–224.

Exercises

Q1: *What are the implications of Werker and Lalonde (1988)'s result that babies do not discriminate a contrast that no natural language uses? Should we test babies younger or older to see if discrimination improves? Why or why not?*

Q2: A famous exception to the eight- to ten-month-old revolution, whereby adults lose the ability to perceive non-native contrasts, comes from velaric imposives (also known as clicks). Best, McRoberts and Sithole (1988) found that monolingual English-speaking adults are still quite good at perceiving contrasts among clicks – and that English-learning 6–14-month-olds are similarly good. *Why might this be?*

Q3: Although babies are getting good at word segmentation already by eight months, they are still rather limited in their abilities. One limiting factor on segmentation is the type of segments found at word edges: before 14–16 months, English-learning kids find it harder to segment V-initial words than C-initial ones – to read more about this result, see Seidl and Johnson (2008) and references therein.... *But why?*

First: speculate about why V-initial words might be harder. Come up with a few different potential hypotheses. Then consider the question of this result should be true for all infants, or whether it is contingent on exposure to L1 English. If you hypothesized that the result is English-specific: *how would you go about testing this hypothesis? What populations of babies would you compare? Using what materials?*

Q4: In a study about the language-specific nature of babbling, de Boysson-Bardies, Sagart and Durand (1984) presented native French-speaking adults with 15-second sequences of babble, produced by French-, Arabic- and Cantonese-learning babies. In one experiment using the babble of eight-month-olds, adults were correct in identifying the French babbles when compared to Arabic babbles 76% of the time, and identifying French rather than Cantonese babbles 69% of the time. With older ten-month-olds, the French vs. Arabic babbles were still distinguishable reliably, but the same French-speaking adults could not pick out French vs. Cantonese babbles, and in one study consistently identified the Cantonese babbles as French! ... *What do you think that suggests (1) about the language-specific nature of babbling and (2) about the development of babble between eight and ten months?*

3 Early Phonology: The Shapes of Syllables

3.1 Preliminaries

This chapter begins the analysis of child phonology in earnest, where you will begin to describe and even explain the grammatical systems that children use to pronounce words. First we have some preliminaries to get in place: for example, we have to decide when a child's speech production begins to involve a phonology.

3.1.1 When Does Phonology Begin?

As a conceptual definition, we might say that a child is using a phonological grammar once they have a stable, core set of pronunciations for lexical items, which is more or less generalized to new items as well. But how can we use that definition in the real world? Unsurprisingly, opinion is mixed as to how systematic a child's productions need to be. The most common such method is to pick a minimum number of words in the child's vocabulary, as it is often claimed that stability and predictability in phonological production emerges when children cross a particular lexical threshold somewhere between 50 and 200 words (for overview and discussion, see Sosa and Stoel-Gammon, 2006; Zamuner, 2009; cf. Vihman and Velleman, 1989; Vihman and McCune, 1994).

Regardless of the criteria used, the earliest phonological outputs often show a considerable degree of variability, and analysts must decide to what extent the variation is a property of a child's grammar, or extra-grammatical factors, or something in between. After we have seen many data sets, Chapter 5.7 will return to these questions of variation in earnest. But to begin, the next few chapters will seek to look past this variation, and find some broader generalizations lurking beneath.

3.1.2 Where Does the Child Get their Inputs?

We must also make some initial guesses as to the representations involved in a child's phonological mappings: that is what are their inputs and outputs?

Since we have the outputs more or less available on the surface, the crucial problem is the correct input, and here Chapter 2's results will be our initial guide. There we learned that by their first birthday, children can perceive (most) native language contrasts adequately; thus we will assume that they have (most) target outputs accurately in mind, at least when attempting to produce familiar words.

We will therefore work with the assumption that early phonological production proceeds by taking target-like, accurately-produced seg-mental strings as *inputs*, and then using the child's current grammar to attempt mimicking those inputs in their own *outputs*. However, we will also assume at the outset that children only encode input proper-ties that they can perceive overtly in the ambient language: concretely, this means inputs will contain stress, whose phonetic correlates are sali-ent, but not syllabification. For example, a child's input for the word 'ice cream' will be something like /ˈaɪskɹˌɪm/: containing all the target segments, as well as primary stress on the initial diphthong and sec-ondary stress on the second vowel. (These assumptions will need to be revisited many times throughout this text, starting already in Section 3.4.2.)[1]

In comparison to their target-like inputs, of course, a child's early outputs will usually fail to be accurate, since their grammar is not yet target-like – and so the child's grammar will make errors, which it is now high time we studied.

3.2   Syllable Shape Inventories

We begin with some early words in four languages – European Portuguese, Greek, Quebec French and American English – produced by children in their second year (ages 1;2–2;0). Our first focus will be on the contents and shapes of <u>syllables</u> in the children's outputs, and how they differ from their tar-get syllable structures. Skim through the following four data sets, and look first just at the children's outputs (in bold). What syllable structures do they contain?

---

[1] For summaries of various alternative views of children's underlying representations, see especially Rose and Inkelas (2011): section 4, Jaeger (1997), and also more discus-sion in Chapters 7.4 and 8. For much more discussion of what it means for the learner to receive 'input' to the learning acquisition procedure, see especially Carroll (2001), which focuses on second language morpho-syntactic acquisition, but is still very help-ful in framing the issues.

(1a)

European Portuguese: Freitas (2003)			
Target	*Child*	*Age*	*Gloss*
/ˈkɾɛmɨ/	[ˈkɛ]	(1;5.11)	*cream*
/ˈabɾɨ/	[ˈabi]	(1;8.2)	*open*
/ˈpɾajɐ/	[ˈpajɐ]	(1;10.29)	*beach*
/tɾiˈsiklu/	[tiˈkiko]	(1;10.29)	*bicycle*
/lɐˈdɾaɾ/	[ˈdal]	(1;5.17)	*to bark*
/ˈgɾẽdɨ/	[ˈgẽːdɨ]	(1;11.10)	*big*

(1b)

Greek: Kappa (2002)			
Target	*Child*	*Age*	*Gloss*
/ˈsakis/	[ˈkaki]	1;11	(proper name)
/baˈbas/	[baˈba]	1;10	*daddy*
/kalˈtson/	[toˈto]	1;11.7	*tights*
/fos/	[po]	2;0	*light*
/bes/	[be]	2;0.7	*come in* (imperative)

(1c)

Quebec French: Rose (2000: 96)			
Target	*Child*	*Age*	*Gloss*
/gasˈpaʁ/	[pəˈpæː]	1;3.07	(proper name)
/ˈɑ̃ˈkɔʁ/	[kæː] [kɔː]	1;3.08 1;3.23	*again*
/paˈtat/	[pəˈtæː]	1;4.07	*potato*
/lwaˈzo/	[lɑzɔᵘ]	1;4.07	*the bird*
/ljɔ̃/	[lɑː]	1;4.07	*lion*
/sɑ̃nˈdal/	[θaˈðæ]	1;4.14	*sandal*
/tuʁˈlu/	[dɣˈlʊ]	1;6.22	*bye-bye*
/ˈflœʁ/	[βœj]	1;7.27	*flower*
/kχɛˈjɔ̃/	[keˈjɔ]	1;7.27	*pencil*

(1d)	English (Trevor: Compton and Streeter, 1977; Pater, 1996)					
	target	*Child*	*age*		*target*	*child*	*age*
	clock	[kæ]	1;2.1		*moon*	[mu]	1;3.11
	puppet	[pʌpə]	1;2.1		*stick*	[tɪ]	1;3.11
	give	[gɛ]	1;2.3		*cracker*	[kækæ]	1;3.11
	pinecone	[gaigo]	1;2,6		*cold*	[ko]	1;3.21
	vacuum cleaner	[gakagaka]	1;2.16		*cup*	[kʌ]	1;3.25
	shoes	[ʃu]	1;2.20		*scissors*	[ʃɪʃɪ]	1;3.25
	owl	[aʊː]	1;2.25		*ice cream*	[aigi]	1;3.25
	blanket	[gækɪ]	1;3.11		*apple*	[æbo]	1;4.6

Looking just at the *outputs*, these children all share one predominant surface syllable shape: CV. (In European Portuguese we see one final [l] coda; in
Quebec French there are some vowel length differences; nevertheless CV is
the overwhelming majority.)

The next question about the grammar is how these CV syllables are being
formed: which syllable structures have been lost from the targets? In (1),
the targets have been transformed into *inputs* so they have no syllabification (since children can't hear syllables) – but all the segments are there,
so recalling the syllabification strategies from Chapter 1 should let you
guess the adult syllabifications fairly accurately. To take Trevor's example of
ice cream: in the adult form, both *ice* and *cream* have a single coda consonant, and *cream* also has an onset cluster; in the child's output, all three are
missing:

(2)   Different syllabifications, in a mapping from (1d):

    Target: /aɪskɹɪm/ → [aɪs.kɹɪm]
    Child: /aɪskɹɪm/ → [ai.gi]

So we have two processes: deletion of some onset segments, and all coda
segments (small exceptions not included). And both processes can be understood intuitively as aiming for a common syllable target: [CV].

All of the languages being acquired by the children in (1) allow much
complicated syllables than [CV] to surface – in that sample of target words,
you can find syllables with the shapes [V], [CVC], [CCV], [CCVC] and
[CVCC]. But there are indeed adult grammars whose syllable shape inventory

looks very similar to (1). For example, here are some representative words from Cayuvava, an extinct language once spoken in Bolivia:

(3)	Cayuvava syllables (Key, 1961)[2]			
	['ko.rã.βa]	large black birds	[ha'tʃo.tʃo.ɛ]	I love
	[a'ri.bo.ro]	he already gave it	[i.'a.ru,a]]	death
	[ta'ka.a.si]	old man	[tu.i'dʒi.ɲi.ka]	on house top
	['ki.tɔ.rɛ]	kind of tick	['ri.mo]	lemon

Words in Cayuvava can get quite long, but each syllable is only of two types: CV or V. Similarly restrictive syllable inventories are found in Hawaiian (whose syllables are all CV or CVV) and Hua (which Blevins, 1995 reports as strictly CV). In other words: some target languages share the same syllable inventory as the child grammars in (1).

What is perhaps equally revealing is the _converse_ fact – that is that no child or adult phonology looks like (4) below:

(4)	**Unattested** syllable structure grammar			
	Target	Output	Target	Output
	/'sakis/	['as.is]	/'krɛmɨ/	['ɛ.ɨm]
	/fos/	[os]	/tri'siklu/	[i.'ik.ol]
	/bes/	[es]	/'praɪɐ/	['a.ɐp]

The unattested language in (4) appears to prohibit what (1) allows and allow what (1) prohibits: all syllables are moulded to the shape [VC], with no onset and an obligatory coda. It's not that such reversals don't occur in certain circumstances, but they never appear in an across-the-board flavour like (4).

Taken together, this cross-linguistic evidence from child and adult languages suggests that phonological grammars prefer CV syllables over the alternatives: they are where child phonologies start, and more complex syllable structures are built from them. How to impose these preferences in the grammar?

One option might have been to define CV as the 'optimal syllable', and then describe the initial state of phonological development as allowing only

---

[2] Details of final vowel devoicing are left out of transcriptions for ease of reading; see also Key (1961: 145 regarding some unstable occasional /gr/ clusters).

the optimal syllable. Thus far, we would then have said that if an input cannot be syllabified only using the optimal syllable, i.e. [CV.(CV).(CV) ...], the phonology will delete input segments until only optimal syllables remain.

This approach turns out to be somewhat unsatisfying, for a number of reasons. Here is one: many children insist that their outputs contain *some* of the optimal syllable's properties, but not all of them. For example, here is another child, G, learning English at around age two:

(5) | G (Gnanadesikan, 1995/2004) |
|---|

clean	[kin]		please	[piz]
sleep	[sip]		friend	[fɛn]
slip	[sɪp]		spill	[bɪw]
skin	[gɪn]			

This grammar's output syllables are *somewhat* optimal, but not entirely so. It imposes the restriction of only one onset segment per syllable, but it also tolerates coda consonants. Likewise there are adult languages that impose this slightly more permissive syllable structure – one clear example is Yakuts, illustrated in (6). Notice too in these words that Yakuts does not *require* a syllable to have a coda: the CV syllable is always an option, but now CV(C) is too (onsetless syllables [V(C)] are also permitted).

(6) | Yakuts (cited in Baertsch, 2002: 54, 92) |
|---|

[bɪ.raa.bɪ.la]	*rule*		[sap]	*thread*		[e.tiŋ]	*thunder*
[se.re.de]	*Wednesday*		[at]	*horse*		[su.rudʒ³]	*to write*
[kin.gie]	*book*		[ba.lik]	*fish*		[im]	*sunset*
[sɪ.ma.la]	*resin, pitch*		[su.lus]	*star*		[dʒil]	*year*

To capture both the very strict CV languages and these more moderate CV(C) languages, we will need something more nuanced than a single optimal syllable. Instead, we need a grammar that makes reference to all the pieces of an optimal syllable – each one describing one desirable property of the syllable, which each language may or may not obey. The property shared

---

[3] This final segment is an affricate, just as in English *judge [dʒʌdʒ]*, and so counts as a single coda segment.

by all our child outputs thus far has been the one in (7); the one that has been varyingly obeyed is in (8):

(7) NoComplexOnset   No onset contains more than one segment
(8) NoCoda   No syllable contains a coda

These descriptions of output properties will become one set of OT *constraints*,[4] which grammars can enforce to varying degrees – and while all the target languages in (1) happily disobey these constraints, we will still find use for them along the way.

To round out a bit more of the syllable structure typology, let's look at two other children: one learning English (9) and the other Dutch (10). Before you continue reading, describe in your own words the property of syllable structure that these two children are imposing on their inputs:

(9)

Amahl at 2;7 (Smith, 1973)[5]			
Target	*Child*	*Target*	*Child*
Elastoplast	ˈlaːtəbl̥aːt	*pleased*	pliːd
book-shelf	buklɛf	*scales*	geil
box	bɔk	*touched*	tʌt
desk	gɛk	**touched*	tʌtʃt
footprint	wutplit	**fact*	wækt

(10)

Dutch (Fikkert 1994: 57-58)			
Target	*Child*		*Gloss*
/ˈoːtoː/	[ˈtaːtoː]	J (1;6.27)	*car*
/ˈaːpiː/	[ˈtaːpiː]	J (1;7.15)	*ape* (dim.)
/ˈoːtoː/	[ˈtoːtoː]	T (1;2.27)	*car*

Continued

---

[4] It is standard OT practice to write constraint names as all one word and in small caps. All the constraints used in this textbook have been previously proposed in the OT literature, in some format; some of them are borrowed verbatim and some are reworked considerably. In most cases, a new constraint will be introduced along with some key references as to its provenance. If a constraint is so basic or universally used that citation has been abandoned, it can be found in the classic OT references listed at the end of this chapter's further reading.

[5] Note that Amahl's prohibition on complex codas was more segmentally-subtle than this; the full pattern is discussed in Chapter 6.

Target	Child		Gloss
/aːp/	[baːp]	T (1;3.24)	ape
/aːp/	[paːp]	L (1;9.15)	ape
/'apəl/	['paːpuː]	L (1;10.29)	apple

The data in (9) suggest that this child's grammar does not permit coda clusters with more than one segment (with a couple of starred *exceptions). The Dutch data in (10) shows a different pattern: comparing the inputs and outputs here, it seems that these children's grammars do not permit a syllable to begin without an onset. Thus we need two more constraints:

(11)   NoComplexCoda   No coda contains more than one segment
(12)   Onset   No syllable lacks an onset

It will now not be surprising that these properties are imposed to varying degrees in other adult languages too – recall Hua's CV-only syllables mentioned above (which requires satisfying Onset) – and the numerous languages that only permit single codas but no coda clusters include Spanish and Cantonese.

We have now begun to describe how a phonological grammar can regulate its syllable structure. The requirements are broken down into a set of local properties, each regulated by a constraint on outputs, and each language decides which ones to obey. To illustrate the options, the following table lists some syllable shapes and their satisfaction or violation of each constraint (try to add other syllables to the table!):

(13)

	NoCoda	Onset	NoComplexOnset	NoComplexCoda
CV	satisfies	satisfies	satisfies	satisfies
CVC	violates	satisfies	satisfies	satisfies
V	satisfies	violates	satisfies	satisfies
VC	violates	violates	satisfies	satisfies
CVCC	violates	satisfies	satisfies	violates
CCV	satisfies	satisfies	violates	satisfies

Note this set of constraints also captures the idea that CV is the optimal syllable. How? Because C violates none of these syllable structure constraints.

A leading idea in the study of syllable structure acquisition is that table (13) not only describes all the properties of child and adult grammars alike, but also that it predicts <u>order</u> of acquisition, so that the more constraints a syllable structure violates, the later it will be acquired. This notion goes back at least to Jakobson (1941) – and we will see many domains where it runs into trouble – but for syllables it has been remarkably accurate. A notable success of this approach comes from 12 Dutch-acquiring children reported in Levelt, Schiller and Levelt (1999) and Levelt and van der Vijver (2004). Below in (14) is a summary chart of the syllable acquisition paths that these Dutch-acquiring children took – and it would seem to show that each successive stage of syllable structure acquisition moved learners from a more restricted, more cross-linguistically preferred set of syllable shapes to a larger set with more options:

(14)   Upshot of Dutch syllable acquisition reported in Levelt, Schiller and Levelt (1999)

Stage		1	2	3	4		5		
Syllables Added to Legal Outputs	Path a)	CV	CVC	V	VC	CVCC	VCC	CCV	CCVC	CCVCC
	Path b)					CCV	CCVC	CVCC	VCC	CCVCC

In broad strokes, these developmental paths are pretty typical, moving from simpler to more complicated output syllables. However it is also clear that these paths are influenced by language-specific factors, with various explanations. In the Dutch data above, the two trajectories differ on whether onset or coda clusters are learned first – some kids produced [CCV] before [CVCC] and others did the reverse. In German acquisition, Lleo and Prinz (1996) provide spontaneous production evidence from five children that onset clusters are acquired before coda clusters, as do Demuth and McCullough (2009a) for the acquisition of French. On the other hand, Kirk and Demuth (2003)'s experimental study suggests that for English-learning children the reverse is true, at least in that coda clusters are more accurately produced before onset ones. Similarly, children learning the Dravidian language Telugu spoken in India (Chervela, 1981), and learning Mexican Spanish (Macken, 1978), are reported to produce certain coda clusters before any onset clusters emerge. Thus, language-specific factors must be interacting with other principles to produce specific paths like in (14): more to come.

In terms of chronological age and development, consonant clusters in particular provide a great empirical testing ground: some two-year-olds learning some languages can produce many clusters correctly, while some eight- and nine-year-olds are still struggling with others (for a review and many key references, see McLeod et al., 2001). And as we have already seen, syllable structure typology is fairly well understood across the world's languages, so the comparisons between child and adult patterns are plausibly accurate. Thus, children's stages of syllable structure provide an excellent empirical area in which to build our theory of developing phonological grammars.

3.3 Optimizing Syllable Shapes

The previous section provided some core data demonstrating grammatical preferences for syllable shapes and a set of constraints that can impose these preferences. Before we can go any further, though, we need a working grammar that uses these constraints, to see what we can account for in children's speech.

Suppose we think of structural constraints as filters, which rule out ungrammatical surface outputs. And what does the grammar do when the input fails to obey one of these structural constraints? The previous section's datasets demonstrated that in the earliest cases, children's grammars impose optimal CV syllables via segmental *deletion*. In Trevor's case: when at 1;3 his grammar is given the input /kʌp/ *cup*, it prefers the surface result [kʌ] without a coda compared to the adult version.

We will keep track of these grammatical preferences in a *tableau*, shown in (15). The first row provides the input to the grammar, and the constraints at issue. Each subsequent row of the tableau indicates how many times each potential output for the top row's input violates each constraint, with one asterisk for every violation as defined in (16) below:

(15)

		/kʌp/	NoCODA
	a)	[kʌp]	*
☞	b)	[kʌ]	

(16) NoCODA defined:
Assign a violation mark (*) for every syllable in the output that contains a coda

The whimsical ☞ indicates the grammar's preference: since [kʌ] violates this grammar's lone structural constraint fewer times than the other output *candidate* under consideration, it is referred to the *optimal* candidate or output.

In the case of Trevor's pronunciation of *stick*, the grammar prefers more deletion – because we have *two* structural constraints that the input disobeys, and each violation must be repaired. Make sure you can define the structural constraint *COMPLEXONSET in the manner of (16) before reading past this tableau:

(17)	/stɪk/	NOCODA	*COMPLEXONSET
	[stɪk]	*!	*!
	[stɪ]		*!
	[tɪk]	*!	
☞	[tɪ]		

The exclamation points in this tableau are a standard way of highlighting why each suboptimal candidate lost out to the optimal one – that is they show which constraint filtered out that row's losing candidate, in favour of the winning optimal one. Notice that the ordering of the rows in a tableau is arbitrary: each one simply lists a potential candidate and its violations.[6]

By now you may be wondering about target English – that is what is the difference between child and adult English grammars? Why does NOCODA not cause Trevor's parents to also pronounce *cup* as *[kʌ]? It can't be because deletion is something special about children's developing phonologies (or their motor control or planning properties or anything similar) because many adult language phonologies also reduce their dispreferred syllable shapes via deletion. An example from the Polynesian language Samoan is illustrated in (18) below. These Samoan <u>perfective</u> verbs all end with the suffix [-ia]; those in (18b) have a consonant-final stem, but all their simple forms have deleted that consonant, so that on the surface all syllables are (C)V:

(18)		Samoan syllable structure (data from Harris, 2011)						
	a)	*Simple*	*Perfective*	*Gloss*	b)	*Simple*	*Perfective*	*Gloss*
		o.lo	olo.i.a	*rub*		a.pi, *a.pit	api.ti.a	*be lodged*
		a.ŋa	aŋa.i.a	*face*		so.po, *so.poʔ	so.po.ʔi.a	*go across*
		tau	tau.i.a	*repay*		mi.lo, *mi.los	mi.lo.si.a	*twist*
						o.so, *o.sof	o.so.fi.a	*jump*
						tau, *taul	tau.li.a	*cost*

---

[6] The questions of how output candidates are created (from an input or elsewhere), and what the order of the columns means, will get addressed as the chapter continues. Keep reading …

Why isn't the simple verb meaning 'be lodged' pronounced *[a.pit]? Because Samoan doesn't tolerate violations of the constraint NoCODA any more than Trevor does.

A very different example comes from prefixing *reduplication* in Tonkawa (a language isolate once spoken in Oklahoma and Texas). All of the verbs in (19) begin with a complex syllable – containing a long vowel VV and some cases an additional coda VVC – but when reduplicated these are both deleted and shortened to CV.[7] (If 'reduplication' is a completely novel term to you, just compare the underlined syllable shapes in the reduplicated forms to their ungrammatical forms, marked with a *, and notice that the former contain only CV syllables. Reduplication will be explained in earnest in Chapter 4.)

(19)		Tonkawa (data from Gouskova, 2007, citing Hoijer, 1933: 12–14)		
		Root	*Reduplicated form*	*Glosses*
a) /CVV-/		naa.to?s	na.naa.to?s *naa.naa.to?s	*I step on it/REP*
		jaa.tso?s	he.ja.jaa.tso?s	*I see him/ several look at it*
b) /CVVC-/		soop.ko?	so.sop.ko? *sop.sop.ko?	*he swells up/I swell up (REP)*

In Samoan and Tonkawa, we can understand deletion as the solution to the coda problem – and Trevor chooses this solution, too, while many languages (like English) do not. More generally: every language has its own surface structures it will tolerate and those it won't. English is willing to disobey NoCODA more than Samoan will, but it won't put up with strings of vowels like [o.i.a] in (18a), nor will it permit Tonkawa's clusters like [m?] or [l?]. Thinking about very early child speech, it may have occurred to you that obeying all the possible structural constraints you have seen in every phonological problem set would result in a very, very simple set of surface forms – maybe just [ba.ba] and [baa]. And how exactly would such a grammar give you enough surface forms to build a lexicon?

So a constraint-based phonological grammar is built to do two things: first to filter out dispreferred output structures, but second to <u>maintain the material that's stored in underlying representations</u>. This is accomplished via a second set of constraints, which each require that properties of the input be faithfully reproduced in the output. And one of these *faithfulness* constraints (as they are called) must be active in target English to preserve the final

---

[7] The transcriptions of [ts] and [m?] should not be understood as onset clusters but as affricates and glottalized singletons respectively.

segment of input '*cup*' by preventing its deletion. In the OT literature this constraint is called MAX, meaning that the input should be *max*imally preserved in the output, but we could also think of it as something more memorable – like Don't Delete.

(20)   MAX (Don't Delete) first definition:
        Assign a violation mark for every segment in the input that is
        not in the output

Now our tableau for any input with a potential coda needs to consider the demands of both NOCODA and MAX – because when considering an input like *cup*, they necessarily require different things! In Trevor's grammar, we know that NOCODA is obeyed – in contrast, MAX must be *violated*. In target English the reverse must be true, where MAX is obeyed at the expense of NOCODA:

(21a)

/kʌp/	NOCODA	MAX
[kʌp]	*!	
[kʌ]		*

(21b)

/kʌp/	MAX	NOCODA
☞ [kʌp]		*
[kʌ]	*!	

In OT terms, the difference between Trevor's grammar and that of his parents is not a question of which constraints they have, but *how they are ranked*. Note that this similarity between (21a) and (21b) is not just because they are both speaking (a version of) English, either. At least with respect to coda production, Trevor is speaking more Samoan than English, because their grammars share the ranking NOCODA >> MAX as in (21a), in comparison to target English in (21b).

The logical extreme of this argumentation is thus that all languages, whether child or adult, share the same set of constraints, both on output structures and on input faithfulness, and that the only difference between languages is the relative *rankings* of those constraints. This very strong hypothesis is a powerful one – it's almost certainly slightly wrong, but we will use the parallels between child and adult languages of the sort already seen to investigate how far it will take us. These continuities also represent key support for the idea that phonologies are driven by output-oriented constraints; they give us a way to describe the goals that children are aiming for when they produce non-target like words.[8]

---

[8] This way of connecting adult and child data is certainly not new; a famous version of it is found in Pinker (1984) under the name of the *Continuity Hypothesis* (Pinker, 1984: 7).

Before we move on, note to yourself that constraint ranking in OT is very all-or-nothing. Ranking Constraint 1 >> Constraint 2 does not suggest a tendency towards preferring candidates that obey C1 over C2, but rather imposes the harsh truth that *any* violation of C1 is worse than *every* violation of C2. In the present case, that means that any amount of deletion may be tolerated in order to satisfy higher ranking constraints, for example:

(22)

/koɫd/	NoCoda	Max
[koɫd]	*![9]	
[koɫ]	*!	*
[kod]	*!	*
☞ [ko]		**

At the broadest level, an OT grammar is a vast compromise between a number of mutually exclusive demands. Among pairs of constraints, though, it is a totalitarian regime.[10]

In another example below, Trevor's mapping of *stick* onto [tɪ] shows that his grammar ranks two structural constraints above Max, but doesn't tell us anything about their *relative* ranking. We indicate this indeterminacy in ranking with a dotted line: the notation in tableau (23) shows that NoCoda >> Max and *ComplexOnset >> Max, but doesn't claim anything else.

(23)

/stɪk/	NoCoda	*CompOnset	Max
[stɪk]	*!	*!	
☞ [tɪ]			**

Our next question: why should deletion be the only route to structural constraint obedience? The definitions of the structural constraint NoCoda in (16) provide no process or repair; NoCoda doesn't tell the learner *how* to avoid codas, it only tells the learner how dispreferred they are (to the tune of one violation per coda). The tableaus in (17) and (22) have already shown how the learner can consider many different potential

---

[9] Did you think this candidate should have two stars? Go read the definition of NoCoda again in (16).

[10] There are other constraint-based grammars which relax this ranking authoritarianism (called *strict domination*). The closest such OT relation is Harmonic Grammar, about which see Jesney and Tessier (2011) and references therein.

output candidates – but thus far they have all undergone varying degrees of *deletion* only. What else could we do to the input to satisfy NoCoda or *ComplexOnset?

One option has perhaps occurred to you from your previous phonology training, and it can be seen at work in some additional data from the beginning of the chapter's (1a) and (1d) children. Note that these output productions are from later in development, in the children's third year of life rather than their second:

(24a)	European Portuguese (data from Freitas, 2003)			
	Target	*Child*		*Gloss*
	/ˈgɾẽdɨ/	[ˈkɨ.ɾẽːdɨ]	Luis (2;5.27)	*big*
	/ˈpɛdɾɐ/	[ˈpɛdiɾɐ]	Luis (2;5.27)	*rock*
	/ˈfɾaldɐ/	[ˈfiɾawdɐ]	Luis (2;5.26)	*diaper*
	/ˈpɾẽdɐ/	[pɨˈɾẽdɨ/	Laura (2;2.30)	*gift*
	/ˈbɾẽku/	[bɨˈɾẽːku/	Laura (2;2.30)	*white*
	/ˈlivɾu/	[ˈliviɾu]	Laura (2;8.23)	*book*
	/bisiˈklɛtaʃ/	[bisikɨˈlɛtaʃ]	Laura (2;11.4)	*bicycles*

(24b)	Trevor at 2;1 (Pater, 1996)					
growl	[gʌwauːz]	2;1.0	*spammeat*	[sʌpæːmiːt]	2;1.15
drip	[dɛwɪps]	2;1.14	*blow*	[bəwou]	2;1.17
plant	[pəwænt]	2;1.14	*squeak*	[gʌwik]	2;1.26
plate	[puwait]	2;1.14	*bright*	[bəwait]	2;1.5

In all of these words, *ComplexOnset is satisfied not by deleting a consonant but rather by *epenthesizing* a vowel.

Epenthesis as a cluster repair is not as common as deletion, both within and across child grammars. For Trevor, only 9/72 of his reported onset clusters at age 2;1 showed epenthesis, and likewise 55/2492 (2%) of the complex onsets in his corpus[11] were repaired with epenthesis. Similarly in Freitas (2003)'s longitudinal study of multiple Portuguese-learning children,

---

[11] As organized by Becker and Tessier (2011).

epenthesis accounted for only 9% of onset cluster attempts. Still, the pattern is clearly seen in many child grammars – and many adult grammars, too.[12] To see this we can return to the Yakuts data from (6). Previously, we saw a set of Yakuts words whose syllable shapes were all (C)V(C); but now we will look at the subset of those words which Yakuts has borrowed from Russian, and compare the Russian source and Yakuts borrowed forms:

(25)	Yakuts: More data (Schönig, 1988; Baertsch, 2002)		
	Russian source	*Yakuts borrowing*	*Gloss*
	[prá.vi.lo]	[bɪ.raa.bɪ.la]	*rule*
	[sre.dá]	[se.re.de]	*Wednesday*
	[kní.ga]	[kin.gie]	*book*
	[smo.lá]	[sɪ.ma.la]	*resin, pitch*

With another potential /input/→[output] change comes the need for another faithfulness constraint: this time one with the effect of Don't Epenthesize. Its standard OT name in the literature is DEP, because it requires that every output segment must *dep*end (in a formal sense to be defined later) on an input segment, and thus that no output segment be novel.

(26) DEP (Don't Epenthesize) first definition:
Assign a violation mark (*) for every segment in the output that is not in the input.

As for its ranking: what is crucial about the ranking of DEP in Trevor's grammar (23) and the Yakuts' grammar (as in 25)? First, (27) establishes the definition of *COMPLEXONSET (that was your task above tableau (17)):

(27) *COMPLEXONSET (defined):
Assign a violation mark (*) for every syllable in the output that contains more than one onset segment.

To determine its crucial ranking compared with MAX and DEP, we can compare violations of some relevant output candidates in an *unranked table*

---

[12] In fact, target English provides some interesting evidence that epenthesis is a possible cluster-simplification strategy, albeit for dramatic effect. When someone over-articulates with disgust a word usually spelled 'puh-LEASE!', this output is understood as a variant of input /pliz/, which suggests that our common grammars understand vowel epenthesis into clusters to be a marginal but possible pattern.

in (28). Note that this is <u>not a tableau,</u> so it is not illustrating any particular grammar – it just assesses a set of potential input → output mappings, and how many violations each one incurs according to each constraint:

(28)

/spæm/	*COMPLEX ONSET	MAX	DEP
spæm	*		
pæm		*	
☞ sʌpæm			*

There are three constraints here, so there are six different rankings possible[13] – but as it turns out, there are only three different grammars. How can that be? Here are the two rankings that could *either* represent Trevor's grammar equally well:

(29a)

/spæm/	*COMPONSET	MAX	DEP
spæm	*!		
pæm		*!	
☞ sʌpæm			*

(29b)

/spæm/	MAX	*COMPONSET	DEP
spæm		*!	
pæm	*!		
☞ sʌpæm			*

Examining the two grammars in (29), you will find they share one crucial ranking: in both cases DEP is ranked beneath the other two constraints. It doesn't matter here what the ranking of MAX and *COMPLEXONSET is; so long as DEP is lowest-ranked, the optimal output is one that epenthesizes and does nothing else. We can consolidate this information with a standard ranking notation, where >> again indicates necessary rankings, and {} encloses constraints whose ranking with respect to each other is unimportant:

(30)   *A fragment of Trevor's grammar at work in (24b)*
       {MAX, *COMPLEXONSET} >> DEP

---

[13] Which is 3×2×1 or 3!, and so in the general case it will be n! for n constraints.

It can also be convenient (and sometimes more accurate) to simply list the crucial pair-wise rankings within a grammar – which are enough to choose the right winners, regardless of other rankings. In this case:

(31)   MAX >> DEP
         COMPLEXONSET >> DEP

Exercise 1: There are four more possible rankings of the constraints in (28), which create two other grammars. Draw a tableau like (29), and then determine the crucial rankings in those other grammars as in (30). Does each one correspond to a child and/or adult language we have already seen?

Exercise 2: This exercise is a topic for your own thought. Given what you have learnt so far in this chapter, consider the extent to which children learn to talk by imitating.

3.4   More Choices in Optimization

3.4.1   A Role for Sonority

We will next tackle more questions of how the grammar and the child deploy their repair strategies, by asking about the range of output candidates they can assess. In the child data where clusters undergo deletion, we have simply noted the disappearance of a consonant as being a method to obey a structural constraint. But how did the grammar choose *which* segment to delete? Why is *stick* pronounced [tɪk] and not *[sɪk]? In most cases, children's productions reveal systematic targets for deletion, and so we must find a way to capture them. We will focus mostly on onset clusters, in part because they are so well studied.

In Chapter 1's discussion of cross-linguistic phonotactics, we saw that grammars often impose restrictions on clusters in terms of their segments' relative *sonority*. Sonority also turns out to be a major determinant of how cross-linguistic learners repair the target clusters which their current grammar rules out. We begin in (32) below with one group of clusters with a similar sonority profile, in English, Hebrew and Dutch. Examine these three data sets, and describe the patterns in terms of sonority: what kinds of clusters are found in these target inputs, and which member of each such cluster is deleted in the output:

(32a)	G (Gnanadesikan, 1995/2004)			
	clean	[kin]	*please*	[piz]
	sleep	[sip]	*friend*	[fɛn]
	slip	[sɪp]	*draw*	[da]
	grow	[go]	*cream*	[kim]

(32b) | SR learning Hebrew (Bloch, 2011: 32–33) | | | |
| --- | --- | --- | --- |
| *Target* | *Child* | *Gloss* | *Age* |
| /ˈglida/ | [ˈgidɑ] | *ice cream* | 1;06.12 |
| /ˈtʁaktor/ | [ˈtaktor] | *tractor* | 1;06.12 |
| /klaˈvim/ | [kaˈvim] | *dogs* | 1;09.09 |
| /bʁeˈxa/ | [beˈxaa] | *swimming pool* | 1;11.02 |
| /blonˈdini/ | [boˈdini] | *blonde* | 2;02.02 |

(32c) | Dutch (Data from Fikkert, 1994) | | | |
| --- | --- | --- | --- |
| *Target* | *Child* | *Gloss* | *Age* |
| /klaːr/ | [kɑ] | *ready* | J 1;4.18 |
| /klɔk/ | [kɒk] | *clock* | J 1;6.27 |
| /trɛintjə/ | [taɪta] | *train* | 1;7.15 |
| /bruːk/ | [buːk] | *trousers* | 1;9.21 |
| /plɑsən/ | [paːsə] | *to pee* | 1;10.15 |

If we create a list of all the target clusters in (32), we will fairly soon find a clear pattern in their featural make-up. All these clusters consist of stops or fricatives, followed by liquids and glides – put more generally, obstruents followed by sonorants.[14] With these two categories in mind, we see all of these clusters are simplified by deleting the sonorant and preserving the obstruent.

Now: what kind of structural constraint should be built to capture this pattern? (We will see its presence in adult phonologies too, in a few pages.) If all we need to do is prefer obstruents over sonorants in onset – why not a constraint that imposes this binary distinction?

(33) *SonorantOnset – *tentative*
   Assign a violation mark for every syllable with a sonorant
   segment in its onset

For all the inputs in (32), this constraint will do the right work, as shown in (34). But can you come up with possible inputs where this won't be enough?

---

[14] It is true that sonorants include nasals, but in fact nasals often pattern somewhat differently than liquids and glides in this cluster environment. We will not say much about nasals in onset clusters in this chapter, although they will make a brief appearance below.

(34)

/slip/	*ComplexOnset	*SonorantOnset	Max
slip	*!		
lip		*!	*
☞ sip			*

Here's the insufficiency of (34): while obstruent+sonorant clusters are no doubt the most common onset clusters across languages, many onsets include more than one member of either class – and (33) will have nothing to say about how they are repaired. Below in (35) are examples of two such cluster types in child speech: French onsets that contain two sonorants, and Polish onsets that contain two obstruents. In the latter case, notice that the clusters include fricatives, stops and affricates in multiple orders. ...Thinking beyond (33), can you see how sonority plays a role in simplifying the clusters below?

(35a)

French (Rose, 2000: 96, 99)			
Target	*Child*	*Gloss*	*Age*
/lwaˈzo/	[laˈzɔᵘ]	*the bird*	C, 1;4.07
/ljɔ̃/	[la]	*lion*	C, 1;4.07
/mjam/	[ma]	*yum*	T, 2;0.21
/pwasɔ̃/	[pɔsɔ]	*fish*	T 2;4.28

(35b)

Polish (Lukaszewicz, 2007: 58)		
Target[15]	*Child*	*Gloss*
/fpatw/	[pat]	*he burst into*
/d͡ʒvi/	[dzi]	*doors* (nom.)
/spɔtkaw/	[pɔtkaw]	*he met*
/xt͡ɕawam/	[tsawam]	*I wanted*
/kɕɔ̃w̃ʃka/	[kɔ̃w̃ska]	*book* (nom.)
/stɔnt/	[tɔnt]	*from here*

What these clusters emphasize is that survival or deletion of segment within a cluster depends not on its *absolute* sonority – but on its *relative* sonority, compared to the other segments around it. Is [l] a bad onset segment? If the alternative is something *less* sonorous, then yes: so [l] deletes in *play*, or *flower* or

---

[15] The segments with tie bars in these inputs are affricates.

sleep (as in 32). But if the alternative to [l] is *more* sonorous, like a [w], then no: [l] won't delete (as in 35a). The upshot is that when reducing an onset cluster, these grammars delete the most sonorous segment *available in the input.*

How do we impose these relative restrictions? All we need is a more articulated onset constraints – one for each step on the sonority hierarchy, so that *SONORANTONSET is replaced by a family like *FRICATIVEONSET, *LIQUIDONSET, *GLIDEONSET and so on. With this constraint family, our existing OT architecture provides the mechanism for relative choices: rankings!

(36a)　The Onset Sonority hierarchy (replacing *Sonorant Onset)
　　　　(see related constraint definitions in Prince and Smolensky,
　　　　　　1993/2004 and Pater and Barlow, 2003)

> *GLIDEONSET　Assign a violation mark for every onset containing a [+vocalic, −syllabic] segment
>
> *LIQUIDONSET　Assign a violation mark for every onset containing a [+approximant, −vocalic] segment
>
> *NASALONSET　Assign a violation mark for every onset containing a [+sonorant, −approximant] segment
>
> *FRICONSET　Assign a violation mark for every onset containing a [−sonorant, +continuant] segment

(36b)　*GLIDEONS >> *LIQUIDONS >> *NASALONS >> *FRICONSET

The order in (36b) is a *fixed ranking*. In other words, we will treat it as a given in <u>every</u> grammar that these constraints are ranked as in (36b), whereby the higher the sonority of a segment, the higher-ranked its *ONSET constraint. The three tableaus in (37) now show how this fixed ranking ensures the effects of *relative* sonority in onset cluster reduction:

(37)

		*COMPLEX ONSET	*GLIDE ONSET	*LIQUID ONSET	*NASAL ONSET	*FRIC ONSET	MAX
a)	/slip/						
	slip	*!					
	lip			*!			*
	☞ sip					*	*
b)	/mjam/						
	ja		*!				*
	☞ ma				*		*

Continued

		*COMPLEX ONSET	*GLIDE ONSET	*LIQUID ONSET	*NASAL ONSET	*FRIC ONSET	MAX
c)	/stɔnt/						
	sɔnt					*!	*
	☞ tɔnt						*

Note: the shading of columns above is a standard way to indicate constraints which are <u>irrelevant</u> to the ranking decisions of a particular tableau. In (37a), the two losing candidates are ruled out by *COMPLEXONSET and *LIQONSET, so all the constraints ranked lower are shaded out; in (37c) however, the lower-ranked *FRICONSET is crucial to choosing between the two potential candidates, so only MAX is shaded out. Shading will be used sporadically through the text, to highlight the importance of constraints in more complicated tableaus, but you are encouraged to use it wherever it helps to clarify your analyses.

Exercise 3: Which of the rankings in (37) are we sure of? For example, to make sure all the right candidates win, does MAX really need to be ranked at the very bottom of this tableau? Given the candidates under consideration here: could you move it higher in the ranking and get the same result? What about the crucial rankings of *COMPLEXONSET?

Notice that in the Polish example (37c), our fixed ranking chooses the least sonorous onset segment (a stop rather than a fricative) even in the exceptional case of reversed sonority, that is where the first segment is *more* sonorous than the second. The data in (35b) demonstrated that Polish allows a myriad of such clusters – but recall that English, Hebrew and other languages also tolerate one such reversed cluster, namely [s]+stop.[16] Returning to the children from (32), the data excerpts below show that those children's grammars also reduce fricative+stop clusters to their least sonorous member (the stop) – at least most of the time. For G, no exceptions to this pattern were reported, while in the two Hebrew-learning children's corpora the pattern holds 85% of the time.

(38a)

	G (Gnanadesikan, 2004)			
	sky	[gaj]	*skin*	[gɪn]
	spill	[bɪw]	*spoon*	[bun]
	straw	[dɑ]	*star*	[dʌ:]
c.f.:	*snow*	[so]	*sleep*	[sip]
	snookie	[sʊki]	*slip*	[sɪp]

---

[16] Hebrew in fact allows many more, as you will soon find out.

(38b)	SR and RM learning Hebrew (Bloch, 2011: 39–40)			
	Target	*Child*	*Gloss*	*Age*
	/ʃtaim/	[taim]	*two (fem.)*	RM (1;09.27)
	/ʃtaim/	[θaim]	*two (fem.)*	SR (2;00.05)
	/ski/	[ki]	*ski*	SR (1;07.17)
	/sguˈlim/	[guˈlim]	*purple (masc. pl.)*	RM (2;02.11)
	/stam/	[sam], [taj]	*purposelessly*	RM (2;04.19
	/spaˈgeti/	[paˈgeti]	*spaghetti*	SR (1;09.12)

Taking a cross-linguistic step back, we can see the influence of this Onset Sonority hierarchy in a variety of target language patterns. A fairly comparable one is seen in Pali, an Indo-Aryan language once spoken in India and elsewhere, and used as the literary language of Buddhist scriptures. Pali's syllable structure restrictions mean that stringing together morphemes in the input often creates illegal surface clusters which must be repaired. Examine the data in (39), and consider which member of those clusters survives:[17]

(39)	Pali (data here from de Lacy, 2002: 483–486, citing Fahs, 1985)					
	Input	*Output*	*Gloss*	*Input*	*Output*	*Gloss*
	/dʰov-ta/	[dʰo.ta][18]	*to clean*	/kar-ja-ti/	[kirːati]	*make*
	/lag-na/	[lagːa]	*join*	/sak-ʃːa-ti/	[sakːʰati]	*be able to*
	/gam-cːa/	[gaːca]	*go*	/lip-ja-ti	[lipːati]	*scrawl*
	/das-ja-ti/	[disːati]	*see*	/kʰan-ja-ti/	[kʰaɲːati]	*dig*

Just as in the child grammars we have been analysing, the Palian grammar handles input consonant clusters by deleting the more sonorous member and keeping the less sonorous one. To see the need for <u>relative</u> sonority, compare the forms meaning 'go' and 'dig' below:

---

[17] A few other processes are going on here as well: first, sometimes the surviving consonant is *lengthened*; second, /n+j/ comes out as a palatal nasal. Both patterns will be echoed in child data to come.

[18] [dhovita] is also cited as an alternative output.

(40) a) /gam-c:a/   → [ga:ca]   /nasal + stop/ → [stop]
      b) /kʰan-ja-ti/   → [kʰaɲ:ati]   /nasal + glide/ → [nasal]

Upshot: relative sonority, encoded via an *Onset hierarchy, will account for a lot of child cluster reduction. So far so good! As it turns out, the Hebrew cluster reduction facts are more complicated than a sonority-only account can handle – but let's put this problem on hold for a section, and get a bit of perspective on what we've done so far.

3.4.2   Thinking Through the Candidate Set

An important piece of any OT analysis is to examine all of the grammatical rankings accumulated for a particular language, to make sure none are contradictory (a sure sign of trouble!) and then to assess whether further output candidates must be considered. This last point is one we will now attempt to address: what IS the range of output candidates that the grammar provides, or that the learner entertains?

In a rule-based grammar, there is no need to imagine the output of a derivation before one applies a rule – if the context of a rule is satisfied, its change occurs, and whatever comes out, comes out. But evaluating an input in OT means considering a range of fully-formed output candidates, in light of each ranked constraint, and so we must define that range. Where do the outputs come from?

The strong(est) OT hypothesis is that *every potential output* is under consideration when mapping any input to its optimal output. Just as every language has the same constraints, but in a different ranking, so every mapping in every language has the same set of potential output candidates – although each mapping is made with reference to a particular input and a language-specific ranking. This may sound terrifying for the learner or analyst or both[19] – but for this text's purposes, we will always try to build a set of limited relevant candidates, with some support from a proven property of OT called *harmonic ascent* (Moreton, 2004).

Speaking somewhat informally, this property tells us that given a particular set of structural and faithfulness constraints in an OT grammar, every input can only be mapped in one of two ways. Either (1) it can be fully

---

[19] Particularly because this output set is, given only what we've seen so far, infinite! If one way a candidate can differ from its input is through epenthesis of a segment, and in many cases multiple segments – then how could there be a principled bound on the number of epentheses possible? If there is none, then the candidate set can grow infinite larger with more and more epenthesis. If this really bothers you, you might want to read Riggle (2004).

faithful (meaning that it doesn't violate any faithfulness constraints, and so no segments are deleted or inserted or otherwise structurally changed) or else (2) it can be mapped to some unfaithful candidate, but only if that unfaithful candidate fares <u>better</u> on one or more structural constraints than it would by simply being faithful. The upshot of harmonic ascent is that when you have an input and a set of constraints, and you are trying to find an output winner, you must always consider the fully faithful output candidate, and then look at those candidates that better satisfy some structural constraint(s), but are otherwise as faithful as possible. From that set, you will find your winner.

To put this into practice, let us consider the constraints we have and their necessary rankings for children like G and others who repair onset clusters by deleting their most sonorant member. We have seen two key groups of rankings for this grammar: the first below ensures that complex onsets are repaired via deletion, and the second encodes the notion that the lower sonority an onset, the better:

(41)   {*COMPLEXONSET, DEP} >> MAX
        *GLIDEONS >> *LIQUIDONSET >> *NASALONSET >> *FRICATIVEONS

We know that when faced for example with the input '*play*', a grammar with the rankings in (41) will map /pl/ → [p]. That winning output candidate [pej] is as good as we need to get, harmonic-ascent-wise, because it violates *none* of the structural constraints we have, and violates the *lowest ranked* faithfulness constraint, MAX.

But what if that liquid onset had been the only one? Suppose the input was '*lay*'? What does this grammar predict? It turns out that we need more rankings between our constraints to decide. For instance, if MAX is ranked at the very bottom of the grammar, look what happens!

(42)	/lej/	*COMPLEXONSET	DEP	*LIQUIDONSET	MAX
	lej			*!	
☞	ej				*

Now '*lay*' also loses its liquid onset! Perhaps it wasn't obvious when these constraints were introduced, because we were only comparing candidates like [pej] vs. [lej] – but now you can see that the onset sonority constraint hierarchy from (36) will in fact insist, if given its way, that <u>every onset be a stop</u>, since stops are the least sonorous manner of consonant and the only one not penalized by any of (36)'s constraints.

Is this prediction at all right? Mostly, no. It is indeed true that some sonorant consonants like [l] and [ɹ] are often acquired quite late, and sometimes they are even deleted (much discussion to follow in Chapter 5). But certainly this is not the general rule. Furthermore, it is certain that the children in (32) produced sonorants as singleton onsets – in fact, G's mother reports that at this stage, all of G's /ɹ/s and /w/s were produced as [w], so clearly onset glides were permitted. So how could these /ɹ/s and /l/s be treated different in for example *lay* versus *play*?

You can probably come up with an intuitive explanation, which goes something like this: In *play*, there is a structural problem to be solved, namely the illegality of onset clusters, but in *lay*, there is no such <u>independent</u> demand for deletion. And this intuition can be captured using our existing constraints, merely by adjusting the ranking. Do you see how? Before you continue, draw a tableau for yourself, replicating (42) but with the opposite result (mapping /lej/ → [lej] faithfully, rather than pushing it to *[ej]) – and then read on.

***

Here is a ranking that does the trick:

(43) {*ComplexOnset, Dep} >> Max >> *Glide/Ons >> *Liquid/Ons
     (and so on).

Sandwiching Max with *ComplexOnset above it and the Onset Sonority hierarchy beneath it will capture both the cluster reduction and singleton preservation facts. When there is just a singleton, the maths is simple: faithfulness is more important than the sonority of any singleton onset:

(44) /lej/	*Complex Onset	Dep	Max	*Glide Onset	*Liq Onset	*Nasal Onset	*Fric Onset
☞ lej					*		
ej			*!				

In a cluster, on the other hand, the highest-ranked structural constraint means that repair is unavoidable (ruling out 45a below). The ranking Dep >> Max means that repair will be deletion (ruling out 45b), so that the lower-ranked Onset Sonority constraints have a say, in which segment to delete:

(45)		/plej/	*COMPLEX ONSET	DEP	MAX	*GLIDE ONSET	*LIQ ONSET	*NASAL ONSET	*FRIC ONSET
a)		plej	*!				*		
b)		pəlej		*!			*		
c)		lej				*	*!		
d)	☞	pej				*			
e)		ej			**!				

Both candidates (45c) and (45d) violate MAX equally – and so the decision is passed down to the lower-ranked sonority constraints, where *LIQUID/ONSET does the work of deleting the input's higher sonority segment, choosing (d) over (c).[20] Finally, notice that (45e) is ruled out by MAX – because while it fully satisfies the top two constraints and the Onset Sonority hierarchy, it fails due to its <u>excessive</u> deletion. No constraint above MAX is better satisfied by deleting <u>both</u> onset segments rather than just one, so candidate (e) loses out to (d) as well.

3.4.3   Other Cluster Reduction Grammars

While sonority-driven reduction is perhaps the most common child treatment of onset clusters, it is by no means the only one. Other structural pressures can compete with sonority considerations to determine which segment gets deleted – and here is one such example, taken from other Hebrew onset cluster types produced by two children, RM and SR. (Note: at this stage, both of these children produce /s/ → [θ] across the board, not just in this phonological environment.)

(46)		More Hebrew cluster acquisition (Bloch, 2011: 36, 45)					
		RM			SR		
		Target	Child	Gloss	Target	Child	Gloss
a)		/tmu'not/	[tu'not]	pictures	/ʃne'hem/	[θe'em]	the two of them
		/ʃnej/	[se]	two	/sna'it/	[θa'ʔit]	squirrel (fem.)
		/kmo/	[ko]	like	/tni/	[ti]	you give (fem.)

Continued

---

[20] This isn't the only approach to making sure singletons survive, mind you. A different problem with deleting the [l] in *lay* is that the output has no onset! Try out that grammar, using the constraint from (12), and think about which rankings you need.

	RM			SR		
	Target	*Child*	*Gloss*	*Target*	*Child*	*Gloss*
b)	/ʃnej/	[ne]	*two*	/ˈʃmone/	[ˈmone]	*eight*
	/kmo/	[mo]	*like*	/kmiˈtsa/	[miˈθa]	*ring finger*
	/smiˈxa/	[miˈxa]	*blanket*	/tmuˈna/	[tmuˈna]	*picture*

These inputs all begin with an obstruent followed by nasal – and the output is decidedly mixed, with both children sometimes deleting the nasal (the more sonorous segment), but often deleting the obstruent instead. Note that the discrepancies in these data do not come from two different stages of development – this variability was seen at 2;02 all the way to 2;10, in one word or another.

How should we analyse these two patterns in (46)? As a first approximation, suppose that there are two grammars at play in this data: one that explains (46a) and another that chooses (46b). (This approach means we will also have to figure out how two grammars exist at once in one child, but one problem at a time.) With respect to (46b) then: [s]+nasal clusters in English are also sometimes reduced to their nasal rather their fricative, so perhaps there is something generally weird about /C+nasal/ inputs.[21] But from the OT perspective, this weirdness must be understood as the result of competing pressures. That is, *NASALONSET prefers the outputs in (46a), but what prefers (46b)?

One final set of data from Hebrew may help us see a pattern. Like Polish, Hebrew allows a variety of obstruent+obstruent clusters, not just [s]- and [ʃ]+stop – and in SR's grammar, there is a consistent explanation for which segment gets deleted, but it is <u>not</u> sonority-driven:[22]

(47)	SR's obstruent+obstruent Hebrew onsets (Bloch, 2011: 53)					
	Target	*Child*	*Gloss*	*Target*	*Child*	*Gloss*
	/kfits/	[fiθ]	*spring*	/ktanim/	[taˈnim]	*small (masc. pl.)*
	/dvoˈʁa/	[vaˈʁa], [daˈʁa]	*bee*	/ktanot/	[taˈnot]	*small (fem. pl.)*

Continued

---

[21] For related arguments see for example Pater and Barlow (2003) on English; Yavaş et al. (2008) especially about Hebrew; Kristoffersen and Simonsen (2006) on Norweigan.

[22] In this way, the Hebrew facts are different from those found for Polish in (35a). Remember, however, that we are looking in depth at a few children, rather than across a large data set, so we cannot say much about language-specific vs. child-specific tendencies. For what it's worth, the dominant pattern here in SR's data also holds, to a lesser extent, in RM's Hebrew data as well.

Target	Child	Gloss	Target	Child	Gloss
/'txelet/	['xelet]	*light blue*	/gdola/	[do'la]	*big*
/gvi'na/	[vi'na]	*cheese*	/gdolot/	[do'lot]	*big (fem. pl.)*
/kvi'sa/	[vi'sa], [ki'sa]	*laundry*	/pkak/	[kak], [pak]	*cork*
/tsvi/	[vi]	*gazelle*	/ktana/	[ta'naa], [ka'na]	*small (fem.)*
/zvuv/	[vuv]	*fly*			
/tsva'im/	[va'ʔim]	*colours*			
/tsvaʁ'de.a/	[fa'de.a]	*frogs*			

In all of (47), it is not the sonority of a segment that determines its fate in a cluster, but its position – the second member of cluster, the one closest to the vowel, is the one which predominantly survives. Can you imagine a constraint that would capture this pattern?

The additional tool that we will use to capture this ordering fact is a faithfulness constraint, proposed in the OT literature to explain other target language patterns, which prefers output strings to be *contiguous* in the input. This constraint (simply called CONTIGUITY[23]) always prefers $/C_1C_2V/$ → $[C_2V]$ in every case, simply because the alternative $*[C_1V]$ involves two segments which are contiguous in the output but not the input.

The contiguity-driven account of SR's onset cluster grammar can be explained informally as follows. When sonority differences between onset cluster members are sufficiently big (i.e. obstruent+approximant), the Onset Sonority constraints conspire to delete the more sonorous one (as in 32b). But when all onset options are fairly low sonority (i.e. all obstruents), then sonority is deemed irrelevant and CONTIGUITY is allowed to choose the second member (47).[24] The case of obstruent+nasal (46) represents a middle ground: sometimes the sonority gap between obstruent and nasal seems big enough to matter, and sometimes it doesn't. (This sketch does not provide the details of this account, but it at least demonstrates the kinds of competing pressures that may drive complicated patterns of syllabification – and faithfulness to input contiguity is a phonological pressure you may see again on your travels.)

---

[23] See McCarthy and Prince (1995).

[24] In this grammar, then, the fact that /s/+stop → [stop] happens to choose the least sonorous output segment, but that is just a happy accident. It is really only because the input /stop/ was contiguous with the vowel that it survives.

3.4.4   More Competition: Word-Medial Clusters

Our last foray into child cluster reduction turns to Spanish, and the relative acquisition of consonant clusters under different syllabifications. The data below introduce two different children's treatment of Spanish consonant clusters in the <u>middle</u> of words – this means that these clusters could either be syllabified as complex onsets (V.CCV) or coda-onset strings (VC.CV).

First we will examine the word-internal clusters of one child, anonymized as BL4[25], recorded at age 2;8. To understand the pattern, you will need to look at word-initial clusters (i.e. onsets), and then the range of word-medial CCs. Before reading on, describe BL4's syllable structure restrictions in your own words. (Recall that [tʃ] is an affricate, a single segment, and so does not violate *COMPLEXONSET!)

(48)		BL4's Spanish at age 2;8 (Barlow, 2005)						
		Target	*Child*	*Gloss*		*Target*	*Child*	*Gloss*
a)		/plato/	[pato]	*plate*	c)	/manzana/	[manzana]	*apple*
		/bloke/	[boke]	*block*		/dulses/	[dulses]	*sweets*
		/fresa/	[fesa]	*straw berry*		/falda/	[falta]	*skirt*
		/tren/	[ten]	*train*		/arbol/	[albol]	*tree*
b)		/tʃikle/	[tʃike]	*gum*		/kumpleaɲos/	[kumpeaɲos]	*birthday*
		/negro/	[nego]	*black*		/sombrero/	[sombelo]	*hat*

At the beginning of words (48a), BL only allows one onset segment, so clearly no complex onsets are permitted. This provides a good understanding of why some clusters are reduced in the middle of words (in 48b) and yet others survive (48c). If you were to syllabify the targets in <u>English</u>, you would already see a difference: words like *chi.cle* would have a complex onset, but those like *fal.ta* would have a coda followed by an onset (compare them to English words like *an.klet* and *fal.ter*). If BL4 is using the same syllabification strategies as English does, then we can understand their grammar as one in which no complex onsets are allowed, but codas are permitted:

(49) BL4's cluster grammar:
   *COMPLEXONSET >> MAX >> NOCODA

---

[25] This child was a Spanish-English bilingual (both were learning Mexican Spanish in southern California), but there is no indication that knowledge of English is necessary to get this pattern.

(As for why 48b words can't hang onto their cluster by syllabify it as *neg.ro* – good question! But wait till Chapter 6.1)

Now, however, compare BL4's productions with those from another child in the same population:

(50)

	Target	Child	Gloss		Target	Child	Gloss
		SD1's Spanish at age 3;4 (Barlow, 2005)					
a)	/plato/	[plato]	*plate*	c)	/kampanas/	[kapanas]	*bells*
	/bloke/	[bloke]	*block*		/fuente/	[fuete]	*water fountain*
	/fresa/	[freda]	*straw berry*		/gantʃo/	[gatʃo]	*hook*
	/tren/	[tren]	*train*		/delfin/	[ofi]	*dolphin*
					/dulses/	[duθes]	*sweets*
b)	/tʃikles/	tʃikles	*gum*		/estreja/	[etreja]	*star*
					/tʃaŋklas/	[tʃaklas]	*sandals*

In word-initial vs. word-medial clusters, this child SD1 appears to be the mirror opposite of BL4!: complex onsets are permitted (50a) and so retained word-medially (50b), while word-medial codas are reduced (c).

However: what is the structural constraint that bans surface forms in (c), like *[gan.tʃo]? The interesting analytic point is that this candidate <u>cannot</u> just be NoCoda (i.e. it is not a mirror image of 49) because words like [tren] and [tʃaklas] demonstrate that nasal and fricative codas are, in fact, grammatical. What is not allowed is a coda-onset *sequence*, or a word-internal coda, and for that precise ban we have as yet no constraint.

The cross-linguistic typology of adult language makes clear that word-internal and word-final codas often pattern differently in the same grammar, which requires that they be targeted by different structural constraints (more on that in a moment). In this case, it appears that there is something especially dispreferred about a word-internal coda (see similar observations in e.g. Fikkert (1994) on Dutch, Freitas (1997) on European Portuguese, and Rose (2000) on Quebec French.) Thus, suppose that we add a structural constraint which prohibits just those codas that precede an onset:

(51)   *SYLLABLECONTACT (first pass)[26]

Assign a violation mark for every coda which is followed by a onset.

---

[26] On this type of constraint, see especially Gouskova (2004) and many pre-OT references therein.

(Notice that this isn't quite the same as banning all word-medial codas – while they are exceptional, there are times when a language might syllabify a string as /VC.V/, which would not violate *SYLLABLECONTACT.)

This constraint can be the one that rules out (50c)'s input clusters in SD1's grammar, while NOCODA can remain low-ranked to allow final codas. To make sure you see how this works, draw in the violations for these two mappings in SD1's grammar, and indicate the winner beside its letter (answers at the end of the chapter):

(52)		/tʃaŋklas/	*SYLLABLE CONTACT	MAX	*COMPLEX ONSET	NOCODA
	a)	tʃaŋ.klas				
	b)	tʃaŋ.kas				
	c)	tʃa.klas				
	d)	tʃa.kla				

Exercise 4: Where must *SYLLABLECONTACT be added to the ranking in (49) to ensure that BL4's grammar still captures the data in (48)?

We now have two constraints against codas in our constraint universe: NOCODA, which penalizes them in all contexts, and *SYLLABLECONTACT, which bans a subset of them. Taking a step back, this means we can now predict three kinds of languages: ones in which languages tolerate codas in *no* contexts, in *all* contexts, or just word-finally. These three patterns certainly exist in target languages – Chapter 1 mentioned Hawaiian as a coda-less language; English is an example of the coda-ful pattern, and Luo (a Nilotic language spoken in Kenya and Tanzania) provides the intermediate case, where only word-final codas are allowed.

But the language we can*not* capture is one in which word-internal codas are <u>allowed</u>, but word-final codas are <u>banned</u>. Do you see why? There is no way to derive the following two mappings simultaneously:

(53) *Impossible grammar given constraints in* (52):
    a) medial codas saved: /VCCV/ → [VC.CV], and not *[V.CV]   *but also*
    b) final codas banned: /VC/   → [V], and not *[VC]

To generate (53a), both constraints against codas must rank below MAX. But if so, nothing can cause unfaithfulness in (53b). (If you can't see it yet, draw the tableaus for yourself!) This is the predictive power of a universal set of constraints: and in this case, it reveals how powerfully wrong we are, because languages like (53) are not hard to find – for example, the not-so-exotic language of Italian.

The upshot, then, is that a full account of coda distributions across languages will need more structural constraints than just NoCODA and *SYLLABLECONTACT. One analytic idea is that in some (or even all!) languages word-final consonants are not actually codas, but rather sit somewhere else in the prosodic hierarchy; maybe they are onsets in disguise (Kaye, 1990; Piggott, 1999; Harris and Gussman, 2002), or maybe they are not part of any syllable at all. Adding this option into the analytic mix allows for adult languages like Italian, but it then also allows for different interpretations of the child grammars seen above for BL4 and SD1 (for more on this topic, see arguments in Goad and Brannen, 2003, also taken up in Barlow, 2005).

3.5   Consequences and Alternatives

This chapter's extended discussion of consonant cluster reduction and sonority-driven accounts has aimed to give you a first in-depth example of OT analysis. In doing so, we have faced some of the crucial questions that must be asked and that also can be answered using the theory's architecture and assumptions.

Let's now take stock! This section deals with three types of discussion points: more about the data, more about the theory, and a first pass at framework-comparison.

3.5.1   More about the Data

One big empirical question we will always return to is the question of individual variability, and the extent to which the syllable structure patterns discussed thus far are universal and exceptionless – which, at the broadest level, you already know they are not. In Section 3.3.3, we already suspended the notion that each stage of development is captured by a single invariant ranking, in trying to understand how Hebrew-acquiring children treat obstruent+nasal clusters.

One kind of between-child variation suggests that the earliest stages of phonological *production* may not coincide with the initial state of phonological *learning*. For instance, the very first stages of speech overwhelmingly prefer CV structures, yet it is certainly the case that some children's earliest words also include VC and CVC syllables – see for example Vihman (1981) on Estonian, Grijzenhout and Joppen (1998) for German, and Khattab and Al-Tamimi (2011) for Lebanese Arabic.

However, there also seem to be some clear language-specific differences in earliest syllable structure preferences, and in particular some which counter the universal syllable pressures encoded in our syllable structure constraint set above. As a striking example, Savinainen-Makkonen (2000a) reports on a process of word-initial consonant omission in very young children especially learning Finnish, typically before age 2; some of the details will be discussed in Chapter 5.2.3. Interestingly, the several children learning European Portuguese (whose cluster reduction and epenthesis we have already seen) also occasionally handled initial clusters by deleting the entire thing:

(54)	European Portuguese (Data from Freitas, 2003)			
	Target	*Child*	*Gloss*	*Age*
	/ˈgɾẽdɨ/	[ˈẽɲi]	*big*	J (2;2.28)
	/bisiˈklɛtɐ/	[pisiˈɛtɐ]	*bicycle*	L (2;0.27)
		[ˈɛtɐ]		J (2;4.30)
	/ˈbɾuʃɐ/	[ˈũgɐ]	*witch*	J (2;2.28)
	/ˈpedɾu/	[ˈpe.u]	*Peter*	J (2;4.30)
	/floɾ/	[ˈolɨ]	*flower*	I (1;9.19

These cases of entire cluster deletion are rare, and unattested in many child-development studies, but they are also as yet unexplained in our theory-building. It might be suggested that these clusters are particularly difficult for children to reproduce because they are *unstressed* – but at the very least, it will do nothing to explain Finnish word-initial deletions, since those all occur in stressed syllables. (For more explanation of that last sentence, wait till Chapter 4.)

A further cause of variability might always come from perception vs. production skills. What if children misperceive more complicated syllable structures as simpler ones? Can that account for cluster reduction and simplification? Looking at the data you have seen thus far, there are a couple reasons to be suspicious about a wholesale appeal to perceptual explanations. For instance: it seems unlikely that BL4 systematically heard *no* onset clusters but *all* medial clusters, while SD1 did precisely the reverse. It may also strike you that misperceiving a cluster by failing to hear a segment is more plausible than misperceiving the existence of a vowel – that is that cluster 'deletion' could be better explained by misperception than cluster 'epenthesis'.[27]

---

[27] This may well be right, although you should know that lots of adult second language learner misperceive clusters as containing illusory vowels – see Dupoux et al. (1999).

However, we will delay this discussion of perception until we have a few more pieces of the empirical puzzle in place.

3.5.2. More about the Theory

This chapter has introduced the workings of Optimality Theory, starting from scratch but moving quickly. There are therefore many areas of the theory currently left very sketchy; the next chapters will do some of the larger fleshing out, but let us at least tackle a couple of big issues.

3.5.2.1 More about Representations

The first issue is all about syllables and representations, and all the questions of where and how syllables are represented in the grammar. The descriptions of child data here have been mostly agnostic about any subtleties of syllable structure, especially concerning nuclei – more must be said in a fuller description of child phonology regarding vowel length and diphthongs, and moraicity, as well as the syllabic constituent called the *rime*, '*extrasyllabic*' segments and so on. For at least a start on syllable structure and its roles in child phonology, see the further readings listed at the end of the chapter.

Another crucial question, necessary to fully implement any OT evaluation, is to determine which strings in the grammar actually contain syllable structure. At the beginning of the chapter, we assumed that inputs come unsyllabified to the learner's grammar: inputs look like /CVCVC/ and outputs look like [CV.CVC]. It is instructive to note that this is also the usual assumption about adult grammars, but for different reasons. The already-mentioned reason for leaving syllable structure out of adult inputs is that syllabification is never *contrastive*: once you know the language-specific grammar, syllabification should always be predictable, and therefore needn't be stored in the lexicon. Regardless of whether this reasoning is sound, the fact that syllabification is never contrastive can be captured simply in OT <u>by excluding any constraints that are faithful to syllabification.</u> If there is no such faithfulness constraint – that is no constraint like 'MAX-ONSETSEGMENTS' – then no amount of syllable structure in the input will have any effect on the choice of optimal output.

Easy enough, as far as it goes – but this question extends to many other questions about whether child and adult inputs are the same type of representation. If we think that children's inputs are taken from the target forms, heard as adult <u>outputs</u>, this puts them in sharp contrast with the usual notion of underlying representations attributed in a phonology textbook to an adult native speaker – in the latter case, we usually posit the input as some abstract mental representation, not a fully-formed output. Such abstract inputs used by adult grammars might have underspecified segments, or archiphonemes or floating features, or no stress, or all of the above – but if a child's <u>input</u> is built from an adult's <u>output</u>, it will never contain any of these unpronounceable things, and will also contain some potentially redundant things too. So perhaps the inputs to a child's phonology are special with respect to syllable structure too? Perhaps! In fact, Chapter 4 will present a pattern whose most promising account <u>requires</u> that syllables be assigned in some way to input representations. But again, it is worth noting that in OT terms, adult inputs can, in fact, contain as much redundant detail as you like, so long as what's crucial to the phonology is captured and regulated by constraints.

3.5.2.2   More about Constraints

A third topic which we will simply flag for now concerns the definitions and the sources of the grammar's structural pressures: what are the limitations on the definitions of constraints? And where do constraints come from?

These are both very big questions, and they loom analogously large for any phonological enterprise, working in or out of acquisition, in any framework. For example: any theory of phonology, governed by rules or constraints or otherwise, is frequently faced with decisions as to which *boundaries* or *junctures* can be referenced in a rule – whether syllable, morpheme, compound stem, word, intonational phrase, syntactic phrase and so on. In the OT literature, there are several different theories of constraint structure: on the faithfulness side, there is a fair degree of consensus (McCarthy and Prince, 1995); on the structural side, there is rather more variation.

In addition, OT phonology has often been associated with views about the <u>source</u> of constraints. For the most part, these sources are seen as giving phonological constraints a 'functional grounding': sometimes implying, and sometimes explicitly asserting, that structural constraints are derived from phonetic facts about articulation or perception, cognitive facts about memory and salience, and other sources (for a somewhat early but comprehensive survey, see the readings in Hayes, Kirchner and Steriade, 2004).

To keep this textbook manageable in size, scope and narrative cohesion, it will side-step the debate over the source of structural constraints almost entirely. Our goal will be to capture production processes using constraints that have been proposed and found descriptively useful in the literature, but we will not have anything to say about how these unifying constraints relate to other mental or physical realities. This is not to suggest that the search for sources is not important! Once having absorbed something of the facts and their interpretation in this book, the reader may well be better equipped to delve deeper into their structure and provenance.

3.5.3   Comparing Frameworks: Constraints vs. Rules Part 1

Even with what little we have now seen of Optimality Theory, it is already useful to step back and compare its workings with the rule-based phonology that this text assumes you already know. To make the comparison concrete, we will contrast two analyses of a coda-less language in which /CVC/ and /CVCC/ → [CV]. In constraint-based terms, our understanding of this pattern is encoded in the following simple ranking:

(55)   {NoCoda, Dep} >> Max

In a rule-based grammar, this pattern might instead be analysed with a simple rule:

(56)   C → 0 / __]$_\sigma$ (delete all syllable-final codas, one at a time)

The first point to emphasize is that rule-based grammars almost always apply in some *serial* fashion – one rule at a time, producing a series of interme-diate strings along the way to final surface product – whereas a core component of OT is that every output candidate is considered at the same time, in *parallel*. Thus in mapping from for example /CVCC/ to [CV], there is no sense in which the grammar removes one member of the coda cluster 'before' the other. This turns out to have many ramifications, both helpful and challenging.

The second focus for now will be the relative emphasis on the *change* imposed by rules (variously also called the process, or the repair, terms used throughout this text) vs. the *targets*, which are the aims of structural con-straints. The constraint-based view of grammar predicts that a single surface configuration will be resolved differently by different languages and children: onset clusters might be resolved via deletion, epenthesis and perhaps many other tricks. On the other hand, rule-based grammars instead focus on the processes of deletion, epenthesis and so on as the primary objects of study.

What's the difference? In one sense, the discomfort with a focus on pro-cess can simply be that rules without targets feel like they 'miss the point' – the <u>analyst</u> knows that the rule in (56) is 'about' avoiding codas, but the <u>grammar</u> knows nothing of this goal. But here is a more important issue: if processes are the primitives, what makes an attested or an unattested rule? In a constraint-based grammar, we expect consonants to be deleted at the ends of syllable and not the beginnings – because there is a constraint NoCoda, and there isn't a constraint NoOnset. What is the rule-based equivalent of this predictive power? What can rule out (57) compared to (56)?

(57):   C → 0 / $_\sigma$[__   (delete all syllable-initial onsets – **unattested!**)

It is not that restrictions on rules can't be written: see especially Selkirk (1982) and Ito (1986, 1989), in which string-based rules like (56) were replaced by rules for manipulating prosodic representations, along with principles for where and when to apply them. Rather, the argument is that the constraint-based approach is inherently made for seeing surface generalizations, and for capturing complicated 'conspiracies' via a simple(r) set of structural pressures, interleaved with faithfulness constraints in a strict ranking. The OT architecture thus provides a well-structured approach to analysing many disparate phenomena with a few tools – like the disparate phenomena of child and adult phonologies.

Before continuing, it might be worth emphasizing that this OT architecture also makes it much easier to directly build a theory of phonological acquisition – that is a method by which a learner could move from one constraint ranking to the next, until finally approximating the target language. This text's final chapter is an introduction to some such methods, and it will aim to connect much of the empirical work from these early chapters on child production data with results from the OT learnability literature.

3.6   Methodology: Longitudinal and Cross-Sectional Studies

To close this chapter, we will talk very briefly about the two most common ways that data on the development of phonological production has been collected: *longitudinal* and *cross-sectional* studies.

Longitudinal studies are about individuals' development over time. They typically follow a small group of children (very often just one, but sometimes a handful or even dozens), starting as early as the babbling stages but usually somewhere around the onset of productive speech, and recording phonological data at intervals, tracking the children's progress over months if not years. Often their goal is to accumulate enough data to evaluate overall phonological development within a small population, encompassing most aspects of the target language's phonology. Data collection usually occurs at least once a month, perhaps for an hour at a time, and often during a play session with favourite toys or storybooks, aimed at eliciting as much spontaneous speech from the child as possible. Some studies of a larger group might only collect data every six months, while those which focus on a single member of the researcher's own family (usually called '*diary studies*') might collect data nearly every day and thus in a much wider range of contexts. The earliest longitudinal data (beginning in the 19th century, and also during a renaissance in the 1960s and 1970s) was transcribed by the researcher straight to paper, as accurately as possible given perceptual and memory constraints. Today, data is usually collected via audio recording, with increasingly good sound quality (lapel mikes are a precious gift), and sometimes with simultaneous video as well.

In contrast, cross-sectional studies are in many ways less about depth and more about breadth. Typically, they focus on the acquisition of a particular structure or process, by gathering single-session data from a large group of children (sometimes into the hundreds of participants) at a pre-chosen stage of development, usually in a specific age range, but also for example with a certain vocabulary size and so on. The session often includes semi-structured tasks or games, asking children to name objects or describe pictures designed to elicit the phonological structures of interest. The goal of many cross-sectional studies is to establish normative, age-related milestones (e.g. by what age does the average typically-developing English-speaking child acquire complex onsets?), and to infer the relative order of acquisition among structures (under the assumption that e.g. if more two year olds produce complex onsets accurately compared to complex codas, then complex onsets must be acquired earlier). The data published from cross-sectional studies is often aggregated in multiple ways, collapsing across items, children or both, and provides sufficient power for statistical comparisons between groups and conditions.

It is hopefully already clear that both longitudinal and cross-sectional studies are necessary to form meaningful generalizations about the acquisition of phonology, or indeed any linguistic knowledge. Longitudinal studies provide the depth and detail to build individual grammars – they provided nearly all of the examples used in this chapter, and to a lesser extent in the ones to come, and they provide an invaluably comprehensive window on development. Especially in the case of diary studies, they can capture developmental stages that only last a few days, or processes unique to a subset of the lexicon (see Chapter 7) and they can be annotated with sufficient context to be sure of the inputs being attributed to the child. With very young children (e.g. below 16 months), these studies may be the only way to gather sufficient data for any kind of analysis at all: sporadic speakers, uncomfortable with strangers and uninterested in imitation tasks, may perhaps only be studied in a longitudinal setting.

On the other hand, cross-sectional studies provide the context to see how individual children fit into the spectrum of developmental possibilities. The age at which one child acquires a structure is fairly meaningless unless we know what other children do, or when learning other languages – especially since that structure's acquisition may be dependent on another aspect of their phonology, whose correlation would only be noticed after multiple children were observed doing the same thing. Cross-sectional data is almost always collected by an impartial observer, which affords less contextual knowledge but also introduces less bias. And while cross-sectional data may not allow in-depth coverage in some respects, its structured data collection may in fact gather more answers to a particular research question in one session than through months of spontaneous speech.

One of the tricky balancing acts for the linguist studying phonological acquisition is to use these two data sources in tandem. How much stock should we put in any one child's data? And then again, how should data averaged across multiple children be interpreted? These questions will become more crucial as we proceed, and as you consider your own interests in studying phonological development.

3.7   Further Reading

Readings on Optimality Theory – to Get Started

Gouskova, Maria. 2010. Optimality theory in phonology. In B. Heine and H. Narrog (eds) *The Oxford Handbook of Linguistic Analysis*. Oxford: Oxford University Press. 531–553.

McCarthy, John J. 2008a. *Doing Optimality Theory: Applying Theory to Data*. Malden, MA & Oxford: Wiley-Blackwell.

Classic OT Readings, Especially for References on Constraint Definitions

Prince, Alan and Smolensky, Paul. 1993. *Optimality Theory: Constraint Interaction in Generative Grammar*. Ms, Rutgers University & University of Colorado, Boulder. Published 2004, Malden, MA & Oxford: Blackwell.

McCarthy, John J. and Prince, Alan. 1993a. *Prosodic Morphology I: Constraint Interaction and Satisfaction*. Technical Report #3, Rutgers University Center for Cognitive Science, 1993.

McCarthy, John J. and Prince, Alan. 1995. Faithfulness and reduplicative identity. In Jill Beckman, Suzanne Urbanczyk and Laura Walsh Dickey (eds) *University of Massachusetts Occasional Papers in Linguistics 18: Papers in Optimality Theory*. Amherst, MA: GLSA Publications. 249–384.

On the Development of Child Syllable Structure

Pater, Joe and Barlow, Jessica A. 2003. Constraint conflict in cluster reduction. *Journal of Child Language* 30. 487–526.

Goad, Heather and Rose, Yvan. 2004. Input Elaboration, Head Faithfulness and Evidence for Representation in the Acquisition of Left-edge Clusters in West Germanic. In René, Kager, Joseph, Pater, and Wim Zonneveld (eds). 2004. *Fixing Priorities: Constraints in Phonological Acquisition*. Cambridge, MA: CUP. 101–157.

Exercises

Q1: One day, at age 2;1.14, Trevor produced the word 'straw' as [dɛwɔː]. *What do you think are the necessary components of a grammar that would produce such a mapping?* Draw a tableau with all the candidates you think need to be considered. Include only those constraints that are strictly relevant to choosing between those candidates. Comment on any difficulties you have in getting the winner to win. (You won't be able to predict vowel quality in any way – you might as well consider the mapping as from /strV/ → [dVwV].)

Q2: Examine the data below, from a child Joe at 4;6 whose phonological development was delayed. Comment on his treatment of word-initial [s]C clusters. *How many repairs does he have? How can you predict them?* You will need to talk about syllabification to understand the patterns. You don't have nearly enough constraint-based tools to capture these pattern as of yet, but try at least to write sufficiently-explicit rules to describe them.

Target	Child	Target	Child	Target	Child
skate	[ksejt]	*hospital*	[hɔspɪɫ]	*suspicious*	[səfɪʃəs]
skunk	[ksʌŋk]	*whisper*	[wɪspɹ]	*explain*	[flejn]
scar	[ksaɹ]	*icebox*	[ajspɔks]	*I spy*	[ajfaj]
spoon	[fuwn]	*mistake*	[mɪsteik]	*Scott's school*	[ksɔtsksuwɫ]
space	[fejs]	*upstairs*	[əpsɛɹz]	*boyscout*	[bɔjksæwt]
spinach	[fɪnɪtʃ]	*lipstick*	[lɪpsɪk]	*rollerskate*	[ɹowɫɪksejt]
stitch	[sɪtʃ]	*understand*	[əndɹsænd]	*telescope*	[tʰɛləksowp]
story	[sɔɹi]				
street	[sɹit]				

Q3: In tableaus (28) and (29), we looked at a grammar fragment that prefers vowel epenthesis over consonant deletion, to satisfy *COMPLEXONSET. But we did not give any account of *where* epenthesis takes place. Notice that either of the epenthesis mappings below satisfy the structural constraint!

	/spæm/	*COMPLEXONSET
a)	spæm	*
☞ b)	əs.pæm	
☞ c)	sə.pæm	

What constraints could choose between candidates (b) and (c)? In the data we analysed in this chapter, candidate (c) should win – however, candidate (b) is a very viable contender. Recall the connection between the English word *Spanish* and the Spanish word *Español?* Cross-lingusitically (and even among children) both epenthesis patterns are possible, so there must be constraints that prefer (b) over (c), too.

***

Answers from table (52) (recall that tʃ is an affricate, and so does not violate *COMPLEXONSET)

(52)		/tʃaɲklas/	*SYLLABLE CONTACT	MAX	*COMPLEX ONSET	NOCODA
	a)	tʃaɲ.klas	*!		*	**
	b)	tʃaɲ.kas	*!	*		**
☞	c)	tʃa.klas		*	*	*
	d)	tʃa.kla		**!		

4 Early Phonology: Word Sizes and Shapes

4.1 Early Word Shapes

This chapter moves from children's restrictions on syllables to their restrictions on larger prosodic units, that is the sizes and shapes of words. We will again look at data from many different children and languages, compare their patterns to those found in target languages, and start to build a set of constraints to capture their commonalities.

The argumentation in the first section of this chapter is quite involved, and there will be many moving parts to put in place, so a more elaborate roadmap may be useful. First we will look at child and adult data to identify two kinds of restrictions on word length and stress placement (4.1.1). Then we will develop a set of constraints to control the location of word stress (4.1.2) that will turn out to explain much of the child data (4.1.3 and 4.1.4). Next we look at a different word length restriction and fit it into our analyses (4.1.5), and then finally we will evaluate the question of how universal these early child stages and generalizations appear to be.

4.1.1 A First Look at the Data

To begin with, let's look at the size of output words for one child learning American English at age two:[1]

(1)	English data from 24f6: (Kehoe, 2000: table 3)	
	baby	[be]
	kitty	[kiː]
	bunny	[bãɪl]

Continued

---

[1] Although we don't spend much time on absolute ages. note that 2;0 is somewhat late for this stage, which might be more often observed at 1;0–1;6.

yellow	[wo]
giraffe	[waɪs], [bas]
shampoo	[pu:]
alligator	[ge], [ge:]

Here is the same pattern, produced by a child just beginning to speak around age 1;9 – but speaking Mohawk (an Iroquoian language, mainly native to Ontario, Quebec and New York state). Note that in this data, [í] and [ì] both represent word stress or accent, marked by rising or falling tone respectively:

(2)	Mohawk data from child 1 (Mithun, 1989)		
	Target	*Child*	*Gloss*
	[satíta]	[ki:]	get in!
	[ʃnekì:ra]	[kí:], [kí:r]	drink!
	[sewahió:waneʔ]	[ió:]	apple

Both of these children have a very clear size restriction: while the English inputs range from two to four syllables, and Mohawk words can be five syllables (or longer), all these outputs contain only one syllable. As we saw in Chapter 1.3, most target languages impose a minimum word length – but these grammars seem to impose a <u>maximum</u>.

To meet this surface requirement when producing a word like *alligator* takes a lot of unfaithfulness; this wholesale deletion of syllables is also referred to as *truncation*. In addition to deciding how much to truncate, this grammar must also choose which segments and syllable to truncate, and which to keep – perhaps you can see a faithfulness preference already in these data? More to come.

Looking across children, the one-syllable-only stage can be a fairly fleeting one. It is reported for various languages with longer words,[2] but there are many children whose earliest grammars do not truncate quite so dramatically. Another perhaps more prevalent early word-shape stage is illustrated in (3):

---

[2] See for example Fee and Ingram (1982) on English; Fikkert (1994) on Dutch; Adam and Bat-El (2009) on Hebrew; Revithiadou and Tzakosta (2004) on Greek.

(3)	More American English early word shapes (Data from Kehoe, 2000, table 3)					
	24m6		18m4		18f4	
bubbles	[ˈbʌbo]	*bunny*	[ˈbʌni]	*baby*	[ˈbebi]	
hammer	[ˈhæmɚ]	*picture*	[ˈpɑkɪs]	*kitty*	[kiː]	
doggie	[ˈdɑɪ.i]					
giraffe	[vɑ], [wɑ]	*giraffe*	[dɛf], [ʔæf]	*giraffe*	[wɑ]	
banana	[ˈnɑnʌ]	*banana*	[ˈnænæ]	*banana*	[ˈnænʌ], [ˈnænæ]	
elephant	[ˈɑɪsə], [ˈæfə]	*elephant*	[ˈɑfɪnt], [ˈɛlbɪnt]	*peekaboo*	[buː]	
alligator	[ˈægɜ], [ˈæde]	*alligator*	[ˈæwe], [ˈægu]	*alligator*	[ˈægi], [ˈɑgi]	

Some of the inputs in (3) are produced with two syllables, while some are truncated to only one. Putting aside one exception (18f4's production of *kitty*, which we will have to leave unexplained) there is a clear predictor, the same for all three grammars, as to whether outputs will retain one or two syllables. It's not input <u>length</u>: compare *picture* vs. *giraffe*, both with two target syllables, or *peekaboo* vs. *banana*, both with three. Before reading on, describe in your own words what determines these grammars' output syllable count.

***

What appears to drive the extent of output truncation in (3) is the placement of <u>primary stress </u>in the input. Those English words which are truncated to a single syllable have their primary stress on the final syllable: *giraffe* and *peekaboo*,[3] while those with primary stress earlier in the word retain two syllables. Notice too that in the bisyllabic outputs, it is always the first

---

[3] If you think that peekaboo has primary stress on its first syllable … well, so did I. Perhaps we should imagine this version of the word as part of the actual game, where the 'peak-a' part is delivered from behind something, and the 'BOO' emerges with primary stress when the surprise interlocutor is revealed? But if this is not convincing, don't worry, more compelling examples of final stress truncation to a single syllable will appear.

syllable that is stressed. In other words, there are two surface output patterns: [S] (monosyllables) and [Sw] (disyllables). In Chapter 1, we saw a common prosodic unit that could be either one or two syllables – the foot – and both of these feet are those in which stress falls on the first syllable (if more than one), that is a *trochee*. Then in Chapter 2, we saw that English-learning children are sensitive to and prefer to segment out trochees from running English speech (Jusczyk, Houston and Newsome, 1999). All put together, these pieces of evidence suggest that the grammars in (2) have a maximal word shape of <u>one trochee</u>.

To what extent is this pattern English-specific? The answer is a matter of some debate. Here are some comparable truncations from children learning German and Spanish:

(4)

German trochaic truncation (Lléo, 2002)			
a) *Target*	*Child*	*Gloss*	
/faːˈzaːn/	[zɐn]	*pheasant*	Thomas (1;8.2)
/karˈtɔŋ/	[tɔŋ]	*cardboard box*	Thomas (1;9.0)
/kaˈpʊt/	[puχ]	*broken*	Marion (1;10.5)
/kaˈkaːo/	[gɔχ], [gɔːχ]	*cocoa*	Johannes (1;8.1)
b) /baˈnaːnə/	[ˈnɑnɛ], [ˈnɑnə]	*banana*	Marion (1;10.5)
	[baːne]		Johannes (1;8.1)
/meˈloːnə/	[ˈjojo]	*melon*	Marion (1:8.3)
/karˈtɔfl̩/	[ˈtofɛl	*potato*	Johannes (1,9.21)
/gəˈbuːɐtstak/	[ˈbudza], [ˈbudas]	*birthday*	Marion (1;11.25)

(5)

Spanish trochaic truncation			
Target	*Child*	*Gloss*	
/koˈnexo/	[ˈðeʁo]	*rabbit*	Miguel (1;8.26)
/peˈlota /	[ˈlɔda]	*ball*	Miguel (1;10.18)
/mariˈposa/	[ˈboza]	*butterfly*	Miguel (1;8.23)
/arˈðiʎa/	[ˈzijɐ]	*squirrel*	José (1;7.27)
/alˈβerto/	[ˈbɛtou]	*(name)*	José (1;9.2)
/esˈpaða/	ˈ[paðɐː]	*sword*	José (1;11.23)

For a different perspective, let's look at early word shapes in Hebrew: which is like English in that the position of its word stress is somewhat predictable from its phonology, but only somewhat. One salient difference between the two languages is that Hebrew words with final stress are much more common than English words like *giraffe*, with roughly 73–75% of Hebrew child-directed words bearing final stress (Adam and Bat-El, 2009, Segal et al., 2009). What effect does this input difference have on Hebrew-learning children's first word shapes? The data in (6) provide some examples from one child we saw a lot in Chapter 3, SR:

(6)	Hebrew data from SR, ages 1;3.14–1;5.29 (Adam and Bat-El, 2009)					
	Target	*Child*	*Gloss*	*Target*	*Child*	*Gloss*
	/ˈsaf.ta/	[ta.ta]	*grandma*	/kaˈpit/	[tik]	*spoon*
	/ˈtu.ki/	[kuki]	*parrot*	/bakˈbuk/	[baˈbu], [buk], [bakˈbuk]	*bottle*
	/ˈge.ʃem/	[ˈge.θem]	*rain*	/taˈnin/	[taˈnin]	*crocodile*
	/ˈpe.rax/	[ˈpe.ax]	*flower*	/aˈgas/	[gaθ]~[aˈgaθ]	*pear*
	/ta.ˈpu.ax/	[ˈpu.ax]	*apple*	/kivˈsa/	[sa],[ˈkisa], [kiˈsa]	*sheep*
	/baˈnana/	[ˈna.na]	*banana*	/agaˈla/	[iˈgja]	*pram*
	/dʒiˈrafa/	[ʒi.ˈja.ja]	*giraffe*	/neʃiˈka/	[ka]	*kiss*
	/goˈrila/	[ˈgila]	*gorilla*	/mitriˈja/	[ˈti.ja]~[ti.ˈja]	*umbrella*

What similarities and differences do we see between the English/Greek/Spanish vs. Hebrew data sets? In the left-hand column we see target words with penultimate stress, either two or three syllables long. With the exception of *giraffe* these outputs are all [Sw], just like the English pronunciation of *banana* as 'nana'. Meanwhile, the right-hand column contains targets with final stress, and these surface with three different output shapes, some of them novel. All three shapes are seen in SR's attempts at /kivˈsa/, *sheep*: one is the English approach, truncating to a monosyllable, another is to maintain the final two syllables [wS], and a third allows stress to shift to the penult, surfacing as [Sw].

So across languages, words with final stress are consistently being treated differently than those with penultimate stress. Another commonality to focus on now is that SR's outputs, and all the others we've seen thus far, are no *bigger* than a foot: (S), (wS) and (Sw) are all possible foot-shapes.

Are such maximal word restrictions found in adult grammars at all? Indeed, they are reflected in a range of cross-linguistic patterns. A good example below can be found in the ways that English creates nicknames or *hypocoristics*. Compare the two columns of names below: what are the possible wordshapes for an English hypocoristic?

(7)	North American English nicknames (Data adapted from McCarthy and Prince, 1986)	
	Cynthia	Cynth; Cindy
	Marjorie	Marge; Margie
	Alexandra	Lex; Alex, Lexie, Sandy, Sandra
	Elizabeth	Liz, Beth, Bess; Lisa, Lizzie, Betty, Bessie
	Angela	Ange; Angie
	Katherine	Kath, Kate; Kathy, Katie
	Victoria	Vic; Vickie, Tory
	Kenneth	Ken; Kenny
	Edward	Ed, Ted; Eddy
	Douglas	Doug; Dougie
	Michael	Mike; Mikey
	Thomas	Tom; Tommy

Regardless of input syllable count or stress pattern, two wordshape options are possible: (i) a single stressed syllable, almost always with a coda, or (ii) two syllables, with stress on the first and typically a reduced [i] as nucleus of the second. As with the child truncations, these two shapes are again both compatible with building a single trochee, whether (S) or (Sw).

To see word maximality in a different language, try describing the shape of these Japanese abbreviations, created from longer words and phrases of many shapes:

(8)	Japanese abbreviations (Data from McCarthy and Prince, 1986, citing Poser, 1984)		
		Abbreviation	*Gloss*
	/paasonaru + koN[4]pju:ta:/	[paso koN]	*personal computer*
	/wa:do + puroses:a:/	[wa: puro]	*word processor*

Continued

---

[4] This capital N is described as a 'placeless nasal glide'.

	Abbreviation	Gloss
/ime:zji tjenzji/	[ime tjeN]	*image change (makeover)*
/paNti: sutok:iNgu/	[paN suto]	*panty stocking*
/konekusjon/	[kone]	*connection*
/sutoraiki/	[suto]	*strike*
/zemina:ru/	[zemi]	*seminar*

In all of these cases, again: each word in the phrase is truncated from the left edge up to a trochee: either a *heavy* syllable (CV: or CVN), or two syllables (CVCV).

Another prominent role for maximal word restrictions in target languages is in *reduplication*, which you probably know as a process in which morphological meaning is marked on a word by repeating some phonological material from its *base* form.[5] (We already saw one reduplication pattern from Tonkawa in Chapter 3.) While some reduplicative morphemes copy all of their bases, many copy only part, and this *partial reduplication* frequently copies as much material as will fit in a prosodic unit, like a syllable or a foot.[6]

Below are two such examples, both from prefixing reduplication patterns in unrelated languages. Examine the data in (9) and (10), and determine the maximal size of the reduplicant (which is underlined) in each case:

(9) | Ilokano Progressive Reduplication (including an [ag-] prefix) (McCarthy and Prince, 1986, citing Bernabe et al., 1971)

Base	Reduplicated	Gloss
/basa/	[ag-<u>bas</u>-basa]	*read/be reading*
/dait/	[ag-<u>da</u>-dait]	*study/be studying*
/adal/	[ag-<u>ad</u>-adal]	*study/be studying*
/takder /	[ag-<u>tak</u>-takder]	*stand/be standing*
/trabaho/	[ad-<u>trab</u>-trabaho]	*work/be working*

---

[5] English doesn't have much reduplication, although many speakers are familiar with a total reduplication process that marks prototypicality, for example 'I don't want soy or almond or rice or anything crazy, just *milk* milk in my latte, please.' See also the patterns in Section 4.2.2.

[6] This connection between prosodic categories and morphological marking within and pre-OT is covered extensively in many works by McCarthy and Prince, starting with McCarthy and Prince (1986); see also especially McCarthy and Prince (1993).

(10) | Lardil verbal reduplication
(McCarthy and Prince, 1986; Wilkinson, 1988)

Root	Simple	Reduplicated	Gloss
/kele<u>t</u>/	[kele]	[<u>kele</u>kele]	*cut*
/keli<u>t</u>/	[keli]	[<u>keli</u>keli]	*jump*
/pareli<u>t</u>/	[pareli]	[<u>parel</u>pareli]	*gather*
/la<u>t</u>/	[lata]	[<u>laː</u>la]	*spear*
/ne<u>t</u>/	[neta]	[<u>neː</u>ne]	*strike*
/ŋaali<u>t</u>/	[ŋaali]	[<u>ŋaali</u>ŋaali]	*thirst*

The Ilokano reduplicant is a *syllable* – as many segments as can possibly be fit into a syllable, even if the material used spans <u>multiple</u> syllables in the base: compare ***tra.ba**.ho* with the reduplicant [trab]. In Lardil, the reduplicant is a *foot*: whether a bisyllabic [CVCV] or heavy monosyllable (CVV or CVVC). Notice that Lardil must only assign syllable weight to vowels and not coda consonants: [CVC] is not big enough to create a foot, so bases that are smaller than a foot like /ne<u>t</u>/ (where [<u>t</u>] is the 'verbal suffix') are reduplicated with a long vowel to make a syllable heavy enough to be a whole foot.

We have now assembled several examples of grammars that impose a one-foot-limit, for children and adults alike. For early learners, this limit appears to emerge as an across-the-board requirement: only one foot per word, whether a trochee (in English, Spanish and German, among other languages), or otherwise (as in Hebrew, which we will finally address in 4.1.3).

And now: how does the grammar impose this one-foot-limit? To build an analysis of children's word shape, we must begin by remembering Chapter 1's discussion of feet and stress patterns in target languages. From there, we will assemble a constraint set that derives footing and foot-based limited in both adult and child languages, including the one-trochee stage, and then we will look at broader and later trends in prosodic development.

4.1.2   A First Analysis of Target Language Stress

In Chapter 1.3.2, we took a whirlwind tour of phonological stress patterns. Here is a reminder of two such systems: what do they have in common?

(11) | Hungarian stress (repeated from Chapter 1) | | | |
|---|---|---|---|
| [ˈʃaːrgɒ] | *yellow* | [ˈtɛlihold] | *full moon* |
| [ˈɛrdøː] | *forest* | [ˈtyːzoltoːʃaːg] | *fire department* |
| [ˈtørveːɲeʃ] | *legal* | [ˈpɒrɒditʃom] | *tomato* |
| [ˈpɒlotɒ] | *castle* | [ˈeːksiːnkeːk] | *sky blue* |
| [ˈʃyːrgøːʃ] | *urgent* | [ˈøsːɛkøtːɛteːʃ] | *connection* |

(12) | Garawa (Furby, 1974, repeated from Chapter 1) | |
|---|---|
| [ˈja.mi] | *eye* |
| [ˈwat.jimˌpa.u] | *armpit* |
| [ˈja.kaˌla.kaˌlam.pa] | *loose* |
| [ˈam.paˌla.inˌmu.kunˌji.na] | *at our many* |

The simplest commonality these two languages share is that they stress the first syllable of every word. In foot-based terms, as we used in Chapter 1, this means they both begin their words with a foot, and our first task will be to account for the overall pattern of languages aligning feet with word edges. To account for this aspect of Hungarian and Garawa, we can use one of a family of constraints that <u>align</u> the edges of phonological objects: here, the edge of a foot, and the edge of a word:

(13) INITIAL-FOOT[7]

Assign a violation for every word in which the initial syllable is not in a foot[8]

---

[7] Throughout this chapter, the names of structural constraints on stress will not necessarily match those found in the literature – partly because the theory being used is a hybrid of many, and partly because some constraint names are more historical remnants than helpful labels. In this case, the family of 'Alignment' constraints that inspires INITIAL-FOOT and those in upcoming sections comes from McCarthy and Prince (1993).

[8] Sidenote: although INITIAL-FOOT is not categorically observed in English, it can be seen to affect the placement of secondary stress, especially in longer mono-morphemic words. Names like Lollapalooza and Winnepesauke are stressed (ˌsw)w(ˈSw), with secondary stress on a word-initial foot; for a lot more on this, see especially Pater (2000).

Getting back to our typology, Chapter 1 also pointed out that the primary stress in an iterative stress system is similarly attracted to word edges. In Garawa, the main stress is word-initial; in Hungarian, the main stress is also vacuously on the initial foot, because the first foot is also the only foot. So both grammars also obey an alignment constraint geared specifically to the *main stress foot*:

(14) INITIAL-MAINSTRESSFOOT (shortened to INITIAL-MSFOOT)[9]
      Assign a violation for every word in which the initial foot does not receive main stress

Both INITIAL-FOOT and INITIAL-MSFOOT are obeyed perfectly in Hungarian and Garawa – but they differ in their stress patterns because Garawa continues to build further feet. We must assume then that there is some kind of structural pressure for rhythm <u>throughout the word</u> – which probably seems quite right, in that one 'ta-DA!' at the beginning of a long word doesn't really sound much like 'rhythm', any more than one bash at the keyboard constitutes a song. You could probably invent several different definitions for this constraint, but here's a common version:

(15) *UNFOOTEDSYLLABLE[10] (*UNFOOTED)
      Assign a violation for every syllable that is not within a foot.

With the three constraints we have, let's see what languages we can capture. This table in (16) is not a tableau, just a way of checking which kinds of footing violate which constraints. (Notice that this candidate set is restricted to the syllabification that Garawa's grammar deems optimal, so that /pau/ is parsed into two syllables):

(16)	/watjimpau/	INITIALFOOT	INITIAL-MSFOOT	*UNFOOTED
	a) wat.jim('pa.u)	*		**
	b) wat.jim.pa.u	*		****
	c) (ˌwat.jim)('pa.u)		*	
	d) ('wat.jim)(ˌpa.u)			
	e) ('wat.jim)pa.u			**

---

[9] This analysis of main stress placement is in the spirit of McCarthy (2003), which in turn is an OT translation of Prince (1983)'s End Rule.

[10] Two comments: one, this constraint is usually called PARSESYLLABLE in the literature. Two, I have chosen to use this constraint for ease of explanation here, but there is good reason to suspect that this definition is the wrong one – see *Lapse as an alternative: Selkirk, 1984; Elenbaas, 1999.

These three constraints work together to build the Garawa stress pattern: as many feet as possible, including one exactly at the left edge, with main stress on the leftmost foot. However, there is no doubt that there must be other, conflicting constraints somewhere in the grammar: for starters, Hungarian will require that something counteract *UNFOOTED, because otherwise a non-iterative candidate will never be optimal. From the candidate set in (16), the Hungarian grammar <u>should</u> choose (16e) with a single foot – but that candidate fares worse than (16d) on *UNFOOTED and does equally well on the other two constraints. In OT terms, we say then that the Hungarian-like candidate (e) is *harmonically bounded* by candidate (d) – and that means we must be missing a constraint.

What could prefer the Hungarian optimal form (16e), then? One option that you might imagine, but turns out not to be the right approach, is a truly opposite constraint that says e.g. *FEET, or *FOOTEDSYLLABLE (for why that makes pathological predictions, see arguments as in Gouskova, 2003).

Instead, here's a hint of a way to understand non-iterative footing: remember that in <u>other</u> languages, the phonology aligns trochees to the <u>end</u> of the word, rather than the beginning – as in Polish, where the main stress was found at the *right* edge of the word. Another such iterative stress pattern is found in Warao (a language isolate spoken in Venezuela), which we can see in its alternating stress below. The specifically right-edge orientation is detectable in words with odd numbers of syllables, where it is the initial syllable which remains unfooted – the table in (18) has added the foot boundaries with (parentheses) to make this clear:

(17)		Warao (Osborn, 1966)[11]	
	a)	('tira)	*woman*
	b)	ji(ˌwara)('nahe)	*he finished it*
	c)	nĩ(ˌhãra)('paka)	*alligator*
	d)	(ˌjapu)(ˌruki)(ˌtane)('hase)	*verily to climb*
	e)	e(ˌnaho)(ˌroa)(ˌhaku.)('tai)	*the one who caused him to eat*

---

[11] The stress pattern of Warao has been simplified here; see Osborn (1966) for causes of exceptional final stress (like Spanish borrowings) and some larger complications, e.g. involving verbal morphology, that cause antepenult stress.

To capture right-edge stress whether in Polish or Warao we will need constraints that operate in opposition to the two initial footing constraints we have invented – both to align feet with the end of the word, and to ensure that the last of these feet (as in Warao) gets main stress:

(18) FINALFOOT
   Assign a violation for every word in which the final syllable is not in a foot

(19) FINAL-MAINSTRESSFOOT (FINAL-MS-FT)
   Assign a violation for every word in which the final foot does not receive main stress

Although the workings of the analysis may not be obvious, these constraints in (18)–(19) combined with the three constraints we used in (16) can be ranked to create a grammar with only a single edge-aligned foot. Do you see how? Before reading on: take an input with four syllables (schematically /σ σ σ σ/) and play with the rankings of these five constraints, and try to work out how this grammar might be built. Here is a sort of hint: *you want the first foot to also be the last foot!*

***

The solution requires only two crucial rankings, shown in the tableau below:

(20) /σ σ σ σ/	FINAL-MS-FT	INITIAL-MS-FT	*UNFOOTED
a) ('σ σ) (ˌσ σ)	*!		
b) (ˌσ σ) ('σ σ)		*!	
☞ c) ('σ σ) σ σ			**
☞ d) σ σ ('σ σ)			**

In order to ensure that only one foot is built, both INITIAL-MSFOOT <u>and</u> FINAL-MSFOOT must be ranked above *UNFOOTED. As (20) illustrates, having both MS-FOOT constraints at the top of the ranking means that main stress must fall on both the first and last foot – and this is only achievable if there is only one foot![12]

---

[12] This method of creating non-iterative stress is not the most common one in the literature, but it avoids both some rather complicated constraints and some typological pitfalls – see especially McCarthy (2003).

Notice that this ranking will choose one foot as optimal, but won't choose the location of that foot – to choose Hungarian stress vs. Polish stress (20c vs. d), we need to choose a ranking of INITIALFOOT vs. FINALFOOT.

Exercise 1: As a quick check of your understanding thus far: here is a set of rankings which describe the stress pattern of a language we've already examined in this chapter. Which one?

(21) MAINSTRESS-INITIAL, *UNFOOTED >> MAINSTRESSFINAL
       INITIALFOOT >> FINALFOOT

Convince yourself of your answer by filling in the violations for each candidate in this tableau, and choosing the correct winner (answers at the chapter's end).

/σ σ σ σ σ σ/	INITIAL -MS-FT	INITIAL-FT	*UNFOOTED	FINAL -MS-FT	FINAL-FT
('σ σ) σ σ σ σ					
σ σ σ σ ('σ σ)					
('σ σ)(ˌσ σ) σ σ					
(ˌσ σ)(ˌσ σ)('σ σ)					
('σ σ)(ˌσ σ)(ˌσ σ)					

4.1.3 Analysing the Child's One-Trochee Stage

And now back to our regularly-scheduled programme: how to analyse the child one-trochee stage seen in Section 4.1.1, using the structural constraints on stress we have just built, and focusing just on the output word shape and not where the segments in that output come from.

To recast the data with our new terminology, we can say that children begin with a non-iterative stress system (since they only build one foot), as in the ranking we just saw in (21). However, clearly (21) is not the end of our foot-based analysis, because its winners do not look like our child data: the child strategy to satisfy structural constraints like INITIAL/FINAL-MSFOOT is not the same as the Hungarian or Polish target grammar. To illustrate, let's look back at the child versions of a target English word like *alligator*:

(22) | *alligator* | ['æg3],['æde] | ['æwe],['ægu] | ['ægi], ['ɑgi] |

In all of these productions, children truncated this word to one Sw foot, of the general format [æCV]; I have chosen one particular segmental version ['æwe] for concreteness:

(23)	/'ælɪˌgerɚ/	FINAL-MS-FT	INITIAL-MSFT	*UNFOOTED
	a) ('æ.we)(ˌge.rɚ)	*!		
	b) ('æ.we)ge.rɚ			*!*
	c) æ.we.ge.rɚ			*!***
☞	d) ('æ.we)			

This tableau reminds us that we should never take for granted the optimality of a candidate: given these constraints, *every* language with non-iterative stress should also be truncating to a single foot! The tableau in (21) looked good because we weren't considering candidates like (d). So what constraint marks the difference between the Polish and child methods of satisfying the two MS-FT constraints? The ranking of a faithfulness constraint we already know well – one that the child grammar is happy to violate, but the target grammar of for example Polish is not: MAX!

(24)	/'ælɪˌgerɚ/	FINAL-MS-FT	INITIAL-MSFT	*UNFOOTED	MAX
	a) ('æ.we)(ˌge.rɚ)	*!			
	b) ('æ.we)ge.rɚ			*!*	
	d) æ.we.ge.rɚ			*!***	
☞	d) ('æ.we)				****

The Polish grammar, on the other hand, ranks MAX >> *UNFOOTED SYLLABLE – so that while only one foot surfaces, the remaining syllables are unfooted, not deleted.

What about children's treatment of a different input like *giraffe?*

(25)	*giraffe*	[vɑ], [wɑ]	[dɛf], [ʔæf]	[wɑ]

What all these child optima have in common is a single heavy syllable, either [CV] with a tense nucleus or [CVC] – so this again looks like one foot, just a monosyllabic one. How does our constraint ranking fare at producing this output? Tableau (26) assesses, again using just one of the segmental options:

26)	/dʒɪˈɹæf/	FINAL-MSFT	INITIAL-MSFT	*UNFOOTED	MAX
	a) (ˌdʒi)(ˈʔæf)		*!		
	b) dʒɪ(ˈʔæf)			*!	
☞	c) (dʒɪˈ.ʔæf)				
☹	d) (ˈʔæf)				*!*

This tableau considers four possible candidates. The first just reminds us of the one-foot-only restriction; it turns the first syllable into something big enough to be its own foot, but the MS-FT constraints prohibit multiple feet. Remaining constraints prohibit deletion and leaving syllables without feet – but the winner that currently satisfies all constraints is (c), in which both syllables surface!

How then can (26d) win, when it is currently harmonically bounded by (26c)? (The sad face indicates the tragedy that (d) is the intended winner, but is not optimal according to the current grammar.) Both contain a single foot – but their foot *types* differ: (26c) begins with an unstressed syllable, while (26d) does not. By now you may see what pair of opposing constraints we have yet to propose that would choose between these two? ... Try writing a foot type constraint or two, to choose (26d) over (26c) and vice versa, before reading on.

***

The constraints we now need are those referring to the shape of each foot in the output: are they trochees or iambs? This again is a matter of preferences across languages: grammars typically choose one foot shape or the other, although there are many examples of somewhat 'mixed' languages (see Hayes, 1995). Thus, our grammars must include two constraints like those below, to be ranked in and around the others:

(27) TROCHEE:
    Assign a violation for every foot that begins with an unstressed syllable

(28) IAMB:
    Assign a violation for every foot that ends with an unstressed syllable

These constraints might be expected to contain a lot more detail, but for our purposes these will do well. An important note: we are assuming that in every possible output candidate, feet only ever include two weight-bearing units (in the terms defined in Chapter 1), so that all these foot type constraints need to do is monitor where stress falls within these proscribed limits.

With TROCHEE ranked high, we can now ensure that our child English grammar will select outputs with the right foot shape, and so *giraffe* gets truncated:

(29)	/dʒɪˈɹæf/	TROCHEE	*UNFOOTED	MAX
	a) dʒɪ(ˈʔæf)		*!	
	b) (dʒɪˈ.ʔæf)	*!		
☞	c) (ˈʔæf)			**

While high-ranking TROCHEE is clearly a crucial component of this grammar, where does IAMB fit in? In fact <u>none</u> of the candidates in (29) violate IAMB, since as it is defined in (28) it only prohibits bisyllabic (Sw) feet. To see where IAMB must be ranked, we need an input candidate where these two foot shape constraints are in direct competition. Look for example at the treatment of a /wSw/ input like *banana* in (30) below:

(30)	/bəˈnænɑ/	TROCHEE	*UNFOOTED	MAX	IAMB
	a) (bəˈnæ)	*!		**	
☞	b) (ˈnæ.nɑ)			**	*
	c) (ˈnæ)			***!*	

Candidates (a) and (b) both contain two of the input's three syllables and no unfooted syllables; it is the ranking TROCHEE >> IAMB that chooses between them. Candidate (c) provides the option of preserving just a monosyllabic foot (as in the winner for *giraffe*), thereby providing an optimal foot shape (for these constraints). Since the (Sw) winner keeps more syllabic material, but in doing so violates IAMB, we know that MAX>>IAMB.

We have now provided an initial account of the child one-trochee stage: all the crucial rankings are provided in (31):

(31) {INITIAL-MSFOOT, FINAL-MSFOOT, UNFOOTED} >> MAX
   TROCHEE >> MAX >> IAMB

Notice that we have no rankings here for INITIALFOOT or FINALFOOT – they were crucial to the adult stress typology we built, but in the child data we have seen, we cannot assess their position in the grammar. Why not? Make sure you see why before moving on.

Before adding to this account, let's take a crack at addressing the child stage that did <u>not</u> provide uniform evidence of single trochees, namely the Hebrew data excerpted in (32):

(32) | Excerpt of (6)'s Hebrew data (Adam and Bat-El, 2009) | | | | | |
|---|---|---|---|---|---|
| *Target* | *Child* | *Gloss* | *Target* | *Child* | *Gloss* |
| /'saf.ta/ | [ta.ta] | *grandma* | /ka'pit/ | [tik] | *spoon* |
| /'tu.ki/ | [kuki] | *parrot* | /bak'buk/ | [ba'bu], [buk], [bak'buk] | *bottle* |
| /ta.'puax/ | ['pu.ax] | *apple* | /mitri'ja/ | ['ti.ja]~ [ti.'ja] | *umbrella* |
| /ba'na. na/ | ['na.na] | *banana* | /aga'la/ | [i'gja] | *pram* |

The first issue in this data is that input stress matters in a way we have not seen before. The treatment of words with final stress means that the child's system must be variable in some way(s) – but in fact handling this variation is rather complicated. Notice that we don't want to build a grammar in which stress can freely fall on the last or second last syllables: if the grammar was underdetermined in that way, it would incorrectly predict that /Sw/ inputs (the lefthand column) should sometimes show stress shift to [wS]. Neither can we say that the input stress pattern always determines the surface stress – because that would incorrectly predict that /wS/ inputs (the righthand column) should never show stress shift.

Since this is a question of *input* stress predicting surface patterns, some of this pattern will require the use of *faithfulness* constraints on stress – which we will turn to in the next section. For now, we can at least determine the necessary rankings for the grammar that builds word-final iambs for Hebrew inputs with word-final stress. To figure them out: here is an <u>unranked</u> table of our constraints on word size and foot shape, and their violations for a three-syllable input with final stress. What rankings are necessary for candidate (a) to win?

(33) /mitri'ja/	TROCHEE	IAMB	*UNFOOTED	MAX
a) (tri'ja)	*			**
b) ('ja)				*****
c) mi(tri'ja)	*		*	

One way of figuring out the answer to this question (which will be central in Chapter 10) is to compare the intended winner (here, 33a) with each of the losing candidates in turn. For every constraint, we can ask: does this constraint prefer the intended *winner* (33a) or the *loser* – say (33b)?

This comparison is tabulated for candidates (a) vs. (b) in (34) below. First up, TROCHEE assigns a star to (33a) but not to (33b), so that means TROCHEE *prefers the Loser* and receives an 'L' in this table. In this same way: we can see that IAMB and *UNFOOTED prefer neither of the two forms (because they assign no stars to either) and finally MAX *prefers the Winner* (because it assigns (33a) only two stars but a full five stars to (33b). Thus we get the following comparison data:[13]

(34)	input	winner vs. loser	TROCHEE	IAMB	*UNFOOTED	MAX
	/mitri'ja/	(tri'ja) ~ (ja)	L			W

From this, we can immediately determine a ranking: if MAX prefers the Winner and TROCHEE prefers the Loser, we just need MAX >> TROCHEE to ensure that (tri'ja) will beat (ja)! To put this ranking into words: in this grammar it is more important to retain input segments than it is to build a trochee.

Performing the same pairwise calculations for (33a) vs (33c) we get the table below. Here it is *UNFOOTED that prefers the winner, because the loser has an unfooted syllable and the winner doesn't, while MAX prefers the fully-faithful loser:

(35)	input	winner vs. loser	TROCHEE	IAMB	*UNFOOTED	MAX
	/mitri'ja/	(tri'ja) ~ mi(tri'ja)			W	L

---

[13] In a format called an ERC vector; see Prince, 2002 and Chapter 10.

This provides another easy-to-interpret result: to prefer the winner over (33c), the grammar must rank *UNFOOTED>> MAX. Putting together the information from (34) and (35), we get the required rankings in this constraint set to map from/mitri'ja/to [(tri'ja)], and in general from /wwS/ to [(wS)]:

(36) *Fragment of the Iambic grammar*
      *UNFOOTED>> MAX >> TROCHEE

You will notice that this ranking actually doesn't specify where IAMB is ranked! … which might seem surprising, but remember that we are just trying here to account for the treatment of inputs with final stress, and none of our relevant candidates violate IAMB. (Recall that we needed a candidate like /wSw/ to argue for the ranking of TROCHEE vs. IAMB in English.) Bear in mind too that this fragment in (36) cannot be the full story, since we know that words with penultimate stress do choose surface with trochees. But this fuller account must be left for another textbook – and as for the additional variability which we have not accounted for, we will return to this particular data set in Chapter 5.7.

4.1.4   Adding Faithfulness into the Analysis

Returning now to the one-trochee stage: what's missing from our analysis? We've said a lot about the structural constraints on stress, but the biggest gap in the account thus far is an understanding of how <u>faithfulness</u> influences children's output word shapes. Child grammars are happy to delete segments to build a preferred output – but how to choose which segments are deleted? And what other unfaithful processes could be applied between input and output to satisfy these structural constraints?

In (30) we saw how English /wSw/ inputs are mapped to (Sw) and not (wS), but we did not consider different options for the syllables to make up that winning (Sw). Why not *[('bʌ.næ)], with a trochee built of the first two syllables instead?

The overall observation about faithfulness in early child English phonologies, exemplified in the data above, is that children are preferentially faithful to the <u>content and position of stress:</u> that is, they resist deleting stressed syllables, and they also resist shifting stress. In broad terms, this is a frequently observed preference across child languages: for example, Vigário et al. (2006) provide early snapshots of two children learning European

Portuguese who truncate to a single (S) or (Sw), always maintaining the input stressed syllable:

(37)

European Portuguese (Vigario et al., 2006)					
João (1;3–1;9)			Ines (1;1–1;4)		
Target	*Child*	*Gloss*	*Target*	*Child*	*Gloss*
/tiˈti/	[ti]	*Auntie*	/bɛˈbɛ/	[bi]	*baby*
/pɐˈpa/	[pa]	*(he/she)threw (it)*	/ʃɐˈpɛw/	[pɐ]	*hat*
/ɐˈki/	[ki]	*here*	/iˈneʃ/	[ne]	*Ines (name)*
/ˈpa.pɐ/	[pa]	*food*	/ˈmẽ̃ntɐ/	[mɐ]	*blanket*
/ˈpa.tu/	[pa]	*duck*	/ˈbaɾku/	[ba]	*boat*
/ˈbɔlɐ/	[u]	*ball*	/ˈmɔʃtɾɐ/	[mɔ]	*show me*

... at least, that's probably what the grammars in (37) are doing. In some cases, it is not exactly clear which syllable is being maintained (for example in the case of *ball* or *hat* above), but the overall pattern is robust. More of this ambiguity is found in the additional Portuguese examples below, followed by some similar Greek ones, where in both cases longer inputs are truncated to a single syllable or foot. Can you determine which bits of the input are preserved in the output?

(38)

Marta, learning European Portuguese (Vigario et al., 2006: 197)		
Target	*Child*	*Gloss*
/mɨˈninu/	[ˈmunu]	*boy*
/muˈr̃ẽguʃ/	[m̃ẽguʃ]	*strawberries*
/kɨˈridu/	[ˈkidu]	*dear*
/sɨˈnoɾɐ/	[ˈsoɾɐ]	*carrot*

(39)

Learning longer Greek words (Data from four children 1;11–2;05) (Revithiadou and Tzakosta, 2004)		
Target	*Child*	*Gloss*
/ɣliˈko/	[ɣo]	*sweet*
/portoˈkali /	[pa]	*orange*

Continued

Target	Child	Gloss
/kra'ta.o/	['ka.o]	*hold* (1st sg)
/pi.e'rotos/	['po.toθ]	*clown*
/friɣa'nula/	['fu.la]	*cracker* (dim.)
/ɣuru'naci/	['ɣa.ci]	*pig* (dim.)

In these data, surface stressed syllables match <u>none</u> of the input syllables perfectly. However, their material is still predictable: they contain the *rime* of the input stressed syllable (which in this case usually consists only of a vowel) and the *onset* of the initial syllable. You may have gleaned from Chapter 1 that stress is really assigned more to the *rime* of a syllable than anything else (recall that quantity-sensitive languages specifically care about weight within the rime, i.e. nucleus and/or coda, when building feet). Thus it is usually assumed that in examples like (38–39), the grammar is being faithful to the stressed syllable, in the form of the stressed rime, but that additional pressures conspire to replace its onset with another – for example that Greek /friɣa'nula/ in (39) surfaces with its last two input syllables, the stressed one and the last one, but that the stressed syllable's onset has been replaced by an earlier one: ['fu.la].[14]

From a rather different perspective, Lewis, Antone and Johnson (1999) also find considerable quantitative evidence of stressed syllable faithfulness in their longitudinal study of one North American English-learning child (see also Johnson, Antone and Hogan 1997). Between 1;0 and 1;6, this child's grammar reduced forms with only one stressed syllable /Sw/ and /wS/ to a monosyllabic output between 70–100% of the time, while bisyllabic inputs with two stressed syllables (e.g. *racoon*, or compounds like *goldfish)* were truncated only 30% of the time or less. The examples in (40) suggest again that truncation, when it occurred, preserved the stressed syllable's rime:[15]

(40)	Stressed syllable faithfulness (Data from Lewis, Antone and Johnson, 1999)			
	Target	Child	Target	Child
	shampoo	[pu]	*tummy*	[tʌm]
	hello	[ho]	*closet*	[kas]
	meow	[aʊ]	*heater*	[hi]
	bottle	[ba]		

---

[14] This pattern is discussed in detail in Section 4.3.

[15] See Lewis et al. (1999) and Johnson et al. (1997) for a somewhat different interpretation of these facts.

It is thus far clear that we need a constraint that preserves stressed rimes. Since it is about preservation, it must be some flavour of faithfulness constraint; the question is what type. Should we use a MAX constraint like (41)?

(41) MAX-STRESSEDRIME: (MAX-STRESSED)[16]
    Assign a violation for every stressed rime in the input which is deleted in the output

Will this constraint be enough to capture the preservation of stress patterns seen thus far? Not quite. Examine the tableau below, in which the three syllables of a /wSw/ input have been truncated to one bisyllabic trochee. The winner we expect to be optimal is (c) – but why is (b) just as good?

(42)

/bə'næ.nɑ/	MAX	MAX-STRESSED
a) ('bə.nɑ)	**	*!
☞ b) ('bə.næ)	**	
☞ c) ('næ.nɑ)	**	

To choose between (b) and (c), we need a constraint to prohibit not stressed syllable *deletion*, but stress *shift*. How might you define this constraint? Try inventing such a constraint before you read on (the details might not all work, but try to get the gist of it in place).

***

To build a constraint that prevents stress shift, we must first remember our representational choices made back in Chapter 1 about how stress is defined. The decision there was to treat stress as a feature – like [voice] or [labial] or any of the others. We will also assume that this stress feature is housed on the segment(s) in the nucleus of a stressed rime.[17]

With this idea of stress in mind, what we need to rule out (42b) is a faithfulness constraint that compares input and output versions of each segment and requires that they *match* for the 'feature' stress – that is either they are both stressed or both unstressed. Such constraints that require featural matching are known in the OT literature as IDENTITY or IDENT constraints, and they will figure prominently in Chapter 5–6's study of segmental patterns.

---

[16] For arguments that support this kind of faithfulness, see Nelson (2000), also Curtin (1999).

[17] This is a rather old idea about how stress works (see Chomsky and Halle, 1968) but it will do for now.

(43) IDENT-[STRESS]

Assign a violation for every input segment[18] whose value for the feature [stress] does not match its output segment's value.

With IDENT-[STRESS], our grammar can now prevent both stress deletion and stress shift:

(44)

/bə'nænɑ/	MAX	MAX-STRESSED	IDENT-[STRESS]
a) ('bə.nɑ)	**	*!	*!
b) ('bə.næ)	**		*!*
☞ c) ('næ.nɑ)	**		

Candidate (a) violates IDENT[STRESS] because the first rime is unstressed in the input and stressed in the output; candidate (b) incurs <u>two</u> violations, because both rimes have switched their input stress values. Notice, however, that IDENT-STRESS seems to have subsumed MAX-STRESSED: (44c) can be ruled out using IDENT[STRESS] alone ... So can we throw out MAX-STRESSED and use IDENT[STRESS] instead? Will this always work? Stay tuned.

Now that we have at least one, maybe two constraints, for retaining a stressed syllable as the S of a (Sw) foot, which constraints decide what is preserved as the weak syllable? For inputs where stress is penultimate, we have seen the last two syllables consistently retained (note again those Greek examples). Perhaps this seems like the only option, as if there is only one syllable following the strong one, you keep it! ... and we will continue with this assumption, that is that the underlying order of input syllables is not altered in the output candidates. But what about forms like *elephant* and *alligator*? If the input stress is followed by multiple additional syllables (with no stress, or perhaps secondary stress), there are multiple options to choose as an output weak syllables. We saw a fair amount of variation in this regard in the various pronunciations for 'alligator' in (22) and giraffe in (25) – but one fairly common pattern is seen in these three-syllable words:

(45)

English: Kehoe and Stoel-Gammon (1997)					
Target	*Child*	*Age*	*Target*	*Child*	*Age*
animal	['æmɑ]	1;10	Pinocchio /pə'no.kjo/	['nekwo]	2;3
elephant	['ɛfɪt]	2;4	binoculars	['nɑkjɚz]	2;3

Continued

---

[18] We might assume that stress can only appear by definition on a nucleus, in which case this definition would talk about 'every nuclear segment'.

Target	Child	Age	Target	Child	Age
	[ˈɑfɪn]	1;10	*rhinoceros*	[ˈnɑsɹɪs]	2;3
octopus	[ˈɑbʌs]	1;10	*hippopotamus*	[ˈpɑmɪs]	2;3

The pattern here is to choose the *final* syllable as the weak one, which we will begin to indicate with indices: $/S_1w_2w_3/$ → (S_1w_3).

This preference for maintaining final over non-final syllables seems well-supported in a variety of child language studies.[19] For example, Echols and Newport (1992) report the results of a detailed corpus study from three children (ages 1;5–1;11), which investigated independently the influence of stress and word position in children's truncations. To focus just on the cases of unstressed syllables in longer words (three syllables or more, like the words in 45), Echols and Newport found that 55% of the 112 medial weak syllables were deleted (as in $/S_1w_2w_3/$ → (S_1w_3) where the medial unstressed w2 is gone) whereas only 10% of the 55 final weak syllables (like w3) were lost. Similar evidence, experimental and anecdotal, is collected variously in Blasdell and Jensen (1970) and Echols (1993), as well as in MacWhinney (1985) on Hungarian and Ota (2001) on Japanese.

We can thus tentatively adopt the following constraint:

(46) MAX-FINALRIME (MAX-FINAL):
Assign a violation for every last rime in the input that is not preserved in the output.

(47)

/ˈæ.nɪ.mət /	MAX	IDENT-STRESS	MAX-FINAL[20]
a) (ˈænɪ)	***		*!
☞ b) (ˈæ.mɑ)	***		

---

[19] Although it is worth noting that some experimental works cited in support of final syllable preservation were strictly speaking designed to address whether learners were better at *perceiving* final syllables in novel words, rather than whether they were preferred in production; see also Section 4.3.

[20] A different view, however, might be that it is often unclear whether final rimes are really being retained in data like (45) – because in addition to being word-medial rather than final, the truncated syllables almost always have schwa as their nucleus. This might mean that final syllables are being interpreted as bearing secondary stress – so that inputs like *elephant* are really /Sws/. Under this view, MAX-STRESS would in fact be crucial, because both input stressed syllables are being retained, but the surface <u>weak</u> syllable was in fact <u>stressed</u> in the input, so its preservation could not be explained by IDENT[STRESS].

To look for other evidence of truncation driven by input stress and/or word-final position, let us look at representative data from two children D and M acquiring Dutch, reported in Wijnen et al. (1994). The table in (48) provides examples of these children's dominant treatment for three kinds of inputs, which are all truncated to a single (Sw) trochee. Can you predict the three output patterns? And are MAX-STRESSED or IDENT-STRESS enough to do so? Think especially about how the output weak syllable is chosen:

(48)

		Dutch truncation at 1;10–2;4: (Wijnen et al., 1994: 71, 73)		
	Target		*Child*	*Gloss*
a)	/ˈSww/	/ˈɑndərə/	[ˈɑn‚ʀə], [ˈɑn‚də]	*other*
		/ˈpɔpəcjə/	[ˈpɔ‚pə].	*doll*
		/ˈjɑnəkə/	[ˈzɑŋ.kə]	*(name)*
b)	/ˈSw‚s/	/ˈsikə‚hʌys/	[ˈsik‚hʌys]	*hospital*
		/ˈkɑŋxu‚ru/	[ˈkɑx.ru]	*kangaroo*
	/ˈS‚sw/	/ˈfʀɑxt‚ɑuto/	[ˈfʀɑ‚xɑu]	*truck*
		/ˈnøːs.‚hɔrən/	[ˈnøːs.‚hɔːr]	*rhinoceros*
c)	/‚sˈSw/	/‚kɑsˈtɑnjə/	[ˈtɑ‚nə]	*chestnut*
		/‚pɑnˈtɔfəl/	[ˈtɔ‚fət]	*slipper*
		/‚ʃiˈrɑfə/	[ˈsɑ‚fə]	*giraffes*

In (48a), the weak syllable could be either w2 or w3 – hard to tell, given that they are both always schwa, but certainly the onset can be taken from either syllable. In (48b), the inputs have an initial primary stress, and a secondary stress later in the word, and the outputs retain both stressed syllables, regardless of whether they are input-final or not. Thus /Ssw/ words like *truck* and *rhinoceros* keep their medial syllable, because it is stressed in the input. But in (48c), the preservation of all stressed syllables fails – the initial syllable receives secondary stress, but in the output that syllable has been deleted, while the final stressless one survives. Why? What constraint prefers mapping /‚kɑsˈtɑnjə/ → [ˈtɑ‚nə] and not [(ˈkɑs.tɑn)]? Try to invent one now for yourself – it will be a variation on a constraint you've already seen; and the answer will appear before the chapter is through.

4.1.5   Minimal Word Shapes

We have now seen many datasets where the one-foot stage imposes a maximality restriction on inputs. As it turns out, grammars that restrict outputs to a single foot can also impose a *minimality* restriction. How so? Well, it depends on how much the grammar needs to build a foot.

As you now know well, feet are *binary* groupings of phonological structure. Their binarity is obvious when they include two syllables; in the monosyllabic cases a syllable's rime can provide this binarity if it contains two *heavy* or 'weight-bearing' segments, and languages differ as to which segments can contribute weight to the nucleus (and sometimes coda) within the rime.

In English, we've seen that tense vowels (*bee*) or lax vowels plus coda consonants (*bit*) are enough to make a monosyllable heavy and thus footable as a word. Other languages, however, are not so flexible as to minimal word size. One example comes from the Muskogean language Choctaw spoken in Mississippi and other southeastern US states, shown in (49) below. The verbs in (a) are shown with and without a prefix; what is different about the stems in (b)?

(49)

		Choctaw (Nicklas, 1974; Lombardi and McCarthy 1991: 46–47)		
		Stem form	*/iʃ-/ prefixed form*	*Gloss*
a)		[ani]	[iʃani]	*(for you) to fill*
		[ona]	[iʃona]	*(for you) to arrive*
		[iʃi]	[iʃiʃi]	*(for you) to fill*
b)		[abi]	[iʃbi]	*(for you) to kill*
		[apa]	[iʃpa]	*(for you) to eat*
		[amo]	[iʃmo]	*(for you) to gather*
		[ala]	[iʃla]	*(for you) to arrive*

As Nicklas (1974: 63–64) observes, the stems in (49a) can begin with any vowel, and that vowel remains when prefixed, but those stems in (49b) all begin only with [a], and that [a] is missing under prefixation. These two observations suggest that it is the grammar, rather than the inputs, that are responsible for the word-initial [a]s in (49b) – that is, some structural constraint prefers that inputs like /bi/, /pa/ and so on be mapped to [abi], [apa] and so on. Notice too that all the (49b) stems are one syllable long. Altogether, this suggests that the problem with [bi] is that it contains only one weight-bearing unit, and so isn't big enough to make a foot. The English [tense/lax] distinction is not part of the Choctaw grammar, so these CV forms have only one segment in their rime – and thus the grammar augments these sub-minimal inputs by adding an initial vowel.

Before analysing the Choctaw pattern, we will look at a different example from Berbice Dutch Creole, a language once spoken in Guyana. In (50a), we see the language's regular pattern of optional stem-final vowel deletion. If this vowel deletion process would result in a voiced obstruent coda as in (50b), roots can lose <u>two</u> final segments. But in (50c), final vowel deletion is blocked: what's blocking it?

(50)		Berbice Dutch Creole (Kouwenberg, 1994; Dow, 2013)				
	a)	plɛkɛ ~ plɛk	*place*	b)	fɪndɪ ~ fɪn	*find*
		koro ~ kor	*descend, fall*		tambu ~ tam	*pound in mortar*
		jefi ~ jef	*eat*		maŋgi ~ maŋ	*run*
				c)	kiba, *ki	*short*
					redi, *re	*ready*
					fragi, *fra	*ask*

As with Choctaw, the fact that vowel deletion cannot apply in (50c) prevents words from getting as small as [CV]. In this case, it appears that the need to build at least one foot outranks whatever constraint(s) cause the final deletion process (which we will not analyse here[21]).

In both of these languages, what structural pressure prevents a CV syllable from being parsed into a foot? Up until now we were simply preventing the grammar from building such candidates, but now let us build such a constraint on single light syllables making feet on their own, defined for our purposes in (51).

(51) FOOTBINARITY (FTBIN)
    Assign a violation for every foot which does not contain at least two weight-bearing units

In Choctaw, FOOTBINARITY conspires with *UNFOOTED (and other pressures ignored here) to drive epenthesis into subminimal roots, violating DEP as in (52).

(52)		/bi/	*UNFOOTED	FTBIN	DEP
	a)	bi	*!		
	b)	(bi)		*!	
☞	c)	(abi)			*

---

[21] For a similar final deletion process and its analysis, see Wilkinson (1988) on Lardil.

Evidence that child grammars are similarly concerned with minimal word requirements come from a couple different sources. One is a case where deletion is prevented (as in Berbice Dutch Creole) reported at the early English one-syllable stage. Kehoe and Stoel-Gammon (2001) and Demuth, Culbertson and Alter (2006) both found that English-learning children were more likely to produce a monosyllable's coda if its nucleus contained a *lax* vowel – as hypothetical examples, this meant they were more likely to maintain the coda of *bit* than that of *beet*. If we assume that these children have already determined that a tense vowel bears two units of weight on its own, this pattern is just like (52): the constraints that insist on footable outputs outrank NoCoda and so block deletion:

(53)		/bɪt/	*Unfooted	FtBin	NoCoda	Max
	a)	bɪ	*!			*
	b)	(bɪ)		*!		*
☞	c)	(bɪt)			*	

What is striking about this blocking pattern is that vowel quality was connected to coda deletion rates only in monosyllables – that is, the word-final coda of a disyllabic input was no more likely to be preserved if it contained a lax vowel rather than a tense one.[22] This makes a strong case for the approach in (53): because an input with two syllables as in (54) is big enough to build a foot <u>with or without its coda</u>, so the top-ranked constraints are satisfied either way and NoCoda gets to choose deletion:

(54)		/ˈpʌpɪt/	*Unfooted	FtBin	NoCoda	Max
	a)	(ˈpʌ.pɪt)			*!	
☞	b)	(ˈpʌ.pɪ)				*

The second example of children's minimal words is a case of triggering (as in Choctaw), coming from Rose (2000)'s diary study of Quebec French as acquired by Clara, and as analysed in Goad and Buckley (2006). Unlike

---

[22] This was strictly true for three of four reported children; for one child, codas in polysyllables were more likely to survive after *tense* vowels, but the authors speculate that this may reflect that fact that more final tense vowels happened to occur later in the sample, that is when the children were older, and therefore when codas were overall more faithfully preserved.

English, French allows many lexical items to be smaller than a foot, only CV. However, other morphemes are frequently obligatory in a phrase, suggesting they play a role in filling the minimal word requirement: for example, French nouns require determiners or articles of some kind, so that while *lait* (milk) is on its own the subminimal word [lɛ], its full noun phrase must be for example *le lait* (the milk) or *du lait* (some milk), beefing up the phrase to two syllables.

The influence of minimal word status on Clara's outputs is most obvious early on, at ages 1;3–1;5. During these months, Clara attempted 28 subminimal lexical items (CV) of which only 7 were transcribed as [CV]. The rest either showed vowel lengthening of some sort (e.g./nɔ̃/→ [nɔʊ], 'no'; /wi/ → [wiː], 'yes') or epenthesis of a pretonic syllable (/wi/ → [əˈɥi], /gi/ → [əˈgi], *Guy (name)*). These data suggest that Clara's grammar, like that of Choctaw, requires every word to be at least a foot. As in the Choctaw tableau (52), the constraints driving this minimal word size outrank DEP, and so vowels are epenthesized. Beyond this example from French, other children are also reported to repair submininal words with lengthening of an existing vowel (see e.g. Stemberger, 1992 for English; and especially Ota, 1999, 2001 for Japanese).[23]

4.1.6   Universals, Tendencies and Early Word Shapes

As Chapter 3 already began to emphasize, Optimality Theoretic grammars are able to unify many disparate phenomena, helping linguists to find what is common among processes and unrelated languages. Thus, their explanations are necessarily cross-linguistic: an OT explanation of child English phonology must in some way be related to other learners and other languages – and so inevitably we turn to the questions of phonological universals. In this section, we will consider two possible universals in the acquisition of stress and word shape, to what extent they hold up empirically, and where they might lead us.

The first question is whether all learners, or learners of all languages, preserve stressed syllables above all others. While stress preservation appears to be very common among children learning completely or even semi-predictable stress languages like English,[24] there are still occasional examples

---

[23] There is some debate in the literature as to whether /CV/ → [CV:] is minimal word augmentation or a process of final lengthening that has nothing to do with feet. For arguments against the latter position see especially Goad and Buckley (2006).

[24] The acquisition of stress in fully lexical languages is, to my knowledge, very understudied.

of stress shift: Demuth, Culbertson and Alber (2006) report a few final stress words which were shifted to trochees by three of the four children in their study.[25] Recall also that we saw several stress shifts away from word-final Hebrew syllables and onto earlier syllables (Section 4.1.1). But might this be a fact about Hebrew and its ambient stress patterns?

As is discussed in detail by Adam and Bat-El (2009), Hebrew has a fair amount of morphologically-sensitive stress, including shifts from root to suffix within morphological paradigms. These stress alternations may cause additional difficulty and confusion for children, so perhaps this confusion causes some over-application of stress shift? A somewhat similar set of stress patterns are found in the target grammar of Spanish, where stress falls somewhere within the last three syllables of a word (as in Hebrew), according to fairly predictable phonological restrictions – but in Spanish, lexical class is also very crucial, so that the noun and verb systems differ on what is a regular or even possible stress pattern for a particular phonological form. For example, vowel-final Spanish nouns regularly receive penultimate stress ([ˈgato], *cat*), and so do all present tense verbs ([ˈha.blo], *I speak*), but the same vowel-final verbs in the past tense must receive final stress ([haˈblo], *I spoke*).

In both Hebrew and Spanish, then: learners may be receiving fairly conflicting evidence as to their target grammar's faithfulness to stress. Nevertheless, it seems that children learning these phonologies do not give up on generalization and simply mimic the correct adult stress. Instead, many such early grammars <u>do</u> attempt to impose phonological generalizations about word shape on their target words, both by restricting word size along the foot-based lines we've already seen, and also by shifting stress. In the case of Spanish, this shift may only become apparent once children begin to produce words with more infrequent stress patterns. Hochberg (1988) quotes Montes Giraldo (1971: 340) as reporting a 'well-known' anecdotal fact that children shift stress from the antepenult (rare) to the penult (much more common), with examples such as in (55):

(55)	Spanish stress shifts (data from Hochberg, 1988)					
	Target	*Child*	*Gloss*	*Target*	*Child*	*Gloss*
	/ˈkaskara/	[kaˈkala]	*(egg) shell*	/ˈfosforo/	[poˈpulo]	*match*
	/esˈtomago/	[toˈmago]	*stomach*	/hipoˈpotamo/	[popoˈtamo]	*hippo*
	/ˈlampara/	[pamˈpala]	*lamp*	/ˈplatano/	[taˈtano]	*banana*

[25] Cf. one child with a persistent word-final stress pattern, and possible atypical phonological development, in Kehoe (2000).

Hochberg (1988) also provides experimental evidence that three- to five-year-old learners are sensitive to the phonotactics as well as relative frequency of Spanish stress. When imitating novel words, children were more likely to make mistakes producing phonologically-illegal vs. legal stress patterns, and irregular (rare) vs. regular stress, and their mistakes showed a tendency to move towards regular and legal stress assignment.[26]

To summarize in broad terms, then, child grammars across languages show a strong preference for faithfulness to stressed syllables – but they also obey pressures to regularize stress according to structural constraints, sometimes at the expense of stress faithfulness. To actually construct a grammar that would impose Spanish stress shifts, however, requires two analytic elements we don't yet have. First we would need a mechanism for choosing antepenult stress in the first place: given our constraint set now there is no way to assign stress to the third last syllable of a word, as is the default in (55)! Second, we need a theory of how morphologically-sensitive phonology is represented, and how it can be that a stress pattern is grammatical for a noun but not a verb within a single language. These topics will be left for more advanced students of prosodic phonology and its acquisition (see further readings at the end of this chapter), although some of these morpho-phonological questions will begin to be addressed in Chapter 8.

The other potential universal at the earliest stages of children's prosodic grammar deals with foot type. It has been suggested in particular that learners are particularly biased to initially build not just a single foot per word, but a single trochee (Allen and Hawkins, 1978, 1980) – that trochees are preferred independent of the target language, though of course they will be outgrown over the course of development if the target is iambic.

In one sense it is now evident that this bias is not truly universal: that is, if the ambient language provides NO evidence of trochees (i.e being strictly stress-final) children's earliest speech does not insist on inventing them. For example, Pye (1983)'s study of children learning Quiché Mayan, a stress-final and morphologically-rich language, found that young children consistently truncated long words to their final, stressed syllable:[27]

---

[26] A different source of stress shift in early speech is suggested by Sónia Frota and colleagues for European Portuguese, a language which uses pitch accents as well as word stress, so that stress is marked predominantly by duration alone; these complications might initially mislead the learner – see for example Frota and Vigario (2008), Frota (2009).

[27] See Pye (1983) for quantitative details and much further discussion.

(56)	Child Quiché word-final stress (Pye, 1983)		
	Target	*Child*	*Gloss*
	/kinwiˈloh/	[loh]	*I like it*
	/kawaˈrik/	[lik]	*he's sleeping*
	/a: kasiˈpaj chuˈweh/	[paj weh]	*will you give it to me?*

A more complicated case is French, whose prosodic acquisition has been much discussed in recent literature. It is clear that stress only ever falls on the last syllable of French words – but it is a matter of some dispute whether stress is assigned via a right-edge iamb or something else.[28] At any rate, early French grammars certainly impose different restrictions than the English one-trochee pattern, although it is perhaps not known how the majority of French-learning children begin. Some children appear to begin by truncating to a monosyllable (Archibald and Carson, 2000), which would be consistent with both final stress and a possible trochee (cf. English monosyllables outputs for *giraffe* and *peekaboo*), while other children begin almost immediately with bisyllables (see Goad and Buckley, 2006). Wauquier and Yamaguchi (2013), while overtly arguing for a French prosodic analysis without iambs, still find that in French children's earliest forms '[a] size constraint on these word forms is clearly evident (they never exceed two vocalic nuclei)' (p. 326). (See Wauquier and Yamaguchi, 2013 for their analysis of how these syllables are chosen from the French 'accentual arc' and how word shape develops in later stages; see also Chapter 7.5.)

Perhaps more clear evidence of early French iambs can be seen in Goad and Buckley (2006)'s analysis of Clara's three-syllable inputs (data from Rose, 2000). Starting at 1;5 (when her attempts at three syllable inputs begin) until at least 1;10, Clara's corpus includes 20/36 forms truncated to two syllables, and only seven forms with a tri-syllabic parse:

(57)	Quebec French: Clara's iambs (Goad and Buckley, 2006; data from Rose, 2000)		
	Target	*Child*	*Gloss*
	/ladəˈdã/	[laˈðæː]	*in there*
	/abʁiˈko/	[kəˈko̩]	*apricot*

Continued

---

[28] It's also the case that some words in an utterance won't receive stress at all, because stress is assigned to the end of entire phonological *phrases* (see e.g. Fonagy, 1980; Jun and Fougeron, 2000).

Target	Child	Gloss
/papiˈjɔ̃/	[bəˈpɔ:]	*butterfly*
/pɑ̃taˈlɔ̃/	[bɔːˈjə]	*trousers*
/salɔˈpɛt/	[bəˈpʰɛ]	*overalls*
/klemɑ̃ˈtsɪn/	[mæˈtsi]	*clementine*
/ɛskaʁˈgo/	[kæˈko̞]	*snail*

In this regard, Demuth and Johnson (2003) find very similar evidence for iambs in French three syllable inputs (more on this child's development in Section 4.2.2):

(58)	European French: Suzanne between 1;4 and 1;7 (Demuth and Johnson 2003; data from Deville 1891)		
	Target	Child	Gloss
	/dɔmiˈno/	[ɔˈjɔ], [bɔˈjɔ]	*domino*
	/ɔmniˈbys/	[byˈby]	*omnibus*
	/pɔʁtmɔˈnɛ/	[meˈne]	*changepurse*
	/paʁaˈplɥi/	[aˈpi]	*umbrella*
	/ʁəgaʁˈde/	[daˈde]	*look!*

... The upshot is that if these French-acquiring children are building feet, they are clearly building iambs not trochees.

In a very different kind of study, Paradis (2001) also found evidence suggestive of iambic parsing among somewhat older children (ages 2;4–3;0) learning Quebec French. When these children were asked to imitate four-syllable nonce words, they overall preserved a word's final syllable 92% of the time, and its penultimate syllable 71% of the time; preserving either the first or second syllables was possible, but both were less likely and with no statistically-significant difference between them (37% and 45% preservation for first and second syllables respectively).

Overall, the evidence from languages such as French suggests that trochees are not a universal given in children's first grammar of prosody: with no evidence, the ranking TROCHEE >> IAMB will not appear in early speech (see also Vihman, DePaolis and Davis, 1998; Rose and Champdoizeau, 2008). However, a weaker version of the trochaic bias might be found in languages with more indeterminate target evidence of footing – and so we return, finally, to the Hebrew truncation data from Section 4.1.1.

What makes Hebrew different from both English and French is that roughly three quarters of Hebrew words in both child and adult speech are stressed word-finally: while this skews the numbers in the iambic direction, it still leaves a good number of words with stress on the second to last (or even third to last) syllables, which are more easily parsed as trochees. Adam and Bat-El (2009) argue that the earliest production patterns from Hebrew, in which penultimate stress inputs are truncated to [Sw] and final stress inputs are treated more variably as [S], [wS] and even [Sw], suggest that a trochaic bias is indeed at play. A different Hebrew-acquiring child (RM) from the same corpus also shows this bias. At ages 1;03.27–1;05.14, RM truncated words with final stress to <u>monosyllables</u> 75% of the time, but truncated the <u>two</u> relevant syllables of potential trochees (i.e. words with penultimate or antepenult stress) only 10.9% of the time (Albert and Zaidenberg, 2012: 170). In sum, it is possible that trochees are indeed preferred over iambs independent of the learner's evidence – but that this bias is weak enough only to emerge when the input (target) stress pattern is highly variable.

In any event, the universals or tendencies discussed in this section cannot yet be implemented in any formal way: we have only built tools to describe grammars that map inputs to outputs, but nothing connects a learner's particular ranking to the frequency or variability of inputs they have heard. These connections will need to be drawn eventually, and the evidence will slowly accumulate in subsequent chapters – but for now we just note their absence, and continue our tour of developmental stages.

4.2   Later Word Shapes

For learners of languages with many multisyllabic words, moving on from the one-foot stage means moving onto bigger and harder word shapes and prosodic possibilities. Bear in mind that progress through these later stages may be much more language-dependent than the one-foot stage, and much more cross-linguistic study will be necessary to flesh out this picture.

4.2.1   Bigger Words

Starting again with English, here are two children (aged 2;3 and 2;4) who have moved past the one-foot stage but have yet to master the full range of multisyllabic words. Can you describe their word shape restrictions using the constraints we have already seen? What previously-obeyed structural pressure has been relaxed?

(59)	English: two and three syllable words (Kehoe, 2000)		
	Target	*27m6*	*28f1*
	raccoon	[ˌɹæˈkun]	
	banana	[ˈbɑni]	[ˈnɛːnʌ]
	tomato	[ˈmedo]	[ˈmedo]

Continued

Target	27m6	28f1
elephant	[ˈɛlɪf]	[ˈɑfɪt]
dinosaur	[ˈdaɪnˌsɔ] [ˈdaɪnəˌsɔ]	[ˈdaɪnˌʃɔ] [ˈdaɪnəˌsɑ]
kangaroo	[ˈkæŋnoˌjɑ]	[ˈkɛŋəˌwu]

The clear output change in these data is that two feet are now possible, though syllable truncation is still found in many words.[29] What determines how many feet can surface? The key is the number of <u>stressed</u> syllables: those outputs with two feet all come from inputs with two stressed syllables: /sS/ (*racoon*), /Sws/ (*dinosaur*) and /swS/ (*kangaroo*). This suggests that MAX-STRESSED is now the high-ranking reason that two feet are now possible, and that it can outrank the MS-FOOT constraint that previously kept outputs so small. The following tableau illustrates such a mapping:

(60)	/ˈdaɪnəˌsɔɹ/	MAX-STRESSED	*UNFOOTED	MAX	FINAL-MS-FOOT	INITIAL-MS-FOOT
☞	(ˈdaɪ.nə)(ˌsɔ)				*	
	(ˈdaɪ.nə)sɔ		*!			
	(ˈdaɪn.sɔ)			*!		
	(ˈdaɪ.nə)	*!		***		

A tableau for *kangaroo* would look just as this one for *dinosaur*, except that it is INITIAL-MSFOOT, instead of FINAL, which is violated to maintain the input stress pattern /swS/.

The tableau in (60) above shows that MAX-STRESSED, *UNFOOTED and MAX all need to at least outrank the main-stress placement constraints – but why does MAX need to be ranked in the middle? To make sure that all longer words with only one stressed syllable still get uniformly truncated. This tableau for *banana* demonstrates that at least *UNFOOTED >> MAX[30]:

(61)	/bəˈnænʌ/	MAX-STRESSED	*UNFOOTED	MAX	FINAL-MS-FOOT	INITIAL-MS-FOOT
	bə(ˈnɛ:nʌ)		*!		*	
☞	(ˈnɛ:nʌ)			*		

---

[29] For another two-foot stage, see Fikkert (1994) on Dutch.

[30] Alternatively, it could be INITIAL FOOT and IDENT-STRESS, ranked above MAX, that keep deleting initial unstressed syllables; try it in a tableau.

Now what does this ranking predict for four-syllable words? Decide how a four-syllable input should be treated according to (60–61), and then see if the predictions are borne out in (62):

(62)	English: two and three syllable words (Kehoe, 2000)		
	alligator	[ˈæbɪˌgɛɾ]	[ˈædəˌgedɚ]
	helicopter	[ˈhɑˌkɑpɚ]	[ˈhɑpˌkɑpdɚ]
	avocado	[ˌɑˈkɑdo]	[ˈkɑdo],[ˌeˈkɑdo]

The generalization for these targets is still that the number of stressed syllables predicts the number of feet – with the exception of one production of *avocado*, the outputs are either (S)(Sw) or (Sw)(Sw).

One problem seen in both data sets, however, is understanding why (S)(Sw) is a possible version of these two-foot words: for example [ˈdaɪnˌsɔ] for *dinosaur* and [ˌɑˈkɑdo] for *avocado*. If two feet are tolerated, why not maintain every syllable? As it stands, our constraint set deems truncation of any weak syllable that can get into a foot as always suboptimal: the unranked constraints in (63) show how (S)(Sw) is harmonically bounded by the fully-faithful option:

(63)		/Swsw/	MAX-STRESSED	*UNFOOTED	MAX	FINAL-MS-FOOT	INITIAL-MS-FOOT
	☞ a)	(Sw)(sw)				*	
	☹ b)	(S)(sw)			*!	*	

The upshot of (63): either our constraint set is flawed, or this pattern is not the doing of prosodic constraints. Keep reading!

Moving from one foot to two is by no means the only next step towards larger words. Here is a different English pattern in (64); this child is only 1;10 but has already begun to produce outputs with more than two syllables. The pattern seems rather different than what we have seen thus far: some words are truncated from three syllables to one, yet a four-syllable output is also possible! So what is predictable here?

(64)	More English: 22m1 (Kehoe, 2000)			
	Target	*Child*	*Target*	*Child*
	banana	[ˈbɑdɪn]	*kangaroo*	[wuː], [huː]

Continued

Target	Child	Target	Child
elephant	[ˈaʔvɛn]	*chimpanzee*	[zɪːŋ]
telephone	[ˈkɛfʌm]³¹	*alligator*	[ˈhɛˌgedə] [ˈʔiˌgeɚ]
crocodile	[ˈdædʌ]	*helicopter*	[ˈaʔgədida]

What's systematic is not the output word shape, but the output stress placement, which in turn predicts truncation for each input stress pattern. Words like *kangaroo* and *chimpanzee* show what drives truncation: <u>the first syllable of the output must be the *main* stressed syllable of the input.</u>

Which of our existing structural constraints could conspire to create that pattern? The tableau below illustrates a couple crucial rankings, using a schematic version of an input like *chimpanzee*. Compared to the winner, the fully faithful output (65b) that keeps all three syllables must be ruled out because its main stress foot is not leftmost; the option of keeping those syllables unfooted is ruled out as usual by *UNFOOTED (65c).

(65)	/ˌswˈS/	INITIAL-MSFOOT	*UNFOOTED	MAX
☞	a) (S)			**
	b) (ˌsw)(ˈS)	*!		
	c) ww(ˈS)		*!	

Why not produce *chimpanzee* with all three input syllables and main stress on the first foot with the pattern [(Sw)(s)]? Looking at the rest of the data set in (64), the problem with [(Sw)(s)] can't be a word-maximality effect, because three- and four-syllable outputs are possible – and underlyingly /Sws/ words at least keep two syllables (*telephone* and *elephant*).

Instead, the truncation of *chimpanzee* must be a stress <u>faithfulness</u> effect: input <u>main</u> stress is preserved as output main stress. A way of analysing this is to (re)define IDENT-STRESS so that it is assessing two kinds of rimes: those with main stress, and all others (secondary or no stress), and it is this dichotomy that the child's grammar preserves:

(66) IDENT-MAINSTRESS

Assign a violation for every input segment whose value for the feature [main-stress] does not match its output segment's value.

---

³¹ This child also produced *telephone* with two strong syllables [ˈɛˈbʌn], which will not be analysed here.

With that definition, we can derive the radical truncation of *chimpanzee* (67) and also the survival of a second foot to the right main stress, meaning that FINAL-MSFOOT is lowly ranked (68). Notice too that IDENT-MAINSTRESS provides a solution to the unresolved Dutch truncation pattern from (48c)!

(67)

		/ˌswˈS/ (like *chimpanzee* in 64)	IDENT-MAINSTRESS	MAX
☞	a)	(S)		**
	b)	(ˈSw)(ˌs)	*!*	

(68)

		/ˈSwˌsw/ (like *alligator* in 64)	MAX	FINAL-MSFOOT
	a)	(Sw)	*!*	
☞	b)	(ˈS)(ˌsw)	*	*

So far so good – but this analysis remains incomplete, similar to the previous discussion of the two-foot stage. Where has *alligator*'s medial weak syllable gone? And where, for that matter, is the middle syllable of /Sws/ words like *elephant* and *telephone*? ... For more on this data set, see exercise 2 at the end of chapter.

Here is a somewhat similar pattern, from child 2 at 2;4 learning Mohawk (Mithun, 1989), who was more advanced in her prosodic acquisition compared to the child reported in Section 4.1.1. Mohawk is a highly polysynthetic language: its words are typically several syllables long, with fairly opaque morphological structure and many suppletive forms. Its word stress is fairly consistently penultimate (and marked with either high or low accent), though epenthesis into underlying consonant clusters sometimes results in antepenultimate stress (Michelson, 1988; Piggott 1995). Mithun (1989) notes that this child had yet to demonstrate any morphological sensitivity to the structure of Mohawk words, but her outputs did vary in size according to the position of word stress in the input:

(69)

		Mohawk data from child 2 (Mithun, 1989)		
	a)	*Target*	*Child*	*Gloss*
		/satá:ti/	[tá:ti]	*talk!*
		/nahò:ten/	[hò:ten]	*what?*
	b)	/sewahió:wane?/	[ió:wana]	*apple*
		/wákeras/	[wáest]	*it stinks*
		/éntene?/	[énte?ne?]	*let's go*

The commonality between these two patterns is that whichever input syllable is stressed begins the output word – INITIALFOOT plus IDENT-STRESS and MAXSTRESSED – which combined with the final syllable provide a disyllabic foot. With respect to the post-stress syllables, Mithun reports that 'when stress was antepenultimate, [the child's] words consisted of the stressed syllable plus one or both of the following syllables,' so the role of faithfulness and of unfooted syllables (since Mohawk is not reported to have any secondary stress) cannot be resolved.

A third pattern for building beyond the one-foot stage is well-documented in Romance languages like Spanish. Rather than building rightwards from the main stress syllable, learners of Spanish often achieve larger words by adding one pre-stress syllable (see Lléo, 1997, 2001, 2002):

(70)		Spanish (data here from Lléo, 2002)		
		Target	*Child*	*Gloss*
a)		/ko'nexo/	[ko'nexo]	*rabbit*
b)		/ˌmari'posa/	[ma'posa]	*butterfly*

These pre-tonic syllables are much more prevalent in Spanish than in the acquisition of English and other Germanic languages (see Lléo, 2002 specifically comparing Spanish and German) – and moreover they are clearly acquired very early. Data in Lléo (2002) show that for three children aged only 1;3–1;6, between 61% and 78% of unfooted syllables were already being preserved in outputs, and given facts of target Spanish stress these were overwhelmingly word-initial.

How to analyse this pattern? The first thing to note is that finally we have evidence of some pressure outranking *UNFOOTED. While words can't get too big yet – only one foot per word, still – MAX now permits an additional syllable to survive:

(71)		/ko'nexo/	MAX	*UNFOOTED
a)	☞	ko('nexo)		*
b)		('nexo)	*!	

When facing a (sw)(Sw) word like *mariposa*, though (70b) – how does the grammar work? Several of the pieces are put together in the tableau in (72) below. Two feet are still too much, so the two MAINSTRESSFOOT constraints still outrank MAX (72b). The fact that the unstressed syllable survives before rather than after the output foot could have different explanations. A likely option is that it's IDENT-MAINSTRESS again (72c) – recall that this constraint as defined in (66) is only violated when *main* stress shifts, so that losing the secondary stress on [ma] is not a violation:

(72)

		/ˌmariˈposa/	INITIAL-MSFOOT	MAX	*UNFOOTED	IDENT-MAINSTRESS
	a)	(ˈposa)		***!*		
	b)	(ˌmari) (ˈposa)	*!			
	c)	(ˈmari)po		**	*	*!
☞	d)	ma(ˈposa)		**	*	

There remain at least a couple of other candidates which need to be ruled out. One is [ri(ˈposa)] – how does the grammar choose which unstressed syllable to keep? Or why not keep all the segments and leave two unfooted syllables? Compared to the winner in (72), these candidates do exactly as well *or better*:

(73)

		/ˌmariˈposa/	INITIAL-MSFOOT	MAX	*UNFOOTED	IDENT-MAINSTRESS
☞	a)	ri(ˈposa)		*!*	*	
☹	b)	mari(ˈposa)		**		
	(72d)	ma(ˈposa)		*!*	*	

You may already have a guess about (73a), involving a more articulated story of stress faithfulness, but this further analysis (as the horrible saying goes) is left as an exercise to the reader.[32]

The next section looks at two other strategies that children use to get more input material into surface forms – and its echoes of adult target language phonologies, too.

4.2.2 Other Attempts at Bigger Words

In Chapter 3, we looked at several children's production of English consonant clusters, including those by G around age two. Here, we will turn to a

---

[32] For part of the story, see the OT analyses in Lléo (2002).

different aspect of G's early phonology: her unusual (but not unique) method of producing pretonic syllables. Before reading past (74), come up with a generalization about G's treatment of these /wS/ and /wSw/ words: in particular, is this grammar faithful to the initial weak syllable?

(74)	More from G: Gnanadesikan (2004)			
	Child	*Target*	*Child*	*Target*
	fiˈbejə	*umbrella*	fiˈbun	*balloon*
	fiˈgido	*mosquito*	fiˈpis	*police*
	fiˈdinə	*Christina*	fiˈbo	*below*
	fiˈvaɪzə	*advisor*	fiˈbɛt	*barrette*
	fiˈtenə	*container*	fiˈmɑwo	*tomorrow*
	fiˈgɛɾi	*spaghetti*	fiˈteɾo	*potato*
	fiˈbɛkə	*Rebecca*	fiˈmon	*Simone*
	fiˈwaɪn	*rewind*		

The answer is: sort of. G's outputs are faithful in some sense to the <u>existence</u> of an input weak syllable; in syllable count terms, her productions are [wSw] and [wS] as the adult forms would be, looking as though she has reached the grammatical stage of the Spanish-acquiring children from the previous section. But G is very unfaithful to initial weak syllables in another way: that is, she does not maintain any of their segmental content, replacing all of their segments with the syllable [fi].[33]

While it may be surprising – *fi? where'd she get fi?* – this pattern of G's is not unheard of. The child Amahl in Smith (1973)'s famous longitudinal study also used a similar strategy of replacing initial unstressed syllables: interestingly, his replacement segments of choice were [ɹi]. And in various different accounts of child speech, researchers have often noted *dummy* or *filler* syllables that seem to take the place of an input's segmental material – holding its spot in the word, somehow (or sometimes holding the spot *of* a word).[34]

---

[33] G is also occasionally unfaithful to the onset of the stressed syllable too, as in *barette*, *police* and *balloon*. On which see Section 4.3

[34] For more English examples and analyses, see for example Peters (1977, 2001); Peters and Menn (1993). Dutch fillers are also discussed in depth by Taelman, Durieux and Gillis. (2009); see also Veneziano and Sinclair (2000) for French; Albert and Zaidenberg (2012) on Hebrew; Aksu-koc and Slobin (1985) on Turkish.

To what extent is such a process attested in adult languages? Dummy syllables, or at least dummy segments, are found in a number of adult grammars – although somewhat confusingly, they are typically observed as part of reduplication. One example comes from a morphological process called 'echo reduplication' in many Dravidian languages, which can be glossed as meaning something similar to '[base] *and the like'*. Some representative examples (across many different lexical categories) are given below from Kannada (a Dravidian language native to several different parts of India). What is the dummy material here?[35]

(75)

Kannada Echo Reduplication (Data collected in Lidz, 2001)		
Base	*Reduplicated*	*Gloss (reduplicated gloss)*
[pustaka]	[pustaka-gistaka]	*books (and related stuff)*
[wo:da]	[wo:da-gi:da]	*run (and related activities)*
[doɖɖa]	[doɖɖa-giɖɖa]	*large (and the like)*
[me:le]	[me:le-gi:le]	*above (and the like)*
[ba:gil]	[ba:gil-gi:gil]	*the door (and related things)*

The invariant segments of Kannada's echo reduplication are [gi-], and it appears they must be overwritten with [g] as onset and [i] as nucleus, at the left edge of the reduplicant. In fact, English also provides an example of this *fixed segmentalism* (as it is often called, see Alderete et al., 1999). The English dummy segments appear in the slightly complicated process that marks what Rice (2006) calls the 'ridiculative mood':

(76)

Examples of the English overwriting reduplication (see especially Nevins and Vaux, 2003)
'Breakfast <u>shmreakfast</u>, look at the score for God's sake. It's only the second period and I'm winning twelve to two'.   *– explanation provided by a character in the movie Mallrats (1995) to his girlfriend as to why he cannot abandon a video game that he's winning.*
'Oedipus, <u>Schmoedipus</u>! What does it matter, so long as he loves his mother?'   *– punchline of an old unattributable joke*

---

[35] Most of the account provided here owes much to Gnanadesikan (2004)'s original analysis of G's 'fi' pattern, and her comparison to a very similar echo reduplication in another Dravidian language, Kolami (Emeneau, 1955; McCarthy and Prince, 1986).

Here the fixed segment is just an onset cluster – [ʃm], an onset otherwise unheard-of in English – which again must be leftmost, overwriting the reduplicant's underlying onset.[36]

Putting aside the complicating factor of reduplication, there is considerable similarity between the Kannada and English target patterns and children's dummy syllable patterns. The common core is that their inputs include some additional material, which competes with segments in a lexical entry for a spot in the output.

To see how this works more clearly in adult languages we will use one more target data pattern, a famous Japanese process called *rendaku*.[37] When two roots are made into a compound, the first segment of the second compound changes featurally – but in what way?

(77)

Japanese rendaku in compounding		
Roots	*Compound*	*Gloss*
/toki-toki/	[toki**d**oki]	*time-time/sometimes*
/jama-tera/	[jama**d**era]	*mountain-temple/*
/te-kami/	[te**g**ami]	*hand-paper/letter*
/ori-kami/	[ori**g**ami]	*fold-paper/paperfolding*
/hira-kana/	[hira**g**ana]	*plain-character/(name of an alphabet)*
/hana-tʃi/	[hana**dʒ**i]	*nose-blood/nosebleed*
/maki-suʃi/	[maki**z**uʃi]	*roll-sushi /nori-wrapped sushi*
/kokoro-tsukai/	[kokoro**dz**ukai]	*heart-using/courtesy*

The change is one of *voicing*: all of the second roots begin with a voiceless obstruents, and when compounded they turn into their voiced counterparts. This change in voicing only happens when two morphemes are brought together to make a compound – so, similar to the Kannada and English cases, it is a particular morphological environment that brings this additional floating [+voice] feature into the input:

(78) Input for 'origami':   /ori-kami, {[+voice]}/

The crucial fact for us is that this floating feature needs somewhere to attach to, a segment on which it can be heard and pronounced – and in *rendaku*, it competes for a spot with the underlying [-voice] feature on the left

---

[36] Although note that in *shmreakfast,* the onset cluster contains the second half of the original base's cluster /br/; for this and many other details, see Nevins and Vaux (2003) and references therein.

[37] For readers who are getting suspicious of this textbook's use of 'famous' – it's famous among phonologists, trust me.

edge of the second root, like the /k/ in *kami*. Since the floating feature wins out, there must be a faithfulness constraint that protects such features. Many definitions of this constraint exist in the literature, but here is a simple one:

(79) MAX-FLOAT (adapted from Wolf, 2005):
Assign a violation for every floating feature in the input that is not attached to a segment in the output

To bring about rendaku, the Japanese grammar must rank MAX-FLOAT above the normal faithfulness constraint that controls regular input/output matches in voicing. This again will be the job of IDENT constraints, like the ones we have seen for stress already, but regulating <u>segmental</u> features too – we will wait to define and flesh out these constraints much more in Chapter 5. The tableau in (80) just sketches the very basics of the analysis:[38]

(80)		/ori-**k**ami, {[+voice]}/	MAX-FLOAT	IDENT-VOICE
	a)	ori-**k**ami	*!	
	b)	ori-**g**ami | [+voice]		*

To finally return to G's dummy syllables: we can now understand overwriting as a similar competition between '*fi*' and the rest of a target word's segmental input. In both cases, the broad reason for this competition is that faithfulness constraints want the grammar to keep corresponding phonological units – such as inputs and outputs – the same size as each other. In Japanese, size is counted in segments: DEP prevents the grammar from adding any new segments into *kami* to house this floating [+voice] feature, so it is forced to overwrite the voicing of some underlying segment like /k/.

The leap from *rendaku* to G's overwriting grammar is to now measure size in terms of <u>syllables</u>: this competition in G's grammar is enforced by versions of familiar faith constraints like DEP, but which hold of syllables[39]:

(81) DEP-σ
Assign a violation for every syllable in the output that is not in the input

---

[38] For much more detail on rendaku and its analysis see e.g. Ito and Mester (1986), Kubuzono (2005) and many references therein.

[39] Although the details of the analysis used here are different than those usually assumed for adult overwriting in reduplication, they share fundamental insights. In the target English and Kannada cases, faithfulness constraints like MAX and DEP hold not between inputs and outputs, but between bases and their reduplicants. For the real beginning of this story, see McCarthy and Prince (1995).

These constraints require that if an input like *advisor* has three syllables, its output will also have three syllables. And if (crucially) floating segments like *fi* <u>are not syllabified</u>, the only way they will surface in *advisor*'s output is if they are fit somewhere into the input's original three. (This approach does, crucially, require that G has syllabification in her inputs, which we explicitly avoided in Chapter 3. We'll get back to this at the end of the section.)

But where does *fi* come from?? The idea behind *fi* as floating segments is that they are G's preferred filler; rather than coming with morphological meaning, they are simply always a part of her underlying forms, providing a default CV to fill in segmental gaps – though only when constraint interaction in her grammar allows. This last point means that MAX-FLOAT is outranked by various other constraints: for example, MAX-STRESSED ensures that *fi* can't overwrite input stressed syllables.

To simplify the illustration of this idea a little, the following tableau uses syllables rather than segments in the input – along with the <u>output</u> syllable hooked up to the floating segments, indicated as σ_{fi} – to show how overwriting comes about. We will also assume that /fi/ has already been determined to be a prefix (like Japanese [+voice] or English /ʃm/) and so the grammar is only considering candidate where /fi/ overwrites at the left edge of the base or else nowhere (for constraints that do this work, see especially Alderete et al., 1999). As you examine this tableau's candidates, <u>do not panic!</u> – each loser is considered below, and compared with the winner:

(82)		/{fi} $\sigma_1'\sigma_2\sigma_3$ /	DEP-σ	MAX-STRESSED	MAX-FLOAT	*UNFOOTED
	a)	$\sigma_{fi}\,\sigma_1('\sigma_2\,\sigma_3)$	*!			**
	b)	$\sigma_1\,('\sigma_2\,\sigma_3)$			*!	*
☞	c)	$\sigma_{fi}('\sigma_2\,\sigma_3)$				*
	d)	$('\sigma_2\,\sigma_3)$			*!	

Candidate (a) is faithful to all three input syllables, <u>plus</u> the floating 'fi', so it is ruled out by DEP-σ for having one extra syllable compared to the input. Candidate (b) simply saves the lexical item's three syllables *advisor*, and so is ruled out by MAX-FLOAT – it is identical to the winner (c) except that it deletes a more prized set of segments, namely the floating ones. Candidate (d) is the normal truncation candidate, previously optimal at the one-foot stage – but in this grammar MAX-FLOAT outranks *UNFOOTED, so truncation to maximize footing is ruled out.

Of course, we should remember that G did not insert *fi* at the beginning of every word: in particular, she never overwrote syllables in normal trochaic inputs of the form /Sw/. This means that in contrast to *advisor*, bisyllabic words like *visor* would not have been overwritten even though under this analysis *fi* was always 'floating' in the input. As seen in (83), the same ranking that created *fi-visor* above does not overwrite this shorter word, because that would mean deleting an input <u>stressed</u> syllable (83c), and it cannot get a new syllable of its own due to DEP (83a):

(83)

		/{fi} $'\sigma_1\,\sigma_2$ /	DEP-σ	MAX-STRESSED	MAX-FLOAT	*UNFOOTED
	a)	$\sigma_{fi}('\sigma_1\,\sigma_2)$	*!			*
☞	b)	$('\sigma_1\,\sigma_2)$			*	
	c)	$('\sigma_{fi}\,\sigma_2)$		*!		

In this account, dummy syllables are a way to move beyond a very limited early word shape (namely a single foot) without committing to full segmental faithfulness. To conclude this discussion, we will examine a related pattern – one that is seen in many places in early phonology, especially the earliest stages. One example comes from Suzanne, the child learning European French reported in Deville (1891) and analysed by Demuth and Johnson (2003). At the early ages of 1;3 and 1;4, Suzanne's grammar would only allow a maximally bisyllabic form – but where did she find the material for these two syllables?

(84)

French: Suzanne at 1;3–1;4 (Data from Demuth and Johnson, 2003: 221)		
Target	*Child*	*Gloss*
/pu'pe/	[pe'pe]	*doll*
/kʀɛ'jɔ̃/	[ɔ'jɔ]	*pencil*
/ʃa'po/	[po'po]	*hat*
/ku'to/	[to'to]	*knife*

In these words, Suzanne was being faithful to syllable count (and producing the iambs her grammar wanted anyway, as we saw in (58)), at the expense of some segmental material. Recalling that French stress is final, we can analyse her pattern as fully faithful to the segments in the input stressed syllable, and faithful to the <u>presence</u> of the input weak syllable. However, what makes this pattern different from G's is that the segmental strategy for filling that weak syllable was not an input dummy like 'fi', but rather a <u>copy of the stressed syllable</u>.[40]

A further data set shows the same process of copying to move beyond the one-foot stage, this time in Catalan. The diary study data in Lléo (1990) provides a number of such examples: longer words with penultimate stress which at early stages were truncated to trochees (85a) were produced at a later stage with one more syllable (85b), with copies of stressed segments:

(85)	Catalan data from Lléo (1990)		
Target	(a) *One foot*	(b) *More than one foot*	
Amélila	['meljia] (2;10)	[me'meljia] (2;10)	
bisikleta	['bɛka] (2;3)	[blɛ'blɛka] (2;9–2;10)	
cervesa		[βɛ'βɛzə] (2;10)	
sabates	['patəs] (2;5–2;6)	[pa'patəs] (2;11)	
taronja	['ʒɔnta] (2;6)	[ʒɔ'ʒɔnta] (2;9–2;11)	
tovallola	['βɔla] (2;6)	[βɔ'βɔla] (2;10)	

The prosodic shape of the (85b) pattern is strikingly like the Spanish *mariposa* → [ma('po.sa)] pattern discussed in the previous section – but instead of preserving more input segments, this grammar copies existing (stressed) segments to at least preserve more syllables.

Such copying processes are by no means unique to these children, or to romance languages like French and Spanish (see for example Johnson and Reimers, 2010: 3–5 for many cross-linguistic examples). As with dummy syllables, copying appears to provide a method to stay faithful to input syllable count, without adopting more segmental complexity. However, their analysis proves a little tricky – for reasons that we will now at least characterize, if not explain away.

---

[40] This pattern was not necessarily driven by the need to create a well-formed iamb: at the same stage, Suzanne was quite happy to faithfully produce subminimal [CV] words from monosyllabic inputs, so it is possible her ideal foot at the time was in fact monosyllabic. If so, her grammar was mapping /CVCV/ → [CV(CV)], meaning that she was copying for the sake of syllable faithfulness alone.

Often, children's copying of entire syllables is referred to as *reduplication* – but there is a crucial sense in which surface forms like Suzanne's *pepe* and *ojo* are not reduplicative, because their copying does not add any additional <u>meaning</u>. In target languages like Kannada – and also the Ilokano and Lardil examples from the very beginning of the chapter, examples (9) and (10) – reduplication adds semantic content to its base, and so that meaning is encoded as a <u>morpheme</u> in the input. The child copying patterns, by contrast, we can describe as driven purely by the grammar's <u>phonological</u> pressures. However, this copying doesn't change the meaning of the word – just as G's *fi* adds no meaning to her over-written words either – so it isn't really like adult reduplication at all. There <u>are</u> target phonology processes which seem more like copying or reduplication for purely phonological reasons, but their unification with the child processes above must await a longer textbook (hints are provided in the further reading section).

To summarize this section, we have seen two approaches by which children can produce more syllables in a word without adding new segmental complexity: either by overwriting with fixed segments, or by copying pre-existing segments. These provide stepping stones to the later stages where children's word shape becomes target-like – tolerating multiple feet, unfooted syllables, more complicated foot types and so on.

After two chapters of OT analyses, you will hopefully now be getting more familiar with this theory's kinds of data-goggles and reasoning. We have continued in this chapter to build up a set of structural constraints which restrict outputs to certain shapes and sizes, without any proscriptions of how to meet those restrictions, and ranked them in and around existing and novel faithfulness constraints, to yield a *typology* of different surface results. As we've progressed, the merit of our analyses has been evaluated as to the extent to which they account for multiple, diverse phonological phenomena – that is, the broader a constraint's application, the better established its place in our constraint set. We have also started to see how levels of representation can interact, with segments and syllable preferences influencing footing decisions; this trend will continue in earnest in Chapter 5.

4.3   An Alternative: Perceptual Accounts of Truncation?

As was true for Chapter 3's discussion of cluster reduction, our treatment of syllable truncation must also consider the extent to which faulty <u>perception</u> rather than production could explain the child data we have seen. What if children delete syllables from targets not because their grammar won't permit them in the outputs, but because they've never made it into the input? In the case of word shape truncation, this explanation may seem particularly intuitive for at least two reasons: first, as pointed out in Chapter 2, infants are particularly attuned to aspects of the input such as stressed syllables and indeed trochees in English; second, the literature on adult misperceptions and word segmentation has found a key role for the dominant stress patterns of the listener's native language (see especially Cutler and Norris, 1988). The argument that children's early word shapes in particular are derived from perceptual biases is made perhaps most comprehensively in Echols (1993).

On the other hand, knowing that the syllables that children truncate the most are those which are hardest to perceive does not in itself prove that their errors are caused by misperception directly. It has often been suggested (especially in connection with the work of John Ohala – see e.g. Ohala, 1981, 1993) that constraints on phonological production develop over time precisely under the influence of perceptual ease and difficulty. Bringing this reasoning to the present case: certain syllables could be missing from children's production <u>either</u> because they have failed to represent those hard-to-hear syllables in their underlying representations, <u>or</u> because their production grammar has constraints against such hard-to-hear syllables.

Given just the data thus far, though, this section will examine two data points on either side of the issue: one pattern where we can be confident that perception is *not* the (sole) cause of syllable truncation, and one where it may well be the most plausible alternative. This will leave the explanation of many remaining patterns undetermined, but discussion will continue (and more research is necessary!).

The clear evidence that truncation is not solely due to misperception comes from outputs which contain segmental aspects of *both* some preserved and deleted syllables. Recall how some examples of 'blended' truncation data (exs. 38–39) led us to define faithfulness to stress as preserving the stressed *rimes* – in part because many times the *onset* of those stressed syllables was in fact a remnant of an otherwise deleted syllable, such as the Greek /por.to'ka. li/ → [pa] and Portuguese /si'nɐ/ → ['sɐ]. It seems unlikely that the child attempting a four-syllable input like /porto'kali/ has in fact perceived that string as [pa], and more specifically that they perceived the word-initial /p/ as contiguous with the third syllable's stressed [a].

If this is unlikely to be perceptual, we must instead search from a plausible <u>grammatical</u> explanation, when such mix-and-match productions are systematic in a child's speech. Assuming a one-trochee-only grammar, what kind of constraint would prefer the blended output in the grammar below?

(86)		/sɨ'nɐ /	*Unfooted	C1??	C2??
	a)	sɨ('nɐ)	*!		
	b)	('nɐ)		*!	
☞ c)		('sɐ)			*

In this case (and most of those cited in 38–39), there are at least two reasons that a grammar might prefer choosing the truncated syllable's onset as in (86b). First, it is first – that is (86b)'s /s/ sits at the left edge of the input, as the first segment of the input string, and in keeping with all the edge effects we have seen thus far in phonological systems, there is considerable evidence that grammars prefer to *anchor* the beginnings of corresponding inputs and outputs. Such a constraint is defined in (87):

(87) ANCHOR-LEFT (ANCHOR-L)
    Assign a violation for each word whose initial segment in the
    input is not the initial segment in the output

Notice that ANCHOR is only one of two constraints needed to understand (86): while some grammars may choose the onset of an initial weak syllable, many other grammars would choose to keep the stressed syllable's onset too! Thus, there must be a conflicting constraint that prefers ['noɾɐ] – and we have seen it before in Chapter 3: CONTIGUITY, which prefers that output segments be contiguous in the input. The relative rankings of ANCHOR-L and CONTIGUITY can therefore derive the difference between children who maintain word-initial onsets even under truncation and those who do not:

(88)		/sɨˈnoɾɐ /	*UNFOOTED	ANCHOR	CONTIGUITY
	a)	sɨ(ˈnoɾɐ)	*!		
	b)	(ˈnoɾɐ)		*!	
☞	c)	(ˈsoɾɐ)			*

What is the second possible explanation for saving the onsets of otherwise deleted syllables? This pressure is a preference for the truncated syllable's <u>segment</u> on its merits alone, regardless of its position. A most compelling example is found in a sub-pattern of G's *fi*-overwriting – the crucial examples are repeated below, where we can see that sometimes *fi* does not edge out an unstressed initial syllable. Examine these outputs, and try to describe the conditions under which deleted syllable onsets are maintained, before reading on:

(74)	partially repeated
Child	*Target*
[fiˈbun]	*balloon*
[fiˈpis]	*police*
[fiˈbo]	*below*
[fiˈbɛt]	*barrette*

The examples in (74) are the only ones in which G's grammar over-rides the pressure of CONTIGUITY and preserves a word-initial onset, and this subpattern is very particular. The following conditions must be met: (1) the initial syllable begins with a labial stop /b, p/ and (2) the stressed syllable begins with a central approximant /ɹ, l/. One understandable aspect of this pattern is that stops are preferred over approximants as onsets – this is a straightforward sonority effect, although implementing its analysis would take some careful work. Looking back at the Greek and Portuguese examples, note that many of them also involved choosing a lower sonority initial segment (usually a stop or fricative) over a higher sonority stressed one (a nasal or approximant).

So overall, the preservation of onsets from otherwise-truncated syllables can often be understood via well-established grammatical pressures. And more fundamentally, this pattern shows that truncated syllables <u>must be perceived</u> and added to children's lexical representations – for only if these stops and initial segments are included in the inputs can they make their way selectively into outputs.

On the other hand, the best example of a pattern we have seen which might be perceptually-driven is the truncation of medial weak syllables. We saw multiple English examples of this pattern in 4.2.1:

(89)	Missing medial syllables? (in bold) (from exs 62 and 64)	
*el**e**phant*	[ˈɑʔvɛn]	
*tel**e**phone*	[ˈkɛfʌm]	
*all**i**gator*	[ˈæbɪˌgɛɾ]	
*hel**i**copter*	[ˈhɑˌkɑpɚ]	[ˈhɑpˌkɑpdɚ]
*av**o**cado*	[ˌɑˈkɑdo]	[ˌeˈkɑdo]

Certainly these syllables are the least perceivable of any in the input – the rest are either stressed to some degree, or else final and so subject to lengthening. A second reason for suspicion about a production account is the dubious evidence of this stress reduction pattern in adult stress typology – on this point, see exercise 2 at the end of the chapter. It might be, therefore, that an extra-grammatical explanation should in fact be sought, and a perceptual one seems close at hand.

Experimental evidence also provides crucial evidence about patterns which are or are not perceptually driven. On the one hand, some studies have shown that truncated weak syllables leave a subtle but measurable 'trace' in the output, in the form of a slightly longer stressed syllable adjacent to the truncation site (Carter and Gerken, 2004). This both confirms that the speaker had perceived at least something of the missing syllable, but also that small phonetic details like duration in milliseconds (such as we have not been representing anywhere in our tableaus and analyses) can be necessary to understanding a child's full language knowledge.

4.4 Methodology: Elicitation Studies

Like Chapter 3, much of the data in this chapter has come from longitudinal diary studies and other contexts in which naturalistic data was collected and later analysed, based on whatever words, phrases and topics the child participant was speaking about that day.

However, much of the English data in particular also came from more controlled experimental conditions, namely *elicitation* tasks where experimenters aimed to get children to produce a set of previous chosen stimuli. Often elicitation tasks are the best (or only) way to collect sufficient evidence of an input pattern in children's speech, particularly if it is infrequent in or absent from everyday discourse. While three-year-olds have well-established English stress patterns in their grammars, they usually do not bring up four- or five-syllable words on their own. (Sadly, we cannot always collect naturalistic data the day after children see the hippopotami at the zoo.) But then how do you get a small child to say what you want? Various experimental options are available, depending on the complexity of the stimuli and the age of the participants.

A very common method is to use storybooks or single pictures with images of the target words, and getting the child and an experimenter (sometimes alongside the mother or guardian, especially if the child is younger than perhaps three) to 'read' the book together, with the adult prompting the child with phrases such as 'What's that?' or 'Can you tell me what that is?' For example, Paradis (2001) describes an experimental method as follows: '*This is a patoolfiga. Can you say "patoolfiga"?. Working with small children in a naturalistic play setting precluded strict adherence to verbal protocol, so occasionally, the name was also presented in midsentence, as in, "The patoolfiga wants you to say his name. Can you say his name?"'* (Paradis, 2001: 26).

With older children, a more fluid method can be used in which children are given a series of connected pictures and asked to recount their story. Usually these latter materials have been designed to test children's narrative skills, but their results can also be very revealing of children's spontaneous phonology, and using the same narrative images with many different children should consistently elicit for example labels for the story's main characters. (Some such samples are cited in the further reading section.)

Spontaneous elicitation via pictures has the benefit of introducing referents without having to use the intended word, meaning that children's utterances will be *spontaneous* rather than *imitated*. If the child does not provide a response or chooses a different lexical item, however, the experimenter can then follow up with a prompt that allows for imitation, for example: 'That's an *alligator*. Can you say that?' It is not well-established in the literature to what extent spontaneous productions differ systematically from imitations, since the same types of effects are found in both types of tasks (see e.g. discussion in Echols and Newport, 1992: 197), but nonetheless many studies indicate whether or not a production token was spontaneous or not (as in e.g. Kehoe, 2000, which contains much of the English data from this chapter). A downside of this approach is that it is limited to those objects which are reliably depicted with images: elicitation of nouns therefore being the easiest, along with some classes of adjectives like colours, then followed perhaps by fairly active verbs. But often researchers are faced with questions like: how to use images to elicit for example *honest* or *future* or *exist*? Another difficulty is knowing whether participants will know the words being targeted – while questionnaires can be used to collect data from parents on their children's vocabulary (see Chapter 7), lexicons vary widely.

Some elicitation tasks directly aim to collect imitations. With very young children (1;6–2;0), the best method will probably be the simplest: for example, Chambless (2006) introduced children to stuffed animals with the target words as names, and asked them to say hello and goodbye to each one with its name: 'Bye-bye, _____'. Various batteries for testing language skills also include nonword repetition as a direct imitation task, in which children listen to and repeat recorded words (e.g. CTOPP: Wagner, Torgesen, Rashotte and Pearson, 1999), to which we also return in Chapter 7.

4.5   Further Reading

On Word Shape and Stress in OT

Hayes, Bruce. 1995. *Metrical Stress Theory*. Chicago, IL: University of Chicago Press.
   – about stress typology, not within OT, but with countless case studies and many concepts that have been subsequently introduced into Optimality Theoretic-approaches.
Chapter 4 of: Kager, René. 1999. *Optimality Theory*. Cambridge, UK: Cambridge University Press.
   – a comprehensive chapter dedicated to the kinds of stress patterns discussed here, and also including many more complications in the typology.
McCarthy, John J. and Prince, Alan. 1986. *Prosodic Morphology*. Technical Report, University of Massachusetts Amherst and Rutgers University.
   – includes an early discussion of Minimal Word requirements.

On Word Shape and Stress in Child Phonology

Kehoe, Margaret. 2000. Truncation Without Shape Constraints: The Latter Stages of Prosodic Acquisition. *Language Acquisition* 8(1): 23–67.

Exercises

Q1: This question deals with a slightly different kind of stress faithfulness, seen in the early speech of a child reported in Johnson, Lewis and Hogan (1997). Up until age 1;5, more than 46% of his multisyllabic targets were reduced to a single output syllable; the faithfulness pattern demonstrated in the examples below are taken from ages 1;2–1;6:

Target	Child	Target	Child
butterfly	[baj]	*belly*	[bi]
hello	[ho]	*pillows*	[poz]
piano	[po]	*rabbit*	[wit]
bunny	[bi]	*crying*	[kajn]

What segmental material is being preserved in these outputs? What constraints might be used to capture the pattern?

Q2: This question returns the topic of whether there is any good grammatical explanation for truncations like /SwSw/ → [(S)(Sw)], as in *alligator* or *helicopter*. *If two feet are possible, why doesn't the grammar preserve all four syllables?* The problematic data is repeated below:

(89)

Missing medial syllables? (in bold) (from exs 62 and 64)		
*el**e**phant*	[ˈɑʔvɛn]	
*tel**e**phone*	[ˈkɛfʌm]	
*all**i**gator*	[ˈæbɪˌgɛɾ]	
*hel**i**copter*	[ˈhɑˌkɑpɚ]	[ˈhɑpˌkɑpdɚ]
*av**o**cado*	[ˌɑˈkɑdo]	[ˌeˈkɑdo]

Here is perhaps the best potential grammatical analogue to this pattern, taken from Gouskova (2003, 2007)'s analysis of vowel deletion in Tonkawa (Hoijer, 1933). As you can see below, the Tonkawa grammar frequently deletes a lot of word-medial vowels (bold in the inputs), and builds trochees which are often only one heavy syllable long (other vowels later in the inputs are deleted for unrelated reasons, so just focus on the bold ones):

Input	Output	Gloss
/not**o**xo-oʔ/	[(ˈnot)(ˈxoʔ)]	*he hoes it*
/we-n**o**toxo-oʔ/	[(ˈwen.to)(ˈxoʔ)]	*he hoes them*
/ke-w**e**-jam**a**xa-o:-ka/	[(kew)(ˈjam)(ˈxo: ka)]	*you paint our faces*
/jam**a**xa-oʔ/	[(ˈjam)(ˈxoʔ)]	*I paint his face*
/he-j**a**kapa-oʔs/	[(ˈhej.ka)(ˈpoʔs)]	*I hit myself*
/ke-n**a**tale-oʔs/	[(ˈken.ta)(ˈloʔs)]	*he licks me*

Gouskova's analysis is that these vowels are deleted under pressure from a structural constraint that requires stressed syllables to be *heavy* – let's just call it *ˈL (see Prince, 1990; Gouskova, 2007: 373). This pressure causes the grammar to delete the second vowel of a /CVCV/ sequence, to add weight to the first syllable's rime:

	/notoxo-oʔ/	*ˈL	MAX-VOWEL
a)	(ˈno.to)(ˈxoʔ)	*!	
☞ b)	(ˈnot)(ˈxoʔ)		*

So the question is: *can this analysis of Tonkawa be used to also explain the truncation in the middle of children's words like alligator and elephant above? If so, how so? If not, why not?*

Q3: This question deals with Japanese prosodic acquisition. Ota (2001)'s quantitative study of a corpus of child recordings found the following asymmetry: when children deleted coda consonants as in (A) below, they produced a measurably longer vowel before the missing consonant (similar to the Carter and Gerken (2004) study reported in Section 4.3). But when children deleted onset consonants, as in (B), they produced no reliable difference in the length of surrounding vowels.

Pattern (A) /CVC/ → [CV:]	*Target*	*Child*	*Gloss*
	/waNwaN/	[wo:wɔ]	*doggie*
	/panda/	[pa:da]	*panda*
	/ampam:aN/	[a:ma:pa:]	*(cartoon character)*
	/nanda/	[na:da]	*what?*
Pattern (B): /CV/ → [V], *[V:]	/koɾe/	[kɤ.e]	*this*
	/aɾe/	[a.e]	*that*
	/hebi/	[e.bi]	*snake*
	/gohaN/	[dɔ.ã:]	*meal*

What does this difference between (A) and (B) tell us about children's prosodic knowledge?

Q4. In Section 4.1.4, we accounted for children's selection of input syllables under truncation via faithfulness constraints, like MAX-STRESSED and MAX-FINAL. Often in OT analyses, we find that *either* structural OR faithfulness constraints can be used and elaborated to capture a pattern. *So, looking back at the data in 4.1, can you explain children's choices of which syllables to preserve at the one-foot stage using structural constraints, rather than faithfulness constraints?*

***

Answer to the question in Section 4.1.2: Garawa. Here is the filled-in tableau:

/σ σ σ σ σ σ/	INITIAL-MSFT	INITIAL-FT	*UNFOOTED	FINAL-MSFT	FINAL-FT
('σ σ) σ σ σ σ			*!***		*
σ σ σ σ ('σ σ)		*!	****		
('σ σ)(ˌσ σ) σ σ			**	*	*
(ˌσ σ)(ˌσ σ)('σ σ)	*!				
☞ ('σ σ)(ˌσ σ)(ˌσ σ)				*	

5 Early Phonology: Consonants

5.1 An Ornithological Introduction to Constraint-Based Featural Phonology

It seems that one of the easiest observations about child language involves the consonantal substitutions that they make – these make up most of what adults think of when they characterize 'baby talk'. For example: if you are familiar with North American cartoons from several decades ago, you will probably be able to identify this character (if not see footnote[1]) whose non-target processes are very similar to those found in the speech of English-learning two- and three-year-olds:

(1) (a)   'This little piggy went to market'
          ['dɪs wɪɾi 'pɪdi wɛn tə 'ma:tʰɪt]

          'This little piggy stayed home'
          ['dɪs wɪɾi 'pɪdi tʰeɪd 'hom]

    (b)   What a hypocrite!
          [wʌɾə 'hɪpotwɪt]!

          'Atta girl, Granny!'
          ['æɾæ dəɫ 'dwæni]

    (c)   I thought I saw a pussy cat!
          [aɪ 'tʰɑɾaɪ tʰɑ ʔə 'pʰʌdi tʰæt]!

For the most part, the segmental processes that the Loony Tunes creators applied to target English to create Tweety Bird's speech in (1) are in fact common among young children. To describe them we could write rules as in (2) – to account for fricatives [s, θ, ð] being *stopped* (turning into stops [t, d]), velar stops /k,g/ being *fronted* (also to [t, d], and /l/ and /ɹ/ turning into the glide [w] (complications to these rules are discussed below):

---

[1] Quotes in (a) are from *A Tale of Two Kitties* (1942); (b) from *Tweety's SOS* (1951) and (c) appears in both.

(2) /s, θ/ → [t]   /k/ →   [t]   /l, ɹ/ → [w]

    /ð/ → [d]   /g/ →   [d]

The other common lay-person's way of looking at consonant acquisition is in terms of *inventories*: usually in terms of sounds that are missing from a child's outputs, as in 'She hasn't got "s" yet' or 'She can't make "th" sounds.' In this way, we can translate the rules in (2) into surface *targets* as well: Tweety Bird's phonological inventory does not include coronal fricatives, velar stops or liquids.

By now you are used to looking at phonological generalizations in these two ways, via output *targets* and input-to-output *processes*, and again in this chapter we will build grammars that constrain and optimize segmental distributions and inventories in child phonology, with reference to cross-linguistic typologies. But before we get to any real child data, let's just look at Tweety's limited data set from these two perspectives. Two initial observations:

(i)   While interdentals are stopped in all contexts, /s/ has a more compli-cated distribution. It appears to be stopped in *onset* position as in *saw* and *pussy,* but survives as a word-final coda in *this.* It is also deleted in the onset cluster of *stayed* (though note that if it had been stopped in that context it would create a highly illegal word-initial geminate [t:]).

(ii) Approximants are also treated differently by syllable position: onset /l/s and /ɹ/s are mapped to [w] as in ***l**ittle* and ***gr**anny,* while in the rime they are vocalized or deleted, in *litt**l**e* and *ma**r**.ket* (in *girl,* the lat-eral survives but the syllabic [ɹ] is mapped to a pure vowel).

One explanation for these differences is that Tweety's phonology is described best in term of syllabic targets: the core fact being that certain seg-ments are prohibited from certain positions in outputs, and the processes by which they are transformed into something else are various (change in man-ner features, or place features, or deletion, etc). From this perspective (which of course will be challenged from time to time), we will be able to describe the acquisition of segmental and featural phonology with the OT grammars we've been building. First, however: let us move from the voice characteriza-tions of cartoons to the speech of their youngest audience members.

5.2   Child Consonant Inventories

The acquisition of consonantal inventories has been studied on a large scale since at least the 1920s and 1930s, and has proved central to research on phonological acquisition. Study of the development of segmental inventories has been particularly tied to the quest for what's universal in phonology (starting most prominently with the influential work of Jakobson, 1941/1968). In addition, much of the large scale data gathering has been driven by clinical goals and needs for norms. To get a small overview of this large field, the goal first will be to determine in broad terms which consonants are typically acquired early and late in various unrelated languages, and consider the implications of these tendencies.

Before we can begin, one key methodological point is what it means to 'acquire' a segment, for which the criteria can vary considerably. One option is to say that for any individual child, a segment is acquired once it is consistently produced accurately in multiple words. Another is to collapse across children, and determine the age at which for example 75% or 90% of children produce a sound reliably in at least one word. A somewhat unresolved issue is whether having a sound in multiple word-positions (onset vs. coda, or more often word-initial/medial/final) is necessary to its being labelled as 'acquired' (see discussion in Dodd et al., 2003: 622); for sounds with rather different allophones by syllabic position, this seems a large barrier to generalization.

Let's start with one of many English data samples, one in which the spontaneous speech of 34 children was recorded in one hour sessions, at the ages of 1;3 and 2;0. For each testing age, table 3 shows which consonants these children produced in multiple words, at the beginnings and ends of words. What generalizations emerge about the classes of sounds they produced? Which sounds are missing? Try thinking in terms of the three types of natural classes: *manners*, *place* and *voicing* – and keeping in mind the range of options provided by target English:

(3)	Early American English consonant inventories (Stoel-Gammon, 1985: adapted from table 1)				
	Word-initial Cs			Word-final Cs	
Age (n)^2	*Acquired by 50% of sample*	*Acquired by 90% of sample*		*Acquired by 50% of sample*	*Acquired by 90% of sample*
1;3 (7)	[bd h]	[bd]		(none)	
1;6 (19)	[bd mn h w]	[bd]		[t]	
1;9 (32)	[btd mn h]	[b]		[tn]	
2;0 (33)	[btdkg mn fsh w]	[bd]		[ptk n s r]	[t]

---

^{2} Here 'n' refers to the number of children in the sample.

To compare with some older children, let's look at a much larger, cross-sectional study of children learning British English. The table below lists the consonants that had been acquired by 90% of children in each age group (between 57–100 children), in any position of the word, starting at age three. What further generalizations can be drawn from this set?

(4)	Early British English consonant inventories (Dodd et al., 2003: adapted from table 14)	
	Age	*Acquired by 90% of sample (new Cs at each age)*
	3;0–3;5	[bp td kg mnŋ fvszh wlj]
	3;6–3;11	[tʃ]
	4;0–4;11	[dʒ ʒ]
	5;0–5;11	[ʃ]
	6;0–6;11	[ɹ]
	> 6;11	[ðθ]

With respect to *manner* features: we can say that the earliest consonants to be produced are stops and nasals; the last to appear are many of the fricatives; some approximants are early [w] and some are late [ɹ]; and laterals and affricates sit somewhere in the middle. In terms of *place* features, labials and coronals appear before velars, and among alveolars the interdentals, palatals and alveo-palatals appear late (although this may be as much a function of English's inventory of options, as we have e.g. no palatal stops). And with respect to position in the word: table (3) suggests that initial inventories contain more segments than final inventories, and that word-initial stops are predominantly voiced while final stops are voiceless (and in fact voicelessness in stops here appears first in final position). To some extent, these generalizations about word position can be extended to describe *syllable* position asymmetries as well, that is that stop voicing is learned first in onsets rather than codas.[3]

Now let us consider how well these featural generalizations hold up among three other widely-spoken languages: Spanish, Arabic and Cantonese (note that these three data sets are taken from only one dialect of each language, just to exemplify). In each case: how similar is the trajectory to English?

---

[3] See also Chapter 6.1.3.

(5)

Early Mexican-Californian Spanish consonant inventories (Jiménez, 1987: Across 120 children)	
Age	*Acquired by 90% of sample (novel Cs added at each age)*
3;3	[b p t]
3;7	[k m n w]
3;11	[l j]
4;3	[f]
4;7	[d g tʃ ɾ]
4;11	[x ɲ]
5;7	[s]
> 5;7	[r]

One discrepancy is that Spanish [d] and [g] seem to be learned rather late compared to English. However, this may be an artifact of this study's choice to group voiced stops together with their approximant allophones [ð] and [ɣ], and their late appearance as voiced fricatives is much more similar to the English facts already seen.

What about Cantonese? The table in (6) below provides the same kind of overview:

(6)

Early Cantonese consonant inventories (So and Dodd, 1995)		
Age	*Acquired by 75% of sample (novel Cs added at each age)*	*Acquired by 90% of sample (novel Cs added at each age)*
2;0–2;6	[p t k m n ŋ h l w]	[p t j n]
2;6–3;0	[pʰ ts f s][	m ŋw]
3;0–3;6	[tʰ kʰ tsʰ]	[k h]
3;6–4;0		[pʰ tʰ kʰ l]
4;0–4;6		[ts f s]
> 4;6		[tsʰ]

Here the later-acquired segments include fricatives, and aspirated obstruents, which in Cantonese are in <u>phonemic</u> contrast with the plain voiceless stops. One surprise compared to English is that [l] begins to appear so early, though it is not 90%-acquired until rather late.

The last data table is from Arabic, whose consonant inventory contains most English segments, and also includes stops and fricatives further back in the vocal tract (uvulars and pharyngeals) and a series of *pharyngealized* stops and fricatives (transcribed here as Cˤ). The table below takes data from 10 children per age group; note that percentage of acquisition is calculated across words, not across participants.

(7) | Early Jordanian Arabic consonant inventories (Adapted from Dyson and Amayreh, 2000: table 1) |

Age	Produced accurately >50%	Produced accurately >75%	Notes on target language
2;0–2;4	[btkʔ mn fsXħh lw]	[btʔ mn Xħh l]	*Arabic has no p, g, ŋ*
2;6–2;10	[btkʔ tˤ mn fsʃXħh lwj]	[btkʔ mn f l]	
3;0–3;4	[btkʔ tˤ dʒ mn fszʃXʁħh r lwj]	[btkʔ mn fʃXħh lw]	
3;6–3;10	[btkʔ tˤdˤ mn fszʃXʁħʕh r [lwj]	[btkʔ mn sfʃXħh lw]	
4;0–4;4	[btkʔ tˤdˤ dʒ mn fszʃXʁħʕh r lwj]	[btkʔ mn sfʃXħ r l]	
Missing segments	[q θð sˤðˤ]		*[q] not common in this dialect*

One perhaps surprising fact here is how early some of the fricatives are acquired, especially uvular [X] and voiceless pharyngeal [ħ]. The later-acquired segments, however, are those with difficult articulations, including pharyngealized segments, interdentals and uvulars.

To summarize, many broad-level English generalizations hold across languages – in that stops and nasals are typically first, fricatives are mostly late, and [+anterior] consonants are usually learned before [-anterior] ones. At the macro level, these characterizations hold up to a great extent: for example, the late acquisition of the majority of fricatives is reported for Spanish, German, Swedish, Japanese, Mandarin and Xhosa.[4] One interesting area of wide variation, however, is the class of rhotics and laterals; we will return to this point later in the chapter.

---

[4] A Bantu language spoken in South Africa, Botswana, Lesotho and elsewhere.

5.3   Constraints on Consonant Inventories

What makes a segment late to appear in a child's production inventory? Take the example of interdental fricatives. In both English and Arabic, interdentals were among the very last to be acquired; they are not found in the target inventory of Cantonese, and only one is found as an allophone in Mexican Spanish[5] and Cantonese. More generally, interdentals are often considered to be a fairly rare and exotic aspect of the English consonant system. The online World Atlas of Language Structures (WALS) reports that of 567 sampled languages, only 43 (7.6%) contained interdentals or dental(like) fricatives, making them among the least common classes of segments. Should these adult and child language facts be connected? And if so, through what analysis? (These questions will take us a few tries to answer, so keep reading.)

From the OT analytic perspective, if a segment does not appear in a target language, it must be ruled out on grammatical terms. In other words, we cannot stipulate that the inventory of Cantonese simply does not contain interdentals or that English does not contain pharyngeals. Why not?

For one thing, recall that the grammar must be able to map the illegal segments of borrowed words to something more palatable to the target phonology. When most native English speakers produce the German name *Bach*, we replace its final word-final fricative with a velar stop /bax/ → [bɑk]. In borrowing Arabic words with voiceless pharyngeal fricatives, English has predominantly mapped them to [h], so that for instance the word *hajj* (meaning a pilgrimage to Mecca) has been mapped /ħaːʒ/ → [hadʒ]. When other languages borrow words with interdentals from English they are most commonly turned into alveolar or dental stops [θ → t, ð → d], so that for example *maths* has been borrowed into Cantonese as [met.si]. Cross-linguistic studies of *loanwords* reveal how native speakers recruit their native phonological knowledge to map illegal sounds to legal ones. To take one example of many, Paradis and LaCharité (2001) find that languages with a glottal-like English /h/ will map most Arabic pharyngeals onto a nearby segment, but those without /h/, like French, will borrow the same words by deleting the pharyngeal altogether.[6]

Thus it would seem that a speaker's phonological grammar should be used not only in controlling the distribution of sounds in native underlying forms, but novel and borrowed ones too. To capture this range of effects we can use the same grammar of constraints that we have been building in previous chapters – but now focusing on surface distribution and faithfulness of *segmental* features. Via ranking, we can use the same structural constraints

---

[5] Though many dialects of Spanish do have voiced [ð] as an allophone, as mentioned above.
[6] See also Paradis and LaCharité (2012) on the cross-linguistic borrowing of interdentals.

to derive the language-specific extent of a natural class such as interdentals: ungrammatical as in Cantonese, grammatical as in English or grammatical only in certain phonological contexts as in Spanish.

A very simple version of this grammar is one with structural constraints that ban natural classes (in 8), ranked among faithfulness constraints which can preserve those natural classes. This is illustrated schematically in (9) (refer back to Chapter 1 if you need reminders of the features used in these definitions):

(8a) *PHARYNGEAL[7]
      Assign a star for each segment in the output with the features
      [-sonorant, +back, +low]

(8b) *INTERDENTAL FRICATIVES (*T)
      Assign a star for each segment in the output with the features
      [+continuant, +anterior, +distributed]

(9)   Schematic ranking to define inventories:
      a) Cantonese: *T >> All relevant Faith
      b) Spanish: Some Faith >> *T >> Other Faith
      c) English: All relevant Faith >> *T

One kind of support for this approach to ruling out natural classes of segments in the grammar can be found among the order of acquisition of natural classes, compared with their cross-linguistic distribution. An example comes from Stoel-Gammon's (1985) data regarding the relative order of acquisition among English manner classes, that is stops, nasals, fricatives and liquids. Across all the children in the sample (for whom sufficient data is available), table (10) reports the percentage of kids whose inventories included one manner before the other, in both word-initial and word-final contexts:

(10)	Order of Manner Acquisition (Stoel-Gammon, 1985: Adapted from table 1)[8]			
Manner		>	*Manner*	*% of Word-initial inventories (n)*
stops			nasals	90% (10)
stops			fricatives	100% (27)

% of Word-final inventories (n)
89% (19)
92% (28)

Continued

---

[7] This kind of *featural co-occurrence* constraint goes back in spirit to Prince and Smolensky (1993) and references therein.

[8] See Stoel-Gammon (1985) for the role of glides, which appear between stops and nasals.

Manner	>	Manner	% of Word-initial inventories (n)	% of Word-final inventories (n)
stop		laterals	100% (32)	96% (24)
nasals		fricatives	92% (24)	85% (20)
nasals		laterals	100% (31)	89% (18)
fricatives		laterals	94% (18)	55% (22)

Again at the macro level, this order of acquisition is quite common. As just one other example, Macken (1978) reports the same order of manner acquisition at least regarding voiceless obstruents (first stops, then nasals, then fricatives, then laterals) for a child learning Spanish.

To see the overall connection in manner features between child development and target languages, compare (10) to the percentages of the WALS sample which are reported to lack each one of these manner features. Describe the similarities in the two tables before reading on.

(11)	Manner	% of Languages in WALS lacking that manner (N = 567)
	Stops	0
	Nasals	1.7
	Fricatives	8.5
	Laterals	16.6

In both the child English and cross-linguistic target languages, the asymmetries are very clear: stops are most common and acquired first, followed by nasals, then fricatives, then laterals. (The exception among children is word-final fricatives vs. liquids, both of which are learned later, and see below.) If those children who showed simultaneous acquisition of multiple manners are included, the main data difference is that stops and nasals for many children appear roughly at the same time, but the delay in other manners does not disappear. In fact, this matches fairly nicely with the target data, as even in those ten languages reported to lack nasals, some include nasal allophones in their outputs (e.g. the Chocoan language Epena spoken in Columbia; Harms, 1984), so the subordination of nasals to stops may be somewhat tenuous in both realms.

A second broad-level observation of this sort can be made about voicing as a class of features, compared to the other major feature types of place and manner. It is uncontroversial that all languages have consonant inventories with contrasts between multiple place features: perhaps the smallest known consonant inventory, that of Rotokas spoken in Papua New Guinea (Firchow and Firchow, 1969), includes labial, coronal and velar stops [p, t, k]. Likewise, nearly all languages have consonants with multiple manners – Clements (2004) lists some languages whose consonants are all stops, but there are at best perhaps a handful such cases. However there is ample evidence of languages which do not use voicing contrastively. As one example, the Zuni language (an isolate still spoken in western New Mexico and Arizona) has the following consonant inventory: stops [p t k, k^j, k^w, ʔ], affricates [ts, tʃ], fricatives [s, ʃ, ɬ, h], nasals [m, n] and approximants [l, j, w] (Kroeber, 1916). While much about this inventory is fairly familiar to an English speaker, it differs significantly from English in that its voicing is all completely predictable from its manners: obstruents are all voiceless, and sonorants are all voiced. In fact, fully 182 of the WALS languages (32%) lack a phonemic contrast in voicing.

The developmental observation about consonant feature classes is that, broadly speaking, laryngeal or voicing features are acquired last, i.e. after contrasts in place and manner. This seems to be especially true for languages in which laryngeal contrasts mean more than [+/-voice] – for instance, learners of Thai and Hindi in which aspiration, pre-voicing and/or breathy voice are used phonemically, are reported to not master these features until at least ages six or seven (see Gandour et al., 1986; Davis, 1995, and recall Cantonese aspiration in (6)). Another illustration comes from the early consonant inventory of an English-learning child Jennika, reported in Ingram (1985) and Ingram and Ingram (2001). Which features does she appear to use contrastively in her inventory?

(12)

Jennika's early inventory mappings (Adapted from Ingram and Ingram, 2001, ex. 4)			
Target	*Child*	*Target*	*Child*
/m/	[m]	/g/	[g]
/n/	[n]	/d, t/	[d]
/b, p/	[b]	/s, ʃ/	[s]
/f/	[f]	/w, l, ɹ/	[w]

While Jennika collapses some place distinctions (s vs ʃ) and manner too (all the approximants coming out as [w]), her outputs distinguish between bilabial, coronal and velar places, and between stops, fricatives nasals and approximant manners. Voicing, however, is as predictable as we saw in Zuni above: though stops are voiced, fricatives are voiceless and sonorants remain voiced (as they nearly always do).

These two child English examples suggest that macro-level implications among natural classes and features in adult languages are recapitulated in their order of acquisition; this view is both well-supported and frequently-challenged in the phonological literature.[9] To round out this introductory discussion, we will take two other looks at this idea.

First we return to the claim that interdentals are both rare and learned late. What other segments appear late in child inventories? Are all cross-linguistically 'exotic' segments acquired late? Let's consider some other consonant types listed in the online WALS as 'uncommon segments' (Chapter 19): in addition to the dental fricatives [θ, ð], the Atlas discusses labio-velar stops like [k͡p] (in 8% of the sample) and pharyngeals (in 4.1%):

- *Labio-velar stops*: One study of consonant acquisition in Igbo (Nwokah, 1986, see below) found that [k͡p] and [g͡b] were two among the last five consonant phonemes to be acquired (out of about 26), and that they were repaired by more than half of the 17 three-year-olds and a third of the 13 four-year-olds. Thus, these seem both rare and fairly late to be acquired.
- *Pharyngeals*: The data from the acquisition of Arabic pharyngeals is rather mixed. On the one hand, the pharyngeal fricatives appear fairly <u>early</u> in the Jordanian Arabic data of (7) – especially voiceless [ħ], which appears in the earliest age group, 2;0–2;4. (See also pharyngeal fricatives acquired by 2;6 in Egyptian Arabic, Saleh et al., 2007.) On the other hand, Arabic consonant inventories also include a series of pharyngealized stops and fricatives, which many studies of Arabic acquisition have found to be acquired late if not last among all segments (see discussion in Dyson and Amayreh, 2000: 94–95).

So to summarize again: the connection between typological frequency and order of acquisition is there, broadly speaking – but there are surely other factors at play.

The second take-home message is about <u>how</u> we might capture a connection between the rarity of a feature or natural class and the relative order of its acquisition. Here we run into the same question from 4.1.6 regarding universals and tendencies: the OT theory of grammar <u>on its own</u> is in no position to explain why children might learn for example the English ranking for interdentals in (9c) starting with the Cantonese ranking in (9a).

---

[9] See first Jakobson (1941/1968), also Brown (1997), and debate in Ferguson and Farwell (1975); Macken and Ferguson (1983); Pye et al. (1987).

However! What <u>can</u> connect these results is a theory of learning which re-ranks constraints, with guidance – and OT has been uniquely effective among learning theories in helping phonologists and developmentalists understand those connections which do exist. ... All this excitement awaits us in Chapter 10! Before that, we have many more pieces of the puzzle to assemble; next are the segmental processes that create child-specific inventories.

5.4   Child Consonant Repairs

The previous section looked at some surface facts about children's early consonant inventories: that is, we discussed which consonants appear in outputs, but without considering what their inputs were. But now we turn to this latter topic – when children attempt to produce consonants or features that are not in their inventory, what happens? What kinds of processes occur? From what we have seen, we should expect that rare segments and featural classes should be replaced by more common ones; this expectation will be met to a moderate degree.

To begin with, here are some representative data from a language rather distant from English: one from Igbo, a Niger-Congo language spoken in Nigeria and elsewhere. (Note that this data set includes samples from the speech of 39 children, so different children might apply different processes to the same segments.)

For each form you can compare the output to its target form (which we continue to take as input), and note what featural changes have occurred in each case. And do they seem like patterns you might find in English too?

(13)	Igbo segmental processes: Nwokah (1986), ages two to four					
	/únèrè/	[únèjè]	*banana*	/èŋʷè/	[èwè]	*monkey*
	/ɛ́zɛ/	[édɛ]	*teeth*	/ŋʷókò/	[wókò]	*boy*
	/áká/	[átá]	*hand*	/áɲá/	[ájá]	*eye*
	/aɣa/	[aja, awa]	*fighting*	/máɲálá/	[mánálá]	*dried fish*
	/égó/	[edó]	*money*	/ák͡pɔ́kpɔ́kʷɔ́/	[ápɔ́pɔ́kɔ́]	*shoe ('leather on leg')*
	/ázʘ/	[aʒʘ]	*fish*	/ákʷɔ́kʷ/	[ákɔ́kɔ́]	*book*

Here is a summary of processes for you to compare with your own notes, grouped according to the class of feature that has changed between input and output:

(14)	Place features	Manner features
	/k/ → [t]	/z/ → [d]
	/g/ → [d]	/ɲ/ → [j]
	/ɣ/ → [w, j][10]	/r/ → [j]
	/ŋ/ → [n]	/kʷ/ → [k]
	/z/ → [ʒ]	/ŋʷ/ → [w]
	/k͡p/ → [p]	

Among the changes in place features, one consistent pattern is the mapping of velars /k, g, ŋ/ to their respective coronals [t, d, n] (and exceptionally to a labio-velar [w], in the case of the voiced fricative). These repairs are typical examples of *velar fronting* – just like Tweety Bird's fronting in '*atta **g**irl **g**randma!*' and 'pussy [**k**]at' in the examples of (1). The changes within coronals /ɲ/ → [j] and /z/ → [ʒ] are perhaps less common, though both target sounds are often inaccurate in early speech.[11]

Among changes in manner features, there are three patterns. The first two are *stopping* of a fricative (/z/ → [d]) and *gliding* of sonorants, as both palatal nasal and /r/ mapped to [j]; both of these are quite common in child speech. Tweety Bird shows signs of both, mapping /s, θ/ → [t], and some /l, ɹ/ → [w] (though not nasals). Fricative stopping and sonorant gliding are reported in a number of cross-linguistic studies – here are some examples from Greek (15a) and English (15b), respectively:

(15a)	Greek fricative stopping (Kappa, 2002: tables 11 and 20)							
	Target	*Child*	*Age*	*Gloss*	*Target*	*Child*	*Age*	*Gloss*
	/peˈði/	[peˈdi]	2;0	*child*	/ˈvolta/	[ˈbota]	2;2	*walk*
	/ˈfeta/	[ˈpeta]	2;2	*slice*	/ˈolɣa/	[ˈoga]	2;3.18	*(name)*
	/ˈvazo/	[ˈbado]	2;3.21	*vase*	/ðes/	[des]	2;5.23	*see*
	/ˈθelo/	[ˈtelo]	2;4.18	*(I) want*	/oçi/	[ˈoci]	2;0-5	*no*

---

[10] Categorizing this as a change in place assumes that what the IPA symbol suggests is a voiced velar fricative is really more of an approximant, which is not an uncommon state for a language to be in. Also see Section 5.7 on rhotics.

[11] It is rather interesting to note that [ʒ] is not part of the target Igbo inventory.

(15b)	English sonorant gliding (Velten, 1943: 288)			
	Target	*Child*	*Target*	*Child*
	smell	[maw]	rubber	[wabu]
	belt	[bawt]	reach	[wuts]
	jelly	[dawa]	sorry	[sawa]
	Wallace	[wawas]	Mary	[mawa]

The final set of segmental mappings in Igbo involve the language's complex consonants – the complicated but not too rare /k^w, g^w/, the rarer /ŋ^w/ and the extremely rare labio-velar stops /k͡p, g͡b/. All three segment types are mapped by children onto a singleton consonant, but the three consonant types each pattern differently. To quantify these differences, here are all the errors reported for these five segments in Nwokah (1986)'s cross-sectional study (n = 34 children):

(16)		Complex segments: Igbo (Tallied from data in Nwokah, 1986)		
		Child		
	Target	[k],[g],[ŋ]	[p],[b]	[w]
a)	/k^w/	8	6	2
	/g^w/	14	5	4
b)	/ŋ^w/	4	–	33
c)	/k͡p/	3	40	–
	/g͡b/	–	33	–

In (16a), we see that labialized stops frequently lose their secondary place e.g. /kw/ → [k], and this kind of simplification can be seen in many child language guises. For example, children's initial attempts at producing Arabic's pharyngealized consonants usually surface as plain stops and fricatives (e.g. Dyson and Amayreh, 2000). In (16b) the labialized nasal most often comes out as [w] – this might be the same process as /ɲ/ → [j], that is another case of nasal gliding, but one in which the complex segment's labial feature is retained in the [w] glide (see more at the very end of this section).

But (16c) shows a different pattern, in which the two-placed stops /k͡p/ and /g͡b/ were nearly always produced as simple <u>labial</u> stops. These segments are not like anything found in English, or indeed any other language whose acquisition we have examined thus far – however, if you think about how these sounds are articulated,[12] you may well be able to make an educated guess as to why Igbo-learning children produce them first as [p] and [b]. (You might also want to come back to this point after reading Section 5.5.6.)[13]

Let's look at a different process affecting consonantal place, this time in Polish, which has a large set of sibilant fricatives and affricates. Without getting too involved in details, we will simply note that Polish contrasts three different places of articulation among coronal fricatives and affricates and that in the child outputs illustrated below, this three-way distinction is *neutralized* to the most anterior place, roughly alveolar:

(18)	Polish sibilant neutralization: Lukaszewicz (2007: 57–58)					
	Target	*Child*	*Gloss*	*Target*	*Child*	*Gloss*
	/juş/	[jus]	*already*	/ɔɕɔw/	[ɔsɔw]	*donkey*
	/zatşarɔvana/	[zatsajɔvana]	*enchanted (fem.)*	/tɕɛb'jɛ/	[tsɛbɛ]	*you (gen. sg.)*
	/kɔlɛʑankax/	[kɔjɛzankax]	*colleague (fem. loc. pl.)*	/ʑarɛnka/	[zarɛnka]	*seed (dim. nom. pl.)*
	/zjɛʑ dʑawa/	[zjɛz dzawa]	*(she) went down*	/lɔ dʑɛ/	[jɔ dzɛ]	*ice (loc. sg.)*

Note that this data also shows the familiar process of gliding both /r/ and /l/ to [j].

---

[12] To learn about producing a doubly-articulated consonant, consult a phonetics textbook like Ladefoged (1993).

[13] A related finding comes from the acquisition of clicks in Xhosa (Mowrer and Burger, 1991). Recall that clicks are velar *ingressive* sounds, and that like [k͡p] and [g͡b] they also require two closures, one at the velum and somewhere farther forward in the mouth. Comparing errors at different places of articulation in Mowrer and Burger (1991)'s data reveals another split: when attempting the dental click [|], children produced a [t], but for the palato-alveolar [!] and lateral [‖] clicks, they most often produced a [k]. Can you imagine what might account for this split?

We have yet to see any examples of repairs involving *voicing* alternations –
but this is not to say that they are not present in early speech. Anecdotal
studies in fact suggest that voicing can be the last type of feature to stabilize in a child's production, though often transcriptions of voicing can be
somewhat unreliable (and we will return to the perceptual issues with voicing
acquisition in Section 5.7).

One general consensus is that at the earliest stages, obstruent voicing is
usually neutralized to what might be a 'neutral' laryngeal specification – that
is voiceless and unaspirated. As we discussed in Chapter 1, this kind of stop in
English can be roughly equivalent to a target 'voiced' (unaspirated) sound –
most closely approximating our stops after /s/ – as in the word '*stop*' itself.
Macken (1980a) points out that in Spanish, VOT is distributed much differently, so that a plain voiceless stop will sound to Spanish native listeners to
be 'voiceless'. Thus, while descriptions of child voicing may differ from language to language, children may well be beginning with the same targets.
After this initial 'default' stage, however, the distribution of voicing features
seems to be very influenced by *position* in the word, or rather the syllable –
and we will treat the acquisition of positional allophones and voicing directly
in Chapter 6.1.3.

5.5   Comparing Consonant Repairs in Children and Adults, and their Analysis

The preceding section drew a series of connections between the sounds
which children add late to their production inventories, and their rarity in
adult languages, to suggest that output-oriented constraints (like the simple
*Pharyngeal) should be used to provide them a common explanation. Now,
we address the question of how child and adult segmental *repairs* of such
sounds match up. We will focus on some common child patterns, and for
each assess their status among adult typologies. After looking at the comparative evidence, we will focus on one particular pattern in place of articulation
repairs that highlights the situation's complexity.

5.5.1   Sonorant Gliding and Liquid/Glide Alternations

Many target grammars show patterns similar to the Igbo /áɲá/ → [ájá] from
(13), or English *rabbit* as ['wæbɪt]. Some examples come from Brazilian
Portuguese, in which coda /l/ has turned into the glide [w] (as compared with
European Portuguese in (19a); in southern dialects the palatal nasal has glided
as well (19b–c):

(19)		Sonorant gliding in Brazilian Portuguese (Data in a) from Flynn, 2006; b) and c) from Harris, 1990)						
	a)	*European Portuguese*	*Brazilian Portuguese*	*Gloss*	b)	*Northern BP*	*Southern BP*	*Gloss*
		[mal]	[maw]	*badly*		[veʎa]	[veja]	*old (fem)*
		[kalda]	[kawda]	*syrup*		[paʎa]	[paja]	*straw*
						[moʎu]	[moju]	*sauce*
					c)	[baɲu]	[bãj̃u]	*bath*
						[soɲu]	[soj̃u]	*dream*
						[viɲu]	[vĩj̃u]	*wine*

The data in (20) shows a more synchronic example; in the Indo-Aryan language Oriya of India, nasal gliding occurs when moving from formal to informal speech:

20)	Nasal gliding in Oriya (Piggott, 1987; Trigo, 1988: 102–103)		
	Formal	*Informal*	*Gloss*
	[bʰumi]	[bʰũj̃ĩ]	*ground*
	[dʰumɔ]	[dʰũw̃ɔ̃]	*smoke*
	[swami]	[sãj̃ĩ]	*lord*

To capture the differences between Oriya's informal vs. formal speech registers, or Brazilian Portuguese(s) vs. European Portuguese (and also English), we will need faithfulness constraints which protect the features distinguishing sonorants. According to the features we adopted in Chapter 1, the crucial properties of laterals are [+consonantal, +approximant] and a change from liquids to glide means being unfaithful to that [+consonantal] feature, since glides are crucially [-consonantal]. With this in mind, we can mint two new constraints: the one in (21) is a structural ban against liquids, and the other in (22) is an IDENT constraint which preserves the liquid/glide distinction. This latter needs a bit of unpacking, so read it carefully before continuing.

(21) *[+cons, +approx.] (*LIQUID)
      Assign a violation for every output segment with the features
      [+consonantal] and [+approximant]

(22) IDENT[+/-CONSONANTAL]   (*IDENT[+/-CONS])
Assign a violation for every input segment with the feature
[α-consonantal] whose output correspondent has the feature
[β-consonantal].

The definition of IDENT[+/-CONS] is more technical than our previous IDENT[STRESS] constraint, but once you understand it, you will realize we've needed this definition all along. The important addition is the notion of *correspondents*: the Identity (in terms of + or − consonantal feature values) that the constraint enforces is between input and output correspondents. Previously, we have been fudging this fact, and saying that faithfulness is violated when something in the input is changed in the output ... but how can you be sure what's changed into what?

In the Correspondence Theory approach to faithfulness (introduced by McCarthy and Prince, 1995), we track changes by giving each segment[14] of the input an index – usually just represented with a number, but anything would do – and similarly indexing all the segments in each output candidate. As you can see in (23), this makes it clear how the input and output are related, and thus lets us formally evaluate when a segment has 'turned into' another one (via featural changes), rather than being deleted and replaced with something else entirely.

The tableau in (23) demonstrates the workings of IDENT[+/-CONS] a little bit. Its relative ranking with *LIQUID and MAX determine which of these three candidates win: resulting in either liquid faithfulness (as in European Portuguese), gliding (as in Brazilian Portuguese, and in child data), or even liquid deletion. The winning candidate in (23c) does not violate MAX – because the /l/ has not been <u>deleted</u>, it has merely changed some of its feature values:

(23)		/mal₃/	*LIQUID	MAX	IDENT[+/-CONS]
	a)	[mal₃]	*!		
	b)	[ma]		*!	
☞	c)	[maw₃]			*

---

[14] Or sometimes more than segments. Recall for example Chapter 4's definition of MAX-STRESSEDRIME. To formalize that constraint, we will need to index syllable rimes, too ... Also recall the DEP-σ used to deal with segmental over-writing.

Notice that in these constraints we have not accounted for any *positional* restrictions yet – recall from both Tweety Bird and Brazilian Portuguese that onset vs. coda liquids can be treated differently.

In the case of nasal consonants (which we can regulate with a constraint similar to (21), but banning instead the featural combination *[+NASAL, -CONTINUANT]), changing into a glide requires unfaithfulness to both [+/-approx] and [+/-consonantal]. On the other hand, notice that at least in the adult data, faithfulness to the actual feature [+nasal] seems to be preserved in (19) and (20) via nasalization of glides and nearby vowels.

Another illustration of alternations between glides and liquids comes from the suffixes of Kipare, a Bantu language of Tanzania. Two of these suffixes, the perfective /-ije/ and the applicative /-ija/, have consonants that can surface as [j] or as either [l] or [r] depending on the featural properties of the roots they attach to. As an exercise, figure out how to predict which allomorphs occur where (the answer will appear in Section 6.3).

(24)	Kipare glide/liquid alternations data from Odden (1994: 315–316); Hansson (2010: 100–101)			
	a) perfective suffix: /-ije/			
	[nikundije]	*I liked*	[nizorije ~ nizorire]	*I bought*
	[nibigije]	*I beat*	[nitalije ~ nitalile]	*I have counted*
	[nivonije]	*I saw*	*[nivonile], *[nivonire]	
	[nirongije]	*I made*	*[nironigre]	
	b) applicative suffix /-ija/			
	[kutetija]	*to say for*	[kuzorija ~ kuzorira]	*to buy for*
	[kubigija]	*to beat for*	[kutalija ~ kutalila]	*to count for*
	[kudikija]	*to cook for*	*[kudikila], *[kudikira]	
	[kurumbija]	*to make pots*	*[kurumbira]	

5.5.2 Other Repairs for Nasals

Although nasals are usually added to children's inventories quite early, they are also segmentally repaired in at least one other way beyond gliding. Two examples from children learning North American English are given below – what is the featural change children are imposing here?

(25) | Sally's nasals: (Bernhardt and Stemberger, 1998: 320) | |
|---|---|
| *mask* | [pæks] |
| *mouthy* | [bʌʊθiː] |
| *music* | [tusɪk] |
| *noise* | [towəs] |
| *plum* | [bapʰ] |

(26) | Joan's nasals (Velten, 1943) | |
|---|---|
| *broom* | [bub] |
| *spoon* | [bud] |
| *jam* | [dab] |
| *home* | [hub] |
| *swim* | [fub] |

In these cases, nasal consonants – of the manner class [+sonorant, –approximant] and also [+nasal] – are becoming oral voiced stops [–sonorant, –nasal, –continuant].[15]

Similarly, there are several target language patterns which show nasals becoming stops, usually voiced ones. One example comes from the historical development of Lushootseed, one of the many Salish languages native to the Pacific Northwest region of North America. Most Salish consonant inventories include voiceless stops and nasals – for example, see the forms in (27a) from Halkomelem – but in Lushootseed (27b), the nasals have become voiced stops (Thompson, 1979; Urbanczyk, 2001).[16]

---

[15] The role of the feature [+/-continuant] is hard to assess in child phonology. On the one hand, it is often assumed that nasal consonants are [-cont] as well, since there is no air flowing through the oral cavity, and thus we could propose that nasal stopping is just a change in [nasal] and [sonorant]. However, there are many patterns where children seem to treat oral stops differently than all other segments, including nasals, and this will be crucial to an analysis of child Polish in Section 6.1.1. This is why Chapter 1 specified nasals as [+continuant].

[16] Interestingly, Urbanczyk (2001) argues that Lushootseed's voiced stops are still treated in the language's phonology as though they were sonorants.

(27) | Nasals vs. voiced stops in Salish cognates
(Data from Hess and Heaman, 1989: 248)

a) Cowichan (Halkomelem)	Gloss	b) Swinomish (Lushootseed)
[mə́qsən]	nose	[bə́qsəd]
[ʔə́ɬtən]	eat	[ʔə́ɬəd]
[ɬə́ptən]	eyelash	[ɬə́ptəd]
[θámən]	eyebrow	[cúbəd]

Another example comes from Hixkaryana, a Carib language native to Brazil, where nasal consonants can turn into voiced stops when they follow an oral stop or fricative – for example, *'I gave him meat'* can be pronounced either [wɪtmænɔ] ~ [wɪtbænɔ], and *'I caught it'* as either [wæhɔsnɔ] ~ [wæhɔsdɔ] (data here from Martlett, 2013).

5.5.3 Fricative Stopping

Target languages also show lots of alternations between fricatives and stops – though they aren't perhaps fully analogous to child stopping patterns. Often particular fricatives (notably the interdentals) will become stops, but not the entire fricative series. The best analogue of the context-free stopping seen in many children's earliest speech, such as the Greek examples of (15a), is probably the treatment of loanwords in languages which lack (at least some) fricatives entirely. For example Dinka, a language of Sudan, has borrowed English words as below:

(28) | Fricative stopping in Dinka borrowings from English
(Data from Idris, 2004: 36–38)

Dinka target	English source	Dinka target	English source
[hoṭpitol]	hospital	[aprïka]	Africa
[nɛkitïp]	negative	[laba]	lava
[ṭukul]	school	[iŋgliṭ]	English

In Dinka, the native grammar ranks the context-free ban on fricatives – *[-SONORANT, +CONTINUANT] – above all relevant faithfulness constraints.[17] These loanword data demonstrate an additional ranking: that among relevant

---

[17] This might be a simplification – it is also reported that [f] may occur in free variation with [p] (at least for some speakers?) and that the language may also include some other fricative allophones.

faithfulness constraints, the one which controls the difference between fricatives and stops is lowest ranked. In our feature system, this faithfulness constraint is IDENT[+/-CONTINUANT], so the tableau below shows how this IDENT
constraint must be ranked below for example MAX, to choose fricative stopping rather than fricative deletion:

(29)		/lav₃a/	*[-SON, +CONT]	MAX	IDENT [+/-CONT]
	a)	lav₃a	*!		
	b)	laa		*!	
☞	c)	lab₃a			*

To connect this treatment of fricatives back to Chapter 3: some children's
distaste for fricatives can also be seen in onset cluster reduction. While the
lowest sonority segment usually survives in an English-learning child's onset
cluster reduction, the data in (30) from one child Julia shows a more complicated treatment of fricatives. Describe the clusters in which Julia preserves
fricatives, and in which she deletes them:

(30)	North American English: Julia's treatment of onset clusters with fricatives (Pater and Barlow, 2003: tables 11 and 13)			
	Target	Julia	Target	Julia
	sleep	[sip]	sneeze	[nis]
	slide	[saːit]	snake	[nek]
	flowers	[faʊwɚ]	smell	[mɛʊ]
	froggy	[fɔgi]		

In the left hand columns, fricative+liquid clusters keep their fricative. But
on the right hand side, fricative+nasal clusters keep their nasal, and lose their
fricative, even though nasals are more sonorous!

Pater and Barlow (2003)'s explanation for this exceptional treatment of [sn]
and [sm] clusters is a combination of two pressures: the hierarchy of onset-
sonority constraints, according to which nasals are better onsets than liquids,
and the general constraint on fricatives. The ranking in (31) shows how Julia's
pattern can be captured. Sandwiching *[-SON, +CONT] in the middle of the onset
sonority hierarchy means that the grammar is willing to tolerate some fricatives, like when the alternative is a liquid onset (31a), but it nevertheless deletes
them when a good enough alternative is available, that is a nasal onset (31b):

(31a)

/slip/	*ComplexOns	*Ons/Liquid	*[-son, +cont]	*Ons/Nasal
slip	*!	*!	*	
☞ sip			*	
lip		*!		

(31b)

/snek/	*ComplexOns	*Ons/Liquid	*[-son, +cont]	*Ons/Nasal
snek	*!		*	
sek			*!	
☞ nek				*

Another context in which target phonologies turn fricatives into stops is illustrated below in Greek, with a group of verbs marked with a passive/perfective affix. Can you predict this morpheme's alternation between the allomorphs [θik] and [tik]? (The morpheme boundaries have been indicated with hyphens to make the forms more readable):

(32)

Greek stop ~ fricative alternation (Spencer, 1991; data here from Flynn, 2012)			
[agape-θik-e]	*he/she/it was loved*	[akus-tik-e]	*he/she/it was heard*
[fer-θik-e]	*he/she/it behaved*	[ðex-tik-e]	*he/she/it accepted*
[stal-θik-e]	*he/she/it was sent*	[γraf-tik-e]	*he/she/it was written*

This alternation seems to be one of fricative *dissimilation*: this morpheme begins with a fricative [θ], except when attached to a root that already ends with a fricative like [s, x, f]. Thus, the structural pressure driving the process must be more specific than *[-son, +cont] – instead, it bans a *sequence* of adjacent fricatives (try writing such a constraint for yourself!).

5.5.4   Repairs for Individual Fricatives

Some errors in 5.3 involved mapping certain fricatives onto others, like /ʃ/→ [s] or /s/ → [θ], and many such mappings are very common in child language. Before we consider their target language reflexes, however, let's look a little more at some child facts, relying on a large cross-sectional study including children with phonological delays and possibly disorders.

Although this data might therefore be non-representative, the patterns are still revealing.

This study looked at the treatment of three English voiceless fricatives: /s/, /f/ and /θ/. After examining the inventories of 160 children, three reliable patterns of errors were observed; we will look at two of them now (the third is an exercise at the end of the chapter). Take a moment to determine the patterns before continuing:

(33) Fricative feature changes in early (North American) English
     (Data from Dinnsen, 2002; Dinnsen et al., 2011)

(a)	Pattern One					
	[bʌs]	*bus*	[fʌndoʊ]	*thunder*	[feis]	*face*
	[soʊp]	*soap*	[maʊf]	*mouth*	[wuf]	*roof*
	[dʒusi]	*juicy*	[fʌm]	*thumb*	[kɔːfiŋ]	*coughing*
	[sʌn]	*sun*	[tuf]	*tooth*	[lif]	*leaf*
b)	Pattern Two					
	[beiθbɔl]	*baseball*	[bæθ]	*bath*	[kɔf]	*cough*
	[maʊθ]	*mouse*	[θif]	*thief*	[hæfin]	*laughing*
	[θoʊp]	*soap*	[maʊθ]	*mouth*	[wuf]	*roof*
	[bʌθ]	*bus*	[tuθi]	*toothy*	[gufi]	*goofy*

In Pattern One, /θ/ and /f/ both surface as [f] in outputs, while /s/ is faithfully preserved; in Pattern Two, /s/ and /θ/ both surface as [θ], while [f] is preserved. So two place-based mappings can be seen in the child data here: one against interdental fricatives (driving 33a), and one against alveolar fricatives like /s/ (driving 33b). An additional common fricative change we saw involved post-alveolars and other coronals becoming alveolar, such as in the Polish data of (18). Summarizing, then:

(34) (some) Common fricative substitutions in child language
     /ʃ/ → [s]   /s/ → [θ]   /θ/ → [f]

But this is not the whole story. First, these targets are all in the front half of the vocal tract – there must also be investigations of for example pharyngeal fricatives, as discussed above for Arabic, and see Section 5.7 below about uvular fricatives. It should also be acknowledged that these mappings in (34) are sometimes reversed (e.g. a child might occasionally map /f/ → [θ]), but these are the predominant trends.

Are the patterns in (34) also found in target languages? Indeed. Both the /ʃ/ → [s] and /θ/ → [f] mappings are fairly well attested. With respect to the former, fronting other coronals to alveolar, this process is quite similar to a featural change seen in Luseño (a Uto-Aztecan language native to the San Diego region of California), when making diminutive forms. Compare the (35a) base forms with their diminutives in (b) – in addition to a [-mal] suffix, notice how the fricatives change:

(35)		Luseño /ʃ/ → [s] in diminutives (Kroeber and Grace, 1960: 23; Flynn, 2012)				
	a)	*Target*	*Gloss*	b)	*Target*	*Gloss*
		[ʃukat]	*deer*		[sukmal]	*fawn*
		[ʃokáːwot]	*tree squirrel*		[sokáwmal]	*small tree squirrel*
		[toːʃexet]	*cottontail*		[toːsexmal]	*young cottontail*
		[maʃla]	*large brake fern*		[masmal]	*small fern*

The mapping /θ/ → [f] is also reported context-free in many different dialects of English – for example, a little bit of internet searching can bring you to a site telling t-shirts from 'Norf London' (to distinguish it from its geographical opposite, Souf London). One interesting difference is that such target English dialects with this mapping transform both the voiceless and voiced interdentals similarly, but children are not usually reported to similarly map /ð/ → [v].

The upshot of these data is that our constraint set must control the /ʃ~s/ and /θ~f/ distinctions each with (at least) one faithfulness constraint. To keep track of the relevant features, (36) provides a little table of all the feature values for these four fricatives, as laid out in Chapter 1:

(36)	Some fricative features			
Major place:		*[+ labial]*	*[+coronal]*	
		[f]	[θ s ʃ]	
Minor place:			*[+anterior]*	*[+distributed]*
			[θ s]	[θ ʃ]
			[-anterior]	*[-distributed]*
			[ʃ]	[s]

From this table, we can determine that changing /ʃ/ to [s] is a violation of IDENT[+/-ANTERIOR], and / θ/→ [f] is a violation of place faithfulness, changing from coronal to labial (to which we return in the next section). One notable fact is that both of these repairs do not change the *stridency* feature of the input fricatives (strident fricatives are also known as *sibilants*) – and perhaps a better featural system would rely on that fact. At any rate, we can now build a grammar of child English where a structural constraint on post-alveolar or interdental fricatives can drive these mappings; since the repair used here is not stopping, IDENT[-SONORANT] and IDENT[+CONTINUANT] will rank higher as well.

Exercise 1: Draw a tableau that ranks a structural constraint against [ʃ] and a set of faith constraints (both violated and satisfied by the winner) to describe the Luseño process in (35).

One notable difference between child and adult production is that the mapping /s/ → [θ] seems conspicuously rare, perhaps absent from adult languages. This may suggest that this child process does not warrant a grammatical account. For now we will put this aside with some caution; but see also Section 5.6 below.

5.5.5 Velar Fronting

Velar fronting is very common in child English, and indeed across many (though not all) child grammars. The big issue in reconciling this pattern with the adult typology is the *contexts* of velar fronting.

Here is one diary study example of velar fronting in North American English, reported in Inkelas and Rose (2008), and illustrated with data from ages 1;07–2;04 below. Before reading on, examine the two sets of columns and determine the phonological conditions in which E does and does not front her velar stops to coronals:

37)		Contexts for velar fronting in E's grammar (Data from Inkelas and Rose, 2008: exs 1–2)					
	a)	*Target*	*Child*	*Age*	b)	*Target*	*Child*	*Age*
		cup	[tʰʌp]	1;09.23		*book*	[bʊkʰ]	1;07.22
		go	[doː]	1;110.01		*padlock*	['pædjɔk]	2;04.09
		cool	['tuwɔ]	1;11.02		*bagel*	['bejgu]	1;09.23
		again	['ədɪn]	1;10.25		*goggles*	['dɑglʸs]	2;0.24
		together	[taˈdɛɾə]	2;01.21		*bucket*	['bʌkɨt]	2;01.11
		helicopter	['hɛwˌtɔptɛə]	2;00.19		*actually*	['æktʃwi]	1;11.22
		alligator	['æwəˌdɛɾɚ]	2.01.18		*octopus*	['ɑktəpʊs]	2;01.05

The velars which map to coronals in (37a) are all the *onsets of stressed syllables*, whether word-initial or medial. In E's corpus 294/352 of stressed velar onsets are fronted, and only 38 such velars were produced (others were omitted or included a different error). On the other hand, the data in (37b) show that velar place is consistently preserved elsewhere, meaning in unstressed onsets and in coda position. In these contexts, E produced a velar stop in 353/384 instances, and applied velar fronting a mere eight times.[18]

This contextual velar fronting is very typical: it is virtually identical to the case study data in for example Bills and Golston (2002) and Chiat (1983). A cross-sectional study of 67 English-acquiring kids by Stoel-Gammon (1996) demonstrated three production patterns for velars: fronting in all contexts, fronting in no contexts or fronting just in stressed or 'strong' prosodic positions, just as E did in (37). It is also widely reported in other languages – for example, see references in Ayyad and Bernhardt (2009) on velar fronting in early Arabic.

And what about target languages?[19] Some languages do not include velar consonants in their inventories at all – at least this is reported of the Austronesian language Tahitian of French Polynesia. More commonly, languages ban velar consonants in certain contexts ... but <u>not</u> the contexts that show positional fronting in E's grammar. Instead, velars in target languages may be banned strictly in coda position (as is the case in the formal register of Kiowa, an American language indigenous to Oklahoma). In addition, velars and labials can pattern together and *both* be neutralized with coronals in codas or final positions. Most varieties of Spanish permit a range of word-final codas, so long as they are all <u>coronal</u> – [d, n, l, r, s] but not [*b, m, f, k, ŋ]. Another example of neutralization to coronal place is found at the end of reduplicants in a Taiwanese secret language (Li, 1985).

Overall, it has been well-established that adult languages do not show velar fronting in just the prosodically strong positions, as children do. This discrepancy will be addressed in a couple different ways throughout the rest of this chapter; stay tuned.

5.5.6   Another Process among Places of Articulation

The final segmental pattern discussed in this section is more complicated, and probably less frequent, but is pervasive and theoretically-interesting enough to warrant analysis. It is illustrated below in two children's

---

[18] See Inkelas and Rose (2008) for a slightly different description of the environment, as well as all the numerical data and much analysis.

[19] This cross-linguistic data below was collected in de Lacy (2002).

simplification of North American English onset clusters; figure out the common patterns and think about their potential featural explanations before reading on.

(38)		Joe at 4;5 – atypical development (Data from Gandour, 1981, citing Lorentz, 1976)						
	a)	*stitch*	[s]itch	(b)	*spoon*	[f]oon	*swoop*	[f]oop
		story	[s]ory		*space*	[f]ace	*swamp*	[f]am
		snap	[sǽ]p		*spinach*	[f]inach	*swollen*	[f]ollen
		snake	[sẽɪ]k		*smooth*	[f]ooth	*Smith*	[f]ith
					smell	[f]ell		

The second example is very much like the first – but it comes from the typically-developing phonology of G, whose onset clusters we examined in detail in Chapters 3 and 4. One class of target clusters was withheld in the previous data sets, though, and (39) shows what it looked like:

(39)	More clusters from G (Gnanadesikan, 2004)			
	tree	[pi]	*drink*	[bɪk]
	cry	[paɪ]	*grape*	[bep]
	quite	[paɪt]	*twinkle*	['pɪkəw]
	sweater	['fɛɾɹ]	*smell*	[fɛw]

What is common to these two grammars? In both cases, clusters are repaired exceptionally under circumstances that can be described in terms of one place of articulation. For Joe, the unusual mapping is from /sm, sw, sp/ to [f]; G shares the mapping /sw, sm/ → [f], but her grammar has two additional patterns: /tr, tw, kr, kw/ all map to [p], and /dr, gr/ to [b].

In all of these repairs, the singleton onset in the output retains features of both input cluster segments. In the case of /sw/ → [f] for instance, the output onset segment has the *manner* (fricative) and *voicing* (voiceless) of the input /s/, but the *place* of the input /w/ – labiodental [f] being as close to a labial as English fricatives permit.[20] To generalize, manner and voicing come from

---

[20] Of course /w/ is also velar, but apparently the fact that English has no velar fricatives precludes this alternative; to my knowledge no English-acquiring child uses the velar fricative [x] to avoid clusters like [sw].

the initial input segment; in Joe's case this pattern only holds of input /s/, while for G it can affect stops and fricatives, coronals and velars. But in every case, the place of the second cluster member also emerges in the output – just when that place is *labial*. The necessary assumption is that English [ɹ] is specified as labial, which is not implausible given the degree of lip rounding that accompanies this central approximant. (If you aren't convinced you round your lips considerably, especially in onset position, while making an [ɹ] – try saying an r-initial word like *radio* with lips spread wide in a grin, and you will find it's really hard![21] If you say such a word naturally, your lips will definitely round.

Exceptional faithfulness to labial place is by no means unique to English. As a very different example: So and Dodd (1995)'s cross-sectional Cantonese study reports that children's /kʷ/maps to [p], for example /kʷa/ → [pa], but simple /k/ maps to [t], as in /kɐj/ → [tɐj]. (See also discussion of [labial] for Dutch in Levelt, 1994; Fikkert and Levelt, 2008.)

A theoretical point: what kind of unfaithfulness are mappings like /kʷ/→ [p]? In Chapter 3, we saw many examples of cluster reduction via deletion, and in correspondence terms we can now define that mapping as $/C_1C_2/$ → $[C_1]$ (usually), where MAX has been violated by the input $/C_2/$ which has no output correspondent. But in this case, your analytic intuition is probably not that for example $/s_1w_2/$ has just been mapped to $[f_1]$, deleting the [w] ... because then the grammar will also have to change $/s_1/$'s place of articulation to labial, with no clear reason. Not <u>every</u> input /s/ maps to [f]! Just the ones followed by a labial! The failure of this account is illustrated in (40) – in addition to violating MAX, the candidate we want to win gratuitously violates an IDENT constraint on place of articulation:

(40)	Failing to map /sw/ → [f]			
$/s_1w_2amp/$	*COMPLEXONS	MAX	IDENT[LABIAL]	
s_1w_2amp	*!			
☞ s_1amp		*		
☹ f_1amp		*	*!	

Instead of being treated as an oddly-triggered deletion, this process is known as *coalescence*, or *fusion*. In this case, the output segment [f] represents

---

[21] For an interesting twist on 'r' rounding, some dialects of British English appear to have mapped this segment onto the <u>labiodental</u> allophone [ʋ] – see especially Foulkes and Docherty (2000).

a mash-up of features in both the /s/ and /w/ input segments, and corresponding to both: /$s_1w_2$amp/ → [$f_{1,2}$amp].

Examples of featural coalescence are not hard to find in target languages. For example, look at what happens to the initial segment of an Indonesian root when it is prefixed with this nasal-final prefix:

(41)

		Indonesian coalescence (here from Cohn and McCarthy, 1994: 40)		
		Root	*Prefix+root*	*Gloss*
a)		[isi]	[məɲisi]	*fill*
		[atur]	[məɲatur]	*arrange*
		[hargai]	[məŋhargai]	*value*
		[bantu]	[məmbantu]	*help*
b)		[potoŋ]	[məmotoŋ]	*cut*
		[tulis]	[mənulis]	*write*
		[kata]	[məŋərikan]	*word/say*

In (41a) the prefix appears as [məŋ-], and before a voiced stop-initial root, its place assimilates [mə**m-b**...]. When the root begins with a voiceless obstruent in (41b), however, we can see segmental coalescence: the output segment retains the *manner* of the first segment (nasality) but the *place* of the root-initial segment.[22]

The upshot is that featural coalescence is a different kind of repair: an alternative to deletion when trying to repair structural constraints. This means that it must be a separate kind of faithfulness violation – it doesn't violate MAX, because no input segments are really gone. Instead it violates a constraint called UNIFORMITY, which prevents multiple input segments from having the same output correspondent:[23]

(42) UNIFORMITY (adapted from McCarthy and Prince, 1995)
Assign a violation for every pair of input segments which have the same output correspondent.

---

[22] For the rest of an analysis of Indonesian nasal coalescence and its other quirks, see especially Pater (2001).

[23] For the reverse faithfulness constraint, see Section 7.4.

To get a handle on this analysis, the table below compares the two candidates that repair the cluster via <u>deletion</u> (b)–(c), as we had already seen, to the two that use <u>fusion</u> (d)–(e). Note that this is NOT a ranked tableau, but simply a table of constraint violations.

(42)		More faithfulness options: Coalescence and /sw/ → [f]				
		/s₁w₂amp/	MAX	IDENT[LABIAL]	IDENT[+APPROX]	UNIFORMITY
a)		s₁w₂amp				
b)		s₁amp	*			
c)		f₁amp	*	*		
d)		s₁,₂amp		*	*	*
e)		f₁,₂amp			*	*

Notice that candidates (b)~(d) and (c)~(e) are in fact homophonous – you can't <u>hear</u> in the output whether an [s] is a correspondent of one or two input segments. However, we can deduce the existence of coalescence via violation profiles. Let's work this out:

If UNIFORMITY >> MAX, then the grammar will resolve this cluster via deletion, and [s₁] will always win: notice how candidate (42b) harmonically bounds (42c), because there's no reason to gratuitously turn a coronal into a labial. But if MAX >> UNIFORMITY, the grammar will choose fusion – in which case a constraint like IDENT[LABIAL], which insists that an underlying [labial] feature not be lost in the shuffle, will always prefer (42e) over (42d). This means that if a child maps /sw/ → [f] as the kids in (38–39) did above, that winner <u>must</u> be the result of fusion (42e) rather than the deletion-plus-feature-change of (42c). (Note that while (42e) does not violate MAX, it certainly has other faithfulness violations not illustrated above, since its output [f] corresponds to both /s/ and also /w/, and /w/ differs from [f] not just in its value for [+/-approximant].)[24]

Returning to the cross-linguistic facts: it is clear that faithful constraints protect the different places of articulation found across the typology of languages. However, it is not common that faithfulness to labial place in particular wins out over others.

---

[24] Gnanadesikan (1995) demonstrates that children who systematically coalesce their clusters to retain certain features of the input must in fact treat all cluster reduction as a case of fusion, but which in certain cases is vacuous because all of one segment's features are retained. To see why this is, try building a ranking that will map for example /k₁l₂/ → [k₁], not fused [k₁₂], but can also drive the labial fusion facts above. It won't work! If /kl /→ [k₁] with simple deletion wins, then so will /kw/ → [k₁].

What is however common is the special treatment of *coronal* place – usually being treated unfaithfully in favour of labials or velars. One such example comes from Catalan's treatment of place in coda nasals.

In English, there is an active structural constraint that insists nasals share the place of a following obstruent, and it affects labials, coronals and velars alike (we will see more on this in Chapter 6.1). Word-internally, we therefore find clusters like *ca[nd]y*, *pri[ns]ess*, *ju[mb]o*, *a[mb]ling*, *ju[ŋk]ie* and *ju[ŋg]le*, but not for example *ca[md]y* or **ju[ng]o*; English also has some alternations between prefix allomorphs as in *i[mp]ossible* vs. *i[nt]olerant*.[25] In Catalan, however, only some of that assimilation takes place:

(43)	Catalan nasal place assimilation across word boundaries (Data here from de Lacy, 2002: 293–294, see Mascaró, 1976; Hualde, 1992)			
	[son əmiks]	*they are friends*	[som əmiks]	*we are friends*
	[som beus]	*they are voices*	[som kuzins]	*we are cousins*
	[soŋ kuzins]	*they are cousins*	[som dos]	*we are two*
			[tiŋ pa]	*I have bread*
			[tiŋ presə]	*I'm in a hurry*

In the left-hand column, word-final [n] assimilates in place to a following stop, but final nasals at other places of articulation, [m] and [ŋ], do not assimilate.

One response to this asymmetry is to add two faithfulness constraints to the grammar: one protecting labial *and* dorsal[26] place, to the exclusion of coronals, and one just to coronals, and then to place them in a fixed ranking as below:

(44) IDENT {[LABIAL], [DORSAL]} (IDENT{K,P})
   Assign a violation for every [+labial] or [+velar] input segment whose output correspondent does not match its place of articulation.

(45) A fixed ranking of place faithfulness
   IDENT{K, P} >> IDENT{T} (meaning coronal).

---

[25] Note that English varieties differ on the extent of their velar assimilation in this affix: some dialects produce the prefix in *incapable* with a velar nasal, to match the following [k], while others resist assimilation and choose [n.k].

[26] Recall from Chapter 1 that [dorsal] is the major place feature we adopted for segments including velars.

Can this constraint IDENT{K,P} be enough to explain the fusion facts in Joe and G's grammars, in which C_1C_2 fuse into a single segment, maintaining the labial place of C_2? ... Perhaps. Since almost all the other C_2s in English onset clusters are in fact coronals, the C_2s with labial place (m, w and maybe ɹ) could be protected by IDENT {K,P} with little ill-effect – that is, there are no dorsal C_2s to worry about incorrectly protecting, because we have no clusters like *[sŋ] or *[px].

On the other hand, the larger typology of child patterns which preferentially protect labial place suggests that the feature [+labial] in particular is special, to the exclusion of dorsal place (see especially Fikkert and Levelt, 2008). This would require that the constraints in (44) be split into two constraints, IDENT[LABIAL] and IDENT[DORSAL], so that IDENT[LABIAL] could be higher.

However, there are a very few solid examples of <u>target</u> languages in which labial faithfulness is preserved over dorsals. One of the very few cases comes from the Himilayash language Hayu spoken in Nepal. Hayu does not tolerate labial-velar consonant clusters, and when they appear at morpheme boundaries labial place always survives, often to the exclusion of the velar (and also demonstrating coalescence):

(46) Hayu preservation of labial features (Michailovsky and Mazaudon, 1973: 146, 148)

/mu<u>m+k</u>oŋ/ → [mũpoŋ]   *'he gave food to you'*
/mu<u>m+ŋ</u>om/ → [mumom]   *'he'll give food to me'*
/di<u>p+k</u>oŋ/ → [dixpoŋ]   *'he pinned you in wrestling'*
/di<u>p+ŋ</u>om/ → [diʔmom]   *'he'll pin me in wrestling'*

Rare patterns like (46) aside, it does seem that the extra faithfulness to labial place in particular may be somewhat special to child phonologies – a fact for which we have no good explanation at present.

5.6   On Alternative Explanations

The take-away message from this section thus far has been that *most* segmental repair patterns show close analogues in target languages, and so featural constraints (both structural and faithfulness) can be used equally to regulate segment distributions in both kinds of grammars. However, the treatment of *place* features – as in velar fronting and labial coalescence – throws a couple of wrenches in our works; we will see this mismatch writ much larger in Chapter 6. Before moving on, therefore, we will take some time to consider the possibility that extra-grammatical factors are to blame for children's segmental repairs.

When people say things such as *'the sound "r" (or whatever sound) is just really hard for children to make'*: what does this mean in phononological terms? Should we assume not that it translates into a constraint against such a structure, but rather that it indicates an articulatory ceiling against which children's early motor efforts bump against? Could it be that the *grammar* maps /s/ → [s] faithfully, or indeed /k/ → [k], and that it is not the cognitive system but the phonetic implementation module that messes up and approximates more of a [θ] or a [t] respectively?

These are not easy questions to answer, and many authors would argue to some or all extents that indeed these repairs are not grammatically regulated. There are, however, a couple of reasons that we will continue here to use our constraint-based tools. One is the observation that often a child's repair pattern seems very *linguistic* in its application, in that it is closely tied with the utterance of real words as opposed to vocal play. A telling quote is from Inkelas and Rose (2008), regarding E's trajectory of velar fronting:

> *E produced velars accurately in his babbling and very early words, but starting at 1;0.27 systematically fronted his velars in strong position all the way through 2;3.0. By the time of the next documentation, five days later at 2;3.5, PVF had ceased categorically; in 30 words with target strong velars [up to 3;9.29], ... VF occurred only in the word "again" (...at 2;3.21). Moreover on two occasions [...] at E's ages 2;01.14 and 2;03.21, E's mother witnessed him producing nonsense words containing velars in stressed syllables (e.g. [gaek], [kæk] [kɑnk]. (Section 8.1)*

The fact that E produced initial velars before 1;0.27, and later produced them in nonce words before real ones, suggests that it was specifically the act of mapping from inputs to outputs that triggered the application of velar fronting – a task a grammar is built to perform. The missing piece of the puzzle, then, is what structural constraint drives children's velar fronting, but never applies in adult grammars – we will take up this challenge again in Chapter 6.3.

If you are a skeptic, this quote about the extent of E's velar fronting may have raised a different objection for you regarding the complexity of speaking. Maybe it's not that E can't produce initial velars at all, you could argue, but rather that he can't produce them when he's trying to coordinate the rest of an input word and its associated complexity! Maybe it's not straight motor control, but motor planning that's getting in the way.

In this particular case, the motor planning argument may not be the most persuasive, since it would have to assume that between 1;0 and 2;3 E <u>always</u> found it hard to plan a velar in an onset and <u>never</u> in a coda. However, many variable segmental repairs might be given either of these alternative explanations. And while we cannot solidly dismiss these alternatives in every case, we can again find individual examples where the alternatives seem implausible.

One remarkable such example comes once more from G's *fi* dummy syllable pattern from Chapter 4.2.2. In (47a), you can remind yourself of how *fi* was used in her grammar to replace initial unstressed syllables, and that initial labial stops (47b) were sometimes retained from that overwritten syllable. Now in (47c), see how *fi* interacted with labial coalescence:

47)		G's labial coalescence + dummy *fi* insertion					
	a)	dummy *fi*		b)	dummy *fi* with initial labial faith	c)	dummy *fi* with labial coalescence
		[fi'gido]	*mosquito*		[fi'pis]	*police*	[fi'bejə]	*gorilla*
		[fi'dinə]	*Christina*		[fi'bo]	*below*	[fi'bæf]	*giraffe*
		[fi'vaɪzə]	*advisor*		[fi'bɛt]	*barrette*	[fi'bɛkʃən]	*direction*

Exercise 2: use the fact that G 's grammar maps *gorilla* to [fi'bejə] and not *[fi'ɹejə] or *[fi'gejə] to discuss whether her labial coalescence was the result of articulatory planning problems.

5.7   Repairs for Rhotics

To conclude our discussion of segmental repairs, we will touch on <u>rhotics</u>: a kind of consonant that appears to show considerable language-specific variation in its acquisition, and consider where this inter-language variation comes from.

Natural classes in the phonological sense can often pick out rather different sounds in different languages – perhaps most obviously among vowels, where an English [i], a French [i] and a Swedish [i] may well sound rather different. Among the consonants, the most disparate such case is probably the rhotics: those sounds which are thought of as 'r'-like. While this may sound like a bizarrely informal definition of a natural class, the output segments treated as 'r' (e.g. spelled or transliterated using the symbol 'r' in the Roman alphabet) fall into at least three quite distinct categories.[27] As summarized

---

[27] And why should we even think all these disparate sounds form a natural class? Because often languages show allophonic variation across the three categories, for example with alveolar trills in one context and uvular fricatives in another. See especially discussion in Bradley (2001a, 2001b), and see also Paradis and LaCharité (2001: 272).

below, it appears that though rhotics are learned late in most if not all languages, the type of rhotic does seem to correlate with the segments that are chosen to *substitute* for 'r'. Thus:

- One rhotic class contains the coronal trills or taps, especially alveolar [r] (as in e.g. Italian, Polish and Scottish English) or [ɾ] (as in Japanese and Korean). Several languages have both trills and taps phonemes (as in e.g. Spanish and Palauan), though they are typically neutralized in many phonotactic contexts (see especially Bradley, 2001a, 2001b); many other languages have trills or taps at multiple coronal sites (e.g. Hindi has both dental [ɾ] and retroflex [ɽ] taps).

  Children learning languages with alveolar trilled /r/ most often replace them with the alveolar lateral /l/ – as reported for Jordanian Arabic, Italian, Spanish, Hindi (see especially Bortolini and Leonard, 1991; Dyson and Amaryeh, 2000), and Xhosa (Mowrer and Burger, 1991). On the other hand, some children learning Cairene Arabic are reported to replace the alveolar trill with [d] (see Ragheb and Davis, 2014).
- A second class consists of the 'central' (non-lateral) alveolar approximant or glide, used in most rhotic dialects of English (as in e.g. most dialects of both North America and Ireland). As mentioned with regard to labial coalescence in English, these rhotics appear to be often accompanied by lip rounding.

  In English /ɹ/ is most often replaced by another glide, either [w] or [j].
- A third class of rhotics are uvular continuants, as in for example many varieties of French, German and Hebrew. Their manner is usually fricative (χ and ʁ), though the voiced rhotic can become more approximant-like, and some languages also use a uvular trill (ʀ).

And what is substituted for uvular rhotics? Options vary. Dyson and Amareh (2000)'s study of Jordanian Arabic acquisition found that /ʁ/ was replaced most often by voiceless [χ], followed by [g] and [ʔ]. A very different repair strategy for /ʁ/ comes from one child's acquisition of Quebec French. There is a lot of variation here – but is there anything predictable about the output rhotic substitute?

(48)		Quebec French rhotics: Clara (Rose, 2000: 228)			
		Target	*Child*	*Age*	*Gloss*
	a)	/ʒiˈʁaf/	[vɛˈwæf]	1;10.04	*giraffe*
		/ʁɔb/	[wɔb]	1;10.10	*dress (n.)*

Continued

	Target	Child	Age	Gloss
b)	/ka'ʁɔt/	[tʰɔ'dɔːt]	1;09.01	*carrot*
	/su'ʁi/	[zʊji]	1;11.06	*mouse*
	/ʁuʒ/	[jʊʃ]	1;11.06	*red*
		[zʊʒ]	1;11.21	

As a first pass generalization, it seems that Clara's grammar can replace rhotics with a stop, a glide, a fricative – but the *place* of the output replacement (usually) comes from another consonant in the word: in (a) the rhotic is replaced by a labial, correlating with another labial; in (b) the rhotic is now a coronal, under the apparent influence of a nearby coronal.

From the perspective we have taken thus far the upshot of this typology is that to predict rhotic substitution patterns, we will need featural machinery to distinguish between rhotic types, and thereby regulate their faithfulness. In particular, there must be some featural similarity between a trill and a lateral that makes the latter a not-too-unfaithful substitute for the former. In the case of English, treating [ɹ] as a glide would make the / ɹ / → [w], [j] mappings fairly faithful, requiring merely a violation of IDENT constraint on place, but not manner. As for /ʁ/, the fact that both [ʔ] and [g] can be used as replacements suggests a pressure to maintain posterior place of articulation, that is satisfying IDENT[DORSAL] – and in the case of Clara, perhaps /ʁ/ is understood to have no place at all (on which see Rose, 2000).

5.8 Methodologies: Phonological Corpora and Acquisition Data

The notion of a linguistic 'corpus' can be very broadly defined: the term is used to describe nearly any collection of language data, given some even minimal degree of linguistic organization. The first corpora of child phonological data in this sense are the raw reports from diary studies, beginning in the 19th century and continuing throughout the 20th, resulting in the wealth of longitudinal, individual data that made possible many early observations about phonological development.

In the digital age, past and present diary studies are being documented electronically. Current diary study sessions are typically recorded, so that transcriptions can be checked and re-evaluated; transcriptions and audio files are organized into searchable databases to be used for a variety of different analyses. A pioneering effort to collect, standardize and disseminate child acquisition data grew into CHILDES (the Child Language Data Exchange

System, http://childes.talkbank.org/), housed at Carnegie Mellon University. As the child language component of the larger TalkBank system, CHILDES contains decades' worth of child language corpora, and these data (largely in transcript format) can be searched electronically with a free software tool called CHAT.

However, many of the projects which created these corpora were focused on morpho-syntactic learning, so they do not include the narrow transcriptions or audio files necessary to study their participant's phonologies. Within CHILDES, the PhonBank project (http://childes.talkbank.org/phon/) was created to specifically collect phonological corpora for the study of acquisition. These corpora are readable in PHON, software developed by Yvan Rose and Greg Hedlund, and thus can be searched for patterns, targets and anything that the transcribers deem code-worthy.

As more and more transcribed acquisition corpora are making their way into the openly-accessible public domain, the study of phonological development across time, children and languages has become much easier and better-informed. At the same time, these corpora are still very focused on a handful of widely-spoken languages (English being the overwhelming front-runner). Building up corpora within PhonBank is also a time- and resource-consuming project, and while transcription and data alignment improves as technologies improve, the field still faces a daunting amount of work before large-scale cross-linguistic research on phonological development reaches its peak.

5.9 Further Reading

Readings on OT Constraints and Segmental Restrictions

Dinnsen, Daniel A. 2002. A reconsideration of children's phonological representations. In B. Skarabela, S. Fish, and A. H.-J. Do (eds) *Proceedings of the 26th Annual Boston University Conference on Language Development*. Somerville, MA: Cascadilla Press. 1–23.

Lombardi, Linda 1999. Positional faithfulness and voicing assimilation in Optimality Theory. *Natural Language and Linguistic Theory* 17: 267–302.

Readings on Phonological Corpora in Acquisition

Rose, Yvan (2014). Corpus-based investigations of child phonological development: Formal and practical considerations. In Jacques Durand, Ulrike Gut, and Gjert Kirstoffersen (eds) *Handbook of Corpus Phonology*. Oxford: OUP.

Exercises

Q1: In Chapter 3's treatment of cluster simplification, we used a series of *Onset Sonority constraints that made reference to different manner classes:

*GLIDEONS >> *LIQUIDONS >> *NASALONS >> *FRICONSET

The only major manner feature not penalized in that set is the stops. *So why don't children simplify their onsets by mapping them all to stops, for example mapping sleep to [tip] or frog to [bɑg]?* You now have constraints to explain why this doesn't happen; use tableaus to illustrate the crucial rankings that prevent this mapping.

Q2: *Examine this data from Alice learning English, who imposed some striking segmental changes on her outputs. Attempt to describe the output restrictions on Alice's words, and the segmental processes she uses to achieve them (data extracted from Jaeger, 1997).*

Child	Target	Child	Target
[pʌpi]	puppy	[tʊti]	dirty
[pʌtʊ]	butter	[pɪki]	piggy
[pikakʰ]	peacock	[pakʰ]	frog
[pukʰ]	cup	[taɪkʰ]	kite
[tiki]	kitty	[pɪti]	T.V.
[piç]	sheep, sweep	[pita]	David
[tuç]	teeth	[kʊki]	cookie
[tikʰ]	cheek	[tukʰ]	duck
[taki]	doggy	[takʰ]	sock

6 Early Phonology: More Consonants and Phonotactics

6.1 Consonants in Codas

As we have already seen in several places, languages often impose strict segmental restrictions on coda and coda clusters, in terms of manner/sonority, place, voicing and combinations thereof. Likewise, children acquiring languages with more complex coda structures – or indeed, ANY coda structures – will often go through early stages of coda simplification.

An example of British English coda cluster development, on which we did not dwell, appeared early in Chapter 3 (ex. 9) from Amahl's data. The table below in (1a) reproduces that data set – but note the new examples in (1b), all taken from the same month of data collection. Looking at both sets together: what are the featural restrictions on Amahl's coda clusters?

(1)	Amahl at 2;7 (Data from Smith, 1973)					
	a)	*Target*	*Child*	b)	*Target*	*Child*
		Elastoplast	ˈlaːtəb̪laːt		*cold*	kuːld
		book-shelf	buklɛf		*dent*	d̪ɛnt
		box	bɔk		*drink*	g̊riŋk
		desk	gɛk		*ink*	iŋk
		footprint	wutplit		*pink*	piŋk
		fox	ʋɔk		*malt*	mɔːlt
		pleased	pliːd		*reins*	rein
		scales	g̊eil		*want*	wɔnt
		touched	tʌt		*won't*	wont
		touched	tʌtʃt		*want*	wɔt
		fact	wækt		*meant*	mɛt

The overall generalization is about manner: this grammar tolerates most sonorant+obstruent codas (mostly found in 1b), but almost never permits two adjacent obstruents (as in 1a). Among at least English learners, Amahl is in good company: McLeod, van Doorn and Reed (2001) report the most common word-final clusters produced by two-year-olds to have been nasal+stop. Typologically, this pattern is also well-supported – indeed if a language has only one type of coda clusters, they are perhaps most likely to be nasal+obstruent or liquid+obstruent.

Altogether, then, it seems clear that coda clusters, like onset clusters, are mediated by structural constraints on sonority. To remind yourself that you know what this means: take the two constraints given in (2) and use them to draw tableaus for Amahl's optimization of coda clusters in *fox* and *pink*. (Note that you will have to choose the faithfulness constraint yourself, but that should not be hard.)

(2a) NoComplexCoda (see Chapter 3 ex. 11)

(2b) *[-son][-son]-Coda[1]

Assign a violation mark for every coda which contains two obstruents.

(3)		Amahl's sonority-driven coda cluster reduction (answers provided at end of chapter)			
a)		/fɔks/	?	?	?
		[ʊɔks]	*!		*
☞		[ʊɔk]		*	
		[ʊɔ]		**!	
b)		/piŋk/	?	?	?
☞		piŋk			*
		pik		*!	

Another factor involved in coda acquisition is position within the word: in general, word-medial codas are slower to emerge than those found word-finally. This fact might be given several different interpretations: for example, that word-final codas are easier to perceive than medial ones, or (as discussed in Chapter 3), that word-final consonants (and clusters) might in fact <u>not</u> be

---

[1] This definition is my own invention; for a rather more nuanced discussion see Morelli (1999).

true codas. To examine the difficulties of word-medial position, we will first compare data from Japanese – where codas and therefore medial clusters are extremely limited – and Polish, where they are remarkably diverse.

In a study of Japanese phonological development, Ota (2001) notes the following stage in the acquisition of coda-onset sequences:

(4)	Japanese medial coda acquisition (Ota, 2001)			
	Target	*Child*	*Gloss*	*Age*
	/ombɯ/	[obbo]	*carry me!*	1;9.28
	/daŋgo/	[dakko]	*dumpling*	1;11.23
	/peŋgiN/	[peppiː]	*penguin*	1;10.2
	/kentʃaN/	[tettʲa]	*name (dim)*	2;0.6
	/otʃintʃiN/	[dziddzi]	*penis*	1;10.26

In Japanese, the only possible coda consonants are nasals (as in (4)'s targets) or the first half of a geminate – and these children appear to only allow the geminate option. Let's contrast this pattern with a data set from a child learning Polish, a language with a rich variety of medial consonant sequences (all Polish data in this section come from Lukaszewicz, 2007).

To begin with, what does the pattern in (4) have in common with (5) below? Focus on the underlined target clusters:

(5)	Polish medial coda acquisition: O at ages 4;0–4;4 (Lukaszewicz, 2007: ex. 20)		
	Target	*Child*	*Gloss*
	/vɛʂwɨ/	[vɛsːɨ]	*(they, fem.) entered*
	/pɔʂwa/	[pɔsːa]	*(she) went*
	/pɔmiçlaw/	[pɔmisːaw]	*(he) thought*
	/kartɔflɛ/	[kantɔfːɛ]	*potatoes (nom.)*
	/zasnɔw/	[zasːɔw]	*(he) fell asleep*

While the processes are different, the output goals are the same: both children are creating surface coda-onset geminates. In Japanese, this repair is triggered by nasal codas, while in the Polish grammar these are triggered by fricative+sonorant clusters, such as /sw, kl, sn/.

What kind of structural constraints should we use to explain these patterns? First, note that we don't want to build constraints that prefer these codas in their own right, because stops and especially fricatives are by no means the most typologically-preferred codas. But what makes them optimal here is their role as the first half of a geminate: they make the best possible codas because they are nothing but an extension of an adjacent onset, and so introduce no additional structure of their own. (Note that a few target languages <u>only</u> allow codas which geminate from a following onset – e.g. the Micronesian language Woleaian, which only allows geminates as codas word-internally; see Sohn, 1975.)

The structural constraints that we will use to capture this pattern go under the name of 'Coda Conditions' (following Ito, 1986, 1989). As defined in (6), these prevent classes of features from being associated *only* with a coda position – thus, codas do not violate CODACOND if they share that feature with a following onset. The original CODACOND bans codas from bearing their own *place* features (6a), but we will also want a CODACOND on manner features too (6b).

(6a) CODACOND-PLACE   *CODA-PLACE
      Assign a violation for every coda which is uniquely associated with a place feature
(6b) CODACOND-MANNER   *CODA-MANNER
      Assign a violation for every coda which is uniquely associated with a manner feature

Tableau (7) shows how these constraints prefer geminate coda-onset clusters in Japanese, and thereby drive unfaithfulness to a number of segmental features. Notice that some familiar constraints have been brought in to rule out alternative methods of satisfying *CODA-MANNER (the input already satisfies *CODA-PLACE, as does target Japanese):

(7)

	/daŋ$_1$ɡ$_2$o/	*CODA-MANNER	*NASAL/ONSET[2]	MAX	IDENT [+/-NASAL]	IDENT [+/-SON]
	daŋ$_1$ɡ$_2$o ∕ ＼ [+son,+nas] [-son,-nas]	*!				
☞	dak$_1$k$_2$o ∨ [-son, -nas][3]				*	*
	daŋ$_1$ŋ$_2$o		*!			
	dak$_2$o			*!		

---

[2] This is not the only possible explanation for why the winning candidate's geminate is a velar (oral) stop and not a nasal. What other constraint might be responsible?
[3] In this text we will not be concerned with the precise representation of this featural sharing – that is whether there are one or two [-son] features in this candidate. We will also disregard the devoicing in these candidates, although see later in this chapter on voicing acquisition.

6.1.1   A Case Study of Polish Coda-Onset Acquisition

Now let us look more carefully at other word-medial clusters in O's grammar: what coda-onset requirements are being imposed here, and how? To make the pattern a bit easier to see, syllabification has been added to the child outputs:

(8)

	Target	Child	Gloss
	More of O's Polish medial clusters: (Łukaszewicz, 2007: 65, 67–68)		
a)	/albɔ/	[am.bɔ]	or
	/tɨlkɔ/	[tɨŋ.kɔ]	only
	/bajk'i/	[baŋ.k'i]	fairy tales (nom.)
	/kartɔflɛ/	[kan.tɔf:ɛ]	potatoes (nom.)
	/star.tsa/	[tsan.tsa]	old man (gen.)

	Target	Child	Gloss
	More of O's Polish medial clusters: (Łukaszewicz, 2007: 65, 67–68)		
b)	/nudnɔ/	[jun.dɔ]	boring (adv.)
	/vɨbraw/	[vɨm.baw]	(he) chose
	/dɔbra/	[dɔm.ba]	good (fem.)
	/upadwa/	[wu.pan.da]	(she) fell
	/ɔgrɔdzɛ/	[ɔŋ.gɔ.dzɛ]	garden (loc.)

Again, these data show a variety of mappings to achieve a single output configuration: a *homorganic*[4] nasal coda+obstruent onset. Put together with the data from (5), it would seem that along the way to acquiring Polish medial cluster phonotactics, O has built a grammar that precisely matches target Japanese!

Before getting too excited about this convergence, we must note that actually O's grammar is only identical to Japanese when combining obstruents and sonorants in medial clusters. Like target Polish (and completely unlike target Japanese), O happily tolerates medial sequences of fricatives and stops:

---

[4]Meaning 'produced at the same place of articulation'.

(9)	O's Polish obstruent clusters: (Łukaszewicz, 2007: 58–59, 63)		
	Target	*Child*	*Gloss*
	/pat.ʂi/	[pat.sɨ]	*(he or she) looks*
	/ɕɔstra/	[sɔs.ta]	*sister (nom.)*
	/mwɔt.si/	[mɔt.sɨ]	*younger (masc.)*
	/kf'jatk'i/	[katk'i]	*flowers*
	/fsistkɔ/	[siskɔ]	*everything*
	/mrufka/	[mufka]	*ant (nom.)*

Thus we have several puzzle pieces to fit together. Given an obstruent-sonorant cluster, O's grammar applies multiple processes to achieve a Japanese-like configuration. First, other sonorant codas are turned into nasals, and their place is matched to their following onset. More drastically, input stop-sonorant clusters also undergo *metathesis*: the sonorant is placed before the stop, where it also must conform in nasality and place as above. However, our analysis must not predict any featural repair of a coda fricative or stop within an obstruent cluster, as in (9). Adding these to the gemination facts above, we are now going to build an analysis of O's grammar that simultaneously derives the following four optimizations:[5]

(10)   Summary of O's medial cluster mappings

i)	/son + obs/	→	[nasal.obs]	/lb/ → [m.b], *lb
ii)	/stop + son/	→	[nasal.obs]	/dw/ → [n.d], *dw, *wd
iii)	/fri + son/	→	[fric.fric]	/sw/ → [s.s], *sw, *ws, *ns
iv)	/obs + obs/	→	faithful	/ts/ → [ts], *tt, *nt

Let's start with the first two patterns, which suggest that in addition to place assimilation (via *CODA-PLACE), the grammar can impose a specific preference for nasal codas in coda-onset clusters. This pressure is encoded directly in the novel constraint of (11) below. In O's grammar, this structural coda constraint causes manner changes among liquids, glides and nasals, meaning that faithfulness constraints to the features [+/- approximant] and [+/- consonantal] are ranked lower than NASALONLY-CODACOND below:

---

[5] Many of the insights in this analysis come directly from Łukaszewicz (2007), although see that work for alternative explanations for some of these patterns, and more data.

(11) NASALONLY-CODACOND

Assign a violation for every coda which is uniquely associated with any manner feature combinations other than [+son, -approx]

To build an account of (10i) and (10ii) together, we need to be sure about O's potential syllabification of these clusters. Łukaszewicz (2007) demonstrates that at this stage, all of O's word-initial clusters were always reduced to singletons in all circumstances. This means that in O's grammar, *COMPLEXONSET outranked all conflicting constraints, so we need only consider output candidates with C.C syllabifications.[6]

With these syllabifications, the drastic unfaithfulness in (10ii) can be understood as a solution to an extreme coda-onset problem, and once again it is a question of sonority. Cross-linguistically, most languages prohibit their codas from being less sonorous than their adjacent onsets. Encoded in (12), this constraint bans for example *Vd.wV as a possible syllabification:

(12) *SONORITYRISE   (*SONRISE)

Assign a violation for every coda which is lower in sonority than its following onset

For our purposes here, we are going to interpret all obstruents as sharing a degree of maximally-low sonority – so that stops and fricatives are equally (non-) sonorous, and stop-fricative sequences do not violate *SONRISE. This is of course a simplification, but only for the sake of space (for a full set of constraints that would precisely define the sonority-rise threshold that O's grammar permits, see Gouskova, 2004).

To modify stop+sonorant clusters so that they obey *SONRISE, O's grammar is unfaithful in a way that we have not previously seen: the input order of segments is reversed, in a process called *metathesis*. Since it is a well-known (if fairly uncommon) method of repairing cluster phonotactics,[7] metathesis must be a possibility included in output candidates for the grammar to assess – and so there must some faithfulness constraint to prevent it, namely:

---

[6] For sake of comparison: Rubach and Booij (1990) report the results of a syllabification study with Polish-speaking adults, which suggests that obstruent+sonorant medial clusters were syllabified variably, though perhaps more often as complex onsets (e.g. V.brV vs. Vb.rV), but sonorant+obstruent medials were treated as coda+onset, for example Vn.dV.

[7] For examples most similar to this one, see Hume (2004: 208) on metathesis in the Cushitic language Sidamo spoken in Ethiopia, in which /stop+nasal/ → [nasal.stop], and also Hume and Seo (2004) – although those works seek to explain such metathesis with quite different mechanisms.

(13) LINEARITY (Adapted from McCarthy and Prince, 1995)
Assign a violation for every pair of input segments x and y, with output correspondents X and Y, where x precedes y but Y precedes X.

Together with *CODA-PLACE, NASAL-CODACOND and *SONRISE conspire to create the repairs in (10i–ii): sonorants become nasals, and they metathesize with stops to get into coda position. These repairs come at the expense of sonorant manner features, place features and LINEARITY. Make sure you understand the ungrammaticality of the first three candidates in this tableau before reading on.

(14)

	/upad₁w₂a/	*SON RISE	NASAL CODA COND	*CODA PLACE	LINEARITY	IDENT [+/-APPROX], [+/-CONS]	IDENT [LAB]
a)	wu.pad₁.w₂a	*!	*	*			
b)	wu.paw₂.d₁a		*!	*	*		
c)	wu.paɳ₂.d₁a			*!	*	**	
☞ d)	wu.pan₂.d₁a				*	**	*

Since we know that creating a geminate is optimal elsewhere in the system (10iv), let's pause now and see if we understand why the mapping /dw/ → [d.d] is <u>not</u> an option in (14). It must be something to do with <u>faithfulness</u>: mapping /w/ to [d] must be unfaithful in some excessive way, and since it can't be faithfulness to <u>place</u> (since the winner in (14d) does violate IDENT[LABIAL]), it must be faithfulness to <u>manner</u>. If you scan the changes to manner features that O's grammar permits, as summarized in (10), you may notice that some sounds become nasals, and others become fricatives, but no other manner of segment is ever transformed into a *stop*. Thus, one way to rule out gemination in a stop-sonorant input is to prevent unfaithfulness to the unique feature of stops, that is their lack of continuancy. If this faithfulness constraint (IDENT[+/-CONTINUANT]) is ranked above LINEARITY, the metathesis-plus-feature change option is better than geminating:

(15)

	/upad₁w₂a/ / \ [-cont] [+cont]	IDENT [+/-CONT]	LINEARITY
a)	wu.pad₁.d₂a \/ [-cont]	*!	
☞ b)	wu.pan₂.d₁a │ │ [+cont] [-cont]		*

Now let us account for those cases where geminates *do* occur, when the inputs contain fricative+sonorant (10iii). Inputs like /sw/ violate the same three structural constraints as /dw/ in (14). However, since both /s/ and /w/ are already [+continuant], IDENT[+/-CONT] does not block the complete featural assimilation solution (as it did in 15a) – and so creating a geminate is a possibility.

The tableau in (16) walks us through this mapping. First, what faithfulness constraints are violated by the creation of a geminate? Here, mapping /w/ to [s] violates faithfulness to place, but moreover there is necessarily a change in sonority – recall that geminates are only created when fricatives are followed by sonorants. Comparing the candidates in (16c–d), we find a ranking argument: LINEARITY must outrank IDENT[+SONORANT], since this /w/ becomes an obstruent (in d) rather than metathesizing (in c):

(16)

		/$v\varepsilon s_1 w_2 \dot{\imath}$/	*SONRISE	NASAL CODACOND[8]	LINEARITY	IDENT [+SON]	IDENT [LABIAL]
	a)	$v\varepsilon s_1.w_2\dot{\imath}$	*!				
	b)	$v\varepsilon w_2.s_1\dot{\imath}$		*!	*		
	c)	$v\varepsilon n_2.s_1\dot{\imath}$			*!		*
☞	d)	$v\varepsilon s_1.s_2\dot{\imath}$				*	*

What may be easy to miss is that this IDENT[+F] constraint violated by the winner (16d) is different than those we have used thus far: examine its definition below carefully!

(17) IDENT[+SONORANT] (adapted from Pater, 2001)
Assign a violation for every input segment with the feature [+sonorant] whose output correspondent has the feature [-sonorant]

In other words, this constraint only prohibits /sonorant/ → [obstruent], and not the reverse. To see why this is crucial, we turn to our final data point (10iv): the obstruent clusters that don't change at all. Using the constraints we have accumulated, can we explain why obstruent+obstruent clusters survive?

As for why obstruent clusters cannot turn into geminates, we have the tools but require an additional ranking. Tableau (18) shows how IDENT[+/-CONT] will prevent any gemination in a fricative+stop or stop+fricative cluster – and

---

[8] Why does the optimal candidate (16d) not violate Nasal-CODACOND? Remember its definition, whereby codas only need to be nasals if they are <u>uniquely</u> associated with manner features, hosting them on their own. This coda gets all of its features from the following onset, and so gets a free ride to vacuously satisfy all CODACOND constraints.

since the faithful cluster is preferred, it must outrank NASAL-CODACOND. (Recall that *SONRISE is only violated by obstruent+sonorant clusters, and so cannot drive unfaithfulness here.)

(18)

/pat$_1$s$_2$i/	IDENT [+/-CONT]	NASAL CODACOND
pat$_1$t$_2$i	*!	
pas$_1$s$_2$i	*!	
☞ pat$_1$s$_2$i		*!

As for why obstruent clusters do not undergo nasalization (and possible metathesis) – this returns us to that picky faithfulness constraint IDENT[+SON]. While O's grammar repairs some phonotactics by mapping sonorants to fricatives, like [sw] → /ss/, it will not tolerate the reverse, meaning it never maps obstruents to sonorants (such as nasals). This means that the mirror image of (17), IDENT[-SON] must also be ranked above NASAL-CODACOND (LINEARITY is included in this tableau only to remind us it is too low-ranked to make this choice):

(19)

/pat$_1$s$_2$i/	IDENT [-SON]	NASAL CODACOND	LINEARITY
pan$_2$.t$_1$i	*!		*
☞ pat$_1$.s$_2$i		*!	

With no other repairs available, then, medial obstruent clusters are optimal, despite their less than ideal codas.

Congratulations on making it to the end of this analysis! To summarize, (20) provides all the rankings that were necessary in tableaus (14–19) to capture all the medial-cluster phonotactics in O's grammar:

(20)

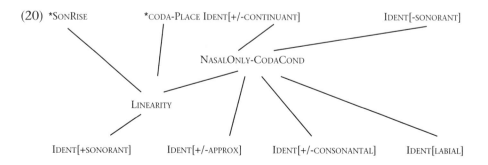

It must be noted that a few loose threads remain. For instance, the input used to exemplify the obstruent-obstruent faithfulness pattern in (18) was carefully chosen to include obstruents *at the same place of articulation*. If we had chosen /fk/ instead, *Coda-Place would insist that the optimal coda-onset cluster should share place, that is /fk/ → *[xk]! In O's grammar, it appears that *CodaPlace is only obeyed when one member of the cluster is a sonorant; this might mean that the constraint needs to be split into multiple *CodaPlace constraints according to manner specifications. For now, we will leave this problem unsolved.

As a final reward for having survived the preceding analysis let us now step back and ask whether cross-linguistic cluster-reduction patterns are ever as complicated as O's many-claused patterns in (10). After carefully constructing the ranking edifice in (20), you should be happy to know that indeed they can be. One well-studied example is from Diola Fogny (a Niger-Congo language spoken in Senegal, described by Sapir, 1965). In this language, coda-onset clusters are restricted in familiar ways – recall your Japanese! – and when reduplication and morpheme concatenation causes illegal clusters to be created, a couple of different repairs are possible.

(21)	Coda-onset clusters in Diola Fogny (Sapir, 1965; data here from McCarthy, 1999)		
	/ni-maŋ-maŋ/	ni.mam.maŋ	*I want*
	/ni-ŋan-ŋan/	ni.ŋaŋ.ŋan	*I cried*
	/najum-to/	na.jun.to	*he stopped*
	/pan-dʒi-maɲdʒ/	paɲ.dʒi.maɲdʒ	*you (pl.) will know*
	/na-tiŋ-tiŋ/	na.tin.tiŋ	*he cut through*
	/ku-boɲ-boɲ/	ku.bom.boɲ	*they sent*
	/ujuk-ja/	uju.ja	*if you see*
	/let-ku-jaw/	le.ku.jaw	*they won't go*
	/kob-kob-en/	ko.ko.ben	*yearn for*
	/a-jaw-bu-ŋar/	a.ja.bu.ŋar	*voyager*
	/na-laɲ-laɲ/	na.la.laɲ	*he returned*
	/na-joken-joken/	na.jo.ke.jo.ken	*he tires*
	/na-waɲ-am-waɲ/	na.wa.ɲa.waɲ	*he ploughed for me*

No analysis will be provided here for this data – all the conceptual tools should be available to you now, even if some constraint definitions will need revising or (re)inventing. If you get stuck, Ito (1986, 1989) provide initial analyses, in a pre-OT framework (see also McCarthy, 1999 analysis).

6.1.2   Geminates

Let's now return to a special structure with a prosodic connection that we've just discussed: consonantal geminates. Phonemic length in consonants is in fact fairly rare: Maddieson (1984) reports only 6% of 317 sampled languages with geminates. Here we will consider the development of geminates in three different languages, and merely touch upon the insights and questions they raise.

Japanese words include many geminates, which are implicated in the phonology's extensive sensitivity to weight among *rimes*, and Ota (2001)'s longitudinal study of prosodic development reveals that children acquire this sensitivity early. At the very beginning of productive phonology, geminates are all reduced to singletons; this can be understood as simply the work of syllable structure constraints, since all coda consonants are in fact deleted, and the first half of a geminate is always part of a coda. At a second stage, two children began to produce only sonorant geminates, but not obstruents.[9] And at a slightly later stage (but still under the age of two!) these same children began creating geminates in a grammatically-controlled way – not only to repair illegal codas as we saw in the previous section, but also to replace the second half of shortened long vowels:

(22)	Japanese geminate acquisition (Ota, 2001: 80)			
	Target	*Child*	*Gloss*	*Age*
	/tʃoːtʃo/	[tʃɯːʃɯ]	*butterfly*	1;10.23
	/niːtʃaN/	[ditːan]	*big brother*	1;11.23
	/çikoːki/	[kokːi]	*plane*	1;10.16
	/keːki/	[kɪkːɪ]	*cake*	1;10.2

---

[9]Note however that the typological study of consonantal geminates suggests that languages actually prefer obstruent geminates to sonorant ones, arguably for good perceptual reasons (see especially Kawahara, 2007).

This latter stage suggests that the acquisition of Japanese geminates is determined by the acquisition of prosody. That is, once the constraints on rime structure are correctly ranked and faithfulness to segmental weight is enforced, children use geminates as part of this system. To think about this a little further, see the first exercise at the end of this chapter.

Another language with prevalent use of geminates is Finnish, and it has been reported that if anything children acquiring Finnish demonstrate a distinct preference for geminates in early outputs. The data in (23), taken from two different learners in their second year, shows geminates being faithfully preserved or even created, while other syllable structure is lost:

(23)	Finnish geminates between 1;1–1;7 (Data from Savinainen-Makkonen, 2000b, 2007)						
	Target	*Child*	*Gloss*		*Target*	*Child*	*Gloss*
	/anːikɑ/	[akːɑ]	*(name)*		/kortːi/	[kotːi]	*card*
	/lusikːɑ/	[uːkɑ]	*spoon*		/irti/	[itːi]	*off*
	/keŋkæ/	[kenːæ]	*shoe*		/keksi/	[kekːi]	*biscuit*
	/aŋkːɑ/	[akːɑ]	*duck*		/nostaː/	[otːɑː]	*carry*

The first 50 words of one Finnish-learning child Joel included 37 words with geminates (74% of his total vocabulary!) Among these words, most include geminates in their inputs – but in some cases, the geminate was of Joel's own making:

(24)	Finnish *inserted* geminates between 1;1–1;7 (Data from Savinainen-Makkonen, 2007)		
	Target	*Child*	*Gloss*
	/æiti/	[ætːi]	*mother*
	/auki/	[akːi]	*open*
	/meni/	[enːi]	*went*
	/nami/	[mamːi]	*candy*

This preponderance of geminates in early Finnish speech has been used as evidence that (some) children's early phonological outputs adhere to phonological *templates*. In this view, surface forms are regulated not by structural constraints against particular structures or features, but rather by prescribed whole word shapes – for example ['VC:V] – and pieces of the input are modified or abandoned in order to fit this desired word shape. This idea will be discussed in more detail in Chapter 7.5.

6.1.3   Positional Allophones and Neutralizations, among Children and Adults

This section will touch very briefly on two types of contextual restrictions on segments and features. Each is found in both child and adult languages alike, but there is some considerable ambiguity and debate as to their connections and similarities.

The first kind of distribution is often observed in early production of laryngeal features, such as voicing. Chapter 5.3 discussed the observation that voiceless, unaspirated stops often show children's first voicing setting, though this output may be interpreted differently by adults depending on the target language's voicing system. As an example of what happens once multiple voicing features emerge, Johnson and Reimers (2010) provide a representative data sample:

(25) British English: early voicing
(Data from Johnson and Reimers, 2010: 12–13)

Target	Child	Target	Child
pig	[bɪk]	*big*	[bɪk]
peg	[bɛk]	*bead*	[bit]
bear	[bɛə]	*flag*	[flæk]
cup	[gʊp]	*Bob*	[bop]
two	[du]		

In this data onsets (word-initial) stops are voiced, and codas are voiceless. The cross-sectional data at the very beginning of Chapter 5 showed a similar pattern in order of acquisition: [b] and [d] were the first word-initial stops, and [p, t, k] were first found word-finally.

In the cross-linguistic typology of voicing, there is a clear asymmetry which partially replicates (25)'s pattern: coda voicing contrasts are commonly neutralized to [-voice], and (nearly?) never to [+voice]. This restriction causes the familiar syllable-final devoicing pattern in languages such as German and Dutch. German data in (26) demonstrates that the voicing contrast seen between vowels (compare *wheels* with *to advise*) is neutralized at the end of these words singular forms:

(26) German syllable-final devoicing (Data here from Flynn, 2012)

Ra[t]	Rä[d]er	*wheel ~ wheels*	Ra[t]	ra[t]en	*advice ~ to advise*
Flu[k]	Flü[g]e	*flight ~ flights*	Vol[k]	Vol[k]e	*people (nom. ~ dative)*

Continued

| akti[f] | afti[v]e | *active (sg. ~ pl)* | Ho[f] | Hö[f]e | *courtyard ~ yards* |
| Gra[s] | Grä[z]er | *grass ~ grasses* | Ro[s] | Ro[s]e | *horse ~ horses* |

On the one hand, these child grammars appear to be imposing coda devoicing, just as in target German and so on. On the other hand, the grammar is similarly restricting onset position to only voiced obstruents – and this pattern is rather or very *un*common in adult typology, if attested at all. (In fact, some theoretical approaches go to considerable lengths to avoid it.) This neutralization in children's onset positions is therefore left unexplained.

The grammar of Amahl provides a different distribution of voicing features, as you can work out from the data below:

(27)	Amahl's voicing at 2;6 (Data from Smith, 1973: 37)					
	Target	*Child*	*Target*	*Child*	*Target*	*Child*
	pen	[pɛn]	*open*	[ubuː]	*bump*	[pʌpʼ]
	ball	[pɔː]	*elbow*	[ɛbuː]	*cube*	[kuːpʼ]
	turn	[təːn]	*naughty*	[nɔːdiː]	*nut*	[nʌtʼ]
	door	[tɔː]	*greedy*	[kiːdː]	*hard*	[aːtʼ]
	come	[kʌm]	*sticky*	[kigiː]	*milk*	[mikʼ]
	grape	[keipʼ]	*lego*	[kɛguː]	*egg*	[ɛkʼ]

In this grammar, we see a three-way distribution of voicing. To see a relevant adult language comparison, determine the voicing patterns of Swampy Cree:

(28)	Voicing in Swampy Cree (See Wolfart, 1975)					
	[asabap]	*thread*	[paskwaw]	*prairie*	[ogik]	*these*
	[mibit]	*tooth*	[ospwagan]	*pipe*	[kodak]	*another*
	[wabos]	*rabbit*	[kogos]	*pig*	[adim]	*dog*
	[nabew]	*man*	[tahki]	*often*	[nisto]	*three*
	[pimi]	*lard*	[mide]	*heart*	[tʃigahigan]	*axe*

What voicing restrictions do both grammars share? First, intervocalic stops (or all obstruents) are uniformly voiced. This process of *intervocalic voicing* is robustly attested around the world (Kaplan, 2010 identifies 26 languages in which voiceless stops are voiced between vowels; see also Gurevich, 2004).

Second, those stops (or obstruents) which are not intervocalic are all voiceless – making voicing in both grammars completely *allophonic*, and this too is common enough (recall the 32% of languages without phonemic voicing contrasts).

An OT grammar is well-equipped to capture allophony – so long as the necessary structural constraints are available. With respect to the distribution of voicing, we have seen (i) that some languages have only voiceless obstruents but none have only voiced, and (ii) that languages like Swampy Cree typically permit only voiceless obstruents, <u>except</u> in one specific context, when they are voiced between vowels. These generalizations suggest two structural constraints: a general one that prohibits voiced obstruents (29), and a more specific one that can impose the 'except'-clause, prohibiting voiceless obstruents just when intervocalic (30):

(29) *[-SON, +VOICE]   *VCDOBS
     Assign a violation for every output voiced obstruent

(30) *V[-SON, -VOICE]V   *VTV
     Assign a violation for every output voiceless obstruent between vowels

Let's build a simple tableau to illustrate. The Swampy Cree word [ogik] has a word-final [k], because of general *VCDOBS, and it has a medial [g] because the specific *VTV is ranked higher:

(31)

/ogik/	*VTV	*VCDOBS
☞ [ogik]		*
[okik]	*!	
[ogig]		**!
[okig]	*!	*

And what about faithfulness? The crucial thing about allophones is that they are totally *predictable* – given their context, you can predict their value <u>regardless of the input</u>. In Swampy Cree (and Amahl's) grammar, if a stop is word-initial, you know it will be voiceless. This means that IDENT[+/-VOICE] must be ranked <u>below</u> the structural constraints that do the work of predicting voicing. To return to Amahl's grammar: this is why *grape* and *sticky* are each unfaithful to voicing, where the structural constraints dictate:

(32)

/stɪki/	*VTV	*VCDOBS	IDENT[+/-VOICE]
[kikiː]	*!		
[gikiː]	*!	*	*
☞ [kigiː]		*	*

(33)	/gɹeip'/	*VᴛV	*VᴄᴅOʙs	Iᴅᴇɴᴛ[+/-ᴠᴏɪᴄᴇ]
	[geip']		*!	
☞	[keip']			*

The upshot thus far is that children's early voicing features are controlled by structural, prosodic pressures, some of which are well-attested in adult languages, but some of which (word-initial neutralization to [+voice]) are not. If we account for onset patterns like (25) using a structural constraint that bans initial voiceless stop, we will be making the incorrect prediction that such neutralizations occur in adult languages too.

A final sidenote regarding Amahl's word-final laryngeal features. Translating from their original description, these segments have been transcribed above as ejectives [C'] (following e.g. Goad, 2010). In featural terms, it is probably reasonable to assume that these final stops were [+constricted glottis], being a feature attributed to ejectives, glottal stop, creaky vowels and various other 'tense' sounds. In languages with *contrastive* [+constricted glottis], this feature is usually <u>neutralized</u>, rather than preserved, in word-final contexts. For example, the Wakashan language Nuu-chah-nulth spoken on the south-western edge of Canada has a phonemic contrast between plain and ejective consonants, but it is preserved only in syllable-initial contexts, and neutralized in codas (Howe and Pulleyblank, 2001) – see also the Korean data set later in this chapter. Thus, Amahl's word-final [+c.g.] stops seem rather odd. On the other hand, however, it appears that word-final voiceless stops can undergo phonetic processes which result in constricted glottis release. In various British English dialects, /k/ in particular is often reported as [k'], at least in utterance-final (pre-pausal) contexts (discussed in Wells, 1982; Cruttenden, 2008) and see also Goad and Brannen (2003) for a discussion of children's early word-final stop release bursts.

The grammar of voicing in target languages like German is an example of the other featural pattern we now turn to, namely *contextual neutralizations*. Such final devoicing is broadly representative of the overall pattern: target languages tend to retain their featural contrasts more often in onsets, and neutralize them in codas. An example that includes both laryngeal and manner features comes from Korean: obstruent onsets can include stops, fricative and affricates, with a three-way voicing contrast, while in coda all obstruents are unreleased stops:

(34)	Coda neutralization in Korean (Data here from Jun and Lee, 2007)[10]					
	Locative	*Isolation form*	*Gloss*	*Locative*	*Isolation form*	*Gloss*
	[ose]	[ot˺]	*clothes*	pape	[pap̚]	*rice*
	[patʰe]	[pat˺]	*field*	ipʰe	[ip̚]	*leaf*
	[natʃe]	[nat˺]	*day*	pakʼe	[pak̚]	*outside*
	[pitʃʰe	[pit˺]	*light*	puəkʰ e	[puək̚]	*kitchen*

Turning now to manner features in child grammars: there is ample data regarding children's positional neutralization of manner, but the results are by no means uniform. Fricatives provide a particularly murky test case. In some cases, fricatives are convincingly acquired first in onset position by some children (Rvachew and Andrews, 2002; Altvater-Mackensen and Fikkert, 2010 – and recall also data at the beginning of Chapter 5). More often, however, it appears that fricatives emerge and stabilize first in <u>coda position</u> (e.g. Dinnsen, 1996; Stoel-Gammon, 2002; McAllister Byun, 2011). As McAllister Byun (2011) emphasizes, this pattern in child production is at odds with the adult typology typified by the Korean data in (34).

The case of positional neutralization among laterals is also somewhat confused. Like the treatment of rhotics discussed in Chapter 5.7, the differing places of articulation for laterals no doubt influences their contextual restriction in language-specific ways. As we saw beginning with Tweety Bird, the velar coda allophone [ɫ] is frequently vocalized in early English, whereas alveolar [l] is much more likely to be glided. Unlike in English, children acquiring French, Italian and Portuguese have all been reported to delete some word-initial /l/s altogether:

(35)	Lateral deletion in French (Data from Ingram, 1986)		
	Target	*Child*	*Gloss*
	/lɑ̃p/	[ɑ̃p]	*lamp*
	/læ/	[æ]	*the*
	/liʁ/	[i]	*read*
	/lɣn/	[um]	*moon*

---

[10] These locative forms represent the 'standard', traditional outputs, which are undergoing some reorganization in modern Korean – see Jun and Lee (2007) for more details.

A larger pattern of onset sonorant deletion has been reported as fairly pervasive in early Finnish across children (see especially Savinainen-Makkonen, 2000a and references therein). The data below show its effect on one child's laterals:

(36)

Sara at 1;10: Finnish lateral deletion (Data from Savinainen-Makkonen, 2000a: 173, 177)					
Target	*Child*	*Gloss*	*Target*	*Child*	*Gloss*
/lampːu/	[ampːu]	*lamp*	/lentokone/	[entoe]	*aeroplane*
/lopːu/	[opːu]	*end*	/lehmæ/	[ehmæ]	*cow*
/lentæː/	[entæː]	*fly*			

Taken as a whole, neutralization in onset position represents a notable discrepancy between child and adult phonologies: whether collapsing laryngeal features to [+voice], stopping fricatives, deleting liquids wholesale – and also the neutralization of coronal vs. velar place seen in velar fronting (Chapter 5.5.5). In any event, this section must end on a necessarily unsettled note; there is much here that we do not yet understand.

6.2   Interactions Between Consonants and Vowels

As noted in this book's introduction, this text does not focus on the acquisition of vowels proper (see further readings). However, this section will introduce you to one interaction between the acquisition of consonants that we've been studying thus far and some featural properties of vowels.

Perhaps the most common or primary consonant-vowel interaction observed in child phonologies is exemplified below, from an early study of child English. Can you describe it featurally, before reading on?

(37)

		Consonant and vowels: child at 1;4 (Fudge, 1969)							
	a)	*Target*	*Child*	b)	*Target*	*Child*	c)	*Target*	*Child*
		ball	[bo]		*drink*	[ti]		*cake*	[kʌk]
		book	[bo]		*again*	[den]		*truck*	[kʌk]
		dog	[bobo]					*garden*	[gʌŋ]
		mummy	[mɔmmo]					*doggie*	[gʌgɯ]

As these words come from a very early production stage, there are many aspects of unfaithfulness to the adult targets here (cluster reduction, coda deletion etc.), but our main interest is the restriction on place of articulation. Perhaps this is most obvious in the two output versions of *dog* or *doggie*: either [bobo] or [gʌguɯ], the first containing two labial consonants and the latter two velars. For every word here, all consonants match in place of articulation – the forms [den] and [gʌŋ] confirm that the consonants needn't be identical in *all* features, but certainly place. But [bobo] or [gʌguɯ] also contain different vowels, and the three data columns in (37) groups outputs both in terms of their output consonant place as well as their output *vowel* place. Outputs in (a) have the vowels [o] and [ɔ]; those in (b) have [i], [e], and in (c) [ʌ], [ɯ]. This is not an accident!

Before we generalize and analyse, let us examine a similar phenomenon in Dutch. Starting with the three vowel groups from (37), attempt to characterize the consonant-vowel co-occurrences below in the initial vocabulary of one child, Eva, also at 1;4. In this Dutch child's grammar, which vowels go with which consonants? You may need to consult an IPA chart for the vowels [œ] and [y].

(38)	Dutch consonant and vowels: Eva at 1;4;12 (Fikkert and Levelt, 2008: table 7)						
a)	*Target*	*Child*	*Gloss*	b)	*Target*	*Child*	*Gloss*
	/'oma/	[oma]	*granny*		/dɪxt/	[diə]	*closed*
	/ɔp/	[ɔp]	*on*		/ent/	[ein]	*duck*
	/'opə(n)/	[opə]	*open*		/'etə(n)/	[eitɪ]	*eat*
	/bœyk/	[bœyp]	*tummy*		/bɛt/	[dɛt]	*bed*
	/brot/	[mop]	*bread*		/prɪk/	[tɪt]	*injection*
	/'slɔfə(n)/	[pɔfə]	*slippers*		/ber/	[dɛ]	*bear*
	/pus/	[puf]	*cat*		/nøs/	[nɛs]	*nose*
	/'sxunə(n)/	[umə]	*shoes*		/ko'nɛin/	[tɛin]	*rabbit*

The most important cases are those like *prik* → [tit], /boeik/ → [bœyp] and /ʃœnen / → [umə], where the place of articulation of input consonants seems to be easily disregarded, but whose vowels remain quite faithful. And thus to understand these patterns, we must look at vocalic *place*.

Taken together, these data require distinguishing three types of vowel articulation. Let's start with the (a) words from both (37) and (38): these forms include the consonants [b, p, m, f], that is only *labial* consonants, and their vowels include [o,ɔ] in English, and [o, ɔ, œ, y, u] in Dutch.[11] And what

---

[11] Ignoring schwa.

do these vowels all have in common? If you had to look up the non-English vowels of Dutch in IPA chart, you may have guessed: because all these vowels are *rounded* – meaning they too, featurally speaking, are [labial].

The (b) outputs include the vowels [i, e, ɪ, ɛ] – these vowels are all unrounded, and they are all also found in the *front* of the vowel space. In consonantal place terms, this 'front' vowel area is roughly located somewhere in the post-alveolar-to-palatal region. (To remind yourself of this, note that the high front vowel [i] can easily turn into the palatal glide [j], if you just raise your tongue a little higher; an emphatic pronounciation of the letter 'e' will probably sound like [iiiiijjjj]). Thus, we can say that in consonantal terms, these vowels would be [coronal] – and note that the consonants in (b) outputs are [t, d, n, s] – all coronals too.

There are no (c) words in this early Dutch lexicon, but the English ones consist of dorsal consonants and back vowels [u, ʊ]. Recalling again that the high back vowel [u] can easily be turned into a velar glide [w], it should not be surprising that back vowels share the [dorsal] place feature as well. (Note that [u] appears to be treated differently in English vs. Dutch – it is both [round] and [labial], and each language prizes one of these features more than the other.)

To sum up: at the very initial stages of production, these two child grammars require place sharing or *assimilation* among their vowels and consonants. In fact, <u>entire words</u> have one place of articulation, and all segments must join in (see again Fikkert and Levelt, 2008). As a first pass, we can try writing a schematic structural constraint that these children's grammars obey:

(39)   AGREE-V/C[PLACE][12]
       Assign a violation for every vowel with the feature [α-place] which is adjacent to a consonant with the feature [β-place]

From this text's theoretical perspective, we should pause to note that this structural constraint demands place agreement between output vowels and consonants, but it does not (and cannot) tell us <u>how</u> to enforce agreement when an input violates it. In the Dutch data, we can see that it is the input *vowel* that determines the one output place feature – for example, /prik/'s input coronal vowel assimilates the place of both adjacent consonant, [tit]. As an alternative, one of the consonants might have driven the place assimilation, and in other child grammars such patterns are indeed observed. A cross-sectional study of early Cantonese (So and Dodd, 1995) reported one consistent error among non-target vowels (30% of cases) in which a vowel

---

[12] For some early versions of AGREE[FEATURE] constraints see Bakovic (1999); Eisner (1999); Lombardi (1999). However, AGREE[F] constraints also have their problems: see especially McCarthy (2003).

assimilated to the place of an adjacent consonant: such as /kœk/ → [kɔk]. The difference between these two repairs is most likely the result of ranking different faithfulness constraints: splitting IDENT[PLACE] constraints into vocalic and consonantal versions, and ranking as in (40). In the first candidate (a), note that AGREE V/C[PLACE] is violated *twice* – once for the adjacent [pɪ] string, labial followed by coronal, and once for the adjacent string [ɪk], with coronal followed by dorsal[13]:

(40)		/prik/	AGREEV/C[PLACE]	IDENT[COR]-V	IDENT[COR]-C
	a	[pɪk]	*!*		
	b	[pyp]		*!	
	c	[tɪk]	*!		*
☞	d	[tɪt]			**

From what cross-linguistic analysis is available, it seems that consonantal place assimilation to input vowel place as in (37) and (38) is only attested in the earliest productive phonologies. However, place assimilation of a different sort can survive for much longer: see Section 6.3 below. In addition, there are some compelling parallels to this C–V place assimilation in adult languages. It is especially common for front vowels and coronal consonants to co-occur and for one to attract the other – many languages have processes (variously called *palatalization* or *assibilation*) in which a dorsal consonant becomes coronal when adjacent to (usually preceding) a coronal vowel. In Acadian French (spoken in New Brunswick and other Canadian provinces) /k/ and /g/ as in (41a) have a coronal allophone [tʃ] and [dʒ], whose distribution in (41b) you should now be able to spot:

(41)	Acadian French C/V interaction (Data from Flynn, 2012; citing Hume, 1994[14])				
	a)	*Target*	*Gloss*	b)	*Target*	*Gloss*
		[kʊt]	*cost*		[ki] ~ [tʃi]	*who*
		[ka]	*case*		[kɥir] ~ [tʃɥir]	*leather*
		[ko'te]	*side*		[okɛ̃] ~ [otʃɛ̃]	*not any*

Continued

---

[13] IDENT[LABIAL] and [DORSAL] constraints will also have to be ranked beneath AGREEV/C[PLACE], to ensure that other place featural changes are permitted.

[14] This is slightly simplified – this coronal allophone may vary between a palatalized kʲ and gʲ and the coronal affricate transcribed.

a)	Target	Gloss	b)	Target	Gloss
	[gar]	*station*		[kœr] ~ [tʃœr]	*heart*
	[gʊt]	*drop (n.)*		[kø] ~ [tʃø]	*tail*
	[sark]	*circle*		[gœl] ~ [dʒœl]	*mouth*
	[griˈʃe]	*ruffled*		[gɛˈte] ~ [dʒɛˈte]	*to watch for*

In Acadian French, like the child Cantonese example, it is the class of front vowels whose place survives, and the dorsal consonant which is fronted to satisfy AGREE-V/C[PLACE]. A very similar pattern is seen among back vowels in Xhosa. Traill (1985: 89–90) reports a productive restriction on the shape of Xhosa roots, whereby dorsal consonants cannot be followed by the language's front consonants, [i] and [e]. Since the language includes a large number of clicks, which all contain a velar closure, this means that the distribution of [i] and [e] is highly restricted in native words. In words borrowed from Afrikaans which violate this prohibition, consonants are fronted to enforce C/V place sharing, for example /dɔŋki/ → [ton**ti**] *donkey*.

These target language patterns resemble the place sharing we observed in children's speech above, though they differ too in a couple of respects. One difference is that the target language patterns require a laxer amount of assimilation, in that vowels tend to trigger assimilation only with *one* adjacent consonant (usually the one preceding), and not both. (In Cantonese, there is also a static restriction whereby back round vowels cannot be flanked by coronal consonants – that is, schematic roots like kut, tuk and kuk are all attested, whereas *tut is not.)

As we will see in the next section, the extent and *directionality* of place sharing in phonological grammar is a tricky question. But as it turns out that place assimilation is a big part of child consonantal phonology, that is now where we turn.

6.3   Consonant Harmony

As you may have learnt in your previous study of phonological analysis, featural assimilation (also called *agreement* or *harmony*) is found all over sound patterns in language. This section deals with a very prevalent type of consonant assimilation in child grammars that has been crucial to much theorizing about phonological development – since it shows many similarities to adult harmonies, but also some fundamental divergence.

6.3.1 Manner Harmonies

We will start with consonant harmony patterns, which find the most direct analogues in target languages. Here is one such common example, again from Amahl:

(42)	Amahl (Data here from Johnson and Reimers 2010: 210)			
	Target	*Child*	*Target*	*Child*
	lollypop	[loliːbop]	*wall*	[wɔː], [wɔːl]
	lorry	[loliː]		
	really	[lili]		
	yellow	[lelo]		
	yelling	[lɛlin]		

What features are agreeing here? The segments involved are all coronals approximant: /r/ and /j/ are becoming [l] – but only when there is another lateral <u>elsewhere in the word</u>. This would suggest the feature [+/-lateral] is harmonizing, at least among coronals.[15] Compare this pattern to the allomorphy from Sundanese (a Malayo-Polynesian language of Indonesia), in which the plural infix [-ar-] seen in (43a) surfaces as [-al-] in (43b):

(43)		Sundanese liquid harmony (Cohn, 1992; Rose and Walker, 2011)						
	a)	*Singular*	*Plural*	*Gloss*	b)	*Singular*	*Plural*	*Gloss*
		[kusut]	[karusut]	*messy*		[dahar]	[dalahar]	*eat*
		[damaŋ]	[daramaŋ]	*well (adj.)*		[hormat]	[halormat]	*respect*
		[poho]	[paroho]	*forget*		[pərceka]	[palərceka]	*handsome*
		[ŋoplok]	[ŋaroplok]	*flop down*		[combrek]	[calombrek]	*cold*
		[gɨlis]	[garɨlis]	*beautiful*		[motret]	[malotret]	*take a picture*
		[mahal]	[marahal]	*expensive*		[bɨŋhar]	[balɨŋhar]	*rich*

This alternation also shows /r/ becoming [l], when infixed into a stem that already contains an /l/. Given these patterns, our constraint set will need to contain some kind of structural constraint that bans a sequence containing

---

[15] It might be safe to say that coronality is not important, but rather that simply (i) there are no labial laterals, and (ii) *wall* does not harmonize to *[ɬal] because the English ban against onset velar laterals is ranked high … keep reading.

both an r and an l. At least in Amahl's case, the harmony is bi-directional – the /r/s in both **lorry** and **really** harmonize – so an initial attempt at constraint definition might look like (44):

(44) AGREE-CORONALAPPROX/[+/-LATERAL]
Assign a violation for every pair of output coronal approximants
X and Y, where X is [α-lateral] and Y is [β-lateral]

Note that this AGREE constraint is constructed with two arguments: the first identifies the natural class of segments that are required to agree (coronal approximants), and the second picks out the feature for which that natural class must agree, [+/- lateral]. Cross-linguistic typological studies of adult consonant harmonies find consistent correlations between these two arguments – that is, it is almost always alveolar [ɹ] and [l] that harmonize for [+/-lateral].[16]

To drive harmony, AGREE[LATERAL] must outrank a faithfulness constraint that typically protects this feature. But of course this only explains some of the pattern – because consider the range of relevant output candidates for an input with both [ɹ] and [l] like *really,* shown in (45):

(45)		/ɹili/	AGREE[LATERAL]	IDENT[+/-LATERAL]
	a	[ɹili]	*!	
☞	b	[ɹiɹi]		*
☞	c	[lili]		*

This AGREE constraint requires harmony, but does not specify <u>which feature wins</u> – an output candidate with two laterals is no better than one with no laterals. How should the grammar distinguish between these two candidates, so that [lili] wins?

To answer this question, you should know that in some target languages [ɹiɹi] does, in fact, win. As an example: there is a benefactive suffix /-il/ or /-el/ in the Bantu language Bukusu spoken in Kenya (Odden, 1994) that provides a mirror image to Sundanese, turning into [ir] or [er] only to harmonize with an [r] earlier in the word, so that for example /te:x/ is suffixed as [te:x-el-a] '*cook for,*' but /re:b/ becomes [re:b-er-a] '*ask for*'. What this should tell you is that the grammar must have some <u>re-rankable</u> way to choose between candidates (45b-c) – try coming up with a constraint that does so![17]

---

[16] There do not appear to be good examples of /j/ and /l/ harmonizing in a target language grammar, representing a small divergence between child and adult patterns.

[17] In both Sundanese and Bukusu, it is the suffix liquid that harmonizes with the root's consonant: see Rose and Walker (2004); Hansson (2001, 2010) for a full account of how to capture these differences that is much more thorough than this section's analyses.

Now we will turn to a second kind of harmony, comparing the child data from Daniel and Trevor's fairly early speech in (46) to the adult language data in (47). What feature is harmonizing, under what circumstances?

(46a)

Daniel at 1;8–2;1 (Menn, 1971)[18]			
Target	*Child*	*Target*	*Child*
broom	[mʌm]	*jump*	[mʌmp]
bump	[mʌmp]	*stone*	[non]
prune	[nun], [mum]	*down*	[naʊn]
blimp	[mɪmp]		

(46b)

Trevor (1;3–2;0) (Data here from Dinnsen and O'Connor, 2001)			
Target	*Child*	*Target*	*Child*
mower	[momə]	*around*	[əmaund]
crying	[kaiːnɪŋ]	*iron*	[aiːnən]
window	[nɪnoː]	*raining*	[neni]
mirror	[mɪmə]	*run*	[nʌn]
ring	[nɪŋ]	*siren*	[saiːnən]

(47)

Harmony in Yaka (Hyman, 1995, data here from Rose and Walker, 2011)					
Root	*Perfective*	*Gloss*	*Root*	*Perfective*	*Gloss*
[sól]	[sól-ele]	*deforest*	kém	[kém-ene]	*moan*
[jád]	[jád-idi]	*spread*	nútúk	[nútúk-ini]	*bow*
[kúːnd]	[kúːnd-idi]	*bury*	méːŋg	[méːŋg-ene]	*hate*

These data sets all exemplify *nasal harmony*, in which the presence of a nasal consonant is the *trigger* that drives another natural class of consonants to become nasal as well. Looking back, you will see that in each grammar, the *targets* (i.e. the class that becomes nasal) are slightly different. For Daniel's

---

[18] We will return to the development of this pattern in Chapter 7.4.

stage in (46a), nasal harmony affects voiced and voiceless stops; for Trevor, it targets laterals and glides; in Yaka, it targets voiced stops and laterals. Lateral and nasal harmonies are thus shared across child and adult grammars – even if they differ somewhat in their scope and targets, they look analogous along the lines of many patterns we have already seen.

6.3.2 More Divergent Harmonies

We now delve, however, into the most common child harmony pattern, a subset of which is shown in Amahl's grammar in (48). First determine what defines this subset of the data, and then describe the triggers and targets for the harmony seen in all these words:

(48)	Amahl at 2;01–2;03 (Smith, 1973; data in part from Goad, 2010)							
a)	*Target*	*Child*	b)	*Target*	*Child*	c)	*Target*	*Child*
	kiss	[gɪk]		*stalk*	gɔːk		*black*	[bæk]
	coach	[guːk]		*dark*	gaːk		*milk*	[mik]
	glasses	[gaːgi]		*duck*	gʊk		*swing*	[wiŋ]
	clean	[giːn]		*sticky*	gigiː		*grape*	[geip]
	skin	[gin]		*snake*	ŋeik		*escape*	[geːp]
				neck	ŋ(g)ɛk		*come*	[gʊm]

The data in (48) all include a velar consonant /g,k,ŋ/ in one position of the input, and either a labial or coronal elsewhere. The columns in (a) and (b) show consonantal place harmony, with the feature [velar] as trigger and [coronal] as target: the coronals at the beginning of *duck* and end of *coach* both become velar, [gʊk] and [guːk] respectively. Those two examples also show that harmony flows in either direction when the target is a coronal <u>obstruent</u>. When it is a <u>nasal</u>, however, harmony is only *regressive*, meaning that the target's feature must follow the target, and so 'regresses' its featural value back earlier in the word: thus *snake* harmonizes, but *clean* and *skin* don't.[19] Column (c) shows that labials are never targets of velar harmony: neither the /b/ of *black* or the /m/ of *come* is affected by the velar consonant elsewhere in the word.

---

[19] Regressive harmony vs. its opposite, *progressive* harmony, also develop differently over time in Amahl's grammar and those of other children; keep reading.

Notice finally the contrasts between this consonant harmony and the V–C place sharing above in Section 6.2. In this grammar, vocalic place is always irrelevant: for example, the coronal vowel [ɪ] surfaces faithfully as a front vowel in harmonic velar output (*kiss*), disharmonic velar-coronal outputs (*skin*) and disharmonic labial-velar outputs too (*milk*). This was similarly true of the lateral and nasal harmonies seen for both children and adults above – in other words, child consonant harmonies often ignore intervening segments, whether vowels or any other irrelevant natural classes (see below for the adult harmony facts).

A rather similar pattern to Amahl's is also reported by So and Dodd (1995) from the acquisition of Cantonese. In that cross-sectional study of two-year-olds, the authors report that 47/51 non-target consonantal productions classified as 'assimilation' involved a 'syllable-initial alveolar being realized as a velar, in the presence of a syllable-final velar, e.g. /tʰɔŋ/→ [kʰɔŋ].'

Now compare Amahl's harmony with some child French harmony data from Clara in (49). Figure out why some words in both columns harmonize and why others do not, and compare the targets and triggers to those in Amahl's data:

(49)		Clara at 1;3–2;03 (Rose, 2000:168–169)						
	a)	*Target*	*Child*	*Gloss*	b)	*Target*	*Child*	*Gloss*
		/də'bu/	[bɑ'buː]	*standing*		/gas'paʁ/	[ba'pæː]	*(name)*
		/ʃə'val/	[væ'væl]	*horse*			[pæ'pæː]	
		/sa'vɔ̃/	[fə'fɔ]	*soap*		/ka'pab/	[pa'pæb]	*capable*
		/ʃa'po/	[pæ'po]	*hat*		/ka'fe/	[pə'fɛ]	*coffee*
		/wa'zo/	[əwɛ'zuː]	*bird*		/abʁi'ko/	[pupæ'koː]	*apricot*
		/mi'nu/	[mə'nu]	*kitty*		/bɪskɥi/	[βi'kiː]	*cookie*
		/ba'lɛ/	[pə'læ]	*broom*		/fʁi'go/	[bʊ'ko]	*fridge*
		/mu'tɔ̃/	[mʌ'to]	*sheep*		/pi'ke/	[pi'keː]	*to prick*

Clara's consonant harmony is both quite similar to, and yet quite different from Amahl's! They are similar in that both choose a predominant featural trigger, but while Amahl's is [velar] place, Clara's trigger is [labial]. In both columns of (49), a labial consonant sometimes compels agreement with a coronal (49a) or a velar (49b), and what predicts harmony is their relative order – all of this grammar's harmony is regressive, so that an input labial can only trigger harmony in a place feature <u>earlier</u> in the word.

A similar case of purely regressive harmony is reported by Tzakosta (2007) in the speech of several different Greek children. Collapsing across kids in this way, we can see two commonalities among all of these place-changing errors – what are they?

(50) | Regressive harmony in Greek (Data from Tzakosta, 2007)

Target	Child	Age	Gloss
/ˈkani/	[ˈtani]	2;02.12	*do (pres. sg.)*
/ˈcita/	[ˈtita]	1;10.18	*lady*
/traˈpɛzi/	[paˈpɛji]	2;0.06	*table*
/arkuˈðaci/	[tuˈðaci]	2;03.29	*bear (dim)*
/ðaˈskala/	[ɣaˈkala]	2;0.22	*teacher*
/ˈxromata/	[ˈfomata]	2;05.16	*colours*
/ˈkabjɛs/	[baˈbɛ]	1;09.29	*grubs*
/ˈstoma/	[ˈpoma]	2;10.02	*mouth*
/poˈtiri/	[toˈtili]	2;04	*glass*
/ˈkunɛlos/	[ˈtulɛloɥ]	2;06.03	*rabbit*

All of these harmonies are *regressive*, and they transfer the major place of articulation of the <u>second onset onto the first</u>. Note that harmony does not hold between consonants in other prosodic positions – between the second and third onsets we see plenty of disharmony, such as /paˈ**pɛ**ji/or [ɣaˈ**kala**] – and that harmony is regressive regardless of whether the first or second syllable is stressed.

Consonant harmony among the major place features – [coronal], [dorsal] and [labial] – is very common in child phonology. In fact, it probably appears in the speech of at least some child learning every language whose phonological acquisition has been studied.[20] However, this pervasive child harmony pattern is also thoroughly unattested in the world's adult languages, which we will now examine.

---

[20] Although it is definitely not universal among all children: Velten (1943) for example provides a very detailed characterization of his daughter's phonological acquisition, which includes at most a few cases of harmony.

6.3.3   Place Interactions in Target Languages

How do target languages restrain the interaction between place features? There are two relevant kinds of harmony. The first involves long-distance assimilation, but of *secondary* place features. To take a very famous example, the Athapaskan language Navajo (spoken in Arizona and other southwestern US states) has two sets of coronal sibilants which differ in minor place features: alveolars (s, z, ts, dz) and post-alveolars (ʃ, ʒ, tʃ, dʒ). Within a word, alternations show that all sibilants must be at one place or the other (51).

(51)	Sibilant harmony in Navajo (Data from McDonough, 1991)		
	Underlying	*Output*	*Gloss*
	/j-iʃ-mas/	[jismas]	*I'm rolling along*
	/ʃ-is-ná/	[sisná]	*he carried me*
	/si-dʒé:ʔ	[ʃidʒé:ʔ]	*they lie (slender stiff objects)*
	/dzi-ʃ-l-ta:l/	[dʒiʃta:l]	*I kick him (below the belt)*
	/dzi-ʃ-l-ts'in/	[dzists'in]	*I hit him (below the belt)*

Supposing that the featural difference between these two coronal places is [+/-anterior], this means that AGREE[+/-ANTERIOR] must outrank IDENT[ANTERIOR], analogous to the ranking we saw for lateral harmony in (45). Notice too that this harmony is again *regressive*, so that the input value of the last sibilant of the word is what surfaces as the [anterior] setting for all sibilants in the output.

The second kind of place assimilation in target languages comes from Korean, in which medial clusters of stops and nasals are compelled to agree for place under certain featural conditions. The harmony in the lefthand column below shows that velar onsets will impose their place on any preceding coda (52a), and labial onsets will trigger harmony on a preceding coronal coda (52b). In the righthand column, however, other place combinations do not harmonize: velar codas never harmonize with a following onset (52c), and labials do not harmonize with coronals (52d):

(52)		Local place assimilation in Korean (Data here from Pater and Werle, 2003)						
		Harmonizing forms				*Non-harmonizing forms*		
	a)	/əp-ko/	[əkko]	*bear on the back (+conj.)*	c)	/paŋ-to/	[paŋto]	*room as well*
		/kam-ki/	[kaŋki]	*a cold/flu*		/kuk-pap/	[kukpap]	*rice in soup*

Continued

	Harmonizing forms				Non-harmonizing forms		
	/pat-ko/	[pakko]	*receive (+conj.)*				
	/han-kaŋ/	[haŋkaŋ]	*the Han river*				
b)	/kot-palo/	[koppalo]	*straight*	d)	/ip-ta/	[ipta]	*wear*
	/han-bən/	[hambən]	*once*		/sum-ta/	[sumta]	*hide*

In some ways, both the Navajo and Korean data are quite similar to the child place harmonies we have seen: both show *regressive* assimilation, and the Korean pattern shows that when major place is at issue, the most likely target is *coronals*. Beyond these two examples, these directional and featural asymmetries are frequently found in the world's languages (see e.g. Mohanan 1993; Jun 1995; de Lacy, 2002; Hansson, 2001; Rose and Walker, 2004) – and you can also look back at Chapter 5 example (43) for the facts of Catalan nasal assimilation.[21]

So what is crucially different between the child and target grammars? The crux of the matter is the domain of harmony: in target languages, major place assimilation as in Korean is *local*, affecting only adjacent consonants, while all the other consonant harmonies we've seen (including lateral and nasal harmonies) is *non-local*, applying at a distance across vowels and syllables.

This generalization – that in child grammars, major place features harmonize at a distance, while target grammars only harmonize major place in adjacent segments – might not look immediately like a deep chasm to cross. But the problem is considerably amplified by the following observation: target languages do show a common interaction between major place features at a distance, but in the *opposite direction*. That is, non-local major place features do not assimilate, they *dissimilate*!

The tendency to dissimilate major place at a distance has been long known to hold in Semitic languages like Arabic and Hebrew, where lexical stems consist of two, three or four consonants only – for example /sm/, /ktb/, /dhrj/ – interspersed with vowels bearing morphological information

---

[21] Pater and Werle (2003) examines Trevor's pattern of English place harmony, which matches Korean more closely than Amahl's: dorsals trigger harmony that overwrites both coronal and labial place, while labials compel harmony in only coronals. Analysing this three-level pattern of faithfulness requires more complicated tools than those presented in the next section's analysis (in particular, it requires multiple AGREE constraints). Much of the insights throughout this section are inspired by Pater and Werle (2003), de Lacy (2002); see also Goad (1997) and references therein.

like word class, inflection and the like. As described in McCarthy (1986): *'An often noted phenomenon of Semitic languages, first characterized rigorously by Greenberg (1960), is the virtually complete absence of nominal and verbal stems of the pattern CiVCiVC'* (p. 208). Thus there are no stems whose first consonants are both labial, velar, pharyngeal or coronal, for example *[tatak], *[sasat] or *[kagam]. Much research over the past decades has revealed that, when studied statistically, this dispreference for matching major place features within the consonants of a word holds not only as a categorical ban, but also gradiently in the lexicon of many world languages: not just in Semitic, but also English and many others (see e.g. Coetzee and Pater, 2008 and references therein). Thus it is clear that place harmony as observed in child phonology is emphatically at odds with the facts of target languages.

6.3.4 Analysing Consonant Harmony

With all of these facts in place, what kinds of explanation should we use to understand child consonant harmony?

On the one hand, the asymmetries in directionality and targets seen in local place assimilation in target languages must be captured in the grammar, and in fact we already acquired some of the relevant tools in Chapter 5 when discussing Catalan. In the example (45) there, we built a fixed ranking of faithful constraints, with IDENT[CORONAL] ranked below a combined constraint IDENT{[DORSAL], [LABIAL]}.

> (45) *A fixed ranking of place faithfulness (repeated)*
>   IDENT{[DORSAL], [LABIAL]} >> IDENT[CORONAL][22]

To drive harmony, we will also need an AGREE constraint that picks out the triggering place feature. In the case of Amahl's grammar this will be AGREE[DORSAL], defined provisionally as in (53):

> (53) AGREE[DORSAL]
>   Assign a violation for every output non-[dorsal] <u>obstruent</u> within <u>the same word</u> as an output [dorsal] consonant

Notice that this constraint has two underlined parameters that might need tweaking: there is the natural class that acts as a target, here defined as

---

[22] This is somewhat simplified – for one thing, Clara's grammar in fact sometimes compelled other places to harmonize with *coronals*, though only under certain prosodic conditions. For analysis, see Rose (2000).

obstruents (but recall that Amahl also showed regressive harmony onto *nasals* as in '*snake*'), and there is also the pesky problem of 'domain,' defined here over the entire word (on which see below).

The two tableaus below show how AGREE[DORSAL] drives Amahl's harmony in words like *duck* but not *black*:

(54)

/dʊk/	IDENT {[K], [P]}	AGREE[DORSAL]	IDENT[T]
[dʊk]		*!	
[dʊd]	*!		
☞ [gʊk]			*
/blæk/	IDENT {[K], [P]}	AGREE[DORSAL]	IDENT[T]
☞ [bæk]		*	
[bæp]	*!		
[gæk]	*!		

Notice that the definition of major place features as monovalent is important here – that is, notice how satisfying AGREE[DORSAL] in *duck* by turning a coronal into a velar does NOT violate IDENT[K]! If you need convincing of this, re-read the definition of the constraint in (45): it penalizes losing an input [+velar] specification, not adding one in the output. In the case of *black*, harmony does not happen because changing <u>either</u> input segment to match the other constitutes a violation of high-ranking IDENT.

For Clara's data in (49), AGREE[LABIAL] must be the active harmony constraint. In cases where labial overwrites coronals, harmony is straightforward, and the ranking looks very similar to Amahl's (be warned that we will revise this grammar in a minute):

(55a)

Clara's grammar – take one			
/ʃa'po/	IDENT {[K], [P]}	AGREE[LABIAL]	IDENT[T]
[ʃa'po]		*!	
[ʃa'ʃo]	*!		
☞ [pa'po]			*

But what about labials overwriting dorsals, as in *café*? The ranking from *chapeau* above will not suffice – because since both features are specifically preserved by the high-ranking IDENT constraint, harmony should be blocked (just as it was for Amahl in *milk*):

(55b)

The problem with Clara's grammar – take one			
/ka'fe/	IDENT {[K], [P]}	AGREE[LABIAL]	IDENT[T]
☹ [kə'fɛ]		*!	
[kə'xɛ]	*!		
[pə'fɛ]	*!		

In fact, Clara's grammar is more committed to labial harmony than the ranking in (55a) describes – AGREE[LABIAL] must in fact *outrank* both faithfulness constraints we have seen thus far ... and the only kind of faithfulness that outranks AGREE[LABIAL] for her is a more specific IDENT constraint, focused *only* on labials. Notice the lower ranking of IDENT{[K], [P]} – and that in (56b), this ranking still captures labial-coronal interactions accurately:

(56a)

Special [labial] faithfulness in Clara's grammar, revised				
/ka'fe/	IDENT[P]	AGREE[LABIAL]	IDENT {[K], [P]}	IDENT[T]
[kə'fɛ]		*!		
[kə'xɛ]	*!		*	
☞ [pə'fɛ]			*	

(56b)

Special [labial] faithfulness in Clara's grammar, revised				
/ʃa'po/	IDENT[P]	AGREE[LABIAL]	IDENT {[K], [P]}	IDENT[T]
[ʃa'po]		*!		
[ʃa'ʃo]	*!		*	
☞ [pa'po]				*

Exercise 3: Where must AGREE[DORSAL] be ranked in Clara's grammar? To determine this, use this constraint in tableaus which compare the winner in (56a) to the loser *[kə'xɛ].

As an interim summary: we can use familiar types of constraints to capture place asymmetries in child consonant harmonies, but there are unresolved issues about how typologically-valid they are. For one thing, recall from the discussion in Chapter 5.5.6 that target languages do not appear to make use of the special labial faithfulness that IDENT[LABIAL] introduces into the range of possible grammars (even though Clara and other children seem to).

Another similarity between child and adult <u>long-distance</u> assimilation is the dominance of regressive over progressive harmony (in the local assimilation cases like Korean, the likely explanation for regressive harmony is a preference for faithfulness to *onsets* rather than *codas*). A common grammatical account would tie together Clara and Amahl's preference for right-to-left harmony with the similar tendency in harmonies like Navajo.[23] But getting an OT grammar that derives regressive assimilation (or in fact any kind of spreading that it is not 100% across-the-board) is in fact not trivial: McCarthy (2011) explicitly describes many such attempts and their problems (and see Exercise 2 at the chapter's end).

Taking a step back: the broadest question is whether AGREE[PLACE] constraints of any sort should in fact be added to our constraint set? While such agreement constraints will capture the child facts of major place harmony, they are diametrically opposed to the major place *disharmony* that target languages impose, and this tension remains unexplained.

One possibility might be to understand pervasive target language patterns, like place dissimilation across Semitic and other languages, to be the real results of human language constraints, and to assume that children use those constraints as 'templates' for some of their own language-specific generalizations. Another approach might be to assume that child consonant harmony is not created by a phonological grammar at all, and that it reflects a child-specific attempt to handle the difficulty of multiple places of articulation within a single output. It remains unclear, however, how the non-grammatical status of consonant harmony might be reconciled with the suspiciously-grammar-like preferences for coronal targets and regressive application of harmony which children's consonant harmony displays.

6.4   Another Look at Misperception

As was done in previous chapters, this section looks at those segmental production facts which might find a perceptual, rather than a purely production, explanation. [...] We learned in Chapter 2 that although infants already have language-specific discrimination skills by their first birthday – many

---

[23] Note that the harmonies in Sundanese and Yaka look progressive, but in fact are controlled by the morphology, spreading from root to suffix; see Hansson (2001) for more.

months before this chapter's production data – we also know that getting that phonetic detail into the input for a specific word can be more challenging. We therefore must assess the possibility that children can correctly perceive all their native language contrasts and allophones, but some of them might end up mis-perceived and mis-stored in one or more lexical items. In the segmental domain, there have been some systematic attempts to tease apart these two explanations for non-target child speech, with important consequences.

One pattern whose explanation was put on hold in Chapter 5 was the treatment of Igbo's labio-velar consonants, /k͡p/ and /g͡b/. Table (13) there revealed the following split: while <u>labialized</u> velar stops k^W and g^W were most often simplified to [k] and [g], almost all of the target labio-velar stops (kp and gb) were produced as simple <u>labial</u> stops [p] and [b]. This latter pattern proba-bly has an excellent perceptual explanation: Ladefoged and Maddieson (1996) report that the velar closure of labio-velars finishes <u>prior</u> to the labial one – so that at the time of the stop's release it sounds most similar to a labial stop.[24]

An English segmental change in child speech which is often attributed to perceptual error is the vocalization of English velarized lateral /ɫ/, as in *ani-mal* → ['amʊ]. Another frequent pattern from child Japanese comes from the treatment of voiceless vowels, which occur between voiceless obstruents (and sometimes word-finally): e.g. [dekita] 'done', [kɯ̊tʃi], 'mouth'. Ota (2001) quantifies the number of missing input syllables whose vowel is voiced vs. voiceless for the four children in his corpus study: in bisyllabic words the dif-ference was particularly striking, with 43.6% of voiceless vowels missing but only 2.3% of the voiced vowels.[25] If voiceless vowels are very hard to hear, perhaps they have simply not yet been included in 43.6% of these children's underlying representations.

While it is true that English [ɫ] and [u] or [ɑ] are easily-confused sounds, and that voiceless vowels are easy to miss entirely: how do we <u>know</u> that misperception is responsible for these errors, rather than the production gram-mar or any other explanation? One approach is to study children's perception directly; while not impossible, such studies are hard and therefore somewhat rare. Often, a sort of one-trial experiment has been carried out informally as

---

[24] Cahill (2006)'s perceptual study of Yoruba, a different language of Nigeria, found that native (adult!) listeners perceived the contrast between [gb] and [b] very accurately, and that they relied on both the *prevoicing* (i.e. negative VOT) and the consonant's effects on the acoustic properties of the following vowel (*CV transitions*) to identify the difference. The question is therefore when learners get sensitive to these special acous-tic properties of [gb].

[25] These percentages represent 129/296 voiceless vowel syllables vs. 165/7150 voiced vowel syllables. While less striking in raw numbers, the asymmetry holds statistically for each individual child, and for longer words as well: see Ota (2001: 89–90).

part of diary studies, with reference to a particular contrast that a child has merged in his or her production. For example, Menn and Matthei (1992) discuss how Daniel (studied in Menn, 1971 and subsequent work) was asked by a researcher's 'accomplice' to show them his [gʌk], at a stage where this output in Daniel's speech matched both the target inputs *duck* and *truck*. Upon hearing *guck* from the adult, Daniel looked 'confused', and crucially did not look at either the duck or truck before him. This tells us at least that he was not calling ducks and trucks *gucks* because he thought that was exactly what they were called, challenging any purely perceptual explanation of this particular consonant harmony pattern.

There is, however, a certain degree of uncertainty that remains after running one such test. If a child's non-target production of a word is due to having perceived it incorrectly, similar in kind to the misperception errors that adults also make when learning new words, then it is surely plausible that these errors would not occur in *every* lexical item. But this reasoning makes a clear prediction: error patterns caused by misperception should be lexically-specific, in the sense that they should be expected to only affect a subset of the child's words that meets their structural description. On the other hand, errors that are caused by the production grammar should be independent of particular lexical items, and only be restricted by phonological context.

With this idea (among others) in mind, Macken (1980b) provides a reanalysis of a process in Amahl's speech (Smith, 1973), in which coronal stops and nasals were backed to velars before the dark lateral (see examples in 57a). Macken (1980b) points out that about a fifth of the targets for this rule were exceptions, in precisely the same phonotactic contexts (57b). The data below are representative of speech up until the end of stage 28 in Smith's study:

(57)	Amahl's coronal backing (Smith, 1973; Macken, 1980b)				
a)	*Target*	*Child*	b)	*Target*	*Child*
	bottle	[bɔkəl]		*beetle*	[bitəl]
	puddle	[pʌgəl]		*cuddle*	[kʌdəl], [kʌgəl]
	journal	[dsəːŋəl]		*tunnel*	[tʌnəl]
	tiddly-winks	[tɪgəli wɪŋks]		*tiddly-pom*	[dɪdəli pɔm]
	gentle	[dɛŋkəl]			
	butler	[bʌklə]			

From Amahl's extensive corpus, Macken (1980b) identifies 47 words which fit the target shape as in (57a): of these 47, seven *never* underwent coronal backing, and three others seemed to stop backing before the remaining 37 – making about 20% of the potential targets exceptional. Macken compares coronal backing to coronal stopping, a process from around the same time in Amahl's development (up until Smith's stage 20) in which strident fricatives and afficates became coronal stops: for example *puzzle* → [pʌdəl]. In Amahl's corpus, Macken finds 21 potential targets for coronal stopping, and not a single exception among them.

In counting exceptions, is 10/47 different enough from 0/21 to argue that the former pattern was in fact caused by 37 misperceptions? This is a pretty tough question to answer – but the perceptual account is bolstered by some evidence at stage 29, when coronal backing became optional so that (57a) words started to surface with their target coronals like (57b). At that point, Macken notes a very interesting change in two other words in Amahl's vocabulary:

(58)

Target	Child before stage 29	Child at stage 29
pickle	[pɪkəl] (stage 23)	[pɪtəl]
circle	[sə:kəl] (stage 28)	[sə:təl]
circles	[sə:kəlz] (stage 21)	[sə:təlz]

What's going on in *pickle* and *circle*? Velars that were previously produced correctly before laterals are now being *fronted* – showing the opposite effect as in (57a)! Why? Macken's answer is that this mapping from /k/ → [t] was precisely what Amahl had to do at stage 29, to <u>all the (57a)-type words</u> in his vocabulary: because he had just detected his previous mistake, in *misperceiving* coronals before laterals as velars, and so now *every* velar before a lateral in his lexicon was suspect. If so, then all such inputs might need revising, and *pickle* and *circle* were victims of a slightly overzealous lexical-repair project (at this stage, Macken finds eight potential targets for this repair process, meaning 2/8 were affected). This explanation is schematized here for three kinds of underlying forms:

(59) Before stage 29   At stage 29:
    beetle   /bitəl/   →   (no change)
    puddle   */pʌgəl/ →   */pʌgəl/ revised to /pʌdəl/
    pickle   /pɪkəl/   →   /pɪkəl/ revised to */pɪtəl/

This account is notable in that it ties together productions that fail to follow a pattern when they should (57b) and those that shouldn't follow a pattern but do anyway (58), explaining both as the result of a perceptual error which affected individual lexical items differently. As such, these analytical criteria remain relevant to any child's systematic but exception-ful pattern.

A final comment must be made in particular about perception in development and the acquisition of target-like voicing. Those pervasive onset reduction mappings like /sp/ →[b] seem to make excellent sense on perceptual grounds – that is, the 'p' in *spoon* is really very similar in VOT terms to an English word-initial [b], so why should the child necessarily distinguish the two? In addition, there is good reason to think that the perceptual problem is in some ways also on the listeners' or transcriber's side, at least with respect to categorization. Suppose a child has two phonemic mental categories for voicing which she produces reliably differently – but the precise VOT targets for *both* categories lie within a single category's range of possible VOT values in their target language. For example, suppose a child learning English produces target /b/ with a VOT of 0 msc, but target /pʰ/ with only a VOT of 15 msc. Native English listeners will have the impression that both stops are being produced as plain and aspirated, that is within the same phoneme, even though the child is reliably producing a voicing difference! This phenomenon is known as *covert contrast*.

In this situation, we must say that the child is making a kind of error, because their speech is sufficiently non-target-like that it will be misperceived (i.e. *pot* will sound like *bought*) – but are they <u>phonological</u> errors? If constraints like *VoicedObstruent or Ident[aspiration] are not at the correct level of detail, should they be supplanted by constraints referencing the kind of phonetic detail that such a child is getting wrong? On the other hand, should covert contrasts indicate that children have indeed acquired the correct grammar, allowing a voicing contrast, and there is some additional phonetic implementation module, which we are ignoring entirely in this textbook, that is making the errors? This book doesn't have enough space to talk about this possibility in any detail, but it's a question that must be addressed especially when considering the acquisition of laryngeal contrasts. For readings on the topic, see for example Scobbie et al. (2000).

6.5   Comparing Rules and Constraints Part 2

This section returns to a fundamental difference in focus between rule-based and constraint-based phonologies: applying a series of ordered processes in the former, vs. satisfying a set of output goals in parallel in the latter. While thus far the parallel application of OT constraints has facilitated many analyses, we now turn to a data configuration where it is rather more of a hindrance than a help.

One example is found among the segmental repairs of some English voiceless fricatives /s, f, θ/ that we saw in Chapter 5.5.4. Two neutralizations were discussed there: one in which both /s/ and /θ/ surface as [θ], and another in which /θ/ and /f/ both surfaced as [f]. But that study also reported a third pattern, observed in 11 out of 160 grammars, illustrated now below:

(60)	Two English fricative mappings in the same grammar (Data from Dinnsen et al., 2011)					
	Target	*Child*	*Target*	*Child*	*Target*	*Child*
	soup	[θupʌɔ]	thumb	[fʌmi]	five	[faɪv]
	sock	[θɔk]	thunder	[fʌndʊ]	fat	[fæt]
	sun	[θʌn]	thirsty	[fʊθi]	face	[feɪθ]

These children use *both* unfaithful mappings seen in the previous two data sets. A way to visualize this grammar is given below in (61a): the inputs and output candidates are lined up vertically, and the arrows track their mappings. A flatter version is provided in (61b):

(61a)　　　/s/　/θ/　/f/　　　(61b)　s → θ → f

　　　　　*[s]　[θ]　[f]

Before considering the analysis of this pattern, let's consider its similarity to two others. One is from Joan, another child learning American English (Velten, 1943), at a stage where her grammar applied two processes in word-final position:

(62)	Stops and nasals in word-final position (Data from Velten, 1943)								
	a)	*Target*	*Child*	b)	*Target*	*Child*	c)	*Target*	*Child*
		swim	[fub]		stove	[duf]		laugh	[zaf]
		jam	[dab]		shoes	[zus]		sauce	[zas]
		spoon	[bud]		bad	[bat]		coat	[dut]
		rain	[wud]		seeds	[zuts]		oats	[uts]

Both of these patterns we have seen before from other children: in (a) nasals are becoming voiced stops; in (b) voiced obstruents become voiceless, and (c) shows us that voiceless stops are retained faithfully. Comparing forms like *spoon* and *bad*, we can schematize this pattern as n → d → t.

A second example comes from So and Dodd (1995)'s account of Cantonese phonological acquisition, which reports that among 42% of children under 2;6, and 18% of children aged 2;6–2;11, /s/ was affricated to [ts], but that the input affricate /ts/ (grammatical in Cantonese) was 'typically being realized as a stop'. Together, these two facts describe the mapping s → ts → t.

In the phonological literature, this type of data pattern is most often called a *chain shift*: each mapping shifts one link in the chain onto the next. Chain shifts have been much studied, debated and analysed for many decades, but the upshot for our purposes is they are frequently reported in child speech, and they are also available in the synchronic grammars of target languages too. Here is just one chain shift from the target phonology of Polish: examine the two data sets in (112), in the context of a following high vowel like [i], and draw the chain before reading on.

(63)

Polish chain shift (Rubach, 1984; Data from Łubowicz, 2003)					
Nom. sg.	*Augmentative*	*Gloss*	*Nom. sg.*	*Augmentative*	*Gloss*
gro[x]	gro[ş]isko	*bean*	gro[ş]	gro[s]isko	*a penny*
gma[x]	gma[ş]isko	*building*	kapelu[ş]	kapelu[s]isko	*hat*
fartu[x]	fartu[ş]isko	*apron*	arku[ş]	arku[s]isko	*sheet*

In this example, the chain shift is x → ş → s.[26]

The rule-based analysis of chain shifts is very commonly part of an introductory class on phonology: in fact, chain shifts are one of the classic reasons for adopting serial *ordering* as a crucial component of rule-based phonology. We will therefore put together a quick analysis of Joan's word-final process using rules, and then turn to constraints.

Since there are two distinct processes in Joan's data from (62), we need two rules: one to stop her nasals, and one to devoice her obstruents. Write these rules (recall that their environment is word-final) and then determine their necessary order, providing derivations that show how the underlying forms *spoon* and *bad* both surface correctly. Then read on.

Here are two rules to account for Joan's data, and derivations that show how devoicing must be ordered <u>before</u> stopping:

---

[26] For some other examples of synchronic chain shifts see for example Donegan and Stampe (1979) and Łubowicz (2002).

(64a) [+sonorant, →   [-sonorant, / __ #   (Nasal Stopping)   e.g /n/ → [d]
       -approx]   -continuant]

(64b) [-sonorant] →   [-voice] / __#   (Obstruent Devoicing) e.g. /d/ → [t]

(65)   UR   /spun/   /bæd/

       Devoicing   –   [bæt]

       Stopping   [spud]   –

       SR[27]   [spud]   [bæt]

And why must these rules be in this order? Consider the effect on *spoon* in the opposite rule order: first it would be affected by Nasal Stopping, /spun/ → [spud]); then it would be affected by Devoicing meaning /spud/ → *[sput]. In other words, the order in (65) is needed to prevent /n/ going more than one step down the chain.[28]

Now: what of the OT approach to chain shifts? As it turns out, they are fundamentally rather incompatible with at least one basic OT concept – namely, the idea of surface-oriented output constraints.

To see this, we need the equivalent of the two rules in (64) to capture these two processes. One constraint must penalize word-final nasals, and one (that we have already discussed) bans word-final voiced obstruents. Both simple mappings are illustrated in (66) below (the constraint in the first tableau is ad hoc, just used here to illustrate the problem):

(66a)

/spun/		*FINALNASAL	IDENT[+/-SON]
	[spun]	*!	
☞	[spud]		*

(66b)

/baed/		*FINALVOICEDOBSTRUENT	IDENT[+/-VOICE]
	[bæd]	*!	
☞	[bæt]		*

---

[27] In Joan's actual grammar, there were also other rules at play – that is those that reduce the cluster in /sp/ (and maybe change its voicing) and change /ae/ → [a].

[28] The classic terms for these interactions are that the chain shift comes about because of a *counterfeeding* order (term from Kiparsky, 1973). If Stopping happened before Devoicing, the rules would be in a *feeding* order: Stopping would create new [d]s from /n/s, which would then be fed to the Devoicing rule, and /n/, /d/ and /t/ would all neutralize to [t] on the surface.

But when we put both of these rankings together in a single grammar, we get an inaccurate result. If you expand the treatment of *spoon* and consider the constraints in both tableaus, we get not a chain shift, but a total merger:

(67)

		/spun/	*FINALNASAL	*FINALVOICEDOBS	IDENT [+/-SON]	IDENT [+/-VOICE]
	a)	[spun]	*!			
☹	b)	[spud]		*!	*	
☞	c)	[sput]			*	*

Where is this problem coming from? Why can't our OT grammar easily create a chain shift?

Recall that a major selling point of this constraint-based approach has been the focus on output goals – encoded in the structural constraints, with no focus on their provenance. This classic OT grammar that we've been building doesn't know where the violations of structural constraints came from: it just fixes them, with as much unfaithfulness as demanded and allowed by the ranking. In contrast, we discussed in Chapter 3 how rule-based grammars are much less focused on their output targets, and emphasize instead their processes. For this reason, a serial rule-based grammar can *order* its processes, in a way that happily captures chain shifts.

The most common OT reaction to the problem of chain shifts is probably the revision of faithfulness constraints. Intuitively, it seems that chain shifts could be preferred by a grammar over total merger (i.e. 67b over 67c) by an overall faithfulness pressure aimed at not changing any one input 'too far' – and in fact Dinnsen et al. (2011) point out that none of the 160 kids in their sample produced a full merger, which would map all three of /s, θ, f/ onto [f]. One promising approach to this type of faithfulness modification is found in Jesney (2005).

There are many other reactions to chain shifts (and related phenomena) that lend support to different constraint-based frameworks beyond classic OT. One suggests that constraints are not strictly ranked as we have been hypothesizing, but *weighted*, so that faithfulness constraints like the two IDENTS in (116) could *gang up* on a higher ranked structural constraint at times (see here especially Jesney and Tessier, 2009, 2011). Another suggests that grammatical evaluation is less parallel than in classic OT, so that faithfulness constraints are in fact violated *in a serial order* that can be tracked and manipulated via ranking (see esp. McCarthy, 2007, 2008b). If these data interest you a great place to start your further reading is McCarthy (2007), an entire book dedicated to the topic!

6.6   Finally Tackling Variation in Child Phonology

To complete this chapter, we will turn to another large question about our overall undertaking: how to account for the variation in children's productions, even within a single child's speech at a single stage of development. We will not reach any definitive answers; the goal is to provide fodder for the reader's own future thought and investigation.

The first empirical topic of debate is the extent of variation within child speech. It is well established that children can vary between multiple patterns of production simultaneously – but how much is variable? How many different patterns exist concurrently, and how systematic or coherent are they? In some sense, these questions are just as hard to pose as they are to answer, because agreeing upon the methods for quantifying variability between and within children is not at all trivial (compare e.g. Ferguson and Farwell, 1975; Macken and Ferguson, 1983; Stoel-Gammon and Dunn, 1985; Goad and Ingram, 1987; Hale and Reiss, 1998).

One approach to variation (which we have adopted for the most part thus far) is to idealize away from it: to find patterns that hold in the majority of cases over a short period of time, and use the majority to represent the whole. In some cases, it is argued that children are very systematic in their non-target patterns, over a long period of time – for example, recall the quantitative extent of velar fronting in E's grammar from Chapter 5.5.5. Lewis et al. (1999)'s study of syllable truncation addresses this question explicitly with the report that over the course of each month in their data, at least 91% of word types showed only one type of truncation pattern. Is 91% close enough to dismiss the remaining 9%?

However, the degree of variability in other children's data has pushed several researchers even to claim that it is impossible, or at least unwarranted, to construct a single phonological grammar as we have been doing to capture child speech. For example, examine the different outputs for the following five very early words in the speech of one child. Can you characterize how inputs are mapped to outputs in this lexicon?

(68)	Variability at 1;0–1;1.15 (Data from Vihman and Velleman, 1989)	
	bang	ba'ŋ, baĩ, pæ:, bæŋ
	down	tæ̃, tæ̃ʔ, tæ̃ŋ, dæ:n
	(a)round	hanʌ
	balloon	by.ɛʰ
	button	bʌʔ

Some connections between target and child forms in this data set are clear, but many are murky. Perhaps the clearest mapping is that initial stops /b/ and /d/ are retained in both manner and place. But elsewhere variation is far-reaching – for example: final nasals can survive, change place, reduce to glottal stop, nasalize preceding vowels and/or delete, in what appears here to be an unpredictable fashion. One potential suggestion is that each lexical *type* (here, word) is handled on its own; that is, that the mechanisms for producing an output for 'bang' is distinct from those which produce 'down', and so on – that what's predictable is the (set of) production(s) word-by-word, not sound-sequence-by-sequence as phonological constraints would assume.

But what does this mean? Does it mean that a child's phonological system does not look anything like an adult one? Or even that this child's speech is not controlled in any meaningful way by a phonological grammar? Another set of questions concerns the variability across children. Given that no other child may have produced these five English words in all and only the ways reported in (68), how much stock should the analyst put in universal tendencies or generalizations about child phonology?

We will return to this issue in various ways in Chapter 7 (see especially 7.5). For now, we will entertain the possibility that this lexically-driven variation is only typical of the very first production stages. Within a couple months of the previous data set, the child in (68) reached a more stable pattern for treating many of these words. While stop voicing appears to still be unpredictable, a bisyllabic trochee with faithfulness to nasals has emerged (for a somewhat different view, see Vihman and Velleman's own discussion):

(69)	Later stages from Vihman and Velleman (1989)		
	at 1;2		at 1;3.24
down	t'ænə	*bang*	pa^{n}nə
(a)round	wa:nə	*down*	t'a^{n}nə
balloon	bʌnə	*Graham*	kɔ^{n}ni
button	pa^{n}nə	*camera*	kam:ə
Ernie	hʌnə	*name*	nɛ^{m}mi
Brian	panə	*green*	kynɪ

How do we understand this increase in systematicity over time? One option is definitional: if having a phonology means applying systematic sound patterns to inputs by virtue of their phonological form, perhaps this data tells us when 'phonology' began! In other words, we might assume that before 1;2 this child had not yet begun to subject their speech targets to a phonological grammar, but was rather attempting individual items with some other mental system – a proto-phonology, or something else that the tools of this text are not equipped to handle.

A second point to be emphasized in light of this text's goals is that some of children's variation does not resemble adult variation in its nature. In target languages, phonological variation is often controlled (whether unconsciously or not) for extra-grammatical purposes – that is in using different variants to signal more or less formality, or to mark membership in a sociolinguistic community of some sort. On the other hand, the kind of variation seen in child speech appears to be uncontrolled in this way. For example, Dodd et al. (2003: 621) discuss an inverse correlation between a word's segmental accuracy and its syllable count, suggesting that variation between more and less correct productions of a particular segment is in part driven by an utterance's number of competing demands. In such cases at least, we would not want to attribute this variation to a target-like grammar (because no adult language shows any such correlation) – but this does not rule out the idea that other, larger aspects of the child's overall production is grammatically-constrained.

Despite any other handwaving efforts, there does seem to be variation within children's individual stages of production that is related to grammatical principles. For example, back at the beginning of Chapter 4, we saw one child's word shape restrictions in the acquisition of Hebrew, repeated again below in (70). We noted several times that trochees vs. iambs were treated qualitatively differently in this grammar, in that iamb targets (words with final stress, in the righthand column) showed three different truncation patterns, sometimes applying all three to the same word (examine *'bottle'*). Meanwhile, target trochees were nearly all treated with the same [(Sw)] truncation:

(70)	Hebrew data from SR at 1;3.14–1;5.29 (Adam and Bat-El, 2009) *repeated from Chapter 4 table (6)*					
	Target	*Child*	*Gloss*	*Target*	*Child*	*Gloss*
	'saf.ta	[ta.ta]	*grandma*	ka'pit	[tik]	*spoon*
	'tu.ki	[kuki]	*parrot*	bak'buk	[ba'bu] [buk] [bak'buk]	*bottle*
	'ge.ʃem	['ge.θem]	*rain*	ta'nin	[ta'nin]	*crocodile*
	'pe.rax	['pe.ax]	*flower*	a'gas	[gaθ]~[a'gaθ]	*pear*

Continued

Target	Child	Gloss	Target	Child	Gloss
ta.ˈpu.ax	[ˈpu.ax]	*apple*	kivˈsa	[sa] ['kisa] [ki'sa]	*sheep*
ba. ˈna.na	[ˈna.na]	*banana*	agaˈla	[iˈgja]	*pram*
dʒi.ˈra.fa	[ʒi.ˈja.ja]	*giraffe*	neʃiˈka	[ka]	*kiss*
go.ˈrila	[ˈgila]	*gorilla*	mitriˈja	[ˈti.ja]~[ti.ˈja]	*umbrella*

This asymmetry in the input phonological properties that cause variability – penultimate stress doesn't, but final stress does – is particularly compelling because no child learning Hebrew is reported to show the reverse pattern, with a consistent treatment of final stress targets and variability among penultimate stress targets. Connecting this locus of variation with the potential cross-linguistic tendency for early trochees (as discussed in Chapter 4) does therefore seem like a task for our grammar, and a topic for future research. In the meantime, we will at least try to tackle the issue of developmental variation between stages explicitly in the final chapter (Section 10.4).

6.7   Further Reading

Readings on the Acquisition of Vowels

Donegan, Patricia. 2013. Normal vowel development. In Martin J. Ball and Fiona E. Gibbon (eds) *Handbook of Vowels and Vowel Disorders*. New York: Psychology Press. 24–60.
  – this chapter tackles this topic with many of the same guiding principles adopted in this text.
Bernhardt, Barbara H. and Stemberger, Joseph P. 1998. *Handbook of Phonological Development from the Perspective of Constraint-based Nonlinear Phonology*. San Diego: Academic Press.
Lieberman, Philip. 1980. On the development of vowel production in young children. G. H. Yeni-Komshian, J. F. Kavanagh, and C. A. Ferguson (eds) *Child Phonology: Volume 1, Production*. New York: Academic Press. 113–142.
McGowan, Rebecca, McGowan, Richard, Denny, Margaret and Nittrouer, Susan. 2014. A longitudinal study of very young children's vowel production. *Journal of Speech Hearing and Language Research* 57(1): 1–14.

Reading on Chain shifts in Acquisition

Dinnsen, Daniel A. and Barlow, Jessica. 1998. On the characterization of a chain shift in normal and delayed phonological acquisition. *Journal of Child Language* 25: 61–94.
Jesney, Karen. 2005. *Chain Shift in Phonological Acquisition*. M.A. Thesis, University of Calgary.

Readings on Variation in Child phonology

Ferguson, Charles A. and Farwell, Carol B. (1975). Words and sounds in early language acquisition. *Language* 51: 419–439.

Goad, Heather and Ingram, David. 1987. Individual variation and its relevance to a theory of phonological acquisition. *Journal of Child Language* 14: 419–432.

Fikkert, Paula and Altvater-Mackenson, Nicole. 2013. Insights into variation across children based on longitudinal Dutch data on phonological acquisition. *Studia Linguistica* 67(1): 148–164.

Exercises

Q1: Here is some data from one child's acquisition of word-final clusters in Cairene Arabic, presented by Ragheb and Davis (2014: table 6):

Target	Child	Gloss		Target	Child	Gloss
/nusˤː/	[ʔusˤː]	*half*		/ħabl/	[ʔalː]	*rope*
/ward/	[wadː]	*flowers*		/ʔism/	[ʔimː]	*name*
/bɪnt/	[bɪtː]	*girl*		/maħl/	[malː]	*salt*
/kalb/	[kabː]	*dog*		/ʔamħ/	[ʔamː]	*wheat*
/ʃiribt/	[ʔitː]	*I comb*		/taħt/	[taħt]	*under*
/miʃtˤ/	[ʔitː]	*drink*		/baħr/	[baħl]	*sea*
/naml/	[ʔalː]	*ants*		/ʃaʕr/	[saʕr]	*hair*

Given what you learned in this chapter, what can you say about this child's current grammatical constraints on word-final clusters? In particular, you may want to think about Section 6.1.2's discussion of Japanese acquisition of geminates.

With respect to the last three pieces of data, Ragheb and Davis (2014) cite previous works which suggest that in Arabic, pharyngeal fricatives have the phonological features of *glides*. Consider if that assumption can contribute to your analysis.

Q2: In this question we return to the idea of specifying the *direction* of long-distance harmonies? The best grammatical option may in fact be the rather clunky type of constraint below, exemplified for [dorsal]:

AGREERIGHT-[DORSAL]
Assign a violation for every pair of input <u>consonants</u> x and y,
for which x precedes y, y is [dorsal], and x and y's outputs
correspondents are not both [dorsal].[29]

Look back at the data from Amahl in (48). First, examine how well
this AGREERIGHT constraint works in capturing Amahls' *snake* (which
harmonizes) vs. *skin* (which doesn't). *Can you get a ranking to do this?*
*Second, can this pattern of regressive harmony between stops and nasals be
reconciled with the analysis of Amahl's obstruent-only words, where velar
harmony flows both directions?* (Look again at the prose below (48).) *Is
there necessarily redundancy in any grammar that captures both patterns?
Can you make it work?*

Answer from (3)

(3)		Amahl's sonority-driven coda cluster reduction			
	a)	/fɔks/	*[-SON][-SON]-CODA	MAX	*COMPLEXCODA
		[ʊɔks]	*!		*
	☞	[ʊɔk]		*	
		[ʊɔ]		**!	
	b)	/piŋk/	*[-SON][-SON]-CODA	MAX	*COMPLEXCODA
	☞	piŋk			*
		pik		*!	

---

[29] This definition is inspired most by Rose and Walker (2004), but it is crucially
somewhat different.

7 Lexical Influences and Interactions in Phonological Learning

7.1 What's in a Word?

Up until now, this textbook has been focused squarely on the <u>phonological</u> predictors of children's systematic errors. While every tableau needed an input to demonstrate how the grammar worked, the choice of actual input word never mattered to the outcome.

Now we will complicate this picture, because children are clearly not learning their phonologies in a semantic vacuum: they are learning not just sound patterns but real <u>words</u>. So this chapter turns to some aspects of phonological acquisition which (might) require reference to more information about the learner's lexicon: its size, shape, organization, categories, development and so on. There has been a tremendous range of research on the interaction between phonological and lexical development, and this chapter will only scratch some of the surfaces, from a phonology-centric perspective.

The general question we will begin with is how aspects of a learner's lexicon might influence their production accuracy, that is the similarity between the learner's output for a word and its target output. You might be able to imagine possibilities from your own experience of recalling and producing words in a second language; while child and adult language acquisition might be rather different in these regards, this mental exercise might get your mind working on the topic. In particular, here are two sub-parts of this question:

Q1: *Does your phonology treat words differently depending on how long you've known them?*

Q2: *Does your phonology treat words differently depending on how many similar words you know?*

Over the years, I have asked these questions of undergraduates in class, and students have consistently come up with predictions that push in both directions. For example: If you've known a word a long time, then you have had time to practice producing it, to perceive all of its phonetic detail and encode it correctly in your mental lexicon of inputs. Upshot: the longer you've known the word, the higher its accuracy. Then again: if you've known a word a long time, you may have originally produced or perceived it incorrectly, with a more immature phonology than you currently have. This might mean the word could get 'stuck' in the past, reflecting the constraints and restrictions of earlier developmental stages. Upshot: the longer you've known the word, the lower its accuracy.

Moving beyond the thought experiment: what do we know about actual phonological development for early vs. late-acquired words? There is evidence for both predictions. On the one hand, Garlock et al. (2001) report that words which have been in the lexicon for longer are produced more accurately overall, at least by school aged children, while in Section 7.4 we will examine cases of longer-known words which are in fact less accurate. Of course, the third option is that experience with a word and its overall accuracy might not correlate in either way: Johnson, Lewis and Hogan (1997) (discussed in Chapter 4.1.4) note explicitly that the length of time an item had been in their subject's lexicon did not correlate with their production accuracy measures.

With respect to Q2 and the knowledge of similar words, how could accuracy be affected? On the one hand, knowing a lot of similar words might result in lots of production 'practice,' which could be inherited by another new, similar word. Upshot, the more similar words you know, the higher a word's accuracy. On the other hand, knowing a lot of similar words might make it easier to get confused between them, whether in online production or in encoding the right details in the input representations. Upshot: the more similar words you know, the lower a word's accuracy.

Experiments in adult speech processing have indeed found that the similarity between a target word and your mental lexicon of similar words can make words either harder or easier to access, depending on the task – these influences are referred to as *inhibitory* and *facilatory* effects respectively. In much of this literature, the measure of what it means for words to be 'phonologically-similar' is defined via a concept called the *phonological neighbourhood*. What makes two words phonological neighbours? Usually, a word's neighbours include all those words which differ from it in only one segment: so, for example the neighbours of *cat* would include *bat, mat, kit, cot, cab,* and *calf.* Thus, we can define how many words are phonologically-similar to *cat* by calculating its *phonological neighbourhood density.*

On the child acquisition side, various connections have been observed between neighbourhood density and word learning. From the perspective of production accuracy, there is evidence of inhibitory pressures in Ota and Green (2012)'s corpus study of three kids learning English consonant clusters up to age 3;0, which found that the more phonological neighbours a word has (i.e. the denser its neighbourhood), the lower its probability of being produced with an accurate cluster. On the other hand, high density neighbourhoods seem to facilitate the acquisition of words themselves. For example, Storkel (2004)'s study of typical words in English-learning children's vocabularies (as reported in the CDI, Fenson et al., 1994b, first discussed in Chapter 2.4) found that words learned earlier have denser neighbourhoods.

As the foregoing discussion has begun to hint, phonological properties are highly interconnected with word learning in a variety of complicated ways. In this chapter, we will touch on only some of these connections, with particular focus of course on the phonological ramifications. But as already warned, there is much, much more out there, and the further readings should help the interested reader get started.

7.2   Lexical Frequency and Phonological Production

The most basic way the lexicon and phonology interact (not just for children) is that the phonology is put to use when a speaker actually wants to produce or perceive a real word of the target language. This means that the *frequency* with which a learner attempts each phonological structure is related to the frequency of that structure in the lexicon – and these are related in several ways, because both 'frequency' and 'lexicon' can mean several different things.

Suppose we are interested in the acquisition of the voiced labiodental fricative [v], and we want to consider its frequency in a child's lexicon. What do we count? We could count how many different words the child says whose input form includes a /v/: *very, love, wave, give, vroom* etc. – this means calculating the *type frequency* of /v/ in their *productive lexicon*. We could ask their parents how many different words with /v/ their child can understand: adding *five, dive, evil, cave, vacuum* etc. to this larger set of their *receptive lexicon*. Or we could count the number of instances the child attempts any word with an input /v/: this calculates *token frequency*, whereby 100 input /v/s matter equally whether they are 50 attempts to say two different words or two attempts each at 50 words. We could also be more nuanced in our counts: we could calculate the type and token frequency of onset /v/ or /coda/; /v/ before stressed vs. unstressed vowels; /v/ adjacent to rounded vs. unrounded vowels; and so on. Finally, we could count the type and/or token frequency of /v/ in their *input*, meaning the ambient speech produced around the child, often focusing specifically on the *child-directed* speech spoken directly to them by parents, caregivers and other adults.

Each of these measures may well be important, but research suggests that child-directed type frequency is probably the most revealing measure in predicting children's speech patterns.[1] Since phonetically-transcribed child-directed corpora are often hard to come by (at least beyond English), and often are not large enough for reliable word counts, researchers often resort to using adult-directed spoken corpora to calculate ambient frequencies, but child-directed corpora are increasingly available.

Before going on, we should note that the many possible predictors are often highly correlated, so it can be very tricky to know which factors are the cause and which are the effects. Here is a summarizing quote from one study that highlights the extent of this challenge: '*words frequent in maternal speech were more frequently attempted by the child, attempted first at an earlier age, found in a phonologically denser neighborhood, and shorter in structure (i.e. had fewer phonemes) than infrequent words in maternal speech*' (Ota and Green, 2012: 12). So: were these words attempted more frequently by the child because they were more frequent in their mother's speech; or for example because they were attempted earlier and so better practised; or for example because they were in denser phonological neighbourhoods and so again better practiced? Teasing all of these factors apart is a complicated task.

The ambient frequency of phonological structures has been largely implicated in predicting relative order of acquisition – particularly when comparing different languages with different lexical frequencies for the same segments, syllable shape and so on. In Chapter 5.3, we saw evidence that the relative <u>typological</u> frequency of structure often correlates with the order of acquisition for natural classes: for example stops are more frequently found in the inventory of the world's languages than fricatives, and the class of stops emerge in child speech before fricatives. We are now considering the contribution of frequencies which each individual child experiences directly – the frequency of sounds in words they've heard.

Many studies have asserted that differences in the order of segmental acquisition between languages is the result of different input frequencies in their lexicons; clear support for these claims is not always provided, but sometimes it has been rigorously investigated. A recent series of studies by Edwards and Beckman have compared the acquisition of coronal and dorsal obstruents in English, Greek, Cantonese and Japanese, investigating whether differences in input frequencies of the same segments correlate with their relative order of acquisition. As one example: English and Greek both use the interdental segment [θ]; however, Greek [θ] occurs much more frequently than English, and it is also produced more accurately in early Greek acquisition than English (Edwards and Beckman, 2008). On the other hand, this study explicitly tested for a correlation between children's

---

[1] Although others would suggest token frequencies are more important, for example Marchman and Plunkett (1989).

production accuracy for these obstruents in each language, as a function of their input ambient frequency in that language – and found only a significant correlation in English, but not for Cantonese, Greek or Japanese.

Returning to the case of /v/: Ingram (1988) compares the acquisition of this fricative in four languages: English, Swedish, Estonian and Bulgarian. Diary studies from the latter three languages suggest that [v] is acquired reliably in these languages before the age of two, which is at least a year earlier than is typical in English. With respect to frequency, /v/ is very infrequent at least in children's early English productive lexicons. But with respect to the other three languages, Ingram (1988) points not to the absolute frequency of /v/, but to its relative role as a bearer of contrast in the languages. In particular, /v/ is the only voiced fricative in both Swedish and Estonian, and this might suggest that it bears more of what is called a *functional load* in the language. In a similar vein, Stokes and Surendran (2005) studied the correlations between input frequency, functional load and segmental acquisition in English, Cantonese and Dutch.[2] Although frequency and functional load were strongly correlated, the results found that both measures were useful predictors of overall order of acquisition, but to differing extents among languages. In Cantonese, the frequency of a consonant was best at predicting the age at which it emerges in production, while in Dutch frequency was instead the best predictor of a consonant's production accuracy at age two. Also in this study, however, frequency was less useful for predicting acquisition than functional load (and other measures).

In the domain of syllables and word shapes, there is perhaps more robust evidence that order of acquisition is guided by lexical frequency in the native language input. As one clear cross-linguistic example: coda consonants appear in the speech of younger English, Dutch and German-learning children compared to children learning Romance languages, while word-initial unstressed syllables appear much earlier in for example Spanish than English (e.g. Gennari and Demuth, 1997; Lléo and Demuth, 1999; Lléo, 2002). With this backdrop, Roark and Demuth (2000) show that these acquisition orders line up with their relative English vs. Spanish frequencies: in a large corpus of child-directed speech (450,000 English utterances and 18,000 Spanish), about 60% of English words contained codas compared to only 25% of Spanish words, while 28% of Spanish words contained a weak first syllable compared to only 4% of English words.

One interesting comparison involves the input frequency of geminate consonants in Japanese vs. Finnish, two languages where consonantal length is contrastive. Multiple sources of input frequencies – both child-directed speech

---

[2] In this study, functional load for a segment x was based on the number of phonemes y at the same place of articulation that x contrasted with, weighted according to how frequent each y was in the language.

corpora as well as word counts from children's books! – suggest that consonant geminates are up to twice as frequent in Finnish children's lexical input
compared to Japanese (Aoyama, 2000; Kunnari et al., 2001). For example, in
15 mothers' recordings of half-hour play sessions with their children, 13.2%
of Finnish mothers' words contained geminates, while only 6.5% of Japanese
mothers' words did. Turning to these same children's own productions,
Kunnari et al (2001) found that Finnish children at around 1;1 were already
producing target geminates with nearly double the closure duration of short
consonants, while at around 1;5 Japanese children were still not reliable in
producing significantly longer target geminates compared to singletons.

What about within a single language? Let's examine one case study on
the connection between the frequency of a structure and its order of acquisition, focusing specifically on American-English learning children's acquisition
of word-final coda segments. To address this question, Zamuner, Gerken and
Hammond (2005) compiled a corpus of 40,000 CVC word tokens taken from
child-directed speech in CHILDES and calculated the relative frequency of
each English consonant phoneme in word-final position. The results are in (1):

(1) American-English word-final Cs in child-directed speech, from most to
     least frequent
     (reported in Zamuner, Gerken and Hammond, 2005)
     t > ɹ > n > d > z > k > s > l > m > v > ʃ > g > p > θ > ŋ > tʃ > f > dʒ > b > ʒ, ð

Then, Zamuner et al. (2005) examined production data from 41 American-
English-learning children under 3;0 to determine which coda segments they
acquired first. To quantify this order with such a large data sample, they tallied
either the child's first coda segment, or the child's five most frequent segments
(depending on the data available), and the ordered results across all 41 kids are
given in (2). Before reading on, compare the rankings of (1) and (2). For this data:
how well does input frequency do at predicting word-final order of acquisition?

(2) Order of acquisition for American-English word-final Cs
     (reported in Zamuner, Gerken and Hammond, 2005)
     t > n > k > d, m > ʔ > p > tʃ, l > b, f, ŋ, ɹ, s

For some segments the frequency and early acquisition of English codas
match up rather well: the first codas to be produced are [t, n, d, k], which are
also four of the six most frequent. For a couple of other segments, there are
clear mismatches: the other two most frequent codas are [ɹ] and [z]; [ɹ] is at
the bottom of the acquisition list, and [z] doesn't even make the list! Here
again there may well be a predictive role for language-specific frequency in
coda acquisition, but there must also be conflicting factors at work.

Before moving on let us consider these results a little further, in the context of previous chapters. How well do the results in (1) vs. (2) fit with the results at the beginning of Chapter 5, concerning the order of acquisition of natural classes? How much of the observed acquisition orders in (2) fit with the view that more cross-linguistically common segments are acquired earlier? One general preference across languages is that coda inventories often contain sonorants rather than obstruents – so, the early acquisition of [t, k, d] might look suspicious. On the other hand, Chapter 3.3.4 showed that word-*final* position is not always a simple *coda* position, so these data probably need to be interpreted with some caution.

7.2.1 Connecting Input Frequency and Order of Acquisition – Implications for Grammar Use

The intuitive idea as to how input frequency could drive order of acquisition is that the more lexical evidence you get for a structure, the quicker you acquire it. We will get back to this in Chapter 10, but note for now that it is still compatible with our overall grammatical view, whereby an input lexical item is fed to a single phonological grammar, which decides how optimally to produce its sound patterns. This is illustrated schematically in (3): count the number of instances of /A/s and /B/s in the 'words' of the language in (3a) compared to the /C/s and /D/s, and you will see why the structural constraints against the former two are ranked low in (3b):

(3) Schematic connection between input frequency and structure:
a) High frequency words in the lexicon: /AAB/   /BAB/   /BABB/   /CAA/
   Low frequency words in the lexicon: /CDD/   /CDC/   /BCCA/   /DACB/
b) First generalizations learned: As and Bs are permitted in the target
                                              (Cs and Ds not as frequently observed)
c) Intermediate grammar ranking: *C, *D >> Faithfulness >> *A, *B

But there is a different potential connection between frequency and acquisition: that the likelihood of a child producing a phonological structure is related to the <u>frequency of the particular word </u>in which it sits. A study on this topic was carried out by Ota and Green (2012), which tracked the longitudinal acquisition of English onset clusters up to age 4;0 in three children, and compared each production token's cluster accuracy to the input frequency of that word. To do this, the authors pre-determined a criterion for counting a cluster as acquired in each word, and divided each child's lexicon into two groups: words whose input frequency lay either above or below the overall mean. At 2;11–3;2, children had acquired onset clusters in about 40%

of the higher frequency words, but only 20% of the lower frequency words; at 3;5–3;8, onset clusters were now acquired in roughly 50% of the high frequency and only 30% of the low frequency words.

It is rather less clear how to reconcile these results with our grammatical story thus far – because it appears MAX outranks *COMPLEX more often for frequent words than for the reverse. However, such studies are as yet few and far between, in large part because these kinds of questions are only answerable with the wealth of child-directed-speech corpora which are just becoming widely available.

7.3 Lexical Avoidance

This sections deals with an interaction between lexicon and phonology that is somewhat harder to observe than the production data we saw in Chapters 3–5. Here, we are looking at inputs which never even make it to the surface – that is <u>potential</u> outputs which are systematically absent from the child's productive lexicon.

Our first example comes from the acquisition of word shape in Hebrew, from the longitudinal study of SR that we have looked at several times. Recall from Chapter 4.1 that Hebrew word stress is most often found on the final syllable (in about 75% of words), but penultimate stress is also common. In Chapter 4, we saw early /… Sw/ words produced with a consistent (Sw) trochee, while /… wS/ words were produced variously as (wS), (S), and even (Sw) (with stress shift). In table (4) below, we are tracking a different kind of data about word shape. Regardless of what his outputs looked like, what proportion of SR's inputs were /…wS/ vs /…Sw/? Examine this table that quantifies the frequency of these two word shapes in SR's productive lexicon[3]:

(4)	SR's development of Hebrew word shape (Data from Adam and Bat-El, 2009)				
		Prosodic Shape of Targets			
	Age	/…Sw/	/…wS/	total	% of / … wS/
	1;02–1;05.08	81	65	146	44.5%
	1;05.15–1;05.29	35	57	92	65%

Continued

---

[3] Note that this table only includes 'major class' lexical items, that is nouns, verbs, adjectives, adverbials and so on. Additionally, some of SR's developmental stages have been collapsed together; see Adam and Bat-El (2009) for details.

	Prosodic Shape of Targets			
1;06.2–1;06.20	49	55	104	53%
1;06.26–1;07.09	51	99	150	66%

The final column of this table suggests a second way in which SR treats words with penultimate vs. ultimate stress differently, especially at the first stage (1;02–1;05.08). Compared to the approximately 75% of /wS/ words in the ambient language, SR chooses /wS/ inputs only 44% of the time – in other words, it seems like he is actively avoiding /wS/ inputs.

This phenomenon is known as *lexical avoidance* or *lexical selectivity*, and it has been observed in numerous diary studies, as well as a few experimental contexts (see especially Schwartz and Leonard, 1982; see also especially Storkel, 2006, and other readings at the end of the chapter).[4] Why would children avoid certain phonological structures in inputs? You will probably already see that there is a connection between the structures children avoid as inputs and those that their grammar bans in the output – in this case, both SR's production grammar and his input choices conspired to produce more surface trochees.

Another tantalizing example comes from Clara's asymmetries in consonant harmony at different places of articulation (Rose, 2000: 168–171). In Chapter 6.3, we saw that Clara imposed regressive *labial* harmony on her CVCV outputs; this pattern held over many months, overwriting both input dorsals and coronals. In Rose (2000)'s corpus, Clara harmonized dorsals with a following labial in 55/59 cases (as in *café*), and coronals harmonized with a following labial in 14/15 cases (as in *chapeau*).

But for inputs with coronal and dorsals, Clara's pattern was different. Between 1;00 and 1;09, she applied regressive coronal harmony to 19 out of 31 targets, as in *gateau* 'cake' [gæto] → [tæto]; and for the reverse order we have no evidence – because in nine months of recording sessions, Clara never attempted a single /Coronal-V-Dorsal-V/ input.

It may be that such inputs are rarer than other place of articulation orders, meaning that this gap might be an accidental one. However, one hint that the gap was phonological in nature is that monosyllabic /Coronal-V-Dorsal/

---

[4] In the domain of morpho-syntax acquisition, it seems that the avoidance of certain structures is much more common – see especially Snyder (2011) on the notion of 'grammatical conservatism'.

words also behaved exceptionally in Clara's grammar. Examine Clara's production of CVC words in (6) below:

(6)

Clara's CVC inputs at 1;7–1;10 (Data from Rose, 2000: 171)					
Target	*Child*	*Gloss*	*Target*	*Child*	*Gloss*
/liv/	[liφ]	*book*	/sak/	[katʃ]	*bag*
/dam/	[dam]	*lady*		[kæːt]	
/bɔt/	[bʌtʰ]	*boot*	/tsɪg/	[kɪːn]	*tiger*
/bɔl/	[pɔl]	*bowl*			
/gʊt/	[gʊtʰ]	*drop (n.)*			

None of these words are harmonized for place within their syllable: but the inputs in which a coronal onset precedes a dorsal coda, *sac* and *tigre*, surface with *metathesis*, resulting in a [Dorsal-V-Coronal] output. Strikingly, this class of input is the only one which undergoes metathesis in all of Clara's production. Overall, then, it seems that Clara's ban on coronal consonants followed by dorsals was in fact grammatically controlled: in /CVC/ inputs it could be repaired, but in /CVCV/ inputs no solution was apparently available, and so the forms were avoided altogether. But why?

One interpretation of this failure to even attempt an input is called *absolute ineffability*: a situation in which the grammar rules out every possible output candidate for a particular input, so that it simply cannot be produced. In target languages, ineffability often results from affixes that will only attach to stems with certain phonological properties. For example, the German diminutive suffix [-çən] causes a featural change (known as *umlaut*) in certain stem vowels when it attaches, as seen in (7a). However, speakers overall report that there is no way to diminutize a stem whose unstressed vowel would undergo umlaut, as seen in (7b)[5] – for the more complicated details in this paradigm, see Fanselow and Féry (2002).[6]

---

[5] It would appear that these diminutive judgements differ between German dialects and/or speaker groups.

[6] There are several English suffixes which cannot attach to many stems you might expect: for example, –*ity* can be used in *curious~curiosity, generous~generosity* but not *envious~*enviosity, glorious~*gloriosity*. However: the explanation for –*ity*'s restrictions doesn't come from the phonology of these stems, but from other members of their morphological paradigm: see Aronoff (1976) for the point that *enviosity* and *gloriosity* are blocked by the pre-existing words *envy* and *glory*.

(7)		Ineffability among German diminutives (Data from Fanselow and Féry, 2002: table 11)						
a)	*Base*	*Diminutive*	*Gloss*	b)	*Base*	*Diminutive*	*Gloss*	
	jaːʁ	jɛːʁ-çən	*year*		moːnat	ʔmoːnɛt-çən ʔmoːnat-çən *møːnat-çən	*month*	
	bʁuːdəʁ	bʁyːdəʁ-çən	*brother*		ɔɪʁoːpa	ʔɔɪʁoːpɛ-çən ʔɔɪʁoːpa-çən *ɔɪʁøːpa-çən	*Europe*	
	mauəʁ	mɔYəʁ-çən	*wall*		vɔtka	ʔvɔtkɛ-çən ʔvɔtka-çən *vœtka-çən	*vodka*	

Though we will not build a formal account of ineffability here, many attempts to explain the phenomenon within OT have built around the idea that the output candidate set contains a 'null parse'. This null parse is a candidate made simply of silence with no content at all, which we will indicate simply with a zero [0]. By definition, the null parse violates no structural or faithfulness constraints; instead, it violates a single new constraint, called 'M-Parse,' which requires some minimal amount of output content for any input.[7] In most grammars M-Parse is ranked fairly high, so that speakers can't simply avoid violating markedness and faithfulness constraints by just not saying anything. But if M-Parse is ranked beneath a large enough set of constraints, one of which must be violated to produce a particular input, the result is that saying nothing becomes optimal.

In some cases, it might be possible to understand children's lexical avoidance as the result of ineffability. Suppose we built a grammar for Clara's data in (6) whereby /TVK/ words like *sac* were mapped to [KVT] to satisfy a constraint against *[COR...DOR][8] sequences. As shown in (8), this would require that LINEARITY be ranked below M-Parse, to ensure that metathesis beat out the null parse:

---

[7] This idea originated in Prince and Smolensky (2004:57ff). If you are interested in how the null parse could possibly just violate M-Parse and nothing else, see McCarthy and Wolf (2007). For a different kind of idea about ineffability within OT, see Orgun and Sprouse (1999).

[8] This is a different way of analysing consonant harmony than the more general AGREE constraints used in Chapter 6.3, but it will work here to sketch a possible analysis.

(8)

		/sak/	*[Cor...Dor]	M-Parse	Linearity
	a)	sak	*!		
☞	b)	kas[9]			*
	c)	0		*!	

As has been noted in many places, metathesis is both uncommon and also usually very local in language patterns, usually affecting strictly or nearly-adjacent segments (see Chapter 5.2.1). This might suggest that Linearity is in fact a set of constraints – the general one from early chapters that penalizes any segmental re-ordering, and more specific ones which penalize metathesis at greater distances, such as across a syllable boundary (shown in (9)). If in a grammar like Clara's this more specific Linearity constraint is ranked high, along with *[Cor...Dor], metathesis will not be a possible repair for those /TVKV/ words that Clara never attempted – and if M-Parse ranks beneath them both, the winner will be the null parse:

(9) Linearity-Syllable
     Assign a violation for every pair of input segments x and y, with
     output correspondents X and Y <u>in different syllables</u>, where x precedes
     y but Y precedes X.

(10)

/sVkV/	*[Cor...Dor]	Linearity-Syllable	M-Parse	Linearity
sV.kV	*!			
kV,sV		*!		*
☞ 0			*	

Notice how regular Linearity, as was violated in monosyllabic words like (8), has to be ranked below M-Parse – or else /CVC/ words like *sac* would be unpronounceable too.

We will leave as an open question how well the concept of absolute ineffability and/or the null parse can captured the full range of children's lexical avoidance. From the broader perspective, the phenomenon demonstrates that either the grammar or the learner has some sense of the phonological 'fate' awaiting inputs that are fed to the grammar. Even if M-Parse is not the right account of lexical selectivity, the learner must have some knowledge of what they are and are not able (or willing) to produce, since they can choose to avoid the latter.

---

[9] In (6), Clara also stopped the /s/ to [t] but that is irrelevant to the current point.

7.4 Exceptions, Regressions and Fossils

Let's now return to the time course of individual children's speech production, beginning with a more detailed look at manner harmony in Daniel's
speech (from Chapter 6.3.1, ex 46a). In this data, nasal consonants caused
oral stops to become nasal too, e.g. *broom* → [mum]. In the previous chapter,
we were only concerned with describing this pattern at one stage, and its similarity to adult consonant harmonies – but now, we will consider a few stages
in its lexical development (from Menn, 1971), summarized in table (11):

(11) | Daniel's nasal harmony: Data abbreviated from Menn (1971) | | | | | |
|---|---|---|---|---|---|
| *Stages 1–2* | | *Stage 3* | | *Stages 4–5* | |
| *broom* | **[mum]** | *train* | **[ŋaɪn]** | *blimp* | [mɪmp] |
| *bump* | [bʌmp] | *prune* | **[nun], [mum]** | *bump, jump* | [mʌmp] |
| *stone* | [don] | *stone* | [don] | *stone* | [non] |
| *down* | [daʊn] | *down* | [daʊn] | *down* | [naʊn] |

At stage 1, nasals trigger harmony in a limited set of labial-initial words (in
bold): the initial C of *broom* nasalizes, but *bump* does not. At later stages, the
harmony affects a larger range of onset segments, including other /Cɹ/ clusters, and by stage 5 harmony affects many coronal stops too – compare *stone*
and *down* across the table.

A similar example comes from a longitudinal study of one child K, whose
grammar imposed *velar fronting* (recall Chapter 5.5.5) in the onsets of stressed
syllables. At the beginning of this study, K fronted velars systematically in all
but six lexical items: *cookie, kitty cat, cow, cookie (ice) cream* and *Gumbi*. The
table in (12) shows how these words nearly always resisted fronting during
the study's first six stages, after which they displayed the majority pattern
and fronted as well:

(12) | K's velar fronting and exceptions (Data from Bleile and Tomblin, 1991) | | | | | |
|---|---|---|---|---|---|
| *Regular pattern* | | | *Initial exceptions* | | *Regression* |
| | | | | *stages 1–6* | *stages 7–22* |
| e.g. *candy* | [tændi] | | *clown* | [kaʊn] | [taʊn] |
| | | | *okay* | [oˈkeɪ] | [oˈteɪ] |
| | | | *cookie* | [ˈkʊki] | [ˈtʊki] |
| | | | *# tokens fronted* | 3/19 (16%) | 58/61 (95%) |

There are at least two broad ways of understanding this trajectory in Daniel and K's phonologies. If nasal harmony is described as a general phonological process, which has the potential to affect all oral stops (as the adult language nasal harmonies in Chapter 5 can), then Daniel's stage 1 includes many *lexical exceptions* to the pattern, which by stage 5 have been grammatically regularized. From this viewpoint, something special must be done in the grammar (or elsewhere) at stage 1 to ensure that for example *down* does not harmonize. If on the other hand Daniel's output lexicon is compared to the targets at each stage, then stages 2–5 contain an increasing number of *lexical regressions*, as forms like *down* which initially were produced without harmony become <u>less</u> faithful over time. From this viewpoint, something special must be done every time Daniel adds more lexical items to the set which harmonize (though again, this something special might or might not be a grammatical something.)

Thus, *exceptions* and *regressions* are two ways to view a phonological process which spreads over time in a child's lexicon. They are not necessarily observed together, however: a child's earliest speech can, for example, begin with most onset clusters reduced to singletons (/CC/ → [C]) but with a few words' clusters produced as faithful exceptions. Later the child will acquire faithful cluster production throughout the lexion (/CC/→ [CC]), and this may occur without ever having shown *regression* among those early faithful words.

Finding the explanation(s) for lexical exceptions and regressions depends a lot on our assumptions about how phonological knowledge is learned and represented. From this text's OT perspective, the first crux of the matter is in the constraint set, which will determine the range of lexical items that should be expected to participate in a process, and therefore determine whether a word should be interpreted as acting exceptionally or not. In Daniel's case, the issues are what counts as a target for nasal harmony: does AGREE[NASAL] refer to just labial voiced stops? Or to all obstruents? Or to something in between? Are there in fact several different nasal harmony constraints, with varying scope?[10]

To make these idea concrete, let's walk through two stages in the speech of one child Morgan learning North American English, as described by

---

[10] Note that this last idea is indeed our approach to the range of *adult* language nasal harmonies with varying scope and targets; recall Section 6.3's data, and see especially Rose and Walker (2004), Hansson (2007).

Stemberger, Bernhardt and Johnson (2001). Here is a representative sample of certain lexical items in Morgan's production between 1;4–1;6.21.

(13)		Morgan: Initial stage (Data from Stemberger et al., 2001)				
	a)	*Target*	*Child*	b)	*Target*	*Child*
		no	nɤː		*me*	miː
		shoe	çɯː		*sockie*	laki
		cow	tʰaɯ		*doggie*	dagi

In addition to vowel lengthening in /CV/ words[11], the words in (13a) demonstrate a notable featural pattern of vowel *unrounding*: target vowels /u/ and /o/ and the diphthong /aʊ/, which are all produced with lip rounding, are mapped to unround vowels [ɤ] and [ɯ] (not found in target English!).

The diary study of Morgan's speech revealed a change in this pattern specifically at 1;6.22. What has changed in Morgan's treatment of final vowels?

(14)		Morgan: Next Stage (1;6.22) (Data from Stemberger et al., 2001)				
	a)	*Target*	*Child*	b)	*Target*	*Child*
		no	nɤː ~ nɤːm		*me*	miː ~ miːm
		shoe	çɯː ~ çɯːm		*sockie*	lakim
		cow	tʰaɯ ~ tʰaɯm		*doggie*	dagim
		yellow	lalɤː, *lalɤːm			

In (14a), word-final round vowels in the input are still unrounded, but they now can also surface followed by an epenthetic [m] (though the word *yellow* is reportedly exempt from this epenthesis). In (14b), we see a few other words which are now also produced with final [m] insertion. ... So what's going on? Are all of these new [m]s a sign of grammatical regression?

There is, in fact, an explanation for (14a)'s pattern, which treats these [m]s as representing an <u>increase</u> in faithfulness, rather than a regression away from the target. In those words which end with input round vowels, inserting a

---

[11] You can probably understand this in the terms of Section 4.1.5: if the grammar is not yet set up to interpret English tense vowels as contributing two weight units, /CV/ must be augmented to meet Minimal Word requirements. Notice how diphthongs as in *cow* do not trigger lengthening, since they are already [CVV].

labial segment provides a method of retaining that [+labial] feature in the output – just not on the target segment. Schematically:

(15)

This is the opposite of fusion or coalescence, as we saw in Chapter 5; in this case features are undergoing *fission*, reproducing the features of one input segment on multiple output segments. This precise type of fission is, in fact, found in adult languages, particularly in diachronic change and loanwords. For example in Bislama, a creole spoken in Vanuatu (Crowley, 2004), the French word *camion* [kæ'mjõ]has become [kamioŋ], in which the French nasalized vowel has been split apart into two segments, a vowel and a nasal consonant:

(16) Bislama nasal vowel fission

So from this perspective, Morgan's mapping from /no/ → [nɤ:m] is driven by a familiar constraint, Max[LAB]. And at 1;6.22, Max[LAB] must have become more important (i.e. ranked above) the constraint against featural fission. What is that constraint? It is another correspondence constraint, the opposite of UNIFORMITY (Chapter 5.5.6) which prevents featural fusion – and it is called INTEGRITY:

(17) INTEGRITY (adapted from McCarthy and Prince, 1995)
Assign a violation for every pair of output segments which have a single input correspondent

The tableaus in (18) below show how re-ranking these two constraints, beneath *ROUNDVOWEL, captures these two different languages:

(18)	Morgan's initial stage				Morgan's next stage			
	/no₁/	*ROUNDV	INTEG	MAX [LAB]	/no₁/	*ROUNDV	MAX [LAB]	INTEG
	no	*!			no	*!		
☞	nɤ:			*	nɤ:		*!	
	nɤ₁:m₁		*!		☞ nɤ₁:m₁			*

So this apparent 'regression' in the output of forms like *no, cow* and *shoe* has been explained along the same lines we have been following throughout this text: different rankings of the same constraints necessary to capture cross-linguistic phonologies, leading to similar trade-offs and repairs.

However, there are clearly missing pieces to this analysis. One is that the word *yellow*, including a word-final round vowel, did not undergo fission – so *yellow* must have been an exception (although since the pattern was variable, we would need to know how many times *yellow* was recorded to know whether it too was variable, but just not produced <u>often enough</u> to demonstrate its alternative pronunciation.)

The other, bigger concern is Stemberger et al. (2001)'s report of at least three words which underwent [m]-epenthesis even though their input vowels are not [+labial]. Our grammatical notion of preserving underlying rounding cannot explain the presence of these [m]s, in *me, doggie* and *sockie*. They constitute regressions, but we have no grammatical explanation for them; they are exceptions that will need to be captured in some other way.

Another kind of lexical exception is seen in words which do not continue to change in their production from stage to stage, but rather appear stuck at an earlier stage of development; these are sometimes referred to as *fossilized* forms.[12] To assess an example of lexical fossilization, we will examine two excerpts from stages of Trevor's phonology.

First consider the processes at work in the first data set (19), when Trevor was 1;7:

(19)	Trevor at 1;7.11–28 (Data from Compton and Streeter, 1977; Pater, 1996)			
	Target	*Child*	*Target*	*Child*
	raisin	[neni]	mirror	[mɪmə]
	iron	[aiːnʌn]	Lorna	[nonæ]
	rake	[wek]	window	[nʌno]
	ring		crying	[kainiː]

---

[12] Their opposite – words that seem to be in advance of a child's current phonology – are referred to by Moskowitz (1980) as 'progressive idioms'. A frequently-cited example from Leopold (1970) involves a child's production of the word 'pretty', which between 0;10–1;8 was pronounced with an initial [pɹ] cluster, but subsequently was brought in line with the rest of the child's onset cluster and reduced to [b]. It is probably important to know that at its earlier stage, this child used this word as a 'vague emotive' (Leopold, 1947: 265), and it was at 1;8 when / pɹ/ → [b] that the word began to be treated as an attributive adjective.

Most of these examples demonstrate Trevor's process of nasal harmony, which target approximants and glides (ɹ, l, j, w) – in the word *raisin,* it also seems to target a medial /z/. There is also some evidence that his word-final coda production is variable: compare the codas in *rake, iron* and *ring* with those missing in *raisin* and *crying.* Now examine Trevor's later data in (20). How would you describe the fate of nasal harmony and word-final codas now?

(20)	Trevor at 1;10–2;0					
	Target	*Child*	*Age*	*Target*	*Child*	*Age*
	pants	[pæːnts]	1;10.11	*running*	[nʌːnɪŋ]	1;10.15
	plants	[pæːnts]	1;10.13	*colouring*	[kʌləˑɪŋ]	1;11.9
	hands	[hæːnds]	1;10.13	*two airplanes*	[tuː pɝˑpeːnz]	1;11.10
	two raisins	[tuː neni]	1;11.9	*raisins*	[neːniz]	2;0.3
	ring	[wɪŋ]	1;11.25	*corns*	[kaːrɪnz]	2;0.3
	iron	[aiːrʌn]	1;11.12	*presents*	[pɛːzɪnts]	2;03

Most of this later data reveals that nasal harmony is almost gone: *running* still shows nasalization of /ɹ/, but *ring, iron, corn* and *colouring* all include surface rhotics, and notice that *presents* retains its medial /z/ as well. In addition, word-final codas are much more stable – and in particular, nasal+obstruent clusters are all produced faithfully: *pants, plants, hands, planes, corns.* ... All except *raisins,* which at 1;10 is still produced as [neni] and at 2;0.3 surfaces as [neniz]. Even if we did not trust Trevor's ability to deploy the final /-z/ plural, this word has fossilized many earlier processes, including singleton coda deletion, and nasal harmony affecting both /ɹ/ and even /z/. In fact, *raisins* does not appear with an initial rhotic until 2;2.7, many months after nasal harmony has otherwise been left behind.

Where do fossils like '*neni*' come from? In this case, it may be necessary to consider a little more about his semantic acquisition and his lexicon – which the intimate detail of a diary study permits us to do. From the transcripts and annotations, it would appear that Trevor was rather fond of raisins, especially in his oatmeal – and starting at age 1;3, he consistently referred to them as '*neni*'. On a few occasions at 1;4, there are notes that he used the term to describe any small snack food, and at 1;5 he occasionally used the term in a context that led the transcribe to believe Trevor was actually referring to the oatmeal itself, not the raisins. These data points might suggest that Trevor had coined a novel word *neni* that was not exactly analogous with English *raisin* – or at least that he had created an underlying form /neni/ meaning 'raisins (and raisin-like things)', and which the transcribers had no better translation for than 'raisins'. If so, this fossilization is not the result of frozen phonology – a grammar which was exceptionally deleting the coda and nasalizing other consonants in /ˈɹeɪzɪn(z)/ – but rather a child-specific underlying form.

Of course, just because one fossilized form in Trevor's speech might well be attributed to his developing grammar does not mean that every fossil has a similar explanation. The larger question – in trying to understanding data from Daniel, Morgan and Trevor alike – is to what extent these patterns are replicated in target phonologies. In other words: what do lexical exceptions look like in target phonologies? To the extent that they are similar to those seen among children, we will look to use similar tools to capture both – but if they are substantively different, we will want to look for explanations outside our grammar of ranked constraints.

To make a long story short: adult phonologies do contain a range of lexical exceptions, with some processes holding absolutely 100% of the time, some holding in only very restricted and unpredictable lexical contexts, and many others lying on a continuum in-between. Here is one of a multitude of examples, taken from Finnish (Anttila, 2002): in this language, stems which end with the vowel [a] can behave in one of three ways when suffixed with plural [-i-]:

(20)	Finnish exceptional allomorphy (Data from Anttila, 2002: ex 19)		
	Underlying	*Surface*	*Gloss*
	/tavara-i-ssa/	[tavaroissa]	*things (inessive)*
	/jumala-i-ssa/	[jumalissa]	*gods (inessive)*
	/itara-i-ssa/	[itaroissa] ~ [itarissa]	*stingy (inessive)*

How can a grammar capture this behaviour? The phonological mapping of /a + i/ → [o] is not so exceptional in itself; [a] and [i] are very disparate vowels at least in height, and [o] is perhaps a compromise between them. But if we build a grammar for Finnish that drives this mapping, how can the ranking hold in (a), but be reversed in (b), and then somehow optionally apply in (c)?!

There are a few different constraint-based approaches to lexical exceptions, but one prominent strategy is to add versions of our familiar structural and faithfulness constraints <u>which only apply to certain words</u>.

If this seems special pleading: let's put the Finnish discussion on hold and think instead about your own experience with borrowed words. If you are familiar with the word *'genre,'* for example, and/or if you know that it is originally a French word, you might pronounce it in English as ['ʒɑn.ɹə]. But if so, this word is unique in your English lexicon in that it contains a word-initial [ʒ] – all other English [ʒ] are found in the middle or ends of words (*azure, leisure, beige, rouge*), and you can compare the English names *'John'* and *'Jack'* which begin with affricate [dʒ] to their French counterparts *Jean* and *Jacques* which begin with a [ʒ]. Thus, *'genre'* is an exception to the otherwise-robust English distributional restriction *#[ʒ].

It may well be the case that if you pronounce this word exceptionally, you also know that it's a foreign word – that is that it was borrowed recently into English from French – and so you are willing to cut it a little phonological slack, so to speak. If someone tried to just invent an English word ['ʒɑn.ɹə] tomorrow, speakers would probably revolt – that is, they'd pronounce it with a word-initial [dʒ] like a well-behaved English word.

A grammatical way to encode this dichotomy is to say that certain words in the lexicon are accorded special faithfulness. Just as we have used special versions of faithfulness constraints that refer only to onsets, these ones will refer only to inputs that are tagged as special in some way: in this case, we could say that *genre* has, in some people's lexica, the tag [Recent]. If we have a version of IDENT[+/-Continuant] (which protects the contrast between affricates and fricatives) which is specific to the [Recent]-tagged inputs, then it can be ranked above *#[ʒ], to maintain the fricative in *genre*, and the general IDENT[+/-CONT] can be ranked below to capture the general English fact:

(21) IDENT[+/-Continuant]-ₚₑCENT[13]
     Assign a violation for every input segment *in a word marked [Recent]* with the feature [α-continuant] whose output correspondent has the feature [β-continuant].

(22)

/ʒak/	IDENT[CONT] ᵣₑCENT!	*#[ʒ]	IDENT-[CONT]
ʒak		*!	
☞ dʒæk			*
/ʒɑnɹə/	IDENT [CONT] ᵣₑCENT!	*#[ʒ]	IDENT-[CONT]
☞ ʒɑn.ɹə		*	
dʒɑn.ɹə	*!		*

---

[13] This definition is mine, but the popular idea of indexing faithfulness constraints to particular sublexicons can be found in Ito and Mester (1995); also for example Pater (2000: 258–260); Jurgec (2010) and in a slightly different approach, Inkelas, Orgun and Zoll (1997). For how these constraints might get learned see further readings in Chapter 10.

Perhaps you now see the connection to other kinds of lexical exceptionality like the Finnish treatment of /a+i/: maybe a word doesn't need to be a recent borrowing to belong to a group of words tagged for special treatment by constraints like (21). If the Finnish word for '*thing*' undergoes vowel change but '*god*' doesn't – maybe '*god*' is part of a group of words, a *sublexicon*, with its own IDENT constraints? And if in Morgan's grammar *shoe* can retain final vowel rounding via epenthetic [m] but *yellow* cannot – maybe one of them is tagged as exceptional too. If it's *yellow* that's part of an exceptional sublexicon, then here's the ranking:

(23)	*Morgan: No Fission in exceptional words like* yellow (cf. 17b)				
/jɛloː/ [lex1]	*ROUNDV	INTEG [LEX1]	MAX[LAB]	INTEG
laloː:	*!			
☞ lalɤː:			*	
lalɤ:m		*!		*

One potentially big difference between target vs. child patterns of lexical exceptions comes from their origin. When learning Finnish, a child observes the various behaviours of suffixes after [a], and is forced by their observations to invent some account, whether in the grammar or otherwise, even just by memorizing all the words where vowels alternate in these ways.[14] But the lexical exceptions that we see in child phonologies, like Morgan and Daniel's, are not forced on them by the observed data: they are exceptions to <u>processes the children have created themselves</u>.

So maybe looking for analogues to adult grammatical processes is not the right way to describe lexical exceptions, regressions and so on. Maybe these data tell us not about how the grammar affects individual words in different ways, but how our learning mechanisms can treat words differently? We will return again to this topic in Chapter 10.4.

---

[14] To tease these options apart, experimental study is required. To use an English example, there is some notable work in the 1970s and 1980s on speaker's intuitions about the English alternations called *trisyllabic laxing*, seen in paradigms like *serene~serenity* and *grade~gradual*, but not in similar paradigms like *obese~obesity* and *brave~bravery*. The overall experimental finding was that adults are not very likely to extend trisyllabic laxing to novel words – see especially Jaeger (1984) and references therein.

7.5   Templates and the Like

The last phenomenon in this chapter is another innovative pattern that learners sometimes impose on a subset of their lexicon. To get a taste of the data, examine the forms in (24) below from a diary study of one English-learning child C (Priestly, 1977), all taken from the same week at age 1;11. Try as best you can to provide a comprehensive description of the input-output mappings in this data before reading on: how much is predictable, and from what?

(24)

C at 1;11, week 4 (Data from Priestly, 1977)			
Target	*Child*	*Target*	*Child*
pɛjas	*bison*	bɛjan	*Brenda*
kijas	*Christmas*	wijak	*whisker*
gajas	*garage*	pajat	*powder*
wijas, wijus	*whistle*	tajak, tajaŋ[15]	*tiger*
pijat	*peanut*	tajak	*turkey*
pijan	*panda*	bajat	*spider*

In terms of word shape, every output surfaces as two syllables, with one initial, medial and final consonant; the inputs are also all bisyllabic but with varying clusters and syllable margins. To create this consistent output shape, input clusters get simplified (*Christmas, spider, Brenda, whisker*) and codas may also be created (as at the end of *panda* and *Brenda*; think also about *whistle*). The initial consonant is always predictably faithful to the input, once any cluster has been reduced, but the medial consonant is always predictably unfaithful, produced 100% of the time as [j]. The final consonant is a little more complicated to predict. Its manner of articulation in these data is always a voiceless obstruent or a nasal, and in most cases it looks like a correspondent of one of the input segments, whether final or medial in the input:

(25)

Sources for output final Cs in (24)					
bison	/'b₁aɪs₂ən/	[p₁ɛjas₂]	*garage*	/g₁aˈɹɑdʒ₂/	[g₁ajas₂]
whisker	/'w₁ɪsk₂əɹ/	[w₁ijak₂]	*peanut*	/'p₁inʌt₂/	[p₁ijat₂]
panda	/'p₁æn₂dʌ/	[p₁ijan₂]			
turkey	/'t₁ɚk₂i/	[t₁ajak₂]			

---

[15] One exceptional production of tiger was [kajaŋ].

As always, we will not have much to say about the vowels (Priestly, 1977 is much more thorough on this point). But it is overall important to note that the two vowels of each output are restricted to a couple of options: first vowel as [i] or [a] and second vowel as [a].

These vowel patterns, combined with the single consistent word shape and the output medial [j], are reminiscent of restrictions we have seen before: segmental over-writing like we saw in Chapter 4.2.2, for both child and adult languages, and shape restrictions on e.g. the size of a reduplicant as in Chapter 4.1.1. These target language phenomena have often been referred to as *templatic* phonology, and C's data has also been provided as a classic example of a child's template, which we might describe informally as [CVjaC]. However, the acquisition literature on children's early templates has taken a fundamentally different stance on their analysis and origin compared to the constraints of Chapter 4 and elsewhere in this text. Before delving into some theory, let's take a closer look at C's patterns.

Wherever the template came from, it wasn't used for every one of C's words – as shown in the outputs in (26) which he also produced during week 4:

(26)	Some of C's non-templatic outputs at 1;11				
puppy	['papi]	*hammer*	['hæmə]	*flower*	['fawə]
kitchen	['kɪkɪn]	*funny*	['fʌni]	*Wendy*	['wɛni]
lion	['lajən]	*coffee*	['kɒfi]	*doggy*	['gɒgi]
deer	['dijə]	*Grandpa*	['bampə]	*Teddy*	['tɛdi]

Can analysing C's lexicon give us any clues as to the source or predictability of this templatic pattern? The table below in (27) tallies the number of C's week 4 words that did or did not follow the template, grouped according to their input medial consonant:

(27)	C's input lexicon and template use at week 4				
Input Medial C	liquids: /ɹ, l/	nasals: /n, ŋ/	fricatives: /s, z/	stops: /p, t, d, k, g/	glides: /j/
templatic words	3	5	6	13	
non templatic	0	12	7	28	17
% templatic	100%	29%	46%	32%	

This table shows that C applied the [j]-medial pattern to words with all sorts of input medial consonants. However, it also reveals that 17/91 or 19%

of his recorded words had a medial [j] in the target: given the dialect he was acquiring, this included words such as *lion, wheel, nail* and *fire*. While in terms of natural classes C's lexicon included more medial stops than glides, in terms of individual segments, [j] was by far the most common. This lexical skew seems to suggest that the medial [j] of the template was derived from the most common input shape in his current lexicon. On the other hand, the final coda of the CVCVC template seems less amenable to a frequency explanation: at week 4, only 19/58 input words ended in a final consonant.

C's templatic phonology pattern lasted from week 4 until at least week 13. During weeks 5–7, 22 new words were produced with the template, while only four templatic words switched to being produced normally (i.e. without medial [j]), and after that no further templatic words appeared. The first significant weakening of the template was between weeks 8 and 10, during which input medial nasals and stops emerged, in words like *doughnut, peanut, panda, spider, rabbit* and *dragon*. Finally during weeks 12 and 13, 27 templatic words returned to normal, including medial liquids and fricatives, as in *berries, porridge, whisker* and *whistle*.

With this fuller data set in mind we return to our fundamental question: how should this [CVjaC] pattern be captured in C's phonological system?

On the one hand, medial lenition to a glide is common in target languages. In North American English, in fact, medial alveolar flaps are often produced in fast casual speech as glides – that is, the medial consonant of *water* can easily surface as something closer to ['wɑjə] (see data in Warner and Tucker, 2011). Thus it seems that target phonologies already need a constraint that prefers medial glides like [VjV] over the other less sonorous consonantal manners seen in the target words in (24). Looking at C's development over time, we can also note that his template disappears in a typologically-reasonable way: stops and nasals are the first to be tolerated, and liquids and fricatives come later. This is in line with the order of acquisition segmental facts from the beginning of Chapter 5.

But there are many aspects of this data that should cause scepticism. One issue is the choice of consonants to preserve word-finally, which we started to consider in (25) above. If we consider this choice of final C as a competition between the non-initial segments in the target, a few patterns via natural classes of manners emerge:

(28)		Predicting word final consonants in C's j-medial pattern words					
	a)	*coronal fricatives and affricates survive as final /s/:*					
		14 examples:				*4 exceptions*	
		bison	[bajas]	*garage*	[gajas]	*orange*	[ajat]
		Jesus	[dʒijas]	*coaster*	[kajows]	*engine*	[ɛjan]

Continued

a)	*coronal fricatives and affricates survive as final /s/:*						
	14 examples:					*4 exceptions*	
	present	[pɛjas]	muskox	[majaks]		whisker	[wijak]
	Christmas	[kijas]	Oscar	[ɔjas]		basket	[bajak]
	whistle	[wijas]	records	[ɹɛjas]			
	music	[mɛjas]	medicine	[mejas]			
	porridge	[pajas]	berries	[bɛjas]			
b)	*among remaining manners, stops survive as final /t/:*						
	14 examples:					*2 exceptions*	
	peanut	[pijat]	powder	[pajat]		Brenda	[bɛjan]
	doughnut	[dɛjawt]	turkey	[tajak]		fountain	[fajan]
	min ute	[mijat]	sucker	[fajak]			
	finger	[fijak]	spider	[bajat]			
	blanket	[bajak]	soldier	[sɔjat]			
	hydrant	[hajat]	shoulder	[sɔjat]			
	parrot	[pajat]	carrot	[kajat]			

While these two descriptions can explain a majority of the word-final output consonants, the effects do not make particularly good phonological sense. In particular: if these segments are codas, why are fricatives best, and stops second best – what's wrong with nasals, which are often the best codas there are? In addition, this pattern does not seem to be derived from input target frequencies either; looking at the lexicon that C had back at week 4, there is no skew towards final fricatives over nasals in targets. And with respect to production at that stage, he was already producing nasal codas – in *lion, iron, kitten, kitchen, Indian* and *bacon* – while only two fricative codas were reported, in *lizzies* and *scissors*. So what else could be the explanation?

Priestly (1977)'s original suggestion for final segment selection in C's pattern concerns *salience* – that certain input segments, like the *stridents* (those coronal fricatives and affricates in 28a), might have made it into the final C position of the [CVjaC] template because they were easy to perceive. More broadly speaking, it might be that templates emerge when the learner's underlying representations for certain words are insufficiently specified.

Suppose that a learner hears the word *bison* for the first time, and does not perceive it all quite enough to store it as /baɪsən/. What might at least get stored was that the word began with a [baɪ...], that it was bisyllabic, and that somewhere it contained a strident. This information, plus a default template which fills in additional content – the syllable structure, and the [j] and [a] – might be sufficient to predict the [bajas] surface form. This is illustrated in (29a), compared to a word whose UR is fully specified and so mapped without reference to the template (29b):

(29) *Two degrees of input specification*

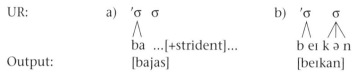

UR: a) 'σ σ   b) 'σ   σ

ba ...[+strident]...   b eɪ k ə n
Output: [bajas]   [beɪkan]

But can this templatic mapping be done solely using the kinds of phonological constraints we have been using thus far? With respect to featural faithfulness: anchoring the initial C (and often V) of the input and output to the left-edge of the word is easily done; something must also ensure that all coronal fricatives and affricates map to [s], and all stops to voiceless [t] or [k], and these too seem like reasonable faithfulness effects. With respect to structural constraints, restricting words to a single trochaic foot with no consonant clusters is also typical! But on the other hand, over-writing the *medial* consonant with [j] seems problematic. For one thing, what's this 'medial position'? It isn't a phonological object that we can grab onto, unlike for example the initial unstressed syllable that G over-wrote segmentally in Chapter 4.2.2.

This section has only scratched the surface of the kinds of idiosyncratic output patterns that have been ascribed to templatic strategies in the child speech literature. In most cases, no explicit attempt has been made to construct and compare accounts of the same data, using both the cross-linguistically motivated constraints of an OT-like grammar and comparing them to the lexicon-specific templates suggested by the child's outputs. In the end, however, examples like C's do emphasize the child-specific nature of some early word shapes; see the further readings below for more radical use of templates and other relevant data and debate.

7.6   Further Reading

On Phonological Neighbourhood Density in Adults and in Acquisition

Stokes, Stephanie F. 2010. Neighborhood density and word frequency predict vocabulary size in toddlers. *Journal of Speech Hearing and Language Research* 53(3): 670–683.

Storkel, Holly L. 2004. Do children acquire dense neighbourhoods? An investigation of similarity neighbourhoods in phonological acquisition. *Journal of Applied Psycholinguistics* 25: 201–221.

Storkel, Holly L. 2009. Developmental differences in the effects of phonological, lexical and semantic variables on word learning by infants. *Journal of Child Language* 36(2): 291–321.

Vitevitch, Michael S., Armbruster, Jonna and Chu, Shinying. 2004. Sub-lexical and lexical representations in speech production: Effects of phonotactic probability and onset density. Journal of Experimental Psychology: Learning, Memory, & Cognition 30: 514–529.

On Lexical Avoidance (and Related Topics)

Adam, Galit and Bat-El, Outi. 2009. When do universal preferences emerge in language development? The acquisition of Hebrew Stress. *Brill's Annual of Afroasiatic Languages and Linguistics* 1: 255–282.

Albright, Adam. 2010. Lexical and morphological conditioning of paradigm gaps. In Curt Rice and Sylvia Blaho (eds) *Modeling Ungrammaticality in Optimality Theory.* Equinox.

– this chapter is not about acquisition, but it provides insight into this topic and those in the next chapter *on templates*.

Menn, L. 1978. Phonological units in beginning speech. In A. Bell, and J. Hooper-Bybee (eds) *Syllables and Segments.* Amsterdam: North-Holland. 157–172.

Schwartz, Richard and Leonard, Laurence. 1982. Do children pick and choose? an examination of phonological selection and avoidance in early lexical acquisition. *Journal of Child Language* 9: 319–336.

Storkel, Holly L. 2006. Do children still pick and choose? The relationship between phonological knowledge and lexical acquisition beyond 50 words. *Clinical Linguistics and Phonetics* 20(7–8): 523–529.

Vihman, Marilyn V. and Tamar, Keren-Portno. (eds.) 2013. *The Emergence of Phonology: Whole Word Approaches and Cross-linguistic. Evidence* Cambridge: Cambridge University Press.

Exercises

Q1: A study by Hollich, Jusczyk and Luce (2002) found a somewhat complicated connection between the neighbourhood density of a novel word and the ease with which infants (at 1;5) learnt that word. If in training infants were briefly exposed to a word, they could only learn its meaning if the word had been presented to them within a high-density neighbourhood – that is if they had heard it in a list with other phonologically-similar words. But if infants were trained for considerably longer, they could now only reliably learn a word's meaning if it had been presented within a low-density neighbourhood, that is in a list with less-similar words. ... *What does this suggest about how children at 1;5 are storing novel phonological strings?*

Q2: The study by Zamuner, Gerken and Hammond (2005) discussed in Section 6.2 calculated the relative frequency of input coda segments using a corpus of CVC words in child-directed speech. Before counting the number of each coda segment, the authors excluded all proper names. *Why do you think they chose to do this? How do you think this choice could have affected their results?*

Q3: Here is a dataset from Claire at 1;10–2;2, who was learning European French (data from Wauquier, 2014: tables 5–6). *How templatic do you think Claire's productions are in this data? Can they be accounted for using the kinds of input-like URs and structural/faithfulness constraints we have assumed throughout this text? Do they require a different kind of analysis? Or some combination thereof? ...* You may find it useful to compare with C's data above in Section 7.5.

Target	Claire	Gloss		Target	Claire	Gloss
/ele'fã/	[ejã]/[eã]	*elephant*		/ʀuʒ/	[ju]	*red*
/vaʃ/	[ja]	*cow*		/oʀɛj/	[oje]	*ear*
/pwasɔ̃/	[pajɔ̃]	*fish*		/wazo/	[jajo]	*bird*
/lamezɔ̃/	[lamejɔ̃]	*the house*		/paʀdɔ̃/	[pajɔ̃]	*pardon, sorry*
/koʃɔ̃/	[kojɔ̃]	*pig*		/ãkɔʀynʃãsɔ̃/	[ãkɔjɔ̃jɔ̃]	*another song*
/mãʒe/	[mãje]	*to eat*		/lekamjɔ̃/	[jajajɔ̃]	*the trucks*

8 Acquiring Morpho-Phonology

8.1 Introduction to the Problem

The last chapter discussed the interactions between a child's developing phonology and the growing set of lexical items they are learning. This chapter is about the child's discovery that some of those lexical items are in fact built of smaller pieces – *morphemes* – and thus how morpho-phonology develops.

Up until now, we have focused almost exclusively on *phonotactics*, meaning that we have built grammars that capture sound patterns that are permitted in output forms, under the assumption that any ambient word that the child hears can be analysed as coming from a faithful input. For example: English words can end in two voiceless obstruents like *tax* [tæks] or with a sonorant plus voiceless obstruent like *dance* [dæns] or *pulse* [pʌɫs] but not in a voiced+voiceless obstruent, such as *[ægs] or *[dæds], and so we have aimed to build rankings that in this case would map as in (1):

(1) a) /tæks/ → [tæks] b) /ægs/ → something else … maybe [æg], [æks]…
    /dæns/ → [dæns]   /dæds/ → something else … maybe [dæd], [dæts]…
    /pʌɫs/ → [pʌɫs]

In any traditional understanding of generative phonology, however, this assumption about (1a) cannot be maintained throughout learning – that is, lots of real words surface <u>unfaithfully</u> compared to their inputs! For this chapter's purposes, the big reason for unfaithful inputs is *alternation*. As soon as words are built from inputs containing <u>multiple morphemes</u>, phonology will cause the same morpheme to surface as multiple phonological variants according to context. For example, compare the clusters in (1) to the ones in English plurals in (2):

(2)		*sing.*	*plur.*				*sing.*	*plur.*
a)	*tack*	[tæk]	[tæks]		b)	*bag*	[bæg]	[bægz]
	boot	[but]	[buts]			*bed*	[bɛd]	[bɛdz]
	ship	[ʃɪp]	[ʃɪps]			*ban*	[bæn]	[bænz]
	laugh	[læf]	[læfs]			*bell*	[bɛɫ]	[bɛɫz]

These two columns of data represent part of what is probably the most frequently-taught alternation in English introductory phonology classes. In the (a) data, plural is marked on nouns with the suffix [-s], but in (b) this same suffix surfaces as [-z]. Under the assumption that suffixes which mean the same thing are stored in the adult speaker's mind as a single *underlying representation* (UR), we can determine from (2) that the English plural morpheme alternates between [-s] and [-z], and therefore that sometimes it is mapped unfaithfully. (Another useful term to describe such patterns is that the English plural here exhibits two *allomorphs*, [-s] and [-z].)

If the input for English plural is /-s/, then the plural words in (2b) all involve mappings like /bæg+ s/ → [bægz]; if the input is actually /-z/, then (2a)'s mappings are unfaithful like /tæk + z/ → [tæks]; either way, one of the two columns must involve violations of IDENT[+/-VOICE]. The phonological pressure driving this alternation must be some flavour of AGREE[+/-VOICE]-OBSTRUENT, operating on adjacent obstruents: notice that if they were faithful, these two hypothesized inputs would end in illegal English clusters *[tæ**kz**] and *[bæ**gs**].[1]

Our purpose here is not to build a full grammar of English plural alternations. For one thing, they are rather more complicated than (2), involving multiple phonological processes and some tricky questions of lexical exceptionality: compare *kiss~kiss[əz]; judge~judg[əz]; leaf~lea[vz], roof~roo[fs]?roo[vz]?; child~children; mouse~mice; octopus...* (We will return to this complexity in Section 8.4.)

Instead, our first focus is on how alternations and other morphophonological interactions are learnt. To do this, learners must fit together three parts of a puzzle presented below, though not necessarily in this order:

One: Build underlying forms that make sense of a language's phonotactically-driven allomorphy.

What does it mean to make sense? In this English example, it leads to adopting a plural UR of /-z/, and using the grammar to derive the surface [-s] by devoicing in words like *tacks*. The alternative assumption, that the English plural UR is /-s/, would not make sense of the voiced allomorph [-z] in plurals like *bans* [bænz], because outputs like *dance* [dæns] are also permitted by our phonotactics.

---

[1] As for which input for the English plural is the right one – that is is it really /s/ or /z/ – you probably already know. If so, move on. If not; consider first what happens when vowel-final words are pluralized. Then compare *bells* vs. *pulse* and *bans* vs. *dance* ... Note that this data set also demonstrates one reason why AGREE[+/-VOICE] cannot apply to sonorants. And make sure you understand the answer here before reading further.

Two: Add new rankings to the phonological grammar to predict
   the precise observed alternations.

Observing isolated words is enough to reveal to an English learner that no word-final obstruent clusters disagree for voicing, so that AGREE[VOICE]-OBSTRUENT is highly ranked. But before a learner knows the morphological composition of complex words like ca[ts] vs. do[gz], they cannot know how to rank the faithfulness constraints around AGREE[VOICE], because they have never seen evidence of repair.

In this way, discovering morpho-phonological alternations can refine a learner's rankings – here to ensure that an input like /kæt + z/ will be repaired by changing voicing, rather than for example deleting one of the offending /t/ or /z/ segments. Note too that the learner may need to adopt different repairs for different allomorphs, depending on their phonological content. In the English plural case, sibilant-final nouns like *kiss* or *witch* cannot solve the phonotactics problems associated with adding plural /-z/ by simple devoicing, since it would result in an equally-ungrammatical surface string like geminate *[kɪs:] or *[wɪtʃs].

Exercise 1: Examine the tableau below and add constraints that will choose the correct winning candidate as indicated. What crucial new rankings can be determined from this tableau? (Answers at end of chapter.)

(3a)	/kæt + z/				
	[kætz]	*!			
	[kæt]		*!		
	[kæz]		*!		
☞	[kæts]				*
	[kætəz]			*!	

What about *kisses* with its epenthesis rule? Here you will need to define a constraint to rule out the geminate candidate, which can be very simple or more complex depending on whether you are ready to also treat forms like *witch* ... and you will have to add a ranking between faithfulness constraints that you didn't have before:

(3b)	/kɪs + z/		NEW!			
	[kɪsz]	*!				
	[kɪs:]		*!			*
	[kɪs]			*!		
☞	[kɪsəz]				*	

Three: Determine the phonological contribution to morphologically-exceptional phonology.

Here, the English plural learner must decide how to cope with [f]-final nouns and their plurals: *laugh~lau*[fs], vs. *leaf~leav*[vz], vs. *roof~roo*[fs]~*?roo*[vz]*?* In each case the plurals' final clusters show voicing assimilation, but they differ in the target of voicing unfaithfulness. In all regular English nouns not ending in [f] it is the suffix voicing which is unfaithful – [kæts] not *[kædz] – and however this is enforced normally, it must be modifiable for certain URs like *leaf.*

In other cases, however, the regular phonology cannot be asked to control allomorphy; no grammar of phonotactic generalizations will map /tʃɪɫd + z/ as *children.* Perhaps most complicated are those cases where allomorphy is clearly related to phonological pressures, but not otherwise observable in the language. One example comes from two Dutch diminutive suffixes [-pje] and [-kje], which appear after stems ending in an unstressed vowel followed by certain labials and velars, so that for example a diminutive broom is a ['bezəmpjə] while a diminutive king is a ['konɪŋkjə]. In most other contexts, the diminutive suffix surfaces as [-tje], so this pattern looks like simple place assimilation – but this is misleading, because nowhere in the phonology of Dutch is a sequence like /...mtjə/ or /...ktjə/ banned or otherwise repaired (Trommelen, 1983; Booij, 2002). How a learner reconciles these patterns with their pre-existing phonology is of course a matter of some considerable debate – for one thing, their representation in the grammars of adults is already controversial, never mind how they might be learned (recall the discussion of lexical exceptions in Chapter 7.4).

At the earliest stages of production, children must have next to no knowledge of alternations because they appear to have no productive control of morphemes independent of words – or perhaps whole phrases, as in many children's earliest one-word stage, which will include phrases like *'all gone'*, treated as a single word. At this stage, any complex morphology must be memorized.

But when do children start using multi-morphemic words productively? Given that children often begin by producing bare roots and stems without affixes (not just in English and related languages, but see also e.g. Adam and Bat-El, 2009 about Hebrew), we might label the onset of a morpheme's productivity as the time when children begin to mark a morphological feature like number of gender *obligatorily*. But even with that assumption, once children reach that stage, how do we know that their inputs include more than one morpheme? Simply producing a word like *bells* [bɛɫz] does not tell us what children have learned about morphology. Is their input /bɛɫ + z/ or an unanalysed /bɛɫz/ or something else altogether?

Many different theories of morpho-phonological acquisition have been proposed. In essence, they differ in their views of how learners attempt to build complex words: through grammatical means (like rules or constraints), with varying degrees of reference to phonological environments and restrictions, and/or through analogical processes (both will be discussed further below). But how can these theories be tested using acquisition data? As we will see, spontaneous speech does provide evidence about the acquisition of alternations, but only when children make mistakes – and as it turns out, almost no child ever produces plural errors like *ca[dz] or *do[gs], and while they do produce plurals such as *foots* and *childs*, they are rather few and far between (see 8.4.1 below).

Thus, studying the acquisition of morpho-phonological learning often requires the kind of data that only experimental work can provide. Enter: the *wug test*.

8.2   Methodology and Data: Wug Tests

The most common experimental approach to determining whether children (or adults) can use morphemes and their attendant phonology *productively* (that is, extend patterns to novel forms) is known as *wug testing*, in honour of a notably adorable test item from a pioneering study by Berko (1958). The protocol is to ask learners to produce morphologically-complex words based on *nonsense* roots, because while a child who can say *dog* and *dogs* may have just memorized two unrelated URs and know nothing about plural morphology, a child who can pluralize a word like *wug* that they have never heard before must know something more.

A classic wug test trial involves two pictures – for example, one of a single novel animal, and the other of two such animals – which the experimenter introduces thusly:

(4)   The classic Wug Test (Berko, 1958)
      'This is a *wug*.'   (pointing to the singular picture).

      'Now there is another one.'   (pointing to the plural picture).
      'There are two of them'.
      'There are two ... ?'   (waiting for child response .... '*wugs!*')

Berko (1958)'s study investigated the acquisition of many different English suffixes: plural allomorphs [s~z~əz], as well as the same allomorphs of the possessive suffix, and the past tense [t~d~əd] as in *walk*[t], *hug*[d] and *want*[əd].[2] She found that children as young as four were able to complete this task and produce novel inflected words, but their accuracy in producing target-like morphology was quite variable.

---

[2] The full study also included several suffixes which do not create any allomorphy: progressive *–ing*, comparative *–er*, superlative *–est*, and derived adjective *–y* (as in *quirky*).

As an introduction to this area we will look at data from three wug tests of plural formation: first in Hungarian, then in Berko's original English study, and then in Dutch.

8.2.1   Plural Wug Testing in Hungarian

Our first wug test data come from an early study of the acquisition of Hungarian plural suffixes by MacWhinney (1975, 1978). The Hungarian plural suffix surfaces as [-k] or [–Vk], but Hungarian has many different phonological processes which create allomorphy within that suffix vowel – rounding and backing harmony driven by the root-final vowel, as well as contextual shortening, lengthening and deletion – so that altogether, the plural suffix can surface as [-k], [-øk], [-e:k] [-ɛk], [-ok], [-o:k], [-ɔk] or [a:k.]

In this wug test, 25 children aged 2;1–3;8 (though most participants were at least 2;8) were first given an object to play with and told its novel name in the singular; then they were shown a second such object, and finally they were asked with regards to the two objects together 'What are these?' to elicit a plural response.

A really interesting aspect of this study was that it aimed to ask directly whether children would create novel plurals via grammatical knowledge (like a rule or a constraint ranking), or via *analogy* with known words. In the latter case, a child who knows that the Hungarian real word *hajó* [hɔjo:] means '*boat*' and that [hɔjo:k] means '*boats*' could draw an analogy between *hajó* and a new nonsense singular *fajó*, and so suppose that the latter ought to be pluralized as [fɔjo:k] – <u>without</u> using a grammar to choose the [-k] allomorph over any other. To look for the potential effects of such analogies, the experiment alternated trial by trial between real and nonce words, so that each nonce singular was preceded by a minimally-different real word like the [hɔjo:] ~ [fɔjo:] pair above.

Tables (5) and (6) below provide an excerpt of this study's wug test results. The data patterns that emerged from this study are very rich, providing examples of many common morpho-phonological learning stages and errors. We will return to these data a few times throughout this chapter, so <u>do not panic</u> if the table at first seems overwhelming.

In (5) there are four pairs of items, in each case with a real singular followed by a very similar nonce word. The first column gives a description of how this real word's plural is created – for example in (a), the singular [hɔjo:] is pluralized simply by adding [-k]. The table provides the singular as given to the children; the target plural (which in the case of nonce words was taken from the responses of 15 Hungarian-speaking adults); the children's plural productions with the proportion of the 25 participants who provided each one; and finally the percentage of null responses (%NR).

In this first examination of the data, note an answer for yourself to the four following questions before reading on. Q1: *How accurate are children at producing the real Hungarian plurals?* Q2: *In comparison, how accurate (i.e. adult-like) are their nonce plurals?* Q3: *What recurring patterns can you find in their errors? Were some errors more common or unique to just real or nonce words?* Q4: *How might phonology be involved in these errors?* (That last question is rather harder than the first three.)

(5)

Excerpt I from MacWhinney (1975: table 2)						
Plural type	*Real Sg.*	*Nonce Sg.*	*Target plural*	*Child plurals*		
				Target	*Errors (%)*	*%NR*
a) [-k]	[hɔjoː]		[hɔjoːk]	100%		
		[fɔjoː]	[fɔjoːk]	84%		16
b) [-k]; root-final /ɛ/ → [eː]	[tʃeːsɛ]		[tʃeːseːk]	67%	tʃeːsɛk (22%), tʃeːsɛ (6%)	5
		[seːsɛ]	[seːseːk]	50%	seːsɛk (39%), seːsɛ (6%)	5
c) [-ɛk], obeying [-back] harmony	[køɲv]		[køɲvɛk]	83%	[køɲvøk] (17%)	
		[øɲv]	[øɲvɛk]	55%	[øɲvøk] (17%) [øɲvɛ] (17%)	11
d) [-ɔk], [-ok]	[hɔl]		[hɔlɔk]	72%	[hɔlok] (22%), [hɔlɔ] (6%)	
		[gɔl]	[gɔlok]	67%	[gɔlɔk] (17%) [gɔlo] (5%)	11

To begin with, children are fairly accurate at real word plurals, but there is a lot of lexical variation: they were 100% accurate at adding just [-k] in (5a) but only 67% accurate at [-k] plus a root-final V change in (5b). In contrast, children are definitely less accurate at nonce words – though they certainly can perform the task, hitting 50–84% accuracy – and their performance in each trial roughly matches the real words, that is best at (5a) and worst at (5b).

In their non-target forms, children made three kinds of errors. The most common difference between target and child forms was in vowel quality, seen consistently in both real and nonce forms. In (5b) the lengthening and raising process /ɛ/ → [e:] was often not applied, even though in Hungarian it is obligatory at the stem + affix boundary, while in (5c) rounding harmony was sometimes spread from the root vowel to the suffix vowel, although harmony is not imposed in the target. A second error, seen almost exclusively in nonce words, was a failure to add the ubiquitous [-k] suffix; this resulted in vowel-final plurals like *[hɔl-ɔ] or nonce *[øɲv-ɛ]. This affixation pattern is particularly interesting since real Hungarian plurals may vary in vowels but always end with a final [-k]! A third error, only seen in nonce words, was to simply provide no response at all.

The errors in vowel quality in particular suggest that some of these young children's grammars have not yet become morphologically-sensitive. For example, the /ɛ/ → [e:] mapping in (5b) is a regular and automatic change in Hungarian – but it is only found at morpheme boundaries, so a child cannot learn it until enough singular/plural pairs like [tʃe:sɛ] ~ [tʃe:se:k] have been analysed and compared. On the other hand, even when children's attempts at productive morphology do not hit their morphological targets, they still obey the phonotactics of Hungarian: no child added the bare [-k] suffix to make an illegal cluster, like *[køɲvk], and no child added a novel vowel in a [-Vk] to an already vowel-final stem, like *[tʃe:se-ok].

Now consider two more trial pairs from this study. What is different here?

(6)		Excerpt II from MacWhinney (1975: table 2)						
	Plural type	*Real Sg.*	*Nonce Sg.*	*Target plural*	*Child plurals*			
						Target	*Errors (%)*	*%NR*
a)	[-ɛk]; root-final /e:/ → [ɛ]	[kɛɲe:r]		[kɛɲɛrɛk]	22%	[kɛɲe:rɛk] (67%) [kɛɲerk] (6%)		5
			[kɛpe:r]	[kɛpe:rɛk] [kɛpɛrɛk]	67%[3]	[kɛperk] (17%), [kɛpe:rɛ] (5%)		11
b)	[-øk]; plus stem V-deletion	[tykør]		[tykrøk]	6%	[tykyrøk] (83%), [tykørk] (11%), [tykørɛk] (5%)		
			[fykør]	[fykørøk]	62%	[fykørk] (11%), [fykørø] (11%), [fykørɛk] (6%)		

---

[3] Adults differed on their responses; this 67% includes 56% for the first 'correct' form and 11% for the 'incorrect' form that many adults nevertheless provided.

The biggest difference in these two trials is that children are much worse at producing the real word plurals than in the previous data – only 22% and 6% accurate!

This difficulty is understandable in that both of the vowel alternations seen here are more complicated than those like (5b) or (5d). Even once a morpheme boundary has been detected, the vowel lowering seen in (6a) and deletion seen in (6b) are much more irregular and lexically-specific among Hungarian nouns; in this way, we might think of them as similar to the irregular *mouse~mice* or *bring~brought* paradigms of English. Notice that this exceptionality affected both adults and children: in the case of vowel deletion (6b), adults did <u>not</u> apply the deletion to [fykør~ fykørøk], even after having just produced [tykør~tykrøk], suggesting that speakers only associate vowel deletion with known lexical items that they have seen alternate.[4] In children's non-target productions, there was more variation in responses – and a new kind of error emerged, in which these [r]-final stems were suffixed with a bare [-k] and no additional vowel. As this final [-rk] cluster does not violate Hungarian phonotactics, this might be a default strategy for marking the plural for when the learner is highly unsure what vowel to use.

Overall, these results demonstrate that children even as young as two or three have made considerable headway into the complicated Hungarian system of morpho-phonological alternations. They also provide clues as to the mechanisms by which learners try to understand how allomorphy works: to what extent they are memorizing full plural stems, or using a rule that uses a particular suffix allomorph as input, or applying one of multiple allomorphs, whether by rule or by analogy to similar, memorized forms. ... Can you find some evidence in Tables (5) and (6) for one or more of these mechanisms at work?

Discussion question 1: What does the fact that children produce real words more accurately than nonce words tell you about their mechanisms of morpho-phonological learning? What about the fact that children only failed to provide a response to some nonce words, never real words?

Discussion question 2: Children's error patterns in the two items of (5d) and (6b) clearly demonstrate that analogy cannot be children's only mechanism for nonce word plural formation. Explain why not.

---

[4] As mentioned in the previous chapter, English studies have found that adults are quite reluctant to apply vowel changes like those in *serene~serenity* and *divine~divinity* even to similar novel words; see for example Jaeger (1984).

8.2.2 Wug Testing in English: Back to Berko

In comparison to the wide range of Hungarian plural allomorphs, the English allomorphs in *cats*, *dogs* and *kisses* may now look quite tame. So let's consider how well these allomorphs were learned in Berko (1958)'s wug tests.

The first Table in (7) below shows the percentage of correct responses in forming novel plurals from two kinds of singulars[5] – those which take [-z] and [-əz] – among 80 children, ages four through seven. Note how much older the English-learning children were, compared to the Hungarian two- and three-year-olds above. How well do they appear to have mastered these two regular plural allomorphs? (Percentages with * indicate items on which older children, ages 5;5–7, were more accurate than younger kids, ages 4–5).

(7)	English plural formation (Berko 1958: table 2)			
		singular	*plural*	*% correct*
[-z] *Nonce words*		[wʌg]	[wʌgz]	91*
		[lʌn]	[lʌnz]	86*
		[tɔɹ]	[tɔɹz]	85
		[kɹɑ]	[kɹɑz]	79*
[-əz] *Real word*		*glass*	[glæsəz]	91*
[-əz] *Nonce words*		[tæs]	[tæsəz]	36
		[gʌtʃ]	[gʌtʃəz]	36
		[kaʒ]	[kaʒəz]	31
		[nɪz]	[nɪzəz]	28

The pattern is pretty clear: children can correctly add the [-z] allomorph to stems with final voiced segments, and this knowledge improves between ages 4 and 7. But while children are quite accurate with the [-əz] allomorph when pluralizing the known word like *glass*, they are most often unable to apply [-əz] productively, and their accuracy has not improved even at age seven!

Can you guess what their most common error was? For example: kids correctly pluralized *tass ~ tasses* only 36% of the time, but what did they do in their remaining 64% of responses? ... In 62% of cases, they simply repeated the singular *tass*. This strategy was <u>not</u> a repair seen in the Hungarian data, where children sometimes provided no nonce word response but did not repeat back the singular.

---

[5] As it turns out, Berko (1958) only tested one [-s] plural – and it was [hif], which forms part of the slightly irregular set of /f/-final stems discussed above – so we will stick to two allomorphs.

So now what do we learn from the English asymmetry between allomorphs, where four-year-olds are competent at creating [-z] plurals but even seven-year-olds have not acquired the [-əz] allomorph? Let us start with the extent to which English phonotactics predict this difference. First, we assume that these four-year-olds have learnt the static surface patterns of their phonology; this prevents them from producing a final [-z] (or [-s]) after *tass*, because that would create an ungrammatical word final cluster *[tsz] or geminate *[tæss].[6] Is it simply that English-learning children are not ready to apply any morphologically-specific pattern, like inserting a schwa between *tass* and its suffix? In one way, they must know more than this – because recall that sonorant-final nonce words like *tor* or *lun* would be grammatical English words with either [-z] or [-s] allomorphs attached – compare with real words *bores* and *horse*, *buns* and *once*. So, children's existing knowledge of their pure phonology is not enough to explain their mastery of [-z]; they must have learned something specific to the plural, such as that /-z/ is its underlying form.

But why is [-əz] in particular so hard? Is it really that rare in the English input? Surely children hear about *kisses* and *wishes*? More data about [əz] comes from other English morphemes with the same three allomorphs, namely third person singulars and possessives. In these cases, children were given the following type of prompt:

(8a) This is a man who knows how to *nazz* ([næz]). He is *nazzing*. He does it every day. … Every day he _____. ('...*nazzes!*')

(8b) This is a nazz who owns a hat. Whose hat is it?
.... It is the _____ hat. ('...*nazz's!*')

Were they any more accurate in these conditions? See below:

(9)	More [-əz] morphemes (Berko 1958: tables 4 and 5)			
	a) *3rd Sg nonce verb*	base	3rd sing	% correct
		[ludʒ]	[ludʒəz]	56
		[naez]	[naezəz]	58
	b) *Singular possessive*	base	possessive	
		[wʌg]	[wʌgz]	84
		[bɪk]	[bɪks]	87
		[nɪz]	[nɪzəz]	49

---

[6] Given the lack of modern recordings of this study, we cannot go back to check whether children actually produced a longer final [s] in the [-ez] environment … maybe they were saying [taes:] but no one knew?

... Moderately so! Compared to the range of 28–36% accuracy in [-əz] plural wugging from Table (7), the same children reached a full 56–58% accuracy in [-əz] 3rd person verb wugging, which at least suggests that the difficulty with these cells of the morphological paradigm is not purely about the sound pattern itself. The singular possessive shows the same trend as plurals – both [-z] and [-s] were target-like most of the time, and [-əz] was only target-like half the time. Thus, the difficulty with the vowel-initial suffix is to some extent UR-specific, but still affects all morphological categories where it is required.

One very intriguing possibility about why children do not affix [-əz] is that the stems which require this allomorph already end in a [-s] or [-z]. If we compare singular/plural pairs like *paw~paws and pause~pauses*: notice how the output [pɑz] is both a plural for *paw* and a singular for *pause*! In other words, singulars that end with alveolar fricatives look like they are already plural. So one hypothesis is that children are not using affixation rules to build morphologically-complex forms, but rather generating phonological constraints on the output shape of complex forms – in other words, children decide whether an input needs to be altered to create a complex output by first checking to see if it ends with a suffix already?![7] This would in part explain the difference between English and Hungarian error patterns, in that none of the singular Hungarian stems already ended in [-Vk], and so none appeared pre-pluralized.

Let us try to flesh this idea out using the theory of constraints we have built thus far. To capture this idea that children only add an overt suffix if they detect its absence, we could suppose that children are inventing morphological constraints as in (10):

(10) 'PLURAL': [+ANTERIOR, +STRIDENT]#
   Assign a violation for every input containing the meaning 'plural' whose output does not end in a [+anterior] strident (...which in English means [s,z])

If children (sometimes?) were to start off learning English plurals by building a constraint like (10), this would mean that their learning strategy was to generalize across just the output phonological forms of plurals – rather than by trying to identify a difference between singulars and their plurals which could then be added to URs. This might have far-reaching consequences! But first let's try to implement it.

---

[7] About this idea, see especially Bybee and Slobin (1982), although with rather different formalism than the one suggested here.

In the case of /wʌg/, our new Plural constraint could drive epenthesis of a coronal fricative, and structural constraints would ensure it had the right voicing:

(11) /wʌg/ + 'plural'	PLURALS: [s, z]	AGREE[+/-VOICE]-OBS	DEP
wʌg	*!		
wʌgs		*!	*
☞ wʌgz			*

In the case of /tæs/, the morphological constraint would already be satisfied by the input, so no additional fricative would be necessary:

(12) /tæs/ + 'plural'	PLURALS END IN [COR FRIC]	AGREE[+/-VOICE]-OBS	DEP
☞ tæs			
tæsəz			*!*

This might look like the beginnings of an analysis, but it has some big holes. To see one of the problems, try to build a tableau for a sonorant-final noun like *lun*. Here is a tableau with the candidates and the constraints; you assign the violations and determine the outcome:

(13) /lʌn/ + 'plural'	PLURALS END IN [COR FRIC]	AGREE[+/-VOICE]-OBS	DEP
lʌn			
lʌns			
lʌnz			

<u>Discussion question 3:</u>   What does the ranking in (11)–(13) predict about other words like *gutch*? Do you think these problems can be surmounted, or is a radically new analysis necessary?

Berko (1958) demonstrated that English-learning four- to seven-year-olds have acquired productive knowledge of some but not all the regular plural allomorphs. We will return to more English wug testing in Sections 8.4 and 8.6, but for now we will turn a third language's plural allomorphy, involving an arguably even simpler alternation pattern.

8.2.3 Wug Testing in Dutch: Production, Comprehension and Frequency

Our final wug test data set involves the word-final voicing alternation of Dutch obstruents. As we noted in Chapter 6.1.3, Dutch is a language in which voiced obstruents are banned word-finally. This means that stems like those in (14) which take the regular vowel-initial plural –*en* [ən] can have a voiced segment in their plural forms, but are devoiced in the bare singular:

(14)	Dutch regular plurals (data from Kerkhoff, 2007: 94)		
Singular	*Plural*	*Gloss*	
[bɛt]	[bɛdən]	*bed~beds*	*c.f. 'pet ~ petten' – cap~caps*
[hut]	[hudən]	*hat~hats*	
[hɑnt]	[hɑndən]	*hand~hands*	
[wɛp]	[wɛbən]	*web~webs*	
[nef]	[nevən]	*nephew~nephews*	
[hɑs]	[hɑzən]	*hare~hares*	

Although there are other irregular plural forms in Dutch just as in English, this [-ən] suffix is the most common and the voicing neutralization seen in (14)'s singulars applies 100% of the time. Perhaps this means that Dutch-learning children master this alternation early?

There is, however, one problem with using wug testing to examine Dutch children's knowledge of this allomorphy. In fact, we will learn next to nothing by giving children nonce word singulars and asking them for the plural. Why? Think it through before reading on …

… because the Dutch alternation we are looking for cannot be seen in the singulars! All of them will simply end in voiceless obstruents. If children are given a nonce singular [slat], it could either be pluralized as [slatən] or [sladən], and so a wug test would in essence be asking children to <u>guess</u> the UR for a novel word, which would be a rather confusing and arbitrary task. If we are trying to determine whether children know that [slat] can be the singular form of [sladən], we can instead wug test them in reverse: presenting nonsense <u>plurals</u> and asking them to produce the singular.

This kind of reverse wug test was used in Zamuner, Kerkhoff and Fikkert (2012) with 32 Dutch-learning children ages 2;4–4;8 (8 in each age group shown below) using plural and then singular pictures: 'These are two (*plural form*)'. 'What is this? _____ (*singular form!*)'.

Each child was asked to produce a singular for 11 plural words. Of these 11, three were real words which take the more exceptional plural suffix [-s], for example *kikker~kikkers* 'frog~frogs,' and eight were nonce words: four with medial [d] which should devoice in the singular, and four with medial [t] which should not alternate.

On trials with the three real words with plural [-s], two-year-olds were already at between 80–83% accuracy, and three- and four-year-olds were right 100% of the time. As for the nonce plurals formed with [ən], the table in (15) gives the average correct production of the singulars for each age group:

(15)		Correct singular responses in Dutch reverse wug production task (Zamuner, Kerkhoff and Fikkert, 2012: table 4)				
		Sample plural item	*Mean % correct (SD)*			
			2;4	2;7	3;7	4;8
a)	*Alternating*	sla[d]en	14% (.15)	13% (.23)	23% (.30)	13% (.13)
b)	*Nonce Non-alternating*	ji[t]en	22% (.28)	17% (.26)	44% (.42)	38% (.30)

Overall, it seems that most Dutch-learning children even at 4;8 were pretty unequipped for this reverse wug test. The authors report that the most common error was in fact akin to the English treatment of [-əz] plurals – when given a plural like [sladən] or [jitən], children would most often choose to repeat it as a singular, even as 'one [sladən],' using the number to show it must be singular. Even though they were fairly poor at the task, children were however significantly more accurate at producing singulars in (15b)'s non-alternating verbs than in (15a)'s alternating ones.[8] As with the previous data sets, note that children's errors showed that their knowledge of Dutch phonotactics was in place – because no child ever produced the singular of [sladən] as *[slad]. Thus it seems likely that the difficulty caused by nonce plurals with medial [d] is indeed connected to children's knowledge that they cannot create the singular of [sladən] by simply removing the suffix – but that they cannot recruit this knowledge to build the correct singular form. (Kerkhoff, 2007 also reports some similar difficulty in German-acquiring five-year-olds.)

---

[8] Although it may look like children were improving with age in the non-alternating forms, this trend was not significant in the ANOVA tests – which is probably due to the very large differences between individuals, seen in the standard deviations.

One hypothesis about this poor showing is that reverse wug production is just too tricky for very young children. A simpler test of the same knowledge can be couched in a comprehension task, as used in Zamuner, Kerkhoff and Fikkert (2006): here children were first shown a plural picture labelled either *slaten* or *sladen* and then given the task of pointing to the *slat* from one of three pictures. The three testing images included the correct answer (one *slat*), an incorrect singular (one of some other creature) and the incorrect plural (repeating the same image of multiple *slaten*). This both tested whether children knew that removing -*en* meant removing plurality, and also whether they could associate final [t] and medial [d] as alternating within a single stem allomorph. The results are given in (16):

(16)		Correct responses on Dutch reverse wug comprehension task (Zamuner, Kerkhoff and Fikkert 2006: table 3)		
		Sample *singular~plural*	*Mean % Correct (SD)*	
			2;6–2;8	3;6;-3;8
a)	Nonce alternating	sla[d]en ~ sla[t]	53% (.17)	42% (.20)
b)	Nonce non-alternating	ji[t]en ~ ji[t]	70% (.06)	51% (.09)

While these data are still quite variable between participants, the study found that both groups of children were better than chance at the task, but that alternating words (16a) were still less accurately identified than non-alternating ones (16b). Even when the task is made simpler, children are less willing to associate a plural and a singular with a change in final voicing.

If children know what [-ən] means, and they know that **slad* is not a possible word of Dutch, why is this plural alternation so difficult to use? One idea is that it is due to input frequency (for this argument and much more data, see especially Kerkhoff, 2007). Remember that the only nouns which provide evidence of the alternation are those ending in underlying voiced obstruents, and they must be seen in the plural as well as the singular to demonstrate the alternation. In addition, various facts about the Dutch lexicon and phonemic inventory mean that nearly all of the noun-final voicing alternations are d~t. So how much d~t evidence do kids get?

A longitudinal child-directed corpus of children ages 1;6–5;2 (van Kampen, 1997) provides some clues. This study found that children's input included 154 different singular noun <u>types</u> vs. only 40 plural noun types, and that of those plurals, only 13 were alternating nouns. This suggests that a rather small proportion of children's input gives them the evidence for the singular of a plural like *sla*[d]*en*: they know that **sla[d] isn't an option, but maybe they don't necessarily know how to repair it.[9] Finally, Dutch three- and four-year-olds are also reported to make errors with known alternating nouns. In one elicitation study by Kerkhoff (2007), three- and four-year-olds produced common real words like [bɛdən] *beds* as *[bɛtən] around 40% of the time!

So the morpho-phonology of Dutch reveals some clear caveats to the phonology-first view of learning alternations. While children learning Dutch clearly obey the phonological constraint against final voiced obstruents, they do not easily produce stem-final devoicing within noun paradigms. The source of this difficulty may well come from a fairly low number of examples in their input, but we will return to other potential explanations later in the chapter (see also a discussion exercise at the end of the chapter).

8.2.4   Summarizing the Beginnings of Morpho-Phonological Acquisition

The three wug tests we have discussed so far tell us that children as young as two are learning a lot about their morpho-phonology, and that children as old as seven may not yet have mastered it. We have seen that they consistently obey the phonotactic patterns they already know, but they make many different kinds of mistakes in attempting to build complex words. Some of their production errors suggest a certain degree of conservatism – not providing nonce word responses, or repeating the target – but others show strategic attempts to follow or extend observed patterns.

We saw with Dutch plurals that even a very regular phonotactic fact of a language does not necessarily make morpho-phonological learning trivial. But it is certainly true that very lexically-specific phonological patterns, restricted to a small set of morphemes or contexts, are usually the slowest to be learnt. Another more direct phonological influence on order of acquisition can come from the phonological pressures created by a morpheme itself. For instance: some children learning the English plural will begin adding [-z] and [-s] affixes to vowel-final nouns before consonant-final ones. Why? Well, consider their output results: if pluralizing *bee~bees*, the plural [biz] has a singleton coda, but pluralizing *dog~dogs* means creating a coda <u>cluster</u> [dɑgz]. Thus, a

---

[9] This corpus also revealed that the frequency of alternating noun tokens in the corpus is in fact almost double the non-alternating ones, in both singular and plural. So it would appear that hearing many instances of the same alternating noun is not good enough to generalize the alternation – recall the discussion of type vs. token frequency in Section 7.2.

child whose production grammar allows codas but not complex codas will only be able to faithfully produce the plural affix in vowel-final words like *bees* (see Song, Sundara and Demuth 2009, and references therein).

8.3 Morphological Paradigms and Phonological Uniformity

8.3.1 The Child Data

This section turns to a different aspect of the Hungarian plural wug test data, in particular the most common error among two of the real/nonce pairs. In all of these cases, children appear in some sense to under-apply aspects of the target language morpho-phonology:

(17)		From tables (5) and (6) above; data from MacWhinney (1975: table 2)		
		Real Sg.	*Nonce Sg.*	*Target Plural*	*Most Common Child Error (%)*
	a)	[tʃe:sɛ]		[tʃe:se:k] (67%)	tʃe:sɛk (22%)
			[se:sɛ]	[se:se:k] (50%)	se:sɛk (39%)
	b)	[kɛɲe:r]		[kɛɲɛrɛk] (22%)	[kɛɲe:rɛk] (67%)
			[kɛpe:r]	[kɛpe:rɛk] (56%), [kɛpɛrɛk] (11%)	[kɛperk] (17%)

As we discussed in Section 8.2.1, the stem-final raising in (17a)'s pairs like [tʃe:sɛ] ~ [tʃe:se:k] is a very regular alternation, though only at morpheme boundaries. In the most common error, children did not apply this raising – perhaps this means they were confused about its morphological context. A similar, lowering alternation occurs at the end of the (17b)'s real word stem, [kɛɲe:r]~[kɛɲɛrɛk]; this pattern is much less predictable in the Hungarian lexicon, and indeed 67% of children failed to apply it as well. In the corresponding nonce word, [kɛpe:r], some adults joined the majority of children in not lowering the stem final vowel in [kɛpe:r]~[kɛpe:rɛk] or [kɛperk]. In each of these examples, children (and sometimes adults) are not applying processes that change the quality of stem-final vowels. Could this type of error have a common explanation?

The effect of this under-application of a phonological change is to simplify an aspect of the morphology, because not applying the vowel change ensures that the noun stem of both the singular and plural remain identical – in particular, the last vowel of the stem remains either [ɛ] or [e:] throughout. As it turns out, this resistance to phonological alternations that could obscure the

identity of a stem or root within a morphological paradigm is found throughout morpho-phonology. Adult language examples will follow, but let's look at
more learner data – this time from spontaneous data, noted in diary studies.

A first case comes from the acquisition of Greek. In the target the velar
fricatives [x, ɣ] and their palatal counterparts [ç,j] are predictable throughout
the language. This allophony is determined by the segment that follows the
fricative: to see this, examine the different inflections of the two Greek verbs
in (18), and describe the pattern:

(18)	Velar [x, ɣ] vs. palatal [ç,j] alternations at verb stem endings						
	to have				*to leave*		
	1sg	[exo]	1pl	[exume]	1sg	[fevɣo]	1pl	[fevɣume]
	2sg	[eçis]	2pl	[eçete]	2sg	[fevjis]	2pl	[fevjete]
	3sg	[eçi]	3pl	[exune]	3sg	[fevji]	3pl	[fevɣune]

A simple description of the pattern is that the final segment of these two
verbs is usually a velar fricative, but except when followed by a front vowel [i]
or [e]. This distribution is similar to some of the consonant-vowel interactions
we saw in Section 6.2: the except-when appearance of palatal fricatives can be
attributed to place assimilation, via a constraint that bans a back (i.e. velar)
fricative before a front (coronal) vowel, which we will call *[x][FRONTV] in the
analysis below.

As this allophonic pattern is exception-less in target Greek, true in simple
and complex words alike, we would expect that children should master the
velar/palatal fricative allophones quite early in learning. Our expectation was
indeed met by Marina, a child learning Greek studied in Kazazis (1969), who
initially produced the pattern without incident. However, for a few weeks at
4;7, Marina began to incorrectly produce velar fricatives where palatals were
phonologically-required – but <u>only in certain verbal paradigms</u>:

(19)	Marina at 4;7 (Kazazis, 1969)		
		Target	*Child*
	2pl, *to have*	[eçete]	[exete]
	2pl, *to leave*	[fev**j**ete]	[fev**ɣ**ete]

Kazazis (1969) noted that Marina's new error on these forms had the morphological effect of reducing verb allomorphy to a single surface form, so that
every inflected form of '*to have*' began [ex-] and every form of '*to leave*' began

[fevɣ-]. In other words, it appears that Marina was imposing the requirement that this verbal paradigm be phonologically 'uniform' – accordingly, this phenomenon is often referred to as *paradigm uniformity*.[10]

To provide a paradigm uniformity explanation of Marina's data, we must assume that this error emerged at 4;7 because it was then that Marina made an overt connection in her lexicon and grammar between all the surface forms of these verbs – that is, at 4;7 she determined their common stem. Notice that Marina's development of fricative allophony followed what is often called a *U-shaped* curve, meaning that she temporarily moved further away from the target, becoming <u>less</u> faithful to the second person forms in (19). Understood from a paradigmatic perspective, this loss of faithfulness was driven by a pressure that only became applicable after she had decomposed these verbs into morphemes; we will get more formal about this trade-off in a couple sections.

As a second example, examine the following data from two Hebrew-acquiring children:

(20)	Two children learning Hebrew vowel~zero alternations (Bloch, 2011: 65)		
Gloss	*Stem*	*Target derived form*	*Child derived form*
small	ka'tan	kta'na (fem.)	kata'na
big	ga'dol	gdo'la (fem.)	gadʊ'la
camel	ga'mal	gma'lim (pl.)	gama'lim
rabbit	ʃa'fan	ʃfa'nim (pl.)	ʃafa'nim

These Hebrew-learning children also seem to be avoiding alternations within the noun or adjective stem – in this case, by not deleting a stem vowel which is usually lost in the feminine or plural forms.

Is this pattern a good example of paradigm uniformity? What if instead these children do not yet know the derived forms of these adjectives and nouns, and so are simply adding a suffix without further phonological consequences? … There are some good reasons to doubt this suffixing-only explanation. For starters, notice that while the children's stems in both base and derived forms are identical in their vowels, the stems do in fact alternate in another way – they shift stress onto the suffix, [ka'tan] vs. [kata'na]. One explanation is that children have learned that suffixes like [-a] and [-im] cause

---

[10] Starting with Venneman (1972); Harris (1973) see also especially Burzio (1994); Kenstowicz (1996); Benua (2000).

stress shift, but not that they cause vowel deletion (which would seem perhaps equally noticeable?); another explanation is that they are imposing paradigm uniformity along the vowel~zero dimension.[11]

The acquisition literature includes a variety of other anecdotal examples of paradigm uniformity in child speech. The most common English example is probably the production of English derived words without flaps: so that *water* contains a flap but *waiting* begins to be produced with a medial [t], presumably due to its association with the base form *wai*[t] (discussed in Bernhardt and Stemberger, 1998). A paradigm uniformity connection can also be made with the following cross-linguistic observation: in languages where a derived form requires both an affix and a within-stem alternation like the umlaut of German plurals, Slobin (1985) reports a common stage in which children apply the affix but fail to apply stem-internal changes. Finally, the very low accuracy rates in Dutch wug testing (reported in 8.2.3) could also be explained in terms of paradigm uniformity – since again it is the noun-final segment that must alternate if plural *sla*[d]*en* is in the same paradigm as singular *sla*[t].[12]

8.3.2 The Adult Data

We have now seen multiple kinds of evidence that children impose – and in fact innovate – phonological similarity among morphologically-related forms. Does this pressure assert itself among adult phonological grammars? Indeed it does, in many different guises.

A frequent domain of paradigm uniformity is the interaction between a word's stress and the distribution or quality of its vowels. Many morphologically-complex English words demonstrate this effect. For example, how do you stress the words *originality* or *phenomenology*? If you transcribe it for yourself (or from the speech of a native speaker if you are not one), you will find secondary stress on the second syllable and primary stress on the fourth: for example [ɔˌɹɪdʒɪˈnælɪˌɾi] (possibly some stress on the last syllable, too). But is this a typical stress pattern for English six-syllable words? Monomorphemic

---

[11] A second question is whether the derived forms without vowel deletion like [kataˈna] are actually ruled out by the phonology – that is, is this vowel deletion pattern as phonologically-automatic as Greek fricative allophony? ... Not exactly. There are not a lot of native Hebrew roots with three syllables; but there are plenty of borrowings, and there are also several stems that don't alternate, mostly (all?) for historical reasons: [kaˈbir ~ kabiˈra] *'immense'*; [taˈbax ~ tabaˈxim] *'cook'*; [gaˈmad] ~ [gamaˈdim] *'dwarf'*, and so on. For lots more on this pattern, see Bat-El (2008).

[12] For more experimental evidence of children imposing paradigm uniformity, see Tessier (2012) and also Section 8.5.

words with so many syllables are fairly rare (nearly always place names) – but try stressing a word like *onomatopoeia,* or a place name like *Apalachicola.* (We used these examples back in Chapter 1's introduction of English stress.)

... Do these words follow the stress pattern of *originality*? If you are a native English speaker, you will certainly agree that they do not. Instead, these latter words' stress falls on every odd syllable, meaning the first, third and fifth, with final stress on the penult. The table below compares these two very different patterns. Try producing each type of word with the other stress pattern; you might find it rather hard to do![13]

(21)		Two six-syllable English stress patterns (Grammatical examples from Pater, 2000)		
			$(ˌσ σ)(ˌσ σ)('σ σ)$	$σ(ˌσ σ)('σ σ)(ˌσ)$
a)		onomatopoeia	[ˌɑnəˌmæɹɪ'pijə]	*[ɑˌnʌmə'tɪpiˌjʌ]
		Apalachicola	[ˌæpəˌlætʃɪ'kʰolə]	*[əˌpʰælə'tʃɪkəˌlʌ]
b)		originality	*[ˌɔɹɪˌdʒɪnə'lɪɾi]	[ɔˌɹɪdʒɪ'næliˌɾi]
		phenomenology	*[ˌfɪnəˌmɪnə'ladʒi]	[fəˌnamə'naliˌdʒi]

Why are these two patterns so different? If you recall the constraints on foot placement that we used in Chapter 4, the (21a) pattern seems quite an optimal one: three trochaic feet, aligned with both the beginning and ends of the word, and no syllable left unfooted. So what is special about *originality* and *phenomenology*? As you might have guessed by now, their special phonology can be attributed to their derived morphological status – that is, their morphological bases are o**ri**ginal and phe**no**menon, with their main stresses marked in bold. The paradigm uniformity effect here is that whatever syllable receives main stress in the base must at least retain <u>some</u> stress in the derived form – in (21b), this means shifting the feet over one syllable.[14]

Here is a second example, from Northern Italian. In this language, [s] is voiced between vowels; this applies in monomorphemic forms (22a) and when at the boundary of many roots+affixes (22b). However, the derived forms in (22c) surface without intervocalic voicing of [s]. Can you put together a paradigm uniformity explanation of these exceptions?

---

[13] In the ungrammatical cases, I have had to invent some vowel qualities for full vowels that one does not usually hear stressed.

[14] Of course, this doesn't tell us why *original* doesn't align its feet properly with the word edges either – but this is another example of why English stress is so complicated. For some OT analysie of many such complications, see Pater (2000) and extensive references therein.

(22) | Northern Italian s/z alternations:
(data from Kenstowicz, 1996: 10–11)

a) *V[s]V within morphemes		c) exceptional V[s]V
a[z]ola *button hole*	*a[s]ola	re[s]entire *to hear again* (c.f. [s]entire)
a[z]ilo *nursery school*	*a[s]ilo	a[s]ociale *asocial* c.f. [s]ociale *social*
ca[z]a *house*	*ca[s]a	bu[s]ino *bus,* dim. c.f. bu[s] *bus*
b) *V[s]V across morphemes		
di[z]-onesto *dishonest* di[z]-uguale *unequal*	c.f. di[s]-parita *inequality*	
pre-[z]entire *to have a presentiment* re-[z]istenza *resistence*		

In the (c) examples, the exceptional [s] that does not become voiced is also found in the derived form's morphological *base*. The *V[s]V constraint has no reason to voice [s] in *sentire*, *sociale* or *bus*, so it is over-ruled in *presentire* and *busino* to keep the paradigm uniform. An interesting comparison can be made between the items which mean '*to hear again*' and '*to have a presentiment*': the first verb acts though it takes '*to hear*' as its base, whereas the second does not. This seems intuitively right, but it also points out the crucial role of UR morphological assumptions – that is, that a learner's grammar (or a target grammar) can only impose paradigm uniformity in this way if some form has been established as the base! We will return to this complication in a couple sections, but first let us spell out the idea using our constraint-based tools.

8.3.3   An Analysis of Paradigm Uniformity

We will sketch this analysis using the Northern Italian data set above, beginning with a structural constraint against intervocalic voiceless [s], which we will simply call *V[s]V. Since Northern Italian usually repairs this structure via voicing, *VsV must rank above IDENT[+/-VOICE] – so that even if we feed the grammar an input like /'kasa/ to mean '*house*' the intervocalic [s] will become voiced:

(23)	/kasa/	*V[s]V	IDENT[+/-VOICE]
	kasa	*!	
☞	kaza		*!

With (23) as the purely phonological grammar, the exceptional behaviour of derived intervocalic [s] must be driven by a constraint that ranks <u>above</u> *VsV. The informal notion of paradigm uniformity that we have been using so far is a pressure to keep derived words faithful to their morphological bases – here, that [s] is retained in atypical contexts because it must match the 's' in its base. Of course, our OT framework provides us with a mechanism for imposing similarity between forms – faithfulness constraints, in fact IDENT[+/-VOICE]! But not the IDENT[VOICE] in (23), which regulates the correspondence between inputs and outputs. Instead, this new IDENT[VOICE] will be relativized to a morphological concept:

(24) IDENT[+/-VOICE] – DERIVED[15]
   Assign a violation for every output segment of a morpheme which does not match the voicing feature of its correspondent in the output of its base

The most surprising part of this definition is that it holds between two *output* strings: the output of a base, and the output of that base within a more complex word. This means that the input of a derived form will need to be associated with whatever the grammar produces as the output of the base on its own – this first calculation is shown in (25a), where the input contains nothing derived and so the highest ranked constraint is irrelevant. In (25b) the output base is simply part of the derived word's input, as a sort of annotation:

(25a)	/bus /	IDENT[+/-VOICE]-DERIVED	*V[s]V	IDENT[+/-VOICE]
☞	bus			
	buz			*!

---

[15] In the literature, these constraints go by many different names, including 'Output-Output' constraints (Benua, 2000; Burzio, 2004). Note too that this is only one such faithfulness constraint – but depending on what phonological process is avoided in derived forms, we will also need MAX-DERIVED, DEP-DERIVED and so on.

(25b) /bu̱s-ino/ *base*: [bus]	IDENT[+/-VOICE]-DERIVED	*V[s]V	IDENT[+/VOICE]
☞ bu̱s̱ino		*	
bu̱ẕino	*!		*

Note again that these faith constraints on derived words are defined so that if a word does not have a morphological base defined in the lexicon, the constraint is vacuously satisfied (you can't be unfaithful to a base you don't have). Thus, these constraints kick in piecemeal, as the lexicon develops: once a base has been identified and associated with a portion of a derived word, paradigm uniformity can emerge.

Let's now return to Marina's treatment of Greek fricatives to see how paradigm uniformity can emerge in learning. In the target phonology which Marina had already acquired by 4;7, the distribution of palatal and velar allophones is controlled by two structural constraints as shown in the two tableaus below. The general structural constraint is a ban on palatal fricatives (26), which is outranked by the specific place-assimilation constraint *[x][FRONTV] doing the work in (27):

(26) /eço/	*[X][FRONTV]	*PALATAL FRIC	IDENT[+/-BACK]
☞ exo			*
eço		*!	

(27) /eç-ete/ (hypothetical)	*[X][FRONTV]	*PALATAL FRIC	IDENT[+/-BACK]
exete	*!		*
☞ eçete		*	

In Marina's grammar, however, these are in turn outranked by an IDENT-DERIVED constraint, which keeps all fricatives in derived forms identical in place to their base. To make this happen, though, we need a base for her verbal paradigms. Note that all the members of these verbal paradigms include an inflectional ending – the verb *to have* never surfaces bare as *[ex], so how does Marina choose a base?

We will continue to wrestle with this question in Section 8.5, but meanwhile there are various strategies given to learners in the literature that would suffice. For example, a verb's base might be found in the infinitival or first person forms – here, both contain the velar fricative, to which Marina seems to be levelling her paradigm:

(28)

/ex-ete/ base: [ex-]	IDENT[+/-BACK] -DERIVED	*[X][FRONTV]	*PALATAL FRIC	IDENT[+/-BACK]
eçete	*!		*	*
☞ exete		*		

Before moving on, it's worth examining the three tableaus (26)–(28) to see how this analysis is made possible by OT's constraint <u>rankings</u>. Reading the tableau from right to left, we can describe Marina's grammar as banning palatal fricatives ... except before front vowels ... except if the base contained a velar fricative – and each exception clause is the result of a ranking between conflicting constraints.

8.4   Morphological (Over)regularization and Allomorph Selection

This section turns to a different kind of morphological learning that can occur once a learner becomes morphologically aware. We began the chapter with the example of English plural marking, via the three allomorphs [s~z~əz] whose distribution can be predicted, to a large extent, by English phonotactics. But we also noted that there are various words which simply cannot be pluralized using any variant of that morpheme:

(29) English plurals beyond /-z/ and its allomorphs
   goose ~ geese   *child ~ children*   *one sheep ~ many sheep*
   tooth ~ teeth   *ox ~ oxen*   *one moose ~ many moose*
   foot ~ feet   *one deer ~ many deer*
   mouse ~ mice   *person ~ people*
   louse ~ lice   *index ~ indices*
   man ~ men   *phenomenon ~ phenomena*
   woman ~ women   *crisis ~ crises* ['kɹaɪ.siz]

What should a learner of English do with these words? There are not that many of them – this list already includes almost all of the common ones – but are they at all grammatically predictable? The only <u>phonological</u> pattern might be similarities among those nouns in the lefthand column that mark plural with a vowel change: [maʊs]~[maɪs], [laʊs]~[laɪs], and [gus]~[gis], [tuθ]~[tiθ]. But the patterns are very limited: *house* ~*hice? moose* ~*meese?*

Given these factors, it seems reasonable that learners simply memorize them as exceptions.

This first example may not seem like a big deal – but the difference between *regular* allomorphy like plural [-s/-z/-əz] and *irregular* morphology of the types in (29) has played a significant role in both classic and recent attempts to understanding children's acquisition of morphology and also morpho-phonology. One reason is that many children show U-shaped development of some irregulars: for example, first producing *feet* correctly, then at a later stage regressing to the form **foots*, or perhaps **feets*, and then eventually returning to *feet*.[16] As with the emergence of paradigm uniformity in the last section, the regression to forms like **foots* suggests that children have realized something about English plural morphology that they did not yet know when they first produced *feet*.

This process of trying to apply regular morphology to an irregular base is known as *over-regularization*, and it is attested among children starting around age two or even earlier. Depending on the kind of morphology being over-regularized, the phenomenon can continue well into the school-aged years. Moe, Hopkins and Rush (1982) report that first-graders produce English past tense over-regularizations at a rate of 2.8% (based on 10,530 target irregulars, collected from more than 300 children); Schaner-Wolles (1988) and Veit (1986) both report evidence that German plural marking continues to be over-regularized at age five (see below).

Returning to the data in (29) above: while there are these exceptions, this English paradigm is overwhelmingly regular. Cross-linguistically, though, many other morphological patterns show much more variability, including multiple frequent methods of marking the same morphological category, and often with only moderate phonological predictability. So once children have begun to break down the morphological components of their words, how do they handle these paradigms? What is the role of the relative frequency of each morphological pattern? What is the evidence that a child's grammar considers a root to be regular or irregular? And where is the child's pre-existing phonology in all this?

8.4.1   A Tale of Two (Ir)regular Paradigms

To take an introductory stab at these questions, the rest of this section will compare two famous cases of irregularity among familiar languages. The first is English <u>past tense</u> marking on verbs, which is considerably more irregular

---

[16] For some quantitative evidence for this U-shape from longitudinal child corpora, see Marcus et al. (1992: 40-43).

than the plural. The regular past tense allomorphs are [-t/-d/-əd] as in *walk*[t], *jog*[d] and *need*[əd]; and here are some of the irregulars, of varying frequencies:

(30) Sample English irregular past tense mappings

/i/ → [ɛ]	/d/ → [t]	/i/ → [o]	/aɪ/ → [o]	/ɪ/ → [æ]
feed ~ fed	build ~ built	speak ~ spoke	drive ~ drove	sing ~ sang
bleed	bend	freeze	dive	ring
read	send	steal	ride	swim
meet	spend	weave	write	sit

Note that there are many other irregular patterns: *bring ~ brought, think ~ thought, swing ~ swung, eat ~ ate, stand ~ stood, was ~ were, go ~ went* ... and also those where the past tense is marked with <u>nothing</u>, such as *fit, hit, quit, beat, let, bid* and several others.

One often-cited study by Albright and Hayes (2003) took a very large corpus of adult-to-adult speech (CELEX: Baayen et al, 1993) and extracted every verb that appeared at least 10 times. Of the 4,253 verbs that resulted, 4,035 verbs were regular in past tense, and 218 did something irregular. This means that about 5% of verb types in this lexicon take an irregular past tense; of course, many irregulars have a much higher *token* frequency than many of the regulars – *go* and *be* being stand-out frequent irregulars, but many others as well.

So how does this irregular 5% of forms impact children's acquisition of the past tense? Marcus et al. (1992)'s extensive study of children's English past-tense over-regularization finds that children typically show their first over-regularization of an irregular past tense verb between 1;8–2;11. It also shows individual correlations between the timing of a child's productive, obligatory use of the <u>regular</u> past tense and the emergence of over-regularization of <u>irregular</u> past tense – in other words, errors like *go-ed* do indeed coincide with children's morphological discoveries about the past tense. As for the frequency of over-regularization, the table below in (31) gives data from nine children in the Marcus et al. corpus study, including the age ranges over which they were studied and the overall proportions of correct vs. over-regularized verbs.

(31)

Past tense over-regularization rates (Marcus et al, 1992: table 2)				
Child (age)	*Correct (e.g. run)*	*Irreg. + ed (e.g. runned)*	*Past + ed (e.g. ranned)*	*Proportion over-regularized*
Abe (2;6–5;0)	1,786	465	99	24.0%
Adam (2;3–5;2)	2,444	44	4	1.9%
Allison (1;5–2;10)	31	2	0	6.1%
April (1;10–2;11)	47	6	1	13.0%

Continued

Child (age)	Correct (e.g. run)	Irreg. + ed (e.g. runned)	Past + ed (e.g. ranned)	Proportion over-regularized
Eve (1;6–2;3)	283	23	1	7.8%
Naomi (1;3–4;9)	378	34	2	8.7%
Nathan (2;3–3;9)	243	11	3	5.4%
Peter (1;3–3;1)	853	17	4	2.4%
Sarah (2;3–5;1)	1717	61	4	3.6%

From a larger sample of 25 children, Marcus et al. (1992) report an overall average of 4.2% over-regularization, although notice that in (31), two children are really bringing up that average. But it is striking that in comparison with this rate of over-regularization, the reverse process is almost entirely unattested, whereby regular verbs would be over-<u>irregular</u>ized. Looking through all of the thousands of verbs recorded from three of these children (Adam, Eve and Sarah), there were a grand total of four potential 'irregularization' errors, and they all applied to irregular verbs, just with the wrong irregular: *beat ~ *bate, *bet, hit ~ *heet, bite ~ *bat*. The overall result is that English past tense over-regularization seems to be an infrequent but robust pattern, and its nature suggests that learners are in some way sensitive to '*regular*' verbal morphology.

Our second example is the German plural, which is marked with four different suffixes and zero marking as well. As a further complication, three of these five categories also include verbs with internal vowel changes (the process known as *umlaut*).[17]

(32)	German plural marking (Marcus et al, 1995: table 4)			
	Marking	Singular	Plural	Gloss
	zero plural	daʊmən	daʊmən	thumb
	zero plural + umlaut	mʊtɐ	mʏtɐ	mother
	[-ə]	hʊnt	hʊndə	dog
	[-ə] + umlaut	kuː	kyːə	cow
	[-əɐ]	kɪnt	kɪndɐ	child
	[əɐ] + umlaut	valt	vɛldɐ	forest
	[-n]/[-ən]	fraʊ	fraʊən	woman
		bɛt	bɛtən	bed
	[-s]	aʊtoː	aʊtoːs	car
		paɐk	paɐks	parks

---

[17] As you probably are aware, it's not an accident that some of the irregular English plurals and past tenses look like they contain umlaut; these vowel changes were once much more regular in English and German's common ancestor language.

This pattern therefore looks quite complicated for the learner – what should they assume about pluralizing new words, or words they have never heard in the plural? What strategies might they rely on?

Let's start with each option's relative frequency. The broad frequency facts about German plural marking are that [-n/ən] is the most common plural suffix, followed by [-ə], while the other three are much less common. In particular, [-s] is definitely rare: for example, Marcus et al. (1995)'s search across multiple corpora found that no more than 9%, and probably closer to 5% of noun types take the [-s] plural, perhaps affecting no more than 30 common nouns.[18] Looking at token frequency the rarity of [-s] is if anything greater: Marcus et al. report that out of the 343, 147 tokens of mono-morphemic German nouns in the CELEX corpus, only 3% (8,701) took a [-s] plural. This relative frequency is also attested in child speech: in the corpus of one child, Simone (reported in Clahsen et al, 1992, and see more below), out of 345 tokens with correct plurals, 38% used [-ə] and 24% used [-(ə)n], while only 8% took [–s].

Why all this focus on one rare group of plurals? As it turns out, this [-s] may be low frequency, but it also has some other special properties: it has no phonological restrictions on the nouns it can attach to; it is used to pluralize names and pronouns, and it is most commonly used to pluralize new borrowings. These and other hints suggest that [-s] is in some sense the 'default' German plural. Does this make it 'regular,' akin to the regular past and plural morphemes in English? Recall that in English, 5% was roughly the number of *irregular* past tense verb types, whereas under this account only 5% of the German nouns would take the *regular* plural suffix.

Several studies of German children's acquisition of the plural have converged on a few key results, summarized especially in Clahsen et al. (1992). First, the most common error in plural marking by far is simply to use the singular form. For example, a corpus study of one child Simone between 1;7–3;9 included 405 plural noun targets, and 42/54 of her errors were the use of singular forms where plurals were required; in wug tests, zero-plural marking is the dominant response found even as late as age five (Mugdan, 1977; Walter, 1975). Second, the most common error of overt marking is to add [-n], but [-s] is also found – in Simone's data, of her 12 incorrect plural affixations, only four used [-n] and four used [-s]. These are small numbers, but there are additional facts which suggest the [-s] affix is special in her plural marking, similar to the target German paradigm. One striking fact is that Simone uses [-s] for all of her own invented nouns, as shown in (33) – in other words, she seems to have settled on [-s] as the default when wug testing herself:

---

[18] On this, see Clahsen's commentary on Marcus et al. (1992).

(33)	Simone's pluralization of invented words (Clahsen et al. 1992: ex 10)		
Child	*Gloss*	*Age*	
lumlums	*balloons*	1;9	
puppas	*dolls*	2;4	
auas	*little hurts*	2;5	
lalas	*pacifiers*	2;5	
wauwaus	*dogs*	2;8	
lilis	*sweets*	3;5	

Taken together, such data suggests that children learning the German plural marking system tend to avoid plurals quite late in acquisition, and they show more variability in their affixation errors than English learners. And yet the low frequency of [-s] compared to [-(ə)n] and other allomorphs does not prevent [-s] from being over-used, and even being used as a default in nonce words.

8.4.2 Phonology and Analyses of Allomorphy Selection

As already hinted above, the literature on how children acquire regular and irregular morphology is rather divided, with regard both to the empirical facts and their proper interpretation. It is uncontroversial that some aspects of these paradigms must be stored in a lexically-specific way: that is that no purely phonological mechanism should be mangled so that it can predict that the past tense of *go* is *went*. So from the perspective of this textbook, the big question is where the learner's phonological knowledge <u>does</u> play a role in choosing allomorphs – whether regular, irregular and anything else. More broadly, though, it turns out that the different mechanisms proposed to capture regular vs. irregular morphology have different overall consequences for how all kinds of morpho-phonology are represented in the mind, so we must grapple with them a little bit more.

Across languages, there are often phonological generalizations about which stems take which regular or irregular allomorphs, though they are usually neither simple nor categorical. In English, one simple generalization is that every verb root ending in a voiceless fricative (all 352 in the Albright and Hayes, 2003 corpus) is <u>regular</u>: there are no verbs like *wish~wush* or *swiff~swaff*. In German, the phonology of a noun's right edge can be used to predict certain aspects of plural allomorphy, with sufficient attention to the noun's gender and other details: the simplest case is that vowel-final neuter nouns take a zero-marked plural if they begin with the prefix *ge-* and the [-ən] suffix otherwise.[19]

At least with respect to <u>adults</u>, experimental data has begun to reveal that native speakers are indeed sensitive to these kinds of phonological generalizations or *subregularities* in morphological paradigms: for example, adult learners of English are especially likely to treat a nonce word as regular if it ends in a voiceless fricative (Albright and Hayes, 2003). So: however it is that learners acquire these morphological alternations, they must end up with some (unconscious) access to their phonological subregularities. How are these acquired? Different accounts of the regular/irregular divide make different predictions about how and where the phonological sub-patterns are known; these are schematized in (34) below.

One view is that a learner finds a morphological default, writes a general rule for that, and then memorizes lots of other patterns which take precedence over the default, 'blocking' it from applying (34a). Another view is that in the face of multiple allomorphs, the learner simply memorizes every pair (34b). In both of these approaches, sensitivity to phonological similarities among the irregulars must come about through a speaker's ability to analogize across subparts of the lexicon; in the latter case, it's also how you know to perform a wug test. In a third view, the learner begins by writing rules for every pair, and then builds more general ones from the specific ones, assigning them greater weight when they work well, and eventually evolving a very general subset of rules that look like the 'regular' (34c).

(34) Three schematic examples of the regular/irregular English past tense

<u>a) One regular rule, many stored irregular pairs (e.g. Prasada and Pinker, 1993)</u>

(i) $0 \rightarrow$ [d] / stem# ___ [+past]   (ii) *bleed ~ bled*   *speak ~ spoke*
                                                  feed ~ fed   *sing ~ sung*
                                                  dive ~ dove   ... etc.

<u>b) All stored pairs, regular and irregular[20]</u>

walk ~ walked   *bleed ~ bled*   *speak ~ spoke*
talk ~ talked   *feed ~ fed*   *sing ~ sung*
jog ~ jogged   *dive ~ dove*   ... etc.
need ~ needed

---

[19] To see the less simple cases, Appendix 2 of Marcus et al. (1995) gives a full summary of Mugdan (1977)'s generalizations.

[20] One body of literature that includes all the memorization of (34b) is associated with *exemplar theory*, or rather the range of exemplar theories, as in for example Pierrehumbert (2001, 2006). A rather different take on morphological alternations that is also similar to (34b) is found in *connectionist* approaches, starting with Rumelhart and McClelland (1986).

c) Many rules, regular and irregular (see Albright and Hayes, 2003)

(i) *walk ~ walked*: $0 \to [t] / w \, \alpha \, k \,\# \rule{1cm}{0.4pt}_{[+past]}$

(ii) *talk ~ talked*: $0 \to [t] / t \, \alpha \, k \,\# \rule{1cm}{0.4pt}_{[+past]}$

(iii) *generalizing across (i–ii)*: $0 \to [t] / \alpha \, k \,\# \rule{1cm}{0.4pt}_{[+past]}$

(iv) *after many generalizations …* $0 \to [t] / [\text{-voice}] \rule{1cm}{0.4pt}_{[+past]}$

(v) *a sub-generalization along the way:* $0 \to [t] / [\text{-voice, +cont}]_{[+past]}$

Setting aside all the many ways these approaches differ: a property that (34a) and (34c) share is the assumption that phonological alternations are encoded in <u>rules</u>. This means that they are fundamentally incompatible with a phonological grammar that encodes its knowledge in constraints, as we have been assuming throughout this text. However, this reliance on rules is understandable – because morphological alternations are indeed <u>changes</u>, and those changes are used not (for the most part) to satisfy a phonological well-formedness condition but to mark semantic content in the underlying form. These may require faithfulness, but they don't seem to be about satisfying structural pressures. Thus, combining constraint-based phonotactics with the processes of allomorphy selection can be a challenge.[21]

In addition to all this analytical debate, a variety of data questions regarding the contributions of phonological knowledge to (ir)regular morphology remain somewhat unresolved. One such question relates to phonological similarity among regulars. Recall that Albright and Hayes (2003) found that nonce words that were phonologically similar to English regular verbs were also more likely to form a regular past tense; that result seems to challenge the (34a) view in which there is no phonology in sight of the regular rule.[22]

However, Albright and Hayes' data comes from adult speakers of English – in child speech, by contrast, it seems that the role of phonological similarity seems to be focused on the behaviour of irregulars alone. On the one hand, a verb's chances of being over-regularized are correlated with the frequency of similar irregular verbs, meaning that the likelihood that a child produces the past tense of sting as **stinged* will be affected by the frequency of *fling~flung*, *cling~clung*, *stink~stunk* and so on, and the more frequent they are, the less

---

[21] The literature here is not for beginners, but advanced students are pointed to Becker and Gouskova (2014), Albright and Hayes (2010) and Wolf (2008).

[22] Prasada and Pinker (1993) found something similar, but had reason to believe it could be explained by the overall phonological well-formedness of their nonce words; Albright and Hayes (2003) ran a ratings task to ensure that their items were all judged quite English-like, and in any event these ratings did not correlate with rate of (ir)regular marking.

likely *stinged will be. On the other hand, Marcus et al. (1992) report <u>no</u> effect of similarity among regular verbs increasing the chance of over-regularization – that is, in their data the chance of *sting~*stinged* is not affected by the frequency of regular verbs like *wing~winged, sink~sinked* and so on.[23] In this domain, more large-scale data (and data from many other languages) will be necessary before these fundamental questions can be answered.

8.5   On Finding Underlying Forms

The previous two sections have discussed two kinds of errors that emerge during children's mastery of morpho-phonology: morphological bases being protected at the expense of other phonological pressures, and irregular allomorphs being incorrectly replaced with more regular allomorphs. In both cases, however, learners can only make these mistakes once they have decided on some structure for morphologically-complex words – in Section 8.3, choosing a *base* to be preserve faithfully; in Section 8.4, choosing a *stem* to which affixes can attach.

The missing piece of the picture thus far is how learners are choosing to store the pieces of morphology they decompose, so they can be used as *inputs* when assembling new words (or building novel ones in a wug test). Once children know that their inputs have more internal structure than they originally assumed how do they build underlying forms for morphemes, whether roots/stems or affixes? This question has been central to phonological theorizing almost from the beginning of the generative programme – and it remains a central problem in characterizing how children acquire phonological knowledge, because it means tapping mental representations, and their development. In other words: we still don't really know how they do it.

8.5.1   The Problems and Methods

We began this chapter with the following idea: since children learn a lot of phonotactic patterns before they begin this morphological process, it seems intuitive and efficient that learners should use their phonology to choose the right underlying form. In the case of Dutch plural marking, for instance, the child comes to this morphological task already knowing from their phonotactic learning that word-final /d/ maps to output [t], but does not map

---

[23] See Marcus et al. (1992: 122-128), and also for example arguments in Bybee and Slobin (1982).

intervocalic /t/ → *[d]. With that information, a learner who has now found the reliable plural suffix [-ən] could observe alternations like *bet ~ beden*, and in some sense 'ask' their phonology which stem allomorph to store as the input form, comparing the options in (35). (The high- and low-ranked structural constraints used here are from Sections 6.5 and 6.1.3 respectively.)[24]

(35a)

Using input /bɛd/to produce *bet~beden* – ***success***			
/bɛd/	*FINAL-VCDOBS	IDENT[+/-VOICE]	*VTV
[bɛd]	*!		
☞ [bɛt]		*	
/bɛd-ən/	*FINAL-VCDOBS	IDENT[+/-VOICE]	*VTV
☞ [bɛdən]			*
[bɛtən]		*!	

(35b)

Using input /bɛt/to produce *bet~beden* – *failure*			
/bɛt/	*FINAL-VCDOBS	IDENT[+/-VOICE]	*VTV
[bɛd]			
☞ [bɛt]		*	
/bɛt-ən/	*FINAL-VCDOBS	IDENT[+/-VOICE]	*VTV
☹ [bɛdən]		*!	*
☞ [bɛtən]			

In this example, our learner is considering only two input hypotheses, /bɛt/ and /bɛd/ – that is, the two surface allomorphs they have observed, [bɛt] and [bɛd-]. This reflects a frequent assumption about UR discovery: that learners at least start with just all the observed allomorphs, and try to choose a single input among them, from which to derive the others.

It is worth pointing out, though, that many morpho-phonological paradigms don't easily permit this kind of analysis. A famous example comes from the

---

[24] For a different approach to this voicing neutralization, see Lombardi (1999).

Austronesian language Palauan (Schane, 1974). Examine the verbs listed below in three different morphological environments, and try to determine what their URs should be (begin by parsing out the prefix and suffixes to find the stem):

(36)	Palauan alternations (data from Schane, 1974)			
	Present	*Future – a*	*Future – b*	*Gloss*
	məˈdanəb	dənəˈball	dəˈnobl	*cover*
	məˈteʔəb	təʔəˈball	təˈʔibl	*pull out*
	məˈnetəm	nətəˈmall	nəˈtoml	*lick*
	məˈtabək	təbəˈkall	təˈbakl	*patch*
	məˈsesəb	səsəˈball	səˈsobl	*burn*

In Palauan (even more so than in English), unstressed vowels are reduced to schwa. This means that underlying vowel quality can only be revealed in a *stressed* syllable – and since each word bears only one stress, whose position shifts depending on the phonotactic environments caused by affixation, you might see the first stem syllable stressed (as in the present tense) or the second (as in the future-b). The upshot is that to find the UR of a word with more than one syllable, the learner will necessarily have to gather data <u>from more than one underlying form</u>: the first stem vowel from the present tense, and the second stem vowel from the future-b tense.

So what can we say about how learners acquire URs? Do they, in fact, begin with an 'ask your phonology first' strategy? Or do they simply choose for example the most frequent surface allomorph they see, and fix things later? (If so, how?) Do they insist on choosing an input that matches some observed surface allomorph (making the Palauan-learning child a bit of a mystery?). And more fundamentally: do we know that learners in fact adopt a single UR form for multiple surface allomorphs?

Trying to answer these big questions must be preceded with another big question: what kind of data could answer these questions? Determining what underlying representations a learner has chosen is always necessarily an indirect process – one cannot *ask* – and performance is always hard to interpret. Production errors may provide clues: if a Dutch-learning child produces a target plural like *beden* incorrectly as *beten* – this <u>might</u> mean that they have incorrectly analysed the UR of the word as */bɛt/, although there is also a different explanation of this error that you may already see coming (keep reading).

In one sense, if a distributional pattern or alternation survives intact for many generations (as is the case in Dutch plurals, for instance), we know at least that learners are all capable of coming to stable and transmittable analysis of stems and affixes – but of course that doesn't tell us how they got there. However, looking at patterns of language *change* can provide additional evidence; looking at how paradigms are *levelled* or at least re-arranged over time can suggest how learners approach the acquisition of inputs.

To discuss this tricky issue, we will look at one extended case study of both child errors and diachronic change in progress resulting from the many stem-final alternations found in Korean nouns and verbs. You may recall from Chapter 6.1.3 that Korean phonotactics cause neutralization among laryngeal and place contrasts before consonant-initial suffixes – but those were only part of the story.

8.5.2 Learning Korean Verb-Final Alternations

The table in (37) contains some representative examples of Korean verbs, showing three allomorphs of each verb, as observed in front of three different suffixes.[25] Examine these data, and decide what the correct 'Korean problem set' answer would be – that is, how would you choose the underlying form for each verb?

(37)		Korean verb stem allomorphy (Data from Do, 2013)		
		Gloss	*Imperative (verb!)*	*Present ('verbs')*	*Progressive (is verbing)*
a)		*to catch*	cab-a	cam-nɨn	cap-k'o
		to pay back	kapʰ-a	kam-nɨn	kap-k'o
		to close	tad-a	tan-nɨn	tat-k'o
		to mix	sək'-ə	seŋ-nɨn	sək-k'o
		to wash	s'is-ə	s'in-nɨn	s'it-k'o
		to chase	c'otʃʰ-a	c'on-nɨn	c'ot-k'o
b)		*to live*	saɾ-a	sa-nɨn	sal-go
		to push	miɾ-a	mi-nɨn	mil-go
		to walk	kəɾ-ə	kən-nɨn	kət-k'o
		to load	siɾ- a	sin-nɨn	sit-k'o
		to pick up	cuw-ə	cum-nɨn	cup-k'o
		to flow	hɨll-ə	hɨɾi-nɨn	hɨɾi-go

---

[25] Note that these are only a subset of the stem-final alternations in verbs – for other parts of the paradigm and other stems, see Albright and Kang (2009) and references therein.

The data in (37a) suggest that the stem UR can be observed best before a verb-initial suffix, as in the imperative: notice that the verbs *to catch* and *to pay back* appear to have the same final consonant when followed by a consonant-initial suffix, but in the imperative they surface with a final [b] and [pʰ],h respectively. However, in (37b) the imperative forms are not sufficient – knowing that a stem ends in a flap is not sufficient to know how it will behave when followed by a consonant-initial suffix, as you can see comparing *to live*, *to push* and *to walk*.

With respect to Korean phonology beyond verb stem endings, these alternations also vary in their predictability. The alternations in (37a) all align with regular Korean phonotactics: stops must be laryngeally plain before consonants, but can contrast intervocalically; coronal obstruents all neutralize to [t] before other consonants; and nasals cause preceding consonants to nasalize as well. However the alternations in (37b) are for the most part lexically-specific: while [ɾ] and [l] are indeed allophonic ([ɾ] appears between vowels and [l] before consonants), the rest of the alternations are specific to each stem (i.e. ɾ~t, ɾ~0, w~p and ll~ɾi).

How are these verbal alternations learnt? Do (2013) reports that Korean-acquiring children often produce verbs only in the imperative -a/-ə suffixed form (citing e.g. Lee et al, 2003), but she also notes that these data come from the very earliest stages of production, before any evidence of allomorphy emerges. So what kinds of errors do Korean-learning children make when they start using verbal suffixes productively?

Some evidence comes from Do (2013)'s elicitation study, in which adults and children saw images of characters performing actions or displaying properties, and were asked to fill in a blank with a verb to describe the scene. This task elicited present tense forms, sometimes also marked as progressive – for example an image of a cartoon character walking might prompt a Korean form meaning '[he] *walks*' [kən-nɨn-da] or '[he] *is walking*' [kət-k'oit-t'a] (the final [-da/t'a] morpheme is a declarative suffix). Note that in both of these forms, the suffixes immediately after the root are C-initial, meaning they trigger one of the stem allomorphs not seen with the -a/-ə suffix.

The data in (38) below illustrate the kinds of production errors that children made in this task; the stems URs are simply listed in their surface -a/-ə form. What do the children's non-target forms suggest about their own verbal stem URs?

(38)	Korean children's morpho-phonological errors (Data from Do, 2013)		
	Stem	*a) Target forms*	*b) Child forms*
	/kəɾ/ 'to walk'	kə**n**-nɨn-da	kəɾ-i-nɨn-da
		kə**t**-k'oit-t'a	kəɾ-i-goit-da

Continued

Stem	a) Target forms	b) Child forms
/cuw/ 'to pick up'	cu**m**-nɨn-da	cu**w**-i-nɨn-da
	cu**p**-k'oit-t'a	
/s'is/ 'to wash'	s'i**n**-nɨn-da	s'i**s**-ə-n-da
	s'i**t**-k'oit-t'a	

In these examples, children appear to be levelling their paradigms in favour of the allomorph found before vowel-initial suffixes. In other words: they appear to have chosen the imperative allomorph as the UR, and are additionally imposing *paradigm uniformity* (Section 8.3) to maintain that stem throughout. (Notice that they are also epenthesizing a vowel between the stem-final consonant and the suffixes? Back to that in a minute.)

In this study, the younger children aged 4;1–5;3 used the target verb allomorph (as in 38a) only about half the time (105/206 tokens); their most frequent non-target approach (65/206 tokens) was to use the V-final allomorph as in (38b). With respect to 'ask the phonology first,' note that two of the three child errors in (38) are on stems from the (37b) set, with the more irregular alternations. In general, the alternations involving well-supported Korean phonotactics were much less prone to error – in fact, there were no stem errors made by any child for alternations simply involving laryngeal features, nasalization or the basic [ɾ~l] alternation. One striking exception came from /s/-final verbs like *'to wash'* above – while this s~t~n alternation is well-represented in Korean phonology, these younger kids used the vowel-initial stem allomorph [s'is] 13/21 times.

The study's older children, aged 5;1–7;8, produced the target (38a) stems a little more often (73/114 tokens, 64% of the time), but their most frequent non-target productions were not the V-initial stems from (38b). Instead, they took a somewhat more difficult route, choosing different or additional suffixes – but always beginning with a vowel-initial suffix or conjunction (glossed as *'conj.'*), as shown in bold here:[26]

(39)	Older Korean children's morpho-phonological substitutions (Data from Do, 2013)			
	Stem	a) Target forms	b) Child forms	c) Child gloss
	/mən/ 'to eat'	mən-nɨn-da	mən-**ə**-<u>pəɾi</u>-n-da	'eat up'
			eat-conj-clean-pres.-dec.	
	/cak/ 'small'	cak-'ta	cag-**a**-<u>boi</u>-n-da	'look small'
			small-conj.-looks-pres. dec.	

---

[26] The simple use of the wrong stem allomorph as in (38b) represented only 7/114 of the older children's productions.

Notice that these conjunction vowels, like the epenthesized vowels in (38b), provide the phonotactic context for the allomorph that we think children have adopted as their underlying form! In other words, these vowels again provided a way of enforcing *paradigm uniformity*.

One take-home message from this study is it is further evidence that morpho-phonological alternations are easier for children to master when they rely on well-supported, language-wide phonotactics. In the majority of the (38a) verbs, four-year-olds were already using the correct underlying forms and their usual errors were only to enforce too much faithfulness to their chosen base allomorph. In the more phonologically-irregular verbs in (38b), however, even seven-year-old children were making frequent errors – and also were adopting some avoidance strategies for dealing with verbs whose exceptional allomorphs they perhaps did not yet know (as in 39).

8.5.3   Learning Korean Noun-Final Alternations

Now we will turn from verbs to nouns, whose stem-final segments can again alternate in a variety of ways. Below is the Korean data from Chapter 6.3.3, example (52), but now including two more cells in the morphological paradigm; in addition to the neutralizations we saw in the verbal domain, here we see some additional complications that can obscure a stem-final segment. Note that these data represent the traditional nominal paradigm, which is also reflected in the Korean spelling of these nouns in their various inflections. Make sure you can explain where the learner should find the 'correct' UR for these nouns before reading on.

(40)	'Traditional' Korean noun stem allomorphy (Data from Jun and Lee, 2007: table 2)			
Gloss	*Isolation form*	*Nominative*	*Accusative*	*Locative*
clothes	otˈ	osi	otɨl	ose
day	natˈ	natʃi	natɨl	nate
field	patˈ	patʃʰi	patʰɨl	patʰe
light	pitˈ	pitʃʰi	pitʃʰɨl	pitʃʰe
rice	papˈ	papi	papɨl	pape
leaf	ipˈ	ipʰi	ipʰɨl	ipʰe
soup	kukˈ	kuki	kukɨl	kuke
outside	pakˈ	pak'i	pak'ɨl	pak'e

Continued

Gloss	Isolation form	Nominative	Accusative	Locative
kitchen	puǝkʔ	puǝkʰi	puǝkʰɨl	puǝkʰe
nose	kʰo	kʰoka[27]	kʰoɾil	kʰoe
work	il	iɾi	iɾil	iɾe

We already knew that many obstruent contrasts are lost in coda position, so clearly the isolation form is not the place to learn a noun's UR. All three suffixes begin with a vowel, so they do not impose coda neutralizations – but there are still more alternations that obscure properties of the base.

The nominative suffix [-i] neutralizes one contrast: compare the suffixed forms for *field* and *light* and you will see that the final segment of *field* looks to be /tʰ/ but is palatalized before nominative [-i]. This palatalization among stem-final [tʰ] is morphologically-restricted – that is it only occurs at morpheme boundaries like this – whereas the rest of these neutralizations are also part of regular Korean phonotactics. The accusative suffix also causes a type of neutralization via its own two allomorphs: [-il] after C-final stems, and [-ɾil] after V-final stems. Recall that /l/ → [ɾ] between vowels, and you will see how the last two stems in (40), *nose* and *work,* are ambiguous in the accusative. Without knowing other forms in their paradigms, the [ɾ] in those two accusative forms could <u>either</u> be stem-final or suffix-initial!

All this taken together, it seems clear that the 'correct' stem UR should be the surface allomorph seen in the locative form – and Korean phonotactics will take care of most of the rest (except for the small addition of palatalization needed in the nominative as in *field*). However, studies starting at least in 1989 suggest that Korean speakers have been learning something different about nominal paradigms for decades. Some clear evidence comes from Jun and Lee (2007), in which ten native Korean-speaking adults were asked to answer questions that put nouns in one of the three case-marking environments. Looking first just at the three stems in (41) below, what is the pattern? (The number in brackets represents how many of the ten participants gave that response.)

---

[27] Due to a slightly odd vowel harmony, the nominative suffix has two separate allomorphs: /-i/ after C-final stems and /-ka/ after V-final stems. Don't let this throw you – it doesn't have any effect on the choice of noun URs we are worried about here.

(41) Some variants of Korean noun stem allomorphy (Data from Jun and Lee, 2007: table 22)

'Stem'	Isolation form	Nominative	Accusative	Locative
/pap/	pap˺	papi	papɨl	pape
/ipʰ/	ip˺	ipʰi	ipɨl (3) ipʰɨl (7)	ipʰe
/puəkʰ/	puək˺	puəki (8) puəkʰi (2)	puəkɨl (9) puəkʰɨl (1)	puəke (6) puəkʰe (4)

In the case of labial-final stems, adults used the expected allomorphs for the most part. But for this stem /puəkʰ/, which traditionally contained an aspirated [k] before vowel-initial suffixes, it appears that the majority of speakers were choosing a plain [k] as the stem-final segment – as though they had built their UR from the isolation form! And what about the coronal-final stems? Here is an excerpt of their data:

(42) Some coronal-final variants of Korean noun stem allomorphy (Data from Jun and Lee, 2007: table 21)

'Stem'	Isolation form	Nominative	Accusative	Locative
/nas/	nat˺	nasi	nasɨl	nase
/os/	ot˺	osi	osɨl (9) otʃʰɨl (1)	ose
/k'otʃʰ/	k'ot˺	k'osi (2) k'otʃʰi (8)	k'osɨl (4) k'otʃʰɨl (6)	k'otʃʰe(9) k'otʰe (1)
/natʃʰ/	nat˺	nasi (3) natʃʰi (7)	nasɨl (4) natʃʰɨl (6)	nase (5) natʃʰe (6)
/patʰ/	pat˺	pasi (1) patʃʰi (9)	pasɨl (2) patʃʰɨl (8)	patʃʰe (1) patʰe (9)
/pʰatʰ/	pʰat˺	pʰasi (5) pʰatʃʰi (6)	pasi (6) patʃʰɨl (3) patʰɨl (1)	pʰase (5) pʰatʃʰe (1) pʰatʰe (4) pʰate (1)

Apart from stems with final /s/, which seem to be relatively stable as such, the variation here away from the traditional stem form is even more obvious. The stems which end in affricate /tʃʰ/ most often retain their affricate – but the most likely alternative is to use a stem-final [s], which does not appear anywhere in the traditional paradigm at all! The stems which end in an aspirated stop also show some exceptional final [s], as well as affrication to [tʃ] in front of vowels other than [i]. In one case, /patʰ-ɨl/ with the accusative suffix, none of the adult participants provided the expected surface allomorph [patʰɨl]!

The upshot here is that in recent years or perhaps generations, Korean speakers have stopped adopting URs for verbs that align with their locative allomorphs, as the problem set answer would have predicted. In some cases, they may have adopted the bare surface allomorphs (as in /puək/ instead of /puəkʰ/). In other (coronal-final) cases, they appear to have adopted an analysis in which the allomorphs used before vowel-initial suffixes is often /s/. Where did this idea come from?

The missing piece of the puzzle is frequency, and in fact two kinds of frequency appear to be influential. The first is the frequency of stem-final segments in the overall lexicon of Korean nouns – because as it turns out, of the only roughly 18% of nouns that end in obstruents, there are some pretty clear skews in the segmental distributions. The data in (43) gives tallies of how many Korean stems end in each possible obstruent (data from Albright and Kang, 2009), using the Sejong corpus of Kim and Kang, 2000). How might these numbers help understand the novel stem allomorphs seen above?

(43)	Frequency of final obstruents in Korean (Data from Albright and Kang, 2009)						
	Labials		*Coronals*				*Velars*	
	p	1360	t	1	tʃʰ	160	k	5994
	pʰ	64	tʰ	113	tʃ'	0	kʰ	18
	p'	0	t'	0	s	375	k'	6
			tʃ	17	s'	0		

Clearly, a handful of final segments are much more common than others – among the labials and velars, the plain [p] and [k] swamp the other two options, and more than half of the coronals are [s].

This asymmetry in frequency puts a different perspective on the indeterminacy that speakers face when choosing an underlying form. When examining the alternation in (40), we decided immediately against using the isolation form as a verbal UR, because it obscures many underlying contrasts like /k ~ kʰ/. But given the whole lexicon view of (43), the learner who adopts the isolation form as the UR of a velar-final stem is not in particular trouble: of the 6,012 stems they have to learn, they will only make mistakes in front of V-initial suffixes for 24 of them! (18 with an aspirated stop, and 6 with an ejective.) In such a case, memorizing those 24 stems as irregular seems fairly doable – and if that memorization is not robust enough, speakers will begin to use plain /k/ alternants in these inflected forms, just as we saw for /puəkʰ/ ~ /puək/ in (41).

It should also be noted that the frequency of each cell within the morphological paradigm may not be what you would expect, because Korean case-marking is reportedly often <u>optional</u>, and so often children and adults alike do often hear the isolation form of at least some verbs, resulting in lots of neutralization.

To focus now on the coronals: all of these distributional facts mean that learners are faced with a number of obstacles in determining the underlying form of verbs like /nas/, /k'otʃʰ/ and /patʰ/. If learners commit to using the locative surface form as the UR from which to derive all other allomorphs, they will need to ignore the considerably more frequent evidence of bare forms and other parts of the paradigm – possibly meaning they will have to memorize bare stems first, and then revise them later once they acquire the right UR. If learners choose to use the isolation form as UR, however, they will need to learn a bunch of morphologically-conditioned patterns that change the stem-final segment before vowel-initial suffixes. Since more than half of coronal stems actually end in /s/, the learner's first guess of such a process would probably be based on stems like /nas/, which surface as [nat] in isolation – and which would require a morphologically-specific process to map /nat/ → [nas...] before the suffixes in [nasi], [nasɨl] and [nase]. Thus, the exceptional use of /s/ at the end of stems like /pʰatʰ/ in (42) looks like the result of UR identification with the isolation form, plus the creation of ad hoc phonological processes to capture the other verbal allomorphs.

... And as for the next generation? What are children learning about noun stem endings? Do (2012) provides some initial experimental results from noun elicitation with children ages four through seven, in contexts that required a final suffix. When tested on sonorant-final stems, children were fairly accurate: suffixes were added most of the time (87%) and the only frequently-observed alternations were those sanctioned by the phonotactics, such as the [ɾ]~[l] alternation. With respect to final coronal obstruents, however, children showed two different patterns. The older children (six- and seven-year-olds) produced a rather simplified version of the results seen in (43): in the nominative and accusative they most often used an [s]-final stem allomorph. The younger, four- to six-year-olds often responding by simply leaving an obstruent-final stem bare: fully 74% of nominative and 62% of accusative obstruent-final nouns were produced in their isolation forms. You might also recall that this zero-change strategy was also observed among Dutch children, who would repeat a plural noun in a singular context rather than remove the plural suffix which would trigger a phonological alternation.

Do (2012)'s experimental results suggests that Korean-acquiring children are not at all sure about the correct URs for the nominal stems – unsurprising, since the ambient language provided by adults in (41) and (42) must be quite variable. Note too that leaners' uncertainty is phonologically-constrained, in that they show no difficulty with sonorant-final stems. More research about this morpho-phonological change in progress may provide us with novel and additional clues as to how each generation re-learns and recreates the UR structures and phonological grammars of their speech community.

8.6 Further Reading

On Morpho-phonological Acquisition

MacWhinney, Brian. 1975. Rules, rote and analogy in morphological formations by Hungarian children. *Journal of Child Language* 2: 65–77.

Skoruppa, Katrin, Mani, N. and Peperkamp, Sharon. 2013. Toddlers' processing of phonological alternations: Early compensation for assimilation in English and French. *Child Development,* 84(1): 313–330.

Tessier, Anne-Michelle. to appear. Morpho-phonological acquisition. In J. Lidz, J. Pater and W. Snyder (eds) *Handbook of Developmental Linguistics.* Oxford: OUP.

On Learning Morpho-phonological Subregularities

Albright, Adam and Hayes, Bruce. 2003. Rules vs. analogy in English past tenses: A computational/ experimental study. *Cognition* 90: 119–161.

Becker, Michael and Gouskova, Maria. 2014. Source-oriented generalizations as grammar inference in Russian vowel deletion. Ms., Indiana University and NYU. Available at: http://becker.phonologist.org/projects/yers/becker_gouskova_source_oriented.pdf

Exercises

Q1: Zamuner, Kerkhoff and Fikkert (2006)'s comprehension wug test (data above in table (16)) showed the following two numerical trends: first, the degree of accuracy between children was much greater in the /d/-alternating forms than the /t/-non-alternating ones (look at their standard deviations in parentheses); second, the children of 2;6–2;8 were more accurate than those a year old! ... *What do you make of both of these results? What do they tell you about children's knowledge of this alternation? Or about this task?*

Q2: In studying a multi-child corpus of spontaneous speech, Kuczaj (1978) found the following two facts:

i) children who produced statistically-longer utterances (measured in terms of mean length of utterance, or *MLU,* see e.g. Rice et al., 2010) were more accurate in producing the correct <u>regular</u> past tense verbs, and MLU was a better way of predicting their mastery of regular verbs than their chronological age.

ii) in predicting accuracy in <u>irregular</u> verbs (instead of e.g. over-regularizing them to look like regulars), however, chronological age was a better predictor than MLU.

What do these results suggest about how children learn and store regular and/or irregular morphology? If we assume that MLU increases as the grammar improves, does that make these results more understandable?

Q3: The table below provides the data from another of Jun and Lee (2007)'s experiments, in which they asked adult Korean speakers to borrow English words with final /d/ and /t/ into the language and inflect them. (Note that in each case, the isolation form would end in a plain unreleased [t].) The full borrowings are not transcribed – just the stem-final segment that speakers produced. (Note also that in several cases, speakers epenthesized a default vowel [ɨ] after the stem-final segment, rather than producing the correct suffix.)

How do these data confirm, expand on or challenge the conclusions drawn about Korean stem allomorphy in Section 8.5.3?

Final segments used in borrowing English nouns into Korean (data from Jun and Lee, 2007: table 24)			
English source	*Nominative*	*Accusative*	*Locative*
'good'	[s]	[s]	[s](6) [tɨ] (5)
'David'	[s]	[s] (8) [tɨ] (2)	[tʰ] (1) [t] (8) [tɨ] (1)
'cut'	[s]	[s]	[s] (8) [tʰ] (1) [t] (1)
'Pat'	[s] (9) [tʃʰ] (1)	[s]	[s] (9) [t] (1)
'Matt'	[s] (8) [tʃʰ] (2)	[s] (8) [tʃʰ] (1) [tʰ] (2)	[s] (4) [tʰ] (2) [t] (4) [tɨ] (2)
'meet'	[s] (7) [tʃʰ] (2) [tʰ] (2)	[s] (8) [tɨ] (2)	[s] (4) [tʰ] (4) [t] (1) [tɨ] (1)

Answer to Exercise 1 above:

(3a) /kæt + z/	AGREE[+/-VOICE]-OBSTRUENT	MAX-C	DEP	IDENT[+/-VOICE]
[kætz]	*!			
[kæt]		*!		
[kæz]		*!		
☞ [kæts]				*
[kætəz]			*!	

(3b) /kɪs + z/	AGREE[+/-VOICE]-OBSTRUENT	NO GEMINATES	MAX-C	DEP	IDENT[+/-VOICE]
[kɪsz]	*!				
[kɪs:]		*!			*
[kɪs]			*!		
☞ [kɪsəz]				*	

Note the ranking between MAX and DEP that is necessary in (3b) but not yet known just looking at (3a).

9 Children's Bilingual Phonological Acquisition

9.1 Conceptual Issues: Bilingual and Second Language Development

This chapter is about children's acquisition of more than one language's phonology – a topic that is worthy of at least an entire other textbook. As it turns out, bilingual acquisition is no doubt <u>more</u> common among the world's children than the monolingual learning scenario that dominates the research literature: if you grew up speaking and hearing only one language, you are part of a global minority. Neither is this predominant multilingual learning experience confined to the well-known linguistic tapestries of India, or the *lingua francas* found across Africa, and the language co-mingling of western European countries like Switzerland and Belgium. Even in predominantly English-speaking areas such as North America and Britain, a significant and certainly increasing proportion of children are learning English only as their second language, at school and in the playground. According to US Census Bureau data, about 20.7% of people over the age of five living in the US speak a language other than English at home (Ryan, 2013); in Canada, 20% of the population in 2011 reported speaking a language other than English or French (Statistics Canada, 2011); for England and Wales, the 2011 Office of National Statistics census reports that 7.7% of those aged three and older lived in households where English or Welsh was not the dominant language of at least one adult.[1] All over the world, in all sorts of circumstances, children are growing up bilingual.

This chapter's discussion will be more of an overview of known results in the field, rather than the in-depth case studies from earlier chapters, but as always our focus will be to understand common learner processes and

---

[1] In large metropolitan centres, the degree of multilingualism can of course be much higher – in at least five London boroughs in 2011, the number of speakers using English as their main language was less than 70%, and the metro regions of Los Angeles, California and Miami, Florida reported more than 50% of population speaking something other than English at home.

patterns and their potential analyses. To begin with, though, there are many foundational questions to address.

The first question is why this chapter exists at all: that is, in what way is a child's acquisition of two phonologies any different than their learning of one? There are a couple facets to this question. One is the distinction we will make between two learnings scenarios: *bilingual first language acquisition* (bL1), in which a learner is exposed to both languages in a nearly-native-like context, though not necessarily 50% of the time or from birth, vs. *child second language acquisition* (cL2), in which a learner begins acquiring a second language at a point where their first language has been acquired to some substantial degree, though they may ultimately appear native-like in their L2.[2] To define these two categories, we must first determine what age is too late to start bL1 acquisition; a related question is how much exposure to the language is needed in either bL1 or cL2 contexts for grammatical learning to begin? A frequently-cited result is that a child must consistently receive at least 20% of their input in a particular language to maintain its acquisition (see especially Pearson et al., 1997: 55–56, although this threshold was not this study's main result; cf. Schiff, 1979).

At the conceptual level, we could imagine many ways to distinguish between bL1 and cL2 learning. One approach would be to begin with an arbitrary age cut-off – say, that bL1 requires continual exposure to both languages starting before age 3;0 or 4;0 – and then compare learning among these two groups, looking for similarities or differences and shifting the age boundary as necessary to best match the data. Another approach would be to find one acquisition outcome which more or less divides these learners into two groups, and which might then correlate with age of exposure. (It might be good to stop and think before continuing which of these approaches you find most compelling, or what else you might do instead.) The best candidate for such a criterion is probably their *ultimate attainment*: that is the phonology that learners ultimately acquire as adults, and whether it is distinguishable (at various degrees of analysis) from that of monolingual native speakers.

In practice, one heuristic for assigning a cut-off for bL1 acquisition is an age past which learners are not reliably able to acquire a fully-native-like phonology. On the production side, many studies find that children can ultimately learn a second language to the point of near-native competence starting as late as age ten and sometimes even much later (see e.g. discussion in Flege, 2009; Flege and

---

[2] Many different terms have been used to describe these two scenarios: for example, some research refers to the first group as *simultaneous bilinguals* and the latter as *sequential bilinguals*. Often, both of the populations being discussed here would be called *early* bilinguals, to distinguish them from *late bilinguals* who are past puberty by their onset of L2 learning.

MacKay, 2011). As for the perception side, we learnt in Chapter 2 how much L1-specific knowledge of phonological structures is acquired by infants before even the onset of productive phonology! Thus it is not surprising that bL1 learners who have not been exposed to both languages from birth, or merely have been exposed to one language more than the other, should demonstrate at least low-level perceptual knowledge that differs from monolinguals. This knowledge might be more or less precise than that of monolinguals, and it appears to influence even very subtle facts about bilingual infant's word learning (see for example Ramon-Casas et al., 2009; Fennell and Byers-Heinlein, 2014).

While there has been substantial research in the morpho-syntactic domain of multi-lingual acquisition for several decades, the study of phonology among young child bilinguals, and especially second language child learners, is still in the early stages. Thus researchers are just beginning to systematically tease apart answers and approaches to these issues, and in many cases the diverse backgrounds of the children included within a study suggest that bL1 and cL2 learners are being studied side-by-side. Here we will focus primarily on bilingual L1 learners' phonologies.

9.2   Early Child Bilingual Phonology

The primary questions we will ask in this chapter are how similar children's acquisition of multiple phonologies is compared to monolingual development, and what types of explanations could account for their differences. The main focus will be on syllabic and segmental production among primarily bL1 learners, and considering how two phonologies within a single mind do or do not influence each other.

9.2.1   Acquiring Two Phoneme Inventories

We begin our data sampling with an example from Fernando, a bilingual child learning American English and Spanish studied in Schnitzer and Krasinski (1994). Fernando was exposed to both languages from birth; both of his parents were highly fluent in both languages, with one speaking consistently to their children in Spanish and the other in English, and while his environmental language input was mostly Puerto Rican Spanish, he also watched American English television, and frequently visited with monolingual English family members.

To track one aspect of his early segmental development, the table below tabulates Fernando's attempts for the two labial segments /f/ and /p/ in English and Spanish, for one or two particular lexical items. For each word, table (1) shows his output for these words' labial segment between 1;11 and 3;0 (in many cases, his pronunciation varied throughout the month).

Examine the data, and try to decide for yourself how similarly or differently his two languages' labial inventories developed before reading on:

(1) bL1 English vs. Spanish labial inventory
(Data from Schnitzer and Krasinski, 1994 table 1b: p. 596)

Age	Spanish [p] 'papa'	English [p] 'apple'	Spanish [f] 'feo' ('ugly')	English [f] 'fish'
1;11–2;0	p	p	P	p
2;1	p	p	P	p f
2;2	p	p	p φ	p
2;3	p	p	φ f	p
2;4	p	p	φ f	p f
2;5	p	p	f	p f
2;6–2;11	p	p	f	p f
3;0	p	p	f	f

For the first three months during which he used these words (from 1;11 to 2;0), /p/ and /f/ are merged to [p] in both languages – no evidence of divergence is available here. But starting at 2;1, each /f/ shows its own trajectory: for the most part, English /f/ continues to undergo stopping until 2;4, and variably stops until 3;0; meanwhile, Spanish /f/ becomes a fricative by 2;3, and after varying between labio-dental and bilabial, it settles into [f] already at 2;5. It is particularly striking that for all of 2;2–2;3, Fernando's English /f/ is always a stop, whereas during both months his Spanish /f/ is already a fricative; and note that [φ] is never used in English as a substitute for /f/. In each of these ways, then – Fernando's production of labial consonants shows a distinct separation of phonological mappings between his two languages at least by age 2;0. Note, too, that this kind of bilingual differentiation makes it plain that perceptual or motor-planning factors cannot explain these output differences – because they are all coming from the same child, with the same ears, mouth and muscles.[3]

A second example comes from the early acquisition of stop voicing, also by a Spanish-English bilingual child in the United States, exposed to both languages since birth. Spanish and English both use two categories of stops distinguished by their relative VOTs – but whereas English stops differ primarily in amount of positive VOT (where /b/ has near-zero or short lag

---

[3] A caveat: the authors of this study do not read the sum of their data as emphasizing the early separation of two phonologies; however, see Johnson and Lancaster (1998).

VOT and aspirated /p/ has a much longer lag), Spanish voicing is in fact cued by lead vs. lag, where /b/'s voicing begins during the closure, creating a negative VOT, while /p/ has a short positive VOT. Representative VOT values from a few monolingual speakers of each language are given in (2):

(2) Target VOT values for English and Spanish stops
(Lisker and Abrahamson, 1964)

	English	Spanish
	Mean VOT (range)	*Mean VOT (range)*
/p/	58 (20–120)	4 (0–15)
/b/	1 (0–5)	−138(−235– −60)
/t/	70 (30–105)	9 (0–15)
/d/	5 (0–25)	−110 (−170– −75)
/k/	80 (50–135)	29 (15–55)
/g/	21 (0–35)	−108 (−165– −45)

If you compare values by place of articulation, you will see the confusing mismatch in categorization of short VOT lag – that is, an English /b/ is clearly in the same VOT range as a Spanish /p/. So what does a bilingual child do with these distributions?

The table below shows the average VOT values from recordings of bilingual Manuela at three stages, starting at age 1;7. You may recall from Chapter 6 that both monolingual English and Spanish-acquiring kids often seem to produce their first stops all within one voicing range, somewhere in the short lag area of the VOT spectrum. From this perspective Manuela's (admittedly limited) production of both languages' stops in her first session (1;7), where every stop has a small positive VOT, seems quite monolingual. But what happens at the next two stages? Compare the target 'voiced' and 'voiceless' versions of stops at each place of articulation in the two languages:

(3) bL1 English vs. Spanish stop voicing: mean VOT (range or SD)
(Data from Deuchar and Clarke, 1996: tables 3–5)

	1;7		1;11		2;3	
	English	*Spanish*	*English*	*Spanish*	*English*	*Spanish*
/p/	–	19 (0–43)	31 (12.8)	22 (14.6)	62 (32.0)	37 (22.0)
/b/	18 (0–39)	–	22 (19.1)	28 (15.3)	17(10.0)	26 (17.3)

Continued

	1;7		1;11		2;3	
	English	*Spanish*	*English*	*Spanish*	*English*	*Spanish*
/t/	35	–	27 (11.0)	32 (21.1)	76 (34.9)	37 (23.1)
/d/	31	17	15 (9.7)	20 (11.8)	22 (9.8)	29 (13.4)
/k/	30 (14–41)	36 (35–37)	65 (36.8)	46 (22.2)	78 (33.8)	42 (17.4)
/g/	16	30 (15–55)	54 (28.7)	40 (16.1)	30 (13.3)	28 (11.1)

At 1;11 English stops have begun to separate out, into longer and shorter positive VOTs for target 'voiceless' and 'voiced' stops, although both still remain far from their target goals (between 15–65ms overall). For Spanish stops, however, nothing really seems to have changed from the single short lag category stage at 1;7. Statistically speaking, there is too much variation to claim that Manuela's VOT values show distinct behaviour in the two languages at 1;11, but the trend seems emergent.[4]

By 2;3, this trend has developed further: the gap between English VOTs at each place have grown larger, while Spanish categories are only barely distinguished (although velars are getting there). Statistical analysis does confirm that stop voicing is different in the two languages – and most interestingly, comparisons of each segment type reveal that the longest lag stops, the English voiceless ones, had significantly longer VOTs than *any* of the other three categories, while no other pair-wise contrasts were significant. This tells us at least two important things: first, Manuela had acquired an English stop voicing contrast – English /p/ and /b/ were now reliably different, although they did not yet have target English VOTs – but she had not acquired a Spanish contrast. But since Manuela's single Spanish VOT stop category was also reliably different from her English /p/, these results also mean that she was not simply using her English /p/ as a default Spanish stop.[5]

Altogether, then, Manuela's bilingual development of English and Spanish voicing shows that she was clearly learning two sets of phonological categories, starting at 1;11 and demonstrably by 2;3. As Deuchar and Clarke (1996) support with much monolingual evidence, the Spanish contrast probably took longer to learn because lead (negative) VOT stops are simply harder to perceive and/or produce – but her acquisition of the English short vs. long lag contrast progressed faster in the meantime, and at 2;3 her English contrast was not simply borrowed into Spanish, but instead developed independently.

---

[4] The only statistical difference is that, across both languages, /t/ had a longer VOT than /d/.

[5] See Deuchar and Clarke (1996) for all of the main effects and interactions they found.

Quite similar results were found by Johnson and Wilson (2002) in a study of two bilingual siblings' acquisition of VOT in English and Japanese. Target Japanese voicing values are fairly similar to those of Spanish, with voicing lead (negative VOTs) for phonemes like /b/ and short voicing lag for /p/. The younger study participant had lived in Japan until age 11 months and then began to be exposed to English as well; at 2;10, this child showed no significant difference between voicing in the two languages, with English-like VOTs in both languages. However, the older sibling at 4;8, with a similar history of language exposure, showed a reliable distinction between VOTs in the two languages: while voicing lead had not yet emerged in Japanese, there was significantly less voice lag in the older child's Japanese /p/ and /t/ compared to English.

9.2.1.1   Bilingual Phonologies and Language Differentiation

These data examples contribute to one of the fundamental issues of bilingual language acquisition: at what point does the learner establish two mental systems for their two languages? It is now fairly well accepted in the current bilingualism literature that learners set up two linguistic constructs in their minds from the earliest stages at which they can be studied. Thus, children who are learning English and Spanish determine from the onset that there is an English phonology to be acquired and a Spanish phonology, as well as an English lexicon and a Spanish lexicon, and so on (see also 9.2.5 below).

Nonetheless, there is still a lot of discussion and debate about how this partitioning of the multilingual learning space is achieved.[6] For example: what do children know about the distinctive nature of their two languages? On the one hand, bilingual children are typically accurate at choosing the right language for the right monolingual interlocutor, as early as age two (Genessee, Nicoladis and Paradis, 1995). What is perhaps striking is children's conscious knowledge of this ability, or rather lack thereof. A child in the author's extended family, who spoke only French to some monolingual older relatives and only English to others as appropriate, once was asked to translate between two adult relatives and got angry at the annoying hassle – it never having occurred to the child that these adults did not speak a common language. Such anecdotes suggest that while children are not necessarily aware of their language differentiation and knowledge states, they must be able to actively control these distinctions at some unconscious level. (For more on this topic, see especially Bialystok, 1988; also Cruz-Ferreira, 2006.)

Of course, the existence of two distinct phonologies does not mean that each system is 100% impervious to the influence of the other – as you may

---

[6] See especially Lleo and Kehoe (2002) – a special volume entirely on the topic – and many references therein; compare with Volterra and Taeschner (1978).

well already know from personal experience. If you have learnt a second language as an adult, you have experienced phonological 'interference' between your native and second languages: for example, when learning a language like Spanish or Italian with a rhotic trill [r], you may *know* that an 'r' should be trilled and be able to articulate it as such, but nevertheless find yourself in the moment trying to speak your L2 and substituting your native 'r' pronunciation instead.

In the next sections we will see the effects of similar interactions between languages, usually referred to as *interference* or *transfer* – terms which we will try to define more carefully below. And as we did with monolinguals, we begin with syllable structure.

9.2.2 Acquisition of Syllable Structure by Bilinguals

Before engaging in detailed L1 vs. bL1 comparisons, we should begin by simply asking whether bilingual acquisition of syllable structure involves the same kinds of repairs as monolingual acquisition. Here are some examples from one cross-sectional study:

(4) | Error bL1 errors (Data from Gildersleeve-Neumann et al., 2008) | | | |
| --- | --- | --- | --- |
| *stove* | [toᵘv] | *dog* | [dak] |
| *spoon* | [bun] | *cat* | [kæ] |
| *glasses* | [gwæsəz] | *jelly* | [dzɛwi] |
| *black* | [bæk] | *swim* | [ɪm] |

Most of these productions look fairly standard from the monolingual L1 perspective: cluster reduction along sonority lines (compare *stove* with *black*), segmental substitution with like features (e.g. /l/ → [w]), coda deletion in *cat*, and the like. Gildersleeve-Neumann et al. (2008) note that among their bilingual learners, uncommon errors like entire cluster reduction (as in *swim*) represent less than 5% of their tokens, suggesting they are similarly rare as with monolinguals. ... So in what ways are bL1 learners special?

In the domain of syllable structure acquisition, the distinguishing aspect of bilingual phonologies appears to be the <u>rate</u> of acquisition of structures compared to monolinguals. Pause to ask yourself what you might predict about a bilingual child, learning for example English and Spanish (the latter having some but not the full range of English onset clusters and codas)?

Your most likely first guess is that bilinguals will be <u>slower</u> to acquire structures compared to monolinguals – either because they have less raw input in each language from which to generalize, or because they have a more confusing input set to tease apart, or both. But you might also imagine, under some approaches to learning, that bilinguals could be <u>faster</u> to acquire a phonological structure, at least one that exists in both languages: what if learning a structure in one phonology facilitates its acquisition in the other? Paradis and Genesee (1996)'s influential work (focused on morpho-syntactic bilingual development) label these two possibilities as *delay* and *acceleration* respectively (we will return to their third category of bilingual-specific developmental pattern below).

The prediction of bilingual *delay* in phonological acquisition, compared to monolinguals, is indeed borne out in some studies of syllable structure. For instance, Gildersleeve-Neumann et al. (2008)'s longitudinal study compared young English-Spanish bilinguals to monolingual English learners along a number of phonological dimensions including syllable structure errors, as reported in the table below. However, these between-group differences in syllable structure acquisition were not statistically significant – can you see why?

(5) | Delayed syllable structure acquisition among bilinguals (Data from Gildersleeve-Neumann et al., 2008: tables 1 and 2) | | |

Group (N)	*Mean age (range)*	*Rate of coda deletion (SD)*	*Rate of onset cluster reduction (SD)*
English monolinguals (10)	3:6 (3;1–3:10)	17.1% (12.8)	24.5% (26.5)
	4:2 (3;9–4;6)	14.9% (13.8)	21.4% (18.4)
English/Spanish bilinguals (3)[7]	3;5 (3;4–3:6)	36.0% (20.8)	47.7% (22.3)
	4;1 (4;0–4;2)	25.4 % (19.3)	43.4% (31.7)

The mean error rates in (5) tell us that, on average, balanced English-Spanish bilinguals produced roughly double the coda deletion and cluster reduction. But with so much variability between participants, and with only three participants in the bilingual group, the data are perhaps just a suggestion that bilinguals' syllable structure acquisition might be slower than their monolingual peers. (Note that this study did find other significant delays among bilingual phonologies among <u>segmental</u> processes, compared to monolingual learners.)

You may find it more surprising to learn that evidence of phonological *acceleration* among bilinguals' syllable structure acquisition is also attested. One example comes from a study by Kehoe and Lléo (2003), reporting on the order

---

[7] The study also included ten English-dominant bilinguals; see the original study for their results, which were very similar on syllable structure to the English monolinguals.

in which bL1 German/Spanish-learning children acquired syllables shapes in their two languages, compared to monolinguals of both languages. The Spanish differences they found in relative orders can be found in (6) below; find out the discrepancies, and consider how acceleration might explain them:

(6) Order of Spanish syllable structure acquisition (Kehoe and Lléo, 2003)
   a) Monolingual Spanish learners (across 3 children)
      CV → V → CVV → CVC
   b) bL1 German/Spanish learners, by child:
      N: CV → V, CVC → CVV
      J: CV → V → CVC → CVV
      S: CV → V → CVV → CVC

Two of the three bilingual learners acquired Spanish coda consonants earlier than the monolinguals: both N and J produced Spanish [CVC] syllables before they produced [CVV] diphthongs. N also acquired codas at the same time as onsetless syllables [V], first seen in the same recording session at 1;4; for the three monolingual Spanish learners the mean time lapse between [V] and [CVC]'s emergence was six months. A possible cause of this acceleration is the bL1's children's experience of German syllable structure, which includes more frequent codas than in Spanish, particularly in word-final position, where both bilingual children N and J acquired their Spanish codas first.

Thus the literature includes evidence that the discrepancies between bilingual children's two phonologies can <u>both</u> speed up or slow down their syllable structure development. Another example of these interactions is found in Keffala and Barlow (2013, 2014)'s study of Amercan English-Spanish bilinguals. This cross-sectional study compared five three-year-old children from each of three populations – monolingual English, Spanish and bL1 learners – and both their onset cluster and coda production in an elicitation task. Examine the table below, and describe which aspects of the bilinguals' syllable structure acquisition were delayed or accelerated compared to monolinguals (values for which means were significantly different between mono- and bilinguals are indicated in bold):

(7)		Mean accuracy (and SD) of syllable structure in English/Spanish bilinguals (Data from Keffala and Barlow, 2013, 2014)			
		English accuracy		*Spanish accuracy*	
		Monolinguals	*Bilinguals*	*Monolinguals*	*Bilinguals*
a)	Onset Clusters	**67%** (47%)	**79%** (41)	**40%** (49%)	**84%** (37%)
b)	Codas	**86%** (35%)	**67%** (47)	67% (47%)	78% (42%)

With respect to onset clusters, the bilingual children were reliably <u>better</u> at producing CC onsets in both of their languages than either group of monolingual learners. But with respect to retaining codas, bilinguals were reliably <u>worse</u> than English monolinguals, and statistically no different than Spanish monolinguals.[8] While only five children were included in each group, the data was carefully collected to include the same or similar targets for each child within a language, with a few hundred tokens each, so these patterns may well be reliable. If so, what do they tell us about delay and acceleration?

It cannot simply be that a large range of syllable structures in one language will generally lead to acceleration in bilingual phonological learning – for one thing, English's wide range of coda consonants does not appear to speed up the acquisition of codas for the bilinguals in (7b) at all, leaving them delayed compared to English monolinguals. One missing piece of these studies is the investigation of syllable accuracy rates as a function of shared <u>segmental</u> structure. To think about this for yourself:

Exercise: Suppose the English-Spanish bilinguals in (7) who show delayed English acquisition of codas are better at producing those coda segments which are also found in Spanish? What would this result suggest about delay and acceleration in the bilingual acquisition of syllable structure?

Here is another example, from Almeida, Rose and Freitas (2012). This longitudinal study reports the syllable structure development of Barbara, a child who was exposed to both European Portuguese and French from birth, but lived primarily in Lisbon in a Portuguese-speaking culture. The data below are representative of her onset cluster attempts at the earlier stages of cluster development; describe her production pattern before reading on:

(8)	Barbara's Portuguese/French onset cluster development at 2;4–2;9 (Data from Almeida, Rose and Freitas, 2012: 1–2)					
	French			*Portuguese*		
	Target	*Child*	*Gloss*	*Target*	*Child*	*Gloss*
	/glas/	[glas]	*ice cream*	/floɾ/	['floɐ]	*flower*
	/plɛ̃/	[plɛ̃]	*full*	/'plutu/	['plutu]	*Pluto*
	/bʀɥi/	[βi]	*noise*	/'livɾu/	['liβu]]	*book*
	/tʀɛ/	[tɛ]	*very*	/'gɾẽdɨ/	['gẽdɨ]	*big*

---

[8] Although it appears the bilinguals were actually more accurate than Spanish monolinguals, the variability among each population was too much for this to be significant.

The quick picture given in (8) is that Barbara appears to have acquired some obstruent-liquid clusters in both languages – /gl, pl, fl/ – but reduces some obstruent-rhotic ones, namely /bʁ, tʁ, vʁ, gʁ/. In addition to this order of /Cl/ clusters acquired before /C-rhotic/ ones (which the authors note is more typical of L1 French cluster development than Portuguese), you may recall from Chapter 3 that Portuguese onset cluster acquisition is notable for at least two repair types beyond deletion. Here is some Chapter 3 data to refresh your memory:

(9)		Monolingual cluster repairs in Portuguese (From Chapter 3 exs 24 and 54; data from Freitas, 2003)		
		Target	*Child*	*Age*	*Gloss*
	a)	/ˈgɾẽdɨ/	[ˈkɨ.ɾẽːdɨ]	Luis (2;5.27)	big
		/ˈpedɾɐ/	[ˈpedɨɾɐ]	Luis (2;5.27)	rock
		/ˈfɾaldɐ/	[ˈfɨɾawdɐ]	Luis (2;5.26)	diaper
	b)	/ˈgɾẽdɨ/	[ˈẽɲi]	J (2;2.28)	big
		/bisiˈklɛtɐ/	[pisiˈɛtɐ]	L (2;0.27)	bicycle
			[ˈɛtɐ]	J (2;4.30)	
		/ˈbɾuʃɐ/	[ˈũgɐ]	J (2;2.28)	witch

Unlike these monolingual Portuguese learners, Barbara showed no evidence of cluster repair via epenthesis (9a) or the typologically-surprising full cluster deletion (9b). Instead, she showed a fairly typical pattern for L1 French cluster acquisition – and at a rate faster than typical for Portuguese monolingual children. Recalling that her dominant language must have been Portuguese rather than French, this seems like a type of bilingual acceleration: faster cluster mastery than is typical, and without adopting Portuguese-specific cluster repairs.

Whatever the explanation for the variable rates of syllable structure acquisition reported here, there are a few key take-home messages to keep in mind. The first is that, on the whole, young children's bilingual phonology is not very different from monolingual phonology: some acquisition processes may be sped up or slowed down, but the broad strokes are similar.

The second point is that in addition to delay and acceleration, we must also include the third type of distinctive bilingual language development discussed in Paradis and Genesee (1996): that of *transfer*. For our purposes, transfer occurs when one language's phonological grammar (or some subset thereof) is used to map an input from the other language onto an output.

As with speed of acquisition, transfer can manifest itself in some initially surprising ways. One example comes from Tessier, Sorenson Duncan and Paradis (2013)'s study of child second language learners (cL2) at age five and six, which compared L1 Hindi/Punjabi and L1 Chinese children's acquisition of English onset clusters. These two L1 phonologies treat onset clusters differently: Chinese languages do not permit any onset consonant clusters, while Hindi and Punjabi phonologies tolerate a range of onset clusters, but also have registers in which such clusters undergo vowel epenthesis (see e.g. Ohala, 1983). Thus, only the L1 Hindi and Punjabi-speaking children have previous experience with clusters before they begin learning L2 English, but they also have a pre-existing repair for onset clusters. Given this background, what might you predict about these two groups' transfer of L1 phonological skills when learning L2 English?

The table in (10) provides onset cluster production data from ten children – five each from L1 Chinese and Hindi/Punjabi backgrounds – who had all been exposed to Canadian English for four to eight months. For each child, the graph shows the proportion of /CC/ clusters that were treated in three ways: (i) retained as a [CC] cluster, (ii) reduced to a singleton [C], or (iii) given an epenthetic vowel, either [vCC] or [CvC] (raw token numbers are given on each bar). What can you determine about the influence of L1 experience on these children's cluster production?

10) cL2 English onset cluster repairs by L1 Chinese (CH) and L1 Hindi/
Punjabi (HP) children
(Data from Tessier, Sorenson Duncan and Paradis, 2013)

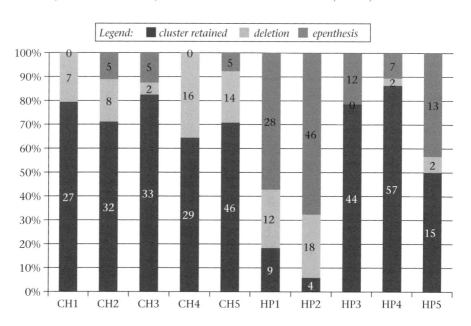

There are two clear differences between these two child L1 populations: their overall *accuracy*, and their most common choice of *repair*. With respect to repair type, the L1 Chinese learners' majority strategy is deletion, making these children look like monolingual English learners; meanwhile, the L1 Hindi/Punjabi children's common repair is vowel epenthesis, which is unsurprising given their first language experience. What is more surprising is the L1 effect on overall accuracy: L1 Chinese-speaking children's proportion of clusters retained faithfully as clusters ranged between 64–83% (mean: 73%), which was much less variable and on average rather <u>more faithful</u> than the L1 Hindi/Punjabi children, who ranged in cluster accuracy from 5–86% (mean: 46%).

Tessier, Sorenson Duncan and Paradis (2013) discuss this difference as a kind of transfer effect – but a surprising one, in that some L1 experience with this structure is <u>delaying</u> the cL2 acquisition of a related structure. Their suggestion is that L1 Hindi/Punjabi experience makes it harder for cL2 English learners to notice and acknowledge that their English cluster production is in fact errorful, whereas L1 Chinese learners are immediately aware that their second language is providing them with a novel, previously ungrammatical structure, from which they can learn quicker.

9.2.3   Acquisition of Word Shape by Bilinguals

Our first data set on the bilingual acquisition of wordshape and prosody comes from a longitudinal study of Spanish-German bilinguals, compared with monolinguals of the same age. In Chapter 4.2.1, we noted a study by Lléo (2002) in which L1 Spanish learners moved past the one-foot-only stage by first acquiring an additional unfooted syllable, that is allowing [w(Sw)][9] surface forms. The graph below charts the development of faithfulness to these unfooted syllables between ages 1;6 and 2;2 for two monolingual children (labelled as M-*name*) and two bL1 Spanish/German children (labelled as B-*name*):

(11) Proportion of faithfulness to unfooted Spanish syllables
       (Adapted from data in Lléo, 2002: tables 2–5)

It is clear from (11) that the monolingual Spanish children begin to produce unfooted syllables far earlier than their bilingual counterparts – particularly between 1;5–1;10 – but that by 2;2 the bilingual children have caught up. This accords with many other accounts, in that the delay in phonological development seen in bilinguals is overcome rather quickly. Indeed,

---

[9] Recall from chapter 4 that this notation indicates a 'weak-Strong-weak' pattern, with a stressed syllable flanked by two unstressed ones.

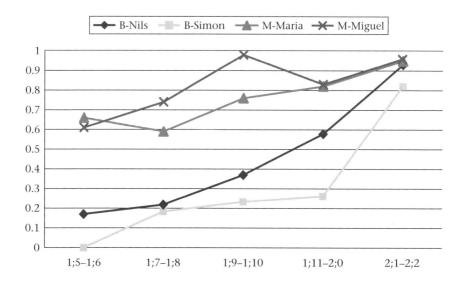

if either bilingual Nils or Simon had been monolingual <u>English</u> speakers, we would have thought their production rates of unfooted syllables at 2;2 to be quite precocious.

In the experimental literature, key evidence of cross-linguistic transfer in syllable truncation comes from Paradis (2001)'s study of English-French bilinguals. We saw some of this data in Chapter 4.1.6, where Quebec French monolingual children (ages 2;4–3;0) truncated novel words in a way that suggested their grammar preferred a single output iamb. However, that data was only one of three conditions in this study, which also included age-matched English monolinguals, and English/French bilinguals. The types of words they were given are illustrated in (12), with both French and English word stress patterns:

(12)	Sample nonce words from Paradis (2001) (**bold** items discussed below)			
	a) *French*		b) *English*	
	Target	*Stress pattern*	*Target*	*Stress pattern*
	/kotima'tœ/	wwwS	**/lə'pætɪˌmun/**	wSws
	/melapo'li/		/pə'tulfɪgə/	wSww
	/pelyma'tan/		/ˌtəm'beɪnɪtə/	sSww
	/ʀamɛli'noz/		**/ˌkoʊmi'gændə/**	swSw

As these children were three or younger, we would expect considerable truncation in most or all of these items. When producing the French items (12a), bilinguals did not look significantly different than French monolinguals:[10] preserving the last strong syllable most often (93%), the penultimate syllable next most often (60%) and the first and second syllables the least often, with no difference between them (32% and 24% respectively).

In the case of (12b)'s English items, however, there were some notable differences between bilinguals and English monolinguals. The table in (13) gives the average rate of syllable preservation for the two groups for the English /wSws/ items like /ləˈpætɪˌmun/. Compare their truncation patterns, and see if you can explain how bilinguals were different and where those differences might come from:

(13)

English <u>preservation</u> rates for monolinguals (M) vs. bilinguals (B) (Paradis, 2001: tables 4 and 5)								
	$\sigma 1$		$\sigma 2$		$\sigma 3$		$\sigma 4$	
Target	M	B	M	B	M	B	M	B
/wSws/	11%	11%	89%	55%	51%	47%	89%	87%

These /wSws/ words present an interesting case for English-French bilinguals, because their syllables could be parsed either into trochees or iambs. If treated with a French phonological grammar, the last two syllables should make a foot – (w_3S_4), probably with truncation of the first two syllables – but when fed into an English grammar the trochaic parse should preserve the second syllable, and perhaps two feet including both stressed syllables.

In (13), the monolingual English-learning children retained the two stressed syllables of /wS$_2$ws$_4$/ each 89% of the time, strongly suggesting they were building two feet. Since they retained the third weak (w_3) syllable 51% of the time, this suggests two different typical outcomes, as in (14a). On the other hand, bilinguals truncated these same words very differently: strikingly, they retained the second, main stress syllable only 55% of the time, not significantly more often than third syllable at 47%.[11] These numbers are aggregated across all 17 bilingual children, so we cannot know how often both or neither medial syllables were retained – nevertheless, these results suggest a couple of bilingual-specific parses, as in (14b).

---

[10] This lack of difference is statistically suggested by a two-way mixed ANOVA, with language group and syllable position as factors: $F(3,99)=1.548$, $p > 0.05$.

[11] Statistically speaking, a two-way mixed ANOVA found that monolinguals and bilinguals treated wSws words differently, and a post hoc Fisher test found that preservation rates of the second syllable (89% vs. 55%) were also reliably different.

(14) Hypothesized output patterns for /wSww/ words:
    a) English monolinguals: /wSws/ →   [(S)(s)]
                                 /wSws/ →   [(Sw)(s)]
    b) Additional parses for English/French bilinguals:
                                 /wSws/ →   [(w₃s₄)],
                                             [(w₂s₄)]

Now compare the two groups' treatment of /swSw/ words in (15) below. What distinguishes monolingual vs. bilingual truncation in these items?

(15)

English preservation rates for monolinguals (M) vs. bilinguals (B) (Paradis, 2001: tables 4 and 5)								
	σ1		σ2		σ3		σ4	
Target	M	B	M	B	M	B	M	B
/swSw/	39%	17%	11%	35%	85%	67%	81%	96%

The general results from the monolingual data are that the final two syllables were nearly always retained – suggesting a final (Sw) trochee – and that although the first two syllables were much less commonly preserved, the first syllable with secondary stress was reliably retained more often than the second, weak one (39% vs. 11%). Thus, the two likeliest truncation patterns for monolinguals are [(Sw)] and [(s)(Sw)]. On the other hand, the overall trend in the bilinguals' productions is most faithful to the final syllable (96%), second most faithful to the penultimate syllable (67%), and so on through the word. While it is perhaps not clear how this truncation profile correlates with output footing (especially without knowing whether e.g. bilinguals who retained the last two syllables also shifted stress to (wS) or not), it must be noted that this pattern looks distinctly like the treatment of <u>French</u> items discussed above and in Chapter 4.

In sum, Paradis (2001)'s elicitation study found evidence that English-French bilingual children showed transfer effects of their French phonological grammar when truncating 'English' words. With respect to those scare quotes: although these were all nonsense words, the bilinguals had at least two excellent reasons to treat these /wSww/ and /swSw/ words with their English phonologies. First, this session was conducted all in English, with their English-speaking parent in the room. Second, the items not only included English-specific segments and allophones, but also their target stress patterns were of course <u>ungrammatical in French.</u> This study therefore provides influential evidence of grammatical 'leakage' between a bilinguals' two systems of linguistic knowledge.

A perhaps more dramatic case of word shape transfer is reported in Brulard and Carr (2003)'s longitudinal study of a British English-European French bilingual learner, Tom. This child spent his first year in northern England, hearing French only at home from his parents, and his second year in France, hearing English only at home from his parents. With this background, you should be able to account for this child's early English words below:

(16)	Stress shift in a French/English bilingual: Tom at 1;8–2;3 (Data from Brulard and Carr, 2003)			
	Target	*Child*	*Target*	*Child*
	rabbit	[ba'bit]	*socket*	[kɔ'kɪt]
	jacket	[da'kit], [ka'kit]	*paper*	[pe'pəp]
	cooker	[ku'kut]	*potty*	[pɔ'ti], [pɔ'tit]

Unlike virtually every monolingual Ll English learner, Tom imposed an *iambic* stress pattern on his English output words, shifting stress from these targets word's first syllable to the last, reflecting the French grammatical pattern. This non-target output pattern was therefore a very clear example of transfer from his French to English phonologies.

A less dramatic example of bilingual stress transfer comes from Keshavarz and Ingram (2002)'s study of an English-Persian bilingual, whose earliest words (at 9–11 months) were in Persian, with target final stress: [ba'ba] *daddy*, [ma'ma] *mommy*, [dæ'dæ] *outside*. Up until age 1;3, the child's language input was deemed more Persian than English, and during this period he produced final stress in English too – though only on a few noted words: *teddy, baby, apple.* Thus this child's prosodic system was clearly more differentiated than the English-French one in (16) above, but some leakage still made its way through to the output.

9.2.4   Bilingual Acquisition of Segmental Phonology

This section now returns to lower-level phonological representations, in terms of segments and features, to consider if, how and why bilingual acquisition is distinct. A place to start is the development of inventories: the order in which natural classes and their contrasts are acquired, compared to monolinguals. Continuing with Keshavarz and Ingram (2002)'s study from the previous section: the table in (17) below presents this English-Persian learner's productive inventory of consonants at age 1;4, when he had reached a lexicon of about 50 words and thus had probably reached a stable early phonology. Recall what you learned in Chapter 5, and decide what aspects of this inventory seem typical or atypical for a monolingual English learner before reading on:

(17)	English-Persian bilingual's consonants at 50 word-stage (Keshavarz and Ingram, 2002: ex 4)					
	Word-initial			*Word-final*		
	Labial	*Coronal*	*Velar*	*Labial*	*Coronal*	*Velar*
	b, p	d	g, k		t	k
					s	
	m					
		l			l	
	w	j				

Some of this inventory looks English-typical: stops are the most common manner in both positions, labials are preferentially initial, and more segments are found in onsets (word-initially) than codas (word-finally). On the other hand, several things are not very common for an English learner: both [l] and [s] have been learned very early, but on the other hand [n] and initial [t] have not yet appeared. Overall the inventory is rather small, totalling 13 segments, whereas for example Ingram (1981) reports 18 segments that are usually acquired by the English 50 word stage. This data therefore give us a hint that consonantal acquisition can again be both delayed and accelerated through the interaction of multiple language inputs.[12]

In the well-studied case of English-Spanish bilinguals, there are several reports of an initial delay in inventory development. Gildersleeve-Neumann et al. (2008) report that their bL1 English-Spanish learners were slower to acquire English interdentals and affricates than monolinguals; Goldstein and Washington (2001)'s study of four-year-old bilinguals also found delays in the acquisition of Spanish fricatives, trills and taps compared to monolinguals.

---

[12] Definitively assessing the degree of transfer effects here would require comparably robust data set on the monolingual acquisition of Persian consonantal inventories, which is as yet not well documented.

To consider this kind of data for yourself, examine table (18) below, listing sounds missing from the inventory of seven English-Spanish bilinguals ages 3;4–3;11. This data was gathered by Fabiano-Smith and Goldstein (2010) using the phonology subtest of the Bilingual English Spanish Assessment (Peña et al., 2005), which includes 31 English and 28 Spanish target items – elicited using photographs of each item – designed to include the full inventory of each language. Come up with some generalizations about these as-yet unacquired sounds among three-year-old bilinguals. You may find it useful to first consider the similarities and differences between English and Spanish target languages, such as you know them. How different do you think this data would look if the speakers were monolinguals?

(18)		Missing sounds from three year old English-Spanish bilingual inventories (Data from Fabiano-Smith and Goldstein, 2010: table 5)			
	Child	*Spanish*		*English*	
		Produced once	*Never produced*	*Produced once*	*Never produced*
	B02		x, ð, ɣ	θ, ð, dʒ	
	B03	ɲ, β, ɣ	x, ð, r	θ, ð, dʒ, ŋ	
	B04	ɣ	r	z, dʒ	ð, v
	B05	ɲ	r		ð, v
	B06	x	ð, r	ʃ, dʒ	v
	B07	β	ð, r, ɾ	ʃ, dʒ	θ
	B08	ɲ, r		j	θ, z, ð

In both of these cases, the inventory gaps among bilinguals are in fact very similar to what we might expect from three-year-old English monolinguals: interdentals and other fricatives and affricates such as [θ, ð, dʒ, v, ʃ] were also missing from some L1 English control group children's inventories. Among the most common missing Spanish segments were the lenition fricatives [β, ð, ɣ] and the trill [r], both known to be late in Spanish monolingual acquisition. Thus, these bilingual children seem to be rather typical in their rate of consonant development compared to monolinguals; neither delayed nor accelerated.[13]

---

[13] Note though that these sounds that the bilinguals are missing also include a number of sounds which are found in only one of the two language's inventories. Teasing apart these two reasons for their slower acquisition requires different language comparisons; see exercise 2 at the end of the chapter.

Despite this relative equivalence, segmental repairs and processes do often show bilingual transfer effects during learning. One common case is the target Spanish process of stop *spirantization* – in which voiced stops become fricatives between vowels, for example *agua* [aɣwa] – which can also appear in bL1 learners' English words:

(19)

Spanish spirantization in English[14]	
Target	*Child*
water	[wæðɚ]
piggy	[pɪɣi]
doggie	[dɑɣi]

Intriguingly, Gildersleeve-Neumann et al. (2008) also report that the bilingual children in their study who applied Spanish spirantization in English also began to extend the use of the voiceless velar fricative [x] to English velar /k/ and other /g/s even outside of the intervocalic context, as in do**g**, roc**k**ing, bi**k**e and tur**k**ey. This might imply that these children had not just transferred a Spanish lenition process, but rather re-arranged their English phonemic inventory as well, and so temporarily acquired a type of *free variation* between velar stops and fricatives.

Another frequent segmental interaction is among English and Spanish rhotics: using the approximant [ɹ] in Spanish words, and conversely the Spanish trill [r] or tap [ɾ] in English words:[15]

(20)

bL1 English-Spanish rhotics (Data from Goldstein and Washington, 2001)			
	Target	*Bilingual Child*	
Spanish	/aˈros/	[aˈɹos]	*rice*
	/floɾ/	[floɹ]	*flower*
English	/tɹen/	[tren]	

---

[14] Data inferred from Gildersleeve-Neumann et al (2008: 321) and Amastae (1982); see also Fabiano-Smith and Barlow (2010).

[15] Also reported in Fabiano and Goldstein (2005); Fabiano-Smith and Barlow (2010) inter alia.

·

While this text has dealt very little with vowel acquisition, it should also be noted that many studies of bilingual phonology report transfer effects among vowels as well. This is probably not very surprising to anyone who has attempted to learn a second language, since vowel targets are notoriously difficult to achieve,[16] and indeed monolingual vowel development includes a lot of non-target productions until years after the 1;0–4;0 range we have been focused on. A memorable example, from a monolingual English-speaker's perspective, is Johnson and Lancaster (1998)'s report of an English-Norwegian bilingual child who produced a Norwegian <u>rounded</u> vowel in place of English front <u>unrounded</u> targets:

(21)

bL1 English-Norwegian vowel rounding (Data from Johnson and Lancaster, 1998)	
Target	*Child*
choo-choo	[tʃʏtʃɪu]
fish	[hyʃ]
baby	[bʏbi]
cheese	[dʏç]
grapes	[bʏp]

Another type of vowel transfer is reported for the English-Persian bilingual child in Keshavarz and Ingram (2002), illustrated in (22). At this age (1;4–1;8), English had become the dominant language in this child's input. Try describing the non-target pattern before reading on:

(22)

Persian words produced by English-Persian bilingual at 1;4–1;8 (Data from Keshavarz and Ingram, 2002: 265)					
Target	*Child*	*Gloss*	*Target*	*Child*	*Gloss*
/ba'la/	[bə'la]	*up*	/'ʔaemu/	['ʔaemə]	*uncle*
/mer'si/	[mə'si]	*thank you*	/bo'r:ow/	[bə'low]	*go*
	[kə'li]	*key*	/po' ru/	[pə'lʊ]	*cheeky*

---

[16] Here is a true, perhaps common, story recounted by a linguist who now passes for a native speaker of English. When learning L2 English as a young teenager, recently arrived in the United States, this L1 Russian speaker had difficulty assigning the vowels /i/ vs. /ɪ/ to English lexical items – thus, she attempted to request a *sheet* of paper in class, but instead requested something rather different. Having learned this lesson, she decided next time to use a different lexical item, but unfortunately tried instead to ask for a *piece* of paper.

As we saw in Chapter 4, Persian has nearly-regular final stress, and its vowel inventory contains no schwa-like element nor is there any vowel reduction. Thus, the pattern in (22) seems a direct transfer effect from English: full input vowels mapped to output schwas when unstressed, as in English. This is particularly notable since many monolingual English children take several years to master English vowel reduction patterns, generally articulating vowels more fully rather than reducing them.[17]

9.2.5   A Sidenote on Bilingual Lexical Development

Although our main focus is the acquisition of multiple phonological grammars, it is important to note that much research in the bilingualism literature has focused on the development of a bilingual's two lexicons. How quickly do bilinguals learn words? Are they delayed in lexical growth compared to monolinguals? Do they acquire words for the same objects in multiple languages from the beginning, or do they appear to build a unified lexicon before splitting their lexicon along language lines?

The short answer, to which we will not do justice here, is that while bilingual children often have smaller vocabularies in each language during their earliest lexical development, this delay is typically short lived and overcome fairly early, that is by the time they reach school age (for discussion see; for example Pearson et al., 1997, and references in Hoff, 2008).

It is also fairly clear that even the earliest bilingual vocabularies can contain two different languages' label for the same thing, aka 'translation equivalents'. In Vihman (1985)'s corpus study, a child learning English and Estonian was reported to have added his first translation equivalents within days of each other at 1;6 (for the word *hat*). In the monolingual literature on lexical and conceptual acquisition, it has been proposed that children initially decide how to connect the words they hear to the objects, properties and actions they observe (and eventually the concepts they know) by using shortcuts to meaning, and that one such heuristic assumes that their target language has no synonyms. Of course this can't be maintained indefinitely, or at least not in any broad sense, but at first it might help you narrow down your

---

[17] It has also been suggested that unstressed vowel reduction is in fact found more generally in the non-target speech of children regardless of their L1 experience – at least, Hochberg (1988) points out the pattern in the monolingual acquisition of Spanish, with a similar lack of vowel reduction. The limited data available here cannot choose between these two accounts.

options.[18] If a child hears the unfamiliar word '*octopus*' while looking at three objects at the aquarium, and the child already knows that two of them are called '*fish*' and '*whale*' respectively, a 'No Synonyms Until Proven Otherwise' principle would help them make an informed guess as to the meaning of *octopus*.[19] With this in mind, it seems that such a principle is not active in preventing young bilinguals from learning for example both *whale* and *baleine* (in French) or *wieloryb* (in Polish) or *livyatan* (in Hebrew). One way to understand this happy tolerance of rampant synonymy, of course, is to assume that they are already building two lexicons from the start, and that the principle should be more accurately described as 'No Synonyms In One Language Until Proven Otherwise'.

Returning to lexicon size, many researchers point out that it is in some sense unreasonable to measure a bilingual's lexicon in comparison to a monolingual's – precisely since many bilingual children do learn multiple names for the same object in multiple languages, meaning that their *total* vocabulary may be at or above age-based norms. At the same time, there are also many case studies that demonstrate a bilingual child acquiring words just as fast as a monolingual even in a single language. For example, Vihman (1985)'s English-Estonian bilingual learner had a productive vocabulary of 490 total words by 2;0, and of these about 34% were terms for the same in both languages. In this case we see clear evidence of two lexicons, and certainly no delay in vocabulary size compared to monolinguals even if we excluded the synonyms, as more than 400 words at 2;0 is well above average.

9.3   The Bilingual Learner and an OT Phonological Grammar

We have now built up a data sketch of some young children's multilingual phonological learning, seeing many commonalities but a few key differences between child monolingual L1, bL1 and cL2 acquisition. We have seen the distinctive effects of bilingualism on the rate at which phonological structures are learned, and the likelihood that knowledge of one phonology

---

[18] Even after learning the tens of thousands of English words you now know as an adult, and thus learning many pairs or groups of words with nearly-identical meanings, there is still a chance you operate under the influence of a No Synonyms-like principle. Among adults there can be considerable idiolectal variation as to what certain pairs of near-synonyms mean: with respect to women's hosiery, *tights* vs. *stockings* is a good example. One explanation for these multitudes of differences is that learners, when faced with multiple labels, will attempt to latch onto some property that permits a meaning distinction between the two terms, and that in the absence of any reliable distinguishing property in the real world, speakers will all invent different distinctions.
[19] For some discussion of this kind of principle in word learning, see Hoff (2008): chapter 5 and references therein.

will transfer to the other. But what can these results tell us about how grammatical knowledge is stored and manipulated in the mind? Before moving on, let us now try to imagine how delay, acceleration and transfer could be understood in OT learning terms.

As Chapter 10 will discuss in detail, the mechanism by which most OT learners are assumed to progress through stages of phonological development works from ambient language-specific evidence. Regardless of how frequency is incorporated into our model, we can also expect, (very) roughly speaking, that the more evidence you get, the more likely you will be to learn. However if the evidence gathered about Language A's structure (like the proportion of words with final codas) means that this structure's speed of acquisition is affected in Language B, this means that evidence must be <u>shared</u> in some way when learning both grammars. How should increased exposure to German CVC affect Spanish rankings of *CODA and MAX?

No well-established answers are provided in the literature. One option at least in the case of acceleration is that experience with errors on German words like /hais/ → *[hai] *hot* simply makes learners better at <u>noticing</u> their Spanish errors on similar structures like /pan/ → *[pæ] *bread*.[20] Another option would be to ascribe these changes in speed as the result of articulatory practice, which will be more or less frequent overall for a bilingual whose other language provides more or less opportunity, or perhaps more perceptual experience with lexical items containing the structure (on this latter point, recall from Chapter 7 that input frequency is usually the better predictor of children's order of acquisition than their own output attempts). One challenge to that view is that while some children show acceleration across languages, some simply show differential speed of acquisition like two monolinguals: recall the bilingual child S in Kehoe and Lléo (2003)'s data whose order of Spanish syllable structure was typical, with coda acquisition delayed. Nevertheless, this child's acquisition of German was monolingual-like as well, with German codas appearing at 1;8 but Spanish codas not until 1;10. In other words, something beyond raw amount of experience with a structure must be mediating their relative acquisition speeds among bilinguals.

How can the prosodic truncation transfer effects in Paradis (2001) be understood within an OT framework? Do they suggest that learners build two word-stress rankings, but sometimes choose the wrong one when producing an output? Note that it cannot simply be an error of feeding for example an English word into the French full phonology, as this would predict that the consonants and vowels of English nonce words in (12) which were truncated to (wS) should also have contained French segments such as initial unaspirated voiceless stops, and no such outputs were reported. What it might suggest instead is that though the bilingual children have built two different phonologies, their English grammar is somewhat less well-defined in its foot structure (and consequent truncation) than

---

[20] Both errors from monolinguals in Keheo and Lléo (2003).

a monolingual's English grammar would be. All English learners are exposed to a variety of word-stress patterns, though with a large frequency skew towards trochees – but these bL1 learners are also exposed to a very consistent iambic pattern in French, and perhaps this <u>consistency</u> in one ranking can influence the other, more <u>variable</u> system. In Section 10.3, we will consider how a *stochastic* OT learner (to be defined in that chapter) could be used to model variability between multiple rankings during learning; this might be the mechanism for implementing quantitative differences in variation between monolingual and bL1 learners.

On the other hand, the Bruland and Carr (2003) data from (16) really does suggest that this child had acquired the same stress ranking in both French and English, whereby IAMB >> TROCHEE, STRESS-FAITH, and so English /Sw/ mapped to [(wS)]. Bruland and Carr (2003) also observe that Tom overcame his English iambic stress pattern in a singular way. On 2;3.20, he produced ten new English words, all correctly as trochees, and one known word *paper,* which he had previously made iambic but now corrected. From then on, he did not produce incorrect iambs in English, including on his previously-learned English words – and neither did he begin to produce French words with ungrammatical trochaic stress. Taken together, this emphasizes first that his English and French lexicons had been distinct, and that secondly it had been his phonological <u>grammar</u> which had previously imposed iambic stress on English words, and which was later re-organized to better approximate the English trochaic system.

In the <u>adult</u> L2 phonological literature, there has been considerable discussion of how grammatical change takes place when transferring from a well-established first language phonology to a new one. One consistent notion has been the potential for *interlanguage phonology* – production patterns which represent neither the L1 nor the L2 targets but rather something intermediate; perhaps as an attempt to better approximate the L2 without making it all the way (see e.g. contributions to Major, 1988). The OT context is very suitable to describing and understanding such interlanguage phonologies, if learning is construed as the re-ranking of many constraints – re-ranking some but not all constraints will cause grammars that resolve structural and faithfulness pressures in a novel way, in between initial (L1) and final (L2) states (see especially Broselow, 2004). With child bilingual acquisition, however, it is much harder to tell whether a non-target pattern might be an interlanguage, or a stage along the regular developmental path – more research into true child L2 phonology will perhaps reveal the extent to which child interlanguage phonology is a helpful construct in understanding their development.

9.4   Further Reading

Meisel, J.M. (2009), Second language acquisition in early childhood. *Zeitschrift für Sprachwissenschaft* 28 (1), 5–34.

Tucker, G.R. (1998). A global perspective on multilingualism and multilingual education. In. J. Cenoz and F. Genesee (eds.), *Beyond Bilingualism: Multilingualism and Multilingual Education.* Clevedon: Multilingual Matters. 3–15.

Exercises

Q1: *When comparing rates of acquisition in some phonological domain, is it appropriate to match monolingual and bilingual children of the same <u>age</u>, or is there some other criteria we could use?* Some studies compare children not of the same chronological age, but with the same vocabulary size in one language, or with the same *MLU* (mean length of utterance, see e.g. Rice et al., 2010.) *Which of these criteria do you think is most appropriate or informative? Does it matter what phonological domain is being studied?*

Q2: Table 18 provided a list of segments missing from a group of English/ Spanish bilingual children's inventories; unsurprisingly most of them were segments which might be expected to be acquired late by monolinguals in each language. However, footnote 12 also noted that these segments also included those found only in one of the two languages, such as the Spanish velar fricatives and the English voiceless interdental. *Could you design a study to tease apart these two factors? The experimental question would be whether or not bilinguals are more likely to acquire a segment later if it is found in only one of their two languages, but factoring out monolingual order of acquisition?* (As this question is a thought experiment, you can try answering it by inventing a language with a phonemic inventory not found in any documented language.)

Q3: Way back in Chapter 2.4 we learnt about monolingual children's ability to learn novel sound-meaning mappings (i.e. words). At 14 months, infants are just acquiring the ability to quickly associate novel words with objects, and they are reliably able to do so if the words are phonologically dissimilar, such as *lif* and *neem. But now – what about bilingual babies? Do you think their performance should be different from that of monolinguals? If so why so; if not why not?* Once you have hypothesized for yourself, see Byers-Heinlein, Fennell and Werker (2013), who tested 14-month-old infants from a wide range of bilingual backgrounds on the *lif/neem* contrast … *Were you right? And what do their results tell us?*

10 Some OT Theories of Phonological Learning

10.1 Framing the OT Learning Problem

This textbook has focused primarily on two goals: describing the observable stages that children go through when learning phonology, and attempting to capture as many of those stages as possible using a constraint-based grammar. What we have left until this last chapter is the actual business of learning – that is, how might a child move from one grammar of ranked constraints to another?

We will frame the learning problem as composed of three interlocking parts:

A. an *initial state* at which all learners begin;
B. a set of *learning data*, the nature of which must be determined; and
C. an *algorithm* by which the learner uses B to progress from A to an *end-state*.

Each of these parts requires a certain amount of conceptual work to be defined; once we have defined them we will try relating them to all the child data we have been studying.

By now the reader will not be surprised that our initial and end-states will consist of constraint rankings: that is, we will take a set of pre-existing constraints at the initial state, and try to explain how learners can move from there through a series of different rankings to the end-state. Of course, this leaves out many other crucial learning questions – perhaps the two biggest are (i) how the learner gets from auditory input to the phonological representations of inputs and outputs that rankings can operate on (cf. Chapter 2), and (ii) how the learner comes to have their constraints in the first place. These topics could fill several other chapters on their own (the further readings section will get you started). However, we will crucially assume that all learners have the same set of basic constraints, at least by the time that they begin building real phonologies.[1]

The *initial state* is the common constraint ranking where every learner begins. We have seen much evidence throughout this text that learners share

---

[1] That is: we will remain agnostic as to what extent those constraints are induced from an infant's experience prior to the onset of phonology, or in some way innately endowed.

many of the same learning stages despite large differences in their target languages, and it is well-established that typically-developing children can learn any natural language to which they are exposed natively, with no regard to their genetic background, so in one basic sense all learners must come to the task from a universal initial state. Again, though, this view of an initial state sets aside some crucial learning questions: the biggest being in the domain of perception, since we know that infants learn a lot of language-specific detail before their productive phonology begins. However, our narrow focus will be on the ranking of phonological constraints which affect output production – and we will continue to assume that by the time productive phonology is being acquired, perceptual learning is complete and perception is fully accurate (though we know there are exceptions, as in Chapter 6.4.)

The final concept to be defined is the *learning data* – what form of evidence do learners use to inform their grammatical development? You may already be familiar with the terms *positive* and *negative evidence* to describe two kinds of potential learning data, but how should these terms apply to a phonological learner? Let's suppose a child hears her father say the word '*ducks*'. She too wishes to discuss ducks, so she repeats the word, which her current grammar produces as [gʌk]. What kind(s) of evidence about English phonology could in principle be extracted from these two speech events? ... Try formulating some possible answers to this question before reading on.

***

The first event, the father's utterance, provides a wide range of potential data points for the learner, by demonstrating that the target phonology allows [dʌks] as an output, and so all of [dʌks]' phonological properties must be optimal (given some input). In other words: hearing [dʌks] gives the learner the *positive evidence* that [dʌks] is a well-formed string of the target language.

But how will this evidence be analysed or used? To a highly conservative observer, it reveals for example that English phonology allows words which consist of an initial voiced alveolar stop, followed by a central low unrounded vowel, followed by a voiceless velar stop, and a final voiceless alveolar fricative. Depending on the learner's willingness to generalize, it might also tell the learner some or all of the following things:

(1)

Potential learning from [dʌks]	
{Words, syllables} can ...	{Words, syllables} can ...
... begin with [d]	... end with [ks]
... begin with an alveolar stop	... end with a velar followed by an alveolar

Continued

{Words, syllables} can ...	{Words, syllables} can ...
... begin with an alveolar	... end with a stop followed by a fricative
... begin with a voiced stop	... end with two voiceless obstruents
... begin with an obstruent	... end with two obstruents
... begin with a single onset	... end with a complex coda
[d] can be followed by [ʌ]	Syllables can be CVCC
a voiced stop can be followed by a low vowel	Words can contain a single CVCC syllable
an alveolar stop can be followed by a back vowel	Words can contain a single syllable

In looking over this list, you will see that some of these generalizations from *ducks* are warranted, but some of them go too far. English words can end in [ks], but not in just any stop+fricative *[kf], and certainly not just any two obstruents, *[pv], *[gʃ], *[zb] and so on. And English words can certainly begin with any alveolar that we have in our inventory, but not every possible alveolar – no alveolar clicks, for instance. In addition, you might have the intuition that some of these generalizations are more helpful than others: for instance, learning from *ducks* that 'syllables can begin with a single onset' is probably not much of an achievement, since in Chapter 3 we established that all known human languages allow singleton onsets.

The second event, the child's own attempt at *ducks*, can also in principle provide evidence to learn from. It shows the learner one difference between their current grammar and the target: namely that the former maps /dʌks/ → [gʌk] and the latter doesn't. To get more specific evidence from this event, suppose we grant the learner the assumption that the father produced the output [dʌks] because his input for this lexical item was also /dʌks/. This will give the learner the following more precise information:

(2) Potential learning from [gʌk]:
   /dʌks/ → [dʌks] is more optimal in the target language than /dʌks/ → *[gʌk]

As we saw in (1), of course, there could be many, many reasons that [dʌks] is preferred to [gʌk], differing in their degree of generalization from this single event. For example:

(3)

Potential learning from [dʌks] → [dʌks], *[gʌk]	
{Words, syllables} cannot …	onset /d/ cannot map to [g]
… begin with a [g]	alveolar stops cannot become velar
… end with a [k]	alveolar stops cannot change place
… begin with a [g] if there is a [d] available	
… end with a [k] if there is an [s] available	[s] cannot be deleted
… contain two stops at the same place	coda fricatives cannot be deleted
… be CVC	word-final segments cannot be deleted

Notice how these facts have already been arranged into two columns: the left side containing structural descriptions of what might make [gʌk] worse than [dʌks] on their own terms, and the right side describing dimensions of faithfulness violated when turning /dʌks/ into [gʌk] that might be ungrammatical.

Another way to describe this evidence is in terms of an OT tableau. From this event, the learner knows that if the input /dʌks/ is fed to the target grammar, the output candidate [dʌks] will beat out every possible output candidate – including [gʌk] but also everything else! In a way, then, this event (coupled with the assumed input) in fact gives an OT learner an *infinite* number of data points: because /dʌks/→ [dʌks] is optimal compared to /dʌks/→ [gʌk], [dʌk], [dʌ], [gʌs], [dʌkɨs] … and so on.

Do all of the descriptions in (2) and (3) constitute positive or negative evidence? … It's a little hard to say. The term *negative evidence* was originally used to describe an explicit learning scenario in which father says to child, for example, '*No, the English pronunciation of* ducks *can't be* guck! *You have to say the coronal stop and obstruent cluster,* ducks!' … And such exchanges appear to be both infrequent and uninteresting to most children.[2] But negative

---

[2] On the former point, parents may well respond to a child's exclamation of '*Guck!'* with '*Yes! I KNOW you love ducks!'* or else '*No, honey, that one's a chicken,'* which proves them a rather unreliable source of praise or correction as regards phonology. On the latter point, many anecdotes demonstrate that young children appear quite happy to ignore all attempts to correct their production errors. However, there is some debate about whether subtle aspects of adults' responses to child errors (syntactic, morphological, but also phonological) do provide useful negative evidence, and whether children attend to it: compare with Brown and Hanlon (1970), Hirsh-Pacek, Treiman and Schneiderman (1984) and Bohannon and Stanowicz (1988). Even if children can take advantage of adult feedback in detecting their own errors, it remains the case that children cannot rely on such feedback in all circumstances, or for all errors.

evidence might also be defined as any evidence of what is <u>not</u> grammatical in the learner's language – and in some sense, the OT architecture does provide that data to the learner for free.

With all this in mind, our OT learner will build their learning data from pairs of events like *ducks ~ guck*: an observed output produced by a reliable speaker of the target language, paired with the learner's current grammar's attempt to reproduce that form when taken as input, as in (4). We will use the term *error* to refer to this pair of events in a technical sense:

(4a) Observed: [dʌks]

(4b)

/dʌks/	AGREE[PLACE]	*COMPLEXCODA	IDENT[COR]	MAX-C
dʌks	*!*	*!		
gʌkx		*!	**	
dʌk	*!			*
☞ gʌk			*	*

Notice that the input to this tableau is the single morpheme /dʌks/, with no recognition that the English word *ducks* contains a plural affix. To keep things simple(r) this chapter will return to the earlier stages of Chapters 3 through 5, when the learner knows nothing of morphological structure or alternations, and so treats every input as an unanalyzed whole (but see further readings.)

Within this OT framework, (4b)'s tableau has probably already made clear how we will extract evidence from errors. The list of all possible generalizations like those in (1) and (3) are filtered through the *constraint set*; all of the positive and negative facts that the learner gleans from an error are found in comparing violation profiles.

We used these comparisons already in Chapter 4 when reasoning about rankings, but we will re-introduce the concepts here since Chapter 4 was a long time ago. The crucial comparisons will always be between two forms: the final state grammar's optimum, here [dʌks], which we will call the *intended winner*, and the current grammar's optimum, here [gʌk], which we will call the *intended loser*. The tableau below compares just these two forms:

(4c)

	/dʌks/	AGREE [PLACE]	*COMPLEX CODA	IDENT [COR]	MAX-C
Intended winner	dʌks	*!	*!		
☞ **Intended loser**	gʌk			*	*

Examining (4c) with just these four constraints, it is fairly easy to see the difference in these candidates's violations; [dʌks] violates the two higher-ranked structural constraints, and [gʌk] violates the two lower-ranked faithfulness constraints. Another way to describe these differences is in terms of the relative *preference* for intended winners or losers that each constraint expresses. AGREE[PLACE] assigns a violation to the intended winner but not loser, so when given the chance to make a decision between these two forms it prefers the intended loser [gʌk]. *COMPLEXCODA also prefers the loser, whereas IDENT and MAX assign violations to that form, so they prefer the intended winner.

In most of the OT learning literature, this terminology for keeping track of these preferences drops the term 'intended,' and thus describes comparisons like (4c) in terms of *winners* and *losers*, abbreviated to W and L. This all boils down to the representation in (5) – a format with various names including a *comparative tableau* (Prince, 2000) – in which W means winner-preferring constraints and L means loser-preferring ones:[3]

(5)	Input	Winner ~ Loser	AGREE[PLACE]	*COMPLEXCODA	IDENT[COR]	MAX-C
	/dʌks/	dʌks ~ gʌk	L	L	W	W

To summarize the story thus far: the learning problem as we have described it is to find a universal initial state constraint ranking and a re-ranking algorithm that together will let a learner re-organize their grammar so as to eventually reach any language's final state ranking, using only their own errors on observed outputs as in (5). ... If you read that again and it makes sense, you are ready to move on.

We will assess our choice of initial states and re-ranking algorithms via two types of results. First, there is the question of end-state success: some combinations of initial state and ranking algorithm will make some languages unlearnable, that is their target ranking will never be reached. To the extent that such languages exist in natural language, we want to build a learner that can learn them![4] Second, we will also consider the trajectory that the learner

---

[3] A crucial point: for this error to be useful to the learner, they must have some access to its component parts, meaning they must 'know' at a certain level both what the observed winner sounds like, and what their own production is like.

[4] Some work takes a somewhat converse track – suggesting that certain classes of languages don't exist precisely because the learning algorithm can't learn them. In a broader sense, that is in fact precisely what we're doing by filtering everything through the constraints – if you don't have a constraint, you can't notice a pattern! See especially Becker, Ketrez and Nevins (2011).

takes along the way to the end-state: different combinations make different predictions about the learner's intermediate rankings over the course of learning. With the kind of cross-linguistic acquisition data we have collected throughout this text, we can compare these algorithmic predictions with empirical evidence.

Before going any further down this rhetorical path, it should be pointed out that this chapter's attempts to use a re-ranking algorithm as defined below (5) to discuss the actual observable development of children is not necessarily a commonplace approach. Prince and Tesar (2004) in fact draw an explicit separation between the language learnability problem of restrictiveness on the one hand, and the early unfaithful child productions which eventually become more faithful on the other. For some literature that attempts to draw connections like this chapter does, however, see the further reading section.

A final caveat: this learning process is focused purely on static phonological knowledge, that is on learning simply to distinguish between possible and impossible surface strings of the target language. What we are not learning is anything about alternations, or how individual inputs are mapped unfaithfully to those surface strings. With this narrow focus, our learner will merely be attempting to reproduce the output forms they hear with their own grammar – so, they will be using the target ambient <u>outputs</u> as their own <u>inputs</u>. The questions of how rankings and underlying forms are revised once allomorphs are discovered and the learner sees that some outputs must not be identical to their inputs are even more challenging than the ones we will try to answer here (but see the further readings section).

10.2   Building an OT Error-driven Learner

10.2.1   The Logic of Re-ranking

The core of this chapter's error-driven learning is the algorithm that takes comparative tableaus like (5) and uses them to change rankings. In fact, this has been part of the OT project from the beginning: the theory's founding document (Prince and Smolensky, 1993: 148) already provides a characterization of how to ensure that a particular winner candidate beats out any particular loser. As rephrased in Prince and Tesar (2004), it says the following:

(6)   *Cancellation/Domination Lemma* (adapted)
    If *every* L-preferring constraint is ranked below *some* W-preferring
    constraint, our grammar will prefer the Winner to the Loser.

                                                    Prince and Tesar (2004: 255)

So in order to build a ranking which prefers a winner over its loser, we will need an algorithm that re-ranks constraints to make (6) true – and the more errors we accumulate, the more re-rankings will be necessary.

As it turns out, this lemma is *necessary* to the success of our ranking algorithm, but it is definitely not sufficient. But first let's see it in action, by using it to resolve the *ducks ~ guck* error from (5), repeated below. Can you re-word (6) requirements using these four constraint names? Try to do so before reading on; using partial rankings plus 'and/or's is probably safest.

(5)	*Input*	*Winner ~ Loser*	AGREE[PLACE]	*COMPLEXCODA	IDENT[COR]	MAX-C
	/dʌks/	dʌks ~ gʌk	L	L	W	W

★★★

Here is what (6) tells us will resolve (5):

(7) *Resolving (5) via the C/D Lemma*
    a) IDENT[COR] >> AGREE[PLACE] OR MAX-C >> AGREE[PLACE]
       AND
    b) IDENT[COR] >> *COMPLEXCODA OR MAX-C >> *COMPLEXCODA

While (7) tells us everything crucial about building a grammar that will prefer mapping *ducks* to itself and not *guck*, it certainly does not give a *total ordering* of the constraints. Here are just four of the total orderings compatible with (7); in each case the **bold** constraint is the crucial W-preferring constraint, and the underlined constraints are the dominated L-preferring ones.

(8) **IDENT[COR]** >> AGREE[PLACE] >> MAX-C >> *COMPLEXCODA
    IDENT[COR] >> *COMPLEXCODA >> AGREE[PLACE] >> MAX-C
    MAX-C >> *COMPLEXCODA >> AGREE[PLACE] >> IDENT[COR]
    MAX-C >> IDENT[COR] >> *COMPLEXCODA >> AGREE[PLACE]

In fact: out of the 4! = 24 possible total rankings of these four constraints, 12 of them – fully half – are compatible with the requirements in (7)! So long as one of the two faithfulness constraints is highest ranked, the three remaining constraints can be in any order below.

So does the choice between these 12 rankings matter? Yes! Because while they all resolve the *ducks~guck* error equally well, they make vastly different predictions about the grammar's treatment of many other words the learner has yet to see. To see this: let's see where we start. (We will get back to this *ducks* dilemma in exercise 1 at the end of the chapter.)

10.2.2 Choosing an Initial State

To begin using the C/D Lemma in learning we need an initial ranking, from which the learner will start making errors, and there are at least two ways we can investigate this initial state. The first is to consider the *learnability* implications of any class of initial states: working out from first principles whether certain initial rankings will block the learner from acquiring certain languages. The second is to look at the earliest production data that we have from children, and see whether hints of this initial state emerge, independent of language-specific influences. Happily, as we will see in a minute, both kinds of evidence converge on the same result.

Let's take the learnability argument first, which we will illustrate by comparing two different rankings of same three constraints in (9). Suppose these two rankings are candidates for the initial state grammar. What kind of errors will they cause?

(9) *Two possible initial states?*
   a)   *PHARYNGEAL >> *CODA >> MAX
   b)   *CODA >> MAX >> *PHARYNGEAL

If the learner is being exposed to English, both grammars in (6) will make errors like the one in (10):

(10)

		/dɑg/	*PHARYNGEAL	*CODA	MAX
a)	☞	dɑg		*!	
		dɑ			*

	/dɑg/	*CODA	MAX	*PHARYNGEAL
b)	dɑg	*!		
	☞ da		*	

(11) Comparative tableau for the errors in (10)

Input	Winner ~ Loser	*PHARYNGEAL	*CODA	MAX
/dɑg/	dɑg ~ da	e	L	W

(Note: In this comparative tableau, 'e' indicates that this constraints prefers the two candidates <u>equally</u> – it assigns them the same number of violations, in this case none.)

With respect to *dog*, (10a) and (10b) have the same effect: since both rank *CODA >> MAX, the grammar maps /dag/ → [da], which the learner will boil down to the comparative tableau in (11). In general: if the error-driven learner is acquiring a language with codas, errors like in (10–11) will demonstrate that the ranking *CODA >> MAX is not in the target language. On the other hand, if the language does *not* contain codas, then errors like (10–11) will never be made, and the initial state ranking of *CODA >> MAX will never be disturbed. Thus this initial state ranking will allow the learner to reach *either* target ranking of *CODA and MAX – either the initial state will be undisturbed, or the learner will make errors that cause their ranking to be flipped.

Looking beyond *dog*, however, the two rankings in (9) do have different consequences as an initial state – because of their relative ranking of *PHARYNGEAL and MAX. What errors can these two orders cause the learner to make?

If the learner is being exposed to for example Arabic, the ranking in (9a) will cause errors like (12a): target pharyngeals will be deleted, and so the learner will see in (13) that *PHARYNGEAL and MAX must be re-ranked. The ranking in (9b) though will *not* cause any errors – pharyngeal segments will be faithfully preserved from the beginning, and no comparative tableau will be built:

(12)		/ħala:/ 'dessert'	*PHARYNGEAL	*CODA	MAX
a)		ħa.la:	*!		
	☞	a.la:			*
b)		/ħala:/	*CODA	MAX	*PHARYNGEAL
	☞	ħa.la:			*
		a.la:		*!	

(13) Comparative tableau for the error in (12a) *only*

Input	Winner ~ Loser	*PHARYNGEAL	*CODA	MAX
/ħala:/	ħa.la: ~ a.la:	L	e	W

But what if you are learning English? Since English contains no [ħ], and indeed <u>no pharyngeals</u>, the English learner will never make any errors like (13). If the initial state is (12a), that's not a problem: the ranking *PHARYNGEAL >> MAX will stay undisturbed in the English learner's grammar until the day when, say, they attempt to parse an Arabic word with a pharyngeal, or borrow an Arabic word into English, and this ranking will assert that the pharyngeal must be deleted.[5] But if the initial state is (12b), this ranking too will stay undisturbed; this English learner's end-state grammar will encode the knowledge that pharyngeal consonants should be *faithfully preserved*. From this learner's perspective, it will be a pure accident that English contains no words with pharyngeal consonants, as the phonology happily tolerates them. … And this characterization is at odds with the intuitions of native adult English speakers, who are well aware that pharyngeal consonants do not form part of their phonological inventories, and will borrow and parse input pharyngeals via some type of repair.

The upshot of this section's learnability analysis is that (9b) is not the right initial state ranking for our error-driven learner. While its ranking of *CODA >> MAX is safe regardless of the status of codas in the target, its ranking MAX >> *PHARYNGEAL is dangerous, because if the target does not contain pharyngeals no errors will be made to reverse it. Taking a step back, we can observe that the crucial rankings in these potential initial states are between structural and faithfulness constraints. In the safe ranking (9a) both *PHARYNGEAL and *CODA rank above MAX; and more broadly this initial state restriction generalizes as follows:

(14) *A first pass at the initial state*
     {Structural Constraints} >> {Faithfulness Constraints}

With respect to any pair of S and F constraints, the ranking S >> F can be described as more *restrictive*, in that the grammar <u>restricts</u> its possible outputs to those which do not violate the structural constraint S. The {all S} >> {all F} initial state is our first way to impose maximal restrictiveness (see especially Smolensky, 1996).

As for empirical evidence of the initial state? By now in this textbook, you have seen ample data to suggest that children's earliest phonologies rank structural constraints above faithfulness, resulting in the simplification and reduction of all levels of phonological structure. Thus the observable facts in production are clearly in line with the learnability results spelled out above: {S} >> {F}.

10.2.3 Restrictiveness and the Re-ranking Algorithm

And now, to finally learn. From the initial state in (15), the learner makes a coda deletion error on *dog*, creates the comparative tableau in (16b), and will then use the C/D Lemma to re-rank:

---

[5] Or, as we saw in Chapter 5, it might undergo some other featural repair like /ħ/ → [h], meaning that MAX in turn outranks another constraint like IDENT[PHAR] beneath it.

(15) *Initial state grammar*
     {*PHARYNGEAL, *CODA} >> MAX

(16a)

/dɑg/	*PHARYNGEAL	*CODA	MAX
dɑg		*!	
☞ dɑ			*

(16b)

Input	Winner ~ Loser	*PHARYNGEAL	*CODA	MAX
/dɑg/	dɑg ~ dɑ	e	L	W

When learning, we will use the term *error archive* to refer to a set of one or more comparative tableaus like (16b) – this will be the official set of data from which we learn. To resolve this particular error in the archive, we know that the W-preferring constraint must be ranked above the L-preferring one – but this allows for any one of the grammars in (17). Which should we choose?

(17) *Five ways to resolve (16)*
     MAX >> *CODA >> PHARYNGEAL
     MAX >> *PHARYNGEAL >> *CODA
     *PHARYNGEAL >> MAX >> *CODA
     MAX >> {*CODA, PHARYNGEAL}
     {*PHARYNGEAL, MAX} >> *CODA

As with the initial state, the deciding factor will be restrictiveness. The error in (16) provides evidence about the relative ranking of L and W-preferring *CODA and MAX (namely that MAX >> *CODA), but nothing about the target's attitude towards *PHARYNGEAL. In the absence of such evidence, the maximally-restrictive learner will continue to impose the initial state's {S} >> {F} ranking – namely, *PHARYNGEAL >> MAX. Thus, we can par down our learning goal:

(18) *The maximally-restrictive way to resolve (16)*
     *PHARYNGEAL >> MAX >> *CODA

Now we will walk through an algorithm that resolves errors and imposes restrictiveness, so that (16) will move the learner from the initial state to the new grammar in (18). The algorithm takes a set of comparative tableaus, and a set of constraints, and builds a new ranking from the top stratum down. To build each stratum, the algorithm follows a series of steps until one or more constraints can be installed. (This approach is based very closely on Prince and Tesar, 2004; Hayes, 2004).

Here is the first step:

(19a)   *Building Stratum One:*
         Step One: Install all Structural Constraints *which prefer no Losers*

What is the point of this step? Well, looking at (16) we see that it means the first stratum of our new grammar will contain one structural constraint:

(19b)   *After building Stratum One*:
         *PHARYNGEAL >> ....

This first step ensures that any structural constraints that have not been implicated in any errors stay high-ranking – staying in their initial state position at the top.

After each stratum is built, the algorithm examines the error archive, and checks whether any errors have now been resolved. But since installing *PHARYNGEAL assigns only an e in (16), nothing has been resolved, and so we move on. Since the archive hasn't changed, Step One will have nothing to do, so we will move on to Step Two:

(20a)   *Building Stratum Two:*
         Step One: Install all Structural Constraints *which prefer no Losers*,
                      unless there are none, in which case:
         Step Two: Install one Faithfulness Constraint *which prefers the most Winners*

Notice that this step installs only *one* F constraint, whereas the first step installed as *many* S constraints as possible. In the case of (16), however, we have only one faith constraint that assigns a W (in fact, only one in total), and so we install it:

(20b)   *After building Stratum Two:*
         *PHARYNGEAL >> MAX ...

Now when we check the archive, we find that our error on *dog* <u>is</u> in fact resolved: now that W-prefering MAX is installed, all remaining L-preferring constraints will have to be ranked below it, so the C/D Lemma tells us it is fixed. As such, the algorithm crosses off that error from consideration – all further constraints can be installed without reference to its violations. In (21), the constraints already installed are greyed out, which will be useful in more complicated examples to come:

(21)	Input	Winner ~ Loser	*PHARYNGEAL	*CODA	MAX
	/dɑg/	dɑg ~ dɑ	e	L	W

In this simple example, this means that *no* errors are left, and so the algorithm can fall back on its bias for being restrictive, namely Step One:

(22a)   *Building Stratum Three*
        Step One: Install all Structural Constraints *which prefer no Losers*

Since there are no errors left in the archive, there are no Ls left, so all remaining markedness constraints prefer no losers! Here:

(22b)   *After building Stratum Three:*
        *PHARYNGEAL >> MAX >> *CODA

Now that all constraints have been installed, the algorithm terminates, and a new (restrictive!) ranking has been learned.

With their new grammar, the learner is now ready to start making new errors! In the case of *dog*, with our mini three-constraint set, there are no more errors to make, so learning is in fact complete. But of course the real constraint set is much, much bigger and there are many more things to learn – so let us now examine a different set of constraints and the kinds of errors they make, as in (23):

(23)	/ɹʌg/	*PHARYNGEAL	*RHOTIC	IDENT[+/-CONS]
	ɹʌg		*!	
☞	wʌg			*

(Notice that now since MAX >> *CODA, we are not entertaining coda-less candidates like *[wʌ], but keep reading.)

Having made this error on *rug*, the learner will add this comparative tableau to the archive. Note that we have expanded our comparative tableau to include all five constraints now, and so added the e-preference for the two new constraints with respect to the *dog* error:

(24)	Input	Winner ~ Loser	*PHARYNGEAL	*CODA	MAX	*RHOTIC	IDENT [+/-CONS]
	/dɑg/	dɑg ~ dɑ	e	L	W	e	e
	/ɹʌg/	ɹʌg ~ wʌg	e	e	e	L	W

Let's now learn again, applying the same steps from the previous learning cycle to see where we end up. Beginning at the beginning:

(25a) *Building Stratum One*
       Step One: Install all Structural Constraints *which prefer no Losers*

(25b) *After building Stratum One:*
       *PHARYNGEAL >> ...

No errors in (24) are resolved by ruling out pharyngeals, so we build stratum two:

(26a) *Building Stratum Two*
       Step One: Install all Structural Constraints *which prefer no Losers,*
                   unless there are none, in which case:
       Step Two: Install one Faithfulness Constraint *which prefers the most*
                   Winners

Here we have a novel bit of indeterminacy. In (24) there are two faithfulness constraints, and they each prefer one winner. So which one does Step Two prefer? ... Here we will say that in fact it's a toss-up; just one of them needs to be installed. Not both! But which one doesn't matter. Suppose we choose [IDENT[+/-CONS]; then we will proceed like this:

(26b) *After building Stratum Two:*
       *PHARYNGEAL >> IDENT[+/-CONS]

By installing this W-preferring faithfulness constraint, the learner has resolved one of their two errors – so the archive is annotated to reflect that one error's Ws and L:

(27)

Input	Winner ~ Loser	*PHARYNGEAL	*CODA	MAX	*RHOTIC	IDENT[+/-CONS]
/dɑg/	dɑg ~ dɑ	e	L	W	e	e
/ɹʌg/	ɹʌg ~ wʌg	e	e	e	L	W

Back to stratum-building we go, with a newly-free structural constraint:

(28a) *Building Stratum Three*
       Step One: Install all Structural Constraints *which prefer no Losers*

(28b)   *After building Stratum Three:*
       * Pharyngeal >> Ident[+/-cons] >> *Rhotic

In (28a), the algorithm's Step One is again enforcing restrictiveness via
{S} >> {F}. While the *rug~*wug* has taught the learner that rhotics cannot be
mapped to glides and so violating Ident[+/-cons], it does not guarantee that
relative position of *Rhotic and any other constraints. Since it is a structural
constraint, Step One allows installs *Rhotic as soon as it can – once its L has
been addressed, it appears in the very next stratum.

Moving on, we have one more unresolved L in (27) to get ranked above
the remaining Ws:

(29a)   *Building Stratum Four*
       Step One: Install all Structural Constraints *which prefer no Losers,*
                   unless there are none, in which case:
       Step Two: Install one Faithfulness Constraint *which prefers the most*
                   Winners

(29b)   *After building Stratum Four:*
       *Pharyngeal >> Ident[+/-cons] >> *Rhotic >> Max

By installing Max, the archive's other error has been resolved – so now it
too can be crossed off the algorith's to-do list, and the final stratum can be
built:

(30)

Input	*Winner ~ Loser*	*Pharyngeal	*Coda	Max	*Rhotic	Ident[+/-cons]
~~/dag/~~	~~dag ~ da~~	e	~~L~~	~~W~~	e	e
~~/rʌg/~~	~~rʌg ~ wʌg~~	e	e	e	~~L~~	~~W~~

(31a)   *Building Stratum Five*
       Step One: Install all Structural Constraints *which prefer no Losers*

(31b)   *After building Stratum Five:*
       *Pharyngeal >> Ident[+/-cons] >> *Rhotic >> Max >> *Coda

All constraints are now installed, the algorithm has succeeded, and a third
new grammar is born. What does this grammar actually do? Well, it retains
codas (as it already did in the last ranking), and it no longer turns its rhotics

into glides. But now that we are looking at all five constraints at once, we see that this new grammar actually makes a different error on underlying /ɹ/:

(32)

/ɹʌg/	*PHARYNGEAL	IDENT[+/-CONS]	*RHOTIC	MAX	*CODA
[ɹʌg]			*!		*
[wʌg]		*!			*
☞ [ʌg]				*	*

But has the learner gone astray? No! Because this new error will again be added to the archive as in (33), and its effect will be to re-order the relative ranking of *RHOTIC and MAX:

(33)

Input	Winner ~ Loser	*PHARYNGEAL	*CODA	MAX	*RHOTIC	IDENT[+/-CONS]
/dɑg/	dɑg ~ dɑ	e	L	W	e	e
/ɹʌg/	ɹʌg ~ wʌg	e	e	e	L	W
/ɹʌg/	ɹʌg ~ ʌg	e	e	W	L	e

After installing *PHARYNGEAL again in Stratum One, the algorithm now has an asymmetry in its W-preferring faithfulness constraints. Recall that in Step Two, the algorithm is required to install a faithfulness constraint *which prefers the most Winners* – and MAX prefers <u>two</u> winners, while IDENT[APPROX] only prefers one, so it is installed next:

(34) *After building Stratum Two:*
    *PHARYNGEAL >> MAX...

This resolves two errors in the archive as in (35):

(35)

Input	Winner ~ Loser	*PHARYNGEAL	*CODA	MAX	*RHOTIC	IDENT[+/-CONS]
/dɑg/	dɑg ~ dɑ	e	L	W	e	e
/ɹʌg/	ɹʌg ~ wʌg	e	e	e	L	W
/ɹʌg/	ɹʌg ~ ʌg	e	e	W	L	e

Given the remaining one error *CODA is now free to be installed, and then IDENT[APPROX] will be ranked above *RHOTIC to complete the ranking.

(36) *Final Stage Three grammar*
      *Pharyngeal >> Max >> *Coda >> Ident[+/-cons] >> *Rhotic

Given this limited constraint set, the ranking in (35) is now target English: pharyngeals are still ungrammatical, but neither codas nor rhotics are deleted, and additionally rhotics are not glided.[6]

This section has shown how an error-driven OT learner can impose the {S} >> {F} bias across stages of learning, from the initial to final states, using a growing accumulation of errors, but these examples have only demonstrated a few of the learner's working parts. Most importantly, many learnability results show that the {S} >> {F} heuristic is only the beginning of keeping the learner restrictive, and that the relative ranking of faithfulness constraints of different types has significant consequences for the learner's eventual success. On these issues, see the further reading section (but also keep reading into the next section)!

This section has demonstrated the workings of a re-ranking algorithm based on a stored archive of errors – but it has been divorced from all the empirical stages we discussed through all the previous chapters of this book. In the rest of this chapter, we will turn back to two of the messier aspects of child phonology as we've seen them, and discuss how different OT error-driven learning algorithms might be used to make sense of that mess.

10.3   Learning Gradually

10.3.1   Why Gradual Learning Is Hard so far

One of the biggest idealizations implied by the previous section's discussion concerns how quickly learners learn, and when this learning is triggered. Does a child update their archive and re-rank constraints every time they produce a word that currently causes an error? Suppose a child at a fairly early stage, quite close to the initial state, has *eggs* for breakfast:

---

[6] Around example (26) above, we reached a choice point about which error in (24) to resolve first, and at the time the choice seemed to make no difference. Either we would rank Ident[+/-cons] >> *Rhotic, and then Max >> *Coda like we did, or we could have first installed Max, and later Ident. In fact, though, choosing to install Max first in (26b) would have sped up learning – because the new Stage Two grammar would never have made the deletion error in (32), and would have simply moved straight to the end-state in (36). ... Does this result have any important consequences? Maybe. Think about it...

(37a) /ɛgz/	Onset	*Coda	*ComplexCoda	Max
ɛgz	*!	*!	*!	
gɛgz		*!	*!	
gɛg		*!		*
☞ gɛ				**

By lunchtime, might she have processed this error already as in (37b)?

(37b)	Input	Winner ~ Loser	Onset	*Coda	*ComplexCoda	Max
	/ɛgz/	ɛgz ~ gɛ	L	L	L	W

Once she has added this comparative tableau to her archive, she will install Max above fully <u>three</u> structural constraints (all those assigning an L above). In this way she moves to the next stage ranking in (38), which will now treat *eggs* as in (39):

(38) *After learning from (37)*

    Max >> Onset, *Coda, *ComplexCoda

(39) /ɛgz/	Max	Onset	*Coda	*ComplexCoda
ɛgz		*!	*	*
☞ gɛgz			*	*
gɛg	*!		*	
gɛ	*!			

That's a pretty big leap for one meal: from no coda consonants at all, the learner has moved directly to a stage where even complex codas are not tolerated![7]

---

[7]A skeptical reader may point out that this sudden faithfulness would be avoided if the learner had more faith constraints than just Max in their constraint set. Assuming Dep and other constraints also begin low-ranked along with Max, won't the learner's next grammar in (38–39) be one in which all codas are avoided with epenthesis, e.g. /ɛgz/→['gɛ.gə.zə]? As it turns out, at this early stage when nearly all S constraints remain high ranked, such epenthesis repairs are usually blocked independently by other structural constraints on word size. If Align and footing constraints prevent words from being bigger than one or two feet, and segments can't be deleted because of now-high-ranking Max, complicated syllable structure like coda clusters will have to survive.

Looking at children's data, development is clearly much more gradual and *incremental* than the move from (36) to (39). In Chapter 3 and elsewhere, for example, we have seen children acquiring singleton codas before complex ones – and indeed at a much more fine-grained level, children acquire new phonological structures one at a time. As another example, Tessier (2007)'s analysis of Julia's early onset cluster development identifies the following three early stages in her trajectory of onset cluster development:

(40)		*Julia's Gradual Acquisition of Onset Clusters* (Tessier 2007: 147–150; raw data from Compton and Streeter, 1977; Pater, 1997)			
		Age	*Cluster Preservation:* /CC/ → [CC]		*Cluster Reduction* /CC/ → [C]
a)		Up to 1;9	none preserved		all clusters reduced
b)		At 1;10	/stop-{ɹ,w}/ preserved (25/34)		/stop-l/, /sC/ reduced (31/34)
			drink	[gwɪŋk]	*spoon*	[pun]
			Grundy	[gwʌni]	*sleep*	[sip]
			crackers	[kwækəs]	*please*	[pis]
c)		1;11 –2;0	/stop-{ɹ,w}/ preserved (55/55) /s-{stop, nasal}/ preserved (56/62)		/stop-l/ reduced (75/79) /s-{l,w}/ reduced (12/14)
			crown	[kwaʊn]	*clap*	[kæp]
			spilled	[spiod]	*slide*	[saɪːt]
			sneeze	[snis]	*swim*	[fɪm]

Looking in this way at one or two months at a time, it's clear that Julia does not overcome her grammar's initial ban on onset consonant clusters in a homogenous way. Rather, some clusters and sonority profiles are acquired at different times – and this despite her own errors, which demonstrate a much wider range of English onset clusters. ... If learners are making and storing errors on all the forms in (40), why aren't they learning from them all?

Below, we'll look at two possible approaches to gradual learning, despite an overabundance of the kind of evidence that could speed them up. As mentioned at the chapter's beginning: the creators of learning algorithms are not necessarily wedded to their use in capturing real-life, natural language phonological learning, and so these algorithms were for the most part designed to get from initial to final stages without reference to what happens in-between. Thus, it is not surprising that the approaches below reflect either a change in how the algorithm is used by the learner, or in how it uses its errors to change the ranking in the first place. This latter possibility is where we start.

10.3.2   Numerical Rankings and Gradual Learning: The GLA

The learning algorithm we used in 10.2.3 to learn from *dog* and *rug* is very global in its effects: it takes an error archive, as a whole, and installs all constraints in a new hierarchy, from top to bottom. If the archive is considerably different than it was the last time the learner learnt, the resulting ranking can be very different; this means it is rather unsuited to learning gradually. A very different and popular approach is to change the grammar in a much more incremental way – to let each error contribute a very small amount to the re-ordering of constraints. To do this, however, requires a new conception of what it means for two constraints to be ranked with respect to each other.

Up until now we have assumed two, or perhaps three, ranking relationships between constraints, namely:

(41) *Classic OT constraint relationships:*

a) C1 >> C2   b)   C2 >> C1   c) {C1, C2}
                                           = C1 >> C2 OR C2 >> C1

For each pair of constraints, one can dominate the other or else they are *unranked* with respect to each other, meaning that either could outrank the other. What other options could there be in principle? What we cannot specify in classic OT is anything about the <u>absolute</u> distance between constraints. Does C1 outrank C2 <u>by a lot</u>? This question is ill-formed in our current framework – because given *strict domination* (introduced as our OT method of winnowing candidates back in Chapter 3.2), C1 >> C2 means that C1 makes ALL the decisions before C2 ever gets involved, and there can be no difference in the strength by which C1 overrules C2.

However! Suppose instead that constraints were ranked not just in an order, as in (41), but along a *number line*. In this view, each constraint is ranked either higher or lower than another, but they also sit above or below each other at a specified <u>distance</u>. As illustrated in (42) below, this means that C1 >> C2 is a shorthand notation for a (potentially infinite) number of grammars. (Notice how zero sits at the <u>right</u> edge of this number-line, to match the left-to-right method of reading constraints in order of importance in a classic OT tableau.)

(42) *Some examples of C1 >> C2, given numerical constraint values*

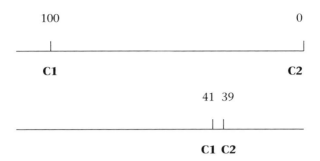

This numerical approach to constraint interactions can be used in a variety of ways, but here we will keep it as close to classic OT as we can. Every time the grammar is used, all the constraint's number values are simply reduced to an ordering as usual, so that when the constraints evaluate a form, all three circumstances in (42) boil down to C1 >> C2.

So if they work the same in the evaluation of input → output mappings, what is the <u>point</u> of numerical rankings? For this chapter's purposes, they are crucial to gradual learning, because instead of *flipping* a ranking between C1 and C2, a learner can respond to errors involving these constraints by *raising and lowering their values*.

Let's look back at the coda deletion error on *dog*, repeated below from (16). How could this error inform a learner with numerical constraint values?

(16b)	Input	Winner ~ Loser	*Pharyngeal	*Coda	Max
	/dɑg/	dɑg ~ dɑ	e	L	W

Rather than *resolving* an error and so changing rankings entirely, this learner can instead change the values of L and W-preferring constraints <u>slightly</u>, so that the new grammar will only approximate the target grammar slightly more than the previous one. Thus, the learner's response to an error will not be an algorithm with multiple stratum building steps, but rather one simple rule roughly like (43). We will refer to this update rule as the *Gradual Learning Algorithm*, or GLA, as it was dubbed in Boersma (1997) and much subsequent work (see further readings section).

(43)   *GLA update rule* (adapted from Boersma, 1998; Boersma and Hayes, 2001)
Lower the value of every L-preferring constraint by x points; and
Raise the value of every W-preferring constraint by y points

To set up our initial state grammar of {S} >> {F} in this framework, suppose that *Pharyngeal and *Coda each begin with a value of 100 and Max begins at zero – just as in the second example of (42) above. Thus the response to a comparative tableau for *dog* as in (16) will be to *lower the value* of *CODA and *raise the value* of MAX. To be concrete, suppose each error caused the learner to demote and promote constraints by two points. Then, after one learning cycle, the error in *dog* would have created the following new grammar:

(44) *After learning from (16b)*

The effect of this learning cycle is not perceivable to anyone but the learner: this ranking will still delete *dog* as much as the last grammar did, and it will take many more errors to change that. But once this learner has learnt from an error, it can be forgotten – that is, no error archive is used – since its trace has been left on the numerical values of constraints. Every time a word with a coda is run through the grammar, its resulting error further demotes *CODA and promotes MAX, until their values reverse:

(45) *After a lot of learning from errors like (16b)*

When the ranking values in (45) are translated into the strict domination ranking that we need to perform our OT evaluation, the grammar will now rank MAX >> *CODA, and so finally codas will be preserved rather than deleted.

10.3.3   Assessing the GLA as a Gradual Learner

An OT grammar with numerical constraint values is inherently designed to change gradually, and the basic GLA as in (43) is a simple method for learning without wholesale changes to the grammar.[8] In what ways then should we compare its properties to the classic, ordered ranking OT and the wholesale learning algorithm of 10.2.3? Here, we will focus on the paths taken by GLA learners between initial and final states, what kinds of *intermediate* stages are predicted along the way, and how well they match our data.[9]

---

[8] It is also very similar (or equivalent) to some pre-existing update rules in the machine learning and psychological literatures: see especially *Perceptron* learning (Rosenblatt 1958), and discussion in Pater (2009).

[9] A different approach to assessment – which is not at all easy – investigates each algorithm's success in *converging* – i.e., determining how likely it is that if a set of comparative tableaus are internally consistent, the learner will eventually settle on a ranking that resolves them all.

The GLA's learning is all error-by-error; in its basic form, promotion and demotion of a constraint is tied exclusively to the number of errors made with an L or W assigned by that constraint. This means that structural constraints which are more frequently violated in the language will be demoted faster – this seems both intuitively reasonable, and in keeping with the kinds of broad frequency facts we saw both in Chapter 7 and elsewhere. It is however important to recall from studies like Zamuner, Gerken and Hammond (2005) and Roark and Demuth (2000) that children's *input* frequency seems often to be the best predictor of acquisition order. For input frequency to translate into speed of constraint adjustment, this must mean that learners are updating their grammars in proportion to the rate at which they *hear* observed forms of different types, not just produce them.

A related question is about GLA's ability to learn *restrictively*, which the algorithm in Section 10.2 achieved in large part by treating structural and faithfulness constraints differently when trying to resolve errors. However, you may have noticed that the update rule in (43) does not treat structural and faithfulness constraints differently: Ls and Ws cause demotion and promotion in the same ways. Does this mean that the GLA can avoid treating particular types of constraints as special, in contrast to the biased OT learner's differential treatment of the two main constraint types?

The short answer is that in fact the GLA still needs biases that make reference to structural vs. faithfulness constraints of various sorts, and here we will walk through a reason why. This particular example comes from the acquisition of onset clusters in Quebec French; both children in Rose (2000)'s study went through a stage like the one in (46) where some but not all onsets are retained.[10] Find the predictive factor as to which clusters survive before reading on:

(46)

Théo 2;05.29–2;11.29 (Rose, 2000: 132)					
a) *onset clusters preserved*			b) *onset clusters reduced*		
/gʁo/	[gʁo]	*'big'*	/tʃak'tœʁ/	[ta'tœᵘ]	*tractor*
/tʃɛ̃/	[kχɛ]	*'train'*	/gʁy'jo/	[kʰœ'jɔ]	*oatmeal*
/kle/	[kxi]	*'key'*	/tʃu've/	[kʊ'βi]	*found*
/plœʁ/	[plœᵘ]	*'(he/she)cries'*	/ˌkχɛmgla'se/	[ˌkχa'na'se]	*ice cream*

---

[10] For different trajectories of French onset acquisition, see Kehoe and Hilaire-Debove (2004); Kehoe et al. (2008).

The deciding factor is stress: onset clusters at the beginning of *stressed* syllables are retained in (46a), but those in unstressed syllables are not in (46b). We have already used special faithfulness constraints to compel preservation of stressed segments, especially in Chapter 4 – so let's now adapt a constraint from Section 4.1.3 as follows (also translating it into correspondence terms):

(47) MaxC-Stressed
    Assign a violation for every input consonant in a stressed syllable which does not have an output correspondent[11]

With *ComplexOnset sandwiched between MaxC-stressed and general Max, we can capture this intermediate stage of cluster faithfulness.

Exercise 1: In (48), fill in the constraint violations to see how this ranking treats clusters in the words meaning *big* and *oatmeal* from (46) (output candidates differ only in their onsets, keeping constant other segmental processes in Théo's actual production):

(48) /gʁo/	MaxC-stressed	*ComplexOnset	Max-C
☞ gʁo			
go			
/gʁy'jo/			
gʁœ'jɔ			
☞ kʰœ'jɔ			

The learning question is now: how might a GLA learner, driven purely by the frequency of constraints violations in errors, move from the initial state to the one in (48)? To figure this out, we need to examine the kinds of errors that the initial state learner is making on onset clusters, and what their comparative tableaus look like. Our initial {S} >> {F} bias means that *ComplexOnset begins ranked above both Max and Max-Stressed, and let's initially assume that both faithfulness constraints begin with a value of zero. At this initial state, the learner will of course obey *ComplexOnset and reduce onset clusters in all contexts; this means they will be making errors with two kinds of violation profiles, shown in (49).

---

[11] Caveat: recall the discussion in Section 3.4.2.1, which should cast doubt on this definition in which inputs necessarily contain syllable structure …

(49)

	Input	Winner ~ Loser	*ComplexOnset	MaxC-stressed	Max-C
a)	/gʁo/	gʁo ~ go	L	W	W
b)	/gʁy'jo/	gʁœ'jɔ ~ kʰœ'jɔ	L	e	W

How will these errors change the GLA learner's ranking? Recall that every time a constraint assigns an L it is demoted a little, and every time a constraint assigns a W it is promoted. Looking at these two errors, then – every *stressed* onset which is deleted will cause <u>both</u> Max constraints to be promoted (49a), and every *unstressed* onset reduction error will cause just the <u>general</u> Max constraint to be promoted (49b). The upshot then is that Max-C will move up the hierarchy faster than Max-Stressed-C ... and so this learner will <u>never reach</u> the intermediate stage ranking in (46) and (48)! Instead, the first constraint to overcome *ComplexOnset will be general Max-C, and so clusters will all be retained regardless of their stress:

(50) Second stage of naïve GLA learning: *all clusters retained*

/gʁo/	Max-C	*ComplexOnset	Max-C-Stressed
☞ gʁo		*	
go	*!		*
/gʁy'jo/			
☞ gʁœ'jɔ		*	
☹ kʰœ'jɔ	*!		

As with so many other child patterns we have studied, this asymmetric pattern of producing clusters only in stressed syllables does have reflexes in adult grammars – Harris (1990) provides examples from Brazilian Portuguese like [li'vre-tu] *'book, diminutive,'* whose onset cluster reduces in the non-diminutive form ['live]) More generally, there is considerable cross-linguistic evidence that phonologies protect structures in certain preferred prosodic contexts – such as stressed syllables and initial syllables – as well as preferred morphological contexts, like roots rather than affixes or nouns over other lexical categories.[12]

---

[12] For example Beckman (1998); Smith (2011); and with respect to learning, Jesney and Tessier (2009).

Thus, in addition to the need to capture intermediate stages like in (46), we must also be concerned with the end-state acquisition of target languages which include such rankings. In this learning scenario, the target language only provides evidence of some phonological structure in the preferred position – for example, if onset clusters only appear in stressed syllables, the only error a learner will be able to make on observed forms will be like (51a). This illustration uses a word of Brazilian Portuguese with a stressed onset cluster, reduced by the initial state grammar and translated into a comparative tableau:

(51a) Positional faithfulness: the only kind of Brazilian Portuguese onset cluster error

/livretu/	*COMPLEXONSET	MAX-C-STRESSED	MAX-C
li'vretu	*!		
☞ li'vetu		*	*

(51b)

Input	Winner ~ Loser	*COMPLEX ONSET	MAXC -STRESSED	MAX-C
/livretu/	li'vretu ~ li'vetu	L	W	W

This evidence provides no asymmetry between the specific and general faithfulness constraints; both versions of MAX are promoted every time an onset cluster is encountered. As a result, the unbiased GLA learner will promote <u>both</u> MAX constraints at the same rate – and so the first observable change to the grammar will occur when both MAXs overcome *COMPLEX:

(52) Second stage of naïve GLA learning: *all clusters retained – unrestrictive!*

/livretu/	MAX-C	MAX-C-STRESSED	*COMPLEXONSET
☞ li'vretu			*
li'vetu	*!	*	
/livre/			
☞ 'livre			*
☹ 'live	*!		

This is clearly not the end-state grammar we want for our Brazilian Portuguese learner. This grammar considers all onset clusters equally grammatical regardless of stress position, meaning that it is purely accidental that no words of the speaker's language contain unstressed onset clusters – and indeed the cluster alternation between the two allomorphs for *book* in (52) is unexplained! In other words, the lack of a bias for MAXC-STRESSED has caused this naïve learner to be less restrictive that the language data requires.

The verdict thus far is that to capture both intermediates and end-state grammars, the GLA learner will need to be equipped with more ranking biases – in particular, with a preference to rank specific, or positional faithfulness constraints like MAXC-STRESSED *above* their general counterparts like MAX-C. To impose this bias *persistently*, the GLA algorithm can be given an additional condition so that all specific versions of a faithfulness constraint must always rank for example 20 points above their basic general version. This condition provides a ranking 'buffer' of sorts, so that every time errors like (49b) or (51b) provide the evidence that MAX-C must be promoted, MAXC-STRESSED will be promoted as well.

10.3.4   More on Ordinal Rankings, Biases and Gradual Learning

Before moving on, we will return to the ordinal rankings of constraints we had been using throughout this book up until the previous section. What of biases and gradual learning for the error-driven ordinal OT learner?

First it must be made clear that the specific vs. general faithfulness bias needed by the GLA learner to capture the last section's intermediate and end-state grammars is also crucial to the OT learner we started building in Section 10.2.3. In that algorithm, we simply stated that once no structural constraints could be installed, the learner should install one faithfulness constraint that prefers the most winners among the currently-unresolved errors – but this turns out to be only part of the necessary biases for faithfulness, and a clause requiring that the learner choose to install a specific faithfulness constraint rather than a general one is also necessary. The study of faithfulness biases in learning is in fact rather fraught (see especially Prince and Tesar, 2004).

Returning to the issue of gradual learning: could a learner whose grammar retains the ordinal rankings of OT still be made more gradual? In the GLA, learning is gradual because every error teaches the learner very little, and so every piece of data can be used to get slightly closer to the end-state. Our OT learner, on the other hand, learns much more from each single piece of data – so, perhaps the way to slow this latter learner down is make them more choosy about the errors they learn from?

This idea is pursued in Tessier (2009) and related work (discussed in the next section). The crucial idea is that instead of immediately updating the grammar from every error made, the learner instead stores errors in an *error 'cache'*, accumulating evidence but not changing their grammar. Learning is only triggered once some threshold of similar errors has been reached, providing the learner with sufficient evidence from different word types that some particular constraint is causing consistent trouble. At this point, the learner uses an *error-selection* algorithm to choose a representative error from the cache and add it to the archive; once an error has been saved in the archive, it triggers learning, constraints are re-ranked and the cycle begins again.

In this kind of framework, the learner's gradual progress is mediated by error selection. What makes the learner choose an error from the cache to learn from? The overall goal is to pick data that will lead the re-ranking algorithm to resolve *one frequent problem*. Let's see this in action, looking back at the initial state error on *eggs* from the beginning of this section. What other errors will that learner's error cache contain, when all syllable structure constraints outrank MAX? Some examples are given in (53):

(53)		An error cache – which one to choose?						
		Input	*Winner ~ Loser*	ONSET	*CODA	*COMPLEXCODA	MAX	DEP
a)	eggs	/ɛgz/	ɛgz ~ gɛ	L	L	L	W	e
b)	*ducks*	/dʌks/	dʌks ~ dʌ	e	L	L	W	e
c)	*dog*	/dɑg/	dɑg ~ dɑ	e	L	e	W	e
d)	*eye*	/aɪ/	aɪ ~ ʔaɪ	L	e	e	e	W

Looking at this table of just three current errors, it is clear that the learner is attempting many target words with codas – notice all the Ls in the *CODA column. How can the learner resolve just their *CODA problem? By learning from an error like *dog*, where *CODA alone assigns an L! If this error in (53c) is added to the archive, MAX will be installed above *CODA, but all other {S} >> {F} rankings will be preserved (for much more on this idea see Tessier, 2007, 2009):

(54) Result of learning just from (53c) – *gradual change*
   ONSET, *COMPLEXCODA >> MAX >> *CODA >> DEP

With these two rather different ideas about gradual learning in mind, we will now turn to a different reality about natural phonological learning: its variability.

10.4   Learning with Variation

Section 6.6 discussed several kinds of variability in child production data, and where it might come from. The conclusion we drew there was that some child production variability <u>did</u> require a explanation connected somehow to the grammar – but that we were not yet prepared to give one. In this final section, we will look at two possible accounts of grammatical variation over time, which ascribe the variability in output patterns to different parts of the learning system.

10.4.1   Variation with Stochastic OT and the GLA

The data we will use comes once again from Trevor and his development of consonant harmony. To keep the data set manageable, we will look at target inputs which contained a coronal consonant followed by a dorsal (abbreviated to /TVK/ below though they also include /TVKV/ targets). Over the course of development from 1;0 to 2;2, these forms showed three primary patterns with respect to place of articulation, illustrated in (54).[13]

(54) *Trevor's output types for /TVK/ inputs* (Data from Pater, 1997)
  K-harmony: /dɔg/ → [gɔg] (1;7)
  T-harmony: /dʌk/ → [dʌtə] (1;3)
  faithful: /tɪkɬ/ → [tɪgul] (1;8)

The graph in (55) below shows the number of these output types in Trevor's corpus, grouped by month. The legend above will let you see how each output type changed in frequency over time; this progression is narrated below:

---

[13] This section does not analyze Trevor's outputs in which the potential trigger or target of harmony was deleted.

(55) Variation in Trevor's /TVK/ harmony by month

Legend:

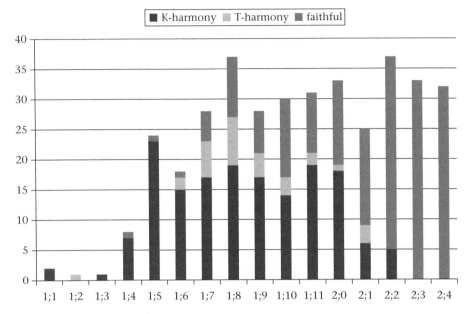

Once Trevor began to attempt /TVK/ words in earnest between 1;4 and 1;5, his first pattern was not variable, in that he produced almost all such inputs with K-harmony. At around 1;7 variation emerged, where some /TVK/ words underwent K-harmony, some showed T-harmony, and others were faithful. Up until 2;0 T-harmony gradually died off while the other two patterns appeared to hold steady; then around 2;1 K-harmony also began a sharp decline. By 2;3, faithfulness became the only output pattern and no further /TVK/ place errors were reported.

To capture these types of variation over time, we will need a learner which can produce multiple outputs for a single input simultaneously. How should this be derived? A simple and popular approach comes from the numerical OT framework used by the GLA in the previous section, to which we now add an additional quantitative dimension. Here is the crucial addition: instead of constraint values being a single point on a number line, we interpret those values as the *mean* of a probability *distribution*. (If this is already two too many statistics terms for you, don't glaze over. All will be explained.)

To illustrate, here is a ranking of some consonant harmony constraints: an agreement structural constraint ranked at 60 and two faithfulness constraints ranked at 50 and 20. In (42) we would have depicted these constraints values as single ticks on a number line; now in (56) we will place *curves* on the number line, with their highest point centered around those ticks:

(56) *Early state of a stochastic OT grammar for TVK harmony*

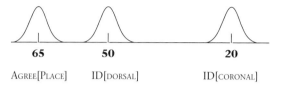

65	50	20
Agree[Place]	ID[dorsal]	ID[coronal]

This *stochastic* OT grammar (proposed originally by Boersma, 1998) will still be translated into an ordinal OT ranking every time the grammar is used, by randomly choosing a one-time value for each constraint from under the probability curve. These curves all represent *normal distributions*, with their mean value indicated on the number line: the higher the curve is, the more likely the constraint is to take on that value in any one use of the grammar, so that for example Agree[Place] is most likely to get its mean value of 65, ID[dorsal] a value of 50 and so on. Given the width of these constraints, there is not much overlap in constraint rankings here – so this stochastic grammar is fairly equivalent to the ordinal OT ranking in (57), where K-harmony is produced, as in Trevor's outputs at 1;4–1;5:

(57) /TVK/	Agree[place] 65	ID[dorsal] 50	ID[coronal] 20
TVK	*!		
☞ KVK			*
TVT		*!	

In theory these curves never flatten out to zero, so that all of these curves overlap to some extent – but when overlap is considerable, then some one-time values will be chosen so that rankings appear to <u>reverse</u>. For example, suppose that from (56) the learner made many errors which caused both Ident constraints to be promoted, and that Ident[coronal] had moved up especially fast (probably due to its interaction with other structural constraints, outside of /TVK/ harmony). As Ident[dorsal] was already ranked fairly close to Agree, the next observable stages might be the one in (58), where Ident has flipped rankings with Agree. What other effects do these constraint distributions have?

(58) *Next stage of a stochastic OT grammar for TVK harmony*

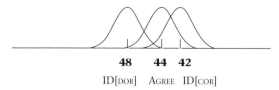

48	44	42
ID[dor]	Agree	ID[cor]

When these constraints are put into the ranking very closely to their mean values, we still get K-harmony as dominant (59). However, if IDENT[COR] and AGREE's values happen to be chosen from the positions in (60a), then the resulting grammar will flip their ranking, resulting in a faithful output (60b).

(59)

/TVK/	ID[DORSAL] 48	AGREE[PLACE] 44	ID[CORONAL] 42
TVK		*!	
☞ KVK			*
TVT	*!		

(60a) *Choosing values from overlapping distributions*

(60b)

/TVK/	ID[DORSAL] 47.8	ID[CORONAL] 43.6	AGREE[PLACE] 42.7
☞ TVK			*
KVK		*!	
TVT	*!		

Exercise 2: Looking back at (55), this variation between K-harmony in (59) and faithfulness in (60) appears in Trevor's speech around 1;6 and 1;7. At the same time, T-harmony forms also emerge – can you see which values must be chosen to make T-harmony optimal? Fill in the tableau in (61) below to do so:

(61)

/TVK/			
TVK		*!	
KVK	*!		
☞ TVT			*

***

In (61)'s tableau, ID[DORSAL] must be the lowest ranked – meaning that both AGREE and ID[COR] must have been assigned values above that of ID[DORSAL]. While this is possible, it's quite unlikely – it will require adding a considerable *noise* to the process of choosing these one-time values.

In this way, a single stochastic grammar of OT constraints with numerical values and noise applied when choosing one-time ranking values can create variation between multiple different ordinal rankings. This approach also makes predictions about the *relative* frequency of each one-time ranking, given a set of mean values. In this case, the mean values chosen in (58–62) predict that K-harmony should be most likely, faithfulness less likely and T-harmony much less likely again. These proportions best represent the stages seen around 1;10–2;0 from Trevor's month-by-month data in (55). However, they also under-predict the amount of T-harmony at 1;7–1;9, but we might well not have enough raw data to interpret these proportions as reflecting the true degree(s) of variability in the underlying grammar.[14]

In the case of target English, the goal end-state grammar is one in which consonant harmony is of course prohibited – so that both IDENT constraints must outrank AGREE[PLACE]. For a stochastic OT learner, this now means that errors will continue to be made until the mean values for faithfulness constraints are sufficiently above AGREE[PLACE] that the likelihood of re-ranking is practically speaking zero, as in (63) below. At this point, errors will stop being made, learning will cease and an end-state will have been reached:

(63) *Final stage of a stochastic OT grammar for TVK harmony – faithfulness wins*

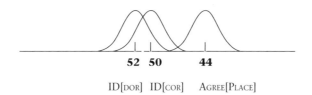

52 50   44

ID[DOR] ID[COR]   AGREE[PLACE]

Along the way, this learner will pass through many more intermediate stages, with the means of each constraint gradually shifting up or down, and with slightly different relative proportions of faithfulness, K-harmony and T-harmony after each learning cycle. (See exercise at the end of the chapter.) Notice that in fact this stochastic OT grammar could also be describing any number of *end-state* grammars – that is any time two conflicting constraints overlap to a noticeable degree, they describe a grammar in which there will

---

[14] It might also suggest different problems with our analysis, for example that our constraint set might be flawed, or at least missing additional constraints. Recall the discussion in Section 6.4 about the uncertainty as to how best to capture this kind of child consonant harmony.

be observable variation in the choices of optimal outputs. To describe variation in end-state grammars with these overlapping constraints, we could decide that at some point the learner stops using errors to push their constraints apart, and simply settles with the overlap they have. To formalize this, we could define the *plasticity* of constraints – meaning the 'x' and 'y' values by which we promote and demote constraints according to (43) – as shrinking over time, so that early errors would have a great impact on the learner and change the grammar quickly, but gradually the grammar would *fossilize* into a steady state in which errors eventually do nothing.[15]

Finally, a word about implementing stochastic OT and its learning. In the examples above, the grammar's values were chosen by hand – in part to make clear that we were only looking at some idealized time slices, not a fully-implemented simulation using all the relevant errors and their crucial relative frequencies. However, you should know several software tools exist for implementing GLA learning (and many related learners); one comes with the free phonetics software kit Praat (Boersma and Weenink, 2015). To implement it, you create data files that feed the learner the definition of your constraints, your initial state values, your errors, each with a relative frequency, and the plasticity – and it will learn! This kind of simulation can be a great tool both for investigating variation among rankings via overlapping constraints, but also simply for assessing the overall workings of a constraint set and its *factorial typology*.

10.4.2   Variation with Ordinal OT, Stored Errors and a Dual Route

This last section goes back to the notion that phonological grammars might be learned gradually not because each error changes the constraint ranking just a little bit, but because only certain errors are used to re-rank. This 'error-selective' approach was introduced at the end of Section 10.3, and now we will see how it might be fleshed out to understand variation between stages as well (this account comes from Becker and Tessier, 2011).

Recall that the ordinal OT learner is accumulating a set of stored errors, here called the error *archive*, which are used altogether to build a new ranking on each learning cycle. In between learning cycles, errors are not used to learn, but simply pile up in an error *cache*, waiting to be archived if and when the time comes. In the case of TVK words and the three constraints we used in the previous section, our biased OT learner will go through three grammatical stages as follows in (64). Note that we have specified that the initial state

---

[15] On the other hand: whether or not the same grammatical mechanism should encode both learner and end-state variation is an open question, left unresolved in Section 6.6.

prefers K-harmony, by ranking Id[DORSAL] >> Id[CORONAL] – this is perhaps not unreasonable given the cross-linguistic place asymmetries we have discussed elsewhere (see Section 6.3), but it is not a *fixed* ranking here, because errors can undo it as in (64b).

(64) *The biased ordinal OT learner's development of TVK harmony*
a) Initial state: AGREE[PLACE] >> Id[DORSAL] >> Id[CORONAL]

/TVK/	AGREE[PLACE]	Id[DORSAL]	Id[CORONAL]
TVK	*!		
☞ KVK			*
TVT		*!	

b) Error archive after (a)

Input	Winner ~ Loser	AGREE[PLACE]	Id[DORSAL]	Id[CORONAL]
/TVK/	TVK ~ KVK	L	e	W

c) Next state, learned from (b):   Id[CORONAL] >> AGREE[PLACE] >> Id[DORSAL]

/TVK/	Id[CORONAL]	AGREE[PLACE]	Id[DORSAL]
TVK		*!	
KVK	*!		
☞ TVT			*

d) Error archive after (c)

Input	Winner ~ Loser	AGREE[PLACE]	Id[DORSAL]	Id[CORONAL]
/TVK/	TVK ~ KVK	L	e	W
/TVK/	TVK ~ TVT	L	W	e

e) Final state, learnt from (d):   Id[CORONAL] >> Id[DORSAL] >> AGREE[PLACE] OR
                                     Id[DORSAL] >> Id[CORONAL] >> AGREE[PLACE]

While this process does include the three stages that Trevor went through – K-harmony, T-harmony and faithfulness – the grammars themselves are not at all variable; each ranking chooses only one optima. To introduce variation let's look back at the role of the error *cache*: those forms created by previous grammars that were simply accumulated in real time, but never archived or actively used. These cached errors might simply be forgotten every time a new grammar is built – but what if instead they were remembered, at least briefly, as remnants of previous rankings? If these cached errors were available, then the learner would have two routes to producing an input form that's been produced before: either to feed it to the newest grammar (whichever of 64a, 64c or 64e is current), or to retrieve a cached output version of that input, as it was produced by some earlier grammar.

This Dual Route approach is schematized below in (65) for a point during stage two of the TVK-harmony acquisition process. Here, the ranking is as in (64c), which ensures that the winner should only be applying T-harmony. However, errors made in (64a) by the previous K-harmony ranking are still rattling around the learner's cache, and the more recently they were made the stronger they are. We implement this property of the cache by *lowering* the strength (defined as a probability between zero and one) for every cached error by a fixed small amount every time the grammar is used. In this case, we will assume that the learner's stage one production of *dog* with K-harmony has sunk to .6 in probability; this means that 60% of the time when the learner intends to say *dog*, they simply produce the older cached form rather than feed the input to the current grammar:

(65) *Using the Dual Route approach during Stage Two:*

Learner intends to say [🐕]

60% of the time via cache: 40% of the time via grammar

Input	Winner ~ Loser	STRENGTH
/dɔg/	dɔg ~ **gɔg**	.6
/dʌk/	dʌk ~ gʌk	.6
/frɔg/	frɔg ~ gɔ	.2

	/dɔg/	ID [COR]	AGREE [PLACE]	ID [DOR]
	dɔg		*!	
	gɔg	*!		
☞	**dɔd**			*

In this view, variation comes about not because the grammar itself is variable as to its choice of optimal candidate, but rather from the competition between multiple ways of getting from inputs to outputs. Over time cached errors get weaker, are chosen less often, and the grammar takes over, but each subsequent grammar also brings about new cached forms to compete. The fragment of error cache in (65) contains two stored forms with K-harmony, but also an output error on *frog*, made by an earlier grammar that for example did not tolerate codas, and which has a lower strength, meaning that the current learner would only have a 20% chance of producing that older error when attempting *frog*.

As with the stochastic OT account, implementing the precise details of Trevor's TVK development is not a complete fit. Since /TVK/ → [TVT] forms as in (65) emerge in his corpus around the same time as faithful [TVK] tokens also begin (between 1;6–1;7), this means that Trevor moves very quickly from Stage One to Stage Three, and that in fact for this particular part of the lexicon his Stage Two errors appear to weaken *more* quickly than his Stage One errors (see Becker and Tessier, 2011 for more).

Overall, this section has explored two possible avenues for incorporating variation between grammatical stages in phonological development. It remains to be seen how well either (or indeed a third, superior approach) works at capturing all and only the attested stages of child development, with respect to how structural and faithfulness pressures are balanced. As with so much child phonology, we are only beginning to have access to sufficiently broad corpora of data and a wealth of longitudinal studies that can provide detailed testing grounds for such theories.

10.5   Further Reading

On Stochastic Constraint-based Learning

Boersma, Paul and Bruce Hayes (2001). Empirical tests of the Gradual Learning Algorithm. *Linguistic Inquiry* 32: 45–86.

Curtin, Suzanne and Kie Zuraw (2002). Explaining constraint demotion in a developing system. In Barbora Skarabela, Sarah Fish and Anna H.-J. Do (eds) *Proceedings of the 26th Annual Boston University Conference on Language Development*. Somerville, MA: Cascadilla. 118–129.

On Constraint Induction

Hayes, Bruce. 1999. Phonetically-driven phonology: The role of optimality theory and inductive Grounding. In Michael Darnell, Edith Moravscik, Michael Noonan, Frederick Newmeyer, and Kathleen Wheatly (eds) *Functionalism and Formalism in Linguistics*, Volume I: General Papers. John Benjamins, Amsterdam. 243–228.

McAllister Byun, Tara. 2012. Positional velar fronting: An updated articulatory account. *Journal of Child Language* 39: 1043–1076.

On Learning Exceptions

This is a topic we have not covered – but it is crucial! What happens when a learner is faced with phonological exceptions, as in the target language patterns of Chapter 7.4? Here are some key OT-related readings.

Pater, Joe. 2010. Morpheme-specific phonology: Constraint indexation and inconsistency resolution. In S. Parker (ed.) *Phonological Argumentation: Essays on Evidence and Motivation*. London: Equinox.

Tesar, Bruce, Alderete, John, Horwood, Graham, Merchant, Nazarré, Nishitani, Koichi and Prince, Alan. 2003. Surgery in language learning. In L. Mikkelson and C. Potts (eds) *Proceedings of WCCFL 22:*. Somerville, MA: Cascadilla Press. 101–114.

On Learning Alternations in OT [not for the novice]

Apoussidou, Diane. 2007. *The Learnability of Metrical Phonology*. Doctoral dissertation, University of Amsterdam.

Pater, Joe, Staubs, Robert, Jesney, Karen and Smith, Brian. 2012. Learning probabilities over underlying representations. In the *Proceedings of the Twelfth Meeting of the ACL-SIGMORPHON: Computational Research in Phonetics, Phonology, and Morphology*, Association for Computational Linguistics. Montreal, Canada. pp 62–71.

Exercises

Q1: This is an exercise in applying the biased ordinal OT algorithm described in Section 10.2. Take the errors on *ducks* that we discussed but never actually learnt from in the text, repeated below, created by an initial state grammar of two structural constraints over faithfulness ones:

(16)

/dʌks/	Agree[place]	*ComplexCoda	Ident[cor]	Max-C
dʌks	*!	*!		
gʌkx		*!	*	
dʌk	*!			*
☞ gʌk			*	*

(17)

Input	Winner ~ Loser	Agree [place]	*Complex Coda	Ident[cor]	Max-C
/dʌks/	dʌks ~ gʌk	L	L	W	W

Feed this error into the algorithm in Section 10.2, step by step, and see what next grammar you come up with. Use that grammar to parse ducks *again, add that new error to your archive, and then feed* both *errors into the algorithm together, and begin again. Continue until your grammar stops making errors on* ducks. *Then comment on the intermediate stages you created and anything about the procedure that you had difficulty with.*

Q2: Look back at Trevor's variability in TVK production in (55). Can you concoct ranking values for the three constraints used in Section 10.4.1 that create Trevor's stages between 1;9 and 2;0? Roughly speaking, Trevor varies between faithfulness and K-harmony as the two common stages, but T-harmony is virtually gone. *Can you use different ranking values to capture the differences between the varying proportions of each pattern across the months?* Comment on any confusions or problems you have.

References

Adam, Galit and Bat-El, Outi. 2009. When do universal preferences emerge in language Development? The acquisition of Hebrew stress. *Brill's Annual of Afroasiatic Languages and Linguistics* 1: 255–282.

Aksu-koc, A. A. and Slobin, Dan I. 1985. The acquisition of Turkish. In D. Slobin (ed) *The Crosslinguistic Study of Language Acquisition Vol I. The Data.* Hillsdale, NJ: Lawrence Erlbaum Associates.

Albert, Aviad and Zaidenberg, Hadass. 2012. Filler Syllables in the Acquisition of Hebrew: A Prosodic Account. *Brill's Annual of Afroasiatic Languages and Linguistics* 4: 162–188.

Albright, Adam. 2010. Lexical and morphological conditioning of paradigm gaps. In Curt Rice and Sylvia Blaho (eds) *Modeling Ungrammaticality in Optimality Theory.* London: Equinox.

Albright, Adam and Hayes, Bruce. 2003. Rules vs. analogy in English past tenses: A computational/experimental study. *Cognition* 90: 119–161.

Albright, Adam and Bruce Hayes. 2010. Modelling productivity with the gradual learning algorithm: The problem of accidentally exceptionless generalizations. In G. Fanselow, C. Féry, M. Schlesewsky, and R. Vogel (eds) *Gradience in Grammar: Generative Perspectives.* Oxford: Oxford University Press. 185–204.

Albright, Adam and Kang, Yoonjung. 2009. Predicting innovative alternations in Korean verb paradigms. In *Current issues in unity and diversity of languages: Collection of the papers selected from CIL18.* Seoul: Linguistic Society of Korea. 893–913.

Alderete, John, Beckman, Jill, Benua, Laura, Gnanadesikan, Amalia, McCarthy, John J. and Urbanczyk, Suzanne. 1999. Reduplication with fixed segmentism. *Linguistic Inquiry* 30: 327–364.

Allen, George and Hawkins, Sarah. 1978. The development of phonological rhythm. In A. Bell and J. B. Hooper (eds) *Syllables and Segments.* Amsterdam: North-Holland Publishing Company, 173–185.

Allen, George and Hawkins, Sarah. 1980. Phonological rhythm: Definition and development. In G. H. Yeni-Komshian, J. F. Kavanagh, and C. A. Ferguson (eds) *Child Phonology: Production.* New York: Academic Press. 227–256.

Almeida, Letícia, Rose, Yvan, and M Freitas, João. 2012. Prosodic influence in bilingual phonological development: Evidence from a Portuguese-French first language learner. In Alia K. Biller, Esther Y. Chung, and Amelia E. Kimball (eds) *Proceedings of BUCLD36.* 42–52.

Altvater-Mackensen, Nicole, van der Feest, Suzanne, V. H. and Fikkert, Paula. 2013. Asymmetries in early word recognition: The case of stops and fricatives. *Language Learning and Development* 10(2): 149–178.

Altvater-Mackensen, Nicole and Fikkert, Paula (2010). The acquisition of the stopfrica-tive contrast in perception and production. *Lingua* 120. 1898–1909.

Amayreh, Mousa M. and Dyson, Alice T. 1998. The acquisition of Arabic consonants. *Journal of Speech, Language and Hearing Research* 41(3): 642–653.

Amastae, John. 1982. Aspects of the bilingual acquisition of English and Spanish. *Jounral of the Linguistic Asscociation of the Southwest* 5: 5–19.

Anttila, Arto. 2002. Morphologically conditioned phonological alternations. *Natural Language and Linguistic Theory* 20: 1–42.

Aoyama, Katsura. 2000. *A Psycholinguistic Perspective on Finnish and Japanese Prosody: Perception, Production and Child Acquisition of Consonantal Quantity Distinctions.* Doctoral dissertation, University of Hawaii.

Apoussidou, Diane. 2007. *The Learnability of Metrical Phonology.* Doctoral dissertation, University of Amsterdam.

Archer, Stephanie L., Ference, Jennifer, and Curtin, Suzanne. 2014. Now you hear it: 14-month-olds succeed at learning minimal pairs in stressed syllables. *Journal of Cognition and Development* 15(1): 110–122.

Archibald, John and Carson, Jana. 2000. Acquisition of Quebec French stress. *Paper Presented at the Annual Meeting of the Canadian Linguistic Association*, University of Alberta.

Aronoff, Mark. 1976. *Word formation in generative grammar.* Cambridge, MA: MIT Press.

Ayyad, Hadeel and May, Bernhardt, B. 2009. Phonological development of Kuwaiti Arabic: Preliminary data. *Clinical Linguistics and Phonetics* 23(11): 794–807.

Baayen, R. Harald, Piepenbrock, R., and van Rijn, H. 1993. *The CELEX Lexical Database.* Philadelphia, PA: Linguistic Data Consortium, University of Pennsylvania.

Baertsch, Karen. 2002. *An Optimality-Theoretic Approach to Syllable Structure: The Split Margin Hierarchy.* Doctoral dissertation, Indiana University.

Bakovic, Eric. 1999. *Harmony, Dominance, and Control.* Doctoral dissertation, Rutgers University.

Barlow, Jessica. 2005. Sonority effects in the production of consonant clusters by Spanish-Speaking children. In D. Eddington (ed) *Selected Proceedings of the 6th Conference on the Acquisition of Spanish and Portuguese as First and Second Languages.* Somerville, MA: Cascadilla Press.

Bat-El, Outi. 2008. Morphologically conditioned V–Ø alternation in Hebrew: Distinction among nouns, adjectives & participles, and verbs. In S. Armon-Lotem, G. Danon, and S. Rothstein (eds) *Current Issues in Generative Hebrew Linguistics.* Amsterdam: John Benjamins. 27–60.

Becker, Michael and Tessier, Anne-Michelle. 2011. Trajectories of faithfulness in child-specific phonology. *Phonology* 28: 163–196.

Becker, Michael and Gouskova, Maria. (to appear). Source-oriented generalizations as grammar inference in Russial vowel deletion. To appear in Linguistic Inquiry.

Becker, Michael, Ketrez, Nihan, and Nevins, Andrew. 2011. The surfeit of the stimu-lus: Analytic biases filter lexical statistics in Turkish laryngeal alternations. *Language* 87(1): 84–125.

Beckman, Jill. 1998. *Positional Faithfulness.* Doctoral dissertation, University of Massachusetts Amherst.

Benua, Laura 2000. *Phonological Relations between Words.* New York: Garland.

Berko Gleason, Jean. 1958. The child's learning of English morphology. *Word* 14: 150–177.

Bernabe, Emma J. Fonacier, Lapid, Virginia, and Sibayan, Bonifacio. 1971. *Ilokano Lessons*. Honolulu: University of Hawaii Press.

Bernhardt, Barbara H., and Stemberger, Joseph P. 1998. *Handbook of Phonological Development from the Perspective of Constraint-based Nonlinear Phonology*. San Diego: Academic Press.

Bertoncini, Josiane, Bijeljac-Babic, Ranka, Jusczyk, Peter, Kennedy, Lori, and Jacques Mehler. 1988. An investigation of young infants' perceptual representations of speech sounds. *Journal of Experimental Psychology* 117(1): 21–33.

Best, Catherine T, McRoberts, Gerald W. and Sithole, Nomathemba M. 1988. Examination of perceptual reorganization for non-native speech contrasts: Zulu click discrimination by English-Speaking adults and infants. *Journal of Experimental Psychology* 14(3): 345–360.

Bialystok, Ellen. 1988. Levels of bilingualism and levels of linguistic awareness. *Developmental Psychology* 24: 560–567.

Bills Shannon and Golston, Chris. 2002. Prosodic and linear licensing in English acquisition. In L. Carmichael, C.-H. Huang and V. Samiian (eds) *Proceedings of the Western Conference on Linguistics*. Fresno, CA: Department of Linguistics, CSU Fresno. 13–26.

Blaho, Sylvia and Szeredi, Daniel. 2011. Secondary stress in Hungarian: (Morpho)-Syntactic, not metrical. In M. B. Washburn, K. McKinney-Bock, E. Varis, A. Sawyer, and B. Tomaszewicz. (eds) *Proceedings of WCCFL 28*. Somerville, MA: Cascadilla Proceedings Project.

Blasdell, R. A. and Jensen, P. 1970. Stress and word position as determinants of imitation in first language learners. *Journal of Speech and Hearing Research* 13: 193–202.

Bleile, Ken M. and Tomblin, J. Bruce. 1991. Regressions in the phonological development of two children. *Journal of Psycholinguistic Research* 20: 483–499.

Blevins, Juliette. 1995. The Syllable in Phonological Theory, *Handbook of phonological theory*, ed. by John Goldsmith, Basil Blackwell, London, 206–4.

Bloch, Tamar. 2011. *Simplification Strategies in the Acquisition of Consonant Clusters in Hebrew*. MA Thesis, Tel-Aviv University.

Boersma, Paul. 1997. How we learn variation, optionality, and probability. *Proceedings of the Institute of Phonetic Sciences of the University of Amsterdam* 21: 43–58.

Boersma, Paul. 1998. *Functional Phonology: Formalizing the Interactions between Articulatory and Perceptual Drives*. Doctoral dissertation, University of Amsterdam.

Boersma, Paul and Hayes, Bruce. 2001. Empirical tests of the gradual learning algorithm. *Linguistic Inquiry* 32: 45–86.

Boersma, Paul and Weenink, David. 2015. Praat: Doing phonetics by computer Version 5.3.23. Accessed August 8, 2012. [Computer program]

Boersma, Paul and Escudero, Paola. 2001. Modeling the perceptual development of phonological contrasts with optimality theory and the gradual learning algorithm. *Proceedings of 25th Penn Linguistics Colloquium*.

Bohannon, John Neil, II and Stanowicz, Laura. 1988. The issue of negative evidence: Adult responses to children's language errors. *Developmental Psychology* 24(5): 684–689.

Booij, Geert. 2002. *The Morphology of Dutch*. Oxford: Oxford University Press.

Bortolini, Umberta and Leonard, Laurence B. 1991. The speech of phonologically disordered children acquiring Italian. *Clinical Linguistics and Phonetics* 5(1): 1–12.

Bradley, Travis. 2001a. A typology of rhotic duration contrast and neutralization. In M. J. Kim and U. Strauss (eds) *Proceedings of NELS 31*. Amherst, MA: GLSA. 79–97.

Bradley, Travis G. 2001b. *The Phonetics and Phonology of Rhotic Duration Contrast and Neutralization*. Ph.D. Dissertation, The Pennsylvania State University, University Park, PA.

Bredberg, G. 1985. The anatomy of the developing ear. In S. E. Trehub and B. Schneider (eds) *Auditory Development in Infancy*. New York/London: Plenum Press. 3–20.

Brent, Michael and Jeffrey, Mark Siskind. 2001. The role of exposure to isolated words in early vocabulary development. *Cognition* 81: B33–B44.

Broesch, Tanya L. and Bryant, Gregory A. 2014. Prosody in infant-directed speech is similar across western and traditional cultures. *Journal of Cognition and Development* 15. DOI: 10.1080/15248372.2013.833923

Broselow, Ellen. 2004. Unmarked structures and emergent rankings in second language phonology. *International Journal of Bilingualism* 8(1): 51–65.

Brown, Cynthia. 1997. *Acquisition of Segmental Structure: Consequences for Speech Perception and Second Language Acquisition*. Doctoral dissertation, McGill University.

Brown, Roger and Hanlon, C. 1970. Derivational complexity and the order of acquisition in child speech. In R. Brown (ed) *Psycholinguistics*. New York: Free Press. 155–207.

Brulard, Ines and Carr, Philip. 2003. French-English bilingual acquisition of phonology: One production system or two. *International Journal of Bilingualism* 7(2): 177–202.

Burzio, Luigi. 1994. *Principles of English Stress*. Cambridge: CUP.

Burzio, Luigi. 2004. Sources of paradigm uniformity. In Laura J. Downing, T. A. Hall, and Renate Raffelsiefen (eds) *Paradigms in Phonological Theory*. Oxford: OUP.

Bybee, Joan L. and Slobin, Dan I. 1982. Rules and schemas in the development and use of the English past tense. *Language* 58(2): 265–289.

Byers-Heinlein, Krista, Fennell, Christopher T., and Werker, Janet F. 2013. The development of associative word learning in monolingual and bilingual infants. *Bilingualism: Language and Cognition* 16(1): 198–205.

Cahill, Michael. 2006. Perception of yoruba word-initial [gb] and [b]. In Olaoba F. Arasanyin and Michael A. Pemberton (eds) *Selected Proceedings of the 36th Annual Conference on African Linguistics*. Somerville, MA: Cascadilla Proceedings Project.

Carroll, Susanne. 2001. *Input and Evidence: The Raw Material of Second Language Acquisition*. Philadelphia, PA. John Benjamins.

Carter, Allyson and Gerken, Louan. 2004. Do children's omissions leave traces? *Journal of Child Language* 31: 561–586.

Chambless, Della. 2006. *Asymmetries in the Acquisition of Consonant Clusters*. Doctoral Dissertation, University of Massachusetts Amherst.

Chervela, Nirmala. 1981. Medial consonant cluster acquisition by Telugu children. *Journal of Child Language* 8(1): 63–73.

Chiat, Shulamuth. 1983. Why Mikey's right and my key's wrong: The significance of stress and word boundaries in a child's output system. *Cognition* 14: 275–300.

Chomsky, Noam and Halle, Morris. 1968. *The Sound Pattern of English*. New York: Harper, Row and somebody.

Clahsen, Harald, Rothweiler, Monika, Woest, Andreas, and Marcus, Gary. 1992. Regular and irregular inflection in the acquisition of German noun plurals. *Cognition* 45: 225–255.

Clements, G. Nick. 2004. The role of features in phonological inventories. Paper presented at the *Symposium on Phonological Theory: Representations and Architecture.*

Coetzee, Andries. Grammaticality and ungrammaticality in phonology. *Language* 84(2): 218–257.

Cohn, Abigail. 1992. The consequences of dissimilation in Sundanese. *Phonology* 9(2): 199–220.

Cohn, Abigail and McCarthy, John. 1994. Alignment and parallelism in Indonesian prosody. Ms., Cornell University, Ithaca, NY, and University of Massachusetts, Amherst.

Compton, A. J. and Streeter, M. 1977. Child phonology: Data collection and preliminary analyses. *Papers and Reports on Child Language Development* 13: 99–109.

Cooper, Robin P. and Aslin, Richard N. 1990. Preference for infant-directed speech in the first month after birth. *Child Development* 61: 1584–1595.

Cooper, Robin P. and Aslin, Richard N. 1994. Developmental differences in infant attention to the spectral properties of infant-directed speech. *Child Development* 65(6): 1663–1677.

Crowley, Terry. 2004. *Bislama Reference Grammar*. Oceanic Linguistics Special Publications, No. 31, University of Hawai'i Press.

Cruttenden, Alan. 2008. *Gimson's Pronunciation of English*, 7th edition. Hodder Education.

Cruz-Ferreira, Madalena. 2006. *Three's a Crowd? Acquiring Portugese in a Trilingual Environment*. Multilingual Matters.

Curtin, Suzanne. 1999. Positional prominence in the acquisition of prosodic structure. *Proceedings of the Annual Meeting of the Canadian Linguistics Society*. 89–100.

Curtin, Suzanne. 2009. Twelve-month-olds learn word-object associations differing only in stress patterns. *Journal of Child Language* 36(5): 1157–1165.

Curtin, Suzanne and Zuraw, Kie. 2002. Explaining constraint demotion in a developing system. In Barbora Skarabela, Sarah Fish, and Anna H.-J. Do (eds) *Proceedings of the 26th Annual Boston University Conference on Language Development*. Somerville, MA: Cascadilla. 118–129.

Cutler, Anne and Carter, C. 1987. The predominance of strong initial syllables in the English vocabulary. *Computer Speech and Language* 2: 133–142.

Cutler, Anne and Norris, D. 1988. The role of strong syllables in segmentation for lexical access. *Journal of Experimental Psychology; Human Perception and Performance* 14: 113–121.

Davis, Barbara L. and MacNeilage, Peter F. 1995. The articulatory basis of babbling. *Journal of Speech, Language and Hearing Research* 38: 1199–1211.

Davis, Barbara. L. and MacNeilage, Peter F. 2000. An embodiment perspective on the acquisition of speech perception. *Phonetica* 57(Special Issue): 229–241.

Davis, Katharine. 1995. Phonetic and phonological contrasts in the acquisition of voicing: Voice onset time production in Hindi and English. *Journal of Child Language* 22: 275–305.

de Boysson-Bardies, Bénédicte, Sagart, Laurent, and Durand, Catherine. 1984. Discernible differences in the babbling of infants according to target language. *Journal of Child Language* 11(1): 1–15.

de Boysson-Bardies, Bénédicte and Marilyn Vihman. 1991. Adaptation to language: Evidence from babbling and first words in four languages. *Language* 67: 297–319.

de Boysson-Bardies, Bénédicte, Halle, Pierre, Sagart, Laurent, and Durand, Catherine. 1989. A cross-linguistic investigation of vowel formants in babbling. *Journal of Child Language* 16(1): 1–17.

DeCasper, Anthony J. and Fifer, William P. 1980. Of human bonding: Newborns prefer their mothers' voices. *Science* 208(4448): 1174–1176.

de Lacy, Paul. 2002. *The Formal Expression of Markedness*. Doctoral dissertation, University of Massachusetts, Amherst.

Delattre, P. C., Liberman, A. M., and Cooper, F. S. 1955. Acoustic loci and transitional cues for consonants. *The Journal of the Acoustical Society of America* 27(4): 769–773.

Demuth, Katherine and McCullough, Elizabeth. 2009a. The acquisition of clusters in French. *Journal of Child Language* 36: 425–448.

Demuth, Katherine, Culbertson, Jennifer and Alter, Jennifer. 2006. Word-minimality, epenthesis, and coda licensing in the acquisition of English. *Language & Speech* 49: 137–174.

Demuth, Katherine and Johnson, Mark. 2003. Truncation to subminimal words in early French. *Canadian Journal of Linguistics* 48: 211–241.

Deuchar, Margaret and Clarke, Angeles. 1996. Early bilingual acquisition of the voicing contrast in English and Spanish. *Journal of Phonetics* 24: 351–365.

Deville, Gérard. 1891. Notes sur le développement du langage II. *Revue de linguistique et de philologie comparée* 24.

Dinnsen, Daniel A. 1996. Context effects in the acquisition of fricatives. In Barbara Bernhardt, John Gilbert, and David Ingram (eds) *Proceedings of the UBC International Conference on Phonological Acquisition*. Vancouver, BC: University of British Columbia. 136–148.

Dinnsen, Daniel A. 2002. A reconsideration of children's phonological representations. In B. Skarabela, S. Fish, and A. H.-J. Do (eds) *Proceedings of the 26th Annual Boston University Conference on Language Development*. Somerville, MA: Cascadilla Press. 1–23.

Dinnsen, Daniel A. and Barlow, Jessica. 1998. On the characterization of a chain shift in normal and delayed phonological acquisition. *Journal of Child Language* 25: 61–94.

Dinnsen, Daniel A. and O'Connor, Kathleen M. 2001. Typological predictions in developmental phonology. *Journal of Child Language* 28: 597–628.

Dinnsen, Daniel A., Green, C. R. Gierut, Judith A., and Morrisette, Michele L. 2011. On the anatomy of a chain shift. *Journal of Linguistics* 47: 275–299.

Do, Young Ah. 2012. Learning alternations in Korean noun paradigms. In Jaehoon Choi, Alan Hogue, Jeffrey Punske, Deniz Tat, Jessamy Schertz, and Alex Trueman (eds) *Proceedings of the 29th West Coast Conference on Formal Linguistics*. Somerville, MA: Cascadilla Proceedings Project. 319–327.

Do, Young Ah. 2013. The early stages of learning alternations. Ms., MIT.

Dodd, Barbara, Holm, Alison, Hua, Zhu, and Crosbie, Sharon. 2003. Phonological development: A normative study of British English-speaking children. *Clinical Linguistics and Phonetics* 17(8): 617–643.

Donegan, Patricia J. 2013. Normal vowel development. In Martin J. Ball and Fiona E. Gibbon (eds) *Handbook of Vowels and Vowel Disorders.* New York: Psychology Press. 24–60.

Donegan, Patricia J. and Stampe, David. 1979. The study of natural phonology. In Daniel A. Dinnsen (ed) *Current Approaches to Phonological Theory.* Bloomington, IN: Indiana University Press. 126–173.

Dow, Michael. 2013. Multiple repairs for voiced obstruent codas in Berbice Dutch Creole. Paper Presented at mfm21, Manchester UK, May 2013.

Dunn, L. and Dunn, L. 2007. *The Peabody Picture Vocabulary Test,* 4th edition. Circle Pines, MN: American Guidance Service.

Dupoux, E., Kakehi, K. Hirose, Y. Pallier, C., and Mehler, J. 1999. Epenthetic vowels in Japanese: A perceptual illusion? *Journal of Experimental Psychology: Human Perception and Performance,* 25(6): 1568–1578.

Dyson, Alice T. and Amayreh, Mousa M. 2000. Phonological errors and sound changes in Arabic-speaking children. *Clinical Linguistics and Phonetics* 14(2): 79–109.

Echols, Catherine H. 1993. A perceptually-based model of children's earliest productions. *Cognition* 46: 245–296.

Echols, Catherine H. and Newport, Elissa L. 1992. The role of stress and position in determining first words. *Language Acquisition* 2(3): 189–220.

Edwards, Jan and Beckman, Mary E. 2008. Some cross-linguistic evidence for modulation of implicational universals by language-specific frequency effects in phonological development. *Language Learning and Development* 4(2): 122–156.

Eimas. Peter D., Siqueland, Einar R. Jusczyk, Peter, and Vigorito, James. 1971. *Science* vol. 171, no 3968: 303–306.

Eisner, Jason. 1999. Doing OT in a straitjacket. Ms., UCLA.

Elbers, Loekie. 1982. Operating principles in repetitive babble: a cognitive continuity approach. *Cognition* 12: 45–63.

Elenbaas, Nine. 1999. *A unified account of binary and ternary stress: considerations from Sentani and Finnish.* Ph.D. dissertation. Utrecht University.

Emeneau, Murray. 1955. *The Kolami Language.* Berkeley: University of California Press.

Fabiano, Leah and Goldstein, Brian. 2005. Phonological cross-linguistic effects in bilingual Spanish-English speaking children. *Journal of Multilingual Communication Disorders* 3(1): 56–63.

Fabiano-Smith, Leah and Goldstein, Brian. 2010. Phonological acquisition in bilingual Spanish-English speaking children. *Journal of Speech, Language, and Hearing Research* 53: 160–178.

Fabiano-Smith, Leah and Barlow, Jessica. 2010. Interaction in bilingual phonological acquisition: evidence from phonetic inventories. *International Journal of Bilingual Education and Bilingualism* 13(1): 81–97.

Fahs, von Achim. 1985. *Grammatik des Pali.* Leipzig: VEB Verlag Enzykopädie Leipzig.

Fanselow, Gisbert and Féry, Caroline. 2002. Ineffability in grammar. In G. Fanselow and C. Féry (eds) *Resolving Conflicts in Grammars: Optimality Theory in Syntax, Morphology, and Phonology*. Special Issue 11 of *Linguistische Berichte*. Hamburg: Buske. 265–307.

Fee, Jane and David, Ingram. 1982. Reduplication as a strategy of phonological development. *Journal of Child Language* 9: 41–54.

Feldman, Heidi M., Dollaghan, Christine A. Campbell, Thomas F., Kurs-Lasky, Marcia, Janosky, Janine E., and Paradise, Jack L. 2000. Measurement properties of the MacArthur communicative inventories at ages one and two years. *Child Development* 71(2): 310–322.

Fennell, Christopher T. 2012. Object familiarity enhances infants' use of phonetic detail in novel words. *Infancy* 17(3): 339–353.

Fennell, Christopher T. and Byers-Heinlein, Krista. 2014. You sound like Mommy: Bilingual and monolingual infants learn words best from speakers typical of their language environments. *International Journal of Behavioral Development* 38(4): 309–316.

Fennell, Christopher T. and Waxman, Sandra R. 2010. What paradox? Referential cues allow for infant use of phonetic detail in word learning. *Child Development* 81(5): 1376–1383.

Fenson, Larry, Bates, Elizabeth, Dales, Philip, Goodman, Reznick, J. Steven, and Thal, Donna. 2000. Measuring variability in early child language: Don't shoot the messenger. *Child Development* 71(2): 323–328.

Fenson, Larry, Dale, Philip S. Reznick, J. Steven, Bates, Elizabeth, Thal, Donna, and Pethick, S. 1994a. Variability in early communicative development. *Monographs of the Society for Research in Child Development* 59(5, No. 242).

Fenson, Larry, Dale, Philip S., Reznick, J. Steven, Thal, Donna, Bates, Elizabeth, Hartung, J. P., Pethick, S. and Reilly, J. S. 1994b. *The MacArthur Communicative Development Inventories: User's Guide and Technical Manual*. San Diego, CA: Singular Publishing Group.

Ferguson, Charles A. and Farwell, Carol B. 1975. Words and sounds in early language acquisition. *Language* 51: 419–439.

Fernald, Anne. 1984. The perceptual and affective salience of mother's speech to infants. In L. Feagans, C. Garvey and R. Golinokoff (eds) *The Origins and Growth of Communication*. Norwood, NJ: Ablex. 5–29.

Fernald, Anne. 1985. Four-month-old infants prefer to listen to motherese. *Infant Behaviour and Development* 8: 181–195.

Fernald, Anne and Kuhl, Patricia. 1987. Acoustic determinants of infant preference for motherese speech. *Infant Behavior and Development* 40: 279–293.

Fernald, Anne and Simon, Thomas. 1984. Expanded intonation contours in mothers' speech to newborns. *Developmental Psychology* 20(1): 104–113.

Fernald, Anne, Taeschner, Traute, Dunn, Judy, Papousek, Mechthild, de Boysson-Bardies, Bénédicte, and Fukui, Ikuko. 1989. A cross-language study of prosodic modifications in mothers' and fathers' speech to preverbal infants. *Journal of Child Language* 16: 477–501.

Fikkert, Paula. 1994. *On the Acquisition of Prosodic Structure*. PhD dissertation, University of Leiden.

Fikkert, Paula and Levelt, Clara C. 2008. How does Place fall into place? The lexicon and emergent constraints in children's developing phonological grammar. In Peter Avery, B. Elan Dresher, and Keren Rice (eds) *Contrast in Phonology: Theory, Perception, Acquisition*. Berlin & New York: Mouton de Gruyter. 231–268.

Fikkert, Paula and Altvater-Mackensen, Nicole. 2013. Insights into variation across children based on longitudinal Dutch data on phonological acquisition. *Studia Linguistica* 67(1): 148–164.

Firchow, I. and Firchow, J. 1969. An abbreviated phoneme inventory. *Anthropological Linguistics* 11: 271–276.

Flege, James Emil. 2009. Give input a chance! In T. Piske and M. Young-Scholten (eds) *Input Matters in SLA*. Bristol: Multilingual Matters. 175–190.

Flege, James Emil and MacKay, Ian. 2011. What accounts for 'age' effects on overall degree of foreign accent? In M. Wrembel, M. Kul, and K. Dziubalska-Kołaczyk (eds) *Achievements and Perspectives in the Acquisition of Second Language Speech: New Sounds 2010*, Vol. 2. Bern, Switzerland: Peter Lang. 65–82.

Flynn, Darin. 2006. *Articulator Theory*. Ms., University of Calgary.

Flynn, Darin. 2012. *Phonology: The Distinctive Features of Speech Sounds*. Ms., University of Calgary.

Fonagy, I. 1980. L'accent en français, accent probabilitaire: dynamique d'un changement prosodique. *L'accent en français contemporain, Studia Phonetica* 15: 123–133.

Foulkes, Paul and Docherty, Gerry. 2000. Another chapter in the story of /r/: 'Labiodental' variants in British English. *Journal of Sociolinguistics* 4(1): 30–59.

Freitas, M. João. 1997. *Aquisição da Estrutura Silábica do Português Europeu*. PhD Dissertation, Universidade de Lisboa.

Freitas, M. João. 2003. The acquisition of Onset clusters in European Portuguese. *Probus* 15: 27–46.

Frota, Sónia. 2009. Early Prosody in European Portuguese. Talk given at UAB. Available at: http://ww3.fl.ul.pt/LaboratorioFonetica/texts/Frota_UAB2_2009.pdf

Frota, Sónia and Vigario, Maria. 2008. Early intonation in European Portuguese. Talk given at TIE3, University of Lisbon.

Fudge, E. 1969. Syllables. *Journal of Linguistics* 5: 253–287.

Furby, Christine E. 1974. Garawa phonology. *Papers in Australian Linguistics 7*. Canberra: Australian National University.

Gandour, Jack. 1981. The nondeviant nature of deviant phonological systems. *Journal of Communication Disorders* 14: 11–29.

Gandour, Jack, Petty, Sorane Holasuit, Dardarananda, Rochana, Dechongkit, Sumalee, and Mukongoen, Sunee. 1986. The acquisition of the voicing contrast in Thai: A study of voice onset time in word-initial stop consonants. *Journal of Child Language* 13: 561–572.

Garlock, V. M., Walley, A. C., and Metsala, J. L. 2001. Age of-acquisition, word frequency, and neighborhood density effects on spoken word recognition by children and adults. *Journal of Memory and Language* 45: 468–492.

Gennari, S. and Demuth, Katherine. 1997. Syllable omission in Spanish. In E. M. Hughes and A. Green (eds) *Proceedings of the 21st Annual Boston University Conference on Language Development*. 1. Somerville, MA: Cascadilla Press. 182–193.

Genessee, Fred, Nicoladis, Elena, and Paradis, Johanne. 1995. Language differentiation in early bilingual development. *Journal of Child Language* 22: 611–631.

Gildersleeve-Neumann, E. Christina, Kester, Ellen S., Davis, Barbara L., and Peña, Elizabeth D. 2008. English speech sound development in preschool-aged children from bilingual English-Spanish environments. *Language, Speech and Hearing Services in Schools* 39: 314–328.

Gnanadesikan, Amalia. 2004. Markedness and faithfulness constraints in child phonology. In Kager et al. (2004). 73–108.

Goad, Heather. 1997. Consonant harmony in child language: an optimality-theoretic account. In S. J. Hannahs and Martha Young-Scholten (eds) *Focus on Phonological Acquisition*. Amsterdam & Philadelphia: Benjamins. 113–142.

Goad, Heather. 2010. *Allophony and Contrast without Features*. Talk given at PhonBank: Future Directions, MUN.

Goad, Heather and Ingram, David. 1987. Individual variation and its relevance to a theory of phonological acquisition. *Journal of Child Language* 14: 419–432.

Goad, Heather and Brannen, Kathleen. 2003. Phonetic evidence for phonological structure in syllabification. In J. Van de Weijer, V. Van Heuven, and H. Van der Hulst (eds) *Issues in the Phonetics-Phonology Interface*. Amsterdam: John Benjamins. 3–30.

Goad, Heather and Buckley, Meaghen. 2006. Prosodic structure in Child French: Evidence for feet. *Catalan Journal of Linguistics* 5: 109–142.

Goad, Heather and Rose, Yvan. 2004. Input elaboration, head faithfulness and evidence for representation in the acquisition of left-edge clusters in West Germanic. In Kager et al. (2004). 101–157.

Goldstein, Brian and Washington, Patricia Swasey. 2001. An initial investigation of phonological patterns in typically developing 4-year-old Spanish-English bilingual children. *Language, Speech and Hearing Services in Schools* 32: 153–164.

Gouskova, Maria. 2003. *Deriving Economy: Syncope in Optimality Theory*. Doctoral Dissertation, University of Massachusetts, Amherst.

Gouskova, Maria. 2004. Relational hierarchies in OT: The case of syllable contact. *Phonology* 21(2): 201–250.

Gouskova, Maria. 2007. The reduplicative template in Tonkawa. *Phonology* 24(3): 367–396.

Gouskova, Maria. 2010. Optimality theory in phonology. In B. Heine and H. Narrog (eds) *The Oxford Handbook of Linguistic Analysis*. 531–553. Oxford, UK: Oxford University Press.

Grijzenhout, Janet and Joppen, Sandra. 1998. First steps in the acquisition of German phonology: A case study. Ms., Heinrich-Heine-Universität, Düsseldorf.

Gurevich, Naomi. 2004. *Lenition and Contrast: The Functional Consequences of Certain Phonologically Conditioned Sound Changes*. Outstanding Dissertations in Linguistics, New York: Garland Publishing.

Hale, Mark and Reiss, Charles. 1998. Formal and empirical arguments concerning phonological acquisition. *Linguistic Inquiry* 29: 656–683.

Hansson, Gunnar O. 2001. *Theoretical and Typological Issues in Consonant Harmony*. PhD dissertation, University of California, Berkeley.

Hansson, Gunnar O. 2007. On the evolution of consonant harmony: the case of secondary articulation agreement. *Phonology* 24(1): 77–120.

Hansson, Gunnar O. 2010. *Consonant Harmony: Long-Distance Interaction in Phonology.* University of California Publications in Linguistics, 145. Berkeley, CA: University of California Press.

Harms, Phillip Lee. 1984. Fonologia del Epena Pedee (Saija). *Sistemos Fonologicos de Idiomas Colombiano*s 5: 157–201.

Harris, James. 1973. On the order of certain rules in Spanish. In S. Anderson and P. Kiparsky (eds) *A Festschrift for Morris Halle.* New York: Holt. 59–76.

Harris, John. 1990. Segmental complexity and phonological government. *Phonology* 7: 255–300.

Harris, John. 2011. Deletion. In Marc van Oostendorp, Colin Ewen, Elizabeth Hume, and Keren Rice (eds) *The Blackwell Companion to Phonology.* Oxford: Wiley-Blackwell. 1597–1621.

Harris, John and Gussman, Edmund. 2002. Word final codas. *UCL Working Papers in Linguistics* 14: 1–42.

Hayes, Bruce. 1981. *A Metrical Theory of Stress Rules.* Doctoral dissertation, MIT, Cambridge, MA. Revised version distributed by Indiana University Linguistics Club, Bloomington, Indiana.

Hayes, Bruce. 1995. *Metrical Stress Theory: Principles and Case Studies.* Chicago, IL; University of Chicago Press.

Hayes, Bruce. 1999. Phonetically-driven phonology: The role of optimality theory and inductive grounding. In Michael Darnell, Edith Moravscik, Michael Noonan, Frederick Newmeyer, and Kathleen Wheatly (eds) *Functionalism and Formalism in Linguistics,* Volume I: General Papers. Amsterdam: John Benjamins. 243–285.

Hayes, Bruce. 2004. Phonological acquisition in optimality theory: The early stages. In Kager et al. (2004). 158–203.

Hayes, Bruce. 2009. *Introductory Phonology.* Malden, MA: Wiley-Blackwell.

Hayes, Bruce, Robert Kirchner and Donca Steriade. (eds.) 2004. *Phonetically Based Phonology* Cambridge, UK: Cambridge University Press.

Hess, Thom and Heaman, Isabel. 1989. *Exercises for Introducing the Study of Language.*

Hirsh-Pacek, Kathy, Treiman, Rebecca, and Scheiderman, M. 1984. Brown and Hanlon revisited: Mothers' sensitivity to ungrammatical forms. *Journal of Child Language* 11: 81–88.

Hochberg, Judith G. 1988. Learning Spanish stress: Developmental and theoretical perspectives. *Language* 64(4): 683–706.

Hoff, Erika. 2008. *Language Development,* 5th edition. Belmont, CA: Wadsworth Cengage Learning.

Hoijer, Harry. 1933. Tonkawa: An Indian language of Texas. In Franz Boas and Harry Hoijer (eds) *Handbook of American Indian Languages* 3. New York: J.J. Augustin. 1–148.

Hollich, George, Jusczyk, Peter, and Luce, Paul. 2002. Lexical neighborhood effects in 17-month-old word learning. *Proceedings of the 26th Annual Boston University Conference on Language Development.* Boston, MA: Cascadilla Press. 314–323.

Houston-Price, C. and Nakai, S. 2004. Distinguishing novelty and familiarity effects in infant preference procedures. *Infant and Child Development* 13: 341–348.

Howe, Darin [Flynn] and Pulleyblank, Douglas. 2001. Patterns and timing of glottalisation. *Phonology* 18(1): 45–80.

Hualde, Jose Ignacio. 1992. *Catalan*. London & New York: Routledge.

Hume, Elizabeth. 1994. *Front Vowels, Coronal Consonants and their Interaction in Nonlinear Phonology*. New York: Garland.

Hume, Elizabeth. 2004. The indeterminacy/attestation model of metathesis. *Language* 80(2): 203–237.

Hume, Elizabeth and Seo, Misun. 2004. Metathesis in Faroese and Lithuanian: From speech perception to optimality theory. *Nordic Journal of Linguistics* 27(1): 1–26.

Hyman, Larry. 1995. Nasal consonant harmony at a distance: The case of Yaka. *Studies in African Linguistics* 24(1): 5–30.

Idris, Hélène Fatma. 2004. Modern developments in the Dinka language. *Göteborg Africana Informal Series* 3. University of Göteborg.

Ingram, David. 1981. The emerging phonological system of an Italian-English bilingual child. *Journal of Italian Linguistics* 6: 95–113.

Ingram, David. 1985. On children's homonyms. *Journal of Child Language* 12: 671–680.

Ingram, David. 1986. Phonological development: Production. In P. Fletcher and M. Garman (eds) *Language Acquisition*, 2nd edition. Cambridge, MA: Cambridge University Press.

Ingram, David. 1988. The acquisition of word-initial [v]. *Language and Speech* 31(1): 77–85.

Ingram, David and Ingram, Kelly D. 2001. A whole-word approach to phonological analysis and intervention. *Language, Speech and Hearing Services in Schools* 32: 271–283.

Inkelas, Sharon, Orgun, Orhan, and Zoll, Cheryl. 1997. The implications of lexical exceptions for the nature of the grammar. In I. Roca (ed) *Derivations and Constraints in Phonology*. New York: Oxford University Press. 393–418.

Inkelas, Sharon and Rose, Yvan. 2008. Positional neutralization: A case study from child language. *Language* 83: 707–736.

Ito, Junko. 1986. *Syllable Theory in Prosodic Phonology*. Doctoral Dissertation, University of Massachusetts Amherst.

Ito, Junko. 1989. A prosodic theory of epenthesis. *Natural Language and Linguistic Theory* 7: 219–271.

Ito, Junko and Mester, Armin. 1986. The phonology of voicing in Japanese: theoretical consequences for morphological accessibility. *Linguistic Inquiry* 17: 49–73.

Ito, Junko and Mester, Armin. 1995. The core-periphery structure of the lexicon and constraints on reranking. In J. Beckman, S. Urbanczyk, and L. Walsh (eds) *Papers in Optimality Theory*. Amherst: GLSA. 181–210.

Jaeger, Jeri. 1984. Assessing the psychological status of the vowel shift rule. *Journal of Psycholinguistic Research* 13: 13–36.

Jaeger, Jeri. 1997. How to say 'Grandma': The problem of developing phonological representations. *First Language* 17(1): 1–29.

Jakobson, Roman. 1941/1968. *Child Language, Aphasia, and Phonological Universals*. The Hague: Mouton. Eng. tr. of *Kindersprache, Aphasie und allgemeine Lautgesetze*. Uppsala, 1941.

Jakobson, Roman, Fant, Gunnar, and Halle, Morris. 1952. *Preliminaries to Speech Analysis*. Cambridge, MA: MIT Press.

Jakobson, Roman and Halle, Morris. 1956. *Fundamentals of Language*. The Hague, The Netherlands: Mouton.

Jesney, Karen. 2005. *Chain Shift in Phonological Acquisition*. MA Thesis, University of Calgary.

Jesney, Karen, and Tessier, Anne-Michelle. 2009. Gradual learning and faithfulness: Consequences of ranked *vs.* weighted constraints. In Anisa Schardl, Martin Walkow, and Muhammad Abdurrahman (eds) *Proceedings of the North East Linguistic Society 38*. Amherst: GLSA. 375–388.

Jesney, Karen and Tessier, Anne-Michelle. 2011. Biases in Harmonic Grammar: The road to restrictive learning. *Natural Language and Linguistic Theory* 29: 251–290.

Jiménez, Beatrice C. 1987. Acquisition of Spanish Consonants in Children Aged 3–5 Years, 7 Months. *Language, speech, and hearing services in schools*. 18: 357–336.

Johnson, Carolyn and Lancaster, Paige. 1998. The development of more than one phonology: A case study of a Norwegian-English bilingual child. *International Journal of Bilingualism* 2(3): 265–300.

Johnson, Carolyn E. and Wilson, Ian L. 2002. Phonetic evidence for early language differentiation: Research issues and some preliminary data. *International Journal of Bilingualism* 6(3): 271–289.

Johnson, Jacqueline, Lewis, Lawrence, and Hogan, Jay. 1997. A production limitation in syllable number: A longitudinal study of one child's early vocabulary. *Journal of Child Language* 24: 327–349.

Johnson, Wyn and Reimers, Paula. 2010. *Patterns in Child Phonology*. Edinburgh, UK: Edinburgh University Press.

Jun, Jongho. 1995. *Perceptual and Articulatory Factors in Place Assimilation: An Optimality Theoretic Approach*. Doctoral dissertation, University of California, Los Angeles.

Jun, Jongho and Lee, Jeehyun. 2007. Multiple stem-final variants in Korean native nouns and loanwords. *Eoneohag* 47: 159–187.

Jun, S. A. and Fougeron, C. 2000. A phonological model of French intonation. In Antonis Botinis (ed) *Intonation: Analysis, Modeling and Technology*. Dordrecht: Kluwer Academic Publishers. 209–242.

Jurgec, Peter. 2010. Disjunctive lexical stratification. *Linguistic Inquiry* 41(1): 149–161.

Jusczyk, Peter W. 1997a. *The Discovery of Spoken Language*. Cambridge, MA: MIT Press.

Jusczyk, Peter W. 1997b. Finding and remembering words: Some beginnings by English-learning infants. *Current Directions in Psychological Science* 6(6): 170–174.

Jusczyk, Peter W., Cutler, Anne, and Redanz, Nancy. 1993. Infants'preference for the predominant stress patterns of English words. *Child Development* 64: 675–687.

Jusczyk, Peter W., Houston, Derek M., and Newsome, Mary. 1999. The beginnings of word segmentation in English-learning infants. *Cognitive Psychology* 39: 159–207.

Jusczyk. Peter, Luce, Paul and Charles-Luce, Jan. 1994. Infants' sensitivity to phonotactic patterns in the native language. *Journal of Memory and Language* 33: 630–645.

Jusczyk, Peter W. and Aslin, Richard. 1995. Infants' detection of the sound patterns of words in fluent speech. *Cognitive Psychology* 29(1): 1–23.

Kager, René. 1999. *Optimality Theory*. Cambridge, UK: Cambridge University Press.

Kager, René, Pater, Joseph, and Zonneveld, Wim (eds). 2004. *Fixing Priorities: Constraints in Phonological Acquisition*. Cambridge, UK,: Cambridge University Press.

Kaplan. Abby. 2010. *Phonology Shaped by Phonetics: The Case of Intervocalic Lention*. Doctoral dissertation, UC Santa Cruz.

Kappa, Ioanna. 2002. On the acquisition of syllable structure in Greek. *Journal of Greek Linguistics* 3: 1–52.

Kawahara, Shigeto. 2007. Sonorancy and geminacy. In *University of Massachusetts Occasional Papers in Linguistics 32: Papers in Optimality III*. Amherst: GLSA. 145–186.

Kaye, Jonathan. 1990. 'Coda' licensing. *Phonology Yearbook* 7(2): 301–330.

Kazazis, Kostas. 1969. Possible evidence for (near-)underlying forms in the speech of one child. In the *Proceedings of the Chicago Linguistic Society* (CLS) 5: 382–388.

Keffala, Bethany and Barlow, Jessica A. 2013. Interaction in Spanish-English bilinguals' acquisition of segments and syllable types. Paper Presented at the International Child Phonology Conference, Nijmegen, The Netherlands.

Keffala, Bethany and Barlow, Jessica. 2014. Frequency and complexity differences predict interaction in bilingual phonological acquisition. Paper Presented at the 88th Annual Meeting of the Linguistic Society of America, Minneapolis, MN.

Kehoe, Margaret. 2000. Truncation without shape constraints: The latter stages of prosodic acquisition. *Language Acquisition* 8(1): 23–67.

Kehoe, Margaret and Lléo, Conxita. 2003. The acquisition of syllable types in monolingual and bilingual German and Spanish children. In Barbara Beachley, Amanda Brown, and Frances Conlin (eds) *Proceedings of BUCLD27*. Somerville, MA: Cascadilla Press. 402–413.

Kehoe, Margaret and Stoel-Gammon, Carol. 1997. Truncation patterns in English-speaking children's word productions. *Journal of Speech, Language and Hearing Research* 40: 526–541.

Kehoe, Margaret and Stoel-Gammon, Carol. 2001. Development of syllable structure by English-speaking children with particular reference to rhymes. *Journal of Child Language* 28: 393–432.

Kehoe, Margaret and Hilaire-Debove, Geraldine. 2004. The structure of branching onsets and rising diphthongs: Evidence from the acquisition of French. In A. Brugos, Linnea Micciulla, and Christine E. Smith (eds) *Proceedings of BUCLD28*. Somervile, MA: Cascadilla Press. 282–293.

Kehoe, Margaret, Hilaire-Debove, Geraldine, Demuth, Katherine, and Lléo, Conxita. 2008. The structure of branching onsets and rising dipthongs: Evidence from the acquisition of French and Spanish. *Language Acquisition* 15(1): 5–57.

Kemler Nelson, Deborah G., Jusczyk, Peter W., Mandel, Denise R., Myer, James, Turk, Alice, and Gerken, Louann. 1995. The headturn preference procedure for testing auditory perception. *Infant Behaviour and Development* 18: 111–116.

Kenstowicz, Michael. 1996. Base-identity and uniform exponence: Alternatives to cyclicity. In J. Durand and B. Laks (eds) *Currents Trends in Phonology: Models and Methods*. Salford: European Studies Research Institute, University of Salford. 363–393.

Keren-Portnoy, Tamar, Majorano, Marinella, and Vihman, Marilyn. 2009. From phonetics to phonology: The emergence of first words in Italian. *Journal of Child Language* 36: 235–267.

Kerkhoff, Annemarie. 2007. *Acquisition of Morpho-Phonology; The Dutch Voicing Alternation.* Doctoral dissertation, University of Utrecht.

Keshavarz, Mohammad Hossein and Ingram, David. 2002. The early phonological development of a Farsi-English bilingual child. *International Journal of Bilingualism* 6: 255–269.

Key, Harold. 1961. The Phonotactics of Cayuvava. *International Journal of American Linguistics* 27. 143–150.

Khattab, G. and Al-Tamimi, J. 2011. *The Role of Geminates in Shaping Early Word Patterns by Lebanese Arabic Speaking Children.* Talk given at International Child Phonology Conference, University of York, York, UK, June 15–18.

Kim, Hung-Gyu and Kang, Beom-Mo. 2000. Frequency analysis of Korean morpheme and word usage. Technical report, Institute of Korean Culture, Korea University, Seoul.

Kimbrough Oller, D. 2000. *The Emergence of the Speech Capacity.* Mahwah, NJ: Lawrence Erlbaum Associates.

Kimbrough Oller, D. and Eilers, R. E. 1988. The role of audition in babbling. *Child Development* 59(2): 441–449.

Kiparsky, Paul. 1973. Abstractness, opacity, and global rules. In Osamu Fujimura (ed) *Three Dimensions in Linguistic Theory.* Tokyo: TEC. 57–86.

Kiparsky, Paul and Menn, Lise. 1977. On the acquisition of phonology. In John Macnamara (ed) *Language Learning and Thought.* New York: Academic Press. 47–78.

Kirk, Cecilia and Demuth, Katherine. 2003. Onset/Coda asymmetries in the acquisition of clusters. In Barbara Beachley, Amanda Brown, and Frances Conlin (eds) *Proceedings of BUCLD 27.* Somerville, MA: Cascadilla Press. 437–448.

Kitamura, C., Thanavishuth, C., Burnham, D., and Luksaneeyanawin, S. 2002. Universality and specificity in infant-directed speech: Pitch modification as a function of infant age and sex in a tonal and non-tonal language. *Infant Behavior and Development* 24: 372–392.

Kouwenberg, S. 1994. *A Grammar of Berbice Dutch Creole.* Berlin: Mouton de Gruyter.

Kristoffersen, Kristian Emil and Simonsen, Hanne Gram. 2006. The acquisition of #/s/C clusters in Norwegian. *Journal of Multilingual Communication Disorders* 4: 231–241.

Kroeber, A.L. 1916. The speech of a Zuñi child. *American Anthropologist* 18(4): 529–534.

Kroeber, A. L. and Grace, George William (eds) 1960. *The Sparkman Grammar of Luiseño.* Berkeley and Los Angeles: University of California Press.

Kubuzono, Haruo. 2005. Rendaku: Its domain and linguistic conditions. In Jeroen van de Weijer, Kensuke Nanjo, and Tetsuo Nishihara (eds) *Voicing in Japanese.* Berlin & New York: De Gruyter Mouton. 5–24.

Kuczaj, Stan A., II. 1978. Children's judgments of grammatical and ungrammatical irregular past-tense verbs. *Child Development* 49(2): 319–326.

Kunnari, Sari, Nakai, Satsuki, and Vihman, Marilyn. 2001. Cross-linguistic evidence for acquisition of geminates. *Psychology of Language and Communication* 5(2): 13–24.

Kyle, John. 1994. The limit of structure preservation in Dakota lexical phonology. *Kansas Working Papers in Linguistics* 19(2). University of Kansas Linguistics Graduate Student Assocation.

Ladefoged, Peter. 1993. *A Course in Phonetics*, 5th edition. Belmont, CA: Thomson/ Wadsworth Publishers.

Ladefoged, Peter and Maddieson, Ian. 1996. *The Sounds of the World's Languages*. Oxford: Blackwell.

Lee, Sam-Hyung, Lee, Phil-Young, and Im, Yoo-Jong. 2003. emalemiuy suptuk kwacengey kwanhan yenkwu ('the study on the process of the acquisition of final endings: A case of korean children under 36 months [translation as given]). *Kwukekyoyukhakyenkwu* 18: 320–346.

Leopold, W. 1947. *Speech Development of a Bilingual Child: A Linguist's Record. Vol. 2. Sound-Learning in the First Two Years*. Evanston, IL: Northwestern University Press.

Levelt, Clara C. 1994. *On the Acquisition of Place*. Doctoral Dissertation 8, Holland Institute of Generative Linguistics, Leiden University.

Levelt, Clara C. 2012. Perception mirrors production in 14- and 18-month olds: The case of coda consonants. *Cognition* 123: 174–179.

Levelt, Clara C., Schiller, Niels O., and Levelt, Willem J. M. 1999. A developmental grammar for syllable structure in the production of child language. *Brain and Language* 68: 291–299.

Levelt, Clara C. and van der Vijver, Ruben. 2004. Syllable types in cross-linguistic and developmental grammars. In Kager et al. 2004.

Lewis, Lawrence B., Antone, Carol, and Johnson, Jacqueline. 1999. Effects of prosodic stress and serial position on syllable omission in first words. *Developmental Psychology* 35(1): 45–59.

Li, Paul Jen-kuei 1985. A secret language in Taiwanese. *Journal of Chinese Linguistics* 13(1): 91–121.

Lidz, Jeffrey. 2001. Echo Reduplication in Kannada and the Theory of Word Formation. *The Linguistic Review* 18: 375–394.

Lisker, Leigh and Abramson, Arthur S. 1964. A cross-language study of voicing in initial stops: Acoustical Measurements. *Word* 20(3): 384–422.

Lléo, Conxita. 1990. Homonymy and reduplication: On the extended availability of two strategies in phonological acquisition. *Journal of Child Language* 17(2): 267–278.

Lléo, Conxita. 1997. Filler syllables, proto-articles and early prosodic constraints in Spanish and German. In A. Sorace, C. Heycock, and R. Shillcock (eds) *Proceedings of the GALA '97 Conference on Language Acquisition*. Edinburgh, UK: University of Edinburgh. 251–256.

Lléo, Conxita. 2001. The interface of phonology and syntax: The emergence of the article in the early acquisition of Spanish and German. In J. Weissenborn and B. Höhle (eds) *Approaches to Bootstrapping: Phonological, Syntactic and Neurophysiological Aspects of Early Language Acquisition*. Amsterdam/ Philadelphia: John Benjamins. 23–44.

Lléo, Conxita. 2002. The role of markedness in the acquisition of complex structures by German-Spanish bilinguals. *International Journal of Bilingualism* 6(3): 291–313.

Lléo, Conxita and Demuth, Katherine. 1999. Prosodic constraints on the emergence of grammatical morphemes: Crosslinguistic evidence from Germanic and Romance languages. In A. Greenhill, H. Littlefield, and Ch. Tano (eds) *Proceedings of the 23rd Annual Boston University Conference on Language Development.* Somerville, MA: Cascadilla Press. 407–418.

Lléo, Conxita and Kehoe, Margaret. 2002. On the interaction of phonological systems in child bilingual acquisition. *International Journal of Bilingualism* 6(3): 233–237.

Lleo, Conxita and Prinz, Michael. 1996. Consonant clusters in child phonology and the directionality of syllable structure assignment. *Journal of Child Language* 23: 31–56.

Locke, J. 1989. Babbling and early speech: Continuity and individual differences. *First Language* 9: 191–205.

Lombardi, Linda. 1999. Positional faithfulness and voicing assimilation in optimality theory. *Natural Language and Linguistic Theory* 17: 267–302.

Lombardi, Linda and McCarthy, John J. 1991. Prosodic circumscription in Choctaw. *Phonology* 8(1): 37–72.

Lorentz, J. P. 1976. An analysis of some deviant phonological rules of English. In D. M. Morehead and A. E. Morehead (eds) *Normal and Deficient Child Language.* Baltimore, MD: University Academic Press. 29–59.

Łubowicz, Ania. 2002. *Contrast Preservation in Phonological Mappings.* Doctoral Dissertation, University of Massachusetts, Amherst.

Łubowicz, Ania. 2003. Counter-feeding opacity as a chain-shift effect. In G. Garding and M. Tsujimura (eds) *Proceedings of WCCFL 22.* 315–327.

Lukaszewicz, Beata. 2007. Reduction in syllable onsets in the acquisition of Polish: Deletion, coalescence, metathesis and germination. *Journal of Child Language* 34(1): 53–82.

Macken, Marlys A. 1978. Permitted complexity in phonological development: one child's acquisition of Spanish consonants. *Lingua* 44: 219–253.

Macken, Marlys A. 1980a. Aspects of the acquisition of stop systems. In Grace Yeni-komshian, James F. Kavanagh and Charles A. Ferguson (eds) *Child Phonology, I: Production.* New York: Academic Press. 143–168.

Macken, Marlys A. 1980b. The child's lexical representation: The 'Puzzle-Puddle-Pickle' evidence. *Journal of Linguistics* 16(1): 1–17.

Macken, Marlys A. and Ferguson, Charles A. 1983. Cognitive aspects of phonological development: Model, evidence and issues. In K. E. Nelson (ed.) *Children's Language* vol 4: Hilsdale, NJ: Lawrence Erlbaum Associates.

MacKenzie, H., Graham, Susan A. and Curtin, Suzanne. 2011. 12-month-olds privilege words over other linguistic sounds in an associative learning task. *Developmental Science* 14(2): 399–410.

MacWhinney, Brian. 1975. Rules, rote and analogy in morphological formations by Hungarian children. *Journal of Child Language* 2: 65–77.

MacWhinney, Brian. 1978. *The Acquisition of Morphophonology.* Chicago: University of Chicago Press.

MacWhinney, Brian. 1985. Hungarian language acquisition as an exemplification of a general model of grammatical development. In D. I. Slobin (ed) *The Crosslinguistic Study of Language Acquisition: Vol 2. Theoretical Issues.* Hillsdale, NJ: Lawrence Erlbaum Associates. 1069–1155.

Maddieson, Ian. 1984. *Patterns of Sound.* Cambridge, UK: Cambridge University Press.

Major, Roy C. (ed.) 1988. Interlanguage Phonetics and Phonology. Thematic Issue of *Studies in Second Language Acquisition* 20(2).

Marchman, Virginia and Plunkett, K. 1989. Token frequency and phonological predictability in a pattern association network: Implications for child language acquisition. In G. Olson and E. Smith (eds) *Proceedings of the Eleventh Annual Meeting of the Cognitive Science Society.* Hillsdale, NJ: Lawrence Erlbaum Associates. 179–187.

Marcus, Gary, Pinker, Steven, Ullman, Michael, Hollander, Michelle, Rosen, T. J., Xu, Fei and Clahsen, Harald. 1992. Overregularisations in language acquisition. *Monographs of the Society for Research in Child Development 57.*

Marcus, Gary, Brinkmann, Ursula, Clahsen, Harald, Wiese, Richard, and Pinker, Steven. 1995. German inflection: The exception that proves the rule. *Cognitive Psychology* 29: 189–256.

Martlett, Steven. 2013. *Phonology from the Ground Up: The Basics.* Ms., Summer Institute of Linguistics.

Mascaró, Joan. 1976. *Catalan Phonology and the Phonological Cycle.* Doctoral Dissertation, MIT.

Mattys, Sven, Jusczyk, Peter, Luce, Paul, and Morgan, James. 1999. Phonotactic and prosodic effects on word Segmentation in infants. *Cognitive Psychology* 38: 465–494.

Maye, Jessica, Werker, Janet F., and Gerken, LouAnn. 2002. Infant sensitivity to distributional information can affect phonetic discrimination. *Cognition* 82: B101–111.

McAllister Byun, Tara. 2011. A gestural account of a child-specific neutralization in strong position. *Phonology* 28(3): 371–412.

McAllister Byun, Tara. 2012. Positional velar fronting: An updated articulatory account. *Journal of Child Language* 39: 1043–1076.

McCarthy, John J. 1986. OCP effects: Gemination and antigemination, *Linguistic Inquiry* 17(2): 207–263.

McCarthy, John J. 1999. *Introductory OT on CD-ROM.* Amherst, MA: GLSA.

McCarthy, John J. 2003. OT constraints are categorical. *Phonology* 20(1): 75–138.

McCarthy, John J. 2007. *Hidden Generalizations: Phonological Opacity in Optimality Theory.* London: Equinox.

McCarthy, John J. 2008a. *Doing Optimality Theory: Applying Theory to Data.* Wiley-Blackwell.

McCarthy, John J. 2008b. The gradual path to cluster simplification. *Phonology* 25: 271–319.

McCarthy, John J. 2011. Autosegmental spreading in Optimality Ttheory. In John Goldsmith, Elizabeth Hume, and Leo Wetzels (eds) *Tones and Features (Clements Memorial Volume).* Berlin: Mouton de Gruyter. 195–222.

McCarthy, John J. and Prince, Alan. 1986. Prosodic Morphology. Technical Report, University of Massachusetts Amherst and Rutgers University.

McCarthy, John J. and Prince, Alan. 1993 *Prosodic Morphology I: Constraint Interaction and Satisfaction.* Technical Report #3, Rutgers University Center for Cognitive Science.

McCarthy, John J. and Prince, Alan. 1995. Faithfulness and reduplicative identity. In Jill Beckman, Suzanne Urbanczyk, and Laura Walsh Dickey (eds) *University of Massachusetts Occasional Papers in Linguistics 18: Papers in Optimality Theory.* Amherst, MA: GLSA Publications. 249–384.

McCarthy, John J. and Wolf, Matthew. 2007. Less than zero: Correspondence and the null output. In Curt Rice and Sylvia Blaho (eds) *Modeling Ungrammaticality in Optimality Theory*. London: Equinox Publishing. 17–66.

McDonough, Joyce. 1991. On the representation of consonant harmony in Navajo. In D. Bates (ed) *Proceedings of WCCFL* 10. Somerville, MA: Cascadilla Press. 319–335.

McGowan, Rebecca, McGowan, Richard, Denny, Margaret, and Nittrouer, Susan. 2014. A longitudinal study of very young children's vowel production. *Journal of Speech Hearing and Language Research* 57: 1–14.

McLeod, Sharynne, van Doorn, Jan, and Reed, Vicki A. 2001. Normal acquisition of consonant clusters. *American Journal of Speech-Language Pathology* 10: 99–210.

Meira, Sérgio. 1998. Rhythmic stress in Tiriyó (Cariban). *International Journal of American Linguistics* 64(4): 352–378.

Meisel, Jurgen M. 2009. Second language acquisition in early childhood. *Zeitschrift für Sprachwissenschaft* 28(1): 5–34.

Menn, Lise. 1971. Phonotactic rules in beginning speech. *Lingua* 26: 225–251.

Menn, Lise. 1978. Phonological units in beginning speech. In A. Bell and J. Hooper-Bybee (eds) *Syllables and Segments*. Amsterdam: North-Holland. 157–172.

Menn, Lise and Matthei, Edward. 1992. The 'two-lexicon' account of child phonology: Looking back, looking ahead. In C. A. Ferguson, L. Menn, and C. Stoel-Gammon (eds) *Phonological Development: Models, Research, Implications*. Timonium, MD: York Press. 211–247.

Michailovsky, Boyd and Mazaudon, Martine. 1973. Notes on the Hayu language. *Kailash* 1(2): 135–152.

Michelson, Karin. 1988. *A Comparative Study of Lake Iroquoian Accent*. Studies in Natural Language and Linguistic Theory. Kluwer Academic Publishers.

Mithun, Marianne. 1989. The acquisition of polysynthesis. *Journal of Child Language* 16: 285–312.

Moe, A. J., Hopkins, C. J., and Rush, R. T. 1982. *The Vocabulary of First Grade Children*. Springfield, IL: Charles C. Thomas Publisher.

Mohanan, K. P. 1993. Fields of attraction in phonology. In John Goldsmith (ed) *The Last Phonological Rule: Reflections on Constraints and Derivations*. Chicago: University of Chicago Press. 61–116.

Montes Giraldo, Jose J. 1971. Acerca de la apropriacion por el niho del Sistema fonologico espanol. *Thesaurus: Boletin del instituto Caro y Cuervo* 26: 322–346.

Morelli, Frida. 1999. *The Phonotactics and Phonology of Obstruent Clusters in Optimality Theory*. Doctoral dissertation, University of Maryland, College Park.

Moreton, Elliott. 2004. Non-computable functions in optimality theory. In John J. McCarthy (ed) *Optimality Theory in Phonology: A Reader*. Malden, MA & Oxford: Blackwell. 141–163.

Moskowitz, Arlene I. 1970. The two-year-old stage in the acquisition of English phonology. *Language* 46: 426–441.

Mowrer, Domald E. and Burger, Sharon. 1991. A comparative analysis of phonological acquisition of consonants in the speech of 2 ½-6-year-old Xhosa- and English-speaking children. *Clinical Linguistics and Phonetics* 5(2): 139–164.

Mugdan, J. 1977. *Flexionsmorphologie und Psycholinguistik*. Tubingen: Narr.

Narayan, Chandan R., Werker, Janet F., and Beddor, Patrice Speetor. 2010. The interaction between acoustic salience and language experience in developmental speech perception: Evidence from nasal place discrimination. *Developmental Science* 13(3): 407–420.

Nazzi, Thierry. 2005. Use of phonetic specificity during the acquisition of new words: Differences between consonants and vowels. *Cognition* 98: 13–30.

Nazzi, Thierry, Bertoncini, Josiane, and Mehler, Jacques. 1998. Language discrimination by newborns: Towards an understanding of the role of rhythm. *Journal of Experimental Psychology: Human Perception and Performance* 24: 756–766.

Nelson, Nicole. 2000. Arguments for stressed rhyme faithfulness: A case study of nancowry. In Roger Billerey and Brook Danielle Lillehaugen (eds) *Proceedings of WCCFL19*. Somerville, MA: Cascadilla Press. 329–342.

Nevins, Andrew and Vaux, Bert. 2003. Metalinguistic, Shmetalinguistic: 'The Phonology of Shm – Reduplication'. In *The Proceedings of the 39th Chicago Linguistics Society*. 702–721.

Newlin-Łukowicz, Luiza. 2012. Polish stress: Looking for phonetic evidence of a bidirectional sytem. *Phonology* 29(2): 271–329.

Nicklas, Thurston. 1974. *The Elements of Choctaw*. Doctoral dissertation, University of Michigan, Ann Arbor.

Nwokah, Evangeline E. 1986. Consonantal substitution patterns in igbo phonological acquisition. *Language and Speech* 29(2): 159–176.

Odden, David. 1994. Adjacency parameters in phonology. *Language* 70: 289–330.

Ohala, John. 1981. The listener as a source of sound change. In: C. S. Masek, R. A. Hendrick, and M. F. Miller (eds) *Papers from the Parasession on Language and Behavior*. Chicago: Chicago Ling. Soc. 178–203.

Ohala, John. 1993. Sound change as nature's speech perception experiment. *Speech Communication* 13: 155–161.

Ohala, M. 1983. *Aspects of Hindi Phonology*. Delhi: Motilal Banarsidass.

Orgun, Cemil Orhan & Ronald L. Sprouse. 1999. From MPARSE to CONTROL: deriving ungrammaticality. *Phonology* 16. 191–224.

Osborn, Henry A. Jr. 1966. Warao I: Phonology and morphophonemics. *International Journal of American Linguistics* 32: 108–123.

Ota, Mitsuhiko. 1999. *Phonological Theory and the Development of Prosodic Structure: Evidence from Child Japanese*. Doctoral dissertation, Georgetown University, Washington, DC.

Ota, Mitsuhiko. 2001. Phonological theory and the development of prosodic structure: Evidence from child Japanese. *Annual Review of Language Acquisition* 1: 65–118.

Ota, Mitsuhiko and Green, Sam J. 2012. Input frequency and lexical variability in phonological development: a survival analysis of word-initial cluster production. *Journal of Child Language* 39(1): 1–28.

Paradis, Carole and LaCharité, Darlene. 2001. Guttural deletion in loanwords. *Phonology* 18: 255–300.

Paradis, Carole and LaCharité, Darlene. 2012. The influence of attitude on the Treatment of Interdentals in Loanwords: Ill-performed Importations. *Catalan Journal of Linguistics* 11: 97–126.

Paradis, Johanne. 2001. Do bilingual two-year-olds have separate phonological systems? *International Journal of Bilingualism* 5(1): 19–38.

Paradis, Johanne and Genessee, Fred. 1996. Syntactic acquisition in bilingual children: Autonomous or interdependent? *Studies in Second Language Acquisition* 18: 1–25.

Pater, Joe. 1996. *Consequences of Constraint Ranking*. PhD dissertation, McGill University.

Pater, Joe. 1997. Minimal violation and phonological development. *Language Acquisition* 6: 201–253.

Pater, Joe. 2000. Non-uniformity in English secondary stress: The role of ranked and lexically specific constraints. *Phonology* 17: 237–274.

Pater, Joe. 2001. Austronesian nasal substitution revisited. In L. Lombardi (ed) *Segmental Phonology in Optimality Theory: Constraints and Representations*. Cambridge, UK: Cambridge University Press. 159–182.

Pater, Joe. 2009. Weighted constraints in generative linguistics. *Cognitive Science* 33: 999–1035.

Pater, Joe. 2010. Morpheme-specific phonology: Constraint indexation and inconsistency resolution. In S. Parker (ed) *Phonological Argumentation: Essays on Evidence and Motivation*. London: Equinox. 123–154.

Pater, Joe and Barlow, Jessica A. 2003. Constraint conflict in cluster reduction. *Journal of Child Language* 30: 487–526.

Pater, Jose, Stager, Christine, and Werker, Janet F. 2004. The perceptual acquisition of phonological contrasts. *Language* 80(3): 384–402.

Pater, Joe and Werle, Adam. 2003. Direction of assimilation in child consonant harmony. *Canadian Journal of Linguistics* 48: 385–408.

Pater, Joe, Staubs, Robert, Jesney, Karen, and Smith, Brian. 2012. Learning probabilities over underlying representations. In the *Proceedings of the Twelfth Meeting of the ACL-SIGMORPHON: Computational Research in Phonetics, Phonology, and Morphology*. 62–71.

Pearson, Barbara, Fernandez, Sylvia C., Lewedeg, Vanessa, and Oller, D. Kimbrough. 1997. The relation of input factors to lexical learning by bilingual infants. *Applied Psycholinguistics* 18: 41–58.

Pegg, Judith. E. and Werker, Janet F. 1997. Adult and infant perception of two English phones. *The Journal of the Acoustical Society of America* 102: 3742–3753.

Pegg, Judith E., Werker, Janet F., and McLeod, Peter J. 1992. Preference for infant-directed over adult-directed speech: Evidence from 7-week-old infants. *Infant Behavior and Development* 15: 325–345.

Peña, E., Gutiérrez-Clellen, V., Iglesias, A., Goldstein, B., and Bedore, L. 2005. *The Bilingual English-Spanish Assessment*. Unpublished assessment instrument.

Peters, Ann M. 1977. Language learning strategies: Does the whole equal the sum of the parts? *Language* 53: 560–573.

Peters, Ann M. 2001. Filler syllables: What is their status in emerging grammars? *Journal of Child Language* 28(1): 229–242.

Peters, Ann M. and Menn, Lise. 1993. False starts and filler syllables: Ways to learn grammatical morphemes. *Language* 69(4): 742–777.

Petitto, Laura Ann and Marentette, Paula F. 1991. Babbling in the manual mode: Evidence for the ontogeny of language. *Science* 251: 1493–1496.

Pierrehumbert, Janet. 2001. Exemplar dynamics: Word frequency, lenition, and contrast. In J. Bybee and P. Hopper (eds) *Frequency Effects and the Emergence of Lexical Structure*. Amsterdam: John Benjamins. 137–157.

Pierrehumbert, Janet. 2006. The next toolkit. *Journal of Phonetics* 34: 516–530.

Piggott, Glyne L. 1987. On the autonomy of the feature [nasal]. In Lynn Macleod and Diane Brentari (eds) *Proceedings of CLS* 23(2): 223–238.

Piggott, Glyne. 1995. Epenthesis and syllable weight. *Natural Language and Linguistic Theory* 13(2): 283–326.

Piggott, Glyne L. 1999. At the right edge of words. *The Linguistic Review* 16(2): 143–185.

Pinker, Steven. 1984. *Learnability and Cognition: The Acquisition of Argument Structure*. Cambridge, MA: MIT Press.

Polka, Linda and Werker, Janet F. 1994. Developmental changes in perception of non-native vowel contrasts. *Journal of Experimental Psychology: Human Perception and Performance* 20(2): 421–435.

Poser, William. 1984. *The Phonetics and Phonology of Tone and Intonation in Japanese*, Doctoral dissertation, MIT, Cambridge, MA.

Poser, William. 1986. Diyari stress, metrical structure assignment, and the nature of metrical representation. In M. Dalrymple, Jeffrey Goldberg, Kristin Hanson, Michael Inman, Christopher Piñon, and Stephen Wechsler (eds) *Proceedings of the West Coast Conference on Formal Linguistics 5*. Stanford, CA: Stanford Linguistics Association.

Prasada, Sandeep and Pinker, Steven. 1993. Generalizations of regular and irregular morphological patterns. *Language and Cognitive Processes* 8(1): 1–56.

Priestly, Thomas. 1977 One idiosyncratic strategy in the acquisition of phonology. *Journal of Child Language* 4: 45–66.

Prince, Alan. 1983. Relating to the grid. *Linguistic Inquiry* 14(1): 19–100.

Prince, Alan. 1990. Quantitative consequences of rhythmic organization. In Karen Deaton, Manuela Noske and Michael Ziolkowski (eds) *Proceedings of CLS 26* vol 2. 355–398.

Prince, Alan. 2002. Arguing Optimality. In A. Carpenter, A. Coetzee and P. de Lacy (eds) *Papers in Optimality Theory* II. Amherst: GLSA. 269–304.

Prince, Alan. 2000. Comparative Tableaux. Ms., Rutgers University. Available as ROA-376.

Prince, Alan and Tesar, Bruce. 2004. Learning phonotactic distributions. In Kager et al. 245–291.

Prince, Alan and Smolensky, Paul. 1993. *Optimality Theory: Constraint Interaction in Generative Grammar*. Ms, Rutgers University & University of Colorado, Boulder. Published 2004, Malden, MA & Oxford: Blackwell.

Pye, Clifton. 1983. Intonational determinants of inflectional development in Quiché Mayan. *Language* 59(3): 583–604.

Pye, Clifton, Ingram, David, and List, H. 1987. A comparison of initial consonant acquisition in english and quiché. In K. Nelson and A. van Kleeck (eds) *Children's Language, Vol. 6*. Hillsdale, NJ: Erlbaum. 175–190.

Ragheb, Marwa and Stuart Davis. 2014. Geminate representation in Arabic. In: Farwaneh, Samira and Hamid Ouali (eds), Perspectives on Arabic Linguistics XXIV–XXV: Papers from the annual symposia on Arabic Linguistics. pp. 3–20.

Ramon-Casas, Marta, Swingley, Daniel, Sebastián-Gallés, Núria and Bosch Laura. 2009. Vowel categorization during word recognition in bilingual toddlers. *Cognitive Psychology* 59: 96–121.

Ramus, Franck, Nespor, Marina, and Mehler, Jacques. 1999. Correlates of linguistic rhythm in the speech signal. *Cognition* 73: 265–292.

Revithiadou Anthi and Tzakosta, Marina. 2004. Alternative grammars in acquisition: Markedness- vs. Faithfulness-oriented Learning. In A. Brugos, L. Micciula, and C. E. Smith (eds) *Proceedings of the 28th Annual Boston University Conference on Language Development: Supplement*. Somerville: Cascadilla Press.

Rice, Curt. 2006. Nothing is a phonological fact: Gaps and repairs at the phonology-morphology interface. In C. Davis, A-R. Deal, and Y. Zabbal (eds) *Proceedings of NELS36*. Amherst, MA: GLSA Publications. 27–38.

Rice, Mabel, Smolik, Filip, Perpich, Denise, Thompson, Travis, Rytting, Nathan, and Blossom, Megan. 2010. Mean Length of Utterance Levels in 6-Month Intervals for Children 3 to 9 Years With and Without Language Impairments. *Journal of Speech, Language and Hearing Research* 53(2): 333–349.

Riggle, Jason. 2004. Contenders and learning. In V. Chand, A. Kelleher, A. J. Rodríguez, and B. Schmeiser (eds) *Proceedings of the 23rd Annual Meeting of the West Coast Conference on Formal Linguistics*. Somerville, MA: Cascadilla Press. 649–662.

Roark, Brian and Demuth, Katherine. 2000. Prosodic constraints and the learner's environment: A corpus study. In S. C. Howell, S. A. Fish, and T. Keith-Lucas (eds) *Proceedings of BUCLD 24*. Somerville, MA: Cascadilla Press. 597–608.

Rosenblatt, F. 1958. The perceptron: A probabilistic model for information storage and organization in the brain. *Psychological Review* 65: 386–408.

Rose, Sharon and Walker, Rachel. 2004. A typology of consonant agreement as correspondence. *Language* 80: 475–531.

Rose, Sharon and Walker, Rachel. 2011. Harmony Systems. In J. Goldsmith, J. Riggle and A. Yu (eds.) *Handbook of Phonological Theory* (2nd ed.). Blackwell.

Rose, Yvan. 2000. *Headedness and Prosodic Licensing in the L1 Acquisition of Phonology*. Doctoral dissertation, McGill University.

Rose, Yvan. (2014). Corpus-based investigations of child phonological development: Formal and practical considerations. In Jacques Durand, Ulrike Gut, and Gjert Kirstoffersen (eds) *Handbook of Corpus Phonology*. Oxford: Oxford University Press. 265–285.

Rose, Yvan and Champdoizeau, Christine. 2008. There is no innate trochaic bias: Acoustic evidence in favour of the neutral start hypothesis. In A. Gavarró and M. J. Freitas (eds) *Language Acquisition and Development: Proceedings of GALA 2007*. Newcastle, UK: Cambridge Scholars Publishing. 359–369.

Rose, Yvan and Inkelas, Sharon. 2011. The interpretation of phonological patterns in first language acquisition. In Colin J. Ewan, Elizabeth Hume, Marc van Oostendorp, and Keren Rice (eds) *The Blackwell Companion to Phonology*. Malden, MA: Miley-Blackwell. 2414–2438.

Rubach, Jerzy. 1984. *Cyclic and Lexical Phonology: The Structure of Polish.* Dordrecht: Foris.

Rubach, Jerzy and Booij, Geert. 1985. A grid theory of stress in Polish. *Lingua* 66: 281–319.

Rubach, Jerzy and Booij, Geert. 1990. Edge of constituent effects in Polish. *Natural Language and Linguistic Theory* 8: 427–463.

Rumelhart, D. E. and J. L. McClelland. 1986. On learning the past tenses of English verbs. In D. E. Rumelhart, J. L. McClelland, and the PDP Research Group (eds) *Parallel Distributed Processing: Explorations in the Microstructure of Cognition. Vol. 2: Psychological and Biological Models.* Cambridge, MA: Bradford Books/MIT Press. 216–271.

Rvachew, Susan and Andrews, Ellen. 2002. The influence of syllable position on children's production of consonants. *Clinical Linguistics and Phonetics* 16: 183–198.

Ryan, Camille. 2013. Language Use in the United States: 2011: *American Community Survey Reports.*

Saffran, Jenny, Aslin, Richard, and Newport, Elissa. 1996. Statistical learning by 8-month-old infants. *Science* 274: 1926–1928.

Saleh, Marwa, Shoeib, Rasha, Hegazi, Mona, and Ali, Pakinam. 2007. Early phonological development in Egyptian Arabic children: 12–30 months. *Folia Phoniatrica and Logopaedica* 59: 234–240.

Sapir, J. David. 1965. *A Grammar of Diola-Fogny.* West African Language Monographs, 3. Ibadan: Cambridge University Press, in association with The West African Languages Survey and The Institute of African Studies.

Savinainen-Makkonen, Tuula. 2000a. Word-initial consonant omissions – a developmental process in children learning Finnish. *First Language* 20: 161–185.

Savinainen-Makkonen, Tuula. 2000b. Learning long words – a typological perspective. *Language and Speech* 42(2): 205–225.

Savinainen-Makkonen, Tuula. 2007. Geminate template: A model for first Finnish words. *First Language* 27(4): 347–359.

Schane, Sanford A. 1974. How abstract is abstract? In A. Bruck, R. A. Fox, and M. W. LaGaly (eds) *Papers from the Parasession on Natural Phonology.* Chicago: Chicago Linguistic Society. 297–317.

Schaner-Wolles, Ch. 1988. Plural- vs. Komparativerwerb im Deutschen: Von der Diskrepanz zwischen konzeptueller und morphologischer Entwicklung. In H. Günther (ed) *Experimentell Studien zur Flexionsmorphologie.* Hamburg: Buske. 155–186.

Schiff, N. B. 1979. The influence of deviant material input on the development of language during the preschool years. *Journal of Speech and Hearing Research* 22: 581–603.

Schnitzer, Marc L and Krasinski, Emily. 1994. The development of segmental phonological production in a bilingual child. *Journal of Child Language* 21(3): 585–622.

Schönig, Claus. 1988. Zum Vokalismus russischer Lehnwörter im Jakutischen. *Ural-Altaische Jahrbücher,* 8: 125–136.

Schwartz, Richard and Leonard, Laurence. 1982. Do children pick and choose? An examination of phonological selection and avoidance in early lexical acquisition. *Journal of Child Language* 9: 319–336.

Scobbie, James M., Gibbon, Fiona, Hardcastle, William J., and Fletcher, P. 2000. Covert contrast as a stage in the acquisition of phonetics and phonology. In M. Broe and

J. Pierrehumbert (eds) *Papers in Laboratory Phonology V: Language Acquisition and the Lexicon*. Cambridge, MA: Cambridge University Press. 194–207.

Segal, Osnat, Nir-Sagiv, Bracha, Kishon-Rabin, Liat, and Ravid, Dorit. 2009. Prosodic patterns in Hebrew child-directed speech. *Journal of Child Language* 36(3): 629–656.

Seidl, Amanda and Johnson, Elizabeth. 2008. Boundary alignment enables 11-month-olds to segment vowel initial words from speech. *Journal of Child Language* 35(1): 1–24.

Selkirk, Elisabeth. 1984. *Phonology and syntax: the relation between sound and structure.* Ph.D. dissertation, MIT.

Selkirk, Elizabeth O. 1982. The syllable. In H. van der Hulst and N. Smith (eds) *The Structure of Phonological Representations*. Dordrecht: Foris. 337–384.

Schafer, Graham and Plunkett, Kim. 1998. Rapid word learning by fifteen-month-olds under tightly controlled conditions. *Child Development* 69(2): 309–320.

Shaw, Patricia. 1985. Modularism and substantive constraints in Dakota Lexical Phonology. *Phonology Yearbook* (2): 173–202.

Skoruppa, Katrin, Mani, Nivedita, and Peperkamp, Sharon. 2013. Toddlers' processing of phonological alternations: Early compensation for assimilation in English and French. *Child Development* 84(1): 313–330.

Slobin, Daniel I. 1985. Crosslinguistic evidence for the language-making capacity. In D. I. Slobin (ed) *The Crosslinguistic Study of Language Acquisition: Vol. 2. Theoretical Issues*. Hillsdale, NJ: Lawrence Erlbaum Associates. 1157–1256.

Smith, Jennifer L. 2011. Category-specific effects. In Marc van Oostendorp, Colin Ewen, Beth Hume, and Keren Rice (eds) *The Blackwell Companion to Phonology*, Malden, MA: Wiley-Blackwell. 2439–2463.

Smith, Neilson V. 1973. *The Acquisition of Phonology: Case Study*. Cambridge, MA: Cambridge University Press.

Smith, Neilson V. 2010. *Acquiring Phonology: A Cross-generational Case-study*. Cambridge, MA: Cambridge University Press.

Smolensky, Paul 1996. On the comprehension/production dilemma in child language. *Linguistic Inquiry* 27: 720–731.

Snyder, William. 2011. Children's grammatical conservatism: Implications for syntactic theory. In N. Danis, K. Mesh, and H. Sung (eds) *BUCLD35 Proceedings*. Somerville, MA: Cascadilla Press. 1–20.

So, Lydia K. H. and Dodd, Barbara J. 1995. The acquisition of phonology by Cantonese-speaking children. *Journal of Child Language* 22(3): 473–495.

Sohn, H. 1975. *Woleaian Reference Grammar*. Honolulu: University of Hawaii University Press.

Song, Jae Yung, Sundara, Megha, and Demuth, Katherine. 2009. Phonological constraints on children's production of english third person singular –s. *Journal of Speech, Language, and Hearing Research* 52: 623–642.

Sosa, Anna V. and Stoel-Gammon, Carol. 2006. Lexical and phonological effects in early word production. *Journal of Speech, Language and Hearing Research* 55: 596–608.

Spencer, Andrew. 1991. *Morphological Theory*. Oxford: Basil Blackwell.

Stager, Christine L. and Werker, Janet F. 1997. Infants listen for more phonetic detail in speech perception than in word-learning tasks. *Nature* 388: 381–382.

Stemberger, Joseph Paul. 1992. A performance constraint on compensatory lengthening in child phonology. *Language and Speech* 35(1, 2): 207–218.

Stemberger, Joseph P., Bernhardt, Barbara H., and Johnson, Carolyn. 2001. U-shaped learning in phonological development. Available as ROA-471 from the Rutgers Optimality Archive.

Stoel-Gammon, Carol. 1985. Phonetic inventories, 15–24 months: A longitudinal study. *Journal of Speech and Hearing Research* 28: 505–512.

Stoel-Gammon, Carol. 1989. Prespeech and early speech development of two late talkers. *First Language* 9: 207–224.

Stoel-Gammon, Carol. 1996. On the acquisition of velars in English. In Barbara Bernhardt, John Gilbert and David Ingram (eds.), *Proceedings of the UBC international conference on phonological acquisition*, 201–214. Somerville: Cascadilla Press.

Stoel-Gammon, Carol. 2002. Intervocalic consonants in the speech of typically developing children: Emergence and early use. *Clinical Linguistics and Phonetics* 16: 155–168.

Stoel-Gammon, Carol and Cooper, Judith A. 1984. Patterns of early lexical and phonological development. *Journal of Child Language*, 11: 247–271.

Stoel-Gammon, Carol and Dunn, Carla. 1985. *Normal and disordered phonology in children*. Baltimore. MD: University Park Press.

Stokes, Stephanie F. 2010. Neighborhood density and word frequency predict vocabulary size in toddlers. *Journal of Speech Hearing and Language Research* 53(3): 670–683.

Stokes, Stephanie F. and Surendran, Dinoj. 2005. Articulatory complexity, ambient frequency and functional load as predictors of consonant development in children. *Journal of Speech, Language and Hearing Research* 48(3): 577–591.

Storkel, Holly L. 2004. Do children acquire dense neighbourhoods? An investigation of similarity neighbourhoods in phonological acquisition. *Journal of Applied Psycholinguistics* 25: 201–221.

Storkel, Holly L. 2006. Do children still pick and choose? The relationship between phonological knowledge and lexical acquisition beyond 50 words. *Clinical Linguistics and Phonetics* 20(7–8): 523–529.

Storkel, Holly L. 2009. Developmental differences in the effects of phonological, lexical and semantic variables on word learning by infants. *Journal of Child Language* 36(2): 291–321.

Stuart-Smith Jane, Pryce, Gwilym, Timmins, Claire, and Gunter, Barrie. 2013. Television can be a factor in language change: Evidence from an urban dialect. *Language* 89: 501–536.

Suomi, K. 2004. Moraic patterns in Finnish prosody and lexicon. In M. S. Peltola and J. Tuomainen (eds) *Studies in Speech Communication*. Publications of the Department of Finnish and General Linguistics of the University of Turku 72; 73–97.

Suomi, K., Toivanen, J., and Ylitalo, R. 2008. *Finnish Sound Structure. Phonetics, Phonology, Phonotactics and Prosody. University of Oulu*. Oulu: University of Oulu.

Swingley, Daniel. 2009. Onsets and codas in 1.5-year olds' word recognition. *Journal of Memory and Language* 60: 252–269.

Taelman, Helena, Gert Durieux and Steven Gillis. 2009. Fillers as signs of distributional learning. *Journal of Child Language*, 36, pp 323–353.

Tessier, Anne-Michelle. Forthcoming. Morpho-phonological acquisition. In J. Lidz, J. Pater, and W. Snyder (eds) *Handbook of Developmental Linguistics*. Oxford: OUP.

Tesar, Bruce, Alderete, John, Horwood, Graham, Merchant, Nazarré, Nishitani, Koichi, and Prince, Alan. 2003. Surgery in language learning. In L. Mikkelson and C. Potts (eds) *Proceedings of WCCFL 22:*. Somerville, MA: Cascadilla Press. 101–114.

Tessier, Anne-Michelle. 2007. *Biases and Stages in Phonological Acquisition*. Doctoral dissertation, University of Massachusetts, Amherst.

Tessier, Anne-Michelle. 2009. Frequency of violation and constraint-based phonological learning. *Lingua* 119, 6–38.

Tessier, Anne-Michelle. 2012. Testing for OO–faithfulness in the acquisition of consonant clusters. *Language Acquisition* 19(2): 144–173.

Tessier, Anne-Michelle, Duncan, Tamara Sorenson, and Paradis, Johanne. 2013. Developmental trends and L1 effecst in early L2 learners' onset cluster production. *Bilingualism: Language and Cognition* 16(3): 663–681.

Thiessen, Erik D. 2007. The effect of distributional information on children's use of phonemic contrasts. *Journal of Memory and Language* 56: 16–34.

Thompson, Laurence C. 1979. Salishan and the Northwest. In L. Campbell and M. Mithun (eds) *The Languages of Native America*. Austin, Texas. 692–765.

Traill, Anthony. 1985. *Phonetic and Phonological Studies in !Xoo Bushman*. Hamburg: Helmut Buske Verlag.

Trigo, Rosario. 1988. *The Phonological Derivation and Behavior of Nasal Glides*. Doctoral dissertation, MIT.

Trommelen, Mieke. 1983. *The Syllable in Dutch, with Special Reference to Diminutive Formation*. Dordrecht: Foris. PhD Dissertation, Utrecht University.

Trubetzkoy, Nikolai S. 1939. *Grundzüge der Phonologie*. Güttingen: Vandenhoeck and Ruprecht.

Tucker, G. R. 1998. A global perspective on multilingualism and multilingual education. In. J. Cenoz, and F. Genesee (eds) *Beyond Bilingualism: Multilingualism and Multilingual Education*. Clevedon: Multilingual Matters. 3–15.

Tzakosta, Marina. 2007. Genetic and environmental effects in L1 phonological acquisition: The case of consonant harmony in Greek child speech. *Journal of Greek Linguistics* 8: 5–30.

Urbanczyk, Suzanne. 2001. *Patterns of Reduplication in Lushootseed*. New York: Garland. Outstanding Dissertations in Linguistics.

van Kampen, N. Jacqueline. 1997. *First Steps in Wh-movement*. Delft: Eburon.

Veit, S. 1986. Das Verstandnis von Plural-und Komparativformen bei (entwicklungs)dysgrammatischen Kindern im Vorschulalter. In G. Kegel et al. (eds), *Sprechwissenschaft und Psycholinguistik*. Opladen: Westdeutscher Verlag. 217–286.

Velten, H. V. 1943. The growth of phonemic and lexical patterns in infant language. *Language 19*: 281–292.

Veneziano, Edy and Hermine Sinclair. The changing status of 'filler syllables' on the way to grammatical morphemes. *Journal of Child Language*, 27, pp 461–500.

Venneman, Theo. 1972. Rule inversion. *Lingua* 29: 209–242.

Vigário, Marina, Freitas, M. João, and Frota, Sónia. 2006. Grammar and frequency effects in the acquisition of prosodic words in European Portuguese. *Language and Speech* 49(2): 175–203.

Vihman, Marilyn. 1981. Phonology and the development of the lexicon: evidence from children's errors. *Journal of Child Language* 8(2): 239–264.

Vihman, Marilyn. 1985. Language differentiation by the bilingual infant. *Journal of Child Language* 12: 297–324.

Vihman, Marilyn M. 2014. *Phonological Development*. Oxford: Basil Blackwell.

Vihman, Marilyn M. and McCune, Lorraine. 1994. When is a word a word? *Journal of Child Language* 21: 517–542.

Vihman, Marilyn M. and Keren-Portnoy, Tamar. (eds) 2013. *The Emergence of Phonology: Whole Word Approaches and Cross-linguistics Evidence*. Cambridge, MA: CUP.

Vihman, Marilyn. M., Macken, Marlys M., Miller, Ruth, Simmons, Hazel, and Miller, Jim. 1985. From babbling to speech: A re-assessment of the continuity issue. *Language* 61(2): 397–445.

Vihman, Marilyn M., DePaolis, Rory A. and Davis, Barbara L. 1998. Is there a 'Trochaic Bias' in early word learning? Evidence from infant production in English and French. *Child Development* 69(4): 935–949.

Vihman, Marilyn M. and Velleman, Shelley L. 1989. Phonological reorganization. *Language and Speech* 32: 149–170.

Vitevitch, Michael S., Armbruster, Jonna, and Chu, Shinying. 2004. Sub-lexical and lexical representations in speech production: Effects of phonotactic probability and onset density. *Journal of Experimental Psychology: Learning, Memory, & Cognition* 30: 514–529.

Volterra, Virginia and Taeschner, Traute. 1978. The acquisition and development of language by bilingual children. *Journal of Child Language* 5: 311–326.

Wagner, R., Torgesen, J., Rashotte, C., and Pearson, N. 1999. *Comprehensive Test of Phonological Processing*.

Walley, A. C. 2005. Speech perception in childhood. In D. B. Pisoni, and R. E. Remez (eds) *Handbook of Speech Perception*. Oxford: Blackwell. 449–468.

Walter, S. 1975. Zur Entwicklung morphologischer Strukturen bei Kindern. Ms., Psychologisches Institut, Heidelberg, Germany: Universitat Heidelberg.

Warner, Natasha and Tucker, Benjamin. 2011. Phonetic variability of stops and flaps in spontaneous and careful speech. *The Journal of the Acoustical Society of America* 130(3): 1606–1617.

Wauquier, Sophie. 2014. Templates and representations, from Semitic to child language. In Sabrina, Bendjaballah, Noam Faust, Mohamed Lahrouchi, and Nicola Lampitelli (eds) *The Form of Structure, the Structure of Form: Essays in honor of Jean Lowenstamm. Language Faculty and beyond 12, John Benjamins*. 219–234.

Wauquier, Sophie and Yamaguchi, Naomi. 2013. 'Templates in French'. In Marilyn May Vihman, and Tamar Keren-Portnoy (eds) *The Emergence of Phonology: Whole Word Approaches, Cross-Linguistic Evidence*. Cambridge, MA: Cambridge University Press. 317–343.

Wells, John. 1982. *Accents of English*. vol 1. Cambridge, MA: CUP.

Whorf, Benjamin Lee. 1946. The Hopi language, Toreva dialect. In C. Osgood (ed) *Linguistic Structures of Native America*. New York: Viking Fund Publications. 158–183.

Werker, Janet F. and Lalonde, Chris E. 1988. Cross-language speech perception: Initial capabilities and developmental change. *Developmental Psychology* 24(5): 672–683.

Werker, Janet F., Fennell, Christopher T., Corcoran, Kathleen M., and Stager, Christine L. 2002. Infants' ability to learn phonetically similar words: Effects of age and vocabulary size. *Infancy* 3(1): 1–30.

Werker, Janet F., Pegg, Judith E., and Mcleod, Peter J. 1994. A cross-language investigation of infant preference for infant-directed communication. *Infant Behavior and Development* 17: 323–333.

Werker, Janet F. and Tees, Richard. 1983. Developmental changes across childhood in the perception of non-native speech sounds. *Canadian Journal of Psychology* 37: 278–286.

Werker, Janet F. and Tees, Richard. 1984. Cross-language speech perception: Evidence for perceptual reorganization during the first year of life. *Infant Behavior and Development* 7: 49–63.

Werker, Janet. F., Cohen, Leslie. B., Lloyd, Valerie L., Casasola, Marianella, and Stager, Christine L. 1998. Acquisition of word–object associations by 14-month-old infants. *Developmental Psychology* 34: 1289–1309.

Wijnen, Frank, Krikhaar, Evelien, and Os, Els Den. 1994. The (non)realization of unstressed elements in children's utterances: Evidence for a rhythmic constraint. *Journal of Child Language* 21: 59–83.

Wilkinson, Karina. 1988. Prosodic structure and Lardil phonology. *Linguistic Inquiry* 19(2): 325–334.

Windfuhr, Gernot. 1997. Persian phonology. In A. S. Kaye (ed) *Phonologies of Asia and Africa*. Winona Lake, Indiana. 675–689.

Wolf, Matthew. 2005. An autosegmental theory of quirky mutations. In J. Alderete, C-H. Han and A. Kochetov (eds) *Proceedings of the 24th West Coast Conference on Formal Linguistics*. Somerville, MA: Cascadilla Proceedings Project. 370–378.

Wolf, Matthew, 2008. *Optimal Interleaving: Serial Phonology-Morphology Interaction in a Constraint-based Model*. Doctoral dissertation, UMass Amherst, Amherst Massachusetts.

Woodward, J., and R. Aslin (1990). Segmentation cues in maternal speech to infants. Talk given at the International Conference on Infant Studies, Montreal, April 1990.

Wolfart, H. Christoph. 1975. Sketch of Cree, an Algonquin language. In I. Goddard (ed) *Handbook of North American Languages Vol 17: Languages*. Washington, DC: Smithsonian Institute. 390–439.

Yavaş, Mehmet, Ben-David, Avivit, Gerrits, Ellen, Kristoffersen, Kristian E., and Simonsen, Hanne G. 2008. Sonority and cross-linguistic acquisition of initial s-clusters. *Clinical Linguistics and Phonetics* 22(6): 421–441.

Zamuner, Tania. 2009. The structure and nature of phonological neighbourhoods in children's early lexicons. *Journal of Child Language* 36(1): 3–21.

Zamuner, Tania, Gerken, LouAnn, and Hammond, Michael. 2005. The acquisition of phonology based on input: A closer look at the relation of cross-linguistic and child language data. *Lingua* 115: 1403–1426.

Zamuner, Tania, Kerkhoff, Annemarie, and Fikkert, Paula. 2006. Acquisition of voicing neutralization and alternations in Dutch. In D. Bamman, T. Magnitskaia, and C. Zaller (eds) *Proceedings of the 30th Boston University Conference on Language Development.* Somerville, MA: Cascadilla Press. 701–712.

Zamuner, Tania, Kerkhoff, Annemarie, and Fikkert, Paula. 2012. Phonotactics and morphophonology in early child language: Evidence from Dutch. *Applied Psycholinguistics* 33: 481–499.

Index of Constraints

Index of Languages

Index of Terms